TENNESSEE RECORDS

Tombstone Inscriptions and Manuscripts

HISTORICAL AND BIOGRAPHICAL

Compiled by

JEANNETTE TILLOTSON ACKLEN
President Nashville Chapter Colonial Dames of America
Vice President-General, N. S. D. A. R.
National Vice-Chairman
Historical Research

Assisted by

KATE WHITE
Honorary State Historian

LENORA WEST BOWEN
State Chairman Preservation of Historic Spots

EMMA ALLENSWORTH DARDEN
Regent Cumberland Chapter

Foreword by

JUDGE JOHN H. DEWITT
Judge of Tennessee Court of Appeals
President of Tennessee Historical Society

JANAWAY PUBLISHING, INC.
Santa Maria, California

Notice

In many older books, foxing (or discoloration) occurs and, in some instances, print lightens with wear and age. Reprinted books, such as this, often duplicate these flaws, notwithstanding efforts to reduce or eliminate them. The pages of this reprint have been digitally enhanced and, where possible, the flaws eliminated in order to provide clarity of content and a pleasant reading experience.

Originally published
Nashville, Tennessee
1933

Reprinted by:

Janaway Publishing, Inc.
732 Kelsey Ct.
Santa Maria, California 93454
(805) 925-1038
www.janawaygenealogy.com

2014

ISBN: 978-1-59641-328-3

Made in the United States of America

FOREWORD

The author and compiler of this book has rendered an invaluable and enduring service. She has done it out of her heart which has long been enlisted in patient and accurate research, in careful and justly appraising study, and in appreciation of the noble people and vital events in our history. She has brought to it a clear understanding and a strong sense of the need of preserving the records and the memorabilia that otherwise would probably be lost. Her distinguished service as a member and an officer in patriotic and historical societies has fitted her eminently for the task which she has so well performed.

In this age of obsession with material things—the problems and the diversions of the times—it is fortunate for us and those coming after us that there are at least a few who seek to study and preserve the history of those who have made our civilization.

The torch of history illumines the pathway before us, for "history is the rival of time, the depository of great actions, the witness of the past, the example to the present, the monitor to the future." It is only by the true interpretation and preservation of the lives of those who have chiefly made the state and nation their ideals of character, their sacrifices to duty, their struggles for independence, their development of an enlightened society, that our history and our ideal destiny can be understood; and thus the life of each worthy person and family and the course of each community becomes important in the story of a great people.

We know much of the lives of the leaders in statesmanship and in war. We know something of the lives and social customs of the wealthy. We yet know but little of the life and thought of the great mass of plain but sturdy people who have not acquired wealth or honors. They have been the human basis of our civilization.

They lie unsung everywhere in quiet graves, under modest tombstones, and yet they live on in the lives of their children to whom they have left the principles of honor and of usefulness. The duty of the historians of the South is to wrest from oblivion the names and records of these people. Such a work will give a new sense of strength and pride, a new confidence and hope, a new inspiration to repeat in the different conditions of the present and the future, the character and the service of those of the long ago.

It is for these reasons that such a work as is here presented will be enduring in quality and importance. It will be a source book for the writers of synthetic history. It is history in itself. It has been brought from family Bibles, from tombstones, from diaries, from letters and other manuscripts, from county records, from other sources which have been neglected and have come but tardily to be appreciated. It is ardently hoped that the publication of this book will stimulate others to engage in this important and fascinating work, to the end that such material may be everywhere rescued and preserved.

All who love our southern history and want it to be brought properly before the world should acclaim this work and give it material encouragement. All who are of kin to those who are here commemorated will delight in these pages and be grateful for them. We are all indebted to Mrs. Acklen and those who have assisted her for this fine contribution to our historical literature.

JOHN H. DEWITT.

Bible Records—Tombstone Inscriptions

OLD CITY CEMETERY, NASHVILLE

Record book copied by Mrs. Joseph Hayes Acklen and Mrs. Oscar F. Noel and checked with inscriptions on tombstones. Pages of names not on Charles Marlin's list or on the "List of Dead" in the office copied. Many stones are illegible and broken.

EXTRACTS FROM "OLD CITY CEMETERY"
BY ELIZABETH PORTERFIELD ELLIOTT, "NASHVILLE TENNESSEAN," SEPTEMBER 18, 1927.

In the early settlement of Nashville the dead were buried on the open ground that overlooked the Sulphur Spring bottom and at two or three country burial places in the neighborhood, and even on the public lot (our Public Square).

Joseph Hay, the first member of the little settlement killed by Indians, was buried a short distance to the east of the Sulphur Spring—not where it now appears, but a hundred yards toward the Capitol where it issued from a rick beneath the surface of the ground. Robert Gilkie, the first who died from sickness, is said to have been buried in this ground.

In a communication to the Tennessee Historical Society, 1850, Nathaniel Cross said: "Being on the bluff immediately above the Sulphur Spring this afternoon, which as is well known was formerly a place of burial for our city, as we now consider it, I observed that there was but one stone left with an inscription on it to tell who lies beneath, as this will disappear like the others.

ERECTED BY COMRADES

"I was induced to copy this sole remaining inscription:
"Erected by Sundry Brother Officers and Comrades—
"To the memory of Richard Chandler, late 1st Lieutenant and Paymaster, 4th Regiment of Infantry. In the Army of the United States, who deceased on the 20th day of December, 1801, aged 37 years, 7 months, and 10 days.
"He lived esteemed an honest man and brave soldier.
"He died regretted by all who knew him.
"Exalted truth, and manly firmness shown.
"Conspicuous in him beneath this stone."

A few of the dead were buried on the Public Square, between the courthouse and the site of the Old Inn. The dear old Thomas

Bible Records—Tombstone Inscriptions

Crutcher, who saw the last one buried there, was heard to say, years after, that the earth was so shallow it was difficult to obtain a sufficient quantity to cover the coffin.

The City Cemetery was first used in 1822, and many bodies were removed from their first resting places for permanent burial there. When located it was thought to be beyond the reach of the city.

The twenty-seven acres inclosed are regularly laid out in streets named like those in a city of the living.

"The soft sunlight here falls through the delicate foilage of Southern evergreens and deciduous trees upon grand monuments, picturesque shrubbery, grassy mounds, and bright green carpets of trailing myrtle. A last palisade of cedar excludes the outside world, whose only approach is through the massive iron gates by which its sleeping tenants enter."

After the War of the States during that terrible readjustment time the Old Cemetery was neglected. Later many families removed their dead to the beautiful new Mt. Olivet. Then an agitation arose to induce the city to remove all the graves and turn the place into a park, or divide it into lots to be sold.

That aroused the sleeping spirit of sentiment and common sense all over the city and county. The fight was on in the City Council. It lasted through many months. The newspapers of that time partially reflect it. In the end, as we thankfully see, the so-called progressive spirits lost, and this precious old "God's Acre" is ours today.

The women of the South Nashville Federation gave the strongest aid in that work. To them also we owe the beautiful entrance gate and through the influence of our present mayor who was the mayor at that time the city built that beautiful and appropriate stone fence.

The names of those who gave freely of their time and money to the cemetery at that time, the workers in the federation and those who planted the roses and some of the trees, will be published later. Mayor Howse is now intensely interested in this movement and is ready to assist in every practical way. Some families have given loving care to their old lots. The Belsnyder, the McCrory, the Winston, the Baxter, the Ewing lots, and several others have been well preserved.

Bible Records—Tombstone Inscriptions

And now the James Robertson Chapter, D. A. R., have taken the cemetery under its special care and protection.

The Gen. James Robertson tomb is the first to receive attention. The work of restoring and beautifying it is now in progress.

A LEGEND

Near the monument of Gov. William Carroll there is a large rock with a graceful iron ornament on top. No name nor date can be found upon either rock or iron to show its meaning. In true legendary style its story has begun to branch out into different versions. Here is one told me when I was a child:

A beautiful young girl lived up the river in the Hermitage neighborhood. On which side of the river I was not told. She had a devoted lover. They were young and very happy. Their favorite place of meeting was among the rocks on top of one of the highest bluffs of the river bank.

The place became very dear to them. It was sweet up there in every season of the year. From it they watched the sunset or the moon rise. They loved it in the sunlight or moonlight or starlight.

There was no objection to their marriage. It gave happiness in the homes of both. But one day something happened; we know not what. A little lover's quarrel followed. It must have seemed to the young girl that the end of all things had come for in her misery and hopelessness she jumped from the bluff into the river below.

Her body was recovered and she was buried in this place. Then the miserable young man had this rock from the top of the bluff removed from its place and hauled to the cemetery. He allowed no name or date upon it. He knew and that was to him sufficient.

This story ended: "And he never . . . "

The other version is in the beginning the same as the foregoing. But it says that they were married and that after a short time the young wife died that she requested that the rock near which "their courting was done" should be placed at her grave. And this the sorrowful young husband did. It is said that she is buried near the bowlder.

Bible Records—Tombstone Inscriptions

INSCRIPTIONS IN CITY CEMETERY

Andrew Ewing; born in the State of Pennsylvania, March 17, 17—. Educated in the Quaker Persuasion. Of the mild and benignant principals of that sect, he was the brightest ornament. Died May 1, 1913. Proverbially good, honest, and charitable. Lived . . . . With all. First Clerk of Davidson County from October, 1783, until April, 1813.

Sacred to the memory of Rev. William Hume. Faithful and devoted minister of the gospel, accomplished and successful instructor of youth, the enlightened and generous philanthropist, the able and intrepid advocate of truth, the humble, consistent, and cheerful Christian.

He was universally loved and respected while he lived and in death mourned and honored by all classes and denominations of the community which he had long and zealously served.

He was a native of Scotland, was educated at the University of Edinborough. Resided in Nashville about thirty years. Died May 22, 1833.

In testimony of their affection and gratitude and profound respect the citizens of Nashville have erected this simple monument under the deep conviction that the memory of his virtues and active goodness will be cherished long after the sepulchral tablet shall be obliterated and forgotten.

To the memory of Duncan Robertson, a native son of Scotland and resident of the United States forty-three years, who died at Nashville the first of May, 1833, in the 63rd year of his age. The citizens of Nashville have erected this monument.

"This loss will be long and severely felt, and his place will not be soon or easily supplied. Always first and best in every work of philanthropy and benificence, to do good to his fellowmen—entirely forgetful of himself seemed to be the great object of his life. In the dungeon of the forsaken prisoner, at the bedside of the wretched and friendless, and in the abode of poverty and distress was he almost constantly found. In imitation of the example of his Divine Master, he literally 'went about doing good.' No personal

Bible Records—Tombstone Inscriptions

sacrifice was too great for him to make when the call of benevolence demanded it.

"He was not only willing but active and efficient in every good work of charity and disinterested beneficience. Such a man is among the wonders of his age—a blessing to any community—and his memory should be embalmed in the grateful recollection of his contemporaries and preserved for the gratitude and veneration of posterity."

George Washington Campbell; born in Tongue Sutherlandshire, Scotland, 1742. Graduated at Princeton College, 1794. Member of Knoxville Bar, 1798. Member of United States Congress, 1803-1809. Member of Court of Errors and Appeals, 1809. United States Senator, 1815. Secretary of Treasury, 1814-1815. United States Senator, 1815. Minister to Russia, 1818-1820. Special Commissioner to France to settle indemnity claims, 1832.

George Thomas Bowen, son of Ephriam and Sarah Bowen. Born in Providence, R. I., March 19, 1803. Rudimented under Dr. Abbot, Phillips Academy, Exeter, N. H. Graduated at Yale College, September, 1822. Studied medicine three years in the University of Pennsylvania. Chosen professor of chemistry in the Nashville University, November, 1825. Died of consumption, October 25, 1828. A gentleman, a scholar, a Christian.

Erected by John Stewart, a merchant of Glasgow, N. B., to the memory of John Stewart, Junior, who died at Nashville, Tenn., where he was residing for the recovery of his health. He was twenty-five years of age. Died, 1836.

Though he was a stranger in a strange land, his relatives had the consolation to know that he was not uncared for. He had found friends among the friends of the common Saviour who felt the influence of his amiable, unobstrusive manner and ministered to him with affectionate solicitude in his sickness and sorrow, but not as those who have no hope over his early grave.

In memory of Thomas W. Erskine. Born in County Antrim, Ireland. Died in Memphis, Tenn., May 20, A.D., 1849, in his forty-fourth year.

Bible Records—Tombstone Inscriptions

Beneath this stone reposes the mortal remains of one endeared to a numerous circle of friends by his brilliant talents, his poetic temperament, his unbending integrity of character, his genial social sympathies, and his loving heart. The broad Atlantic rolls between this spot and his bereaved kindred, and this monument is erected by those to whom he had bound himself by ties as strong as those of blood. His errors were few and lie buried with him. His virtues will live forever.
"He is not dead— . . ."

JERRY

This story is told because we wish to show gratitude and to give honor to the ancestors of one colored citizen. They, too, have a part in our cherished history. So many of them were like the Scotch clansmen who devoted their lives to their chieftain. We are reminded of that grand old man in one of Scott's novels, who, with his twelve sons, surrounded their young chief on a battlefield, and as he saw one after another fall dead, only cried out, "One more for Hector."

A toll gate on the Franklin Pike stood where the road skirts around what is now the Reservoir Hill. The sides of the hill has been cut down to make the grade less steep. It is difficult now to realize how steep the hill up to the toll gate used to be. Along the eastern side of the road a deep gully had been dug to drain off the rain water.

One day Jerry Porterfield was driving his master to town. He was an excellent driver and a kind, good manager of horses. That morning he was driving a young sorrel horse. His estimate of the sorrel was: "This is a fast strong one, but he has not much sense."

Just before reaching the top of the toll gate hill the horse shied and jumped to one side. The buggy turned over into the ditch. Before his master knew what was happening Jerry threw both arms around him. He was a much smaller man than Jerry. They fell together into that ditch with Jerry underneath.

The toll gate keeper ran to them. How he ever managed it with that struggling horse the story does not tell. It was miraculous though. The master was taken up unconscious but soon revived. Jerry was dead—killed instantly the doctor said by striking the back of his head on a rock.

IN HONOR OF
COLONEL JAMES ROBERTSON
BORN 1742 IN VIRGINIA.
DIED 1814 IN TENNESSEE.

HE CAME FROM EASTERN NORTH CAROLINA TO THE WATAUGA SETTLEMENT IN WHAT IS NOW EASTERN TENNESSEE 1769-1770, WHERE HE WAS A LEADER IN CIVIL AND INDIAN AFFAIRS.

CONDUCTED THE "LAND PARTY" OF SETTLERS TO THE FRENCH LICK IN 1779-1780, BUILT THIS FORT NASHBOROUGH AND DEFENDED IT IN ALL THE VARIOUS INDIAN ATTACKS. REMAINED WITH THE COLONY WHEN MANY HAD FORSAKEN IT DURING A PERIOD OF GREAT STRESS, SUFFERING AND DISCOURAGEMENT, AND GAVE TO IT A WHOLE LIFE-TIME OF PATRIOTIC SERVICE.

THE VERDICT OF HISTORY WELL ENTITLES HIM TO THE NAME OF:
"THE FATHER OF WEST (NOW MIDDLE) TENNESSEE"
AND THE
"FOUNDER OF NASHVILLE."

"HE POSSESSED TO AN EMINENT DEGREE THE CONFIDENCE AND ESTEEM OF ALL HIS CO-TEMPORARIES, AND MERITED ALL THE EULOGIUM AND AFFECTION WHICH THE MOST ARDENT OF HIS COUNTRYMEN HAVE EVER BESTOWED UPON HIM. HIS SERVICES IN PEACE AND WAR ARE GRATEFULLY REMEMBERED." (HAYWOOD.)

TABLET IN FORT NASHBOROUGH

Bible Records—Tombstone Inscriptions

He was buried with all honor. His funeral was attended by a large number of his friends—white and colored. Among the white people were many of the best and most prominent citizens of the city and county.

The epitaph on Jerry's tomb was known by all to be a true estimate of his life and character.

CHARLES A. MARLIN'S LIST OF NOTED DEAD IN CITY CEMETERY

Notes on Map.   Sec.   Lot.
Memorial Gate.
Office.
Marlin Dial.
Robertson Dial.
Carroll Monument.
Johnson Valut.
Shelby Vault.
Morris Lanier and Cooley Vault.
McNairy Vault.
Whiteman Vault.
Curran Vault.
Clark Vault.
Baxter Vault.
Mallory Street Gate.
Size: 1176.4 feet on Seventh Avenue.
  817.6 feet on Oak Street.
  1175 feet on Railroad.
About 18 acres.
Contains about 30,000 bodies
Open officially January 1st, 1822.
The third graveyard of Nashville; first was east of Public Square; next was a hill west of French Lick Sulphur Spring (Cabbage Hill).

PROMINENT PEOPLE BURIED THERE

General James Robertson, founder of Nashville, Father of Tennessee, Indian fighter and leader of the settlers. Born, 1712; died, 1811. Moved here from Chickasaw Agency, now Memphis, Tenn. Charlotte Reeves Robertson, wife of above "Hero of the Battle of the Bluffs." Born, 1751; died, 1812.

Dr. Felix Robertson, fourth child of Gen. James and Charlotte Robertson; first white child born in Nashville; mayor of Nashville, 1818-1827-8; professor of medicine, University of Nashville (so designated by Gen. A. Jackson).

His wife, Lydia Robertson. Born, 1788; died, 1832.

Alfred Hume, Father of the Public School System of Nashville. Born, 1808; died, 1853.

His grandfather, Rev. Wm. Hume, pioneer minister of the Presbyterian Church. Born in Scotland, 1769; died in Nashville, 1833.

Capt. John Bradford. Born, 1762; died, 1857.

His wife, Elizabeth Bradford. Born, 1767; died, 1837. "Parents, Alfred Hume"—from monument.

Judge John McNairy—McNairy Vault. This vault contains now (1824) 29 bodies of the McNairy family. Judge and landowner.

Peter Jonte; first Odd Fellow to die in Nashville. Born, 1796; died, 1840.

Robert Baxter, founder of Cumberland Furnace. Died, 1850. Baxter vault.

Richard Claiborne Napier, founder of Napier Furnace, "Oldest Iron Master in State." Born, 1773; died 1834.

Samuel Chapman, Revolutionary Soldier. Died, 1836.

Joseph Norvell; born, 1793; died, 1847. Masonic Emblem. Grand Master of Grand Lodge of Tennessee.

Lipscomb Norvell, Revolutionary Soldier; officer, lieutenant, 1776-1783. Died, 1843.

Bible Records—Tombstone Inscriptions

Archibald Marlin, Revolutionary Soldier. Born, 1763; died, 1818. North Carolina Volunteer, 1777-83. Granted 640 acres of land, Stones Creek, Davidson County, for bravery.

His son, same lot, Henry Marlin, member of Nashville Blues War, 1812. Through Creek and at Battle of New Orleans.

Duncan Robertson, philanthropist. Monument erected by citizens of Nashville. Originator of Caladonian Society for aiding suffering humanity. Born in Scotland; died, 1833.

Gen. Samuel G. Smith, Secretary of State, 1832-1835. Signed first Tennessee bonds. Born, 1791, in North Carolina; died, 1835.

Col. W. B. A. Ramsey, Historian and Secretary of State. Born in Knox County, 1799; died, 1874, at Edgefield. John Somerville, banker. Born, 1770; died, 1846.

Rev. Obadiah Jennings, pastor of the First Presbyterian Church. Born in New Jersey, 1778; died in Nashville, 1832.

Robt. B. Curry, second postmaster, 1800-1826 of Nashville. Mayor, 1822-23. Died, 1848.

George R. Foresyth. Born, 1816; died, 1844. First Grand Treasurer of I. O. O. F.

Col. John Tipton, champion of North Carolina in contest with State of Franklin. Monument erected, 49th General Assembly of Tennessee. Born in Washington County; died October 8, 1831.

Gen. Robert Armstrong. Born in Virginia, 1791; died, 1854. General Jackson bequeathed this man his sword.

Wm. Armstrong, four times mayor of Nashville, 1829-30-31-32. No monument.

Anthony Foster, "one of the oldest citizens of Nashville." Died, April 8, 1825. Age, 60 years.

Admiral Paul Shirley, U. S. Navy. Died, November 24, 1876. Aged, 55 years.

Thomas Crutcher, Treasurer Miro District, 1803-1836. Mayor of Nashville, 1819. Born in Virginia, 1760; died, 1844.

Joseph Coleman, first mayor of Nashville, 1806-07-08. No monument. T. B. Coleman, son of above. Mayor of Nashville, 1842. Cedar head piece.

Wilkins Tannehill, editor, mayor, 1825-26. Grand Master, Odd Fellows and Masons. Born, 1787; died, 1858. Monument erected by Masonic Fraternity.

James Arthur Diggins, first male member of Christ Church. Born, 1805; died, 1855.

Charles C. Trabue. Born, 1798. First Deputy Grand Sir Odd Fellows Instituted Grand Lodge of the body. Mayor of Nashville, 1839-40.

William Edward West, artist; painted Henry Clay pictures, famous one of Lord Byron. Born, Lexington, Ky., 1788; died, 1857.

Robt. Bell Castleman, mayor of Nashville, 1854-55. Born, 1809; died, 1886.

Andrew Allison, mayor of Nashville, 1847-48. Born, 1799; died, 1862.

Alexander Porter, U. S. Senator; Louisiana Judge, Supreme Court.

P. W. Maxey, mayor of Nashville, 1843-44. Born, 1805; died, 1873.

Gen. Richard Stoddard Ewell, Commander of Lee's center at Battle of Gettysburg; Lieutenant-General, C. S. A. Born, 1817; died, 1872.

Same lot, George Washington Campbell. Bought Capitol Hill for a cow and calf and a pair of leather breeches. Sold to the City of Nashville for $30,000. Presented to State for Capitol site by city. Born in Tongue Sutherlandshire, Scotland. Born, February 9, 1762; died, February 17, 1848. Graduate of Princeton College, 1794; member of Knoxville bar, 1798; member of U. S. Congress, 1803-09; Court of Appeals and Errors, 1809; U. S. Senator, 1811-14; Secretary of Treasury, 1814-15; U. S.

Bible Records—Tombstone Inscriptions

Senator, 1816; Minister to Russia, 1818-20; 1832, Special Commissioner to France to settle indemnity claims.

Same lot, Harriet Campbell, his wife, daughter of Ben Stottard. Born, 1789; died, 1849. First Secretary of the Navy.

Same lot, Rebecca Hubbard, wife of Hon. Davis Hubbard, another daughter of Benjamin Stottard. Born, 1797; died, 1872.

Prof. Collins D. Elliott, Nashville Female Academy. Born, 1810; died, 1899.

Col. George Wilson, first editor west of Cumberland Mountains; first Grand Patriarch of I. O. O. F. Born, 1778; died, 1848.

Anthony W. Johnson, capitalist, owned 300 acres in Edgefield.

Joseph Vaulx, capitalist and banker.

Capt. Alpha Kingsly, first sexton of City Cemetery. Born in Vermont, 1778; died, 1846.

John L. Marling, editor, Nashville Union. Born, ...; died, 1854. Minister to Gautamala under President Pierce. Marling-Zollicoffer duel.

His mother, Clara Cole, author of Clara's Poems. Born, 1807; died, 1883. Tennessee Robertson, daughter of William Blount Robertson and granddaughter of Gen. James Robertson. Born, 1808; died, 1857.

Capt. William Driver. Born in Salem, Mass., March 17, 1803; died in Nashville, March 3, 1886. Named U. S. Flag "Old Glory." "His ship, his state, his flag, Old Glory." "A master mariner, sailed twice around the world, once around Australia. Removed Pitcalm Island people from sickness and death in Tahieta to their own Island Home, September 3, 1831; then 69 in number; now 1,200 souls."

Gen. Felix Zollicoffer; killed at Mill Spring, Ky. Born, 1812; died, 1862. Edited Nashville Banner; comptroller of Tennessee, 1843-49. Marling-Zollicoffer duel, 1852.

John Coltart; Born, 1819; died, 1876. Tennessee Lodge No. 1, I. O. O. F., was instituted in his restaurant.

Thomas Nicholson Morgan, Judge of Louisiana. Born, 1814; died, 1844.

Mrs. Hester Jefferson McKenzie, aunt and foster mother of Joe Jefferson, the actor. Born, February 3, 1844; age, 36.

Parmella A. Kirk, first lady school teacher of Nashville. Died, 1860.

Gen. Wm. Carroll, Commander of General Andrew Jackson's right wing through Creek War and at Battle of New Orleans. Born in Pennsylvania, March 3, 1788; died in Nashville, March 20, 1855. Governor of Tennessee for 12 years; chairman of Democratic Presidential Convention, 1844; longest termed Governor of Tennessee. Monument erected by the State.

Timothy Kezer, first Grand Master of I. O. O. F. of Tennessee; elected August 10, 1841. Died, March 9, 1845. Erected by Grand Lodge.

W. H. Wilkinson, second mayor of town of South Nashville, 1853. Born, 1812; died, 1873.

Wm. B. Shepard, banker. Born in Caswell County, N. C.; died in Nashville, 1870. Mayor of Nashville, 1854, three days; installed at regular election; salary not enough; shortest term mayor of Nashville; resigned.

Col. Wm. B. Reece; born, 1891. Author of History of Nashville; judge of courts, etc.

Francis B. Fogg, lawyer and first president of Nashville Board of Education. Hume-Fogg High School named for him. Born, 1825; died, 1848.

Henry Middleton Rutledge, only son of Edward Rutledge of South Carolina, a signer of the Declaration of Independence. Born in Charleston, April 5, 1775; died, January 20, 1844.

His wife, Septima S., wife of Edward Rutledge, and daughter of Arthur Middleton, a signer of the Declaration of Independence. Born, October 15, 1783; died, June 12, 1865.

Bible Records—Tombstone Inscriptions

Abram Husle. This monument is erected by the State of Tennessee to the memory of Abram Hulse, member of the lower branch of the legislature from the counties of Sullivan and Hawkins. Died in Nashville, December 14, 1837.

Charles Longenotti, interpreter for General Jackson at New Orleans. Burned to death, April 21, 1854.

Robt. Farquharson Alderman. Born in Scotland, 1776; died, 1856.

Porter Howard, child of M. H. Howard, after whom Howard school is named. Born, 1855; died, 1856.

W. S. Whiteman, first paper manufacturer in Nashville. Whiteman vault. Born, 1808; died, 1889.

Philip Harsh, first homepathic physician of Nashville; age, 73 years, 2 months.

John Kane; died, July 1, 1848, in 38th year of his age. Erected by stone cutters of the Capitol Monument; designed by Strickland, architect of the Capitol.

Sarah Ann Gray, wife of John W. Walker. Monument designed by Strickland.

Judge Robert Whyte; born in Scotland, 1767; died in Nashville, 1844. Judge of Court of Errors and Appeals, 1816-35.

Rebecca Eakin Ewing, wife of Edward H. Ewing, orator, who laid corner stone of Capitol. Born, 1817; died, 1844.

Dr. Samuel Hogg, son of the woman who made the curt reply to General Tarleton after the Battle of Cowpens in regard to Col. Wm. Washington. Tarleton remarked that he would like the pleasure of meeting Colonel Washington. This woman replied, 'If you had looked behind you, General, at the Battle of Cowpens, you would have had that pleasure." Tarleton did not have time. Colonel Washington wounded him there. Inscription gone by decay.

Joseph D. McEwen, Alderman. Died, July 6, 1855.

Robert P. Curran, in Curran vault; second Commissioner of Public Instruction, 1840-41.

Slab, first monument to James K. Polk. Grundy lot. Polk was buried here from June, 1849, to May 22, 1850.

Thomas W. Erskin, Irish essayist. Born in County Antrim, Ireland, 1805; died in Memphis, May 20, 1849.

Rev. John Rains, son of pioneer preacher. Born, 1796; died, July 4, 1879.

Andrew Hynes; born, December 22, 1786; died, January 21, 1848. Hynes school and street named for him.

His wife, Ann Hynes, first female member of First Presbyterian Church, August 10, 1794-February 12, 1837.

Gerard Troost, first geologist of Tennessee. Born in Holland, March 15, 1776; died in Nashville August 1, 1850. Professor of chemistry of University of Nashville, 1828-1850.

Frederick Smith, first rigger on Capitol Hill; Masons' lot. Died, February 20, 1848; age, 43 years.

Terry H. Cahal, State Senator and Speaker; Chancellor of Tennessee; served in first Florida War. Born in Virginia, 1802; died, 1851.

Joseph B. Knowles, after whom Knowles school is named.

Isaac Paul, first mayor of town of South Nashville, 1851-1853; Pearl vault.

David Shelby bought the whole of South Edgefield for a cow and calf. In vault of his son, John Shelby, capitalist, who is in the same vault.

William Gilliam monument. He was lost on the steamer Arctic, 1851. Cenetapth.

First monument to John Sevier, first Governor of Tennessee, on Tennessee soil, put up by Albigence W. Putnam, historian of Tennessee history.

Ephriam H. Foster; born, September 17, 1794; died, September 6, 1854; lawyer, Tennessee Senator.

Robt. C. Foster; three times candidate for Governor. Died, September 22, 1854; age, 75 years.

Bible Records—Tombstone Inscriptions

Geo. W. Harris, author of Sut Lovingood Yarns.

Lieut. J. W. Gould; died, 1863; shot by Gen. Bedford Forrest at Columbia, Tennessee.

Rev. Alexander A. Winbourne; monument put up by Tennessee-Alabama M. E. Church Conference.

HONOR ROLL OF CITY CEMETERY
Nashville Tennessean, September 18, 1927

A partial list of noted people buried in the City Cemetery follows:

MAYORS OF NASHVILLE
Joseph Coleman, 1806-7-9; Wilkins Tannehill; Robert B. Curry, 1822-23-25; Charles C. Trabue, 1839-40; P. W. Maxey, 1843-44; W. B. Shapard, three days, in 1854; Felix Robertson, 1818-27-28; Thomas Crutcher, 1819; Wm. Armstrong, 1829-30-31-32; T. B. Coleman, 1842; Andrew Allison, 1847-48; Robt. L. Castleman, 1854-55.

MAYORS OF SOUTH NASHVILLE
Isaac Paul, 1851-53; W. R. Wilkerson.

Andrew Ewing, clerk to the government of the notables, 1783-1813; Nathan Ewing, son of Andrew, clerk of Davidson County Court for many years.

EDUCATIONAL
Ann Robertson Cockrell. She taught the little school on board the Adventure and was the first teacher here.

Dr. Felix Robertson, professor of medicine, University of Nashville.

The Rev. Wm. Hume, second president of Nashville Female Academy.

Thomas Crutcher, Nashville Female Academy.

C. D. Elliott, President, N. F. A., 1840-61.

Francis B. Fogg, first president of education, city schools.

Robert P. Curran, commissioner of public instruction.

Dr. Charles Winston, medical department, University of Nashville.

Gerard Troost, first geologist of Tennessee; professor of chemistry, University of Nashville.

Pamella Kirk, a noted teacher, primary school.

Andrew Hynes, Hynes school.

Joseph Knowles, Knowles school.

Porter Howard, son of M. H. Howard, Howard school.

Frederick F. Foy, student in medical department of University of Nashville, 1858.

George Thomas Bowen, professor of chemistry, University of Nashville, 1825.

FRATERNAL LEADERS
George R. Forsyth, first Grand Treasurer.

Col. George Wilson.

Timothy Kezer, first Grand Master, Tennessee.

John Coltart.

Wilkins Tannehill, Past Grand Master, Masonic Fraternity of Tennessee.

Charles C. Trabue.

Joseph Norvell, Grand Master of the Grand Lodge of Tennessee Free Masons.

Moses Stevens, by Grand Lodge of Tennessee, Grand Royal Arch Chapter.

James L. Howell, Woodmen of the World Memorial, and many others.

WAR
Gen. James Robertson.
Capt. John Bradford.
Samuel Chapman, Revolution Soldier.
Lipscomb Norvell, Revolution Soldier.

Bible Records—Tombstone Inscriptions

Anthony Foster, Revolution Soldier.
Col. Joel Lewis, Revolution Soldier.
A. Marlin, Revolution Soldier.
Henry Marlin, Nashville Blues, 1812, Creek War, New Orleans.
Gen. Samuel G. Smith.
Col. Wm. B. Ramsey.
Col. John Tipton.
Gen. and Gov. John Sevier.
Gen. Robert Armstrong.
Gen. Wm. B. Carroll.
Charles Longenotti, interpreter, Battle of New Orleans; now called Charles Maddis. Tablet, Daughters of 1812.
Terry H. Caral, Florida War.
Dr. Samuel Hogg (see remark of his mother to General Tarlton after the Battle of the Cowpens).
Capt. William Driver.
Admiral Paul Shirley, U. S. A.
Gen. Felix K. Zollicoffer, C. S. A.
Gen. R. S. Ewell.
Col. William B. Reese, C. S. A.
C. D. Elliott, C. S. A.
Lieut. J. W. Gould, C. S. A.
Capt. Alpha Kingsley.

___

ORIGINAL PIONEERS
James Robertson.
John Cockrell.
Ann Robertson Johnson, widow, afterward Mrs. John Cockrell.
David Shelby.
Andrew Ewing.

___

LAWYERS, BANKERS, PUBLIC SPIRITED MEN
Judge John McNairy.
Judge Robert Whyte.
Judge Thomas N. Morgan.
Alexander Porter, Judge of Supreme Court.
George W. Campbell (served in a great many ways).
Francis B. Fogg, lawyer.
Ephriam H. Foster, lawyer and senator.
Terry H. Cahal, chancellor of Tennessee.
John Somerville, banker.
Joseph Vaulx, banker.
James Woods, banker—Iron Furnace.
William B. Shapard, banker.
Robert Baxter, Cumberland Furnace.

Richard C. Napier, "Oldest Iron Master in State."
A. Johnson.
Judge William B. Reese.
Anthony Foster.
David Shelby and John Shelby.
Captain Belsnyder.
Robert B. Curry, second postmaster, 1800.

___

EDITORS, WRITERS, ARTISTS
John L. Marling, Nashville Union.
Felix Zollicoffer, Nashville Banner.
Col. George Wilson, first editor west of Cumberland Mountains.
Wilkins Tannehill, editor and famous book store.
Col. W. B. A. Ramsey, historian.
Col. and Judge William B. Reese, historian.
Thomas W. Erskine, Irish essayist.
George W. Harris, author of Sut. Lovingood.
Wm. Edward West, famous artist.
Edward Ewing.

___

MONUMENTS ERECTED BY THE PUBLIC
Wilkins Tannehill.
Timothy Kezer, by Grand Lodge.
Dr. Duncan Robertson, by City of Nashville.
Gen. William Carroll, by State of Tennessee.
Abram Husle, by State of Tennessee.
John Sevier, by A. W. Putnam.
John Tipton, by 49th General Assembly.
John Kane, stone cutter of State Capitol (designed by Strickland).
Robert Wilson, by fellow workmen.
Robert Armstrong, by a friend.
The Rev. Alexander A. Winbourn, M. E. Church Conference.
Alexander G. Brown, by Nashville Fire Co. No. 1, 1839.
William Sneed, by a numerous circle of friends, 1827.
The Rev. William Hume, by the citizens of Nashville.

Bible Records—Tombstone Inscriptions

CHURCH

Rev. William Hume, Presbyterian.
Rev. Obadiah Jennings, First Presbyterian Church.
Rev. John Rains, son of Pioneer John Rains.
Rev. Aex. A. Winbourn, M. E. Church.
James A. Diggons, first male member of Christ Church.

A FEW OF THE NOTED WOMEN

Charlotte Reeves Robertson.
Mrs. Hester Jefferson McKenzie, aunt and foster mother of Joseph Jefferson.
Tennessee Robertson.
Rebecca Ewing, wife of Edward Ewing.
Harriet Campbell, daughter of first Secretary of Navy.
Hannahetta West Norvell.
Bamella Kirk.
Mothers of many of us.
An old Southern "Mammy."

The City Cemetery contains monuments to the following persons who are not buried there:
William Gilliam (lost at sea).
John Sevier.
John Tipton.
David Crockett. (Was this the famous David or his son? The lot is owned by Mr. Putnam, the historian.)

INSCRIPTIONS

A

Abernathy, Mrs. L. B., 1823-1908.
Abernathy, Ann Louisa B., May 10, 1821-1850, wife of C. Abernathy; September 18, 1848.
Abston, Margaret A.
Abston, Pattie.
Achor, M.
Adams, Alfred A., March 6, 1801-July 1, 1854.
Adams, Eliza, 1787-1831.
Adams, Martha, 1768-1861.
Adams, Susan Porterfield, wife of A. G. Adams.
Adams, Tommy, 1883-1887.
Adams, T. T.
Adcock, Jennie, 1867-1870.
Adcock, Rebecca G., March 15, 1846-June 9, 1879.
Albertson, Sarah, 1853-1857.

Akin, John A., 1848-1851.
Akin, John W., January 17, 1817-August 22, 1868.
Akin, Mary A., 1855-1862.
Akin, Rebecca J., May 26, 1846-November 8, 1847.
Akin, Guilford W., 1841-1861.
Akin, Alex, 1862-1897.
Allen, Allis M., 1854-1855.
Allen, Annie M., 1852-1853.
Allen, Margaret S., 1849-1851.
Allen, John Taylor, March 8, 1847-1848.
Allen, Theo F., 1841-1845.
Allen, E. F., 1842-1845.
Allen, M. S., May 18, 1807-July 26, 1865.
Allen, Mary G., 1812-1886.
Allen, T. J., 1814-1824.
Allen, Mary E. Sadler, December 12, 1820-December 26, 1867.
Allen, Manier R., 1873-1888; daughter of W. H. and M. E. Allen.
Allen, Fannie E. S., 1844-1845, April 25.
Allen, Francis A., August 28, 1819-May 1, 1880.
Allen, S. M., 1846-1877.
Allen, Benjamin, 1773-1846.
Allen, Ann, 1778-1846.
Allen, (Infant), died 1842.
Allen, Helen Ann, January 24, 1838-August 30, 1839.
Allen, J. H., 1842-1865.
Allen, Robert F., October 29, 1839-May, 1865.
Allen, George E., 1803-May 9, 1830.
Allen, William, 1756-August 10, 1822; age, 66 years; born in Virginia.
Alexander, C.
Alley, C. J. B., 1858-1861.
Alley, F., January 15, 1813-April 9, 1845; wife of Joseph Alley.
Alley, Mary, 1840-November 24, 1841.
Alley, Martha A., July 24, 1824-July 19, 1849; wife of J. B. Alley.
Alley, Rebecca, 1802-1877.
Alley, T. R.
Allison, Robert V., 1841-August 31, 1864.
Allison, William Bascom, age,1 year.
Allison, William G., 1802-August 18, 1874.
Allison, Alexander, November 3, died, 1862.
Allison, John Allcorn, 1833-June 22, 1856.

13

Bible Records—Tombstone Inscriptions

Allison, James Hart, 1824-September 21, 1846; fell at Monterey, Mexico; son of Alexander and Madeline T. Allison.
Allison, Madeline T., 1810-February 16, 1876.
Alloway, Mrs. Irena, died, November 26, 1832; age, 37 years.
Altmeyer, Conrad, 1797-September 3, 1846; born in Germany.
Ament, Lemuel S., December 8, 1832-July 2, 1833.
Ament, George, Jr., May 26, 1831-March 6, 1833.
Ament, J. D., 1796-1851.
Ament, Olivia, March 21, 1845-September 2, 1855.
Ament, Beulah, March 31, 1840-December 24, 1842.
Anderson, Mary A., 1810-1887.
Anderson, Jasper, 1811-Aug. 25, 1834.
Anderson, Jane, January 11, 1788-March 17, 1845; born in Virginia, wife of John E.
Anderson, Mary Eliza, 1845-1847; daughter of Gen. S. R. and Mary J. Anderson.
Anderson, Mary J., February 4, 1812-July 13, 1854.
Anderson, Robert J., August 28, 1842-November 4, 1854; son of Gen. S. R. and Mary J. Anderson.
Anderson, Andrew, 1795-1867.
Anderson, Eliza, January 26, 1807-February 28, 1849.
Anderson, Felix R., 1840-1841.
Anderson, J. M., 1842-1843.
Anderson, Nancy, December 26, 1803-January 25, 1874.
Anderson, Nancy E., died, July 31, 1817.
Anderson, N. S., June 2, 1799-August 22, 1849.
Anderson, Wm. H. N. (infant), died, July 31, 1846.
Anderson, Mary Pamelia (infant), died, October 1, 1836.
Anderson, Alex.
Anderson, son of H. and M. E.
Andrews, A., 1834-September 27, 1841; daughter of John and Eliza Andrews; age, 7 years.
Argo, Percy E., October 16, 1882-August 16, 1883.
Armstrong, Dr. F. W., 1831-1868.
Armstrong, R. H. M., 1819-1846.
Armstrong, Robert, 1801-July 4, 1850.

Armstrong, Mrs. Margaret D.; died, June 29, 1834; age, 56 years.
Armstrong, General Robert, 1791-February 23, 1854; born in Virginia; died in Washington, D. C.
Austin, Pattie Patrick, Bedford City, Va.; age 53 years.
Ashley, Maria Louise, 1808-March 5, 1871.
Aykloyd, Wm. James, November 5, 1832; age, 6 years, 3 months, 8 days.

B

Bailey, C. H., February, 1853-1878.
Bailey, Frederick T., October 11, 1832-August 3, 1898.
Baird, John; died, January 9, 1825.
Baird, John W., 1843-July 24, 1848.
Baird, W. H., 1840-August 28, 1844.
Baker, L. D.; died, March 26, 1866.
Baker, Sarah Ann, 1821-July 18, 1840; wife of L. D. Baker.
Baker, James S.
Baker, James Leonard (infant); only son of L. D. and S. A. Baker; October 12, 1840.
Baker, "Our Willie."
Baker, Emelia, 1846-1847.
Ball, Harrison, March 13, 1821-May 31, 1848.
Ball, G. W., July 11, 1846-September 21, 1848.
Bandy, R. G.
Barbour, George V., 1831-1882.
Bargozie, S.
Barker, Mrs. Alley, 1798-1830, February, 1831.
Barker, Nathaniel, 1815-August 31, 1825; from Massachusetts (age, 25 years, tomb says).
Barner, Sarah L.; born, April 5; died, April 6, 1839.
Barr, George M., July 30, 1837-March 31, 1838.
Barrell, Charles C., 1833-1833.
Barrett, Matthew.
Barrett, three infants.
Barrow, Willie, July 24, 1770-June 7, 1825.
Barrow, Ann H., July 27, 1789-August 6, 1831.
Barry, Mrs. Nancy, died, January 3, 1856; wife of W. L. Barry.
Bass, Fannie.
Bass, Mary Ann, June 22, 1816-October 11, 1832.
Bass, Susan H., 1821-1849.

14

Bible Records—Tombstone Inscriptions

Bass, Queeny, 1833-1851.
Bass, Peter, 1769-May 19, 1829; died in Smithland, Mo.
Bass, Anna Stone, 1779-May 9, 1809; consort Peter Bass.
Bass, William James, May 19, 1809-March, 1828; son of Peter and Anna Stone Bass.
Bass, Malvina Grundy, May 31, 1840-March 4, 1848; daughter of John M. and Malvina Bass.
Basson, Sophie, 1806-1864.
Bateman, Mary, 1782-1858.
Bateman, Johann, 1818-1847.
Bateman, B. S.
Bateman, Addie, March 2, 1855-December 25, 1857.
Bateman, David R.
Bateman, Emmett A., August 19, 1848-August 30, 1864; son of J. L. and L. A. Bateman.
Bateman, Malinda, June 24, 1817.
Bateman, Idia, no dates.
Bateman, Mrs. E., 1822-1845.
Bates, Ann J.
Bates, Robert F., 1815-1822.
Bates, Mary J, 1835-1910.
Bates, Thomas L., 1891-1903.
Bauer, Lillie E., 1877-1881.
Bauman, Henry S., January 23, 1814-September 15, 1846; born in Lancaster County, Pa.; son of Peter and Mary B. of Cincinnati.
Baxter, Rebecca B., 1796-1840.
Baxter, Robert, 1785-1850.
Beach, James W., 1840-1840.
Bear, Nancy, 1806-1855.
Beasley, J. P., 1880-1882.
Beck, George, died, August 29, 1845; age, 43 years.
Becker, Katey, October, 1868-August 15, 1870.
Beckwith, Ann W., 1788-March 31, 1818.
Bedford, Wm. W., January 6, 1789-July 13, 1869; born in Mecklenburg County, Va.
Bedford, Ann M., April 7, 1835-December 6, 1843.
Bedford, Lucinda, 1802-1893.
Bedford, W. H. H., September 15, 1840-June 23, 1862.
Bedford, Wm. H., 1789-1869.
Beguin, Dolly R.
Beguin, J. Frederick, died, 1859.
Belcher, Mary F., 1846-1847.

Belfield, Susannah, October 2, 1814-March 10, 1841.
Bell, Ernest, born, 1878.
Bell, Eugene, 1872-1773.
Bell, Myrtle Louise, July 23, 1900-July 16, 1902.
Bell, M. J.
Bell, John, November 18, 1808-June 21, 1851.
Bell, Mrs. Mary M. W., 1837-1873.
Bellsnyder, James Johnston, June 20, 1847-June 11, 1849.
Bellsnyder, Polly M. Hutchinson; wife of Thomas; daughter of Chris. and Sally Hutchinson Brooks, Burkville, N. Y.; February 19, 1809-June 17, 1854.
Bellsnyder, Samuel D. Lanby, November 13, 1839-August, 1859.
Bender, Frederick, September, 1822-August, 1865; born in Germany.
Bengiff, Sarah.
Bennett, Samuel, 1826-August 9, 1852.
Benoit, E., 1776-1831.
Benson, Isaac C., 1787-March 7, 1854.
Benson, Ned, 1818-October, 1838;
Bentley, Samuel, died, June 7, 1835.
Benton, Lizzie, 1783-1843.
Berryhill, Mary Craig, December 28, 1789-March 20, 1857.
Berryhill, Wm. McLean, 1785-1836; died, October 13; age, 51 years, 11 months, 24 days.
Bertrand, Henry W., 1849-1850.
Beth, Elizer.
Biggs, John A., December 23, 1856-October 2, 1889; date on monument, 1886.
Biggs, Sarah A.
Bigley, Amelia, 1804-1843.
Biglow, Dr. Luther, January 13, 1794-October 6, 1832; born in New Ispwich, N. H.
Bipe, James, 1806-1856.
Birchett, Luvinia.
Black, Ferrebe, 1806-January 17, 1845; age, 39 years, 9 months, 24 days.
Black, P. A., 1828-November 19, 1844; age, 16 years, 10 months, 12 days.
Blackmore, Andrew G., March 16, 1817-July 13, 1849.
Bland, Henrietta C. Hughes, March 3, 1836-January 23, 1863.
Bland, Jackie, March 29, 1856-July 30, 1857; daughter of Jos. H. and H. Bland.
Bledsoe, James, 1833-July 17, 1839.
Bledsoe, James M., 1802-April 4, 1839.

15

Bible Records—Tombstone Inscriptions

Bledsoe, Lydia M., 1844-March 25, 1854.
Bledsoe, Robert, August 7, 1857-April 12, 1867.
Bloodworth, Amelia E., February 22, 1833-June 3, 1835; daughter of Alfred and Mary B.
Boardman, Wm. Z., 1806-1855.
Bobbett, Wm. L., March 9, 1810-January 25, 1837; born in Mississippi.
Bohney, Clara Gerth, October 19, 1843-September 23, 1866; wife of G. H. Bohney.
Bolton, Alice, October 2, 1855-January 14, 1856.
Bolton, Georgie, January 12, 1867-August 28, 1867; daughter of G. and M. Bolton.
Bolton, George W., March 20, 1828-August 2, 1883.
Bolton, Jeffie, May 16, 1868-August 23, 1869.
Bolton, Julia, August 15, 1858-July 19, 1859; daughter of G. and M. Bolton.
Bolton, Martha, May 6, 1862-August, 1862; daughter of G. and M. Bolton.
Bon, N. H., 1799-September 28, 1862; age, 63 years; born in Verlon, Belgium.
Bosher, Charles, died, November 16, 1831.
Bosley, John B., December 27, 1839-August 20, 1841.
Bosley, Mary Jane, 1841-1847.
Bosley, Samuel B., 1838-February, 1847.
Bosley, Samuel B., 1849-1850.
Bostick, D. F., died, 1835; age, 18 years.
Bostick, M. R., 1804-1897.
Bosworth, A. J., April 22, 1855-March 10, 1857.
Bosworth, H. and E.
Bosworth, P., 1784-1860.
Bowdis, Marion, 1861-1863.
Brown, Percy, March 5, 1843-June 12, 1853.
Brown, Mary W. P., 1822-1849.
Brown, J. R., 1823-1853.
Brown, Nettie S.
Brown, Annie E.
Brown, Wm. D.
Brown, S., 1844-1909.
Brown, Susannah, 1774-October 5, 1841; age, 67 years.
Brown, Sally, October 13, 1774-August 23, 1843; wife of Henry Brown.
Brooks, Christopher, August 8, 1775-June 20, 1854.
Brooks, Christeann, March 14, 1845-November 25, 1857.
Brooks, Melyina Rebecca, 1848-June 15, 1849.
Brooks, Malissa, July 15, 1816-May 9, 1837; consort of M. D.
F. H. Brooks; daughter of Robert and Elizabeth McGowan.
Brooks, "My Boy."
Browne, Julia May Wheat, February 5, 1820-June 15, 1843; wife of J. Steen Browne of Virginia.
Bruce, Emily A., 1856 (infant).
Bruce, Henry C., 1836-1859.
Bruhold, Peter, 1856-1857.
Bryan, Jessee Avritt, December 2, 1815-July 19, 1843.
Bryan, T. J., died, 1860.
Bryant, Jonny, 1868-1869.
Bryant, Mrs. Mary Macon.
Buck, Mary W., 1792-1854.
Buckner, Wm. L.
Buddeke, Auguste M. F., December 1, 1841-August 20, 1843.
Buddeke, Charles B., 1846-1847.
"Buddie, Our."
Buist, Ellen Douglas, October 22, 1873-June 13, 1874.
Burgess (infant), died, August 29, 1834; son of Daniel and Elizabeth.
Burlington, John B., 1804-1861.
Burnett, C.
Bowen, Prof. George Thomas, March 19, 1803-October 25, 1828; born in Providence, R. I.
Bowling, M. J., 1843-1843.
Boyd, John, May 2, 1764-December 4, 1847.
Boyd, Martha B., November 3, 1798-February 8, 1856; age, 58 years.
Boyd, Mary Jane, February 6, 1823-November 13, 1855; daughter of M. and J. Buck.
Boyd, Joseph B., July 10, 1818-August 17, 1835; born in Bedford County.
Bradford, John W., 1824-May 3, 1860.
Bradfute, Burwell Mortimer, August, 1832-June, 1833.
Bradfute, Lucy A., April 1, 1794-April, 1826; consort of Robert; daughter of Wm. and Elizabeth Vasser.
Bradford, "My Little Jennie."
Bradshaw, Wm. A., 1818-1842.
Bradshaw, Elizabeth.
Brady, Angeline, 1827-1853.
Brandon, George, 1827-1859.
Brandon, Richard.

Bible Records—Tombstone Inscriptions

Brandon, Thomas.
Brazier, M.
Bransford, A., 1803-1845.
Breathitt, Edward, March 2, 1790-January 30, 1837.
Breathitt, Mary P., April 15, 1790; died, in Memphis, February 5, 1817; born in North Carolina.
Britt, Martha, 1809-June 2, 1865.
Bridges, Elizabeth L. Robenson, 1804-1855; wife of H. Bridges.
Brown, Alex C., 1820-1839; Philadelphia, Pa.
Brown, B. F.
Brown, Charlotte T., April 18, 1813-June 12, 1853; wife of James Thomas Brown.
Brown, George B., April 3, 1822-January 4, 1865.
Brown, Jane W. W., August 10, 1828-October 26, 1882; wife of George B. Brown; daughter of Robert F. Williams.
Brown, Sammy (infant).
Brown, James Percy, April 9, 1812-April 2, 1844.
Brown, Mat., January 9, 1787-1847.
Brown, Mrs. A., 1833-1849.
Burnett, Arietta.
Burns, V. A., 1862-1863.
Burke, R. W. (infant).
Burrroughs, Theodore, July 7, 1850-September 27, 1850.
Burton, Margaret Adalaid, daughter of George H. and Elizabeth Burton; born, January 18, 1836; died, May 22, 1849.
Burton, Charles P., December 15, 1826-November 25, 1856; removed.
Burton, Fannie Martin, July 10, 1864-July 15, 1865.
Burton, Fannie A. McGaughey, February 18, 1838-July 21, 1864.
Burton, George H., 1803-July 28, 1846.
Burton, Georgietta E., August 7, 1842-June 10, 1865.
Burton, Jos. G., April 7, 1840-October 28, 1857.
Burton, Lydie Elizabeth, died, August 3, 1835 (infant); daughter of George H. and Elizabeth Burton.
Burton, Mary A., April 1, 1831-May 3, 1858; wife of W. F. Jones.
Burton, Nancy Octavia C., 1841-1857; dates on monument, December 14, 1844-December 26, 1860.
Burton, Ann, 1766-1843.
Burton, Samuel C., 1805-1842.
Burton, 1847-1848.
Butler, Susan, 1834-1864; daughter of J. and C. Correy.
Byram, Charlie, July 29, 1868-May 18, 1872; son of C. W. and M. O. Byram.
Byram, Fannie Jackson, February 26, 1862-July 14, 1864; daughter of C. W. and M. O. Byram.
Byram, Jesse Hugh L., April 26, 1858-January 27, 1863; son of C. W. and M. O. Byram.
Byrd, James; died, 1861.
Bust, Peter.
Bust, Mrs.

C

Cabler, Ammon D., April 20, 1845-August 25, 1870; son of C. G. and S. E. Cabler.
Cabler, Christiana.
Cabler, Emily.
Cabler, Mattie C.
Cabler, Thomas W.
Cabler, Wm. W.
Cahal, Ann C., wife of Terry H.; died, July 2, 1855; age, 40 years.
Cahal, Elizabeth, mother of T. H. Cahal; February 27, 1858; age, 80 years.
Cahal, James S.
Cahal, Terry H., of Virginia, September 4, 1802-April 15, 1854.
Cain, Mary Sophia, 1836-May 9, 1886; wife of Robert B.; daughter of Dr. Wm. P. Lawrence.
Cain, Paul J., 1847-1861.
Cain, Oscar M., 1845-1859.
Calcote, Mary B., September, 1843-July 11, 1850.
Callender, Mary Catherine, April 13, 1836-October 15, 1837.
Callender, Mary, wife of Thomas; no dates.
Callender, Sarah J., daughter of Thos. and Mary C.; wife of James W. Owen, 183..-1859.
Callender, Thomas, 1796; moved to Nashville, 1819; died, June 11, 1851.
Campbell, S. E.; died, January 29, 1838; age, 25 years; born in Fayetteville, N. C.
Campbell, Thomas, 1785-January 21, 1828.
Campbell, Caroline.
Campbell, James; died, January 19, 1847; age, 38 years.
Campbell, James A.; died, November 19, 1850; age, 12 years, 5 months.

17

Bible Records—Tombstone Inscriptions

Campbell, James.
Campbell, Fanny, 1845-1864.
Campbell, Wm. W., —— 1864.
Campbell, Granville O.
Campbell, Martha E., 1820-1850.
Campbell, George Washington, 1742-1848; son of Dr. Archibald Campbell and Elizabeth Mackay.
Campbell, Harriet, 1789-1849.
Campbell (infant), 1822; age, 5 months; G. W. and H. Campbell; infant grandson of George McGehee.
Campbell, Ann, November 28, 1778-June, 1825.
Campbell, A. W., 1848-1850.
Campbell, Robert R., 1846-1850.
Cameron, Robert Daniel, August 11, 1827-June 10, 1839; son of Daniel and Sarah Cameron.
Cameron, Amelia A., 1885-1898.
Cameron, Grace Bruce, 1805-June 24, 1883.
Cannon, Mrs. F., 1786-1823.
Cannon, J. R., 1819-1820.
Cannon, T. V., August 4, 1800-February 11, 1849; born in Mecklenburg County, Va.
Cannon, Mary M., January 11, 1804-March 22, 1849.
Cantrel, Jane, July 21, 1771-1840.
Capington, Lorissa, 1799-1832.
Card, Milton E.
Capps, Caleb, September 22, 1808-August 22, 1864.
Carns, Emma M.; age, 2 years.
Carroway, C. C. P., 1793-1816.
Carpenter, B., 1813-1839.
Carroll, Annie Florence, November 6, 1856-July 9, 1858.
Carroll, John J., July 13, 1850-December 24, 1896.
Carroll, Mary Cooley, March 27, 1852-June 16, 1853; daughter of Hugh and Elizabeth Carroll.
Carroll, Elizabeth E., December 25, 1826-October 16, 1899; daughter of John and Martha Cotton; wife of Hugh Carroll.
Carroll, Hugh, 1814-1845.
Carroll, Gov. Wm., 1788-1844.
Carroll, Charles Simms, April 7, 1874-January 29, 1877.
Carroll, Maud Evylina, July 3, 1876-June 23, 1877.
Carroll, Robert Henry Lee, September 28, 1863-October 11, 1879.
Carroll, Teresa A., 1825-1827.
Carroll, E. J., 1845-1852.
Carson, Martha Ann.
Carroll, Hugh, September 19, 1819-February 23, 1895.
Carson, N. D., 1808-1849.
Carlisle, Burlington, 1833-1873.
Casper, S., 1778-1852.
Caster, M. A.
Cartmell, Sarah; died, September 26, 1854; age, 51 years; wife of H. B. Cartmell.
Caseday, Araminter F., 1806-July 23, 1829.
Castleman, Annie W., January 8, 1825-March 19, 1854; wife of R. B. Castleman and daughter of James and Elizabeth Woods.
Castleman, Maggie, May 1, 1852-April 28, 1856.
Castleman, Robert Bell, 1809-July 29, 1886.
Castleman, Anthony Wilkinson; died, July 10, 1846; age, 49 years.
Carter, Phillis, 1780-1840.
Catron, Minerva, 1846-1847.
Cauvin, Fanny, March 31, 1862-June 29, 1876; daughter of Secondo and Catherine Cauvin.
Cauvin, Lewis Felix, December 14, 1879-October, 1881; son of Horace and Sarah Cauvin.
Cavender, John, 1867-1869.
Chaemer, James H., October 27, 1858-September 30, 1866; son of C. and Rebecca Chaemer.
Chapman, J. M. N.
Chapman, Ophelia.
Chapman, Sallie P., March 6, 1822-February 19, 1846.
Chapman, S., 1757-September 25, 1826; age, 70 years.
Chapman, J. McN., 1835-July 16, 1836; age, 9 months.
Cheek, Beverly H., 1819-1863.
Chemault, Augusta, 1861-1866.
Chemault, Margaret C., 1859-1866.
Childress, Monroe, 1819-May 16, 1836; son of Dilson Childress.
Childress, Sarah, September 27, 1836-July 28, 1837; daughter of Elisha and Mimey Childress.
Christian, Elizabeth A.
Churchill, Henry; died July 26, 1867; age, 38 years, 9 months.
Claiborne, Anastasia L.; died, July 17, 1812; age, 27 years.

Bible Records—Tombstone Inscriptions

Claiborne, Charlotte, 1821-1848; date on monument, July 17, 1818; age, 27.
Clark, George Hatch; died, September 27, 1833; age, 2 years, 29 days.
Clark, James, 1793-May 21, 1832.
Clark, Smith C. (vault), September 12, 1833-February 8, 1863; born in Ithica, N. Y.
Clay, Woodson, October 14, 1797-August 17, 1824; born in Lunenburg County, Va.
Clayton, W. D.
Clements, Jesse B., February 4, 1799-June 18, 1877.
Clements, B. N., June 1, 1824-September 4, 1865.
Clements, Lucinda, August 2, 1802-July 23, 1857; wife of Jesse B.
Clements, Sarah, March 15, 1781-August 4, 1849; wife of Benj. Clements.
Click, Reuben, 1819-1851.
Clinard, Mary, 1755-1850.
Clinton, 1803-1848.
Cloud, Mariah, August 21, 1839-June 15, 1849; daughter of Daniel G. and Harriet Cloud.
Cobb, Orville L., 1901-1902.
Cockerill, James, April 22, 1815-April 12, 1853; son of Nathaniel and Catharine Cockerill.
Cockerill, Nathaniel, March 9, 1812-June 28, 1860; son of John and Louisa Cockerill.
Cockerill, Sarah; died, February, 1853; age, 42 years; wife of James Cockerill.
Cockerill, W. N., 1818-December 21, 1837; age, 21 years, 1 month, 2 days.
Cockrill, Martha, June 18, 1817-May 23, 1864; wife of Milton; born in Kentucky.
Cockerill, Milton Boone (infant), January 23, 1891.
Cockerill, Cornelia, February 20, 1859-January 30, 1860; daughter of B. F. and Sarah E. Cockerill.
Cockerill, Dicie; died, 1866.
Cockrane, Wm., 1803-June 13, 1830; drowned; age, 27; born in Ireland.
Cockson, Isaac Will, January 29, 1798-August 8, 1849.
Coffman, Susan E.
Cogswell, Nathaniel W., 1827-1846.
Cole, Mary Catherine, June 22, 1846-June 25, 1847.
Cole, Samuel R. A., February 3, 1825-April 29, 1847.

Cole, Sarah Ann, January 21, 1852-February 1, 1853.
Cole, Willis W., January 28, 1817-December 19, 1847.
Cole, Clarence E.
Cole, C. Clara, February 3, 1807-April 30, 1883.
Coleman, Ellen D.
Coleman (infant).
Coleman, Joseph H.
Coleman, Nannie.
Coleman, Thomas G.
Coleman, Annie G.
Coleman, Edmund; five infant children of R. D. and M. J. Coleman; one marble slab.
Coleman, Medora, infant child of R. D. and M. J. Coleman.
Coleman, Matthew, infant child of R. D. and M. J. Coleman.
Coleman, Thomas, infant child of R. D. and M. J. Coleman.
Coleman, Corinna, infant child of R, D. and M. J. Coleman.
Coleman, Dr. Anthony, 1793-January 25, 1816.
Colladay, Jacob W.
Collier, J. McDaniel, April 17, 1832-April 20, 1854.
Collinge, George Washington, December 11, 1835-March 17, 1853.
Collins, Lydia, 1791-December 26, 1849.
Coltart, Margaret, April, 1824-August, 1853; consort of John Coltart; daughter of Abraham and Sarah McIntyre.
Colvert, Ada, 1859-1861.
Colvert, Bettie M., March 6, 1854-March 14, 1859; daughter of J. L. and Johanne E. Colvert.
Colvert, Wm. I., August 10, 1792-September 21, 1859.
Colwell, Oliver, 1810-May 30, 1829; drowned.
Condon, Catherine A., 1817-1855.
Condon, James W., August 23, 1815-July 27, 1852; born in New York.
Connelley, J. B., 1859-1860.
Connor, Cornelia, November 3, 1831-July 22, 1836; child of C. and M. A. Connor.
Connor, John M.; died, May 12, 1811; age, 12 months; child of C. and M. A. Connor.
Cooke, Margaret; died, 1893.

Bible Records—Tombstone Inscriptions

Cooney, Darby, 1812-May 2, 1834; born in Enniscorthy County, Wexford, Ireland.
Cooper, Edmund, 1760-January 5, 1822.
Cooper, J., 1840-1843.
Copeland, Henry, February 13, 1869-July 20, 1871.
Copeland, Mary Alice, September 7, 1874-August 24, 1876.
Copeland, Sarah J., November 10, 1878-August, 1879.
Copeland, Walter, August 19, 1872-September, 1873.
Corbitt, Caroline, 1826-1903.
Corbitt, Samuel, 1823-1885.
Corbitt, Eliza J.
Corbitt, Felix M.
Corbitt, Lucinda F., June 3, 1813-May 7, 1878.
Corbitt, W. A., March 6, 1818-March 28.
Corbitt, J. H., 1834-November 3, 1836.
Correy, James, March 1, 1795-August 1, 1863; born in Philadelphia; died in Memphis.
Correy, Mrs. Caroline; died, November 3, 1854; age, 52 years.
Cotton, Eugene C.
Cotton, Cynthia J., August 27, 1825-May 25, 1850.
Cotton, James R., July 31, 1830-June 26, 1849.
Cotton, Martha, 1777-1849.
Cotton, Sally, January 9, 1820-December 9, 1890.
Cotton, William R., August 21, 1827-July, 1843.
Cowan, Ada L., February 22, 1865-September 15, 1885.
Cowan, A. L.
Cowan, Shelly R., February 8, 1865-August 9, 1893.
Cowan, Gracie May, January 31, 1867-March 26, 1881.
Cowan, John R., August 7, 1830-December 3, 1868.
Conn, George, 1838-1839.
Couch, John Allen, September 29, 1813-October 2, 1870; born in Virginia.
Couch, Maria A, October 25, 1792-January 9, 1864.
Couch, James A., 1843-1843.
Couch, James M., 1837-1838.
Couch, John W., 1844-1847.
Coussens, Nathaniel P., 1844-1845.
Crabb, Henry, October, 1793-November 28, 1827; born in Virginia.

Craddock, Sarrah L., October 20, 1819-July 18, 1850; wife of W. C. Craddock.
Craft, W. H., April 19, 1828-April 6, 1882.
Craighead, Anthony, S. M. C., October 27, 1854-August 21, 1856.
Crandall, Carrie; died, November 14, 1877; daughter of Ira and B. Crandall.
Crawford, Maggie R., January 12, 1862-October 12, 1863.
Crawford, Charles D., April 24, 1807-November 5, 1863.
Crenshaw, Robert E., 1851-1852.
Crockett, David, 1798-September 28, 1828; and infant daughter.
Crockett, Richard, November, 1812-1833; born, Parish Lithrod, County Donegal, Ireland, emigrated to America in 1832; died in New Orleans of yellow fever, 1853.
Cross, Wm. B., 1836-1838; son of Nathaniel and Ann Cross.
Cross. A. H., 1835-1843.
Cronk, Mary M.; died, 1861.
Crosthwait, Lucy A., April 2, 1843-February 26, 1886; wife of J. W. Baker.
Crosthwait, Malinda L., September 12, 1800-November 16, 1883; wife of W. H. Crosthwait.
Crosthwait, Thomas I., February 17, 1880-March 13, 1900.
Crow, Franklin S., 1803-July 9, 1836; age, 33 years, 4 months, 21 days.
Crutcher, Elizabeth J., February 12, 1809-August 22, 1898.
Crutcher, Edmund, 1774-July 2, 1846.
Crutcher, Jane, 1780-February 27, 1845.
Crutcher, Mary Jane, 1810-April 11, 1847; daughter of E. and J. Crutcher.
Crutcher, Thomas, February 18, 1760-March 8, 1844; born in Virginia.
Crutcher, T. H., December 22, 1802-August 10, 1829.
Currey, Elijah, July 8, 1792-November 13, 1864.
Currey, Margaret, 1807-1847.
Currey, A. D., 1811-1813.
Currey, R. H., 1774-1848.
Currey, W. H., 1828-1831.
Cuvney, Milley; died, 1833.

D

Dalton, F.
Dance, Russell; died, October, 1838.
Daniel and Elizabeth.

Bible Records—Tombstone Inscriptions

Daniels, John, 1824-1853.
Dashazer, J. J.
Dashazer, M. W., 1837-1850.
Dashiel, Eleanor Virginia, 1831-August 28, 1842; daughter of Daniel and Jane Dashiel.
David (infant).
Davidson, Lauretta H., 1822-1829.
Davis, Helen, 1795-1817.
Davis, J.
Davis, Jane, 1830-1858.
Davis, K. J.
Davis, Richard S., 1811-December 7, 1854.
Davis, Samuel.
Davis, Tennessee R., 1808-1857.
Deadrick, A. L. B.; born, 1816.
Deberry, Joseph, 1823-September 22, 1844.
DeGrove, Emelia W., December 15, 1810-November 12, 1859.
DeGrove, Julia Emma Hunt, January 24, 1834-July 23, 1854; wife of Quincy C. DeGrove (second).
DeGrove, "Our Little Jonny," October 1, 1853-December 6, 1859.
Delworth, Annie; died, 1859.
DeMoville, Andrew J., 1832-1852.
DeMoville, Mary A., born October 9, 1802, ——; in Hanover County, Va.; died, June, 1855.
DeMoville, Peter, born February 22, 1796, in Charles City County, Va.; died June, 1855.
Derrick, Mary Ann, 1825-November 9, 1855; wife of Henry B.
Devinney, E. Roseline, 1843-April 21, 1844; daughter of H. F. and M. I. Devinney.
Devinney, J. M., April 13, 1791-1815.
Dickinson, Catherine R. T., 1796-1848.
Dickinson, Mrs. Belinda G. P., 1816-1844.
Dickinson, Henry, 1813-1845.
Dickinson, John, 1781-1815.
Dickinson, M.
Dickson, Michael, 1777-1859.
Dickson, N. W., 1825-January 1, 1851.
Dickson, Thomas, 1796-August 23, 1833; age, 27 years; from Kentucky.
Diffee, Lucy, March 9, 1814-June 6, 1833; consort of Wm. Diffee.
Diffee, Robert, December 19, 1831-May 31, 1833.
Diggons, Albert Ward, 1854-July 3, 1855.
Diggons, Henry; died, 1834.
Diggins, Lilla, 1835-1836.
Diggons, James Arthur, 1825-May, 1855.
Diggons, William M., 1816-September 7, 1824.
Diggons, William H., 1830-November 18, 1832.
Dillon, N.
Dittmer, Jacob, 1805-1848.
Dix, Mrs. Frances, February 21, 1810-June 25, 1881.
Dix, William.
Dobson, Albert.
Dobson, Effie.
Dobson, J. N.
Dobson, Jennie.
Doke, James, October 12, 1816-August 11, 1853.
Dorris, Samuel T., November 20, 1787-October 16, 1875.
Dorris, Susannah, April 23, 1791-August 24, 1870.
Dorris, Samuella.
Dorris, Elizabeth.
Dorris, Elizabeth M., 1743-1811; wife of John Irvin.
Dorris, John I., October 22, 1773-August 1, 1822.
Dorris, John J., 1830-1848.
Dorris, John L., April 17, 1830-June 26, 1848.
Dorris, Joseph, March 24, 1837-1838; son of W. D. and Rebecca Dorris.
Dorris, Rebecca, May 1, 1835-July 10, 1850.
Dorris, Rebecca Shivers, January 9, 1710-1881.
Dorris, William D., August 23, 1802-January 30, 1892.
Dorris, William M., October 14, 1833-November 25, 1847.
Dougal, John B., Feb. 9, 1827-August 9, 1837; son Joseph and Nancy.
Dougle, Amelia A.
Doughty, Bushrod, 1814-1854.
Doughty, George, 1782-1846.
Doughty, Helen Foley, 1782-1832; wife of George Doughty.
Doughty, Townsend, 1816-1875.
Doughty, Jos. A., 1811-1850.
Doughty, William B. F., 1823-1850.
Douglas, Porter, 1805-1859.
Douglass, Mrs. Jemima, August 20, 1780-December 3, 1844; consort of late Wm. Douglas of Kentucky.
Douglass, Tabitha L., April 22, 1805-April 17, 1856; daughter of Wm. and

Bible Records—Tombstone Inscriptions

Jemima Douglass.
Dowd, S. C.; age, 26 years.
Downs, Catherine, 1798-1865.
Dowyers, William Thomas, 1848-1848.
Drain, John A., 1855.
Driver, Eban R., September 7, 1836-September 7, 1882.
Driver, Ed. M. R.
Driver, William, March 17, 1803-March 3, 1886; born in Salem, Mass.
Duckworth, Amanda A.; died, 1860.
Duff, Joseph.
Duncan, Anna.
Dunton, William, 1791-1830.
Duval, Lucy J., August 15, 1825-September 5, 1841.
Dyas, H. J. (infant).
Dyas, John Gordon, September 7, 1845-March 24, 1862.
Dyas, Sarah Bell, 1820-1850.
Dyer, H., 1831-1834.
Dyer, John Decker, 1829-July 29, 1930; son of Isham and Harriet Dyer.

E

Eakin, Rebecca.
Earborhart, Ella, 1862-1863.
Earborhart, Kate, 1858-1859.
Earborhart, Molly, 1851-1856.
East, Lillie P., January 11, 1856-June 8, 1887.
East, Addison, April 28, 1786-December, 1833.
East, H.; died, 1830.
Eastham, William, 1812-1831.
Edmondson, James, 1763-1851.
Edmondson, Elizabeth, 1767-1849.
Edmondson, Thomas, 1789-1851.
Edmundson, Ellen Kirkman; died, August 19, 1895.
Edmundson, John K., September 19, 1809-October 28, 1876; F. L. T.
Edmundson, Matilda G., December 16, 1819-March 27, 1876; wife of J. K. Edmundson.
Egan, Charlotte Emily, 1844-1851; daughter of Thomas and Harriet Egan.
Eggleston. E. M., 1834.
Elliott, Willie and Annie, 1818-1869.
Elliot, Thomas; died, September 25, 1869.
Elliot, Alice.
Elliot, Arthur M., 1851-1894.
Elliot, Collins D., December 20, 1810-July 28, 1899.
Elliot, Elizabeth, 1818-1877.
Elliot, Susan R., 1844-1885.
Ellis, George M., 1863-1864.

Ellis, Mary A.
Ellison, James M., May 7, 1844-April 6, 1880; born in Pulaski, Ky.
Ellison, Katie, dates illegible.
Elmore, Elizabeth, ——, 1831.
Elsworth, Elmer E., January 31, 1861-February 13, 1862.
Embric, Mrs. Augusta, 1836-1857.
Emmerson, Sarah Jane, November 2, 1830-July 22, 1863.
Emmie, D. M.
Ensley, Elizabeth, 1761-1829.
Ensley, Thomas J., February 28, 1831-July 4, 1850.
Erskine, Thomas W., 1805-May 20, 1849; born in County Antrim, Ireland.
Estell, J. P.
Esters, H., 1774-1839.
Esters, Martha, 1779-1847.
Evans, Ann W.; daughter of E. and Mary Evans of Frankfort, Ky.; age, 15.
Evans, William C.
Everett, James, November 29, 1823-March 29, 1893.
Everett, Thomas, April 6, 1835-February 1, 1851.
Everett, Mary, July 11, 1833-December 6, 1850.
Everett, Walter N., 1873-1878.
Eves, Jeff Davis, December 12, 1861-December 1, 1864.
Eves, John Silas, March 5, 1855-October 3, 1884.
Eves, Silas, 1825-1853.
Evins, Eliza, January 8, 1819-January 22, 1846; wife of John Evins; daughter of James and Lucy Warren.
Evins, R. R. M.
Ewell, Luzinka C., 1820-1872.
Ewing, Martha Vaulx, August 3, 1805-July 1, 1880.
Ewing, John L., October 18, 1833; son of Randall M. and Martha N. Ewing.
Ewing, Sarah, 1848-1863.
Ewing, Andrew, June 15, 1815-June 17, 1864.
Ewing, A. W.
Ewing, Margaret.
Ewing, Milbrey H., 1815-September 27, 1864; wife of Orville.
Ewing, Our Margaret, 1819-1841.
Ewing, Orville, February 6, 1806-October 10, 1876.
Ewing, Rebecca P., 1817-1844.
Ewing, Rowena J., 1820-1903.
Ewing, Thomas.

Bible Records—Tombstone Inscriptions

Ewin, Susan H., December 28, 1822-May 22, 1849; wife of John H. Ewin.
Ewin, William H., 1824-1867.
Ewing, Charlie, October 24, 1858-September 29, 1866.

F

Fachtzehner, 1801-1866.
Fall, Ellen.
Fall, M. E.
Falpz, Catherine, 1820-1847.
Farquharson, Eliza, 1791-May 7, 1864; wife of Robert; born in Kentucky; age, about 73.
Farquharson, Robert, 1776-June 23, 1856; born in Banff, Scotland.
Farrar, Marvine E., 1868-August 27, 1889; wife of L. H. Farrar; age, 21 years, 6 months, 18 days.
Farrell, Ernest Rossier, January 10, 1847-1870.
Farrell, John, October 12, 1809-February 9, 1854 or 59; born in County Down, Ireland; died in Edinburg, Scotland.
Farrell, Norman, 1st son; died, 1830.
Farrell, Norman, 2nd son, 1840-1842.
Farriss, Charles, January 10, 1848-October 15, 1849; son of Charles and Amanda Farriss.
Felts, Capt. J. W., 1811-1878.
Ferguson, John G., 1821-July 11, 1859; son of James B. and Eliza Ferguson.
Ferriss, Mary Alice, 1844-1855; daughter of Josiah and Mary Ferriss.
Fields, Susan Jennett, April 3, 1844-April 12, 1846.
Fisher, R. F., 1828-1829.
Fisher, Thomas B.
Fite, Amanda F., 1819-January 30, 1849.
Fite, Virginia G. L. Randall, September 23, 1826-July 6, 1853.
Fleming, Ebenezer, 1846-1849.
Fleming, John McKnight, 1842-1849.
Fleming, Thomas S., 1816-1849.
Fletcher, Amanda M., 1828-June 13, 1880; wife of G. Fletcher.
Fletcher, Mrs. Harriet; died, 1864.
Fletcher, Robert H.; died, 1864.
Fletcher, William R., May 22, 1854-March 7, 1901.
Fluker, Sarah, and infant Sarah, 1835-1885.
Flenz, Jacob, July, 1811-June 19, 1850.
Fly, Nancy M., October 1804-February 12, 1825; consort of Micajah Fly.

Fogg, Elizabeth, 1799-March 19, 1832.
Fogg, Frances B.
Fogg, Henry M. R.
Fogg, Mary M., 1801-1872.
Fogg, Septima M.
Fogg, James, 1837-1849.
Forbes, B. S., 1803-1836.
Ford, Dr. John Pryor, June 7, 1810-August 17, 1865; born in Cumberland County, Va.
Ford, James, 1843-1862.
Forest, James, no dates.
Forest, Martha M., no dates.
Foster, M. P., 1836-1837.
Foster, S. W., 1814-1839.
Foster, Charles V., 1812-1832.
Foster, Anthony, 1765-1825; 60 years old in April.
Foster, Eleanor, 1778-1825; 48 years old on June 11.
Foster, Ann H., 1830-1850.
Foster, Ann S., 1770-1850.
Foster, Ephraim H., September 12, 1794-September 6, 1854.
Foster, E. H. (infant), July 29, 1849; first child; age, 7 weeks.
Foster, Jane M., 1792-November 12, 1847; age, 55; wife of Ephraim Foster.
Foster, James H., October 1, 1798-October 26, 1876.
Foster, Narcissa H., January 28, 1805-December 17, 1845; wife of James H. Foster.
Foster, Robert Coleman, 1768-1844.
Foster, Robert S., 1828-1847.
Foster, Susan Cheatham, August 26, 1822-August 16, 1853.
Foster, William Lytle, July 14, 1820-March 5, 1889.
Foster, Susan; wife of W. E. Foster.
Foster, Ellen, 1871-1872.
Foster, Fanny, February 21, 1870-1870; children of Andrew and M. Foster.
Forsyth, G. R., 1816-1844.
Foy, Frederick, August 19, 1839-December 21, 1858.
Fraley, J. W., July 12, 1843-June 26, 1847.
Fraley, M. C., July 22, 1845-June 24, 1846.
Fraley, Mrs. A. M., April 18, 1818-February 25, 1862; wife of J. M. Fraley.
"Frank, Little."
Franklin, E. A., 1839-1840.
Franklin, J. W., 1777-1858.

Bible Records—Tombstone Inscriptions

Frasch, Charles, March, 1863-February 2, 1866.
Frasch, John, August 29, 1833-February 17, 1861.
Frasch, Thomas, April 26, 1864-September 4, 1865.
Frazer, Robert E., 1850-1865.
Freeman, Tommy, 1845-1849.
"Our Eugene."
"Our Carrie."
Frensley, Lorena.
Frick, J. B.
Frindsley, Elizabeth, October 25, 1831-November 25, 1872; wife of C. W. Frindsley.
Frindsley, G. W., March 18, 1820-December 23, 1894.
Fry, Trimon, ——, 1843.
Fuller, Olive L., 1838-January 4, 1866; wife of Geo. W. Fuller, Indiana.
Fuller, Wm. H., 1829-April 19, 1864; born in New York.
Furguson, J. W., November 7, 1825-April 23, 1860.
Furguson, Rebecca, 1820-1867.
Furtwangle, E., 1814-1835.

G

Gaines, Wm., ——, 1864.
Gaines, J. E. (infant), 1865.
Gale, Annie M. G. (R).
Gale, Anna, date illegible.
Gale, Thomas, March 31, 1852, ——.
Gale, Eliza G. (R.).
Gale, Mary K. (R), (Mary K. Knox), 1829-1861?
Gallaghan, R. P. Miles, 1840-1866.
Gallaghan, Maria, 1804-1845.
Gallaghan, Philip, 1790-1850.
Gallaher, Wm. J., April 23, 1828 or 3-February 17, 1846.
Gally, Jos. G.
Garrett, Morgan, 1885-1886.
Garrett, Betsy C., 1777-July 16, 1850; wife of Rev. Wm. Garrett.
Garrett, Elizabeth C. Z., December 20, 1821-1846.
Garrett, Rev. Wm., December 10, 1774-November 20, 1853; born in Coosa County, Ala.
Gannaway, M. E.; died, 1849.
Gaither, Mary D. Zollicoffer, October 19, 1849-1871; wife of Nat Gaither.
Garrett, Green M., June 7, 1812-December 24, 1878.
Garrett, Minerva, 1825-1847.
Gash, Basil, 1812-August 21, 1844.

Geiger, Frederick, 1863-July 22, 1864; son of Jacob and Catherine Geiger.
Genie, Little.
Gennett, Andrew, 1809-1858.
Gennett, John (infant), 1850-1852.
Gennett, Vincent, 1841-1844.
Gennett, Josephine L., 1847-1866.
George, Little.
Gibson, Mary.
Gibson, Mary Alice, September 11, 1833-June 23, 1886.
Gibson, Nathan, June 1, 1827- September 9, 1878.
Gibson, Jane, 1815-September 21, 1836; age, 31 years; wife of Robert Gibson.
Gibson, Nathan, 1820-1831.
Gibson, Rosanna, 1800-January 7, 1856; age, 56 years.
Gibson, T. S., 1828-1829.
Gibson, Wm., 1788-May 2, 1828; age, 40 years.
Gilbert, Capt. Thomas; died, January 14, 1862; age, 72 years.
Gilbert, Nancy.
Gilbert, Wm.
Gilbert, M. E. H., 1900-1904.
Gilbert, Idella Cathron; died, 1847; daughter of John V. and Mary Gilbert.
Gilchrist, Frances A.
Gill, James J.
Gilliam, Wm., March 23, 1791-September 27, 1854; born in Dublin, Ireland.
Gilliam, Frances, 1786-1851.
Gilliam, John W.
Gilliam, Wm., 1821-1851.
Gilliam, Jane E., 1802-1837.
Gilliam, Thomas, 1811-1852.
Gillman, Henry C., 1821-1856.
Gillman, Mary Susannah, 1822-1855.
Gillman, Wm. Carroll, 1830-1848.
Glenn, Robert F.; died, July 21, 1829.
Glover, Wm.
Glover, Wm. R., 1850-1852; son of James and Elvira Glover.
Goad, Bell; died, 1889.
Goad, Fannie.
Goad, George; died, 1855.
Goad, Maggie A.; died, 1865.
Goad, Martha; died, 1859.
Godshall, Webb, 1855-1855.
Gooch, Priscilla G., 1822-1851.
Goodloe, Edward A., 1849-1873.
Goodwin (infant).
Goodwin, S. H.
Goodwin, Wm W., 1825-1850.
Goodwin, Alsenia J. B., 1825-1848.

Bible Records—Tombstone Inscriptions

Goodwin, J. V. J., 1817-December 13, 1822.
Gordon, M., 1810-1831.
Gore, Albert P., June 23, 1830-February 26, 1850.
Gore, Geo. W., 1822-1847.
Goss, John D., Sr., 1747-1867.
Goss, Mary A.
Gould, Abagail, December 11, 1793-January 6, 1838.
Gould, Jos. H., October 21, 1813-1845, F. L. T.
Gould, Jas. S., October 6, 1790-August 1, 1866.
Gould, Martha W., June 25, 1804-March 6, 1859.
Gould, A. W., July 12, 1840-June 26, 1863.
Gower, Martha J., April 21, 1837-March 5, 1861; wife of Oliver Gower; daughter of Robert Work.
Gowdey, Napoleon, December 28, 1828-July 6, 1829.
Gowdy, Margaret Victoria, November 16, 1836-October 18, 1838.
Graham, Andrew, 1788-May 15, 1822.
Graham, Eliza, 1839-1855.
Graham, George, 1774-1844.
Graham, George, Jr., 1822-1825.
Granger, Ann, November 13, 1860; age, 34 years.
Grace, Little.
Grant, G., 1823.
Grant, Mary A., 1823-1824.
Gray, Oscar, 1820-1840.
Green, Elizabeth Hetty, 1812-August 28, 1834; age, 22 years.
Green, Jacob; died, 1854.
Green, Judith, 1761-1856.
Green, S. W.; died, 1838.
Green, T., 1837-1854.
Greene, Thomas, June 10, 1810-July 31, 1838.
Green, J. L., 1835-1837.
Green, E. N., 1838-1838.
Green, Rebecca A., 1828-1849.
Green (infant); died, February 19, 1836; son of A. and E. Green.
Green, Mary, 1836-June 11, 183—.
Green, Virginia, January 2, 1833-May 2, 1863; wife of Samuel Green.
Green, Rebecca, March 18—— August 21, 1839; daughter of Abraham and Elizabeth Green.
Greenhalgh, S. A., 1828-1832.
Greenhalgh, W. W., 1821-1822.
Greenfield, Fanny, 1840-1847.
Greenfield, Thomas, 1846-1846.
Greenfield, Wesley, 1844-1845.
Greenwood, L. J.
Greer, John, January 4, 1796-September 25, 1847.
Greers, T.
Griffice, Maria, September 1, 1818-May 28, 1881.
Griffice, Durham; died, October 30, 1848; age, 63 years.
Griffice, Nausey; died, July 27, 1850; age, 58 years.
Griffin, Eliza, 1817-1851.
Griffin, Thomas, 1830-1850.
Griffis, S. A., 1815-1850.
Grizzard, Hulon H., July 9, 1817-September 5, 1818; son of James and Charlotte Grizzard.
Groomes, Cordelia E., 1845-June 1849.
Groomes, Elizabeth, December 23, 1793-July 26, 1860; born in Virginia.
Grosse, Ludw., December 1833-December 6, 1866.
Grubbs, Bessie.
Grubbs, Daniel R.
Grubbs, Wm. H., May 24, 1848; infant son of Cordelia Grubbs.
Grubbs, Malinda J., May 22, 1837-March 14, 1866.
Gussman, M. C., March 27, 1828-March 9, 1842.
Gussman, Godfried H., 1854-1855.
Gussman, P. J., 1828-1869.

H

Hall, Elihu, December 14, 1786-March 5, 1857; born in Cecil County, Md.
Hadley, Isaac, 1810-1858.
Haggart, J. K., 1846-1864.
Hager, Mrs. C., 1755-1861.
Hager, T. J., 1811-1833.
Hager, Henry, 1791-October 7, 1846.
Haile, Evaline, 1842-1859.
Haile, G. M. D., 1844-1870.
Halley, John W., 1824-1857.
Hailey, Adda T., 1853-1854.
Hailey, Ader K.
Hailey, Francis A., 1851-1852.
Hailey, Frances R., 1865-1866.
Hailey, Julia E., 1863-1864.
Hailey, Quintilla T. G., 1823-1824.
Hailey, Wm. H., 1817-1883.
Hailey, Wm. Z., 1817-1849.
Haile, Evaline, March, 1807-April 6, 1863; wife of Thomas J. Haile.

Bible Records—Tombstone Inscriptions

Hale, Peter A., September 9, 1826-May 10, 1855.
Halfer, F. W., 1861-1864.
Halfer, H. M. C., 1863-1864.
Hall, Sophia W., 1790-1816.
Hall, Elihu W., 1813-1815.
Hall, Elihu S., 1786-1857.
Hall, Mary, 1805-1839.
Hall, H. John, September 30, 1765-August 24, 1827.
Hall, Mrs. E., December 5, 1770-March 24, 1836.
Hall, Mary E., 1770-1836.
Hall, J., Jr., 1826-1828.
Hall, Charlie.
Hallum, Elizabeth, 1796-April 10, 1839; consort of Wm. Hallum.
Hamilton, Nancy J., August 15, 1811-September 12, 1858.
Hamilton, Felix V.
Hamilton, Thomas, 1828-August 1, 1855; age, 27 years; born in Strabene, Ireland; died in Memphis.
Hanks, W. B., 1813-1833.
Hare, Mary J. Depp, 1823-August 31, 1859; wife of S. E. Hare.
Harlow, W. H., 1846-September 12, 1866.
Harman, Richard G., 1771-1822.
Harman, Isabella H.; died, January 3, 1845.
Harman, Henry Gibben, June 2, 1853-November, 1856; son of W. J. and M. E. Harman.
Harman, Capt. W. J., February 8, 1826-November 28, 1883.
Harman, Charles C.
Harman, Eliza.
Harman, George E.
Harman, Sarah.
Harmey, Lucy A., 1833-1850.
Harris, A. W., 1844-1846.
Harris, J. W.
Harris, G. W.; died, January 12, 1848; age 59 years; 3 months.
Harris, Lizzie.
Harris, George, February 23, 1827-August 21, 1844; son of R. P. and Lydia Harris.
Harris, M. A. W., 1839-1863.
Harris, Adam G., August 23, 1775-October 10, 1840; born, Leipsic Saxony.
Harris, Elizabeth S.; born, 1834.
Harris, Emma A., November 25, 1841-August 22, 1843.
Harris, Medora F., January 25, 1837-March 9, 1837.
Harris, Wm., June 10, 1808-April 6, 1846.
Harrison, Wm.; age, 55 years.
Harsh, Dr. Philip; age, 73 years.
Harsh, L. A., October 11, 1834-July 4, 1887.
Harsh, Madaline, 1808-1888; wife of Dr. P. Harsh.
Hartshorn, Robert H.
Haslam, Sallie M., November 18, 1862-August 22, 1864.
Haslam, Sarah Ann; died, June 21, 1848; daughter of H. and Ann Ebaugh.
Haslam, Willie W., 1874-1874.
Haslam, C.
Hatham, J. W. (infant).
Hawkins, George K. (C), 1806-1863.
Hawkins, Mary Ann R., 1843-1845.
Hawkins, Virginia, 1847-1865.
Hawkins, Mary E.; died, March 29, 1828; age, 4 years; daughter of A. B. and J. H. Hawkins.
Hawkins, Abner B.; died, August 8, 1828; age, 33 years.
Hawkins, S., 1839-1840.
Hay, John De La, 1789-1857.
Hay, Catherine, 1801-1886.
Hay, John G., February 21, 1809-1837; monument, June 25, 1835.
Hay, George, December 17, 1833-July 11, 1846; son of Preston and Sarah Hay.
Hay, Preston, 1807-1849.
Hayes, Malinda.
Hayes, N. C., 1798-1828.
Hayes, R. P., 1828-1829.
Haynie, Adilade, 1854 ——.
Haynie, Calista S., 1850-1852.
Hard, J. F.
Hefferman, Wm., 1817-1865.
Heiss, Mrs. Anna, 1813-August 20, 1838; age, 25 years, 2 months.
Henderson, Adam T., 1852-1853.
Hensley, Merritt S. P., October 31, 1825-October 13, 1854.
Henderson, Adam, 1809-May 15, 1852.
Hensley, J., 1829-February 18, 1842.
Henness, Elizabeth J., June 25, 1802-October 18, 1858.
Henning, Joseph, 1798-May 14, 1862; born in Newry, Ireland.
Henning, Eliza, March 18, 1813-March 9, 1891.
Henning, Richard Alexander, 1840-Oc-

Bible Records—Tombstone Inscriptions

tober 14, 1841; son of Joseph and Eliza Henning.
Henning, James S., 1842-December 14, 1857; son of Joseph and Eliza Henning.
Hergel, Henry, January 22, 1818-December 15, 1872; born in France.
Herndon, Wm., 1792-1830.
Herriges, Barbara Ann.
Herriges, Wm.
Herriges, Groff.
Herriges, John Joseph.
    Lizzie Rachel.
    Annie Laurie.
    Lucy Ella.
Hewlett, Wm. E., March 8, 1814-1847.
Hewlett, Mary, 1813-1830.
Higginbotham, Martha.
Hicks, Alfred H., December 22, 1814-March 5, 1876.
Higgins, Bernard, 1828-1878.
Higgins, Rebecca Ann, December 4, 1813-January 17, 1881.
Higgins, Harriett, 1783-1833.
Hildebrand, Maria M.
Hill, Mary, 1815-1839.
Hill, Mary Catherine, 1809-April 20, 1829; wife of Wm. Hill.
Hill, Mary Sophia, 1826-December 11, 1832; daughter of Wm. G. and Mary C. Hill.
Hill, J. D. (vault).
Hill (infant), 1837; 2nd infant, 1839.
Hill, Jane Ann, 1816-1843; wife of Samuel Hill.
Hill, S. February 20, 1811-February 18, 1856.
Hill, Rebecca S., March 12, 1812-1851.
Hillman, Daniel, 1849-1849.
Hillman, Elizabeth H. M., 1824-March 18, 1849; wife of Charles E. Hillman.
Hines, Willie R., 1865-November 9, 1865; age, 2 weeks.
Hobbs, Wm. S., —— 1851.
Hobbs, N. J. H.; born, 1856.
Hobbs, Theodocia, 1799-1876.
Hobbs, Collin S., November 20, 1822-August 25, 1848.
Hobbs, Mrs. A. D., 1825-1840.
Hodge, Elizabeth M., 1833-1854.
Hogan, Catherine, 1827-1829.
Hogg, Dr. Samuel E., April 18, 1783-May 28, 1842.
Hogg, Samuel E, April 14, 1817-February 3, 1842.
Holley, Fred, 1810-1849.
Holliday, Wm. J., 1829-1830.

Hollingsworth, Mrs. Eliza, October 10, 1818-May 19, 1839; consort of Henry Hollingsworth.
Holmes, Mary Maria Elizabeth, 1830-September 23, 1835; daughter of Phineas and Eliza Jane Holmes.
Homes, James.
Hood, Julia Ann.
Hood, Capt. Chesley, 1809-1876; born in Virginia.
Hood, John G., 1843-1889.
Hood, J. P., 1817-1882.
Hooper, James A., January 25, 1825-November 5, 1854.
Hopkins, A. (daughter).
Horn, Martetia, 1845-1846.
Horn, Jesse, 1841 (illegible).
Horn, Mary E., 1840-1847.
Horn, Nancy Alvira, 1843-August 23, 1844; age, 9 months.
Horn, Philadelphia, 1848-1850.
Horn, Jane B., April 21, 1832-July 21, 1854; consort of Wm. L. Horn.
Horn, Nancy F., 1799-1869; consort of Wm. H. Horn.
Horn, J. H.
Hood, Sarah L. Read, December 17, 1841-April 20, 1884.
Horton, Sophia W. (Davis), July 11, 1799-March 23, 1874.
Horton, Joseph W., August 15, 1792-October 31, 1846.
Hossbein, Capt. D.
Hotten, Margaret.
Hough, Junius.
Hough, Ellen D. A.
Hough, Joseph H.
Houchens, Mary E., 1824-1868.
Houser, John G., November 19, 1813-July 8, 1850.
Houser, A. N.
Howard, Porter P., April 16, 1835-August 10, 1836; son of M. H. and R. P. Howard.
Howard, Mary M., 1879-1887; daughter of Mike and Annie Howard.
Howard, Mrs. Susan, 1798-July 4, 1868. 1868.
Howell, L. S.
Howell, Demanda; died, 1861.
Howell, C. S.
Howell, Birdie, 1874-1876.
Howell, Willie, 1888-1888.
Hubbard, Rebecca S., July 9, 1797-March 26, 1872; wife of Hon. Daniel Hubbard; daughter of Benj. Stoddard, first Secretary of the Navy.

Bible Records—Tombstone Inscriptions

Hudgins, James S., 1816-1845.
Huff, Ann R.; died, July 23, 1829; age, 18 years; wife of John Huff.
Hughes, Olivia.
Hughes, Andrew J., January 3, 1837-December 27, 1885.
Hughes, David, 1788-1828.
Hull, Lawrence, Jr., of New York; 1814-March, 1842; age, 28 years.
Huse, Abram V.
Hume, Rebecca, 1788-September 30, 1861.
Hume, Rev. W., 1772-May 22, 1833.
Hume, J. W., 1822-1854.
Hume, Louisa H., August 25, 1811-December 21, 1861.
Hume, Dr. Wm.
Hume, Alfred, November 2, 1808-October 29, 1853.
Hume, Alfred.
Hume, Mary E., June 24, 1843-March 3, 1858; daughter of Alfred and Louisa Hume.
Hume, Edward B., May 11, 1871-January 2, 1875; son of Wm. and M. L. Hume.
Hummer, C. W., January 16, 1828-September 27, 1871.
Hummer, Ann Brown, August 19, 1836-March 1, 1865; wife of V. C. W. Hummer.
Hummer, Charles Breckinridge, January 21, 1865-July 16, 1865.
Hundley, Robert Martin, June 17, 1841-February 13, 1848.
Hundley, George R., March 20, 1849-June 28, 1849; T. N. and Martha A.
Hundley, Laura Jane, June 4, 1845-1852.
Hunt, Addie, —— 1903.
Hunt, Sarah W., —— 1904.
Hunter, Matilda, 1808-May 29, 1880; born in Ireland.
Hunter, Mary, 1777-June 7, 1853.
Hurry, Eiza J., 1846-1849.
Hurt, Harriet E.; died, March, 1845; age, 22 years, 6 months, 6 days.
Hurst, James, 1812-September 5, 1834; age, 22 years; Philadelphia.
Hutchison, Anna M., 1850-1851.
Hynes, Ann, 1796-1837.
Hynes, Ann, 1825-1833.
Hynes, Andrew, 1823-1827.
Hynes, Laura, 1830-1833.
Hunt, Wm. G., February 21, 1791-August 13, 1833.

I

Ignatz, Anne.
Ignatz, Clara.
Ignatz, Frank
Ignatz, Julius.
— Children of C. and B. Ignatz.

Irwin, Robert, July 18, 1848-June 2, 1879.
Irwin, Mary, 1778-1816.
Irwin, D., 1776-1828.

J

Jackson, Alice M., 1857-1858.
Jackson, Andrew.
Jackson, Frances, 1820-1821.
Jackson, Daniel B.
Jackson, John, January 28, 1819-February 4, 1860.
Jackson, Mrs. Mary W., 1800-July 9, 1847.
Jackson, Andrew Bell, October 11, 1822-July 5, 1843.
Jackson, Alicia Frances, August 14, 1796-October 15, 1877.
Jackson, Hugh, September 3, 1824-November 8, 1846.
Jackson, J., 1835-1845.
Jackson, R. G., 1859-1864.
James, Dice, —— 1858.
James, Elizabeth, 1788-February 13, 1853; born in North Carolina.
James, Orville N., February 2, 1849-July 2, 1850.
Jefferson, Ann S.; died, 1877.
Jefferson, Amanda McNairy, 1824-1855.
Jefferson, John R., March 8, 1816-March 9, 1845.
Jenkins, Alex; died, October 9, 1860; age 11 years; born in Strathmore, Ireland.
Jenkins, David, 1814-May 26, 1840; born in Strabane County, Tyrone, Ireland.
Jennings, M.
Jennings, Rev. Obodiah, December 13, 1778-January 12, 1832; born in New Jersey.
Jewett, Lydia C., 1811-October 19, 1836; age, 24 years, 11 months, 19 days; wife of Isaac Jewett; born in New Hampshire.
Jobe (infant); died, 1821.
Jobe, Wm. J.
Johnson, Andrew.
Johnson, Capt. Bailey, 1815-1887.
Johnson, J.

Bible Records—Tombstone Inscriptions

Johnson, James G., December 25, 1842-September 30, 1866.
Johnson, J. P., 1848-1849.
Johnson, Elizabeth S., July 10, 1804-December 11, 1837.
Johnson, Anthony W., Jr., November 5, 1826-July 11, 1828.
Johnson, Nicholas H., June 26, 1831-August 9, 1832.
Johnson, Mary E.
Johnson, Charles, January 11, 1806-July 20, 1836.
Johnson, Mrs. Sarah C. A., September 15, 1812-November 26, 1835; consort of Charles Johnson.
Johnson, Elizabeth, June 7, 1859; age, 29 years.
Johnson, Lucius P., 1810-185—.
Johnson, Rev. Moses R., May 22, 1845-April 30, 1877.
Johnson, Mary A. C., 1825-July 15, 1865; Fryeburg, Maine.
Johnson, Miss Parnel; died, January 25, 1820.
Jones, W. F., December 30, 1818-March 1, 1858.
Jones, Cabber; daughter of Malan Jones.
Jones, Jovsey, 1775-September 16, 1835.
Jones, Wm. H., December 4, 1859-December 16, 1859; son of E. W. and M. C. Jones.
Jones, Ira.
Jones, Louisa C., 1815-May 6, 1854; age, 39 years; wife of W. E. Jones.
Jones, Lillie Harrison, 1861-July 6, 1862; daughter of Hiram J. and Cornellia Ford Jones.
Jones, Elizabeth F., 1843-1868.
Jones, Lucinda C., 1823-1864.
Jones, F. M., —— 1860.
Jones, J. F., —— 1850.
Jones, Andrew J., 1845-1847.
Jones, Preston B., 1838-1840.
Jones, Allen, 1818-1880.
Jones, James Henry, 1849-1855; son of Y. B. and Eliza Jones.
Jones, Wm. L., 1853-1854; son of Y. B. and Eliza Jones.
Jones, Young B., 1821-1891.
Jones, Lela and Lula, —— 1867.
Jones, Sophia, 1871-1873.
Jones, Catherine, 1835-December 5, 1858; age, 23 years; wife of J. C. Jones.
Jones, William, February 14, 1858-June 27, 1858; son of J. C. and C. Jones.
Jonti, P., 1796-1840.
Julius, Oscar, September 28, 1846-May 15, 1848.
Jones, Little Sophia, November 5, 1871-July 27, 1873; daughter of J. C. and F. E. Jones.

K

Kaiser, Marcus, 1825-October 4, 1867.
Kane, John, 1810-July 1, 1848.
Kelly, J. D.
Kelly, Mrs. E., 1764-1856.
Kelley, E. J.
Kendrick, James, 1824-1886.
Kendrick, Sarah H.; died, 1855.
Kessling, Mary E. 1871-1872.
King, Robert, June 7, 1826-March 4, 1859.
King, Catherine S., 1833-1864.
King, Sarah Ann, 1838-1855; daughter of Ann Granger.
King, Mary E., 1835-1848; daughter of Ann Granger.
King, David, 1827-1840.
Kingsley, Capt. A.
Kingsley, Wm. Bissell, December 20, 1810-March 15, 1836.
Kingsley, A., 1812-1813.
Kirk, Pamilla; died, 1860.
Kirkman, Ellen, August 9, 1863-July 13, 1864; daughter of S. and E. Kirkman.
Kirkman, Elizabeth, April 25, 1838-October 18, 1865; wife of Samuel Kirkman; daughter of James Woods.
Kirby, John M., 1812-1848.
Kirby, Susanna C., 1837-1838.
Kirby, Mr.
Kirby, Sarah J., 1842-1844.
Kirby, Wm. B., 1844-1850.
Kirby, L. P., 1844-1850.
Kirby, Irvin G., 1848-1850.
Kirkpatrick, Malvina, 1825-April 23, 1826.
Kleiser, James Ely, 1847-December 21, 1876.
Kleiser, George S., July 26, 1846-January 10, 1873.
Kleiser, Jos. H., 1845-1882.
Klooz, Henry, 1848-1859.
Klooz, Louisa, —— 1872.
Knight, Eliza F., April 6, 1821.
Knowles, Mary T., 1803-October 6, 1823; wife of Joseph Knowles.
Knowles, James; died, February, 1824.

Bible Records—Tombstone Inscriptions

Knowles, R. L., 1835-1887.
Knowles, Celeste, March 21, 1837-May 7, 1901.
Knox, James Adams, 1813-1846.
Kuhn, Mary A., 1813-1873.
Kyle, James, August 18, 1825-August 4, 1875.
Kyle, Josephine Smith, June 21, 1834-July 12, 1903.

L

Laird, Sarah Jane, 1830-November, 1851.
Laird, James A., April 2, 1827-October 29, 1861.
Langford, Wm.
Langley, Anna M.; died, October 11, 1856.
Lanier, Rev. E.
Lanier, Frank G.; died, April 17, 1828; age, 19 years.
Lanier, Emma, 1806-September 6, 1831.
Lanier, Van B., 1777-1833.
Lanier, Wm. H., February 22, 1822-June 2, 1891.
Lanier, John T., 1847-1849.
Lanier, Isaac, August 1792-January 3, 1847.
Lapsley, Mary P.; died, June 20, 1842; daughter of Robert A. and Catherine R. Lapsley.
Lapsley, Catherine Rutherford, April 17, 1804-March 22, 1844; daughter of John M. Walker; consort of Rev. Robert A. Lapsley.
Lapsley, Joseph W., 1824-May 19, 1852.
Lapsley, Elspa, 1842-1842; twin of Mary P. Lapsley.
"Larned, My Little."
Lassiter, Dora Hughes, November 13, 1866-September 18, 1891.
Lattiner, Jane A., January 19, 1806-March 30, 1874.
Laurent, Theresa B., May 5, 1813-July 1, 1850.
Law, Sophia.
Lawrence, Emmer Lavinia, August 5, 1850-January 3, 1854; daughter of Ed. and Mary J. Lawrence.
Lawrence, Henry E.; died, 1895.
Lawrence, Benj. R., 1817-August 30, 1836; age, 19 years.
Lawrence, Charles P., December 25, 1830-November 8, 1832.
Lawrence, Mary, 1749-1829.
Lawrence, Nancy Pomeroy, August 11, 1791-March 19, 1846.
Lawrence, Dr. Wm. Pitt, September 26, 1784-January 30, 1853.
Leake, Mrs. Sarah, 1791-December 25, 1858.
Leake, G. S., 1816-1849.
Lee, A. P.
Lee, K. B.
Lebow, Elizabeth S., 1826-1862.
Lee, R.
Lehmann, Anna, November 26, 1855-August 18, 1856.
Lehmann, Anna H., August 14, 1864-April 16, 1865.
Lehmann, J. Albert, May 1, 1866-March 19, 1871.
Lester, Andrew M., 1841-1903.
Lester, Ann M., 1842-1847.
Lesueur, E. M., 1846-1850.
Lesueur, M. M.
Lesueur, Sarah L., March 20, 1819-July 13, 1850.
Lesueur, Mary Ann, November 11, 1829-June 20, 1851; consort of C. H. Lesueur, and daughter of J. P. and Mary A. Calhoun.
Lesueur, M. E., August 26, 1831-June 2, 1866; wife of E. C. Lesueur.
Levin, Ann C.
Lewis, Mary M., 1805-1852.
Lewis, Richard W., September 5, 1788-July, 1855.
Lewis, Augustus, April 3, 1826-March 31, 1860.
Lewis, Emily.
Linert, Mary.
Linert, Wm. (infant).
Lincoln, Elizabeth; died, 1849; age, 22 years.
Lincoln, Georgianna, no dates.
Lincoln, Wm., 1822-1849.
Lindsley, Hannah, 1790-1846.
Littlefield, Edward B., 1785-February 18, 1849, age 50 years; Newport, R. I.
Littlefield, S., 1808-1862.
Litton, Jacob A., May 19, 1817-July 7, 1835.
Litton, A. H., 1788-May, 1836; born in Dublin, Ireland.
Litton, Richard J., 1817-February, 1853.
Litton, Joseph, July 19, 1808-August, 1841.
Litton, J., May 1, 1778-June, 1846; born in Dublin, Ireland.

Bible Records—Tombstone Inscriptions

Litton, Rebecca, 1819-1843; consort of Isaac Litton.
Litton, Catherine, —— 1845; wife of I. J. Litton, born in Ireland.
Livingston, John, 1809-1859.
Livingston, Eleanor R., 1813-1841; age, 27 years.
Livingston, Rachel, 1837-1843.
Lockalier, Major Jeffrey, 1808-September 2, 1850.
Lockhart, Mary, 1792-1853.
Lockett, John Bell, 1817-1850.
Locket, Helen A. J., January, 1831-September 25, 1847.
Lomas, Georgianna, 1863-1869; daughter of G. and E. W. Lomas.
Lomas, Mary Amelia, 1853-1857; daughter of G. and E. W. Lomas.
Lomas, Charlie, —— 1852.
Long, Philip W., December 22, 1826-March 2, 1850.
Loomis, Solomon H., 1829-1855.
Loomis, Archer H., 1851-1855.
Longinotti, James Polk, October 23, 1844-1854; burned to death, April 21.
Longinotti, Charles, October 26, 1849-1854; burned to death, April 21.
Longinotti, Albert, April 9, 1817-June 19, 1819.
Longinotti, Augustine; both names on same stone.
Lovell, J. H., 1845-1849.
Loving, Ruth F., September 23, 1822-January 21, 1893; dates on monument, 1820-1903.
Long, Robert, 1864-1864.
Lovisson, Francis, June 14, 1847; native of Denmark, F. L. T.
Lowrey, Ruthy; died, August, 1841; wife of Peter Lowrey. "Little Lulu."
Luster, Dr. T. J., 1800-August 27, 1838.
Lyons, James P., June 25, 1810-March 22, 1885.
Lyon, Luke K., 1847-1847.
Lynch, John Bowman, 1814-May 3, 1842; born in South Carolina.
Lynch, Henry C., 1828-October 24, 1843; born in Virginia.

M

Mace, Frank R., 1851-1860.
Mace, Wm. R., February, 1835-September 21, 1872.
Mace, Charlie, 1868-1873.
Maddux, Sadie B., September 23, 1883-April 28, 1884; child of Wm. and N. C. Maddux.
Maddux, Helen O., January 22, 1881-January 11, 1882.
Magar, E.
Magar, R. A.
Magar, R. L., 1867-1887.
Mahan, John Brown, 1861-August 25, 1863; son of James and Cassandia Mahan.
Malone, Alfred A., 1856-1858.
Malone, Lee, 1862-1864.
Malone.
Mandley, Nancy.
Manning, Kate, November 23, 1862-January 5, 1863; daughter of Mary A. Manning.
Manning, Jos. George, October 3, 1827-January 6, 1832.
Marlin, M. R.
Marlin, A., May-August.
Marlin, Alice.
Marlin, Charles, 1854-1855.
Marlin, Joseph Leake, 1825-1856; Minister to Guatemala.
Marlin, Jos. P., December 19, 1854-March 14, 1860.
Marlin, George W., February 4, 1859-February 5, 1860; son of W. C. and M. L. Marlin.
Marlin, Mary L., April 23, 1833- February 13, 1903; wife of W. C. Marlin.
Marlin, October 7, 1867; infant daughter of W. C. and M. L. Marlin.
Marlin, Wm. C., November 18, 1833-April 7, 1897; Protection Lodge No. 155, K. of H.
Marlin, J. W., 1825-1885.
Marling, Samuel C., 1796-1841.
Martin, Sallie, 1863-September 27, 1864.
Martin, Laura, 1861-September 15, 1864.
Martin, Thomas, November 15, 1835; age, 55 years.
Martin, Irene, 1890-July 11, 1892.
Martin, Jos. P.
Martin, Cornelia F., 1826-1850.
Martin, Thomas, 1830-1854.
Martin, Peter; died, 1867.
Marshall, Lieut. W. W.; died, 1848; age, 48 years; born in East Tennessee.
Marshall, Jos. H., 1796-June, 1815; born in Powhatan, Va.
Marshall, Eliza Jane.   Children of
         Jos. H. Marshall.
Marshall, John.

31

Bible Records—Tombstone Inscriptions

Marshall, Samuel M., November 21, 1858-August 25, 1859; infant son of Theo. J. and Sarah H. Marshall.
Marshall, Catherine Williams, November 28, 1813-January 16, 1844; married November, 1837.
Marsh, Sarah, 1810-1844.
Marlow, S. J., 1837-1839.
Masterson, Maria G., October 7, 1815-January 8, 1820.
Massengill, John C., November 4, 1806-1831.
Aunt Matilda.
Matthews, W. W., 1829-January 12, 1846; age, 17 years, 4 months, 4 days.
Maxey, P. W., May 2, 1810-August 8, 1876.
Maxey, Wm. O., March 14, 1837-July 5, 1862.
Maxwell, Frances; died, December 24, 1878; age, 30 years.
Maxey, John A., 1813-1878.
Mayer, L., 1795-1815.
Mayo, Caroline M., August 25, 1818-January 1, 1867.
Mayo, Walter, August 20, 1860-April 6, 1861; son of W. and M. B. Mayo.
Maynor, Nancy, November 17, 1788-May 28, 1836.
Mayson, Frances Marion, February 24, 1811-February 1, 1846.
McAlister, Wm. K., November 17, 1804-November 30, 1891; Jonesboro.
McAlister, Frances Rhea, November 8, 1812-May 27, 1856.
McAlister, Florence, July 22, 1852-September 7, 1853.
McAlister, Samuella Rhea, November 10, 1848-September 12, 1849.
McAlister, James, December 18, 1811-December 22, 1817.
McAlister, Sarah Lacky, May 3, 1812-April 2, 1814.
McAlister, J. H.
McAlister, Frances Akin, June 20, 1838-September 27, 1841.
McAlister, John Audley, July 15, 1831-December 22, 1838.
McAllister, W. E.
McAllister, Willie, 1866-1867; child of J. H. and E. C. McAllister.
McBride, C. P., 1863-1864.
McBride, W. W., 1860-1861.
McC., W. I.
McCampbell, Eli, 1826-1847.
McClellan, John.
McCluggager, Robert; died, July 15, 1851; age, 28 years; born in Carduff, County Antrim, Ireland.
McClung, Malvina, January 15, 1802-December 3, 1831; Knoxville.
McComb, T. H., 1821-1821.
McComb, M. J., 1822-1825.
McComb, S. H., 1827-1829.
McComb, J. H., 1827-1829.
McComb, Eliza, 1789-June, 1852.
McComb, J. W., 1788-1880.
McComb, James Royle, January 11, 1826-September 14, 1858.
McConnell, Jane, 1780-1829.
McCrory, Martha Douglas, 1857-November 10, 1862.
McCroy, Samuel M., 1861-1864.
McCurdy, J. L., 1797-1831; born in Norwich, Conn.
McDaniel, John H., 1853-1854.
McDaniel, Booker, 1823-1845.
McDaniel, Margaret, 1833-1857.
McDaniel, Ellen, 1818-1858.
McDaniel, Mary D., 1822-July 19, 1827.
McDaniel, Sarah Ann, 1827-July 19, 1829.
McDaniel, Charles M., 1802-April 18, 1852.
McDaniel, Edward, 1820-1854.
McDaniel, Patience, 1804-1854.
McEwen, Dr. J. W., 1826-1863.
McFarland, Frances.
McFadden, Bobbie; died, January 28, 1864.
McFillen, F. M.
McGar, Florence, July 17, 1856-March 18, 1857; daughter of G. C. and M. J. McGar.
McGar, Fanny L., May 22, 1854-June 20, 1856; daughter of G. C. and M. J. McGar.
McGavock, Nancy.
McGavock; died, 1832.
McGavock, Hester, 1833-November 26, 1852.
McGowias, Maria, 1818-1856.
McGuire, Mary E., June 21, 1827-December 9, 1849; consort of John G. McGuire.
McGuire, John H.
McGuire, Walter S.
McIndoe, R., 1814-1834.
McIntire, Abraham, 1791-July 30, 1831.
McIntire, James, 1822-August 4, 1824; F. L. T.

32

Bible Records—Tombstone Inscriptions

McIntosch, John, October 15, 1794-May 31, 1859; born in Fayette County, Ky.
McIntosch, Foster.
McIntosh, Margery McG., 1821-1850.
McIntosh, twins, December 24, 1850; infants of Wm. and Isabella McIntosh.
McIntosh, Albert G., June 16, 1827-January 28, 1831.
McKay, Ella M. H., 1844-1870.
McKeon, Miles; died, June 5, 1844; born in Longford County, Ireland.
McKenzie, Hester J., 1808-1844.
McKenzie, Mrs. Mary; died, 1853.
McLaughlin, Mrs. Ann, 1800-October 3, 1861.
McLaughlin, James L., 1820-1823; son of James and Mary C. McLaughlin.
McLaughlin, James Law, January 15, 1823-March 20, 1848.
McLean, A., infant.
McLemore, E. D.
McMinn, Elizabeth; died, August 21, 1826; consort of Robert McMinn.
McNeal, Wm.
McPherson, Alice and Elizabeth, December 22, 1858-March 10, 1860; daughters of John and M. J. McPherson.
McQuade, Peter; died, August 8, 1843; born in Monaghan County, Ireland.
McQuade, Henry; died, March 15, 1844; age, 1 month; son of Michael and Nephew of Peter McQuade.
McWright, Wm. A., April 25, 1871-July 6, 1872; child of A. T. and E. C. McWright.
McWright, James M., November 9, 1869-December 29, 1869; child of A. T. and E. C. McWright.
McWright; born, 14, 1867; infant son of A. T. and E. C. McWright.
Mead, Martha, April 13, 1789-May 28, 1850.
Meadows, Cordelia Frances, August 11, 1850-April 20, 1851; daughter of John O. and Martha C. Meadows.
Meadows, J. O.
Merriman, John G., 1824-November 24, 1844; age, 20 years, 12 days.
Merritt, Leroy C. C., May 23, 1836-April 24, 1859.
Merry, Sidney, 1856 (infant).
Merry, Eli, —— 1850.
Meyer, Louis, 1861-1872.
Meyer, Rose, 1816-1871.
Our Mike, 1839-1860; on Mitchell and Bradsute lot.
Miles, J. N., August 17, 1838-January 6, 1843.
Miller, E.
Miller, Capt. Jos., 1791-December 31, 1846; born in Lancaster County, Pa.
Miller, Nancy E. W. (removed), 1832-1870.
Mills, Annie C., June 19, 1837-March 1, 1859; wife of John E. Mills; daughter of Samuel and Jemima Casey.
Mills, Mary E., September 22, 1793-March 28, 1850; wife of Robert Mills.
Mills, Mary A.
Minnick, Joseph P., December 11, 1770-May 7, 1835.
Minor, Philip T., November 13, 1831-December 25, 1835.
Mitchell, C. H., 1794-1842.
Moffat, Alice Josephine, March 10, 1846-March 8, 1859; J. K. and C. R.
Monday, Rachel.
Monnahan, Michael M., 1796-1865.
Moore, Isaac, 1806-1864.
Moore, T. P.
Moore, Susan
Moore, Elizabeth.
Moore, Rice.
Moore, Alexander, —— 1860.
Moore, David M., 1794-1847.
Moore, Mary, 1800-April 6, 1854.
Moore, Samuel M.
Moore, Louisa H., 1821-April 10, 1840.
Moore, Robert I., 1791-1849.
Moore, Isabella C., 1802-April 25, 1851; late consort of Robert I. Moore.
Moore, Martha, 1809-January 22, 1835; wife of Robert I. Moore.
Moore, J. R.
Moore, R., 1828-1829.
Moore, Robert V., February 18, 1841-May 16, 1896.
Moore, Rachel, —— December 2, 1825; consort of Frances Moore.
Moore, John N., July 4, 1776-March 12, 1828.
Moore, Wilmirth F., August 31, 1803-February 11, 1831.
Moore, Araminta, 1776-August 22, 1837; age, 61.
Moore, Sarah S. (infant), January, 1835.

33

Bible Records—Tombstone Inscriptions

Moore, W. H., Jr., February 11, 1836-April 25, 1841.
Moore, Robert R., October 23, 1842-March 13, 1844.
Moore, Wm. C., 1809-1844.
Morefield, T.
Morgan, Dicie, 1841-1878.
Morgan, Robert F., 1801-1845.
Morgan, Nancy, 1777-1857.
Morgan, Elizabeth.
Morgan, Hon. Thos. Nicholson, 1810-October 3, 1844; New Orleans.
Mortimore, Henry, 1843-1854.
Morris.
Morris, Calista G., 1810-1862.
Morrison, A.
Morrison, DeWitt C., 1827-1830.
Morton, W. H., 1827-1854.
Mosher, Charles E., September 22, 1837-November 30, 1845.
Mosher, Ed. C. April 30, 1844-December 3, 1845.
Moseley, Chas. O.; died, November 24, 1864; age, 23 years.
Mosley, Benj. F., 1846-1848.
Mosby, Elizabeth Ann, June 8, 1812-November 29, 1833.
Moser, Mary.
Moss, Dr. J.
"Our Mother."
Mulhall, Jane, 1790-1860.
Munroe, Virginia A.
Murphy, Geo. W., April 8, 1816- February 14, 1879.
Murray, Henry, May 31, 1813-March 2, 1872; born in Newcastle, County Down, Ireland.
Murrell, J. P., 1840-1842.
Myers, Caroline, July 5, 1848-October 12, 1848.
Myers, Edwin Newell, April 4, 1854-July 12, 1854.
Myers, Frances Eliza, May 31, 1844-June 21, 1845.
Myers, Henry Neat, April 29, 1811-December 26, 1878.
Myers, Louis McChesney, July 19, 1846-November 11, 1871.
Myers, Father.
Myers, Mother.
Myers, Susie E.; age, 27 years, 4 months, 14 days; daughter of Sarah and Samuel Myers.

N

Napier, G. F., September, 1829-July 13, 1873.
Napier, Willie, 1854-1879.
Napier, John G., August 17, 1856-July 16, 1905.
Napier, William.
Napier, Julia E. (infant), June 4, 1838.
Napier, Mary Eliza, 1813-September 22, 1842; age, 29.
Napier, Frances, January 8, 1835-February 3, 1846.
Napier, Ann Elizabeth (infant), May 26-June 10, 1852.
Napier, J. B., August 1833-October, 1834.
Napier, James R., 1801-July 12, 1832; 31 years, 10 months, 23 days.
Napier, Richard Claiborne, 1773-March 20, 1834; native of Virginia.
Napier, Richard; died, July 6, 1851; age 19 years; son of James R. and Hannah Napier.
Neal, Mary E., 1832-1833; daughter of R. P. and C. R. Neal.
Neal, R. P., 1803-May 27, 1839; age, 36 years, 9 months.
Neely, Harriet, March 2, 1808-June 13, 1842; wife of George W. Neely.
Nell, Lavinia.
New, Martin, 1789-April 20, 1848.
Newbern, Thomas, September 20, 1800-May 13, 1863.
Newbern, Elizabeth, October 9, 1809-May 29, 1865; wife of Thomas Newbern; born in North Carolina.
Newell, J. D., 1836-1869.
Newell, Duncan (infant), 1910.
Newell, Jane C., 1847-1848.
Newell, G. D., 1836-1844.
Newell, G. D., 1834-1855.
Newell, J. R., 1839-1855.
Newman, Catherine, April 12, 1812-April 6, 1855; wife of Andrew Newman.
Newman, Mrs. Martha, January 27, 1822-February 16, 1847; wife of Dr. C. M. Newman; daughter of Ed. B. and Cornelia L. Littlefield.
Newman, M. A., 1835-1863.
Nichol, Lydia T., 1818-October 2, 1902; wife of Charles Nichol.
Nichol, Chas. McAllister, 1805-1867.
Nichol, R., 1795-1824.
Nichol, E., 1814-1824.
Nichol, M., 1823-1842.
Nichol, J. D., 1819-1842.
Nichol, Josiah, Jr., 1809-1836; monument, December 15, 1830; age, 27 years.

Bible Records—Tombstone Inscriptions

Nichol, Joseph, 1771-May 31, 1833; died of cholera.
Nichol, James B., 1793-1827.
Nichol, F. R., 1828-1867.
Nichol, Mrs. Adelaid Stokes, December 30, 1812-January 27, 1845; wife of James Nichol; daughter of Benj. and Sarah McCulloch.
Nichol, Mary E., December 1, 1808-April 10, 1845; daughter of Josiah and Eleanor Nichol.
Nokes, Willie, October, 1852-June 13, 1854.
Nokes, Lucy Walker, July 27, 1819-February 22, 1896.
Nokes, E. B., October 17, 1819-July 14, 1854.
Noles, Lucy, November, 1776-May 10, 1855; wife of Corben.
Norvell, Joseph, June, 1793-January, 1847.
Norvell, James Washington, November 26, 1831-July 15, 1843; son of Moses Norvell.
Norvell, Moses.
Norvell, Henrietta W.
Norvell, Martha, November 25, 1810-May 25, 1830.
Norvell, Hendrick, September 29, 1808-March 18, 1837.
Norvell, Joseph, December 17, 1836-June 9, 1837.
Norvell, L., 1776-March 2, 1813.
Norvell, J. D.

O

O'Bryan, Kyrn, 1817-August 22, 1846; age, 29 years; born in County Kilkenny, Ireland, survived by wife, Anastasia.
O'Harris, Frances Ann, August 23, 1818-November 26, 1861; wife of Wm. O'Harris (Bartee).
O'Rilley, T. T., 1817-1839.
Ochrle, J. C. W., 1824-1850.
Oliver, D. A., 1823-1849.
Omohundro, Wm. B.; died, July 3, 1849.
Oney, Francies E.; died, November, 1877; age, 3 months.
Oney, Mary F., died June 1873; age, 18 months.
Oney, Susan D., 1868-1891.
"Our Mother," Oney lot, 1838-1879.
Oscar, Carl, September 25, 1844-June 18, 1849.
Otto, Gohanna Frederick, November 20, 1819-June 18, 1849.
Otto, William, November 6, 1848-July 3, 1849.
Owens, Mary R. E., 1860-1861.
Owen, Jane Gray, February 4, 1792-May 13, 1867; wife of Robert Brownlee Currey.

P

Page, M. W.
Parish, Martha.
Parish, Mary.
Parish, Fanny; age, 39 years; wife of Frank Parish.
Parish, James.
Parish, Woodson.
Parker, Joseph, June 21, 1852-July 30, 1852.
Parker, Fanny, 1845-1846.
Parker, W. L., 1833-1893.
Parker, Cynthia A., 1841-1888.
Park, Ann Elizabeth, 1826-October 12, 1827; age, 15 months.
Park, Joseph, May 20, 1828-October 30, 1828; age, 5 month, 10 days.
Parmer, Hattie, 1837-1864.
Parminter, K., 1872.
Parminter, M. B., 1857-1879.
Parrish, S., 1801-1828.
Parrish, T. K., 1819-1821.
Parrish, L., 1822-1824.
Parrish, Georgianna C., 1842-1844.
Parrish, Marietta R., October 19, 1846-October 9, 1847.
Parrish, Thos. H.; born, 1818.
Parrish, John M., 1847-1856.
Parrish, John Marshall, October 19, 1843-May 4, 1865; son of Thos. H. and Maria A. Parrish.
Parrish, Catherine A., 1854-1855.
Parrish, Ann E., 1835-1869.
Parrish, Jolly, February 14, 1833-August 22, 1899.
Parrish, John M., 1867-1868.
Parrish, James B., 1856-1861.
Parrish, Sarah A., December 25, 1829-May 30, 1881.
Parrish, Catherine C., 1799-1878.
Parrish, Jolly, 1787-1838.
Parrish, Alexander, 1836-1809.
Parrish, Martha and Mary, 1841.
Parrish, Martha C. 1791-1873.
Parrish, Jessie, July 2, 1791-September 15, 1853.
Parrish, Margaret, 1860-1862.
Patton, Francis L., 1844-1845; daughter of Y. S. and F. M. Patton.
Patton, Selina.

Bible Records—Tombstone Inscriptions

Patton, Mary A.
Patrick, Elizabeth W., 1800-1841.
Patrick, Eliza J., 1830-1846.
Paul, Lucy H., March 1, 1831-May 2, 1857; wife of W. P. Paul; daughter of John and Sally McIntosh; died in Memphis.
Paxendale, Mary J., 1834-1866.
Payne, Susan Jane; died, March 17, 1851; wife of Albert Payne.
Peach, J. T., June 27, 1847-July 31, 1848.
Peach, E. A. Z.
Peach, Susan, January 5, 1813-March 14, 1865; wife of Wm. Peach.
Peach, W. H., 1839-1864.
Peach, Houston, 1857-1862.
Peach, Emmerson, 1859-1862; sons of H. S. and Mary Peach.
Peach, Bettie F.
Peacock, Martha C., 1823-1864.
Pearl, Clara.
Pearl, Wm. E., July 8, 1827-December 27, 1854.
Pearl, Martha A. Goodwin, December 22, 1826-July 28, 1850; wife of Elbridge G. Pearl.
Peay, Sarah E., January 19, 1823-September 4, 1868; daughter of Sam and Mary Winfred, Buckingham County, Va.
Pearson, M. C. Kittie, March 16, 1850-January 29, 1900; wife of B. A. Pearson.
Pentecost, Lucinda, 1834-1864.
Perkins, S. E., 1816-1837.
Person, Alice, 1794-1860.
Person, Francis, April 16, 1808-February 11, 1870.
Person, Alicia, 1784-June 30, 1860.
Person, Emily, 1820-1889.
Perry, Sarah, 1808-1874.
Perry, Mamie, March 18, 1881-June 15, 1883.
Perry, Leana or Laura, September 26, 1879-June 6, 1883.
Perry; children of W. P. and R. D.
Perry—Willie Perry, May 3, 1866; Jesse E. Perry, June 21, 1867-August 31, 1869.
Perry, Mrs. Wm.
Perry, J. B., August 20, 1820-September 14, 1886.
Perry, John B., August, 1813-March, 1869.
Perry, Jesse H., 1847-1848.
Perry, Pamelia, 1823-1850.

Petit, James B., lodge 279 I. O. O. F.
Pettit, Jos. P.
Petty, Sarah.
Petty, Sarah.
Petty, Eliza S.
Petty, Mary.
Petre, M., September 28, 1829-July 31, 1867.
Pew, J. W. H., 1817-1850.
Pew, J. W. H., February 20, 1835-August 3, 1858.
Pfeiffer, Selastian Neukirk.
Phillips, B. A., 1801-1855.
Phillips, Johnny, 1849-1864.
Phillips, Jimmy, August 30, 1856-November 22, 1857; son of J. C. and J. G. Phillips.
Pickett, Margaret, 1828-1858.
Pickett, Maria, 1836-1863.
Pickett, Rev. Calvin P., August 4, 1825-April 29, 1898.
Pickett, Mary (his wife), July 18, 1826-May 8, 1872.
Pickett, Mary.
Pickett, Calvin, Jr., born and died, December 2, 1866.
Pike, J. B., 1850-1851.
Pike, John, December 22, 1800-August 2, 1876.
Pike, Adolphus, September 17, 1830-July 17, 1855.
Pike, Matilda, July 20, 1828-July 11, 1845.
Pilcher, Catherine B., February 14, 1802-October 10, 1828.
Pillow, Louise, 1846-1865.
Pinchum, J.
Pitcairn, Jane.
Pitcairn, George Wilson.
Pitcairn, Delila Ann.
Pitcairn, Thomas.
Pittman, Asa, 1786-1837.
Phelps, Mary A.
Plummer, John.
Plummer, Mrs. B.
Plummer, Mrs. Eliza, no dates.
Plummer, Erle H., 1876-1877.
Plummer, Susan.
Plummer, Mrs. J.
Polk, C. P., 1828-1830.
Pollard, Lieut. Joseph, no dates.
Poteet, Sarah A., 1869-1873.
Porter, S.
Porter, Cynthia, 1797-1866.
Porter, Alex, September 7, 1825-February 12, 1905.
Porter, M. A.

Bible Records—Tombstone Inscriptions

Porter, Robert, 1764-June 8, 1833; age, 69 years; born in Ireland.
Porter, A., 1771-1853.
Porter, Susan, 1777-January 2, 1853.
Porter, James A., Jr., May 5, 1849-August 1, 1866; drowned.
Porter, Martha Watson, January 29, 1830-June 7, 1860; wife of Alexander Porter.
Porter, Sallie Ann; died, 1848; date on tomb, July 14, 1849.
Porter, Evilina, 1747-October 20, 1819; wife of Alex Porter, Jr., of St. Martinsville, La; born in Washington, Ky.
Porter, Alexander, 1785-1849.
Porter, James, 1793-1849; son of Rev. James Porter.
Porterfield, Percy, 1790-1846; tomb, September 22, 1797.
Porterfield, Jennie.
Porterfield, Frank, July 22, 1831-June 18, 1864.
Porterfield, Bettie Kay Castleman, August 8, 1847-July 15, 1885; wife of Frank Porterfield.
Porterfield (infant of Bettie), infant daughter of Elizabeth.
Porterfield, Mary, 1845-1846; daughter of R. R. Porterfield.
Porterfield, Frank, March 15, 1843-April 11, 1901.
Porterfield, Robert R., 1822-March 14, 1846.
Porterfield, Malinda, September 21, 1795-October 31, 1869.
Porterfield, Francis, September 28, 1785-June 3, 1833.
Post, George W., December 26, 1830-June 18, 1858; New York.
Powell, Elias K., 1822-1850.
Powell, W. E.
Powell, E., 1802-1840.
Powers, Myra L., March 12, 1818-October 27, 1877; wife of S. H. Powers.
Powers, S. H., June 20, 1813-June 15, 1863.
Powers, Susan W., 1818-1843.
Powers, F. G., August 30, 1843; infant son of J. H. and S. W. Powers.
Price, Grief; died, 1829.
Price, Reuben F., 1840-1890.
Price, Sarah J.; died, 1903.
Price, Jesse W., 1812-1880.
Price, Allice M., 1879-1880.
Price, Marie, February 20, 1896-February 18, 1900; daughter of H. P. and B. L. Price.
Price, Jos. W., February 12, 1844-June 27, 1867; son of Levi and Sarah Price.
Prige, Mary E.
Pritchet, James Robert; son of James and Jane E. Pritchet.
Pritchet, Willie; son of James and Jane E. Pritchet.
Probart, William; died, 1819.
Pugsley, C., 1773-1832.
Putnam, Ann Eliza, 1829-July 23, 1836; age, 8 years; daughter of Dr. J. R. Putnam.
Pyle, Alex W., 1857-1884.
Pyle, Willie Hedric, 1870-1872.
Pyle, Alexzine.
Pyle, Mary.
Pyle, Annie.
P'Pool, Laurence Dayton.

Q

Quinn, A. J.

R

Radford, Joe.
Rahm, Laura, 1858-1864.
Rains, Sarah Eveline, October 24, 1829-April 14, 1837.
Rains, John, May 2, 1796-July 4, 1879; Mason County, Ky.
Ramage, Christina (infant), April 11, 1847; age, 4 months; daughter of John and Mary Ramage.
Ramsey, Susan P, 1810-1849.
Ramsey, Col. Wm., B.A., 1799-1874.
Ramsey, Charlotte P., 1812-1887.
Ramsey, Mary E. W.
Ransom, Agnes, 1805-April 6, 1858; daughter of Hulday Ransom.
Ransom, Hulday, 1767-May 27, 1857.
Rawley, W. B.
Rawlings, Dr. Ed., 1800-1832.
Rawlings, Margaret G., 1805-1831.
Rawson, Gracie Bell; died, June 21, 1878; age, 6 months, 11 days; daughter of W. S. and M. A. Rawson.
Ray, Henry, September 20, 1844-October 13, 1846.
Read, Harriett H.
Read, G.
Read, Grace Million, June 15, 1856-August 16, 1884.
Read, David B., Jr.; age, 10 weeks.
Read, Harriett A., September 11, 1816; age, 1 days; daughter of James and Sarah Read.

37

Bible Records—Tombstone Inscriptions

Read, David, March 10, 1799-May 15, 1872.
Read, Mrs. Sarah A., October 11, 1824-February 17, 1858.
Read, James Henry, February 28, 1848-June 16, 1849; son of James and Sarah Read.
Read, Harriet A., October 6, 1804-November 24, 1876.
Read, Martha L.
Read, Edney Eugene, July 2, 1846; age, 22 years; son of David and Harriett Read.
Reddy, Mrs. Ann; died, January 19, 1848.
Reddick, Winnie A., December 4, 1845-December 1, 1884.
Reed, Clara; died, January 13, 1850; age, 23 years; wife of Marvin Reed.
Reese, Wm. B.
Reeves, Virginia Walton, July 19, 1840-October 10, 1885.
Reid, A. H. L., 1841-1861.
Reyburn, S. J., 1828-1828.
Reyburn, J. B., 1820-1828.
Reyburn, G. L., 1824-1828.
Reyburn, M. E., 1823-1829.
Reinberger, H., 1861-1862.
Reynolds, Henry G., August 5, 1820-June 14, 1849.
Reynolds, Sarah G., February 9, 1828-June 11, 1849.
Reynolds, H., 1787-1839; age, 51 years, 10 months.
"Little Richard."
Richards, Henry, March 26, 1769-November 19, 1846.
Richards, Corintha A., 1862-1863.
Richardson, Wm.
Richardson, Alex., February 12, 1776-January 1, 1825; born in Ireland.
Richie, Helen; died, November 11, 1832; age, 40 years, 10 months; consort of John Ritchie.
Riddle, Mary A., 1830-1833.
Rieff, Annie L., ⸺ 1831.
Rieff, Mrs., ⸺ 1831.
Risely, G.
Riggs, Mary C. Napier, 1821-July 25, 1841; consort of James L. Riggs.
Riva, Andrew, 1833-1867.
Rives, Charles W., November 2, 1852-July 13, 1853.
Rives, George N., August 17, 1851-July 6, 1852; age, 10 months.
Rives, John A., October 25, 1848-April 1, 1852.
Rives, Richard G., January 1, 1816-March 1, 1852; son of R. G. and M. A. Rives.
Roane, A., 1774-1821.
Roane, Ann, 1779-April, 1851; age, 72 years; relict of Judge Roane.
Roane, Laura H., June 17, 1815-November 18, 1823.
Roane, Mary H., February 1, 1791-1824.
Robb, John H.
Robb, S. E. C., 1844-1845.
Robert, I., 1848-1848.
Robert, E. T., 1820-1840.
Robert, A. D.
Robertson, Sarah Stonelake, May 17, 1845-September 4, 1904.
Robertson, Gen'l James, 1742-1814.
Robertson, Mrs. C. R., 1751-1843.
Robertson, Dr. Felix, 1781-1865.
Robertson, Mrs. Lydia, 1788-1832.
Robertson, Duncan, April 29, 1771-May 1, 1833; born in Scotland.
Robertson, Wm., November 7, 1799-1822.
Robertson, Jonathan Freel, son of Gen. Robertson; moved to this cemetery by Gen. James Robertson Chapter.
Robertson, Catherine, February 14, 1771-August 15, 1834; widow of Duncan Robertson; born in Chester County, Pa.
Roberts, Luella J., 1863-1865.
Robeson, George H.
Robinson, Ishmael, 1808-January 3, 1847.
Robinson, Catherine, 1842-1862.
Robinson, 1831-1832.
Robinson, Wm., died May 8, 1833; age, 24 years; born in Liverpool, England; died in Nashville.
Robinson, Benjamin L., 1847-March 27, 1855.
Robinson, J. L., 1834-1852.
Robinson, J. C., 1795-1852.
Robinson, J. C., 1827-1862.
Robinson, A., 1829-1861.
Robinson, S., 1802-1863.
Robinson, M. L., 1839-1865.
Rockwood, Elizabeth Ann, 1814-1853.
Rockwood, Walter, 1810-1851.
Rogers, Sallie Edmundson; died, October 26, 1904; wife of J. W. Rogers.
Rogers, N. E., 1774-1847.
Rogers, Luretia Adelaide Clay, May 23, 1842-September 7, 1843.
Rogers, Mary A. S.

Bible Records—Tombstone Inscriptions

Roger, Foster.
Roger, George W., no dates.
Roler, Margaret F., 1858-1859.
Roler, Elizabeth D., 1856-1860.
Roland, M. A., 1821-1837.
Roser, John, 1817-1865.
Roser, Catherine, 1814-1855.
Rowan, John Hamilton, January 1, 1819-February 20, 1862.
Rowe, Julia Elizabeth (infant), August 31, 1825-September 26, 1826; daughter of James and Rosina.
Royle, M.
Royster, Thomas W., November 12, 1801-April 13, 1837.
Ruhm, Theodor, Geb, June 13. 1832, Zu Liegenhof Deutschland; Gest, August 10, 1864.
Ruckle, Margaret, 1795-1859.
Ruckle, Robert, 1796-1885.
Ruth, Hannah Ann, 1824-September 28, 1853; wife of Robert B. Ruth.
Rutherford, David, 1827-1846.
Rutledge, Alice W., 1838-1854.
Rutledge, Septima S., 1783-1865.
Ryman, Mary E., 1822-1888.
Rymer, Jos. W., 1840-November 23, 1862; age, 23 years; born in Frederick County Va.
Rutledge, Henry, 1775-1844.

S

Sadler, Elvington A., 1828-February 28, 1848.
Sadler, J. H., 1796-1851.
Sadler, Rebecca S., 1805-January 24, 1844; wife of James Sadler.
Sadler, Mrs. M., 1766-1833.
Saffrans, H., 1832-1833.
Sagalay, E.
Sagalay, D.
Sanders, Ann Rawlings, 1815-1836.
Sanders, John W., 1807-1842.
Sanders, Robert H., 1797-December 29, 1829.
Sanders, Margaret, 1831-1840.
Sanderson, R., 1794-1822.
Sandhouse, G. Arnold, January 29, 1847-January 10, 1848; son of A. and L. Sandhouse.
Sandhouse, M. L., January 2, 1843-January 2, 1845; daughter of A. and L. Sandhouse.
Sandhouse, J. Arnold, February 17, 1845-October 24, 1846; son of A. and L. Sandhouse.
Sandhouse, Caroline E.
Sandhouse, John B. E.
Sandhouse, Wm. E.
Sandhouse, Mary C. E.
Sandhouse, A. J.
Sawyer, Mrs. Martha Jane; died, June 20, 1843; age, 31 years; consort of Rev. Seymour R. Sawyer.
Sayers, Robert D., December 15, 1880-March 7, 1902.
Sayers, Stephen, April 10, 1849-June 22, 1881.
Sayers, Mary A., September 1, 1850-February 15, 1904; wife of Stephen Sayers.
Sayres, Maria E., June 16, 1809-October 9, 1852; wife of Charles Sayres.
Sayrs, Foster; died, June 4, 1820.
Scharenberger, C., March 2, 1813-June 26, 1854.
Scharenberger, Louisa Francis, May 1, 1851-April 26, 1852; infant daughter of M. and C. Scharenberger.
Schloss, Augusta, 1851-1852.
Schloss, Henrietta, 1854-1858.
Schnell, M.
Scott, Mattie.
Scott, Mary; died, February 5, 1865; wife of S. M. Scott.
Scott, Ruth, September 21, 1806-December 5, 1875; born in Virginia; wife of Flemming Scott.
Scott, Henry.
Scruggs, Margaret, and babies, February 10, 1838-April 12, 1870; wife of W. A. Scruggs.
Seabury, Alex M., dates illegible.
Seabury, Edward R., 1819-May 10, 1843.
Seay, Rachel Douglass, February 27, 1806-February 1, 1879; relict of Samuel Seay.
Seay, Jane M., August 1, 1804-1847.
Seay, Samuel, March 1, 1784-January 28, 1864.
Seek, Simeon, 1752-1845.
Seibert, George; born in Baden, Germany.
Selleck, George G.
Sewanski, Josephine A., 1840-1867.
Shaffer, Richard W., September 12, 1811-July 4, 1883.
Shaffer, Catherine F., March 20, 1818-February 23, 1883.
Shaffer, D. Ella, 1847-1848.
Shaffer, Margaret, August 4; infant daughter of R. W. and C. Shaffer.
Shannon, Elizabeth, 1846-April 25, 1873; wife of Thos. S. Shannon.

Bible Records—Tombstone Inscriptions

Shapard, Margery Childress, November 2, 1801-October 22, 1879; wife of Wm. B. Shapard; Caswell County, North Carolina.
Shapard, Wm. B., November 5, 1797-January 19, 1870.
Shapard, Thos. C., September 22, 1838-December 17, 1864.
Shapard, Maggie, 1833-1840.
Shapard, Martha J., 1831-1849.
Shapard, "Little Maggie."
Shapard, "Little Gardner."
Sharpe, Benjamin, January 1, 1800-March 17, 1848; born in Philadelphia.
Sharpe, Victoria A., 1841-September 23, 1844; daughter of Benjamin and Ann Sharpe.
Sharpe, Chas. Thomas, August 9, 1843; infant son of Benj. and Ann Sharpe.
Sharpe, Elvira, 1824-1861.
Sharpe, Thos. A., 1825-1865.
Shelby, John, Shelby vault, built in 1855.
Shelby, David.
Shaw, Nancy, —— 1825; age, 56 years; consort of Major B. Shaw.
Shaw, J. T., 1826 ——.
Shaw, Sarah, 1825-1850.
Shaw, George W., 1848-1848. "My Boy."
Shelton, G. L., 1841-1894.
Shelton, Susan, October 8, 1823-January 28, 1850; wife of M. L. Shelton.
Shelton, M. L., March 7, 1822-September 7, 1863.
Shelton, Amelia, 1857-1859.
Shelton, Cimmy, 1862-1863.
Shelton, Susan W., 1854-1855.
Sheffield, Henry, March 31, 1874-June 23, 1874; son of Eugene R. and Winnie Smith Sheffield.
Sheffield, Mrs. Henry, —— 1872.
Sheppard, J. O., 1865-1867.
Sheppard, Matilda S., 1813-November 19, 1882.
Sheppard, Mary Frances, 1843-April 20, 1844.
Sheppard, Chas. Ed., 1847-1849.
Shearon, Rose (infant).
Sherwood, Edwin E., 1830-March 5, 1858; New Orleans.
Sherwood, Mrs. Rachel, —— June 10, 1862.
Shields, James, February 25, 1832-1834; age, 2 years, 2 months, 15 days.
Shields, Mrs. Maria, 1811-March 24, 1836; age, 25 years, 2 months, 13 days; consort of Wm. Shields.
Shirley, Paul, died April 16, 1834; age, 43 years.
Shirley, Mrs. S. C., 1776-January 13, 1876.
Shirley, James A., 1825-June 21, 1847.
Shirley, Paul Admiral, 1821-November 24, 1876; U. S. Navy.
Shirley, Jimmie P.; died, 1881.
Shirley, Wm. Riley, November 30, 1858; age 1 month; son of Wm. and M. E. Shirley.
Shivers, Jonas, no dates.
Shivers, Elizabeth Fleming; wife of Jonas Shivers; no dates.
Shivers, John C., March 18, 1842-October 4, 1853.
Shivers, N., 1806-1833.
Shouman, Frederick, 1784-September 24, 1828; age, 44 years, 35 days; native of Leipsic, Saxony.
Sigler, Elizabeth P.
Simms, Millington, September 17, 1783-January 17, 1848.
Simms, Armice, November 24, 1802-August 6, 1849.
Simms, Anthony, 1786-1852.
Simms, Capt. Wiley, January 8, 1827-March 1, 1879.
Simms, Nancy, March 9, 1827-December 8, 1880.
Simpson, Robert H., August 1, 1825-July 4, 1850.
Simpson, Mary J., 1833-1847.
Simpson, Thomas, 1827-1890.
Sippy, James, 1831-1869.
Skeggs, Mary J., June 13, 1818-October 8, 1899.
Skeggs, Thos. L., August 17, 1810-July 26, 1880.
Skeggs, Frank H., May 6, 1841-November 11, 1845.
Skeggs, Edwin E., 1845-1869.
Skeggs, Maggie E.
Slade, John N., 1856-1858.
Slade, Martha A., 1825-1859.
Slade, Children.
Sleage, J. H.
Sloan, Rebecca L., 1842-July 24, 1863; daughter of E. and Jane Wise.
Slocum, Caledonia J. Moffat, September 4, 1854-August 30, 1879.
Smiley, Robert, 1783-September 11, 1823; born in Ireland.
Smith, Joshua, January 12, 1830-July 5, 1858; son of Robert and Ann Smith.
Smith, Charlotte O., 1808-1877.

Bible Records—Tombstone Inscriptions

Smith, O. B.; died, 1853.
Smith, Matty C., March 10, 1851-1857.
Smith, E. W.
Smith, Louisa M. H.
Smith, Albert J.
Smith, John H., April 10, 1812-December 24, 1849.
Smith, Alice M.; died, 1847.
Smith, Wm. H.; died, 1836.
Smith, Sarah C.; died, 1841.
Smith, Elizabeth; born in North Carolina, August 17, 1795-June 25, 1848 in Philadelphia; consort of O. B. Smith.
Smith, Jane, 1810-June 2, 1863.
Smith, Jennett, —— March, 1848; born in Glasgow, Scotland.
Smith, Sarah, 1832-1833.
Smith, John H., 1778-June 22, 1834; born in Scotland.
Smith, Gen. Sam G., September, 1794-September, 1835.
Smith, Frederick, 1805-1848.
Smith, Mortimer W.
Smith, Rocksey, 1806-December 10, 1827.
Smith, Z. W., 1824-August 16, 1827.
Smith, Richard, May 1, 1827-May 27, 1830.
Smith, Capt. Joseph, 1787-February 28, 1837.
Smith, Elizabeth K., April 21, 1802-October 16, 1877.
Smith, Minor, July 3, 1832-January 11, 1862.
Smith, Joseph V., October 5, 1825-October 25, 1867.
Smith, Wm. N., 1842-1846.
Smith, Tim E., 1817-1818.
Smith, James K. R., 1844-1846.
Smith, Nancy D., 1846-1846.
Smith, Ann; died, September 11, 1844; age, 6 months.
Smith, Henry C.; died January 19, 1848; age, 2 years, 2 months, 13 days.
Smith, Sallie.
Smith, Elizabeth, 1821-1864.
Smith, Eva J., 1859-1862.
Smith, Ursey L., May 20, 1838-1841; daughter of Widow Jane.
Smith, Ralph, 1787-September 24, 1860.
Smith, Tullula, —— 1861.
Snead, Jas. Norvell, May 23, 1820-December 26, 1862.
Sneed, E., 1776-March 5, 1842.
Sneed, Col. John, March 24, 1778-September 9, 1844.
Sneed, Burwell B., 1778-August 22, 1829.
Sneed, Mary.
Sneed, Susanna, 1776-1828.
Snedekum, Johanna Pless; born in Hamburg, Germany, January 19, 1805; died, 1859; wife of August Snedekum.
Snell, Louisa M., August 27, 1811-May 29, 1818; wife of R. S. Snell.
Snider, W. D.
Snow, H., 1779-1821.
Sophia.
Spain, Berry, April 7, 1854-January 12, 1864; son of L. K. and S. G. Spain.
Spain, W. G., 1821-1834.
Speece, Lewis, 1765-April, 1829.
Speece, Alfred M., 1802-March 1, 1828.
Speece, W. J., infant.
Speece, S., 1766-January 19, 1827.
Speece, Jackson (infant).
Spenge, John, 1768-1838.
Spiegelhalter, George, April 23, 1821-February 22, 1855.
Spottswood, Isaac F., 1816-1856.
Springfield, Mary C., November 11, 1843-May 16, 1864; wife of H. J.
Stagg, P., 1801-1836.
Stainback, Martha, 1813-March 14, 1835; consort of James W.
Stainback, Ann J., 1847-1849; daughter of J. W. and M. E., June 5, 1840.
Stalcup, Marcus L., 1826-January 30, 1844; age, 18 years.
Stall, Jacob.
Stanley, William B., January 6, 1792-May 17, 1848.
Stanley, William E., 1847-1847.
Stanley, Luvisa, August 3, 1832-June 6, 1849.
Staton, Chas. F., 1838-1842.
Staub, Felix.
Steane, Michael, 1797-1829.
Stearns, Frances, August 31, 1847-September 19, 1850; daughter of Aaron and Mary Stearns.
Stephens, E. J.
Stephens, George W., 1844-1866.
Stephens, Caroline Minerva, 1815-April 17, 1845.
Stephens, Rev. Abenego, 1782-February 27, 1811.
Stephens, J. C., 1776-1849.
Stevens, Sarah B., 1827-1839.
Stevens, Moses, October 1, 1790-March 23, 1841; born in Andover, Mass.

41

Bible Records—Tombstone Inscriptions

Stevens, John B., May 19, 1827-June 14, 1855.
Stevens, William Henry, 1818-1843.
Stevens, Charlie, April 2, 1862-July 20, 1863; son of James and Amanda.
Stevenson, Elizabeth, February 10, 1827-July 12, 1834.
Stevenson, A.
Stewart, John, Jr., 1811-April 10, 1836.
Stewart, Robert.
Stewart, Mary E.
Stewart, Frances E.; born, 1825.
Stewart, M. S., 1825-1872.
Stewart, Drucilla; died, November 18, 1862.
Stewart, John, August 19, 1840-February 16, 1855.
Stewart, William.
Stewart, J., Jr., 1811-1836.
Stewart, Sallie, April 1, 1814-January 13, 1862.
Stewart (infant of Wm.); died, 1829.
Stodder, Sarah Ellen, 1827-1835.
Stodder, Mary P., 1816-1841.
Stodder, Mary, 1790-1841.
Stodhard, N. G., 1809-1827.
Stone, Tandy S., September 4, 1827-1856.
Stothard, Sarah P.
Stothard, Hugh Kirkman, June 10, 1854-May 19, 1858.
Stothard, Anna Augusta, March 30, 1860-July 11, 1860.
Stothard, Cornelia, August 6, 1846-December 21, 1882.
Stothard, Walter, September 18, 1847-March 15, 1865.
Stothard, Eugene Leonidas, February 28, 1857-November, 1879.
Stothard, Jerry, August 15, 1815-September 17, 1866.
Stothard, Ann, September 19, 1827-February 24, 1899; wife of Jerry.
Stothard, Mary D., July 17, 1809-July 15, 1827.
Stothard, M. P.
Stothard, Samuel P., May 16, 1856-August 15, 1853; son of Jerry and Ann.
Stothard, E. P.
Stothard, Charlotte, 1796-1841.
Stothard, Charlotte.
Stout, George H., July 18-August 18.
Stout, Andrew A., 1824-1828.
Stout, John W., October 17, 1833-July 19, 1834.
Stout, Augustine Frances, 1826-April 3, 1829; daughter of V. D. S. and C. S. Stout.
Stout, Ira, 1790-March 18, 1817.
Stretch, Elizabeth, 1738-1833.
Studley, Inez P., 1864-1865.
Sullivan, W. W., 1810-1849.
Sommerville, M., 1799-1879.
Sommerville, John, June 25, 1770-April 26, 1846; born in York, Pa.
Sommerville, Elizabeth, January, 1778-November 22, 1815; married May 22, 1794.
Sommerville, Pierce Butler, 1802-January 2, 1838; age, 36 years; son of John and Elizabeth.
Sumner, Wm. H.
Sumner, Wm. H., from New Orleans; member of Convention held in Nashville; died, August, 1810.
Sweeney, Edward H., June 11, 1857-September 3, 1861.
Sweeney, L. J.; died, April 10, 1845.
Sweeney, Sarah J., January 19, 1841-May 11, 1848.
Sweeney, E. F., July 6, 1844-June 10, 1848; daughter of G. and J. F. Sweeney.

T

Tait, Margaret, 1806-1842; consort of Richard Tait.
Tannehill, Eliza, 1789-April 3, 1843.
Tannehill, F., 1840-1843.
Tannehill, Virginia Wilkins, July 24, 1838-August 24, 1841; daughter of W. F. and E. A. Tannehill.
Tannehill, Wilkins, March 4, 1787-1858, by Masonic Fraternity; born in Pittsburgh.
Tardiff, Martha, 1782-1857.
Tarver, J. B., 1839-1852.
Tarver, H. S.
Tate, Eugenia A., 1837-1837.
Tate, Othelia, 1838-1840.
Taylor, Josiah, 1821-May 7, 1849.
Teal, Charles H., 1838-October 28, 1847; age, 9 years.
Tebow, Elizabeth Stevens, April 3, 1826-December 7, 1862; Orange County, Ind.; wife of Theodore.
Telton, O. E., 1828-1838.
Terry, G. W., 1831-1854.
Terry, G. M., 1851 ——.
Terry, M. J., 1825-1845.
Terrass, Ann T., 1811-July 2, 1826; daughter of Henry and Amey Terrass.
Temple, Mary A., 1866-1884.
Temple, Col. Liston Elliott, September 25, 1797-January 13, 1851; born in

Bible Records—Tombstone Inscriptions

Virginia Carolina Co.
Tessier, Mrs. Catherine; died, June 16, 1843; consort of Judge Tessier.
Thomas, Lucinda.
Thomas, Sally, 1787-1850.
Thomas, E.
Thomas, Frances.
Thomas, Caroline, April 12, 1811-January 28, 1827; daughter of Sarah Thomas.
Thomas, Philip, 1783-December, 1831.
Thomas, C. W.
Thomas, Eliza, 1818-1849.
Thomas, M. O.
Thomas, J., 1805-1846.
Thomas, S. K., 1844-1846.
Thomas, J., 1800-1836.
Thomas, John, June 4, 1798-March 1, 1842.
Thomas, Nancy; died, November, 1810; wife of Philip Thomas.
Thomas, Jonathan, 1804-1863.
Thompson, J. S., 1846-1851.
Thompson, Harriett; died, September 22, 1879; age, 58 years.
Thompson, James H., August 1, 1815-July 3, 1865.
Thompson, James, 1841-August 13, 1841.
Thornburg, W. P., October 8, 1832-December 27, 1869.
Tilford, Mary, 1787-1853.
Tilford, S. J., 1829-1829.
Tilford, Margaret S., 1825-1832.
Tindall, John, —— 1795-1863.
Tipton, Col. John, October 8, 1831; born in Washington County, Tenn., Erected by 49th General Assembly.
Titus, Jonas; died, September 27, 1837; age, 28 years; Cayuga County, N. Y.
Todd, Mary J. (infant).
Todd, John N., 1787-1844.
Todd, John N., Jr., 1837-1878.
Toombs, J.
Toney, Elizabeth Goodwin, February 21, 1821-August 26, 1846; wife of Wm. Toney.
Toney, Cascenda L., September 26, 1811-1840; daughter of Wm. and Elizabeth Toney.
Toney, Parmelia, December 7, 1843-October 19, 1841; daughter of Wm. and Elizabeth Toney.
Townsend, Edward Penn, 1830-May 20, 1832.
Trabue, Chas. Clay, August 27, 1798-November 21, 1851.

Trabue, Agness G., November 7, 1799-March 12, 1849; born in Virginia.
Trimble, Anna W. (Horton), 1821-1852.
Trabue, Wesley F., 1806-1861.
Troost, Gerard, M.D., Ph.D., March 15, 1776-August 14, 1850; born in Holland.
Tully, Milton, June 15, 1824-August 4, 1845.
Tully, N., —— 1844.
Turbeville, W. W., 1861-1883.
Turbeville, Amanda, 1842-1874.
Turbeville, M. E., 1852-1886.
Turner, Annie, 1841-1860.
Turner, Wm. W., 1796-1853.
Turner, W. C., 1821-1873.
Turner, "Our Boy."
Turner, Sarah E. H., 184—-1862.
Turner, Julia E., 1845-1857.
Turner, Martha, 1764-1839.
Turpin, White, July 15, 1843-January 11, 1865; son of Jos. A. and Laura Turpin, Jefferson County, Miss. Member of Darden's Battery, C. S. A.; died from wounds received at Battle of Nashville.

U

Ullian, Lucia, 1861-1862.

V

Valentine, Lizzie.
Vance, Thos. M., 1832-1856.
Vance, Jerry, —— 1863.
Vaughn, Virginia.
Vaulx, Mary A., July 5, 1850-July 13, 1851.
Vaulx, Mary, September 3, 1852-June 24, 1853.
Vaulx, Daniel, July 6, 1843-July 13, 1844.
Vaulx, Roberta, April 10, 1842-December 16, 1850.
Vaulx, Joseph, September 13, 1835-February 25, 1908.
Vaulx, Susan E., 1808-October 13, 1835.
Vaulx, Wm. H., 1829-1851.
Vaulx, Ellen C., July 14, 1830-April 9, 1852.
Vaulx, Susan J., July 7, 1832-July 18, 1853.
Vaulx, Samuel.
Veador, W. S., 1805-1827.
Vines, Polly; died, December 29, 1837.
Vines, Mary L., October 2, 1850-August 5, 1852.

Bible Records—Tombstone Inscriptions

Vogel, John, March 18, 1863-September 21, 1864.
Vogel, Emili, March 3, 1870-April 5, 1870.

W

Waggoner, Veria.
Wade, Mary G.
Walker, Mary E. G., 1817-1845.
Walker, Mrs. Sarah W., 1791-April 4, 1835; consort of Wm. Walker.
Walker, James T. C., 1830-November 4, 1835; son of Wm. and Sarah W. Walker.
Walker, Margaret, September 13, 1781-July 19, 1841; relict of John Moore Walker.
Walker, Adeline, April 5, 1829-August 11, 1791; daughter of Robert and Adeline Walker.
Wallace, James Herney, 1809-March 11, 1834.
Wallace, Eliza A.; died, December, 1835.
Wallace, Benj. R. B., October 10, 1808-June 17, 1849.
Wallace, Margaret, 1822-January 20, 1842; wife of Stewart Wallace; born in Ireland.
Waller, Ada Eugenia, July 1, 1855-February 13, 1859; daughter of John P. and Mary E. Waller.
Walling, Andrew T., July 10, 1855-March 9, 1856.
Walton, Robert J., 1833-1852; born in Chester County, Pa.; date on monument, December 17, 1862.
Waldron, Charles, 1838-1875.
Waldron, Willie, 1871-1874.
Wand, Sarah.
Wand, James, 1766-1845.
Ward, Rachel, 1828-December 2, 1865; age, 37 years, 8-9 months.
Warder, M. T., 1851-1857.
Warder, Tennessee R. F., 1852-1856.
Warder, James H., 1850-1859.
Warfield, Mrs. S. B., 1814-1837.
Warren, Roberts Soule, 1830-June 17, 1852.
Warren, Isaac, 1793-November 23, 1862.
Warren, Emeline.
Ward, Julia M.
Washington, James G., September, 1798-January 21, 1834; Brunswick County, Va.
Washington, Albert.

Washington, Sarah Alexander, 1784-August 29, 1846; consort, Nedham Longhorn Washington; King George County, Va.
Washington, C.
Washington, Sarah Janett, July 1, 1826-April 17, 1847; daughter of Gilbert and Elizabeth Washington.
Washington, Gilbert Gray, October 7, 1785-December 1, 1846.
Washington, Thomas, September 22, 1823-September 13, 1855; son of Gilbert and Elizabeth Washington.
Watkins, Philip, 1817-May 21, 1851; age, 34 years; son of Gilbert and Elizabeth Washington.
Watkins, Robert B., September 10, 1842-January, 1846.
Waters, Margaret A.
Waters, Eunice Healy.
Watson, Elsey, 1786-1866.
Watson, Marcus M., 1842-1843.
Watson, Anna M., 1827-1844.
Watson, Alice L., 1841-1844.
Watson, Mary Frances, 1826-August 17, 1841; daughter of M. and R. Watson.
Watson, Susan Emma, June 11, 1829-October 11, 1833; child of Matthew and Rebecca Watson.
Watson, John Dexter, June 11, 1840-November 18, 1844.
Watson, Susanner, May 12, 1793-June 7, 1849.
Webb, Mary L., 1817-1817.
Webb, N. E., October 24, 1813-January 7, 1848.
Webber, Nancy, 1802-1824.
Webber, Eliza, 1820-August 25, 1820; age, 9 months, 22 days.
Webber, Wm. C., 1821-July 4, 1822; age 1 year, 6 months, 12 days.
Webber, Elizabeth S., 1822-October 1, 1823; age 1 year, 12 days.
Webber, John A., 1824-1825.
Weaver, Ann Magon Ford, June 11, 1807-February 24, 1859; wife of John G. Weaver.
Ween, D.
Welborn, Jane, 1801-1839; consort of Cal Enoch.
Weller, Elizabeth A., 1825-1836.
Weller, Elizabeth Ann, June 5, 1828-July 11, 1846; born in Russellville, Ky.
Weller, Lucintha, April 6, 1806-March 15, 1860; wife of Ben S. Weller.
Welcker, Frederick, April 5, 1815-May

44

Bible Records—Tombstone Inscriptions

27, 1841; born in Roane County.
Wells, Walter, 1855-1857.
Wells, Elizabeth H. Garrett, July 27, 1820-October 1, 1856.
Wells, Eliza P., 1808-1830.
West, J. C.
West, T. J., 1824-1828.
West, Wm. Edward (artist), 1788-1857; born, in Lexington, Ky.
West, Mary E., March 29, 1829-May, 1854.
West, Chas. Burton, August, 1814-May, 1854.
West, Wm. E., September 13, 1819-December 12, 1856; monument, 1854.
Wersner, S. A. (infant).
Weston, Sophia L., 1801-1830.
Weston, Thomas, 1772-1830.
Weston, Clement, 1826-1844.
Weston, H. N.
Wetterou, John C., 1826-1860.
Wetzel, Joseph; died, August 16, 1837.
Wetzel, Lewis, March 31, 1804-April 14, 1848.
Wharton, Araminta Jane, November 24, 1832-November 4, 1861; tomb, 1867.
Wharton, Pricilla P., 1810-1847.
Wharton, Ellen J., 1843-1844.
  Sons of Henry and Mary Wharton:
Wharton, Miner (infant), January 23, 1845-May 31, 1846.
Wharton, Wm. Henry (infant), December 8, 1840-March 6, 1841.
Wharton, Frederic (infant), August 6, 1842-July 23, 1843.
Wheat, Reginald H.
Wheeless, W. T., 1847-1908.
Wheeless, Ellen Shapard, December 30, 1836-February 19, 1863.
Wheeless, Ellen S., 1862-1864.
White, Maria, 1851-1908.
White, Carter.
White, Fanny.
White, Ella Kenton, November 12, 1840; wife of John W. White; daughter of Rev. John and Lucinia Rains.
Wehrley, Elizabeth, 1816-March 22, 1833.
Whiteman, Catherine, 1818-August 29, 1855; age, 37 years.
Whiteman, Mrs. L., 1844-1910.
Whyte, Robt., 1767-1844.
Wiles, Annie.
Wiles, Ottie.
Wiles, Roy.
Wilkerson, B.
Wilkinson, J. E., —— 1840.

Wilkinson, J., 1816-1840.
Wilkinson, Wm. H., Jr., May 28, 1842-April 12, 1894.
Wilkinson, Georgetta C., November 13, 1816-September 1, 1884; wife of Wm. H. Wilkinson, Sr.
Wilkinson, Wm. H., November 2, 1812-March 21, 1873, F. L. T.
"Our Willie," 1851-1852.
"Our Willie."
Williams, M. A. C., —— 1859.
Williams, D. D., 1836-1836.
Williams, Sarah A.; died, June 14, 1861.
Williams, Col. Thos. H., January 20, 1773-August 7, 1850.
Williams, Mary C., 1801-1874.
Williams, Jacob, 1807-March 5, 1842.
Williams, Isaac, 1790-1850.
Williams, Matilda E. (infant).
Williams, Caledonia P., July 17, 1850-June 22, 1852; daughter of A. and M. J. W. Williams.
Williams, Martha J., February 16, 1816-November 29, 1859; wife of Alex.
Williams, E., 1792-1818.
Williams, F. A.; died, 1864.
Williams, S. E.; died, 1864.
Williams, Nellie, 1884-1885.
Willis, Sarah Preston, February, 1823-October, 1842.
Wilson, Cresa, January 8, 1839-December 3, 1859.
Wilson, Eleanor V., February 27, 1799-January 7, 1871.
Wilson, Syrus A., 1828-1848.
Wilson, Geo. A., March 12, 1808-May 11, 1846.
Wilson, Col. Geo. W., September 28, 1778-November 8, 1848, F. L. T.
Wilson, Elinora, April 5, 1847-1847.
Wilson, Robert; died, May 28, 1859; age, 39 years.
Wilson, Albert.
Wilson, Luticia, 1833-1842.
Wilson, William.
Wilson, Eugenia G.; died, March 13, 1841; age, 26 years; consort of George Wilson.
Willis, Julia H., December 4, 1800-April 22, 1878.
Willis, John, January 8, 1788-June 20, 1848.
Winbourn, Maud, 1862-March 30, 1862; age, 6 months; daughter of J. R. and M. E. Winbourn.
Winbourn, Mary E. Brown, July 14,

Bible Records—Tombstone Inscriptions

1842-August 14, 1863; wife of J. R. Winbourn.
Winbourn, Agnes, 1863-May 24, 1863; age, 3 months, 15 days.
Winbourne, Rev. Alex A., 1809-1840.
Winder, Van Perkins, June 3, 1809-November 8, 1854, at Ducross Plantation, La.
Winder, Martha Grundy, wife of V. P. Winder, June 25, 1812-December 16, 1891.
Winder, Martha Grundy, February 10, 1837-August 8, 1853.
Winder, Elizabeth R., 1834-1842.
Winder, Margaret Rawlings, July 5, 1832-August 30, 1842.
Winder, John Davidson Smith, May 28, 1835-May 31, 1838.
Winder, Ann G., 1830-1831.
Winder, William Shields, August 1, 1850-June 21, 1851.
Winder, Malvina Bass, March 30, 1841-February 18, 1852.
Wing, A., 1810-1829.
Wingfield, Francis, 1833-1848.
Wingfield, Samuel Henry, 1803-June 16, 1834.
Winston, A. W.
Winston, Dr. C. K.
"Our Baby."
Winston, L. B.
Winston, C. K.
Winston, W. B.
"Little Brother."
Winston, E. B.
Winstead, Hugh; died, 1848.
Wise, Edward H., 1836-February 6, 1870.
Wise, Henry A., 1846-1847, November 19.
Witty, Maria S., 1842-1850.
Wood, J. E.
Wood, John.
Wood, William.
Wood, Mary.
Wood, Andrew W., March 15, 1857-July 15, 1899.
Wood, Addie P.; died, April 5, 1920; wife of Andrew Wood.
Woods, Samuel, 1779-July 31, 1838.
Woods, Henry, 1824-1862.
Woods, B. A.
Woods, M. B.
Woods, E. W.
Woods, Joseph, June 22, 1779-April 20, 1859.
Woods, Joseph, Jr., January 10, 1829-March 18, 1857; son of James and Elizabeth Woods.
Woods, Penelope Porter, May 13, 1805-May 29, 1852; wife of James Woods.
Woods, Elizabeth A., November 7, 1803-March 22, 1844.
Wolf, Samuel, February 12, 1801-March 1, 1848; born in Pennsylvania.
Woodhead, John, 1807-1849.
Woodfin, Cordelia A., 1831-1832.
Woodfin, Frances M., 1807-1832.
Woodfolk, W. W., 1799-1890.
Woodfolk, Ellen D., December 23, 1819-December 24, 1851; wife of Wm. Woodfolk W.; daughter of J. and S. Horton.
Woodfolk, Richard, November 15, 1851-January 18, 1852.
Woodfolk, Lucius H., January 18, 1845-July, 1850; son of Wm. and Ellen Woodfolk.
Woodfolk, M. W., 1776-1831.
Woodward, Mrs. Lindamior, 1796-July 11, 1850.
Woodward, Hezakiah W., July 19, 1795-February 2, 1858; born in Virginia.
Woodward, Elizabeth Harris, January 12, 1802-March 10, 1858; wife of C. G. Washington.
Woodward (infant).
Woodward, M. A., 1838-1865.
Work, Julia, 1804-January 17, 1869.
Wray, Susie H. C., 1849-1875.
Wrigglesworth, Benjamin, 1804-November 25, 1852; born in London, England.
Wright, Mrs. J.
Wright, Ansil Howell; died, June 4, 1818; age, 3 months, 17 days.
Wyatt, Nancy E., 1832-1858.
Wyne, W.
Wynne, Albert H., March 8, 1800-June 29, 1849.
Wright, Amelia A.; died, 1841.
Wright, John Williams; died, 1841; father and daughter.

Y

Yarbrough, F. A., 1846-1872.
Yarlin, Mary E., 1837-1838.
Yeatman, John, February 17, 1793-August 2, 1859; born in Pennsylvania.
Yeatman, Eliza Schooley, August 1, 1797-May 25, 1870; born in Ohio; died in New York; wife of John Yeatman.
Yeatman, Louisa, 1829-1842; born in

Bible Records—Tombstone Inscriptions

Cincinnati, Ohio.
Yeatman, Mary L., 1825-1828.
Yeatman, E. K.
Yeatman, Martha, 1796-May 14, 1815; age, 19, consort of Thomas.
Young, Martha Ellen, January 29, 1837-April 21, 1855; wife of Wm. Dodson.
Young, Joseph Robert, May 13, 1814-April 1, 1849.
Young, E. K.
Young, C. H.

Z

Zachary, E. A., May 3, 1835-May 18, 1864; daughter of W. and S. Peach.
Zollicoffer, Louisa P. Gordon, February 21, 1819-July 13, 1857; wife of Felix K. Zollicoffer.
Zollicoffer, Gen. Felix K., 1812-1862.
Zollicoffer, Ridie; died, October, 1902; daughter of F. K. and L. P. Zollicoffer.

SUPPLEMENT FROM NOVEMBER, 1908, TO NOVEMBER 20, 1911

Argo, H. S.
Argo, J. C.

Bean, B. A.
Barbour, Mrs. S. A., September 16, 1842-March 4, 1910.
Bates, Mrs. M. A.
Birchett, D. A.
Birchett, W. V., 1907-1911.
Burnett, O. F. (I).
Birchett, D. A., 1822-1910.
Bradley, Mrs. M. E., 1850-1909.
Burton, J. A., 1844-1910.

Cunningham, Mrs. M. H.
Clements, R. A., 1869-1910.
Cain, Ira, 1873-1909.
Carroll, Miss L. E., 1893-1911.
Champion, G. W. (infant).
Chilton, J. H.
Combs, Wm. R., 1861-1909.
Cooper, Mrs. J. P., 1870-1910.
Cross, H. B., 1898-1909.
Connor, Mrs. Z., 1835-1910.
Crosswait, J. H.
Crosswait, Mrs. H.

Davis, R. L. (infant).
Dickens, Lee (infant).
Duff, Mrs. M. E., 1848-1910.
Dennis, P. (infant).

Edmondson, R. G. (infant).
Edmonson, Mrs. M. E., 1891-1909.
Elliott, Mrs. M. P.
Ellison, J. M. (infant).
Enoch, B. E., 1888-1911.
Eubanks, Gene (infant).
Evans, Omah.
Everett, Stonewall J., 1865-1911; monument, April 23, 1867-July 29, 1911.
Enoch, G. H. (infant).

Fawcett, Mrs. C., 1840-1910.
Felts, W. (infant).
Funk, Henry, —— 1911.

Gaines, J. E. (infant).
Goodwin, L. (infant).
Graves, Mrs. C.
Green, Chas. R., 1826-1908.
Griffis, Mrs. S. J.

Hailey, Wm. (infant).
Hale, Chas. (infant).
Harman, W. H.
Hawks, Mrs. L. S.
Hood, Mrs. S. A.
Huff, D. L.; died, 1909; infant, died, 1910.
Hume, Miss R. J. 18?6-1910.
Hamilton, Mrs. N. E., 1825-1911.
Harris, Peter.
Hawks, L. S., 1875-1909.

Johnson, J. W. (infant).
Johnson, Mrs. S. A.
Jacobson, Mrs.

Keezer, T.
Kiernan, Mrs. R. B.
King, Mrs. H. W.
King, H. W., 1837-1908.

Lassiter, Mrs.
Lawrence, R. E. (infant).
Lovell, Mrs., and infant, 1865-1911.

Mallory, Wm. (infant).
Miller, H. B., 1855-1909.
Mooreland, T.
Myers, Mrs. S., 1848-1911.
McCaslin, Charles, May 18, 1850-September 23, 1910.
McCaslin, H., 1894-1897.
McCaslin, Katherine, 1889-1890.
McKnight.
McKierman, Mrs. R. B.; died, 1911.

Nevins, R. P. (infant).
Nevins, T. A. (infant), (D), 1910.

47

Bible Records—Tombstone Inscriptions

Newell, W. G. (infant).
Newburn, Mrs. S. A.

Paragan, Mrs. N., 1870-1910.
Parriah, Amanda.
Parrish, Jas. M.
Parrish, Mrs. S.
Parrish, T. K.
Plummer, S. P.
Poole, L. P.
Price, Mrs. F. E., 1841-1910.

Reese.
Rose, J. A. J., 1833-1909.

Savage, Mrs. A. B., 1856-1909 (?)
Shaeffer, Mrs. M. T.
Sinclair, J. M.; died, 1911.
Sevier, John.
Shelton, T. F. (infant).
Steel, G. (infant).
Smith, Joel M., 1786-1864.
Stewart, 1856-1909.

Thompson, Mrs. K. P., 1853-109.
Turner, Mrs. E. A.

Warder, Mrs. E. P., July 4, 1833-February 11, 1911.
Watkins, Mrs. M. D.
Watkins, Robert B.
Watkins, Robert N., 1852-1908.
Watkins, R. M.
Watkins, S. D., 1820-1874.
Wessells, John, 1817-November 29, 1859.
Whiteman, Mrs. L.
Williams, Mrs. B. D.
Wilson, Robert.
Woods, J. C.
Wyatt, Capt. James, September 15, 1826-October 25, 1910; F. L. T.

Young, Miss Lizzie.

ADDITIONAL LIST COPIED FROM STONES BY MRS. ACKLEN, MRS. NOEL, AND MRS. DARDEN

Nathan Ewing, Feb. 17, 1776-May 1, 1830.
Henry Neat Myers, Feb. 1, 1842-July 11, 1870.
Chloe Drake Wilkinson, Sept. 8, 1891-Feb. 28, 1916.
G. W. Craft, Feb. 16, 1857-June 8, 1859.
M. Craft, Jan. 31, 1860-June 28, 1862.
Mary W. Edmundson; their daughter (John and Matilda Edmondson) rests beside her husband, James Parkes, Franklin, Tenn.
Sarah Wheat McIver, Alabama, Nov. 4, 1895.
Matilda B. Edmundson, daughter of John and Matilda Edmundson, buried in Tuskaloosa, Ala.
Elizabeth Porterfield, Feb. 22, 1818-Sept. 19, 1877.
Josephine Nichol Shearon, wife of W. M. Shearon, Nov. 26, 1832-April 21, 1921.
Mary K. Bailey, Feb. 19, 1850-May 30, 1929.
Leonard P. Thornburg, Dec. 27, 1868-July 6, 1921.
His mother, Mary Kate Bailey, Feb. 19, 1850.
R. J. Bates, 1859-1883.
Paul A. Skeggs, May 11, 1863-Aug. 4, 1931; F. L. T.
F. Skeggs, July 12, 1815-Aug. 25, 1869.
Mary Loving Vaughn (mother), Mar. 19, 1847-Mar. 31, 1930.
John D. Vaughn (father), Mar. 5, 1837-Sept. 28, 1886.
Wm. Loving Vaughn, Feb. 15, 1868-May 10, 1906.
Martha L. Wyatt, Jan. 1842-Oct., 1921.
Joseph G. Dally, born in City of New York, Sept. 21, 1801-Oct. 18, 1813.
Mary Miller, July 26, 1837-July 6, 1873; widow of R. J. Walton; wife of W. R. Bell.
Catherine C., late consort of Reuben Foltz, March 1, 1820-June 7, 1847.
Flora Miller, May 1813-Sept. 6, ——.
Samuel A. Otis, born in Newburyport, Mass., 1799-Aug. 9, 1883.
Augusta Yeatman, wife of J. M. Embree, Arkansas; daughter of John and Eliza Yeatman; died, Oct. 15, 1837; age, 21 years.
Amanda M., wife of Latechas Waldron, Nov. 22, 1842-Jan. 4, 1907.
Charles B. Hall, 1818-1897.
Matilda Ann, wife of Chas. B. Hall, 1820-1900.
Wm. T. Hall, 1857-1923.
——. ——., Carpenter; died, July 18, 1839.
Bathenia Wills, wife of Jesse Wills; born in Pittsylvania County, Va., March 29, 1793-August 16, 1830 or 1850.
Isaac Drake, no dates.

Bible Records—Tombstone Inscriptions

Isabella, wife of James L. Hodge, Feb. 9, 1823-April 12, 1859.
Infant daughter of Wm. and Isabella Smith; died, Sept. 11, 1844.
Henry C. Smith; died, Jan. 19, 1818; age, 2 years.
Wm. Smith; born in England.
R. P. Smith, 1796-1862.
Ann Nicholson Smith, 1805-1882.
Currin Smith, 1844-1845.
Ann Hamilton Currin, no dates.
Mary Franois Stewart, daughter of Miranda Johnson and Wm. Stewart.
Sarah Lee Arthur, daughter of Mary Franois Stewart and Chas. H. Arthur.
Andrew J. Moulton, 1828-1895.
Mary N. Wheeler, 1837-1906.
Maria Callaghan, 1801-1815.
Philip Callaghan, 1790-1850.
Wm. F. Elliott, July 12, 1818-Dec. 2, 1869.
Margaret Harmon, wife of John Allen Couchm; born in North Carolina, Sept. 10, 1811-Feb. 4, 1870.
J. S. Hollowell, Feb. 3, 1840-April 1, 1908.
Green Lee Jones, 1845-1926.
Annie L. Jones, 1859- ———.
Mary Doran Watkins, 1823-1908.
Theodore Baxter Watkins, 1851-1925.
Annie Jackson Watkins, 1849-1923.
Wm. A. Goodwin, son of Wm. W. and Anna Goodwin, March 20, 1825-July 24, 1850.
Frankie Pickett, born and died, Feb. 14, 1869.
Kingsley Pickett, Nov. 1, 1870-Sept. 16, 1871.
John W. Pickett, Sept. 11, 1929.
W. H. C. Toney, March 4, 1812-May 4, 1852.
Mrs. Margaret McGregor, wife of Alexander McIntosh; died, Aug. 14, 1830; age, 30 years.
Hiram S. Argo, July 23, 1858-March 11, 1911.
John Crosthwait, Dec. 18, 1869-March 13, 1911.
His wife, Lena, 1869-1825.
A. L. Crosthwait, Jan. 26, 1839-May 27, 1927.
Helen Harley, wife of A. L. Crosthwait, Oct. 2, 1841-June 17, 1911.
A. L. Sutfin, Aug. 10, 1829-July 15, 1835. (?)
Martha C. Peacock, March 7, 1829-April 21, 1861.

Mary P., wife of G. F. Napier; died, April 23, 1912.
James A. Chilton, 1834-1910.
Emily C. Chilton, 1833-1864.
Berta A. Chilton, 1859-1884.
James A. Chilton, 1863-1864.
Jeanetta S. Chilton, 1861-1863.
J. F. Dillen, 1815-1864.
Mary E., wife of G. H. Harris, Jan. 25, 1824-Aug. 16, 1849.
Sarah Ann Gray, wife of John W. Walker; died, March 16, 1845; age, 28 years.
Mrs. Lass Hartman Lee; died, Aug. 9, 1932; age, 59 years.
W. S. Whiteman, II, Sept. 4, 1808-Aug. 26, 1889.
Lucy Ella Robertson, daughter of J. and G. Robertson; March 22, 1858-Oct. 17, 1867.
Henry and David Rix, no dates.
Martha E. Slack, May 18, 1820-May 7, 1922.
Joseph A. Bland, Oct. 18, 1830-July 20, 1905.
Andrew J. Coleman, Oct., 1826-July 26, 1857.
Martha Cotton, Oct., 1796-June, 1840.
John Cotton, Oct. 10 ———.
Thomas H. Savage, Aug. 14, 1845-July 15, 1932.
Ada Blanch, wife of Harry Savage, Feb. 22, 1852-Oct. 29, 1909.
Rosa Floeck, May 4, 1859-Sept. 15, 1860.
Julia T. Knapp, Aug. 12, 1845-Sept. 16, 1904.
James M. Knapp, Dec. 13, 1840-Sept. 29, 1897.
Frederick Jonte, Sept. 26, 1823-Feb. 11, 1858.
James A. Smith, Oct. 3, 1856-April 26, 1858.
Alice J. Smith, April 27, 1852-May 6, 1852.
Eliza J. Smith, 1821-Feb. 5, 1864.
Maria Price, 1790-Sept. 5, 1860.
Elizabeth Stevens, mother and grandmother and relict of the late Colonel Abram Stevens, Fayetteville, N. C.; died, June 26, 1849, in 62nd year.
Blake Willy, Nov. 1, 1849-June 23, 1850.
Nathaniel Cross, Basking Ridge, N. J., June 15, 1802-Dec. 19, 1866.
Thomas J. Allen, March 29, 1812; age, 28 years, 21 days.

Bible Records—Tombstone Inscriptions

Nancy Ferns, June 14, 1828-May 25, 1892.
Effie Haslam, June 3, 1870-Nov. 5, 1881.
John H. Smith, 1778-June 22, 1834.
John Beverly Rayburn, Dec. 25, 1820-Dec. 22, 1828.
Green Lafayette Rayburn, Oct. 28, 1824-Dec. 23, 1828.
Sarah Ann Rayburn, Jan. 8, 1828-Sept. 12, 1828.
Mary Elizabeth Rayburn, April 1, 1823-March 31, 1829.
Alexander Ramsey, son of James and Rachel Irwin, Oct. 8, 1822-June 30, 1824.
Susan Wells Armstrong, wife of James Armstrong; trooper; died, May 3, 1833; about 72 years; born in Maryland.
William McNeill Armstrong, June 27, 1830-April 22, 1856.
Jane C. Newell, Dec. 13, 1839-Sept. 20, 1869.
Gideon Mortimer Martin, May 1, 1855-June 22, 1857.
Alicia Sarah Gibson, 1862-1931.
Wm. H. A. Bang, son of W. F. and J. P. Bang, Aug. 21, 1837-Nov. 8, 1841.
Martha J. Stewart, wife of Arthur Stewart; died, Feb. 14, 1843; age, 22 years.
Rebecca Adams Gibson, wife of Wm. Gibson, Dec. 31, 1793-April 20, 1852.
Mary Elizabeth Fell; died, March 16, 1814; age, 11 years, 7 days.
Caler Fagalay; died, June 17, 1837; age, 39 years, 1 month, 6 days.
David Fagalay; died, July 12, 1836; age, 10 years.
Nicholas S. Parmantick, native of France; died, July 15, 1835; age, 59 years.
Alexander King; born in Ireland; died, April 30, 1839; age, 29 years.
George R. Forsyth; died, March 26, 1811; age, 28 years.
John Estell; age, 17 years.
Edwin Alexander Ruthven Royster, April 6, 1833-Sept. 16, 1833.
Charles Colborn; died, Nov. 11, 1835; age, 4 months, 1 day.
Mary Webb, consort of K. Webb; died, May 13, 1834; age, 32 years.
Anne Elizabeth Yeatman, daughter of Thomas and Jane; died, Nov. 7, 1822; age, 2 years, 3 months, 4 days.
Chas. T. Yeargin, May 27, 1849-March 13, 1922.
Florence Rutland, wife of Chas. T. Yeargin, March 3, 1853-July 23, 1920.
Mrs. Mary E. Hall, wife of Allen A. Hall; died, Nov. 22, 1829; age, 24 years.
James Thompson, infant son of J. D. and Sarah March, Aug. 13-Aug. 21, 1844.
Sarah March, consort of J. D. March, Sept. 1810-June 15, 1844.
Jefferson Cartwright; died, Sept., 1833; age, 26 years.
John Spence; died, Dec. 19, 182—; age, 46 years.
Anna L. Deadrick, consort of Fielding Deadrick, daughter of Edmund and Patsy Cooper, Aug. 27, 1816; age, 49 years.
Infant son of James and E. A. Woods, April 2, 1827.
Elizabeth, wife of John C. McLemore, Nov. 22, 1796-July 2, 1836.
Rachel Nichol, consort of John Nichol; died, Aug. 9, 1824; age, 28 years, leaving a husband and five children.
Elizabeth, daughter of John and Rachel Nichol, Sept. 29, 1823; age, 8 years, 2 months.
Bernard Vanleer, Sept. 7, —— Jan. 17, —33.
Hannah, wife of Bernard Vanleer; died, —33; age, 58 years; stones broken, mended at place of dates.
Marjory, daughter of John and Rachel Nichol; died, March 21, 1812; age, 18 years.
Sarah Elizabeth, daughter of John and Sarah Elizabeth Campbell; born in Fayetteville, N. C., Oct. 29, 1835-June 14, 1849.
Mrs. Oliva F. Glasscock, Jan. 23, 1815-Nov. 3, 1837.
Jane W. Tarver, March 28, 1815-April 26, 1856.
Frank C. Clark; age, 19 months.
James Trimble Clark; age, 17 years.
Mary Martin, wife of Russell Dance, July 22, 1815-June 20, 1837.
Infant son of Mrs. Maria E. Coen; age, 6 years.
Susan Carper, 1778-Feb. 23, 1852.
Nathan and Thomas P., infant sons of Thomas P. and Ann Adams.
Nathan; died, Aug. 8, 1821; age, 11 months.

Bible Records—Tombstone Inscriptions

Thomas P.; died, June 4, 1834; age, 23 months.

Wm. Loman and Jonathan, his brother, infant children of Alfred and Polly Loman; Wm. died June 21, 1821; age, 1 year, 2 months; Jonathan died June 22, 1821; age, 2 years.

James L. Howell, Oct. 19, 1847-Dec. 18, 1918.

Alice A. Howell, April 29, 1850-Nov. 4, 1922.

William Eastham of Virginia, Jan. 23, 1788-Aug. 30, 1834.

Wm. Napier; age, 42 years.

M. A. E. Allen; died, 1842.

Elizabeth, infant daughter of Nancy Smith, Nov. 3, 1824.

Fred E. Fisher, born in Pennsylvania, Jan. 3, 1789-June 15, 1856.

George Washington Campbell, son of G. W. and Harriot Campbell; born in St. Petersburg, Russia, Oct. 1, 1818; died in Rochefort, France, Aug. 6, 1853.

Thomas J. Barker; died, July 11, 1855; age, 51 years.

Manoah James Bostick, no dates.

Sue Bostick, 1844-1862.

T. H. Bostick, 1833-1871.

C. B. Habert, 1828-1916.

Mary Litton, wife of S. F. Wilson, 1858-1920.

Ellis M. Gunn, 1881-1902.

John Waters, M.D., 1794-1867.

Ann Rawlings Williams, wife of John Waters, 1826-1910.

Malvina Bass Waters, daughter of John and Ann R. Waters, 1847-1860.

Lyman C. Gunn, 1846-1914.

Richard Stoddert, Lt.-Gen. C. S. A., Feb. 8, 1817-Jan. 25, 1872.

Julia A. Maxey, Dec. 13, 1—1—; died, April 29, 1—7—; dates almost illegible.

P. C. Maxey, May 13, 1841-Feb. 17, 1864.

Ann Bennett, Oct. 7, 1809-May 23, 1858.

James A. McAlister, Jan. 18, 1814-April 4, 1904; born in Jonesboro, Tenn.

Maria A. Parrish, 1822-1895.

Miss Betty Holt, 1843-1916.

Infant son of W. R. and Blanche McNabb; born and died April 24, 1912.

Sarah L. Newman (mother), Aug. 28, 1843-Aug. 12, 1918.

Joseph A. Newman (papa), Dec. 26, 1836-May 28, 1914.

Ora Elmo Newman, Nov. 23, 1876-June 25, 1877.

Alexander Francis Marian Parrish, June 9, 1836-April 8, 1839.

Dorothy Parrish, June 7, ——Nov. 22, 1822.

Sarah E. Swiney, infant daughter of Mary E. Swiney, April 13-April 15, 1831.

William Denton, Massachusetts; died, August, 1830; age, 29 years.

Eliza R. Price, infant daughter of Thomas K. and Eliza J. Price.

Letitia Price, Maryland, 1758-1832.

Margaretta Eliza Hill Price, infant daughter of Thomas K. and Eliza J. Price, June 8, 1840-March 22, 1841, at New Orleans.

Addie Hunt; died, Dec. 26, 1903.

Sarah W. Hunt; died, July 20, 1904.

Samuel Read Anderson, 1804-1883.

Ella T. H. Elliston, Feb. 2, 1845-May 30, 1899.

John Adrian Gilbert, son of John B. and Mary Gilbert, 1855.

William Hiter Elliston, July 3, 18——April 25, 1852.

John W. Saunders; died, Aug. 31, 1842; age, 35 years.

Miss Toy Holman, 1839-1911; daughter of James T. and Clementina Holman.

James T. Holman, Prince Edward County, Va., Feb. 20, 1802-Feb. 16, 1839.

Mary Mackenzie, Sept. 15, 1853; age, 29 years.

Mrs. M. Dickson; died, July 22, 1843; age, 23 years, and her daughter.

Mary L. Dickson; died, Feb. 6, 1843; age, 3 years, 6 months.

Sarah Bigley, Aug. 17, 1842; age, 69 years.

Minerva C. Hays, daughter of Hammond and Elizabeth Hays; died, May 2, 1855; age, 6 years.

Sally, wife of Preston Hay, May 10, 1807-Nov. 19, 1849.

Elizabeth Harper; age, 68 years.

Ralph Henry Martin, son of Ralph and Sejus Martin, Dec. 12, 1800-July 19, 1818.

Ralph William Hank, Oct. 6, 1835; age, 11 months.

John F. Hawkins, son of W. N. and E. M. Hawkins, Jan. 13, 1842; age, 7 months, 4 days.

Bible Records—Tombstone Inscriptions

Benjamin Alley, Sept. 24, 1775-Feb. 19, 1830.
John Coltart, 1819-1876.
Roanna Duff Duncan, 1862-1869.
John McIntire; died, 1871; stone mended at place of dates.
Jennie Wise Rose, Sept. 10, 1837-May 20, 1918.
Jacob W. Golladay, Sept. 28, 1843; age, 43 years.
Rosina Domido, March 11, 1779-March 3, 1843.
Tennessee, daughter of William Blount Robertson and Leadocia Irwin, granddaughter of Gen. James Robertson, Aug. 15, 1808-July 28, 1857.
Paul Blanchi, native of Milan; died, May 17, 1835; age, 55 years.
James Moncrief; born in Scotland; died, Oct. 3, ——; age, 29 years.
A Revolutionary Soldier of 1776; sacred to the memory of Capt. John Bradford; born May 14, 1762, and departed this life Jan. 27, 1827.
Elizabeth Blackwell, wife of Capt. John Bradford, June 27, 1767-April 24, 1837.
Parents of Mrs. Alfred Hume.
Children were (these are listed on the large slab):
Ann, born, 1786.
Elizabeth, born, 1788.
Armistead Blackwell, born, 1789.
John Alexander, born, 1791.
Hiram, born, 1793.
Judith, born, 1795.
Robert, born, 1797.
William Ashton, born, 1800.
Edward, born, 1802.
Frederick, born, 1805.
Evalina Matilda, born, 1807.
Louisa Harner, born, 1811.
Mary Margaret, born, 1813.
Children of Mary and William Hume:
Earle, Sept. 7, 1879-1881.
John Orr, Oct. 27, 1875-June, 1876.
William Richardson, great-grandson of Rev. William Hume, Nov. 7, 1861-Sept. 29, 1891.
Joseph B. and Rebecca Hume; died, 1826; died, 1829; infants of William Hume.
Essie Hume, March 8, 1822-Aug. 16, 1854.
Rachel Jackson Hume, 1827-1910.
Auguste Emilie Hauser, April 6, 1840-March 11, 1843.

William Sneed, late of Lynchburg, Va.; died, Sept. 14, 1827; age, 22 years.
Robert McIndole; died, Feb. 11, 1839; age, 25 years.
Johnny, infant of D. and M. Bryant, Aug., 1868-Sept. 17, 1869.
E. Furtwangler, native of Schwarzwald; died, April 11, 1835; age, 21 years.
Homer N. Smith; died, Nov. 11, 1836; age, 18 years.
S. V. W. Stout, April 13, 1787-Aug. 8, 1850.
Mary W. Corsaw, Nov. 11, 1825-Oct. 11, 1912.
Craven Jackson, Nov. 1770-Oct., 1821.
Joseph F. Hard, July 12, 1813-June 18, 1855; born in Arlington, Vt.
James Halliday; died, Oct. 31, 1830.
Henry Fly, son of Micajah and Nancy Fly, Feb. 11, 1821-May 21, 1821.
Amanda A. Page, wife of S. P. Plummer, Dec. 15, 1834-Jan. 7, 1895.
S. P. Plummer, Sept. 31, 1831-May 21, 1909.
Lizinka Campbell, daughter of George Washington and Harriot Campbell; born in St. Petersburg, Russia, Feb. 21, 1820; married James Percy Brown, who died in 1841; in May, 1863, she married Lt.-Gen. Ewell, Richmond, Va.; died, Springhill, Tenn., Jan. 22, 1872.
Harriot Campbell, daughter of Benjamin Stoddert, Secretary of Navy undes; born in Georgetown Disct. April des; born in Georgetown Disct April 12, 1788; married, July 18, 1812; died, July 17, 1842.
Kate Ferris Thompson, Feb. 3, 1853-Dec. 3, 1909.
John B. Ewin, Feb. 3, 18—; illegible.
William F. Elliott, July 12, 1818-Dec. 2, 1869.
Maria Callaghan, Feb. 4, 1815-1861.
Andrew J. Moulton, 1828-1895.
Mary N. Wheeler Moulton, 1837-1906.
Claudine Mabel, youngest child of W. H. and Eleanora Carroll, June 13, 1878-Aug. 26, 1892.
Lizinka Campbell, wife of Richard Stoddert, Lt.-Gen. C. S. A., Feb. 24, 1820-Jan. 22, 1872.
Our Maggie (Hicks), Oct. 29, 1851-May 31, 1852.
Jane and her children; Driver lot;

Bible Records—Tombstone Inscriptions

Sept. 18, 1878; George Wilson, Delilah, Thomas Pitcairn.
Polly Hill, mother of Sarah Es—11; died, Nov. 6, 1849.
Albert J. Tully, Oct. 1, 1826-Aug. 4, 1845.
Elizabeth McEwen Boyd, Feb. 28, 1788-Dec. 29, 1861.
Joseph McEwen; died, July 6, 1855.
Sophia Elizabeth McEwen; died, July 13, 1843.
Esther Maria and Robena A., infants of Liston and Wm. Elizabeth McEwen Stones.
John Cockrill, Dec. 19, 1757-April 11, 1837.
Ann Cockrill, formerly Ann Robertson, Feb. 10, 1757-Oct. 13, 1821.
Col. B. F. Cockrill, Nov. 1, 1852-April 28, 1903.
His wife, Sarah Foster Cockrill, Oct. 20, 1836-Nov. 12, 1902.
Mrs. Ellen Cheatham, wife of Col. B. Cheatham, daughter of Ephraim Foster.
Mrs. Julia Ann Hood, daughter of Ephraim Foster, wife of John M. Hood; died, Oct. 11, 1849; age, 19 years, mother and daughter.
Robert C. Foster; died, Sept. 27, 1844; age, 75 years.
Ann S. Foster, Nov. 17, 1850; age, 80 years.
Frances Ann, wife of M. J. Gilchrist, daughter of J. H. and N. H. Foster, Aug., 1825-April, 1850.
Charles Francis Adams; died, July 3, 1866; age, 11 years, 3 months.
Susan Jane Marlow, Feb. 10, 1837- Dec. 1, 1839.
Jacob Stoll, no dates.
Sarah Ann Poteet, daughter of Brice and Sarah D. Poteet, May 16, 1867-July 15, 1873.
Rev. E. I. Fitzgerald, Nov. 5, 1793-Oct. 8, 1844; age, 60 years.
Frank A. Scheuerman, Sept. 10, 1853-Aug. 23, 1924.
Mary Ida Scheuerman, April 1, 1855-Jan. 20, 1924.
Mark A. Cooper, May 1, 1851-Dec. 19, 1883.
Elizabeth Bateman, April 22, 1822-Jan. 23, 1815. (?)
Dr. G. F. Helfer and M. M. Helfer, born in Arinz.
F. W. Helfer, June 17, 1861-Aug., 1864.
H. M. C. Helfer, July 24, 1863-July 23, 1864.
Phyllis Carter; died, Jan. 21, 1840; age, 60 years.
Calop B. Commander, March 8, 1804-Sept. 9, 1837.
Mary Emma Kissing, Feb. 2, 1871-March 18, ——.
Mrs. H. H. Jones, Dec. 1, 1818-June 23, 1880.
Aleen Jones, Aug. 19, 1810-Feb. 2, 1875.
Maria Ann Stout, no dates.
J. C. Woehrle, Dec. 14, 1821-Nov. ——.
George Haller, Germany, Sept. 23, 1866; age, 29 years.
Emma M. Wallace; died, April, 1866; age, 13 months, 14 days.
John Wallace, Sept. 24, 1866; age, 8 years, 9 months, 11 days.
Y. B. Jones, 1828-1860.
Celia Page Jones, wife of Y. B. Jones, 1839-1897.
Henrietta Schorr, Aug. 8, 1834-Jan. 10, 1858.
Henry Schorr, Hanover Germany, no dates.
Augusta Seibert, Germany, March 30, 1821-Jan. 22, 1884.
Augusta Schorr, March 30, 1851-July 11, 1852.
Johanna Louise Schorr, July 14, 1853-July 22, 1853.
Margaret, wife of Alfred McGavock, Oct. 20, 1830-Jan. 25, 1862.
Hannah Lindsley; died, Sept. 17, 1846; age, 56 years.
Susan Person, 1814-June 26, 1821.
Eugenia Ann Tait, Jan. 11, 1837-Sept. 18, 1837; daughter of A. L. and A. A. Tait.
Othelia Ann Tait, July 1, 1838-Jan. 12, 1840; daughter of A. L. and A. A. Tait.
Samuel Bentley Boseley, Feb. 11, 1814-July 22, 1850.
Catherine Lawrence, wife of Granderson Lawrence; died, Oct. 1, 1838.
Little Queenie, daughter of James and Sarah Bass, May 16, 1853-Aug. 23, 1854.
Charles I. Love; died, July 29, 1837; age, 63 years.
Mrs. Hannah Claiborne, July 19, 1788-March 31, 1808.
Percy Sharpe Goodwin, July 9, 1844-Nov. 27, 1919.
Mary C., daughter of T. H. and Sarah

Bible Records—Tombstone Inscriptions

Claiborne, June 10, 1814-June 12, 1814.
C. C. P. Conway; died, Oct. 11, 1816; age, 23 years, 1 month, 15 days.
William C. Dickinson, M.D., Aug. 11, 1791-Nov. 14, 1844.
Catherine Richardson, Feb. 19, 1796-March 11, 1848.
Belinda G. Polk, Dec. 31, 1816-March 26, 1844.
Berry M. Franklin, 1832-1883.
Frances Peyton Love, consort of Chas. I. Love, Gloucester County, Va., 1785-June 17, 1855.
Peter Harris, 1836-1899.
Sarah F. Harris, 1838-1898.
Jackson Green of County Down, Ireland, erected monument for his son, Thomas, June 25, 1850, age, 20 years, and his beloved wife, Eliza, daughter of Wm. Johnson, County Down, Ireland, Oct. 7, 1854; age, 43 years.
Henrietta Rimberger, May 18, 1861-Nov. 2, 1862.
Joseph L. Garrett, Nov. 15, 1847-Sept. 21, 1866.
Elizabeth Keesee; died, June 5, 1865; age, 73 years.
Mary A. Jennings Miller, 1848-1926.
Margaret Thomm, Sept. 17, 1866; age, 45 years; Sophia Bassow, Aug. 7, 1861; age, 38 years.
Robert L., died, March 20, and Huston N, April 24, 1870; sons of —— and M. C. Britt; stone badly broken.
Maria F. Jennings, 1822-1893.
Wm. H. Jennings, 1814-1850.
J. K. F. Jennings, 1844-1847.
Wm. H. Jennings, 1846-1847.
J. Willima H. Jennings, 1851-1873.
Lucy A. D. Adams, 1838-1858.
Nathan J. Adams, 1830-1856.
Ella Dallas, wife of Triv. B. Dallas; died, Pensacola, Fla., March 20, 1873.
Booker; died, Sept., 1845; age, 22 years.
Margaret; died, Dec., 1857; age, 24 years.
Patience, May 23, 1854; age, 50 years.
John Henry, June 25, 1854; age, 14 months, 8 days.
Edmond, June 25, 1854; age, 34 years.
No surname for these five.
Robert Buckle, Dublin, Ireland; died, 1855; age, 60 or 69 years.
James, son of Frank Parish; age, 19; no dates.
Martella, infant daughter of Edmond and Malinda Howe, Aug. 6, 1845-Aug. 16, 1846.
Elizabeth, daughter of Lelly Bradshaw, wife of Anderson Hardeman; died at age of 44 years.
Emily L., daughter of A. Herbert and Mary Levi; died, July 9, 1819.
Robert Evers, Nov. 8, 1827-April 23, 1881.
Margaret Murray, Nov. 25, 18——June 14, 1849.
Ann Smith Jefferson, wife of John Proyor Ford; born in Cumberland County, Va., May 31, 1877.
Martha Pentecost; died, Feb. 10, 1923; age, 68.
Mary Elizabeth Hougins, Oct. 27, 1824-Jan. 25, 1868.
Wm. Gilliner, March 3, 1821-Nov. 11, 1851.
Samuel Vanleer, June 23, 1802-Nov. 11, 1844.
Amelia Wood Terrass, wife of Samuel Vanleer, 1807-1894.
John Peabody, Sept. 9, 1792-July 4, 1850.
Mary C. Cooper, Aug. 2, 1823-Dec. 15, 1877; Hopkinsville, Ky.
Ben S. Weller, Hopkinsville, Ky.; died in Nashville.
Elis M. Campbell, Aug. 7, 1826-June 22, 1847.
Elizabeth Beasley, Oct. 24, 1796-July 21, 1853.
Ethelred Williams, Jan. 29, 1791, in Halifax, a Mason, marker in honor of service in War of 1812.
Sarah Ann Hodge, July 31, 1853-June 6, 1895.
Wm. B. Hodge, Feb. 22, 1829-June 10, 1895.
Elizabeth M. Hodge, wife of James L. Hodge.
Rebecca A. Green, June 14, 1828-March 18, 1849.
Marinda W., daughter of J. J. and P. A. Deshazer, Lunnenburg County, Va., Dec. 29, 1837-July 8, 1850.
Laura M. Argo, Feb. 18, 1853-July 4, 1928.
James Alexander of Scotland; age, 25 years.
Wm. C. White, 1875-1931.
Cora B. White, 1884-19——.
Joseph H. Fuller, 1841-1915.
Amanda M. Fuller, 1848-1916.

Bible Records—Tombstone Inscriptions

Elizabeth G. Cotton; died, Oct. 13, 1884; age, 52 years.
Ernest, son of G. A. and M. C. Marlin, Feb. 4, 1859-Feb. 5, 1860.
A. May, Aug. 27, 1894-May 31, 1895; child of W. L. and N. R. Marlin.
Nettie, May 12, 1900-Sept. 12, 1901; daughter of W. I. and N. R. Marlin.
Little Mother, Victoria Green, 1890-1932.
S. J. Norman; died, 1873; wife of H. H. Norman; died, 1875.
Leon S. Buck, April 20, 1889-Oct. 25, 1927.
Joney K. Brown, daughter of Wm. and Nancy Whaley, wife of Joseph P. Brown, Jan. 27, 1823-April 16, 1853.
Jonathan Thomas, June 1, 1804-Oct. 30, 1863.
Jos. Caldwell McCrory, Jan. 17, 1832-July 6, 1912.
Emma J. Boone, wife of J. C. McCrory, Oct. 18, 1833-Dec. 12, 1918.
P. F. Lawrence, 1835-1904; infant children of P. F. and Emma; L. F. L., 1873-1875; L. L. L., 1876-1879.
Robert B. Lawrence, 1878-1922.
Infant children of R. B. and Ella Lawrence: R. H., died, 1905; J. P., died, 1905; M. C., died, 1908.
C. A. Lawrence, 1881-1825.
Emma Lawrence, 1845-1927.
Shakespeare, son of Francis Person, 1830-Nov. 20, 1835.
Alice Vanney; died, April 26, 1856.

Marian, daughter of James T. and Catherine M. Growdis, Aug. 31, 1861-May 7, 1863.
Thomas M. Frensley, March 21, 1864-Nov. 16, 1919.
Sussie Phelps, 1839-Jan. 12, 1920.
Thomas Weaver, son of Calvin and Sarah E. Gabler, June 21, 1850-March 17, 1845.
John Corbitt, Oct. 20, 1790-Nov. 8, 1862.
Rachel C., wife of John, July 9, 1794-April 18, 1821.
G. G. Gabler, 1815-1895.
Emily Newherne, wife of G. G., May 13, 1827-Sept. 21, 1853.
James Sanders, Sept. 27, 1838-March 26, 1860.
Susan H. Bass, wife of Augustus, born in Ohio, Aug. 21, 1821-June 9, 1849.
Beverly H. Cheek, Nov. 8, 1819-July 13, 1863.
Julia M. Ward, May 10, 1861-April 17, 1863.
Sarah J. Neal, Feb. 6, 1849-Dec. 22, 1928.
Nannie J. Williams, wife of J. M., Feb. 6, 1869-Sept. 18, 1928.
Louise M. Sinclair, 1830-1870.
Sarah Parker, wife of Richard, Amelia County, Va., Sept. 30, 1811-July 11, 1852.
Mary Parker; died, July 8, 1816; age, 3 years.

Mount Calvary Cemetery
Established in 1868

Persons dying previous to the period of 1868 were buried in the old Catholic Cemetery, which was abandoned in 1910, and the dead removed to Calvary. These are interment dates.

This report was compiled by Elizabeth C. Breen and Delia S. Brew, appointed by the Colonna Club.

David Moran, 1842.
Mary Manning, 1843.
William Lowe, 1847.
Thos. F. Burns, 1848.
George Bergin, 1850.
John Bergin, 1850.
Phillip Ryan, 1851.
Francis Cox, 1852.
Sister Jane Francis Kennedy (Sisters of Charity buried on Thos. Farrell lot) in 1854, died of cholera.
Sister Ellen Davis buried on Farrell lot; died of cholera in 1854.
Mary Jane Breen, died, 1855.
Thos. Breen, 1855.
Maria Breen, 1861.
William M. Dwyer, 1863.
Bridget Hailey Breen, 1863.

Bible Records—Tombstone Inscriptions

Bridge Goyle Lowe, 1854.
Mary Brady, 1855.
Patrick Foley, 1856.
Martin Ward, 1856.
Rev. Augustine Murphy, 1856.
Michael Glenn, 1856.
Maurice Geary, 1858.
Johanna Shea, 1858.
Thos. Ward, 1858.
Joyn Flannagan, 1859.
Thos. Flannagan, 1859.
Michael Gegan, 1859.
Patrick Lally, 1859.
Mary Patterson, 1859.
Michael Regan, 1859.
Patrick Shea, 1859.
Jas. Glenn, 1859.
John Gough, 1859.
Jerry Buckley, 1859.
William Dalton, 1859.
Mary Kelley, 1859.
Conrad J. Schund, 1859.
Henry Gillespie, 1859.
Julia Ann Whelan, 1859.
Austin Burns, 1860.
Martin Dalton, 1860.
John Fitzgerald, 1860.
Dan Ward, 1860.
Mary Driscoll, 1860.
Catherine Hagerty, Feb. 20, 1860.
Johnny Hagerty, Feb. 20, 1860.
Bridget Hayes, Feb. 20, 1860.
Ann Bergin, April, 1860.
Willie Allen, 1860.
Edward Jennings, 1860.
Emma Dalton, Sept., 1860.
Mary Ryan, 1860.
Willie Murphy, Oct. 21, 1860.
Mary Ann Murphy, Oct. 5, 1860.
Mary Burke, 1861.
Margaret Fitzgibbon, 1861.
Margaret Jane Fitzgibbon, 1861.
Michael Heheir, 1861.
William Jacobs, 1861.
Patrick Murphy, 1861.
Catherine O'Connell, 1861.
Joseph Whelan, Jan. 11, 1861.
Ellen Donnelly, 1861.
Bridget Farrell, 1861.
Maggie Sutherland, 1861.
Maggie Flanagan, 1861.
George E. Wright, 1861.
Mary Plummer, 1861.
Patrick and Francis Gilride, July 15, 1861; moved from old Catholic Cemetery, 1901.
Mary C. Walsh, 1861.
Thos. Whelan, 1861.
Lawrence Olwill, 1861.
Philip Olwill, 1861, children.
Patrick Brady, Dec., 1861.
Mary Lally, 1862.
John Morrissey, 1862.
Ann Geary, Jan., 1862.
Jas. Hardeman, Feb., 1862.
A. H. Archibald, 1862.
James Hughes, 1862.
Edgar Ryan, 1862.
Patrick Buckley, Nov., 1862.
John Collins, 1863.
Ellen Cox, 1863.
Leonard Fitzgerald, 1863.
Thos. Fitzgerald, 1863.
Patrick John Hughes, 1863.
Michael Patterson, 1863.
Margaret Quinn, 1863.
John Brady, 1863.
Thos. Whelan, 1863.
Damian Jacobs, 1863.
Mary Ann Nogianna, 1863.
Mary Riley, 1863.
Patrick Archibald, 1864.
Mary Halloran, 1864.
Francis Kinney, 1864.
Harry Quin, 1864.
Thos. Walsh, 1864.
Patrick Archibald, Jan., 1864.
Charles Wright, 1864.
Elizabeth Wright, Jan., 1864.
Florence Wright, 1864.
James Donelly, Feb., 1864.
Winnifred Murphy, Feb. 20, 1864.
James Plummer, Feb., 1864.
Timothy Donnelly, Apr., 1864.
Margaret Buckley, May, 1864.
Patrick Taylor, June, 1864.
Edward P. Hickey (old Catholic family), died, 1864.
John Plummer, 1864.
Christopher Hennot, 1864.
Mary Vaughn, 1864.
Solomon Wymer, 1864.
Mary Cronin, 1865.
Michael Davis, 1865.
Margaret Donnelly, 1865.
Bessie Kerrigan, 1865.
Elizabeth Kerrigan, 1865.
James Ryan, 1865.
John Walsh, 1865.
Bridget Callahan, 1865.
Euclid Burke, 1865.
Jas. Heheir, 1865.
Timothy Murphy, 1865.
Mary O'Donnell, 1865.

Bible Records—Tombstone Inscriptions

Albert Cox, 1866.
Matthew Dillon, 1866.
Owen Finnegan, 1866.
Bridget Halloran, 1866.
Mary McGovern, 1866.
Thos. McGovern, 1866.
Mary Murray, 1866.
Florence Sullivan, 1866.
Francis Dorgan, 1866.
Michale Brady, 1866.
Nicholas Maloney, 1866.
Jas. McGovern, 1866.
John Kenelly, 1866.
Hannah Brady, 1866.
Peter Hanson, 1866.
Ellen Hines, 1866.
John Hines, 1866.
Johanna O'Callahan, 1866.
Tim Ryan, 1866.
John O'Connor, 1866.
Mary Heverin, 1869.
Patrick Madden, 1867; age, 58 years.
Kate Madden, 1867; age, 14 years.
John Quinn, 1870; age, 42 years.
John Quinn, 1870; age, 42 years.
Jas. Powers, 1867.
Michael Callahan, 1867.
Kate Powers, 1867.
Catherine Connors, 1867.
Patrick O'Hagerty, 1868.
Jas. and Thos. Farrell, 1868.
Dan O'Leary, 1866.
Mary Ann Joyce, 1868; age, 29 years.
Emma Meir, Aug., 1868.
Richard Lally, Sept., 1868.
Patrick McGuire, 1868.
James Ryan, 1868.
Michael Dalton, 1868.
Malachy Molloy, 1868; age, 50 years.
Sarah Sheilds, 1868; 40 years.
Thos. Hussey, 1868; age, 26 years.
Delia Halloran, 1869.
Clara Sinnot, 1869.
Emele Latelle, 1869; age, 22 years.
John Flyn, 1869; age, 65 years.
Ann Strobel, Jan. 3, 1869.
Cornelius Murphy, 1869; age, 45 years.
Mary Ann Reynolds, 1869.
John O'Bryan, 1869; age, 60 years.
Rosalie Fay, Jan. 20, 1869; age, 40 years; born in Germany.
Annie French, 1869.
Jas. Doyle, Jan., 1869.
Miles Gillespie, Feb., 1869.
Hannora Breen, infant.
Margaret Breen, 1869, infant.
Kate M. Brown, 1869.

Wm. Dalton, 1869.
Mary L. McGath, 1869.
Patrick Fay, 1869.
Michael Fitzgerald, 1869.
Catherine Doherty, 1869.
Margaret Chapman, 1869; age, 35 years.
John Schreider, born in Germany; died, 1869; age, 39 years.
Thos. G. Lee, 1869.
John M. Joyce, 1869.
David Coleman, born in Ireland; died, 1869; age, 65 years.
Patrick Farrell and family, removals, 1869.
Eliza Kenny, 1869.
James Kenny, 1869.
Patrick Kenney, 1869.
Patrick O'Brien, 1869.
Jeremiah Murray, 1869.
John Judkins, 1869.
Kate Kerrigan, 1869.
William Laffey, 1869; age, 40 years.
Patrick Cridden, 1869.
Catherine McCormack, 1869.
Dan Gillespie, June 6, 1869.
Anne Mack, 1869.
Jas. Farrell, 1869.
Frank Martin, 1869.
M. H. Matthews, 1869.
Cornelius Burns, 1869.
George McNulty, 1869.
David Leck, 1869.
Michael Clonan, 1869.
John Kenney, 1869.
Michael Maeher, 1869.
Martin Cressen, 1869; age, 17 years.
John Flanigan, 1869; age, 65 years.
Norman Murray, 1869; age, 18 years.
Bridget Murphy, 1869.
Christopher Andrews, died, 1869; age, 40 years.
Thos. Larvis, 1869; age, 32 years.
Margaret Dalton, Aug. 14, 1869.
Catherine Hyde, 1869.
Wm. Maher, 1869; age, 52 years.
Mary O'Connor, 1869.
Anne Gorman, 1869.
Jos. Schneider, 1869.
Jennie Sinnott, 1869.
Peter Carney, died, 1869; age, 48 years.
David Dalton, 1869.
Peter Halloran, 1869.
Jas. Halloran, 1869.
Hugh French McAllister, 1869; age, 4
Jas. Sennett, 1869; 36 years.
Thos. Heffernan, died, 1869; age, 55 years.

Bible Records—Tombstone Inscriptions

Thos. Lomasney, 1869.
Mary Rowley, 1869.
Maurice Moriarity, 1869.
Annie Dodd, 1869.
Von Hurston, 1869; age, 37 years.
William Elliot, 1869; age, 29 years.
Timothy Holony, 1869.
Martin Hession, 1869.
Patrick Hagerty, 1869; age, 26 years.
Margaret Brew, 1869; age, 13 years.
Anne Corcoran, 1869.
Patrick Calvin, 1869.
Margaret Lomasney, 1869.
Margaret Wright, 1869; age, 7 years.
Thos. Edgar, 1869; age, 10 months.
John Andrews, 1869; age 100 years.
John Casey, 1869.
Phillip Breen (infant), 1869.
Julia Halloran, 1869.
Bridge Hanson, 1869.
Anne Hughes, 1869.
Patrick Burns, 1869.
John Frances Gilvain, 1869.
Jas. Cronin, 1869; age, 4 years.
Timothy Gary, 1869; age, 1 year.
Dennis Treacy, 1869; age, 40 years.
Michael Joyce, Dec. 25, 1869,
William Barrett, 1869.
Dennis Horan, 1870.
Lizzie Galvin, 1870.
Edward Jones, 1870.
Patrick Sullivan, 1870.
Hanora Martin, 1870; age, 75 years.
William Martin, 1870.
John W. Gilmore, 1870.
Bernard Evers, 1870; age, 9 years.
Mark Grady, 1870; age 20 years.
Charlotte Sinnot, 1870.
Dennis Horan, 1870.
Mary A. Keegan, 1870.
Starnes Gaskin, 1870; age, 70 years.
John Dwyer, Sr., 1870; age, 35 years.
Edward Manning, 1870; age, 50 years.
Bernard Murphy, 1870; age, 55 years.
Margaret Brett(infant), 1870.
Albert Capps, 1870; age, 3 years.
John Davy, 1870; age, 40 years.
Bridget Naughton, 1870; age, 37 years.
Mary Marton, 1870; age, 32 years.
Hanora Joyce, 1870; age, 35 years.
Jas. C. Laffy, 1870; age, 45 years.
Ellen Creighan, 1870.
John Brackley (single grave), 1870; age, 40 years.
Margaret Ryan, 1870.
Thos. Burns, 1870.

Lizzie Nolan, 1870.
Mary Nolan, 1870; age, 26 years.
Berth Shea, July 9, 1870.
Thos. Neal, July 13, 1870.
Thos. Gloster, July 14, 1870.
Mary Jane Courfman, 1870; age, 48 years.
Margaret Kendrickan, died, July, 1870; age, 15 years.
Alice Kelly, 1870; age, 52 years.
Jerome Lucius Byrne, July 23, 1870.
Johnney Keanon, Aug. 1, 1870.
Ann Cox, Aug. 8, 1870; age, 62 years.
Michael McNulty, Aug. 18, 1870.
P. W. Henley, Aug. 18, 1870.
Anne Mulray, Aug. 2, 1870.
Thos. Egan, Aug. 28, 1870.
Joseph Martin, Aug. 28, 1870.
Mary Shermin, Sept. 4, 1870.
Frances Hynes, Sept. 7, 1870.
Mary E. Dale, Sept. 9, 1870.
Annie Egan, Sept. 13, 1870.
Edward Glennon, Sept. 16, 1870; age, 25 years.
Arthur Allen, Sept. 22, 1870.
Anne Britt, 1870; age, 25 years.
Edward Hugh Benner, Oct., 1870.
E. H. Connor, Oct., 1870.
Thos. Rooney, 1870; age, 65 years.
Johanna Kingsley, 1870.
Patrick McMullen, Oct. 8, 1870.
John Edgar, 1870; age, 40 years.
Margaret Rodes, 1870; age, 38 years.
Elizabeth Parker, 1870; age, 30 years.
Joseph Galvin, Nov. 6, 1870.
Patrick Stack, Nov. 21, 1870; age, 31 years.
Margaret Farrell, Nov. 25, 1870; age, 18 years.
Andrew Burke, Nov. 25, 1870; age, 35 years.
Mr. Moggiana, Nov. 25, 1870.
Martin Costello, 1870; age, 32 years.
Thos. Burns, 1870; age, 42 years.
Lawrence Maddin, 1871; age, 42 years.
Patrick Malloy, 1871; age, 60 years.
Susan Slaman, 1871.
M. Garolin, Jan. 1871.
Jean J. Bertheal, 1871; age, 75 years.
Bettie Lomasney, July 17, 1871.
James Walsh, July 24, 1871; age, 60 years.
Ellie J. Donavan, Aug. 3, 1871.
Mary Joachim O'Connor, Aug., 1871.
Andrew Brady, Sept., 1871.
Anna E. Cullen, 1871.
Thomas Vaughn, Sept., 1871.

Bible Records—Tombstone Inscriptions

Chustin Egly, Sept. 5, 1871; age, 49 years.
Anne Goodrich, Sept. 5, 1871; age 13 years.
Timothy Finney, 1871; age, 28 years.
Patrick McTigue, Sept. 22, 1871; age, 47 years.
Annie Eugenie, Sept. 25, 1871.
Eliza Hughes, 1871; age, 42 years.
James Murphy, Oct., 1871.
Patrick McTigue, 1871.
Patrick Berry, 1871; age, 35 years.
Margaret Quinn, Oct. 23, 1871; age, 50 years.
Kate Coughlin, Nov., 1871.
Robt. O'Shaughnessy, Nov., 1871.
Patrick Derr, March 24, 1872; age 40 years.
Michael Foley, March 24, 1872; age, 50 years.
Catherine Maloney, March 24, 1872; age, 45 years.
Patrick Malloy, March 25, 1872; age, 66 years.
Mary McCarthy, March, 1872; age, 29 years.
Adelina Bauman, April, 1872.
Nellie Powers, April, 1872.
Nellie Hynes, April, 1872.
John Walsh, April, 1872; age, 22 years.
Henry Bustard, April 3, 1872; age, 72 years.
Magdalena Mocker, April 5, 1872; age, 36 years.
Mary Anne Brice, April 6, 1872; age, 4 years.
Bridget Cochran, April 8, 1872; age, 2 years.
Jerry Buckley, April 9, 1872.
Six children of Eugene Ottenville, April 9, 1872.
David Lytle, April, 1872.
Salina Caulfield, April 22, 1872; age, 3 years.
Catherine C. Clark, April 23, 1872; age, 23 years.
Richard Curran, Feb., 1872.
James Regan, 1872; age, 19 years.
Ellen Hynes, April 23, 1872; age, 3 years.
Veronica Bauman, May, 1872; age, 20 years.
Frances Cunningham, May, 1872.
Charlotte Bauman, May, 1872; age, 20 years.
James Kane, May 6, 1872; age, 15 years.
McCarmock Family, May 7, 1872.
Mary Clunan, 1872; age, 55 years.
Ellen Crehan, June, 1872.
John Driscoll, 1872.
Ella Johnson, 1872.
Theodore Seifried, June 6, 1872.
Kate Lasky, June 7, 1872; age 24 years.
Ellen Mulloy, June 14, 1872.
Alice Kuigley, June 14, 1872; age, 12 years.
Mary Ann Kearns, June 15, 1872; age, 18 months.
Roberta Martin, June 15, 1872.
Edward Gloster, June 16, 1872; age 7 years.
Johnnie McKee, 1872; age, 11 years.
William Wright, June 22, 1872.
John Quinn, 1872; age, 31 years.
Anne Dugan, 1872; age, 17 years.
James Rafferty, 1872; age, 6 months.
Matilda Stout, 1872.
Rodger Doyle, 1872; age, 28 years.
Katherine Burns, 1872; age, 35 years.
Rebecca Isman, July 6, 1872; age, 25 years.
Hannah Kelley, July 7, 1872; age, 45 years.
Mary Curren, July 8, 1872; age, 18 years.
Ida Moore, July 17, 1872; age, 1 year.
Margaret Lynch, July 21, 1872; age, 4 years.
Anne Morissey, July 22, 1872; age, 21 years.
Catherine Manning, 1872; age, 2 years.
Maggie Halloran, July 27, 1872.
John Callaghan, July 30, 1872; age, 66 years.
John Hess (infant), 1872.
Michael Quinn, Aug. 4, 1872; age, 34 years.
Patrick Henry Griffin, Aug. 6, 1872.
Patrick Madden, Aug. 7, 1872; age, 50 years.
Margaret Farrell, Aug. 7, 1872; age, 8 years.
Thos. Baine, 1872; age, 43 years.
John Swords, 1872; age, 55 years.
Kate O'Donnell, 1872; age, 55 years.
Rosa Sharenberger, 1872; age, 10 months.
Mary Ellen Burke, 1872; age, 3 years.
Mary Timon (infant), 1872.
Anne Tracey, 1872; age, 5 years.
Michael Brady, 1872.
Mary Lecky, 1872; age, 40 years.
Roderick Mogan (infant), 1872.
Catherine Farrell, 1872; age, 67 years.

Bible Records—Tombstone Inscriptions

Margaret Killea, 1872; age, 50 years.
Michael Hefy, 1872; age, 50 years.
Genevera Arnold, 1872; age, 57 years.
Michael Devany, 1872; age, 15 months.
Michael Cox, 1872; age, 30 years.
Ellen Fitzpatrick, 1872; age, 27 years.
Michael McNarmara, Oct., 1872.
Michael Fahey, 1872; age, 100 years.
Catherine Flynn, 1872; age, 80 years.
Julia Moran (infant), 1872.
Henry Plum, 1872; age, 40 years.
William Langan, 1872; age 40 years.
Thos. Brown, 1872; age, 48 years.
Catherine Gaffney, 1872; age, 53 years.
Patrick Sherfly, 1872; age, 38 years.
Sabina Hynes, 1872; age, 13 years.
Martin Joice, 1872; age 59 years.
Mary Landers (infant), 1872.
John Nicholson, 1872; age, 5 years.
James Sullivan, 1872; age, 26 years.
Katie Evans, 1872; age, 5 years.
Mary Hopert, 1872; age, 2 years.
John Clees, 1872; age, 50 years.
Andrew Connelly, 1872; age, 41 years.
Katie Harahan, 1872.
Margaret Ryan, 1872; age 48 years.
Mary Heheir, 1872; age, 5 years.
Michael Reilly, 1872; age, 58 years.
James Tyne, Dec. 31, 1872.
Thos. Smith, 1873.
Patrick Dawson, Jan. 1, 1873; age, 23 years.
Edward McGrath, Jan. 2, 1873.
Thos. Ryan, 1873; age, 1 year.
Margaret Costello, Jan. 4, 1873; age, 30 years.
Chas. Gallagher, Jan. 5, 1873; age, 54 years.
Thos. Connolly, Jan. 10, 1873; age, 52 year.
Mary Halloran Farrell, Jan. 10, 1873.
Mocker Children, Jan. 14, 1873; ages, 6 and 8 months.
George W. Turner, Jan. 15, 1873; age, 57 years.
James Credon, 1873.
Margaret Devine (infant), Jan. 21, 1873.
Edward Kelley, Jan. 22, 1873.
Josie Dwyer, Feb. 8, 1873; age, 11 years, 9 months.
Mary Cady, Feb. 11, 1873; age 2 years.
John Quinn Neylan, 1873; age, 21 months.
Mary Ellen Neman, 1873; age, 21 months.
William Thomas Daughtery (infant), 1873.
Patrick McKee, 1873.
Arthur Mulloy, 1873.
James Murray, June 22, 1873; age 26 years.
May Walsh (infant), 1873.
John Ryan, 1873; age 70 years.
John Kearns, March 12, 1873; age 15 years.
Anne Kelley, 1873; age 50 years.
Albert Brisbo, 1873; age 5 years.
Patrick Lomasney, 1873; age, 45 years.
Anne Martin, 1873; age, 39 years.
Bridget Halloran (infant), 1873.
John Jacob Floersh, 1873.
Mary Callahan, May, 1873.
Martin Buhler, 1873; age, 3 years.
Mary Ford, 1873; age 29 years.
George Hamilton, May 30, 1873; age, 40 years.
Ellen Morgan, 1873; age, 12 years.
Joseph Reid, June 2, 1873.
Annie Fahey (infant), 1873.
Mary Hurst, 1873; age, 9 years.
Sarah Hurst, 1873; age, 4 years.
Catherine Jones, 1873; age, 37 years.
Michael T. Nogan, 1873; age, 9 years.
Jacob Kuhn, June 6, 1873.
Bernard Leichleiter, June 6, 1873; age, 38 years.
James Glouster (infant), June 8, 1873.
Maurice Lomasney, July 9, 1873.
Otto Valentine, 1873; age, 73 years.
Edward Farrell, 1873; age, 12 years.
Ellen McFadden, June 12, 1873; age, 13 years.
Chas. Buhler, June 14, 1873.
Alice M. Browne, June 16, 1873.
Alice Ann Flanagan, 1873.
Timothy Kelley, 1873; age, 8 years.
Margaret Barrett (infant), 1873.
Mary Dorgan, 1873; age, 37 years.
Eliza Ryan, 1873; age, 4 years.
George Gresiac, 1873; age 20 years.
Maria McDonnell, June 21, 1873; age, 42 years.
Mary Ann O'Neill, 1873; age, 56 years.
Mary Anne Regan, 1873; age, 6 years.
Anne Cox, 1873; age, 27 years.
Patrick Quinn, June 22, 1873.
Jas. T. Treber (infant), 1873.
Mary Dorsey, June 23, 1873; age, 55 years.
Alice Fogarty, 1873; age, 3 years.
Margaret, June 23, 1873; age, 33 years.
Patrick H. Joice (infant), 1873.

Bible Records—Tombstone Inscriptions

Julia Larkin, June 23, 1873; age, 25 years.
Elizabeth Fitzwilliams, 1873; age 15 years.
Tiimothy Flanigan, 1873; age, 65 years.
Ellen Edgar, 1873; age, 16 years.
Mary Martin, 1873; age, 26 years.
Owen McGovern, 1873; age 2 years.
Celia Scanlan, June 24, 1873.
Elizabeth B. Hogan, 1873; age, 22 years.
John Keanan, 1873; age, 1 year.
Louis Batter, 1873; age, 45 years.
John Donnelly, 1873; age, 32 years.
Edward Kenny (infant), 1873.
Jas. O'Brine, June 29, 1873.
Lawrence Spear, June 29, 1873; age, 53 years.
John Connor, 1873.
Thos. Plummer, 1873.
Patrick Morgan, 1873.
Thos. Farrell, July 2, 1873; age 4 years.
Professor Chas. Bauman, 1873; age, 33 years.
P. M. Ryan, 1873; age, 42 years.
Zella Weir, July 4, 1873; age, 30 years.
John Martin, 1873; age, 70 years.
Margaret Reilly, July 7, 1873; age, 22 years.
Margaret Martin, July 9, 1873; age, 12 years.
Patrick Fahy, 1873; age, 50 years.
Bernard McCabe (infant), July 11, 1873.
Brigid Lynch, 1873; age, 26 years.
Claudius Nave, 1873; age, 3 years.
John Nicholson (infant), July 16, 1873.
Mary Rodger and child, 1873; age, 30 years.
John Russey, 1873; age, 63 years.
Sarah Byrne, July 21, 1873.
Michael Lynch, 1873; age, 11 years.
Timothy Fahey, 1873; age, 60 years.
Anne Valentino, 1873.
Michael Breen, Aug. 2, 1873; age, 46 years.
Richard Trihy, Aug. 6, 1873; age, 45 years.
John Ward, 1873; age, 19 years.
Mary Eliza Hogan (infant), 1873.
John Hannapen, 1873; age, 1 year.
Mary Fant, 1873; age, 42 years.
Catherine Caffey, 1873; age, 19 months.
Henry Cox, 1873; age, 55 years.
John Galvin, 1873; age, 7 years.
Michael Grady, 1873; age, 23 years.
Bolan Winter, 1873; age, 2 years.
John Burke (infant), 1873.
Thos. Gorman, 1873; age, 36 years.
Catherine McTague, 1875.
John Callahan, 1873; age, 28 years.
Gabriel Herdel, 1873; age, 45 years.
Anne Holland, 1873; age, 2 years.
Michael Carney, 1873; age, 25 years.
John Fitzwilliam, Sept. 20, 1873; age, 82 years.
Maggie Rooney (infant), 1873.
Mary Lee, 1873.
H. Leffering, Oct., 1873.
Mary Anne Murray, 1873.
John De Lee, 1873; age, 26 years.
Mary Gillen, 1873; age, 40 years.
William Langan, 1873; age, 40 years.
Debora Connor (infant), 1873.
Kate Marah, 1873.
Matilde Keegan, 1873; age, 53 years.
Martin Joice, 1873; age, 50 years.
Johanna Walsh, 1873; age, 73 years.
William Keegan, 1873; age, 23 years.
Martin Ferrick, 1873; age, 63 years.
Thos. Kelley, 1873.
Thaddeus Brew, Nov., 1873; age, 73 years.
Mary Brisbo, Nov. 14, 1873; age, 30 years.
Annie Fugaggi, Nov. 17, 1873; age, 1 year.
Bridget Bains, Nov. 28, 1873; age, 50 years.
Albert Rivin (infant), Nov. 27, 1873.
Antonio Moggiana, Dec. 5, 1873; age, 48 years.
Margaret Murphy, Dec. 3, 1873; age, 73 years.
Michael Carland, Dec. 4, 1873; age, 35 years.
Herman Laporing, Dec. 5, 1873; age, 40 years.
Ellen Fitzgerald, Dec. 18, 1873; age, 51 years.
Michael Dannaher, Dec. 27, 1873; age, 63 years.
Barney Hynes, Jan. 30, 1874.
Patrick Dannaher, 1874.
Frank Hyronemous (Fr.), May 29, 1874; age, 64 years.
Patrick Mitchell, 1874.
Sarah Mitchell (infant), 1874.
Thos. Mitchell, 1874.
John Kemmess, Jan. 3, 1874.
John H. A. Neill, Jan., 1874.
William Keegan, Jan. 10, 1874; age, 51 years.

Bible Records—Tombstone Inscriptions

William Mulloy (infant), Jan. 12, 1874.
Julia Farrell, Jan. 16, 1874; age, 17 years.
Maggie Broderick, Jan. 17, 1874; age, 25 years.
John Langan (infant), Jan. 27, 1874.
Henry Woods (infant), Jan. 30, 1874.
Adelaide Burkhard, Feb. 11, 1874; age, 16 years.
Martin Varley, Feb. 16, 1874; age, 48 years.
Elizabeth Hartnett (infant), 1874.
Thos. McCauley, Feb. 27, 1874.
Michael Hayes, March 2, 1874; age, 50 years.
Alice Heffernan, Dec. 1874; age, 18 years.
Patrick Brett, March 3, 1874; age, 45 years.
James Powers, March 3, 1874.
Blanche Burton (infant), March 6, 1874.
Dennis Connor, March 7, 1874; age, 44 years.
Julia Connor, March 11, 1874; age, 36 years.
Thos. Jennings (infant), 1874.
T. T. Mahoney, March 29, 1874; age, 44 years.
Dennis Mullin, March 29, 1874; age, 20 years.
Kate Morrison, March 30, 1874; age, 27 years.
Patrick Fitzgibbon, April, 1874.
Joseph Metz, April, 1874; age, 29 years.
Mary Millitt, April, 1874.
John Vaughn, April, 1874.
Simon Crimmons, April, 1874; age, 40 years.
William Henry Davis (infant), April 2, 1874.
Martin Landers, 1874; age, 45 years.
Ellen Writesman, 1874; age, 27 years.
O'Keefe, April 22, 1874; age, 35 years.
John Callahan, April 25, 1874; age, 19 years.
Edward McGrath, April 27, 1874; age, 28 years.
Conrad Leonard, May, 1874.
John Powers, May, 1874.
Eugene Leonard, May 3, 1874; age, 30 years.
Maurice Egan, May 7, 1874; age, 31 years.
Julia Hardeman, May 7, 1874; age, 57 years.
Nicholas Hanley, May 13, 1874; age, 40 years.
James Curlin, 1874; age, 17 years.
Thos. Frances Hogan (infant), May 30, 1874.
Patrick Tyrell, June 2, 1874; age, 62 years.
Ferdinand E. Kuhn, Sr., June 9, 1874; age, 51 years.
Henry McGonegal (infant), June 9, 1874.
John Mahan, June 9, 1874; age, 42 years.
Michael Murphy, June 10, 1874; age, 36 years.
Jane Lechliton (infant), June 20, 1874.
Julia Walsh (infant), June 22, 1874.
Frances Walford, June 24, 1874; age, 52 years.
William Watson (infant), June 24, 1874.
Mary Anne Kerrigan (infant), June 25, 1874.
James Cullen (infant), June 28, 1874.
Serofina Puecetti, June 28, 1874.
Tim O'Shaughnessy, June 29, 1874; age, 2 years.
Nora Sayers, 1874.
Chas. Dowd (infant), July 2, 1874.
Matthew Shey, July 3, 1874; age, 40 years.
Jane Elizabeth Dunn, July 4, 1874; age, 8 years.
Kate Fogarty, July 7, 1874; age, 42 years.
Patrick Lehart, July 7, 1874; age, 55 years.
Margaret McKeon, June 10, 1874; age, 5 months.
Catherine S. Timon, June 13, 1874; age, 9 months.
Elizabeth Dowd, July 17, 1874; age, 6 years.
Mary Patricia Lyston, July 21, 1874.
Michael Kenny (infant), July 24, 1874.
Mary Fant, Aug. 2, 1874; age, 1 year.
Matilda Manhard, Aug. 4, 1874; age, 10 years.
Nathan Schio (infant), 1874.
Michael Burke, Aug. 9, 1874; age, 50 years.
Frederick Buehan, Aug. 10, 1874; age, 38 years.
Elizabeth Canon, Aug. 13, 1874; age, 55 years.
Mitchena Bealer (infant), 1874.

Bible Records—Tombstone Inscriptions

Daniel McGuire, Aug. 15, 1874; age, 8 years.
James O'Donnell, Aug. 22, 1874; age, 50 years.
Michael McCarthy (infant), 1874.
Kate Pendergast, Oct. 9, 1874; age, 15 years.
Mrs. Donnard, Oct. 11, 1874; age, 35 years.
John Shorferk, Oct. 11, 1874; age, 35 years.
Patrick McCabe (infant), 1874.
Delia Brew (infant), Oct. 19, 1874.
William McNulty, Aug. 10, 1874; age, 19 months.
Margaret Caffery (infant), Aug. 12, 1874.
Thomas Edward Mitchell, Oct. 20, 1874; age, 1 year.
Michael N. Gorman, Oct. 22, 1874; age, 2 years.
William Morse, Nov., 1874; age, 40 years.
Mary McKinly, Nov. 15, 1874; age, 40 years.
Mary Kane, Nov. 12, 1874; age, 15 months.
Catherine Jones, Nov. 25, 1874.
Catherine Conely, Nov. 30, 1874; age, 30 years.
Mary Connor, Nov. 30, 1874; age, 37 years.
Daniel O'Leary, Nov. 30, 1874; age, 35 years.
Ella Coughlin, Dec., 1874.
Mary Ryman, Dec., 1874; age, 57 years.
Patrick Kerrigan, Dec., 1874.
Mary Kirban, Dec. 6, 1874; age, 8 years.
William Dwyer, Dec. 15, 1874; age, 50 years.
Bridget Burton (infant), Dec. 16, 1874.
George Lecky (infant), Nov. 16, 1874.
Morton Allen, Nov. 18, 1874; age, 76 years.
E. E. Mulvihill, March 31, 1875; age, 32 years.
Mrs. Kohee, April 4, 1875; age, 35 years.
Thomas Francis Lee, April 4, 1875; age, 18 months.
Solomon O'Brien, April 5, 1875; age, 40 years.
David Lomasney, April 8, 1875; age, 2 months.
George Martin, April 12, 1875; age, 2 weeks.
James McGovern, April 12, 1875; age, 31 years.
Bridget Cain, April 20, 1875; age, 40 years.
Mrs. Carney, April 22, 1875.
Patrick Fitzgibbons, April 22, 1875.
James Fitzgerald, May 8, 1875; age, 22 years.
Travis Mooney, May 9, 1875; age, 20 months.
Francis P. Chapman, May 15, 1875; age 8 years.
Mrs. Dunn, May 13, 1875; age, 52 years.
John Tassi, May 18, 1875; age, 8 days.
Lida Ferring, May 24, 1875; age, 7 months.
Stephen Costella, June 2, 1875; age, 43 years.
Mary Morrissey, June 6, 1875; age, 40 years.
Inez Morrissey, June 5, 1875; age, 3 weeks.
Maurice Scalon, June 5, 1875; age, 45 years.
Bridge Barrett, June 8, 1875; age, 2 weeks.
John Carvin, June 18, 1875; age, 1 year.
Matthew McLoughlin, Dec. 29, 1874.
Elizabeth Foot, Jan., 1875.
William Hanifin, Jan. 2, 1875; age, 38 years.
Bridget O'Donnell, Jan. 9, 1875; age, 15 years.
Ellen Fitzgerald, Jan. 12, 1875; age, 60 years.
James Manning, Jan. 15, 1875; age, 14 years.
Thomas Hynes, Jan. 29, 1875; age, 42 years.
R. P. Miles Burns, Feb., 1875.
John Nolan, Feb. 3, 1875.
Ankenbaner, Feb. 4, 1875.
Henry D. Griffin, Feb. 7, 1875; age, 16 months.
Ernest O'Connor, Feb. 9, 1875; age, 3 years.
M. Halloran, Feb. 22, 1875.
Michael Carney, March, 1875.
John Williams, March 2, 1875.
James Morrissey, March 3, 1875; age, 9 days.
Mary Suiter, March 3, 1875; age, 20 years.
John Myers, March 8, 1875; age, 52 years.

Bible Records—Tombstone Inscriptions

Timothy Coughlin, March 9, 1875.
Martin Bains, March 13, 1875; age, 70 years.
Mary McDoyle, March 13, 1875.
Michael McCarthy, March 26, 1875; age, 37 years.
Michael Crommons, March 27, 1875; age, 2 years.
Helen Horan, March 30, 1875; age, 2 years.
Eugene Ottenville, June 20, 1875; age, 27 days.
Sullivan (infant), June 25, 1875.
James Leonard, June 27, 1875; age, 36 years.
Michael Ryan, July, 1875.
Andrew Rue, July 2, 1875; age, 27 years.
Mary Knight, July 3, 1875; age, 4 weeks.
John McDonald, July 3, 1875; age, 9 years.
Martin Deveny, July 8, 1875; age, 34 years.
Mary Elizabeth Ankenbaner, July 12, 1875; age, 5 months.
Annie O'Keefe, July 12, 1875; age, 2 years.
Michael Ryman, July 12, 1875; age, 78 years.
Susan Russell, July 13, 1875; age, 30 years.
William Riley, July 22, 1875; age, 2 years.
Thomas Connor, July 27, 1875; age, 4 years.
Robert Brown, Aug. 4, 1875; age, 20 years.
Henry Grady, Aug. 13, 1875; age, 17 months.
Mary Jacobs, Aug. 15, 1875.
Michael Lomasney, Aug. 15, 1875; age, 5 years.
Leonard Joseph Kennelly, Aug. 16, 1875; age, 11 months.
Henry McGonigoe, Aug. 19, 1875; age, 3 years.
Robert Bevington, Aug. 20, 1875.
William Franklin, Aug. 20, 1875; age, 14 months.
John Joyce, Aug. 20, 1875; age, 44 years.
Hugh McMullin, Aug. 20, 1875; age, 14 months.
Frederick Brockman, Aug. 22, 1875; age, 15 months.

Ellen J. Donovan, Aug. 24, 1875; age, 50 years.
Susan McGonagoe, Aug. 30, 1875; age, 5 years.
Mary Gillespie, Sept. 4, 1875; age, 6 years.
Albert Bevington, Sept. 6, 1875; age, 2 years.
H. Eisenborg, Sept. 8, 1875; age, 32 years.
Annie O'Donnell, Sept. 9, 1875; age, 35 years.
Annie Egan, Sept. 10, 1875; age, 8 months.
Alice Tracy, Sept. 10, 1875; age, 77 years.
John Kerney (infant), Sept. 12, 1875.
Julia Kemes, Sept. 13, 1875; age, 3 years.
John Harrington, Sept. 15, 1875; age, 16 years.
Martin Darcy, Sept. 19, 1875; age, 23 years.
Margaret Dalton, Sept. 20, 1875; age, 2 years.
Catherine Mason, Sept. 22, 1875; age, 8 months.
Percy H. Johnson, Sept. 23, 1875; age, 2 years.
Peter McGovern, Sept. 24, 1875; age, 2 weeks.
Barthelmas Scanlon, Sept. 27, 1875; age, 9 years.
Mary Abbott, Sept. 28, 1875; age, 38 years.
Maggie Coen, Sept. 28, 1875; age, 18 months.
George Edgar, Sept. 28, 1875; age, 5 years.
Annie Gilmore, Oct., 1875.
Michael Hayes, Oct. 1, 1875; age, 9 months.
Joseph Eggansperger, Oct. 4, 1875; age, 65 years.
Mary Hainbly, Oct. 6, 1875; age, 1 day.
Annie Gilmore, Oct. 7, 1875; age, 5 years.
Patrick Hegherty, Oct. 8, 1875; age, 19 years.
Hanora Lynch, Oct. 8, 1875; age, 49 years.
Edmond Daveon, Oct. 9, 1875; age, 55 years.
Martin Moran, Oct. 9, 1875; age, 40 years.
Agnes Riley, Oct. 9, 1875; age, 4 years.

Bible Records—Tombstone Inscriptions

Michael Hannon, Oct. 10, 1875; age, 74 years.
Patrick Callahan, Oct. 11, 1875; age, 16 years.
Martin Fahey, Oct. 13, 1875; age, 48 years.
James Lanon, Oct. 17, 1875; age, 9 years.
Auguste Winnie, Oct. 19, 1875; age, 20 months.
James Nenon, Oct. 20, 1875; age, 3 years.
Charles Lanon, Oct. 21, 1875; age, 6 years.
Little Katie Gerraty, Oct. 28, 1875; age, 8 years.
Robert McKinley, Oct. 28, 1875; age, 26 years.
Solomon Wymer, Oct. 28, 1875.
Margaret Kiggins, Nov. 1, 1875; age, 14 days.
Francis Harrison, Nov. 4, 1875; age, 22 years.
Brigid Skelly Hughes, Nov. 4, 1875; age, 60 years.
Henry Wessel, Nov. 5, 1876; age, 36 years.
Charles Coffing, Nov. 8, 1875; age, 6 months.
James Leehe, Nov. 10, 1875; age, 70 years.
Mary Whelan, Nov. 11, 1875; age, 40 years.
Thomas Whelan, Nov. 11, 1875; age, 35 years.
Bridget Halloran, Nov. 17, 1875;age, 22 years.
Bridget McCormack, Nov. 20, 1875; age, 5 years.
William Hyde, Nov. 21, 1875; age, 16 years.
Richard Monohan, Dec. 1875 Nov. 22, 1875; age, 55 years.
Mary, Tim, and Jim Murphy, Nov. 22, 1875.
Susan Hanly, Nov. 24, 1875; age, 2 years.
Julia Burrall, Nov. 25, 1875; age, 20 months.
Timothy Mattimore, Nov. 27, 1875; age, 33 years.
Francis Greenfield, Nov. 28, 1875; age, 6 years.
Henry Thomas McKeon, Nov. 29, 1875; age, 13 months.
James O'Donnell, Nov. 29, 1875; age, 4 years.

Bridget Hynes, Dec. 7, 1875; age, 8 years.
Mary Sanders, Dec. 8, 1875; age, 4 months.
James Brown, Dec. 12, 1875.
James Brown, Dec. 13, 1875; age, 30 years.
Annie O'Donnell, Dec. 13, 1875; age, 33 years.
Patrick McCarthy, Dec. 16, 1875; age, 35 years.
George Kemes, Dec. 19, 1875; age, 19 years.
Mr. Morrison, Dec. 20, 1875; age, 62 years.
Child of Morris Moran, Dec. 30, 1875; age 2½ years.
D. J. Fahey, 1876; age, 13 months.
John Kinney, 1876.
Robt. Taylor, 1876.
Edward Mulvihill. 1876.
Ellen Fitzgerald, Jan., 1876.
Thos. Fitzgibbons, Jan., 1876.
Eliz. Skelly, Jan., 1876.
Thomas Keenan, Jan. 15, 1876.
Henry Joseph McGonnigoe, Feb. 9, 1876; age, 3 years.
Sarah Mulloy, Feb., 1876; age, 4 years.
Mary Geenan, Feb. 16, 1876; age, 7 years.
Maggie Lynam, Feb. 19, 1876; age, 1 week.
William Fallon, Feb. 22, 1876; age, 35 years.
Sarah Nicholson, Feb. 27, 1876; age, 2 years.
Mary Fitzgerald, March 10, 1876; age, 45 years.
Patrick Fitzgerald, March 10, 1876; age, 35 years.
John Quinn, March 11, 1876; age, 19 years.
John Ecklecamp, March 13, 1876; age, 22 months.
Michael Fox, March 25, 1876; age, 1 day.
Michael Carr, March 27, 1876; age, 48 years.
Bridget McHugh, April 2, 1876; age, 3 years.
Wm. McHugh, April 2, 1876; age, 5 years.
Mary S. Wade, April 3, 1876; age, 7 years.
Aloysius Schneider, April 10, 1876; age, 37 years.

Bible Records—Tombstone Inscriptions

James Devine, April 12, 1876; age, 3 years.
Michael Quinn, April 13, 1876; age, 66 years.
Walter Cleanevsil, April 14, 1876; age, 3 months.
Sarah McLaughlin, April 19, 1876; age, 25 years.
Mary Rose, April 21, 1876; age, 35 years.
Catherine Maloney, April 23, 1876; age, 60 years.
Peter Murphy, April 25, 1876; age, 9 weeks.
John Murray, April 27, 1876; age, 5 years.
Wm. Martin, May, 1876.
May Winters, May 4, 1876; age, 1 week.
Joseph Glennon, May 6, 1876.
James Ryan, May 9, 1876; age, 6 years.
Minerva Currin, May 11, 1876; age, 64 years.
Wm. Davis, May 11, 1876; age, 10 months.
John Molloy, May 11, 1876.
Eliz. Carthy, May 12, 1876; age, 5 years.
Wm. Martin, May 23, 1876; age, 9 years.
Chas. Plummer, May 24, 1876; age, 52 years.
Mary and Margaret McCarthy, May 26, 1876; ages, 3 years and 1 year.
Paul Rosacher, May 26, 1876; age, 6 months.
Thos. Mulray, May 27, 1876; age, 46 years.
John H. Rose, June 2, 1876; age, 46 years.
Emile Power, June 10, 1876; age, 8 months.
Mary Anne McGonnegle, June 11, 1876; age, 13 months.
Clotilda Bertheal, June 12, 1876.
John Edw. Mulloy, June 12, 1876; age, 9 months.
Mary Augusta Smart, June 17, 1876; age, 1 month.
Wm. Griffin, June 19, 1876; age, 6 years.
Mary Nolan, June 20, 1876; age, 40 years.
Serena Ankenbaner, June 24, 1876; age, 4 hours.
Mary Hughes, June 25, 1876; age, 80 years.
Ellen Foley, June 26, 1876; age, 4 years.
Joseph O'Connor, July, 1876; age, 2 years.
Mary Ann Quinn, July, 1876.
Alice Holland, July 3, 1876; age, 2 months.
Patrick Sullivan, July 3, 1876; age 11 years.
Mary Ann Quinn, July 4, 1876; age, 22 years.
Thomas Kelly, July 6, 1876; age, 17 years.
Patrick Foley, July 7, 1876; age, 2 years.
Mary Ann Quinn, July 4, 1876; age, 22 years.
Thomas Kelly, July 6, 1876; age, 17 years.
Patrick Foley, July 7, 1876; age, 2 years.
Ellen Grady, July 7, 1876; age, 9 months.
Thos. McHugh, July 7, 1876; age, 38 years.
James Kedy, July 11, 1876.
John Patrick Bohan, July 12, 1876; age, 13 months.
John Brennan, July 14, 1876; age, 4 months.
Bridget Deveny, July 15, 1876; age, 74 years.
Sabina O'Donnell Sutherland, July 16, 1876.
Margaret Mundy, July 23, 1876; age, 40 years.
Victoria Clements, July 26, 1876; age, 3 weeks.
Eli Jennings, July 27, 1876; age, 6 years.
Theresa Prunty, July 30, 1876; age, 8 months.
Martin Corcoran (Fr.), Aug., 1876.
Clate Harding, Aug. 1, 1876; age, 70 years.
Kate E. Davis, Aug. 2, 1876; age, 34 years.
Mary Malone, Aug. 3, 1876; age, 1 year.
Judith McDonald, Aug. 3, 1876; age, 64 years.
James Egan, Aug. 5, 1876.
John Hamington, Aug. 18, 1876; age, 2 years.
Jane Cairns, Aug. 19, 1876; age, 9 months.

Bible Records—Tombstone Inscriptions

Patrick Mitchell, Aug. 22, 1876; age, 18 months.
Mrs. Mary Harris, Aug. 27, 1876; age, 35 years.
Bridget Frickster, Aug. 29, 1876; age, 40 years.
Arthur Allen, Sept., 1876.
John A. Leckey, Sept. 5, 1876; age, 41 years.
Frank Wernet, Sept. 7, 1876.
Susan McKeon, Sept. 11, 1876; age, 56 years.
Annie Connor, Sept. 18, 1876; age, 45 years.
Robt. E. Olwill, Sept. 12, 1876; age, 6 years.
Robt. Ryan, Sept. 12, 1876; age, 3 years.
Catherine Mahoney, Sept. 14, 1876; age, 47 years.
Mary Gallagher, Sept. 15, 1876; age, 42 years.
James Heston, Sept. 23, 1876; age, 48 years.
Edmund O'Connell, Sept. 23, 1876; age, 8 months.
John Dwyer, Sept. 28, 1876; age, 60 years.
Ellen Kelley, Sept. 29, 1876; age, 1 year.
John Casey, Sept. 30, 1876; age, 35 years.
Martin McCarthy, Oct. 3, 1876; age, 50 years.
Mary O'Shea, Oct. 5, 1876; age, 30 years.
Catherine Hines, Oct. 6, 1876.
Thomas Dorsey, Oct. 9, 1876; age, 60 years.
Mary Leahy, Oct. 10, 1876; age, 50 years.
Nora Bakean, Oct. 13, 1876; age, 1 year.
Ellen Dohoney, Oct. 14, 1876; age, 2 years.
John A. Bakean, Oct. 15, 1876; age, 4 years.
John Cox, Oct. 20, 1876.
James P. Carr, Oct. 26, 1876; age, 7 years.
James J. Fitzgerald, Nov., 1876.
John Kinefie, Nov. 3, 1876; age, 60 years.
Charles McKinley, Nov. 8, 1876; age, 1 day.
Chas. Seifried, Nov. 5, 1876; age, 1 month.
James C. Kelley, Nov. 17, 1876; age, 27 years.
John Mulloy, Nov. 17, 1876; age 24 years.
Ellen Donovan, Nov. 18, 1876; age, 5½ years.
Wm. Eglone, Nov. 18, 1876; age, 3 years.
Jeremiah Donovan, Nov. 20, 1876; age, 1 year.
Patrick McKeon, Nov. 28, 1876; age, 53 years.
Winnie Ryan, Dec. 2, 1876; age, 7 years.
Clementine Embush, Dec. 6, 1876; age, 8 years.
Bessie Browne, Dec. 9, 1876; age, 2 years.
Annie Rooney, Dec. 9, 1876; age, 1 year.
Marie Cummins, Dec. 15, 1876; age, 2 years.
Samuel Lynch, Dec. 15, 1876; age, 67 years.
James Burns, Dec. 19, 1876; age, 5 years.
Winfred Henry, Dec. 24, 1876; age, 50 years.
Dennis Murphy, Dec. 27, 1876; age, 40 years.
Margaret Lynch, Dec. 29, 1876; age, 11 months.
Mary Allen Mahoney, 1877.
James Melody, 1877.
Michael Scally, 1877.
Francis A. Horan, Jan. 9, 1877; age, 1 year.
James Ford, Jan. 11, 1877.
Annie McCue, Jan. 12, 1877.
James Brady (Fr.), Jan. 13, 1877; age, 73 years.
John D. Loger, Jan. 25, 1877; age, 17 years.
Thomas Phillips, Jan. 29, 1877; age, 4 years.
John Murphy, Feb. 1, 1877; age, 2 months.
Dolphire Mory, Feb. 9, 1877; age, 65 years.
Isaac Winningham, Feb. 15, 1877; age, 47 years.
Kate Ellen Baines, Feb. 16, 1877; age, 3 years.
Delia Corcoran, March 18, 1877.
Patrick Geary, March 7, 1877; age, 36 years.

Bible Records—Tombstone Inscriptions

Michael Dohoney, March 9, 1877; age, 50 years.
Edward Meaghen, March 10, 1877; age, 2 years.
Bridget Reynolds, March 11, 1877; age, 70 years.
James H. O'Connell, March 14, 1877; age, 52 years.
Thomas Mannion, March 19, 1877; age, 6 years.
Albert Foley, March 21, 1877; age, 7 years.
Mary Buckley, March 25, 1877; age, 75 years.
Patrick Gilea, March 30, 1877; age, 40 years.
Lizzie Hogan, March 30, 1877; age, 5 years.
John Heston, April 4, 1877; age, 3 years.
Jennie W. Smith, April 6, 1877; age, 3 years.
James Dallinger, April 8, 1877; age, 50 years.
James Cairns, April 9, 1877; age, 1 week.
Cornelius O'Donnell, April 18, 1877; age, 63 years.
Matthew Golden, April 14, 1877; age, 24 years.
Johanna Bradley, April 17, 1877; age, 43 years.
Anna Eliza Cullen, April 21, 1877; age, 2 years.
David Moran, April 21, 1877; age, 15 months.
McKenzie, April 25, 1877; age, 43 years.
Andrew Harris, April 27, 1877; age, 4 years.
John Joseph Danger, May 2, 1877; age, 11 years.
John M. Flanigan, May 3, 1877; age, 21 years.
Michael Dougherty, May 3, 1877; age, 2 years.
Michael Flanigan, May 3, 1877; age, 40 years.
Hattie Mitchell, May 5, 1877; age, 4 years.
Sarah Nestor, May 7, 1877; age, 2 years.
Annie Brady, May 8, 1877; age, 9 years.
Mary Ann Smith, May 9, 1877; age, 12 years, 4 months.
John F. Gray, May 10, 1877; age, 20 years.
Mary Nolan, May 10, 1877; age, 40 years.
John O. O'Shea, May 10, 1877; age, 6 years.
Thomas McManus, May 11, 1877.
Mary Ellen Leche, May 13, 1877; age, 1 day.
Morristown two children, May 14, 1877.
Wm. Morrison, May 14, 1877; age, 75 years.
Andrew Morrison, May 14, 1877; age, 68 years.
James McLaughlin, May 15, 1877; age, 6 months.
John McLaughlin, May 15, 1877; age, 30 years.
Thos. McLaughlin, May 15, 1877; age, 33 years.
Patrick Quinn, May 15, 1877.
Owen Corcoran, May 17, 1877; age, 50 years.
James Ryan, Jr., May 18, 1877; age, 21 years.
Samuel G. Erb, May 21, 1877; age, 10 months.
Thomas Solen, May 26, 1877; age, 5 days.
Michael Haley, June 6, 1877.
Wm. O'Shea, June 6, 1877; age, 4 years.
Julia Fitzgerald, June 13, 1877; age, 18 years.
Alice Lavelle, June 13, 1877; age, 1 day.
Mary Jane McKinley, June 13, 1877; age, 6 years.
Edward Mooney, June 14, 1877; age, 18 months.
Ellen Burke, June 15, 1877; age, 6 months.
Kate Ryan, June 15, 1877; age, 8 months.
Annie McDonate, June 16, 1877; age, 30 years.
Martin Devine, June 21, 1877; age, 7 months.
Emelia Brisboe, June 22, 1877; age, 1 year.
Kate Annie Myers, June 26, 1877; age, 19 years.
E. E. Jones, June 27, 1877; age, 64 years.
Kate Bentley, June 29, 1877; age, 15 years.

Bible Records—Tombstone Inscriptions

Alphonse Jonnard, June 30, 1877; age, 50 years.
Catherine Deubler, Aug. 20, 1877; age, 10 years, 6 months.
Annie Meier, July, 1877.
Martin O'Rourke, July 2, 1877.
Mary Rothenberg, July 7, 1877; age, 37 years.
Bridget Bentley, July 8, 1877; age, 1 year.
Catherine Keefen, July 10, 1877; age, 87 years.
Catherine Kobbs, July 14, 1877; age, 77 years.
Margaret Burns, July 16, 1877; age, 9 months.
Margaret Frank, July 16, 1877; age, 3 years.
Edward May, July 17, 1877; age, 43 years.
Anne Barbara Meyer, July 21, 1877; age, 10 months.
Mrs. McMillan, July 23, 1877; age, 65 years.
Frank Jacob Frank, July 25, 1877; age, 4 years.
Mary Cosgrove, July 26, 1877; age, 23 years.
James Sanders, July 30, 1877; age, 7 months.
Charlie Harahan, Aug., 1877.
W. H. Fitzsimmons, Aug. 1, 1877; age, 39 years.
Wm. Henry Frank, Aug. 1, 1877; age, 6 years.
Maria Crescencia Mehne, Aug. 4, 1877; age, 40 years, 7 months.
Patrick Edw. McGovern, Aug. 8, 1877; age, 12 years.
Barnard Willy, Aug. 10, 1877; age, 1 month.
Lizzie Farrell, Aug. 11, 1877; age, 18 months.
Mary Ann Carney, Aug. 14, 1877; age, 21 years.
Thos. Broderick, Aug. 14, 1877; age, 4 days.
Austin McLaughlin, Aug. 15, 1877; age, 45 years.
Harahan, Aug. 16, 1877; age, 1 year.
Wm. F. Mayes, Aug. 16, 1877; age, 14 months.
Mary McTigue, Aug. 17, 1877; age, 53 years.
Carolina Gorman, Aug. 20, 1877; age, 11 months.
Mary Cannody, Aug. 21, 1877; age, 48 years.
Dora Kohlis, Aug. 22, 1877; age, 15 years.
Isabela Boyd, Aug. 24, 1877; age, 14 months.
Mary Fahey, Aug. 24, 1877; age, 2 hours.
Lizzie Kohlie, Aug. 24, 1877; age, 47 years.
Martin Phillips, Sept., 1877.
Peter Boyle, Sept. 3, 1877; age, 80 years.
Alois Meyer, Sept. 5, 1877.
Mary J. Morrissey, Sept. 5, 1877.
Margaret Lomasney, Sept. 6, 1877; age, 6 years.
John Murphy, Sept. 6, 1877; age, 76 years.
A. Mary Knop, Sept. 9, 1877; age, 11 months.
Patrick Bradley, Sept. 10, 1877; age, 50 years.
Joseph Brionatk, Sept. 12, 1877; age, 55 years.
Patrick Clark, Sept. 12, 1877; age, 51 years.
James Connelly, Sept. 12, 1877; age, 44 years.
Mary Ford, Sept. 12, 1877; age, 3 years, 1 month.
Catherine Connelly, Sept. 13, 1877; age, 55 years.
Thomas Myers, Sept. 14, 1877; age, 20 years.
Catherine Murray, Sept. 19, 1877.
Hannah Keenan, Sept. 22, 1877; age, 70 years.
Bridget Martin, Sept. 24, 1877; age, 9 years, 3 months.
Bridget Crommins, Sept. 28, 1877; age, 3 years.
Catherine Louise Glassar, Oct. 3, 1877; age, 2 years.
Martin Timon, Oct. 5, 1877.
James Burke, Oct. 7, 1877.
James Sullivan, Oct. 10, 1877; age, 6 days.
Anthony Breen (Fr)., Oct., 1877; age, 70 years.
Patrick Martin, Oct. 19, 1877; age, 27 years.
Winifred Davis, Oct. 27, 1877; age, 17 months.
Michael Daughney, Nov., 1877.
Mary Farrell, Nov. 8, 1877; age, 35 years.

Bible Records—Tombstone Inscriptions

James Kelly, Nov. 9, 1877; age, 47 years.
W. B. Singleton, Nov. 12, 1877; age, 41 years.
Thos. Laffey, Nov. 13, 1877; age, 22 years.
Alice Murray, Nov. 15, 1877.
John O. Neylan, Nov. 15, 1877; age, 1½ years.
Joseph Laffey, Nov. 30, 1877.
Sarah Laffey, Nov. 30, 1877.
Thomas Laffey, Nov. 30, 1877.
Sarah Duffy, Dec. 3, 1877; age, 40 years.
Johanna Mahoney, Dec. 5, 1877; age, 2 years.
John Joseph Meyer, Dec. 6, 1877; age, 47 years.
Josephine Klein, Dec. 14, 1877; age, 50 years.
Wm. Cross, Dec. 15, 1877; age, 6 years.
Josephine Marquet, Dec. 17, 1877; age, 56 years.
Mary McCue, Dec. 18, 1877; age, 30 years.
John H. Ryan, Dec. 20, 1877; age, 4 months.
Thomas Dannaher, Dec. 30, 1877; age, 38 years.
Thomas Walsh, Dec. 30, 1877; age, 2 days.
Edward Davis, Jan. 5, 1878.
Robert Davis, Jan. 5, 1878.
Michael Lyons, Jan. 5, 1878; age, 46 years.
Sarah Sullivan, Jan. 5, 1878; age, 74 years.
Mary Fahey, Jan. 1878; age, 22 years.
Michael Murray, Jan. 9, 1878; age, 2 years.
Rose Dowd, Jan. 19, 1878; age, 3 years.
Patrick Sanders, Jan. 21, 1878; age, 90 years.
Josephine Hensley, Jan. 24, 1878; age, 2 years.
Damil Murphy, Jan. 25, 1878; age, 3 days.
Mary Kelly, Jan. 29, 1878; age, 58 years.
Martin Landers, Jr., Feb. 13, 1878; age, 5 days.
Edward Fitzgibbons, Feb. 18, 1878 (removal).
John Fitzgibbons, Feb. 18, 1878; age, 50 years.
Margaret Fitzgibbons, Feb. 18, 1878; age, 24 years (removal).
Mary Fitzgibbons, Feb. 18, 1878; age, 30 years.
David Fitzgerald, March 1, 1878; age, 8 days.
E. G. Breen, March 2, 1878; age, 34 years.
Mrs. Margaret McKee, March 7, 1878; age, 56 years.
James H. Rodes, March 10, 1878; age, 78 years.
Mrs. Katie Butler, March 12, 1878; age, 23 years.
John Egan, March 13, 1878; age, 50 years.
Clara McGovern, March 22, 1878; age, 4 years.
John McGovern, March 22, 1878; age, 8 years.
Eugene McGinnis, March 25, 1878; age, 15 months.
Patrick Moran, March 28, 1878; age, 4 years.
John Sheehan, April, 1878.
Mrs. Nolan, April 3, 1878; age, 40 years.
Mary Murphy, April 24, 1878; age, 55 years.
Michael Grady, April 25, 1878; age, 27 years.
Peter Burke (Fr.), May 4, 1878; age, 43 years.
Thomas Muller, May 9, 1878; age, 16 years.
John Stanley, May 11, 1878; age, 3 months.
Jerry Powers, May 23, 1878; age, 2½ years.
Mary Kilcoin, May 24, 1878; age, 52 years.
Bridget McGarry, May 26, 1878; age, 45 years.
Miss Bradley, June 1, 1878; age, 15 years.
Edward Dillon, June 1, 1878; age, 35 years.
Elizabeth Fennell, June 3, 1878; age, 70 years.
Willie Cook, June 6, 1878; age, 2 years.
Jessie Sharpe, June 6, 1878; age, 5 months.
John T. Hussey, June 10, 1878; age, 4 years.
Thomas O'Brien, June 29, 1878; age, 60 years.

Bible Records—Tombstone Inscriptions

James Rogers, July 1, 1878; age, 35 years.
Kate Hussey, July 2, 1878; age, 5 years.
Henry A. Nolan, July 2, 1878; age, 20 years.
Mary Kate Robterb, July 7, 1878; age, 8 months.
Annie Deveny, July 13, 1878; age, 10 years.
Aloysius Huppert, July 15, 1878; age, 14 years.
James Nolan, July 16, 1878; age, 15 months.
Martin W. Keon, July 23, 1878.
Martin Kearns, July 23, 1878; age, 30 years.
Daniel Callahan, July 27, 1878; age, 18 years.
Maggie Jennings (infant), Aug. 1, 1878.
Catherine Railly, Aug. 1, 1878; age, 58 years.
John Cox, Aug. 3, 1878; age, 32 years.
Mary Jane Hudson, Aug. 3, 1878; age, 46 years.
John Myers, Aug. 10, 1878; age, 25 years.
Nora Crocking, Aug. 12, 1878; age, 3 months (colored).
Bridget Broderick, Aug. 14, 1878; age, 25 years.
John Clark, Aug. 16, 1878.
Mary Davy, Aug. 18, 1878; age, 42 years.
Ellen Brockley, Aug. 22, 1878; age, 41 years.
Michael Flynn, Aug. 27, 1878; age, 27 years.
H. A. Ankenbaner, Sept. 9, 1878; age, 1 year.
M. A. McDonald, Sept. 10, 1878; age, 15 years.
Ann Mogan, Sept. 16, 1878; age, 5 weeks.
Edmond Murry, Sept. 17, 1878; age, 30 years.
Thomas G. Lee, Sept. 19, 1878; age, 49 years.
Catherine Hensley, Sept. 25, 1878; age, 26 years.
Daniel Donahue, Sept. 28, 1878; age, 42 years.
Anthony Vollinco, Sept. 28, 1878; age, 84 years.
H. C. Sheetz, Oct., 1878; age, 45 years.
W. T. Carlin, Oct. 8, 1878; age, 1 week.
Mary Donahue, Oct. 8, 1878; age, 58 years.
Four Mogan children, Oct. 8, 1878.
Leo Smith, Oct. 11, 1878.
Ellen Murray, Oct. 12, 1878; age, 65 years.
Mrs. R. O'Donnell, Oct. 13, 1878; age, 86 years.
James Corcoran, Oct. 21, 1878; age, 13 years.
Andrew Morgan, Nov. 1, 1878; age, 2 years.
John Foley, Nov. 2, 1878; age, 64 years.
Winifred McCook, Nov. 6, 1878; age, 35 years.
Michael Kelly, Nov. 17, 1878; age, 55 years.
Patrick McAnderson, Nov. 28, 1878; age, 25 years.
Catherine Julee, Nov. 30, 1878; age, 25 years.
Mary Fahy, Dec., 1878; age, 63 years.
Mary L. Wiley, Dec. 3, 1878; age, 4 days.
Furtuno Bonfuerlo, Dec. 5, 1878; age, 51 years.
Child of J. Reynolds, Dec. 8, 1878; age, 8 days.
Catherine Meagher, Dec. 11, 1878; age, 5 years.
John Tassi and child, Dec. 11, 1878.
Sarah Farrell, Dec. 13, 1878; age, 52 years.
Malachy McCormack, Dec. 15, 1878; age, 40 years.
William Ford, Dec. 20, 1878; age, 24 years.
Edmonica Fant, Dec. 23, 1878; age, 11 months.
Thomas Bohan, Dec. 24, 1878; age, 3 weeks.
Michael Glenn, Dec. 27, 1878; age, 75 years.
Elizabeth McKeon, Dec. 29, 1878; age, 23 years.
Catherine Ford, Dec. 31, 1878; age, 36 years.
John Whelan, Dec. 31, 1878; age, 49 years.
Mary Burke, 1879.
Ruth Erb, 1879.
Grady (infant), 1879.
Mary Timon, 1879.
Margaret Callahan, Jan., 1879; age, 47 years.
John J. Hood, Jan. 1879; age, 33 days.
Infant of John Grady, Jan. 16, 1879.

Bible Records—Tombstone Inscriptions

Mary Hagerty, Jan. 16, 1879; age, 38 years.
Patrick Hogan, wife, 1 child, Jan. 30, 1879.
Thomas Broderick, Feb., 1879.
Ellen Conlon, Feb., 1879; age, 22 years.
Mary Jane Consadine, Feb., 1879; age, 18 years.
Jeremiah Syers, Feb. 1, 1879; age, 11 days.
Lizzie Hogan, Feb. 3, 1879; age, 4 years.
Margaret Sullivan, Feb. 3, 1879; age, 72 years.
Sarah Jane O'Connor, Feb. 4, 1879; age, 55 years.
John Murphy, Feb. 6, 1879; age, 38 years.
George Smith, Feb. 8, 1879; age, 28 years.
Anthony McAndrews, Feb. 14, 1879; age, 85 years.
Thomas Ahearn, Feb. 15, 1879; age, 45 years.
Bridget O'Connor, Feb. 15, 1879; age, 77 years.
Herman Loubheimes, Feb. 15, 1879; age, 4 days.
William Murphy, Feb. 15, 1879; age, 40 years.
Austina Dooley, Feb. 17, 1879; age, 75 years.
Ellen Fitzgibbons, Feb. 24, 1879.
Doughterty, March, 1879.
T. P. Harbin, March 2, 1879; age, 6 weeks.
John Gambert, March 4, 1879; age, 19 years.
Mary McMahon, March 4, 1879; age, 40 years.
Mrs. Connors, March 7, 1879; age, 67 years.
John Hynes, March 10, 1879; age, 45 years.
Kinney (4 removals), March 10, 1879.
Patrick J. Keegan, March 14, 1879.
Michael Philbin, March 23, 1879; age, 18 years.
Mary A. Burke, March 29, 1879; age, 75 years.
T. F. O'Donahue, March 30, 1879; age, 22 years.
Edward Murphy, April 1, 1879; age, 54 years.
Ruth Asite, April 12, 1879; age, 31 years.
Child of Frances Plummer, April 18, 1879; age, 6 years.
Neva E. Walsh, April 19, 1879; age, 10 months.
Lizzie Sullivan, April 25, 1879; age, 32 years.
Dennis Neylan, May 1, 1879; age, 5 months.
Susan Dowd, May 6, 1879; age, 68 years.
Mamie Rotterman, May 5, 1879; age, 11 years.
James Mattimore, May 9, 1879; age, 10 months.
T. Sullivan, May 11, 1879; age, 5 months.
Thomas O'Shaughnessy, June, 1879.
Capt. Chas. H. Ryman, June 5, 1879; age, 70 years.
Bridget Tansey, June 5, 1879; age, 5 years.
Joseph Pollak, June 6, 1879; age, 54 years.
James K. Morrissey, Jr., June 7, 1879.
Infant of Timothy and Margaret Kelly, June 11, 1879; age, 6 months.
Julia Ford, June 16, 1879; age, 6 months.
Michael Grady, June 16, 1879; age, 6 months.
William Quinn, June 17, 1879; age, 6 years.
Patrick Grady, June 22, 1879; age, 12 years.
John P. Dowling, June 23, 1879; age, 20 years.
Margaret Mulligan, June 25, 1879; age, 75 years.
Martin Wm. Ankenbaner, June 26, 1879; age, 1 year.
Albert Merri, June 26, 1879; age, 6 months.
John Millitt, July, 1879; age, 52 years.
Dilida Rizzetto, July 1, 1879; age, 20 months.
Johanna Keegan, July 3, 1879; age, 40 years.
Michael Ryan, July 4, 1879; age, 6 months.
Maggie B. Nenon, July 8, 1879; age, 6 months.
Annie Cody, July 12, 1879; age, 31 years.
James Leeahy, July 16, 1879; age, 21 years.
Alice Solan, July 16, 1879; age, 10 months.

Bible Records—Tombstone Inscriptions

William Ambush, July 22, 1879; age, 30 years.
Mary Ann Noonan, July 22, 1879.
Brantley Fontine, July 22, 1879; age, 15 months.
Patrick Walsh, July 22, 1879.
Timothy Kelly, Sr., Sept. 6, 1879; age, 40 years.
Bridget Agnes Coer, Sept. 8, 1879; age, 24 years.
Charles G. Bailey, Aug. 11, 1879; age, 14 months.
James Friel, Aug. 21, 1879; age, 18 years.
Rosemary Mitchell, Aug. 22, 1879; age, 40 years.
Thomas Cain, Aug. 26, 1879; age, 18 Years.
Thomas Heheir, Sept. 2, 1879; age, 24 years.
Margaret Hanson, Sept. 3, 1879; age, 81 years.
Peter Dunn, Sept. 5, 1879; age, 56 years.
David Miller, Sept. 5, 1879; age, 70 years.
Oerig Huneycutt, Sept. 9, 1879; age, 3 months.
Frank Duffy, Sept. 16, 1879; age, 19 years.
Ellen Maleaby, Sept. 17, 1879; age, 45 years.
Maggie Flanagan, Sept. 18, 1879; age, 15 years.
Thomas Patrick Keogh, Sept. 18, 1879; age, 6 months.
Child of G. W. Carlin (unbaptized), Sept. 30, 1879.
Martin Deveny, Sept. 30, 1879; age, 4½ years.
Martin Fahey, Oct., 1879.
John D. Mahoney, Oct. 12, 1879; age, 3 months.
John Murray, Oct. 13, 1879.
Patrick O'Maley, Oct. 24, 1879; age, 60 years.
Michael Halloran, Oct. 25, 1879; age, 20 years.
Jerry Sullivan, Oct. 26, 1879; age, 22 years.
Mary (W. F.) Brady, Nov. 3, 1879; age, 25 years.
Edward Beehan, Nov. 6, 1879; age, 11 months.
Ellen B. McMillan, Nov. 7, 1879; age, 1 month.
Mary Ankenbaner, Nov. 11, 1879; age, 53 years.
Mary Davey, Nov. 11, 1879.
James Reynolds, Nov. 12, 1879; age, 4 years.
Thomas Farrell McGovern, Nov. 15, 1879; age, 3 months, 15 days.
Margaret Lynch, Nov. 20, 1879; age, 2 years.
Mary Cairns, Nov. 24, 1879; age, 31 years.
Annie Mary Diamond, Dec. 8, 1879; age, 1 week.
William Plummer, Dec. 9, 1879; age, 22 years.
Thomas Burrows, Dec. 15, 1879; age, 56 years.
Eugene Quinn, Dec. 15, 1879; age, 41 years.
John Dohoney, Dec. 20, 1879.

HISTORY OF SPRING HILL CEMETERY
By Louise Allen Ogden

Spring Hill Cemetery, one of the oldest and most historic of the county's burial grounds, is on the Gallatin Pike, six miles from Nashville.

In 1775 the Rev. Thomas Craighead was called by the community settled at Hayesboro to preach in the Spring Hill meeting house. The next year Davidson Academy was chartered and the Rev. Thomas Craighead appointed "to hold school" in the Spring Hill meeting house. In 1799 Davidson Academy was merged with the Federal Academy and moved to Nashville and Mr. Craighead gave ten acres of ground from his home place (now know as the

Bible Records—Tombstone Inscriptions

Walton Place), adjoining the Spring Hill meeting house, to be used as a cemetery.

The oldest marked grave in the cemetery is that of Margaret Brown, born in Virginia in 1700; died, 1801; but there has been evidence of older unmarked pioneer graves.

When the turnpike was built the foundations of the old Spring Hill meeting house were destroyed. Some time after the Civil War a group of ladies formed the Woman's Craighead Association to care for the graves of the Craighead family and the cemetery. In 1885 the Spring Hill Association was chartered (referred to in the old cemetery minutes as the Craighead's Spring Hill Cemetery) by J. E. Sloan, W. C. Dibrell, M. T. Stratton, David Stratton, and R. E. Love. Permanent organization was not effected until 1888 when M. T. Stratton was made president; W. C. Dibrell, vice president; David Stratton, secretary and treasurer.

In 1913 a 99-year lease of the old Spring Hill burying ground was acquired. James A. Sloan was president and J. Taylor Stratton, secretary and treasurer. Edwin L. Morris, son-in-law of the late J. Taylor Stratton, is president of the Spring Hill Association. The cemetery extends from Craighead or Love's Branch for a half a mile on the Gallatin Road and back to the Cumberland River.

Spring Hill Cemetery
Gallatin Pike, Nashville, Tennessee

Copied by Mrs. Finley Dorris, Mrs. Wm. Ogden, Mrs. Emmett Pryor, Mrs. J. H. Acklen, Mrs. Robert E. Landis. Typed by Mrs. J. F. Draughon.

Annie Elizabeth Cain; died, Oct. 20, 1899; age, 40 years.

Susan Buchanan; died, July 27, 1902; age, 76 years.

Francis Buchanan; died, July 23, 1901; age, 76 years.

Mary Alice Mayberry, Dec. 27, 1893-March 31, 1911.

Lou Anna Allen, 1854-1917.

Oscar D., son of A. C. and L. A. Allen, April 18, 1884-July 1, 1896.

Mary E. McEwen, wife of Albert A. McEwen; died, Nov. 15, 1895.

S. S. Wheeler, Feb. 15, 1900-June 21, 1901.

Rebecca, wife of S. Yeargin, March 15, 1833-June 5, 1901.

John Bridges, June 20, 1843-May 5, 1911; son of Mr. and Mrs. Thomas Bridges.

Jane Ellen, wife of John Bridges, Nov. 5, 1849-May 13, 1896; daughter of Mr. and Mrs. John Martin.

G. B. Padgett, Aug. 6, 1830-July 4, 1909.

Addie W., wife of G. B. Padgett, March 2, 1844-July 15, 1901.

Delia M. Ekhardt, wife of George E. Carlisle, Jan. 27, 1878-June 13, 1907.

Bible Records—Tombstone Inscriptions

James E. Carlisle, Sept. 4, 1897-May 24, 1902.
J. P. Carlisle, 1849 ——.
Sarah, his wife, 1855 ——.
Mary V. Daughter, 1889-1905.
Samuel H. Carlisle, Sept. 23, 1842-April 7, 1903.
David F. Condra, Nov. 24, 1850-Jan. 5, 1923.
Vesta L. Stewart, May 18, 1859-Nov. 2, 1902.
Emmett Hendrix Condra, Feb. 1, 1882-May 8, 1906.
Permelia, wife of Frank Duffy, Oct., 1836-Aug. 3, 1904.
Nancy, wife of Henry Boyle, Oct., 1841-June 23, 1904.
Thos. J. Moore, June 17, 1841-Dec. 24, 1907.
Clarence B., son of E. B. and Marietta Davis, March 14, 1897-March 16, 1897.
Martha, daughter of E. B. and Marietta Davis, Aug. 16, 1901-Aug. 21, 1901.
Marietta, wife of E. B. Davis, Feb. 18, 1866-Feb. 10, 1904.
John W. Bobbitt, July 10, 1855-April 4, 1922.
Hester A. Bobbitt, Nov. 15, 1861-Aug. 3, 1924.
Gus C. Henning, 1890-1917.
Emma S. Bobbitt, June 22, 1859-Aug. 14, 1904, "Sister."
Addie J. Scott, 1879-1909.
Leland J. Scott, 1907-1908.
August Henning, 1840-1904.
Pearl Eve Karl, Jan. 20, 1883-Feb. 25, 1904.
Edna Lee Karl, Sept. 1, 1884-Jan. 30, 1899.
Mary L. Karl, Jan. 13, 1899-June 13, 1899.
Ida Gertrude Karl, Dec. 15, 1880-March 30, 1901.
Terry Monument.
Jane Sobrina, 1845-1919.
Valleye Terry Franklin, 1883-1922.
Lassie Gregsby, 1878-1902.
Julia Ann Johnson; died, Feb. 5, 1908.
Thomas A. Johnson; died, July 7, 1901.
Eliza Harris, 1830-1923.
T. A. Harris, 1815-1904.
Date Milam Cantrell, May 20, 1842-May 7, 1904.
James M. Cantrell, Feb. 7, 1837-Sept. 13, 1924.
F. W. Lawrence, "Our Brother."
Henry S. Lawrence, April 6, 1854-Aug. 16, 1931.
Mattie A. Lovell, 1835-1905.
Capt. T. A. Lovell, 1835-1903.
Evelyn Harriett Hill, 1921-1923.
John Bumpas Hill, 1852-1901.
John Talley, March 25, 1832-July 6, 1921.
Isabella O. Luton, wife of J. M. Talley, Sept. 5, 1832-Nov. 16, 1910.
Millie Ruth, daughter of W. L. and S. W. Talley, April 8, 1897-Dec. 15, 1899.
Annie Smith, 1854-1905.
Albert Wills, 1851-1925.
Mary Bell, 1912-1912.
Annie Bell, 1872.
Thomas H., son of A. J. and J. L. Graves, May 14, 1876-Dec. 25, 1880.
Booker L. Foster, 1875-1905.
Mollie M., his wife, 1874.
Egbert J. Foster, April 14, 1900; age, 67 years, 10 months.
Jessie L. Lenden, Oct. 19, 1890-June 23, 1928.
Pink L. Lenden, Jan. 12, 1893-July 15, 1925.
John Charles Johnson, 1862-1927.
James Martin Utley, April 9, 1908-July 20, 1908.
Margaret Marie, little daughter of Wm. and M. M. Utley, Dec. 25, 1908-March 7, 1909.
Wm. M. Utley, Dec. 12, 1869-Aug. 23, 1912.
John Utley, Confederate Soldier, Oct. 20, 1838-Feb. 13, 1903.
Martha E. Utley, Aug. 21, 1871.
L. L. Utley, Aug. 28, 1876-Dec. 18, 1924.
Leonard L. Doubleday, 1905-1927.
Delmore R., son of Paul and Marie Hunt, Nov. 28, 1913-May 30, 1915.
Susie Belle Doubleday, 1904-1904.
Lameta Dean, daughter of Paul and Marie Hunt, June 10, 1916-Aug. 16, 1918.
Thos. M. Doubleday, 1900-1900.
August Claus, Jr., Oct. 1897; age, 17 months.
Ruth Claus, May 4, 1902-Feb. 5, 1920.
Alice, daughter of J. D. and C. Cantrell, Jan. 18, 1893-Sept. 8, 1893.
Carrie, wife of J. D., April 20, 1862-Sept. 13, 1903.
Carrie, daughter of J. D. and C. Cantrell, April 1, 1882-April 2, 1882.
Hubert, son of J. D. and C. Cantrell,

Bible Records—Tombstone Inscriptions

July 27, 1885-April 26, 1896.
Mary, daughter of J. D. and C. Cantrell, Dec. 22, 1896-July 5, 1897.
Ulysses S. Brent, 1894-1930.
Bertha E. Brent, 1893 ——.
Jane Gilliam, Oct. 18, 1828-Sept. 21, 1899.
John W. Gilliam, Feb. 28, 1821-Feb. 21, 1907.
John H. Matthews; born, Aug. 14, 1846.
Ellen J. Matthews; born, June 6, 1852.
J. J. Holzappel, Dec. 5, 1850-May 11, 1919.
Minnie S. Holzappel, Oct. 6, 1844-May 26, 1919.
Maud L. Matthews, Feb. 19, 1886-July 20, 1904.
Arthur Matthews, Oct. 9, 1883-Sept. 24, 1891.
A. G. Langham, 1858-1911.
Jessie G., daughter of A. F. and Nannie Langham, 1895-1905.
W. H. Draper; died, April 29, 1902; age, 82 years.
Amie Louise Brown, March 31, 1902-Sept. 10, 1902.
Wm. D. Reed, Jan. 21, 1884-June 12, 1918.
J. A. Hill; born, Dec. 10, 1835 ——.
Mary Ann, wife of J. A. Hill, March 20, 1838-June 8, 1905.
Ida Bell, 1867-1924.
G. P. Ferguson, 1863-1917.
Sciota Ferguson, Dec. 8, 1857-April 23, 1881.
A. J. Ferguson, Feb. 22, 1830-Dec. 16, 1889.
Mary J. Ferguson, Dec. 21, 1839-Jan. 9, 1903.
Earnest M. Jackson, Oct. 3, 1899-May 14, 1903.
James F. Waggoner, 1833-1904.
Mary L. Waggoner, 1833-1904.
Henry J. Waggoner, 1873-1901.
Annie Waggoner Schneider, 1867-1930.
Wm. N. Waggoner, 1861-1912.
Livingston Hadly, May 12, 1854-Mar. 6, 1918.
Annie Allen, wife of L. Hadly, Mar. 8, 1865-June 20, 1908.
Oliver C. Cunningham, 1857-1925.
James Edgar McHenry, 1925-1927.
Edgar Pierce Mann, 1888-1904.
John McGavock Kenning, 1896-1912.
Mary Alfred Kenning, 1900-1902.

Maud Horn, June 16, 1883-Mar. 6, 1904.
Paul A. Grizzard, Jan. 2, 1850-Mar. 4, 1902.
Charles W. McCoy, Confederate Soldier, 1845-1929.
Gellie A. McCoy, Dec. 13, 1843-July 13, 1912.
James Bell, 1816-1897.
John H. Page, 1856-1904.
John D. Robinson, 1846-1907.
Lulu J. Bledsoe, April 19, 1876-Mar. 21, 1916.
William Duncan Bledsoe, June 16, 1866-Mar. 17, 1918.
Mary J. Harmon, Dec. 25, 1828-Feb. 28, 1901.
H. P. (Hank) Bledsoe, June 10, 1869-Sept. 15, 1917.
Henry Melburn Lurner, 1856-1904.
Ernest J., infant son of J. G. and Hattie Jones, April 29, 1899-Feb. 6, 1901.
Catherine Arbuthnot, Oct. 6, 1899-Dec. 9, 1907.
Howell Woodside Arbuthnot, Oct. 24, 1899-Oct. 25, 1899.
Jonas Taylor, July 24, 1844-April 20, 1897.
Dorothy Davis, daughter of Mr. and Mrs. Robert L. Monroe, Feb. 23, 1917-July 20, 1918.
Wm. T. Davis, Jan. 18, 1854-Aug. 5, 1926.
Willeria DeBow, wife of Wm. T. Davis, Mar. 11, 1858-July 25, 1897.
Thomas B. Davis, June 14, 1929-Oct. 14, 1918.
Susannah, wife of Thos. B. Davis, Jan. 31, 1835-June 27, 1908.
Willie May McConnico, 1873-1919.
Henry James Loser, 1859-1919.
William W. McConnico, June 28, 1828-Jan. 19, 1899.
Francis Carter Kruder, 1842-1901.
Susan Iron Wells Kruder, 1840-1898.
Emma Dean, daughter of Thomas and Emma McNish, April 3, 1898-Jan. 9, 1900.
Sarah O. Moore, 1837-1913.
Robert W. Moore, 1898-1911.
Minnie Loyd Moore, 1874-1931.
Isaac W. Moore, 1869 ——.
Frank D. Moore, 1912-1915.
Fred W. Gibson, Aug. 16, 1871-April 28, 1912.
V. Blanche Bloodworth, Jan. 27, 1888-May 13, 1906.

Bible Records—Tombstone Inscriptions

Wm. Henry, son of W. H. and S. E. Bloodworth, Nov. 28, 1893-Sept. 26, 1895.
W. H. Bloodworth, Nov. 5, 1842-Jan. 7, 1900.
S. Emma, wife of W. H. Bloodworth and Gran Stargel, Oct. 13, 1865-July 20, 1906.
Lellen Leona Bloodworth Benton, Sept. 5, 1899-July 8, 1919.
Emma Stargel, Blanch Bloodworth, no dates.
Carl, son of R. E. and A. D. Alexander, May 7, 1899; age, 9 years, 7 months.
G. A. Murphey, Dec. 22, 1852-Dec. 20, 1903.
Lewis Y. Craig, April 18, 1806-Sept. 9, 1871.
Mary E. Craig, July 4, 1818-Sept. 14, 1898.
Mother—Nannie L. Craig, Mar. 1852-Jan., 1918.
Lewis M. Craig, April 3, 1846-Jan. 15, 1874.
Our Brother—Louis Thomas, Son of Wm. and Nannie Craig, Nov. 19, 1875-Aug. 29, 1887.
John S. Hitt, May 18, 1842-Jan. 2, 1920.
Lucy Craig Hitt, Sept. 11, 1845-Nov. 24, 1920.
Laura Craig Cato, Jan. 7, 1874-July 9, 1911.
Ruth, daughter of W. G. and Josie Bowers, June, 1889-July 1889.
Bessie Lee Gory, Dec. 22, 1883-March 4, 1884.
Susan Gore Powell Hutchinson, June 26, 1855-Feb. 17, 1929.
Mother—Anna Hicks Russell, 1863-1923.
Robert Chadwell, Sept. 20, 1820-May 14, 1900.
Mary Ann Chadwell, Mar. 7, 1824-Feb. 22, 1896.
T. W. Chadwell, Feb. 27, 1849-Oct. 17, 1907.
Love Chadwell Love, May 17, 1857-June 25, 1927.
Mary Louise Chadwell, Nov. 10, 1907-July 6, 1919.
Sacred to the memory of James Norment; born in Carolina County, Va., Dec. 12, 1768; died, April 27, 1844, in the 76th year of his age.
To the memory of William T. Norment; died, Jan. 23, 1827; age, 28 years, 8 days.

SHRYER MONUMENT

M. W. Shryer, Dec. 23, 1823-Aug. 28, 1907.
M. I. Shryer, Nov. 11, 1824-June 19, 1904.
Annie L. W., daughter of M. W. and M. I. Shryer, April 8, 1867-April 25, 1882.
John Patton Shryer, 1847-1923.
Sallie Hayes Shryer, 1851-1924.
Bessie Marie, 1890-1897.
Mary Louise, 1873-1877.
Daisy Dean, 1875-1877.
Johnnie M., 1877-1878.
Lycurgus W. Gee, born in Trenton, Gibson County, Tenn., July 25, 1836-Aug. 27, 1866.
Rosanna P. Gee, Sept. 18, 1834-Mar. 7, 1863.
Laura L. Gee, Jan. 18, 1833-Dec. 2, 1861.
Josephine C. Gee, wife of F. M. Mitchell, Jan. 21, 1838-June 12, 1878.
Henry Case, born in Canton, Hartford County, Conn., May 15, 1829; died, Mar. 22, 1870.
Marietta B. Case, June 30, 1836-Nov. 13, 1871.
Willie N. Case, Nov. 26, 1856-Mar. 31, 1866.
Jennie W. Case, July 30, 1860-Feb. 17, 1866.
In memory of Benjamin Morgan, Oct. 10, 1762-Sept. 29, 1841. He was a native of Virginia—a soldier of the Revolution. Fought in defense of liberty. A constant friend to the honest poor. He married Elizabeth Kemper of Fouquier County, Va., in 1782. They migrated to South Carolina in 1805.
 "They in silent distance wait
  Their solemn Judge to meet."
Elizabeth Kemper Morgan died in South Carolina in 1821.
Infant daughter of John and Ann W. Morgan; born, October, 1834.
Infant daughter of John and Ann W. Morgan, June, 1835.
H. Leonard, Sept. 22, 1825-Nov. 18, 1888.
Ezekiel Leonard, Mar. 13, 1857-June 4, 1895.
Mary Ella Leonard, Jan. 8, 1865-Mar. 5, 1905.

Bible Records—Tombstone Inscriptions

Robert Edward Leonard, Jan. 14, 1896-May 2, 1912.
Emma F. Alley, Feb. 28, 1848-March 28, 1887.
Matilda W. Atkinson, Mar. 2, 1833-Sept. 3, 1883.
In memory of Chas. Wm. Dixon Cowley, July 22, 1850-Feb. 16, 1861.
William Roberts, born in Berlin, Conn., June 6, 1800-Jan. 31, 1889.
Mrs. Sarah Roberts, wife of Wm. Roberts, Dec. 4, 1807-Mar. 1, 1863.
Clay Roberts, son of Wm. and Sarah Roberts, May 1, 1833-June 7, 1880.
Cornelius L., son of Clay and Mattie L. Roberts, Aug. 26, 1863-Dec. 26, 1876.
Mattie L., wife of Clay Roberts, June 6, 1836-Dec. 12, 1872.
Infant son of M. A. and E. L. Turner
Charlie R. Roberts, April 13, 1851-July 4, 1854.
In memory of Anna P. Condon, consort of James Condon, July 6, 1782-Sept 6, 1844.
Jacamine J. Cartwright, wife of Wm. Glasgow, Oct. 27, 1803-Oct. 16, 1872.
Her daughter, Elizabeth E., Oct., 1831.
Edna Glasgow, Jan. 18, 1857-Feb. 26, 1920.
D. H. Lockart, May 28, 1808-May 18, 1867.
Amasa Witt Lockart, Jan. 4, 1852-Feb. 25, 1877.
L. B. Boyd, Oct. 14, 1847-Sept. 15, 1882.
Cecelia Burkinbine, Jan. 23, 1828-Dec. 6, 1906.
E. D. Richards, born in Fairfax County, Va., Aug. 9, 1804-Dec. 31, 1867.
To the memory of A. McWilliams of Louisiana, who departed this life Aug. 1st, 1834; age, 34 years.
Rev. B. H. Ragsdale, Jan. 18, 1801-Oct., 1862.
Sacred to the memory of the Rev. James H. Bowman, Feb. 8, 1765-Feb. 18, 1812; age, 77 years, 10 days.
Eliza S. Bowman, wife of Rev. James H. Bowman, Aug., 1784-1834; age, 50 years.
In memory of James T. Love, Feb. 2, 1777-Sept. 20, 1850.
In memory of Hannah A. Love, Jan. 10, 1813-Oct. 10, 1835.
Sacred to the memory of James Hanna, who departed this life June 5th, 1817, in the 57th year of his age.
Sacred to the memory of Mary Anne Hanna, who departed this life April 14th, 1817, in the 16th year of her age.
Betsey Hudson departed this life in strong hope of a better inheritance; age, 63 years; Nov. 11, 1819.
Here lies the remains of Mr. Oliver Johnson, who died on the 23rd of April, 1816; age, 59 years, 1 month.
Elizabeth Pirtle, who was born the 26th of June, 1800, and died Sept. 1, 1836.
Jane E. Walters, July 4, 1831-April 9, 1884.
Ebenizer W. McCance; died, June 14, 1852; age, 56 years, 3 months.
Sallie Latta, wife of Ebenizer McCance, Feb. 8, 1803-Mar. 16, 1847.
Wm. N. McCance, Sept. 9, 1822-June 3, 1851.
Matthew McCance.
Ann Walker, wife of Matthew McCance.
Jane Neely departed this life June 6, 1889, in the 91st year of her age.
In memory of William Neely, 1772-May 27, 1842.
1809-Aug. 11, 1829.
In memory of D. D. Neely, Feb. 6,
In memory of W. S. Neely, Aug. 28, 1816-Aug. 11, 1829.
In memory of Thomas C. Neely, Mar. 25, 1827-Nov. 13, 1841.
In memory of Samuel Neely, Nov. 7, 1785-May 6, 1855.
G. F. Hall, Oct. 27, 1840-April 9, 1859.
Edwin Ewing Hall, Nov. 18, 1852-June 10, 1892.
Bryan Kendall Lee, May 1, 1855-Mar. 16, 1883.
Sallie McCance, wife of S. A. Baker, Jan. 29, 1838-Dec. 12, 1888.
Willie F., daughter of Sam and Sallie Baker, Dec. 1, 1865-Nov. 4, 1881.
John Brace; died, Mar. 21, 1889; age, 79 years.
Ellen J., wife of John Brace; died, Mar. 26, 1889; age, 76 years.
Sarah Dautel, born in Hartford, Ohio, Oct. 25, 1823; died in Edgefield, Mar. 5, 1884.
John Harris, July 5, 1831-June 17, 1887.
Louis C. Lischey, April 7, 1813-Feb. 19, 1894.
Ida J. Luster, Sept. 3, 1864-Oct. 20, 1888.
Rev. Thomas B. Craighead, born in Mecklenburg County, N. C., A. D.,

Bible Records—Tombstone Inscriptions

1750; first pastor of the First Presbyterian Church of Nashville, Tenn.; founder of the Davidson Academy and first president of the Academy and successor of Davidson College from which sprang the University of Nashville; man of fine talents and capable of close thoughts. He did the cause of religion much service. Died, A. D., 1825.

Mrs. Elizabeth B. Craighead, wife of Rev. Thomas B. Craighead, is supposed to lie in double vault (box) beside her husband in Spring Hill Cemetery.

Sacred to the memory of Jane Craighead, only daughter of the Rev. Thomas B. and Elizabeth B. Craighead. This tomb is close by the Craighead vault.

HARDING LOT IN SPRING HILL CEMETERY

These bodies were moved from Belle Meade fifteen or eighteen years ago.

Sacred to the memory of Giles Harding, June 30, 1784-Jan. 7, 1843.
Charlotte Harding, consort of Giles Harding, Nov. 20, 1790-April 15, 1836.
Eliza Davis Harding, Oct. 26, 1813-Sept. 13, 1840.
George Harding, Aug. 13, 1818-Dec. 25, 1847.
Charlotte Morris Harding, July 2, 1816-June 11, 1835.
William M., son of Giles and Charlotte Harding, Feb. 2, 1821-Dec. 29, 1848.
Henry Perkins Harding, Sept. 18, 1825-May 8, 1848; age, 22 years, 7 months, 21 days.
David Harding, May 26, 1829-July, 1846; age, 17 years.
Giles H. Page, Aug. 27, 1792-Aug. 12, 1850.
Alexander Waits, April 26, 1794-May 1, 1850.
To the memory of Samuel R. Dismukes; died, April 30, 1844; age, 13 months.
To the memory of William E. Dismukes; died, July 29, 1845; age, 4 years.
To the memory of John T. Dismukes, May 25, 1791-Sept. 16, 1846.
Lizzie B. Rogers, daughter of E. P. and M. P. Bondurant, Oct. 15, 1861-April 2, 1903.

Edward P. Bondurant, Nov. 10, 1836-Dec. 30, 1902.
Fannie May, daughter of J. F. and F. P. Bondurant, July 4, 1892-Nov. 5, 1899.
James F. Bondurant, Sept. 4, 1867-Mar. 17, 1893.
In loving memory of my dear wife, Annie Elizabeth Cain; died, Oct. 30, 1899; age, 40 years.
Jennie N. Billings, May 18, 1855-Mar. 1, 1915.
In memory of Elizabeth Porter, daughter of William Miller and Judith Ann Dismukes, May 14, 1846-Nov. 20, 1898.
Susan C. Dismukes, Dec. 12, 1848-May 13, 1906.
Wm. M. Dismukes, Nov. 18, 1850-Oct. 26, 1919.
Herbert M. D. Trull, Oct. 23, 1883-Mar. 11, 1927.
Sacred to the memory of Sallie M., daughter of Wm. M. and Judith Dismukes, March 18, 1842-May 10, 1864; age, 22 years, 2 months, 8 days. "Not dead, but sleepeth."
In memory of Paul Dismukes, May 1, 1762-Feb. 22, 1828.
In memory of Sarah Dismukes, Feb. 5, 1771-Sept. 12, 1839.
In memory of Ann, daughter of M. T. and Ann Dismukes; died, July 19, 1839; age, 4 years, 9 months.
Ruben B. Kemper, 1838-1899.
Rebecca Ann Kemper, 1843-1918.
Robert Lee Kemper, 1866-1926.
Ruben B. Kemper, Jr., 1873-19—.
My son, Wm. W. Whittle, Nov. 28, 1821-Sept. 19, 1902.
John Bridges, June 20, 1843-May 5, 1911.
Jane Ellen, wife of John Bridges, Nov. 5, 1849-May 13, 1896; daughter of Mr. and Mrs. John Martin.
Nannie, daughter of Paul and Elizabeth Dismukes, May 17, 1865-July 9, 1903.
In memory of Judith Ann, wife of William Miller Dismukes, daughter of David Johnson and Elizabeth Porter Burks, Aug. 31, 1816-Jan. 1, 1880.
In memory of William Miller, son of Paul and Sarah Richardson Dismukes, May 30, 1806-Nov. 11, 1878.
Sacred to the memory of George T., son of William M. and Judith A. Dis-

Bible Records—Tombstone Inscriptions

mukes, March 3, 1840-Oct. 4, 1858; age, 18 years, 7 months.
E. Marvin Deaver, 1878-1930.
Susan D., wife of E. A. Brewer, Oct. 31, 1841-June 27, 1898.
Ann Horn, Sept. 23, 1853-June 30, 1893.
Eliza Bryant, wife of J. W. W. Bryant, Oct. 19, 1866-Nov. 9, 1904.
J. Wesley W. Bryant, Dec. 27, 1906; age, 40 years, 9 months. (St. Charles Lodge, 1866-1906.)
Edna Bryant, Feb. 28, 1890-Aug. 18, 1899.
J. Wesley Bryant, July 10, 1893-Aug. 19, 1900.
Emiley Bryant, Jan. 1, 1831-July 16, 1899.
William C. Campbell, Oct. 16, 1819-May 22, 1899; age, 80 years.
Sarah Campbell, 1825-Sept. 29, 1901; age, 76 years.
Odie W. Johnson, 1866-1889.
Louise B. Johnson, 1848-1900.
Charles J. Johnson, 1843-1903.
Annie B. Grigg, 1869-1907.
James R. Grigg, 1859-1914.
John M. Tulley, 1842-1901.
Mary E., his wife, 1845-1901.
Clara A. Orvyl, 1888-1904.
Wm. M. Patton; born, May 17, 1828.
Eliza J., his wife, Nov. 4, 1847-Oct. 10, 1900.
Susan Buchanan; died, July 27, 1902; age, 76 years.
Francis Buchanan; died, July 23, 1901; age, 76 years.
Mary Alice Mayberry, Dec. 27, 1893-Mar. 31, 1921.
Rebecca, wife of S. Yeargin, Mar. 16, 1833-June 5, 1901; age, 68 years, 2 months, 20 days.
Lou Anna Allen, 1854-1917.
Oscar D., son of A. C. and L. A. Allen, April 18, 1884-July 1, 1896.
In memory of Sabina Bowman Dismukes, daughter of John B. and Ann B. Lynch; born in South Carolina, Sept. 22, 1812-Sept. 30, 1844; an humble follower of the Cross of Christ.
Sacred to the memory of James Henry, son of Paul and Sabina Dismukes; born, Oct. 16, 1842; died at White Sulphur Springs, Va., Nov. 3, 1861; age, 19 years, 17 days.
Elizabeth D. Burks, wife of Paul Dismukes, Aug. 9, 1814-Aug. 25, 1892.

Paul Dismukes, son of Paul and Sarah Dismukes, Dec. 12, 1809-Mar. 23, 1869; age, 59 years, 3 months, 12 days.
In memory of Susan T. Dismukes, daughter of John T. and Ann L. Dismukes, Mar. 12, 1837-Dec. 27, 1856.
Matthew P. Walker, Aug. 16, 1787-Aug. 12, 1849.
Agnes R. Hope, wife of Matthew P. Walker, July 20, 1790-Aug. 17, 1872.
Ann B. Winbourne, Sept. 1, 1809-Oct. 13, 1884.
Elizabeth Pirtle, June 28, 1800-Sept. 1, 1836.
Betsey Hudson, who departed this life in strong hope of a better inheritance; age, 63 years; Nov. 11, 1819.
Oliver Johnson, who died 25th of April, 1816; age, 59 years.
Henry M. Stratton, Jan. 30, 1832-Nov. 22, 1881.
Hannah A. Love, Jan. 10, 1813-Oct. 10, 1835.
James T. Love. Feb. 22, 1777-Sept. 20, 1850.
Rev. James H. Bowman, Feb. 8, 1765-Feb. 18, 1812; age 77 years, 10 months. Wife, born, 1784 (stone broken off).
Rev. B. H. Ragsdale, Jan. 18, 1801-Oct, 1862.
Matt Allen,1805-March 21, 1891.
Tennessee Walker Allen, Jan. 24, 1824-Sept. 19, 1865.
Margaret Brown departed this life Sept. 17, 1801; age, 100 years, 5 months, 17 days.
Jane Porter; died, Aug. 30, 1806; age, 61 years, 12 days.
Mary Ann Hanna; died, April 14, 1817, in 16th year of her age.
James Hanna; died, June 5, 1817, in the 57th year of his age.
William Winboune, 1804-1887.
Mary B. Winboune, 1819-1886.
May C. Preston; died, May 13, 1846; age, 23 years.
Agnes H., wife of C. A. Harbert; died, June 25, 1862; age, 31 years.
Chas. W. Dixon, Lieut, Company H, Mexican War, 1826-1856.
Tennie, wife of D. S. Sanders, Mar. 14, 1845-April 17, 1874.
Bettie L. Hurly, wife of J. J. Hurly, Jan. 2, 1855-Aug., 1885.
John Taylor, Oct. 2, 1809-Oct. 19, 1883.
Agnes R. Taylor, 1822-1850.

Bible Records—Tombstone Inscriptions

David S. Graves, Nov. 30, 1825-Jan. 16, 1886.
Elizabeth R. Graves, Oct. 13, 1829 (McFaddens' Bend)-Aug. 8, 1876.
J. M. Goodrich; born, March 23, 1809; age, 67 at death.
Susan (wife), July 4, 1809-July 9, 1851.
Barah New, Jan. 17, 1791-Feb. 15, 1857.
Catherine M. Elam, June 18, 1821-Sept. 13, 1850.
Rebecca Lingrow, April 10, 1830-Dec. 28, 1845.
Mary A. Nelson, born in Virginia, April 16, 1838-July 7, 1860.
Lucy A., wife of Thomas J. Caruthers, born in Granville County, N. C., Dec. 27, 1804; died in Jackson, West Tennessee, Oct. 26, 1857.
Thomas Jefferson Caruthers; born, Feb. 1, 1801, in Rockbridge County, Va.; died, Aug. 19, 1836, in Davidson County; an exemplary member of the M. E. Church.
Mary Cleveland, April 22, 1756-Oct. 15, 1843.
Joshua I. Gee; died, Aug. 18, 1850; age, 83 years.
Willis Swann; died, April 15, 1802. Father, son, and daughter reinterred in one grave: Willis, Jr., and Jane.
William Swann; born in Powhattan County, Va., 1790; died in Davidson County Aug. 6, 1853.
Peter M. Winston; born in Louisa County, Va., Feb. 10, 1785; died in Davidson County, Tenn., May 31, 1846.
Ann Jettun, Nov. 1, 1815-July 2, 1903.
Fred Berger; died, Dec. 29, 1910; age, 79 years.
Walter Wright, Oct. 26, 1904-Oct. 8, 1910.
Henry L. Graves, May 17, 1889-May 11, 1910.
Sister Ella Gerstle, June 3, 1881-May 20, 1910.
Jason D. Shockney, Nov. 3, 1867-Aug. 11, 1910.
Lucy A., wife of D. C. Norman, June 20, 1848-Aug. 2, 1910.
Sue Ada Watson, Aug. 2, 1861-May 11, 1912.
Octie G. Alexander, Jan. 8, 1886-June 26, 1911.
Joseph Clifton, Oct. 19, 1812-Feb. 18, 1887.
Walter Johnson, 1839-1898.

B. Minnie May Johnson, 1866-1876.
William Landon McInturff, Feb. 22, 1845-Aug. 17, 1880.
Mrs. N. E. McInturff, July 27, 1823-Feb. 12, 1879.
Seth Burke, Mar. 7, 1839-July 21, 1929.
Daisy E. Burke, May 18, 1884-May 22, 1927.
Florence E. Burke, Sept. 27, 1878-Aug. 22, 1824.
Mary E. Crowder, Jan. 20, 1840-Sept. 9, 1883.
Wm. J. Cleveland, July 31, 1835-Mar. 19, 1888.
Monroe H. Notgrass, Mar. 8, 1865-Aug. 6, 1925.
Laura P. Notgrass, May 12, 1865.
Emma Elam McGuire, July 14, 1854-Jan. 6, 1916.
Lizzie Ella Clinton, Feb. 12, 1896-May 23, 1912.
Lou Jane Boyd, wife of W. C. Boyd, April 15, 1848-June 5, 1912.
Mattie Viola Adcock, Mar. 7, 1893-Sept. 7, 1913.
Martha A. Jones, Oct. 13, 1849-June 29, 1912.
Mildred Lee Taylor, June 17, 1912.
Amanda J. McGregor, May 22, 1850-Dec. 8, 1912.
Isaac S. Ridge, June 1, 1843-Jan. 15, 1905.
Sarah E. Ridge, Mar. 25, 1849-May 19, 1903.
In memory of my father, Horatio Hite, Feb. 20, 1809-Oct. 23, 1898.
N. B. Britt; died, Feb. 8, 1898; age, 58 years.
Edward P. Kiger, July 15, 1877-Feb. 5, 1906.
William H. Andrews, Oct. 5, 1852-Mar. 12, 1914.
Mattie Rainey, wife of Samuel Rainey, Oct. 18, 1850-Jan. 23, 1914.
Delia Hale; born in New York, April 28, 1833; died in Nashville, Dec. 20, 1914.
Eunice Fuqua, Feb. 18, 1908-Mar. 19, 1915.
Wm. P. Bowers, Aug. 20, 1865-July 12, 1908.
Samuel Cross, Age, 75 years.
Mary B. Cross, Sept. 3, 1907; age, 93 years.
Mary E. Watkins, 1862-1913.
R. Howell Seay, Aug. 14, 1879-Nov. 23, 1923.

Bible Records—Tombstone Inscriptions

W. H. Hayes, May 24, 1866-Aug. 11, 1910.
Bessie Jones, July 17, 1872-Feb. 17, 1877.
J. H. Stites, July 27, 1875-July 28, 1896.
Father—Rev. John W. Hunter, 1824-1914.
Mother—Harriett Susan Wall, 1829-1897.
Sarah A. Vaughan, June 30, 1823-Sept. 19, 1878.
Nicholas Osborn Love, 1822-1897.
Dorothy Jane Love, 1824-1897.
Wm. E. Love, Dec. 18, 1857-Dec. 17, 1911.
James Benjamin Love, 1853-1858.
Newton Herbert Love, 1850-1881.
Minora Love, 1855-1889.
Jennie Love Anderson, July 20, 1861-Aug. 7, 1893.
John B. Sumner, Dec. 24, 1851-Jan. 10, 1879.
Mary D. Sumner, consort of J. B. Sumner, and daughter of John and Temperance A. Bass, Dec. 8, 1831-Mar. 12, 1858.
J. J. Maddox, son of W. C. and B. A. Maddox, July 4, 1874-Aug. 2, 1879.
Papa and Mama's Pet, Ogden S., son of W. C. and B. A. Maddox, Dec. 7, 1876-Sept. 7, 1877.
John H. Strange, Mar. 8, 1849-Jan. 18, 1878; age, 29 years, 10 months, 10 days.
Elizabeth All Arthurs, wife of Newton C. Hare, Feb. 22, 1827-Nov. 27, 1877.
M. M. Hare, April 15, 1850-July 15, 1887.
Melissa Nancy Arthur; died, Mar. 26, 1902; age, 84 years.
Mariah S. Carlile, Nov. 14, 1815-July 6, 1880.
Louise E. Starnes, wife of C. P. Jones, Aug. 1, 1893-May 24, 1913.
Alice Elizabeth Freese, Nov. 23, 1856-Aug. 6, 1913.
T. B. Horn, Jan. 17, 1847-April 8, 1913.
J. P. Brown, 1861-1930.
Georgie E. Frazier, his wife, 1864-1913.
Sebastian Miller, 1834-1909.
Pamelia, his wife, 1848-1931.
Amanda Unisa Humphreys, 1832-1907.
Susan C. Turner, Jan. 9, 1821-Sept. 7, 1878.
Steve N. Williams, April 10, 1861.
Mattie A. Williams, April 26, 1861-April 26, 1919.
Anna Madeline Williams, Aug. 23, 1893-May 15, 1896.
Robert Thomas Stone, 1852-1904.
Corinne Hudson Stone, 1860-1927.
W. H. Bowers, Dec. 20, 1851-Dec. 18, 1918.
Mary E., wife of W. H. Bowers, Feb. 21, 1853-Nov. 25, 1916.
Ellen, wife of J. C. Gilliland, July 17, 1849-Mar. 29, 1895.
J. C. Gilliland, 1849-1927.
Annie M. Gilliland, 1893-1927.
Mother—Louisa B. Duncan, Mar. 3, 1832-Nov. 25, 1908.
Husband—S. J. Buchanan, Feb. 21, 1843-Nov. 28, 1912.
John C. Clark, Feb. 11, 1834-Oct. 10, 1885.
James Bugg, Sept. 26, 1883; age, 40 years.
Peggy Bugg; age, 5 days.
Mary Liza Bugg; age, 19 years.
Benn Bugg; age, 18 years.
Kattie Bugg; age, 13 years.
Lou Ellen Bugg; age, 13 years.
Martha Bugg; age, 1 year, 9 months.
Maj. J. O. Owsley, 1826-1894.
Eliza R. Page, 1868-1906.
S. B. Harrington, April 5, 1854-Sept. 7, 1918.
Wm. Edwards, son of James O. and Emma Maurey, July 8, 1886-Dec. 31, 1895.
James M. Suit, June 7, 1845-Mar. 6, 1911.
Wilson Suit, July 17, 1880-Nov. 19, 1887.
Mary E. Suit, Dec. 15, 1842-Oct. 16, 1905.
Mother—Anna Suit Patrick, June 7, 1870.
Father—Joseph B. Patrick, Oct. 17, 1859-Sept. 1, 1924.
Babe Stanfield, 1852-1928.
H. B. Stanfield, 1847-1905.
Daisy S. Marfield, 1879-1909.
P. E. Paschall, Dec. 22, 1858-Feb. 5, 1910.
Olga F. Hughes, 1872-1914.
Madison D. Hughes, 1877-1906.
Thomas Good, Aug. 25, 1829-Dec. 7, 1905.
Matilda, wife of Thos. Good, 1824-Dec. 24, 1904.

Bible Records—Tombstone Inscriptions

Luther Eugene Glymp, Mar. 18, 1892-May 1, 1915.
John W. Parks, 1872-1915.
Nannie Lee Weaver, May 25, 1894-April 9, 1914.
Samuel Harvey Vaughan, Mar. 23, 1851-Jan. 7, 1892.
Olive J. Lischey, 1864-1918.
Robert Warnack, Feb. 2, 1895-Oct. 1, 1907.
Archie Warnack, May 2, 1897-Oct. 11, 1907.
Thomas Warnack, Mar. 11, 1907-Oct. 11, 1907.
Elizabeth McCutchen, 1815-1900.
Susanna Johnston, 1822-1893.
Myrtle Price, 1870-1908.
Wm. F. Snyder, 1865-1927.
Fannie M. Snyder, 1867-1930.
Ida Lanier Etheridge, 1861-1930.
Wm. J. Sanders, Oct. 2, 1906; age, 65 years.
W. H. Kiger, 1868-1918.
Hattie Kiger, 1878.
Charlie S. Allison, May 17, 1897-July 25, 1907.
Mabel I. Allison, July 15, 1900-Nov. 3, 1900.
C. T. Allison, July 29, 1854-Dec. 16, 1912.
William Hamill, 1855-1914.
Eugene Buttersworth, 1835-1908.
Georgia E. Linker, July 7, 1891-June 5, 1908.
A. J. York, Aug. 11, 1854-Feb. 22, 1910.
Matilda Abernathy, Sept. 22, 1823-July 30, 1908.
Sarah E. Rice, Nov. 24, 1853.
N. B. Rice, Dec. 9, 1845-Dec. 25, 1926.
Lillian Rutherford, April 4, 1903-Dec. 4, 1905.
Harris Rutherford, Sept. 23, 1898-Nov. 15, 1907.
Leonard S. Rice, Mar. 2, 1889-June 26, 1908.
Robert L. Rice, Jan. 2, 1886-Oct. 24, 1909.
Etta B. Gibbs, Aug. 1, 1895-June 7, 1903.
Green B. Horn, Nov. 27, 1844-May 22, 1908.
Pauline Horn, July 20, 1843-July 11, 1926.
Rosa L., wife of E. G. Glenn, June 10, 1882-May 6, 1908.
Theresa Schnelder, Nov. 30, 1860-July 9, 1906.
Benjamin Waller, Sept. 10, 1879-April 1, 1905.
Henry N. Mullen, Nov. 29, 1840-April 8, 1903.
Bettie J., wife of B. M. Morton, Oct. 15, 1866-Nov. 13, 1905.
S. H. Graves, May 29, 1905; age, 32 years.
A. G. Rutherford, Feb. 6, 1832-Mar. 11, 1907.
Margaret May Cutrell, May 21, 1893-May 20, 1923.
Almeba Luella, daughter of R. E. and Esther Yeargin, 1911-Sept. 4, 1912.
Robert C. Yeargin, Dec. 27, 1858-Oct. 10, 1919.
Luella A., wife of Robt. C., June 1, 1860.
Margie L., daughter of J. W. and M. J. Patton, June 15, 1890-July 18, 1907.
David Griffice, April 25, 1822-Feb. 26, 1908.
Myrtle Louise, daughter of G. M. and Lillie Graft, July 19, 1907-Sept. 12, 1907.
Bynum Graft, Dec. 13, 1894-June 30, 1914.
Mother—Elizabeth Monch Harrison, Jan. 7, 1830-April 19, 1908.
W. H. Rice, Oct. 6, 1865-Sept. 11, 1917.
Mary E., wife of Jesse M. Hammers, Nov. 19, 1867-Dec. 29, 1911.
Jesse M. Hammers, April 26, 1907-May 7, 1907.
Elizabeth Coggin, wife of John A. Hamblen, April 29, 1833-July 22, 1910.
Wm. G. James, Nov. 4, 1839-Feb. 15, 1907.
James Russell, son of J. R. and M. S. Terry, Dec. 31, 1910-Jan. 22, 1917.
Homer E., son of J. R. and M. S. Terry, June 18, 1908-July 21, 1909.
Annie Katie Cunningham, wife of T. J. Peacock, Jr., Sept. 20, 1892-June 24, 1913.
Henrietta A. Childress, Feb. 1, 1853-Feb. 29, 1909.
Wm. Rainey, May 24, 1840-Dec. 5, 1912.
Elizabeth Rainey, Sept. 15, 1840-May 31, 1917.
Morgan L. Ford, April 9, 1832-Feb. 17, 1913.
Nancy Louise Oliphant, wife of M. L.

Bible Records—Tombstone Inscriptions

Ford, Sept. 25, 1834-May 12, 1908.
Campbell W. Jeffreys, 1866-1908.
Mrs. L. D. Redmond, Oct. 9, 1837-April 19, 1908.
Wm. Peet Daugherty, Nov. 20, 1928.
Mollie E. Bland, Feb. 15, 1886-Aug. 3, 1908.
Josie L. Bland, May 21, 1880-Sept. 20, 1912.
Marquis W. Thompson, 1853-1916.
Nancy Ann Thompson, 1853 ——.
Wm. T. Edwards, 1860-1926.
R. P. Bell, Dec. 10, 1859-Oct. 20, 1909.
David Wm. King, Mar. 27, 1883-Mar. 30, 1926.
Horace, son of Wm. N. and Etta McPherson, Nov. 13, 1910-Jan. 18, 1911.
John Allison Roger, Dec. 23, 1822-Nov. 27, 1911.
Eliza Jane Roger, Nov. 16, 1832-Nov. 18, 1909.
Robert Napper, April 16, 1893-Nov. 24, 1909.
Eliz. B. Jones, 1843-1921.
Bulah, wife of J. W. Wood, Aug. 31, 1871-May 29, 1909.
Alex Bland, Aug. 26, 1845-Mar. 30, 1916.
Margaret Evans Bland, 1851-1928.
W. A. Clower, 1877-1909.
Fred Gray, 1869.
His wife, Mary E. Gray, 1871-1910.
Lelia Ruth Gray, 1897-1920.
Wm. F. Shan, 1878-1916.
Wm. T. Shan, Feb. 15, 1858-July 16, 1930.
Harry G. Shan, Jan. 24, 1880-Mar. 15, 1917.
Henry M. Scott, 1850-1913.
Emma L. Scott, 1845-1927.
John S. Williams, Jan. 24, 1878-Jan. 28, 1918.
Wm. J. Cox, Feb. 17, 1856-Feb. 15, 1916.
Lewis Carl Griffin, 1855-1930.
Amelia Bates Griffin, 1858-1915.
Lou Anna Beard, Sept. 2, 1872-Oct. 16, 1927.
H. P. Avrill, Aug. 2, 1852-May 16, 1927.
Tennessee Paradise, Feb. 1, 1849-Feb. 15, 1927.
Jennie Buckingham, Jan. 2, 1873-Feb. 27, 1928.
John T. Shannon, 1862-1927.
Harvey Franklin Hughes, Sept. 5, 1865-Nov. 7, 1927.
Harry L. Wilson, 1874-1929.
John T. Talley, Dec. 18, 1854-Nov. 6, 1929.
J. Samuel Green, May 25, 1871-Feb. 25, 1930.
Adeline Eberhard Weiss, 1858-1929.
Clifton Reynolds, 1866-1925.
Sethe P. Saunders, 1842-1925.
Mary C. Saunders, 1850-1931.
Walter L. Lallemand, 1866-1924.
W. L. Lewis, 1848-1927.
James Theo Oliphant, 1847-1928.
Pittie Orgain Oliphant, 1846-1924.
Jim Talley, 1863-1923.
John K. Roberts, Jan. 3, 1837-Jan. 2, 1927.
Sarah Hembree, 1875-1928.
James W. Richardson, 1871-1929.
Joseph E. Tyler, 1861-1927.
James W. Clark, 1847-1927.
W. H. Slonecker, 1870-1925.
Chas. F. Roach, 1872-1928.
Sarah T. Vick, 1847-1924.
Isaiah L. Vick, 1866-1931.
Irene Tully Alexander, 1871-1925.
John Isaac Alexander, 1869 ——.
W. W. Nellums, 1876-1928.
Lou C. Nellums, 1853-1930.
Isaac A. Swadler, 1866-1926.
William Reed, April 26, 1855-May 3, 1929.
Martha Jane Reed, June 22, 1851-Mar. 25, 1928.
Della Bradford, 1865-1928.
Charlie M. Estes, Sr., 1864-1924.
Diza Moss, 1844-1926.
Julia E. Jones, 1871-1925.
James O. Simpkins, 1874-1925.
Jas. Taylor Combs, 1871-1928.
Louisa J. Spann, Sept. 25, 1853-July 2, 1931.
Susie Robinson Young, Jan. 31, 1872-Dec. 16, 1927.
Walter W. Naylor, 1862-1927.
John C. Sneed, 1854-1928.
Lizzie A. Sneed, 1875 ——.
Dr. Clara E. Harris, 1862-1929.
Elsie Jane White, Oct. 7, 1846-June 26, 1927.
Ida Ferguson Slater, 1861-1930.
Ophelia Gannon, 1859-1929.
Lena Rissel, 1883 ——.
Lucien C. Bowers, 1855-1929.
Frank Warren, July 22, 1862-Sept. 14, 1926.
Cornelius N. Herron, 1864-1929.
Margaret E. Herron, 1867-1926.

Bible Records—Tombstone Inscriptions

Fredonia B. Batson, 1871-1927.
McClellan Taylor, 1867-1927.
Alfred Thomas Jackson, 1864-1928.
S. M. Dewitt, 1844-1926.
Sirena R. Dewitt, 1855-1931.
Adeline T. McCool, wife of W. B. Cross, 1850-1928.
Harriette Vandervart, 1868-1925.
Nettie Brown, 1885-1921.
R. L. Brown, 1882-1928.
William A. Hailey, 1864-1921.
Mattie J. Hailey, 1865-1930.
John T. Rutherford, Mar. 25, 1852-May 2, 1919.
Wm. W. Patton, Oct. 20, 1873-Jan. 29, 1917.
G. Adolph Rissel, 1864-1918.
Kurt Hess Rissel, 1896-1917.
John D. Naive, 1851-1927.
James T. Heath, July 20, 1871-May 7, 1919.
John H. Hare, 1885-1918.
Francis E. Cockrill, 1852-1917.
Benjamin H. Cockrill, 1886-1929.
James R. Cockrill, 1833-1912.
John W. Gowans, 1875-1930.
Clara F. Gowans, 1877-1918.
Wm. H. Jackson, Jan. 7, 1845-Nov. 12, 1922.
Louisa Stulle Frierson, wife of Wm. H. Jackson, 1843-1915.
Ruth M. Moore, wife of E. U. Buchi, Nov. 17, 1895-Oct. 14, 1918.
Era J. Buchi, wife of E. U. Buchi, Oct. 23, 1892-Nov. 20, 1915.
David M. Larkin, Mar. 28, 1865-Mar. 17, 1916.
G. L. Thompson, Aug. 21, 1872-Jan. 20, 1917.
Eulala Thompson, May 16, 1876 ——.
O. V. Anderson, Nov. 25, 1893-Feb. 1, 1917.
Sam. J. Campbell, 1885-1918.
Martha Craig Knox, 1856-1918.
Rome T. Warmack, Feb. 8, 1859-May 6, 1919.
Harry W. Alley, 1883-1916.
Ruth Hayes Hendrix, Jan. 28, 1876-Feb. 14, 1916.
Charles Taylor, Jan. 24, 1889-Feb. 3, 1916.
Lucy H. Bayers, wife of J. M. Bayers, Aug. 6, 1852-April 28, 1916.
W. E. Russell; died, Aug. 31, 1915; age, 33 years.
William D. Lester, 1888-1925.
Fannie Lou Lester, 1889 ——.
Jane, wife of W. F. Mabury, June 12, 1873-Oct. 23, 1916.
Cora Elizabeth Wood, July 25, 1899-Oct. 11, 1915.
Martha E. Baker, Jan. 3, 1849-April 2, 1928.
Henry C. Baker, Aug. 8, 1851-Dec. 31, 1914.
James D. Hudson, 1877-1914.
F. Reed Minton, July 4, 1891-Aug. 22, 1914.
Mary Lille Minton, Mar. 29, 1896-June 15, 1920.
Russell Odis Minton, Aug. 21, 1898-Jan. 27, 1921.
Joel W. Minton, Jr., 1863-1928.
Millie Hitch, Jan. 8, 1858-May 14, 1929.
Nettie Hitch, April 29, 1891-May 29, 1915.
Henry Clay Marlow, April 15, 1842-Jan. 6, 1916; 1st Lieut., Company I, 17th Kentucky Inf.
Emma Cassidy, his wife, June 2, 1849-June 24, 1924.
James H. Alley, June 30, 1854-May 30, 1927.
Anderson S. Campbell, 1860-1918.
Morris W. Whiteley, 1890-1930.
Mary E. Wells, April 2, 1857-April 14, 1916.
Rev. W. T. Dye, Mar. 8, 1931-May 8, 1916.
James Haskell Vaughn, 1887-1909.
Samuel A. Dickerson, 1882-1916.
Nancy E. Dickerson, 1853-1919.
Alice Harding, wife of W. T. Dye, Oct. 25, 1851.
J. H. Peebles, June 1, 1868-July 9, 1918.
Charles H. Harrison; died, Dec. 18, 1917; age, 48.
T. S. Pittard, 1872-1930.
T. O. Dillard, 1888-1921.
John M. Smith, Nov. 18, 1888-July 16, 1917.
Robert A. Holman, 1846-1917.
Hearn Turner, 1897-1918.
Jennie H. Turner, 1870-1920.
Grandmother Hearn, 1838-1920.
Frank M. Sweeney, Sept. 7, 1892-April 17, 1918.
Lee Gardner, 1841-1918.
Mary Jane Gardner, 1842-1928.
N. Burkhalter, July 2, 1876-Aug. 12, 1918.

Bible Records—Tombstone Inscriptions

Dora A. Coatney, Jan. 14, 1870-Mar. 26, 1931.
Boyd Dutton, Oct. 16, 1877-Jan. 30, 1919.
Mary Gertrude Pearsoll, Nov. 17, 1857-Mar. 26, 1919.
Fred H. Bartlett, 1860-1929.
Eula M. Lancaster, 1875-1929.
Lizzie Shepherd, 1864-1930.
Clarence Elvin Biggs, May 31, 1880-June 3, 1930.
Carrie Riel Biggs, July 18, 1889.
John W. Groome, 1866-1928.
Chas. C. Edens, June 4, 1875-Oct. 27, 1924.
Stella A. Edens, 1877-1927.
Josie Price, 1863-1925.
Elizabeth Price, 1859 ——.
Marion DeKalb King, July 19, 1843-May 22, 1925.
Charlie T. Marshall, 1870-1925.
Isabella Moore Holderfield, 1855-1927.
Edgar M. Prince, 1868-1931.
Mary E. Glasgow, 1841-1926.
Ellen Lou Atkins, April 19, 1862-Dec. 24, 1926.
Jas. M. Stout, 1843-1926.
Julious H. Mount, 1858-1927.
W. O. Gowan, Oct. 11, 1847-May 30, 1927.
Z. Taylor Wheeler, 1874-1923.
G. R. Brooks, 1849-1928.
Charles Wood Harman, 1853-1910.
Anne Warwick Harmon, 1860-1929.
Mary E. Harmon, 1855-1914.
Dr. Harvey Shannon, Jan. 18, 1831-May, 14, 1906.
Lucy T. Shannon, Mar. 24, 1838-Nov. 20, 1928.
Anna Goodson, July 23, 1874-Nov. 10, 1929.
Aaron Goodson, Dec. 31, 1873-June 18, 1923.
Nannie E. Boone, 1852-1911.
Gury Quarles, Aug. 28, 1930-Mar. 24, 1931.
Martha Ann Quarles, Oct. 4, 1836-Dec. 1, 1919.
Sallie W. Booth, Aug. 29, 1870-Sept. 8, 1911.
A. H. Cleveland, Nov. 30, 1869-June 21, 1911.
R. A. Dillard, May 17, 1870-Jan. 14, 1918.
Helen Dillard and baby, Nov. 17, 1874-Mar. 25, 1911.

Edward H. Klugman, Jan. 5, 1874-Dec. 1, 1913.
William R. Kernall, 1848-1919.
Margaret A. Kernell, 1864-1929.
John Pittman Roberts, 1861-1912.
Minor M. Young, May 28, 1859-Sept. 19, 1913.
Aley Young, Nov. 15, 1889-Dec. 16, 1918.
J. Ed., 1850-1926.
Thos. J. Overby, May 12, 1854-Oct. 11, 1920.
John S. Barnett, Mar. 16, 1860-Oct. 7, 1920.
Biddie F. Barnett, Mar. 28, 1862.
James Henry, 1872-1925.
Martha Overby, 1868-1917.
Fannie Zula, 1895-1919.
William F. Binkley, Nov. 15, 1854-May 12, 1917.
F. H. Sanderson, 1854-1929.
Missouri C. Jarrell, May 8, 1846-July 23, 1928.
Ellie H. Hughes, Dec. 6, 1864-April 15, 1926.
Bettie Waters Priest, 1859-1925.
John F. Briggs, 1861-1926.
Alice Cole Briggs, 1871-1929.
Douglas Dobie, Oct. 28, 1856-May 16, 1926.
Martha A. Dobie, Sept. 29, 1852-Aug. 10, 1931.
A. J. Howington, Mar. 31, 1857-Feb. 14, 1930.
Fannie Moore, Sept. 9, 1866-May 26, 1926.
Laura Oldham, wife of R. A. Cartwright, 1853-1927.
R. B. Overby, Sept. 11, 1870-May 3, 1931.
Rembardt Gasser, 1868-1931.
Margaritha Gasser, 1873-1926.
Mrs. Ophelia Connor Mooring, 1847-1931.
J. T. Pitt, 1853-1925.
Irene Pitt, 1862-1926.
Ella McDonald Johnson, 1859-1929.
Ora J. Nolen, 1874 ——.
James W. Gee, Nov. 2, 1873-April 1, 1926.
Mary Elizabeth Farrell, 1865-1926.
F. H. Sanderson, listed before.
William Evans, Jan. 31, 1835-April 17, 1918.
Emma B. Evans, May 6, 1837-Sept. 8, 1918.
C. Henderson Cole, 1851-1917.

Bible Records—Tombstone Inscriptions

A. J. Morgan, 1857-1917.
Eliza Smith, May 14, 1840-Mar. 6, 1928.
John Watkins, 1827-1918.
Lucinda S. Watkins, 1850-1929.
James Scott Watkins, Sept. 26, 1883-Aug. 26, 1927.
Gus Gerstle, 1850-1928.
A. L. Phipps, Feb. 16, 1845-Mar. 17, 1913.
Louise Valide Latsch, 1871-1918.
John M. Woodard, Aug. 22, 1852-Mar. 27, 1925.
Archie B. Wood, 1872-1924.
Wm. J. Lancaster, 1841-1924.
Joe S. Roler, 1869-1925.
Harden H. Nolen, 1874-1925.
J. F. Carrell, 1868-1926.
Rev. Lawrence Hosale, 1871-1925.
Andrew Alexander; died, Jan. 30, 1925; age, 66 years.
Minter P. Davis, 1861-1925.
His wife, Anna Frizzell, 1865 ——.
Anne Baxendale, Aug. 27, 1845-Mar. 15, 1922.
J. T. Johnson, 1869-1928.
J. B. Marable, 1838-1924.
James McAlister, 1855-1926.
Hulda Peyton Stacey, 1851-1929.
J. T. Williams, 1861-1926.
W. W. Jones, 1861-1927.
Amelia Turner, Mar. 10, 1844-Nov. 10, 1925.
Annie M. Evans, Nov. 25, 1852-Oct. 9, 1921.
Hardy Nokes, Aug. 4, 1865-Mar. 1, 1926.
Nannie Nokes, Oct. 28, 1861.
S. W. Graves, Jan. 27, 1837-June 22, 1925.
Anna, wife of Thos. Byars, Aug. 22, 1846-April 24, 1920.
Houston F. Jackson, Feb. 15, 1846-Oct. 1, 1928.
James W. Smith, Jan. 1, 1854-Dec. 8, 1926.
Nora Smith, Aug. 5, 1861 ——.
Jesse B. Martin, Feb. 1, 1869-Nov. 15, 1926.
Emily Jane Brooks, Aug. 23, 1847-Aug. 14, 1920.
Mattie May Waggoner, Dec. 3, 1861-Aug. 7, 1920.
Phillip A. Walker, Sept. 25, 1841-June 19, 1924.
Mary J. Flack, May 2, 1857-Aug. 9, 1924.

Alice E. Beard, Sept. 11, 1850-Jan. 16, 1926.
Jesse Cuzzort, June 11, 1866-July 29, 1926.
Tillie F. Fowler, 1875-1926.
Mary C. Frazier, Jan. 27, 1859-Jan. 17, 1924.
John Etta Glymp, July 13, 1865-Dec. 28, 1922.
Frank M. Richmond, 1865-1920.
J. R. Pate, 1859-1919.
Hugh P. Campbell, May 30, 1860-May 12, 1919.
Taylor Myers, 1849-1931.
Amanda E. Myers, 1858-19—.
John Kellum, Sept. 30, 1868-Dec. 7, 1931.
Martha Ellen Kellum, Dec. 12, 1873.
John Maynard, 1859-1927.
Mary Maynard, 1867-19—.
W. H. Ring, 1856-1928.
Josie Ring, 1869 ——.
W. H. Spann, 1855-1928.
Sarah Spann, 1857 ——.
Martha A. Thompson, 1874-1929.
Permelia Thompson, 1841-1920.
Sarah A. Berry, 1854-1927.
Elizabeth Spicer McDougall, wife of William C. McDougall, 1840-1928.
Della Townsend, 1871-1927.
Mrs. M. C. Kimbro, Jan. 21, 1834-Mar. 7, 1928.
Elizabeth A. Chestnut, 1884-1927.
W. R. Carter, Dec. 29, 1849-Aug. 31, 1927.
Jessie J. Leach, Oct. 6, 1854-July 15, 1929.
James N. Elam, July 12, 1865-June 30, 1927.
Pink Vitetoe, June 29, 1871-July 19, 1925.
Sidney E. Kernel, 1870-1926.
George Gottlieb Ruff, Nov. 12, 1844-Feb. 27, 1917.
Conrad H. Bergman; died, Oct. 25, 1918; age, 52 years.
John Glutingers, Feb. 4, 1834-May 25, 1879.
Alonzo Thompson, Sept. 5, 1854-Feb. 26, 1883.
Hinton Grizzard, June 8, 1879; age, 67 years, 2 months, 19 days.
Elizabeth Grizzard, wife of Hinton Grizzard, July 29, 1886; age, 72 years, 11 months, 3 days.
Robert Grizzard, M.D., Oct. 17, 1847-June 9, 1908.

Bible Records—Tombstone Inscriptions

H. Earl Grizzard, Jan. 4, 1883-July 4, 1909.
Joshua Neely, April 6, 1823-June 4, 1904.
Ann Harvey Neely, Aug. 27, 1835-Feb. 21, 1902.
W. F. Gray, 1824-1908.
Mary J. Winbourne, wife of W. F. Gray, 1830-1887.
Agnes Gray, wife of Edwin A. Coles; died, July 8, 1904.
Annie Gray, wife of Church Lanier, Feb. 23, 1899.
Church G. Lanier, July 7, 1855-May 23, 1903.
Mary A., wife of G. W. G. Payne, Dec. 1, 1824-Feb. 24, 1896.
G. W. G. Payne, Aug. 12, 1813-Jan. 13, 1887.
Lear Deartin; age, 50 years.
Andrew Williams, born in Fauquier County, Va., 1835; died in Davidson County, Tenn., 1884.
Florence E. Love, July 22, 1870-Feb. 16, 1894.
Emma T. Love, June 27, 1863-June 4, 1883.
Olive J. Lischey, 1864-1918.
Joe Brown, 1860-1917.
Callie, his wife, 1860 ——.
Mrs. J. Ann Butcher, Aug. 16, 1817-June 22, 1899.
Rebecca E. Blakemore, Sept. 17, 1832-April 15, 1894.
Samuel J. Anderson; born, Dec. 18, 1874.
Rhoda E. Anderson, Jan. 1, 1859-May 23, 1907.
Emma Stephenson, May 12, 1853-Aug. 5, 1892.
Josephine Stephenson, Feb. 6, 1861-Sept. 21, 1929.
William A. Stephenson, 1861 ——.
Kate Colquette Stephenson, 1873-1924.
Joseph S. Kirkwood, Mar. 23, 1842-June 1, 1899.
Margaret A. Kirkwood, Feb. 8, 1853-Feb. 22, 1915.
Minnie L. Traughber, Jan. 22, 1875-Nov. 18, 1916.
W. S. Sesler, April 16, 1863.
His wife, Ziporah, Dec. 18, 1866-Aug. 25, 1920.
James Overton Walker, Nov. 5, 1824-Oct. 10, 1851.
Jesse B. Pitts, born in South Carolina, Dec. 14, 1796-Oct. 6, 1868.
Winnie S. Ridge, wife of Smith McKinnie; died, Aug. 3, 1868; age, 30 years.
Jones A., son of Mary A. and M. T. Grizzard, April 16, 1871-Mar. 17, 1895.
Marion S. Grizzard, 1873-1898.
Mary A. Grizzard, 1848-1922.
Johnnie J. Jones, 1881-1919.
C. B. Barthell, Nov. 2, 1857-July 26, 1876.
Abram Joseph, May 31, 1829-Mar. 21, 1894.
Ella C. Joseph, Jan. 3, 1838-June 7, 1892.
Rev. W. S. Harwell, April 12, 1845-April 4, 1915.
John Morrow and sons.
John A. Cunningham, wife and daughter.
John Henry Guthrie, May 23, 1848-Dec. 3, 1907.
Mary Elizabeth Guthrie, Mar. 27, 1858-May 22, 1913.
M. W. Shryer, Dec. 23, 1823-Aug. 28, 1907.
M. F. Shryer, Nov. 11, 1824-Jan. 19, 1904.
Joe N. Hows, Mar. 24, 1851-Oct. 9, 1927.
Nannie S. Hows, June 8, 1840-Jan. 27, 1929.
Stephen H. Hows, Mar. 16, 1844-April 21, 1928.
Capt. John Wilson; died, July 24, 1870.
Sarah W., wife of John Wilson; died, July 29, 1877; age, 73 years.
Tennie, wife of W. M. Perry; died, Aug. 12, 1913; age, 58 years.
Laura E. Buchanan, 1847-1917.
John M. Buchanan, 1844-1925.
Dock Henry White, 1839-1889.
Nancy Wallace White, 1840-1901.
Oscar Henry White, 1864-1927.
W. T. Lanier, April 19, 1831-Feb. 26, 1908.
Margaret J. Lanier, April 20, 1841-May 5, 1917.
Alsa Harris; died, Nov. 13, 1871; age, 75 years.
Leonora Tulley, 1867-1885.
Hugh C. Thompson, April 22, 1829-July 24, 1919.
Ellen M. Thompson, Oct. 20, 1837-July 21, 1920.

Bible Records—Tombstone Inscriptions

George W. McGinnis, Mar. 21, 1843-June 9, 1880.
John McGinnis, Nov. 4, 1834-Sept. 27, 1865.
Jane McGinnis, July 12, 1812-June 4, 1877.
James McGinnis, Feb. 14, 1802-Oct. 20, 1879.
Wm. W. Maynor, 1848-Aug. 10, 1899.
Mrs. Hanna, wife of Mr. J. Fredale; died, Dec. 1, 1854; age, 82 years.
John Fredale; died, Feb. 12, 1841; age, 76 years.
Pleasant T. Maynor, Oct. 17, 1797-June 2, 1862.
Jane M. Maynor, Feb. 8, 1807-Aug. 3, 1880.
I. C. Loftin, May 25, 1840-Mar. 20, 1920.
Mary M. Loftin, Mar. 6, 1843-Dec. 20, 1889.
William A. Rawls, April 21, 1858-Oct. 19, 1928.
James Jones Pryor, 1839-1922.
His wife, Nannie E. Brazelton, 1850-1920.
Henry Driver, July 19, 1809-May 22, 1892.
Elizabeth C. Driver, May 30, 1816-Aug. 3, 1900.
John Maclin Driver, Dec. 29, 1837-Mar. 6, 1893.
Margaret Donelson Davis, May 3, 1850-Oct. 4, 1877.
W. H. Williams, Mar. 16, 1861-April 23, 1897.
Wm. Williams, Feb. 25, 1819-Feb. 12, 1888.
Lizzie B. Williams, Aug. 25, 1831-Aug. 30, 1918.
Martha A., wife of C. Lanier and daughter of E. F. and Tempy Sumner, Nov. 1, 1818-Aug. 26, 1857.
Chl. Lanier, Sept. 22, 1806-Sept. 14, 1889.
James McFerrin Wright, Nov. 27, 1829-Aug. 16, 1896.
His wife, Thyrza Wortham, Feb. 14, 1833-Sept. 17, 1897.
George G. Bradford, Feb. 8, 1825-Dec. 20, 1866.
Mary Narcissa, wife of G. G. Bradford, July 31, 1850-Dec. 11, 1896.
Grace Bradford, 1862-1905.
Irene Bradford, 1866-1904.
P. S. Shute, Feb. 12, 1857-May 2, 1921.
Henry B. Bradford; died, Dec. 20, 1875; age, 18 years.
A. D. McClure, Jan. 21, 1885.
Clinton Cantrell Elam, Feb. 27, 1839-July 17, 1909.
Dan W. Elam, 1814-1890.
Juliet C., wife of Dan W. Elam, 1818-1895.
Mary E. Jackson, 1861-19—.
Burrell F. Jackson, 1858-1929.
Augustus L. Lee, May 1, 1866-Feb. 27, 1920.
Caroline R. Lee, Aug. 24, 1840-May 22, 1921.
Samuel L. Lee, June 20, 1838-Feb. 23, 1892.
C. B. Brooks; died, Jan. 18, 1892.
A. A. Brooks; died, Oct. 30, 1906.
W. D. Brooks; died, Feb. 22, 1926.
George W. Etheredge, Mar. 23, 1830-Mar. 14, 1895.
Christopher Lock Huckman, Oct. 21, 1839; died at Somerset, England, Jan. 14, 1900.
Emma Mary Huckman, June 25, 1838, Somerset, England; died, Dec. 30, 1896.
Eugene Dumont, July 13, 1873-Sept. 15, 1914.

Mt. Olivet Cemetery

These names were taken from tombstones in Mt. Olivet Cemetery by Mrs. E. C. Pryor. Copied by Mrs. J. F. Draughon, Chairman of Genealogical Research.

Dr. R. M. Buddeke, 1856-1886.
John H. Buddeke, 1808-1887.
Mary Jane, his wife, 1816-1879.
Bernard V. Buddeke, 1855-1862.
Mamie E. Buddeke, daughter of K. and L. Karsch, 1872-1876.
Richard Miles Buddeke, M.D., June 19, 1856-Sept. 19, 1886.
Mary Ann Seifried, 1804-1887. Grandma.
Frederick Seifried, 1871-1872. Brother.
David T. McGavock, April 19, 1813-Jan. 9, 1866.
Caroline E., wife of David T. McGavock, Mar. 12, 1815-Jan. 7, 1863.

Bible Records—Tombstone Inscriptions

Albert T. McGavock, 1814-1836.
Mary T. McGavock, 1834-1843.
Eliza L. Cockrill, 1836-1862.
David McGavock, Feb., 1763-Aug., 1838.
Mary T., wife of David McGavock, 1778-1834.
Charles F. McGavock, 1843-1843.
Annie R. McGavock, 1847-1849.
David A. McGavock, 1857-1862.
Albert T. McGavock; died, 28th of Oct., A. D., 1836, in the 22nd year of his age.
Eleanor Cabler, who departed this life June 21, 1824; age, 72 years.
Harvey Cabler departed this life Nov. 26th, 1830; age, 75 years.
Sacred to the memory of Capt. John Nichol, who departed this life Sept. 17th, 1842; age, 67 years.
S——, consort of John Nichol, departed this life Aug. 6, 1838.
F. W. Baker, April 21, 1833-May 25, 1893.
W. C. Baker, relict of Bartholemew Cole, Oct. 6, 1825-July 25, 1885.
Bartholemew Cole, July 12, 1817-June 30, 1869.
Charles Henry, son of Henry and Louise S. Baker; born in San Francisco, Cal., May 15, 1852; died at Cincinnati, Ohio, Sept. 10, 1863.
Oscar W., son of Henry and Louise S. Baker; born in San Francisco, Cal., Aug. 8, 1855; died at Thomasville, Ga., Feb. 22, 1886.
Louis Wetzel, Mar. 31, 1804-April 14, 1848.
Johonna, relict of Louis Wetzel, Dec. 27, 1803-Dec. 7, 1871.
Willouby Williams, June 14, 1798-Dec. 8, 1882.
Sacred to the memory of Emma and Anna, infant daughters of Gen. W. and Mrs. N. Williams; died, Mar. 18, 1829; age, 20 days.
Sacred to the memory of Mrs. Nancy D. Williams, wife of Willouby Williams, who departed this life on the 18th of July, 1814; age, 37 years.
Araminta E. Smiley, Dec. 11, 1792-Aug. 11, 1880.
Mary Ann R. Smiley; died, Jan. 8, 1881; age, 58 years.
Thos. S. Hayes, May 9, 1846-Oct. 28, 1881.
Louise Jane, wife of Chas. M. Hays, April 11, 1824-Dec. 4, 1868.
Susan Jonte; died, Aug. 7, 1859; age, 52 years.
P. Schwarz; died, June 4, 1890; age, 68 years.
Christian Schwarz, Jan. 12, 1837-Dec. 20, 1891.
W. P. Graham, native of County Down, Ireland; died in Nashville, Nov. 17, 1861.
Adaline Criddle Hurton, 1802-1890.
Edward S. Winham, 1853-1881.
Maria Louise, wife of Vernon K. Stevenson, daughter of John Meredith and Malvina Grundy Bass, 1835-1858.
Anthony Warner, June 12, 1804-Sept. 20, 1867.
Theressa Warner, wife of A. Warner, Aug. 12, 1812-Nov. 1, 1879.
Conrad Aultmeyer, Oct. 22, 1830-Oct. 8, 1868.
Joseph Fetz; died, May 21, 1869; age, 92 years.
Mary Fetz; died, Mar. 8, 1871; age, 89 years.
Die Siebe Hier Ruhet Gervas Haury gebin Alt Breisach Baden. Am 12 Feb., 1783, gest 13 Aug., 1869; 86 years was the time of his noble activities; father of 14 children. We bless his memory.
Rev. Otis Oliver Knight; born in Oxford, Ghewango County, N. Y., Nov. 2, 1823; died in Nashville, Tenn., Dec. 24, 1885.
Agnes, wife of William Montgomery; died, Feb. 5, 1871.
In loving memory of Annie M. Carroll, July 23, 1797-Jan. 21, 1874.
Lydia H. Watkins, Mother, 1831-1872.
Catherine Mary Norvell, wife of C. C. Norvell, Dec. 8, 1816-Oct. 2, 1842.
Elizabeth B. McGavock, Dec. 7, 1809-May 1, 1860.
John McGavock, Jan. 30, 1792-July 6, 1877.
John B. McFerrin, June 15, 1807-May 10, 1887.
Almyra A. Probart, wife of J. B. McFerrin, June 20, 1813-May 12, 1854.
Frederick Kempkau, Aug. 14, 1799-July 5, 1875.
Maria D. Kempkau, Nov. 11, 1816-Oct. 11, 1891.
Henry S. Norvell, 1818-1874.

Bible Records—Tombstone Inscriptions

Louise Hamilton, beloved wife of James M. Hamilton; born in Gallatin, Tenn., 1822; died at her home in Nashville, Tenn., 1889.
James M. Hamilton, 1821-1895.
Anthony Wayne Van Leer; born at Reading Iron Works, Chester County, Pa., Mar. 3, 1783; died at Nashville, Tenn., July 9, 1863.
Hugh Van Leer Kirkman; died, Aug. 29, 1846; age, 18 months, 4 days.
Rebecca Brady, wife of Anthony W. Van Lear; born in Franklin County, Pa., Feb. 3, 1793-Oct. 7, 1826.
Here lieth the body of Thomas Kirkman, who departed this life on the 3rd of March, 1813; age, 55 years, 88 days; native of England and an honest man; major in the British Army and Paymaster-General to the troops in Ireland.
Barbara Carroll, wife of Maj. Thomas Kirkman; died, Jan. 12, 1842.
Mrs. Catherine Cook; born in Philadelphia, Pa., Oct. 28, 1793; died at Cumberland Furnace, Dickson County, Tenn., Aug. 30, 1882.
Hugh Kirkman; born in Nashville, Tenn., May 25, 1810; died at Cumberland Furnace, Tenn., Nov. 9, 1861. Our Father.
Eleanor C. Van Lear, beloved wife of Hugh Kirkman; born at Nashville, Dec. 21, 1821; died, June 1, 1848; age, 27 years, 5 months, 10 days.
Thos. Kirkman, only son of Maj. Thomas and Barbara C. Kirkman, departed this life at Nashville, April 7, 1826; age, 47 years.
Ellen Jackson, wife of Thomas Kirkman; born at Bally Bay, Monaghan County, Ireland, Nov. 18, 1774; died at New Orleans, May 30, 1850.
William H., son of Jas. M. and Gigily M. M. Murrell, July 3, 1853-Jan. 17, 1876.
A. H. Hurley, Oct. 2, 1832-Jan. 1, 1891.
His wife, N. C. Hurley, Oct. 10, 1841-Dec. 9, 1908.
Addie, daughter of A. H. and N. C. Hurley, Dec. 11, 1861-Feb. 28, 1862.
W. P. Hurley, Mar. 28, 1842-May 30, 1881.
James H. Murrell, Feb. 15, 1807-Dec. 23, 1872.
Gigily M. M., wife of J. M. Murrell, Jan. 12, 1815-Dec. 17, 1872.

James A. Porter, Sept. 23, 1800-Mar. 20, 1853.
Amanda J. Porter, Jan. 5, 1809-Aug. 1, 1886.
Andrew Allison Porter, April 5, 1868-June 30, 1873.
Dixon W. Porter, Sept. 18, 1871-Mar. 30, 1888.
Rev. Rickard Owen Currey, M.D., born at Nashville, Aug. 28, 1816-Feb. 17, 1865. While faithfully ministering to the sick and dying in the Confederate Hospital at Salisbury, North Carolina.
Rachel Eastin, wife of Dr. R. O. Currey; born, Nov. 11, 1822; died at Nashville, Tenn., Nov. 21, 1865.
Robert, son of Richard O. and Rachel Currey, 1842-1850.
William, son of Richard O. and Rachel Currey, Nov. 30, 1852-Jan. 15, 1853.
Katie Sumpter Currey, April 12, 1861-Sept. 28, 1862.
Preston Currey, Mar. 22, 1870-April 22, 1872.
Dr. G. W. Currey, Sept. 13, 1823-Jan. 25, 1886.
Emily D. Martin, wife of G. W. Currey, Sept. 15, 1825-Feb. 23, 1892.
Jennie G. Currey, July 26, 1855-Feb. 9, 1875. The voice of the song bird is finished.
Sylvanus Jerome Stine, Sept. 15, 1836-June 26, 1874.
John Porterfield, Aug. 21, 1819-Dec. 28, 1874.
Mary E. Shapard, wife of John Porterfield, Dec. 13, 1820-Aug. 11, 1898.
Maj. Wm. Terrell Lewis, 1757-1808.
His wife, Mary Hipkins, 1760-1806.
William B. Lewis, 1790-1866.
His wife, Margaret, 1793-1815.
His wife, Adelaide Stokes, 1800-1840.
His son, Wm. Henry Lewis, 1820-1843.
Godfrey Malbone Fogg, born in Wyndham County, Conn., Dec. 26, 1800-Dec. 30, 1875.
Ellen Stevenson Fogg, wife of G. M. Fogg; died in Louisville, Mar. 30, 1881.
Leonard B. Fite, Nov. 17, 1811-Oct. 7, 1882.
Martha C., wife of L. B. Fite; died, June 21, 1891; age, 51 years.
Daniel Adams, born in Ireland, Mar. 10, 1810; died in Nashville, Sept. 11, 1885.
John Felix Demoville, 1823-1884.

Bible Records—Tombstone Inscriptions

Julia Morgan Demoville, 1859-1877.
Lady Gennett, June 13, 1869-Dec. 11, 1876.
Andrew Gennett, Oct. 7, 1829-May 23, 1858.
Martha Gennett, Nov. 1, 1819-July 3, 1884.
Laura White Hicks, 1853-1883.
William G. White, 1856-1879.
Henry G. Shepard, Feb. 20, 1835-July 11, 1877.
Luther R. Davis, July 20, 1848-Jan. 23, 1882.
Annie W., wife of Luther R. Davis, Dec. 7, 1852-Sept. 23, 1882.
William Nichol, Feb. 12, 1800-Nov. 2, 1873.
Julia M. Lytle, wife of William Nichol, Sept. 17, 1801-Aug. 22, 1890.
Mary Wyche, wife of R. W. Jennings, Oct. 20, 1842-July 18, 1871.
Tyre, son of R. W. and M. W. Jennings, July 4, 1871-July 29, 1871.
Mary E., wife of Thos. W. Evans, Sept. 10, 1821-May 10, 1856.
Josephine Elliston, daughter of T. W. and M. E. Evans, Jan. 11, 1847-Sept. 8, 1855.
Maud H., daughter of R. W. and N. R. Jennings, June 26, 1876-Feb. 11, 1882.
Charles A. Campbell, May 3, 1840-July 3, 1871.
Celia J., wife of C. A. Campbell, Mar. 1, 1847-July 3, 1871.
Clara Agnes Bryan, May 5, 1874-July 23, 1875.
Lawrence Edward Bryan, Sept. 14, 1877-Aug. 26, 1878.
Our Father and Mother.
Michael Campbell, Feb. 22, 1757-Mar. 17, 1830.
Sarah B., his wife, Aug. 20, 1768-Aug. 19, 1852.
Mary Louise C. Patterson, Oct. 14, 1808-Nov. 25, 1864.
W. G. M. Campbell, Aug. 18, 1797-Nov. 3, 1869.
M. A. Norfleet, wife of W. G. M. Campbell, Sept. 14, 1818-Dec. 24, 1876.
Children of W. G. M. and M. A. Campbell: Thomas Ford died June 5, 1852; Philip Ford died May 24, 1854; Gordall Norfleet died June 16, 1878.
Lewis Judson Davies, born in Watertown, Conn., July 10, 1802; died in Nashville, Tenn., Feb. 22, 1873.
Harriett Bishop, wife of Lewis Judson Davies, born in Durham, Conn., Nov. 11, 1799; died in Nashville, Tenn., July 30, 1881.
Eunice Waters, wife of E. L. Davies, April 19, 1844-Oct. 14, 1877.
Anton Lienert, Jan. 17, 1826-Aug. 18, 1878.
Julius S. Woodford; died, July 3, 1878; age, 54 years.
Mrs. Ruth Fowler; died, March 14, 1879; age, 79 years.
Dr. Edmund B. Smith, born in Garrard County, Ky., Feb. 26, 1798; died in Edgefield, Tenn., Jan. 19, 1876.
Mrs. Sallie H. Smith, April 29, 1805-Dec. 10, 1888.
Sacred to the memory of Joseph William Fulcher, born in Richmond, Va., May 16, 1827-April 3, 1872.
G. W. Lanier, Jan. 2, 1840-April 15, 1884.
Molly Lanier; died, Jan. 13, 1880; age, 33 years.
T. J. Slinkard, died August 14, 1881; age, 51 years.
Mary A. Slinkard, died Nov. 26, 1874; age, 37 years.
Henry B. Morris, Oct. 17, 1821-Dec. 25, 1858.
Cornelia A. Willis, wife of H. B. Morris, died Aug. 23, 1853; age, 30 years.
Martha H. Garner, second wife of H. B. Morris, Sept. 16, 1830-Aug. 28, 1860.
Walter M., son of K. J. and Jane M. Morris, Sept. 8, 1843-Jan. 1, 1861.
Cornelia, wife of A. W. Putnam, April 24, 1816-July 30, 1846.
Eliza T. Baxter, April 25, 1844-Dec. 17, 1875.
Beneath this marble slab rest the remains of Zachariah Stull; died on the 26th day of Feb., 1819; age, about 63 years.
Lady C. Head, May 29, 1849-Mar. 13, 1870.
Sarah Jane Drake, wife of R. L. Weakley, Jan. 19, 1835-April 30, 1876.
Temple O. Harris, April 13, 1814-April 1, 1889.
Martha M. McGregor, wife of Temple O. Harris, Dec. 4, 1824-Nov. 28, 1846.
William O. Harris, June 28, 1812-Aug. 27, 1868.
Frances A. Bartee, wife of Wm. O. Harris, Aug. 23, 1818-Nov. 26, 1861.
John McKenzie, 1798-1867.

Bible Records—Tombstone Inscriptions

Dr. Thomas B. Jennings, July 13, 1807-July 6, 1874.
Margaret A. Jennings, wife of J. M. Cantrell, Nov. 7, 1832-Aug. 20, 1886.
D. P. Richardson, Feb. 4, 1835-Mar. 6, 1876.
Catherine W. Heston, Aug. 3, 1812-Nov. 13, 1883.
Mary G. Reynolds, Dec. 22, 1800-Jan. 3, 1875.
John Hendly Stone, Sr., Nov. 26, 1812-Aug. 8, 1883.
Susan Unity Stone, Aug. 27, 1816-Aug. 31, 1889.
In memory of Louis Ehrhard, born in Zell by Offenbury, Aug. 24, 1829-Nov. 30, 1880.
Howell Huddleston, Sept. 6, 1805-June 22, 1876.
Indiana Stone, wife of Josial Mallory, Feb. 1, 1840-Feb. 20, 1875.
In memory of Robert Ross, born in Edinburgh, Scotland, July 15, 1839; died in Nashville, Feb. 3, 1873.
Elder Jeremiah Stevens, Jan. 14, 1814-Sept. 30, 1884.
Andrew J. Harding, Dec. 28, 1848-Dec. 21, 1872.
John Austin, Nov. 23, 1797-Feb. 12, 1840.
Mary Ann, wife of John Austin, June 18, 1799-June 1, 1868.

The following names were taken from an old record book at Mt. Olivet Cemetery by Mrs. J. B. Newman and Mrs. E. C. Pryor. Copied by Mrs. J. F. Draughon and credited to Cumberland Chapter, D. A. R., Nashville, Tenn. The Burial date, name, and age appear in order named:

Dec. 24, 1862; Andrew Allison, 55.
April 19, 1866; Mrs. Katherine Ambrose, 52.
Sept. 19, 1866; Rudd Adama, 50.
July 2, 1868; Mrs. Mary A. Austin, 69.
Mar. 28, 1869; Mrs. Akroyd, 65.
June 14, 1870; Thos. J. Anderson, 79.
June 14, 1870; Mrs. M. N. Anderson, 58.
May 27, 1872; Matthew Anderson, 51.
May 27, 1873; Jas. Anderson, 75.
May 27, 1873; Mrs. Sarah C. Anderson, 74.
June 20, 1873; E. W. Adams, 53.
June 25, 1873; Rachael M. Alexander, 63.
May 14, 1874; Mrs. Susan L. Abbey, 57.
Mar. 26, 1875; Mrs. Martha R. Allen, 52.
June 27, 1875; G. W. Anthony, 63.
Aug. 29, 1877; Leroy Armstrong, 60.
Aug. 22, 1878; Church Anderson, 60.
Feb. 8, 1879; Lucinda Anderson, 64.
April 29, 1879; Martha Andrews, 77.
July 6, 1879; Mrs. Mary Ament, 79.
Oct. 26, 1879; R. B. Alford, 68.
April 25, 1880; Mrs. M. Armstrong, 75.
Oct. 17, 1880; H. J. Anderson, 79.
Sept. 12, 1885; Daniel Adams, 76.
Sept. 15, 1885; Mrs. Parthenia Allen, 76.
April 21, 1890; A. S. Abbey, 94.
June 5, 1889; Mrs. K. E. Allen, 84.
Mar. 14, 1859; Gov. A. V. Brown, 63.
Jan. 22, 1860; Mary Bailey, 81.
Oct. 6, 1860; Samuel W. Banke, 53.
July 20, 1863; Mrs. Malvina Bass, 54.
Sept. 13, 1864; Robt. Bell, 70.
Oct. 8, 1864; Wm. Bohme, 65.
July 11, 1870; Hon. John Bell, 74.
Feb. 20, 1877; Mrs. Mary L. Bruce, 78.
Oct. 15, 1877; Mrs. John Bell, 79.
June 3, 1863; James P. Clark, 65.
April 3, 1867; Mrs. Rachel Cannon, 71.
Feb. 6, 1868; Mrs. Addie G. Cain, 100.
Nov. 24, 1869; W. G. M. Campbell, 72.
Aug. 2, 1870, Robert Caldwell, 72.
Feb. 3, 1875; Mrs. Fannie Cage, 91.
April 17, 1875; Bailey Carter, 80.
April 27, 1876; Mrs. Clooar, 86.
April 14, 1880; Eleanor Crawford, 80.
April 5, 1881; Mrs. Ann Cunningham, 81.
Dec. 26, 1881; Elizabeth D. Cheatham, 86.
April 25, 1870; A. U. Dixon, 80.
May 2, 1870; Mrs. Maria David, 80.
Sept. 4, 1877; Mrs. Nancy B. Daughal, 74.
June 6, 1878; Mary A. Duling, 78.
Oct. 3, 1878; Dr. P. W. Davis, 86.
Oct. 27, 1880; David Drake, 75.
July 31, 1881; Harriett B. Davis, 82.
March 5, 1883; Mrs. Rhoda Drake, 84.
Dec. 1, 1870; James Erwin, Sr., 73.
April 7, 1871; Mrs. Catherine Edwards, 75.
Sept. 23, 1872; Mrs. Francis L. Erwin, 75.
May 4, 1876; Mrs. Ann T. Elliston, 88.
Sept. 4, 1860; Elizabeth B. Farris, 68.

Bible Records—Tombstone Inscriptions

June 2, 1868; Joseph Fetz, 92.
Feb. 11, 1875; Joseph Fulcher, 78.
April 14, 1878; William N. Ferriss, 85.
Mar. 15, 1879; Mrs. Ruth Fowler, 80.
Jan. 15, 1881; Mrs. Hannah F. Ferguson, 91.
July, 8, 1859; James Gordon, 79.
May 22, 1860; John Green, 62.
May 16, 1862; Mrs. Gertrude Gierr, 75.
April 21, 1864; Thomas Gowdy, 67.
Aug. 14, 1866; Mrs. Charlotte Gardner, 77.
Nov. 26, 1867; George Greig, 71.
Sept. 1, 1871; Mrs. Jane Gallagher, 77.
Nov. 2, 1858; O. B. Hays, 75.
July 6, 1860; Mrs. Catherine Hollins, 66.
July 28, 1864; Mrs. C. Henning, 76.
Feb. 17, 1865; John Hyde, 70.
Oct. 22, 1865; Mrs. Catherine W. Hagen, 70.
Aug. 16, 1869; Gervas Haury, 86.
Sept. 28, 1871; Miss Sarah C. Hayes, 78.
Mar. 29, 1865; James Johnson, 76.
Aug. 4, 1872; Evalina Johns, 73.
April 3, 1876; Mrs. M. Jackson, 77.
July 15, 1880; Wilhemi Jeck, 80.
Sept. 8, 1881; Frederick Jones, 81.
May 17, 1888; Col. A. W. Johnson, 92.
May 28, 1860; Patrick Kinney, Capt., 67.
July 30, 1859; Sarah Kerbey, 71.
July 2, 1865; Francis Kughn, 82.
Oct. 4, 1868; Mrs. Agnes Kughn, 79.
July 6, 1875; Fred Kemphan, 76.
Dec. 27, 1878; Wm. H. Kirkpatrick, 83.
Oct. 29, 1889; Catherine King, 89.
Oct. 1, 1866; Benj. L. Lytton, 67.
Feb. 7, 1869; Joseph Locken, 79.
Jan. 11, 1875; Mrs. Ann Logan, 75.
Sept. 24, 1875; Easter Long, 83.
Oct. 6, 1881; Alphaeus Lyon, 83.
Feb. 12, 1883; Jane Levene, 90.
Aug. 21, 1886; Henerietta Lumsden, 90.
April 11, 1864; Thomas Maney, 69.
July, 17, 1870; Mrs. A. M. M. Muller, 73.
Dec. 29, 1872; Gibson Merritt, 72.
Dec. 31, 1873; Mrs. Mary J. Manier, 86.
June 21, 1874; Thomas Madden, 79.
Feb. 5, 1878; John Moore, 85.
Mar. 31, 1880; John B. Minor, 84.
May 16, 1882; George Morgan, 94.
May 12, 1884; John Myers, 95.
June 1, 1884; Mrs. Susan Martin, 93.
Dec. 25, 1866; Frank McGavock, 72.
Jan. 16, 1868; Col. Robert H. McEwen, 77.
April 30, 1869; Mrs. Annie M. McNairy, 81.
Oct. 8, 1869; Dr. Alex McCall, 74.
Dec. 12, 1869; John McNamara, 71.
Jan. 4, 1873; George F. McWhirter, 84.
Feb. 22, 1873; Mrs. Caroline McLean, 84.
April 21, 1873; Mrs. C. B. McNairy, 86.
July 8, 1877; John McGavock, 86.
Jan. 22, 1881; Miss Hattie K. McEwen, 86.
Mar. 17, 1863; John W. Napier, 80.
June 1, 1869; Mrs. Jane Nutt, 84.
Nov. 24, 1878; William Nichol, 79.
Oct. 6, 1857; Archibald W. Overton, 74.
Dec. 14, 1862; Mrs. Mary Overton, 80.
Oct. 10, 1865; Dr. James Overton, 80.
June 20, 1860; S. M. Phelps, 67.
Oct. 7, 1862; Mrs. Eliza Pugsley, 69.
Aug. 10, 1865; Dyer Pearl, 70.
Sept. 6, 1875; William M. Patton, 76.
Nov. 20, 1877; Samuel Piete, 84.
April 10, 1862; Maj. Moses Ryan, 65.
Sept. 24, 1866; Mrs. Mary Richards, 71.
April 2, 1867; Mrs. Elizabeth Russell, 83.
May 17, 1868; Miss M. R. Ridley, 78.
Aug. 27, 1872; Richard Richards, 88.
June 12, 1862; John Sanders, 76.
June 19, 1866; Mrs. Rebecca Smith, 69.
Sept. 20, 1868; Mrs. Catherine Simmons, 73.
Nov. 24, 1868; Brent Spence, 72.
Sept. 6, 1872; Mr. James Stockell, 78.
Jan. 20, 1875; Mrs. Belinda Scott, 77.
Feb. 13, 1876; Mrs. R. B. C. Spence, 83.
July 8, 1863; Mrs. Esther Taylor, 72.
Sept. 20, 1866; Solomon Taylor, 76.
Oct. 15, 1868; Mrs. Elizabeth Thompson, 76.
Aug. 22, 1869; Mrs. Mary Tanksley, 73.
April 18, 1875; Benjamin, Sr., 81.
June 15, 1878; Mrs. Lucy Thomas, 87.
June 29, 1878; B. B. Trousdale, 85.
Aug. 21, 1882; Mrs. C. M. C. Trabue, 89.
Feb. 15, 1872; Mrs. Sally C. Worley, 77.

REPLICA OF THE OLD FORT BUILT VERY NEAR THE ORIGINAL ON THE BLUFFS OF THE CUMBERLAND RIVER, NASHVILLE, TENNESSEE

Bible Records—Tombstone Inscriptions

Nov. 15, 1872; Dr. Timothy Walton, 79.
May 15, 1873; Mrs. Ann Wilkerson, 74.
June 30, 1874; James Walker, 76.
July 6, 1874; John W. Wilson, Sr., 82.
April 3, 1879; Mrs. Sarah Woods, 89.
April 28, 1879; Mrs. Clara Weatherford, 80.
April 3, 1880; Richard White, 84.
Aug. 12, 1904; Sarah Ann Yeatman, 89.
Nov. 26, 1905; John Y. Yearout, 94.
Jan. 20, 1898; Mrs. Martha Zachery, 93.
Record copied by Mrs. Finley Dorris.
Rev. Thomas Madden, D.D., Feb. 8, 1796-June 20, 1874. Methodist preacher for 57 years. In word, in conversation, in character, in spirit, in faith, in purity and example of the believers, abundant in labors by his ministry much people was added unto the Lord henceforth.

Sarah Moore Maddin, April 16, 1795-Feb. 5, 1863; married Oct. 20, 1819.
Frances E. H. Steger, Oct. 4, 1810-Jan. 3, 1907.
Mary Madden Steger, Mar. 13, 1823-April 17, 1898.
Thos. L. Madden, M.D., Sept. 4, 1824-April 27, 1908.
John W. Madden, M.D., 1834-1908.
His wife, Annie Downs Madden, July 26, 1835-Oct. 20, 1915.
Margaret Madden Connally, daughter of Thomas and Sarah Moore Madden, wife of Andrew Jackson Connally.
Davis G. Tuck, July 28, 1863-Sept. 7, 1889.
Robert W. Steger, Jan. 12, 1858-Jan. 8, 1906.
John Lindsay Watkins, M.D., 1861-1930.
Ida Belle Madden Bass, 1858-1907.
William J. Bass, Jr., only child of Wm. J. and Ida Madden Bass.

John Sevier, "Nolichucky Jack"

The following records copied by Mrs. Finley Dorris:

John Sevier, "Nolichucky Jack," Sept. 23, 1744-Sept. 24, 1815; pioneer soldier-statesman and one of the founders of the Republic; the typical pioneer who conquered the wilderness and fashioned the State—1892. A protector and hero of "King's Mountain"; 35 battles, 35 victories; his Indian war cry, "Here they are—come on, boys, come on." Governor of the State six terms; four times elected to Congress.
Katherine Sherrell Sevier, "Bonny Kate"; died in Russellville, Ala., Oct. 7, 1836.

Rev. Thomas H. Nelson

The Rev. Thomas H. Nelson was born in Guilford County, N. C., on the 22nd of April, 1776, and died on the 25th of Oct., 1838. He became a member of the Presbyterian Church at the age of 11 and died in his communion in the 63rd year of his age, having been a professor and teacher of the same faith more than a half century.
Drury P. Armstrong, Nov. 7, 1799-Sept. 24, 1856.
Amelia H. Armstrong, consort of Drury P. Armstrong, Nov. 2, 1799-Sept. 24, 1856.

Blunt

William Blunt, died 21st of March, 1800; age, 53 years.
Mary Blunt, died Oct. 7, 1802; age, 41 years.
Annet Harvey, died June 3, 1805; age, 51 years.
Blunt Wiatt, son of Edwin and Elizabeth Wiatt, Sept. 23, 1820-Dec. 12, 1820.

Bible Records—Tombstone Inscriptions

WHITE

General James White, died Aug. 15, 1821, in the 74th year of his age; an active and useful elder of this church. The "James White Chapter," D. A. R., of Knoxville is named in honor of this man, and they are contemplating enclosing his tomb in a concrete monument.
James White was a captain in the Revolutionary War, a general in the Mexican War, and the founder of Knoxville, Tenn.
Mary L. White, consort of James White, died 10th of March, 1819; age, 77 years.
To the memory of Hugh L. White, "The Just," who was born Oct. 29, 1773; departed this life April 10, 1810. "Composed in suffering, and in joy, sedate."
Elizabeth Carrick White, wife of Hugh Lawson White; she died on the 25th of March, 1831, in the Natural Bridge Tavern, Virginia, 320 miles distance from Knoxville. Her remains were brought home to Knoxville and buried.

KIRKPATRICK

Sacred to the memory of Rev. Hugh Kirkpatrick, May 8, 1774-Dec. 3, 1863. For many years he was an able minister of the Gospel in the Cumberland Presbyterian Church. "Blessed are the dead who died in the Lord."
This monument marks the resting place of Isabella Kirkpatrick, consort of Rev. Hugh Kirkpatrick, Aug., 1777-Mar., 1859.
Sacred to the memory of James Kirkpatrick, July 18, 1768-Nov. 24, 1852.
Sacred to the memory of Mary Kirkpatrick, wife of James Kirkpatrick, Nov. 11, 1773-Oct. 22, 1852.
Sacred to the memory of Samuel Kirkpatrick, Nov. 29, 1798-Sept. 11, 1853.
Sacred to the memory of Evaline Kirkpatrick, consort of Samuel Kirkpatrick, who departed this life Sept. 7, 1841; age, 39 years.
In memory of Stewart Kirkpatrick, April 15, 1802-Mar. 20, 1844.
Elizabeth, wife of Stewart Kirkpatrick, wife of Peter Ketrine, Aug. 3, 1805-May 25, 1895.
Miss Elizabeth Kirkpatrick, daughter of Stewart and Elizabeth Kirkpatrick, Dec. 1, 1837-June 20, 1854; age, 16 years, 6 months, 19 days.

MCMURTRYE

John McMurtrye, S. V., departed this life Mar. 16, 1841; age, 89 years.
"O my friends, dry up your tears;
I must lie here till Christ appears."
In memory of Margaret McMurtrye, Aug. 1, 1763-April 14, 1846.
The McMurtrye's and Kirkpatrick's records were found in the graveyard in the old "Beech Church" (C. P. Church) grounds on the Long Hollow Highway between Goodlettsville and Shackle Island.

LEWIS

Meriwether Lewis was born in Charlottesville, Va., Aug. 18, 1774, and died Oct. 11, 1809, in Lewis County, eight miles from Hohenwald, Tenn., on the Natchez Trace. He was found sitting by the side of a large tree dead—shot by some unknown person. He had been made Governor of Louisiana and was on his way to Washington to make his report. In 1848 Tennessee erected a splendid monument 25 feet high in Lewis' memory. This monument, which covers his grave, lies in the center of a beautiful, well-kept park owned by the United States Government.

Bible Records—Tombstone Inscriptions

POLK

The mortal remains of President James Knox Polk are resting in the vault beneath. He was born in Mecklenburg County, Va., and emigrated with his father, Samuel Polk, to Tennessee in 1806. "The beauty of virtue was illustrated in his life. The excellence of Christianity was exemplified in his death." Asleep in Jesus. Sarah Childress Polk, wife of James Knox Polk; born in Rutherford County, Tenn., Sept. 4, 1803; died at Polk Place, Nashville, Tenn., Aug. 14, 1891. "A noble woman, a devoted wife; a true friend; a sincere Christian; blessed are the dead which die in the Lord." President and Mrs. James Knox Polk are resting beneath a beautiful tomb on the east side of the Capitol grounds.

SAUNDERS

"Sacred to the family of H. M. and E. M. Saunders."
Rev. Hubbard Saunders, died in 1829; age, about 64 years.
Chloe, wife of Hubbard Saunders, died in 1850; age, about 74 years.
In memory of John A. Walker, Dec. 9, 1790-Aug. 15, 1861.
In memory of Mrs. Elizabeth M. Walker, born Sept. 8, 1795; "departed this life Sept. 16, 1840, in the full triumph of a living faith and beloved by all her acquaintances."
In memory of John H. Read, Feb. 14, 1825-Nov. 22, 1836.
Madison Martin, Nov. 22, 1813-Aug. 5, 1862.
In memory of Anna E. Duncan, Dec., 1826-July 29, 1851.
Anna-lizzia; age, 3 years; child of C. W. and Clara Callender.
Ada Turner; age, 1 year; died July 27, 1855; child of C. W. and Clara Callender.
In memory of Hubbard Wilkins, M.D., son of Robert and Nancy A. Harper; died, Oct. 28, 1856; age, 23 years.
In memory of Nancy A., wife of Robert Harper, 1793-Nov. 11, 1857; age, 64 years.
In memory of Robert Harper, born in Dinwiddie County, Va., Jan. 27, 1785-Oct. 23, 1866. "I know that my Redeemer liveth."
John Gray (colored), died June 2, 1854; age, about 36 years.
Mr. Ed Saunders and Mr. Will Saunders have been buried in this graveyard in the last three or four years, Saundersville, Tenn., on the Nashville and Gallatin Highway.

LINDSAY

Old Family Graveyard of Rev. Isaac Lindsay; situated on the River Bluff off the Gallatin Highway, near Sundersville, Tenn. Copied by Mrs. Dorris.

Rev. Isaac Lindsay, died Dec. 15, 1840; age, 56 years.
Sallie Gussie Crittenden, died Sept. 19, 1864; age, 27 years. (Both on the same stone.)
Mary E. D., wife of Rev. Isaac Lindsay, died Feb. 9, 1863; age, 68 years.
Mary E. D. Crittenden, died Jan. 13, 1864; age, 31 years.
Sallie R. Crittenden, died Oct. 4, 1880; age, 47 years.
Tommie Crittenden, died April 11, 1873; age, 1 year.
Carrie Crittenden, died May 13, 1871; age, 11 months.

Bible Records—Tombstone Inscriptions

HOGGATT

This graveyard lies about a hundred yards off the highway on the Clover Bottom Farm on the Nashville and Lebanon Highway. Copied by Mrs. Dorris.

Captain John Hoggatt, Nov. 28, 1750-July, 1824; commanded a company in the Revolutionary War.
His wife, Diana Hoggatt, Dec. 1, 1766-July 10, 1828.
Abram Sandefur Hoggatt, Aug. 6, 1796-Aug. 21, 1824.
James W. Hoggatt, M.D., Sept. 6, 1798-Mar. 17, 1863. "One of Nature's noblemen."
His wife, Mary Jane Walker, May 12, 1810-Feb. 22, 1829.
His wife, Mary Ann, April 2, 1813-April 28, 1887.
Mary D., wife of Hardy M. Burton, daughter of James W. and Mary J. Hoggatt, July 20, 1828-Oct. 22, 1849.
Harriet Sanders, June 24, 1794-May 7, 1867.
Joseph Gould departed this life Dec. 25, 1823; age, 26 years.

CAGE

Old family graveyard in Cage's Bend, Sumner County, Tenn.

William Cage, died Mar. 12, 1811; age, 66 years; major in Revolutionary War.
Elizabeth Cage, died July, 1792; age, 38 years.
Ann Cage, died Nov., 1800; age, 38 years.
Edward Douglas, Oct. 3, 1713-Feb. 2, 1795.
Sarah Douglas, wife of E. D., 1714-Jan. 2, 1795.
"Cisco" gives Edward Douglas Colonel in the War of the Revolution.

CARTER

Old family graveyard in Wilson County on Cumberland River-Bend Road.

In memory of N. G. Carter, died Feb. 6, 1846; age, 58 years.
Kiziah Carter, wife of N. G. Carter, Nov. 11, 1799-Sept. 9, 1833.
Sarah Carter East, June 3, 1827-Oct. 14, 1844.
In memory of Lucy Carter, Oct. 22, 1816-Sept. 8, 1818.
James Lee, son of E. W. and J. M. Carter, Mar. 3, 1854-Aug 7., 1856.
James M. Carter and family are buried in this burying ground, but have no markers.

SMITH

This old family graveyard contains ancestors and relatives of Mrs. Horatio Berry of Hendersonville, Tenn., and is located near the famous old Rock Castle.

General Daniel Smith, born on the 29th day of Oct., 1748, and died on the 16th day of June, 1818.
In memory of Sarah Smith, Jan. 30, 1755-April 12, 1831.
In memory of Col. George Smith, born on the 12th day of May, 1776, and died on the 17th of Feb., 1849.
In memory of Tabitha Smith, July 17, 1781-Feb. 12, 1854.
Harry Smith, Oct. 19, 1806-July 10, 1888.

Bible Records—Tombstone Inscriptions

Sallie E. Smith, wife of H. Smith, Jan. 2, 1837-Oct. 29, 1863.
Tabitha, daughter of H. and S. E. Smith, June 4, 1863-Oct. 15, 1872.
Easter Smith, died Feb. 17, 1884; age, 57. Be thou faithful unto death.
Alfred Smith, died Aug. 16, 1886; age, 74 years. Well done, thou good and faithful servant.
Daniel S. Sanders, died Jan. 26, 1823. In memory of our Father and Mother.
William Murray, born in Pogomoke City, Md., Oct. 4, 1823-Aug. 18, 1883.
Mary Bugg, wife of William Murray, June 15, 1828-Sept. 1, 1872.
Armfield Murray, Aug. 15, 1862-Mar. 5, 1901.
In memory of Tabitha Bugg, daughter of Col. George and Tabitha Smith, wife of Amselm D. Bugg, Nov. 13, 1803-Sept. 18, 1869.
Samuel Bugg, Sept. 18, 1823-Nov. 23, 1899.

These records are copies from the tombs in the old, splendidly kept graveyard near the historical "Rock Castle" on the Berry home place at Hendersonville, Tenn.

WHERRY

"There will be no sorrow there."

John J. Wherry, June 19, 1817-Nov. 14, 1875.
Jane E. Wherry, April 27, 1818-Aug. 2, 1899.
Mary J. Wherry, Feb. 19, 1853-July 26, 1883.
John M. Wherry, Mar. 2, 1841-Oct. 8, 1862; died at Perryville.
Emily J. Wherry, July 24, 1860-Aug. 4, 1863.
William Wherry, April 18, 1854-July 17, 1863.
Augusta K. Wherry, wife of W. D. Hamilton, Dec. 14, 1858-July 28, 1887.
In memory of Daniel S. Wherry, Sept. 8, 1845-Aug. 21, 1846.
In memory of Evalina Wherry, Mar. 12, 1843-Oct. 21, 1846.

HILL

This old graveyard in which the grave of the Rev. Green Hill of Williamson County is found is now owned by the Tennessee Methodist Conference. In the upper room of the old house, then owned by Rev. Green Hill, the first conference of this section was held.

Rev. Green Hill, born in the old county of Bute, N. C., Nov. 3, 1741; died, Sept. 11, 1826. He was a major in the Provincial Army and a member of the first and each successive sessions of the Provincial Congress of North Carolina. "Blessed is the man that trustest in Thee."
Mary Sewell Hill, daughter of Benjamin Sewell, of the old county of Bute, N. C., and wife of Col. Green Hill, Aug., 1751-Mar. 27, 1821.
Sallie Hicks Hill, daughter of Col. Green and Mary Sewell Hill, Dec. 16, 1783-July 27, 1810.
W. H. S. Hill, Mar. 17, 1817-Jan. 6, 1894.
Hon. Robert F. Hill, Mar. 10, 1826- July 2, 1859. "Blessed is the man who makes the Lord his trust."
Rev. Joshua C. Hill, Aug. 10, 1795-May 12, 1827. "Blessed are the dead who are in the Lord."
Lemiza Hill, daughter of William and Penelope Lanier and relict of Rev. J. C. Hill; born near Williamston, N. C., Jan. 16, 1801; died, Feb. 10, 1860.
James G. Hill, July 13, 1819-Aug. 11, 1841. "Blessed are they that do His commandments."
Rev. John L. Hill, Sept. 6, 1821-Aug. 13, 1852. "Henceforth there is laid up for me a crown of righteousness."

BURR

In memory of Mary E. G., wife of Rev.

Bible Records—Tombstone Inscriptions

W. Burr, of the Tennessee Conference, Oct. 10, 1823-Oct. 19, 1855. "She made him happy."

In memory of Betty, daughter of Rev. W. and Mary E. G. Burr, Sept. 19, 1855-Nov. 3, 1855. "The Lord gave thee, the Lord took thee, and He will restore thee."

Rev. L. Cannon, July 28, 1776-Jan. 31, 1832. "Blessed are the pure in heart."

Mary S. Cannon, Nov. 19, 1813-July 29, 1833. "Behold the lamb of God."

Richard B. B. Cannon, Feb. 16, 1810-Feb. 6, 1873. "The memory of the just is blessed."

Old Shiloh Church Graveyard

Located a few hundred yards off the Hartsville Highway, one and one-half miles from Gallatin, Tennessee. Copied by Mrs. Dorris and Mrs. Oscar Noel.

In memory of Joseph Robb, April 11, 1781-Nov. 11, 1861; age, 80 years, 6 months. "The steps of a good man are ordered by the Lord."

In memory of Anna Robb, consort of Joseph Robb, who departed this life July 3, 1846, in the 56th year of her age. "Thy are gone in the grave. We no longer behold thee, nor tread the rough path of the world by thy side. But the wide arms of mercy are spread to enfold thee and sinners may hope in the Saviour who died."

William Robb, Sr., departed this life Jan. 1, 1830; was born Mar. 2, 1751. "By long experience have I know Thy sovereign power to save. At Thy command I venture down securely in the grave. When I lie buried deep in dust, my flesh shall be Thy care. These withering limbs with Thee I trust, to raise them strong and fair."

To the memory of Mrs. Jane W. Blackmore, wife of J. A. Blackmore. She was born Mar. 29, 1856; age, 35 years, 2 days.

Sacred to the memory of Joel Parish, who departed this life on the 14th day of Sept., 1859; age, 76 years.

Jo M. Parish, June 14, 1819-May 10, 1870.

Richard Alexander, Aug. 21, 1843-May 10, 1868.

Our Mother—Hariet M. Hodge, wife of James M. Bryan, Feb. 1, 1819-June 20, 1877.

Our Father—James M. Bryan, Mar. 2, 1811-July 20, 1884.

To the memory of Mrs. Jane M. Hodge, wife of Robert Hodge, and mother of two surviving children. Was born the 24th of Mar., 1793, and departed this life the 8th of Feb., 1829.

Sacred to the memory of Elizabeth Glover, consort of William Glover, who departed this life June 17, 1820; age, 25 years.

William Glover, Jr., born April 13, 1818, and departed this life September next ensuing.

Here lies the body of Sarah Hudson, who departed this life April 3, 1826, in the 60th year of her life.

Stewart (stone broken), June 15, 1790; age, 12 years.

Born ———, departed this life 11th month, 1837. Oh ——— Sepulchre. Stone ——— her story tell. World sings she lived for God and home. She is gone to heaven with Christ to dwell.

ELI KNI. (Stone broken badly.)

Foot stone, J. M. B. All that can be found of this monument.

Here lies Joseph Motheral, born May 5, 1759, and departed this life Feb. 28, 1816.

    Must friends and kindred die?
    Kind helpers be withdrawn?
    While sorrow with a weeping eye
    Counts all our comforts gone.

Robert Forster, born April 25, 1787, and departed this life Feb. 9, 1806, in the 19th year of his age. "In youthful bloom death laid me down here to wait the trumpet's sound. Prepare for death while you have him, for I was taken in my prime.

Bible Records—Tombstone Inscriptions

SHILOH PRESBYTERIAN CHURCHYARD

Seven miles east of Gallatin, Tenn., on the Scottsville Highway.

B. B. M. L. Barr, April 18, 1836-Feb. 18, 1875.
Annie, daughter of B. B. M. L. and M. L. Barr, Oct. 7, 1865-Oct. 8, 1870.
Lizzie, daughter of B. B. M. L. and M. L. Barr, Dec. 8, 1866-Oct. 1, 1876.
James Milan Barr, 1881-1924.
Kate Milan, wife of R. W. Barr, 1857-1921.
James B. Vance, April 16, 1820-Jan. 11, 1897.
Thomas J. Franklin, Feb. 16, 1813-Oct. 9, 1880.
Amanda J. Franklin, April 12, 1823-Jan. 25, 1887.
J. J. Franklin, Sept. 15, 1847-Aug. 18, 1912.
Emeley J. Franklin, Dec. 26, 1847-Jan. 19, 1919.
James Peyton, Oct. 23, 1815-May 2, 1908.
Kate Peyton, Nov. 2, 1846-Jan. 20, 1870.
Maria, wife of Stephen G. Johnson, Mar. 16, 1844-April 9, 1893.
Mintie, wife of J. N. Bullard, died Aug. 19, 1904; age, 45 years.
Ben J. Franklin, son of W. N. and O. B. Anderson, died July 9, 1901; age, 17 months.

FERRELL

Maj. Burtis W. Ferrell, born in Franklin County, N. C., Feb. 15, 1794; came to Tennessee in 1806; died here at home Jan. 29, 1873. A member of the Methodist Church over 67 years. Bore without abuse that grand old name of a Gentleman.
"Tread softly, friend; my pure-hearted wife sleepeth here." Sarah F. Ferrell, Feb. 15, 1804-Aug. 19, 1846.
Kind stranger, preserve this grave; my daughter rests here. Louisiana D. Ferrell, Feb. 28, 1828-Jan. 5, 1849.
L. S. Ferrell, Nov. 24, 1831-Nov. 11, 1901.
Mollie White Ferrell, Nov. 12, 1833-Sept. 28, 1904.
Charlie D. Ferrell, June 7, 1867-Oct. 1, 1872.
J. W. Ferrell, June 1, 1858-Sept. 1, 1891.
Julia Seay Ferrell, Sept. 5, 1862-Sept. 22, 1891.
Howard Ferrell, Dec. 30, 1862-Feb. 24, 1927.
Mrs. H. S. White (no dates).
Miss Lou Ferrell, Miss Amanda Ferrell (no dates).
Martha Brown White, Feb. 27, 1799-April 30, 1875.

This graveyard can be found in Cage's Bend, Sumner County, on the George Wright Place.

JACKSON

Gen. Andrew Jackson, Mar. 15, 1767-June 8, 1845.
Here lies the remains of Mrs. Rachel Jackson, wife of President Jackson, who died the 22nd of December, 1828; age, 61 years. "Her face was fair; her person pleasing; her temper amiable; her heart kind. She delighted in relieving the wants of her fellow creatures and cultivated that divine pleasure by the most liberal and unpretending methods. To the poor she was a benefactor; to the rich an example; to the wretched a comforter; to the prosperous an ornament. Her piety went hand-in hand with her benevolence, and she thanked her Creator for being permitted to do good. A being so gentle and so virtuous, slander might wound, but could not dishonor, even death when he bore her from the arms of her husband, could but transport her to the bosom of her God."
Andrew Jackson, adopted son of Gen. Andrew Jackson, who died at the Hermitage April 17, 1865, in the 57th year of his age.
"Thou has gained a brighter land,
    And death's cold stream is past;
Thine are the joys at God's right hand

Bible Records—Tombstone Inscriptions

That shall forever last."
Sarah Yorke Jackson, wife of Andrew Jackson, adopted son of Gen. Andrew Jackson; born in Philadelphia July, 1805; died at the Hermitage Aug. 23, 1887.
Capt. Samuel Jackson, son of Andrew and Sarah York Jackson; born at the Hermitage June 9, 1837; died Sept. 27, 1863, of wounds received at the Battle of Chicamauga.
Here lies the remains of Thomas, infant son of Andrew and Sarah York Jackson.
Also Robert Armstrong Jackson, who died the 11th of Nov. 1843; age, 4 months, 23 days.
Rachel Jackson Lawrence, born at the Hermitage, 1832-1923, wife of Dr. J. M. Lawrence, daughter of Andrew Jackson, Jr., and Sarah York Jackson; only granddaughter of Gen. Andrew Jackson. "Her children rise up and call her blessed." Our Mother.
Col. Andrew Jackson, born at the Hermitage April 4, 1834; died, Dec. 17, 1906; graduate of West Point, 1859; Colonel of 1st Tennessee Heavy Artillery—C. S. A.
Amy A. Jackson, wife of Col. Andrew Jackson, Aug. 31, 1851-Jan. 9, 1821. "To live in hearts we leave behind is not to die."
Dr. J. M. Lawrence, Sept. 6, 1823-Nov. 30, 1882; died near the Hermitage. "Sweetly rest beneath Life's wondrous tree."
John Marshall Lawrence, son of Rachel Jackson and Dr. John M. Lawrence, 1859-1926. "A good name is rather to be chosen than great riches."
—Prov.
Mrs. Marion Adams, born in Philadelphia July 23, 1805; died, June 28, 1877.
Sadie Lawrence, wife of Dr. G. W. Winn, and daughter of Dr. J. M. and R. J. Lawrence; born at the Hermitage Mar. 15, 1854; died in Maury County, Tenn., May 6, 1882. "Blessed are the dead which die in the Lord."
In memory of R. E. H. Earl, artist friend and companion of Gen. Andrew Jackson, who died at the Hermitage Sept. 16, 1837.
Uncle Alfred, died Sept. 4, 1901; age, 98 years; faithful servant of Andrew Jackson.

The Horn-Stratton Graveyard

One and one-half miles off the Gallatin Highway, two and one-half miles west of Gallatin.

In memory of Thomas P. Horn, Aug. 9, 1820-July 21, 1857. "Blessed are they that mourn, for they shall be comforted. Blessed are the pure in heart, for they shall see God."
Mrs. T. P. Horn; died, 1908.
John Stratton; died, Oct. 6, 1894.
Mrs. John Stratton; died, Oct. 17, 1916.
Mrs. Carroll, daughter of John and Charity Stratton; died, 1926.
James E. Stratton, Feb. 7, 1870-Jan. 15, 1923. "He is not dead, but sleepeth."
Benjamin F., son of Mosley and Nancy A. Stratton, April 7, 1860-Aug. 20, 1860.
In memory of John A. Horn, born the 2nd day of June, 1856, and died the 26th of March, 1858; age, 1 year, 10 months.
Sacred to the memory of Mary Lawrence, who departed this life Oct. 10, 1852; age, 71 years.
Sacred to the memory of Penelope Daughtry, daughter of Henry and wife, Mary Daughtry; died, Oct. 19, 1857.

McTyeire

H. N. McTyeire, born July 28, 1824. Ordained Bishop, 1866. First President of Board of Trust, Vanderbilt University. Died, Feb. 15, 1889. "A leader of men, a lover of children."
Amelia Townsend, wife of Bishop H. N. McTyeire, Nov. 12, 1827-Jan. 14, 1891. A silent but golden link in the

Bible Records—Tombstone Inscriptions

chain that bound this University to Methodism.
T. O. Summers, D.D., LL.D., Oct. 11, 1812-May 6, 1882. "My body with my charge lay down and cease at once to work and live."
William McKendree; born, July 6, 1757; ordained Bishop, May 18, 1808; died, Mar. 5, 1835. Revolutionary Soldier.
Joshua Soule; born, Aug. 1, 1781; ordained Bishop, May 28, 1824; died, Mar. 6, 1867.
Landon Cabell Garland, LL.D., Mar. 21, 1810-Feb. 12, 1895. ——— First Chancellor of Vanderbilt University, 1875-1893. "He rests from his labors and his works do follow him."

These records are taken from the monument erected to these great men on the Vanderbilt Campus.

WILLIAM STRICKLAND
(Architect for the State Capitol)

William Strickland (architect for the State Capitol), died April 7, 1854; age, 64 years. By an act of the Legislature of Tennessee his remains are deposited within this vault. (North side of building.)
Samuel D. Morgan, died June 10, 1880.

The State here gives repose to the remains of this eminent and useful citizen in recognition of the valuable services rendered by him in the building of the Capitol. (South side of building.)

THOMAS

In the memory of William Price Thomas, born in Westmoreland County, Va., the 2nd of Sept., 1792; died, Feb. 6, 1844. He moved to Sumner County in the fall of 1818, where he taught school 25 years near this place, and two years south of Gallatin with singular success. He was an honest and useful citizen.
To the memory of Elizabeth D. Thomas, wife of William P. Thomas, born, 1794, in England; died in Davidson County, Tenn., July 11, 1855.
To the memory of James Thomas, son of William and Elizabeth Thomas, July 20, 1825-April 11, 1826.
To the memory of Catherine A., the only daughter of William and Elizabeth Thomas, April 4, 1827-Oct. 4, 1828.
To the memory of Elizabeth P. Thomas, daughter of William P. and Elizabeth D. Thomas, Aug. 2, 1840-Sept. 27, 1840.

PARNELL

Henderson Parnell, Oct. 10, 1813-April 29, 1833. "An honest man is the noblest work of God."
Sophia G., wife of H. Parnell; died July 31, 1887; age, about 69 years.
Leroy N., son of H. and S. Parnell, Mar. 15, 1846-Oct. 27, 1857.

GRIMM

Elizabeth, consort of Abram Grimm, July 12, 1786-May 1, 1863.
Mary E., wife of A. Grimm, April 27, 1847-Aug. 17, 1906. "A loving wife and mother dear, lies buried here."
A. Grimm is buried beside his wife, Mary E., but has no marker.

This record of the Thomas', Parnell's, and Grimm's was copied from the tombs in the old Grimm graveyard on the Long Hollow Highway, a mile west of Douglas Chapel, by Mrs. Finley Dorris, Nashville, Tenn., Aug., 1931.

Bible Records—Tombstone Inscriptions

STEVENSON

The Stevenson-Rutland Graveyard is located one mile from the old Rutland Church, between Mt. Juliet and Leeville, Wilson County, Tenn.

Moore Stevenson, born in Northampton County, N. C., Dec., 1759; married Sarah Berry Sept., 1779; moved to Tennessee in 1790; began preaching in 1800. Established his first Baptist Church at Leeville, 25th of April, 1801 (Mt. Olivet Baptist Church) and became its first pastor. Died at the age of 59 years, March 18, 1818.

Sarah Perry, wife of Moore Stevenson; born in North Carolina; married Sept., 1779; died at the age of 84 years.

Christian Rutland, daughter of Moore and Sarah Stevenson, consort of Rutherford Rutland, July 4, 1792-Dec. 11, 1854.

Alexander Brett, Feb. 13, 1815-May 9, 1881.

Charity Sophia Brett, wife of A. Brett, April 23, 1825-Sept. 2, 1881.

In memory of Rutland, son of Alex and C. Sophia Brett, June 30, 1858-July 15, 1858.

Sophia Ann Rice, Oct. 21, 1894-Aug. 11, 1898. Her own words: "Mama, I want to go to heaven and live with God."

—— 1, 11 —— 17 —— 15th, 1845. "Lips I have kissed ye are sealed and cold—
Hands I have pressed you are covered with mold."
(Stone crushed badly.)

WHITE

Grave of Lucinda "Granny White"; pioneer who settled here in 1803—200 feet to the left stood historic Granny White Tavern, famous stopping place for travelers. She died in 1816; age, about 73 years. Grave restored by the Gen. James Robertson Chapter, D. A. R. (Marker.) On her tombstone we find the following: 1816, L. W.

BENDER

Burden Bender, Feb. 1, 1803-June 26, 1884.

Ann Elizabeth Bender, May 12, 1812-Nov. 19, 1888.

Bernice Bender, June, 1802-Sept. 4, 1866.

Elizabeth F. Knowles, wife of Joseph Knowles; died Jan. 20, 1880; age, 49 years. Her husband's truest friend, her children's only confidant, her virtues are known to them and God.

DOUGLAS

In memory of James Douglas, Mar. 15, 1762-Mar. 29, 1851. "Blessed are the dead who die in the Lord."

In memory of Catherine Douglas, consort of James Douglas; born Mar. 29, 1771; married 29th of Jan., 1790; died April 30, 1851.

Sacred to the memory of Robert George Douglas, son of James and Catherine Douglas, Jan. 9, 1808-Sept. 29, 1844; age, 36 years, 8 months, 20 days.

In memory of Elizabeth S. Douglas, wife of R. G. Douglas; born 3rd of Feb., 1807; married 20th of May, 1830; died Jan. 7, 1847. "Died as she lived, a Christian."

To the memory of A. D., eldest son of R. G. and E. S. Douglas, May 2, 1831-April 3, 1859; age, 28 years, 11 months, 1 day.

In memory of A. H. Douglas, who departed this life Sept. 9, 1835; age, 44 years, 11 months, 6 days.

Sacred to the memory of Louisa Douglas, consort of Alfred H. Douglas, who departed this life Jan. 17, 1821; age, 28 years.

In memory of Matilda C., daughter of

Bible Records—Tombstone Inscriptions

J. S. and L. H. Douglas; age, 6 months, 9 days.
In memory of James Franklin Douglas, son of James S., and Lucy H. Douglas, who departed this life Aug. 4, 1827; age, 11 month, 27 days.
In memory of Y. N. Douglas; died, 1865; age, about 35 years.
In memory of Mrs. Bennetta E. Douglas, consort of Y. N. Douglas, Sept. 28, 1813-Jan. 28, 1847.
Sacred to the memory of Little Emma, daughter of Thomas C. and E. A. Douglas, Feb. 16, 1857-Jan. 16, 1860.
In memory of M. G. Parrish, daughter of J. and K. Douglas, Oct. 28, 1792-Sept. 23, 1860.
In memory of Mrs. Mary McMurry, consort of William McMurry, Sept. 15, 1821-Feb. 16, 1864.
Rev. Thomas Lloyd, Mar. 17, 1806-Nov. 12, 1849; age, 43 years.
Infant children of T. and C. Lloyd.
Louise F. Allen, Oct. 27, 1816-May 12, 1846; consort of G. W. Allen.
Joseph J. Jenkins departed this life Dec. 14, 1849; age, 27 years, 16 days.
Helen, daughter of J. J. J. and R. L. Jenkins, departed this life Feb. 4, 1850; age, 6 months, 22 days.
In memory of Young Norval, son of G. W. and L. E. Allen, departed this life June 13, 1840.
"Could fondest hopes have stayed the flight,
Or aught detained thee here below,
Thou love had lived to bless our night,
And cheer is in this vale of woe."
Sacred to the memory of James D. Cook, son of Jacob and Matilda G. Cook, Dec. 20, 1822-Aug. 2, 1840. "Man that is born of women is of few days and full of trouble."
Susie Miller, youngest daughter of Dr. Elmore and Eliza Allen Douglas, died Jan. 19, 1879. "Perfect Rest."
Dr. Elmore and Eliza Allen Douglas are resting by the side of their youngest daughter in the Gallatin Cemetery, as pointed out by the cemetery keeper, but have no markers.
Harriett Louise, daughter of Elmore and Eliza H. Douglas, Sept. 2, 1843-Sept. 26, 1853.
William K., son of Elmore and Eliza H. Douglas, June 23, 1848-Feb. 25, 1849. These two children are buried in the old lot in the Gallatin Cemetery. Mrs. Eliza Allen Douglas was the first wife of Gov. Sam Houston.
To the memory of William Edwards, Sr., July 31, 1752-Jan. 14, 1828. He was one of the pioneers of this country. Brave and active in its defense against the invading tomahawk and scalping knife of the savage. As a husband and parent he was affectionate and indulgent. As a man he was honest and hospitable.
To the memory of Sarah Edwards, wife of William Edwards, Sr., Mar. 31, 1752-Jan. 21, 1826. She was one of nature's best efforts, industry, energy, perseverance, and uniform devotion to domestic duty was her distinguished excellence.
Sacred to the memory of Richard Edwards, oldest son of William and Sarah, Jan. 27, 1781-Nov. 1, 1823. He lived beloved and respected by his acquaintances and died lamented by all who knew him. Funeral preached by the Rev. Hardy M. Crier.
Cullen Edwards Douglas, May 29, 1825-Dec. 3, 1899.
His wives, Harriet Newell Bain, May 9, 1825-Dec. 20, 1892; Mary Elizabeth Estes, Aug. 15, 1836-Mar. 17, 1905.
In memory of William Howard, son of C. E. and H. B. Douglas, April 15, 1852-Aug. 27, 1871.
In memory of Little Hattie, daughter of C. E. and M. E. Douglas, June 7, 1866-Jan. 24, 1867.
John B. Bain, son of Cullen E. and Harriet Douglas, Dec. 8, 1854-April 8, 1855.
Henrietta L. Douglas, 1849-1926.
Miss Nannie Douglas, died Jan. 24, 1928.
In memory of William Howard, son of E. and E. N. Douglas, Oct., 1782-July, 1834.
In memory of Sarah Genette, wife of William H. Douglas, 1792-1865.
In memory of Robert Boyers, son of William H. and S. G. Douglas, 1827-1871.

These records are copied from the tombs in the old Cullen E. Douglas graveyard, located off the Red River Pike, near Gallatin, Tenn., by Mrs. Finley Dorris, Nashville, Tenn., Aug., 1931.

Bible Records—Tombstone Inscriptions

HENDERSONVILLE, TENNESSEE

Near the Highway on the Berry Place. Copied by Mrs. E. C. Pryor and Miss Jean Bradford.

To the memory of Henry Bradford, who departed this life July, 1815; age, 57 year.
Priestley Bradford, Feb. 7, 1795-May 7, 1854.
Elizabeth Genette, wife of Priestley Bradford, Mar. 26, 1799-Sept. 14, 1853.
Norman Bradford, son of Priestly, Mar. 14, 1820-April 11, 1854.
Cecilie Bradford, Oct. 27, 1830-Aug., 1849.
Jane, daughter of Priestley and Elizabeth Bradford, wife of Edward P. Darlington of Pittsburg, Pa., Mar. 14, 1833-1858.
Mrs. M. E. Shute, Mar. 3, 1823-Aug. 9, 1865.
Philip Shute, July 29, 1787-Oct. 28, 1862.
Sallie G. Willis, Mar. 12, 1857-Sept. 1, 1865.
Jane Willis, Feb. 8, 1859-Sept. 2, 1865.
Lizzie Willis, July 9, 1861-Sept. 9, 1865.
Stephen C. Willis; died, March 19, 1881; age, 61 years, 7 months, 4 days.
Mary Sophia, wife of Stephen C. Willis, July, 1827-Aug. 30, 1872.
William E. Willis, Dec. 24, 1854-Sept. 22, 1857; age, 2 years, 8 months, 28 days.
Mary Lizzie, daughter of Philip and M. E. Shute, Nov. 12, 1852-July 12, 1867.
Sallie J. Bradford, May 26, 1835-Dec. 24, 1865.

FREDERICK BINKLEY GRAVEYARD

Located in Davidson County, Tennessee, about ten miles from Nashville on a crossroad between Stewart's Ferry Road and Central Pike on the old Frederick Binkley Farm, where he raised a large family. There are also many slaves buried there.

Frederick Binkley; born Feb. 15, 1774; married Adeline Shackelford Dec. 24, 1804; died Sept. 18, 1857.
Adeline Shackelford Binkley, May 17, 1789-Sept. 15, 1868.
John H. Binkley, Sept. 16, 1807-July 24, 1818.
Pleasant H. Binkley, infant son of John Henry and Mary Walker Binkley; age, 36 days.
Lucy A. Bass, Oct. 13, 1861-Dec. 22, 1864.
James Binkley, son of F. M. Binkley; age, 6 years.
Lou Binkley, infant daughter of J. N. and Cornelia Binkley.
James H. Binkley, July 25, 1831-Dec., 1861; C. S. A.
John M. Binkley, April 1, 1843-Dec. 12, 1861; C. S. A.
Cornelia N., wife of William Binkley, June 9, 1814-Jan. 20, 1864.
William B. Binkley, May 11, 1808-Sept., 1892.

JOSEPH SHACKLEFORD BINKLEY GRAVEYARD

Located sixteen miles from Nashville, one mile from the Central Pike on the old Joseph S. Binkley homestead.

Joseph Shackleford Binkley, Nov. 19, 1810-Aug. 21, 1887.
Wife—In loving memory of Martha Buchanan Steele Binkley, Dec. 9, 1811-July 28, 1859.
In memory of Elizabeth Ivey Holland Binkley, wife of Joseph S. Binkley, daughter of Jaret and Elizabeth Ivey; died July 15, 1879.
Sacred to the memory of Elizabeth

Bible Records—Tombstone Inscriptions

Clark, daughter of Joseph and Elizabeth Ivey Binkley, May 5, 1862-Dec. 6, 1879.
Sacred to the memory of Patience Shane Steele, wife of Samuel Steele, Sept. 2, 1787-June 4, 1852.
In memory of Samuel Steele, May 13, 1782-Mar. 7, 1864; soldier in War of 1812.
Frederick Sumerfield, infant son of Joseph and Martha Binkley, June 22, 1836-June 23, 1836.
Sacred to the memory of Malvina, daughter of Joseph and Martha S. Binkley, May 1, 1839-June 12, 1852.
In memory of Martha Elizabeth, daughter of Joseph and Martha S. Binkley, Dec. 24, 1849-June 18, 1852.
Ree J. McGee, wife of Henry Clay Binkley, April 13, 1848-April 15, 1928.
Samuel Steele, son of Joseph and Martha Binkley, Oct. 2, 1851-Mar. 7, 1833.
Joseph Pitts Binkley, son of Joseph and Martha Binkley, May 14, 1854-April 8, 1921.
Alice Moss, wife of Joseph Pitts Binkley; married April 30, 1876.

Joshua Smith Beadle, husband of Ann Leedy Binkley, Aug. 2, 1836-May 2, 1916.
John Dement, Jan. 20, 1826-June 26, 1911; married June 18, 1846.
Nancy Jane Morrow, wife of John Dement, Dec. 30, 1828-July 12, 1906.
Other children of Joseph S. and Martha Steele Binkley are:
Benjamine Franklin, May 3, 1837-Dec. 17, 1903; wife, Mollie Markham (Mary Matilda), buried at Mt. Olivet.
Almeda Adeline Binkley, Nov. 18, 1843-April 14, 1887; husband, Alexander J. Carver, buried at New Hope Church, Hermitage, Tenn.
Amanda Rebecca, Oct. 21, 1841-Jan. 18, 1925; husband, Frederick Binkley, son of William Binkley, buried at Critton, Ky.
Dr. D. Kelley C. Binkley, June 30, 1857-Aug. 14, 1928, buried at Hurtsburg, Tenn., in Big Bottom.
Captain Bejamine F. Binkley was wounded at the Battle of Franklin.
Dr. Kelley Binkley received the Founders Medal at Vanderbilt in 1878.

Carmack Burying Ground

These names were furnished by Hinton Philips from the old Carmack Burying Ground on his farm and copied by Mrs. J. F. Draughon and credited to Cumberland Chapter, D. A. R., Nashville, Tenn.

In memory of Daniel W. Carmack, June 29, 1795-July 11, 1858.
In memory of Therza Carmack, wife of D. W. Carmack, July 5, 1803-Sept. 25, 1852.
Betsey L. Cummins, wife of David Cummins; died Sept. 12, 1831; age, 51 years.

Old City Cemetery

This inscription appears in the Old City Cemetery on Fourth Avenue, South, and Bass Street, and copy was made May 25, 1931. This monument was originally at Manchester, the ancestral home of Colonel Lewis, where now stands the City View Sanitarium, and was located by Miss Mollie Claiborne. It was moved to this cemetery to make way for a hospital building. Copied by Mrs. J. F. Draughon, Chairman of Genealogical Research.

Sacred to the memory of Col. Joel Lewis, who was born Aug. 28, 1760. He was an officer of the United States during the Revolutionary War and contributed his full share of patriotism, prudence, and bravery towards the

Bible Records—Tombstone Inscriptions

Independence of his country. He reared a numerous and respectful family and set them a striking example of the life of a virtuous man and useful citizen. He was a firm and practical believer in the doctrines of revealed religion, and with unwavering faith and Christian hope he died on the 22nd of Nov., Anno Domini, 1816.

GENEALOGICAL RECORDS

Copied by Robert Cartwright, Chapter D. A. R., Nashville, Tenn. Mrs. E. E. Pearson, Regent.

Committee in charge: Mrs. B. D. Bell, Mrs. P. P. Littlefield, Mrs. John R. Stewart, Mrs. E. E. Pearson, chairman.

Inscriptions from the following old graveyards in and near Nashville, Tenn., and Middle Tennessee:

1. Murfree family, near Thompson's Station, Williamson County.
2. Keeling family, Mansker's Creek, Sumner County.
3. Stark family, Sumner County, near Hendersonville, Tenn.
4. Hooper family, Ewing's Creek Road and Dickerson Road, Nashville.
5. Hyde family, Hyde's Ferry Road, near Nashville, Tenn.
6. Robert Cartwright family, Dickerson Road, Davidson County.
7. Ogden, White, and Bowman families, Nashville, Tenn.
8. Ewing and Drake, Ewing's Creek Road, Nashville, Tenn.
9. Hutchings family, near Florence, Ala.
10. Hart family, Robertson County, Tenn.
11. Church yard of Old Mill Creek Baptist Church, Nashville, Tenn.
12. Douglas family, four miles west of Gallatin, Tenn.
13. Rickman family, near Hartsville, Trousdale County, Tenn.
14. Gleaves family, near Nashville, Tenn., on Love's Road.
15. Bethpage Churchyard.
16. Old Shiloh Churchyard, north of Gallatin, Tenn.
17. Hopewell Chuchyard, ten miles from Gallatin, Tenn.
18. Castalian Springs, near Bledsoe's Fort.
19. Mexican War Monument, Gallatin, Tenn.

OLD FAMILY GRAVEYARDS

Murfree Family

Near Thompson's Station, Williamson, County, Tenn.

Col. Hardy Murfree was born on the 5th day of June, 1752. He died on the 6th day of April, 1809. In peace the citizen, the soldier in war, reverential to God, respectful to man. (Masonic emblems, the Square and Compass.)

Col. Isaac Hilliard, Sr., was born in Nash County, North Carolina, May 19, 1775; removed to Tennessee, 1828; died, April 18, 1832.

This monument is erected to the memory of William H. and Elizabeth M. Murfree by their children, who deprived, alas, too early in life of their fostering care, feel the magnitude of their loss in the veneration with which their memory is regarded by all who knew them. (East face of monument.)

William Hardy Murfree was born in Hertford County, N. C., Oct. 2, A. D., 1781. Emigrated to Tennessee, A. D., 1823, and departed this life January 19, A. D., 1826. Able and honest at the bar and in Congress; just in all things, kind in temper, devoted to his family and friends, he lived beloved and died lamented. (South face.)

Elizabeth Mary Murfree, daughter of James and Mary Maney, was born in

Bible Records—Tombstone Inscriptions

Hertford County, N. C., October 28, A. D., 1787, and departed this life July 13, A. D., 1826. Devoted to her husband and children, affectionate to her friends, kind to all, she was beloved by all who knew her, and, it is hoped, is now happy in heaven. (North face of monument.)

Sacred to the memory of William Hardy Murfree and Elizabeth Mary, his wife. United in their lives, in death they were not long divided. They were married in North Carolina, A. D., 1808, shared with constant affection the joys and sorrows of life, and, it is hoped, are again united in heaven. (West face of monument.)

KEELING GRAVEYARD
Near Goodlettsville, Mansker's Creek, Sumner County, Tennessee

Leonard Keeling, Esq.; died, Nov. 5, 1832.
Andrew Keeling; died, Nov. 30, 1837.
In memory of Dr. George Keeling, Sept. 8, 1807-May 30, 1841; age, 33 years, 8 months, 22 days. He lived the life and died the death of a Christian.
In memory of Mary Keeling, June 11, 1811-July 26, 1841; age, 30 years, 1 month, 15 days. She lived the life and died the death of a Christian.

STARK GRAVEYARD
Sumner County, Tennessee, Near Hendersonville

This graveyard is located in Sumner County, Tennessee, near Hendersonville, on the Anderson farm. The land was originally owned by Capt. John Stark, a Revolutionary Soldier and a native of Stafford County, Virginia. The plot contains the graves of Captain Stark and his wife, Sarah English Stark, daughter of Capt. John English. The graves of Captain Stark and his wife are unmarked. There are also graves of other members of the family connection.

Elizabeth Shelton, wife of M. B. Shelton, born Sept. 30, 1802.
Thornton Stark, Feb. 8, 1780-July 29, 1855.
Sarah H. Stark, wife of Thornton Stark, Dec. 5, 1778-Jan. 1, 1857; married July 25, 1813.
Tabitha C., wife of M. B. Shelton, Nov. 17, 1830-Feb. 28, 1870.
Martin B. Shelton, Jan. 3, 1799-Jan. 31, 1871.

HOOPER GRAVEYARD
Dickerson Road and Ewing's Creek Road. Davidson County, Tenn.

The Hooper family burying ground is located about four miles from Nashville on Ewing Lane, approximately one-quarter of a mile from the Dickerson Road.

Among the graves in this plot are those of Ennis Hooper, Revolutionary Soldier, and his wife, Anne Young Hooper, both unmarked; their son, Claiborne Young Hooper; his second wife,

Bible Records—Tombstone Inscriptions

Mary Ann Keeling Hooper; his third wife, Cynthia Walker Hooper; several of the children of Claiborne Young Hooper; Martha Sugg Keeling, mother of Many Ann Hooper and wife of Leonard Keeling; and graves of several relatives.

The graveyard is on land owned by Ennis Hooper, which was formerly the property of his father, Absalom Hooper. One-half of this tract was conveyed to Ennis Hooper by his father by deed of gift. Ennis Hooper agreed to purchase the other half; but his father-in-law, Daniel Young, advanced the money for this purpose as a gift to his daughter and son-in-law.

This tract was part of extensive holdings owned by Absalom Hooper in that vicinity. The nucleus of this estate was a land grant from Gov. Richard Caswell of the State of North Carolina of two hundred and thirty acres. This tract was granted Absalom Hooper in 1787 as assignee of Col. Martin Armstrong for the latter's services as surveyor of the lands allotted the officers and soldiers of the North Carolina Continental Line.

About half a mile distant, on the opposite side of the creek, is an older graveyard, located on land formerly owned by Capt. Joseph Hooper, another son of Absalom Hooper. Only one grave is marked, that of Martha Hooper and her infant daughter. Martha Hooper was the daughter of Capt. Jos. Hooper and Elizabeth Sugg Hooper, and the first wife of Claiborne Young Hooper.

Sacred to the memory of Mrs. Martha Hooper, an affectionate wife, a tender mother, who departed this life December 30, 1824; age, 20 years, 11 days. On the 11th her infant daughter.

In memory of Mrs. Mary Ann Hooper, who died March 28, 1840, in the 35th year of her age.

My infant daughter, March, 1834.

My infant son, August, 1836.

Leonard K. Hooper, June 6, 1827-May 21, 1877.

Mrs. Cynthia Hooper, who died Sept. 17, 1845, in the 47th year of age.

In memory of Claiborne Y. Hooper, April 21, 1799-June 27, 1848; age, 49 years, 2 months, 6 days. An affectionate husband, a tender father, a resigned Christian. He died in the hope of a blissful immortality. This stone is erected by his children, who cherish his memory.

Erected to the memory of Martha Keeling, age, 84 years, by her grandchildren.

In memory of Mrs. Nancy K. Moore; died May 4, 1843, in the 29th year of her age.

Leonard H. Mizell, Aug. 17, 1858-Nov. 22, 1875.

Hyde Family Graveyard
Hyde's Ferry Pike, Near Nashville, Tenn.

Henry Hyde departed this life the 12th of March, 1812; age, 59 years.

In memory of Taswell Hyde, who died May 3, 1838; age, 43 years, 1 month, 17 days. He leaves a wife and six children to mourn his loss.

Bible Records—Tombstone Inscriptions

Jordan Hyde departed this life December 10, 1827, in the 31st year of his age. (Son of Henry and Rebecca Hyde.)

Felix R., son of Taswell and Susan Hyde, Feb. 6, 1817-Jan. 14, 1832.
Martha L. Young, ―――.

CARTWRIGHT GRAVEYARD
Near Goodlettsville, Tenn., Davidson County

The Robert Cartwright burial ground is located about ten miles from Nashville on the Dickinson Road, overlooking the old road, and about one-quarter of a mile from the new highway on Dry Creek.

In this plot is the grave of Robert Cartwright, a native of Princess Anne County, Virginia, who, after serving his country in various civil and military capacities, both in Virginia and North Carolina, joined the expedition which left Fort Patrick Henry on the Holston River, in December, 1779, and successfully navigated the Tennessee River to its mouth and the Cumberland River as far as the present site of Nashville, arriving at the latter place in April, 1780, after one of the most perilous voyages in the annals of history.

The land, of which this graveyard forms part, was granted Robert Cartwright by the State of North Carolina as a "Preemption," the legislature of that state, in 1782, having passed a bill granting rights of preemption of 640 acres to each family, or head of family, and every single man of twenty-one years of age or upwards on the Cumberland who were settled on these lands before the first day of June, 1780.

Another graveyard is located about half a mile distant on the old turnpike, on land which was inherited by Robert Cartwright's son, Jacob Cartwright. Here are buried Jacob Cartwright, his wife, Patience Hobdy Cartwright, and many of their descendants.

Robert Cartwright, Feb. 22, 1722-Dec. 24, 1809.
    A wit's a feather,
    A chief's a rod;
    But an honest man
    Is the noblest work of God.
David Cartwright, 1782-Jan. 25, 1814.
Elizabeth Powell Cartwright, Oct. 26, 1786-Mar. 8, 1856.

OGDEN, WHITE, BOWMAN FAMILIES
Lischey Ave. (Joy's Floral Plant) Nashville, Tenn.

In memory of B. W. Ogden, M.D., 1828-Feb. 21, 1854.

Sacred to the memory of Eliza Hall Ogden, youngest daughter of the Rev. John W. Ogden, Nov. 3, 1835-May 19, 1850. She was amiable, obliging, affectionate, intelligent, and pious. She loved the Saviour and kept his commandments.

In memory of Arthur G. White, Dec. 11, 1848-July 26, 1849.

Sacred to the memory of Catherine L. White, wife of William F. White, deceased, who departed this life on the 26th of Jan., 1846, in the 39th year of her age. She left a husband and four little children to mourn their loss, but

Bible Records—Tombstone Inscriptions

their loss is her eternal gain. She was an humble, pious, and consistent Christian. In all the relations of life she had no superiors and but few equals. Her sufferings were long and severe, which she bore with Christian fortitude. The conflict is now over. All her sorrows left below, and earth is changed for heaven.

Affections and last tribute. Sacred to the memory of Gen. William White, son of William and Catherine White of Louisa County, Va., Oct. 9, 1783-Aug. 6, 1833. He was a pious, exemplary member of the Protestant Episcopal Church.

In memory of Laura White Bowman, infant daughter of Jos. A. and Lucy G. Bowman, Nov. 24, 1853-July 23, 1855; age, 1 year, 8 months.

To the memory of Lucy G., wife of Jos. A. Bowman, Sept. 6, 1823-Aug. 25, 1856; age, 32 years, 11 months, 19 days. America W. Bowman, Sept. 3, 1829-May 24, 1863.

Joseph A. Bowman, M.D., July 19, 1812-Feb. 15, 1875. In God is salvation. And my glory the Rock of my strength. Dr. W. L. White, Feb. 22, 1827-Oct. 6, 1867.

Arthur G., son of Gen. Wm. G. White, Dec. 3, 1815-Mar. 4, 1877; age, 61 years, 3 months, 3 days.

Mrs. Mary A. White, wife of Arthur G. White, Oct. 23, 1823-Jan. 18, 1877; age, 53 years, 2 months, 18 days.

In memory of Eliza C. Ogden, Feb., 1898-Dec. 24, 1873, in the 75th year of her age. Blessed are the dead which die in the Lord.

EWING FAMILY
Ewing's Creek Road, Near Nashville, Tenn.

In memory of Sarah, relict of Alexander Ewing, Aug. 12, 1761-June 5, 1819.

F. B. Drake, Aug. 9, 1817-May 14, 1853.

HUTCHINS FAMILY
Near Florence, Ala.

In memory of Col. Andrew J. Hutchings, who departed this life Jan. 15, A. D., 1841; age, 28 years. He was reared and educated by his uncle, Andrew Jackson, in virtue and morality, became a useful man in society; respected by all who knew him; was raised to some of the highest honors in his adopted state. A sincere friend, a pious Christian, a tender husband and father, an honest man, the noblest work of God. Cut off in the morning of his glory, the prime of life, his soul rests in the bosom of his God. Peace to his remains.

Sacred to the memory of Mary Hutchings, daughter of General John and Mary Coffee; born Sept. 24, 1812, and departed this life Dec. 11, 1839. I am going to my Lord and Master.

HART GRAVEYARD

This graveyard is located in Robertson County, Tennessee, about seven miles from Springfield on the Adairville Road. The land of which this graveyard forms part was formerly the property of Joseph Hart, a Revolutionary Soldier, and a native of Edgecombe County, North Carolina. Here are buried Joseph Hart's wife, Anna Sugg Hart Robertson, his son, Henry Hart, Henry Hart's wife, Judith Pickering Hart, and many of their descendants.

Bible Records—Tombstone Inscriptions

Edwin Hooper Hart, Nov. 2, 1850-Sept. 27, 1863.
H. N. Hart, July 18, 1844-Feb. 7, 1920 (Father).
Mary F. Hart, Oct. 30, 1844-Feb. 1, 1918 (Mother).
Jimmie, son of J. S. and M. A. Hart, Sept. 2, 1857 ——.
Martha A., wife of John S. Hart, Mar. 19, 1819-June 25, 1872.
Ann B. Hart, daughter of John Spencer and Martha Memorford Hart; age, 12 years.
Sarah Mumford, mother of Mrs. M. A. Hart; died, Aug. 26, 1873; age, about 90 years.
Albert Farmer; died, Mar. 20, 1877; age, 14 years.
Jessie A. Hart, April 10, 1880-Dec. 9, 1919 (mother).
J. S. Hart, Feb. 13, 1869 —— (father).
Note: He must be still alive when this was copied, May 30, 1931.

Nancy Hart, Aug. 21, 1824-Sept. 23, 1832.
Judith T. Hart, wife of Henry Hart, Aug. 17, 1792-June 3, 1865.
Joseph Hart, June 4, 1814-Nov. 4, 1818.
Mary A. Hart, wife of Daniel G. Baird, July 27, 1816-Sept. 16, 1878.
Daniel Gould Baird, July 21, 1808-Sept. 8, 1856.
Dr. Samuel Bowling Brown, Sept. 12, 1829-Nov. 27, 1891.
Ann J., wife of Dr. S. B. Brown, daughter of D. G. and Mary Baird, Sept. 4, 1821-June 17, 1882.
Nancy Robertson, mother of Henry Hart, Sr.; died, Feb., 1845; age, about 70 years.
T. H. Gunn, Feb. 26, 1837-Jan. 26, 1931.
C. C. Gunn, Mar. 7, 1849-July 16, 1915.
Eli Chapman, died June 29, 1828.

Mill Creek Churchyard
Near Nashville, Tenn.

James P. Downs, died July 31, 1819; age, 43 years, 2 months.
Elizabeth Sanders, Nov. 14, 1769-May 29, 1845; age, 77 years, 6 months, 16 days.
Sarah Ridley, wife of Hance H. Ridley, Aug. 7, 1811-Sept. 17, 1834.
Samuel Ham, died Oct. 29, 1854; age, 79 years. He was a native of Amherst County, Va., moved to Tennessee in early life and settled near this spot, where he spent the remainder of his days.
Joseph Vick, died Dec., 1844. He was a Revolutionary Soldier and an honest man.
William Osment, died May 3, 1811. An upright man and devout Christian.
George Goodwin, April 28, 1796-Nov. 1, 1836.
Jane Goodwin, Mar. 28, 18——May 6, —— (stone broken).
Drucilla R. Allen, wife of Shadrack Allen, died April 24, 1838; age, 28 years, 4 months.
Carroll Corbitt, the Soldier, born July 13, 1827; joined the 1st Tennessee Regiment in Captain Cheatham's Company; was in the Battle of Monterey, at the siege of Vera Cruz and the battle of Maddine Bridge, eight miles from Vera Cruz, and in the battle of Cere Gordo. Returned home to the beloved parents in July, 1847. Departed this life June 20, 1858.
William P. Wilkes, June 11, 1827-Sept. 10, 1852.
Andrew Baker, Sr., Jan. 28, 1762-July 15, 1845; age, 83 years, 5 months, 17 days.
W. C. Turberville, died Feb. 3, 1818; age, 53 years, 3 months. Remember me as you pass by. As you are now, so once was I; as I am now, so you will be; remember this, and follow me.
Mary B., wife of W. C. Turberville, Mar. 4, 1796-July 8, 1885; age, 89 years, 4 months, 4 days.
A. T. Hite, Jan. 16, 1819-Jan. 16, 1851.
William Tanksley, Sept. 9, 1817-Feb. 24, 1830.
Mary Leath, consort of W. Leath, died Feb. 16, 1851; age, 39 years, 4 months, 10 days.
Mrs. M. W. Fly, consort of E. Fly, and daughter of Wm. and S. Harwood; died Nov. 28, 1844; age, 37 years, 11 months, 6 days.

Bible Records—Tombstone Inscriptions

Enoch Fly, Sept. 23, 1799-Sept. 16, 1866.
Mrs. Nancy Perry, Nov. 28, 1817-May 5, 1875.
John Topp, died Oct. 3, 1835; age, 65 years.
Thomas Everett, died Mar. 29, 1854; age, 71 years.
Elizabeth Everett, Dec. 29, 1795-May 8, 1875.
Chas. B. Buchanan, Oct. 28, 1809-April 17, 1856.
In memory of Jacob Martin, who died in 1822. A youth of amiable manners and highly—(unreadable).
George Ridley and his wife Sarah Ridley. He died Nov. 29, 1835; age, 98 years, 10 months, 19 days.
She died Mar. 20, 1836; age, 81 years, 10 months, 19 days.
In memory of Christians DeMonbreun, wife of Timothy DeMonbreun, and daughter of Capt. John Rains; died April 9, 1850; age, 63 years, 2 months, 20 days.
William, son of T. N. and Mary Cartwright, Oct. 3, 1827-May 23, 1848.
Mary, wife of T. N. Cartwright, June 20, 1800-April 25, 1847.
Ann C. L., wife of T. N. Cartwright, Dec. 12, 1812-Jan. 31, 1851.

WILLOW GROVE CHURCHYARD

Rickman family buried in Willow Grove Churchyard, near Hartsville, Trousdale County, Tenn.

Mark Rickman, 1762-Aug. 14, 1805. He fought a good fight.

GLEAVES BURIAL GROUND

Love's Road and Brick Church Road, four miles north of Nashville, Tenn.

Here lie the remains of James Gleaves, who fell a victim of congestive fever, June 29, 1841; age, 23 years. Let tears of grief flow for virtue and hope of ——— have fallen.
Note: Other graves and stones were formerly in this burial plot, but have been removed.

BETHPAGE CHURCHYARD

Sacred to the memory of James Bryson, Nov. 28, A. D., 1745-Sept. 3, A. D., 1853.

BARR GRAVEYARD

Near Present Shiloh Church

Sacred to the memory of Joseph Hodge, who died in the triumph of Christianity on the 28th of Feb., 1822; age, 67 years.
Euphrima Hodge; died Sept. 1843; age, about 80 years.
In memory of Mrs. Jane Motherwell Hodge, wife of Robert Hodge; mother of two surviving children; was born March 21, 1793, and departed this life Feb. 8, 1829.
In memory of Anna Robb, consort of Joseph Robb, who departed this life July 3, 1846, in the 56th year of her age. Thou art gone to heaven; we no longer behold thee, nor tread the rough path of this world by my side, but the wide arms of mercy are spread to enfold thee, and sinners may hope since the Saviour hath died.
James M. Parish, June 14, 1817-May 15, 1870.
To the memory of Mrs. Jane M. Blackmore, wife of J. A. Blackmore. She was born March 21, 1821, and died March 29, 1856; age, 35 years, 8 days.

Bible Records—Tombstone Inscriptions

Mary E. King, Aug. 14, 1828-July 3, 1844.

HOPEWELL CHURCHYARD

Ten miles from Gallatin between the Scottsville and Hartsville Roads.

In the memory of Mary Graham Gillespie; was born May 31, 1751, and died Sept. 10, 1815; age, 65 years, 1 month, 9 days.

Sacred to the memory of George Gillespie Bryson, who was born Aug. 6, A.D., 1815, and departed this life in the triumph of Christianity, Sept. 9, 183—; age, 16 years, 1 month, 5 days.

Sacred to the memory of Jane Bryson, consort of Peter Bryson, May 28, 1789-Sept. 22, 1843. A member of the Christian Church.

Sacred to the memory of Peter Bryson, born in Surry County, N. C., Feb. 14, 1780; died, June 25, 1855.

To the memory of Peggy Bledsoe, Oct. 2, 1781; died, Aug. 18, 1831.

BLEDSOE'S FORT

Near Castalian Springs, Near Gallatin, Tenn.

Col. Anthony Bledsoe, born in Culpepper County, Va., 1733; killed by Indians about 200 yards west from this spot, July 20, 1788; married Mary Ramsey in 1760. He was captain in the Colonial Army, a justice by the Peace for Batetourt, Fincastle, and Washington Counties; was the first representative from Washington County in the Virginia legislature; major of Virginia militia in the Revolutionary War; was in the battle of the Flats, Commander of the Troops at Long Island from Dec., 1776, to April, 1777; removed to Sumner County, Tenn., in 1781. One of the first justices of the peace for Davidson County; first colonel of the Davidson County militia; one of the three commissioners appointed to run the "Commissioner's Line"; one of the first Trustees of Davidson County Academy; first representative in the North Carolina legislature from Sumner County; left 5 sons and 6 daughters. (North side of monument.)

Colonel Isaac Bledsoe was born in Culpepper County, Va., about 1735; married to Katherine Montgomery about 1771; was one of the "Long Hunters"; one of the first explorers of the Cumberland Country. Discovered Bledsoe's Lick which was so named for him. Removed to Sumner County, Tenn., in 1780. Was one of the justices of the peace for Davidson County and Sumner Counties, first Major of Davidson County Militia; was killed by Indians about 300 yards west from this spot on April 9, 1773; left 3 sons and 5 daughters. The Indians gave him the name Tullatoska." (South side of monument.)

Sacred to the memory of Col. Anthony Bledsoe and Mary Ramsey Bledsoe. Col. Isaac Bledsoe and Katherine Montgomery Bledsoe; inseparable in life; united in death. (West side of monument.)

Erected in 1908 by descendents of two brothers. Five-sevenths of its cost was contributed by Col. Oscar F. Bledsoe of Grenada, Miss., great-grandson of Col. Anthony Bledsoe. (East side of monument.)

GALLATIN CEMETERY

Monument to the soldiers who were killed in the Mexican War, in Gallatin Cemetery, east side of monument.

This monument was erected by the citizens of Sumner County to the memory of her patriotic sons who sacrificed their lives in defense of the flag of their country in the war with Mexico in 1846, 1847, and 1848. Glory followed their train and by their

Bible Records—Tombstone Inscriptions

death was increased. Their fame is all that survives them. In their graves all their remembrances are buried. Virtuous and esteemed in life, they have become glorious and immortal in death. May our country never feel the want of such heroes.

John F. Ralphfile, born in Philadelphia, Pa., received wound in Battle of Montgomery, Sept. 21, 1846, and died Sept. 24, 1846; age, 30 years.

Briscoe Hatchett, born in Sumner County, Tenn.; died in Camargo, Sept. 24, 1846; age, 21 years.

Joseph Marshall, born in Sumner County, Tenn.; died in Camargo, Sept. 4, 1846; age, 21 years.

Richard Lathan, born in Sumner County, Tenn.; died in Jallappa, Sept. 3, 1847; age, 26 years.

Thomas Young, born in Macon County, Tenn.; died in Lomita, Aug. 9, 1846; age, 28 years.

King Carr, born in Sumner County, Tenn.; died in Camargo, Sept. 10, 1846; age, 23 years.

Booker H. Dalton, born in Sumner County, Tenn.; killed in Battle of Monterey, Sept. 21, 1846; age, 30 years.

Thomas E. Harris, born in Smith County, Tenn.; died in Camargo, Nov. 8, 1846; age, 27 years.

George Barker, born in Sumner County, Tenn.; died at his father's in Sumner County, Tenn., on Dec. 12, 1848, of a disease contracted in service of the U. S. Army; age, 21 years.

William Gambell, belonged to Capt. Hatton's Company; born in Sumner County, Tenn.; died at his uncle's in Sumner County, Tenn., about Nov. 16, 1846, of a disease contracted in the service of the U. S. Army; age, 21 years.

WEST SIDE MONUMENT

Tenth Legion, Capt. Wm. M. Blackman's Company, First Regiment of Tennessee Volunteers.

First Corporal Julius E. Elliott, born in Sumner County; died at Monterey, Nov. 3, 1846, of wounds received in battle on Sept. 21, 1846; age, 21 years.

Peter Hynds Martin, born in Sumner County, Tenn.; killed in the Battle of Monterey, Sept. 21, 1846; age, 22 years.

Edward Pryor, born in Sumner County, Tenn.; was killed in the Battle of Monterey, Sept. 21, 1846; age, 23 years.

Benjamin Soper, born in Sumner County, Tenn.; killed in the Battle of Monterey, Sept. 21, 1846; age, 21 years.

Isaac I. Elliott, born in Sumner County, Tenn.; killed in the Battle of Monterey, Sept. 21, 1846; age, 22 years.

Samuel W. Lauderdale, born in Sumner County, Tenn.; killed in the Battle at Gerro Gordo on April 18, 1847; age, 21 years.

John D. Watson, born in Sumner County, Tenn.; died at Matamoras, Aug. 18, 1846; age, 22 years.

Wm. L. Cantrall, born in Sumner County, Tenn.; died at his father's home in Sumner County, Oct. 20, 1846, of disease incurred in service of U. S. Army; age, 21 years.

William Bradley, born in Sumner County, Tenn.; died in Camargo, Sept. 11, 1846; age, 24 years.

Zaccheus D. Wilson, born in Sumner County, Tenn.; died in Camargo, Aug. 31, 1846; age, 23 years.

Thomas Jones, born in England; killed at Monterey, Oct. 2, 1846; age, 43 years.

SOUTH SIDE MONUMENT

Legion Second, Captain Wm. S. Hatton's Company, Third Regiment of Tennessee Volunteers.

Pleasant V. Bell, born in Sumner County, Tenn., died in City of Mexico, Jan. 10, 1848; age, 28 years.

Powhattan Childress, born in Sumner County, Tenn.; died in City of Mexico, Dec. 31, 1847; age, 19 years.

Joseph Henry, born in Sumner County, Tenn.; died in City of Mexico, Jan. 1, 1848; age, 19 years.

Henry W. Perry, born in Pennsylvania; died in City of Mexico, Jan. 5, 1848; age, 22 years.

Patrick Saunders, born in Sumner County, Tenn.; died at Vera Cruz, Dec. 19, 1847; age, 18 years.

Joseph S. Tennison, born in Sumner County, Tenn.; died in City of Mexico, Jan. 13, 1848; age, 19 years.

Bible Records—Tombstone Inscriptions

Marley Young, born in Sumner County; died at Molino Del Rey, May 5, 1848; age, 22 years.
John G. Kirby, born in Sumner County, Tenn.; died at Penal, Mexico, April 10, 1848; age, 26 years.
Joseph Rhodes, born in Sumner County, Tenn.; died in hospital in New Orleans, June 5, 1848; age, 21 years.
Joseph Blair, born in Sumner County, Tenn.; died here at his father's home, Aug. 6, 1848, of disease incurred in the service of the U. S. Army, Age, 23 years.
William Curry, born in Sumner County, Tenn.; died here at his father's home Aug. 5, 1848, of disease incurred in the service of the U. S. Army; age, 19 years.
Alexander Schell, born in Sumner County, Tenn.; died at Jalappa, Dec. 17, 1847; age, 17 years. Buried here.
Albert King, born in Sumner County; died at Jalappa, May 14, 1848; age, 33 years.
Richard C. Ainsworth, born in Sumner County, Tenn.; died at City of Mexico, June 29, 1848; age, 26 years.
Josephus Zarecor, born in Sumner County, Tenn.; died on the Gulf of Mexico, June 29, 1848; age, 22 years.
Aser Lemons, born in Sumner County, Tenn.; died on the Mississippi River, July 10, 1848; age, 21 years.
Stephen Goarley, born in Sumner County, Tenn.; died at Memphis, July 19, 1849; age, 18 years.
James T. Leddy, born in Sumner County, Tenn.; died at Memphis, July 21, 1848, of disease incurred in service of the U. S. Army; age, 20 years.
William Turner, born in Sumner County, Tenn.; died at Memphis, July 21, 1848, of disease incurred in service of the U. S. Army; age, 22 years.
Eli Robertson, born in Sumner County, Tenn.; died at his father's home in Sumner County, Aug. 5, 1848, of disease incurred in service of the U. S. Army; age, 22 years.
James H. Hagon, born in Sumner County, Tenn.; died at his father's in Sumner County, Aug. 23, 1848, of disease incurred in service of the U. S. Army; age, 21 years.
William Henry, born in Sumner County, Tenn.; died at his father's in Sumner County of disease incurred in service of the U. S. Army, Dec. 20, 1848.

Wray Graveyard

Near the Neely's Bend Road, one mile north of the mouth of Stone's River, on the old Wray-Hamblen place in Davidson County, Tennessee. Most of these have been removed to Spring Hill Cemetery. Copied by W. H. Hamblen, Nashville Post Office.

In memory of William Wray, Dec. 23, 1760-Sept. 8, 1843; age, 82 years, 8 months, 16 days.
In memory of Mary Menees (daughter of James Menees, Revolutionary Soldier; see grant from State of North Carolina, Book C, p. 80, Register's Office; also see Will Book No. 11, p. 80, County Clerk's Office), wife of William Wray (see Book D., p. 266, Register's Office), 1772-1825.
Sacred to the memory of James M. Wray (see Book R., p. 18; all Davidson County, Tenn.), May 3, 1794-June 4, 1864.
In memory of Mildred E. Wray, wife of James M. Wray; died Nov. 11, 1851; age, 39 years, 1 month, 24 days.
Mary Agnes (widow of Richard Jordan, nee Bagwell), wife of James M. Wray, Aug. 6, 1822-June 23, 1889.
In memory of Lewis White, who was born Sept. 11, 1779, and departed this life A. D., 1824.
Sacred to the memory of Sarah White, who departed this life Aug. 23, 1815; age, 22 years, 2 months, 7 days, and two babies with her. (Long inscription illegible.)
Sacred to the memory of Eliza W. G. Wray; age, 22 years, 4 months, 7 days.
Richard W. Jordan (her son), Aug. 22, 1843-Jan. 15, 1870.
Pleasant Ann Wray, Feb. 17, 1854-Oct. 13, 1873.

Bible Records—Tombstone Inscriptions

"She has gone to God, angels greet her,
Gone to join the Seraph band,
Who are springing now to meet her
In the glorious spirit land."
J. K. Polk Hamblen (mother of W. Henry, Annie W., R. Lee, and Mattie Hamblen), Dec. 7, 1844-June 6. 1901.

Mattie G. Wray, wife of J. K. P. Hamblen, Aug. 6, 1859-Aug. 7, 1889.
Mary Agnes, daughter of J. K. P. and Mattie W. Hamblen, Jan. 11, 1878-July 16, 1878. "Of such is the Kingdom of Heaven."

Hamblen Graveyard

Nearly equally distant from Hall's Lane, Dry Creek, Dickerson and Gallatin Pikes, on the old Hamblen Place, Davidson County, Tenn.

In memory of Wm. H. Hamblen (Major of State Militia and in War of 1812), born in Prince Edward County, Va., Oct. 29, 1794; died in Davidson County, Tenn. (moved to Davidson County, Tenn., 1817; see Book L., p. 442, Register's Office, Davidson County), Nov. 17, 1869; age, 75 years, 19 days.
In memory of Verrinia H. Fowlkes (daughter of Capt. Joe Fowlkes, Captain of Virginia State Militia and soldier in War of 1812; granddaughter of "Col." William Cross Craddock, Revolutionary Soldier of Virginia; see R. S. of Va., McIlwain, p. 260), wife of Wm. H. Hamblen, June 15, 1802-Nov. 13, 1881.
In memory of Frances O. Hamblen, Mar. 13, 1823-Feb. 13, 1850.
In memory of Elizabeth A. Hamblen, Sept. 10, 1826-Dec. 24, 1848.
In memory of John A. Hamblen, June 26, 1828-May 1, 1886.
Joseph Caswell Hamblen, Aug. 18, 1835-Dec. 26, 1887. "An honest man's the noblest work of God."

In memory of Violante Hamblem, who departed this life Jan. 27, 1837; age, 12 years, 3 months, 21 days.
In memory of Rebekah F. Hamblen, who departed this life Aug. 13, 1831; age, 1 year, 1 month, 16 days.
Infant daughter of W. H. and V. H., born Oct. 20, 1837-Nov. 3, 1837.
Infant daughter of W. H. and V. H., May 7, 1839-May 20, 1839.
In memory of Wm. H. Hamblen, Mar. 9, 1841-May 14, 1842.
In memory of Thomas F. Hamblen, Aug. 13, 1842-Sept. 28, 1842.
To the memory of Wm. Thomas Hamblen, infant son of John A. and Sarah; age, 7 months, 18 days.
To the memory of Mr. Thomas Fowlkes (grandfather of Wm. H. Hamblen who emigrated with him from near Burkeville, Va., in 1817; see W. B., No. 7 in C. C. Office, Davidson County, Tenn.), who departed this life Nov. 17, 1817; age, 66 years.
To the memory of Mrs. Thomas Fowlkes, who departed this life July 27, 1827; age, 49 years.

Cemetery of Christopher Strong

On the Poor Farm, near Dickson, is the Cemetery of Christopher Strong, a Revolutionary Soldier. The farm was originally his property. Copied by Mrs. Darden, Mrs. Draughon, and Mrs. Landis.

Sacred to the memory of Christopher Strong, Jan 20, 1760-Nov. 22, 1850; age, 90 years, 10 months, 2 days. An honest man and in his last will bequeathed liberally to the advancement of the Redeemer's Kingdom.
Letigah Strong, May 1, 1776-Nov. 29, 1837; age, 71 years, 6 months, 29 days.
Elizabeth Strong, died Dec. 28, 1828; age, 60 years.
Reece Bowen, born in South Carolina, 1788; died, Oct. 2, 1844.
M— Sarah Bowen, Sept. 14, 1787-Sept., 1827.

Bible Records—Tombstone Inscriptions

Elizabeth Bowen Bitts, Aug. 21, 1810-Nov. 20, 1827.
Joseph A. Dickson, Nov. 2, 1807-Aug. 18, 1835.
James R. Pavatt, Aug. 7, 1857-Aug. 1, 1858.
James S., infant son of Reece and Ann I. Bowen, June 1, 1832-Jan. 20, 1836.

RAINS FAMILY

On the country place of J. W. Russworm are several headstones of the Rains Family. Most of the graves were removed several years ago.

W. R. died June 9, 1812.
Sacred to the memory of our daughter, F. R. and M. E. H. Rains, who was born Aug. 2, 1840-Oct. 15, 1840.
Mrs. M. E. H. Rains, late consort of
F. R. Rains, Oct. 6, 1809-June 27, 1841.
Christiana R. Quimby, daughter of Burrell and Susan Quimby; died May 10, 1837; age, 11 years.

BURYING GROUND ON EDMONSTON AND WILSON PIKES

Tombstone inscriptions copied by Mrs. Oscar F. Noel and Mrs. Robert E. Landis. Burying ground on road connecting the Edmonston Pike and the Wilson Pike, Nashville.

Here lies the infant daughter of John and Mary Swain, Oct. 15, 1821-Oct. 23, 1821.
Sarah Lindsley was born Nov. 27, 1773, and departed this life Nov. 21, 1834.
William D. Hopkins was born July 2, 1803, and departed this life Aug. 13, 1834.
Cynthia Hopkins died May 14, 1834; age, 32 years.
Mary Copeland died Mar. 20, 1833; age, 56 years.
Nancy Swain, infant daughter of J. and M. Swain, Nov. 9, 1822-Aug. 19, 1824; age, 1 year, 9 months, 10 days.
In memory of John F. Swain, the infant son of John and Mary Swain, who was born May 12, 1820; died, Aug. 5,
1824; age, 4 years, 2 months, 24 days.
Geo. W. P., son of S. B. and M. E. Frost, May 3, 1854-July 19, 1879. Footstone, G. W. P. F.
Martha E., wife of Dr. S. B. Frost, May 1, 1829-Mar. 2, 1883.
In memory of John Frost, Jan. 27, 1775-June 21, 1836.
In memory of Rebecca Night, June 8, 1779-Sept. 21, 1856.
In memory of James J. B., son of S. B. and M. E. Frost, Aug. 14, 1850-Nov. 25, 1854.
In memory of John S. M., son of S. B. and M. E. Frost, born, Mar. or May (last letter uncertain) 31, 1849; died, Nov. 27, 1854.
James Copeland, died May 9, 1819; age, 48 years.

TOMBSTONE INSCRIPTIONS

Tombstone inscriptions copied by Mrs. J. H. Darden and Mrs. R. E. Landis. Located on a lane off the Gallatin Pike. These stones are in the yard of a house on the right side of the lane.

Pavatt Cuffman who departed this life Sept. 14, 1840; age, 58.
Benjamin Cuffman, Jan. 13, 1823-Sept. 7, 1841.
Jane Cuffman departed this life May 19, 1835; age, 45 years.
Julia J. Cuffman, Aug. 8, 1819-Oct. 6, 1842.
Josephus Cuffman, Mar. 19, 1814-Oct. 27, 1869.
Mary Jane Gooley died in her 26th year, 1871.

Bible Records—Tombstone Inscriptions

Julia Ann Vick, Aug. 1854-April, 1876. One grave unmarked.

Short distance farther on the right side of the lane on a farm owned by Oscar Bainbridge:

John Gibb, born in Kirkaldy Fife Cty, Scotland, Jan. 5, 1779; died, Nov. 21, 1823.

Mary, wife of Harvey Shannon, Aug. 6, 1796-Oct. 11, 1895.

Harvey Shannon, Jan. 9, 1830-Mar. 14, 1830.

Nancy, wife of W. A. Whitworth, Jan. 6, 1821-Jan. 10, 1892.

W. A. Whitworth, July 27, 1814-Nov. 7, 1886.

William D., son of John and Jane Cardwell, July 11, 1853-June 28, 1856.

John R. Cardwell, July 19, 1823-Sept. 22, 1865.

Other graves with field stone, head and foot markers, no names.

On top of a hill back of the house are graves of Michael and Margaret Shannon, no dates.

CEMETERY ON THE FARM OF T. S. PAYNE

Hartsville Pike. Copied by Mrs. Acklen.

E. L. Payne, Feb. 29, 1813-July 25, 1872.

Sarah E., wife of E. L. Payne, May 6, 1821-Feb. 13, 1864.

Thos. K., son of E. L. Payne, Sept. 13, 1845-Dec. 7, 1868.

Charles H., son of M. and D. E. Head, Sept. 24, 1875-July 3, 1876.

Mattie E., daughter of B. E. and L. A. Robertson, April 12, 1882-Dec. 4, 1884.

Wm. Bailey, son of Ed. S. and S. E. Payne, July 27, 1879.

Edwin B., son of E. S. and S. E. Payne, Feb. 5, 1875-July 30, 1890.

Ellen, wife of E. S. Payne, May 24, 1855-Nov. 1887.

Juanita Mitchner, wife of T. S. Payne. Farm next to Payne farm, owned by his sister, there was a vault but only one headstone remains:

Permilia H. Carson, second wife of J. L. Carson, Sept. 22, 1825-Mar. 26, 1876; age, 50 years, 8 months, 4 days.

PITT BURYING GROUND

Cross Plains Road, Eighteenth District. Farm owned by Thomas Pitt of Springfield, Tenn., who says this is an original land grant. Copied by Mrs. Acklen. The first grave there is a rude stone somewhat diamond shaped, with the name:

J. Pitt, died, 1837. This is the great-grandfather of the present owner.

Annie, daughter of G. W. and Mattie Walton, Mar. 10, 1885-April 25, 1887.

Wilson Pitt, Mar. 20, 1814-April 14, 1880.

William Pitt, Aug. 5, 1807-Aug. 25, 1877.

Mary, wife of G. W. Walton, Sr., May 5, 1837-May 21, 1862. She was the daughter of Wm. and Nancy Pitt, so Thomas Pitt says, also that her husband was buried in Florida.

Mary E., daughter of G. W. and Mary Walton, May 11, 1862-Aug. 15, 1862. These are twin stones.

Jeremiah Pitt, July 18, 1811-Jan. 28, 1855.

Mrs. Susan Pitt, wife of Jeremiah Pitt, March, 1817-June 1, 1855.

Nancy Pitt, wife of William Pitt, Dec. 6, 1813-Dec. 27, 1889.

Martha, wife of F. W. Stark, Oct. 18, 1833-Sept. 17, 1880.

R. F. Pitt, Oct. 30, 1859-Oct. 1, 1891.

Mary A., wife of Wilson Pitt, Feb. 22, 1824-May 14, 1883.

Hubert Clour, Mar. 18, 1810-Oct. 15, 1869. Hubbardsville, Tenn., was named for him. (Thomas Pitt told me.)

E. K. Edwards, Dec. 9, 1821-May 28, 1875.

Allie Pitt, wife of W. H. Huddleston, Nov. 17, 1841; Sept. 10, 1885.

Alonzo Pitt, May 5, 1856-Oct. 4, 1909 (son of George Pitt, who is buried here in an unmarked grave).

Bible Records—Tombstone Inscriptions

Marian F. Chandler, Feb. 13, 1875-Feb. 22, 1875.
Lower on the hillside is Arthur Woodard, July 27, 1838-July 2, 1840.

Lone grave in a pasture on the Hartsville Pike. Marble headstone: Minerva Hallum, wife of Bluford Hallum, Sept. 21, 1812-Sept. 22, 1883; age, 71 years.

Across the pike is a well-kept cemetery belonging to John Gilmore.
Mrs. Lucy Belle Bodily, died Mar. 30, 1928; age, 40 years.
Robert W. Angelea, May 4, 1875-Dec. 18, 1919.
Billie Anthony, Dec. 14, 1868-Oct. 17, 1891.
Durrett B. Anglea, April 7, 1832-Sept. 17, 1904.
Mrs. Mary P. Anglea, May 18, 1848-Mar. 10, 1912.
Margaret Anglea Jackson, 1808-1925.
E. G. Walton, no dates.
M. E. Walton, no dates.
J. A. Walton, no dates.
William Rufus Anglea, Dec. 12, 1833-June 25, 1904.
Mattie Cryer Anglea, Aug. 13, 1836-Feb. 6, 1917.

Rachel Jackson Cryer, Feb. 24, 1829-Jan. 12, 1895.
Josephine, wife of J. T. Gilmore, Feb. 19, 1853-Sept. 3, 1912.
Mary, wife of S. B. Gilmore, Mar. 15, 1873-Sept. 15, 1908.
S. B. Gilmore, Mar. 10, 1865-Aug. 8, 1914.
Willie, wife of M. V. Preuett, Dec. 23, 1870-Aug. 10, 1916.
Martin V. Preuett, born July 2, 1861.
Joseph H. Gilmore, Sept. 6, 1824-Dec. 7, 1864.
Lucy A. Gilmore, April 27, 1828-July 27, 1891.
Gwinnetta Duval Anglea, July 8, 1852-June 15, 1877.
Frank P. Mitchner, died Oct. 27, 1886; age, 1 month, 15 days.
Infant son, born Sept. 13, 1897.
Atlanta G. Mitchner, died Oct. 28, 1895; age, 8 months, 12 days.
Gladys D. Mitchner, Oct. 25, 1904-Mar. 25, 1905.
John A. Mitchner, June 24, 1857-Mar. 22, 1918.
Buck Anglea, died Jan. 31, 1921.
A Baby.
John L. Anglea, Oct. 23, 1874-Aug. 19, 1905.

Gladeville Cemetery

Cemetery located at Gladeville, near Lebanon, Tenn. Copied by Mrs. Acklen.

Nimrod F. Bomar, son of Isaac F. and Harriet E., Nov. 22, 1840-Sept. 5, 1841.
John Samuel Sherrill, Nov. 18, 1871-Jan. 11, 1893.
Elizabeth Bomar, wife of Rev. W. J. Bomar, 1785-Oct. 6, 1841.
Nancy Emeline Sherrill, wife of J. F. Huddleston, Oct. 6, 1839-Jan. 1, 1883.
Wm. A. Sherrill, June 9, 1841-July 20, 1880.
Elizabeth Jane Jones, May 11, 1837-1914.
Samuel W. Robinson, Dec. 2, 1859-May 2, 1884.
Nettie Cleo Robinson, wife of T. F. Robinson, Mar. 10, 1867-Aug. 3, 1926.
Wm. H. Robinson, Mar. 20, 1835-Oct. 10, 1876.
Gladys G., daughter of T. F. and Nettie Robinson, Feb. 24, 1892-Aug. 9, 1892.
Eva Ridley Robinson, July 25, 1893-Aug. 11, 1894.
Luke, son of Luke and Alice McMenaway, Nov. 13, 1897-Oct. 20, 1899.
Little John William, son of Luke and Alice McMenaway, May 12, 1907-June 6, 1909.
Luke McMenaway, 1866-1923.
Alice McMenaway, 1870 ——.
E. A. Sherrill, wife of S. W. Sherrill, Jan. 6, 1819-Sept. 2, 1897.
S. W. Sherrill, Nov. 19, 1807-Nov. 19, 1895.
Samuel B. Sherrill, June 11, 1854-Feb. 24, 1895.
R. H. Sherrill, April 12, 1861-June 21, 1898.
George T. Baggarly, Nov. 10, 1904-Dec. 22, 1925.

Bible Records—Tombstone Inscriptions

Bettie G. Steed married L. L. Sherrill Dec. 7, 1881, born Sept. 24, 1865; daughter of N. G. Steed; died, April 17, 1896.
R. H. Sherrill, April 12, 1861-June 21, 1898.
Infant son of L. L. and Bettie Sherrill, July 4, 1892-Aug. 9, 1892.
Infant son of L. L. and Bettie Sherrill, July 4, 1892-Aug. 5, 1892.

Private Burying Ground Near Gladeville

Rev. Joseph Camper, Oct. 31, 1812-Feb. 15, 1894.
Mrs. E. A. Camper, Feb. 15, 1826-May 11, 1901.
Sailiee, daughter of Jos. and Elizabeth A. Camper, born Oct. 4, 1854; married Sept. 28, 1879; died Oct. 3, 1889.

Carver Graveyard

Located fourteen miles from Nashville on the Central Pike on the old Isaac Carver homestead. Given by Mrs. Carver Graves, Nashville.

Isaac Carver, son of Thomas and Clara Carver, Oct. 19, 1791-July 16, 1858; married Oct. 12, 1817.
Wife—Mary Hummer Hughley Carver, born near Alexandria, Va., May 6, 1789; died, Oct. 13, 1877.
Thomas and Clara Carver came to Tennessee about 1800 from North Carolina. Thomas Carver's will was probated in 1821.
Henry Carver, son of Isaac and Mary Carver, Jan. 20, 1820-Aug. 18, 1868; married, Dec. 24, 1840.
Wife—Elizabeth Annas Hamblen, daughter of Joseph and Martha Hill Hamblen, Aug. 21, 1820-June 3, 1866.
Abashaba Moss, daughter of Moore S. and Diana Moss, Dec. 19, 1837-Feb. 1, 1866.
Henry Alton Foutch, infant son of Rose Carver and Alton Foutch, May 6, 1908.
Inez E. Cook Carver, wife of Henry Gilliam Carver, 1887-1924.
Mrs. Kate Cook, 1864-1923.
Isaac Henry Carver, son of Henry and Elizabeth Carver, Nov. 27, 1852-June 12, 1927.
First Wife—Araminta A. Carver, daughter of George W. and Burnetta Carver, Feb. 13, 1854-Mar. 31, 1885.
Second Wife—Elizabeth Steele Carver, daughter of Samuel and Mary Steele, April 23, 1854-Mar. 29, 1926.
Joseph Madison Carver, son of Henry and Elizabeth Carver, 1844-1863, while in Confederate service.
Martha Jane Carver, the beloved daughter of Henry and Elizabeth Carver, July 13, 1848-Mar. 19, 1870.
Pleasant S. Carver, son of Henry and Elizabeth H. Carver, Nov. 24, 1846-April 1, 1902.
James H. Carver, son of Henry and Elizabeth H. Carver, April 5, 1855-May 21, 1911.
James Edwin Carver, Mar. 9, 1917-Mar. 13, 1917.
Thomas B. Carver, son of James H. and Fannie H. Carver, Feb. 20, 1882-June 8, 1902.
Mallie E. Wright Anderson, wife of John H. Anderson, daughter of William and Mattie Hurt Wright, Dec. 6, 1891-Mar. 6, 1916.
Levi W. Wright, Dec. 11, 1836-April 26, 1914.
First Wife—Mary E. Carver Wright, daughter of Isaac and Mary Carver, Feb. 3, 1833-July 13, 1877.
Second Wife—Martha A. Wright, June 17, 1833-July 22, 1899.
W. G. Sweeney, Sept. 24, 1844-Dec. 14, 1911.
Wife—Mary Hester Sweeney, June 26, 1841-April 23, 1911.
George Washington Carver, son of Isaac and Mary Carver, May 6, 1818-Dec. 21, 1890.
Wife—Brunetta P. Carver, Sept. 23, 1818-July 8, 1864.
Elijah W. Carver, son of G. W. and

Bible Records—Tombstone Inscriptions

Brunetta Carver, Feb. 10, 1857-Dec. 7, 1868.
Verdie Carver, Sept. 9, 1882-June 19, 1924.
Julia A. Carver, Mar. 3, 1851-Sept. 9, 1917.
Belle Franklin Smart, April 22, 1859-Oct. 18, 1913.
Wife—Annas Carver Smart, daughter of Henry and Elizabeth Carver, Mar. 20, 1860-Jan. 15, 1913.
James E. Hays, July 18, 1871-April 7, 1900.
Gertie Hays Thompson, daughter of James E. and Lorena Carver Hays, June 27, 1892-Mar. 4, 1920.
Norvella Hays, daughter of James E. and Lorena Carver Hays, Oct. 31, 1894-Sept. 1, 1913.
Mrs. S. C. Bond, 1840-1929.
W. A. Bond, Mar. 6, 1854-Sept. 25, 1923.
John J. Bruce, Sept. 4, 1845-Nov. 30, 1900.
Sarah J. Bruce, Aug. 15, 1846-Dec. 23, 1923.
John Huston Bruce, son of John J. and Sarah Bruce, Oct. 8, 1882-Oct. 1, 1906.
S. W. Cook, July 7, 1824-April 29, 1911.
Mary Emily Carver, daughter of Henry and Elizabeth Carver, Oct. 11, 1850-Nov. 1, 1880; wife of James E. Bridges; married, Dec. 19, 1867.
James E. Bridges, who is buried in Jacksonville, Fla.
Sarah Ellen Carver, daughter of Henry and Elizabeth Carver, Oct. 11, 1850-Aug. 20, 1892; wife of Albert Hardy Ellis; married, Nov. 6, 1870.
Albert Hardy Ellis, Jan. 14, 1845- Jan. 12, 1907.
The above two people are buried in the Old Ellis Graveyard on the Stewart Ferry Road.
Nicie Carver Cook, daughter of Henry and Elizabeth Carver, 1858-1900; wife of James Cook.

New Hope Baptist Church Graveyard

Located twelve miles from Nashville on the Central Pike.

Almeda Adeline Binkley Carver, wife of Alexander Jefferson Carver, Nov. 18, 1843-April 14, 1887. "As wife, mother, and friend she glorified God." "Her children arise up and call her blessed."
Alexander Jefferson Carver, son of Henry and Elizabeth Hanblin Carver, Mar. 5, 1842-Mar. 23, 1930. Buried in the Confederate Circle at Mt. Olivet Cemetery, Nashville, Tenn.
Martha Elizabeth Carver, daughter of Alexander J. and Adeline B. Carver, Feb. 11, 1867-Sept. 21, 1883.
"The Lord hath taken her not,
   Lost, blest thought;
But gone before where we shall meet
   To part no more."
Allie Cawthorn Carver, daughter of Alexander J. and Adeline B. Carver, June 16, 1873-April 19, 1889. "Gentle, unselfish Christian spirit; she was God's messenger of love to the home." "Blessed are the dead which die in the Lord."
Alexander Jefferson Carver, Jr., son of Alexander J. and Adeline B. Carver, Mar. 4, 1876-Nov. 7, 1896. "He that believeth on me, though he die yet shall he live."
Iona Carver, infant daughter of Alexander J. and Lucy Dement Carver, Feb. 16, 1905-Mar. 5, 1905.
G. W. Hagar (Baptist preacher), Aug. 12, 1818-Aug. 8, 1898.
Manervie Jane Hagar, Feb. 13, 1815-June 11, 1878.
Thomas J. Hagar, Jan. 9, 1842-Aug. 19, 1863.
James Franklin Peek, Jan. 21, 1848-Jan. 1, 1896; married, Feb. 28, 1871.
Sarah Elizabeth Peek, wife of James Franklin Peek, daughter of John and Nancy Morrow Dement, Oct. 3, 1847-Nov. 1, 1921.
There are also several other graves in this graveyard which have no inscriptions.

Bible Records—Tombstone Inscriptions

Burial Ground of Rutland Baptist Church
Located in Wilson County, near Mt. Juliet, Tenn.

Joseph F. Hamblen, born in Prince Edward County, Va., 1790; died, May, 1861; married, 1815, to Martha Hill.
Martha Hill Hamblen, born in Virginia, 1796; died, June, 1871.
Permelia S. Hamblen, daughter of Joseph and Martha Hamblen, Mar. 11, 1830-April 12, 1899.
Sallie (twin to Permelia).
Elizabeth Annis Hamblen, wife of Henry Carver, Aug. 21, 1820-June 3, 1866; buried in Carver Graveyard.
Other children of Joseph and Martha Hamblen buried in Wilson County are:
William Daniel.
Watkins F.
John.
Eliza Emily Hamblen Webb.
Joseph F. Hamblin was a soldier in the War of 1812. He came to Tennessee in 1815 and located in Wilson County where he lived his entire life.

Graves and Teele Graveyard
Located in Jackson County, fourteen miles from Gainesboro, Tenn., on the old Teele farm on Jennings Creek.

George Teele, son of Adam Teele, Sept. 19, 1791-April 9, 1847; married, April 29, 1839. He fought in the War of 1812.
Wife—Edna Graves Teele, daughter of Reuben and Elizabeth Y. Graves, Aug. 20, 1797-Oct. 10, 1854.
Elvira Elizabeth Teele Graves, daughter of George and Edna Graves Teele, July 29, 1840-Jan. 22, 1912; married, Jan. 1, 1857.
Husband—Wade Hampton Graves, son of Beamon and Susannah P. Graves, Nov. 10, 1832-Aug. 28, 1901. He fought in the War between the States.
Infant daughter of Elvira T. and Wade Hampton Graves, born and died, 1858.
Josephine Graves, daughter of Elvira T. and Wade Hampton Graves, April 27, 1862-July 9, 1862.
Cortez Henry Graves, son of Elvira T. and Wade Hampton Graves, Mar. 21, 1864-Jan. 5, 1874.
Lee Hatton Graves, son of Elvira T. and Wade Hampton Graves, Mar. 3, 1872-Feb. 28, 1875.
Albert Monroe Crabtree, son of Josie Teele and Dock Crabtree, Sept. 18, 1880-Sept. 8, 1892.
Willie George Pate, daughter of Lena Graves and J. J. Pate, Oct. 24, 1897-July 28, 1902.
James Radford Draper, husband of Nettie Graves Draper, Mar. 8, 1859-April 8, 1888.
Eliza Jane Richardson Jenkins, daughter of Sarah Teele and James Richardson, Aug. 26, 1837-Jan. 11, 1912.
John Samuel Jenkins, husband of Eliza Richardson Jenkins, Aug. 7, 1836-Nov. 29, 1919; buried at Red Boiling Springs.
Patsey Graves, sister of Edna Graves Teele, 1790-1850.
Susannah Graves, orphan niece of Edna Graves Teele, 1828-May 16, 1844.
Sidney Graves, orphan nephew of Edna Graves Teele, 1825-Jan. 29, 1852.
Marshall Graves, Jr., orphan nephew of Edna Graves Teele, 1823-1867. He was serving in the Tennessee Legislature at the time of his death.
There are also many slaves of the Graves and Teele family buried in the family burial grounds.
Reuben and Elizabeth Yarbrough Graves were married Nov. 28, 1786. Their children were:
Rice, who lived and died near Lebanon, Tenn.
Harrison married a Miss Cunningham and moved to Texas.
Marshall.
Nancy, who married a Mr. Moreland.
Lucy, who married a Mr. Sweezy.
Patsey, who died unmarried.
Edna, who married George Teele.
Adam Teele's children were:
George Teele, who married Edna Graves.
Riley Teele.
John Teele.
William Teele.
Peter Teele.

Bible Records—Tombstone Inscriptions

Peggy Teele, who married——Brooks.
Prissy Teele, who married—Lee.
Sally Teele, who married—Lee.
Eliza Teele, who married—Brooks.

There were two other daughters who married Saunders; also two daughter who married Richardsons.

James Buchanan Graveyard

Located nine miles from Nashville on the Elm Hill Road on the old James Buchanan farm.

In memory of James Buchanan, July 16, 1763-Feb. 14, 1841. "A kind husband and affectionate father."
"Farewell, me friends, as you pass by;
As you are now so was I;
As I am now so must you be;
Prepare to die and follow me."
Sacred to the memory of Lucinda East Buchanan, consort of James Buchanan, Dec. 11, 1792-April 15, 1865.
"As thou hast said I shall follow you,
As all the rest must shortly do;
Then be not guilty of any crime,
So you may live in the heaven sublime."
Archibald Buchanan, son of James and Lucinda Buchanan, Mar. 21, 1811-Sept. 7, 1843.
"Away from his home and the friends of his youth;
He died a man of energy and truth."
At Rest—James Buchanan, July 4, 1813-Nov. 26, 1896.
Mary Jane Buchanan, daughter of James and Lucinda Buchanan, May 16, 1821-Jan. 28, 1842.
W. A. Buchanan, 1826-1902.
A. L. Buchanan, Jan. 7, 1820-July 13, 1913.
M. M. Buchanan, 1826-1902.
M. M. Buchanan, 1852-1858.
Joseph A. Fleming, 1874-1878.
Dr. E. E. Buchanan, Dec. 20, 1818-Oct. 8, 1876. "He lived the life of the righteous."
Sallie B. Buchanan, wife of Dr. E. E. Buchanan, May 30, 1830-Nov. 3, 1901. "A devoted wife-mother."
Nancy Louzaner Buchanan, daughter of E. E. and Sarah Buchanan, Dec. 19, 1852-July 11, 1853.
Daniel Blanford Buchanan, died, Oct. 19, 1926; age, 23 years.
In memory of Sarah Marshal Buchanan, consort of Adison Buchanan, daughter of William and Mary Fleming, born in Ross City, Ohio; died,
July 12, 1850; age, 27 years, 10 months, 15 days. "She died to live."
Thomas B. Moss, Sept. 9, 1798-Sept. 11, 1859.
Sarah Moss, Feb. 26, 1810-Mar. 13, 1864.
Joseph H. Watkins, Nov. 4, 1856-April 13, 1857.
Plummer G. Watkins, Jan. 24, 1858-Feb. 17, 1858.
Maggie E. Hite, wife of G. E. Sheets, Mar. 2, 1871-Nov. 24, 1904.
James W. Brown, died, Mar. 23, 1927; age, 75 years.
Sarah F. Harris, 1849-1927.
Samuel J. Frazier, 1846-1925.
Edmond D. Whitworth, Mar. 22, 1824-Dec. 2, 1901.
Miriam Whitworth, Sept. 19, 1827-Aug. 13, 1908.
John T. Whitworth, May 20, 1858-Feb. 2, 1906.
Missouri Whitworth, Nov. 5, 1828-July 13, 1902.
Mary Alice Whitworth, daughter of E. D. and Miriam Whitworth, Jan. 1, 1860-Feb. 1, 1861.
Edmond D. Whitworth, Jr., son of E. D. and Miriam Whitworth, June 30, 1862-June 2, 1871.
Alvin C. Whitworth, April 24, 1878-June 12, 1918; Woodman of the World.
Annie E. Whitworth Goodlet, Oct. 23, 1857-Mar. 23, 1921.
Lucy J. Ridley, Oct. 5, 1853-July 15, 1919.
William B. Ridley, Jan. 28, 1850-Mar. 16, 1904.
H. Beasley Ridley, Sept. 8, 1899-April 4, 1900.
Mary Louise Ridley, June 28, 1885-Jan. 7, 1911.
Mrs. L. T. Ridley, Aug. 12, 1854-July 13, 1912.
James Ridley, June 25, 1846-Aug. 25, 1916.
In memory of Martha Spivey Bowen,

Bible Records—Tombstone Inscriptions

daughter of Jeremiah and Rebekah Bowen, Oct. 17, 1849-Aug. 12, 1850. "Lovely babe how brief thy stay, short and hasty"—remainder illegible. Other inscriptions shaled off.
Inez Elizabeth Buchanan, July 13, 1912-July 21, 1912.
Father—John M. Fleming, Jan. 24, 1843-June 14, 1928.
Mother—Almira Fleming, Aug. 25, 1846-Nov. 20, 1915.
John W. Steele, son of Samuel and Mary Binkley Steele, Nov. 23, 1851-Jan. 20, 1909. "Asleep in Jesus."
Annie M. Steele, daughter of John W. and Molly Buchanan Steele, Sept. 24, 1887-June 9, 1907.
Ann McMurray, daughter of G. W. and E. McMurray, July 7, 1856-Aug. 6, 1861.

G. W. McMurray, Jan. 27, 1815-Sept. 26, 1899.
Jimmie McMurray, Sept. 2, 1904-Dec. 18, 1905.
Leoner McMurray, Aug. 20, 1895-Feb. 25, 1896.
Margaret Sarah Hurt, July 24, 1905-Dec. 1, 1908. "Gone but not forgotten."
J. W. Hurt, Mar. 13, 1872-June 29, 1910.
"Since thou can no longer stay
To cheer me with thy love,
I hope to meet with thee again
In yon bright world above."
Martin L. Cooper, 1870-1892.
Joseph W. Cooper, 1835-1892.
W. A. Ross, July 5, 1854-Jan. 10, 1918. "A christian gentleman well beloved." Woodman of the World.

BUCHANAN HISTORICAL FACTS

James Buchanan, son of Agnes Bowen McFerrin and Archibald Buchanan, came to Tennessee with his parents about 1785 from Augusta County, Southwest, Va., and settled on a 640-acre section of land near Donelson, a part of which is now "Clover Bottom" Farm.

Archibald Buchanan built what is known as the "Old Blue Brick" before 1800. It is located just off the Lebanon Pike on the Stewarts Ferry Road and is still occupied.

Agnes Bowen McFerrin Buchanan was the widow of James McFerrin and had one son, John McFerrin, who is the ancestor of the McFerrin Methodist ministers. Archibald Buchanan was made the guardian of John McFerrin.

Archibald and Agnes Buchanan were buried in the garden of the Old Blue Brick. There their bodies remained until the home was sold; at which time James Buchanan, their son, had them moved to his cousin's, Major John Buchanan, farm, located on Stone's River which was originally "The Buchanan Fort." It is now known as the Knapp Farm.

On March 20, 1932, Anne Carver Graves visited with Tom Wright, a distant cousin, who is 84 years old, and he told her the above facts—he having heard them from both his mother and grandmother in his youth. Mr. Weaver Whitworth, who is also a Buchanan descendant, told her the same facts. Mr. Wright lives

Bible Records—Tombstone Inscriptions

on Stewarts Ferry Road and Mr. Whitworth lives on the Elm Hill Road.

James Buchanan built a large two-story log house on the Elm Hill Road early in 1800, which is still standing and is owned and occupied by Mr. L. L. Payne.

James Buchanan married Lucinda East, and they had sixteen children.

The children of Archibald and Agnes Buchanan were:
James Buchanan who married Lucinda East;
Martha Buchanan who married Andrew Steele;
Mary Buchanan who married a Mr. Jones;
Rebecca Buchanan who married a Mr. Shannon;
Ellen Buchanan who never married;
Nancy Buchanan who married a Mr. Drew;
Lillie Buchanan who married a Mr. Wills.

Agnes Bowen McFerrin Buchanan was the daughter of Dillie McIlhaney and John Bowen. The McIlhaney family came from Ireland to Augusta County, Va., in 1730.

John Bowen was the son of Moses and Rebecca Reese Bowen. Rebecca Reese came from Wales in 1698.

Mountain View Cemetery

Mountain City, Tenn.; Mountain City Chapter, Mrs. Eugene McDade, Regent.

Rev. A. Murphey, 1796-1882.
Catherine Wills Murphey, wife of Rev. A. Murphey, 1812-1904.
Hon. H. P. Murphey, 1816-1899.
Capt. Kemp Murphey, 1841-1916.
Susan Wills Murphey, wife of Capt. Kemp Murphy, 1853-1902.
Lieut. Elbert Murphey, 1846-1884.
James Hawkins Murphey, 1870-1925.
May Murphey Wagner, 1874-1918.
Samuel Dorsey Jackson, 1827-1893.
Alzenia P. Jackson, wife of Samuel Dorsey Jackson, 1833-1911.
J. A. Elliott, 1834-1903.
Martha Elliott, wife of J. A. Elliot, 1844-1904.
Jacob Norris, 1832-1883.
R. A. Donnelly, 1824-1905.
Matilda Donnelly, wife of R. A. Donnelly, 1834-1893.
Alfred Parry, 1846-1914.

Sophronia Parry, wife of Alfred Parry, 1854-1912.
Amanda Ray, 1845-1846.
Alfred Crosswhite, 1858-1891.
Thomas Crosswhite, 1827-1912.
Rebecca Donnelly Crosswhite, wife of Thomas Crosswhite, 1829-1909.
Rev. C. B. Yarbrough, 1837-1903.
Laura Elvira Yarbrough, wife of Rev. C. B. Yarbrough, 1848-1903.
Frederic Slimp, 1824-1904.
Naomi Slimp, wife of Frederic Slimp, 1834-1888.
C. V. Moore, 1842-1858.
H. A. Jenkins, 1845-1918.
Wm. C. Emmitt, died, 1856; age, 56 years.
Hon. Roderick R. Butler, 1827-1902.
Emeline J. Butler, wife of Hon. Roderick R. Butler, 1825-1899.
Dr. J. C. Butler, 1849-1921.

Bible Records—Tombstone Inscriptions

Joseph G. Fuller, died, 1892; age, 72 years.
Lieut. Charles Lefler, 1826-1886.
Esther Tulbert, wife of Lieut Charles Lefler, 1826-1897.
Thomas S. Smythe, 1827-1895.
Margaret C. Smythe, wife of Thomas S. Smythe, 1828-1906.
W. K. Donnelly, 1827-1921.
Rachel A. Donnelly, 1843-1903.
W. S. Stone, 1863-1893.
Wm. Donelly, McClain's Company, M, C. Mil., War of 1812, 1792-1842.
Rebecca Grace, wife of T. J. Barry, 1850-1887.
Benjamin W. Jenkins, 1831-1902.
Nancy D. Jenkins, wife of Benjamin W. Jenkins, 1832-1905.
I. S. Rambo, 1871-1923.
H. K. Thomas, 1846-1926.
W. M. Howard, 1863-1930.
Robert E. Berry, 1831-1906.
Rachel McQuon Berry, wife of Robert E. Berry, 1825-1908.
J. S. Jenkins, 1856-1926.
Capt. Thomas Barry, 1835-1909.
Robert Swain McDade, 1851-1916.
Ollie Jackson McDade, wife of Robert L. McDade, 1853-1912.
Dr. James Doran Donnelly, 1823-1903.
Frances Orr Donnelly, wife of Dr. James Doran Donnelly, 1841-1900.
J. R. H. Smythe, 1852-1932.
Parlee Lewis, 1855-1910.
Retta Crosswhite Fritts, 1860-1922.
David Cress, 1853-1926.
Josiah Parker Pless, 1858-1930.
Mary Adams, 1823-1853.
D. A. Crawford, 1867-1922.
Philip M. Kiser, 1825-1902.
Joseph Asbury Sutherland, 1841-1904.
Nannie Wright Sutherland, wife of Joseph Asbury Sutherland, 1864-1931.
Marian Reece, 1862-1930.
Mattie Howell, 1872-1925.
John Adams, 1853-1928.

PROSPECT CEMETERY

Records from Prospect Cemetery at Prospect Baptist Church, near Loudon, Tenn. Compiled by Miss Elizabeth Jane Taliaferro.

David J. Ballard, son of H. and H. Ballard, May 30, 1858-July 26, 1858.
John W. Ballard, Sept. 9, 1868-Jan. 29, ——.
Samuel C. Ballard, Dec. 14, 1855-Sept. 18, 1856.
Thomas J. Ballard, born, July 16, 1869; age, 33 years.
Washington Ballard, Feb. 10, 1808-Sept. 7, 1860.
Sarah Ballard, wife of Washington Ballard, May 25, 1815-Jan. 16, 1856.
Amanda Ballard, daughter of W. and S. Ballard, Nov. 28, 1816-Feb. 4, 1851.
Leniza Hopkins, died, Sept. 19, 1886; age, 61 years.
Stephen A. Porter, Nov. 17, 1834-June 30, 1888.
Henry H. Lewis, Dec. 5, 1800-Oct. 6, 1863.
Cassela Lewis, Oct. 11, 1807-Sept. 6, 1873.
J. B. Matlock, 1828-1907.
His wife, 1841-1928.
J. D. Taliaferro, July 6, 1862-Oct. 17, 1909.
John W. Taliaferro, Feb. 25, 1823-May 15, 1907.
Mary J., wife of J. W. Taliaferro, June 4, 1828-Mar. 20, 1907.
Charles Wm. Taliaferro, Oct. 26, 1852-Nov. 22, 1875.
Belle MacNabb, May 27, 1848-Dec. 11, 1908.
John Grassham, died, April 1836; age, 50 years.
James R. Scott (Co. C., 3rd Tenn. Cav.), Dec. 4, 1831-Feb. 3, 1906.
Pornick Johnson, died, Oct. 16, 1908; age, 60 years.
William Erwin (Co. A, 2nd Tenn. Inf.), born ——.
Wright Erwin (Co. A, 2nd Tenn. Inf.), born ——.
Benjamin A. Taliaferro, Jan. 6, 1853-July 18, 1854.
Another grave, probably another child.
Melissa Josephine, daughter of Mitchell and Sophia E. Rose, Sept. 7, 1853-Aug. 8, 1875.
Charles Walker, son of Mitchell and Sophia E. Rose, May 24, 1859-July 10, 1875.
Elizabeth H. Show, Feb. 15, 1894; age, about 80 years.
Sarah L. Burnett, wife of Wm. F.

Bible Records—Tombstone Inscriptions

MacCarrell, June 19, 1848-Nov. 17, 1912.
Four infant children of D. A. and C. Bacon:
D. A. Bacon, Dec. 4, 1807-Aug. 7, 1881.
A. S. Bacon, June 17, 1819-Feb. 21, 1885.
C. Bacon, wife of D. A. Bacon, Mar. 3, 1817-Oct. 15, 1887.
S. M. Rose, son of M. and S. E. Rose, Dec. 29, 1813-June 13, 1815.
An infant buried near.
Charles Taliaferro, Mar. 5, 1799-May 23, 1856. (He was an Elder of the Missionary Baptist Church.)
Jane Whitlock Taliaferro, first wife of Rev. Charles Taliaferro, 1801-1837.
Jesse E. Taliaferro, Dec. 31, 1850-Nov. 4, 1866.
Double stone.
Elizabeth Eldridge, second wife of Rev. Charles Taliaferro.
W. J. Simmons, Aug. 25, 1830-Mar. 23, 1892.
Mark Harden Taliaferro, Dec. 9, 1824-Jan. 31, 1900.
His wife (double stone), Louisa Rebecca Taliaferro, Dec. 22, 1840-Mar. 31, 1926.
David V. Marney, Company H, 5th Tennessee Inf.
W. E. Purdy, Company A, 5th Tennessee Inf.
Sam L. Hines, Company B, 5th Tennessee Inf.
Emma, daughter of W. B. and E. E. Rose, July 3, 1888-Feb. 13, 1901.
Flora Rambo, wife of G. R. Rambo, Oct. 7, 1868-July 1, 1893.
J. MacCarrell, Oct. 19, 1808-Mar. 16, 1887.
James M. Robinson, July 12, 1818-Dec. 4, 1884.
Nancy A. Robinson, wife of James Robinson, July 12, 1823-Mar. 12, 1905.
Robert L. Wilson, Sept. 24, 1871-Feb. 6, 1900.
Sarah I. Eldredge, wife of Rufus Wilson, May 18, 1836-Mar. 21, 1906.
Rufus Wilson, Feb. 28, 1834-July 21, 1893.
J. B. Edwards, Oct. 22, 1803-April 20, 1884.
Sarah A., daughter of J. C. and Mary J. Matlock, May 3, 1866-Sept. 9, 1878.
Infant daughter of James and Lavinia Oliphant, Mar. (or May), 1862.
G. W. Matlock, Dec., 1870-July, 1884.
John C. Matlock, 1828-1907.
His wife, Mary J. Matlock, 1841-1928.
Minnie O. Matlock, June 15, 1881-Oct. 27, 1905.
Three Matlock children.

County Line Cemetery

Records from County Line Cemetery, McMinn-Monroe Counties, Tenn. Compiled by Mrs. C. O. Browder, Sweetwater, Tenn.

Infant son of D. A. and R. L. Browder, Jan. 17-Jan. 18, 1872.
Julia E., daughter of J. J. and E. J. Browder, Feb. 16, 1862-Sept. 25, 1873.
Sarah A., daughter of J. J. and E. J. Browder, Aug. 13, 1852-Sept. 4, 1867.
Sacred to the memory of Samuel T. Lotspeich, Mar. 5, 1812-April 2, 1847.
Sacred to the memory of John Lotspeich, Nov. 9, 1782-April 19, 1845.
Ann Lotspeich, Dec. 23, 1789-Jan. 27, 1878.
William L., son of J. J. and E. J. Browder, Nov. 29, 1850-July 7, 1878.
Nancye, daughter of J. J. and E. J. Browder, Feb. 19, 1858-Mar. 26, 1882.
Samuel E. Armstrong, son of James M. and Lizzie A. Browder, July 8, 1882-May 1, 1883.
Sarah S., wife of John H. Pickel, Dec. 25, 1823-May 19, 1852.
Elizabeth Pickel, born, 1796.
Jonathan Pickel, Feb. 15, 1790-Sept. 20, 1854.
Polly, wife of T. C. (or G.) Goddard, Dec. 22, 1793-Aug. 15, 1884.
Hugh Goddard, Nov. 28, 1796-Sept. 8, 1885.
Martha Goddard, Feb. 7, 1821-Oct. 26, 1859.
Laura Goddard, Mar. 25, 1829-Sept. 13, 1897.
Alvin Goddard, May 13, 1832-July 13, 1851.
In memory of Hugh Goddard, May 13, 1819-April 18, 1873.
Gen. Jas. H. Reagan, Feb. 12, 1800-Oct. 15, 1864.

Bible Records—Tombstone Inscriptions

Franklin, son of J. H. and M. A. Reagan, July 14, 1851-1862.
Sarah E. Welcker, daughter of B. F. and S. E. Welcker, Dec. 31, 1813-Jan. 15, 1844.
Welcker (stone fallen), similar to that of Sarah. Inscription indistinct. Two persons probably buried in this grave.
The Rev. Irby Holt was born Jul. No. the 7, Munth and 20 day, in the Yeare of Our Lord, 1783, and departed this life the 12: January, 1829.
Stone near Irby Holt, similar, but not decipherable.
Robert A. Goddard, Feb. 25, 1828-Mar. 27, 1830.
Harris B., son of B. G. and L. J. Glaze, Jan. 21, 1864-April 22, 1865.
Hattie E., daughter of B. G. and L. J. Glaze, —— 1, 1870-Nov. 26, 1871.
Thomas Wallis, April 8, 1809-June 16, 1901.
G. W. Martin, Company F, 4th Tennessee Cav.
Nancy, wife of Thomas Wallis, June 15, 1815-Nov. 8, 1865.
Nancy E., second wife of Thomas Wallis, May 6, 1839-April 16, 1900.
Fidello, son of Prior L. and M. Wallis, April 18, 1853-July 10, 1856.
Tempy, wife of Wm. Wallis, died, Sept. 23, 1855; age, 83 years.
Biddy, wife of James Wallis, Jan. 6, 1802-Oct. 19, 1854.
James Wallis, Mar. 14, 1798-Mar. 27, 1842.
Oty, infant of J. B. and Josie Hansard, June 1, 1906.
Infant of S. and M. A. Thomas, Born, May 7, 1859.
Cirvilla Garen, 1820-Mar. 23, 1859.
Perdita Ritchie, July 6, 1871-Aug. 4, 1871.
Mary L., wife of Alex Ritchie, Feb. 5, 1849-Oct. 15, 1876.
Charles Atkin Ritchie, Oct. 4, 1869-Aug. 19, 1870.
Rev. James Axley, died, Feb. 22, 1837; age, 62 years. He was P. E. of the M. E. Church for 30 years.
Cynthia Axley, died, Sept. 30, 1882; age, 82 years.
T. F. Green, died, June 22, 1867; age, 26 years.
Thos. J. Frazier, Feb. 14, 1833-Oct. 5, 1866.
Josie M. Lowe, wife of James L. Lowe, Aug. 19, 1853-Jan. 26, 1887.
David Asbury Browder (Confederate Marker, also), Mar. 2, 1835-April 6, 1883.
Rachel Letitia Dickey Browder, April 27, 1837-Jan. 21, 1912.
William Browder, Feb. 10, 1792-June 29, 1890.
Elizabeth Lackey, wife of Wm. Browder, Aug. 28, 1793-Nov. 11, 1862.
Infant son of Hugh and Martha A. Lybarger, born and died, Feb. 6, 1876.
David Lowe, Oct. 2, 1802-Oct. 1, 1871.
Margaret, wife of David Lowe, Dec. 2o, 1808-Aug. 18, 1895.
Nancy, wife of James Orr, Feb. 15, 1788-Sept. 24, 1863.
Martha A., wife of Hugh Lybarger, Nov. 20, 1839-Oct. 21, 1879.
J. J. Browder (Confederate Marker, also), Nov. 9, 1818-July 14, 1903. His wife, Elizabeth J., is buried by his side.
John W., son of J. J. and E. J. Browder, April 1, 1854-April 18, 1890.
Hannah W., wife of F. M. Woods, Mar. 1, 1819-April 3, 1885.
Fannie, consort of Robert D. Hook, May 27, 1857-Mar. 9, 1885.
Mary Josie Janeway, wife of J. B. Hansard, Sept. 30, 1871-July 14, 1907.
Hubert Owen Lee.
James E. Burns, June 22, 1909-April 7, 1916.
Arley Earl Burns, Mar., 1916-April, 1916.
John Wylie, no stone, just a Confederate Marker.
Lenoir Reagan, no stone, just a Confederate Marker.
Emma Pyoon Laycock, July 21, 1847-Jan. 25, 1920.
G. W. Laycock, May 31, 1829-April 1, 1915.
Malissa, wife of G. W. Laycock, Oct. 22, 1836-Oct. 22, 1888.
Carl A. M., infant son of J. P. and J. Janeway, Sept. 8, 1892-Sept. 12, 1892.
Charles Alfred Beardsley, April 8, 1805-Sept. 28, 1890.
Joseph Bushing, June 23, 1844-July 10, 1900.
James M. Browder, also Confederate Marker, Oct. 16, 1824-Sept. 10, 1902.
Robert L. Browder, July 27, 1874-April 16, 1908.
Lizzie A., wife of James M. Browder,

Bible Records—Tombstone Inscriptions

Sept. 16, 1850-May 17, 1909.
Sylvia Jane Lybarger, 1878-1897.
Benj. Glaze, Nov. 22, 1830-Jan. 4, 1902.
Lucy J., wife of Benj. Glaze, Sept. 9, 1831-Jan. 12, 1902.
M. W. Glaze, Sept. 9, 1857-April 19, 1922.
Mary Jane Glaze, 1859-1929.
Myrtle (Laycock Cleveland), wife of W. R. Jenkins, July 21, 1881-Jan. 30, 1915.
William Cleveland, Aug. 25, 1879-Nov. 10, 1909.
Mary, wife of J. H. Schneider, Feb. 18, 1855-Jan. 21, 1893.
John L. Reagan, Jan. 11, 1895; age, 3 years, 3 months.
Bessie J. Reagan, died, Aug. 25, 1899; age, 3 years, 6 months.
T. C. Richeson, July 6, 1854-April 7, 1908.
Floreta, daughter of P. L. and Alehea Stiles, May 15, 1915-June 9, 1916.
Horace Edward Frank, April 20, 1919-April 24, 1919.
Thornton G. Goddard, Nov. 10, 1794-Aug. 23, 1884.

Harrison Family Cemetery

Located in the bend of the Tennessee River, near Loudon, Tenn. Compiled by Elizabeth J. Taliaferro.

Casander Lanston, died, Sept., 1869; age, 65 years.
James Harrison, died, Oct. 20, 1861; age, 71 years.
Eliza Harrison, wife of James Harrison, died, Dec. 27, 1865; age, 72 years.
Susannah Harrison, died, April 17, 1837.
John Harrison, died, April 8, 1856; age, 72 years, 3 months.
Dr. R. W. Adams, July 14, 1833-Mar. 11, 1861.
Lieut. John H. Harrison, C. S. A., June 22, 1832-June 5, 1864. Killed at the Battle of Piedmont, Va.
Dr. James F. Harrison, 1809; died, summer of 1861.
James M. Harrison, May, 1836-Sept. 13, 1866.
Child, Henry Mayo, son of J. M. and L. H. Harrison.
Dr. Henry MacCray Harrison, son of Dr. J. J. and M. B. Harrison, May 31, 1873-June 6, 1897.
Robert A., son of Dr. J. F. and S. D. Harrison.
Mary E. E., daughter of J. F. and S. D. Harrison, Dec. 7, 1845-May 7, 1854.
Infant son and daughter of James and Lula Harrison Calloway; James, Aug. 21, 1893-Aug. 12, 1896; daughter, Lavinia Merrick, Aug. 26, 1900-May 27, 1901.
Frank R. Harrison, attorney-at-law, May 11, 1871-Aug. 2, 1922.
Emmett Merrick Harrison, Jr., Feb. 2, 1909-Sept. 17, 1923.
Dr. Josiah Jackson Harrison, Feb. 13, 1834-Oct. 25, 1917.
His wife, Mary MacCray Harrison, Sept. 9, 1846-Mar. 14, 1918.
Rev. William Harrison, June 7, 1821-Sept. 26, 1891.
Martha Evaline Lowe, wife of Rev. William Harrison, Mar. 6, 1832-Mar. 11, 1915.
J. L. Lowe, Dec. 12, 1837-Nov. 18, 1918.
Elizabeth Harrison, wife of J. L. Lowe, April 10, 1828-Sept. 22, 1916.
Addie C. Lowe, wife of Arthur E. Robinson, Feb. 13, 1867-Oct. 12, 1897; married, May 6, 1886.
Ben T. Harrison, Oct. 12, 1832-Nov. 13, 1906; married, Sept. 30, 1860.
Martha R. Clark Harrison, Mar. 26, 1841-April 23, 1924; married, Sept. 30, 1860.
James Harrison, Sept. 23, 1823-Feb. 19, 1900; married, Oct. 18, 1854.
Ann E. Holston, wife of James Harrison, Dec. 1, 1831-Dec. 23, 1899; married Oct. 18, 1854.
Ida Harrison MacGuire, Oct. 23, 1857-Jan. 26, 1888.
Mary Scott, daughter of Mr. and Mrs. W. S. Harrison, Feb. 3, 1919.

Bible Records—Tombstone Inscriptions

OLD GREENEVILLE CEMETERY
BY MRS. LEROY BROWN, ROCKY HILL, GREENVILLE

The deed to this plot of ground was made by James Galbraith to the trustees of Mount Bethel Church in 1792. It adjoined the building in which they then worshipped, and interments were undoubtedly made before this date. No stones were erected at that time, and the limestone which was used at a later date has not survived the ravages of time. Many old graves, including at least one Revolutionary Soldier, are unmarked. They cannot be positively identified. The old church was long since destroyed by fire, and the congregation having divided, two new buildings were erected in other localities.

TOMBSTONE INSCRIPTIONS FROM OLD CEMETERY

In memory of our grandmother, Mary Dougherty, died, Feb. 13, 1856; age, 64 years; widow of Jacob Johnson and mother of Andrew Johnson, 17th President.

Hexehiah Balch, D.D., 1741-1810; pioneer educator and preacher; founder of Greeneville (Tusculum) College in 1794; erected by Tusculum College and Nolichucky Chapter, D. A. R., 1931.

Rev. Charles Coffin, D.D., born in Newburyport, Mass., Aug. 15, 1775; died, June 3, 1853.

To the memory of Margaret, wife of Robert J. McKinney, and daughter of Rev. Charles Coffin, D.D., Aug. 15, 1775-June 3, 1853.

To the memory of our parents; pious, affectionate, and faithful they lived in the daily discharge of duty and died in the hope of a blissful immortality: Valentine Sevier, July 8, 1780-April 24, 1854; Nancy Sevier, Dec. 27, 1786-Mar. 26, 1844.

Vinerah C. Sevier, born in Wallingford, Conn., Sept. 26, 1814; died in Greeneville, Tenn., July 25, 1879.

Sacred to the memory of Joseph Sevier, Mar. 30, 1830-July 22, 1864.

Robert Valentine, infant son of Chas. L. and Julia Brown Sevier, 1878.

Infant daughter of Edward and Mary N. Sevier.

Canzaty (?), wife of A. Sevier, Oct. 26, 1841-June 16, 1880; age, 39 years, 7 months. "Blessed are the dead which die in the Lord."

Charles Francis, son of G. W. and N. Coffin, Aug. 11, 1850-July 13, 1859.

Daniel L., infant son of G. W. and N. Coffin, died, July 30, 1856; age, 10 months.

Rev. Samuel V. McCorkle, May 8, 1840-Dec. 1, 1897; married, Sept. 24, 1862. Asleep in Jesus.

—harine Ann McCorkle, Sept. 27, 1843-July 30, 1844.

In memory of James McCorkle, who died Oct. 21, 1840; age, 10 years, 7 months.

Charles Francis, son of F. A. and I. McCorkle, died Dec. 24, 1855; age, 7 years, 4 months, 19 days.

In memory of our father, Psalm 112:6; the righteous shall be in everlasting remembrance; Rev. F. A. McCorkle, M.D., Sept. 1, 1795-Mar. 17, 1869. A lover of humanity—of his country—above all, of his God. He still lives in greatful remembrance here, and in the enjoyment of the glorious reward beyond. Blessed are the dead which die in the Lord from henceforth; yea, saith the Spirit, that they may rest from their labors, and their works do follow them.

In memory of Isabel McCorkle, daughter of Valentine Sevier, and consort of Rev. F. A. McCorkle, Jan. 10, 1805-Feb. 21, 1867. "Blessed are the pure in heart, for they shall see God. And God shall wipe all tears from their eyes; and there shall be no more death; neither sorrow nor crying, neither shall there be any more pain."

In memory of Robert McCorkle, Nov.

Bible Records—Tombstone Inscriptions

26, 1832-Jan. 30, 1875. He giveth his beloved sleep.

In memory of Emily G. Moffett, wife of Robert McCorkle, Oct. 23, 1837-Sept. 3, 1925.

In loving memory of Willie Alison, son of Robert and Emily G. McCorkle, Nov. 14, 1863-May 5, 1884. Neither shall there be any more pain.

Nannabel, daughter of Robert and Emily G. McCorkle, Sept. 20, 1858-Nov. 29, 1885.

Sacred to the memory of Agnes Woods Mitchell, a native of Ayrshire, Scotland, who departed this life on the 22nd of March, 1844; age, 42 years. Jesus saith unto her, I am the resurrection and the life; he that believeth in me, though he were dead, yet shall he live. Erected by the citizens of Greeneville in token of their high respect for her many shining virtues, and also as an expression of their feelings that her death is a public calamity.

Sam Milligan.

Children of Sam and E. R. Milligan: Howard, age, 6 years; Sallie K., age, 17 months.

Joseph Brown, Aug. 9, 1767-Nov. 1, 1845.

In memory of Peggy R., consort of David Alexander, deceased May 13, 1833; age, 30 years, 11 months, 25 days.

J. W—— Newton Alexander, July 13, 1838-Aug. 29, 1844.

John A. Brown, Aug. 10, 1804-Dec. 2, 1880; age, 76 years.

In memory of Charles P. Rabe, son of Dr. Charles and R. L. Rabe, born Nov. 5, 1854, in Franklin, La.; died, Mar. 6, 1873, having a little while before repeated the lines: "On Jordan's stormy banks I stand, and cast a wishful eye," etc. He will long be remembered as generous, kind, affectionate.

Rebecca L., wife of John A. Brown, Nov. 1, 1827-Mar. 3, 1891; age, 63 years.

Here lies the body of William Brown, deceased, 18——; age, ——.

Jessie W., daughter of J. W. and F. A. Brown, Mar. 23, 1873-June 15, 1889.

Mordcai Lincoln, born in Rockingham County, Va.; died, April 29, 1851, in Greeneville, Tenn.

Sophia Williams Heiskell, wife of Mordcai Lincoln, born in Hagerstown, Md., 1800; died in Greenville, Tenn., 1873.

In memory of Elizabeth C., wife of Rev. Jonathan Lyons, born in Armaugh County, Ireland, Oct. 28, 1828; died in Greeneville, Tenn., Sept. 9, 1854.

Also William, infant son of J. and E. C. Lyons, Mar. 25, 1854-July 11, 1854.

Alexander Williams, M.D., born in Surry County, N. C., April 28, 1793, and died in Greeneville, Tenn., Aug. 4, 1852.

In memory of William Dickson, born in the County of Antrim, Ireland, May, 1775; immigrated to the United States in early life; died on the 2nd of Jan., 1843, in his 68th year.

In memory of Eliza Dickson, consort of William Dickson, born in Laudon County, Va., June, 1766; died on the 30th of Oct., 1836, in her 71st year.

In memory of Sarah Dickson, consort of John Dickson, born in Greenock, Scotland, May 6, 1781; died, Mar. 1, 1864. A kind friend and devoted Christian.

In memory of William D. Dickson, a native of Ireland, who departed this life Sept. 9, 1851; age, 63 years.

In memory of William G. Dickson, Jan. 23, 1841-June 3, 1865; age, 24 years, 4 months.

To the memory of James D. Dickson, a native of Ireland, who departed this life Feb. 14, 1849. He lived to die, and died to live.

In memory of John McKee, born Nov. 1, 1773, in the County Donegal, Ireland; immigrated to the United States in 1793; died, Jan. 28, 1860.

Elizabeth W., wife of John McKee, June 22, 1809-Oct. 28, 1890.

Robert McKinney McKee, Dec. 20, 1834-Dec. 25, 1918.

Sarah P., wife of R. M. McKee, Nov. 25, 1837-April 12, 1912. So kind, so true, so gentle.

Sam McKee, Mar. 6, 1873-April 14, 1906.

Our darling boy, Joseph, son of Robt. M. and Sallie P. McKee; died, Sept. 5, 1867; age, 4 years, 1 month, 12 days.

Leonora, infant daughter of Robt. M. and S. P. McKee, 1870.

John Mitchell McKee, June 10, 1840-May 2, 1923.

My mother, Mrs. Jane Fowler, Feb. 16,

Bible Records—Tombstone Inscriptions

1817-Aug. 15, 1869; age, 52 years, 5 months, 29 days.
Our Angel Child, Ella May, April 19, 1866-Jan. 10, 1871.
James Mason, Oct. 20, 1831-Aug. 22, 1853.
This dark abode proclaims the truth, To bending age and blooming youth. You must your active limbs resign And be a moldering corpse—.
Joseph Powell, Oct. 8, 1801-Mar. 7, 1873. (Double stone.)
Mary M. Powell, Sept. 6, 1796-Feb. 18, 1879. Gone, but not forgotten.
In memory of Mrs. Matilda D. Martin, a native of Ireland, died, Feb., 1865. A benevolent and devoted Christian.
Henry B. Baker, Dec. 4, 1811-Aug. 14, 1883.
Will H. Baker, Jan. 5, 1841-Mar. 9, 1871.
David F. Baker, April 20, 1836-Feb. 12, 1865.
Minnie Bell Baker, Nov. 24, 1861-Aug. 15, 1863.
Mary E. Baker, June 17, 1847-Sept. 7, 1851.
Annis Baker, Jan. 21, 1850-May 22, 1851.
Frank Baker, Aug. 6, 1862-Sept. 3, 1865.
William Alexander, infant son of John W. and Elizabeth Cunningham; died, Sept. 28, 1842; age, 1 year, 6 months, 2 days.
Infant children of John W. and E. J. Mathes, beloved all of life, and blossomed on earth and passed away:
John Elmer, Aug. 3, 1829-Oct. 21, 1829.
Charles Earl, Aug. 3, 1829-Nov. 9, 1829.
Robert T., son of W. A. and Emily G. Harmon, Dec. 31, 1847-Dec. 21, 1854.
Elizabeth G. Johnston, Aug. 25, 1841-Nov. 26, 1845.
Martha E. Johnston, June 30, 1844-July 27, 1844.
Sarah J. Johnston, June 30, 1844-July 9, 1844.
In memory of Eliza Jane Russell, May 19, 1824-Jan. 8, 1855; age, 30 years, 7 months, 19 days.
In memory of our father, Blackston McDannel, Jan. 15, 1811-July 27, 1888; age, 77 years, 6 months, 12 days. Died in the triumph of faith. His many virtues form the noblest monument to his memory.
Elizabeth McDannel, wife of Blackston McDannel, April 9, 1811-May 22, 1848; died a Christian.
In memory of my mother, Louisa Britton, wife of Blackston McDannel, Dec. 27, 1824-April 8, 1876. Died in the triumph of faith. Blessed are the pure in heart.
In memory of our grandmother, Sarah Whitesides; died, April 27, 1854; age, 60 years.
Mother—Dorcas Payne; died, Mar. 15, 1874.
Merryman Payne; died, Feb. 10, 1844; age, 56 years.
W. D. McClelland, Aug. 15, 1822-Aug. 5, 1864.
Jennettie, wife of W. D. McClelland; born, Aug. 1, 1824. Gone to rest.
J. D. McClelland, April 28, 1851-Oct. 14, 1873.
Tabitha Dryden; died, Mar. 9, 1844; age, 67 years.
Richard M. Wood; died, June 20, 1845; age, 58 years.
Ephraim Wilson; died, Feb. 9, 1849; age, 64 years.
Alexander A. Lane, June 5, 1837-Oct. 25, 1872; age, 35 years, 4 months, 20 days.
Josiah Clowson, Aug. —— -Dec. 27, 182—.

TOMBSTONE INSCRIPTIONS FROM
LEBANON-THE-FORK

Copied by Mrs. LeRoy Brown.
First Presbyterian Church in Knox County, 1791, Rev. Samuel Carrick, founder and first pastor; earliest burial ground in this section. (Marker by Bonny Kate Chapter.) 1828.
Elizabeth M. Carrick, consort of Rev. Carrick, died Sept. 1795.

(Large tomb)
Sacred to the memory of Col. Francis Alexander Ramsey, May 31, 1764-Nov. 5, 1820. In his 20th year he was Secretary of the Franklin Convention and held civil and military appointments under that and the succeeding Federal and State Governments till his death. He was one of the founders and elders of Lebanon Church. The old stone church was erected by his munificence and consecrated by his prayers. These

Bible Records—Tombstone Inscriptions

grounds were his gift to this Presbyterian congregation, which in commemoration of his liberality and his private and public virtues, has erected this monument to his memory.

(On one side)

Sacred to the memory of Peggy Alexander Ramsey, wife of Col. F. A. Ramsey, and daughter of J. M. McKnitt Alexander, Esq., Secretary of the Mecklenberg Convention, May 20, 1775; born, April 3, 1766; married, April 7, 1789; died, July 7, 1805.

(Other side)

Sacred to the memory of Mrs. Ann Agnew Ramsey, wife of Col. F. A. Ramsey; married, Aug., 1806; died, Dec., 1816.

Sacred to the memory of Reynolds Ramsey, Esq., born at Newcastle, De., Oct. 24, 1736. He was with Washington at Trenton and Princeton. He died Mar., 1816; age, 80 years. And of Naomi Alexander, born Dec. 13, 1736; married, Sept. 24, 1761; died, Sept. 10, 1813; age, 77 years. Rest in heaven.

Husband, John M. A. Ramsey, Oct. 16, 1807-July 6, 1864.

Daughter, Margaret E. Ramsey, July 28, 1840-Aug. 30, 1862.

Arthur G. Ramsey, Feb. 28, 1846-June 15, 1864; died at Piedmont, Va.

Sacred to the memory of Gen. John C. Ramsey, born at Mecklenburg, June 7, 1824; died at Knoxville, Jan. 1, 1869. A dutiful son, an affectionate brother, a tried soldier, an honorable gentleman, distinguished for his public and private virtues, his chivalry and patriotism.

Sacred to the memory of J. G. M. Ramsey, A.M., M.D., Mar. 25, 1707-April 11, 1884. Author of Annals of Tennessee; a patriot, a scholar, and a Christian.

Margaret B. Crozier, wife of J. G. M. Ramsey, Sept. 18, 1802-Oct. 14, 1889.

J. G. M. Ramsey, Jr., June 30, 1835-April 26, 1900.

Elizabeth Breck, daughter, Feb. 4, 1823-June 8, 1911.

Charlotte Barton Ramsey, daughter of Dr. J. G. M. and Peggy Barton, Crozier Ramsey, Sept. 10, 1838-April 16, 1863.

SOLDIERS BURIED IN OAK GROVE CEMETERY, GREENVILLE, TENN.

Sent by Mrs. Le Roy Brown.

Confederate

Major Thos. Arnold
Dr. R. L. Dobson
Joseph Fields
James Fields
M. H. Hankal
Capt. John C. Marshall
James M. Morey
A. F. Naff
L. W. Morris
James H. Robinson
Capt. Wm. D. Williams
Capt. Thos. Williams
H. C. Yost
Wm. Cregger of North Carolina.
Capt. Robert L. Francisco, Virginia.
T. B. Pickering, Virginia.
Capt. Porch, Georgia.

Union

James Britton
W. D. McClellan
J. W. McCoy
John Naulty
Elisha Laughters
A. W. Walker

OLD CEMETERY

Confederate

Thomas Rumbough.
—— Howard.

WAR OF 1812

James Rumbough.
Thomas Lane.

REVOLUTION

Wilson McAmis.

PRESIDENTS OF GREENEVILLE COLLEGE

Rev. Hexehiah Balch, 1794-1810.
Dr. Charles Coffin, 1810-1827.

Bible Records—Tombstone Inscriptions

Old Cemetery at Jonesboro

Records in the Old Cemetery at Jonesboro sent by Mrs. J. M. Scott and Mrs. W. P. Diehl, Jonesboro.

To the memory of David Nelson, son of John and Jane Nelson, born in Rockbridge County, Va., Feb. 11, 1780; died in Elizabethton, Tenn., Sept. 2, 1850; age, 70 years, 6 months, 21 days.
Col. Matthew Aiken, Mar. 27, 1775-Oct. 6, 1860.
Blanche B. Aiken, Oct. 21, 1789-Nov. 29, 1862.
Sacred to the memory of Enoch Brown, 1806-Sept. 15, 1878.
Ann Rebecca, wife of Enoch Brown, born in Baltimore, Md., Jan. 7, 1799; died in Jonesboro, Tenn., Feb. 6, 1855.
John Blair, born in Washington County, Tenn., Sept. 13, 1790; died in Jonesborough, Tenn., Mar. 22, 1863; an elder in the Presbyterian Church more than 30 years; member of Congress 11 years.
Mary H. Chester, wife of John Blair, born in Jonesborough, Tenn., May 12, 1797; died in Bristol, Tenn., Nov. 11, 1872.
Sacred to the memory of Elizabeth P., wife of Dr. Worley Embree, and daughter of John and Mary Blair, born at Jonesboro, Tenn., Mar. 31, 1818; died at Chattanooga, Aug. 27, 1892. A tribute of a brother's love.
Jeremiah Gibson, Feb. 23, 1786-July 17, 1868.
Pheobe Gibson, June 16, 1782-May 4, 1864.
In memory of Catherine, relict of Thomas Emerson, born in Wilkes County, N. C., Nov. 19, 1789; died in Jonesboro, Dec. 10, 1858; age, 69 years, 21 days.
Sacred to the memory of John Kennedy Chester, who departed this life Oct. 20, 1828.
In memory of Elizabeth Chester, who departed this life Jan. 18, 1812; age, 69 years.
Elizabeth Conway Byers, wife of Charles P. Byers, and daughter of John Sevier, July 24, 1812-Oct. 19, 1845.
James Dillworth, born in Petersburg, Va., Nov. 7, 1897; died in Jonesboro, Tenn., May 9, 1877; age, 79 years, 6 months, 2 days.
Mary Charlotte Dillworth, born in Hagerstown, Md., Jan. 6, 1802; died in Jonesboro, Tenn., Nov. 19, 1881; age, 19 years, 5 months, 13 days.
Jacob Broyles, Dec. 10, 1804-Nov. 3, 1896.
Lucinda Broyles, Sept. 14, 1804-Oct. 4, 1891; married Dec. 13, 1827.

Fairview Cemetery
(Near Jonesboro)

Martha Borcroft, 1813-1872.
Jonathan Borcroft, Jan. 8, 1771-June 3, 1849.
W. M. Carmichael, May 8, 1792-April 8, 1841.
Cynthia McAdams, April 30, 1817-Oct. 20, 1874.
Thomas C. McAdams, Dec. 5, 1806-Jan. 1, 1881.

Fairview Quaker Cemetery

Rachel West Bales, June 19, 1775-July 7, 1840.
David Bales, June 4, 1771-Oct. 1, 1870.
Elizabeth Marsh, April 2, 1805-Dec. 20, 1878.
Hannah Marsh, Jan. 1, 1812-Jan. 12, 1887.
Henry Jones, Feb. 14, 1820-Nov. 21, 1885.

New Hope Cemetery
(Near Jonesboro)

David Garber, Dec. 26, 1821-Dec. 6, 1852.

Uriah Cemetery
(Near Jonesboro)

J. E. T. Harris, June 23, 1823-Dec. 19, 1885.
John G. Harris, Sept. 10, 1773-1842.
Rev. George Eakin, born in Tryone County, Ireland, May 23, 1782; died in Abington, Va., in his 75th year.
John Walter, Mar. 30, 1830-Oct. 23, 1873.
Susan Walter, Jan. 10, 1821-Feb. 1, 1899.

Old Dutch Graveyard
(Six Miles South of Jonesboro)

Cassimore May, 1751-May 31, 1836.

Bible Records—Tombstone Inscriptions

WASHINGTON COLLEGE CEMETERY
Samuel Doak, Aug., 1749-Dec. 12, 1829.
Agnes Wood; died, April 3, 1824; age, 57 years.
John Blair, New Jersey Line Revolutionary.
William Greenway, War of 1812.

CHEROKEE CEMETERY
(Near Jonesboro)
Joseph Booth; died, Dec. 5, 1828; age, 48 years.
Sarah Booth; died, June 7, 1849; age, 63 years.
Hannah Hoss, Sept., 1774-June 30, 1859.
Rev. Resse Bayless, Aug. 22, 1787-Oct. 29, 1864.
Robert Million, April 20, 1781-Aug. 21, 1856.
Mary, wife of Robert Million, Sept. 8, 1787-Jan. 12, 1855.
Elizabeth West, Aug. 29, 1771-Oct. 23, 1839.
Dan Bayless, April 16, 1777-Feb. 14, 1867.
Mary Bayless, consort of Dan Bayless; died, March 8, 1863; age, 83 years.
Reuben Bayless, June 17, 1754-Nov. 7, 1826.
Isaac Henley, Jan. 6, 1785-Dec. 4, 1846.
Elizabeth Henley, wife, July 26, 1789-Nov. 18, 1869.

W. D. Asher, husband of Agnes Asher, Dec. 8, 1808-Jan. 27, 1859.

LEESBURG CEMETERY
(Near Jonesboro)
Isaac Morrell, May 18, 1799-Oct. 7, 1870.
Susanna Morrell, Jan. 6, 1802-May 29, 1876.
Moses D. Rice, born in Newhaven County, Conn., April 1, 1809; died, April 1, 1835.
Jacob Fetter, May 18, 1814-Sept. 26, 1885.
Sam Lyon, Feb. 9, 1816-Nov. 23, 1887.
Esther Duncan, Feb. 4, 1835-Oct. 16, 1887.
Robert Duncan, Oct. 8, 1810-May 28, 1898.
Mary Ann Buchanan, July 10, 1813-Mar. 8, 1893.
J. W. Slonaker, born in Tryone, Pa., Feb. 6, 1826; died, Dec. 29, 1889.
Mary Slonaker, born in Leitersburg, Md., June 12, 1824; died, July 31, 1893.
Sarah Carson, June 22, 1821-Jan. 15, 1882.
Rebecca Cochran, Nov. 22, 1799-Aug. 13, 1870.
Ezekiel Lyons, April 22, 1782-Jan. 2, 1845.
Mary Lyons, Nov. 18, 1782-Aug. 10, 1855.

JORDAN FAMILY BURYING GROUND

Tombstone inscriptions from family burying ground of Jordan family, Triune, Tenn.

Erected to the memory of Dr. Clement J. Wood, Mar. 13, 1836-Nov. 1, 1852; age, 26 years, 7 months, 18 days.

In memory of Stephen A. Jordan, son of W. E. and Elizabeth O. Jordan, May 29, 1851-Oct. 16, 1856.

CAGE CEMETERY

Cemetery records sent by Mrs. George Harsh, Memphis, family data. Inscriptians on the tomb of Col. Edward Douglas, his wife, Sarah George Douglas, and their daughter, Elizabeth Douglas Cage. These graves are in the old Cage Cemetery at the Cage home which was owned and occupied by Maj. Cage from the time that he came to Sumner County, then Davidson, until his death.

Edward Douglas, 1713-1773.
Sarah Douglas, 1714-1777; wife of E. Douglas.

Elizabeth Cage; died, July, 1772; age, 38 years.
Wm. Cage; died, Mar. 12, 1811; age,

Bible Records—Tombstone Inscriptions

66 years; a major in the Revolutionary War. Wm. Alexander, Dec. 25, 1746-Aug., 1830. See inscription on tomb in Alexander graveyard on land originally granted Wm. Alexander for Revolutionary services, located near Hartsville in Trousdale County, formerly Sumner County. Wm. Alexander married Mary Brandon in Rowan County, N. C., Jan. 21, 1769.
Mary Brandon, Nov. 11, 1749-Sept., 1834. See Bible Records, Judge Wm. Hall of Gallatin, Tenn., and Mrs. Sam Young of Dixon Springs. The graves of Maj. Wm. Hall and Thankful Doak Hall are on the old Hall homestead near Castalian Springs and are marked by stones of the limestone rock quarried on the place. This land was granted to Maj. Hall for Revolutionary services. There are no inscriptions on these stones, but the record was kept by the late Judge Wm. Hall of Gallatin who was the great-great-grandson of Maj. Hall and Thankful Doak Hall.
Capt. John Morgan, who married Mary, the eldest daughter of Maj. Wm. Hall and Thankful Doak Hall, before leaving North Carolina, moved with the Halls to Sumner County, but later settled in Mulberry, near Fayetteville, Tenn. Capt. Morgan died in the '30's and was buried near Mulberry. His wife, Mary Hall Morgan, survived him until 1850 and was buried in the old Cemetery at Fayetteville where their grandson, Gen. John Morgan Bright, lived.
John Cage, son of Maj. Wm. Cage, and Elizabeth Douglas Cage, married Thankful Morgan, daughter of Capt. John and Mary Hall Morgan. Mary Pricilla Cage, daughter of John and Thankful Morgan Cage, married David Barry; their son married Lutie Chenault; and their daughter, Thankful Barry, married George Harsh of Menphis.
Jane Alexander, daughter of Wm. and Mary Brandon Alexander, married Redmond Barry; David Barry, son, married Mary Pricilla Cage; their son, David F. Barry, of Gallatin married Lutie Chenault; their daughter, Thankful Barry, married George Harsh of Memphis.

Salem Christian Church Graveyard

Six miles from McMinnville, Tenn. Sent by Mrs. James Elkins, McMinnville.

Ann Hixey, wife of G. N. Lowery, Mar. 29, 1831-Nov. 19, 1886.
Roler Dempsey, 1821-1887.
Harriet Richardson, wife of J. B. Tubb, later wife of W. B. Cope, 1834-1912.
Nancy Golden, 1817-1907.
T. J. Romans; died, 1931; age, 74 years.
Margaret, wife of John Blackwell; died, 1913; age, 74 years.
Dr. T. W. Potter, 1847-1914.
Abenida Lowery, May 4, 1798-Aug. 24, 1884.
Wm. Lowery, May 15, 1798-May 9, 1877; age, 78 years.
Martha, wife of Howard Smith, Jan. 9, 1828-Feb. 10, 1897.
Martha Jane Reeder, June 24, 1842-Nov. 28, 1926.
Elizabeth Reeder, June 28, 1824-1897.
H. J. Christian, Jan. 25, 1848-Sept. 6, 1889.
Wm. J. Patton, Feb. 24, 1849-Oct. 22, 1896.
Maggie Patteon, Mar. 31, 1854-May 1, 1913.
W. L. Hart, Sept. 18, 1878-Oct. 24, 1898.
Joe Byars, Oct., 1849-Dec. 6, 1913.
May Byars, Dec. 28, 1850-June 25, 1917.
Fannie Cantrell, Feb. 18, 1828-May 5, 1908.
Alice, wife of H. S. Safley, April 28, 1826-Feb. 25, 1910.
Flora, wife of L. P. Sanders, Dec. 22, 1861-June 9, 1900.
Nettie, wife of J. P. Evans, Feb. 9, 1879-Sept. 10, 1904.
Mary, wife of W. J. Fuston, June 15, 1840-Dec. 5, 1909.
Eliza E., second wife of M. C. Green, June 24, 1858-Oct. 21, 1911.
M. C. Green, Sept. 12, 1845-Dec. 2, 1926.

Bible Records—Tombstone Inscriptions

J. D. Lewis, Feb. 29, 1852-Jan. 3, 1928.
Marrion Simmons, Jan. 21, 1868-May 1, 1905.
Josie Florence, wife of G. W. Drake, June 6, 1861-Jan. 31, 1903.
Mary Lou, wife of George Simmons, Aug. 21, 1848-Feb. 4, 1913.
Sarah, wife of J. W. Sanders, Sept. 24, 1846-Feb. 28, 1918.
J. W. Sanders, May 29, 1845-Mar. 6, 1924.
Joe Roland, 1859-1930.
Lydia Ann Roland, 1856-1930.

CONCORD BAPTIST CHURCH YARD
Seven miles north of McMinnville, Tenn.

Nancy, wife of James Byars, Nov. 8, 1817-Mar. 16, 1865.
William Lowery, May 15. 1798-May 9, 1877.
Abenida Lowery, May 4, 1798-Aug. 24, 1888.
Martha, wife of Howard Smith, Jan. 9, 1828-Feb. 10, 1897.
William A. Smith, June 14, 1820-June 25, 1864.
Lucy, wife of W. A. Smith, Nov. 11, 1809-Aug. 20, 1889.
Isaac Denton, Dec. 23, 1906-April 7, 1889.
Nancy, wife of Isaac Denton, Nov. 13, 1810-Aug. 23, 1883.
Mrs. Mary Jane Patterson, died Feb. 14, 1932; age, 75 years old.
Thomas Bright, April 25, 1847-Oct. 18, 1911.
Lizzie, wife of Thomas Bright, Sept. 16, 1851.
Wm. Bright, May 19, 1870-June 19, 1911.
Stephen Smith, Dec. 2, 1850-Mar. 12, 1890.
Mary Ann Smith, Nov. 14, 1837-Jan. 24, 1913.
Elizabeth Smith, wife of Wm. Smith, Oct. 4, 1820-July 12, 1876.
Wm. Smith, Jan. 2, 1801-Oct. 31, 1878.
W. A. Smith, May 14, 1820-May 25, 1864.
Octa, wife of J. T. Webb, Aug. 19, 1858-Aug., 1885.
J. G. Tompkins, June 20, 1856-Mar. 10, 1921.
T. J. Davis, June 10, 1835-Feb. 10, 1914.
Charlie Crain, Jan. 11, 1783; age, 97 years.
Mary Crain, wife of A. M. Crain, Oct. 16, 1831-June 21. ——; age, 65 years.
A. M. Crain, July 11, 1825-June 22, 1907.
T. A. Glenn, 1859-Dec. 12, 1914.
Hanner Glenn, wife of T. A. Glenn, 1859.
J. D. Glenn, Dec. 11, 1873-June 28, 1911.
Emma Glenn, wife of J. D. Glenn, Mar. 30, 1863-April 17, 1909.

OLD SHILOH CHURCH GRAVEYARD
Eight miles east of McMinnville, Tenn.

Wm. Lusk, 1774-1860.
Sarah, wife of Wm. Lusk; died, 1846.

OLD BRYAN FAMILY CEMETERY

Sarah Bryan, born in North Carolina, May 15, 1782; died, Dec. 1, 1849.
John Bryan, born in North Carolina, March 7, 1780; died, Oct. 28, 1854.
Sarah E. Bryan, wife of C. D. F. Browne, 1820-1858.
Cyrus D. F. Browne, 1817-1859.
Abner Bryan, born in North Carolina; died in Coffee County, Tenn., Mar. 4, 1873.

Bible Records—Tombstone Inscriptions

BASCOM CEMETERY
Near Vervilla, Tenn.

Dr. Jesse Hill, Jan. 15, 1835-July 17, 1914.
Josie, wife of Dr. J. Hill, June 13, 1850-Mar. 28, 1921.
Thomas Springs, born in Cape Hatteras, Dec. 19, 1808; died, June 13, 1877.
John H. Chapman, June 18, 1823-July 12, 1874.
Elijah Anderson, Jan. 12, 1826-Jan. 13, 1898.
Elizabeth, wife of Elijah Anderson, Oct. 19, 1827-Jan. 5, 1905.
L. B. Brown, Oct. 14, 1844-Sept. 28, 1899.
W. L. Brixley, Feb. 20, 1850-May 8, 1890.
J. W. Rodgers, Aug. 7, 1852-Nov. 24, 1913.
Eliza Badgers, Nov. 22, 1854-Sept. 17, 1912.
W. H. Kell, Mar. 15, 1822-Dec. 28, 1886.
Martha Brixey, Sept. 14, 1833-Mar. 10, 1895.
Elizabeth, wife of J. C. Wheeler, Feb. 22, 1792-Feb. 20, 1879.
J. C. Wheeler, July 10, 1802-Sept. 8, 1890.
W. A. Hood, 1831-Sept. 21, 1908.
Mary Hood, June 7, 1842-June 12, 1915.
C. S. Thompson, April 5, 1855-July 13, 1930.
Amanda C., wife of C. S. Thompson; born, Jan. 1, 1849.
John Gowen, April 16, 1851-Nov. 9, 1926.
Callie Hankins, wife of N. L. Hankins, May 27, 1882-Sept. 11, 1908.
G. M. Finger, Dec. 27, 1845-Mar. 16, 1926.
Jane Henegar, wife of G. M. Finger, Feb. 22, 1856-Oct. 3, 1904.
Mrs. Frances A. Parker Paty, Dec. 7, 1809-Aug. 7, 1877.
Ann E. J., wife of G. L. Sain, daughter of J. W. and F. A. Paty, Aug. 28, 1844-May 8, 1871.
John W. Sain, son of G. L. and A. E. J. Sain, Sept. 1, 1866-May 29, 1885.
Mary Jane, wife of Lorenzo Paty, June 11, 1836-Aug. 14, 1907.
Lorenzo Paty, Mar. 18, 1826- Oct. 23, 1891.
H. M. Finger, Mar. 16, 1825-Oct. 23, 1891.
M. A. Finger, Nov. 10, 1833-July 8, 1902.
John Swann, Sept. 13, 1803-Oct. 31, 1862.
Peggy, wife of John Swann, Oct. 21, 1806-Mar. 25, 1868.
Abner L. Comer, Mar. 16, 1823-Mar. 18, 1919; married, Oct. 20, 1844.
Nancy Parker, wife of Abner L. Comer, Mar. 16, 1823-Dec. 24, 1892.
William J. Swann, Mar. 28, 1801-Mar. 27, 1872.
Lucy Ann Bonner, wife of William James Swann, Oct. 26, 1843-Dec. 22, 1881.
W. T. Swann, Aug. 10, 1838-Feb. 24, 1888.
Nannie K. Swann, wife of J. W. Snipes, Sept. 4, 1866-Aug. 14, 1912.
Hattie G., wife of James H. Edwards, Dec. 28, 1857-Feb. 18, 1883.
Frank P. Mone, Dec. 12, 1857-Sept. 12, 1881.
T. T. Peay, born in Williamson County, Feb. 29, 1812-Oct. 3, 1895.
Nancy, wife of T. T. Peay, Sept. 8, 1823-Sept. 15, 1850.
Joseph Hollis, Dec. 22, 1805-Feb. 2, 1833.
Elizabeth, wife of Joseph Hollis, Aug. 3, 1790-Aug. 3, 1850.
George Shannon, 1836-Mar. 18, 1920.

STUBBLEFIELD GRAVEYARD AT VIOLA

William Stubblefield, 1772-Dec. 25, 1858.
Wilmath, wife of Wm. Stubblefield, 1785-Jan. 11, 1850.
A. L. Stubblefield, Feb. 18, 1824-Nov. 20, 1909.
Mary Jane Catherine, wife of A. L. Stubblefield, Jan. 1, 1830-Mar. 5, 1926.

Bible Records—Tombstone Inscriptions

RAMSEY GRAVEYARD
Near Viola, Tenn.

Jane McCaslin Ramsey, wife of David Ramsey, 1764-1821.
Wm. Ramsey, son of David and Jane Ramsey, Jan. 8, 1795-July 9, 1865.
Elizabeth Stroud, wife of Wm. Ramsey, Dec. 16, 1795-Sept. 5, 1880.
Samuel Ramsey, April 23, 1798-Aug. 28, 1810.
Polly, wife of Samuel Ramsey, Dec. 23, 1803-Sept. 1, 1877.
David, son of Wm. and Elizabeth Ramsey, Jan. 6, 1818-Nov. 22, 1901.
Sarah Tilford, wife of David Ramsey, born in Murfreesboro, Tenn., Dec. 30, 1817-Sept. 5, 1877.
Mary Stubblefield, Jan. 17, 1783-April 18, 1879.
David Ramsey, Jan. 16, 1802-May 2, 1861.
Lucy, wife of David Ramsey, Dec. 26, 1804-Sept. 18, 1879.
Rachall, wife of Wm. Ramsey, Oct. 12, 1835-Mar. 15, 1882.

GRAVEYARD AT PIKE'S HILL
Two miles north of McMinnville, Tenn.

Asa Faulkner, Sept. 1, 1808-Oct. 3, 1872.
Anna Faulkner, Feb. 24, 1806-Mar. 25, 1851.
Benjamine Faulkner, Jan. 18, 1832-Sept. 18, 1865.
Wm. Faulkner, Sept. 17, 1814-May 27, 1875.
Edwin Finley Pennebaker, Dec. 8, 1858-Dec. 30, 1872.
Elizabeth Cope, July 2, 1842-June 18, 1908.
James Greer, Aug. 10, 1877-Mar. 25, 1902.
Bettie Greer, Sept. 25, 1852-Mar. 19, 1901.
Josie Zwingle, Sept. 7, 1857-Nov. 25, 1878.
Bennie Zwingle, Nov. 11, 1858-May 23, 1879.
Mary Owen, Dec. 28, 1828-Mar. 3, 1910.
Samuel Mitchell, May 10, 1814-Jan. 7, 1890.
Elizabeth Mitchell, Nov. 2, 1824-Aug. 19, 1900.

PHILADELPHIA GRAVEYARD
Near Vervilla

Redding Bonner, born in North Carolina, Mar. 15, 1787.
Mary M. Faulkner, Oct. 30, 1852-Jan. 9, 1870.
Mary E. Faulkner, Dec. 26, 1826-Sept. 24, 1857; wife of L. L. Faulkner, daughter of Mary and Redding Bonner.
Mary Bonner, wife of Redding Bonner, July 26, 1792-Sept. 1, 1857.
Victoria Logan, Feb. 9, 1858-May 20, 1879.
L. Nix Murphree, Mar. 25, 1814-Oct. 16, 1857.
Redding Bonner, May 16, 1820-Nov. 30, 1899.
Bettie, wife of Redding Bonner, May 29, 1829-Feb. 26, 1893.
E. J. Darnell, Aug. 26, 1843-Feb. 6, 1912.
Mary Lou, wife of A. J. Bonner, Aug. 15, 1855-April 14, 1887.
Josephine Ramsey, wife of H. B. Bonner, Sept. 5, 1855-April 19, 1885.
John McAfee, Nov. 27, 1819-Aug. 13, 1878.
Sarah Ann Faulkner, Jan. 29, 1846-Mar. 30, 1864.
Bilbrey Bonner, Nov. 4, 1852-Mar. 29, 1861.
Mrs. Fatima, wife of J. F. St. John, Oct. 13, 1833-Jan. 26, 1865.
Matilda, wife of Wm. Smoot, Nov. 25, 1822-Nov. 20, 1885.
Mary Rutledge, Oct. 19, 1806-Jan. 22, 1895.

Bible Records—Tombstone Inscriptions

BLUE SPRINGS CHURCHYARD

What was once a Primitive Baptist Church in Viola, Tenn. Most of the stones are gone, or illegible.
William Wooten; died, Dec. 1, 1836; age, 90 years.
George Layne; died, Nov. 28, 1848; age, 72 years.
Patsy, wife of George Layne.
Polly McGehee, daughter of William McGehee, June 26, 1875; died 82 years later.

GWYN FAMILY GRAVEYARD
Near Viola, Tenn.

Ransone Gwyn, son of Fames and Amelia Gwyn; died, Feb. 8, 1872; age, 82 years.
Elizabeth Sheppard, first wife of Ransone Gwyn; died, July 19, 1834; age, 38 years.
Margaret M. Davidson, wife of Hugh Davidson, second wife of Ransone Gwyn; died, April 24, 1868; age, 66 years.

ANTIOCH CEMETERY
Two miles south of Viola, Tenn.

W. H. Wooten, Oct. 11, 1832-Oct. 8, 1862.
Jonathan Wooten, Dec. 20, 1794-April 15, 1877.
Nancy Hampton Wooten, Mar. 3, 1803-Jan. 9, 1885.
Cyrus A. Brown, Feb. 8, 1856-Oct. 2, 1888.
Dr. A. B. Davis, Nov. 18, 1811-Feb. 14, 1873.
Mary E., first wife of Dr. A. B. Davis, Mar. 14, 1825-Nov. 15, 1854.
Martha J., second wife of Dr. A. B. Davis, Sept. 16, 1827-June 19, 1896.

CUNNINGHAM PRIVATE BURYING GROUND
Near Viola, Tenn.

John Cunningham, 1747-Dec. 18, 1842.
Kiziah Cunningham, consort of John Cunningham, Mar. 6, 1758-April 22, 1839.
Langdon Cunningham, born in Charlotte County, Va., April 14, 1783-June 24, 1835.
B. W. Cunningham, April 11, 1788-Aug. 7, 1838.
Langdon Cunningham, Aug. 18, 1813-Oct. 24, 1870.
John Perry Philips, Sept. 8, 1845-Feb. 10, 1896.
Mary J., wife of J. P. Philips, Sept. 11, 1848-Mar. 7, 1912.
Nancy Cunningham, Dec. 2, 1823-Sept. 7, 1873.
John Cunningham, son of L. N. Cunningham, June 6, 1808-Nov. 17, 1868.
Mary, daughter of N. and Martha Mabry, wife of John Cunningham, born in Brunswick County, Va., Nov. 17, 1816-Dec. 15, 1861.
J. L. Cunningham, son of John and Martha Cunningham, Oct. 1, 1840-Mar., 1865.
Ida R., wife of S. H. Gardner, daughter of J. and Martha Cunningham, Dec. 24, 1854-Oct. 14, 1880.
M. Josephine Garritson, daughter of John and Martha Cunningham, June 29, 1838-Aug. 27, 1885.
John R. Cunningham, May 27, 1825-June 16, 1889.
Helen C., daughter of J. and M. Cunningham, wife of C. J. Berry; died, Aug. 17, 1888; age, 39 years.
John R. Fletcher; died, Sept. 17, 1885; age, 36 years.
Mattie, wife of J. R. Fletcher, Mar. 25, 1854-July 17, 1906.
George H. Cunningham; died, June 1, 1887; age, 26 years.
S. A. Cunningham, Mar. 12, 1856-Sept. 19, 1891.
Sarah Elizabeth, daughter of N. W.

Bible Records—Tombstone Inscriptions

and E. W. Williams, and wife of J. E. Cunningham, Dec. 11, 1840-April 24, 1872.
Harrison Kinnard; died, Aug. 13, 1840.
Martha Kinnard, wife of William Kinnard, Mar. 25, 1801-Sept. 7, 1843.
Joseph Kinnard, Mar. 28, 1823-June 22, 1844.
Hinchia, son of N. E. and M. Mabry, born in Virginia, 1817-Aug. 12, 1876.

Janie Albritton, born at Snowhill, Wilcox County, Ala., Oct. 10, 1850; married E. H. Williams of Warren County, Jan. 14, 1874; died near Viola, Mar. 13, 1880.
M. F., wife of E. H. Williams, Dec. 1, 1843-Aug. 30, 1867.
E. H. Williams; died, Feb. 25, 1890; age, 54 years.

OLD WALLING GRAVEYARD
One and one-half miles from Doyle, White County, Tenn.

Thomas Marning Walling, June 10, 1778-Oct. 6, 1855.
Nancy Jones Walling, Jan. 1780-Mar. 29, 1863.
James Walling, Sr., May 17, 1773-Oct. 15, 1849.
Phoebe Jones Walling, 1771-Aug. 17, 1843.
James Walling, May 12, 1793-July 22, 1831.
Phoebe Gist, Oct. 6, 1824-Sept. 12, 1904.

Arethusa Green, May 8, 1838-May 9, 1857.
W. P. Green, Dec. 1, 1832-Dec. 5, 1863.
Isham Rogers; died, 1863.
Rachael Bryant, July 2, 1817-Nov. 15, 1844.
Churchal Randall, Oct. 1806-Sept. 2, 1857.
James Randall, dates illegible.
Polly Randall, dates illegible.

HARDEMAN COUNTY, TENNESSEE
Two and one-half miles from Toone, Tenn.

(Rev. Sol) William Yarbrough, Sr., 1766-Mar. 26, 1859.
Rachael Shelby Yarbrough; died, 1855.

OLD TOWLES FAMILY BURYING GROUND
Near McMinnville, Tenn.

Mary, wife of Arthur Towles, Dec. 25, 1823-Nov. 18, 1879.
Sarah, wife of Joseph Towles, Mar. 18, 1785-Jan. 8, 1848.

Joseph Towles, Feb. 2, 1836-Jan. 15, 1893.
Salie S. Towles, Dec. 23, 1842-Jan. 15, 1899.

BYARS FAMILY BURYING GROUND
Six miles north of McMinnville, Tenn.

Nathan Byars, Dec. 12, 1808-Jan. 12, 1894.
Nancy, wife of Nathan Byars, Mar. 12, 1812-Sept. 9, 1887.
Charlotte, wife of F. P. Byars, Nov. 24, 1856-July 12, 1889.

OLD GRAVEYARD
In southwest suburb of McMinnville, Tenn.

A list as nearly as can be recorded of burials. Records taken from notes of Mrs. Blanche Spurlock Bentley, and from remaining stones. According to tradition, the first burial in this cemetery was that of Samuel Colville,

Bible Records—Tombstone Inscriptions

son of Joseph Colville, born Feb. 8, 1789-June 4, 1813.
Stokeley Donaldson Rowan, son of Henry Rowan, April 14, 1789-1870.
Lucretial Hord, wife of Stokeley D. Rowan, born in Hawkins County; died, 1842.
Jane Caswell Grundy, second wife of Stokeley D. Rowan, widow of James Grundy, son of Hon. Felix Grundy, and great-grandson of Gov. Caswell of North Carolina.
Col. Samuel Henderson, born Feb. 25, 1742, in Granville County, N. C., defender of Boonsboro, Ky., under Daniel Boone. Rescued from the Indians Elizabeth Calloway, whom he afterwards married. Colonel in the Revolutionary War. Brother of Jurist Richard Henderson of North Carolina. In old age lived with his son, Pleasant Henderson, in McMinnville. Died, 1816.
Pleasant Henderson, born in Granville County, N. C.; son of Samuel Henderson, and wife, E. Calloway; married Agnes Robards; died, 1837.
Agnes Robards, wife of Pleasant Henderson; died, 1870.
George Tunley Purvis, born in Amherst County, Va., Dec. 4, 1806-1896, son of Charles Purvis and Wife, Mary Crisp.
Sarah Morris Herndon, wife of George Purvis; died at an advanced age.
Mrs. Sarah Herndon, mother of Sarah H. Purvis; died, Oct. 1, 1851.
Joseph Colville, born in Washington County, Va., July 6, 1764-Jan. 7, 1834.
Samuel Colville, son of Joseph Colville and wife, Sarah Lusk, Feb. 8, 1789-June, 1813.
Mrs. Settle.
M. L. Settle; died, Feb. 23, 1891; age, 75 years.
Elizabeth Settle, wife of Oliver Clark.
Mary Ann Clark Smith, wife of Alexander Black, and daughter of Col. Meriweather Smith and wife, Sally Payne.
Polly Gorden Black; died, 1815; mother of Alexander Black and first woman mentioned in records of Warren County.
Robert B. Cain, son of Wm. and Hannah Cain; born, Feb. 25, 1808, in Kentucky; died in McMinnville, Feb. 25, 1889.
Mary L. Lawrence, wife of Robt. B. Cain; died, 1832; daughter of Dr. Wm. Pitt Lawrence and wife, Nancy Pomroy. (Close relative of the Jackson-Donalson families of Davidson County, Tenn.)
Capt. Wm. White, born in North Carolina, 1750-June 28, 1816; refused pension or to have bullet, received in Revolutionary War, removed from body.
William White, son of Capt. Wm. White and wife, Bathia Lyne, Jan. 20, 1800-July 5, 1863.
Martha, daughter of Thomas Edmondson and wife, Martha Buchanan, wife of William White, Jan. 20, 1800-July 7, 1861.
Martha, daughter of Wm. White and wife, Martha Edmondson; wife of M. D. Hampton, Jan. 19, 1832-June 29, 1863.
George R. Smartt, Dec. 5, 1790-Oct. 30, 1854.
Athelia, wife of George R. Smartt, daughter of Isham Randolph and wife, Sally Payne, 1792-Oct. 4, 1861.
Mary V. Smartt Hill, daughter of George R. and Athelia Smartt, and wife of Brig.-Gen. B. J. Hill, June 13, 1825-Jan. 5, 1880.
Josiah Furman Morford, born in New Jersey, April 4, 1799-April 27, 1869.
Jane Taylor Morford, wife of Josiah Morford, daughter of Col. Edmund Taylor and wife, Polly Robards, Feb. 28, 1808-Aug. 7, 1864.
Comfort Mullins, wife of Mathew Mullins; died, 1816.
Dr. John S. Young, April, 1804-July 7, 1857; Secretary of State of Tennessee.
Walter S. Young, son of John S. Young and wife, Jane Colville Young, Sept. 20, 1832-Oct. 25, 1864.
Archibald Stone, June 5, 1798-July 19, 1868.
Sarah Wood Stone, wife of Archibald Stone, July 12, 1800-Dec. 20, 1879.
John Stone, 1820-1867.
James B. Stone, 1828-1871.
Dillard G. Stone, 1820-1859.
Charity Paine, wife of B. J. Argo, Oct. 3, 1829-Oct. 9, 1875.
J. B. Argo, Mar. 5, 1819-June 6, 1861.
Dr. M. Hill, Nov., 1804-Oct. 8, 1861.

Bible Records—Tombstone Inscriptions

Mary, wife of Dr. M. Hill, 1813-Sept. 9, 1835.
Robert E. Titus, Oct. 10, 1815-Sept. 3, 1843.
Joshua M. Coffee, 1789-Oct. 3, 1842.
Jane Trousdale, wife of J. Coffee.
Ellen Langdon Powell, wife of Rev. John Powell, born in Middlebury, Vt., Mar. 7, 1826-Feb. 20, 1873.
Miss Bettie Langdon, born in Middlebury, Mass., Jan. 18, 1797-July 2, 1863.
Sarah Allen Shaw, wife of James Clare Spurlock, and daughter of John Lyle Shaw and wife, Sarah Davidson; died, 1884.
Drewy Clare Spurlock, son of James C. and Sarah S. Spurlock, Jan. 23, 1835. Killed at battle of Murfreesboro, Dec. 3, 1862; Captain of Company C, Savage's 16th Regiment, Tenn.
Chamberlain J. Spurlock, son of James C. and Sarah A. Spurlock, April 15, 1842-Mar. 5, 1873. In Savage's Reg., 16th Tenn. C. S. A.
Rebecca Brown Wharton, wife of Samuel Wharton; Revolutionary War soldier. (Statement of historian, Shawnee Chapter, Murfreesboro, Tenn.)
John S. Shaw, 1780-1852. In War of 1812.
Elizabeth, wife of J. M. Evans, Jan. 25, 1818-Nov. 5, 1853.
Jane Armstrong, wife of Landy Waters; married, 1845; died, 1884.
Dr. J. L. Jones, Mar. 16, 1831-Sept. 16, 1902.
Fannie, wife of J. L. Jones, born in Overton County, Tenn., April 16, 1836-Jan. 12, 1861.
Thomas North Clark; died, 1834.
Elizabeth Clark, wife of T. N. Clark; died, 1831.
Addison B. Howell.
Elizabeth Etter Howell.
Dr. Thomas Boyd; died, 1831.
Mary Hopkins French, wife of Robt. French, daughter of Col. John Hopkins and wife, Mary King, of Nelson County, Va.; died, 1850.
Landon A. Kincannon.
Cyrena Robertson Kincannon.
Sion Spencer Read, son of Capt. John Nash Read and wife, Elizabeth.
Julia Spencer, born in Charlotte County, Va., April 22, 1791-Aug. 27, 1843; married his cousin Hardenia Jefferson Spencer.

Hardeman J. Spencer, wife of Sion Spencer Read; died, Sept. 6, 1889; age, 83 years. (Married a second time to Dr. M. Hill.)
Harriet Read, wife of Dillard Stone. (Married a second time, Samuel Pennybaker.)
Samuel Pennybaker, born Mar., 1834-Sept. 11, 1867.
John Cain; died, 1836.
Beersheba Porter Sullivan, wife of John Cain.
Hiram B. Stubblefield, Sept. 25, 1814-June 17, 1861.
Jane Bowie, wife of Elisha B. Hammer, June 26, 1858-Oct. 30, 1873.
Joseph Brown, Oct. 8, 1824-Nov. 11, 1875.
Lucinda Tabitha Atnip, Mar. 18, 1840-July 8, 1870.
Lorenza Dow Mercer, born in Wayne County, Ky., Nov. 23, 1810; died, ——; son of Richard and Mary Mercer.
Anne Hord, wife of L. D. Mercer, born in Hawkins County, Tenn.; died, Feb. 18, 1851; age, 28 years.
Elza H. Mercer; died, Feb. 18, 1857; age, 40 years. (Lieut. in Capt. Andrew Northcutt Company in 1st Tennessee Reg., Mexican War.)
John L. Stubblefield; died, Dec. 13, 1859; age, 47 years.
Philo Risley Lyon, July 4, 1870-Jan. 8, 1869; wife of James Lyon, daughter of Benj. Risley and wife, Eunice Grant; a noted New England family.
Laura Matilda Lyon, daughter of James and Philo Lyon, born in Saratoga, N. Y., Jan. 5, 1796-Nov. 21, 1840; wife of Wood Furman.
Eliza Jane Lyon, daughter of James and Philo Lyon, born in Washington City, Nov. 17, 1801; wife of Edward J. Cotton; married second time to Solomon Mitchell.
John Wesley Mitchell, June 4, 1821-June 9, 1885.
Nancy Mitchell, wife of J. P. Lively, daughter of Salmon Mitchell; died, Feb. 15, 1863; age, 33 years.
Phily Hoodenpyl, Sept. 29, 1818-Oct. 29, 1873.
John Mabry; died, Oct. 1, 1841. (Set his Negroes free that they might be sent to Liberia.)
Wm. T. Lone, born in Virginia, Dec. 18, 1834-May 27, 1869.

Bible Records--Tombstone Inscriptions

Isham Randolph and wife, Sally Payne.
James Rodgers, son of John Rodgers and wife, (Mrs.) Ann Clendenning; born in Greenbriar County, Va.; married first Jane Brown; second, Margaret Campbell, daughter of Judge David Campbell of Campbells Station, E. Tennessee; died in McMinnville.
Robert Alexander Campbell, born in Richmond, Va., in 1812; son of James Austen Campbell and wife, Massie Vaughn, of Nelson County, Va.; died in McMinnville about 1843.
Wife of Robert A. Campbell.
Andrew Jeffries Marchbanks, born in Jackson, Tenn.; died, Jan. 6, 1867.
Catherine, wife of A. J. Marchbanks, daughter of George Savage and wife, Elizabeth Kenner Savage.
Martha Camp (widow Flournoy), second wife of Andrew J. Marchbanks.
Rachael Shebby Edmondson, wife of James Powell Thompson, born in Davidson County, Tenn., in 1804; daughter of Thomas Edmondson and wife, Martha Buchanan; died in McMinnville, 1859.
Capt. John Lucas Thompson, born, 1833, son of James P. Thompson and wife, Rachael Shebby Edmondson; died in McMinnville, 1886. In Savage's 16th Tenn. Reg. C. S. A.
Joshua Stone Harrison, born in Pittsylvania County, Va.; son of Amworth Harrison and wife, Dolly Coleman Stone; died in McMinnville.
Judith Turner Harrison, wife of Joshua Stone Harrison.
From Records of Mrs. Blanche S. Bentley.

RIVERSIDE CEMETERY
McMinnville, Tenn.

C. R. Morford, Nov. 25, 1840-Jan., 1900.
Florence Spurlock, wife of C. R. Morford; died, Nov. 17, 1881.
Josiah Furman Morford, Mar. 25, 1835-Sept. 19, 1897.
Ann Lusk, wife of J. F. Morford, Mar. 25, 1835-Sept. 19, 1897.
W. F. Whitson.
Rebecca Morford, Oct. 19, 1849-Mar. 29, 1892.
J. E. Jones, Mar. 3, 1843-Feb. 6, 1922.
N. R. Taylor, May 31, 1851-April 23, 1886.
Dr. John B. Armstrong, Jan. 20, 1819-Dec. 18, 1873.
His wife, Maria Ready, 1813-1885.
Phillip Hoodenpyl, 1830-1881.
James H. Smith, 1838-1899.
His wife, Sarah Fite, 1833-1911.
William G. Brittain, 1827-1904.
His wife, Mary, 1833-1890.
Martha Jane Bain, 1814-1881.
William Clark, 1846-1929.
Lou Goodbar Clark, 1851-1918.
Patrick Coffee, Sept. 21, 1821-Feb. 27, 1895.
Hannah Black, June 22, 1856-May 26, 1881.
Harriet Reams Leftwich, Dec. 8, 1838-Mar. 1, 1892.
Chatham Coffee, Dec. 14, 1825-Mar. 6, 1889.
Mary Evelyn Coffee, Sept 22, 1831-June 25, 1890.
Alex. Coffee, Feb. 10, 1835-Mar. 24, 1909.
Leila Coffee, wife of G. W. Lewis, Aug. 14, 1858-Dec. 12, 1929.
W. P. Brewer, Mar. 4, 1855-Sept. 17, 1883.
Joseph Newton, 1802-1893.
His wife, Mary Maguire, 1824-1889.
Mrs. Nancy Jones, 1800-1881.
W. P. Faulkner, 1838-1904.
Mary A. Faulkner, 1846-1912.
Martha Walling, wife of W. R. Faulkner, 1844-1896.
Leonard Owen, 1831-1904.
Margaret Owen, 1830.
James DeBard, 1800-1883.
Eliza DeBard, 1814-1887.
Legil Smith, 1810-1891.
Lucinda Smith, 1817-1887.
David Wallace, 1828-1918.
Susan Murray Wallace, 1835-1893.
Jesse Walling, 1841-1930.
Bettie Winton Walling, 1847.
Judge S. J. Walling, 1813-1891.
H. L. Walling, 1832-1923.
Nancy Ann Miller, his wife, 1838-1916.

Bible Records—Tombstone Inscriptions

Capt. L. H. Meadows; died, Oct. 12, 1888; age, 54 years.
Edward Munford, Oct. 16, 1820-Nov. 4, 1887.
Mary Elizabeth Mumford, Aug. 15, 1822-July 2, 1900.
James DeBard, Mar. 30, 1846-Feb. 8, 1907.
Nancy Fitzpatrick DeBard, Dec. 19, 1808-June 4, 1894.
Dr. J. B. Ritchey, Dec. 2, 1830-Mar. 24, 1909.
Myra Smartt Ritchey, Dec. 10, 1837-Aug. 18, 1925.
James J. Womack, July 7, 1834-July 18, 1922.
Jennie G. Womack, Mar. 14, 1844-July 18, 1905.
Clara, wife of W. S. Gillespie, daughter of W. D. Chadwick, July 26, 1853-Aug. 24, 1882.
Wm. Henry Meadows, Aug. 17, 1848-Aug. 31, 1914.
Susan Argo, Mar. 18, 1820-Nov. 22, 1887.
Irin Argo, Feb. 17, 1817.
Rev. Wm. D. Chadwick, D.D., Jan. 22, 1817-Sept. 4, 1878.
May J. Chadwick, Aug. 21, 1818-Oct. 28, 1905.
Cynthia Colville Ramsey, May 22, 1829-Dec. 16, 1878.
Andrew Brown Ramsey, May 22, 1862-Sept. 18, 1926.
Elizabeth Brown Ramsey, Nov. 10, 1856-Dec. 29, 1912.
Robert B. Womack, Jan. 21, 1849-Sept. 5, 1902.
H. Hacket Ross, April 1, 1862-April 1, 1932.
Julia Cannon Ross, June 4, 1870-April 4, 1910.
John F. Brown, Sept. 22, 1828-April 3, 1888.
Nancy A. Brown, Jan. 23, 1826-May 26, 1906.
Susan Colville, wife of J. C. Ramsey, 1822-1903.
J. C. M. Ross, June 21, 1830-Jan. 19, 1914.
Laura Colville Ross, Dec. 19, 1835-Dec. 9, 1904.
Thomas Christian Lynn, 1842-1903.
Clara B. Davis, July 19, 1815-June 3, 1882.
Dr. Thomas Black, June 13, 1837-Feb. 27, 1904.
Emma Young, wife of Thomas Black, May 6, 1845-Feb. 26, 1918.
O. H. Ruster, 1824-1899.
Jane Ramsey Rusber, 1828-1909.
James H. Haggard, 1808-1895.
Parmelia Haggard, 1824-1906.
M. D. Smallman, 1838-1928.
Cornelia A. Magness, wife of M. D. Smallman, 1850-1893.
Asabel R. Hammer, 1858-1917.
Sallie Hammer, 1859-1924.
Joseph Tuck, May 1, 1831-May 22, 1888.
Laura Tuck, June 20, 1845-May 25, 1914.
Martin A. Morrow, Jan. 2, 1828-June 7, 1907.
Ann Morrow, May 9, 1828-Sept. 25, 1906.
Wm. Henry Meadows, Aug. 17, 1848-Aug. 31, 1914.
James H. DeBard, Mar. 30, 1846-Feb. 8, 1907.
Dr. J. B. Ritchey, Dec. 10, 1837-Aug. 4, 1925.
Mary Dozia Walling Parmer, July 1, 1836-April 17, 1876.
Mrs. Nancy Jones; died, Sept. 17, 1881; age, 81 years.
H. H. Faulkner, 1840-1913.
Harriet Green, wife of Joseph Walling, Feb. 16, 1835-July 16, 1899.
Eliza J. Smallman, wife of N. W. Griswold, Mar. 8, 1834-Mar. 14, 1904.
Lucinda Jones, wife of O. M. Thurman, Sept. 27, 1835-Nov. 11, 1924.
O. M. Thurman, April 22, 1827-July 4, 1895.
Martha Evelyn Howard, Feb. 13, 1845-Jan 22, 1920.
J. W. Howard, Oct. 11, 1843-Mar. 31, 1902.
A. L. Howard, Jan. 14, 1837-Feb. 28, 1880.
Eliza Howard A. Howard, 1818-1893.
Thomas Burroughs, Nov. 25, 1831-May 9, 1893.
Nancy Burroughs, July 27, 1838-Mar. 16, 1919.
Cyrus McClarty, April 13, 1838-Aug. 26, 1890.
Sarah Elizabeth McClarty, Mar. 6, 1847-June 21, 1897.
Francis Bell, Mar. 17, 1816-Sept. 11, 1873.
Bettie Colville, Feb. 21, 1823.

Bible Records—Tombstone Inscriptions

W. M. Gross, Dec. 2, 1815-Sept. 19, 1877.
Mollie Green, wife of I. A. Gross, April 9, 1847-Oct. 2, 1886.
Susan, wife of J. G. Brooks, July 8, 1845-Jan. 2, 1882.
Anglina, wife of P. H. Price, daughter of George and Amelia Smartt, mother of George Stroud, Jan. 2, 1823-June 23, 1908.
Wm. H. Smith, Nov. 2, 1832-Mar. 23, 1873.
Henry Smith, Sept. 24, 1802-Oct. 3, 1880.
Robert Park, Nov. 29, 1826-May 23, 1902.
Eliza Park, July 22, 1834-May 23, 1910.
Louisa Stroud, wife of G. W. Hoodenpyl, Feb. 18, 1839-July 17, 1870.
George W. Hoodenpyl, Mar. 25, 1833-Nov. 10, 1907.
Isaac Thurman, Aug. 14, 1858-Aug. 27, 1920.
Ella Brown, wife of James L. Witten, July 22, 1837-Jan. 31, 1914.
Margaret Bonner, Sept. 22, 1836-Dec. 22, 1916.
Rufus Bonner, May 9, 1823-May 3, 1911.
Hyson McAfee, Feb. 13, 1844-Feb. 12, 1911.
Lucy McAfee, Dec. 31, 1846-Oct. 17, 1921.
Lerr Smith, 1835-1911.
Laura Argo Harwell, July 2, 1843-May 14, 1917.
Mary Jane Faulkner, Nov. 26, 1847-Sept. 7, 1925.
Thomas H. Faulkner, April 19, 1842-Nov. 27, 1889.
Elvan Potter, Oct. 29, 1845-May 26, 1914.
Mollie A. Fisher Potter, June 26, 1847-Jan. 7, 1920.
Elizabeth Cantrell, wife of H. P. Cantrell, April 2, 1850-Dec. 2, 1922.
Isaac Lister, Feb. 15, 1849-Sept. 10, 1925.
Sarah E. Lister, Mar. 31, 1853-Mar. 24, 1923.
Samuel Alexander, Mar. 22, 1833-Feb. 5, 1918.
Ruth Sewell Alexander, Oct. 1, 1842-April 23, 1895.
G. A. Davey, Feb. 19, 1843-Dec. 20, 1915.
Anna Cummings Davey, June 30, 1826-June 30, 1904.
G. G. Davey, Jan. 18, 1822-Nov. 30, 1881.
G. G. Davey, Jr., July 1, 1858-July 13, 1916.
James A. Jones, Sept. 15, 1838-June 21, 1917.
Harriet M. Martin, wife of James A. Jones, Sept. 6, 1839-Sept. 15, 1900.
Lutie Ann Northcut, wife of James A. Hughes, Dec. 16, 1835-Jan. 15, 1891.
James Hamilton Hughes, born in Rockingham, Va., Dec. 15, 1837-Jan. 15, 1891.
John F. Wilson, Mar. 15, 1830-Feb. 22, 1910.
Nathaniel Patterson; died, July 2, 1917; age, 70 years.
Joshua Reynolds, Oct. 13, 1837-Nov. 20, 1907.
Belle Faulkner Reynolds, Oct. 30, 1843.
A. J. Bonner, Nov. 11, 1831-Sept. 20, 1914.
James Ewing Clift, Sept., 1853.
Olie Clife; died, Mar. 25, 1879.
Maj. Joseph Goodbar, July 12, 1837-Dec. 10, 1861; major of 16th Tenn. C. S. A.
Jane McKinney Goodbar, Oct. 7, 1811-Nov. 28, 1867.
Mary Goodbar, wife of Thomas Murray, 1829-1878.
Wm. L. Swan, Dec. 22, 1828-Dec. 26, 1922.
Cynthia, wife of W. L. Swan, 1828-1902.
Amanda, wife of W. A. Connell, 1855-1925.
Mary Colville Womack, 1848-1923.
Mrs. Nuttie Colville, Feb. 12, 1797-Jan. 23, 1884.
Amanda Colville, wife of Samuel Colville, and daughter of Young and Nuttie Colville, Oct. 16, 1825-Oct. 4, 1887.
Samuel Colville, born in McMinnville, Aug. 4, 1819-1896.
Thomas Turner, born in Windsor County, Vt., May 4, 1797-Feb. 16, 1882.
Abbey E. Turner, born in Chatham County, N. C., July 28, 1803-Oct. 9, 1883.
Jane, wife of A. B. Brown, Nov. 25, 1822-Dec. 15, 1894.
Absolem Duskin Brown, Jan. 26, 1848-Sept. 12, 1889.
Hannah, wife of J. L. Garrett, Feb. 5, 1843-Mar. 13, 1893.

148

Bible Records—Tombstone Inscriptions

James Garrett, Feb. 22, 1843-Aug. 2, 1926.
Thomas Hubble; born, 1845.
Anne Walling Hubble, 1854-1895.
Elizabeth Thompson, wife of Col. Ed. J. Wood, Dec. 27, 1831-Nov. 16, 1898.
Edmund J. Wood, May 15, 1828-May 12, 1894.
Robert Thompson, 1828-1895.
Hattie, wife of Prof. W. E. Bell, 1860-1888.
Sallie Wood, wife of J. S. Doyle; died, Feb. 24, 1888.
Wm. H. Magness, 1824-1891.
Elizabeth West Magness, 1826-1887.
Ella Magness Sims; died, 1901.
Edgar Magness; died, 1914.
Emma Young Seitz, 1842-1909.
A. P. Seitz, 1832-1898.
Mary, wife of P. B. Gingrich, born in Canada, 1841-1888.
George Savage; born, 1786, in Woodstock, Va.; died, 1873.
Elizabeth Kenner Savage, 1791-1887.
Abram Monroe Savage, 1818-1857.
Owen Watkins Davis, 1826-1884.
Elizabeth Savage Davis, 1831-1909.
John H. Savage, 1815-1904.
Andrew J. Marchbanks, 1804-1867.
John Barclay Armstrong, born in Giles County, Tenn., 1819-1878.; son of John Armstrong and wife, Mary Armstrong McCall; G. G., son of Col. Martin Armstrong (Revolutionary soldier).
Maria Ready, wife of Barclay Armstrong, and daughter of Hon. Charles Ready of Readyville, Tenn., and wife, Mary Palmer.
Alfred Payne, son of Wm. and Orpha Payne; born in East Tennessee; died in McMinnville, 18—.
Myra Billingsley Randolph, wife of Alfred Payne, and daughter of Isham Randolph and wife, Sally Payne. (Only a small stone to the memory of Orville Sydenham Payne, infant of Alfred Payne and wife Myra, remains intact.)
James Powell Thompson, born in Amherst County, Va., Feb. 2, 1792-Feb. 2, 1882; son of John Thompson of County Antrim, Ireland and wife, Rebecca. Edwards Powell, descendant of Wm. Edwards, Burgess of Surry County, Va. James Powell Thompson once owned the land upon which "Riverside Cemetery" is located. Rebecca Thompson, daughter of James Powell Thompson, and wife, Rachael Shebby Edmundson, is buried here.
John Lyle Spurlock, Nov. 11, 1829-June 12, 1871; son of James Clare Spurlock and wife, Sarah Allen Shaw, and grandson of Drewry Spurlock and wife, Olive Clare.
Louise Thompson, wife of John Lyle Spurlock, and daughter of James Powell Thompson and wife, Rachel Shebby Edmundson, Aug. 21, 1831-Oct. 10, 1910.
Lyle Spurlock; born, Nov. 12, 1856; son of J. L. Spurlock and wife, Louise Thompson.
John Eldridge Bentley, born in Huntsville, Ala., Nov. 11, 1846-Nov. 5, 1890; son of John Gay Bentley and wife, Judith Bolling Bentley.

Viola Cemetery
Sent in from Miss Sarah Robinson

Mary Esther Bonner, July 2, 1847-Dec. 12, 1910.
Andrew H. Bonner, 1856-1911.
Hanna W. Bonner; born, 1856.
L. P. Sain, Feb. 11, 1853-Oct. 12, 1906.
John L. Prater, 1858-1930.
Nannie Prater, 1865-1911.
Sarah Stubblefield, July 21, 1862-Feb. 1, 1925.
James R. Stubblefield, born March 8, 1861.
Frank Mitchell, born in Germany, Aug. 7, 1817-Mar. 3, 1897.
William Ramsey, Mar. 9, 1832-April 30, 1908.
Mary Taylor, wife of William Ramsey, Feb. 22, 1841-May 6, 1913.
Mary A., wife of H. J. Thaxton, Aug. 3, 1841-Oct. 30, 1923.
Sarah Hiltson, Mar. 9, 1836-Aug. 8, 1918.
W. R. Cunningham, May 19, 1858-Jan. 17, 1929.
John M. Ramsey, Nov. 7, 1864-July 1, 1911.
J. G. Mitchell, Dec. 28, 1833-Mar. 12,

Bible Records—Tombstone Inscriptions

1898.
M. J. Mitchell, June 18, 1844-Mar. 22, 1901.
David W. Ramsey, Aug. 6, 1868-Sept. 21, 1895.
E. W. Smartt, 1841-1913.
Chas. C. Ramsey, Mar. 5, 1846-May 14, 1917.
Clariss Bragg, wife of Chas. Ramsey, Jan. 29, 1842-Dec. 5, 1918.
T. W. Laurence, Dec. 22, 1843-Feb. 21, 1912.
Mary J. Laurence, Dec. 25, 1845-Dec. 19, 1919.
John Rutledge, Mar. 28, 1835-June 27, 1912.
Nannie Rutledge, Dec. 7, 1848.
A. J. Ramsey, Sr., Mar. 1, 1828-Nov. 9, 1895.
Lou A. Ramsey, June 27, 1843.
Lockey Smith, Sept. 29, 1821-Nov. 28, 1905.
Amanda Bradford, 1845-Feb. 13, 1908.
Louise, wife of J. F. Bogle, July 19, 1841-July 20, 1920.
J. F. Bogle, 1840-Dec. 11, 1903.
Charlie M. Turner, Nov. 8, 1859-Nov. 8, 1905.
N. C. Brewer, wife of J. T. St. John, July 29, 1850-Oct. 3, 1901.
J. T. St. John; born, Sept. 20, 1829.
Christian Brewer, Feb. 14, 1830-Nov. 1, 1898.
S. M. Beadford, June 9, 1870-Aug. 13, 1897.

David Ramsey, Dec. 1, 1828-Feb. 13, 1911.
Emma Macon, Nov. 12, 1858-Aug. 27, 1910.
Nannie M. Gannawey, Sept. 3, 1860-Mar. 16, 1905.
Dr. I. E., son of J. F. and Fatima St. John, Oct. 26, 1862-July 25, 1899.
Mary D. Hill Hughes, Sept. 28, 1866-Mar. 12, 1911.
J. P. Hughes, Mar. 14, 1860-Dec. 11, 1914.
P. H. Winton, 1841-1918.
Andrew George Brown, Jan. 21, 1865-Aug. 28, 1903.
Joe A. Doyle, Feb. 15, 1847-Feb. 21, 1899.
Dr. W. H. Moore, Mar. 14, 1853-Feb. 11, 1910.
Jennie Witherspoon, Sept. 18, 1858-Jan. 26, 1903.
Hattie G. Ramsey, Oct. 26, 1851-May 18, 1910.
David A. Ramsey, Jan. 30, 1840-Nov. 23, 1906.
George W. Ramsey, Dec. 22, 1833-July 24, 1912.
Elizabeth King, wife of George Ramsey, Sept. 12, 1838-Feb. 12, 1926.
R. G. Wooten, May 25, 1856-Mar. 6, 1926.
Tillie W. Wooten, Dec. 8, 1858-Jan. 23, 1923.
J. R. West, Oct. 27, 1858-June 7, 1904.

DIBRELL BURYING GROUND

Ten miles north of McMinnville, Tenn. Sent by Miss Sarah Robinson.

Jim Haley, 1854-1920.
Didama Badger, Sept. 20, 1831-Jan. 10, 1899.
Telisha Webb, July 8, 1823-Dec. 21, 1882.
John B. Webb, Mar. 25, 1823-April 1, 1900.
J. B. Grissom, Mar. 31, 1858-Nov. 30, 1906.
H. G. Stevens, Aug. 18, 1842-Oct., 1919.
Tennessee Stevens, April 24, 1844-Sept. 22, 1927.
J. F. Reeder, Sept. 22, 1858-June 6, 1931.
Nancy H. Reeder, May 3, 1852-April 18, 1920.

E. L. Guntrie, Jan. 30, 1854-Sept. 11, 1922.
Lucinda Guntrie, Mar. 10, 1856-June 16, 1906.
J. B. Cantrell, April 18, 1862-Aug. 25, 1910.
Lissie Goodson, 1884-1930.
Daniel Odum, May 5, 1827-Oct. 12, 1904.
Mary B. Odum; died, Jan. 16, 1904.
John F. Sullivan, July 24, 1863-July 23, 1926.
Rev. T. L. Kidwell, Mar. 9, 1854-July 6, 1906.
Maude Phillips, April 30, 1871-April 7, 1921.

Bible Records—Tombstone Inscriptions

Thomas Mullican, July 28, 1864-Dec. 26, 1899.
Rachel Bass, Jan. 9, 1831-Mar. 17, 1911.
John W. Bass, Nov. 24, 1824-Feb. 17, 1907.
Elder T. P. Potter, Mar. 14, 1854-May 22, 1911.
Irvin Gribble, Aug. 16, 1823-Aug. 30, 1890.
Mary Gribble, Aug. 17, 1823-June 16, 1904.
Mrs. Malvinie Potter, June 15, 1848-Mar. 2, 1911.
Della Bryant, May 18, 1881-June 20, 1894.
G. L. Bryant, June 11, 1847-Jan. 25, 1885.
Belle Webb, wife of Isham Gribble, Feb. 14, 1866-Jan. 5, 1927.
Mrs. F. C. Slatton; born, July 8, 1931; age, 88 years.
J. H. Slatton; died, Dec. 4, 1912; age, 39 years.
Preshia, wife of Wm. Sparkman, Sept. 16, 1813-Dec. 23, 1857.
Wm. Sparkman, July 21, 1881-June 24, 1883.
James Webb, Dec. 25, 1815-Sept. 6, 1902.
Mary Webb, Mar. 31, 1828-Aug. 31, 1897.
John R. Grizzell, Dec. 16, 1850-May 20, 1913.
Jane Webb, wife of John Grizzell, Oct. 10, 1845-Oct. 5, 1895.
G. G. Fisher, M.D., Feb. 19, 1888-Oct. 10, 1915.
P. G. Potter, Sept. 27, 1842-Mar. 16, 1924.
Osel, wife of S. T. West, May 28, 1866-Oct. 30, 1898.
Thomas Davis, April 16, 1840-Jan. 17, 1892.
Eliza Davis, Dec. 18, 1842-Oct. 20, 1906.
Isaac Glenn, Aug. 3, 1852-Mar. 26, 1913.
Elizabeth, wife of Isaac Glenn, Mar. 20, 1850-Nov. 30, 1916.
H. J. Webb, Jan. 1, 1851-Oct. 11, 1904.
Nelson Aecorn, Oct. 14, 1842-Feb. 24, 1923.
Mary H., wife of Nelson Aecorn, Nov. 29, 1850-Feb. 28, 1923.
S. W. Anderson, July 4, 1829-Aug. 13, 1919.
Perry G. Green; died, Jan. 8, 1929; age, 41 years.
W. M. Harden; died, Feb. 20, 1933; age, 80 years.
Isaac Glenn, Aug. 3, 1852-Mar. 26, 1913.
Elizabeth, wife of Isaac Glenn, Mar. 20, 1850-Nov. 30, 1916.
H. J. Webb, Jan. 1, 1851-Oct. 11, 1904.
Mary H., wife of Nelson Aecorn, Nov. 29, 1850-Feb. 28, 1923.
Mrs. W. M. Pinegar; died, Feb. 7, 1931; age, 72 years.
John L. Byars, Nov. 10, 1846-Mar. 18, 1902.
Wm. Pinegar, Oct. 5, 1844-June 19, 1931.
R. L. Reynolds; died, Mar. 29, 1927; age, 70 years.
Mary L. Reynolds; died, April 24, 1932; age, 72 years, 6 months, 20 days.
Melvinia Van Hooser; died, June 10, 1933; age, 86 years.
Chas. Harden, Oct. 16, 1887-July 13, 1927.
T. B. Bounds, July 1, 1824-Dec. 23, 1895.
Mary Bounds, Sept. 6, 1826-Dec. 17, 1906.
W. C. Bounds, April 22, 1847-Sept. 22, 1922.
H. J. Mullican; died, July 25, 1932; age, 83 years, 10 months, 5 days.
Mrs. Ophie Dunlap; died, Jan. 31, 1930; age, 35 years.
James N. Cope, Dec. 21, 1857-Sept. 12, 1930.
Mrs. Cymantha Boren; died, Aug. 16, 1933; age, 68 years, 6 months, 28 days.
Josie Tittsworth, June 15, 1859-Mar. 15, 1913.
Mattie Bass Webb, wife of I. G. Webb, June 20, 1859-Mar. 19, 1919.
Nannie Helen, wife of W. H. Flanders, April 29, 1857-Oct. 12, 1905.

Bible Records—Tombstone Inscriptions

PINE BLUFF, MCMINNVILLE

Pine Bluff is one and one-half miles west of Rock Island on the old Campaign Road. By Mrs. James Elkins.

Mary M. Sherrell, Mar. 14, 1838-May 17, 1916.
Mark M. Sherrell, Oct. 30, 1841-Dec. 9, 1910.
William M. Hash, 1827-1898.
John Hash, 1856-1878.
Mary E. Mason, Jan. 2, 1846-Sept. 25, 1860.
Mrs. S. G. Mason, June 19, 1825-April 20, 1897.
Mrs. Mary Lettice Mason, Aug. 14, 1835-June 18, 1920.
Lewis Chapel Mason, Feb. 22, 1825-Mar. 3, 1913.
John A. Sesson, June 30, 1841-Aug. 1, 1868.
Mrs. T. A. Crawford, Oct. 30, 1832-Dec. 19, 1901.
T. E. Hash, Dec. 16, 1866-Jan. 10, 1925.
Melvin Hash, April 11, 1818-May 7, 1880.
L. V. A. Hash, Feb. 14, 1841-June 26, 1905; wife of Melvin Hash.
Alice G. Moore, Sept. 28, 1866-June 19, 1914; wife of James Crawford, saved Aug. 19, 1882, married Jan. 4, 1905.
S. (?) L. Crawford, Feb. 25, 1874-Feb. 24, 1904.
J. A. Jones, June 17, 1849-June 25, 1918.
Mrs. M. J. Jones, Mar. 25, 1851, ——.

SHILOH

The land was given by Frederick Stepp for the Shiloh Cemetery. The first church was built in 1809 and was a Primitive Baptist and Methodist. Bishop Asberry visited this church. Two other churches have been built and the third church is now standing. Henry Waterhouse preached in the present church when he was a circuit rider. Later he was president of Emory and Henry College.

Copper Scott, 1805-1886.
Sara McCallum, 1808-1850; wife of Copper Scott.
David Coppinger, 1822-1883.
Mary Stepp, 1813-1857.
Jacob Wanamaker, Mar. 5, 1793-Dec. 23, 1893.
Sanford Perry, Dec. 2, 1816-Nov. 25, 1880.
John Madewell, Mar., 1818-Jan. 31, 1901.
Sarah Cagle, Jan. 28, 1813-Aug. 16, 1869.
R. N. Cartwright, 1801-1871.
Elizabeth Cartwright, 1810-1863; wife of R. N. Cartwright.
C. W. Clendenen, 1838-1900.
Eliza (Barnes) Clendenen, 1842-1912.

BROWN CEMETERY

Near the Shiloh Cemetery is the old Brown Cemetery. Absolem Brown and wife, Mary, and the Lovelards are buried here.

PHILADELPHIA

Philadelphia is thirteen miles south of McMinnville in Grundy County. This church is Primitive Baptist and Methodist.

John Dykes, Dec. 15, 1814-Mar. 16, 1862.
Nellie Dykes, Jan. 13, 1818-April 5, 1902.

Bible Records—Tombstone Inscriptions

Susana South Lane, June 30, 1822-Sept. 28, 1874.
Losson Gross, Dec. 25, 1812-Sept. 5, 1894.
Hannah Gross, 1825, ——.
William Morton, 1808-Dec. 8, 1880.
Nancy Smith, 1799-1879.
Asa Gross, July 25, 1821-Dec. 30, 1885.
Sara Louise Bost, Feb. 8, 1833-Feb. 8, 1918; wife of Asa Gross.
Holman Lockhart, Feb. 9, 1824-Mar. 24, 1914.
Nancy Lockhart, May 16, 1830-Feb. 8, 1914.
Mary Wimberly (Cain), 1838-1912.
John Wimberly, 1834-1905.
William S. Cain, 1856-1918.
J. L. Coppinger, 1848-1928.
Sarah Coppinger, 1839-1878.
Rachel (Nunelly) Coppinger, 1817-1874.
Jesse Coppinger, 1812-1865.
Alexander Coppinger, 1838-Mar. 4, 1865; killed in the Civil War.
Adam Moffitt, 1841-1866.
J. B. W. Bond, 1831-1911.
Nancy Nunelly, 1840-1856; wife of W. C. Nunelly.
J. J. Nunelly, 1836-1868; son of Jesse and Belle Nunelly.
Robert Dugan, 1814-1861; born in Buncomb County, N. C.
Prudence Dykes, 1782-1862.
Isom Dykes, 1773-1871.
John Hobbs, 1832-1882.
Rachel Williams, 1835-1909.
Jeremiah Walker.
Mary Dugan, 1791-1829; wife of Wm. Dugan.
Wm. Dugan, 1785-1867; born in South Carolina.
Wm. Patrick, 1828-1886; son of E. D. and M. A. Patrick.
Wm. Morton, 1808-1880; born in North Carolina.
Prudie Lockhart, 1866-1898.
Squire Monroe Lockhart, 1856-1885.
James Lockhart, 1875, ——.
Elijah Walker, 1811-1882.
Mary C. Walker, 1831-1913.
Samuel Walker, 1839-1912.
Sarah E. Barnes, 1863-1885; wife of N. B. Barnes.
Polly Ann Killian, 1841-1891; wife of J. D. Killian.
A. H. Killian, 1814-1891.
Major James Tate, ——, April 19, 1849.
Mary Tate, wife of J. W. M. Tate.
J. W. M. Tate, 1827-1873.
Sarah Gross, 1790-1868; wife of John Gross.
John Gross, 1780-1874.

Liberty

Liberty is a Cumberland Presbyterian Church. It lies two and one-half miles south of McMinnville.

Thomas Hopkins, May 13, 1764-Mar. 16, 1836; born in Goochland County, Va.; came to Tennessee early in life; soon became a speculator in land.
Major Lusk Colville, May 27, 1791-July 5, 1865.
James Colville, Jan. 22, 1822-Aug. 18, 1859; son of Lusk.
Ann Caroline Colville, Feb. 2, 1824-Dec. 1, 1843; daughter of Lusk Colville and Cynthia Hacket Colville.
Cynthia Hacket, Dec. 14, 1792-Sept. 26, 1842.
Martha Colville, second wife of Joseph Colville, first wife of Francis Smartt; mother of Wm. Cheek Smartt.
David Vance McLean, Nov. 28, 1801-April 29, 1871; second husband of Margaret Davidson Smartt.
Margaret Davidson Smartt McLean
Gwynn, Dec. 26, 1807-May 14, 1881.
(Francis) Frank Smartt, Aug. 8, 1805-Mar. 17, 1843.
Gen. Wm. Cheek Smartt, Nov. 13 1785-June 8, 1863.
Peggy Colville (Margaret) Smart — Feb. 22, 1827; first wife of Wm. Cheek Smartt, about 40 years of age at death
Elizabeth Smartt, Feb. 22, 1791-May 1, 1864; second wife of Wm. Cheek Smartt.
Octavia Smartt, Oct. 20, 1829-Mar. 13, 1857; first wife of S. McRamsey.
S. McRamsey, Jan. 13, 1831-Dec. 3, 1897.
Martha E. McRamsey, Jan. 12, 1833-June 19, 1880.
Mary Clarke Lauflin, June 11, 1801-Nov. 11, 1840; wife of Samuel Henry Lauflin.

Bible Records—Tombstone Inscriptions

Mary Robinson, Mar. 31, 1806-April 26, 1880; wife of B. G. Thomas.
Margaret W. Humble, Oct. 23, 1796-April 22, 1881.
Isaac Humble, Sept. 10, 1795-Nov. 24, 1882.
Zachariah Humble, Jan. 26, 1847-May 8, 1863.
Willy Humble, Mar. 16, 1862, ——.
Sidney Ross, 1796-Aug. 16, 1880.
Drusilla, June 20, 1808-Oct. 30, 1893; daughter of John Christian McLemore; wife of Sidney Ross.
Martha, Nov. 20, 1833-Aug. 21, 1894; wife of John R. Locke.
Elizabeth Ross, 1842-1864.
Mary E. Ross, June 29, 1828-Oct. 5, 1877; wife of Jones Locke.
Jones Locke, June 30, 1819-Aug. 19, 1865; married Mary Ross, 1848.
Wm. Carter, Feb. 17, 1817-Sept. 17, 1863.
Nancy, wife of Wm. Carter, Feb. 16, 1817-April 19, 1862.

Samuel G. Smartt, son of Wm. Cheek Smartt and Margaret Colville Smartt, Mar. 30, 1816-Feb. 23, 1880.
Martha, first wife of S. G. Smartt, ——, 1840.
Elizabeth, second wife of S. G. Smartt, ——, May 27, 1854.
Martha, third wife of S. G. Smartt, July 6, 1826-1871.
Dr. Thos. Calhoun Smartt, Nov. 8, 1811-Dec. 24, 1891.
George Madison Smartt, ——, May 22, 1904; age, 90 years.
Ann Waterhouse, first wife of George Madison Smartt, ——, Dec. 2, 1870; age 50 years.
Cornelia Smartt, second wife of George Madison Smartt.
Wm. Davidson Smartt, June 23, 1832-Jan. 14, 1888.
Josephine C. (Savage) Smartt, first wife of Wm. D. Smartt, Oct. 6, 1834-Nov. 5, 1881.

Armstrong Cemetery
Irving College

Harriet Etter, Aug. 8, 1807-July 21, 1887.
Rev. Enoch Woodlee, Nov. 3, 1825-April 16, 1870.
Mary Woodlee, wife of Enoch, Mar. 20, 1831-April 2, 1914.
Jacob Woodlee, Nov. 9, 1789-Feb. 15, 1850.
Mary Woodlee, Mar. 29, 1798-April 16, 1878.
Jacob Woodlee, Mar. 6, 1824-Sept. 20, 1857.
Louisa Woodlee, May 4, 1819-April 7, 1857.
Levi Woodlee, Nov. 24, 1818-Sept. 10, 1878.
Tabitha Woodlee, Nov. 6, 1825-Feb. 2, 1878.
Elijah Martin, April 22, 1820-April 18, 1900.
Harriet Etter, May 24, 1838-Dec. 7, 1926.
H. R. Etter, Nov. 5, 1808-1879.
Elizabeth Etter, April 20, 1821-June 22, 1859.
Add Moffitt, Nov. 10, 1825-July 29, 1863.
Bettie Latham, Mar. 20, 1824-June 5, 1854.

Harriet Etter, 1845, ——.
George W. Etter, May 10, 1850-Jan. 8, 1881; killed by a train near Kingston, Tenn.
Elijah Rodgers, 1808-1873.
Grace Rodgers, 1827-1913.
Isiah Rodgers, 1835-1886.
Wm. Sims, 1797-1857.
Charlotte Sims, 1803-1857.
Watson Moffatt, 1847-1883.
Phillip Hughes, Mar. 14, 1806-Sept. 23, 1863.
Phasha Hughes, 1840, ——.
Isabel Moore, 1847-Oct. 16, 1870.
Jothan Woodlee, 1718, ——.
David Woodlee, son of John Woodlee, Jan. 30, 1800-Oct. 4, 1855.
Elijah Woodlee, ——, ——.
Archibal Northcutt, son of Sarah and Gen. A. Northcutt, May 20, 1828-Sept. 19, 1856.
R. E. Mitchell, Feb. 5, 1824-Sept. 14, 1878.
Sallie Tate, Aug. 12, 1784-Sept. 30, 1883.
Mirah Woodlee, 1830-1855.
Solomon Masey, April 11, 1796-Nov. 25, 1861.

Bible Records—Tombstone Inscriptions

Soloman Masey, Feb. 12, 1808-Mar. 25, 1851.
Sarah Northcutt, Nov. 23, 1803-Jan. 24, 1872.
Gen. Adrien Northcutt, Sr., ——, Jan. 19, 1869; age, 70 years.
Henry T. Spong, ——, ——.

SMYRNA

Smyrna Church lies six miles southeast of McMinnville.

William Rogers, 1818-1905.
Tubithy Rogers, 1808-1871.
A. E. Moffitt, Sept. 14, 1814-June 15, 1885.
Elizabeth Moffitt, July 30, 1821-Jan. 24, 1872.
Martha Ware, Dec. 2, 1799-Oct. 21, 1874.
Margerite Curtis, June 15, 1824-Mar. 7, 1903.
Chesley Curtis, Aug. 6, 1795-Aug. 6, 1866.
M. B. Bullen, Jan. 20, 1799-Sept. 14, 1847.
Elvira Ford, wife of Wm. Ford, Feb. 1, 1827-Nov. 13, 1878.
Wm. Ford, 1813-1897.
Elza or Eliza Dodson, 1819-1878.
Richmond Dodson, 1818-1872.
Martha McGregor, 1828-1890.
Henderson McGregor, June 15, 1821-Oct. 27, 1887.
Ezekiel McGregor, 1781-1856.
Sara McGregor, Dec. 15, 1786-April 20, 1856.
Henry Powell, Sept. 4, 1837-Mar. 13, 1915.
J. T. Hayes, 1838-1896.
Sallie Wagner, Sept. 12, 1826-Sept. 24, 1910.
David Fairbanks, Sept. 30, 1823-May 30, 1911.
Julian Fairbanks, Jan. 25, 1830-Feb. 10, 1900.
H. C. Hardenband, 1802-1878.
Phatha Safley, wife of Jesse Safley, 1788-1870.
Jesse Safley, 1781-1861.
Mira Safley, married Anderson Safley Mar. 1, 1832, Oct. 18, 1812, ——.
Anderson Safley, Nov. 17, 1811-April 13, 1885.
Henderson Safley (his wife, Millery, died, 1863), 1816-1884.
Wm. Phillips, Sept. 10, 1788-Oct. 2, 1877.
Sara Phillips, wife of Wm. Phillips, ——, ——.
Wm. B. Barnes, Nov. 23, 1812-Jan. 16, 1882.
Martha Kesey, wife of Wm. Kesey, 1829-1884.
William Kesey, Dec. 25, 1833-April 29, 1901.
Ella Kesey, wife of John Kesey, July 4, 1840-Feb. 18, 1921.
John D. Kesey, consort of Ella Kesey, Aug. 14, 1835-April 30, 1894.
Dion A. Kesey, Nov. 3, 1865-July 25, 1890.
W. V. Kesey, Dec. 19, 1861-Oct. 18, 1881.
Malinda Cartwright, Nov. 22, 1811-Feb. 19, 1899.
John Meyers, Jan. 30, 1892-Nov. 13, 1875.
Mary Meyers, July 15, 1790-Nov. 7, 1875.
Crawford McDaniel, 1801-1881.
Amy Solomon, wife of Bennett Solomon, 1778-1857.
Temperance Ware, wife of Roland Ware, 1771-1844.
Isom Ware, 1793-1855.
Jacob Martin, 1775-1860.
Neely Martin, 1825-1900; born in England, wife of Mose Martin.
Mose Martin, 1811-1874.
Rebecca Curtis, 1806-1865.
J. M. Myers, 1830-1892.
Jesse McGregor, 1825-1883.
Ruthie McGregor, wife of Jesse McGregor, 1822-1899.
Mary Sargent, 1812-1892; born in England; had two sons, John Powell and Henry.
Richmond McGregor, 1804-1856.
Willis McGregor, 1784-1861.
Susan McGregor, 1787-1871.
Margaret McGregor, 1827-1864.
Phoebe McGregor, 1822-1851.
Melgene McGregor, 1830-1854.
Clinton McGregor, 1824-1874.
Charlotte Etter, wife of W. G. Etter, 1843-1877.
Jacob Akeman, 1797-1866.

Bible Records—Tombstone Inscriptions

Martha Akeman, wife of Jacob Akeman, 1804-1824.
Samuel Worth Hill, son of W. and
Mary Hill, 1849-1867.
Mary Waggoner, 1847-1867.
Jacob Waggoner, 1825-1860.

HILL BURYING GROUND

Isaac Hill, July 22, 1748-July 28, 1825; buried at the old Hill Tavern on Hill's Trace on Cumberland Mountain.
Henry Alexander Hill, Feb. 7, 1774-Aug. 1, 1825.
Ervin Hill, July 17, 1796-1836.
Isaac Hill, Jr., 1797-1871.
J. P. Hill, 1803-1881.
Dr. Dick Hill, 1804-1868.
Hugh L. W. Hill, 1810-1892.
George Washington Hill, 1814-1866.
Wm. Carrol Hill, 1818-1870.
Lafayette Hill, 1824-1869.
Johnston Hill, 1833-1888.
Susannah Hill (Barnes), 1834-1879.
Polly Johnston, 1787-1870.
Eliza Hill, 1800-1859.
Louvice Hill, 1822-1839.

Susannah (Swales) Hill, 1767-1846.
Francis, 1804-1834.
Aaron Moffitt, 1802, ——.
Vesta Hill, 1837-1878.
Susan (Brock) Hill, 1825-1903.
Elover (Morgan) Hill, 1799-1860.
Basil Bess, 1804-1881.
Mary Williams, wife of Wm. Williams, 1822-1863.
Isaac Smith, Feb. 2, 1788, ——; married to Britania Savage, Dec. 25, 1811.
Britania Savage, June 20, 1793, ——.
Susannah Smith, Oct. 22, 1812, ——.
A. J. Smith, Jan. 1, 1815, ——.
Isaac Carrol Smith, May 27, 1817, ——.
Jacob Woodlee, Nov. 9, 1789-1850.
Adrian Northcutt, 1790-1860.

SHELLSFORD GRAVEYARD
Baptist Church

Aaron Burlison, May 28, 1812-Jan. 1, 1891.
Lucinda Burlison, Mar. 13, 1815-Jan. 31, 1868.
Nancy Clendenen, July 27, 1824-Sept. 4, 1867.
James Clendenen, July 21, 1848-June 21, 1890.
W. J. Stubblefield, Mar. 5, 1805-Oct. 9, 1890.
Rebecca Stubblefield, Aug. 2, 1815-Mar. 22, 1906.
T. J. Stubblefield, May 27, 1833-Jan. 23, 1859.
Esther Jones, daughter of John McGee, wife of Isaac Jones, Nov. 24, 1833-Jan. 19, 1880.
Martha McGee, wife of John McGee, Nov. 9, 1801-July 14, 1878.
John McGee, Mar. 5, 1804-Nov. 12, 1878.
Martha, daughter of John and Martha McGee, 1817-1870.
Mahala Thompson, wife of Rev. Wm. Thompson, July 6, 1800-June 6, 1871.
Wm. Thompson, pastor of Shellsford Church when he died, ——, Jan. 10, 1852.

Levina Eady, June 12, 1812-July 12, 1864.
Musula Smith, May 12, 1818-July 14, 1859.
Wm. Quick, 1800-Dec. 2, 1884.
Wm. Smith, Jan. 26, 1782-Aug. 26, 1881.
Reetha Smith, wife of Wm. Smith, Jan. 6, 1796-Jan. 9, 1878.
Richard Forest, Oct. 4, 1783-1878.
Sarah Forest, wife of Richard Forest, Sept. 22, 1783-Sept. 16, 1827.
John Drake, April 19, 1818-Aug. 9, 1905.
Disa (?) Drake, Mar. 15, 1817-Aug. 10, 1898.
Malinda Eperson, daughter of Aaron and Lucinda Burlison, Nov. 18, 1831-April 12, 1855.
Asa Smith, ——, June 27, 1852.
George Harrison, Dec. 10, 1810-Sept. 22, 1859.
Elizabeth Harrison, ——, Feb. 2, 1856.
Audrey Harrison, June 5, 1794-Nov. 30, 1856.
Jessie Jennings, Dec. 23, 1802-July 27, 1884.

Bible Records—Tombstone Inscriptions

J. A. Bottom, Nov. 22, 1830-Aug. 6, 1893.
Miranda Bottom, daughter of Wm. Smith, Feb. 11, 1828-Dec. 12, 1913.
John Cardwell, Feb. 24, 1815-Jan. 17, 1884.
Sarah Cardwell, wife of John Cardwell, June 23, 1821-Oct. 19, 1917.
Christian Shell and his wife, Bradford, are buried in this cemetery, but there is no stone to mark the place.

WESLEY CHAPEL
Near Viola, Tenn.

Salie, widow of William Lusk, Feb. 22, 1814-Nov. 30, 1894.
Sarah, wife of James Parks, Feb. 2, 1811-May 24, 1893.
Michael Hoover, Oct. 11, 1806-Oct. 4, 1891.
Charlotte, wife of M. Hoover, Feb. 15, 1815-Oct. 1, 1882.
William Hoover, Jan. 1, 1834-Aug. 15, 1881.
J. B. Hoover, Dec. 7, 1844-July 31, 1895.
Mary J., wife of Fred Hoover, Nov. 12, 1820-Aug. 30, 1875.
Frederick Hoover, Nov. 3, 1809-Aug. 14, 1882.
A. W. Hoover, July, 1840-Sept. 10, 1887.
J. R. Hoover, Aug. 22, 1871-Aug. 14, 1887.
William Hoover, July 8, 1874-June 4, 1900.
Nancy Green; died, Oct. 10, 1887; age, 60 years.
William Simmons, Mar. 23, 1807-June 26, 1889.
Salina Simmons, Dec. 26, 1807-June 26, 1887.
S. D. Porter, 1849-1923.
A. K. Knott, May 2, 1827-June 27, 1899.
Tom Sain, April 14, 1824-June 19, 1898.
Mary A. Sain, Oct. 25, 1829-Aug. 14, 1895.
Tom Sain, July 11, 1860-Nov. 25, 1890.
Sarah E. Adam, April 19, 1833-April 21, 1908.
Jennie Adam, May 6, 1867-Sept. 6, 1906.
John Samuel Sain, Oct. 22, 1855-Sept. 28, 1829.
Bettie J., wife of W. H. Sain, April 9, 1860-Sept. 17, 1896.
Ruth H., wife of John H. Fletcher, June 19, 1807-Mar. 9, 1893.
Eliza J., wife of J. B. Thaxton, July 29, 1838-Mar. 9, 1880.
Sarah Elizabeth; died, Aug. 9, 1809.
J. B. Thaxton, Dec. 27, 1835-May 22, 1905.
Alfred Leaird; died, Nov. 23, 1871; age, 31 years.
Susan L., wife of A. Learid, June 8, 1845-April 3, 1885.
N. B. Sain, Feb. 22, 1817-Oct. 4, 1902.
M. W., wife of N. B. Sain, April 30, 1822-April 24, 1904.
Josephine Sain Cook, Sept. 30, 1850-Feb. 23, 1903.
Margaret L. Christian, daughter of J. Y. and Nancy Brawley, and wife of W. W. Christian; born, June 10, 1857; married, 1879; died, Oct. 22, 1895.
S. J. Christian, June 26, 1822-Jan. 19, 1894.
Babbathy Christian, Feb. 14, 1827-Aug. 14, 1881.
Stephen Winton, June 4, 1829-Aug. 22, 1886.
Mary Elizabeth Winton, May 13, 1835-Dec. 11, 1894.
Parlee, wife of L. Griswold, and daughter of S. and M. E. Winton, Oct. 24, 1868-Oct. 28, 1928.
Winton, Oct. 24, 1868-Oct. 28, 1928.
Thursly, wife of J. J. Winton, June 22, 1873-Oct. 11, 1894.
S. Leagania, Jan. 15, 1843-Oct. 13, 1889.
W. Harrison Lusk, Dec. 27, 1841-Oct. 6, 1927.
Bethamy, wife of John Umbarger, Dec. 8, 1820-April 15, 1890.
Sallie, wife of William Lusk, Feb. 22, 1840-Sept. 30, 1894.
Martha Garriston, 1839-1906.
I. G. Garretson, July 21, 1813-June 5, 1895.
Andrew Stotts, Jan. 6, 1824-Dec. 5, 1900.
Thomas McColloch; died, May 5, 1867; age, 81 years.

Bible Records—Tombstone Inscriptions

Millard McColloch; died, Sept. 17, 1888; age, 84 years.
Isaac Thomas Berry, Jan. 4, 1873-May 1, 1902.
Flora Lorena, wife of Isaac Berry, Oct. 12, 1872-Nov. 25, 1926.
J. D. Berry; died, Jan. 19, 1903; age, 82 years.
Sallie, wife of J. D. Berry, July 29, 1829-May 1, 1902.
A. C. Lusk, Aug. 22, 1834-Sept. 8, 1912.
Lucy A. Lusk, Jan. 16, 1825-June 25, 1916.
James C. Lusk, Sept. 29, 1868-Aug. 29, 1922.
D. B. Hoover, June 30, 1837-Aug. 18, 1909.
James Hoover, Dec. 10, 1835-Aug. 29, 1917.
Lucy Ann, wife of James Hoover, Mar. 19, 1845-Dec. 30, 1913.
Thomas Martin, Aug. 18, 1836-Aug. 17, 1911.
W. B. Winton, Sept. 28, 1839-Sept. 18, 1910.
Lizzie, wife of W. B. Winton, June 25, 1846-April 21, 1916.
James Rhea, Mar. 30, 1833-April 15, 1912.
Mary Rhea, Feb. 6, 1839-Sept. 3, 1913.

VILLINES BURIAL GROUND

Near Cross Plains, Robertson County, Tenn. Records sent by Mrs. William H. Simmons, Springfield.

T. J. Villines, April 20, 1839-May 26, 1908.
Sallie, wife of T. J. Villines, Mar. 24, 1842-Aug. 3, 1913.
Mary Strother, July 16, 1812-April 28, 1889.
S. G. Strother, Oct. 22, 1804-Aug. 21, 1886.
John Strother, born in Culpepper County, Va.; age, about 65 years.
Calista Villines, Mar. 23, 1854-Aug. 5, 1879.
Lydia K., wife of Jas. W. Villines, daughter of S. G. and Mary Strother, Dec. 23, 1837-Oct. 13, 1862.
J. W. Villines, Nov. 11, 1833-Oct. 29, 1877; a Mason.
A. J. Cole, Oct. 30, 1816-Sept. 13, 1868; a Mason.
Ellen M. Cole, daughter of William and Mary Villines, wife of A. J. Cole, Jan. 6, 1832-Jan. 3, 1860.
M. E. Cole, daughter of A. J. and E. M. Cole, Mar. 9, 1851-July 13, 1852.
W. S. Cole, son of A. J. and E. M. Cole, Dec. 7, 1851-Jan. 14, 1857.
Capt. W. S. Winfield, Nov. 29, 1831-Mar. 6, 1892.
Robert M., oldest son of Wm. and Mary Villines, April 20, 1830-Oct. 2, 1860.
Susan Hollis, daughter of Wm. and Mary M. Villines, Jan. 25, 1828-Oct. 5, 1854.
Elizabeth A. Davis, daughter of Wm. and Mary M. Villines, July 21, 1826-Nov. 17, 1854.
William Villines, born in Caswell County, N. C., Nov. 14, 1814-Jan. 9, 1876.
Mary, wife of Wm. Villines, Oct. 1, 1887-June 26, 1890.
William E., son of W. H. and N. J. Villines, April 4, 1865-Sept. 19, 1879.
Nancy J., wife of W. H. Villines, July 17, 1838-Nov. 26, 1879.
Elizabeth Bell; born, Jan. 15, 1867; age, 73 years.
William Orville Cranor, son of W. O. and Edna Cranor, Nov. 19, 1902-Jan. 21, 1903.
Thomas Kilgore, born in Virginia or North Carolina, about 1715; age, about 105 years; served in Revolutionary War.

COOK CEMETERY

Near that of Villines'

Clara, wife of Jacob Zeck, Oct. 24, 1819-Jan. 11, 1897.
Angeline, daughter of Jacob Zeck, Feb., 1853-Nov. 8, 1871.

Bible Records—Tombstone Inscriptions

Ann, wife of W. F. Kusle; born, 1840; married, 1855; died, 1886.
George W. Cook, 1824-1911.
Catherine Cook, wife of George W., 1827-1875.
Sarah G., wife of G. W. Cook, Aug. 26, 1827-Mar. 1, 1875.
Ann E. Empson, Nov. 28, 1851-Jan. 13, 1927.
Kate Smelling, wife of George T. Cook, May 2, 1857-June 2, 1915.

TURNER GRAVES
Copied by Mrs. Wm. Simmons

James Atlas Stark, 1833-1890.
Narcises Wright Stark, 1842-1923.
James Madison Wright, May 26, 1815-May, 1898.
Lucy West, wife of J. M. West, Jan. 13, 1823-June 28, 1898.
F. W. Wright, Feb. 19, 1852-Jan. 23, 1882.
Stephen H. Turner, Aug. 17, 1798-May 2, 1848.

Stephen Turner in 1848 drove in a wagon a pair of mules to Alabama, taking his bedding and food and a drove of hogs. When they broke down he would haul them. In Captain Wright's yard now stands the Oche Orange trees that were old trees in 1848 and are still green and wonderful in 1933.

MT. ZION CHURCH CEMETERY
Thirteenth District. Sent by Mrs. Wm. Simmons.

Col. J. Thomas Farmer, born in Hillsboro, N. C.; died, April, 1818; charter member of Mt. Zion Church; served in the Revolutionary War; was a member of the House of Burgesses of North Carolina.
Samuel, son of Col. J. Thomas Farmer, June 9, 1784-May 22, 1866; served in the War of 1812.
Sarah Childress, wife of Samuel Farmer, married in 1835, Jan. 13, 1790-Nov. 15, 1876.
Thomas H. Martin, son of Rev. Patrick and Mary Martin, April 20, 1816-Feb. 15, 1888; married Elizabeth Malinda Farmer, daughter of Samuel Farmer, Jan. 14, 1816-Oct. 5, 1885; tombs together.
George Anderson Farmer, son of Samuel Farmer, Nov. 28, 1825-May 20, 1890.
Nancy Ann Farmer, wife of John Fugnor, Oct. 26, 1830-Mar. 23, 1910.
Elizabeth Childress, wife of Rev. Thomas Martin, Jan. 24, 1798-Oct. 20, 1869.
Thomas H. Farmer, son of Samuel Farmer, Feb. 13, 1818-Dec. 15, 1852.
Catherine Martin, wife of Thomas H. Farmer, daughter of Rev. Thomas and Nancy Martin, Jan. 22, 1818-Sept. 8, 1887.
Rev. George Martin married Rebekah McVeigh, daughter of the Governor of Alabama.
Rebekah McVeigh, wife of Rev. George Martin, no dates.

BATTS BURIAL GROUND

Lucinda Darden, June 7, 1848-Feb. 21, 1925.
Agnes Burnes, daughter of R. F. and M. M. Biggers; died, June 2, 1892; age, 14 years.
James H., son of G. N. and L. B. Darden, Jan. 7, 1871-1895.
George M. Darden; died, 1907.
Harrison Long, Jan. 12, 1835-May 22, 1907.
James Henry Long, Sr., April 9, 1828-Feb. 18, 1920.
Sallie Ann Long, 1834-Mar. 17, 1914.
James H., son of J. M. and L. B. Darden, July 7, 1871-July 8, 1895.
Sarah Margaret, wife of W. J. Batts, June 5, 1857-Jan. 8, 1888.
Jeremiah Batts, born in North Carolina, Aug., 1804-1886.

Bible Records—Tombstone Inscriptions

Mary Ann, wife of Jeremiah Batts, May 8, 1810-Feb. 8, 1869.
Capt. Jeremiah Batts, Nov. 22, 1840-Dec. 9, 1864; killed at Battle of Franklin.
R. L. Powell, May 25, 1841-Nov. 30, 1864; killed at Battle of Franklin.
Nancy, wife of Jeremiah Batts, Dec. 25, 1820-Aug. 2, 1872.
Willie Onnan, son of J. O. and Josie Rice, 1868-1884.
L. Batts, 1845-1922.
Virginia, wife of John T. Batts, April 6, 1850-1870.
Laurana Artemiss, wife of J. G. Batts, Mar. 24, 1831-Jan 25, 1867.

Woodard Burial Ground

Dr. T. M. Woodard, Jan. 15, 1828-Jan. 4, 1878; married Dec. 24, 1852, to Catherine Woodard; again, Dec. 8, 1817, to Mrs. M. D. Pepper; practiced medicine 26 years.
Catherine Woodard, wife of Dr. T. M. Woodard, Jan. 12, 1828-Dec. 17, 1861.
James Woodard, Mar. 8, 1799-Nov. 5, 1875; prominent Baptist.
Margaret, wife of James Woodard, June 24, 1803-June 3, 1883.
Franklin Woodard, son of James and Margaret, Sept., 1831-July 4, 1862.
Zadok W. Bell, Sept. 27, 1892-Aug. 14, 1872.
Gustavus A. Woodard, Mar. 5, 1840-Feb. 13, 1877.
Marens L. Woodard, July 16, 1836-Nov. 30, 1883.
Julia W. Bell, July 24, 1849-May 20, 1921.
J. G. Woodard, July 4, 1833-Aug. 2, 1918.
Virginia Woodard, Dec. 22, 1845-July 13, 1911.
William Woodard, son of James and Margaret Woodard, May 19, 1826-Aug. 16, 1840.
M. E. Patterson, Oct. 8, 1830-June 20, 1896.

Mt. Sharon Church Cemetery
Sixteenth District

Samuel Crockett, born in Carlisle, Pa., Dec. 4, 1759-April 21, 1841; married Sarah Wilson, Sept. 25, 1787, in Pennsylvania; served in the Revolutionary War in 3rd Co., 3rd Massachusetts Reg.

Hart Burial Ground

Henry Hart, June 22, 1792-Dec. 24, 1856.
Judith Hart, Aug. 15, 1792-June 3, 1865.
Mary A. Hart, wife of D. G. Baird, July 27, 1816-Sept. 16, 1878.
Daniel G. Baird, July 21, 1808-Sept. 8, 1858.
Samuel Bowling, Sept. 12, 1829-Nov. 27, 1891.
Ann, wife of Dr. S. B. Brown, Sept. 4, 1831-June 17, 1882.
Nancy Robertson, mother of Henry Hart, Sr.; died, Feb., 1845; age, about 70 years.
Martha Robertson, wife of A. Gunn, 1801-1861.
T. H. Gunn, Feb. 26, 1837-Jan. 26, 1931.
C. C. Gunn, Mar. 7, 1849-July 16, 1915.
Jesse A. Hunt, April 10, 1880-Dec. 9, 1919.
Wife of J. S. Hart; born, Feb. 13, 1869.
Lizzie G. Davis, Dec. 16, 1856-Sept. 17, 1905.
Albert Farmer; died, Mar. 20, 1877; age, 14 years.
Sarah Mumford; died, Aug. 26, 1873; age, about 90 years; mother of Mrs. M. A. Hart.
Ann S. Hart, daughter of John and Martha A. Hart; age, 12 years.
Martha A., wife of John S. Hart, Mar. 19, 1849-July 25, 1872.
Jimmy, son of J. S. and Martha Hart, Sept. 27, 1857-Jan. 13, 1892.

Bible Records—Tombstone Inscriptions

Mary F. Hart, Oct. 30, 1844-Feb. 1, 1918.
Wife of H. N. Hart, July 16, 1841-Feb. 7, 1925.
Edwin Hooper, son of Henry and Huldah Hart, Feb. 3, 1850-Sept. 27, 1863.
Alice Baird, daughter of D. G. and Mary A. Baird, and wife of Rev. W. R. Warren, July 8, 1848-Feb. 23, 1876.
W. F. Borthick, May 22, 1869-Aug. 9, 1901.
Eliza, wife of M. Barbee; died, Oct. 22, 1873; age, about 95 years.

REVOLUTIONARY SOLDIERS

List of Revolutionary Soldiers whose graves are located in Robertson County. Sent by Mrs. Wm. Simmons, Regent, Charlotte Reeves Robertson Chapter, Springfield.

SAMUEL CROCKETT

Samuel Crockett, born in Carlisle, Pa., Dec. 4, 1759; died, April 21, 1841, in Robertson County, Tenn.; married Sarah Wilson, who was born Feb. 27, 1766; died, May 20, 1849; married Sept. 25, 1789, at Carlisle, Pa. Samuel Crockett service in War Department, Adjutant-General's office, Mar. 15, 1929, records show he served in the Revolutionary War in the 3rd Co., 3rd Massachusetts Regiment, commanded by Col. Michael Jackson. His name appears only on the muster roll of 20 months and 12 days. Records dated Oct. 14, 1783. Children: Wilson, born July, 1788; William, born April, 1790; John, born Dec. 20, 1791; James, born Nov. 3, 1793; Nathaniel, born Mar. 15, 1795; Samuel, III, born Nov. 10, 1799; Elizabeth, born May 11, 1809; Margaret, born July 3, 1797; Sarah, born ——; Martin, born May 11, 1809; Mary, born Dec. 20, 1806. He is buried in Mt. Sharon Burying Ground, 18th District, Robertson County, Tenn., seven miles from Springfield, Tenn. Most of the above is recorded, "War Books of N. C.," page 576, in Crockett History by French and Armstrong in possession of Tony Dowlen of Springfield, Tenn. Samuel Crockett was one of the commissioners to lay off Springfield, Tenn. He built a block house or fort a few miles south of Springfield in 1788.

WILLIAM YATES

William Yates, Lieutenant-Col., Dept. of Muster Master General, 11th of April, 1777, found in History Register of Continental Army of Revolution. This record is from L. B. Heitman of the War Department. Married Agnes Price in Virginia; moved to North Carolina, Taswell County, in 1780 or 81; then moved to Cross Plains and died there at the age of 110; is buried in "Carr" Burial Ground, one and one-half miles north of Cross Plains in the 15th Civil District; son of John Yates.

THOMAS FARMER

Thomas Farmer was born 1763; died, 1815; served in the Revolutionary War in pay roll of Capt. James Thackston's Company; enlisted the 1st day of Mar., 1781, and discharged the 29th day of June following, Vol. 22 of the State Records of North Carolina, signed by Robert F. Hughes, Jr., Acting Librarian, and Claud R. Moore, Notary. He was also a member of Assembly in 1783, Vol. 19 of State Records of North Carolina, pages 234 and 235. He was of Hillsboro, N. C.; moved to Robertson County, Tenn., where he lived and died; is buried in 13th Civil District; married Frances Toller; second wife, Lorene Harper. He was the ancestor of Mrs. J. S. Freeman of Charlotte Reeves Robertson Chapter, Springfield, Tenn.

WILLIAM STARK

William Stark, buried in "Stark" Cemetery on the farm of Joe Couts, two miles north of Springfield, Tenn.; his commission in North Carolina, Continental troops; was in battle of Kings Mountain; ancestor of Mrs. Farmer McIntosh, Charlotte Reeves Robertson Chapter, D. A. R., Springfield, Tenn.

DR. MARTIN WALTON

Dr. Martin Walton of Louisa County, Va., entered the Revolutionary Army,

Bible Records—Tombstone Inscriptions

1777, on his 16th birthday. He served a year. He wanted to join early and took physical exercise in order to grow rapidly that he might join sooner. Later he studied medicine, also received the degrees of Doctor of Divinity and Law. Married Elizabeth Johnson, a niece of Thomas Johnson and granddaughter of William Johnson, who were members of the House of Burgesses from 1762 to 1765. Standard Colonial Register on file in Virginia State Library, pages 157 to 169. Her father, David Johnson, was a Continental soldier, page 231, in manuscript volumns known as was 4 in Virginia State library. His grave is near Springfield, Tenn. He is an ancestor of Mrs. Frances Walton Simmons of Springfield, Tenn.

DUDLEY BROOKE

From papers in the Revolutionary War Pension Claim S-3055 it appears Dudley Brooke was born July 3, 1762, in Chesterfield County. He enlisted from Buckingham County, Va., in the spring of 1781, and served seven months as private in Robert Carey's Company, Col. Combe's Virginia Regiment. He was pensioned May 15, 1833, while a resident of Robertson County, Tenn. He enlisted Oct., 1777; served in Capt. White's Company as private, Taylor's Virginia regular. In 1778 he enlisted and served 3 months; officer not stated. In 1779 he enlisted and served 3 months under Lieut. Henry Johnson, Col. Anthony New's Regiment. He enlisted in 1781 and served 3 months in Capt. Richard Phillips' Company. Enlisted in 1781 and served in Capt. John White's Company 1 month. He was allowed pension on application May 16, 1833, while resident of Robertson County, Tenn. He had resided here since 1802 when he left Louisa County, Va.
Children: Elizabeth, Sarah, Mary, Harry, John Frances, Dudley Brooke, Jr. He is the ancestor of Mrs. Frances Walton Simmons of Springfield, Tenn. His grave is near Cross Plains, Robertson County, Tenn.

RICHARD NUCKOLLS

Richard Nuckolls was born in Virginia, Feb. 26, 1762; married Temperence Walton, who was born in Virginia, Jan. 21, 1839, moved to Tennessee in 1797. He died June 20, 1835. Was a member of the Baptist Church. Children: Lewis married Wells, Nellie married Long, Dorcas married Jones, Tobitha married Foote.

DAVID HENRY

From Revolutionary War Records, pension claim S-2287, it appears that David Henry was born in 1753 in Pittsylvania County, Va. He enlisted in the spring of 1777, and served six months as an orderly sergeant in Captain John Donelson's Company, Col. Evan Shelby's Virginia Regiment, and was in an expedition against the Cherokee Indians. He enlisted early in 1778 and served as an orderly sergeant in Captains Thomas Dillard and Montgomery's Companies in Colonel George Rogers Clark's expedition to Illinois, and captured Oakhaw Towns and was discharged Aug. 29, 1778. He stated that his brother, Hugh Henry, was lieutenant in both tours of his service. He was pensioned on his application executed Aug. 15, 1832, at which time he was living in Robertson County, Tenn.
Children: Isaac, Lemuel, Elizabeth, Catherine. His grave is east of Springfield, Tenn.

HENRY JOHNSON

Henry Johnson was born in 1738 of Scotch-Irish parentage. In Mar., 1763, he married Rachel Holman in Pennsylvania, both being residents of that state at that time. To them was born ten children, six sons and four daughters; all lived to be grown and married except one daughter who died in early womanhood.
Some time after his marriage he removed to North Carolina; he passing through Virginia possibly tarried there for a while. In North Carolina he settled a short distance from the town of Salisbury, near the Yadkin River. History tells us there were other Scotch-Irish from Ulster who settled in that section.
On May 29, 1777, he enlisted as a private for a period of time (three years) in the service of his country in the Revolutionary War, his name appear-

Bible Records—Tombstone Inscriptions

ing on the roll of Capt. Ingles Company, dated Sept. 9, 1778. Also in Capt. Clements Hall's Company of the same regiment. He was commissioned drummer or fifer in 2nd North Carolina Regiment commanded by Col. Patton.

In 1796 he removed to Robertson County, Tenn., and purchased property about 3½ miles east of Springfield, farm now in possession of John Durham. From time to time he acquired other lands in Robertson County, as appears on the early records of the county. He died in 1815; Rachel, his wife, passing away about the same time. They, with perhaps a few others of their immediate family, are buried on the farm of John Durham. The graves are unmarked, but can be located, which is going to be done soon.

APPLICANTS FOR PENSIONS

Applicants for pensions for Revolutionary Service of men living in Robertson County, June 1, 1804.

The list of soldiers living in Tennessee June 1, 1840, who applied for pensions for Revolutionary service, by counties and age given. The Robertson County are the following: John C. Coon, age 85; Charles Gent, age 85; James Jones, age 88; David Jones, age 86; Martin Walton, age 79; William Walker, age 85; David Henry, age 89; Fendal Roland, age 76; and Ann White, evidently a widow. Copy can be obtained from the Pension Office, Washington, D. C. (There are quite a few others.)

THOMAS KILGORE

Book A, page 14, in archives of Robertson County, Springfield, Tenn. Thomas Kilgore transfers a part of 640 acres granted to said Kilgore by North Carolina, Grant No. 2511, on Aug. 27, 1795.

Thomas Kilgore was born in Virginia or North Carolina about 1715 and died near Cross Plains, Tenn. He left North Carolina in the spring of 1778 with some ammunition, salt, and a few grains of corn to take advantage of the pre-emption law passed by the legislature of North Carolina, securing to settlers of Tennessee, 840 acres of land, provided it was settled before 1780. Traveling on foot, he passed through East Tennessee and plunged into the wilderness beyond. Guided alone by the sun and the North Star, he pushed on, seeing no white people until he reached Bledsoe's Lick, where he found a colony of six or eight families. After resting a few days he went on some 25 miles west when he selected a cave from which issued a bold stream of water running into the middle fork of Red River. By wading the stream he could enter the cave without leaving a trail. He kicked up some of the rich alluvial soil of the cane break and planted a few hills of corn. He watched and tended his little crop, living in the meantime on game he killed. In the fall he gathered two or three ears of corn, returned to North Carolina and had the title to his land confirmed. In the spring of 1779 he, with a few families, returned to the spot where he had passed the previous summer. A stockade fort was immediately erected on a commanding eminence about three-fourths of a mile from Cross Plains, and named Kilgore's Station. It was a landmark for years in the overland emigration to Tennessee. Probably the first mill was built on the middle fork of Red River, three-fourths of a mile northwest of Cross Plains, between 1785 and 1790 by Thomas Kilgore. (From History of Tennessee, published by Goodspeed in 1886, page 820.

Thomas Kilgore, after living half a century on the lands thus acquired, died at the advanced age of 108 years. (See Goodspreed, p. 830.)

Thomas Kilgore was a major in Washington's Army at Yorktown. The record sent to Mrs. Walter F. Yates, Memphis, Tenn., Oct. 5, 1898, by Miss Flora Creech, Pension Clerk, North Carolina, follows: "This certifies that there appears the name of Thomas Kil-

Bible Records—Tombstone Inscriptions

gore in the Revolutionary records in this office. A soldier in the Revolutionary War. Said name appears on page 19, Book No. 21, in pay roll of Comptroller's office, North Carolina Militia. The said Thomas Kilgore was in active service."

Signed Hal. W. Ayer,
State Auditor.

Thomas Kilgore married Phoebe Lee, daughter of Lieut.-Col. Harry Lee and Lucy Grimes, in Virginia. His death was caused by a trip by foot from Cross Plains to Gallatin to have his gun repaired. He made the trip in a day and at his advanced age it was too much for him.

Children: Phoebe Lee Kilgore married Dawson Moore; Lydia Kilgore married James Yates; Anice Lee Kilgore married John Strother and later married Mr. Payne; Frances Kilgore married Thomas Gunn; Gabriel Kilgore and Thomas Kilgore were unmarried.

FORT BURYING GROUND

On the farm of W. H. Simmons, near Springfield, Tenn. Mrs. Simmons is the Regent of the Charlotte Reeves Robertson Chapter. Copied by Mrs. Acklen.

Corporal Elias Fort, in C. Regt., Revolutionary War., S. A. R. Marker.
John D. Fort, Mar. 18, 1804-Oct. 28, 1829.
Wm. E. Dancy, April 2, 1792-Oct. 31, 1854.
Mrs. Annie Parks Sinsebaugh, July 3, 1843-May 31, 1903.
John D. Parks, Mar. 3, 1845-Mar. 5, 1913.
L. P. Parks, Oct. 27, 1807-Dec. 10, 1890.

Mrs. C. A. Parks, July 4, 1816-May 14, 1895.
Eliza P. Parks, Feb. 2, 1855-Mar. 24, 1861.
Alonzo T. Parks, Dec. 5, 1857-Sept. 18, 1866.
W. L. Parks, June 3, 1847-July 10, 1912.
Bettie L. Parks, Dec. 5, 1849.
Mrs. Harriet Parks Mille, Sept. 27, 1852.

CLEVELAND FAMILY CEMETERY

Records from Cleveland Family Cemetery, Sweetwater, Mt. Harmony, Chestua. Located near Philadelphia, Tenn., Sweetwater, Madisonville, Tenn. Copied by Mrs. Richard Jarnigan Yearwood.

Capt. Robt. Cleveland, son of John Cleveland; born, ——; died, ——.
Elder Eli Cleveland, son of Capt. Robt. Cleveland, Oct. 1, 1781-Nov. 23, 1859.
Polly Ragon Cleveland, wife of Eli Cleveland, July 30, 1786-Jan. 21, 1862.
Robt. R. Cleveland, Sept. 15, 1808-April 7, 1868.
Sydney G. Nelson Cleveland, wife of Robt. R. Cleveland, July 15, 1811-Oct. 23, 1884.
Aley Mathis Cleveland, May 7, 1813-May 30, 1855.
Clarrisa Cleveland, Sept. 6, 1815-Mar. 11, 1880.
David H. Cleveland, Nov. 5, 1824-Aug. 10, 1900.

Elizabeth Johnson Cleveland, wife of David H. Cleveland, Jan. 5, 1827-Dec. 31, 1882.
Jesse F. Cleveland, July 11, 1845-Oct. 27, 1846.
Mary Katherine Cleveland Walker, wife of Seth McKinney Walker, Jan. 4, 1847-April, 1906.
Louis J. Cleveland, Feb. 17, 1853-Oct. 4, 1853.
Presley Cleveland, son of Capt. Robt. Cleveland, Sept, 14, 1779-May 31, 1861.
Elizabeth Johnson Cleveland, wife of Presley Cleveland, Feb. 17, 1792-Nov. 20, 1854.
Aley Cleveland, Oct. 14, 1816-Nov. 3, 1824.

Bible Records—Tombstone Inscriptions

William Cleveland, Oct. 11, 1820-Aug. 22, 1835.
Franklin King Berry, Mar. 25, 1809-Oct. 28, 1845.
Emily Laughlin Berry, wife of Franklin King Berry, Jan. 26, 1823-Oct., 1884.
Frank K. Berry, Jr., Dec. 4, 1841, ——.
Caroline Cleveland Berry, wife of Frank K. Berry, Jr., Feb. 2, 1843-Sept. 16, 1910.
Lodusky Caroline Jones, Oct. 6, 1834-June 30, 1862.
Walter Franklin Lenoir, Nov. 21, 1816-Sept. 1, 1878.
Elizabeth Campbell Goddard Lenoir, first wife of Walter Franklin Lenoir, April 2, 1821-Jan. 10, 1855.
Martha Neely Yearwood, wife of William Yearwood, Oct. 24, 1789-Feb. 14, 1867.
Col. Horace Burton Yearwood, son of Wm. and Martha Neely Yearwood, Mar. 13, 1820-June 17, 1897.
Elizabeth E. Scruggs Yearwood, wife of Horace Burton Yearwood, Sept. 26, 1827-Oct. 25, 1905.
John Scruggs Yearwood, Jan. 12, 1850-Aug. 1, 1903.
Lavinia Ida Yearwood, June 12, 1856-Dec. 10, 1890.
Hugh Yearwood, Dec. 19, 1868-Aug. 21, 1889.
Thomas Yearwood, April 2, 1810-May 24, 1889.
Lavinia Walker Scruggs Yearwood, wife of Thomas Yearwood, Feb. 3, 1832-Aug. 4, 1899.
Elder John Scruggs, Mar. 14, 1797-Nov. 11, 1867.
Theresa Newell Carter Scruggs, wife of Elder John Scruggs, Oct. 8, 1806-Nov. 9, 1888.
Richard Francis Scruggs, Feb. 1, 1834-Dec. 28, 1903.

Frank Heiskell Scruggs, Sept. 15, 1862-July 8, 1895.
Susan Newman Scruggs, Sept. 13, 1871-Nov. 6, 1890.
Francis Jackson Carter; died, 1857.
Esther Crocket Carter, wife of Francis Jackson Carter; died, July 9, 1870.
William Yearwood, Jan. 8, 1780-Aug. 5, 1865.
Sarah Pennington, April 25, 1848-Dec. 5, 1848.
Alpha Davis Pennington, wife of John Pennington, 1802-1872.
Lucinda Elizabeth Pennington, July 4, 1823-Dec. 9, 1828.
Daniel Ragon, —— 6, 1792-July 26, 1860.
Elizabeth Ragon, wife of Daniel Ragon, Sept. 18, 1798-Dec. 29, 1864.
J. E. Ragon, Sept. 6, 1828-Nov. 22, 1906.
Mary E. Ragon, daughter of J. E. and L. J. Ragon, May 1, 1854-Sept. 6, 1870.
Clarrisia E. Ragon, daughter of J. E. and L. J. Ragon, Mar. 10, 1864-July 3, 1865.
Caroline Cleveland, Nov. 25, 1827-Nov. 10, 1896.
Harvey H. Cleveland, Mar. 18, 1830-Sept. 25, 1854.
William Johnson, Mar. 24, 1766-Dec. 27, 1837.
Louis Johnson, Jan. 29, 1799-April 17, 1890.
Catherine Pennington Johnson, wife of Luis Johnson, May 29, 1805-Sept. 5, 1865.
William Pennington, Dec. 13, 1777-April 22, 1838.
Elizabeth Eller Pennington, wife of Wm. Pennington, Oct., 1776-Dec. 7, 1844.
John Pennington, son of William Pennington, Oct. 27, 1801, ——.
W. J. Pennington, July 10, 1827-Oct. 27, 1854.

FIRST PRESBYTERIAN CHURCH GRAVEYARD

Bonnie Kate Chapter, Knoxville. By Kate K. White.

William Blount.
Mary Blount.
James White.
Mary Lawson White.
Hugh Lawson White.
Elizabeth Carrick White.

Thomas Dunn, first grave, Revolutionary Soldier.
Christopher Acklen, 185—.
Donald McClanahan, 1848, Revolutionary Soldier.
Anthony Crush, 1859.

Bible Records—Tombstone Inscriptions

Samuel R. McClannahan, 1838.
William Crush, 1831.
Rebedda Hodges, 1831.
Capt. John Crozier, 1850.
Hannah Crozier, 1838.
Blanch Crozier, 1812.
John Crozier, Jr., 1805.
James Campbell, born in Scotland, 1771; died, 1837.
Annie Campbell, 1834.
Donald McIntosh, born in Scotland; died, 1837.
Majorie McIntosh.
George Harris, 1846, Revolutionary Soldier.
Josephine Harris, 1846.
James M. Roberts, 1836, Revolutionary Soldier.
Jane Boyd, 1838.
A. J. Roberts, 1809.
M. F. Boyd, 1821, Revolutionary Soldier.
James Conner, Revolutionary Soldier.
William Carr, Revolutionary Soldier.
Peggy Heiskell, 1818.
Joseph Heiskell.
Mary Brown, 1824.

Margaret Ramsay, 1834.
Thomas Humes, 1811.
James Cowan, 1811.
Eliza Morgan, 1850.
Sarah Bearden, 1847.
Calvin McClung, 1845.
Rachell McClung, 1843.
James White, son of Hugh L. White, 1831.
Robert Campbell; age, 77 years.
—— Campbell; age, 71 years.
James Scott, Revolutionary Soldier, North Carolina.
Jane Scott, 1837.
Jenefee Scott, daughter of Frances Ramsay.
Stelle, 1852, Revolutionary Soldier, North Carolina.
John Formalt, 1819.
John Anthony, 1838, Revolutionary Soldier.
John Scott, 1819.
Betsy Scott, 1821.
William T. Pryor, Revolutionary Soldier, Virginia.
William Arthur, 1822.
Wait Blount, 1820.

SIMPSON GRAVEYARD

South of the river, oldest in Knox County, first known as Cunningham, then Flenniken, then Baker, now Simpson.

Robert Cunningham, 1752-1797, Revolutionary Soldier, Lieut.
Betsy Cunningham, mother of Robert, 1733-1778.
John Flenniken, son of signer of Mecklenburg Protest, 1808.
Mary Flenniken, 1775-1836.
Samuel Flenniken, son of signer.

Joseph Flenniken, Elizabeth Flenniken, children of Samuel.
John Mc. Simpson, 1859.
Sarah Jett, 1835.
John Davis, 1839.
Roady Anderson, 1870.
John Young, 1757-1829, Revolutionary Soldier.

TOMBSTONE RECORDS

This graveyard is situated in Lincoln County, Tenn., about one and one-half miles from Fayetteville, which is the county seat of Lincoln County. It is on the right-hand side of the highway leading from Fayetteville to Shelbyville and can easily be seen from the highway. (The condition of this graveyard is such that it is just beginning to become dilapidated.) · Copied by Louise Harrison.

E. M. Anderson, April 14, 1836-Jan. 22, 1863.
Amos Anderson, Aug. 22, 1809-July 28, 1876.

Malinda Anderson, wife of Amos Anderson, May 20, 1801-Dec. 8, 1884.
William M. Anderson, Oct. 6, 1832-July 25, 1905.

Bible Records—Tombstone Inscriptions

Martha Jane Blankenship, wife of Willis Blankenship, and daughter of Hugh and Jane C. Thomison, Nov. 15, 1830-Oct. 2, 1859.
Fannie Broadway, wife of J. E. Broadway, Feb. 18, 1854-Dec. 1, 1907.
Son of G. B. and Julia Ann Cowan, born and died Sept. 9, 1855.
Cora Ann Gray, June 23, 1872-July 1, 1877.
Martha E. Gammill, wife of J. J. Gammill, daughter of A. and M. Anderson, Oct. 26, 1835-Jan. 12, 1879.
Blount W. Grigsby, 1846-1867.
Elizabeth, wife of J. W. Jean, Oct. 12, 1833-Mar. 30, 1902.
Samuel Lee Jones, son of W. H. and M. C. Jones, Aug. 27, 1866-Sept. 30, 1880.
Mary L. K. Jewell, Mar. 12, 1840-Mar. 1, 1854.

Robert Campbell Kennedy, Aug. 25, 1761-Feb. 25, 1815.
Esther Edminston Kennedy, April 12, 1766-Aug. 16, 1823.
Sallie Buchanan Kennedy, Aug. 1, 1806-July 25, 1818.
Mary M. Kercheval, Feb. 14, 1799-Nov. 29, 1854.
Annie Lizzie McKinney, Mar. 11, 1851-May 4, 1877.
James Z. Motlow, son of Z. and Mary E. Motlow, Sept. 7, 1830-Aug. 28, 1892.
(Bad condition and may be a little different, but best as can be made out.)
Arih(K) McO'Naway, Dec. 25, 1801-Feb. 20, 1854.
Bettie Jenkins Renfro, wife of B. F. Renfro, June 15, 1863-June 7, 1913.

New Providence Graveyard

Tombstone records from New Providence Graveyard, Lenior City, Tenn., R. F. D. Copied by Louise Harrison.

C. M. Hotchkiss, Sept. 22, 1802-Jan. 26, 1892.
Sallie Wyly Hotchkiss, Sept. 4, 1811-Aug. 4, 1889.

John Lauderdale, Dec. 27, 1835-Oct. 24, 1904.
Louisa Lauderdale, Nov. 23, 1845-Dec. 6, 1912.

Mt. Harmony Cemetery

Copied from tombstones in Mt. Harmony Cemetery, about four miles east of Niota, McMinn County, Tenn. By Mira Love Lowry (Mrs. J. W.) and J. Walker Lowry.

Our mother, Susan Lowry, wife of Daniel Lowry, Sept. 26, 1805-Nov. 23, 1878.
In memory of Daniel Lowry, Mar. 15, 1797-Mar. 1, 1861.
Rebecca J. Davis; age, 25 years.
Rebecca Janes, wife of John Cunningham, Sept. 10, 1813-Oct. 27, 1856.
In memory of James Lowry, Nov. 28, 1771-Dec. 4, 1849; born in Ireland.
In memory of Nancy Lowry, Jan. 15, 1773-Oct. 19, 1851.
Esther I. Lowry, Sept. 19, 1841-Jan. 5, 1859.
Ellen Lowry, Mar. 13, 1812-April 30, 1865.
Capt. John D. Lowry, June 15, 1810-Jan. 5, 1897.
Robert P. Lowry, May 13, 1853-Feb. 26, 1868.

Mary Ellen Lowry, Nov. 25, 1843-Mar. 2, 1902.
Lodusky C., daughter of J. H. and M. C. Lowry, Sept. 25, 1874-Oct. 29, 1874.
Cornelia Lowry, Feb. 13, 1844-Dec. 20, 1887.
Corrinna M. A., wife of James Lowry, Sr., Sept. 14, 1809-Feb. 2, 1885.
James Lowry, Nov. 19, 1806-Nov. 10, 1877. (Born 3 months after family came to U. S. A. from Ireland.)
Maggie F. Hardin, Oct. 26, 1843-April 6, 1903.
James C. Lowery, Sept. 23, 1844-Oct. 20, 1879 (Masonic Emblem).
Clarissa, wife of T. J. Lowry, June 3, 1830-Nov. 19, 1916.
Samuel N. Lowry, Oct. 9, 1862-Dec. 23, 1890.

Bible Records—Tombstone Inscriptions

Nancy B. Lowry, Nov. 23, 1823-April 20, 1857.

James McGill, Oct. 28, 1830-Aug. 14, 1865.

BLACKMAN GRAVEYARD

Located in Seventh Civil District of Rutherford County, Tennessee, seven miles west of Murfreesboro, Tenn., almost at the end of Manson Pike. Copied by Mrs. Alfred Battle. The following graves and tombstones are to be found.

Alfred Blackman, Nov. 14, 1790-June 29, 1872; moved to Rutherford County in 1808.

Elizabeth Blackman, wife of Alfred Blackman, died Sept. 20, 1865, in 74th year of her age.

Elizabeth Blackman, mother of Alfred Blackman; died, 1845, in the 75th year of her age.

Lazarus Blackman, son of Alfred and Elizabeth Blackman; died, 1842, in 34th year of his age.

Hilary Oats Blackman, son of A. B. Blackman, Jan. 4, 1824-Sept. 15, 1872.

Temperance Blackman Fanning; died, 1854; age, 27 years.

Sarah Jane McLane; died, 1842; age, 23 years.

Allen M. Blackman; died, 1840; age, 31 years.

Benjamin Blackman, died, 1843; age, 17 months.

James Blackman, Dec. 25, 1832-May 1, 1853.

William Blackman, Sept. 16, 1834-Aug. 21, 1853.

Mary Ellen Batey, wife of James M. Batey, and daughter of Hezekiah and Julia A. Howse, Dec. 3, 1829-Dec. 12, 1853.

Other graves, but unmarked, are those of Hezekiah Howse, died about 1843; married Nov. 13, 1828; his wife, Julia Ann Howse, June 7, 1813-June 3, 1891.

ANDREW EWING GRAVEYARD

Inscriptions on stones in the graveyard of Andrew Ewing, Revolutionary patriot, whose ancestral home is now known as the E. T. Noel farm, four miles south of Nashville, Tenn., on the Granny White Pike; copied in 1911 by Albert Ewing, Jr., great-great-grandson of Andrew Ewing, I. Sent by Mrs. Albert Ewing, III, Nashville.

Andrew Ewing, born in the State of Pennsylvania, Mar. 17, 1740; educated in the Quaker persuasion of the mild and benignant principles of the sect, he was the brightest ornament; he died May 1, 1813; age, 75 years; proverbially good, honest, and charitable. He lived as he died, in peace with all men; the first clerk of Davidson County, from Oct., 1783, until April, 1813.

Sacred to the memory of Susannah Ewing, consort of Andrew Ewing, buried by her side; born in Philadelphia Dec. 25, 1737-Oct. 31, 1818; age, 80 years, 10 months, 5 days.

To the memory of Nathan Ewing, Feb. 17, 1776-May 1, 1830. This monument is dedicated by his surviving wife and sons as a testimony of their love for his person and their respect for his virtues. By his virtues he raised to himself a monument more precious than gold, more durable than marble.

Dr. John O. Ewing, a native and citizen of Nashville, Tenn., June 16, 1800-Feb. 28, 1826; age, 25 years, 8 months, 12 days. He leaves his parents, Nathan and Sarah Ewing, and his wife, Lamaria A.

Hill, infant son of J. O. and L. S. Ewing, born and died Feb. 27, 1825.

Bible Records—Tombstone Inscriptions

Susannah Ewing, July 15, 1813-Sept. 13, 1814.
Dan H. Ewing, born 26th of May, 1817, and died the same day, son of Nathan and Sallie Ewing.
John Ewing, infant son of J. M. and Charlotte C. Smith, Aug. 19, 1826-Sept. 19, 1826; age, 1 month.
Martha Ann, only daughter of Joel M. and Charlotte C. Smith, June 30, 1824-Dec. 11, 1835; age, 11 years, 6 months, 19 days.
Sacred to the memory of Henry Bateman, our dear father, born June 14, 1781.
Erected in memory of Elizabeth Sluder, consort of A. B. Sluder, and daughter of Wm. and Lucinda Garner, who departed this life 1835; age, 46 years, 4 months, 20 days.
To W. G. E., infant son of A. B. and Elizabeth Sluder, who departed this life Aug. 14, 1835; age, 5 months, 6 days.
"To Mac Bean."

GRAVESTONES OF TWO REVOLUTIONARY SOLDIERS

John Chambers, died Dec. 30, 1841; age, 102 years. He was a Soldier of the Revolution and served. (This stone is in the cemetery in Wright City, Lincoln County, Mo.)
Sacred to the memory of William Barnhill, who departed this life May 4, 1810; age, 75 years.
Isabella Barnhill (wife) who died Aug. 7, 1826; age, 67 years.
Isabella Barnhill, daughter, who died Feb. 13, 1826; age, 23 years.
The large stone under which the three were buried is in the Bersheba Burying Ground, York County, S. C.

BARNHILL GRAVEYARD
Near Guys, McNairy County, Tenn.

John N. Barnhill, Oct. 21, 1811-Aug. 14, 1881.
Elizabeth, wife of J. N. Barnhill, Oct. 11, 1809-April 27, 1893.
William N., son of J. N. and Elizabeth Barnhill, May 13, 1840-Aug. 30, 1871; Capt. of Co. A, 19th Tenn. Cav., C. S. A.
Virgil Decalb Barnhill, born Aug. 7, 1837; killed in battle of Perryville, Ky., Oct. 8, 1862; Lieut-Col. G., 31st Tenn. Reg., C. S. A.
Samuel Barnhill, Mar. 5, 1833-May 2, 1835.
Cynthia Ann Barnhill, May 25, 1843-Aug. 16, 1854.
Henry R. Sharp, Oct. 21, 1809-April 25, 1875.

GRAVEYARD OF THE CLYNE HOMESTEAD
Six miles southeast of Nashville on the Chattanooga Road

Daniel Vaulx, born in Maryland, died Aug. 15, 1815; age, about 65 years.
Catherine Vaulx, wife of Daniel Vaulx, born in Caroline County, Va., July 20, 1755-Nov. 12, 1851; age, 96 years, 8 months, 23 days.
Sacred to the memory of Mary Vaulx, consort of Wm. Vaulx, and daughter of Charles and Ann Hays, April 22, 1799-Dec. 31, 1829; age, 30 years, 8 months, 9 days.

DILLAHUNTY-McFADDEN GRAVES

Inscriptions in graveyard located in a field southwest of the Belle Meade Golf and County Club, to the right of Belle Meade Boulevard going toward Percy Warner Park entrance.

John Dillahunty, Dec. 8, 1728-Feb. 9, 1816; was for 60 years a minister of the gospel, Baptist Order.
Sally Beaton Dillahunty died on Sun-

Bible Records—Tombstone Inscriptions

day, June 10, 1817, in 10th year of her age.
Hannah Dillahunty, Mar. 30, 1732-May 5, 1816.
Dorcas Beaton died Mar. 22, 1813; age, 69 years.
Lucy McFadden died Aug. 11, 1843; age, 45 years.
William McFadden, Oct. 7, 1824-Dec. 4, 1830.
James Branch McFadden, Nov. 13, 1832-Jan. 23, 1837.

GREEN HILL PLACE GRAVEYARD

Inscriptions in graveyard on the old Green Hill place near Brentwood, in Williamson County, Tenn. Information from Mrs. George Waters, Belmont Boulevard, Nashville, Tenn.

Rev. Green Hill, born in the old county of Bute, N. C., Nov. 3, 1741; died, Sept. 11, 1826. He was a major in the Provincial Army of North Carolina and a member of the first and each successive session of the Provincial Congress of North Carolina. "Blessed is the man that trusteth in Thee."
Mary Seawell Hill, daughter of Col. Benj. Seawell, of the old County Bute, N. C., wife of Col. Green Hill, Aug. 1, 1751-Mar. 29, 1821.

Rev. Joshua C. Hill, Aug. 10, 1795-May 12, 1827. "Blessed are the dead which die in the Lord."
Lemiza Hill, daughter of Wm. and Penelope Lanier and relict of Rev. Joshua C. Hill, born near Wilmington, N. C., Jan. 16, 1801; died, Feb. 10, 1860. "Blessed are they that keep His testimonies and that seek Him with the whole heart."

GRAVEYARD OF "SYLVAN HALL"

Inscriptions on stones in the graveyard of "Sylvan Hall," home of Captain Joseph Philips who fought in North Carolina during the Revolution. The farm is located on the Dickerson Pike, six miles north of Nashville, Tenn.

Joseph Philips, Oct. 31, 1763-May 22, 1822; born in North Carolina and settled on this place in 1791.
Milbiry Philips, wife of J. Philips, Dec. 4, 1764-Dec. 19, 1851; born in North Carolina and settled on this place in 1791.
William D. Philips, son of Joseph and Milbiry Phillips, born on this farm, April 19, 1804; died where he was born and lived, June 15, 1879.
Eliza Dwyer, wife of William D. Philips, daughter of Daniel and Bridget Dwyer, born at Roscrea, Tipperary County Ireland, Aug. 3, 1801; died, May 10, 1871.
Margaret Thomas, wife of Josiah F. Williams, daughter of Joseph and Milbrey Philips, Sept. 30, 1799-1844.
To the memory of Josiah F. Williams; this monument is erected by his children; he was born on the 2nd day of Feb., 1780, and died on the 29th day of Nov., 1851. His life was characterized by inflexible honesty, sterling ———, the most unpretending ———.
Sally Philips, Aug. 1, 1783-Jan. 19, 1859.
Wm. Williams and Sally Philips married Feb. 11, 1807.
Wm. Williams, April 15, 1776-Mar. 6, 1872.
In memory of Charlotte Philips, who died July 23, 1811, in the 16th year of her age.
Henry Williams, a moral and intelligent youth, May 3, 1814-July 14, 1826.
Elisha Williams; died, Aug. 17, 1811; age, 62 years. Married Mar. 25, 1775, and had six children: William, Betsey, Joshua, Elisha, Josiah, Martha.
Sacred to the memory of Eliza N., daughter of Wm. Williams, wife of Evander McIver, departed this life Mar. 28, 1826, in the 19th year of her age.

Bible Records—Tombstone Inscriptions

Mary, daughter of William and Sarah Williams, and wife of Robert M. Porter; born, Oct. 26, 1816; married, Dec. 4, 1838; died, Mar. 21, 1839.
Martha H. Williams, Nov. 29, 1809-Nov. 3, 1833.
Robert, infant son of J. F. and M. T. Williams.
Evander McIver Williams, May 25, 1829-Dec. 27, 1855.
David D., son of J. F. and M. T. Williams, Jan. 11, 1829-Feb. 17, 1829.
William, son of Wm. D. and Eliza Philips, Sept. 3, 1846-July 11, 1862.
Father—William P. Harding.
Mother—Milberry C. Philips.
Sarah, infant child of Wm. D. and —.
Joseph Philips, who died July, 1823; age, 6 months.
Beneath this inscription lies the unfortunate Joseph John Sumner who was born Aug. 14, 1780, and perished in the Gulf of Mexico on the morning of Dec. 28, 1813. Oh! Gulf of Mexico, why hast thou thus deprived us of this our most affectionate friend. As the —— of spring fadeth away the leaves, etc., etc.
William Henry Sumner, son of the above, Sept. 24, 1813-June 30, 1816.

Gower Church Graveyard

On the Gower Road, which turns off the River Road; the River Road begins at the Charlotte Pike about eight miles from Nashville.

Charlotte Gower, July 1, 1782-April 16, 1860.
Rev. William Gower, Oct. 6, 1776-Oct. 11, 1851.
Lorenzo D. Gower, Sept. 27, 1803-July 11, 1892. Asleep in Jesus, blessed thought.
Nathan Gatlin, Jan. 30, 1782-Mar. 8, 1855.
Obedience Gatlen, Dec. 16, 1787-June 18, 1866.
Susan L. Bradford; died, July 26, 1904; age, 60 years.
Mary E. Robertson, Nov. 24, 1828-June 28, 1910. Gone home.
A. J. Johnson, Sept. 24, 1842-Jan. 28, 1910.
Henry E. Kimbro, Nov. 22, 1850-Sept. 12, 1890.
Walter S. Johnson, June 13, 1879-May 28, 1924.
Ina Christine Johnson, Feb. 8, 1906-May 23, 1927.
Lonnie H. Johnson, May 3, 1907-Oct. 13, 1923.

Mount Moriah Church Graveyard

Six miles from Pulaski, Giles County, Tenn.

Sacred to the memory of the Rev. John Wray who was a native of Ireland; was educated at Cole-rain; emigrated to U. S. A. in 1816; became a member and minister of the C. P. Church in the worship of which he lived a consistent member and a useful minister until his death which occurred the 20th of Dec., 1856. The religion he commended to others during his life and ministry was his consolation in death. His toils are passed, his work is done; and he is fully blessed, he fought the fight, the victory won.

Pleasant Grove Cemetery

The following inscription is on the stone over the only child of the above Rev. John Wray, and was found in the Pleasant Grove

Bible Records—Tombstone Inscriptions

Cemetery, four miles from Selmer, McNairy County, Tenn., on the Highway to Corinth, Miss.:

In memory of Mary Jane, wife of Rev. Robert Young, died June 3, 1855; age, about 33 years, 5 months.
Other inscriptions in the Pleasant Grove Cemetery are:
Brice P. Ray, Feb. 20, 1838-Nov. 28, 1921.
Margaret Ann, wife of B. P. Ray, Dec. 24, 1846-May 31, 1868.
N. F. Ray, wife of B. P. Ray, Nov. 5, 1848-Aug. 26, 1914.
Nancy A., daughter of B. P. and M. A. Ray, May 27, 1868-Oct. 17, 1868.
Edmona, daughter of R. and J. J. Young, July 2, 1860-Aug. 31, 1873.

The following inscriptions on stones in an old graveyard about eight and one-half miles out the Granny White Pike, from Nashville:

Harriet Tucker, Jan. 22, 1821-Sept. 22, 1862.
Stephen Tucker, Oct. 21, 1821-Feb. 6, 1871.
Oliver H. Hayes, Sr., 1857-1916.
Stephen T. Hayes, 1891-1915.
Fannie T. Hayes, 1857-1899.
Henry B. Hayes, 1882-1899.
Ella C. Carpenter, Sept. 3, 1871-1892.
M. C. Carpenter, Dec. 25, 1851-Sept. 8, 1904.

PASCO CHRISTIAN CHURCH GRAVEYARD
Fifteen miles out Harding Road

Martha Cartwright, Jan. 11, 1842-Sept. 16, 1917.
Thomas Jefferson Spears, Feb. 23, 1858-Mar. 14, 1914.
Nancy Ellen Barnes, Sept. 15, 1842-May 4, 1912.
Lucy Wilkins, daughter of A. R. and Della Castleman, Mar. 21, 1917-Feb. 18, 1918.
Annie Pearl, daughter of Walter W. and Missouri B. Jones, Aug. 14, 1902-July 11, 1913.
Howard Grover, son of Cleveland and Lura Peach, June 8, 1914-Dec. 31, 1914.
Mr. and Mrs. W. M. McNeill; he was born Mar. 22, 1845, and died May 25, 1919; she was born May 8, 1855, and died Mar. 19, 1930.
James G. Harrison, 1833-Jan. 4, 1913.
William Carroll Potts, July 21, 1831-Aug. 25, 1915.
M. J. Potts, Jan. 12, 1862-April 26, 1914.
S. E., wife of M. J. Potts, Jan. 8, 1864.
I. F. Newson, June 17, 1890-Jan. 5, 1917.
Hardy Douglas, son of Albert and Odell Potts, June 17, 1913-June 18, 1913.
I. M. Potts, Feb. 27, 1838-Oct. 13, 1910.
Lucinda A. Potts, Dec. 2, 1825-Jan. 2, 1913.
Cynthia Velony Potts, Mar. 19, 1845-Feb. 5, 1923.
Infant son of Flaud and Lena Burnett, born and died Oct. 4, 1910.

ALLISON PLACE GRAVEYARD
About seventeen miles from Nashville, Tenn., on the Harding Road

ALLISON

Thomas Brown, born at Brentsville, Prince William County, Va., April 7, 1800; died at his home, Old Town, Williamson County, Tenn., Jan. 13, 1870.
Mrs. Nancy Brown, wife of Thomas Brown, daughter of Hugh and Lydia Allison, Oct. 6, 1810-Jan. 21, 1838.
Joseph A. Brown, Oct. 10, 1829-Sept. 6, 1857.
Hugh Allison, Oct. 21, 1767-Sept. 3, 1837.

Bible Records—Tombstone Inscriptions

Lydia Allison, wife of Hugh Allison, Sept. 16, 1777-Mar. 26, 1834.
Richard H. Allison, Jan. 1, 1804-Feb. 7, 1837.
Margaret Walker, daughter of Hugh and Lydia Allison, Aug. 3, 1801-Feb. 22, 1847.
Infant son of W. T. and Tennie Castleman, Feb. 5, 1903-Feb. 5, 1903.
John W., son of W. T. and Tennie Castleman, Sept. 10, 1901-Nov. 20, 1903.
Lydia Allison, daughter of Alexander and Mary Allison, Mar. 23, 1834-Sept. 1, 1854.
Hugh Allison, Jan. 31, 1835-July 27, 1900.
Margery Venable, wife of H. B. Venable, Dec. 31, 1797-April 1, 1858.
Sarah H. Allison, wife of Thomas J. Allison, April 1, 1816-Sept. 9, 1836.
Thomas J. Allison, April 9, 1808-Jan. 2, 1897.
W. H. Allison, Aug. 27, 1845-July 10, 1919.
Nannie M. Allison, May 17, 1855-Jan. 26, 1926.
E. M. Mayberry, Aug. 19, 1828-May 14, 1916.
Hugh Allison, Aug. 23, 1877-July 5, 1911.
Tabitha Newson, wife of Thomas Allison, Nov. 7, 1819-Aug. 23, 1910.
Nannie L., daughter of Thos. and Tabitha Allison, and wife of Hugh Allison, May 28, 1846-Jan. 13, 1864.
Cornelia N., daughter of Thomas and Tabitha Allison, Sept. 12, 1849-July 31, 1865.
Maude E. Newsom, Sept. 30, 1843-Nov. 15, 1873.
Sallie C., daughter of Thomas and Tabitha Allison, Nov. 15, 1841-Sept. 8, 1891.
Mattie A., wife of John W. Baugh, May, 18, 1858-Sept. 29, 1897.
Hattie Lou Allison, Aug. 2, 1900-Feb. 23, 1911.
Willie D., daughter of John W. and Matilda Sept. 2, 1888-June 24, 1889.
The above Allison inscriptions are to be found on the old Allison Place, about 17 miles from Nashville, Tenn., on the Harding Road.

CLEARWATER BEACH GRAVEYARD

At the old entrance to Clearwater Beach, about twenty miles from Nashville, Tenn.

LINTON

Margaret, daughter of Benj. and Morning Pritchett, and wife of Silas Linton, Sr., April 7, 1803-Oct. 9, 1878.
Silas Linton, Aug. 8, 1790-Aug. 1, 1873.
Silas Linton, Sr., Oct. 30, 1848-Aug. 3, 1916 (father).
Kate Anderson Linton, Feb. 22, 1851-July 5, 1916 (mother).
Silas Linton, Jr., Dec. 26, 1873-Sept. 26, 1914.
Betty P. Linton, Mar. 11, 1840-Aug. 5, 1895.
Rosa, wife of J. V. Linton, daughter of Thomas and Lucie Hughes, July 21, 1844-Feb. 9, 1873.
Tommie, son of J. V. and B. P. Linton, Jan. 8, 1879-Jan. 21, 1879.
Mary Jane, second wife of William J. Linton, daughter of Elizabeth and P. W. Moss, Sept. 15, 1834-June 25, 1855.
Eustacia A., daughter of W. J. and
E. A. Linton, Sept. 6, 1875-Oct. 14, 1877.
Willie R., daughter of W. J. and E. A. Linton, April 19, 1862-Nov. 2, 1877.
Janie Linton, Jan. 25, 1869-Nov. 27, 1885.
W. J. Linton, Oct. 22, 1822-Nov. 29, 1885.
Eustacia Ann Linton, nee Hughes, 1862-1912 (mother).
J. V., son of W. J. and M. E. Linton, Jan. 8, 1884-Nov. 8, 1895.
W. J. Linton, Mar. 4, 1858-July 7, 1918.
Mary Frances Linton, May 26, 1852-May 21, 1929.
Nathan G. B. Greer, Feb. 2, 1832-Sept. 10, 1883.
Margaret, daughter of W. J. and Jarutio J. Linton, and wife of Nathan G. B. Greer, Dec. 21, 1845-Jan. 29, 1879.
Martha T., daughter of Nathan and Margaret Greer, Aug. 1, 1863-April 2, 1866.

Bible Records—Tombstone Inscriptions

William J. Linton, son of Nathan G. B. and Margaret Greer, April 28, 1875-May 6, 1875.
Infant daughter of W. M. and Janie Alexander, died May 24, 1835.
Fred, son of W. M. and Janie Alexander.
Katie Anderson Joslin, 1906-1907.
Anna Louise Joslin, 1902-1906.
Annie Lou Linton Joslin, 1876, ——.
Charles L. Joslin, 1873-1929.
John D. Allen, Aug. 23, 1869-Dec. 23, 1904.
E. Lee Vaughan, May 19, 1855-July 7, 1886.

Jarutio Jane, wife of Wm. J. Linton, Dec. 8, 1825-July 10, 1853.
Thomas H. Linton, son of Wm. J. and Jarutio Jane Linton, May 17, 1853-May 20, 1853.
Saley F., daughter of Nathan G. B. and Margaret Greer, June 15, 1876-June 16, 1876.
Lucy Minor, daughter of W. J. and E. A. Linton, June 10, 1858-July 15, 1876.
(Above inscriptions in graveyard at the old entrance to Clearwater Beach, about 20 miles from Nashville, Tenn.)

Smith Graveyard

About sixteen miles from Nashville on the Harding Road Chapter.

Smith

William H., son of Byrd F. and Lucy J. Smith, Oct. 27, 1861-Jan 7, 1890.
Lucy L. Mays, Dec. 23, 1863-July 12, 1886.
McPherson, George W., 1874-19—;
Lucy G., 1863-1931.
James H. Smith, July 13, 1788-Sept. 26, 1840; age, 57 years, 2 months, 13 days; a member of the Christian Church.
Lucy Smith, wife of James H. Smith, Mar. 16, 1793-Aug. 3, 1872; age, 79 years, 4 months, 17 days; a member of the Christian Church.
Nathan G. Smith, Feb. 25, 1834-Feb. 26, 1914.
Eunice Elizabeth Ragan, wife of N. G. Smith, Aug. 14, 1841-April 24, 1915.
Walter S. Smith (father), Dec. 12, 1831-Feb. 15, 1899.
Mary Elizabeth Neal, wife of Walter S. Smith, Oct. 29, 1842-May 24, 1914.
Byrd F. Smith, Feb. 1, 1824, ——.
Lucy J. Smith, Jan. 6, 1832-Feb. 9, 1915.
James T. Mays, April 13, 1840-April 16, 1895.
Emily P. Smith, wife of James T. Mays, Dec. 30, 1838, ——.
J. T. Mayes, Oct. 9, 1863-Mar. 26, 1903.
Jennie Smith, wife of Z. T. Pegram, Aug. 25, 1866-Dec. 24, 1907.
A. P., son of Billy and Ida Greer, July 3, 1900-Oct. 31, 1903.

James A., son of John A. and Margaret Couch, Jan. 22, 1843-July 30, 1843; age, 6 months, 8 days.
James M., son of J. A. and M. Couch, Jan. 2, 1837-Sept. 29, 1838.
Robert F. Glenn departed this life July 24, 1820; age, 6 months.
Infant daughter of William and Mary Stewart, 1829.
Thomas Weston; died, July 18, 1830; age, 48 years.
Horatio Nelson Weston, Oct. 21, 1805-Feb. 8, 1849.
Miss Sophia J. Western, Nov. 27, 1801-May 13, 1830.
Clement Weston departed this life Jan. 3, 1844; age, 18 years, 6 months.
Frances M. Woodfin, May 6, 1807-Jan. 29, 1832.
Cordelia Ann Woodfin, Dec. 22, 1831-Sept. 4, 1832.
John N. Moore, July 4, 1776-Mar. 12, 1828.
Wilmirth F. Moore, Aug. 31, 1803-Feb. 14, 1831.
Catherine Hogan died Oct. 23, 1822; age, 2 years, 9 months.
Sarah Burgie died Aug. 15, 1829; age, 3 months, 9 days.
Darby Cooney, a native of Enniscorthy, County Wexford, Ireland, died May 2, 1834; age, 22 years.
Sarah E. Swiney, infant daughter of M. and Mary E. Swiney, born the 13th and died the 15th of April, 1822.
Eliza, IV, daughter of J. and N. Web-

Bible Records—Tombstone Inscriptions

ber, died Aug. 23, 1820; age, 9 months, 22 days.
William C., son of J. and N. Webber, died July 4, 1822; age, 1 year, 6 months, 12 days.
Elizabeth S., daughter of J. and N. Webber, died Oct. 10, 1823; age, 1 year, 12 days.
John A., son of J. and N. Webber, died July 7, 1825; age, 1 year, 6 months, 1 day.
Nancy Webber, consort of John Webber, departed this life Mar. 26, 1828;
age, 24 years, 6 months, 6 days.
Wm. A. Bradshaw, Aug. 17, 1818-Nov. 17, 1842. Erected by his brother-in-law, B. R. B. Wallace.
Will M. Diggons departed this life Sept. 7, 1824.
Lilla Diggons, 1835-1836.
Amelia A. Dougle.
My wife, Ann C. Hays Levin.
Rachel Moore, consort of Francis Moore, departed this life Dec. 2, 1825.
Luticia, daughter of Robert and Matilda Wilson, Oct. 28, 1833,——.

Cedar Grove Cemetery

At Athens, McMinn County, Tenn. Sent by Alexander Keith Chapter.

A

Rebecca E. Alexander, June 14, 1840-Sept. 25, 1857.
Sarah G. Atlee, Dec. 29, 1807-Jan. 13, 1891.
Rev. Edwin A. Atlee, Dec. 7, 1804-April 18, 1869.
Delilah G. Atlee, Sept. 27, 1809-July 10, 1885.
Daniel B. Agnew, Dec. 13, 1803-Aug. 19, 1852.
Nora Sehorn, wife of B. G. Atlee, July 8, 1849-June 5, 1871.
Wm. W. Alexander, M.D., born in Robersville, Tenn., 1830; graduated from University of New York, 1854; died, 1876.
Mrs. Ann M. Anderson, wife of Colpearo B. Anderson, died July 13, 1846.

B

E. J. Gettys, wife of J. L. Bridges, 1831-1854.
J. G. Bridges, 1854-1883.
Archibald Blizard, 1818-1897.
Martha Brazzelton, wife of T. M. Burkett, Oct. 31, 1830-Feb. 22, 1901.
George G. Blanghard, born at Rushford, N. Y., Aug. 4, 1862; died at Athens, Tenn., April 24, 1890.
Margaret D., wife of Geo. W. Bridges, Mar. 23, 1829-Aug. 14, 1853.
J. L. Blackwell, born Dec. 1, 1834.
Julius B. Bridges, Aug. 15, 1847-Jan. 3, 1876.
Cornelius Brown, June 15, 1782-Feb. 26, 1864.
Julia A. Baker, Nov. 16, 1813-July 16, 1890.
James Baker, May 4, 1811-Nov. 18, 1888.
James A. Baker, July 11, 1856-April 5, 1881.
Victoria Banks, April 22, 1868-Mar. 10, 1889.
A. B. Brown, May 20, 1809-Jan. 11, 1860.
Ann W., wife of Charles Malfour, daughter of Robert and Elizabeth King of Montgomery County, Va., May 28, 1795-Aug. 19, 1854.
Mrs. Abigail Brown, died Jan. 20, 1832; age, 67 years.
Elizabeth V. Brown, consort of Joel K. Brown, July 17, 1794-Feb. 4, 1855.
Eliza Ann Crawford, wife of Wm. H. Briant, died May 15, 1895; age, 52 years, 10 months, 12 days.
George W. Bridges, Oct. 23, 1847-July 3, 1883.
Erminta E. Burger, Jan. 12, 1853-Oct. 5, 1877.
Nancy E., wife of T. E. Black, July 20, 1849-April 5, 1892.
J. Ross Black, Dec. 5, 1877-July 9, 1900.
Lucinda, wife of L. L. Ball, Oct. 28, 1810-July 6, 1893.
Francis Boyd, died May 20, 1857; age, 58 years.
William Burns, April 17, 1790-Mar. 6, 1869.
Rebecca, wife of Wm. Burns, died Nov. 14, 1878; age, 82 years, 3 months, 13 days.
James F. Bradford, died July 17, 1852; age, 52 years.
Mary B. Boyd, 1812-1899.

Bible Records—Tombstone Inscriptions

Wm. T. Blackwell, son of J. W. and M. Blackwell, Dec. 16, 1827-Nov. 1, 1857.
Nancy Bridges, died May 24, 1887; age, 46 years.
George Branan, Aug. 26, 1872-Sept. 11, 1898.

C

Rev. Seth Church, of Winsted, Conn., Oct. 5, 1852; age, 30 years.
J. C. Calhoun, Dec. 10, 1839-Feb. 25, 1890.
M. E. Calhoun, Oct. 15, 1834-Mar. 3, 1899.
Milly L. Carr, Mar. 30, 1849-Sept. 23, 1892.
Mary C. Cardin, Feb. 15, 1867-Dec. 7, 1900.
Charlotte M., wife of Dr. N. E. Cobleigh, April 21, 1826-Oct. 10, 1893.
Alex. Cleage, Mar. 30, 1801-Jan. 4, 1875.
Jemima Hurst Cleage, Dec. 25, 1813-Aug. 11, 1896.
Margareta, wife of W. R. Carmack, Aug. 22, 1833-Aug. 24, 1881.
Eliza G. Fisher, wife of Bishop R. J. Cooke, 1854-1904.
L. S. Caldwell, 1822-1899.
Fred H. Caldwell, Aug. 7, 1871-June 12, 1893.
Sallie Truley Cleveland, and infant, 1865-1886.
C. K. Crouch, April 5, 1814-July 3, 1884.
Carrie E. Crow, Oct. 6, 1856-May 11, 1891.
Richard R. Crow, Mar. 28, 1870-Nov. 16, 1893.
Nancy, wife of Thomas Caldwell, died April 25, 1877; age, 65 years, 18 days.
A. H. Crow, Aug. 10, 1818-July 22, 1873.
Tennie B. Crow, Sept. 13, 1857-April 17, 1880.
T. J. Cox, Feb. 9, 1865-April 18, 1890.
John Crawford, June 28, 1797-Mar. 26, 1862.
Eliza A. Crawford, Oct. 1, 1809-Jan. 1, 1868.
George G. Crawford, June 2, 1836, died, age, 16 years.
Anna Pocahontas, wife of Rev. J. L. Cook, born at Wythville, Va., June 22, 1871-April 18, 1897.

D

Bessie F. Dodson, July 27, 1879-July 13, 1900.
John J. Dixon, May 6, 1806-Jan. 6, 1874.
Belle Howard, wife of C. B. Davis, Oct., 1860-July 13, 1898.
Charlie B. Davis, Dec. 26, 1860-July 9, 1898.

E

Margaret, wife of Robt. Engledow, died April 3, 1857; age, 80 years.
Mark Ester, May 8, 1818-April 25, 1891.
T. M. Evans, Oct. 31, 1843-Sept. 24, 1899.
Thomas Evans, Dec. 25, 1804-Aug. 2, 1877.

F

Rev. John Foster, 1802-1894.
Margaret E. Fisher, 1847-1915.
R. M. Fisher, 1817-1883.
J. H. Fox, Jan. 9, 1824-Nov. 5, 1892.
Nancy, consort of the late Dr. A. P. Fore, Mar., 1785-June 21, 1858.

G

Elizabeth Gilbert, Sept. 1, 1814-June 17, 1900.
Jackson Grubb, born in Wyth County, Va., June 21, 1816; died in Athens, Tenn., May 7, 1879.
Virginia C. Grubb, April 9, 1842-April 14, 1896.
Maggie V. Gibson, 1847-1873.
Susan K., daughter of Chas. and Margaret Gibson, April 10, 1849-June 15, 1856.
Nancy Brazzleton, wife of J. W. Gillespie, Nov. 10, 1829-Oct. 20, 1887.
Sallie White Grant, 1837-1899.
Dorothy B. R., wife of J. Gettys, 1807-1864.
James Gettys, 1799-1879.
Hannah D., wife of J. Gettys, 1798-1833.
W. L. Gettys, 1835-1860.
R. T. Gettys, 1827-1863.
John M. Gresham, May 22, 1821-April 4, 1856.
Nancy Gresham, wife of John M. Gresham, May 4, 1828-May 9, 1851.
T. M. Gass, Aug. 10, 1818-Mar. 7, 1888.
Dora Gass, Dec. 15, 1860-Oct. 9, 1886.
Wiley S. Gaston, Nov. 28, 1848-Sept. 4, 1900.

Bible Records—Tombstone Inscriptions

Mrs. Hattie H. Gaston, died July 27, 1889.
Sarah Jane, wife of G. R. Gilbert, daughter of Alvan and Mary Jones, July 9, 1820-Aug. 9, 1851.
Bernhart Gilbert, Esq., of Gettysburg, Pa., died Oct. 27, 1868; age, 82 years.
Susanna, consort of Bernhart Gilbert, died July 21, 1863; age, 77 years, 6 months.
Mary, wife of —— Gardiner, Sept. 6, 18—-April 12, 1874.
John P. Griffin, April 24, 1830-Feb. 16, 1871.
Bernhart Gilbert, Sept. 23, 1837-Nov. 6, 1892.

H

Julia A., wife of S. G. Hoge, Jan. 19, 1814-Dec. 16, 1882.
George W. Hoge, Dec. 10, 1838-Nov. 2, 1886.
Emma C., wife of Alfred S. Haley, Aug. 12, 1844-June 25, 1881.
Cornelia M., wife of W. F. Henderson, Dec. 15, 1850-Aug. 25, 1872.
James Henry Hornsby, Major 9th Tenn. Cav. U. S. A. from 1861-1865, Oct. 23, 1823-Mar. 12, 1917.
J. N. Hicks, June 13, 1842-Nov. 30, 1895.
Mrs. P. C. Horton, wife of W. E. Horton, June 4, 1828-May 16, 1875.
Meredith Helm, Oct. 7, 1879; age, 64 years.
James Daniel, son of W. G. and P. C. Horton, Dec. 26, 1857-June 27, 1859.
Lucinda E. Tongray, wife of Holton Humphreys; age, 68 years.
John Wilson Harbison, Mar. 16, 1866-Aug. 17, 1891.
E. W. Hyden, Feb. 22, 1820-July 14, 1884.
A. L. Henderson, Mar. 17, 1795-July 9, 1879.
J. Horace Hickox, Sept. 5, 1852-Aug. 15, 1879.
W. H. Howard, Jan. 28, 1822-Jan. 24, 1879.
James Howard, Feb. 18, 1889; age, 38 years.
W. G. Horton, Jr., Dec. 16, 1859-Feb. 17, 1899.
Mary C. Hunt, died May 5, 1842; age, 25 years.
Mary C. Henninger, Nov. 8, 1840-Nov. 22, 1860.
Wm. Hyden, Sr., 1761-1858.
Elizabeth H., consort of S. B. Harris, Jan. 13, 1819-Dec. 15, 1849.

I

Sam Powell Ivins, Aug. 2, 1811-June 17, 1887.
Mary E. E. Ivins, July 8, 1851-Oct. 28, 1895.
J. L. Ivins, Aug. 12, 1848-Aug. 12, 1916.
Andrew J. Irvin, June 20, 1837-Feb. 23, 1894.

J

Susan A. Joins, born in Knoxville, Sept. 16, 1847; died in Athens, Tenn., Jan 30, 1866.
R. C. Jackson, Sept. 27, 1809-June 18, 1892.
Julia Brazzelton, wife of R. C. Jackson, Dec. 11, 1823-April 13, 1880.
Mary M., daughter of W. A. and A. A. Jones, died Dec. 1876; age, 22 years.
Nathaniel C. Jones, July 16, 1827-Dec. 30, 1891.
Sarah M., wife of A. C. Jones, June 19, 1839-Feb. 1, 1881.
Mart A. Johnson, wife of E. P. Johnson, Mar. 10, 1843-July 13, 1881.
H. E. Johnson, Dec. 28, 1865-Aug. 18, 1887.
Mary Bell Jones, Jan. 15, 1888-May 24, 1899.

K

Peter Kinser, Dec. 27, 1779-Nov. 4, 1837.
Jamima Kinser, Jan. 27, 1784-June 11, 1854.
M. F. Kilzoe, Aug. 14, 1866; age, 45 years.
Mrs. M. A. Keyes, died Dec. 21, 1883; age, 72 years.
A. D. Keys, died April 21, 1829.
Julia, daughter of C. L. and Julia R. King, Dec. 13, 1861-Mar. 30, 1883.
Julia R., wife of C. L. King, Jan. 8, 1813-April 26, 1889.
Charles L. King, Nov. 13, 1810-Mar. 6, 1892.
W. B. Kelley, husband of Eliza Kelley, July 26, 1836-Mar. 31, 1892.
D. N. Kyker, July 14, 1862-Aug. 3, 1889.

L

Catherine Atlee Lane, 1830-1881.
Mary Atlee Lester, June 13, 1868-Feb. 1, 1893.

Bible Records—Tombstone Inscriptions

Pleasant A. Lawson, Nov. 23, 1847-May 16, 1900.
Wm. Lasater, Mar. 5, 1820-Oct. 19, 1891.
Nancy Lasater, Dec. 20, 1824-April 25, 1895.
Mary J., wife of W. L. Lafferty, daughter of F. and Mary B. Boyd, died June 23, 1861; age, 24 years.
John W. Lide, M.D., Mar. 22, 1792-April 10, 1842.
Tennie, daughter of Wm. and N. A. Lasater, Nov. 28, 1852-Nov., 1890.
Rev. Carroll S. Long, Ph.D., Jan. 3, 1850-Sept. 4, 1890.
Sarah E. Long, April 4, 1829-Dec. 5, 1889.

M

James L. Matthews, July 29, 1862-Nov. 23, 1881.
McCulley Vault, 1892.
Gideon R. Matthews, April 27, 1860-July 29, 1887.
Sarah Jane Rankin, wife of J. H. Magill, Nov. 1, 1826-Dec. 15, 1885.
James H. Magill, Sept. 3, 1823-Nov. 9, 1897.
Rev. John B. Meek, born Sept. 24, 1821; installed as pastor of Mars Hill Church, June 18, 1848, died Oct. 18, 1848.
Elizabeth J. Murrell, wife of Onslow G. Murrell, June 8, 1807-Mar. 31, 1947.
Margaret Lipscomb, wife of G. H. Mayo, June 18, 1823-Feb. 14, 1890.
John Moss, Dec. 24, 1786-June 7, 1857.
Virginia Lane Moss, Dec. 25, 1840-Mar. 12, 1900.
Andrew W. McKeldin, born in Cookstown, near Belfast, Ireland., Feb. 14, 1805-Jan. 19, 1867.
Margaret L., wife of E. H. McDowell, Feb. 15, 1873-Feb. 25, 1898.
H. A. McAffrey, son of J. W. and N. A. McAffrey, Mar. 17, 1856-April 9, 1889.
John B. Marston, born in Halford, England, May 29, 1852; died in Knoxville, Tenn., Mar. 23, 1886.
Jas. W. McAffrey, May 30, 1827-July 5, 1864.
Anna, wife of H. A. McAffrey, May 30, 1853-May 6, 1881.
W. J. Miller, May 31, 1863-May 12, 1887.
Mary, daughter of J. C. Vaughn, wife of F. B. McElwee, Mar. 6, 1854-July 30, 1892.
James T. McClaskey, Sept. 17, 1839-July 27, 1899.
Lizzie McRoberts, died Aug. 30, 1888; age, 39 years.
Nelson McKamey, May 1, 1806-April 14, 1858.
James A. McMurray, Aug. 1, 1857-Oct. 2, 1891.
William L. Mardith, 2nd Lieut., Company H, 3rd Reg., T. E. T. V. I., U. S. A., Nov. 2, 1839-May 14, 1864.
M. R. May, Oct. 18, 1816-April 15, 1880.
W. B. McKeldin, June 17, 1841-Jan. 8, 1882.
Emley Brazzleton McKeldin, Mar. 6, 1890; age, 69 years.
Martha Cannon McGaughey, Dec. 12, 1808-April 22, 1891.
John McGaughey, Feb. 1, 1797-Jan. 29, 1865.
John G. McGaughey, April 14, 1838-July 11, 1867.
Mattie McGaughey, Jan. 28, 1852-Feb. 26, 1869.
Mary Hattie McKinney, Jan. 3, 1866-Dec. 20, 1876.
Mary Adaline Mayo, daughter of G. W. and M. H. Mayo, died Sept. 3, 1829; age, 11 months, 16 days.
George W. Mayo, April 25, 1801-April 16, 1886.
Sarah G. McEwen, daughter of Charles C. and Ann W. Balfour, wife of R. N. McEwen, May 24, 1827-Sept. 13, 1885.

N

Ross Neil, Aug. 20, 1851-Sept. 5, 1886.
William G. Nice, M.D., born in Manchester, Va., Oct. 5, 1820-July 27, 1853.

P

Mary G. Peck, July 22, 1859-May 1, 1895.
John Campbell Parsons, June 25, 1835-Feb. 4, 1899.
Fannie Parkison, Mar. 22, 1849-Dec. 7, 1894.
Martha J. Harris, wife of J. A. Parsons, June 22, 1870-Mar. 8, 1889.

R

Lavinia Wasson, wife of C. T. Riddle, Dec. 6, 1861-April 17, 1899.
Mrs. Harriet Record, Sept. 26, 1824-Mar. 9, 1900.

Bible Records—Tombstone Inscriptions

Wm. R. Rider, June 19, 1835-Jan. 30, 1896.
Fannie Fisher, wife of C. M. Reed, 1865-1900.
Mary E. Rumple, daughter of A. H. and M. Gamble, May 29, 1835-Nov. 25, 1869.
John F. Reeder, April 28, 1813-Dec. 27, 1848.
W. T. Reed, Mar. 22, 1867-Oct. 20, 1900.
C. L. Rice, Aug. 16, 1836-Mar. 4, 1882.
Margaretta, wife of C. L. Rice, Dec. 26, 1844-Mar. 17, 1891.
Emma S., wife of G. T. Russell, Sept. 10, 1851-Oct. 31, 1880.
John N. Rogers, Jan. 2, 1855-Feb. 2, 1877.
Callie, wife of A. G. Robeson, Dec. 28, 1838-June 8, 1864.
Mrs. Margaret Rice, Died Nov. 23, 1876.
Lewis Wood Rose, Jan. 18, 1856-Oct. 26, 1899.
Mary P. Reid, died May 10, 1853.

S

Rev. Charles B. Smith, Oct. 15, 1820-July 11, 1899.
Mrs. Diadama, wife of C. B. Smith, Oct. 2, 1822-Dec. 11, 1900.
Sallie Cochran Sherlin, Dec. 12, 1877-July 3, 1899.
James A. Stevens, Dec. 13, 1863-June 12, 1888.
Mary C. Slover, 1826-1888.
John F. Slover, 1825-1878.
Emma Watson Smith, 1859-1898.
Caroline Rowena, wife of T. B. Sample, Nov. 26, 1832-June 2, 1858.
Elizabeth, wife of E. B. Shugart, May 9, 1809-Dec. 27, 1865.
E. B. C. Shugart, born in Lee County, Va., May 12, 1807-Jan. 5, 1878.
Dora V., son of Calvin and Lucinda Shoemaker, April 23, 1862-Nov. 21, 1886.
Lynn B. Scott, Jan. 10, 1882-Oct. 7, 1886.
Anna H. Scott, June 12, 1888-Oct. 8, 1888.
Richard Scott, Mar. 31, 1816-Aug. 11, 1884.
James L. Scott, Oct. 8, 1846-May 30, 1887.
Elizabeth P., wife of E. B. J. Sugart, May 9, 1809-Dec. 27, 1865.
E. B. G. Sugart, born in Lee County, Va., May 12, 1807-Jan. 5, 1878.
Jeremiah Seever, of Fairfield County, Ohio, Aug. 17, 1852; age, 25 years, 4 months.
M. J. Sims, wife of W. H. H. Sims, June 29, 1837-Mar. 21, 1891.
Farlee, daughter of W. H. and M. J. Sims, July 21, 1866-Feb. 26, 1891.
W. M. Sehorn, Dec. 29, 1817-July 14, 1876.
Ann Eliza Coleman Sehorn, wife of W. M. Sehorn, Sept. 8, 1821-Nov. 22, 1895.
William Monroe Sehorn, Jr., July 6, 1858-Aug. 31, 1880.
George Covington Sehorn, July 10, 1860-Sept. 28, 1900.
Joseph H. Smith, Jan. 14, 1836-Feb. 18, 1891.
Ephraim Sautell, born in Hollis, N. H., Aug. 12, 1808-Oct. 12, 1878.
Mary, wife of E. Sautell, May 6, 1808-July 8, 1866.
Martha L. Sautell, Sept. 12, 1836-Aug. 1, 1862.

T

Rebecca E. Moss Taylor, wife of James B. Taylor, daughter of John and Rebecca Moss, May 10, 1825-Sept. 16, 1850.
James A. Tucker, of Cumberland County, Va., Sept. 22, 1800-July 2, 1880.
James Turner, Oct. 10, 1812-April 14, 1887.
Harriet A. Turner, consort of James Turner, Mar. 23, 1820-June 20, 1895.
Louise, wife of J. R. Tuell, Oct. 19, 1837-Feb. 28, 1892.
Joseph W. Tuell, Mar. 7, 1859-May 26, 1879.

V

Eliza Ann, wife of Thomas Nixon Van Dyke, May 1, 1814-Jan. 26, 1896.
Thomas Nixon Van Dyke, Jan. 22, 1803-Mar. 3, 1891.

W

Ernest Atlee Wright, Mar. 6, 1831-Sept. 17, 1895.
Letitia Atlee, wife of P. C. Wilson, Sept. 21, 1841-Sept. 18, 1871.
O. B. Wattles, 1802-1875.
Eliza Wattles, 1705-1884.
W. G. C. Williams, died Mar. 29, 1893; age, 24 years, 6 months, 6 days.

Bible Records—Tombstone Inscriptions

Mary A., wife of G. G. Wester, Jan. 12, 1830-June 18, 1873.
Lula Wilds, wife of Peter Wilds, 1851-July 26, 1885.
Elias Walker, Sept. 17, 1830-July 12, 1897.
Addie McGaughey Witcher, Oct. 17, 1831-Mar. 28, 1888.

Y

Col. Wm. Yearwood, born Dec. 24, 1816. After serving a tour of 10 months and 2 days in Mexico as first Lieutenant of Company H, 2nd Reg., Tenn. Vols., fell mortally wounded while commanding company in charge at Cerro Gordo on the 18th day of April, 1847; died of his wound April 24, 1847; age, 30 years, 4 months. Interred in Athens, Aug. 16, 1848.

Z

Esther Ziegler, July 1, 1811-May 24, 1855.

CEDAR GROVE CEMETERY
At Athens, Tenn. Sent by Mrs. Richard Yearwood, Knoxville.

James, son of F. and Mary Boyd, Jan. 2, 1845-May 9, 1846.
John, son of F. and Mary Boyd, July 17, 1842-June 9, 1849.
Julius B. Bridges, Aug. 15, 1847-Jan. 3, 1876.
Thomas J., husband of Martha Greenwood, Mar. 1, 1830-Oct. 25, 1888.
John H. Grubb (Uncle John), July 6, 1844-May 27, 1905.
Emma A. Grubb (Aunt Emma), May 6, 1846-Dec. 17, 1927.
Peter Kinder, Dec. 27, 1779-Nov. 4, 1837.
Jamima Kinder, Jan. 27, 1784-June 11, 1854.
Lucinda E. Tongray, wife of Hilton Humphreys; age, 68 years.
Elizabeth Ann, daughter of H. H. and Margaret C. Rider, Sept. 26, 1840-Nov. 3, 1855.
Lennis Wood Rose, Jan. 18, 1856-Oct. 26, 1899.
Julia A. Baker, Nov. 18, 1819-July 16, 1890. There is joy on the other side.
Rebecca E., wife of James B. Taylor, and daughter of John and Rebecca Moss, May 10, 1825-Sept. 16, 1850.
In memory of John Ross, Dec. 24, 1786-June 7, 1857.
Aaron Mathews, Mar. 11, 1794-May 5, 1836.
Martha E. Cleage, wife of C. A. Beard, 1858-1915.
Mary L. Weir, wife of John B. Weir, and daughter of David and M. M. Cleage.
John B., son of David and Martha M. Cleage, born at Pikesville, Tenn., Sept. 27, 1847-April 21, 1857.
Alexander Cleage, Mar. 30, 1801-Jan. 4, 1825.
Father—H. Schumann, Mar. 4, 1847-Jan. 15, 1930.
Frances E. Schumann (mother), Aug. 31, 1854-Nov. 2, 1904.
Kate, wife of W. L. Davis, Dec. 7, 1888-June 28, 1911.
J. F. Davis, Jr., Jan. 17, 1883-Mar. 31, 1910.
Elizabeth, daughter of F. and Mary Boyd, Aug. 5, 1840-Sept. 30, 1841.
Martha, daughter of F. and Mary Boyd, Oct. 12, 1854-Aug. 15, 1856.
Our mother—Margaret, wife of I. W. Allen, Nov. 11, 1843-Jan. 5, 1894.
In memory of Ereminta E., daughter of J. M. and A. M. Burger, Jan. 12, 1853-Oct. 6, 1871.
In memory of Eva M., daughter of J. M. and Ann Burger, Jan. 12, 1853-Oct. 6, 1871.
C. M., wife of W. F. Henderson, Dec. 15, 1850-Aug. 25, 1871.

THE DIXON'S CREEK BAPTIST CHURCH
BY LAURA GASTON GARRETT

Organized in 1799 as an arm of the Station Camp Church in Sumner, at the home of Capt. Grant Allen, and separating from

Bible Records—Tombstone Inscriptions

that church and "going on its own" on March 8, 1800, under the ministry of Rev. Daniel Burford, this became the first Baptist Church between Station Camp and the settlements in East Tennessee.

From a letter in my father's collection, written in 1804 to the Cumberland Baptist Association on Harpeth, I learn that Thomas Banks (son of Richard) was then clerk and that the membership at that time totaled forty-nine.

The first log building stood at the mouth of Scatty Branch of Dixon's Creek on Col. Wm. Martin's land. Later he gave five acres or more for the church site, at the lower end of his home tract, several hundred yards above the point where the Ft. Blount Road crosses Dixon's Creek. Much later, around 1850, I believe, the second building was discarded as a church and the third and present building of brick erected on the site. It still stands and in 1900 its members celebrated its centennial, and in 1930 its one hundred and thirtieth birthday.

Literally hundreds of Baptist Churches of Tennessee descend directly and indirectly from the Dixon's Creek Church.

Many faithful slaves were members of the church before the war and as is shown by the minister's letter, etc., integrity and high conduct were required of the colored members as well as of their masters.

The old church has held membership in various associations throughout its long history, as deemed expedient from the increasing numbers of people and churches in Cumberland.

Among its prominent early members were: Richard and Thomas Banks, Capt. Grant Allen, Col. Wm. Martin, Jefie Sitten, Richard Britten, Benjamin Johns, Harris Grisham, Sr.; and as one of the early clerks I find the name of Thomas T. Young, the father-in-law of Senator George of Mississippi, whose statue has been placed in the National Hall of fame.

John McGee's Tombstone

The first Methodist Church in Smith County stood for many years near and to the northeast of the graveyard on John McGee's land. There were other graves in the graveyard, but John McGee's is the only one now marked. The grave is on a knoll a few hun-

Bible Records—Tombstone Inscriptions

dred yards southeast of the house occupied and owned for many years by Wilson W. Jenkins, near Dixon Springs, Tenn.

In memory of Rev. John McGee, June 9, 1763-June 16, 1836. Was a preacher of the gospel in the M. E. Church nearly half a century; was honored of God in beginning and carrying on the great revival of religion which commenced in 1799; died as he lived, in peace with God and all mankind; his body rests beneath this stone; well done, good, and faithful servant, enter thou into the joy of thy Lord.

ROBERT WRIGHT'S TOMBSTONE

On left of old road from Brattontown, Macon County, Tenn., to Thompkinsville, Ky., near Brattontown, on old Wright place.

In memory of Mr. Robert Wright, a native of Virginia; born in 1759, died Aug. 7, 1—31. A hero of the Revolution under Generals Washington and Green nearly the whole of the war; he died as he had lived, an honest, high-minded, honorable man.

DAVID BURFORD GRAVEYARD

Tomb inscriptions from David Burford Graveyard, near Dixon Springs, Tenn., on the land first settled by Col. Wm. Saunders, next owned by his heirs, then by Richard Alexander, who married his widow, and by various others, including W. Y. Clay, Hugh Wright, Robert D. Douglas, and now by Bell Gregory.

David Burford, Nov. 5, 1791-May 23, 1864; age, 72 years.
In loving memory of our mother, Elizabeth W. A., wife of David Burford, Dec. 9, 1808-July 15, 1894.
To the memory of Nancy A. Burford, Jan. 27, 1810-Jan. 13, 1812.
Sacred to the memory of Mary Ann and Daniel L. Burford; the former born Oct. 10, 1828, and died Jan. 20, 1834; the latter born Nov. 24, 1830, and died Jan. 25, 1834; both children of David and Elizabeth Burford.
Daniel L. Burford, son of David and Elizabeth Burford, Sept. 25, 1835-Dec. 18, 1867; age, 32 years.
To the memory of Fanny M. Burford, Aug. 28, 1843-Aug. 5, 1853.

Jonathon Burford.
Robert Allen Burford, son of David and Elizabeth Alexander Burford, Feb. 23, 1827-Jan. 28, 1904. "I feel that I have done my duty by my family, my country, and my God, and am not afraid to die."
Mary E., wife of Robert A. Burford, and daughter of E. P. and Nancy Lowe, Jan. 18, 1833-Jan. 27, 1879.
Laura, daughter of Robert A. and Mary E. Burford, Feb. 9, 1851-Oct. 25, 1861.
David, infant son of Robert A. and Mary E. Burford, May 13, 1863-Oct. 20, 1863.
In memory of Little George, son of Rom C. and Bettie H. Wright, Dec. 27, 1850-April 30, 1852.

CAPT. WM. ALEXANDER GRAVEYARD

Inscriptions from tombs in Capt. Wm. Alexander Graveyard, one-half mile southeast of Hartsville, Tenn., on his original land grant, now owned by Ben Jones.

Wm. Alexander, died Aug. 4, 1830, in the 84th year of his age.
Mary Alexander departed this life on Sept. ——, 1834, in the 86th year of her age.
In memory of Mary Jane, daughter of

Bible Records—Tombstone Inscriptions

Wm. L. and Mary Allen Alexander, July 24, 1839-Aug. 10, 1842. Darling J. Ervin, son of M. and A. L.

(P.) Jones, Nov. 11, 1867; —— 2, 1868.

Dr. Redmond Barry Graveyard

Inscriptions of tombs of Dr. Redmond Barry Graveyard (in bad condition), about one-sixteenth of a mile northwest of the point where the Andrew Jackson Highway crosses East Station Camp Creek, Sumner County, Tenn.

In memory of Dr. Redmond D. Barry, a native of Ireland, Dec. 22, 1766-Feb. 16, 1821.
William A. Barry, Feb. 5, 1805-Mar. 13, 1805.

John B. Barry, 1806-1806.
Sacred to the memory of Jane Barry, born Oct. 19, 1780; married Dec. 23, 1803; died Mar. 20, 1841.

Saunders-Cunningham-Alexander Graveyard

Inscriptions of tombstones remaining in the old Saunders-Cunningham-Alexander Graveyard on Colonel Saunders' original grant, called "Old Bledsoesborough." Maj. Wm. Cunningham and wife also were buried there, as they were the parents of Colonel Saunders' second wife, but some of the tombstones, as well as the rocks from the wall surrounding the graveyard, were removed by a one-time owner of the land and used in "walling up" a milkhouse.

To the memory of William Saunders, April 20, 1759-Oct. 20, 1803; commissioned a lieutenant in the North Carolina line in the army of the United States, Feb. 8, 1779, a member of the North Carolina Cincinnati.
To the memory of Nancy Alexander, Dec. 17, 1777-Dec. 1, 1839. This monument is erected by her children.

To the memory of Richard Alexander, Jan. 11, 1769-Oct. 15, 1855. Monument erected by his children.
This covers the remains of Frances Cunningham, who died April 15, 1849; age, 63 years.
W. G. Hamilton, 1816-1849.
Susanne Hamilton, wife of J. M. Hamilton, 1784-1853.

Marks Place Graves

Inscriptions on graves in small plot on the Marks Place (formerly Moore's place, near New Middleton, Tenn. The field the graves are in joins the tract on which old Clinton College was located.

In memory of Ann Jinkins, died May, 1829; age, 36 years.

In memory of Wilson Jinkins, died July, 1830; age, 65 years.

Lone Grave

On Thomas Place, formerly Clinton College, in a field is one

Bible Records—Tombstone Inscriptions

lone grave, under a clump of trees, with this inscription (as far as I was able to read):
John Minton Synoh or Lynch, of ——— County, Pa., died, Clinton College, 1834.

GRAVEYARD ON FARM OF BRADLEY MADDUX

In a graveyard on a beautiful hill on the farm owned by Bradley Maddux of Rock Spring Valley, near Buffalo Valley, Smith County, Tenn., are a number of very old seeming box tombs, all in very bad repair, some with no inscriptions, and most of them now broken and falling. I was able to copy the following from them:

Martha Ann Kerr, Feb. 20, 1832-Feb. 15, 1853.
Rebecca McDaniel, Oct. 10, 1795-Sept. 19, 1851.
Henry ———, Jan. 14, 1792-Dec. 21, 1851.
Dr. Edward R. McDaniel, Nov. 23, 1828-Dec. 21, 18—0.

GEORGE T. WRIGHT GRAVEYARD

Tomb inscriptions from graveyard of George T. Wright, on Scanty Branch, Trousdale County, Tenn (or Macon County?).

In memory of George T. Wright, Feb. 27, 1787-Aug. 24, 1847.
In memory of Sarah H. Wright, consort of George T. Wright, June 12, 1800-Aug. 25, 1856.

DIXON SPRINGS CEMETERY

Some of the tomb inscriptions from the Wright lot in the Dixon Springs Cemetery.

Romulus C. Wright, born in Amelia County, Va., 1818; died at his home near Dixon's Springs, July 15, 1892. "His life was gentle and the elements so mixed in him that Nature might stand up and say to all the world, 'This was a man!'"

Betty Burford Wright, wife of Romulus C. Wright, Sept. 21, 1832-April 4, 1898.
A heart and mind of rarest mold,
  An instinct true;
Her soul found nature's streams of gold
  And richly drew.

ISHAM BEASLEY GRAVEYARD

In Sullivan's Bend, Smith County, now owned by John Jellicorse.

Isham Beasley and Polly Andrews were married Nov. 27, 1782.
Isham Beasley, Jan., 1760-May 20, 1855; age, 95 years, 4 months, 9 days.
Polly, wife of Isham Beasley, May 19, 1767-Mar. 26, 1851; age, 83 years, 4 months, 7 days.
William Beasley, Mar. 1, 1815-May 18, 1880.
Harriet D. Beasley, Oct. 6, 1826-April 9, 1875. "Blessed are they which die in the Lord."
Grave a few yards from left side of residence of Mr. Jarrel Burrough of Carter Branch, near Hilsdale; both Mr. Burrough and Mr. Tom Perkins, both Confederate Soldiers, told me that Wm. Carter was a Revolutionary Soldier.

Bible Records—Tombstone Inscriptions

In memory of William Carter, June 9, 1760-Feb. 21, 1847. He professed religion Mar. 12, 1812, and lived a consistent member of the Methodist Church up to his death.
In memory of Mary Carter, Jan. 6, 1764-May 22, 1835. She professed religion in the year 1795 and lived a consistent member of the Methodist Church up to her death.
Joseph L. Carter, April 28, 1805-Mar. 23, 1870.

The grave of Prior Carter, descendant of Wm. and Mary Carter, is also within the rock wall or at least in the graveyard, but has never been marked by his heirs.

On the Millard Holland place (on Salt Lick Creek, near old Bagdad and the present Gladys), the place on which Maj. Thomas Draper lived and died, is a graveyard. Two graves in it are enclosed by a high rock wall, and Mr. Holland says that it has always been told by older members of his family who should know that "Old man Draper and his wife were buried in these graves—the first Draper that lived here." There are many other graves there with "box tombs" and other kinds.

CORLEY GRAVEYARD

Near Corley's School House, Trousdale County, Tenn., owned first by Francis Corley, Revolutionary Soldier.

Joyce P., wife of B. W. Burford, Nov. 7, 1814-May 19, 1891; one of earth's purest and best.
Little Jerry, etc.
Little Jim, etc.
Maj. John H. Burford, May 26, 1796-Feb. 7, 1863.
Fanny Burford, daughter of John H. and Nancy Burford, Mar. 16, 1837-Sept. 18, 1856.

Mary H. Burford, born Oct. 6, 1820; married D. H. Burford Mar. 18, 1841; died Aug. 8, 1856.
(Many other graves, some old box tombs, probably of the Corley family, many markers down and broken and some covered by earth; all enclosed by a tall wire fence, erected by Phil D. Shaw.

MADDEN GRAVEYARD

On place near house now owned by Dave Merryman, Trousdale County.

Mary H. Thompkins, Mar. 16, 1811(?)-July 10, 1846. She closed her eyes and stood in peace before a smiling God.
John M. Madden, Mar. 13, 1813-Dec. 13, 1889. His many virtues form the noblest monument to his memory.

(On other side of the large monument):
Mary H. Thompkins, ——.
Violet Madden.
Joel Madden.
Footstones read: V. M., J. M., J. M. M., M. H. T.

Bible Records—Tombstone Inscriptions

GRAVEYARD NEAR HARTSVILLE

Graveyard on place now owned by Mr. Duncan on Tilman Dixon Highway, one mile from Hartsville.

In memory of Joseph Gifford, Sept. 20, 1775-July 23, 1853; age, 77 years, 11 months, 28 days.

In memory of Jabes Gifford, Nov. 28, 1802(?)-Mar. 22, 1855; age, 47 years, 3 months, 26 days.

In memory of E. P. G. Gifford, April 5, 1815-Nov. 9, 1856; age, 41 years, 7 months, 4 days.

GRAVES FAMILY GRAVEYARD

On road above Kempville. Enclosed with good rock wall, four graves marked. The following inscriptions are not verbatim, but dates are accurately copied:

Susan Graves, died 1891; age, about 99 years.

Beman Graves, 1788-1863.

—— Graves, son of S. and B. Graves, 1827-1840(?).

DIXON-VAUGHAN-SEAY GRAVEYARD
Near Dixon Springs

Major Tillman Dixon, June 26, 1750-April 2, 1816; a member of the North Carolina Cincinnati.

Mary Dixon, his wife, May 16, 1767-Aug. 26, 1806; stone erected by her daughter, M. G. Overton.

Many other graves, some with stones decaying and falling to pieces. The Negro graveyard of the faithful slaves in close proximity.

JOHN BREVARD'S GRAVEYARD

At John Brevard's Graveyard on the top of a beautiful knoll on Goose Creek I could find only one grave marked, and that was not inside of the large wall. There are shrubs planted and the wall still stands partially, but the only tombstone was that of Polyxina Brevard (daughter of John, I have been told, who did not marry).

BELLVIEW GRAVEYARD

Home of Col. Wm. Martin, on Dixson's Creek, three miles north of Dixon Springs, formerly Smith, now Trousdale, County.

Sacred to the memory of Col. William Martin, a pioneer of the West, Nov. 26, 1765-Nov. 4, 1846. He was a Christian in the true sense of the word. He visited the sick, clothed the naked, and fed the hungry. He filled various stations in both the civil and military departments, and in every way acquitted himself like a man. Possessing a mind of very superior power. He retained his faculties unimpaired until he fell asleep in the arms of Jesus. He was a member of the Baptist Church fifty-six years. He settled at this place Nov. 4, 1798.

In memory of Mrs. Frances Martin, wife of Col. Wm. Martin, June 30, 1770-July 27, 1831.

Bible Records—Tombstone Inscriptions

ANDREW GREER GRAVEYARD
On Goose Creek

Sacred to the memory of Major (?) Andrew Greer was born the 4th (?) of Mar., 1763, and departed this life the 17th of Feb., 1819. Truth and manly firmness ——(?) conspicuous in him beneath this stone.
Sacred to the memory of Mrs. Sarah Greer, Aug. 15, 1775-Mar. 15, 1851. "Blessed are the dead that die in the Lord."
Sacred to the memory of Andrew Wiley Greer, son of Andrew and Sarah Greer, Nov. 29, 1805-Sept. 15, 1822.
In memory of Mrs. Sarah S. Martin, June 5, 1808-April 6, 1842. Loved in life, honored in death; she died the death of the righteous. This is erected by her husband, Wm. L. Martin.
This stone is erected to the memory of Hall Greer Martin, Nov. 3, 1857-Mar. 27, 1842; and of Thomas Hamilton Martin, July 11, 1841-Jan. 5, 1842; sons of Wm. L. and Sarah S. Martin. Sweet little boys rest in peace.
In the triumph of faith, the elevated virtue of this amiable lady will long be remembered by all who knew her.
In the same enclosure (high wall) are the graves of Col. Martin's sister, Mary (Polly) Hammack, who died in 1852, and her husband, Daniel Hammack, who died in 1829; of Mrs. Malinda, wife of Col. Martin's brother, Brice; she died in 1825; of Col. Martin's son, Brice F. (Ferriss) Martin, who died in 1843, and his wife, Susan T., who died in 1857; of Col. Martin's youngest son, Norval Douglas; of his daughter, Mrs. Betsy Brooks, wife of Dr. Henry Brooks; of Mrs. Parmelia D. Drake, wife and infant son of E. B. Drake. There are also several graves not marked, or with stones gone. Jacob Burrus is buried here also, and most probably Wm. Cleveland, son of Col. Benjamin of King's Mountain fame.
In an enclosure adjoining this graveyard are the graves of Capt. Lemuel Hammack, son of Daniel and Polly Hammock, and his wife and infant daughter. Outside the enclosure stands the grave and stone of Gustavus C. Newton of Mystic, Conn., an Odd Fellow who died at the home of Wilson Y. Martin on Jan. 14, 1847.

REVOLUTIONARY SOLDIERS' MARKED GRAVES

Memorial Gate Way, near Bristol, at Weaverville Cemetery, where more than two hundred Revolutionary Soldiers are buried. Memorial Tablet, with the names of the Revolutionary Soldiers buried in McMinn County, was placed on Enterprize Building in Etowah, Tenn. The Unveiling ceremonies were on May 30.

Marker on grave of W. H. Cook, pioneer soldier, buried in Cook Cemetery, Etowah, Tenn.
Jacob Franklin Peck, soldier of War of 1812, buried at Sink Creek, marked by D. A. R. and 1812 Chapters.
Thomas Cochran, buried at Englewood, marked by D. A. R. and 1812 Chapters.
Thomas Cantrell, buried at Williamsburg Cemetery, near Etowah.
Return Jonathan Meigs, buried at Calhoun, Tenn.
Lieutenant Isaac Lane, buried near Nioto, Tenn.
Dr. James Cosby, buried in Falling Water Cemetery, near Red Bank, Chattanooga.
Captain Robert Patterson, buried in Cemetery near Sale Creek.
General George Rutledge, buried in Blountville Cemetery, Sullivan County.
Jacob Kimberly, buried — near Knoxville.
Marcus Tulloch, buried in Blount County.
William Lipton, buried in Blount County.
Robert McKay, buried in Blount County.

Bible Records—Tombstone Inscriptions

James Henry, buried in Blount County.
James White, Revolutionary Soldier and founder of Knoxville, buried in Knoxville. He served in the Revolutionary War as Captain and Colonel, and after that was appointed Brigadier-General of State Militia by Governor Blount.
Kenneth Anderson, buried at Shelbyville. Unveiling, Oct. 12, Shelby Chapter.
Marker at grave of Nathan Burchfield. Grave marked by Spencer Clack Chapter, Sevierville, name not reported.
Christopher Taylor, buried in cemetery near Jonesboro, marked.
John McFerin, buried in Shelby County, marked.

REVOLUTIONARY SOLDIERS' UNMARKED GRAVES
By Mrs. Rhea Garrett

Thomas McAmis, located in the old cemetery at Greeneville.
Michael Hyder, Sr., died in 1790, buried in Hyder Cemetery, Powder Branch, Carter County.
Edmund Williams, buried in old Williams Cemetery, Buffalo Creek, Carter County.
John Tipton, Tipton Cemetery, Sinking Creek, Washington County.
Samuel Tipton, Green Hill Cemetery, Elizabethton, Carter County.
Isaac Taylor, Taylor Cemetery, Milligan College.
James Edens, Edens Family Cemetery, Gap Creek, Carter County.
Hugh Harris, New Salem Church, Washington County.
Jacob Acres, Fair View Cemetery, Washington County.
Le Roy Taylor, Fair View Cemetery, Washington County.
John Blair, Old Salem Cemetery, Washington County.
Henry Hardin, family cemetery, Beaver Creek, Ashe County, N. C.
Joel Friel Robertson, eldest son of James Robertson, buried on farm on Charlotte Pike; moved to Old City Cemetery in Nashville and placed beside his illustrious father.
Jesse Lincoln, nephew of President Lincoln, buried in —— County; reported by Rock House Chapter.
Grave of little Indian girl marked, Sarah Elizabeth Ross, niece of John Ross, buried at Calhoun, Tenn.
Government marker at grave of A. M. Taylor, Chickamauga, Ga., a confederate veteran who was great-grandson of James Taylor, a Revolutionary Soldier.
Burgess Witt, died Dec. 17, 1843; buried at Ironsburg, Monroe County, Tenn.; married Elisabeth Mayo; service with North Carolina troops; was in battle of Kings Mountain and Cowpens; discharged May 4, 1782.
John Oliphant, born in New Jersey, Jan. 2, 1850; died in Greene County, 1823; married Hannah Amos; he was a gunsmith.
Captain William Bean, Jr., was born in Virginia about 1745; died in Grainger County, 1799. Court records of that county prove time of death. He was Captain under Col. John Sevier.
Captain William Bean, Sr., born about 1720; died in Washington County in 1782, his will being probated that year. Russell, the first white child born in the state, is mentioned in his will. William Bean built the first cabin; he was a member of the Committee of Safety and a member of the Watauga Association.
John Bowen, born in Virginia about 1766; died in Grainger County, 1823; he was at the battle of Kings Mountain, although only sixteen years old.
John Gibson, born in Orange County, N. C., 1760; died in Lincoln County, Tenn, 1844. His service was with North Carolina Regiments under Col. Paisley and others. He was out against the Tories. He was a member of Donelson's Voyage.
William Cocke, buried in Pold Presbyterian Cemetery, Rutledge. He was a member of the first Congress, Soldier of the Revolution.

Bible Records—Tombstone Inscriptions

ROGAN BURYING GROUND
Near Gallatin; sent by Mrs. Charles Rogan

Hugh Rogan and wife, Nancy Duffy Rogan, are buried here. Near a large oak tree is a weathered stone to Richard Parkerville, died Oct., 1838; age, 68 years.

Charles Duffy, born, 1770; died, Oct. 5, 1826. "A True Republican." Charles Duffy was a brother-in-law of the pioneer Hugh Rogan.

Following records were sent by Mrs. George Oster.
NETU VIEW CEMETERY
Sent by Willie McSutherland Rambo

J. A. Sutherland, Aug. 17, 1841-Mar. 24, 1904.

Nannie Wright Sutherland, June 2, 1865-Mar. 7, 1931.

KEYS CEMETERY

James Keys, died Sept. 3, 1851; age, 76 years, 10 months, 8 days.
Margaret, cousin of James Keys, died Feb. 10, 1867; age, 83 years, 11 months.

Benjamin, son of D. L. and S. J. Keys, died Feb. 12, 1863; age, 4 years, 1 month.

WILLS CEMETERY
Sent by Bess Wills

James N. Wills, 1855-July 25, 1919.

WAGNER CEMETERY

Col. David Wagner, died Mar. 29, 1845; age, 85 years, 11 months, 19 days.
His wife, Margaret Wagner, May 2, 1790-Sept. 13, 1883.
Matthias Wagner, died Aug. 19, 1835; age, 68 years, 6 months, 9 days.

His wife, Susanah Wagner, died Jan. 11, 1850; age, 76 years, 5 months, 26 days.
Isaac Reece, Mar. 12, 1789-Jan. 1, 1864.
Elizabeth Reece, May 22, 1793-Aug. 22, 1847.

MOUNTAIN VIEW CEMETERY
Sent by Miss Smythe, Mrs. Joe C. Muse, Mrs. Joe J. Lefler, and Carrie Wagner Donnelly.

Dr. James C. Smythe, born July 7, 1790, in Washington County, Va.; died in Henry County, Tenn., Oct. 21, 1850.
Thomas S. Smythe, June 29, 1827-July 4, 1895.
Margaret Donnelly Smythe, Dec. 2, 1828-Dec. 10, 1906.
Richard Donnelly, Aug. 17, 1790-Aug. 26, 1870.
Rebecca Loran Donnelly, Sept. 9, 1796-Dec. 28, 1876; married Oct. 1, 1817.
Rhoda Louvenia Crockett Berry, Mar. 12, 1862-April 18, 1924.

Robert Edmonson Berry, Feb. 1, 1831-Mar. 12, 1906.
Rachel Wills Berry, July 18, 1825-Jan. 25, 1908.
Rebecca Wills Faw, Jan. 15, 1823-Dec. 17, 1913.
Same cemetery, sent by Margaret Butler Brown:
R. R. Butler, April 8, 1827-Aug. 18, 1902; Congressman 10 years.
E. E. Butler, Senator, Feb. 6, 1864-Dec. 13, 1930.

Bible Records—Tombstone Inscriptions

Emeline Butler, Sept. 2, 1895-Oct. 10, 1899.
William Edward Butler, Jan. 13, 1894-June 21, 1927. (Ten years in Congress, Lt.-Col. of 13th Tenn. Cavalry.)
Charles Lefler, May 1, 1826-April 22, 1886.
Esther U. Lefler, July 23, 1826-Mar. 14, 1897.
Kendrick H. Lefler, Oct. 29, 1862-Nov. 22, 1925.
Charles Tulburt Lefler, July 23, 1869-Feb. 6, 1927.

Daniel Wagner, 1746-1827; buried in Bethany Reform Cemetery in Davidson County, N. C.
Mathias Wagner, son of Daniel, Feb. 10, 1765-Aug. 19, 1835; buried in Wagner Graveyard, four miles south of Mountain City, Tenn.
Mathias Miller Wagner, son of Mathias, Feb. 15, 1801-June 30, 1887.
His wife, Mary Fyffe, 1804-1887.
Noah Jacob Wagner, April 16, 1844-Jan. 26, 1931.
His wife, Nellie King, Aug. 25, 1842-Nov. 10, 1921.

Brown Cemetery
Sent by Ruth W. McQueen

James Brown, Oct. 23, 1811-Oct. 31, 1894; captain in the Home Guards of Civil War.
Harriet Newel Farthing Brown, Mar. 22, 1816-May 17, 1897.
Joseph Hamilton Brown, June 14, 1838-Feb. 19, 1852.
Mary Eugenia Brown Shull, Mar. 24, 1845-Jan. 21, 1886.
Sally Lucinda Brown, Dec. 30, 1846-April 25, 1850.
Anna Evaline Brown, July 4, 1849-Feb. 15, 1931.
James Julian Monroe Brown, July 21, 1854-May 6, 1895.
William Finley Shull, Aug. 1837-Jan. 12, 1912; first Lieutenant in 37th North Carolina Infantry.

Polly Shoun, Jan. 30, 1808-Mar. 4, 1892. Mrs. Jenkins' grandmother is buried at Little Doe, Tenn.
Washington Cole, May 8, 1819-April 30, 1870.
Sarah A. Cole, Jan. 2, 1829-July 13, 1909.
Benjamin W. Jenkins, Dec. 27, 1831-Jan. 24, 1902.
Nancy E. Jenkins, May 7, 1832-May 21, 1905.
(Mrs. Jenkins' father and mother are buried in Shady Valley, Tenn.)
(Mr. Jenkins' parents are buried in Mountain View Cemetery, Mountain City, Tenn.

Shouns Cemetery

The following is a list of the names of the settlers here as shown in the Shouns Cemetery and on the monument to the Shouns erected by Uncle Ross and Grandmama Donnelly. Sent to Mrs. Oster by Edith Hill.

Leonard Shoun, Nov. 10, 1773-June 9, 1845.
Barbara Shoun, May 3, 1775-April 20, 1851.
David Henderson Shoun, Jan. 9, 1817-Oct. 30, 1850.
Sarah Baker Shoun, April 11, 1817-Aug. 6, 1888.
Elihu A. Shoun, Nov. 15, 1820-Dec. 16, 1851.
James L. Shoun, Jan. 10, 1825-Nov. 2, 1842.

Daniel L. Shoun, Dec. 29, 1846-Oct. 18, 1852.
Macon R. Wills, 1842-1929.
Jennie Mc. Wills, 1847-1924.
H. T. Grant, Aug. 9, 1843-Aug. 27, 1920.
Robert Campbell Rhea, April 19, 1837-Nov. 3, 1911.
Caroline McQueen Rhea, May 10, 1846-Oct. 16, 1930.
Samuel Robert Rhea, Mar. 22, 1868-Sept. 28, 1930.

Bible Records—Tombstone Inscriptions

Joseph S. Donnelly, Dec. 30, 1869-Mar. 12, 1915.
Mary Rhea Donnelly, Nov. 21, 1869-May 16, 1924.
Harrison Carter Donnelly, May 14, 1840-Feb. 8, 1905.

ROGERSVILLE GRAVEYARD

Sent by Miss Margaret Pierce of Rogersville to Mrs. George Oster.

Joseph Rogers, born in the County of Tyrone, Ireland, Aug. 21, 1764; came to U. S. of America in 1784; settled here and founded the village of Rogersville, 1786, where he lived until his death, Nov., 1838.
Mary Rogers, daughter of Thomas Amis, and consort of Joseph, born in County of Duplin, N. C., Aug. 22, 1770; died, Nov. 30, 1833.
Elizabeth Mary Rogers, daughter of Joseph and Mary Rogers, Oct. 26, 1790-April 23, 1809.
Memorial Tablet, "Here lies David Crockett and his wife, grandparents of David Crockett, who were massacred near this spot by the Indians, 1777. Division of the State of Tennessee." About three miles from New Market are the graves of the maternal ancestors of Miss Pierce. It was in their home that the first Sunday school was organized in the State of Tennessee. The graves are:
Anthony Caldwell (born in Virginia and immigrated to Tennessee, perhaps just after the close of the Revolutionary War. This is not on the tombstone), born, 1764; died, 1832, and His wife Elizabeth Akin Caldwell. "They were Christians and Patriots during the Revolution."

OLD TURNER HOME GRAVEYARD

At Turnersville, Robertson County. Sent by Mrs. J. Hughes Darden.

Mrs. Wealthy S. Turner, died June 4, 1830; age, 29 years, 6 months.
Maj. Jack E. Turner, Dec. 22, 1774-Dec. 22, 1825; age, 51 years.
Julia Glover, Sept. 6, 1792-Dec. 1, 1850.

DARDEN GRAVEYARD

Near Turnersville, Tenn.

James Darden, May 4, 1799-May 19, 1869.
Jesse Darden, May 1, 1801-Dec. 20, 1859.
Oliver G., son of James and Lucinda Darden, 1845-1848.
Other children of James and Lucinda Carr Darden buried here, but not marked are: Mrs. Lucinda Clinard, Robert Darden, and Mrs. Elizabeth Rozell and her daughter, Etta Rozell.

RECORDS

Sent by Edythe R. Whitley, Nashville, Tenn.

Sallie E. Thomison, Feb. 24, 1849-Mar. 6, 1871.
Susie Thomison, Oct. 16, 1861-Nov. 6, 1883.
Elizabeth C. Thomison, Nov. 23, 1832-Aug. 9, 1853.
Jane C., consort of Hugh Thomison, May 13, 1808-Nov. 10, 1834.

Bible Records—Tombstone Inscriptions

Hugh Thomison, Sr., July 11, 1805-Sept. 19, 1878.
Elizabeth Thomison, second wife of Hugh Thomison, Dec. 14, 1814-July 3, 1895.
William Carroll Thomison, June 18, 1838-Feb. 9, 1854.
Sarah A. Thomison, Dec. 29, 1838-June 24, 1843.

WARDEN

Robert Warden, Sept. 29, 1855-Mar. 23, 1911.

Daniel Warden, June 3, 1828-May 31, 1905.
Sallie Landers Warden, wife of Daniel Warden, Dec. 8, 1837-Nov. 16, 1896; joined Primitive Baptist Church, 1870.
Mary Warden, wife of Daniel Warden, born Nov. 19, 1835; joined Primitive Baptist Church, Oct., 1856; died, April 21, 1891.
Holman Frost, son of J. W. and K. E. Warden, Mar. 26, 1882-Mar. 25, 1893.
Travis Warden, Sept. 8, 1853-Mar. 18, 1899.

TOMBSTONE RECORDS
Copied from tombstones at Winchester, Tenn.

Mark Hutchins White, Aug. 26, 1851-Mar. 3, 1933. Son of Col. George W. White and Mary Hutchins White.
Whitmel Ransom, Mar. 1, 1824-Nov. 18, 1890.
Martha Jane Ransom, April 20, 1832-Feb. 5, 1912.

Thomas Ransom, Nov. 7, 1849-Jan. 7, 1893.
Nannie Ransom White, April 1, 1852-April 25, 1924.
Mark Hutchins, born in Windsor County, Vermont, Oct. 28, 1793; died at Winchester, Tenn., Jan. 9, 1849.

JULIUS C. WADE GRAVE
Send by Rebekah Jetton

On the farm of Homer Gannon, Nashville Highway, near Stones River National Park, in a cornfield is a handsome seven-foot monument bearing the inscription: Julius C. Wade, born June, 1820; died April 11, 1871. All other headstones were hauled away.

CEMETERY NEAR GRANNY WHITE PIKE

Cemetery about seven miles out on right side of Granny White Pike shows many graves have been moved. Those still there are listed. Copied by Mrs. Patton and Mrs. Acklen.

Mrs. Mary P. F. Sanders, April 11, 1818-May 20, 1908.
Sterling Smith, July 22, 1867-Mar. 16, 1902.
Mary B., daughter of J. A. and R. R. Cotton, April 18, 1869-July 27, 1884.
Rachel P. Cotton, wife of J. H. Cotton, May 16, 1841-May 23, 1885.
John H. Cotton, Jan. 21, 1834-Aug. 8, 1911.
W. E. Bush Taggart, Jan. 19, 1908-Mar. 6, 1916.
Harvey Lee, son of Emmett and Agnes Taggart, Mar. 6, 1906-Oct. 13, 1907.

Lucy Pitts, daughter of E. W. and Martha Farley, April 16, 1898-Dec. 2, 1900.
Mary Elizabeth, daughter of E. L. and Agnes Taggart, Mar. 3, 1898-Dec. 3, 1900.
Robert Weakley, son of E. W. and Martha Farley, Jan. 3, 1900-July 7, 1900.
Son of J. H. and E. L. Perry, April 1, 1898-April 4, 1890.
Wm. Thomas Austin, Jr., April 18, 1922.

Bible Records—Tombstone Inscriptions

OLD CEMETERY ON PROPERTY OF DR. W. A. BRYAN

On the property of Dr. W. A. Bryan is an old cemetery in very bad condition. The vault has fallen in and the once fine rock wall is partially destroyed. Marble tombstones are down and badly defaced. There are many interesting epitaphs there.

Thomas N. Cotton, Feb. 12, 1808-April 3, 1854.
Napoleon Bonaparte Moore, infant son of B. W. and E. A. Moore, June 11, 1851-June 19.
Susan Cartwright, 1766-Oct. 20, 1849.
Rufus M. Waller, son of R. M. and Rachel Waller, Aug. 3, 1850-Aug. 15, 1851.
Louisa J. Tanksley, Nov. 15, 1818-Feb. 23, 1852.
Martha Elizabeth Parrish, July 4, 1834-June 11, 1854.
Tennessee Parker, June 28, 1821-Nov. 12, 1845.
Fleming Mosley, Dec. 5, 1794-Dec. 11, 1845.
William Mosley, Mar. 18, 1823-Sept. 21, 1845.
Albert G. Parker, Aug. 28, 1819-Aug. 31, 1845.
James A. F. McCrory, Mar. 6, 1831-June 7, 1849.
William A. McCrory, Jan. 12, 1829-June 6, 1849.
—— A. G. Mosley, July 11, 1794-July 7, 1836.
Geo. T. Burnet, Aug. 17, 1836-Mar. 20, 1839; age, 2 years.
Michael L. McCrory, Mar. 15, 1797-June 6, 1849.
Sally L. McCrory, Oct. 18, 1804-May 25, 1830.
Thos. McCrory, Nov. 18, 1824-May 17, 1862.
——es Moore, Feb. 15, 1764-July 12, 1838; age, 74 years, 7 months, 3 days.
Elizabeth Johnston, born in Bucks County, Pa., 1742-June 15, 1815; age, 73 years.
John Johnson, Tyron County, Ireland, Mar. 17, 1734-Mar. 4, 1816.
Betty Ward Osborn, died Oct. 4, 1833; age, 74 years.
J. Cox, 1800.
T. Cox, 1806.
Rebecca Cox, born in Burks County, Pa., Aug. 24, 1770-Sept. 8, 1827.

Francis Campbell, died Jan., 1854, in the 77th year of his age.
Thos. Cox, born in Baltimore County, Md., June, 1761-Dec. 15, 1850.
Thos. T. Campbell, Oct. 21, 1820-June 10, 1851.
Margaret Cunningham, Aug. 26, 1817-Sept. 1, 1855.
Abraham Crockett, Nov. 1795-Sept. 5, 1827.
Sara Crockett, daughter of J. and N. Crockett, Mar. 18, 1824-Oct. 15, 1824.
Alexander Campbell, June 25, 1829, in the 77th year of his age.
Margaret Campbell, Dec. 22, 1756-July 7, 1816.
Martha A., wife of Alfred Waller, Sept. 10, 1827-Dec. 3, 1845.
Alfred Waller, July 25, 1811- —— 26, 1850.
John H. Rives, April 2, 1809-July 21, 1849.
Rachel McCrory, born in Mecklenburg County, N. C., Mar. 4, 1772-April 17, 1830.
Mary S., wife of John P. Waller, June 7, 1818-Aug. 6, 1849.
Delilah Roy, consort of John Roy, born in Franklin County, N. C.; age, 77 years; died, Feb. 27, 1854.
Richard Mathis, 1774-Mar. 10, 1854.
Wm. Bumpass, Jr., son of Wm. and Elizabeth Bumpass, Mar. 31, 1815-Aug. 23, 1835.
In memory of Mary Cotton.
John S. Mosley, Oct. 2, 1826-April 25, 1830.
Robt. E. McCrory, June 6, 1813-June 21, 1843.
Thos. C. McCrory, Aug. 24, 1827-May 19, 1831.
Amanda M. McCrory, daughter of Thomas and Polly McCrory, Aug. 11, 1821-Oct. 25, 1825.
Melvin G. Cox, son of E. A. Cox, Aug. 17, 1840-Dec. 4, 1840.
Eliza Crockett, daughter of J. and N. Crockett, Sept. 10, 1811-Oct. 4, 1821.

Bible Records—Tombstone Inscriptions

SMALL BURYING GROUND ON HARPETH HILLS ROAD

Husband and Father, Oliver Hayes Gardner, April 16, 1861-June 24, 1929.
J. F. Gardner, June 22, 1862-Dec. 8, 1915.
M. S. Gardner, Jan. 16, 1866-Feb. 17, 1897.
Sallie M. Gardner, Mar. 10, 1871-Oct. 9, 1887.
Abby Gardner, Mar. 7, 1831-Jan. 11, 1917.
James Gardner, Nov. 13, 1828-July 16, 1900.
W. T. Gardner, July 1, 1850-Feb. 22, 1913.

WHEELER BURYING GROUND OR MEADES CHAPEL

On the Antioch Pike or the Creek Valley Road. Copied by Mrs. Alfred F. Battle, Nashville, Tenn.

Clara Mai Martin, daughter of R. G. and Annie Martin, May 2, 1905-Oct. 31, 1923.
Mother—Annie Vicy Martin, Nov. 16, 1866-July 17, 1927.
Joe Griggs, Mar. 23, 1854-June 26, 1922.
Ellen Davis, wife of R. C. Mullen, Nov. 17, 1843-May 21, 1913.
Ira (Dick) Vick, 1888-1929.
Epham C. Jackson, Jan. 14, 1875-Sept. 16, 1912. Killed by train.
Eugene L. Mims, Feb. 3, 1897-Mar. 22, 1905.
Annie Lou Mims, Feb. 2, 1900-Nov. 15, 1901.
J. Pleasant Mims, 1856-1929.
Sallie Mims, 1852-19—.
A. L. Mims, Oct. 31, 1854-June 26, 1932.
Aaron Lemuel Mims, Jan. 2, 1834-April 13, 1913.
Sue Rieves, wife of W. H. Wheeler, April 27, 1859-Mar. 18, 1912.
Ophelia S. Adams, Jan. 9, 1882-Sept. 7, 1900.
Ernest A. Adams, 1891-1921, Rainbow Division.
Maggie Epps, Sept. 5, 1854-July 29, 1913.
James A. Epps, Jan. 2, 1854, ——.
James I. Gay, 1866-1926.
Susan J. Mims, Nov. 13, 1830-Feb. 14, 1911.
J. K. Lane, June 11, 1839-May 29, 1913.
Mrs. L. E. Lane, Sept. 30, 1844-Mar. 13, 1927.
George A. Wheeler, Sept. 29, 1892-Sept. 5, 1930.
Baby, July 5, 1899-July 17, 1899.

T. J. M. Wheeler, July 26, 1862-Sept. 21, 1929.
Minnie L. Wheeler, Dec. 2, 1886-Jan. 1, 1926.
Nellie Wheeler Rush, 1888-1918.
Sally Morton, 1865, ——.
F. N. Morton, 1838-1932.
Walter E. Denton, Mar. 31, 1886-June 11, 1922; World War Veteran.
Lovie May Horton, Nov. 24, 1892-June 5, 1912.
Ed Horton, July 9, 1869-Oct. 7, 1930.
J. G. Horton, June 6, 1856-Dec. 22, 1932.
Daisy Mai Willard, Oct. 21, 1911-April 28, 1913.
William Lemuel Cutchin, 1849-1914.
Martha Goodman Cutchin, 1846-1930.
Mary Walker Wheeler, April 5, 1830-Aug. 13, 1902.
Annie Bess Hill, Mar. 4, 1905-June 14, 1907.
Ruby Pickard Hill, May 14, 1896-Dec. 9, 1900.
Bettie Thompson, 1850-1926.
Mary Thurman, wife of Frank Hill, May 1, 1850-April 2, 1932.
Bessie Morton, wife of H. B. Hill, Feb. 22, 1882-Oct. 29, 1921.
Maggie O'Neal, 1906-1929.
Everett Simpson, 1894-1931.
Jolley, no dates.
Roger T. Pickford, Aug. 20, 1876-Jan. 3, 1928.
Martha E., wife of J. F. Dunn, May 1, 1868-Jan. 12, 1923.
Arlie A. Abernathy, 1889-1928.
Ansil G. Abernathy, 1917-1930 (shield "G. S." on monument).

Bible Records—Tombstone Inscriptions

Charlton McWhorter, June 5, 1887-Oct. 31, 1924.
George Dunn, 1900-1928.
James R. Willard, Nov. 9, 1866-Oct. 31, 1929.
H. G. Carley, 1879-1930.
Mary A., wife of R. W. McWharter, Dec. 2, 1845-Mar. 1, 1922.
R. W. McWharter, Feb. 17, 1849-July 19, 1915.
David A. Woodall, Feb. 14, 1875-April 25, 1920.
Lizzie, wife of T. C. Whitley, Sept. 25, 1885-June 25, 1914.
Emma J. Woodall, born in Chester County, England, 1844-Nov. 11, 1908.
J. R. Woodall, June 12, 1869-April 8, 1903.
Sophia Lane, May 9, 1911; age, 58 years.
John E. Jarrell, June 29, 1887-May 23, 1912.
James Walkup, Dec. 21, 1838-Jan. 6, 1910.
Lavinia Walkup, Dec. 25, 1844-Dec. 31, 1910.
Mary Hatton Trail, Oct. 31, 1907-Nov. 3, 1910.
Jimmie Mossell Trail, daughter of Mr. and Mrs. F. C. Trail, Oct. 16, 1905-Oct. 13, 1913.
R. O. Hill, July 3, 1898-Aug. 17, 1918.
C. W. Brewer, Mar. 6, 1849-Jan. 19, 1912.
Ella B. Brewer, Oct. 19, 1929; age, 72 years.
Albert S. Lane, Nov. 14, 1866, ——.
Martha Ann Lane, June 25, 1874-Aug. 22, 1830.
Lenna D. Lane, Nov. 4, 1895-Nov. 5, 1906.
Willie B. Brewer, July 24, 1883-July 17, 1887.
Lillie Ruth Redmond, July 12, 1914-Oct. 21, 1918.
Lulu Wheeler McAbee, 1882-1933.
Elijah D. Wheeler, July 10, 1854-Feb. 13, 1933.
Ada B. Wheeler, May 30, 1856, ——.
Mary E. Wheeler, Oct. 13, 1877-Feb. 13, 1913.
Susan Truett Gay, wife of Wm. Gay, Feb. 26, 1886-Dec. 4, 1904.
Wm. R. Gay, Nov. 11, 1833-Mar. 18, 1908.
Mattie Prichitt, wife of J. P. Hill, June 17, 1879-Sept. 1, 1908.
Johnie Hill, Aug. 9, 1907-Oct. 6, 1908.
Sallie R. Hill, wife of Samuel G. Ivey, Feb. 11, 1872-Mar. 16, 1912.
Wm. Franklin Gay, Oct. 28, 1861-Mar. 26, 1927.
Mary Franklin Gay, Oct. 1, 1853-Aug. 6, 1928.
Annie, wife of A. R. Davidson, Mar. 25, 1905; age, 35 years.
James E. Ragan, Aug. 13, 1850-Dec. 11, 1909.
Elizabeth, wife of W. H. Adams, May 10, 1853-April 17, 1894.
Beulah Adams, June 28, 1886- Nov. 1, 1914.
Mary Thompson, wife of J. H. Adams, July 10, 1817-Feb. 15, 1900.
J. J. Rader, Oct. 23, 1867-Mar. 1, 1929.
Kate Ezell Rader, Mar. 18, 1866, ——.
Wm. Cool Rieves, Feb. 28, 1851-Aug. 6, 1928.
Susan Elizabeth Rieves, Jan. 10, 1849, ——.
G. W. Wheeler, Jan. 29, 1851, ——.
Ellen Waldron Wheeler, Jan. 7, 1856, ——.
Sarah, wife of J. W. Jarrett, Mar. 29, 1854-June 28, 1901.
Eva May Jones, June 18, 1886-April 17, 1908.
Willie, son of W. M. and Minnie Jackson, Aug. 9, 1904-Dec. 12, 1904.
Mary Long, daughter of W. M. and Minnie Jackson, Nov. 6, 1911-Nov. 6, 1912.
Charley B. Lane, Aug. 15, 1872-Nov. 5, 1908.
John Robt. Lane, Sept. 5, 1899-April 25, 1909.
Eliza W., wife of E. J. Wheeler, May 28, 1824-Jan. 3, 1897.
E. J. Wheeler, Jan. 13, 1821-Jan. 26, 1898.
Evie, no date.
Eva Clements, date illegible.

CEMETERY RECORDS

Tennessee N. S. D. A. R. Records, Spencer Clack Chapter, Sevierville, Tenn., Mrs. Stanley McMahon, Regent.

Bible Records—Tombstone Inscriptions

The Sevierville Cemetery, known as the old Baptist Church Cemetery, in which the body of Spencer Clack, for whom the Spencer Clack Chapter is named, is buried; and others, including Rogers, Dickeys, Andes, and Catletts. This burying ground is located on the banks of the East Fork of Little Pigeon River and about one block from the center of the town. This cemetery is said to be seventy-five years old by older residents of the town.

Shiloh: A church cemetery south of Sevierville, Sevier County, Tenn., near the Gatlinburg (Park Road) about five miles out of town. Many of Sevier County's oldest settlers and prominent families were buried there, including the Nichols, Catletts, Mullendores, Rambos, Thomas, Wynns, Montgomerys, Hendersons, etc.

The Fox Cemetery on the Sevierville and Newport Highway is another old graveyard, and many of the descendants of our early settlers are buried there; it is about twelve miles east of Sevierville.

The Riverside Cemetery, located about two miles east of Sevierville on the Sevierville and Newport Highway and on the East Fork of Little Pigeon River, is also an old cemetery. In this cemetery the bodies of Adella C. (Huffaker) Chandler and her daughters, Kate C.) Mrs. Miles B. McMahan and (Dixie Lee) Mrs. W. A. Bowers are buried, direct descendants of Spencer Clack. And others are: McMahans, Hendersons, and Yetts, ancestors of some of the town and county's most influential citizens and early Settlers of the county.

The Richardsons' Cove Graveyard, located on the east Fork of Little Pigeon River and about nine miles east of Sevierville, is a very old burying ground; and many of the McMahans, some of the county's earliest settlers, are buried there.

Shiloh Cemetery

Records from Shiloh Cemetery sent by Mrs. Stanley McMahon, Sevierville.

Flay'll Nichols, F—N—D— 4-17, A. D., 1823.
Mitchell Porter, Thurston's Va. Co., Revolutionary War, 1760-1836.
Jane M., wife of Richard Lanning, April 22, 1800-July 10, 1885.
Richard Lanning, June 7, 1789-Feb. 4, 1877.

William Montgomery, Jan. 12, 1797-Mar. 29, 1840.
John Andes, Nov. 27, 1797-June 5, 1880.
M. W. McCowan, died April 14, 1889; age, 71 years, 5 months, 23 days.
William Catlett, May 3, 1817-Mar., 1895.

Bible Records—Tombstone Inscriptions

The following are from the Old Baptist Church Cemetery:
Spencer Clack, Mar. 28, 1740-July 9, 1832.
Katherine Clack, born Sept. 9, 1778.
In Sevierville the Spencer Clack Chapter have erected a magnificent boulder and marker in honor of Spencer Clack. This was completed during the Regency of Mrs. McMahon. (Note by Mrs. Acklen.)

THOMSON FAMILY BURYING GROUND

Inscriptions on headstones in family burying ground on the old Matthew Thomson Place, Clark County, Ky., near Thomson Station. Sent by Mrs. Charleton Rogers.

Matthew Thomson, Dec. 15, 1773-Feb. 13, 1839.
Nancy M. Thomson, consort of William N. Thomson, daughter of Joel Quisenberry, June, 1821-May 19, 1843.

RICHMOND (KY.) CEMETERY

Inscriptions in Oldham lot at Richmond (Ky.) Cemetery.

Abner Oldham, born in Caswell County, N. C., Dec. 2, 1783; died in Madison County, June 15, 1852. Removed with his father to Madison County, Ky., in 1795. In character, frank and decided, he discharged with marked fidelity his duty to his family, his friends, and his country. Indulging in a fondness for reading, he became one of the most intelligent farmers in the county, which he represented in the legislature.

Hannah Oldham, Mar. 21, 1786-Jan. 20, 1859.
Rachel White, Jan. 3, 1787-Dec. 19, 1864.
Helen Oldham, Dec. 6, 1820-April 3, 1843.
Lavinia Oldham, Jan. 5, 1827-April 13, 1843.
Ulysses Oldham, Nov. 24, 1810-Oct., 1822.

RICHMOND (KY.) CEMETERY

Inscriptions in the William Chenault plot of the Richmond (Ky.) Cemetery.

William Chenault, Oct. 2, 1773-June 19, 1834.
Susannah Phelps Chenault, Dec. 25, 1785-Sept. 10, 1848.
William Chenault, 1805-1858.
Josiah Phelps Chenault, May 8, 1811-Nov. 29, 1863.
Narcissa Oldham, wife of J. P. Chenault, May 26, 1814-Jan. 29, 1873.
Anne, June 20, 1848-Oct. 16, 1862.
Mary S., Mar. 28, 1854-Nov., 1862.
Ulysses, Oct. 12, 1833-Feb. 18, 1854.
Robert, son of J. P. and N. Chenault, Sept. 28, 1855-Mar. 13, 1880.
Jason Walker Chenault, Aug. 31, 1841-Dec. 29, 1896.
Ellen Thomson, his wife, Jan. 1, 1843-Jan. 20, 1912.

Bible Records—Tombstone Inscriptions

ROGERS FAMILY BURYING GROUND

Inscriptions on the tombs of the Rogers family of "Bryant Station" in the family burying ground there.

Susan Darnaby, died Feb. 16, 1856; rest in peace.

Sacred to the memory of Joseph Rogers, born, 1742, who departed this life on the 13th day of July, 1834; age, 92 years, 4 months.

No more, my God, I boast no more,
  Of all the duties I have done.
I quit the hopes I held before
  To trust the mercy of Thy Son.
Now, for the love I bear his name,
  What was my gain, I count my loss.
My former (pride?) I count my shame
  And nail my glory to the cross.

Bernard F. Rogers, Dec. 24, 1816-May 28, 1845.

TOMBSTONE OF COL. RICHARD CLOUGH ANDERSON, SR.

Inscription on tombstone of Col. Richard Clough Anderson, Sr., in the family burying ground of his old home, "Soldier's Retreat," now Hurstbourne Farm, near Louisville, Ky.

Richard Clough Anderson, son of Robert and Elizabeth Anderson, born Jan 12, 1750, at Gold Mines, Hanover County, Va.; died, Oct. 16, 1826, at Soldier's Retreat, Jefferson County, Ky. A patriotic soldier, he served his country through the War for Independence, in Virginia Continental Line, having entered the army a captain and retired when liberty was secured a lieutenant-colonel. He was wounded at Trenton, seriously injured at Savannah, taken prisoner at Charleston, acted as aid de camp to Lafayette in his campaign in Virginia, and to Governor Nelson at the siege of Yorktown. After the war he was appointed by the officers of the Line surveyor-general of the Virginia Military Lands (and) retained the office during life. In 1784 he removed to Kentucky. One of the patriarchs of his adopted state, he lived a life of usefulness and honor, leaving to his children and country the memory of a good citizen, a true patriot, and a just man.

On the west side of the monument is the inscription:

Elizabeth Clark Anderson, daughter of John and Anne Clark, and wife of Colonel Richard Anderson; born, 1768; married, 1787; died, 1795.

On the south side is this inscription:

Sacred to the memory of Sarah Marshall, Nov. 20, 1779-Aug. 25, 1854, daughter of William Marshall of Caroline County, Va., and Ann Clark McCleod; married at Fair Hope, Jefferson County, Ky., Sept. 17, 1797, to Lieut.-Col. Richard Clough Anderson of Soldier's Retreat—his second wife.

ANDERSON FAMILY BURYING GROUND

Other inscriptions on tombstones in the Anderson family burying ground at "Soldier's Retreat." Within a foot of the east side of the base of the marble shaft are two small and comparatively modern granite markers. On the larger one is carved the following:

In memory of Frances Marshall, Oct. 29, 1800-Dec. 2, 1802; Hugh Roy, Aug. 20, 1811-Feb. 7, 1812; Lucelia Poindexter, Sept. 19, 1817-Aug. 20, 1820; Matthew, April 3, 1819-Oct. 29, 1820—children of Richard Clough and Sarah Marshall Anderson.

On a smaller granite marker is:

Charles, son of Robert Anderson, grandson of Robert Anderson, of Gold Mine, Va.; died, 1824.

MARY NOAILLES MURFREE
(*Charles Egbert Craddock*)

Bible Records—Tombstone Inscriptions

NEW PROVIDENCE PRESBYTERIAN CHURCH

From Miss Jessie E. Turner, member of John Ross Chapter, D. A. R., Chattanooga, Tenn.

One of the oldest churches in Tennessee is New Providence Presbyterian Church at Maryville, Blount County, Tenn., whose history dates from 1786, and at present date, 1933, is in sound condition.

The church was organized by the Rev. Gideon Blackburn, D.D., in 1793, from a group which had formed itself for religious worship in the new settlement in 1786. Its people heard sermons from early preachers like Samuel Doak and Samuel Carrick. The Rev. Isaac Anderson became pastor in 1812 and remained so until his death, 1857, in the meantime becoming the founder of Maryville College and its president for thirty-eight years. Co-operation between church and college was and is so close that one is a part of the other.

New Providence churchyard, now bordering a chief street of the thriving town of Maryville, has thus far withstood encroachment from commerce and industry. Because of the age of the burying ground and the contribution to the building of the Volunteer State made by the brave pioneers who lie sleeping there, it is to be devoutly hoped that the graves will never be disturbed. Inscriptions on the tombstones there tell a story of the past better than might be engraved upon any modern monument.

The burial grounds had been open free to the dead of all creeds, denominations, and citizens generally, and continued so until about 1880, when they had become so full that it was difficult to dig a grave without going down on old ones. The trouble was largely due to the fact that the graves had been dug without system or order, the only rule observed being that the foot of the grave be toward the sunrise.

According to the late Maj. Will A. McTeer, an elder in the church for years, the custom of placing the graves toward the sunrise affected nearly all old cemeteries, the Christian pioneers following a "superstition originating from sun worship which they condemned but observed unawares."

Bible Records—Tombstone Inscriptions

Many graves are unmarked, says Maj. McTeer in his "History of New Providence Church," published in 1921, adding, "In the early settlements it was difficult to get stones to mark the graves, especially with inscriptions; so a great majority of the older graves have either only rough limestone boulders or no marks at all. Many bodies of soldiers of the Revolutionary War, as well as the War of 1812, are buried in our cemetery, the particular spot being often unknown; and others worthy of the highest commendation and even of a place in the hall of fame cannot be identified, but their ashes mingle with the soil of New Providence Church."

A few years also, following a suggestion made by Mrs. T. J. Wallace, of Franklin, Tenn., the New Providence Churchyard Association was formed to care for this historic graveyard. Many persons who had kindred buried there warmly welcomed the plan. Mrs. Wallace was made president; Mrs. Narrie T. Maxey, of Maryville, treasurer; and Maj. Will A. McTeer, secretary.

A permanent fund of about five hundred dollars was contributed, principally by non-residents of Maryville whose forefathers sleep in the old cemetery. The fund was placed on deposit to the credit of the association, and the interest only is being used for improving and preserving the place. Among those active in promoting the association and collecting the endowment fund were: Gen. L. D. Tyson, representing the Charles M. McGhee estate; George A. Toole, of Maryville; Mrs. J. C. M. Bogle, of Lenoir City; and Mrs. Harriet C. J. Henry, of Baker's Creek.

Two bronze markers given by the Sons of the American Revolution have been placed on the graves of William and Jessee Wallace, patriots, who gave civil and military service in the Revolution. Ceremony was sponsored by Mary Blount Chapter, D. A. R., of Maryville; and Maj. McTeer and Will A. Parham were the speakers.

NAMES OF PERSONS BURIED TAKEN FROM INSCRIPTIONS

The following is the list of names and dates of persons who were buried in the grounds, as appears from the gravestones, so far as

Bible Records—Tombstone Inscriptions

the same can be read. The dates following the names give the births; the second dates give the deaths.

Anderson, Rev. Isaac, D.D., Mar. 26, 1780-Jan. 28, 1857.
Anderson, Florence, June 3, 1782-Nov. 18, 1852.
Anderson, Samuel E. H. B., Mar. 11, 1810-Nov. 15, 1841.
Arbeely, Mary J. A., born in Damascus, Syria, in 1832; died in Maryville, Tenn., June 9, 1883.
Alexander, Martha Flora, wife of Rev. James H. Alexander, Oct. 16, 1836-May 5, 1861.
Alexander, Sarah Mildred, wife of Dr. James H. Alexander, Mar. 29, 1850-Oct. 25, 1869.
Cannon, Robert W., died Sept. 3, 1849; age, 33 years, 2 months, 13 days.
Virginia Godfrey, wife of Benjamin Chairs, died Sept. 26, 1849; age, 24 years.
Craig, Malinda Hester, daughter of John S. Craig, Mar. 15, 1851-Sept. 26, 1860.
Dowell, Rev. William T., April 27, 1821-July 28, 1867.
Dowell, Brownlow; age, 25 years.
Duncan, Mary, Nov. 22, 1792-July 11, 1825.
Duncan, Andrew, Oct. 16, 1800-May 1, 1883.
Eagleton, John, Oct. 20, 1785-July 12, 1865; he was one of the elders and a strong support to Dr. Anderson.
Eagleton, Lavinia, wife of John, Jan. 11, 1793-Dec. 5, 1880.
Elliott, Mary Ann, wife of Adam Haun, Aug. 13, 1818-Dec. 5, 1848.
Ford, Jesse, born in Woodford County, Ky., May 3, 1796-Nov. 24, 1873.
Godfrey, Francis H., of Bibb County, Ga.; died at Montvale, Sept. 30, 1835.
Greer, Darthula K., wife of James M. Greer, May 5, 1845-Feb. 2, 1875.
Greer, Sallie H. Greenway, wife of James A. Greer, Oct. 8, 1848-Dec. 27, 1881.
Greer, Nellie, Feb. 23, 1880-Mar. 22, 1887.
Greer, Mamie, June 19, 1878-April 14, 1879.
Greer, William Arthur, Feb. 18, 1870-Sept. 16, 1872.
Greenway, William David, Dec. 19, 1845-July 10, 1870.
Greer, Norma, June 7, 1876-Nov. 28, 1894.
Grisham, Sarah Alzena, Mar. 20, 1847-Dec. 22, 1859, daughter of A. and A. M. Grisham.
Gibbs, Margaret Virginia (stone sunk until dates cannot be seen).
Hart, Elizabeth, died Nov. 9, 1849; age, 53 years, 9 months, 12 days.
Haines, Daniel T., of Philadelphia, died May 8, 1832.
Hart, Edward, died Oct. 24, 1858; age, 70 years, 1 month, 10 days.
Hart, John, May 18, 1823-April 2, 1874.
Haun, Mary Ann Elliott, wife of Adam Haun, Aug. 13, 1818-Dec. 10, 1848.
Hooke, Robert, Mar. 16, 1773-1848.
Hooke, Elizabeth Kilbourne, 1784-Feb. 27, 1847.
Hoyt, Rev. Darius, Nov. 11, 1804-Aug. 11, 1837.
Hood, Francis M., June 18, 1818-April 9, 1881.
Hood, Eliza, wife of Francis M. Hood, June 11, 1832-April 5, 1891.
Hood, John, Feb. 7, 1799-Dec. 18, 1856.
Houston, James S., May 1, 1842-Aug. 15, 1842.
Irwin, Margaret J., wife of James B. Irwin, Aug. 26, 1832-July 22, 1854.
Morton, James, Feb. 9, 1800-July 6, 1859.
Morton, Rebecca, July 10, 1811-Mar. 4, 1883.
Montgomery, Andrew C., Mar. 23, 1793-June 25, 1884.
Montgomery, Ann M., wife of Andrew C. Montgomery, May 22, 1803-Feb. 8, 1834.
Montgomery, Evalina, Sept. 20, 1809-July 18, 1853.
McGhee, Barclay, died Aug. 17, 1819; age, 59 years, 11 months, 20 days, one of the original pioneers of Maryville.
McGhee, Jane, wife of Barclay McGhee, May 17, 1767-Sept. 8, 1835.
McGhee, Dr. Alexander, died June 3, 1841; age, 54 years.
McKenzie, Sallie A., Nov. 4, 1856-June 23, 1887.
McKenzie, John G., Sept. 11, 1849-April 5, 1905.
McGinley, Col. James, one of the pi-

201

Bible Records—Tombstone Inscriptions

oneers and a noted man, Nov. 20, 1763-Mar. 26, 1834.
McGinley, James, Jan. 3, 1822-April 14, 1859.
McGinley, Martha Eliza, wife of James McGinley, Nov. 12, 1825-Sept. 5, 1854.
McCulloch, Eliza Jane, wife of John A. McCulloch, May 22, 1851-Jan. 21, 1873.
Nunn, Martha Elizabeth, wife of Eli Nunn, Nov. 9, 1824-July 29, 1854.
Patton, Theresa Charlotte, wife of Robert S. Patton, Sept. 5, 1852; died at Adairsville, Ga.
Pride, Ruth, died Dec. 25, 1824; age, 56 years.
Pope, Theresa Charlotte, died May 24, 1856; age, 57 years, wife of Rev. Fielding Pope.
Pruner, Mrs. Mary E. McGhee, Jan. 21, 1828-Aug. 25, 1870.
Robinson, Margaret, wife of Rev. John J. Robinson, D.D., Mar. 8, 1824-Mar. 8, 1856.
Scruthin, Florida, April 8, 1852-Aug. 31, 1853.
Scott, Minerva; age, 52 years; Feb. 3, 1882.
Spencer, Calvin M., died Oct. 25, 1838; age, 8 years, 1 month, 10 days.
Tedford, Joseph T., Mar. 26, 1846-July 15, 1868.
Tedford, John N., May 15, 1840-May 6, 1859.
Tedford, Robert, Feb. 10, 1799-Feb. 19, 1859.
Tedford, Phoeba M., June 11, 1800-July 4, 1888.
Tedford, Kate Bond, Jan. 13, 1830-Mar. 2, 1877.
Tedford, John N., Feb. 17, 1803-Mar. 16, 1869.
Toole, William, Jan. 4, 1792-May 16, 1860.
Toole, Martha Jane, wife of Col. James M. Toole, died Feb. 18, 1850; age, 32 years, 2 months.
Thompson, Jesse, Mar. 6, 1795-June 1, 1842.
Thompson, Elizabeth, June 9, 1802-June 30, 1850.
Thompson, Rebecca, Nov. 4, 1789-April 12, 1845.
Tucker, Richard C.
Walker, J. J., died July 12, 1842.

Wallace, Mary, wife of Gen. William Wallace, and sister of Gen. Sam Houston, Mar. 4, 1797-April 29, 1854.
Wallace, Matthew, died July 1, 1840; age, 76 years.
Wallace, Elizabeth, wife of Matthew Wallace, died Aug. 3, 1845.
Wallace, Jesse, Oct. 4, 1767-Feb. 13, 1854.
Wallace, Martha George, wife of Jesse Wallace, Sept. 14, 1776-Dec. 26, 1848.
Wallace, Mary, died Nov. 15, 1844; age, 60 years.
Wallace, Gen. William, Sept. 8, 1894-April 21, 1864.
Wallace, Margaret, Aug. 17, 1792-Nov. 8, 1844.
Wallace, Cynthia Eliza, wife of J. George Wallace, died December 21, 1848; age, 18 years, 9 months, 18 days.
Wallace, Samuel W., Mar. 22, 1831-April 10, 1855; died in Eufaula, Ala.
Wallace, Caroline C., 1829; age, 64 years, June 30, 1893.
Wallace, Octavia, wife of Alexander Wallace, Mar. 24, 1825-May 15, 1852.
Walker, Eliza Woods, wife of William A. Walker, Dec. 8, 1830-Oct. 24, 1854.
Walker, William A., Feb. 9, 1823-Feb. 28, 1890.
Wear, James M., Mar. 13, 1828-April 20, 1846.
Wear, Lucretia, wife of John S. Wear, Mar. 6, 1794-July 31, 1825.
Wright, Nelson S., Jan. 30, 1790-July 8, 1862.
Wright, Jane B., wife of Nelson S. Wright, Aug. 21, 1793-Feb. 9, 1856.
Wilson, Oscar, Sergeant Co. I, 1 U. S. Hy. Art.
Wilson, Mary E., wife of Oscar Wilson; age, 47 years.
Wilson, Sarah E., wife of Richard I. Wilson, April 3, 1828-Aug. 8, 1854.
Wilson, Richard Wilson, a prominent and leading man of the county, public-spirited and greatly beloved, is known to have been buried by the side of his wife; and his son, James K. Wilson, was also buried there, but there are no stones or inscriptions to mark their graves.

Bible Records—Tombstone Inscriptions

OAKLAND CEMETERY

Names of those buried in Oakland Cemetery, Trenton, Tenn. (Born prior to 1900.) Sent by Mrs. G. W. Wade, Trenton, Tenn.

Alley, Agnes S., wife of Jonah Alley, June 1, 1851-Nov. 4, 1901.
Atkins, Emma, wife of J. A. Atkins, May 13, 1862-Aug. 8, 1888.
Attry, Sarah J., wife of J. W. Attry, Feb. 24, 1845-Aug. 2, 1886.
Aslin, Sue, Mar. 14, 1853-July 28, 1914.
Alexander, Mary B., Nov. 19, 1839-Feb. 13, 1916.
Alexander, J. W., Dec. 28, 1828-Jan. 4, 1902.
Barker, Jas. S., Feb. 16, 1859-April 1, 1905.
Barrett, Walter F., Nov. 10, 1850-June 30, 1897.
Blakemore, Frances, 1843-1894.
Bennett, Sara F., Jan. 1, 1840-Mar. 6, 1878.
Bennett, Sallie, Sept. 21, 1844-Mar. 12, 1918.
Bennett, Jas. F., Mar. 17, 1835-Feb. 21, 1907.
Bennett, Robt., Jan. 2, 1867-Oct. 25, 1894.
Birmingham, Green, Mar. 12, 1826-April 25, 1880.
Birmingham, W. E., June 25, 1859-April 4, 1914.
Birmingham, Emma, Dec. 20, 1859-Sept. 23, 1914.
Brett, A. M., 1884-1917.
Brett, Mary M., 1839-1916.
Borsch, G. F., April 2, 1831-June 1, 1891.
Buck, Church, May 13, 1843-Dec. 3, 1918.
Brown, Rosie A., Jan. 16, 1849-May 20, 1918.
Crawford, Benoni, 1797-1857.
Carthel, J. T., May 14, 1831-Oct. 5, 1912.
Carter, Sarah Carthel, 1827-1918.
Carthel, Minnie Neely, wife of J. T.
Carthel, June 11, 1837-Jan. 26, 1891.
Caldwell, W. C., May 14, 1847-Dec. 23, 1924.
Carne, J. D., 1842-1888.
Carne, S. A., 1854-1888.
Carne, Rev. J. B., 1848-1885.
Chester, Elizabeth, 1841-1899.
Choate, P. H., Nov. 1, 1848-Nov. 22, 1922.
Choate, Sallie B., June 14, 1858-June 12, 1912.
Cowan, Seth, Mar. 7, 1822-Jan. 26, 1878.
Cowan, Mrs. T., Sept. 20, 1839-Jan. 15, 1879.
Crisp, Annie, 1876-1885.
Coley, Martha Ann, Feb. 24, 1826-Nov. 24, 1901.
Conner, Nannie, ——, Aug. 15, 1883.
Curry, A. S., Jan. 8, 1825-Feb. 2, 1897.
Curry, Martha, Jan. 8, 1826-Feb. 2, 1897.
Davis, John L., Aug. 15, 1807-Feb. 3, 1882.
Davis, Elizabeth, ——, April 4, 1884.
Davis, Elizabeth, ——, Jan. 8, 1882.
Davis, R. N., June 21, 1830-Sept. 25, 1901.
Davis, Belle, Oct. 11, 1841-Oct. 19, 1920.
Davis, Herbert, Nov. 4, 1870-May 6, 1912.
Doyle, Sue, ——, Dec. 20, 1890.
Dew, R. J., 1842-1917.
Dew, Amanda, 1849-1903.
Deason, David G., Sept. 18, 1822-1876.
Elder, Horace M., Aug. 20, 1847-Nov. 28, 1910.
Elder, Sallie H., Sept. 20, 1853-July 26, 1910.
Elder, Chas. A., Sept. 21, 1838-Sept. 6, 1899.
Elder, Robt., Feb. 12, 1811-Sept. 16, 1852.
Harlan, Tilson, 1843-1917.
Harbert, Thos. T., April 12, 1832-Mar. 20, 1915.
Hill, Spl., 1843-1910.
Hill, Annie, 1847-1911.
Hays, Minnie Elder, 1859-1899.
Hannah, John M., Sept. 12, 1839-Oct. 25, 1905.
Hannah, Elizabeth, Oct. 6, 1854-June 7, 1912.
Hicks, E. J., 1843-1910.
Hicks, G. B., 1826-1902.
Herron, J. M., Nov. 29, 1846-April 19, 1898.
Herron, William, Oct. 10, 1810-Feb. 16, 1891.

Bible Records—Tombstone Inscriptions

Herron, Kathryn, Feb. 25, 1818-Jan. 12, 1904.
Holmes, Marion, Sept. 15, 1832-Mar. 18, 1905.
Hunt, Robert, Sept. 21, 1842-Sept. 19, 1889.
Harper, Henry, 1815-1898.
Hunt, Margaret, 1839-1917.
Happel, Dr. T. J., ——, 1902.
Hicks, Mattie M., 1858-1887.
Happel, Mary G., 1826-1908.
Hackl, Adalbert, May 26, 1885-Nov. 13, 1897.
Hill, J. D., 1802-1871.
Hillsman, Rev. Matthew, Aug. 7, 1814-Oct. 22, 1892.
Harwood, Thos. S., 1852-1931.
Hillsman, Ann., 1818, ——.
Harper, H. D., Nov. 23, 1815-Dec. 20, 1896.
Harrison, Sarah, 1829-1912.
Hess, Anna, 1850-1894.
Jarrell, Dr. Joseph, 1811-1872.
Jarrell, Lucy, 1809-1868.
Jones, L. M., Sept. 26, 1817-Sept. 24, 1895.
Jones, Cassandra, June 15, 1830-May 12, 1878.
Jones, W. S., Sept. 9, 1868-April 21, 1899.
Jetton, Dan. B., Aug. 24, 1818-Sept. 8, 1895.
Jetton, Martha C., June 28, 1826-Oct. 7, 1905.
Johnston, Robt., 1784-1859.
Johnston, Mary B., 1785-1828.
Kyle, Benj., 1861-1869.
Keenan, Sallie Hicks, 1859-1929.
Lassiter, A. J., Dec. 4, 1823-Nov. 18, 1898.
Lassiter, Bettie, Dec. 25, 1836-Jan. 21, 1912.
Lee, William A.; age, 45 years.
Landis, Ben, 1821-1879.
Levy, Dr. Lewis, 1806-1879.
Little, A. J., 1839-1905.
Morgan, Annie G., June 2, 1867-April 6, 1895.
Morgan, C. W., 1860-1927.
Morgan, Bettie, 1850-1926.
Morgan, Lulu E., Aug. 23, 1863-Sept. 2, 1906.
Morgan, L. W., Aug. 5, 1868-Jan. 13, 1905.
Marshall, Rev. Matt, ——, Aug. 23, 1874.
Marshall, Eliza M., Jan. 1, 1808-July 31, 1878.
Marshal, A. A., 1838-1902.
Marshal, Julie, 1843-1916.
McGee, G. R.
McGee, Sallie V., 1842-1900.
McCulloch, Lizzie, 1843-1879.
McRee, Maggie M., 1858-1897.
Moody, Thos., 1714-1803.
Moore, Amanda, 1843-1870.
McDearmon, A. J., Sept. 28, 1842-Sept. 19, 1889.
Neilson, Mrs. H. D., 1817-1892.
Neilson, Thomas, 1843-1862.
Neilson, Jas. Willis, 1848-1884.
Nimmo, Allen, Nov. 22, 1785-Feb. 25, 1899.
Nimmo, Cassandra, Sept. 24, 1832-May 20, 1867.
Partee, B. L., Sept. 18, 1831-Feb. 25, 1899.
Partee, Martha, Nov. 6, 1834-Jan. 13, 1918.
Patton, William, Aug. 15, 1815-Jan. 15, 1885.
Patton, Newton C., 1820-1888.
Peeples, Mildred, April 23, 1832-Jan. 17, 1879.
Russel, William Alex, 1854-1875.
Reese, DeWitt, Aug. 8, 1828-Nov. 31, 1876.
Reese, Ann, Aug. 8, 1828-June 28, 1851.
Skiles, James M., Nov. 9, 1851-June 28, 1927.
Skiles, Martha, Dec. 27, 1850-Nov. 28, 1914.
Strong, Nannie, Feb. 3, 1841-Oct. 20, 1910.
Smith, Conrad, 1837-1897.
Smith, Alice, 1848-1877.
Smith, Sarah, 1833-1888.
Seat, Robt., 1800-1871.
Seat, Sarah, 1816-1887.
Smith, William, 1848-1901.
Smith, Joe Hope.
Shackelford, Sara, Jan. 20, 1800-Jan. 20, 1870.
Senter, Mollie, May 15, 1841-April 27, 1892.
Taylor, Mettie T., 1852-1917.
Taylor, Basil Manley, 1811-1887.
Taylor, Dicie W., 1817-1891.
Taylor, Donald C., Oct. 25, ——; Mar., ——.
Thompson, Richard, 1820-1871.
Taylor, R. Z., 1846-1922.
Turner, James, 1793-1849.
Tiner, J. N., 1832-1877.

Bible Records—Tombstone Inscriptions

Taylor, A. J., Oct. 12, 1862-Sept. 26, 1922.
Taylor, Emma, Sept. 16, 1860-Nov. 27, 1900.
Torrence, W. G., 1849-1888.
Torrence, Durotha, 1829-1899.
Vick, J .W., 1857-1917.
Vick, Mattie, 1863, ——.
Vaden, Martha, ——, 1876.
Walker, John R., Dec. 3, 1855-Feb. 3, 1919.
Wofford, Emma, May 1, 1839-Nov. 27, 1885.
Wright, W. T., Sept. 17, 1838-1855.
Willis, S. L., 1852-1915.
Willis, Carolin, 1855-1928.

Watkins, Thos. S., Feb. 6, 1848-Oct. 3, 1876.
Watkins, Mosella C., Dec. 26, 1844-July 6, 1909.
Wood, William A., July 25, 1838-Jan. 3, 1877.
Wood, E. G., Nov. 8, 1813-Sept. 19, 1881.
Wood, Mary, Dec. 10, 1816-May 23, 1875.
Wade, Major William, 1807-1884.
Wade, Rebecca, 1861-1903.
Wade, Alex, 1825-1911.
Wade, Eliz, 1867-1883.
Wright, 1826-1898.

RECORDS FROM OLD CEMETERIES IN UNICOI COUNTY, TENN.

Contributed by Mrs. J. M. Ferguson, Erwin.

Mary McInturf, wife of James Johnson, May 20, 1819-July 20, 1888. Inscription: "Behold God is my salvation, I will trust and not be afraid."
James B. Johnson, May 6, 1810-June 17, 1876; age, 66 years, 41 days.
Henry Jones, Mar. 4, 1804-Feb. 12, 1877.
Elizabeth Feathers, wife of Henry Jones, Feb. 2, 1818-Nov. 18, 1869.
Hannah Constable, died Mar. 2, 1843; age, 67 years.
Mary Baker, wife of Ezekiah Birchfield, June 12, 1807-May 1, 1874.
Ezekiah Birchfield, —— 13, 1814-Jan. 22, 1883.
Charlie Nelson, died Mar. 17, 1866; age, 25 years, 6 months, 18 days.
Will Tipton, Company B, 13th Tenn. Cavalry.
Corporal J. W. Ramsay, Company A, 3rd North Carolina 2nd line.
C. A. Smith, Company G, 4th Tenn. Infantry.
Charles Nelson, Company B, 12th Tennessee Cavalry.
William P. Love, 1813-June 18, 1876; age, 58 years.
Jacob D. Love, Nov. 9, 1842-May 10, 1907, Co. I, 63rd Tenn. Inft.
Pheobe Stout, wife of J. D. Love, April 10, 1840-June 26, 1923.
J. R. Love, 1844-Mar. 28, 1912.
M. A. Birchfield, wife of Robert Birchfield, April 12, 1850-Feb. 26, 1908.
Maggie Welborn, wife of J. A. Freeman, born Aug. 12, 1870.
Nathan Birchfield, Revolutionary Soldier, said to be one hundred and seven years of age at his death, 1863.
William McInturf, Jan. 14, 1837-Oct. 25, 1902.
Rhoda McInturf, April 11, 1838-Feb. 8, 1882; age, 43 years, 9 months, 37 days.
Mary E. McInturf, May 5, 1862-Nov. 14, 1886.
Mary E. Hodge, June 3, 1866-Jan. 28, 1885.
W. S. Willock, Aug. 7, 1820-May 20, 1885.
G. W. White, Mar. 13, 1864-July 15, 1921.
Hester A. White, 1872, ——.
Ellene Roberts, May 12, 1861-April, 1891.
George W. Yarbrough, Oct. 12, 1833-Mar. 25, 1905.
Eunice Brown, Mar. 6, 1824-July 24, 1906.
Jasper Brown, Co. C, N. C. Inf.
Elizabeth, wife of Hugh Harris, died Dec. 5, 1910; age, 84 years.
Polly Davis, Mar. 5, 1878-Oct. 29, 1914.
Wilson Edwards, June 6, 1847-Mar. 12, 1918.
Feldon Edwards, Oct. 20, 1877-Feb. 27, 1901.
Pheobe A. Banner, Oct. 28, 1850-Sept. 3, 1918.
Henry C. Banner, Aug. 22, 1850-Aug. 30, 1904.

Bible Records—Tombstone Inscriptions

Elizabeth Banner, Sept. 19, 1817-Oct. 30, 1892.
W. H. Harris, Aug. 2, 1846-Nov. 6, 1922.
Hiriam Bailey, June 15, 1825-June 14, 1906.
Sarah Bailey, July 6, 1825-April 14, 1905.
Jennie Crosswhite, June 16, 1829-Jan. 10, 1894.
William Daniel Dougherty, April 1, 1859-Dec. 8, 1901.
Thomas E. Bowman, Jan. 26, 1886-July 6, 1915, 110 Co. U. S. A. C.
William McInturf, Jan. 14, 1837-Oct. 25, 1902.
Sarah Huskins, Feb. 28, 1836-June 5, 1878.
John Huskins, Mar. 15, 1839-Mar. 4, 1914.
Laura Pippin, Oct. 5, 1869-Oct. 26, 1885.

Robert Birchfield, Mar. 3, 1872-Feb. 4, 1914.
Serena, wife of R. W. Gilbert, Jan. 8, 1856-Jan. 10, 1926.
Rachel Hughes, wife of Wm. Hughes, Jan. 6, 1862-June 8, 1922.
Rachel Hensley, Jan. 24, 1832-Sept. 12, 1891.
Nancy A. Love, July 12, 1823-Dec. 21, 1913.
Wm. Huskins, April 28, 1859-May 14, 1926.
Sallie Hensley, April 16, 1841-Mar. 9, 1925.
Mary Grindstaff, Nov. 18, 1828-Dec. 22, 1915.
Barbara A. Britt, 1819-Dec. 4, 1889.
Rev. C. G. Johnson, 1848-1919.
His wife, Elizabeth, 1848-1921.
Mrs. Liddia Rowe, Dec. 8, 1840-May 17, 1902.

Abstracts of the Will of Major Peter Helphenstine

Abstracts of the will of Major Peter Helphenstine was probated in the Courthouse, Frederick County, Va., May 4, 1779.

I, Major Peter Helphenstine, of the town of Winchester, County of Frederick and Colony of Va., make this my last will and testament.

I will the third part of my estate to my dear wife, Catherine Helpenstine, with all wearing apparel, plate and the two-thirds to be equally divided between my sons, Phillip, Peter, William, and Henry, and my daughters, Catherine, Rosanna, Charlotta, and Elizabeth, sons to be paid at age of twenty-one, daughters paid at age of eighteen or days of marriage.

In witness hereunto, I set my hand and seal. This 24th day of March, 1876.

Abstracts of the Will of James Black

Abstracts of the will of James Black of the Township of Martic, County of Lancaster, State of Pennsylvania.

I bequeath to my dearly and well-beloved wife, Jane, her bed and furniture, all pewter and two pots, one cow and four sheep of her own choosing. I also allow her one-third of my real estate during her life in the manner the law directs. To my dutiful and beloved daughter, Mary, I bequeath twenty pounds in which is to be included, her saddle and bridle, bed and bed clothes. To my beloved son, Thomas, I give two pounds, ten shillings. To my beloved son, James, I give five pounds. My beloved children David, Margaret, and John, are yet in their minority and will require more education.

It is my will that David receives schooling to the value of five pounds, Margaret to the value of five pounds, and John to the value of ten pounds. I also bequeath Margaret twenty pounds.

It is my will that David and John go to a trade as they arrive at the age of sixteen.

It is my will my books be divided between my wife and children, my wife to choose her own.

The residue of my estate after everything else is paid, to be divided among my sons, Hugh, David, and John.

It is my desire that Mary and Mar-

Bible Records—Tombstone Inscriptions

garet receive each an additional ten pounds. My sons, Thomas, Black, and James Black are appointed executors of this my last will and testament. I have set my hand and seal this 23rd day of August in the year of our Lord, 1805. Probated Feb. 7, 1806, Lancaster County, Pa., Martic Township.

Abstracts of the Will of Thomas Harry

Abstracts of the will of Thomas Harry of the Township of Pennsbury, County of Chester, State of Pennsylvania. I give and devise unto my two sons, Amos Harry and Isaac Harry, all the plantation of land I live on in the Township of Pennsbury, they to pay the following legacys:

To my sons, Evan Harry and Jacob Harry, and daughters, Mary Hollingsworth, Hannah Walter, Betsey Harlen, and Sarah Vernon, the sum of one hundred dollars each. My daughter Lidia Walker the sum of five dollars, grandson Samuel Harry, son of my daughter Lidia Walker, the sum of ninety-five dollars. My daughter Rachel the sum of six hundred dollars. I give and bequeath unto my son Amos Harry the sum of four hundred dollars to be paid from my personal estate. To my daughter Rachel one hundred dollars worth of my household and kitchen furniture of her own choice. To my two sons, Amos and Isaac, all the residue of my estate to be equally divided between them. My two sons, Amos and Isaac to be executors of this my last will and testament.

I hereunto set my hand and seal the 12th day of the 8th month in the year of our Lord, 1824.

Wills in possession of Julia Elizabeth Sprint Ferguson, descendant.

Carrie Harper Cheek, Data

Carrie Harper Cheek (Mrs. H. D.), descendant of John Harper, Sr., who was born 1740; died, Sept., 1812, in Sumner County, Tenn. The daughter of James George Harper and Emma Hunt Harper. George, the son of Thomas, who was the son of John Harper, Jr., who married Martha Snead Oldham, daughter of Major George Oldham, who was born Feb. 25, 1779; died, April 25, 1845. John Harper, Jr., the son of John Harper, Sr., and Margaret Morrow, born, 1750; died, Dec. 6, 1835; married, 1772. He was of English descent. Margaret Morrow's parents came from Ireland. Children of John Harper, Sr., and Margaret Morrow:

Rebecca Harper, born May 16, 1773.
William Harper, born Jan. 1, 1775.
Hugh Harper, born Sept. 22, 1776.
John, Jr., Harper, born Feb. 25, 1779.
Anna Harper, born Sept. 8, 1781.
Andrew Harper, born Oct. 3, 1784.
James Harper, born June 6, 1786.
Elizabeth Harper, born Mar. 25, 1788.
Asa Harper, born Aug. 4, 1790.
Enos Harper, born July 2, 1793.
Jesse Harper, born Dec. 1, 1795.
Margaret Harper, born Nov. 29, 1799. John Harper, Jr., owned a large tract of land in Anderson County; he was for many years a Justice of the Peace. An old account book, a hundred years old, contains an account of these transactions, in possession of his grandson, James George Harper, Seneca, S. C. He and his wife are buried at Big Creek Cemetery.

John Harper, Jr.'s will is on record at Anderson Courthouse. A letter written by Wm. L. Harper from Tennessee to South Carolina relative in 1851, July 17th, says he is the son of Jesse Harper, who is the son of John Harper, married Sarah Gregory in 1826. Six children were born to them: Wm. Lafayette, Leander Franklin, Mary Ann Elizabeth, Eliza Caroline, Sarah Louise, and Margaret Catherine Harper. This letter is in possession of Carrie Harper Cheek, was mailed at Gallatin, Tenn., July 17, 1851, to John Harper or family, Anderson, S. C.

Bible Records—Tombstone Inscriptions

OLD (ORIGINAL) CEMETERY AT FRANKLIN

The inscriptions on the tombstones of my great-grandfather and mother whose remains lie in the Old (Original) Cemetery at Franklin are as follows:

Sacred to the memory of Col. Guilford Dudley, Sr., who was born in Caroline County, Va., April 17, 1756, and departed this life the 3rd of Feb., 1833. Sacred to the memory of Anna Bland Dudley, wife of Col. Guilford Dudley, and daughter of Gen. Tho. Eaton of North Carolina, Dec. 21, 1763-Dec. 6, 1847.
Col. Dudley was first a private in the company of his father, Capt. Christopher Dudley, of Caroline County, Va. Later he was captain, then major, then colonel in another command. His wife, Anna Bland (Eaton) Dudley, belonged to the Bland family whose estate was in Prince George County, Va., and whose place was called "Cawsons." They emigrated to this (Williamson) County in 1806 and settled six miles south of Franklin. Later they moved to Franklin. Colonel Dudley very shortly before his death received a pension from the U. S. under Act of 1832. (From a letter to Miss Gentry.)

Park Marshall,
Mayor of Franklin, Tenn.

REVOLUTIONARY SOLDIERS

Sent by Mrs. Mary Nichols Britt

Alexander McCowan, Jr., and Elizabeth McCown Nichols, parents. Annie McCown Bochms and Margaret McCown are the children of Alexander and Susanna (Uncell) McCown, of Bardstown, Ky. These four are buried in the "Old Cemetery" at Franklin, Williamson County, Tenn.
Alexander McCown, Sr., was born in Lancaster County, Pa., on the 25th day of November, 1755, and died in Bardstown, Ky., on the 23rd day of September, 1835. He served in the Revolutionary War. His wife, Susanna Uncell, was born June 1, 1765; died, May 2, 1854; was married to Alexander McCown, Aug. 22, 1786. They are buried at Bardstown, Ky., in the "Old City Cemetery."
Reference: Department of Interior of War, Washington, D. C.; Bureau of Pensions, Washington, D. C.; Bardstown City Cemetery. I am the great-granddaughter of Alexander and Susanna Uncell McCown.

John Atkinson, Sr., was born Sept. 18, 1755, in Cumberland County, Va.; he died near Franklin, Williamson County, Tenn., April 2, 1837. He was married to Mary Armstead, Nov. 6, 1777; she was born Feb. 17, 1758; died, ——.

Samuel Atkinson, oldest son, was born Dec. 20, 1778.
Fannie (Atkinson) Hogan, ——.
Sarah (Atkinson) Cravendel, ——.
Betsy Atkinson, ——.
John Atkinson, Jr., 1789-1845.
Armstead Atkinson, 1787-1860.
William Atkinson, born 1781.
All buried in the family graveyard on the Atkinson farm, now called the "Jessie Short" place, except John, Jr. John Atkinson, Sr., served in the Revolutionary War; enlisted in Pittsylvania County, Va., Sept. 1, 1780; served two years.
References: A letter from the Department of the Interior, Bureau of Pensions; Wheeler's History, N. C., page 85.
Observations: In the vestibule of the courthouse in Franklin, Williamson County, Tenn., is a tablet containing names of Revolutionary Soldiers buried in Williamson County, and the name of John Atkinson, my great-grandfather, is found.
Major Anthony Sharp was born in Sumner County, N. C., in 1746, and died in Franklin, Tenn., on the 9th day of June, 1812. He married Margaret Nelson, of Maryland, in 1791. Moved from Sumner County, N. C., in 1809 to

Bible Records—Tombstone Inscriptions

Franklin, Williamson County, Tenn. He enlisted in Sumner County, N. C., 1776, and served to close of the war. From Lieutenant to rank of Major; he died June, 1812. He and his wife, Margaret, and daughter, Ann (Sharpe) McPhail, who was born Aug. 24, 1798, married Augusta McPhail, Dec. 10, 1812, my great-grandmother.
Margaret Sharp was married the second time, May 16, 1813, to George Hulme of Williamson County, Franklin, Tenn.; was born Oct. 25, 1761, in Amelia County, Va. He was also a Revolutionary Soldier. He died Mar. 29, 1835, and is buried in the "Sharp Family Cemetery," later called the "Lockridge Place," on the Boyd Mill Road.
Reference: Pension Bureau, Washington, D. C., received from Adjt. Gen. office; and on tablet at courthouse at Franklin, Tenn.

John Nichols, Sr., was born June 24, 1743, in Yorkshire, England. He came to America in 1764, joined the American Army in Orange County, N. C., March 11, 1777. He was married to Mrs. Sarah Stout Lytle, of Philadelphia, Pa., the widow of Gen. Lytle, in 1788. Went to Nashville, N. C., then, in 1791, and settled on a grant of land of 600 acres at East Nashville, Tenn.; both are buried in the McNairy Vault, Nashville, Tenn.
John Nichols, Jr., oldest son, is buried in the Old Cemetery at Franklin, Tenn. Alfred, the youngest son, and Lucy Nichols Engrim, and Nancy Nichols Deprew are all buried in the family cemetery in Williamson County, Tenn. Reference: Vol. 25, Records of N. C., page 30. War Department, Washington, D. C. John Nichols is my great-grandfather.

REAL DAUGHTERS

Colleced by Miss Susie Gentry. Miss Gentry in an interesting collection of Revolutionary material reports the graves of nine Real Daughters in Tennessee.
1. Anne McCown Bochms.
2. Margaret McCown.
3. Fannie Atkinson Hogan.
4. Sarah Atkinson Cravendel.
5. Betty Atkinson.
6. Anne (Sharpe) McPhail.
7. Lucy (Nichols) Engrim.
8. Nancy Nichols Deprew.
9. Mrs. Guilford Dudley.

REVOLUTIONARY SOLDIERS—5
1. Alexander McCown.
2. John Atkinson.
3. Maj. Anthony Sharp.
4. John Nichols.
5. George Hulme.

AUTHORITIES ON MARTIN-CHILES-PAGE LINEAGE

Showing relationship to Henderson, Hughes, McGavock, Perkins, etc. Vol. XIX, pages 104, 211, 324, 437 of the Virginia Magazine of History and Biography; Standard's Colonial Virginia Register; Tombstone of Col. John Page at Bruton Church, Williamsburg, Va.; Annual Report of the American Historical Association for year 1893, article entitled, "Gen. Joseph Martin and War of the Revolution in the West"; Family History, including Hughes, Dalton, Martin, Henderson, all originally of Virginia, by Lucy Henderson Horton; Two Old Colonial Places, page 217, by Thomas Nelson Page, Vol. 8, Virginia Magazine of History and Biography.

Bible Records—Tombstone Inscriptions

MT. HOPE CEMETERY

Inscriptions on graves in Mt. Hope Cemetery, Franklin, Tenn. The first three graves are in Williamson County at Meadow Brook.

John Hughes, born Aug. 3, 1776, in Patrick County, Va.; married Sallie Martin, Feb. 7, 1798; died, Dec. 26, 1860.

Sallie Martin, born 1777; married John Hughes Feb. 7, 1798; died Sept. 10, 1842.

Lt.-Col. William Martin, 2 W. Tenn. Vols., War of 1812. He was born 1781; died, 1843. This stone was furnished by the United States Government.

Samuel Henderson, born Oct. 8, 1804; married Mar. 14, 1844; died, Dec. 9, 1884; 64 years a Methodist; 48 years a Mason. He giveth his beloved sleep.

Rachel Jane, his wife, Feb. 27, 1818-Jan. 16, 1858.

John Hughes Henderson, son of Dr. Samuel and Jane Hughes Henderson, Dec. 18, 1849-Feb. 26, 1915.

Lizzie Ewen Perkins, wife of John H. Henderson, May 11, 1860-Dec. 4, 1918.

Samuel Henderson, son of John H. and Lizzie P. Henderson, July 24, 1880-July 21, 1881.

John Hughes Henderson, son of John H. and Lizzie P. Henderson, June 27, 1888-June 20, 1896.

Sarah Martin Henderson, daughter of John H. and Lizzie P. Henderson, Oct. 25, 1892-Sept. 2, 1912.

Infant son of Edward James and Theresa Henderson Hamilton, born Jan. 7, 1915.

Dr. Samuel Henderson, son of Dr. Samuel and Jane Hughes Henderson, June 27, 1852-Sept. 15, 1913.

Florence Morton Henderson, daughter of George W. and Lou Copeland Morton, Aug. 3, 1856-Feb. 25, 1888.

William Warren Henderson, son of Dr. Samuel and Florence Morton Henderson, Sept. 3, 1887-Jan. 25, 1908.

Henry Hollis Horton, April 10, 1811-July 26, 1881; saved through great faith.

Henry Claiborne Horton, 1835-1914; "Shelby Greys" Co. A, 4th Tenn. Inf.

Gaston Reedy Buford, son of James Leslie and Mary Gillespie Buford, born at College Hill, Miss., Jan. 1, 1875; died at Atlanta, Ga., Feb. 17, 1917; husband of Evelyn Caffey Buford, by whom this stone is erected to his precious memory. G. R. B.

Mary Gillespie Buford, May 8, 1848-Mar. 29, 1908.

James Leslie Buford, Mar. 31, 1845-July 5, 1891.

William R. Warren, born Dec. 27, 1830; joined the Tennessee Conference of the M. E. Church, South, Oct., 1848; died July 8, 1898.
Servant of God, well done,
Thy glorious warfare's past;
The battle is fought, the race is won,
And thou are crowned at last.

Mary Jane Henderson, wife of William R. Warren, Jan. 17, 1849-May 29, 1915.

Capt. Geo. W. Smithson, 1837-1900.

Sallie Martin Henderson, wife of Geo. W. Smithson, 1847-1899.

In memory of Mrs. Susan V. Winstead, daughter of Dr. Samuel Henderson and Rachel Jane Henderson, and wife of M. P. G. Winstead, born June 9, A. D., 1855; joined the M. E. Church, South, at Douglass Aug. 18, A. D., 1868; married Oct. 18, A. D., 1888; died Dec. 5, A. D. 1889. Companion of my soul, farewell, M. P. G. W. S. V. W.

Winder McGavock, July 13, 1857-June 3, 1907.

Susie Lee McGavock, April 4, 1863-Oct. 25, 1931.

Martha McGavock, Dec. 24, 1890-Jan. 3, 1909.

Sara McGavock, Dec. 7, 1885-Dec. 11, 1911.

Bettie B. Henderson, 1855-1908.

Brown H. Henderson, 1890-1912.

John H. Harrison, Jr., 1875-1914.

John H. Harrison, Sr., 1846-1910.

Bettie Scruggs Harrison, 1846-1910.

Samuel Feon Perkins, 1833-1885.

His wife, Theresa Ewin, 1836-1916.

Thomas F. Perkins, Mar. 12, 1809-Dec. 2, 1887. Was a consistent member of the Cumberland Presbyterian Church and loved by all who knew him, especially by the poor.

Bible Records—Tombstone Inscriptions

Thos. F. Perkins and wife, Leah America Cannon, and seven children: Samuel Feon, Newton Cannon, Louisa, Laura Susan, Leah Letitia, Thomas Feon, and William Cannon Perkins.
Henry Ewin, infant son of H. E. and S. B. Perkins, April 10, 1899-Aug. 15, 1899; age, 4 months, 5 days.
Laura Susan, daughter of Thomas F. and Leah A. Perkins, Aug. 1, 1845-Feb. 7, 1863.
Thos. Feon Perkins, Jr., Dec. 6, 1842-Jan. 15, 1893. He sleeps here in the hope of the resurrection. He served his state with devotion as a soldier and a citizen and his friends with never failing fidelity. A captain of Confederate Cavalry, County Court Clerk, State Senator, Clerk and Master in Chancery, Brig.-Gen. Confederate Veterans, and President of Association of Confederate Soldiers of Tennessee.
Louisa H. Cochrane, loving wife of Thomas F. Perkins, Jr., 1846-1928.
In memory of Leah America Perkins, daughter of Gov. Newton and Leah Cannon, wife of Thomas F. Perkins, Nov. 14, 1814-April 16, 1878; age, 60 years, 5 months, 2 days. She was the mother of seven children, leaving at her death three sons, Samuel F., Newton C., and Thos. F. Perkins.

Some Inscriptions on Martin Tombstones

Inscription on tombstone of Lucinda Martin, who lies buried in the Settle-Martin burying ground near Reidsville, N. C.:
Lucinda Martin, daughter of Robert Martin (1784-1848), died Sept. 15, 1846, in the bloom of girlhood. (Robert Martin was brother of Governor Alexander Martin of North Carolina.) Inscription on marble stone which marks her grave is as follows:
"Rest, sainted spirit, with thy God,
 Thy cross alone is neath this sod;
 In memory, love, thou shalt be kept,
 Not less than if thou only slept."
Inscription on tombstone of Martha Martin, daughter of Robert Martin (1784-1848), died Jan. 19, 1853; age, 25 years. On April 7, 1847, she married Stephen A. Douglas, then Senator in Washington, D. C. Stephen A. Douglas had carved on his wife's tomb in the Settle-Martin burying ground, near Reidsville, N. C., the following tribute:
"Yes, loved one while in heaven supremely blessed,
 Thou are more than wife and mother to us here;
 Thy memory woos us upward and is blest;
 And thou, our guardian angel, still art near."
Stephen A. Douglas, April 23, 1813-June 3, 1861. He lies buried on a beautiful spot overlooking Lake Michigan in Chicago. A magnificent monument, built by State of Illinois, marks his grave.
(Note: For much information in regard to ancestry and history of antecedents of these two Martin sisters—Lucindia Martin and Martha Martin Douglas—see "Family History, including Hughes, Dalton, Martin, and Henderson," by Lucy Henderson Horton, under head of Martin.)
Col. John Martin of Caroline County, Va., was a member of the House of Burgesses, 1738 and 1740, and later for King William County, where he lived 1752-53-54-55-56 (see page 198, Virginia Magazine of History and Biography for Oct., 1905). Col. John Martin and Joseph Martin, whose wife was Susanna Chiles, were of the same family of Martin, and their wives were both kinswomen of the Col. John Page (1627-1691) family (see page 123, etc., of "Family History, including Hughes, Dalton, Martin, Henderson," by Lucy Henderson Horton.
Inscription of tomb of Martha Burnell Martin at "Clifton" in Caroline County, Va.:
Interred beneath this stone lies the body of Mrs. Martha Martin, wife of Col. John Martin of Caroline County, and daughter of Lewis Burwell, Esq., of Glosster County, who departed this life May 27, 1738, in the 36th year of her age and left three sons and four daughters.
(Note: See William and Mary Quarterly, XI, 146; also Virginia Magazine

Bible Records—Tombstone Inscriptions

of History and Biography for Oct., 1905, page 199.

Inscription on tombstone of Colonel John Page at Bruton Church in Williamsburg, Va.:

Here lieth, in hope of a joyful resurrection, the body of Colonel John Page, Esq., of Bruton Parish—one of their Majesty's Council in the Dominion of Virginia, who departed this life on the 23rd of January, in the year of our Lord, 1691; age, 65. Colonel John Page gave the land on which old Bruton Church is built. He was vestryman. Bishop Meade, in "Old Churches and Families of Virginia," tells us on page 146 that the pew in Bruton Church of Colonel John Page was by the chancel.

Some Inscriptions on Henderson Tombstones

Inscriptions on tombstones of Samuel Henderson (1759-1828) and his wife, Lucy Henderson (1765-1843). Their bodies rest in a little graveyard on land given to a Henderson heir by Governor Alexander Martin of North Carolina in his will. This graveyard is near Bethseda, in Williamson County, Tenn. One can see in the books at the courthouse in Franklin, Tenn., that Governor Alexander Martin had a large grant of land from North Carolina in what is now Williamson County, Tenn.

Samuel Henderson, Nov. 27, 1759-Dec. 5, 1828.

Lucy Henderson, Nov. 16, 1765-July 14, 1843. Lucy (Ryckman) Henderson (1765-1843) was born in Cumberland County, Va. She had New York ancestry. Many New York families, we are told, came to Virginia to live. On page 19, "An American Epoch," by Odum, it is said that two hundred families from New York alone settled in a single Virginia County. She came of an old Dutch family in New York. Harme Janse Ryckman was a resident of Albany between 1666 and 1667. Ary Ryckman owned a farm which included what is now Astor Place.

Samuel Henderson (1759-1828) was son of Nathaniel Henderson, born Dec. 1, 1736, and grandson of Samuel Henderson, born 1700; died 1783, and his wife, Elizabeth Williams.

Graves of Members of This Family Connection

Henderson Graves

Samuel Henderson, 1700-1783, and his wife, Elizabeth Williams, both lie buried at the place of their grandson, Chief Justice Leonard Henderson, in Williamsboro, N. C. Their graves are marked by tombstones.

Colonel Judge Richard Henderson, 1735-1785, son of Samuel Henderson (1700-1783), and his wife, Elizabeth Williams, was one of the founders of Nashville, Tenn. Col. James Robertson, Col. John Donaldson, Judge Richard Henderson were founders of Nashville, Tenn. He was author of the Cumberland Compact. He lies buried in what is now Vance County, N. C. (formerly Granville County), near the old village of Williamsboro.

Nathaniel Henderson, born Dec. 1, 1736. From Wheeler's History of North Carolina we learn that at the time of his death he was a member of the Tennessee Legislature. He was son of Samuel Henderson (1700-1783) and his wife, Elizabeth Williams. He was one of the signers of the Cumberland Compact, May 13, 1780, of which his brother, Richard Henderson, was author. He lies buried in Hawkins County, Tenn., on his land grant from North Carolina, consisting of 640 acres, Grant No. 321. This grant can be seen at War Memorial Building in Nashville, Tenn.

Pleasant Henderson, son of Samuel Henderson (1700-1783) and his wife, Elizabeth Williams, signed the Cumberland Compact of which his brother, Judge Richard Henderson, was author on May 13, 1780. He had pre-emption of land which included French Lick near Nashville, Tenn. This was No. 2 (see Nashville Banner of May 3, 1931, page 3). He lies buried in Carroll County, Tenn.

John Henderson, son of Samuel Henderson (1700-1783), and his wife, Elizabeth Williams, lies buried near Grendal Shoals Pawlet, S. C.

Bible Records—Tombstone Inscriptions

Samuel Henderson, son of Samuel Henderson (1700-1783), and his wife Elizabeth Williams, lies buried in Rockingham County, N. C.

William Henderson, son of Samuel Henderson (1700-1783), and his wife, Elizabeth Williams, lies buried in Spartanburg District, S. C.

Hughes Graves

Colonel Archelaus Hughes, born in Goochland County, Va., in 1747; died, 1798, in what is now Patrick County, Va. He is buried here on his estate, "Hughsville." He was married to Mary Dalton, daughter of Samuel Dalton of Mayo (1699-1802) in Rockingham County, N. C., Sept. 20, 1769. In War of the Revolution he became Colonel of a Virginia Regiment (see page 415, Vol. IX, Virginia Magazine of History and Biography). He was the father of Capt. John Hughes (1776-1860) spoken of above.

Mary Dalton, wife of Colonel Archelaus Hughes (1747-1798), and daughter of Samuel Dalton of Mayo River, Rockingham County, N. C., is buried beside her husband, Colonel Archelaus Hughes, on their estate, "Hughesville," in Patrick County, Va. She was born in 1748; died, 1841. She married Sept. 25, 1769. Lucy Henderson Horton is Daughter of the American Revolution through Col. Archelaus Hughes, Capt. William Martin, and Samuel Henderson.

Martin Graves

Captain William Martin (1742-1809), son of Joseph Martin and his wife, Susanna Chiles, was born in Albermarle County, N. C. He lies buried at "Hughesville" in Patrick County, Va., beside his wife, Rachel Dalton Martin (daughter of Samuel Dalton (1699-1802) of Mayo. Before the Revolutionary War he was County Lieutenant. He was appointed by Committee of Safety on Sept. 27, 1775, Captain of Militia in Pittsylvania County, Va. (see American Monthly Magazine for June, 1812, page 255; here quotation is made from original county records. He fought at Guilford Courthouse, Yorktown, etc. (See pages 225-229 of American Monthly Magazine for June, 1912.)

Samuel Clark and his wife, Virginia Martin, daughter of Capt. Wm. Martin, lie buried on Sumners Knob in Williamson County, Tenn. He was born in Albermarle County, Va.

In the old family burying ground at "Belmont," home of General Joseph Martin (1740-1808) in Henry County, Va., lie the bodies of four Joseph Martins in one line: General Joseph Martin, his son, Colonel Joseph Martin, who married Sally Hughes, and his grandson who married Susan Pannell, and great-grandson Joseph Martin. These last three lived at their home, "Greenwood." "Belmont" overlooks Leatherwood Creek in Henry County, Va.

Horton Grave

Joshua Horton, the explorer, who came to what is now Tennessee with Col. James Smith in 1766, lies buried at his home place, "Green Hill," near Watauga River. He was the first patentee of land of the Watauga Association. He was lineal ancestor of Henry Claiborne Horton (1835-1914), mentioned above, whose wife was Lucy Henderson, daughter of Dr. Samuel Henderson (1804-1884).

Sent in by Mrs. Lucy H. Horton, 2302 Dixie Place, Nashville, Tenn.

Gravestones, Monuments, Old Cemeteries, and Family Bibles in Williamson County Tenn.

Memoranda and copies of inscriptions and records from gravestones and monuments in old cemeteries and family Bibles in Williamson County, Tenn., contributed by "Old Glory" Chapter, Daughters of American Revolution, Franklin, Tenn.

Mrs. Robert Hugh Crockett, Regent;

Bible Records—Tombstone Inscriptions

Mrs. George I. Briggs, First Vice Regent;
Mrs. Marvin T. Regen, Second Vice Regent;
Mrs. John H. Truett, Recording Secretary;
Miss Frances Stewart, Corresponding Secretary;
Mrs. John W. Hanner, Treasurer;
Mrs. Jennie Kinnard, Chapain;
Mrs. Frank Gray, Registrar;
Mrs. Jesse E. Short, Historian.

Some account of the old Municipal Cemetery, located at Fourth Avenue and North Margin Street, Franklin, Tenn.

This old burial ground, located at the corner of Fourth Avenue and North Margin Street, in area approximately two acres, was laid off and established by the town of Franklin, in Williamson County, about the year 1811, and was the only community burying ground until about 1858, when the "New Cemetery," now referred to as Rest Haven, was opened and established.

The land was acquired and the cemetery established by orders of the municipality, and small burial lots donated to the heads of families.

The plan of this burial ground appears to have been—we say appears to have been, for no record has been preserved, and the information here recorded is gathered from tradition and an inspection of the premises—somewhat as follows:

1. For the use of white citizens the area from Indigo Street (now Fourth Avenue) to a line beginning five feet west of the (south) gate, and running parallel with the street. This includes about two-thirds of the whole area. This area is subdivided by parallel lines, running north and south, and parallel with the street, ten feet apart, and these strips are divided into lots fifteen feet long, each lot being ten feet wide and fifteen feet long. No boundary marks appear to have been set up and boundaries are more or less uncertain, and in many instances graves are found crossing lot lines and encroaching upon walk ways.

2. Adjacent to the dividing line, above mentioned, five feet west of the gate, there appears to be a strip, twenty feet wide, left for a walk way.

3. Adjacent to this walk way there appears to be a strip, forty feet wide, reserved for persons without local family connections, strangers, and travelers.

Bible Records—Tombstone Inscriptions

4. All of the residue (the easterly side of the area) reserved for the burial of Negro slaves.

5. Though not mentioned in any of the by-laws, with reference to the cemetery, there appears to have been laid off a narrow walk way, extending from the twenty-foot walk way, and at right angles with it, to the fence at Indigo (Fourth Avenue) Street. There was no gate opening on Indigo Street (now Fourth Avenue) until 1917. Some graves are found within this narrow walk way, near the twenty-foot walk way above described.

While enclosed by a substantial stone wall, without encroachment by adjacent roads, buildings, or other structures, many of the old box tombs, monuments, head and foot stones and markers have been overturned by storms and subsidence of the soil; and inscriptions, in many instances, are entirely obliterated by erosion, and in others are illegible by reason of the poor workmanship and the overgrowth of moss and other like conditions. No record has been kept, or at least no record can now be found of the interments.

Several years ago Mrs. Adelicia McEwen German, her daughter, Mrs. Samuel R. Webb (formerly a Regent of this Chapter), and Mrs. Freeman J. Hyde, with very great labor, compiled from inscriptions on the gravestones and made a record of the names of a great many persons here interred. Due to the condition of the inscriptions, it was impossible to make a complete list and to decipher each and every name and date, and further research and effort would probably add many names. However, we deem the work already accomplished worthy of a place in the Chapter's Archives, and we have been furnished with a copy of the names compiled, which have been verified as far as possible and arranged alphabetically as follows:

Where only one date is given it is the date when the person died:

Allen, Mrs. Elizabeth, 1862.
Andrews, Mary Louisa, 1904.

Badger, Catherine, 1843.
Bailey, Charles, 1854.
Bailey, John Hartwell, 1845.
Bailey, Virginia M., 1838.
Bailey, Virginia.
Bain, Wm. M., 1854.
Baltishweiler, Ann Carter.
Baltishweiler, Bernard.
Baltishweiler, Frank H., 1869.
Barham, Mrs. Mary, 1842.
Barham, William P., 1856.
Beech, Eddie and Alice.
Beech, John B., 1860.
Beech, Sarah, 1859.
Berson, Gillaume, 1838.
Berson, William (Jeweler), 1844.
Binford, Mrs. Mary (Perkins), 189—.
Black, James, 1855.
Blackburn, Elizabeth, 1847.
Blackburn, John R., 1843.
Bradley, Mrs., 1843.
Bradley, W. M. Duncan, 1886.
Branch, John.

215

Bible Records—Tombstone Inscriptions

Branch, Maj. Joseph (1812), 1827.
Brown, Lucy R., 1831.
Brown, Mrs. Mary, 1870.
Brown, Rosa, 186—.
Brown, Wm., 1847.
Boehms, Catherine, 1846.
Boehms, Mrs. Elizabeth, 1839.
Boehms, James H., 1840.
Boehms, Mary Ann, 1858.
Boehms, Samuel, 1853.
Boon, Martha A., 1852.
Booth, William, 1826.
Boyd, Harrison.
Boyd, Virginia Cliffe.

Caldwell, Andrew B., 1847.
Caldwell, infant of Andrew Caldwell, 1848.
Caldwell, Lou.
Caldwell, Nancy, 1811.
Caldwell, Rachel, 1850.
Cameron, Ewen, 1846.
Cameron, Mary C., 1845.
Cameron, Mary L.
Campbell, Andrew, 1818.
Campbell, Carrie, 1835-1852.
Campbell, Frances Ann, 1838.
Campbell, child of John and Eliza Campbell, 1847.
Campbell, Mrs. Jane B.
Campbell, Jane A., 1839.
Campbell, Mary.
Carter, Fountain Branch, 1871.
Carter, Frances, 1841.
Carter, James F., 1859.
Carter, Mary A., 1852.
Carter, Newton, 1834.
Carter, Nisan R., 1827.
Carter, Orlando H., 1828.
Carter, Maj. Robert, 1839.
Carter, Samuel A., 1837.
Carter, Theoderic, 1838.
Carter, William A., 1830.
Chapel, Sarah C., 1844.
Cody, Walter, 1863.
Cody, W. H., 1867.
Cody, Yancey, 1848.
Courtney, Eliza, 1896.
Courtney, James, infant, no dates.
Courtney, Philip, 1863.
Courtney, Robert, 1857.
Courtney, Robert, 1859.
Craig, Alexander, 1855.
Craig, Alex, 1864.
Craig, John K., 1858.
Criddle, J. Mat., 1861.
Crockett, Charles (son of Dr. Samuel), 1844.

Crockett, Frances B., 1836.
Crockett, Dr. Samuel, 1775-1853.
Crouch, Barton S., 1850.
Crouch, Charles W., 1872.
Crouch, Elizabeth, 1849.
Crouch, John H., 1858.
Crouch, W. H., 1874.
Crouch, Wm. H.
Crutcher, Charity Louisa Parks, 1857.
Cunningham, Eva C., 1850.
Cunningham, John D., 187—.
Cunningham, Mrs. John D., 1854.

Davis, C.
Davis, Joseph F.
Davis, Sarah, 1845.
Dempsey, Hugh, 1849.
Dempsey, Nancy, 1837.
Doyle, Michael, 1843.
Doyle, Nancy, 1841.
Drake, Catherine.
Dudley, Caroline, 1802-1832.
Dudley, Col. Guilford (Rev.), 1833.
Dudley, Helen, 1848.
Dudley, Helen Lord, 1843.
Dudley, Sallie B., 1796-1815.
Dudley, Thomas Eaton, 1836.
Dwyer, Mary, 1836.
Dwyer, William, 1820.

Eelbeck, Henry E., 1856.
English, Jane Ophelia, 1839.
Erwin, Margaret.
Estes, Maria B., 1808-1843.
Ewing, Dr. A. B., 1881.
Ewing, A. B., Jr., 189—.
Ewing, Andrew G., 1853.
Ewing, Anna M.
Ewing, Eliza McGavock, 1876.
Ewing, Dr. Felix.
Ewing, Joseph.
Ewing, Louisa.
Ewing, Mamie.
Ewing, Mary.
Ewing, Rachel McCrory, 1890.
Ewing, Sarah Amanda, 1846.
Ewing, Wm. and Lida, 1865.

Farrington, Abegail K., 1830.
Ferguson, Martha J., 1857.
Figuers, Mrs. Nancy, 1836.
Fisher, Eli A., 1839.
Fisher, Stanford Burney, 1840.
Foster, Ben J., 1853.
Foster, George W., 1840.
Foster, James H., 1836.
Foster, Laura, 1843.

Bible Records—Tombstone Inscriptions

Foster, Louisa T.
Fry, Amanda.
Fry, Joseph, M.D.
Gadsey, Sarah A., 1810-1862.
Gault, Mary J., wife of James Gault, 1841.
Gilliam, Eloisa, 1807-1866.
Glass, Margaret Cameron, 1855.
Glass, Robert, M.D., 1850.
Gohlson, M., 1812-1815.
Gordon, Sallie Carter.
Gordon, Sarah H., 1865.
Gray, child of James and Mary Gray, 1839.
Gunter, Abegail, 189—.
Gunter, Felix G., 1857.
Gunter, Frances, 1848.
Gunter, Frances, 1840.

Hall, James, 1842.
Hall, John C., 1846.
Hall, Mary M., 1837.
Hall, Sarah G., 1850.
Hall, Wm. H., 1846.
Hanlon, Mrs. Anna Brown, 186—.
Hanner, Rev. J. W., 189—.
Hanner, Mrs. J. W., 1841.
Hanner, William (soldier), 1863.
Hansbrough, Mary, 1842.
Hardeman, Geo. W. L., 1836.
Hardeman, Nicholas Perkins, 1772-1818.
Haynes, J. W., 1818.
Haynes, Rachel Elizabeth, 1833.
Haynes, Susan, 1853.
Haynes, Thomas, 1863.
Hicks, Ann, 1817.
Hightower, Dr., 1865.
Hightower, Mrs. Ann, 1845.
Hightower, Louisa, 1878.
Hildreth, Hattie E., 1859.
Hill, James C.
Hill, Mary James, 1836.
Hobbs, John Patrick, 1839.
Hobbs, Hartwell, 1842.
Hollins, Miss Susan, 1850.
Hutton, Eli P., 1835.

Jenkins, Thomas, 1814.
Johnson, Mrs. Louisa, 1797-1833.
Johnson, Martha Jane, 1842.
Johnson, Mary and Joanna, 1833.
Johnson, Miss Nancy, 1817.
Johnson, Mrs. Rebecca, 1821.
Johnson, Robert C., 1831.
Johnson, Mrs. Sallie A., 1831.

Johnson, Sallie King, 1854.
Johnson, Samuel C., 1823-1845.
Johnson, Sarah Louisa, 1839.
Johnson, ——.

Lanny, Avery, 1853.
Lester, C. H., 1816.
Lewis, Mrs. Lewis of Virginia.
Long, George R., 1823-19—.

Manning, Mrs. Ann, 1820.
Marr, Annie, 1849.
Marr, Mary E.
Marshall, Elizabeth, 1853.
Marshall, Margaret Campbell, 1842.
Martin, Jas. C. Hardy, 1831.
Mays, F. H., 1907.
Mays, Nettie Beech, 1869.
McAlister, Charles.
McAlister, John.
McClellan, Charity, 1856.
McClellan, Infant, 1832.
McConnico, Adeline, 1844.
McConnico, Elizabeth B., 1838.
McConnico, J. M. DeKalb, 1847.
McCown, Margaret, 1795-1873.
McDaniel, Nancy, 1841.
McGann, Alfred, 1850.
McGann, Eli, 1855.
McGann, Malinda, 1809-1875.
McGann, Mary, 1851.
McGann, William, 1850.
McPhail, Daniel, M.D., 1846.
McPhail, Mary A., 1869.
McPhail, Mary Carter.
McPhail, Sarah.
McPhail, Sarah, 1861.
Miller, Ann J., 1852.
Miller, Wilburn W., 1869.

Neely, George T.
Neely, George W.
Neely, Henrietta Park, 1847.
Nichol, Elizabeth J., 1850.
Nichol, Matilda, 1854.
Nichols, Elizabeth, 1799-1881.
Nichols, John, 1789-1863.
Nichols, Sarah Douglas, 1848.

O'Bryan, Dr. Lawrence D. G., 1845.
O'Bryan, Lawrence, 1847.
O'Bryan, Susan, 1844.
Otey, James, 1916 (?).
Otey, John H., 186—.
Otey, Mildred, 1841.
Otey, Mrs. Sallie M., 186—.
Owen, Mrs. Ann Augusta.

Bible Records—Tombstone Inscriptions

Pankey, James Edward, 1835.
Pankey, Oscar Mills, 1842.
Pankey, Mrs. Susan, 1844.
Parkes, Elizabeth, 1858.
Parkes, Mary E., 1886.
Parkes, Selena Campbell, 1837-1856.
Parkes, Wm. J., 1886.
Park, Fanny Bland, 1847.
Park, William, 1848.
Parrish, Abram Maury, 1828.
Parrish, Eugenia, 1881.
Parrish, James Harvey, 1803-1881.
Parrish, Joel, 1811.
Parrish, Hannah, 1890.
Parrish, Harvey, 187—.
Parrish, Mrs. Mary M. B., 1831.
Parrish, Robert, 1829.
Parrish, Mrs. Susan.
Peebles, Infant.
Peebles, Mary C., 1833.
Perkins, Mrs. Mary, 1865.
Perkins, Mary Malonia, 1852.
Perkins, Mrs. Martha, 1881.
Perkins, Nicholas, 1856.
Perkins, Nicholas P., 1833.
Perkins, Slaughter, 1856.
Perkins, Wm. O'Neil, 1895.
Perkins, Wm. O'Neil, Jr., 1850.
Plunkett, Eugene Collet, 1845.
Porter, George C., 1833.
Pointer, Madison, 1835.
Porter, Susan Madison, 1833.
Potts, Louisa, 1866.

Ragsdale, Martha E., 1851.
Ragsdale, Penelope, 1851.
Rice, James, 1834.
Richardson, Eliza Ann, 1841.
Richardson, J. O., 1904.
Ripley, Miss Riley of Boston, Mass.
Robinson, Frances C., 1816.
Robinson, Richard, 1850.
Rodgers, Susan C., 1852.
Rothrock, Margaret E., 1845.

Sample, William, 1786-1816.
Scott, Eli Davis, 1872.
Scruggs, John H., 1854.
Scruggs, Wm. Edward, 1855.
Searight, George, 1847.
Sessions, Ferdinand Hardeman.
Shehan, Mrs. Doyle, 187—.
Shehan, James V., 1853.
Short, J. J.
Short, Malissa McGann.
Short, Thomas Albert, 1883.
Simmons, Eliza, 1853.

Sinclair, James, 1847.
Sinclair, John A., 1863.
Sinclair, Julia, 1865.
Sinclair, Wm. H., 1862.
Slaughter, Mary Frances, 1838.
Smith, Mrs. Agnes, 1832.
Smith, Asa, son of Mrs. I. Smith, 1850.
Smith, Isabella (Dr. Cliffe's mother), 1891.
Smith, infant of D. C. Smith, 1855.
Smith, infant of D. C. Smith, 1859.
Spivey, Nancy, 1846.
Spann, Mrs. Susan P., 1837.
Spann, Rev. William, 1836.
Squier, David (Revolutionary Soldier), 1762-1818.
Stovall, Calliope M., 1868.
Stuart, Margaret, 1835.
Stuart, Judge Thomas, 1838.

Taylor, Elizabeth, 1858.
Taylor, W. D., 1852.
Tillett, Sarah, 1854.
Toon, Miss Margaret, 1851.

Vanpelt, Ann H., 1837.

Watkins, Martha Jane, 1848.
Wells, Eliza D., 1852.
Wells, infant of W. T. Wells, 1858.
West, Elizabeth C., 1849.
White, Moses B., 1850.
Williams, Franklin M. J., 1855.
Williams, Willis L., 1855.
Wilson, Louisa, 1845.
Woldridge, Ferd, M.D., 1870.
Woldridge, Lizzie Reese, 1854.
Wren, Alphonsus W., 1850.
Wren, infant of C. A. Wren, 1850.
Wrenn, Cicero A., 1850.
Wren, Elizabeth, 1864.
Wren, John Z., 1861.
Wright, Nancy, 1859.
Wright, Nancy Louisa, 1854.

Some years ago this Chapter, in harmony with the movement throughout the country, undertook the work of locating the graves of soldiers of the American Revolution, in Williamson County, reports of which have been heretofore made, and record of these locations, compiled by Miss Susie Gentry, of Franklin, will be found in the State Library at Nashville. A tablet, set in the front wall of the courthouse at Franklin bears the following inscriptions:

Bible Records—Tombstone Inscriptions

1910
This tablet is placed commemorative of the Revolutionary Soldiers buried in Williamson County by "Old Glory" Chapter, D. A. R. Organized by Miss Susie Gentry, November, 1897.
Mrs. Eliza B. Wallace, Regent.
Mrs. Sophia C. Fitts, Secretary.
Mrs. Fannie W. Roberts, Treasurer.
Miss Susie Gentry, Registrar and Chairman of the Committee.
Mrs. Bettie W. Thomas, Vice Regent.
Mrs. Pattie C. Rodes, Corresponding Secretary.
Mrs. Lucy H. Horton, Historian.
Mrs. Julia P. Eggleston, Chaplain.

John Allen.
William Allen.
John Anderson.
Mark Andrews.
Frederick Bass.
John Beard.
Anson Burke,
Minos Cannon.
Henry Cook.
William Crutcher.
Col. Guilford Dudley.
John Echols.
John Evans.
Thornton Fergeson.
Henry Garrett.
Watson Gentry.
Andrew Goff.
Jacob Grimmer.
Robert Guthrie.
Laban Hartley.
Samuel Henderson.
Daniel Hill.
Major Green Hill.
George Hulme.
John McCallister Hutton.
William Kennedy.
Peter Leslie.
Tarpley Lightfoot.
William Lockridge.
Samuel McCutcheon.
Daniel McMahon.
Roger Mallory.
William Marshall.
Col. William Martin.
Col. Hardy Murfree.
Nelson R. Nailling.
George Neely.
Robert Osborn.
Lieut. Hardin Perkins.
Joseph Phillips.
Miles Priest.
Moses Priest.
James Potts.
James Ragsdale.
Jacob Scott.
John Secrest.
Major Anthony Sharp.
Henry Sledge.
Sherrod Smith.
David Squires.
Edward Swanson.
James Turner.
Richard Vernon.
Daniel White.
Moses Lindsley.
Rev. John Atkinson.
Joshua Pearre.
Col. William White.
Jason Wilson.
William Redford.
James Sheppard, First Lieut.
Richard Puckett.

NAMES INSCRIBED

During the year 1931 descendants of Lieutenant Andrew Crockett, interred in the Crockett family cemetery, reported to the Chapter evidence that he served as a soldier in the Virginia Militia during the period of the Revolution. The location of his grave in the Crockett cemetery has long been known, but evidence of his service was lacking until recently, and during the year 1931 when the facts were ascertained.
It is contemplated that the name of Lieutenant Andrew Crockett will be inscribed on this tablet in the near future.
Some account of the life and service of Lieutenant Andrew Crockett:
Son of Samuel (1690-1750) and Esther Thompson (1710-1770) Crockett, born in 1745 in that part of Orange County, Va., out of which Augusta County was that year established (later successively Botetourt, Fincastle, Montgomery, and Wythe County); married (1770) Sarah (Sallie) Elliott (1750-1821), daughter of Robert Elliott of Prince Edward County, Va. Farmer, merchant, and manufacturer. Recommended County Court, Montgomery County, October, 1777; Second Lieutenant under Captain Draper (McAllister, p. 217). Commissioned First Lieutenant Jan. 10, 1782, to take rank from April 5, 1781 (Summers, p. 815). Captain

Bible Records—Tombstone Inscriptions

Wythe County Militia, 1790 (Summers, p. 1357). Major Wythe County Militia, 1797 (Summers, p, 1362). Acquired large bodies of land in Virginia, Kentucky, and Tennessee. Emigrated to Williamson County, Tenn., 1799, where he had acquired fertile lands on the Little Harpeth, part of which are still owned by his descendants. Died May 29, 1821. His wife, Sarah Elliott Crockett, died June 28, 1821. Both are interred in the Crockett Family Cemetery, located on part of his estate, and many of his descendants rest with him. Inscriptions on grave stones:
In memory of Andrew Crockett, died May 29, 1821, in the 76th year of his age.
In memory of Mrs. Sally, consort of Andrew Crockett, died June 28, 1821, in the 71st year of her age. "Blessed are the dead that die in the Lord."
The will of Lieutenant (later Major) Andrew Crockett was admitted to probate at the July term, 1821, of the County Court of Williamson County, at Franklin, Tenn., and is of record at page 241, Will Book, 1819-30. Many descendants of Lieutenant Crockett reside in Williamson and adjoining counties of Tennessee.
Other inscriptions from grave stones in the Crockett Family Cemetery:
Samuel Crockett, Nov. 1, 1772-Jan. 31, 1827.
Joanna Crockett, wife of Samuel Crockett, Nov. 20, 1772-Sept. 17, 1812.
Andrew Crockett, born Nov. 15, 1793, in Wythe County, Va.; died, Sept. 12, 1852.
Catherine Bell Crockett, born Feb. 21, 1798, in Davidson County, Tenn.; died, Feb. 14, 1890.
Andrew Crockett was married to Catherine Bell April 2, 1818.
On top slab of box tomb: In memory of Andrew Crockett, son of Samuel and Joannah Crockett, born in Wythe County, Va., Nov. 15, 1793; moved to Williamson County, Tenn., in 1799; died, Sept. 12, 1852.
"I am the resurrection and the life. He that believeth in me, though he were dead, yet shall he live."—John xi:25.
James Crockett, born in Wythe County, Va., Dec. 9, 1790-Nov. 17, 1874.
Martha E. Crockett, born Jan. 15, 1804.

FAMILY CEMETERY OF COL. HARDY MURFREE

Inscriptions taken from the family cemetery of Col. Hardy Murfree, located on lands now owned by the heirs of Samuel P. Cannon, in Williamson County, south of Franklin, and contributed by his daughter, Mrs. William C. Jones.

Col. Hardy Murfree was born the 5th of June, 1752; he died the 6th day of April, 1809. In peace the citizen, the soldier in war, reverential to God, respectful to man.
William Hardy Murfree was born in Hertford County, N. C., Oct. 2, A.D.. 1781. Emigrated to Tennessee, A. D., 1823. and departed this life Jan. 19. A. D., 1826. Able and honest at the bar and in Congress, just in all things, kind in temper, devoted to his family and friends, he lived beloved and died lamented.
Elizabeth Mary Murfree, daughter of James and Mary Maney, born in Hertford County, N. C., Oct. 28, A. D., 1787, and departed this life July 13, A. D., 1826. Devoted to her husband and children, affectionate to her friends, kind to all, she was beloved by all who knew her, and it is hoped is now happy in heaven.
This monument is erected in memory of William H. and Elizabeth M. Murfree by their children, who, deprived alas too early in life of their fostering care, feel the magnitude of their loss in the veneration with which their memory is regarded by all who knew them.
Sacred to the memory of William Hardy Murfree and his wife, Elizabeth Mary, united in their lives, in death they were not long divided. They were married in North Carolina in

Bible Records—Tombstone Inscriptions

A. D., 1808, shared with constant affection the joys and sorrows of life, and it is hoped are again united in heaven.

Gray Cemetery

In the heart of the City of Knoxville, Tenn., on North Broadway Street. Sent by Miss Kate White.

Oliver Temple, Jan. 27, 1820-Nov. 2, 1897.
Boyce Mary Temple, died May 15, 1929; age, 72 years.
David Hume, born in Scotland, 1794-Feb. 23, 1830.
Eliza Sanderson Hume, born in Scotland, wife of David Hume, May 26, 1788-Aug. 18, 1872.
Wm. E. Bauman, Mar. 9, 1842-Feb. 18, 1921.
Catherine Schendier, wife of Wm. E. Bauman, Dec. 9, 1821-Nov. 16, 1913.
Kate Welker McNutt, 1851-1872.
George McNutt, Oct. 29, 1822-Dec. 16, 1900.
Cornelia Ramsay, May 13, 1849-Dec. 17, 1880.
Frank A. M. D. Ramsay, April 7, 1821-May 24, 1834.
Mary Kennedy, wife of Wm. Boyd, Oct. 21, 1834-Oct. 11, 1877.
Anne M. Ramsay, Mar. 25, 1834-May 29, 1868.
Cornelia Williams, wife of Thomas Humes, May 22, 1817-Nov., 1847.
Dr. James King, Aug. 21, 1787-Aug. 29, 1835.
Mary J. King, wife of James King, Feb. 10, 1798-Dec. 18, 1816.
George Churchwell, Jan. 22, 1802-Aug. 12, 1864.
Sophrira Moody Churchwell, Jan. 5, 1817-May 9, 1898.
Seraphina Deery Pettibone, wife of Maj. A. H. Pettibone, died Mar. 2, 1918.
Robert Armstrong, Nov. 14, 1844-May 17, 1837.
Frank Mills Armstrong, July 1, 1850-Mar. 24, 1895.
James H. Armstrong, July 18, 1815-Dec. 27, 1872.
Anne E. Armstrong, Oct. 11, 1815-Mar. 6, 1886.
Jennie Fouche, wife of George McTeer, Feb. 3, 1862-Oct. 29, 1911.
Dr. John Fouche, June 18, 1817-Mar. 13, 1898.
Marcus Bearden, June 4, 1854; age, 51 years.
Sarah McLin, wife of Wm. B. Reese, second daughter of John and Sarah Cocke, Jan. 13, 1801-April 10, 1829.
Wm. Brown Reese, Nov. 27, 1793-July 7, 1860.
Eliza Amy, wife of Marcus Bearden, died Mar. 20, 1835; age, 32 years.
Elizabeth, wife of Robert King, Sr., died July 26, 1817; age, 63 years.
Robert King, 1782-Jan. 4, 1845.
Patsy King, wife of Robert King, died June 9, 1841; age, 41 years.
Dr. James A. Cocke, Oct. 22, 1855-July 23, 1910.
Maj. Robert Morrow, U. S. A., April 13, 1846-Nov. 22, 1873.
Samuel Morrow, Jan. 23, 1816-May 16, 1864.
Malinda, wife of Samuel Morrow, daughter of Robert Armstrong, Mar. 28, 1817-July 12, 1884.
Mary Reed, wife of W. A. Reed, Feb. 3, 1812-April 10, 1862.
George H. Smith, Mar. 31, 1826-Dec. 20, 1876.
Annie Wintermutt, wife of George H. Smith, Nov. 9, 1829-Feb. 18, 1874.
Edward Sanford, Nov. 23, 1831-Oct. 10, 1897.
Emma Chavannes, wife of Edward Sanford, Mar. 20, 1831-Oct., 1885.
Robert N. Hood, May 21, 1849-Feb. 1, 1852.
Jackson Smith, July 2, 1862-Jan. 2, 1910.
Amy Maxwell Rogers, wife of Jackson Smith, Feb. 2, 1867-May 2, 1888.
Dr. M. L. Rogers, Feb. 27, 1826-Dec. 4, 1871.
Maj. T. G. Webb, Sept. 26, 1840-Sept. 24, 1930.
Blanche McClung, wife of T. G. Webb, April 10, 1846-Oct. 5, 1894.
Thomas Mitchell, Sept. 25, 1810-Jan. 4, 1870.
Rowena, his wife, Aug. 28, 1813-July 3, 1874.

Bible Records—Tombstone Inscriptions

Edwin Akers, Aug. 21, 1836-Aug. 20, 1907.
Calvin Morgan McClung, son of Franklin McClung and Elizabeth Mills McClung, May 2, 1855-Mar. 12, 1919.
Annie McGhee McClung, daughter of Charles and Cornelia White McGhee, wife of C. M. McClung, Nov. 7, 1862-Sept. 1, 1898. (On same stone.)
Lucy Grahame Crozier, Aug. 7, 1856-Nov. 30, 1930.
Wm Swan, Aug., 1789-Mar. 13, 1853.
Wm. G. Brownlow, Aug. 29, 1805-April 29, 1877. Governor of Tennessee, 1865-69; U. S. Senator, 1869-1875.
Eliza O'Brien, wife of Wm. G. Brownlow, Sept. 25, 1819-Feb. 2, 1924.
Lillian Sawyers Long, Sept. 9, 1858-Feb. 6, 1897.
Dr. James H. Sawyers, Mar. 10, 1832-May 26, 1858.
Susan Brownlow Boyton, July 25, 1837-Mar. 12, 1913.
Annie Brownlow Patrick, 1854-1893.
Callie Brownlow Hale, 1854-1903.
David Boyton, Feb. 8, 1837-Jan. 1, 1888.
(All on Brownlow lot.)
Mary M. Stuart, daughter of James and Mary Sevier, April 8, 1814-Feb. 2, 1887.
Matilda D., daughter of Rev. E. E. Sevier, Sept. 3, 1854; age, 10 years.
Samuel Shepard, May 14, 1823-July 6, 1899.
Lazarous C. Shepard, June 2, 1815-Feb. 15, 1902.
Thomas Powell, 1821-1900.
Eben Alexander, Mar. 9, 1851-Mar. 11, 1910.
Jesse Addison Rayl, Mar. 2, 1825-Jan. 13, 1893.
Ann Elizabeth Rayl, April 1, 1830-June 24, 1896.
Nearby is this grave:
Grac Abbott, born a slave, died a child of Jesus.
Susan M. Moser Sept. 29, 1802-Aug. 28, 1861.
Eben Alexander, Dec. 6, 1815-April 29, 1858.
Margaret McClung, his wife, Oct. 26, 1812-July 27, 1864.
John Parker, April 9, 1800-Dec. 6, 1859.
James Boyd, Oct. 23, 1811-June 9, 1884.

Sarah, daughter of John and Sarah Boyd, 1816-1877.
McMullen Boyd, Mar. 25, 1840-Mar. 14, 1907.
Wm. Stephenson, Nov. 25, 1812-June 7, 1865.
Samuel Becket Boyd, June 3, 1827-Jan. 3, 1920.
Isabella Reed, wife of S. B. Boyd, June 8, 1813-Sept. 25, 1907.
Samuel and Martha Rhea, Oct. 28, 1862-Dec. 27, 1910.
Robert Love Taylor, July 31, 1850-Mar. 31, 1912.
Sarah L. Baird, wife of Robert L. Taylor, Oct. 27, 1857-June 14, 1900.
Ruth, wife of G. J. Collins, Mar. 10, 1828-May 31, 1844.
Edward Clark, Dec. 1, 1827-Mar. 18, 1880.
Eliza, wife, Dec. 21, 1840-July 24, 1884; was daughter of Wm. and Sallie Trent.
Cornelia G. Anderson, Mar. 3, 1820-Aug. 3, 1912.
Frank A. R. Scott, Oct. 12, 1827-Mar. 3, 1909.
Margaret Deaderick, wife of F. A. R. Scott, April 22, 1833-July 20, 1909.
Daniel Deaderick, Mar. 23, 1797-Aug. 2, 1873.
Elizabeth, wife of D. Deaderick, April 16, 1801-April 14, 1887.
William Kennedy, Nov. 26, 1833-Nov. 18, 1897.
Malinda, wife, Oct. 25, 1848-Dec. 3, 1926.
Nancy Baker, wife of Wm. Baker, Oct. 19, 1810-Feb. 2, 1833.
Dr. Chalmer Deadrick, Aug. 22, 1847-April 14, 1927.
Rebecca Williams, wife of C. Deadrick, Jan. 20, 1858-Dec. 25, 1919.
Margaret, wife of W. G. C. Humes, June 25, 1828-April 17, 1859.
William Rule, May 10, 1839-July 25, 1928.
Lucy Ann Rule, Feb. 12, 1838-Dec. 24, 1928.
D. H. P. Rogan, Dec. 5, 1815-Feb. 26, 1894.
Catherine Powell, his wife, Aug. 2, 1812-July 10, 1890.
Father and Mother—John B. Simpson, 1844-1921; Margaret Simpson, 1847-1921. (Flat stone.)
Reuben Roberts, 1840-1928.

Bible Records—Tombstone Inscriptions

Mary Barkly Roberts, 1842-1924.
Alice D. McClung, Sept. 18, 1841-Dec. 2, 1916.
Charles McClung, Mar. 13, 1824-Mar. 30, 1899.
Belinda, wife of Charles McClung, daughter of Dr. Connolly, June 21, 1838-Feb. 24, 1905.
Margaret, wife of Charles McClung, daughter of James Cowan, Sept. 5, 1832-Nov. 17, 1883.
Charles McClung, Aug. 26, 1826-Mar. 17, 1908.
Eliza, daughter of A. L. Miller, wife of Frank H. McClung, June 12, 1833-Sept. 4, 1884.
Frank McClung, Nov. 28, 1828-May 4, 1898.
Matthew McClung, Mar. 11, 1833-April 6, 1933.
Julia Anderson McClung, Jan. 14, 1839-Sept. 19, 1918.
Matthew McClung, Oct. 10, 1795-Oct. 5, 1844. (His mother was Margaret White.)
Pleasant McClung, son of Charles and Malvina Mills McClung, Aug. 19, 1824-June 20, 1862.
Mary G. McClung, daughter of James W. and Sarah Mitchell McClung, and wife of Pleasant McClung, Dec. 6, 1825-July 29, 1874.
Thompson Andrew McClung, Sept. 28, 1865-Oct. 19, 1915.
Charles McClung, May 13, 1761-Aug. 19, 1830. He died in Harrisburg, Ky. Lee McClung brought his remains to McClung plot, Gray Cemetery.
Carrick White Park, Oct. 2, 1826-Sept. 28, 1890.
Eliza Baird, wife of Edward Hodgeson England, Aug. 12, 1810-Mar. 23, 1870. (Mother of writer.)
(Flat stone) Louisa, wife of William Bienter, Oct. 28, 1855; age, 39 years.
(Flat stone) Anne Gillespie McClung, Jan. 28, 1825-Dec. 29, 1873.
Charles Lyon, Nov. 23, 1823-Mar. 20, 1829.

First Presbyterian Church Cemetery

The first church built in Knoxville. This cemetery is one of the oldest in Knox County. Sent by Miss Kate White.

Gen. James White, Revolutionary Soldier, 1747-1821. His wife, Mary Lawson White, died May 10, 1819; age, 77 years.
Margaret White McClung, April 10, 1770-Oct. 27, 1827.
Hugh Lawson White, Oct. 29, 1773-April 10, 1840; married Elizabeth Carrick, second Mrs. Peyton.
Moses White, born April 22, 1775; married Isabella McNutt, daughter of George McNutt.
Mary McConnell White, born Nov. 11, 1782; married Dr. F. May, second, Judge John Overton.
Cyntha Barry White, born April 7, 1786; married Gen. Thomas A. Smith, U. S. A.
Melinda White, born Feb. 15, 1789; married Col. John Williams.
Hugh Lawson White and Elizabeth Carrick White had twelve children, 8 daughters and 4 sons. Only two of them survive, to wit: Isabella, who married General William French, and Samuel A., who both lived in Knoxville. Betsy married Newton Scott, also lived in Knoxville. All the above long since dead, Hugh L. Craighead of Nashville was one of the four descendants of Hugh Lawson and Elizabeth Carrick White; his mother, Sophia, being the daughter of C. A. C. White, son of Judge White. Father, mother, and all the children died of consumption.
Margaret White McClung was born in Iredell, N. C., April 1, 1770-Aug. 17, 1827.
Charles McClung.
Andrew Carrick, Dec. 22, 1797-Nov. 16, 1828.
Betsy Moon White, Aug. 25, 1803-July 2, 1828.
Polly Lawson White, Oct. 4, 1805-May 15, 1818; married William Swan.
Lucinda Blount White, Sept. 19, 1807-Nov. 20, 1827.
Peggy Ann White, Nov. 17, 1809-Aug. 2, 1831; married Ebenezer Alexander.
Cyntha Williams White, July 29, 1812-Jan. 20, 1829.

Bible Records—Tombstone Inscriptions

Malinda McDowell White, May 21, 1815-1830.
On one stone: Sophia, Elizabeth, Hugh, and James Park, all children of A. C. C. White, all died in 1827.
Rev. Samuel Ramsay, died Dec. 27, 1827.
Betsy Jones McClung, May, 1803-April 8, 1829.
Matthew McClung, June 18, 1805-Oct. 5, 1844.
W. C. McMillian, Oct. 17, 1795-Oct., 1844.
James White McClung, Jan. 6, 1798-May 21, 1848.
Hugh Lawson McClung, May 26, 1818-May 31, 1849.
Margaret Malinda McClung, Oct. 26, 1812-July 17, 1868.
Mary Blount, wife of Governor Blount, died 1802.
William Blount, Governor of the Territory, died Mar. 21, 1800; age, 55 years.
Rev. Samuel Carrick, July 17, 1765-Aug. 17, 1800.
Christopher Acklen, died 1852.
Donald McClannahan, 1848.
Samuel McClanahan, 1838.
Andrew J. Crush, 1839.
William Crush, 1831.
Robert Carr Hodges, 1850.
Capt. John Crozier, 1838; his wife, Hannah Crozier, 1839, both dying in a winter of extreme cold.
Blanch Crozier, 1812.
John Crozier, Jr., 1803.
James Crozier, 1801.
James Campbell, born in Scotland, 1771; died in Knoxville, 1837; his wife, Anne, died 1834.
Dr. Donald McIntosh, died 1837; born in Scotland; his wife, Marjorie, died 1837.
George Harris and wife, Jane, 1846.
James Roberts, 1809-1836.
A. J. Roberts, 1822-1838.
Jane Boyd, 1821.
H. F. Boyd, 1821.

Peggy Heiskell, 1827.
Mary Brown, wife of Joseph Brown, 1824.
Jane A., 1854. This stone is so badly broken could not decipher all.
Margaret Ramsay, 1776-1854; three times married—James Cowan, Thomas Humes, F. A. Ramsay.
Thomas Humes, 1811.
Leah Humes, T. S. Humes, S. E. Humes on same stone; cannot decipher dates.
James Cowan, 1804.
Eliza D. Morgan, daughter of Col. Rufus Morgan, 1850.
Sarah Bearden, wife of Marcus Bearden, 1847.
Calven A. Morgan, 1845.
Rachell McClung, Kerby Trigg, 1812.
Campbell; age, 77 years.
Campbell; age, 71 years.
James Ramsay, 1858.
William Steele, born in Virginia, 1852.
John Formwalt, Jr., 1819.
Polly Swan, wife of William Swan, 1825.
William Carr, Revolutionary Soldier, 1833.
John Sacott, 1819.
Betsy M. Scott, wife of John Scott, Jr., 1824.
John Webb, 1845.
John D. Anthony, 1838.
W. T. Pryor, 1841.
Arthur Williams, 1822.
Waitt Blount, 1820.
A. P. White, 1827.
Ann Harvey.
The Blount stone and Ann Harvey are the two brick ones with stone top in this cemetery.
William McCllen, a Revolutionary Soldier. See McClellan.
Rev. Thomas Nelson, teacher and minister.
Rev. Stephen Foster, one of the first teachers in State University.
Abner Baker, shot on Gay Street right after the Civil War by Union men.

EUSEBIA CEMETERY, BLOUNT COUNTY
Sent by Kate White

Robert McTeer, 5th son of the Emigrant James McTeer, born in Pennsylvania, Jan. 25, 1740; died in Blount County April 6, 1825; a Revolutionary Soldier.
Martin Agnew, April 26, 1740-Aug.

Bible Records—Tombstone Inscriptions

5, 1826, 1823; a Revolutionary Soldier. Where McTeer Fort was located a family by the name of McCampbell were massacred by Indians, 1792, on the Indian Trail by McTeer Fort, is seen plainly today, where the trail goes. The Campbell family were buried in one grave in Euesbia Graveyard.

WASHINGTON PIKE PRESBYTERIAN CHURCH GRAVEYARD
Knox County. Sent by Miss Laura Luttrell.

Richard M. Harris, Jan. 15, 1840-Oct. 21, 1881.
Infant son of J. P. and S. C. Adair, Sept. 3, 1892.
Curtis Alexander Sprouell, son of D. L. S. and Sue Adair, July 19, 1880-Jan. 26, 1862.
Daniel Birchie, son of D. L. S. and Sue Adair, May 27, 1877-July 30, 1879.
David Adair, July 23, 1806-July 8, 1887.
David A., son of J. B. and S. E. Adair, Mar. 11, 1860-July, 1879.
In memory of infant son of J. H. and L. B. Anderson. Gone before.
In memory of Hester Anderson, relict of the late Colonel James Anderson, formerly the wife of Captain J. B. Jarnagin.
Her end was peace; Lula Bell, wife of J. Henry Anderson, Jan. 20, 1876-Aug. 30, 1922.
W. M. C. Bean, Aug. 22, 1828-Feb. 1, 1907; served in Company C, 6th East Tenn. Reg. of infantry from April 1861 to 1863. When my life work was done.
Mary J. Bagiotte, Nov. 11, 1848-July 5, 1883.
Barbara, first wife of David Booher, Sr., Oct. 9, 1796-June 22, 1848. As in Adam all die, even so in Christ all shall be made alive.
David Booher, July 4, 1804-Nov. 13, 1892. I have fought a good fight; I have finished my course; I have kept the faith.
Isabella, second wife of David Booher, Sr., April 1, 1813-June 26, 1888. Her children arose and called her blessed; also her husband praised her.
James Alford, infant son of Samuel and M. J. Booher, Nov. 4, 1885-July 5, 1886. Of such is the kingdom of heaven.
At rest, father—Bryson Burton, Mar. 29, 1829-Feb. 18, 1911.
Beulah, daughter of A. C. M. and

Cora Clapp, Oct. 28, 1913-Oct. 28, 1913.
Cora, wife of A. C. Clapp, Oct. 29, 1876-Dec. 29, 1914.
Margaret, daughter of A. C. and Cora Clapp, Oct. 29, 1911-Nov. 11, 1912.
Rachel A. C. Clapp Sawyers, Nov. 11, 1842-July 13, 1923.
William A. Clapp, June 2, 1859-Mar. 23, 1910.
Viola, wife of T. S. Clapp, June 6, 1880-Dec. 10, 1910.
First Sergeant William A. Clapp, Company S, East Tenn. Milt. Infantry.
Martha Jane, wife of S. D. Cole, Jan. 17, 1830-Aug. 12, 1860.
Mother—Nancy J. Crawford, wife of S. D. Cole, Nov. 2, 1831-Dec. 11, 1912.
Sarah, daughter of Sampson D. and Nancy J. Cole, April 15, 1862-April 21, 1862.
In memory of Charles M. Collins, Oct. 11, 1872-July 18, 1893.
In memory of Andrew Crawford, April 19, 1790-Mar. 25, 1856.
Andrew Samuel Crawford, June 6, 1852-Feb. 20, 1914. At Rest.
Drusilia M. Crawford, Nov. 8, 1843-Feb. 22, 1899. Asleep in Jesus.
Elen, daughter of H. F. and R. Crawford, May 12, 1841-Sept. 1, 1883.
Gideons, son of John P. and H. E. Crawford, July 4, 187—May 31, 1874.
Henrietta E., wife of John F. Crawford, daughter of P. H. and N. Roberts, Dec. 3, 1846-Oct. 10, 1874.
In memory of Hugh Crawford, Nov. 13, 1806-July 14, 1835; age, 76 years.
Hugh Reynolds, son of Hugh and Rebecca M. C. Crawford, Feb. 11, 1845-Oct. 5, 1855; age, 9 years.
In memory of Nancy, wife of Samuel Crawford; age, 67 years.
Nancy Isabella, daughter of Hugh and Rebecca M. C. Crawford, born April 10, 1839; age, 19 years.
Farewell—Rebecca Crawford, wife of Hugh Crawford, daughter of A. and I.

Bible Records—Tombstone Inscriptions

Forgey, Dec. 18, 1818; age, 68 years.
Rena D., wife of A. S. Crawford, Sept. 21, 1861-April 12, 1894. Joy cometh in the morning.
In memory of Samuel Crawford, a soldier of 1776; died May 14, 1822; age, 84 years.
Eva Cole, wife of Michael Dameron, Aug. 17, 1870-Mar. 7, 1904.
David Donagan, Company C, 1st Tenn. Cavalry.
In memory of David Dunagon, April, 1827-Nov. 10, 1894; age, 67 years.
John G., son of David and Margaret Dunagon, April 27, 18——-Aug. 25, 1892; age, 32 years.
Rebecca, wife of David Dunagon, ——, 1814-Feb. 27, 1819.
Ganun Duncan, Company E, 6th Tenn. Iniantry, born Mar. 4, 1828.
B. J. Duncan, January 14, 186—.
His wife, Mary E. Booher, July 11, 1853-Dec. 15, 1922.
In memory of Polly Emeline, daughter of J. B. and P. Edmondson, Feb. 28, 1836-April 5, 1860.
Isabel, daughter of W. T. and Iva Ellis, Feb. 9, 1920-Sept. 1, 1928. (Woodman of the World.) Memorial.
J. T. Foust, Aug. 4, 1866-Oct. 10, 1925. Gone, but not forgotten.
John Fulton, son of Hugh and Elizabeth Fulton, Aug. 5, 1839-Aug. 27, 1913; age, 74 years. Veteran of Civil War, Co. D, 2nd Regt. Tenn. The Lord is our Shepherd, we shall not want.
Sister—at rest. Martha Roberts Fulton, wife of John Fulton, born Mar. 7, 1850.
H. C. Mc. L. Hall, June 10, 1862-Feb. 13, 1863; son of G. W. and M. D. Hall.
Monument erected in 1873—Jennie, born Jan. 3, 1840. Susan, born Jan. 6, 1851-July 1, 1851. John M. Harris, Dec. 1, 1833. J. J. Harris, Sept. 24, 1810-July 4, 1852. R. Eva Harris, born Aug. 8, 1838. In memory of Rachel L., wife of J. J. Harris, daughter of John L. Sawyers, Mar. 4, 1812-Mar. 16, 1872.
Our Sister—Drusilla Harris, Feb., 1802-Feb. 13, 1893.
Elizabeth Harris, July, 1818-July 30, 1872.
Jacob Harris, Nov. 8, 1812-Jan. 15, 1894. Father.
Rebecca, wife of Simon Harris, Mar. 5, 1777-June 15, 1863.
Sergt. Richard M. T. Harris, Company T, East Tenn. Inft., Jan. 15, 1840-Oct. 21, 1881. May he rest in peace. Brother.
On gate of Washington Pike Cemetery: Richard M. Harris, Jan. 5, 1840-Oct. 21, 1891.
Patriot of 1776. Simon Harris, 1766-Mar. 1, 1831; age, 65 years.
In memory of two infants of Ance and Mary Johnson, E. A. and A. I., born and died Feb. 1, 1891.
Ance G. Johnson, June 8, 1836.
Mary Rhodes, his wife, Dec. 26, 1828-Jan. 3, 1909. Father and Mother.
Nancy Johnson, Jan. 14, 1812-Jan. 13, 1894. Gone but not forgotten. Our Mother.
Mollie, wife of R. H. Johnson, daughter of W. G. and T. A. Barem, Sept. 1, 1876-April 6, 1906.
Solom Johnson, Oct. 17, 1853-Mar. 10, 1860.
Thomas Johnson, 1801-Jan. 14, 1868.
In memory of Mrs. R. Johnson, Aug. 13, 186—-Jan. 7, 1880. Gone but not forgotten.
Here rests my wife, Nancy C. Johnson, Mar. 23, 1726-April 25, 1875. As the Father has loved you, continue in my love.
In memory of James Lea, Mar. 1, 1840-Sept. 1890.
In memory of Nancy Lea, Dec., 1852-June 9, 1854.
In memory of Rev. Samuel Love, a Baptist minister, Jan. 5, 1802-Aug. 19, 1840. Whose praise is in all churches.
Alexander, son of D. S. and L. R. McAbee, Jan. 7, 1868-July 7, 1872.
James Moore McCampbell, Oct. 1, 1829-Dec. 21, 1903.
M. Malvina McCampbell, June 25, 1835-Sept. 8, 1922. Asleep in Jesus.
In memory of Mary McIntosh, Jan. 21, 1863-May 25, 1888-6. Her lot on earth was lovely; her spirit must rest with God.
In memory of Elizabeth Meek, June 1, 1831-Mar. 7, 1859.
In memory of James Meek, Esq., June 11, 1788-Oct. 24, 1851.

Bible Records—Tombstone Inscriptions

Joseph M. Meek, Mar. 15, 1831-May 5, 1852.
In memory of Barbara Meek, wife of Joseph Meek, May 7, 1792-April 9, 1870. In God is my salvation and my glory.
Lead Kindly Light. James M. Nuebert, Dec. 28, 1874-Dec. 26, 1912. Blessed are the peace of heart, for they shall see God.
Mary Nuebert, Oct. 13, 1840, ———.
Mary Jane Nuebert, Feb. 21, 1873-May 3, 1908. Gone but not forgotten.
Four infants of James and Dora Oaks.
Maj. Andrew Roberts, Oct. 30, 1795-Mar. 22, 1860.
Sister—Amida Roberts, Oct. 1, 1847-Dec. 6, 1915.
Emma Sawyers Roberts, Sept. 20, 1836-Dec. 1, 1914.
Franklin Roberts, May, 1835-Dec. 19, 1933. Served in the Civil War to save the Union.
Henry Roberts, Oct. 24, 1811-May 23, 1868; age, 85 years.
Col. John Sawyers, patriot of 1776, died Nov. 20, 1837; age, 86 years.
John Sawyers, April 9, 1786-Oct. 1, 1851.
In memory of Josiah Sawyers, June 6, 1797-Aug. 18, 1847.
Margaretta Sawyers, daughter of William and A. E. Sawyers, died Jan. 28, 1845, in the fifth year of her age.
Martha E. Sawyers, daughter of Wm. E. and Elizabeth Sawyers, in the first year of her age.
Mary, wife of Josiah Sawyers, Nov. 17, 1802-Aug. 21, 1872.
Mary J. Sawyers, daughter of Wm. and E. Sawyers, died in the fourth year of her age.
Nancy, wife of J. Sawyers, Feb. 18, 1788-May 20, 1841.
Rachel Sawyers, 1779-Sept. 18, 1805.
Rebecca Crawford Sawyers, consort of Col. John Sawyers, died Feb. 25, 1841; age, 88 years.

Farewell, dear sister—Rowena Sawyers, Oct. 17, 1858-July 1, 1870.
W. C. Sherritz, Company C, 6th Tenn. Infantry.
Malinda Jane Channaberry, Aug. 20, 1857-Nov. 14, 1895; was married to George M. Shipe Aug. 2, 1877.
H. F. Smith, Jr., Mar. 11, 1918-Oct. 20, 1924.
John Smith, Company G., Tenn. Cavalry.
Elizabeth, daughter of John Smith, 1832-1897.
John E. Smith, Dec. 16, 1854-Feb. 2, 1880.
J. M. Stair, died Oct. 10, 1895; age, 41 years.
Mollie, wife of J. L. Stairs, Aug. 10, 1862-Jan. 20, 1885. By grace we are saved.
Charles H. Thompson, Jan., 1869-Dec. 18, 1919.
John J. A. Thompson, Feb. 2, 1824-July 4, 1890.
Sarah Johnson, consort of J. J. A. Thompson, June 18, 1823-April 19, 1857.
Sarah Thompson, Dec. 2, 1797-Sept. 11, 1863.
Elizabeth, wife of J. Trout, July 5, 1865-Nov. 6, 1911. "Blessed are the dead which die in the Lord."
N. E. Johnson, wife of W. N. Trout, Jan. 20, 1859-Jan. 16, 1911. Gone but not forgotten.
In memory of Gedion White, born in Granville, N. Y., April 16, 1805; ordained to the office of Holy Minister April 1, 1850; labored from 1850 to 1855 in Sabbath School Agent; preached in Washington and Strawberry Plains Churches from 1835 to 1862; died July 28, 1865.
W. L. Trout, May 10, 1855-July 18, 1925.
Nancy C. White, Feb. 11, 1845-June 30, 1898. We shall meet again.
Infant daughter of Dr. T. A. and S. B. Wiser.

BAKER'S CREEK CEMETERY
Blount Count, Tenn. Sent by W. E. Parham.

Margary Armstrong, wife of William A. D., April 30, 1845; age, 63 years.
John Black, Nov. 7, 1776-June 29, 1845.
His wife, Nancy Black, Feb. 4, 1789-Aug. 5, 1855.
A. T. Dunlap, Feb. 21, 1821-Oct. 14,

Bible Records—Tombstone Inscriptions

1906. His wife is Louise, born April 21, 1870.
Catherine Hammontree, Aug. 16, 1807-Jan. 2, 1900.
Philip Hammontree, Mar. 7, 1803-April 15, 1877.
Sarah Kiser, Oct. 25, 1829-Jan. 2, 1900.
Hannah G. McClung, Jan. 12, 1803-Mar. 14, 1898, wife of Patrick McClung, July 5, 1793-Aug. 10, 1869.
Absolom McNabb, Jan. 27, 1779-Aug. 10, 1858.
Mary McNabb, Mar. 5, 1780-Mar. 4, 1836.
Elizabeth McNabb, Dec. 8, 1811-Jan. 22, 1880.
John McNabb, Aug. 25, 1805-Aug. 15, 1876.
Emma Sanderson, wife of Thomas Sanderson, born in Gasport Hampshire, England, Oct. 16, 1817; died at Well's Grove, Blount County, Tenn., May 12, 1858.
Robert Thompson, Mar. 3, 1801-Mar. 8, 1876. His wife was Nancy Thompson, Jan. 6, 1805-May, 1876.
Robert Thompson, Oct. 23, 1776-Jan. 25, 1854; age, 77 years.
Rachell Thompson, died Oct., 1836; age, 55 years.
A. M. Wilson, died April 1, 1830; age, 22 years.
Isabella Wilson, died April 9, 1808; age, 62 years.
John Wilson, 1776-Jan. 8, 1852; age, 76 years.
Margaret Woods, Oct., 1836-Nov. 1, 1879; wife of Samuel Woods, Jan. 24, 1826-Dec. 8, 1902.
Jane Woods, Feb. 2, 1802-Oct. 2, 1884.
Andrew D. B. Vance, born in Abingdon, Va., July 23, 1793; died Nov. 1, 1872, at Pleasant Hill, Blount County, Tenn.; pastor of Baker Creek Presbyterian Church for 42 years. His wife was Nancy Vance, died Dec. 24, 1844; age, 41 years.
Margaret I. Bond Humphrey, died April 17, 1860; age, 71 years.

Brickly Graveyard

East end of Tuckalechee Cove in Chilhowee Mountains, Blount County, Tenn. Sent by W. E. Parham.

John Abbal, 6th Tenn. Infantry.
Dick Brewer, Company B, 4th Tenn. Infantry, Spanish War.
W. S. Brickley, Sergt., Company H, U. S. Infantry.
William Dickrey, Company D, 2nd Tenn. Infantry.
Capt. John Burns, Company B, Tenn. Infantry, Spanish War.
G. W. Lemmons, Company C of Mounted Infantry.

Clark's Cemetery

Blount County, Tenn., four miles north on Knoxville Highway. Sent by W. E. Parham.

Joseph Ambrister, Aug. 8, 1817-Mar. 28, 1882. His wife, Margarey McCulloch, Aug. 27, 1827-Sept., 1873.
Mary Ann (Dearmond) Clark, Feb. 8, 1832-Oct. 21, 1867. Her sister was Jane and they were the first and second wives of P. Harvey Clark.
Cowans, several old markers.
Elizabeth Eagleton, July 1, 1796-Oct. 22, 1882. (She was a McCroskley, and wife of Robert Eagleton, Dec. 16, 1798-June 5, 1865.)
Elizabeth Hitch, Dec. 24, 1828-Aug. 29, 1903; wife of Arcabald Hitch, Aug. 15, 1828-June 26, 1888.
Samuel Houstan George, Jan. 24, 1846-April 20, 1872. His first wife was Mary E. Lawrence.
Elenore Gillespie, wife of James Gillespie, born Nov. 23, 1831; age, 37 years.
Elizabeth Gillespie, on same stone as her parents, and her husband was Dr. J. H. Gillespie, born 1799; age, 82 years; her parents were Samuel and Ann Tucker.

Bible Records—Tombstone Inscriptions

W. C. Gillespie, died —— 25, 1860; age, 65 years.
Jennie (Holliday) Harris, Oct. 24, 1840-June 30, 1907. Her husband, James M. Harris, died 1925, a Confederate Soldier, no marker; his mother was Pauline McCullough.
Alexander McCulloch, Mar. 28, 1813-July 6, 1847.
Samuel McCulloch, 1822-1845.
Sib. McCulloch, 1785-Sept. 12, 1840; age, 55 years.
Nancy Jane (Thompson) McKeehan, Nov. 9, 1829-Mar. 2, 1906, wife of E. B. McKeehan, who is buried by the side of his second wife in the Cupp Cemetery on Crooked Creek.
Alexander McNutt, 1791-1867.
Margaret McNutt, 1793-April 8, 1873.
Rebecca N. (Thompson) Montgomery, Jan. 18, 1873-May 19, 1886, third wife of Andrew Coville Montgomery, who is buried in New Providence Cemetery, Maryville.
David Mitchell, Mar. 5, 1779-Dec. 15, 1861. His wife was Dolly Peek, 1788-1860; parents of Jasper Mitchell.
Sarah Parks, died Sept. 20, 1864. She was a Sharp.
P. Jane Porter, May 4, 1826-Jan. 18, 1902; married, 1843, W. S. Parker, a daughter of A. C. and Ann Montgomery.
Robert Porter, died April 6, 1849; age, 45 years.
Tedfords, several are here that I cannot decipher.
Almira Thompson, Dec. 8, 1827-July 23, 1895.
Margaret Thompson, Feb. 1, 1827-July 25, 1895.
James Thompson, Feb. 28, 1792-Feb. 3, 1866. His wife was Martha Thompson, June 9, 1799-April 1, 1872.
Alexander Sharp, died 1839, and enclosed in Puline Sharp, April 20, 1827-Nov. 3, 1852.
James D. Wear, Sept. 19, 1810-June 13, 1882.
John Clark and William McNabb, both Revolutionary Soldiers, were buried in this cemetery before Blount County was formed in 1796. There was nobody living in this place, but it has the first body that died in Blount County. Unknown person was drowned.

Clover Hill Cemetery
Blount County. Sent by W. E. Parham.

Martha Baldwin, Feb. 18, 1817-Aug. 4, 1805, wife of Merchant Baldwin, Sept. 5, 1797-Mar. 4, 1885.
Charlotte Baldwin, Mar. 10, 1847-Aug. 11, 1896.
James A. Culton, Sept. 19, 1811-May 14, 1900.
Mary Culton, April 13, 1781-Jan. 16, 1860.
P. W. Culton, Sept. 1, 1781-Jan. 8, 1861.
Ann Eliza Dunn, daughter of Robert Boyd, died Aug. 18, 1865; age, 41 years.
James Frow, Dec., 1802-Aug. 12, 1878.
Abraham Heartsell, born 1777. His wife, Mary, 1782-1864.
James Henry, Feb., 1803-1864.
James Logan, 1803-1871.

Forest Hill Cemetery
Three and one-half miles below Maryville, Blount County, Tenn. Sent by W. E. Parham.

Andrew Anderson, Jan. 5, 1805-Mar. 11, 1882.
Sarah Blair, Aug. 22, 1812-Sept. 2, 1858.
Joseph Broady, died Nov. 9, 1876.
Mary Broady, wife of Joseph, Feb. 17, 1799-1873.
Thomas Broady, April 24, 1827-Aug. 23, 1871.
William G. Broady, died Feb. 16, 1863; age, 26 years.
Newton McConnell, Oct. 10, 1808-July 16, 1898.
Mary Broady McConnell, his wife, Dec. 15, 1808-Aug. 3, 1875.

Bible Records—Tombstone Inscriptions

Thomas Ross, July 14, 1803-Dec. 5, 1875.
William Scott, died Aug. 1875; age, 78 years.
Miles Scroggs, April 3, 1800-Nov. 30, 1867.
Elizabeth Scroggs, July 19, 1797-April 12, 1875.

Sarah Scroggs, Sept. 2, 1836-Sept. 3, 1858.
Jesse Wallace, died Dec. 28, 1858; age, 45 years.
Riseana Wallace, wife of Jesse Wallace, Jan. 9, 1834-Dec. 21, 1879.

FRIENDVILLE CEMETERY
Blount County. Sent by W. E. Parham.

John Hacky, Jr., died Sept. 31, 1834; age, 32 years.
Janes Hacky, wife of the above, died ——— 13, 1814.
John Hacky, Sr., died May 6, 1809; age, 64 years.
Rebecca Hacky, wife of the above, died Nov. 11, 1820; age, 67 years.
William Griffith, died April 23, 1832; age, 50 years.

Mary Griffith, second wife of Wm. Griffith, April 6, 1770-Oct. 30, 1862.
Jane Matthews, Dec. 10, 1750-Jan. 15, 1802.
Susannah Matthews, Oct. 8, 1759-April 25, 1802.
Sarah Beals, died Jan. 10, 1865; age, 98 years.
James Binford, Sept. 5, 1815-Aug. 16, 1890.

HOLSTON COLLEGE CEMETERY
Blount County. Sent by W. E. Parham.

Professor W. A. Blair, Dec. 18, 1835-Mar. 19, 1867.
Jane Bright, Aug. 12, 1812-Feb. 16, 1867.
John Finger, April 1, 1812-May 1, 1875.
Jane Finger, Aug. 5, 1826-Sept. 11, 1896.
John Gillespie, 1774-Mar. 14, 1842; age, 67 years.
Susan Henderson, June 19, 1776-Aug. 6, 1846.
Robert Matlock, April 4, 1854-Mar. 15, 1870.
Layette Prater, Jan. 8, 1832-May 24, 1904.
Jane Prater, 1817-1917.
Sarah Prater, 1832-1850.
Margaret Queener, 1824-1922, wife of T. U. Queener, 1842-1903.
John Russell, Jan. 2, 1796-Aug. 3, 1879.
Ann Russell, June 3, 1796-Aug. 31, 1841.

Matthew Russell, Jan. 3, 1796-Nov. 2, 1862. His wife was Sarah Montgomery, Sept. 28, 1834-July 1, 1892.
Margaret Sterling, 1811-1850.
John Talleferro, Dec. 12, 1796-July 20, 1873.
Martha Talleferro, daughter of John Wright, Jan. 16, 1810-Sept. 9, 1869.
W. H. Talleferro, Mar. 15, 1832-Dec. 8, 1876.
Samuel Tarbett, faded at age of 76 years.
Mary Warren, June 16, 1807-Mar. 10, 1802.
Corley Williams, Feb. 15, 1783-June 24, 1865.
Jane Williams, wife, Mar. 16, 1786-Mar. 9, 1863. Ten children named; she was Jane Corley.
Samuel Saffell, died Sept. 28, 1850; age, 73 years.
Elizabeth Saffell, Mar. 4, 1783-May 26, 1806.

Bible Records—Tombstone Inscriptions

MIDDLE SETTLEMENT CEMETERY

One of the oldest cemeteries. The First Methodist Church was formed here, 1784-1788.

Martin Boham, Aug. 9, 1773-Nov. 3, 1861.
Orpha Boham, 1780-1873.
Henry Bowerman, dates unknown.
Michael Bowerman, died 1864; age, 80 years.
Mary Bowerman, his wife, died 1840; age, 50 years.
Pleasant Bowerman, Dec. 12, 1818-Dec. 19, 1861.
Elizabeth Cox, wife of Medern Cox, a daughter of John Russell, died July, 1867; age, 39 years.
Madern Cox, Dec. 16, 1813-Oct. 3, 1909.
John Cox, died July 4, 1842; age, 65 years.
Henry Madern Cox, Dec. 16, 1813-Oct. 13, 1909.
John Cox, died July 4, 1832; age, 65 years.
Susannah Cox, died Mar., 1863; age, 80 years.
George William, Feb. 26, 1830-Feb. 8, 1864.
John J. J. Hoover, April 29, 1800-May 28, 1842.
Rev. John Hunt, May 28, 1813-June 3, 1887.
Polly Hunt, 1813-1887.
Anne Jeffries, July 15, 1803-Feb. 9, 1866, wife of Thornton Jefferies, Mar. 27, 1795-Nov. 13, 1846.
Here lies the body of P. B. M., May 24, 17—8-Feb. 15, 1835.
Here lies the body of J. W. B. M., died Feb. 7, 1815; age, 18 years. (I think the M. is for Moore; nearby are several stones of Moore.)
This cemetery is 35 miles southeast of Singleton Station on the L. & N. R. R.

MORGANTON CEMETERY, BLOUNT COUNTY

Malinda Leiper, 1789-1857; age, 53 years.
Moses Scruggs, June, 1782-1855; age, 73 years.
Margaret Wayman, died Jan. 1, 1851; age, 82 years.

MOUNT MORIAH CEMETERY, BLOUNT COUNTY

Rendolph Kidd, Oct., 1796-May 8, 1852.
David Chandler, Sept. 5, 1804-Jan. 8, 1894. His wife, Rena K., June 3, 1803-1899.
Edward Kidd, May 24, 1828-Feb. 20, 1904.
David Chandler, Sept. 5, 1814-Jan. 2, 1894. His wife, Mary Jane Porter, 1828-Aug. 8, 1887.
Richard Chandler, April 3, 1850-Nov. 4, 1902.
Edward George, Jan. 20, 1806-July 14, 1872.
Mary Jane George, Jan. 15, 1820-June 14, 1892.
Cathrine Chandler, May 6, 1818-Feb. 9, 1845.
Samuel L. George, Jan. 27, 1844-July 26, 1851.
Joseph Luttrell George, Aug. 31, 1848-May 5, 1893.
Samuel Ballard, 1816-Jan. 12, 1865. His wife, Nancy, 1817-1835; age, 65 years.
Mrs. Nancy B. Rodgers, May 9, 1807-Dec. 12, 1877.
R. N. Badgett, 1820-Sept. 4, 1909.
Salina Chandler Ambrister, died Feb. 11, 1845; age, 26 years; first wife of Joseph Ambrister.
Jane Johnson, Nov. 9, 1811-June 18, 1889.
Andrew McSpadden, June 8, 1815-July 10, 1869.
Martha Jane McSpadden, May 31, 1826-May 13, 1904.
Elizabeth McNutt Singleton, June 19, 1831-Nov. 23, 1899, wife of Dr. John Singleton, Aug. 12, 1840-Feb. 6, 1864.
Nancy Cox Singleton Burem, Mar. 8, 1818-Oct., 1907.
Cassie, wife of Dr. J. P. Russell, died June 22, 1908; age, 69 years.
Nancy Jane Harris, June 1, 1844-Sept. 9, 1888.
Harriet A., wife of Allen Taylor, Oct. 4, 1823-Feb. 20, 1885.

Bible Records—Tombstone Inscriptions

WEAR OR HART CEMETERY

Three and one-half miles west of Deaver Station on an old farm.

James K. Orr, Dec. 13, 1839-Oct. 27, 1887.
Sarah Rebecca Wear, wife of David Wear, April 15, 1839-Jan. 13, 1899.
Margaret L. Wear, wife of Hugh Wear, Mar. 12, 1798-May 2, 1884.
Nora May Young, Nov. 15, 1878-June 27, 1885.

WILDWOOD OR LYON CEMETERY, BLOUNT COUNTY

Eliza Jane Martin, daughter of John and Sarah Martin, June 6, 1824-Dec. 2, 1894.
Elizabeth Nimon Davis, May 26, 1814-Sept. 22, 1884, wife of Jacob Nimon, June 22, 1819-Feb. 23, 1891.
Samuel McCamey, April 10, 1824-April 8, 1864.
Matthew Reeder, Jan. 10, 1780-Dec. 11, 1847.
Enoch Waters, April 12, 1786-Sept., 1835. His wife was Mary Bird Waters, April, 1790-Mar. 6, 1865.
Wm. B. Williams, died Nov. 3, 1858; age, 55 years.

UNITA PRESBYTERIAN CHURCH CEMETERY

Julia A. Bilderlock, Aug. 1842-April 17, 1873.
Griffith Burnett, died 1858; age, 40 years.
James B. Carroll, Company G, 3rd Tenn. Cavalry, Civil War, 1861 to 1865.
Nanie Carter, Feb. 19, 1836-Dec. 15, 1917.
Addison Donaldson, Feb. 22, 1865-Sept. 23, 1924.
Freeling Donaldson, Nov. 12, 1849-Dec. 15, 1917.
Harlin Donaldson, Aug. 1, 1852-Nov. 6, 1921.
Rachell Donaldson, July 29, 1827-1860.
Samuel Donaldson, Mar. 22, 1816-Jan. 5, 1891.
Hannah Fortner, April 4, 1844-Mar. 26, 1906; wife of Rev. Josiah Fortner, May 18, 1844-June 10, 1916.
A. V. Griffith, 1850-1912; wife of J. M. Griffith, 1831-1909.
George Griffith, Dec. 11, 1809-1875.
Martha Griffith, Feb. 27, 1811-June 17, 1887.
Hester J. Griffith, Jan. 3, 1846-June, 1919.
Ramsay Griffith, June 26, 1837-Nov. 3, 1907.
Lucy Griffith, Jan. 3, 1879-Feb. 17, 1910.
William Griffith, May 18, 1875-May 17, 1884.
Mary Griffith, wife of J. D. Griffith, Mar. 19, 1817-Dec. 18, 1900.
Eliza Griffith, Nov. 14, 1847-Oct. 26, 1882; wife of J. L., Sr., May 1, 1840-Dec. 3, 1920.
John G. Griffith, Aug. 7, 1809-Dec. 27, 1890.
Nancy Griffith, wife of J. G. Griffith, June 21, 1815-Feb. 15, 1871. Another wife was Mary, Aug. 27, 1802-June 27, 1845.
Margaret Griffith, wife of John, Jr., died Oct. 24, 1851; age, 50 years.
Nancy Griffith, died Feb. 6, 1852; age, 72 years.
Alexander Humphries, June 29, 1849; age, 52 years.
John Kenson, Aug. 25, 1819-Oct. 27, 1819.
Agnes Hope, Oct. 19, 1793-May 2, 1865.
Nomie Hope, June 9, 1815-Dec. 21, 1889.
John E. Humphries, May 6, 1849; age, 4 years.
Martha B. Humphries, Sept. 11, 1811-Jan. 16, 1873.
Samuel Humphries, Aug., 1879; age, 65 years.
Isabella Humphries, Dec. 30, 1869; age, 50 years.
Martha B. Humphries, born Sept., 1849; age, 4 years.
Martha Humphries, wife of Samuel, Mar. 3, 1843-Mar. 6, 1896.
William Humphries, Sept. 25, 1837-Jan. 26, 1868.

Bible Records—Tombstone Inscriptions

James Matthews, Jan. 26, 1821-Dec. 11, 1901.
Sarah Matthews, July 10, 187— -1816.
Joseph Matthews, July 10, 1871; age, 56 years.
Harlin Matthews, April 5, 1816; age, 78 years.
Nancy Matthews, July 9, 1863; age, 63 years.
Mary McCall Matthers, —— 1, 1858-1921.
Madison LeFayette Matthews, 1852-1919.
S. Matthews, 1828-1893.
Artie Ann Fortner Matthews, wife of J. H. McCaslin, 1873-1916.
Arminta McCaslin, wife of Jerry McCaslin, died 1898; age, 40 years.
John McCaslin, Aug. 10, 1796-1867.
Elizabeth McLin, wife of William McLin, 1782-1855.

NEW PROSPECT PRESBYTERIAN CHURCH CEMETERY

Five miles east of Knoxville on the Sevierville Pike, Blount County. Sent by W. E. Parham.

J. W. Anderson, 1829-1909; his wife was Elizabeth Ford, 1836-1920.
Margaret Bounds, 1810-1880.
Elizabeth Brown, 1825-1907.
Paul Cunningham, 1794-1868.
Mary Cunningham, 1806-1883.
Cyntha Doyle, 1825-1896; wife of John Doyle, 1821-1884.
Joseph Ford, 1830-1898; his wife was Martha, 1826-1921.
C. J. Giffin, 1832-1894; his wife was Bastley Giffin, 1819-1902.
G. B. Gilbert, 1813-1837.
Katrine Houser, 1844-1886; wife of William Houser, 1822-1902.
Esther Johnson, 1840-1897; wife of Robert B. Johnson, 1835-1922.
Joseph King, 1808-1849.
Mary King, wife of Joseph, 1813-1888.
Joseph L. King, 1827-1911; his wife was Sarah E., 1842.
B. S. Love, 1838-1911; on same stone, Mary Love, 1836-1915.
John Mickels, 1811-1892.
Suannah Simpson Mickels, wife of John Mickels, 1818-1890.
Suanna Mickels, 1840-1901.
Margaret Simpson, 1816-1892.
P. P. Simpson, 1820-1909.
Sinia Walker, 1871; age, 74 years.
Barbara Willoughby, 1825-1925.
John Willoughby, 1808-1885.
Mary Willoughby, 1817-1880.
M. J. Wrinkle, 1833-1805.
Robert King, who died in Knox County, Tenn., 1845. Left land in Tennessee, Georgia, Alabama, Missouri to his children, Joseph, John, and Will R. His home in Knoxville was on the east side of Gay Street, next to Calven Rufus Morgan store, Blount County.

Old Salem Church is seceded from Presbyterian Church; it is on the pike from Knoxville to Sevierville, and on the old Elijah Dunn farm (no building there now).
Martha B. Cowan McCammon, Nov., 1815-Nov. 4, 1876.
Samuel McCammon, May 8, 1808-April 1, 1865; married Martha Bearden, Jan. 6, 1851.
Thomas McCammon, June 12, 1868-Jan. 16, 1843.
Thomas J. McCammon, June, 1833-1841.
James Wilson, Nov. 8, 1841-Dec. 19, 1848. He was a member of the seceded church. His son-in-law was Marsh Walker; no issue. Another son-in-law was J. H. Giffin; no issue; also William Houser, John Harvey King, and Wm. Reed, son of Lewis Aprangler. He had a daughter to marry a Dunn; her name was Vina Caroline Wilson Dunn; he died, and she marred Columbus Gamble. William Wilson married a Ford. Capt. Joseph Wilson of the police force of Knoxville is a descendant of Wm. Wilson.
This cemetery was often called the McCammon Cemetery.

Bible Records—Tombstone Inscriptions

MADISONVILLE CEMETERY, MONROE COUNTY
Sent by W. E. Parham

John Agnew, Jan. 30, 1799-Aug. 20, 1854.
Rebecca Agnew, Feb. 15, 1796-April, 1855.
Willton Bradbury, April 24, 1797-Aug. 20, 1841.
Mary Bayless, wife of Col. Samuel Bayless, died Mar. 21, 1843; age, 59 years.
Miles Cunningham, Jan. 11, 1798-April 28, 1852; his wife, Peggy Ann, April 31, 1806-Oct. 13, 1852.
William G. Cunningham, Jan. 7, 1824-Jan. 26, 1852.
Evan Cunning, Feb. 6, 1836-1855.
James Ewing, father of Nathaniel, Mar. 7, 1765-1856.
Martham, daughter of Nathaniel Eding, 1850-1858.
Nanthal Magill, Feb. 27, 1797-1878; his wife, Jane, 1801-1883.
Martha J., wife of John Montgomery, 1821-Oct. 7, 1887.
John Calvin Montgomery, 1823-1911. On same stone is Lena L. Montgomery, 1854-1912.
Susan, wife of John Tolburt, died Oct. 12, 1875; age, 78 years.
Mrs. Emily A. Stephens, daughter of George and Mary Yoakman, Dec. 12, 1816-Aug. 12, 1854.
Aurela Martha, wife of James A. Wright; born, Oct. 9, 1827; married May 25, 1848; died, Aug. 19, 1852.

ROGERSVILLE CEMETERY, HAWKINS COUNTY
Sent by W. E. Parham

First is children of D. S. and A. Alexander, namely: Julia Wilson, 1846-1872; Laura F., second daughter of Laura F., 1836-1877; Mary H., 1842-1867; Miss Cornelia, wife of Audley Anderson, 1832-1890.
Alexander Dicks, born in York, Lancaster County, Pa., Aug. 7, 1790; died at Rogersville, 1875.
James K. Neil, Dec. 22, 1806-April 24, 1860; his wife, Catherine, daughter of George Hale, Dec. 10, 1819-May 25, 1845.
Catherine, wife of Rev. J. W. Elliott, and daughter of H. McCullen of Philadelphia; died, 1849.
Joseph Hoffmeister, April 3, 1784-1872; his wife, Elizabeth, Aug. 1, 1787-Feb. 1, 1872.
Frederick Steillinger (Stamger), 1786-1882; was editor of the Knoxville Register, 1816-1835.
Jane McCampbell, Jan. 5, 1798-1875.
Hon. Samuel Powell, 1776-1841.
James Simpson Sevier, Mar. 1840-1909.
Jane Simpson Sevier, wife of James Sevier; died, 1862.
George Jones, 1844-1905; on same stone, Ann S., 1848-1850.
Robert Sevier, 1859-1862.
W. H. Simpson, born in Antrim County, Ireland; died, 1844; age, 63 years.
Col. John Walker, 1800-1872; his wife, Mary W., 1799-1885.
Dr. Hugh Walker, 1802-1865.
Fanny Walker, 1795-1888.
Celia, wife of Rev. J. M. Wilson, daughter of Rev. T. Rogers, 1828-1865. Her father was born in Abermarle County, Va.

LOONEY, NOW LONAS, CEMETERY
Sent by Kate White and Laura Luttrell

This cemetery is about six miles southwest of Knoxville on an Arrowhead Trail, on a high hill above the Tennessee River. Over 100 old graves have broken stones, with all inscriptions washed off by long years of weather. Absolm Looney, a Revolutionary Soldier, once lived there. Looney Island is right across from this cemetery.
Nancy Looney, wife of J. P. Johnson, Jan., 1840-Mar. 16, 1920.
Alexander Looney, Dec. 10, 1824-Aug. 4, 1885.
Absolm Looney, May 3, 1818-April 19,

Bible Records—Tombstone Inscriptions

1893.
Eleanor Looney, died 1861; age, 42 years.
John Looney, April 9, 1804-May 11, 1870.
Zebella Looney, wife of John Looney, Mar. 18, 1804-April 18, 1854.
Moses Looney, died 1817.
David Badgett, Mar. 6, 1825-Mar. 4, 1919.
Badgett, Feb. 7, 1865-1899.
Lina Lonas, 1812; age, 13 years.
Andrew Sharp, April 4, 1863-Oct. 1, 1875.
Senia Sharp, Oct. 11, 1810-Feb. 5, 1825.
W. W. Stanton, Oct. 29, 1882-April 25, 1920.
Meigs, infant son of A. B. Johnson, 1917-1917.
J. C. Johnson, Oct. 19, 1840-Nov. 5, 1923.
Geneva Johnson, wife of J. K. Kidd, Jan. 7, 1870-July 25, 1906.
Dennis Courtney, June 27, 1929; age, 45 years.
Susan Mary, wife of Joseph Mary, May 10, 1850-1930.
Sarah Looney, wife of Absolm Looney, died, 1833.
Absolm Johnson, June 3, 1863-Sept. 8, 1864.
Nancy Looney, died, 1827.
Sarah Mullen, April 1, 1837-Jan. 9, 1873.

Eusubia Graveyard

Twelve miles northeast of Maryville, near the Old McTeer Fort and near the Old Indian War Path, Blount County.

John S. McCroskey, Aug. 21, 1819-April 10, 1854.
Mirander Armstrong, Sept. 15, 1826-April 15, 1899.
William Johnson, Sept. 25, 1817-Aug. 31, 1887.
Alexander McCallie, May 7, 1781-Oct. 9, 1851.
Martha Johnson, Mar. 2, 1824-Mar. 5, 1901.
Robert Houston, June 11, 1802-1865.
Dorothy, his wife, June 26, 1807-Nov. 7, 1886.
Robert L. Houstan, Jan. 6, 1844-May, 1896.
Samuel Bogle, died July 11, 1857; age, 80 years.
Ann Bogle, June 14, 1797.
Josiah Bogle, died April 1, 1811; age, 54 years.
Andrew Bogle, 1753-Nov. 20, 1813; age, 60 years.
Eliza Bogle, 1750-Sept. 1845; age, 90 years.
John Martin, born Oct. 15, 1843; age, 5 years.
John Williams, died, 1844.
Lucinda Williams, died, 1855; age, 25 years.
Andrew Bogle, Feb. 1, 1802-June 1, 1880.
McCroskey, his wife, Dec. 23, 1830-June 19, 1883.
Buchie McCampbell, Nov. 10, 1825-Nov. 11, 1845.
Andrew McTeer, Sept. 5, 1822-June 16, 1885.
James A. McTeer, May 30, 1823-Nov. 8, 1894.
Louisa Pitner, his wife, Dec. 9, 1819-May 30, 1888.
Ruth Jefferies, wife of Andrew J. McTeer, 1862-1909.
William McTeer, June 4, 1780-May 29, 1862.
Mary, first wife of Wm. McTeer, died, 1814; age, 56 years.
W. Houstan Gamble, Dec., 1848-Nov. 14, 1871.
Elizabeth McTeer, wife of W. S. Gamble, Sept. 9, 1845-Sept. 1, 1889.
Mary McTeer, Oct. 2, 1856-Feb. 25, 1872.
Mary Bogle, second wife of Wm. McTeer, May 5, 1785-Nov. 16, 1866.
Dianah De Lozier, May 26, 17—3-June 30, 1851.
Ann Sheddan, 1771-Jan. 22, 1852; age, 81 years.
James G. Shields, July 15, 1813-Jan. 19, 1884.
Letita Henderson, July 18, 1813-May 10, 1878.
James B. Kountz, died, Oct. 5, 1858; age, 20 years.
Nick Knootz, 1806-1878.

Bible Records—Tombstone Inscriptions

Samuel Knootz, Aug. 8 —— -May 1, 1811.
Mary McTeer, his wife, died Jan. 19, 184—.
O. P. Cunnining, May 5, 1855-Jan. 6, 1910.
Elizabeth Donaldson, wife of Wm. Donaldson, died Aug. 21, 1866; age, 80 years.
Sarah Brackwell, wife of Wm. Donaldson, died Dec. 24, 1847; age, 41 years.
Wm. Donaldson, died July 22, 1856; age, 63 years.
Wm. D. Donaldson, Dec. 4, 1855; age, 56 years.
James Kirkpatrick, Nov. 3, 1798-Feb. 12, 1845.
Andy Kirkpatrick, Feb. 17, 1801-June 28, 1862.
Betsy Kirkpatrick, wife of John Halfly, May 4, 1813-May 20, 1885.
Andrew Halfly, Dec. 17, 1838-June 6, 1907.
Euphrasia Godard, wife of Andrew Halfly, Feb. 27, 1842-Sept. 20, 1881.
James Madison McCroskey, Aug. 8, 1838-Oct. 16, 1873.
Margaret F. B. Snoddy, Mar. 24, 1794-June 12, 1876.
Ann Creswell, wife of Andrew Creswell, Feb. 1, 1820-Mar. 3, 1874.
Mary Johnson, wife of D. R. Pitner, Feb. 4, 1850-Aug. 21, 1905.
James Boyd, Sept., 1812-Jan. 16, 1862.
Jennie Burem, Oct. 28, 1830-1862.
John McCullough, Oct. 17, 1830-June 22, 1862.
J. A. Ambuster, July 31, 1842-Jan., 1898.
Carden Brakbill, 1856-1914.
Diana Miller, daughter of Wm. Jefferies, who was lost on the Sultana, Jan. 27, 1844-April 1, 1900; was a sister to Mrs. McTeer.
Wm. M. Davis, Oct. 23, 1820-May 17, 1897.
(Note: This graveyard is supposed to be one of the oldest in this section.)

Old Zion Graveyard

One of the oldest graveyards in White County, located eight miles from Sparta, two miles off the Sparta to Smithville Highway. Sent by Rock House Chapter, Sparta; Mrs. F. H. Thompkins.

Susan Cloyd, April 14, 1842-June 19, 1914.
Jane Cloyd, Aug. 6, 1847-May 31, 1911.
Rebecca Erwin, Nov. 14, 1849, ——.
W. L. Erwin, Feb. 5, 1841-Sept. 1, 1914.
May Brock, Jan. 26, 1831-April 16, 1914.
Margaret A. Glenn, Jan. 11, 1836-Aug. 16, 1911.
John W. Glenn, July 2, 1833-Feb. 23, 1909.
Jane S. Lansden, Dec. 20, 1810-Jan. 16, 1876.
James F. Lansden, Mar. 31, 1803-Jan. 14, 1877.
Thomas A. Fancher, Jan. 24, 1799-April 3, 1844.
Jennie Lansden Fancher, April 7, 1849-May 18, 1881.
James A. Polk Fancher, Feb. 26, 1841-June 18, 1912.
A. Jordan Robbins, Aug. 24, 1841-Jan. 26, 1913.
Susan Gracy Robbins, May 26, 1841-Sept. 9, 1918.
P. A. Hennessee, June 23, 1838-June 7, 1917.
Loucinda Hennessee, Dec. 29, 1839-May 4, 1919.
R. T. Smith, Nov. 21, 1843-Jan. 18, 1928.
George W. Myers, Aug. 12, 1845-Feb. 16, 1924.
Rosannah Hicks, April 19, 1829-May 13, 1909.
Mary Stewart, Mar. 8, 1832-Mar. 30, 1904.
Isaac Hicks, Dec. 25, 1831-Mar. 9, 1908.
M. J. Slatton, Dec. 21, 1826-Dec. 28, 1905.
Berry Slatton, April 6, 1824-Mar. 31, 1889.
Douglas B. Goodwin, June 26, 1849-Sept. 1, 1883.

Bible Records—Tombstone Inscriptions

Martha A. Goodwin, Mar. 18, 1821-May 28, 1892.
Sarah E. Jones, Aug. 20, 1803-Sept. 8, 1882.
J. T. Goodwin, Nov. 7, 1842-Mar. 16, 1905.
M. E. Goodwin, June 20, 1841-Mar. 8, 1914.
E. D. Hutson, April 9, 1817-Nov. 4, 1885.
W. H. Hutson, Oct. 7, 1814-Oct. 8, 1887.
Ann E. Baker, May 5, 1819-Dec. 5, 1863.
Dr. T. H. Baker, Sept. 17, 1811-Aug. 11, 1874.
Mary Brow Baker Davis, Feb. 1840-May 18, 1907.
Levi Jarvis, Dec. 18, 1802-Mar. 16, 1877.
Martha Jarvis, Mar. 22, 1805-Oct. 6, 1879.
Louisa Boyd, Nov. 25, 1829-Mar. 9, 1910.
B. T. Boyd, April 25, 1822-April 29, 1884.
J. T. Martin, Mar. 2, 1838-July 14, 1915.
John M. Whitley, May 24, 1816-Mar. 2, 1883.
W. L. Lowrey, July 29, 1842-May 9, 1909.
Milanda Lowrey, June 1, 1840-Sept. 30, 1909.
Miles Washington McConnell, April 25, 1810-Dec. 4, 1893.
Martha Jane McConnell, Oct. 9, 1828-July 17, 1898.
Nannie Cass, May 18, 1841-April 2, 1871.
L. W. Cass, May 5, 1846-Jan. 26, 1885.
Mary A. Broyles, April 1, 1833-Sept. 17, 1924.
John S. Broyles, Mar. 16, 1832-Jan. 12, 1892.
Wm. H. Boyd, Jan. 10, 1812-Mar. 15, 1875.
Alta Zara Martin, Dec. 22, 1806-April 4, 1881.
Henry J. Lyda, Dec. 31, 1821-Oct. 1, 1891.
Daniel Lyda, July 31, 1824-Mar. 14, 1845.
Caroline Hudgens, May 11, 1840-Sept. 7, 1921.
Samuel Hudgens, Aug. 20, 1837-Feb. 28, 1872.

L. G. Lisk, June 25, 1819-Aug. 3, 1880.
R. M. Lisk, Nov. 11, 1830-June 11, 1899.
Elmore Brock, Feb. 1, 1829-Nov. 11, 1886.
Isaac T. Erwin, Aug. 12, 1814-July 22, 1864.
William Lowrey, July 12, 1839-May 1, 1918.
Daniel S. Lowrey, Sept. 24, 1817-Sept. 25, 1877.
James Lowrey, Jan. 27, 1806-Jan. 26, 1879.
Thomas Lowrey, Oct. 24, 1833-Nov. 17, 1878.
Eliza H. Fancher, May 27, 1830-Nov. 1, 1880.
Crocket Hudgens, June 28, 1827-Aug. 15, 1900.
Capt. E. P. Sims, Dec. 28, 1829-Sept. 5, 1891.
F. M. Sims, Jan. 19, 1827-May 11, 1889.
John A. Templeton, Nov. 22, 1821-May 8, 1881.
Helen Templeton, Jan. 23, 1830-Jan. 25, 1876.
Amanda Sims, Oct. 14, 1812-July 7, 1875.
Eli Sims, Feb. 1, 1776-Sept. 14, 1862.
William Cope, Nov. 7, 1842-Jan. 31, 1862.
Jane Cope, Mar. 4, 1825-July 1, 1869.
M. E. Cope, April 19, 1828-1898.
Sallie A. Cope, Sept. 28, 1817-Dec. 5, 1902.
John W. Cope, Mar. 9, 1813-Aug. 27, 1853.
I. Lanier Hudson, Nov. 1, 1817-May 27, 1827.
Rachel Cope, Jan. 12, 1840-Feb. 26, 1901.
Sarah White, April 8, 1800-Feb. 8, 1885.
William White, May 14, 1786-Nov. 9, 1870.
Isaac N. Erwin, May 17, 1824-Jan. 25, 1859.
A. P. Erwin, May 22, 1808-Oct. 30, 1881.
Alexander Jarvis, Nov. 22, 1836-May 17, 1908.
W. A. Hennessee, July 28, 1744-Mar. 14, 1807.
Nancy Smith, Mar. 15, 1796-June 27, 1873.

Bible Records—Tombstone Inscriptions

Rachael Sims, Mar. 20, 1791-Mar. 6, 1870.
Mary Kelly, very old grave, no dates.
M. E. Martin, Nov. 24-Jan. 28, 1805.

The following stones are very old; dates invisible: Curdid Simpson, Mary Simpson, John Simpson.

LOWERY FAMILY CEMETERY

Three miles east of Sparta, Tenn., at the foot of the mountain, Bear Cove. Sent by Mrs. H. J. West.

James Hudgens, 1787-1847.
Mary Hudgens, Nov. 11, 1789-1878.
Charles Lowrey, Mar. 10, 1820-Sept. 2, 1884.
Kitty Lowrey, wife of Charles, Nov. 20, 1826-Oct. 15, 1918.
David Crocket Lowrey, Jan. 24, 1850-Aug. 14, 1889.
Sarah Hudgens, Sept. 1823-1847.

John Hudgens, Sept. 17, —— -Dec. 5, 1850.
James Hudgens, Sept. 11, 1836-Sept. 11, 1868.
Charley Hudgens, Nov. 20, 1848-Nov. 3, 1869.
Dudley Hudgens, May 25, 1814-Mar. 24, 1838.
Shelby Hudgens, Feb. 1846-Oct., 1866.

SCOTT FAMILY CEMETERY

Three miles east of Sparta, Tenn., on the Memphis-to-Bristol Highway. Sent by Mrs. Robert Hill.

James Scott, Mar. 24, 1810-Sept. 14, 1881.
Amanda Lowrey Scott, wife of James

Scott, Jan. 18, 1815-Sept. 12, 1894.
Sallie Scott, born Nov. 4, 1844.
Jonathan Scott, Oct. 1, 1841-1862.

THE OLD CEMETERY, SPARTA, TENN.

Known as "The Old Cemetery on the Hill." But few of the inscriptions are now decipherable. Sent by J. H. Potter and Eugene Pearson.

Alexander Lowrey, Jan. 30, 1767-Aug. 20, 1846.
Mark Lowrey, 1790-July 15, 1879.
Anthony Dibrell, Jan. 4, 1738-July 25, 1825.
Jessie Lincoln, born in Rockingham, Va., July 12, 1784; died in Clarktown, Tenn., July 13, 1852. (Nephew of President Lincoln.)
Wayman Leftwich, born in Wythe County, Va., Dec. 2, 1798; died, April 28, 1873.
Rebecca Leftwich, wife of Wayman Leftwich, Mar. 10, 1799-May 11, 1874.
Thomas Clark, died in White County, Aug., 1809.
Wineford Clark, wife of Thomas Clark, born in Culpepper County, Va.; died in White County, Mar. 21, 1850; age, 84 years.
Daniel Clark was born in Shannadrah

County Va., Sept. 23, 1797; died in White County, Jan. 29, 1879.
Mourning Hembree Clark, wife of Daniel Clark, Sept. 20, 1800-April 14, 1876.
Dr. Madison Fisk, May 25, 1794-Oct. 19, 1854; age, 60 years.
Berry Jones, Nov. 5, 1782-Aug. 25, 1855.
Sorah Jones, Sept. 14, 1793-Mar. 24, 1856.
James Snodgrass, Dec. 26, 1798-Jan. 29, 1853.
Margaret Snodgrass, wife of James Snodgrass, Nov. 21, 1806-Feb. 24, 1861.
John Young, Sept. 20, 1798-Aug. 12, 1856.
Elizabeth, consort of William M. Young, daughter of Woodson and Nancy White, May 21, 1813-June 20, 1842.

Bible Records—Tombstone Inscriptions

Edward Murray, 1812-1835.
Martha, wife of Edward Murray, 1821-1896.
Samuel Carrick, May 17, 1800-May 10, 1852.
Susan, wife of J. A. Carrick, June 16, 1813-Feb. 8, 1825.

Pleasant Hill Cemetery

Three miles south of Sparta, Tenn., on the Old Simpson Mill Road. Sent by Mrs. Robert Hill.

Col. Sevier Evans, Mar. 8, 1802-Nov. 27, 1847.
Nancy Rotan Evans, his wife, Sept. 24, 1806-1855.
Wm. Rotan Evans, Sept. 24, 1834-Sept. 24, 1857.
Sevier Evans, Dec. 21, 1852-Oct. 18, 1875.
Mary Lou Snodgrass Carrack, 1855-1918.
Vance Carrick, 1854-1920.
Willie Ann Carrick Cunningham, Jan. 29, 1876-Mar. 7, 1924.
John Cunningham, July 14, 1875-Mar. 8, 1924.
Talman Davis, Aug., 1842-1920.
Elutha Davis, Aug., 1846-1927.

Rock Island, Tenn.
Copied by Miss Mary Noel

G. H. Campen, Sept. 13, 1846-Nov. 27, 1927.
James E. Campen, Sept. 9, 1867-Oct. 3, 1874.
Martha L. Campen, Dec. 26, 1868-Sept. 29, 1874.
Mrs. S. E. Campen, Feb. 27, 1850-Oct. 26, 1920.
Mozell Dunlap, daughter of C. E. and C. M. Dunlap.
Rachel E. Jones, Dec. 11, 1857-Mar. 5, 1926.
Nancy Hash, June 30, 1822-Sept. 30, 1905.
Martha Laurence, Oct. 23, 1822-July 28, 1903.
Elma Katherine Moonyham, Oct. 11, 1922-Jan. 6, 1923.
Billie Louise Powers, daughter of H. G. and L. N. Powers, Mar. 17, 1927-Dec. 27, 1927.
James Ewen Powers, son of H. and Lula Powers, Sept. 29, 1925-Mar. 18, 1926.
Sid Powers, April 14, 1867-Feb. 11, 1925.
Margaret L. Rowland, June 6, 1851-May 5, 1928.
Mary E. Rowland, July 25, 1874-Aug. 20, 1922.
W. T. Rowland, Aug. 9, 1851-Jan. 24, 1932.
B. C. Swah, Nov. 5, 1892-Dec. 24, 1923.

Sikes Graveyard

Sikes' home on Murfreesboro Pike, eight miles north of Murfreesboro. Copied by Mrs. Oscar Noel.

Mary Sikes Moseley, daughter of Thos. Green and Mary Tennessee Moseley, Feb. 26, 1854-Jan. 30, 1855.
Mary Tennessee Moseley, wife of Thos. Green Moseley, daughter of Jesse and Martha Louise Sikes; born, Oct. 14, 1829; married, Dec. 16, 1846; died, May 9, 1864.
John R. Raines, son of J. and M. E. Raines, died Feb. 7, 1863.
J. Sikes Raines, son of J. and M. E. Raines, died Feb. 8, 1863.
Maggie E. Raines, daughter of J. and M. T. Sikes, wife of John Raines, died Mar. 24, 1862.
Ambrose T. Sikes, Jan. 18, 1814-May 10, 1873.
Bettie Sikes, wife of Wm. H. Sikes, daughter of John B. and Mary A. Thompson; born in Green County,

Bible Records—Tombstone Inscriptions

Ala., Sept. 23, 1847; married, Dec. 18, 1866; died, Jan. 14, 1884.
Elizabeth Sikes, daughter of J. W. and B. C. Sikes, born and died Oct. 21, 1884.
Infant son of Wm. H. and B. T. Sikes, born and died May 29, 1879.
Jesse Sikes, Sr., Oct. 13, 1787-Feb. 25, 1869.
Lieut. Jesse W. Sikes, Jr., son of J. and

M. L. Sikes; died at Decatur, Ala., Sept. 10, 1863.
Mary Louise Sikes, daughter of Jesse Sikes, Jan. 9, 1809-May 8, 1886.
Thomas A. Sikes, R. Winston's Co., 14, Va. Regt., Rev. War, Sept. 5, 1835.
William H. Sikes, April 27, 1834-Feb. 21, 1892.

ZION CHURCH
BY FLORENCE NAPIER OF ASHWOOD

Zion Church, situated in Maury County, Tenn., six miles west of Columbia and three miles northeast of Mt. Pleasant, midway between the Jackson and Hampshire-Columbia Highways. Zion is a Presbyterian Church, associated with the Southern Presbyterian Church in the United States.

The pioneer settlers of the Zion community, or Frierson Settlement, as it was for a long time called, were of Scotch-Irish descent. They came from Dumfries, Scotland, and the north of Ireland to Kingstree, South Carolina, Williamsburg District, about 1730-1734.

In the spring of 1805 four of these families left their friends and relatives in Kingstree and set forth to seek a new home in the strange and little explored country to the west. After a hard and perilous journey of six weeks they arrived in the vicinity of Nashville and made this their temporary home.

In the fall they removed to Williamson County, near Franklin, and rented places for themselves and some of their friends who joined them about the middle of April, 1806.

An early tradition is that this last company was divided into two parties, one having their own teams, the other having hired teams and teamsters. The party having their own teams rested on the Sabbath day while the party using hired teams traveled on the Sabbath day. Those who traveled on the Sabbath day met with misfortunes of many kinds, while the other party reached their destination just one hour later with fresh teams and with no misfortunes to relate.

After living near Franklin a little more than a year, they became anxious to find permanent homes.

Bible Records—Tombstone Inscriptions

A deputation was sent into different parts of the western country, and in August, 1807, they negotiated with the heirs of Gen. Greene and purchased from them 5,120 acres, eight square miles, for $15,360. This was a part of the 25,000 acres which was donated to Gen. Greene for his services by the State of North Carolina. At this time the country was a perfect wilderness with but few inhabitants in the bounds of Maury County and no settlements older than one year.

After making the purchase a day was set and every man was requested to come and bring all the assistance he could for the purpose of dividing the land and erecting a large log house as near the center as water could be procured. This house was for public worship and was built before any plans were made for building homes. In less than a week the meeting house was finished and the land divided into eight equal shares.

In September a number of the men came to the purchase again; they built cabins and opened the way to their new habitations. In January, 1808, these families came to occupy their new homes.

About this time the Rev. James White Stephenson, who was pastor of Bethel Church, the church where these pioneers worshipped before they left South Carolina, came to Williamson County to live. He frequently visited and preached for the Zion settlers. In 1809 the Rev. James W. Stephenson came to the community to live and became the first pastor of Zion Church and continued as pastor until his death in January, 1832.

Mr. Robert Frierson, who died in 1808, was the first person to be buried in the Zion Cemetery.

In August, 1812, five years after the erection of the original log church, the first stone of the second church was laid; it was completed in the spring of 1813. This was a brick structure of curious architectural design. The pulpit was in the north end of the building with a door on each side; the south end had two doors for the entrance and exit of the white members of the congregation; on the east and west sides wings were built opening into the main building; these wings were for the use of the Negro slaves who were members of the congregation. The wings were entered through doors on the east and the west. The main part of the building was floored; the wings had dirt floors except that the seats were rested upon puncheons.

Bible Records—Tombstone Inscriptions

In 1847 plans were made for the erection of the third church on practically the same site; this is the church in which the members of Zion worship today. The building, which is made of brick, with stone foundation, is eighty feet long, fifty feet wide, three stories high, including the basement, the second story of the white people and the third story or gallery for the black people, with an open vestibule thirty-four feet long and ten feet wide, with two large doors for entrance into the church, with two square brick pillars in front running up to the commencement of the gallery to support it, and four large windows on both the first floor and in the gallery on both sides of the building.

The only difference in the internal arrangement of the church now and at the time it was built is that the choir formerly stood at the rear of the church facing the pulpit; this was changed about fifty years ago, and the organ and the choir are now located in the rear of the pulpit.

Just recently the old lamps in the two large chandeliers, together with the lamps and candle holders on the choir rail, have been wired for electricity, and a motor has replaced the hand bellows for pumping the organ. A furnace has been installed for heating the church.

The gallery is not used as it orginally was, as it is very occasionally that we see a black face there. Some of the young people's Sunday school classes are taught in the gallery, and on special occasions when the weather does not permit the serving of lunch out of doors long tables are placed in the gallery and lunch is served there.

In Aug., 1809, after Zion had called Rev. James W. Stephenson to become pastor, elders were elected and ordained and the Lord's Supper was celebrated for the first time in Zion congregation. The communion service had been brought from South Carolina, the cups are pewter and the plates blue and white willow ware. These with the lead "tokens" are in the church today and greatly valued by the congregation as sacred relics of the past. The tokens were given by the elders at the Saturday service, which was held as a preparatory service in connection with the communion service to those whom they considered worthy to partake of the Lord's Supper.

Ministers, teachers, lawyers, senators, congressmen, legislators,

Bible Records—Tombstone Inscriptions

chancellors, and judges have gone out from this church and won honor for themselves and Zion.

Zion today has a full-time pastor and most of the membership is composed of lineal descendants of these pioneers from South Carolina.

REVOLUTIONARY SOLDIERS BURIED IN ZION CHURCHYARD

Copied by Mrs. Oscar Noel. Record given by Mr. Cooper Frierson.

Sacred to the memory of John Macon, who was born Mar. 10, 1755-Feb. 9, 1829; age, 73 years, 10 months, 29 days.

In memory of Apt. Wm. Tullifield, died Nov. 1, 1822; age, 70 years.

Revolutionary Soldier David Matthews. Mr. Cooper Frierson said that this was the soldier who roasted the potatoes that were served to Gen. Marion and a British officer who were conferring with him at camp. The officer said when he went back to his company that men who lived on such fare could not be beaten. The story is in many histories and Mr. Frierson is authority for the story of David Matthews.

In memory of William Walston, Soldier of the American Revolution.

William Linn, May, 1750-Oct. 19, 1835.

Robert Frierson, born in South Carolina, Mar. 6, 1743; died near Franklin, Tenn., June, 1808; age, 65 years.

Sacred to the memory of Dr. Samuel Mayes. He was born in Salem Sumpter District, S. C., July 5, 1759. At an early age he entered the Revolutionary Army and was engaged in the battles of Savannah, Cowpens, King's Mountain, and Blackstocks. In 1806 he emigrated to this county and was from the period of its organization to his death a ruling elder in Zion Church. He died full of years and in the hopes of the gospel, June 22, 1844; age, 81 years, 11 months, 17 days. The memory of the just is blessed. Prov. 10:7.

In memory of James Armstrong, born in Salem Sumpter District, S. C., April 6, 1764; died, Nov. 11, 1837, in peace and hope of a joyful resurrection; age, 73 years. In early life he was engaged in the War of the Revolution under the command of General Marion. He moved to this state in 1805 and was for many years preceding his death a ruling elder in Zion Church. "Mark the perfect man and behold the upright for the end of that man's peace."—Psa. 37:39.

Lt. Joshua Frierson.

Sacred to the memory of James Stephenson, D.D., who was born in Augusta County, Va., Jan., 1756; ordained to the work of the ministry, 1789. After 45 years of service as an able and faithful minister of the New Testament, peacefully yielded up his life ministry to Him who gave them on Jan. 6, 1832, at the advanced age of 76 years. Mr. Frierson states that he was a teacher of Andrew Jackson.

SOLDIERS OF THE WAR OF 1812

Major John D. Fleming.
Gen. Samuel H. Williams.
Mather D. Cooper.

CONFEDERATE SOLDIERS BURIED IN ZION CHURCHYARD

Copied by Mrs. Oscar Noel, records given by Mr. Cooper Frierson.

Capt. Gray Armstrong.
M. Gordon Armstrong.
Samuel Henry Armstrong.
George D. Armstrong.
Willie Arnell.
Thomas Bonds.
Willie Bonds.
Sam T. Brown.

Bible Records—Tombstone Inscriptions

Capt. Sam Brallom.
Cas. E. Burton.
Col. D. B. Cooper.
Addison Cooper.
Thomas S. Cooper.
Gordon T. Cecil.
Alex Dobbins.
Albert Dobbins.
Dr. Jos. E. Dickson.
Willis B. Embry.
S. Wickley Frierson.
F. Legarde Frierson.
J. Henry Frierson.
Fount W. Frierson.
R. Luther Frierson.
Dr. Theodore Frierson.
Henry Frierson.
Ed. C. Frierson.
James A. Frierson.
W. J. Frierson.
James Hill.
E. Hunter.
Willis C. Jones.
W. E. Jones.

Capt. A. A. Lipscomb.
Junius Mayes.
A. W. Mayes.
H. S. Mayes.
Col. Mat Martin.
A. A. McMillin.
A. McMillin.
W. H. McFall.
D. H. Porterfield.
John J. Robertson.
W. W. Robertson.
Capt. John J. Stephenson.
Samuel H. Stephenson.
W. W. Stephenson.
John J. Sellers.
A. F. Sevell.
Major W. V. Thompson.
J. W. B. Thomas.
S. R. Watkins.
John J. Wilson.
R. G. Walker.
D. F. Watkins.
F. Youree.
Unknown.

CHURCHYARD OF ZION CHURCH

Inscriptions from the Churchyard of Zion Church, Mount Pleasant, Tenn. Copied by Miss Florence Napier and Mrs. Oscar Noel, typed by Miss Mary Noel.

Charles E. Burton, Mar. 24, —— -June 25, 1898.
Wm. A., son of E. C. and M. J. Frierson, Feb. 28, 1848-June 2, 1860.
Martha J. Wilson, wife of Col. E. C. Frierson, Jan. 10, 1829-May 19, 1865.
Elias Currin Frierson, Jan. 21, 1807-July 29, 1883.
R. W. Dobbins, Mar. 3, 1810-Feb. 24, 1886.
Rebecca M. Frierson, wife of Robert Wilson Dobbins, July 3, 1811-April 21, 1893.
Mary Witherspoon, daughter of R. W. and R. M. Dobbins, Oct. 7, 1837-Sept. 21, 1873.
John F., son of R. W. and R. M. Dobbins, Mar. 7, 1842-Jan. 6, 1860.
Leah Conyers Dobbins, Sept. 15, 1835-Oct. 20, 1855; age, 20 years.
Rebecca Wilson, daughter of R. W. and R. M. Dobbins, April 2, 1851-July 14, 1853.
James White, son of R. W. and R. M. Dobbins, Oct. 25, 1854-Mar. 17, 1858.

Quintilla E., daughter of R. W. and R. M. Dobbins, wife of G. T. Cecil, Sept. 10, 1846-Sept. 6, 1875.
Lewis Shanks Frierson, Aug. 12, 1849-Dec. 2, 1890.
Gordon Cecil, C. S. A., 1845-1915.
Mrs. Ruth Williams, relict of Gen. Samuel H. Williams, Nov. 7, 1777-May 23, 1849; born in Burke County, N. C.
Gen. Samuel Williams, June 27, 1769-April 24, 1835.
Sarah Quincy, daughter of Gen. S. H. and Ruth Williams, wife of Col. Matt Martin, born in Maury County, June 17, 1818; died in Smithland, Ky., April 15, 1850.
Gen. Matt Martin, June 18, 1812-Jan. 11, 1892.
Matt Q., son of Matt and Sarah Q. Martin, Mar. 1, 1842-July 1, 1861.
Blake B. Jones, born in Buckingham County, Va., Aug. 16, 1793-July 28, 1842; a resident of Warsaw, Sumpter County, Ala.

Bible Records—Tombstone Inscriptions

Mrs. Margaret Fleming, Feb. 8, 1801-Nov. 30, 1842.
Margaret M. W., daughter of John D. and Margaret M. Fleming, Nov. 29, 1842-Jan. 1, 1844.
Mary R. B., daughter of John D. and Margaret M. Fleming, Nov. 11, 1840-Sept. 17, 1856.
Maj. John D. Fleming, born in Williamsburg District, S. C., Mar. 2, 1792; immigrated to Tennessee, 1805; to Maury County in 1807; died, Aug. 12, 1882.
Infant daughter of D. F. and Sarah S. Fleming, 1913.
Samuel Haywood, son of D. F. and Sarah S. Fleming, 1910-1912.
Robert G. Fleming, July 22, 1859-May 29, 1909.
Julius Fulton Fleming, Mar. 11, 1850-Aug. 3, 1901; elder in Zion Church.
Whitney Fleming, Feb. 20, 1854-Aug. 31, 1890.
James A. Fleming, July 3, 1820-Feb. 14, 1890.
Sarah Louisa, wife of J. A. Fleming, Nov. 22, 1826-Aug. 19, 1891.
John U. Wilson, July 16, 1830-Oct. 10, 1907.
Rebecca Fleming Wilson, Oct. 11, 1830-Sept. 19, 1887.
Lucretia Adams Fleming, July 15, 1853-Nov. 11, 1912.
Sidney Nelson Fleming, April 24, 1858-June 5, 1896.
Thomas S. Fleming, July 18, 1822-Oct. 1, 1866.
C. L. Fleming, June 3, 1825-April 16, 1902.
James Jones Fleming, Dec. 19, 1848-Oct. 21, 1923.
John J. Fleming, April 18, 1828-July 23, 1866.
Cornelia G., wife of John J. Fleming, July 26, 1835-Oct. 2, 1905.
Infant son of D. F. and L. G. Fulton, Mar. 29, 1901.
George Stubblefield, son of D. F. and L. G. Fulton, Jan. 10-Feb. 2, 1908.
Robert Willis Kennedy, Jan. 12, 1829-Sept. 23, 1841.
Elizabeth O. Kennedy, Dec. 9, 1805-Oct. 7, 1841.
William E. Kennedy, April 18, 1794-Dec. 17, 1863.
Ann M. Kennedy, daughter of Wm. E. and E. O. Kennedy, Sept. 23, 1831-Dec. 20, 1834.
Infant son of Wm. E. and E. O. Kennedy, Sept. 28, 1830.
Francis Henry Kennedy, Mar. 13, 1834-Feb. 27, 1837.
William Edwin Kennedy, Nov. 28, 1836-Aug. 20, 1837.
Junius Dawson Kennedy, Aug. 6, 1838-June 12, 1840.
Mary Emma Kennedy, July 9, 1840-July 20, 1852.
Mrs. Jane Arnell; age, 49 years.
James M. Arnell, pastor of Zion Church from April, 1832 to Mar., 1850; born in Goshen, N. Y., Sept. 25, 1808; died in Maury County, Mar. 4, 1850.
William Arnell, C. S. A.
George Mayes, son of J. T. and Mary F. Hendrick, Sept. 5, 1861-Nov. 22, 1874.
Rev. Joseph T. Hendrick, June 2, 1835-Mar. 15, 1863.
Mary F., wife of Joseph T. Hendrick, Aug. 23, 1835-Nov. 10, 1903.
Jennett W. Hunter, Dec. 4, 1806-Jan. 28, 1884.
James Hill, C. S. A.
W. Vance Thompson, died Oct. 13, 1873; age, about 40 years.
Mary F., wife of Wm. Vance Thompson, daughter of John J. Stephenson, Sept. 3, 1836-Aug. 3, 1866.
Jennie, daughter of Wm. Vance and Mary F. Thompson, Dec. 17, 1860-Aug. 9, 1864.
Dr. Wm. A. Nicholls, Aug. 25, 1857-April 6, 1867.
Fannie, wife of C. G. R. Nicholls, Oct. 7, 1828-Mar. 4, 1885.
Dr. C. G. R. Nicholls, Nov. 13, 1826-Jan. 9, 1888.
Maria R., daughter of M. A. and E. E. Martin, Aug. 26, 1869-July 10, 1870.
Albert Dobbins Watkins, Jan. 13, 1872-Aug. 15, 1895.
Emily Bills, infant of D. F. and Lily Watkins, April 3, 1874-Mar. 22, 1875.
David Milton Brown, June 30, 1850-Mar. 21, 1931.
Alice G., wife of David M. Brown, June 8, 1853-Sept. 22, 1890.
Frederick Watkins Brown, Aug. 9, 1874-Aug. 12, 1875.
James Hugh Brown, Oct. 8, 1875-May 10, 1931.
John L. Isom, Nov. 14, 1848-Oct. 14, 1875.

Bible Records—Tombstone Inscriptions

David Frierson Watkins, 1844-1929.
Lillias Dobbins Watkins, 1849-1927.
A. J. Stanfill, June 13, 1833-May 30, 1872.
His wife, Fannie A. Cates, Mar. 10, 1845-Oct. 2, 1920.
Albert Watkins Hawes, Aug. 3, 1906-Aug. 2, 1907.
Margie Martin Sowell, Mar. 14, 1844-Feb. 12, 1922.
Augustus F. Sowell, Dec. 6, 1844-Sept. 29, 1931.
Elizabeth Sowell McComb, Jan. 17, 1879-June 26, 1922; married, Oct. 2, 1901.
Little Henry, son of A. F. and M. F. Sowell, July 27, 1868-July 30, 1870.
Sam R. Watkins; age, 21 years. "It is finished."
Samuel R. Watkins, "Co. Aytch," June 26, 1839-July 20, 1901.
Virginia Mayers Watkins, July 16, 1839-Jan. 10, 1920.
Dr. J. E. Dixon, Aug. 14, 1831-April 7, 1902.
Emily W. Dixon, Jan. 4, 1841-July 13, 1930.
Louise, daughter of Dr. Joe and E. W. Dixon, Feb. 20, 1869-Dec. 27, 1873.
H. B. Edmiston, Jan. 30, 1850-Mar. 3, 1891.
James Sidney Fleming, born in Williamsburg District, S. C., July 1, 1797-Aug. 9, 1886.
Louisa G. Watkins Fleming, born in Lunnenburg County, Va., June 21, 1811-May 15, 1896.
Emma C. Frierson, 1847-1914.
Samuel Wickliffe Frierson, son of John Frierson, July 4, 1814-Jan. 2, 1865.
Rebecca W., daughter of C. M. and S. H. A. Frierson, April 15, 1859-Nov. 28, 1861.
William A. son of C. M. and S. H. A. Frierson, July 18, 1853-Dec. 10, 1861.
Mary E., daughter of C. M. and S. H. A. Frierson, July 2, 1855-June 26, 1870.
John Marshall, June 27, 1852-July 3, 1854.
In memory of the three little children of W. D. and M. J. Mayes.
Florence Dilla, Sept. 30, 1850-Nov. 22, 1853.
Porter, July 25, 1853-July 1, 1854.
Sarah D. Mayes, Dec. 13, 1840-Dec. 30, 1841.
Rebecca S. Mayes, Aug. 18, 1799-Aug. 17, 1827; age, 28 years.
J. M. S. Mayes, May 29, 1796-April 19, 1888.
Susan M. Mayes, 1804-Mar. 8, 1888.
Maria Ruth, daughter of Gen. S. H. and R. Williams, wife of Barclay Martin, Nov. 26, 1812-Dec. 27, 1867.
Hon. Barclay Martin, Dec. 17, 1802-Nov. 8, 1890.
Mother, Sallie Clay, wife of W. J. Armstrong, Aug. 7, 1840-Dec. 27, 1903.
R. S. M., no dates.
Ann Willis, consort of Nathaniel Willis, Sept. 21, 1769-June 26, 1834.
Nathaniel Willis, April 15, 1770; Brunswick County, Va.; died, Aug. 9, 1846.
Mrs. Mary E. Willis, consort of F. H. Willis, July 23, 1812-Dec. 30, 1834.
Francis H. Willis, son of Nathaniel and Ann Willis, July 26, 1810-April 11, 1834.
Nathaniel Willis, April 15, 1770-Aug. 9, 1840.
Ann Willis, Sept. 21, 1769-Jan. 26, 1834.
Mary E. Willis, July 23, 1812-Dec. 30, 1834.
Mary Hendrick Frierson, Mar. 15, 1840.
Joshua James Frierson, Dec. 22, 1835.
Clyde Johnson, Dec. 2, 1879-Mar. 2, 1924; pastor of Zion Church, 1913-1923.
Margaret Annie Watkins Cecil, 1870-1930.
Charles Ingram Cecil, 1860-1901.
Alberta McFall, Jan. 17, 1894-July 6, 1918.
Albert Wingfield Mayes, 1833-1908.
John Thilman Hendrick, Nov. 30, 1859-April 19, 1895.
My Grace, beloved wife of John T. Hendrick, April 24, 1890; age, 28 years.
Theodore Grace Hendrick, Dec. 5, 1889-April 24, 1906.
Theodore Frierson, April 5, 1826-Mar. 19, 1898.
Harriet A. Frierson, Sept. 4, 1833-May 27, 1900.
Isaac Cooper Milner, son of George C. and Fanny Cooper Milner, April 3, 1875-May 5, 1894.
George Cross Milner, Dec. 19, 1852-Sept. 25, 1833; died of yellow fever,

Bible Records—Tombstone Inscriptions

buried in the city of Culiacan, Mexico.
Fanny Cooper, wife of George C. Milner, April 2, 1855-Nov. 12, 1881.
Emma Sweet Cooper, daughter of Matthew D. and Marian Brown Cooper, Mar. 24, 1850-Dec. 30, 1894.
Alice Jane Cooper, daughter of Matthew D. and Marian Brown Cooper, May 15, 1816-June 29, 1901.
Martha Ann Cooper, daughter of Matthew D. and Marian Brown Cooper, Mar. 27, 1842-April 21, 1928.
Wm. Frierson Cooper, son of Matthew D. and Mary Agnes Cooper, Mar. 11, 1820-May 7, 1909.
Flavel Fleming Cooper, son of Florence Fleming and Duncan B. Cooper, 1868-1905.
Mary Polk Jones, wife of Duncan B. Cooper, 1856-1893.
Col. Duncan Brown Cooper, son of Matthew Delamere and Marian Brown Cooper, April 21, 1845-Nov. 4, 1923.
Florence, wife of D. B. Cooper, daughter of W. S. and F. Mc. Fleming, June 17, 1843-Sept. 2, 1870.
Marian, wife of M. D. Cooper, 1876-1910.
George Patrick Feris, Nov. 3, 1831-Sept. 25, 1822.
Jane Robinson, born in the State of South Carolina, 1768; emigrated to the State of Tennessee, 1811; died, Dec. 12, 1841.
James Robinson, Mar. 30, 1771-June 18, 1833; age, 62 years.
Alexander Feris, Mar. 24, 1755-Mar. 11, 1821.
Mary Linn, June 28, 1767-June 18, 1842; age, 76 years.
James R. Linn, Dec. 25, 1798-Oct. 2, 1827.
William L. Linn, June 28, 1806-July 3, 1843; age, 37 years.
Rebecca Linn, Feb. 4, 1873-June 6, 1852.
Joseph Linn, Oct., 1766-Mar. 27, 1849; age, 82 years.
Hugh Douglass, Mar. 12, 1778-July 28, 1860.
Jane Douglass, wife of Hugh Douglass, Feb. 4, 1780-Dec. 10, 1857.
Jane Esther Douglass, May 15, 1811-May 29, 1851.
Infant daughter of Edward R. and Mary A. Douglass, Sept. 12, 1840-Sept. 15, 1840.

Robert R. Linn, Nov. 9, 1798, ——.
Wm. McFadden, born in Chester District, S. C., Jan. 20, 1846.
John McFadden, Nov. 21, 1790-July 19, 1832.
William Edmund Sansom, April 16, 1856-July 25, 1876.
Mary Ann W., consort of Matthew D. Cooper, Aug. 12, 1822-Mar. 16, 1861.
Matthew Delamere Cooper, born in Chester District, S. C., Oct. 30, 1792-Dec. 20, 1878; died in Columbia, Tenn.
Elizabeth Jane, consort of Matthew D. Cooper, Oct. 6, 1819-Oct. 17, 1838; married, July 7, 1835.
Mary Agness, consort of Matthew D. Cooper, Oct. 1, 1801-May 20, 1834.
Mrs. Elizabeth D. Sansom, consort of Wm. Sansom, Mar. 19, 1775-Aug. 20, 1817.
Jennette W. Swenson, daughter of D. N. and Jennette Sansom, Sept. 24, 1816-Nov. 20, 1850.
Elizabeth Kennedy, consort of J. M. Kennedy, Jan. 17, 1836; age, 34 years.
Mary A., wife of John M. Burns, Mar. 14, 1811-Dec. 22, 1851; age, 39 years.
William C. Sansom, June 2, 1842; age, 42 years; he was the only surviving child of Judge Sansom and Eliza Sansom of Georgia.
Dr. Dorrel N. Sansom, Jan. 10, 1791-April 30, 1834.
Mrs. Mary E. Sansom, Jan. 28, 1805-May 11, 1833.
Jane C. Brown, daughter of Rev. D. and S. Brown, Dec. 25, 1813-Mar. 26, 1818.
William T. Brown, Dec. 30, 1811-Sept. 28, 1826.
Susanna Brown, wife of Rev. D. Brown, Sept. 29, 1782-Sept. 13, 1822.
Infants of Wm. G. and S. A. Armstrong.
Moses G. Frierson, born in Williamsburg District, S. C., Jan. 1775-June 13, 1843.
Elizabeth McCauley, consort of Robert Frierson, Dec. 11, 1746-Feb., 1822.
Mary Brown, consort of Rev. D. Brown, April 9, 1783-Sept. 5, 1848.
Flevel Wilson Fulton, son of J. O. and M. W. Fulton, Sept. 26, 1866-Nov. 15, 1887.
Sallie Witherspoon Boughton, wife of William Boughton, Feb. 4, 1838-Aug. 9, 1868.

Bible Records—Tombstone Inscriptions

Paul White Fulton, son of J. O. and M. W. Fulton, Feb. 25, 1863-Sept. 22, 1887.
Sydenham Minto Fulton, Aug. 9, 1849-Oct. 11, 1874.
Martha Louisa White Fulton, wife of J. O. Fulton, died Sept. 26, 1867.
Robert M. Fulton, Feb. 4, 1844-Mar. 7, 1862.
Elvira Fulton, child of J. O. and M. E. Fulton, Feb. 21, 1859-July 30, 1860.
Margaret Elvira Fulton, wife of J. O. Fulton, Dec. 11, 1822-Mar. 1, 1859.
Mrs. Mary A. P. Fulton, wife of J. O. Fulton, June 9, 1813-Aug. 12, 1856.
J. O. Fulton, May 5, 1813-April 18, 1894.
Martha Emily Dobbins, wife of James G. Dobbins, Dec. 3, 1816-June 28, 1864.
Robert Marshall Dobbins, son of J. G. and M. E. Dobbins, July 25, 1859-Aug. 12, 1866.
James Gardiner Dobbins, July 22, 1811-Dec. 2, 1886.
Foster W. Armstrong, Aug. 5, 1860-Dec. 13, 1899.
Myra E. Armstrong, wife of M. G. Armstrong, July 1, 1835-July 22, 1903.
Samnie, April 2, 1859-July 5, 1865.
Mary Lowrinda, died Feb. 10, 1862.
Infant daughter of J. A. and M. D. Frierson, born and died April 27, 1859.
Infant daughter of M. G. and Kate F. Armstrong, died, 1857.
Robert Austin Frierson, son of Benj. R. and Jennett L. Frierson, June 25, 1846-Feb. 7, 1850.
Kate F. Armstrong, wife of M. G. Armstrong, Oct. 25, 1830-Mar. 6, 1861.
Capt. James Gray Armstrong, Dec. 25, 1829-Jan. 4, 1863.
Kate Gordon Armstrong, child of M. G. and K. F. Armstrong, Dec. 26, 1860-1861.
Rachel Amanda Harris, wife of Wm. L. Harris, Oct. 14, 1825-Aug. 23, 1861.
Children of D. F. and R. L. Wilson:
John Addison Wilson, Feb. 19, 1851-July 21, 1851.
Charles Henry Wilson, Mar. 26, 1849-June 8, 1851.
Samuel Wilson, Oct. 11, 1854-Dec. 17, 1862.
John James Matthews, son of E. M. and S. E. Matthews, Mar. 17, 1842-Jan. 17, 1845.
Elizabeth Adaline Matthews, daughter of E. M. and S. E. Matthews, Dec. 1, 1837-July 7, 1842.
E. F. Smith, wife of E. J. Smith, Sept. 14, 1820-Feb. 5, 1854.
Elias J. Armstrong (Salem, S. C.), Oct. 11, 1787-Aug. 7, 1855.
Elizabeth M. Armstrong, wife of Elias J. Armstrong, April 10, 1794-Aug. 12, 1841.
George M. Dickey, son of J. M. and M. A. Dickey, Nov. 20, 1852-Aug. 24, 1853.
William E. Dickey, July 1, 1827-Feb. 19, 1852; member of the Ashwood Division of the Sons of Temperance.
Frances J. Dickey, wife of W. E. Dickey, Sept. 5, 1831-Oct. 23, 1849.
Thomas Barnes, C. S. A.
George Augustin McFall, Feb. 16, 1848-Sept. 29, 1848.
Margaret J. A. McFall, July 9, 1832-June 5, 1848.
David D. McFall, born April 26, 1807.
Mary L. McFall, July 28, 1811-Sept. 9, 1853.
Sallie W. McFall, Feb. 13, 18— -Dec. 13, 1862.
George A. McFall, Feb. 16, 18— -Sept. 29, 1849.
Mary L. McFall, consort of David D. McFall, July 28, 1811-Sept. 9, ——.
George Dickey, May 23, 1778-Nov. 30, 1847.
Sarah G. Kirkpatrick, consort of T. J. Kirkpatrick, Dec. 14, 1823-Mar. 14, 1846.
Sarah W. Dickey, consort of George Dickey, Nov. 16, 1791-Mar. 9, 1845.
Harriet J. A. Ferguson, Aug. 22, 1815-July 22, 1837.
Samuel G. Dickey, June 22, 1819-Sept. 7, 1841.
N. B. Dickey, July 4, 1834-Mar. 8, 1858.
Samuel Archibald McMullen, son of James P. and Martha L. McMullen, Aug. 18, 1839-May 24, 1840.
John G. Fulton, died Jan 22, 1834; age, 26 years.
John D. Frierson, Dec. 9, 1829-Dec. 5, 1856.
Margaret A. Frierson, wife of J. A. Frierson, Jan. 14, 1805-May 5, 1861.
James A. Frierson, Dec. 9, 1802-April 22, 1858.
Children of J. A. and M. A. Frierson:
Moses G., Sept. 4, 1824-Jan. 11, 1828.
David, Mar. 17, 1826-Dec. 31, 1829.

Bible Records—Tombstone Inscriptions

Mary M., July 12, 1832-Aug. 12, 1833.
Martha W., July 25, 1837-Mar. 22, 1845.
Mary Ann Frierson, wife of W. R. Frierson, June 8, 1829-Sept. 14, 1877.
Thomas J. Frierson, Oct. 16, 1784-Nov. 16, 1846.
M. A. E. Frierson, wife of Thomas J. Frierson, 1796-Feb. 5, 1865.
Sidney M. Wingfield, daughter of A. M. and S. A. Wingfield, May 25, 1837-Jan. 16, 1861.
Cornelia Wingfield, daughter of A. M. and S. A. Wingfield, Feb. 8, 1848-Jan. 3, 1860.
Selina Mayes Wingfield, died Aug. 13, 1882.
Albert Monger Wingfield, died July 5, 1877.
Mary Mayes Martin, wife of Thomas G. Martin, Jan. 25, 1835-June 26, 1859.
Ellen J. Wingfield, daughter of A. M. and S. A. Wingfield, May 7, 1839-July 1, 1855.
Henrietta Seymour Wingfield, daughter of A. M. and S. A. Wingfield, April 12, 1831-Nov. 26, 1835.
Dr. Samuel Mayes (Salem Sumpter District, S. C.), July 5, 1759-June 22, 1841. At an early age he entered the Revolutionary army and was engaged in the battles of Savannah, Cowpens, King's Mountain, and Blackstocks. In 1806 he emigrated to this county and from the period of its organization to his death a ruling elder in Zion Church.
Mary Mayes, wife of Dr. Samuel Mayes, Jan. 1, 1776-June 21, 1855.
James Charles O'Reilly, M.D. (Dublin, Ireland), Jan. 16, 1776-Sept. 9, 1850.
Margaret Armstrong, daughter of E. J. and Elizabeth M. Armstrong, Aug. 1, 1824-Aug. 18, 1840.
James Armstrong, son of E. J. and E. M. Armstrong, June 22, 1829-Oct. 18, 1844.
William Osgood Armstrong, June 27, 1811-Aug. 20, 1885.
Mary E. Armstrong, wife of W. D. Armstrong, Jan. 28, 1815-May 29, 1859.
Samuel Armstrong, an elder in Zion Church for 35 years, Nov. 25, 1800-Nov. 29, 1869.
Martha E. Armstrong, wife of S. H. Armstrong, May 25, 1807-Mar. 17, 1860.
Margaret Armstrong, infant daughter of S. H. and M. E. Armstrong, Mar., 1835-1836 (double tomb; tomb erected to infants of S. H. and M. E. Armstrong).
James Arnell Dobbins, infant son of J. G. and M. E. Dobbins, Sept. 24, 1851-July 26, 1852.
Martha A. Dobbins, daughter of J. G. and M. E. Dobbins, Feb. 7, 1842-Sept. 13, 1843.
Agnes Armstrong, wife of James Armstrong (Williamsburg District, S. C.), Nov. 7, 1759-Oct. 18, 1837.
James Armstrong (Salem Sumpter District, S. C.), April 6, 1764-Nov. 11, 1837. In early life he was engaged in the War of the Revolution under the command of Gen. Marion. He removed to this state in 1805 and was for many years preceding his death a ruling elder in Zion Church.
Wallace Eugene Armstrong, son of W. T. and M. E. Armstrong, Dec. 19, 1853-Feb. 25, 1856.
A. S. Armstrong, Oct. 2, 1802-Feb. 18, 1875.
Wm. G. Armstrong, Sept. 22, 1795-April 17, 1869.
Addy Armstrong, May 15, 1839-Aug. 31, 1856.
Alfred H. Armstrong, son of Wm. G. and S. A. Armstrong, June 7, 1824-May 19, 1832.
Addeline W. Armstrong, daughter of W. G. and A. S. Armstrong, July 28, 1826-June 3, 1838.
An infant.
Agnes E. Armstrong, July 29, 1833-April 22, 1846.
William Alfred, son of G. D. and Lizzie Armstrong, Sept. 25, 1851-April 23, 1853.
George Dickey Armstrong, May 12, 1862-Mar. 25, 1863.
George D. Armstrong, Mar. 13, 1829-May 3, 1862.
Elizabeth Armstrong Sellers, Nov. 28, 1827-Dec. 9, 1903.
Infant of Horace and May W. Armstrong.
May W. Armstrong, daughter of H. A. and May Armstrong, 1911-1914.
May Watkins Armstrong, wife of H. A. Armstrong, 1867-1911.
Elizabeth A. Witherspoon (Wilkes Count, N. C.), July 26, 1802-Jan. 4, 1853.

Bible Records—Tombstone Inscriptions

Martha E. Thompson, wife of Wm. Vance Thompson and daughter of Robert and Charlotte Wilson, Aug. 17, 1835-Mar. 7, 1854.
Robert Wilson (Williamsburg District), Oct. 10, 1774-Oct. 20, 1861.
James Dobbins, April, 1776-Dec. 24, 1862.
Mary Leonora Dobbins, Dec. 26, 1789-July 5, 1856.
Robert Wilson Dobbins, died Sept. 16, 1854.
John D. Dobbins, July 27, 1828-June 21, 1849.
Mary Frierson, Jan. 2, 1780-July 9, 1849.
James Frierson, Sept. 14, 1783-Sept. 28, 1846.
Abner B. Frierson, April 23, 1820-May, 1828.
Mary Frierson, wife of Dr. James H. Frierson, Dec. 17, 1815-Nov. 7, 1868.
James H. Frierson, M.D., Nov. 23, 1812-Jan. 26, 1846.
Maud A. Frierson, died Feb. 28, 1848 (tomb erected by son, Madison S. Frierson).
Mary Frierson, second daughter and youngest child of Dr. J. H. and M. Frierson, Mar. 10, 1846-Jan. 7, 1868.
Dewitt C. Witherspoon (Tuscaloosa County, Ala.), Mar. 9, 1828-Aug. 21, 1849 (died on a visit to Maury County, Tenn.).
Madison Frierson, eminent lawyer, April 27, 1814-Mar. 28, 1871.
Mary E. Frierson, wife of Madison Frierson, Oct. 31, 1821-Jan. 19, 1869.
William Newton Hill, Mar. 5, 1805-Aug. 2, 1856.
Margaret Louisa Dobbins, wife of D. G. Dobbins, Sept. 11, 1815-July 5, 1901.
Helen S. Armstrong, Dec. 26, 1846-Oct. 10, 1895.
Delia Sloane Beecher, 1873-1882.
John Sloane Beecher, 1827-1884.
Eliza Armstrong Beecher, Jan. 22, 1842-Aug. 6, 1927.
Lewis Randolph Amis, pastor in the Methodist Episcopal Church, South, died Dec. 16, 1904.
Robert Gale Walker, C. G. A., 1847-1927.
Mattie Fulton Walker, 1852-1899.
Twin sisters, children of J. A. and M. D. Frierson, born April 27, 1859.
Infant, April 27, 1859.
Martha Blakely, Feb. 19, 1809-Feb. 17, 1858.
Sarah Blakely, Oct. 23, 1781-Mar. 22, 1850.
James Blakely, Feb. 6, 1775-Jan. 30, 1830.
White Frierson Fleming, son of W. S. and M. W. Fleming, April 30, 1856-Jan. 15, 1861.
Mary Witherspoon, daughter of W. S. and M. W. Fleming, Mar. 20, 1858-July 10, 1870.
Mary W. Fleming, daughter of J. W. and Mary S. Frierson, and wife of W. S. Fleming, Jan. 18, 1830-Nov. 8, 1858.
William Stuart Fleming, April 23, 1816-July 13, 1898; elder in First Presbyterian Church, Columbia, 1856-1896; Chancellor, 1870-1888.
Frances McL. Fleming, June 4, 1820-April 30, 1849.
Martha Adaline Oatman, wife of Lemon Oatman, Oct. 10, 1843 (died; age, 20 years, 6 months, 20 days).
Margaret E. Fleming, wife of Thomas F. Fleming, Aug., 1798-Aug. 14, 1866.
Thomas F. Fleming, Aug. 21, 1789-Nov. 16, 1838.
John W. Stephenson, April 17, 1785-Oct. 29, 1847. One of the pioneers that emigrated in 1806 from South Carolina, his native state, to the wilds of Tennessee, assisted at the organization of Zion Church in 1808.
Infant son of William S. and Frances M. Fleming, died July 12, 1840.
Thomas Franklin Stephenson, son of John and Mary Stephenson (Alabama), May 17, 1822-April 30, 1826.
Margaret Muldrow Fleming, daughter of J. S. and S. F. Fleming, June 26, 1839-Feb. 28, 1845.
Mrs. Sarah F. Fleming, wife of J. S. Fleming, supposedly born about Oct. 1, 1800-July 7, 1845.
Mary E. Brooks, daughter of Alfred and Lydia Brooks, Jan. 9, 1828-Feb. 28, 1838.
George W. Brooks, son of Alfred and Lydia Brooks, Jan. 16, 1830-Mar. 12, 1838.
William J. M. Brooks, son of Alfred and Lydia Brooks, Oct. 23, 1832-Mar. 15, 1838.
James W. Brooks, April 20, 1843 (died; age, 1 year, 10 months).

Bible Records—Tombstone Inscriptions

Martha T. J. Jackson, daughter of John and Susan Jackson, Dec. 19, 1837 (died; age 2 years).
George Whitfield Mayes, Mar. 11, 1811-July 15, 1874.
Mary Elvira Stephenson, wife of George W. Mayes, Sept. 10, 1814-Jan. 28, 1897.
John James Mayes, son of George W. and Mary E. Mayes, May 9, 1837-Nov. 2, 1862.
Elizabeth N. Embry, Jan. 25, 1852-Aug. 15, 1855.
Edwin Wallace Embry, son of E. S. and W. B. Embry, Sept. 25, 1853-Dec. 28, 1854.
Mattie Fulton Walker, wife of R. G. Walker, April 23, 1852-Jan. 8, 1899.
Tommie Fulton Walker, son of R. G. and M. L. Walker, July 7, 1882-Dec. 27, 1882.
Eugene Minto Walker, son of R. G. and M. L. Walker, Aug. 22, 1877-Sept. 29, 1882.
Ida D. Armstrong, 1855-1926.
Annie O. Armstrong, April 10, 1852-July 23, 1921.
Minor Goodloe Frierson, May 8, 1854-Jan. 16, 1896.
Sarah Hartley O'Reilly, widow of James C. O'Reilly, M.D. (Philadelphia, Pa.), June 1796-Feb. 19, 1851.
Martha White Fleming, second daughter of J. S. and S. F. Fleming, May 29, 1833-Aug. 11, 1834.
Joseph Fleming, April 17, 1831-July 2, 1852.
Samuel G. Fleming, Feb. 28, 1835-Nov. 6, 1852.
Algernon S. Fleming, Dec. 21, 1841-Sept. 22, 1853.
Little Teddy Fleming; age, 21 months.
Samuel E. Dickey, Sept. 3, 1780-Sept. 30, 1835.
Elizabeth Dickey, wife of Edward Dickey, April 25, 1784-May 16, 1851.
Margaret Mulherrin, 1773-April 18, 1856.
Thomas J. Cayce, Oct. 5, 1859 (?).
Sarah Marshall Cayce, April 17, 1853-Mar. 11, 1923.
Mary Stephenson, wife of Rev. James W. Stephenson, Nov. 27, 1830 (died; age, 61).
Rev. James W. Stephenson, D.D. (Augusta County, Va.), Jan., 1756-Jan. 6, 1832. Ordained to work of the ministry, 1789; 43 years of service.
John James Stephenson, Sept. 10, 1811-Aug. 26, 1838.
Jennet W. M. Stephenson, Jan. 19, 1831 (died; age, 67 years).
Mary B. Stephenson, wife of Thomas Stephenson, 1769-Feb. 27, 1845.
Thomas S. Stephenson, May 5, 1766-April 16, 1848. He was the last of the pioneers that assisted at the organization of Zion Church and the last one of the ruling elders that were chosen at that early day.
John Elihu Stephenson, Sept. 20, 1795-July 24, 1856.
Samuel Bradley Mayes, son of George W. and Mary E. Mayes, April 8, 1848-Feb. 16, 1868.
James Morrison Arnell Mayes, son of George W. and Mary E. Mayes, July 29, 1850-April 8, 1893.
Alice Mayes, July 15, 1841-Mar. 18, 1926.
Samuel H. Stephenson, May 10, 1810-April 22, 1884.
Mary I. Stephenson, Sept. 1, 1846-June 13, 1858.
Theodore Stephenson, Mar. 3, 1856-Feb. 11, 1872.
Sarah Elmira Frierson, wife of Samuel H. Stephenson, July 27, 1815-Nov. 8, 1893.
Emily S. Fulton, April 27, 1825-May 12, 1889.
Willis B. Embry, Aug. 20, 1825-Aug. 11, 1864.
Mary F. Embry, Sept. 5, 1855-June 20, 1921.
Frances J. Embry, wife of M. W. Embry, Dec. 31, 1836-Oct. 31, 1885.
Merrell W. Embry, Nov. 17, 1831-Jan. 19, 1890.
A. Gertrude Walker, died Aug. 12, 1918.
Mary Walker, Jan. 18, 1854-Sept. 9, 1895.
Eliza Gale, wife of T. C. Walker, 1824-1907.
Thomas C. Walker, Oct. 15, 1803-Feb. 2, 1885.
Robert Armstrong, son of C. F. and L. W. Armstrong.
James Dobbins, Mar. 11, 1857-July 16, 1925.
Elizabeth Sowell Dobbins, Sept. 19, 1853.
Dr. G. S. Fain, 1830-1884.

Bible Records—Tombstone Inscriptions

Margaret Eliza Wilson Fain, daughter of Robert and Charlotte A. Wilson, wife of Dr. G. S. Fain, Aug. 19, 1840-July, 1872.
Susan Wharton Thompson, wife of W. D. Thompson (Davidson County, Tenn.), Feb. 8, 1808-Sept. 25, 1870 (Williamsport, Tenn.).
S. Haywood Stephenson, son of Samuel and Aletia Stephenson, Dec. 6, 1872-Mar. 16, 1876.
Whitney S. Fleming, Aug. 18, 1887-Jan. 26, 1906.
Sallie Reams, Aug. 6, 1881-Sept. 9, 1881.
Sallie D. Reams, Nov. 3, 1869-Aug. 6, 1881.
John Dickey Blakely, Mar. 21, 1814-Oct. 26, 1878.
Harriet G. N. Blakely, wife of J. D. Blakely, Aug. 10, 1827-Feb. 22, 1862.
Infant, Feb. 11, 1862-Feb. 21, 1862.
Frederick H. Watkins (Virginia), Feb. 16, 1816-Sept. 17, 1895.
Margaret Ann Watkins, wife of F. H. Watkins, Mar. 8, 1817-Jan. 15, 1879.
Frederick Watkins, July 21, 1819-Oct. 13, 1830.
Penelope E. Watkins Williams, youngest daughter of Dr. G. B. Williams, Sept. 5, 1822-July 9, 1842.
Mary Mayes Lipscomb, 1839-1896.
Archibald A. Lipscomb, 1839-1911.
Mrs. Hariet P. Patillo, Oct. 25, 1852 (died; age, 61 years).
Susan Jane Patillo, April 11, 1853 (died; age, 22 years).
Jesse Harper Patillo, July 6, 1853 (died; age, 24 years).
John Franklin Patillo, July 26, 1853 (died; age, 75 years).
John Pomphrett, Aug. 30, 1852 (died; age, 4 days).
Benj. Franklin, July 12, 1853 (died; age, 10 years).
Mary Frances, July 24, 1853 (died; age, 19 years).
Mrs. Eliza W. Webb, July 24, 1853 (died; age, 40 years).
Wm. Henry, Aug. 26, 1853 (died; age, 3 years).
Louisa Catherine, July 20, 1853 (died; age, 8 years).
Ann Smith, July 21, 1858 (died; age, 14 years).
Virginia Carolina, July 21, 1853 (died; age, 17 years).

Sarah G. Hughes, wife of A. M. Hughes, Oct. 21, 1811-Dec. 21, 1842.
Infant, son of J. W. S. and M. S. Frierson, died July 6, 1837.
Alestia Frierson, Aug. 24, 1833 (died; age, 18 months, 9 days).
Wm. J. Frierson, July 8, 1841-Oct. 8, 1862.
John Neill Hughes, son of A. M. and M. B. Hughes, born Dec. 6, 1845.
Rebecca M. Hughes, daughter of A. M. and S. C. Hughes, July 30, 1838-April 18, 1851.
Franklin Frierson, son of John and Mary Frierson, July 27, 1817-July 30, 1835.
John Frierson, April 16, 1778-Mar. 29, 1841.
Mary Witherspoon Frierson, wife of John Frierson, born in South Carolina, June 2, 1780; married, Nov. 12, 1799; migrated to Tennessee, 1812; died, July 30, 1851.
John Witherspoon Frierson, July 17, 1828-May 26, 1901.
Alice Elizabeth Frierson, Sept. 20, 1833-Sept. 9, 1900.
Grace Frierson, daughter of John W. and A. E. Frierson, Mar. 22, 1883 (died; age, 19 years).
John Witherspoon Frierson, April 11, 1807-Nov. 14, 1828.
John Frierson, infant son of Gardiner and Lavinia T. Frierson, Sept. 1828-Oct 14, 1928.
Samuel Humphreys Williams, son of Gardiner and Lavinia T. Frierson, Sept. 13, 1829-Oct. 4, 1834.
Infant, son of J. L. and J. D. Smith, died July 25, 1838.
Roenna Jane Smith, Nov. 21, 1836-July 15, 1839.
Infant, son of Mr. and Mrs. S. H. Bunch, 1859.
Infant, son of John L. and Jane D. Smith, born Nov. 25, 1828.
Jane Jones, daughter of J. and L. A. Jones, Dec. 26, 1829-June 29, 1832.
Samuel H. W. Jones, son of James and L. A. Jones, Sept. 11, 1831-Dec. 8, —.
Rachel R. Jones, daughter of J. and L. A. Jones, Jan. 30, 1841-May 29, 1849.
Mary T. Hoge, daughter of James H. and L. A. Hoge, May 3, 1858-Aug. 7, 1859.
James H. Hogue, son of James H. and

Bible Records—Tombstone Inscriptions

L. A. Hogue, July 27, 1862-Aug. 23, 1862.
Samuel Williams Martin, infant son of Matt and Sarah Quincy Martin, Oct. 3, 1836-Sept. 28, 1837.
Ruth Williams, widow of Gen. Samuel H. Williams (Burke County, N. C.), Nov. 7, 1777-May 23, 1849.
Gen. Samuel H. Williams.
Jane Eliza Stephenson Frierson, wife of R. L. Frierson, born Sept. 23, 1807; married, July 20, 1826; died, Feb. 4, 1864.
Robert Luther Frierson, born in Williamsburg District, S. C., Jan. 1, 1802; moved to Maury County, Tenn., in 1812; died, Mar. 13, 1857.
Luther Robert Frierson, son of R. L. and Jane E. Frierson, Dec. 8, 1844-Feb. 25, 1863 (Smithville, Miss.).
Mitchner, Oct. 27, 1872-April 12, 1877.
Emma Frierson, July 1, 1852-Feb. 5, 1925.
Leonidas Frierson, May 12, 1827-Feb. 11, 1908.
Jane Eliza Frierson, Aug. 1, 1842-Sept. 24, 1930.
Sarah Catherine Witherspoon Frierson, wife of Leonidas Frierson, July 11, 1837-Dec. 13, 1901.
Claiborne Gee (Lunnenburg County, Va.), Oct. 18, 1805-Mar. 15, 1845.
Infant, daughter of J. and Cornelia C. Fleming, Sept. 9, 1860-Dec. 2, 1860.
Franklin Witherspoon Frierson, Oct. 23, 1836-Mar. 17, 1899.
Mary M. Carthell, wife of Capt. T. J. Carthell, Mar. 14, 1832-Oct. 8, 1923.
Infant, daughter of M. and K. King, born and died Nov. 1, 1869.
Infant, daughter of Meredith and Kate King, born and died Dec. 6, 1870.
Mary L. King, daughter of M. D. and Kate King, Sept. 3, 1886 (died, age, 11 years, 4 months).
C. T. J. Smith King, wife of M. D. King, Aug. 28, 1843-Feb. 7, 1897.
Jennie King, wife of Meredith King, Aug. 4, 1866 (died; age, 21 years).
Meredith David King, July 28, 1836-April 4, 1909.
Iley Brown, Feb. 23, 1870 (age, 56 years).
Archibald M. Williams, Mar. 27, 1809-Nov. 1, 1868.
Mary Frances Dale Williams, wife of A. M. Williams, May 18, 1818-Jan. 19, 1883.
Charles M. Williams, Sept. 28, 1848 Dec. 9, 1883.
E. Hunter.
A. McMillan.
D. H. Porterfield.
F. Youree.
E. Jones.
W. H. Cates, Sept. 5, 1847-Jan. 31, 1892.
Mollie L. Cates, daughter of G. W. and H. J. Cates, Sept. 24, 1862-Sept. 19, 1877.
Annie Green Cates, Sept. 25, 1875-Sept. 23, 1879.
G. W. Cates, July 7, 1825-July 14, 1886.
H. J. Cates, wife of G. W. Cates, July 25, 1839-Aug. 11, 1878.
Wm. B. Cates, Nov. 16, 1865-Oct. 22, 1830.
Annie E. Jones, April 28, 1846-Oct. 6, 1894.
Willis C. Jones, Feb. 22, 1847-Dec. 5, 1893.
Anne Jones, daughter of W. G. and A. E. Jones, Aug. 3, 1884-Feb. 19, 1886.
Elizabeth Lyndad Renick, Sept. 29, 1898-May 18, 1914.
Dr. Benj. J. Harlan, Oct. 25, 1848-May 25, 1889.
Jennette M. Coleman, wife of Wm. W. Coleman, June 27, 1814-Sept. 3, 1880.
Emma Porter Jones, daughter of Thomas and Indie V. Jones, Sept. 3, 1858-July 24, 1870.
Lucretia Jones, infant daughter of T. and I. V. Jones, May 7, 1861-July 22, 1862.
Infant daughter of Mr. and Mrs. S. H. Bunch.
Lucretia Adams Jones, wife of James Jones, Jan. 29, 1803-Nov. 22, 1863.
James Jones (Wake County, N. C.), Jan. 6, 1800-Nov. 24, 1871 (Maury County).
Eliz. A. Williams, Sept. 9, 1827-May 23, 1883.
Rev. C. Foster Williams, April 20, 1819-Nov. 5, 1893.
Charles D. Williams, April 15, 1855-Aug. 22, 1900.
Samuel Wilson Frierson, 1842-1895.
Geraldine Turpin, July 27, —— -Sept. 29, 1902.
Joshua James Frierson, Dec. 22, 1835-Sept. 24, 1898.

Bible Records—Tombstone Inscriptions

Mary Hendrick Frierson, Mar. 15, 1840-Aug. 8, 1914.
Mary D. McFall, 1867-1931.
Emma Florida McFall, 1841-1914.
Wm. Hamlett McFall, 1836-1902.
Wm. K. Jones, July 16, 1826-Oct. 4, 1886.
Willie Polk McFall, son of W. H. and Emma McFall (age, 8 months and 2 days).
Archie Bryan Lipscomb, son of A. A. and A. B. Lipscomb, June 5, 1863-April 1, 1864.
Amanda Bryan Lipscomb, daughter of Joseph and Elizabeth Harlan, wife of Archie A. Lipscomb; born, Aug. 14, 1843; married, May 12, 1861; died, Oct. 16, 1868.
Willie Lipscomb, son of A. A. and Amanda Lipscomb, April 26, 1862-Oct. 2, 1862.
John Caldwell Harlan, Mar. 25, 1797-Feb. 8, 1854.
Martha Anderson Harlan, wife of J. C. Harlan, May 15, 1802-Aug. 16, 1886.
Sarah A. Harlan, wife of Benj. Harlan, daughter of John C. and Maria Harlan (Todd County, Ky.), Feb. 11, 1828-Mar. 1, 1868.
Benj. Harlan, Oct. 28, 1804-June 18, 1887.
John G. Harlan, Feb. 19, 1851-Aug. 5, 1875.
Jane M. Thomas, wife of J. W. B. Thomas, Oct. 31, 1819-May 5, 1870.
J. W. B. Thomas, Sr., Jan. 8, 1807-Jan. 26, 1832.
Job H. Thomas, Dec. 16, 1780-June 14, 1860.
Annie Jones, Aug. 3, 1884-Feb. 19, 1885.
Wickerson Barnes, Sept. 22, 1853 (age, about 80 years).
Eddie W. Thomas, Oct. 14, 1862-Dec. 27, 1887.
Fannie S. Thomas, wife of W. F. Thomas, June 1, 1855-July 24, 1886.
Fannie M. Thomas, daughter of W. F. and F. S. Thomas, June 24, 1886-Aug. 12, 1886.
Alice W. Tindall, Oct. 18, 1832-Nov. 15, 1910.
Clark Tindall, Jan. 15, 1828-Mar. 8, 1897.
Samuel H. Bratton, Feb. 28, 1837-Mar. 13, 1885.
E. H. Sellers, July 29, 1812-May 14, 1878.
Sarah S. Sellers, wife of E. H. Sellers, Mar. 6, 1814-Dec. 17, 1875.
John James Sellers, son of E. H. and Sarah S. Sellers, Dec. 9, 1844-Oct. 6, 1865.
Joseph J. Robinson, Dec. 5, 1842-Jan. 21, 1868.
Mary A. J. Robinson, Sept. 12, 1839-Sept. 16, 1868.
S. W. Robinson, wife of Enos Robinson, May 8, 1813-Jan. 22, 1878.
Enos Robinson (South Carolina), Aug. 11, 1811-May 24, 1881.
John Cabe Hart, April 14, 1881 (age, 68 years).
Wm. Hemphill Robinson, Dec. 16, 1844-Feb. 22, 1930.
N. B. Tindall, April 23, 1786-Sept. 26, 1844.
Elizabeth Tindall, wife of N. B. Tindall, Nov. 10, 1790-June 28, 1848.
Matilda C. McGaw, daughter of John P. and M. J. McGaw, Mar. 26, 1849-Jan. 22, 1878.
Amanda E. McGaw, daughter of John P. and M. J. McGaw, Jan. 29, 1853-Nov. 1, 1877.
Mary Jane McGaw, wife of John P. McGaw, Sept. 20, 1828-May 18, 1867.
Children of G. C. and E. R. Dixon:
Joseph Frierson Dixon, June 18, 1862-April 12, 1864.
Mary Emily Dixon, July 20, 1872-July 8, 1882.
Infant daughter of J. W. B. and Jane M. Thomas, died Oct. 27, 1859.
Jane D. McGaw, wife of David McGaw, daughter of John and Mary Torhit of Chester, S. C.; born, Oct. 8, 1818; married, April 13, 1839; died, June 10, 1858.
Elizabeth Harlan Walker, wife of J. A. Walker, Jan. 8, 1819-Feb. 20, 1888.
Jacob Harlan (Lincoln County, Ky.), April 14, 1786-July 22, 1866.
Willie Clegett Harlan, son of W. G. and Lettie D. C. Harlan, Oct. 1, 1874-Nov. 7, 1874.
Samuel J. Harlan, son of H. G. and J. Z. Harlan, June 2, 1870-June 9, 1870.
Infant son of H. G. and Josephine S. Harlan, born and died May 29, 1872.
Lettie D. C. Harlan, wife of W. G. Harlan, April 18, 1852-Mar. 24, 1825.
Mary Ann Frierson Bledsoe, daughter

Bible Records—Tombstone Inscriptions

of Thomas J. and Annie Blakely Frierson, wife of Enoch Bledsoe, Mar. 24, 1823-Feb. 20, 1887.
Medora E. Brown, Mar. 2, 1845-Dec. 21, 1902.
Hattie E. Brown, daughter of S. T. and M. E. Brown, Dec. 8, 1882-Jan. 20, 1886.
Joseph Henry Brown, Aug. 20, 1838-Mar. 10, 1840.
Clotilda G. Brown, wife of David C. Brown, Feb. 22, 1812-Aug. 27, 1838.
David Caldwell Brown, Jan. 21, 1810-June 31, 1882.
Sarah Harriet Brown, wife of David C. Brown, Jan. 1, 1819-Feb. 11, 1848.
Genie Brown, eldest daughter of D. C. and S. H. Brown, died Feb. 16, 1875.
Harriet Brown Fulton, died Nov. 12, 1896.
Infant children (2 sons and 2 daughters) of S. D. and M. W. Frierson, 1854.
Wm. Newel Frierson, son of S. D. and M. W. Frierson, Aug. 17, 1845-Sept. 2, 1854.
David D. Frierson, son of S. D. and M. W. Frierson, Aug. 21, 1847-Oct. 5, 1854.
S. Doddridge Frierson, Feb. 16, 1811-April 5, 1860.
Martha W. Frierson, wife of S. Dodderidge Frierson, Feb. 10, 1811-Jan. 31, 1879.
Mary Emeline Frierson, 1833-1893.
Mary Cayce, wife of Henry Cayce, Dec. 27, 1857 (died; age, 39 years, 11 months, 7 days).
Mary E. McGaw, daughter of Benj. and Jane McGaw, Sept. 8, 1842-Oct. 22, 1859.
Samuel P. McGaw, May 24, 1825-Sept. 21, 1864.
Mrs. E. P. McGaw, April 24, 1832-May 6, 1867.
Henry C. McGaw, Oct. 26, 1844-Sept. 26, 1867.
Kezia Jane McGaw, July 8, 1839-Oct. 8, 1868.
Addie Virginia Armstrong, wife of E. T. Armstrong, Feb. 25, 1861-Dec. 25, 1902.
Mary Gale Armstrong, daughter of E. T. and A. V. Armstrong, July 23, 1888-May 22, 1899.
Aleyne Armstrong, daughter of E. T. and A. V. Armstrong, July 1, 1894-Nov. 9, 1898.
Josephine Whitworth, daughter of James and A. N. Whitworth, April 19, 1862-Aug. 5, 1865.
Joe C. Cayce, July 23, 1857-July 3, 1911.
Clifford C. Cayce, Aug. 10, 1889-Aug. 19, 1914.
Goode Watkins Fulton, son of D. F. and L. G. Fulton, Jan. 26, 1904-Aug. 18, 1905.
George S. Frierson, Nov. 18, 1809-July 28, 1816.
George Frierson, Mar. 3, 1774-April 3, 1819.
Elizabeth Frierson, June 5, 1775-Dec. 26, 1830.
John J. Frierson, Sept. 16, 1808-Aug. 17, 1827.
Anna Jane Blake, daughter of M. H. and S. A. Blake, Dec. 28, 1815-Mar. 9, 1818.
Duncan B. Frierson, July 2, 1835-Dec. 8, 1853.
Infant son of J. B. and A. E. Frierson, Oct. 11, 1830.
Ann Frierson, wife of Joshua B. Frierson, Mar. 31, 1808-June 7, 1845.
Joshua B. Frierson, Sept. 9, 1806-Feb. 3, 1876.
Cornelia Jones, wife of Thomas N. Jones, daughter of J. B. Frierson, July 28, 1849-June 24, 1879.
Cornelia Dobbin, daughter of A. and M. E. Dobbin, Jan. 25, 1884-Sept. 22, 1885.
Alexander Dobbins, Jan. 11, 1840-Dec. 23, 1887.
Elizabeth Dobbins, Sept. 1, 1842-Aug. 27, 1907.
The Degraffenreidt family were killed by a tornado on night of Mar. 21, 1835:
Mrs. Sarah Degraffenreidt, 1796-Mar. 21, 1835.
Francis G. Degraffenreidt, Mar. 21, 1835.
John K. Degraffenreidt, Mar. 21, 1835.
Thomas L. Degraffenreidt, Mar. 21, 1835.
Infant son of Sarah Degraffenreidt, Mar. 21, 1835.
Dr. Thomas Degraffenreidt, Aug. 4, 1810-Aug 4, 1832.
George A. Degraffenreidt, Feb. 22, 1831-Sept. 1, 1831.
J. K. Degraffenreidt, born June, 1820.

Bible Records—Tombstone Inscriptions

T. L. Degraffenreigdt (age, 2 years, 6 months).
F. G. Degraffenredt, Oct. 22, 1815.
Susan Snipe, Feb. 11, 1796-Feb. 12, 1840.
Charity Snipes, wife of John Snipes, Aug. 7, 1775-Nov. 16, 1843.
David Snipes, Jan. 22, 1797-April 12, 1860.
Nancy Snipes (Granville County, N. C.), Feb. 4, 1806-Sept. 23, 1866.
Joseph Samuel Strayhorn, 1845-1881.
Joseph Bingham Strayhorn, 1879-1905.
James Henry Askew, son of J. and S. Askew, July 29, 1845-Sept. 7, 1847.
A. N. D. Gunn, infant son of H. G. and Martha Gunn, Sept. 24, 1845.
Infant daughter of Baxter and Nancy Ruten, Nov. 10, 1844-Nov. 14, 1844.
Chauncy Haskins, Feb. 8, 1837 (age, 22 years).
Benjamin Harper, Jan. 23, 1793-Jan. 27, 1813.
Wm. Frierson, Dec. 16, 1767-May 8, 1820.
Jane Frierson, wife of Wm. Frierson, Aug. 26, 1773-June 23, 1817.
Elizabeth M. Sellers, wife of Isom Sellers, daughter of H. and J. Duglas, Nov. 28, 1817-June 21, 1883.
A. W. I. Sellers, son of H. D. and M. J. Sellers, Jan. 26, 1812-July 16, 1812.
Judah Jane E. Sellers, Jan. 10, 1847-Oct. 7, 1859.
Elisa Ottilie Hiller, Mar. 24, 1847-Sept. 9, 1848.
Rosalia Emilia Hopman, May 29, 1823-April 13, 1844.
Jennie E. McGaw, daughter of J. P. and Mary J. McGaw, Jan. 29, 1858-July 5, 1859.
Martha J. McGaw, daughter of J. P. and M. J. McGaw, Dec. 23, 1846-Sept. 1, 1853.
Nancy C. McGaw, Sept. 24, 1836-July 10, 1852.
Wm. C. McGaw, Feb. 20, 1824-Aug. 7, 1851.
Jane McGaw, wife of Benj. McGaw, Oct. 9, 1798-Nov. 22, 1846.
Susan B. Oatman, Mar. 27, 1839 (age, 28 years).
Flavel Frierson, Sept. 6, 1812-Sept. 11, 1836.
Wm. James Frierson, Feb. 22, 1834 (died; age, 59 years).
Thomas Frierson, son of W. J. and E. M. Frierson, Nov. 20, 1806-June 2, 1815.
Mary Elmira Frierson, daughter of W. J. and M. E. Frierson, June 4, 1800-June 24, 1815.
Mrs. Mary W. Dickey, Jan. 1848(?)-Dec. 29, 1821.
Mary A. E. Frierson, daughter of R. J. and S. A. Frierson, Mar. 25, 1850-Sept. 9, 1851.
Robt. W. Frierson, Nov. 29, 1821-Nov. 20, 1900.
Thos. Gadsden Frierson, Feb. 4, 1813-Oct. 23, 1874.
Sarah Frierson, Mar. 28, 1794-Nov. 20, 1867.
David Frierson, June 23, 1778-Feb. 29, 1828.
Elizabeth A. Frierson, wife of David Frierson, Sept. 3, 1782-June 17, 1810.
Martha F. Frierson, wife of John W. Frierson, April 30, 1806-June 21, 1835.
Lucy Ann Frierson, wife of J. W. Frierson, June 3, 1807-Nov. 16, 1838.
Luthbury Mosley Frierson, son of J. W. and L. A. Frierson, Nov. 4, 1838-Dec. 29, 1838.
Susan Elizabeth Frierson, daughter of John Wilson and Martha Frierson, June 27, 1827-Oct. 6, 1841.
John Willison Frierson, Aug. 8, 1802-Dec. 26, 1859.
Edward C. Frierson, July 15, 1841-Sept. 4, 1869.
Rev. Wm. James Frierson, 1837-1917.
Lillian Johnson Houser, wife of John F. Houser, 1873-1905.
Rebecca Frierson, wife of Rev. W. J. Frierson, Aug. 2, 1834-May 28, 1898.
Johannah Amelia Houser, wife of John Goodloupe Houser.
Moritz Wm. Houser, Dec. 26, 1821-April 25, 1851.
Christianna Houser, wife of Henry D. Houser.
Henry David Houser (Saxony, Germany), Jan. 28, 1795-Oct. 20, 1854.
Johannah A. Houser, wife of John Frederick Houser.
John F. Houser, Mar. 15, 1824-Oct. 7, 1892.
A. Johanna Houser, Feb. 5, 1872 (died; age, 47 years).
Carrie Bingham Armstrong, wife of Sam Armstrong, Sept. 8, 1864-Sept. 14, 1930.

Bible Records—Tombstone Inscriptions

Lawrence Ludlow Dickey, Oct. 29, 1813-Aug., 1828.
Margaret Gordon Dickey, April 5, 1793-Sept. 25, 1815.
Wm. Stuart Fleming, Mar. 15, 1795-May 27, 1816.
Mary J. Frierson (Williamsburg District, S. C.), Jan., 1777-Jan. 24, 1864.
Robert Frierson (South Georgia), Mar. 6, 1743-June, 1808 (Franklin, Tenn.).
Rev. Duncan Brown, D.D. (Robertson County, N. C.), Oct. 3, 1771-July 6, 1861.
D. A. Davidson, 1826-1907.
Josephine Davidson, wife of D. A. Davidson, Aug. 3, 1894 (died; age, 52 years).
W. O. Davidson, 1866-1904.
Jos. Dobbins Davidson, 1862-1903.
James Bingham, companion of E. H. Bingham, Oct. 15, 1794-Sept. 21, 1841.
Ella Walton Brown, daughter of I. E. and S. E. Brown, Mar. 3, 1850-Sept. 1, 1900.
Foster Brown, Nov. 27, 1931 (died; age, 54 years).
Sally Ann Brown, wife of F. Brown, Sept. 4, 1883-June 28, 1903.
Sarah Elizabeth Brown, wife of Ira E. Brown, Jan. 28, 1828-Sept. 8, 1898.
Stella Coffey, Mar. 26, 1884-Nov. 16, 1897.
Sarah E. Cooper, wife of Thos S. Cooper, Aug. 24, 1828-Nov. 22, 1904.
Thomas S. Cooper, Sept. 5, 1834-Feb. 6, 1923.
M. A. Duke, Feb. 2, 1930 (died; age, 78 years, 4 months, 18 days).
Francis Stephenson Fleming, wife of James H. Fleming, June 26, 1879-Aug. 6, 1908.
James Sam Foster, son of Wm. M. Foster, Oct. 3, 1860-Sept. 16, 1887.
M. J. Foster, Dec. 28, 1885-July 29, 1906.
W. M. Foster, June 17, 1835-June 1, 1906.
Cora E. Frierson, 1858-1892.
Harriet A. Frierson, Sept. 4, 1833-May 27, 1900.
Harriet Nuel Frierson (Washington County, Mo.), Nov. 8, 1822-Oct. 17, 1898 (Irondale, Mo.).
James H. Frierson, May 8, 1885-Aug. 30, 1899.
Rev. J. Simpson Frierson (Maury County, Tenn.), July 22, 1825-Feb. 23, 1889.
Samuel Frierson, Dec. 15, 1765-July 9, 1815.
Sarah Frierson, July 15, 1768-Jan. 4, 1820.
Theodore Frierson, April 5, 1826-Mar. 19, 1898.
Grace Hendrick, wife of John T. Hendrick, April 24, 1890; age, 28 years.
John Thilman Hendrick, Nov. 30, 1859-April 19, 1895.
Theodore Grace Hendrick, Dec. 5, 1889-April 24, 1906.
Dora C. Houser, daughter of C. E. and E. J. Houser, Aug., 1859-July, 1922.
Eleanor J. Cooper Houser, daughter of Col. R. M. and Katie Cooper, wife of Charles E. Houser; born, Oct. 26, 1824; married, Dec. 25, 1848; died, Aug. 16, 1914.
Mrs. Mary Johnson, Mar. 31, 1931 (died; age, 69 years, 8 months, 10 days).
William Linn, May, 1750-Oct. 10, 1835.
Catherine G. Littlefield, wife of Dr. John Littlefield, died June 19, 1832.
Elizabeth Littlefield, died Oct. 1, 1827.
Mrs. Elizabeth Littlefield, Aug. 19, 1822 (died; age, 60 years).
Francis B. Littlefield, Jan. 4, 1826 (died; age, 15 years).
Dr. John Littlefield, July, 1801-Feb. 21, 1848.
Capt. William Littlefield, Nov. 1, 1822 (died; age, 70 years).
Dr. John J. Long, Mar. 2, 1773-Oct. 21, 1816.
Burchet T. Macon, Dec. 25, 1791-Sept. 21, 1851.
Eliza J. Macon, Nov. 8, 1821-Jan. 30, 1844.
Gabriel L. Macon, Aug. 6, 1795-Sept. 23, 1840.
Maj. John Macon, Mar. 10, 1755-Feb. 12, 1828.
Albert Winfield Mayes, 1863-1908.
M. G. McKnight, April 7, 1849-Aug. 13, 1898.
Mrs. Levinia B. Newsum, wife of Robert B. Newsum of Halifax, N. C.
David W. Peeler, Oct. 17, 1817-Aug. 15, 1893.
Martha Ann Perry, wife of Wm. Perry, Jr. (Warren County, N. C.), Oct. 10, 1817-June 23, 1852 (Wayland Springs, Lawrence County, Tenn.).

Bible Records—Tombstone Inscriptions

Sophronia Perry, Nov. 28, 1851-Nov. 22, 1862.
Isaac A. Robinson, Nov. 2, 1818-Sept. 2, 1846.
Enoch B. Stephenson, 1880-1920.
James M. A. Stephenson, May 18, 1850-July 17, 1890.
Mary Bledsoe Stephenson, Sept. 29, 1850-Sept. 14, 1920.
William White Stephenson, Sept. 24, 1844-Aug. 17, 1915.
William James Thomas, Oct. 20, 1879-Oct. 31, 1912.
John H. Turnbow, son of T. H. and M. A. Turnbow, Mar. 5, 1857-Feb. 17, 1872.
William Walston, soldier of the American Revolution.
Ann Eliza Wilkes, died, 1878.
Clement J. Wilkes, died, 1852.
Jane Clement Joanna Wilkes, daughter of James and Mary J. Wilkes, Oct. 19, 1848-Sept. 28, 1852.
James H. Wilkes, Nov. 5, 1808-June, 1879.
Leila Ada Wilkes, infant daughter of James H. and Mary J. Wilkes, July 12, 1855-Aug. 28, 1855.
Mary J. Wilkes, died Sept., 1873.
Infant son of Duke and Mary Williams, Sept. 2, 1825.
John Young, Aug. 21, 1929 (died; age, 87 years, 6 months, 10 days).

John Matthews Cemetery

Six miles south of Columbia, Tenn. Presented to the Maury County Historical Society, Columbia, Tenn., Dec. 1, 1909, by the compiler, Lizzie J. Hart, age, 73, daughter of James W. Matthews and Sarilda Katherine Matthews.

Agnes S. Patterson, Nov. 2, 1824-Aug. 7, 1853.
Ella Spain Barnett, Sept. 19, 1855-Aug. 29, 1894.
Nevel Spain, Nov. 9, 1796-June 6, 1856.
Sarah L. Spain, Sept. 5, 1814-June 4, 1892.
John A. Benderman, Nov. 17, 1808-Sept. 20, 1811.
Margarette Matthews, died, 1811.
Agnes Matthews, Mar. 2, 1792-Oct. 7, 1847.
Sarah Tennessee Davis, died Oct. 4, 1847.
Jennie Matthews, Dec. 12, 1792-May 24, 1864.
In memory of infant daughter of Abner and Asena Matthews; age, 28 hours.
Sacred to the memory of James Matthews, Aug. 12, 1739-Mar. 15, 1825.
In memory of Mary Matthews, who departed this life Mar. 4, 1853, near 84 years.
Sacred to the memory of Joseph N. Matthews, June 9, 1836-May 7, 1837.
Willie K. Matthews, born Feb. 15, 1822; age, 22 years.
Samuel Matthews, born Oct. 18, 1821; age, 6 years.
Annie Baldridge, Mar. 2, 1807-April 2, 1837.
Andrew Hanna, Sept. 24, 1810-July 24, 1852.
Here lies the infant son of Andrew and Naomie Hanna, born and died Dec. 25, 1835.
Samuel Hanna departed this life Dec. 1, 1834; age, 33 years.
Samuel Scott, who departed this life Nov. 4, 1824; age, 22 years.
Here rests the body of Elizabeth Scott, who died May 4, 1829.
To the memory of Sarah, daughter of Samuel and Sarah Scott, Feb. 10, 1794-Nov. 4, 1853.
Here lies the body of Sam Scott, who died Mar. 2, 1829, in the 66th year of his life (grandfather of S. Walker Scott).
Dedicated to Sarah Scott, died Dec. 21, 1845, in 84th year of her age.
R. R. Matthews, Jan. 21, 1820-Sept. 28, 1890.
Sarah Jane, daughter of R. R. and Mary E. Matthews, died Jan. 21, 1855; age, 4 years, 9 days.
Infant son of R. R. and Mary E. Matthews, died Sept. 29, 1844.
Sacred to the memory of Joseph E. Matthews, born Oct. 10, 1827.
James Washington Matthews, Oct. 16,

Bible Records—Tombstone Inscriptions

1811-June 20, 1876.
Edwin Scott, son of J. W. and S. K. Matthews, June 14, 1847-Sept. 3, 1853.
Margaret Ann, daughter of J. W. and S. K. Matthews, May 5, 1842-Nov. 29, 1848.
Elisha F., son of J. W. and S. K. Matthews, lies here, Dec. 25, 1836-Sept. 4, 1837.
James K., son of J. W. and S. K. Matthews, lies here, who was born on the 6th and died on the 19th of Mar., 1834.
Here lies the body of Wm. K. Matthews, son of R. F. and Sarah E. Matthews, Jan. 2, 1825-Aug. 8, 1827.
Robert Matthews, born Oct. 20, 1802; was murdered by some unknown person Mar. 18, 1867.
Sarah Matthews (nee Bills), wife of Robert Matthews, June 9, 1805-April 14, 1884.
Dedicated to the memory of Israel P. Davis of Waxhaw, Mecklenburg County, N. C., who on returning home from viewing the Western District of Tennessee, departed this life Nov. 5, 1826; age, 45 years.
Hellen B., wife of J. H. Courtney, May 25, 1855-Sept. 18, 1897.
Sarah Ann Courtney, born in Dunganon, County Tyron, Ireland, in the year of 1810, and departed this life April 2, 1891.
Sacred to the memory of James Leach, Esq., who was born in the year 1775; died, Aug. 5, 1835.
Sacred to the memory of C. Leach, son of James Leach, May 11, 1820-Jan. 20, 1842.
Rev. R. M. Galloway, Dec. 25, 1796-Oct. 9, 1840.
Mary Ann, daughter of Rev. R. M. Galloway.
In memory of William E. H. Craig, Oct. 23, 1832-Jan. 20, 1852.
Jennie Galloway, wife of James Galloway, June 15, 1802-Oct. 5, 1863.
James Galloway, Mar. 4, 1796-April 18, 1878.
In memory of John S. Craig, July 26, 1834-July 22, 1869.
In memory of Mary Craig, daughter of John and Elizabeth Sellars, and consort of Robert Craig, Nov. 13, 1803-Oct. 4, 1864.
Mary D. Scott, daughter of J. and M. Matthews, and wife of Andrew Scott,
Jan. 24, 1797-Dec. 6, 1869.
Andrew Scott, Jan. 25, 1796-July 31, 1870; age, 74 years, 6 months, 6 days.
Infant son of Andrew and Mary D. Scott, Sept. 6, 1830-July 9, 1832.
Sallie Kerr, wife of Whit Kerr, and daughter of Andrew and Mary D. Scott, Jan. 5, 1837-April 2, 1860.
In memory of M. Agnes Scott, daughter of Andrew and Mary D. Scott, April 9, 1841-May 27, 1862.
Rev. Mrs. A. H. Betts departed this life Nov. 14, 1870; age, 36 years.
William James Walker, Oct. 23, 1851-April 23, 1868.
Martha L. Walker, Oct. 23, 1851-Aug. 28, 1854.
Wm. M. Walker, Dec. 13, 1811-Oct. 2, 1874.
Kisiah V. Walker, consort of Wm. M. Walker, who departed this life Oct. 5, 1845.
Margaret B. Alexander, born Dec. 27, 1822; married to Wm. M. Walker, Sept. 30, 1847; died, June 29, 1901.
Martha J., daughter of A. B. and M. D. Walker, July 24, 1842-Oct. 2, 1845.
Mary A., infant daughter of A. B. and M. D. Walker, Aug. 22, 1845-Jan. 18, 1847.
John A., infant son of A. B. and M. D. Walker.
Joseph N., infant son of A. B. and M. D. Walker, Aug. 18, 1836-Aug. 23, 1837.
Robert B., infant son of A. B. and M. D. Walker, June 3, 1838-June 14, 1839.
Calverte, infant son of A. B. and M. D. Walker, Feb. 11, 1840-Sept. 8, 1849.
Agnes L., daughter of A. B. and M. D. Walker, May 3, 1851-Feb. 1, 1858.
Mary D., wife of A. B. Walker, May 8, 1808-Mar. 30, 1884.
A. B. Walker, July 16, 1805-Mar. 22, 1890.
Eliza Walker Harlow, Dec. 31, 1843-April 15, 1906.
Maggie A. Hanna, wife of J. B. Galloway, Oct. 23, 1834-Aug. 23, 1903.
Infant daughter of J. B. and M. A. Galloway, May 18, 1866.
Infant daughter of J. B. and M. A. Galloway, Dec. 18, 1862.
Samuella Jennie, daughter of J. B. and M. A. Galloway, Dec. 23, 1856-Aug. 11, 1858.
Willie D., son of Wm. D. and M. J.

Bible Records—Tombstone Inscriptions

Matthews, Nov. 30, 1854-Aug. 24, 1856.
Dedicated to the memory of Sarah Matthews, who departed this life Aug. 29, 1855; age, 71 years.
Joseph Matthews, Jan. 13, 1779-June 7, 1847.
W. D. Matthews, Oct. 14, 1822-Sept. 21, 1869.
Martha J. Matthews, wife of W. D. Matthews, Sept. 19, 1822-Nov. 13, 1892.
W. C. Hart, died July 25, 1892; age, 65 years.
William J. Davis, Jan. 7, 1834-June 10, 1860.
Ethleen Davis, Dec. 20, 1859-Oct. 9, 1908.
Charles Wilson, son of Wm. S. and Sarah A. Henderson, died Mar. 15, 1858, age, 13 months.
In memory of Robert C. Davis, born May 20, 1839, and departed this life in military camp at Bowling Green, Ky., on Dec. 10, 1861 (in Capt. Jones Co., 3rd Tenn.).
In memory of James S. Davis, Aug. 22, 1837-Oct. 16, 1859.
Dedicated to the memory of Mary Davis, consort of James Davis, who departed this life Aug. 23, 1846.
James Davis, born in Mecklenburg County, N. C., July 24, 1806-May 12, 1879; age, 72 years, 3 months, 18 days.
Eliza Kennedy, second wife of James Davis, July 24, 1820-Jan. 28, 1901.
Martha M. Burney, Sept. 11, 1835-July 1, 1861; age, 25 years, 9 months, 14 days.
M. Beauregard, infant son of Martha M. Burney, June 4-July 4, 1861; both sleep here.
Mary Agnes, daughter of W. J. and M. T. Scott, Feb. 19, 1868-May 10, 1878.
John M. Scott, Jan. 20, 1820-Nov. 14, 1900.
Eliza L. Scott, Nov. 5, 1824-Feb. 8, 1892.
Died May 30, 1862, infant son of John M. and E. L. Scott, who was born Mar. 16.
David Amis, son of D. C. and S. E. Scott, June 23, 1863-Aug. 5, 1865.
Harris Scott, infant son of Wm. H. and M. J. Ramsey, Aug. 15, 1864-Nov. 5, 1865.
Infant son of W. H. and M. J. Ramsey, June 19, 1868-July 20, 1868.
Wm. H. Ramsey, Oct. 15, 1820-Nov. 25, 1870.
Mary E. Mack, May 10, 1849-Feb. 19, 1875; died in Texas.
Luther Matthews, Nov. 19, 1847-July 4, 1864.
John Thomas Matthews, Jan. 1, 1842-July 4, 1864; died in Mississippi in hospital (in 3rd Tenn. Inf., or was in Capt. Murphy's Co.).
T. Jeff Coleburn, June 10, 1828-Feb. 21, 1899.
Thelma, infant girl of Mr. and Mrs. W. P. Hardin.
Samuel S. Matthews, Oct. 1, 1821-Mar. 4, 1899.
Ann M. Matthews, Mar. 29, 1829-Dec. 14, 1900.
Infant sons of G. D. Matthews, born and died Mar. 30, 1884.
Eugene F. Matthews, Oct. 12, 1867-Mar. 12, 1868.
Gilbert D. Matthews (in J. B. Murphy's Co.), Dec. 12, 1840-Aug. 20, 1897.
R. M. Scott, Nov. 30, 1822-Aug. 15, 1897.
Sarah M. Scott, Nov. 9, 1828-Nov. 11, 1908.
R. N. Scott, July 21, 1864-Oct. 2, 1894.
James M., infant son of W. I. and M. E. Goad, April 21, 1872-Nov. 7, 1873.
Emma E., infant daughter of W. I. and M. E. Goad, Sept. 27, 1809-Oct. 12, 1881.
Willie I., infant son of W. I. and M. E. Goad, born and died July 28, 1883.
Mary M., daughter of W. W. and M. E. Scott, Aug. 23, 1885-Aug. 24, 1885.
Maggie Lu, daughter of W. W. and M. E. Scott, Aug. 10, 1886-July 30, 1887.
Edward McCoy, Oct. 4, 1829-May 22, 1902.
Harvey E. Scott, Jan. 11, 1832-Feb. 5, 1892.
Infant son of H. E. and F. V. Scott, May 7, 1877-May 11, 1877.
In memory of Melvin A., wife of J. E. Walker, Sept. 28, 1848-June 4, 1887.
David B. Walker, Jan. 26, 1880-Nov. 20, 1880.
Maggie E. Walker, Sept. 24, 1877-Nov. 16, 1880.
Wm. R. Walker, Feb. 21, 1833-Aug. 27, 1880.

Bible Records—Tombstone Inscriptions

M. E. Scott, Dec. 14, 1858-Dec. 31, 1899.
Emett B., son of M. E. and M. H. Scott, Nov. 13, 1882-Oct. 30, 1883.
S. M., wife of J. W. Matthews, Mar. 1, 1862-Aug. 26, 1904.
Luther, son of J. W. and S. M. Matthews, Oct. 8, 1882-Jan. 27, 1899.
In memory of Russel, son of J. W. and S. M. Matthews, Mar. 19, 1888-Oct. 3, 1889.
Elven, son of J. W. and S. M. Matthews, Dec. 16, 1880-Sept. 15, 1881.
James Sellars, son of R. A. and S. J. Galloway, Dec. 3, 1880-Dec. 10, 1881.
Adelia Walker, wife of Andrew B. M. Walker, and daughter of P. H. and N. A. Nelson, Aug. 19, 1851-Jan. 1, 1876.
Ella Eugenia, daughter of A. B. M. Walker and A. J. Walker, Aug. 19, 1874-Nov. 5, 1874.
Katy A. Walker, Dec. 17, 1875-July 15, 1876.
Cora Jane Walker, Nov. 7, 1880-Mar. 21, 1894.
Joseph Walker, Nov. 23, 1844-Nov. 11, 1874.
W. T. Walker, April 11, 1849-Jan. 3, 1881.
Sarah W., wife of John J. Walker, Sept. 22, 1824-Sept. 12, 1891.
Annie E., daughter of J. H. and E. O. Morgan, Aug. 28, 1861-July 27, 1898.
Louisa J., wife of J. A. Matthews, July 26, 1828-Sept. 30, 1893.
Joseph Anderson Matthews, born Oct. 22, 1902.
Our Esther, daughter of Joseph and Louisa J. Matthews, Mar. 25, 1859-Sept. 9, 1899.
In memory of Andrew L. Scott, son of Andrew and Mary D. Scott, Feb. 14, 1828-Aug. 12, 1861, in his 33rd year.
Mary Frances, wife of A. M. Davis, July 17, 1848-June 7, 1873.
Addison M. Davis, Jan. 23, 1845-June 21, 1876.
John Matthews, Esq., Oct. 24, 1768-July 20, 1839.
James Matthews, Aug. 12, 1739-Mar. 15, 1825.
Mary Matthews departed this life Mar. 17; age, 84 years.
Here lies the body of James Hanna, Sr., Dec. 25, 1768-Sept. 16, 1854.
Here lies the body of Martha Hanna, wife of James Hanna, Sr., Dec. 11, 1770-Aug. 19, 1859; age, 64 years, 8 months, 8 days.
Here lies the body of Rachel Virginia, daughter of A. H. and M. J. Hanna, Sept. 12, 1849-Aug. 26, 1851; age, 1 year, 11 months, 14 days.
Sacred to the memory of Israel P. Davis, of Waxhaw, Mecklenburg County, N. C., who on returning home from visiting the western district of Tennesse, departed this life Nov. 5, 1826; age, 45 years.

The above is a copy of the inscription on one of the early tombs in the Matthews Cemetery located near the present residence of T. H. Neeley. This was originally the home of Esq. John Matthews, who gave the cemetery grounds and whose descendants have composed some of the best citizenship of Maury County.

The traveling companion of Mr. Davis was my father, Richard Peeples, of Mecklenburg County, N. C. The two friends had traveled through the mountains of Western North Carolina and West Tennessee as far as the Chickasaw Bluffs, the site of the present city of Memphis. On their return home they stopped on a Saturday night at the home of their mutual friend and former neighbor, John Matthews, to rest and to resume their journey on Monday morning. But here, far from his home and family, Mr. Davis was taken seriously ill, and after some days, in spite of the tender care of friends true and tried, he died, and his remains were laid to rest in the cemetery near by, there to rest until the resurrection. With feelings of sadness and loneliness that can easily be imagined, but cannot be expressed, my father resumed the homeward journey alone, taking with him the horse and saddle and saddle-bags and other valuables of his deceased friend to break the sad news to his family.

Some years afterwards the family removed to Maury County, Tenn., and settled near Bigbyville, became identified with the Associate Reformed Church at Hopewell, filling useful and honored places in church and state.

Among these many will remember the late James Davis, whose home was

Bible Records—Tombstone Inscriptions

the present farm of Jonas T. Amis. He was long a ruling elder in Hopewell Church, and a highly esteemed citizen of the county. He with his two wives and several sons and daughters lie in God's Acre near the spot where his father, Israel Davis, was laid 83 years ago. Quite a number of other relatives and decendants sleep near his grave.

Oftimes in my boyhood days here I heard my father tell of the incidents of that trip, of the sickness and death and burial of his traveling companion, Mr. Israel Davis, and of his sad and lonely jorney homeward, all of which occurred eight years before my birth and eighty-three years ago. Nov., 1909.

(Signed) J. H. Peeples.

This record of the John Matthews Cemetery was furnished by Mrs. Oscar Noel and copy of record was made by Mrs. J. F. Draughon, members of Cumberland Chapter, D. A. R., Nashville, Tenn.

LAWRENCE FAMILY BURYING GROUND

On the Jackson Highway, near Mt. Pleasant. Sent by Mrs. George McKennon.

It would be difficult to find a family in this country with any more carefully worked-out pedigree than the Lawrence, and still more difficult to find a family with a more ancient coat of arms. The family in this country was founded by John Lawrence. He was the 16th in descent from the crusaders; he and his wife, Elizabeth, came to this country from England, 1635. The family won no little distinction in this country and has counted among its members generous benefactors to colleges and various New England institutions.

(Copied by Mrs. McKennon, Mrs. Noel, and Mrs. Acklen.)

Johns Long, July 26, 1873-July 2, 1920.
Chalers Q. Long, Feb. 2, 1883-Aug. 3, 1919.
Olivia Harris Long, wife of Johnson Long, Jan. 10, 1843-May 3, 1930.
Johnson Long, Sept. 1833-July 11, 1913; member of Bigby Gray, 3rd Reg. Tenn. Inf., C. S. A.
Harris Long, Nov. 21, 1875-Sept. 17, 1906.
Lucile Gray, Wilie Lawrence, children of Johns and M. O. Long.
Harry, infant of H. A. and A. W. Collon; age, 17 months.
Johnson Long, infant son of C. A. and Martha L. Browlow, Sept. 3, 1904-June 17, 1906.
Lemuel Long was born in North Hampton County, Bryans Crossroads, N. C., Oct. 10, 1799; died, Nov. 14, 1865, near Mt. Pleasant, Maury County, Tenn.
Note: He was the son of Cyrus Long.

His first wife was Tilda, daughter of Ricks Lawrence. Major Long, June, 1831, married Mary B. Craig; children are: Martha (Mrs. James Goodloe), Johnson, a farmer, Drs. Henry and Wash Long. In 1842 Major Long married Saccharissa M. Martin, whose father had removed from Cumberland Gap to Columbia about 1810. Century Review of Maury County.
Eugenie C. W., daughter of F. and L. R. Wilson, wife of Dr. W. Long, Oct. 26, 1845-July 19, 1880.
John Long, son of Lemuel and Matilda Long, his wife, departed this life Sept. 24, 1829; born, Oct. 11, 1828.
Joseph Long, son of Lemuel and Mary M. Long, Feb. 29, 1837-June 25, 1840; killed in a cotton gin and millhouse.
Mary M. Long, wife of Lemuel Long, and daughter of Wm. and Mary Craig, Nov. 8, 1813-Dec. 1, 1841.
Susan Virginia, wife of Rufus Long, Sept. 19, 1859-Aug. 24, 1893.

Bible Records—Tombstone Inscriptions

Kate and Joseph, children of Dr. H. and Fannie Long: Kate, July 16, 1878-July 21, 1885; Joseph, June 16, 1877-Sept. 12, 1879.
Rufus, son of Rufus and Virginia Long, May 19, 1887-May 20, 1889.
Nicholas Hardy, Jan. 6, 1850-Feb. 22, 1914.
Thomas Barrow, Jan. 21, 1818-May 11, 1890.
T. D. Barrow, Mar. 7, 1827-Feb. 20, 1905.
Saccharissa M. Long, wife of Lemuel Long Sen. and daughter of David S. and Sarah Alston Martin, April 9, 1819-Nov. 24, 1910.
Sabra Harris Dickson.
Martha L. Harris, 1814-1884.
Benjamin R. Harris, 1801-1887.
Ben. W. Harris, April 22, 1851-April 8, 1905.
Will H. Harris, Mar. 3, 1878-July 18, 1912.
Infant son of Dr. and Mrs. C. Y. Clarke, died Jan. 22, 1809.
On one stone is "Mother"—"Daughter."
Mary P. Dobbins, June 26, 1831-Sept. 28, 1916.
Nomie Agnes, April 28, 1858-June 6, 1906.
Hunter G. Harris, Oct. 12, 1873-Mar. 24, 1903.
Willis B. Harris, 1841-1872.
Sabra Tool Lawrence, born in North Carolina, Feb. 22, 1787-Aug. 17, 1867.
Matilda L. Long, wife of Lemuel Long, daughter of Peck and Sabrena T. Lawrence, his wife, departed this life July 18, 1830; born, Jan. 26, 1806.
Lawrence Jordon Frierson, Mar. 1, 1892-May 25, 1925; World War Vet.
Mary Louise, Dec. 22, 1868-Feb. 14, 1923.
Luther Lawrence, May 1, 1857-Jan. 19, 1911.
Sydney Goodloe, 1843-1908.
Genevieve Goodloe, May 13, 1890-1891.
Wm. B. Long, June 23, 1855-Mar. 3, 1916.
William A. Long, Feb. 22, 1871-May 29, 1914.
James M. Goodloe, Jr., May 21, 1864-Aug. 28, 1907.
—— Long Goodloe, Mar. 4, 1832-Feb. 15, 1913.
James M. Goodloe, Nov. 18, 1830-Jan. 27, 1872.
Mary M. Hail Temple, Feb. 25, 1857-June 7, 1924.
Joshua Kittrell Hail, Mar. 10, 1848-July 16, 1912.
Mann Dawson Long, June 16, 1876-Nov. 19, 1908.
W. B. and E. T. Long married Nov. 17, 1852.
Willis B., son of Emanuel and Matilda Long, Sept. 12, 1829-April 22, 1881.
Elizabeth Tharp Long, daughter of John and Martha Dawson, Aug. 22, 1833-Dec. 12, 1886.
Mateline, daughter of W. V. and Mamie Wilson, Dec. 22, 1890-Nov. 28, 1895.
Mumford Smith, 1842-1923.
Annie Cecil Smith, 1849-1903.
Alexander Orr, Aug. 3, 1805-Sept. 11, 1889.
Loretto Kittrell Orr, Mar. 13, 1824-June 28, 1911, daughter of Michle John and Ann Hunter Kittrell.
Edwin Alston Orr, April 29, 1863-Jan. 9, 1922.
Maggie Elvira, wife of E. A. Orr, Feb. 16, 1866-Sept. 7, 1897.
Alexander McElwain, son of Edwin A. and Maggie J. Orr, Aug. 27, 1896-April 18, 1900.
John L. Parker.
Same stone: Mary E. Walker, Nov. 5, 1825-Dec. 7, 1898; Walter Parker, July 13, 1838-Oct. 27, 1892.
W. P. Stockard, M.D., May 15, 1815-Dec. 29, 1874.
Margaret Ann, daughter of Benjamin and Mary D. Jones, Feb. 17, 1824-May 12, 1845.
Benjamin William, son of William and Margaret Stockard, May 1, 1845-Nov. 7, 1846.
Mary Lawrence Parker, Feb. 8, 1800-Mar. 26, 1865.
John Green Ingram, Oct. 22, 1829-Jan. 19, 1885.
Rebecca Lawrence Ingram, May 23, 1835-Feb. 20, 1899.
Robert W. Watkins, July 1, 1856-April 11, 1901.
Rebecca Parker Ruhm, daughter of Herman David and Margaret Ingram Ruhm, Oct. 15, 1900-Aug. 10, 1901.
Willis Henry Boddie, son of Willis and Jane Boddie, born in Hampton County, N. C., July 10, 1888; age, 53 years.

Bible Records—Tombstone Inscriptions

Simon P. Jordan, born in Stokes County, N. C., Oct. 1, 1794-Jan. 9, 1887.
Mrs. Martha J., consort of Rev. J. Stephenson Frierson, and daughter of Dr. S. P. and Mrs. J. T. Jordan, Dec. 23, 1831-Sept. 10, 1866.
Emily Susan Jordan, daughter of S. P. and J. T. Jordan, Oct. 11, 1829-April 8, A. D., 1831.
Mary Jane, daughter of Simon P. and Jane T. Jordan, Feb. 11, 1834-Dec. 16, 1854.
Wiley Broddie Francis, son of John M. and Sarah B. Francis, died July 7, 1853; age, 16 years, 10 months, 10 days.
Wm. Jordan Howard, died Aug. 6, 1910; age, 31 years.
Mary J. Frierson, wife of J. W. Howard, died July, 1880, in her 25th year.

Graveyard Adjoining the Lawrence Graveyard

On the Jackson Highway, near Mt. Pleasant. Copied by Mrs. McKennon, Mrs. Noel, and Mrs. Acklen.

Mrs. M. E. Anderson, 1838-1868.
J. M. Anderson, 1829-1905.
Mrs. M. J. Anderson, 1833-1898.
Albert Thomas, son of A. S. and E. T. Allen, Aug. 10, 1906-Oct. 6, 1906.
Willis William Connor, 1846-1915.
Sallie Cecil Connor, 1854-1901.
May, daughter of Newton and Mary Wright, May 10, 1882-Nov. 12, 1898.
Jennie Gray Bostick, 1863-1910.
Merry Bostick, wife of B. 'R. Holbrook, Feb. 9, 1888-May 24, 1908.
Gertrude E., daughter of G. C. and Emma Collins, Dec. 12, 1882-Oct. 4, 1896.
Infant daughter of Dr. W. H. and Pearl Kittrell, 1911.
Sim Wall Kittrell, infant son of Dr. W. H. and Pearl Wall Kittrell, April 22, 1914-May 15, 1914.
Major, son of J. J. and Mary B. Jones, Oct. 8, 1905-June 23, 1906.
Mary B. Akin, wife of J. J. Jones, Sept. 15, 1865-Oct. 8, 1906.
A. R. Kittrell, Dec. 21, 1821-Nov. 10, 1907.
A. Leroy Thompson, 1921-1927.
William S., son of E. M. and M. S. Kindel, Nov. 2, 1885-May 28, 1902.
S. A. Kindel, Aug. 29, 1818-July 22, 1897.
W. R. Kindel, July 6, 1820-Oct. 7, 1897.
Ethel Ingram Irwin, Aug. 8, 1886-Aug. 14, 1910.
Willie Dawson McGavock, Mar. 7, 1921.
Hinton G. Kittrell, June 24, 1845-Feb. 14, 1904.
Floyd Ingram, son of Mr. and Mrs. L. S. Irwin, Aug. 20, 1901-Nov. 7, 1907.
Andrew Walter Ligon, April 24, 1856-Mar. 23, 1906.
Ella Johnson, wife of Geo. C. Boyd, July 6, 1872-Sept. 3, 1905.
Katie Kittrell Harlam, July 4, 1858-April 24, 1923.
Frederic Hardy, May 29, 1849-April 27, 1929.
Harry Green Harlan, Dec. 2, 1860-Jan. 14, 1932.
Infant son of Harry and Kate Harlan.
Dr. D. B. Dobbins, Nov. 23, 1830-Aug. 25, 1903.
Martha L. Dobbins, Sept., 1836-Dec. 23, 1921.
Mary L. Regenold, 1859-1925.
Leslie Regenold, 1891-1916.
W. C. Ingram, April 19, 1837-July 1, 1903.
Hilary Ward, Sept. 9, 1824-Dec. 27, 1910.
H. Ward, Nov. 29, 1832-Aug. 22, 1902.
John Gordon Frierson, M.D., Feb. 23, 1864-Jan. 5, 1906.
Edgar O., son of Lewis and Tennie Coleburn, July 18, 1890-May 1, 1906.
T. M. Halloway, Aug. 11, 1870-Mar. 25, 1908.
Father—John M. Kittrell, July 19, 1834-Dec. 25, 1893; born in Granville County, N. C.
Charity Alston Dawson Kittrell, Feb. 9, 1836-Feb. 8, 1914.
Len H. Bullock, Nov. 6, 1848-July 3, 1890.
Gus Hoge, 1848-1907.
Moses Hoge, 1799-1858.
Cornelius Hoge, 1843-1875.
Gertrude Hoge, 1853-1857.
Eliza A. Hoge, 1816-1909.
Mannie Beattrice, daughter of J. R.

Bible Records—Tombstone Inscriptions

and Martie Rippy, Oct. 11, 1898-Jan. 7, 1901.
Willie Dawson McGavock, Mar. 7, 1921.
Hinton G. Kittrell, June 24, 1845- Feb. 14, 1904.
Seth R., son of H. G. and Mollie M. Kittrell, Aug. 28, 1883-Dec 24, 1900.
Melvin Dawson, May 24, 1887-Oct. 22, 1927.
Mary E. Eichelberger Dawson, Aug. 21, 1855-Dec. 28, 1931.
Mam Dawson, Oct. 10, 1838-May 8, 1921.
Virginia Mai, daughter of Albert and Hinton Y. Kittrell, 1911-1925.
Pattie Jennings Brook, Jan. 9, 1847-May 23, 1903.
Wm. Jennings, infant son of W. D. and P. J. Brook, June 12, 1888-June 15, 1889.
Mary E. Jennings, 1828-1906.
Henry G. Weaver, son of J. H. and Mattie E. Weaver, Jan. 8, 1885-Dec. 11, 1887.

C. B. Walker, 1845-1915.
J. F. Walker, 1836-1913.
Mary Sue, daughter of J. W. and B. D. Hensley, June 24, 1896-Aug. 14, 1897.
Pattie Jennings Harden, 1874-1904.
C. M. Jennings (Cordelia), Dec. 22, 1844-Jan. 10, 1927.
Capt. W. S. Jennings, Sept. 15, 1838-Feb. 6, 1922.
Hershel B. Howard, 1883-1919.
Parlea Blakely, 1824-1908.
Bithea Howard, 1844-1907.
Fannie M., daughter of W. S. and C. M. Jennings, Feb. 27, 1876-June 19, 1891.
Emma Leonora, wife of S. Earnest Irwin, Aug. 7, 1876-Dec. 2, 1905.
Pearl, wife of R. E. Cooper, May 1, 1876-Nov. 6, 1923.
Samuel W. Irwin, Feb. 12, 1841-Nov. 12, 1926.
Mattie Ruth Irwin, July 18, 1849-Mar. 28, 1933.

EBENEZER CHURCH REGISTER

Register of members of the church, giving name of the head of the house, his wife, and their family, dates of births, baptisms, communion, marriage, death, and removal from church. Sent by Mrs. McKennon. Copied by Mrs. Elder.

James Reece, Sen., died Nov. 17, 1824.
His wife, Elizabeth, died Aug. 24, 1821.
Family:
Thomas B. Reece, Asenath, George, Sarah, Ruth, Elizabeth, Flavy, Joel Reece, James H. Reece, Susannah.

Richard Henderson, removal, 1833.
His wife, Jean.
Family:
Rufus Giles, May 18, 1807; dismissed, Oct., 1833.
John Osmon, born Dec. 3, 1808.
William Ramsey, born Jan. 31, 1811.
Ezekiel Alexander, born Feb. 28, 1814.
Tirza Egnew, born July 9, 1816; communicant, 1832; removed, 1833.
James Frankford, born Mar. 3, 1819.
Samuel Caldwell, born Nov. 17, 1821.
Mary Jane, born May 2, 1824; baptized Feb. 6, 1825.
Isabella Caroline, born Mar. 16, 1828; baptized May 1, 1824.
Richard Baldridge, born May 30, 1832; baptized May 19, 1833.

Plum, a black man, and his wife and family: Phill, Philas, all communicants..

Isaac J. Thomas.
His wife, Asenath, born Jan. 11, 1784-Aug. 23, 1821 or 24 (indistinct).
Family:
James Houston, born Sept. 22, 1808; dismissed, 1836.
John Adison, born May 28, 1810.
Isaac Jetton, born June 12, 1817.
Charles Harris, born Aug. 16, 1819.
Martha Patience Green, baptized May, 1830.

William E. McKee, April 7, 1784; married, Sept. 18, 1806; removed, 1834.
His wife, Sarah M., born Feb. 10,

Bible Records—Tombstone Inscriptions

1786; removed, 1834.
Family:
Assenath Caroline, born Aug. 11, 1807; married, May 11, 1830; removed, June 21, 1831.
Rachel Martha, born Dec. 29, 1809; removed, Jan., 1834.
James Hiram Houston, born Jan. 29, 1811.
William Frederick, born Dec. 29, 1813; communicant, Oct., 1831.
Richard Franklin, born April 12, 1816.
Edward Hamilton, born June 10, 1818.
Lydia Sarah, born Feb. 17, 1822; died, June 14, 1831.
Mary Ann, born Feb. 5, 1824; baptized, Mar. 28, 1824; died, July 9, 1831.
Harriet Newell, born Nov. 3, 1825; baptized, Feb. 5, 1825.

Samuel, a black man, baptized, communicant, dismissed.

William Steel Henderson, communicant; died, June 3, 1860.
His wife, Elizabeth, communicant; died, May 29, 1867.
Family:
Alexander Sidney, born July 18, 1805; communicant; married, Aug., 1825; died, Jan., 1861.
William Franklin, born Mar. 28, 1807; communicant, 1832; married, June 9, 1836; died, Jan. 29, 1871.
John Lawson, born Mar. 20, 1809; married, Jan. 16, 1834; died, Sept. 1, 1839.
Marcus Young, born Jan. 15, 1811; died, Nov. 23, 1848.
Eliza Mariah, born Dec. 19, 1812; communicant, 1829; married, Jan. 8, 1835.
Jean Caroline, born Jan. 16, 1815; communicant, 1833; married, Nov. 27, 1845; dismissed, 1847.
Edward Houston, born Jan. 11, 1817; communicant; married, Oct. 31, 1839; died, Jan. 16, 1852.
Michael Baldrige, born Jan. 19, 1819; communicant; died, July 19, 1851.

Lawrence, a black man; communicant; died, June 20, 1854.
Peg, a black woman; communicant.
Mariah, a black woman; communicant.

James Stockard, communicant; died, 1828.

His wife, Susanna, communicant.
Family:
James Reese, April 22, 1810-Jan. 24, 1833.
William, Sept. 25, 1811-April 6, 1863.
Silas Alexander, Jan. 11, 1813-July, 1837.
Joel Brevard.
Samuel Jones, born Jan. 7, 1816.
Ellenor, born Oct. 6, 1817.
Assenath, born May 19, 1820.
Avelina, born Oct. 23, 1821.
Susannah.

Thomas Ramsey, communicant; died, Aug. 31, 1845.
His wife, Susanna, communicant; died, April 24, 1840.
Family:
John Dunwooddy, communicant; dismissed.
Esther Lamirah, communicant; removed, 1831.
Rufus Giles, communicant, Sept. 1835; dismissed, 1847.
Harriet Narcissa, communicant, 1833; removed, Oct., 1855.
Tirzah Catharine, communicant, 1833; married, Sept., 1834; dismissed, 1855.
James Marshal, communicant; married, 1835; dismissed, 1847.
William Henderson, communicant.
Duncan Brown, born Dec. 23, 1826; baptized, May 21, 1827.

Sarah, a black woman; baptized; communicant; died, Aug. 30, 1845.

Franklin R. Houston, communicant; moved in 1829 and returned Oct., 1831.
His wife, Elizabeth P., communicant.
Family:
John M. Dozier, born April 29, 1813; removed, 1833.
David F. Dozier, born Nov. 28, 1814.
Joel Brevard, born Jan. 26, 1820.
James Forbes, born Dec. 26, 1821.
Elizabeth Caroline, born Dec. 23, 1824; baptized, April 5, 1825.
Franklin Hiram, baptized May 21, 1827.
William Sidney, baptized Oct. 5, 1829.
Margaret Emily, baptized, 1833.

James Boyd, communicant; died, Sept. 15, 1825.
His wife, Elizabeth P., communicant.
Family:

Bible Records—Tombstone Inscriptions

Anderson Tate.
Nancy Lamira, born May 4, 1844; received on certificate; communicant; dismissed.
John Parker, born May 4; received on certificate; baptized, Nov. 21, 1824; removed Sept. 16, 1850.

Jane Ames, born May 4, 1844; received on certificate; communicant.
Nancy Ames, received on certificate; communicant; dismissed, 1854.

Tabitha, a black woman; baptized, May, 1831; communicant, 1831.

Mrs. Elenor Forgey, communicant.
Family:
Hugh, married Sept. 25, 1824.
Mary, communicant; married, Sept. 29, 1825.
Nancy.
Andrew.
John.
Samuel Scott.
James, born Aug. 18, 1797; married, Jan. 24, 1819; died, Oct. 10, 1835.

Edward R. Houston, communicant; removal, 1833.
His wife, Mary, communicant; died, May 15, 1828.
Family:
James F. Houston, born Sept. 7, 1818; removal, Jan., 1833.
William Henderson, Mar. 31, 1821-May 15, 1828.
John Tate, born July 28, 1823.
Mary, Assenath, Lydia, born Jan. 5, 1827; baptized, 1827.

Andrew McCarty, removal, 1824.
His wife, Ruth, communicant.
family:
Minerva Cowan, born June 23, 1809; removal, 1824.
David Franklin, born July 1, 1810.
James Reese, born Dec. 12, 1811.
William Wriley, born Jan. 6, 1813.
Andrew Hervey, born Mar. 9, 1814.
Ruth Lovenah, born Dec. 4, 1815.
John Leroy, born Jan. 10, 1817.
Elizabeth L., born Sept. 29, 1818.
Sarah Susannah, born April 24, 1820.
Nancy Caroline, born Aug. 2, 1821.
Jane Moriah, born Sept. 4, 1823.

Edward Hudson, communicant; died, Feb. 25, 1826.
His wife, Assenath, communicant.
Family:
Prudence, born Feb. 24, 1800; communicant; died, Oct., 1824.
Syrene, born Nov. 28, 1801.
Nancy, born April 6, 1803.
Richard Davis, born Dec. 23, 1805.
Elizabeth Brevard, born Dec. 3, 1807.
Charlotte McCauly, Nov. 27, 1809; communicant; married, Dec. 19, 1832; died, June 3, 1833; removal, Dec. 1832.
Greenup, born Jan. 27, 1812; married, July 31, 1834.
Assenath Reese, born Nov. 18, 1813.
Esther, born May 18, 1816.

Silas Alexander, communicant; removal, 1827.
His wife, Sarah, communicant.
Family:
James Orvell, born July 12, 1799; removal, 1827.
William Reese, born Jan. 22, 1803.
George Logan, born Jan. 1, 1805; married, Mar. 17, 1825.
Matilda Sharp, born July 18, 1806.
Peggy Logan, born Feb. 19, 1808.
Elizabeth Caroline, born Sept. 19, 1809.
Daniel Americus, born Sept. 7, 1811.
Silas Grandison, born July 7, 1813.
Sarah Louiza, born Jan. 7, 1815.
Esther Brown, born Nov. 20, 1816.
Franklin Houston, born Nov. 25, 1819.
Rachel Priscila, born Oct. 11, 1821.

Moses D. Harper, communicant.
His wife, Mary, communicant; removal, Nov., 1829.
Family:
Elizabeth Lynn, born Mar. 27, 1814.
Martha, born, July 7, 1815.
Benjamine, born Oct. 29, 1816.
Jane M. Bride, born Oct. 19, 1818.
John Harper, born Dec. 18, 1819.
William Brown, born May 16, 1821.
Samuel Lemmins, born Feb. 4, 1823.
Mary Dickey, baptized Mar. 6, 1825.
James Blair, born Oct. 23, 1826; baptized, Mar. 25, 1827.
Agnes Missinah, born Dec. 28, 1828; baptized, June, 1829.

William Benderman, communicant; died, July 15, 1829.
His wife, Elizabeth, communicant; died, Nov. 20, 1834.

Bible Records—Tombstone Inscriptions

Family:
Margaret Bowman, married Oct. 3, 1822.
Rebeccah.
Elizabeth.
John Anderson.
William.

James Boyd, Com., d Sept. 15, 1825.
His wife, Elizabeth, Com.
Family.

Ephraim E. Davidson, communicant; removed, Nov., 1837.
His wife, Mary B., communicant, Nov., 1837.
Family:
John Franklin.
Margaret Tennessee, communicant; married, Jan. 19, 1836; removal, Feb. 19, 1837.
Ruth Clemens, communicant; married, Dec. 11, 1832.
Robert B., communicant, May 19, 1833.
Curren.
Junius Davidson, born Feb. 28, 1825; baptized, Aug. 7, 1825.
George Washington, baptized June, 1829.
Edward Chaffin, born Dec. 17, 1832; baptized, May, 1832.

George Reese.
His wife, Mary, communicant; removal, Dec., 1827.
Family:
Elizabeth Johnston, communicant.
Alvira Brevard, communicant.
James Madison.
George Monrow, communicant.
John J. Reese.
Mary Billoo.
Ruth Roeinda.
Joseph Reese.
Cyrus Blackburn.
Calvan Watts, baptized June 26, 1825.

Alexander C. Crawford, died, 1850.
His wife, Esther, communicant.
Family:
Alexander Brown.
William Harris, died, 1834; communicant, 1832.
James Madison, communicant.
Prudence Almira, communicant.
Silas Josephus.
Elizabeth Rachel.

Robert Ramsey, communicant; dismissed, Nov., 1834.

His wife, Jane, communicant; dismissed, Nov., 1834.
Family:
Almanse Barthena, dismissed Nov., 1834; removed, 1854.
Esther Oliva.

Mrs. Esther Alexander, communicant; died, 1825.
Daughter, Prudence, communicant.
Mrs. Abernathy, communicant, 1831.
Margaret Doak, communicant; removal, 1822.
Dr. Zebina Conkey, communicant; married, Dec. 18, 1828, removed.
Miss Rachel Reany, communicant; removal, Dec. 5, 1827.
Eliza Henderson, communicant; married, Sept. 6, 1828.
Mrs. Mary Harper, communicant.
Miss Winebeth Boyd, communicant; died, April 27, 1830.
Miss Sarah Boyd, communicant, dismissed.
Fanny, a black woman, communicant, 1834.
Mrs. Fanny Curry, communicant; removal, 1827.
Mrs. Mary Curry, communicant.
Daughter, Sally Emily; baptized, Nov. 21.
Mrs. Sarah Moore, communicant.
Sarah, a black woman; baptized, May, 1827; communicant.
James Harvey Reese, communicant, Oct., 1831; dismissed, April, 1840.
Amelia Thirsa Reese; communicant, Oct., 1831.
Rachel Elizabeth Reese; communicant, Oct., 1831; removal.
Mary M. Reese, communicant, 1833.
Joel Reese, communicant, dismissed.
His wife, Sarah, by certificate on May 15, 1842; communicant; removal, Dec. 1, 1846.

Alexander S. Henderson, born July 18, 1805; communicant; died, Jan. 11, 1861.
His wife, Esther Lamirah, communicant; died, June 20, 1832.
Family:
James Franklin, born Oct. 21, 1826; baptized, April 22, 1827.
Harriet Eliza, born Nov. 15, 1828; baptized, June, 1829.
Susanna Amanda, born Feb. 12, 1831; baptized, May, 1831.

Bible Records—Tombstone Inscriptions

Elizabeth Lamirah, born April 28, 1833; baptized, Sept. 1, 1833.
Mary Jane, born, 1837; baptized, 1837.

David Foster, communicant; died, Aug. 17, 1857.
His wife, Sarah, communicant.
Family:
Elizabeth, communicant, 1833; dismissed, 1850.
Lydia, communicant, April 28, 1850.
Robert Brevard, baptized, 1828.

Angus McDuffee, communicant; died, 1835.
Family:
Margaret, communicant, 1832; died, 1835.
Elizabeth.
John Alexander.
William Niel.
Duncan Brown.

William Therrhis, died Oct. 10, 1838.
His wife, Margaret, communicant; dismissed, June, 1843.
Family:
Nathaniel Green, born May 16, 1828; baptized, 1829.
Andrew Craig, born April 10, 1829; baptized, 1829.
Mary Jane, born Oct. 12, 1830; baptized, July 17, 1831.
Margaret Angeline, born Feb. 2, 1832; baptized, April, 1832.
Luiza Graham, born Feb. 19, 1833; baptized, Sept. 1, 1833.
Samuel James; baptized, Sept. 5, 183—.

James O. Alexander.
His wife, Drucilla, communicant; died, 1830.
Family: not given.

James Ozni Alexander; dismissed, 1834.
His wife, Mary, communicant.
Family:
James Daniel, born July 1, 1822; baptized, May 1, 1828.
Amanda Eliza, born Nov. 11, 1826; baptized, May 1, 1828.
Martha Evaline; baptized, May, 1830.
Wm. Franklin; baptized, May 19, 1833.

Mary Hall, communicant; died, 1839.
Family:

Martha, communicant; dismissed, Sept. 16, 1850.

A. B. Alexander; married, Oct. 5, 1822; died, 1853.
His wife, Margaret, communicant; died, Oct. 23, 1832.
Family: not given.

Zebina Conkey, communicant; married, Dec. 18, 1828; dismissed, Nov., 1837.
His wife, communicant.
Family:
Joseph Joshua, born Oct. 11, 1829; baptized, Oct., 1830.
Sarah Ann Milicent, born Aug. 21, 1831; baptized, Nov., 1831; died, Oct. 10, 1834.

James Magown, baptized, 1830; communicant; dismissed, 1835.
His wife, Nancy, by certificate afterwards; communicant.
Family:
Eliza Jane; baptized, 1830; communicant.

John D. Ramsey, communicant; dismissed, 1831.
His wife, communicant.
Family, communicants.

Robert D. Waid.
His wife, Mary, communicant; dismissed, 1836.

Murell Booker; died, 1863.
His wife, Martha F.; communicant, 1833.

John Galbreth.
His wife, communicant, May, 1833; died, 1844.
Family:
Washington, communicant, 1834; dismissed, Nov. 15, 1849.

Jeremiah J. Stegall, communicant, 1833; removed, Mar., 1835.
His wife, Margaret C., communicant, 1833.

David Turvines, communicant, 1834; dismissed, Oct. 25, 1851.
His wife, Elizabeth, communicant, 1834; dismissed, Oct. 25, 1851.
Family:

Bible Records—Tombstone Inscriptions

Deborah Turvines, communicant, 1842; dismissed, Oct. 25, 1851.

James M. Thompson, communicant.
His wife, Ruth C., communicant.
Family:
Ephraim Woodville, baptized, 1835; dismissed, 1839.
James Nathaniel, born May, 1838; baptized, 1838.

John A. Baldridge, received on examination, 1843; communicant; suspended.

Andrew Wanna, communicant, 1847; dismissed, July 30, 1852.
His wife, Naoma, communicant; removal, 1860.
Family:
William James, born July 15, 1838; baptized, June 27, 1847.
Hugh Brown, baptized, July 18, 1847.

James Brison, communicant; died, July 7, 1852.
His wife, Anna, communicant; died, July 29, 1854.
Family:
William Leonidas, born Aug. 28, 1837; baptized, Mar. 9, 1840; communicant.
John Lawson, born Mar. 29, 1841; baptized, May 15, 1841; died, July 9, 1841.
Lucy Ann, born Feb. 22, 1843; died July 23, 1843.
Mary Leona, born Feb. 27, 1845; baptized, Aug. 3, 1845; died, April 3, 1849.
Elizabeth Frances, born Nov. 8, 1846; baptized, April 18, 1847; communicant.
Malinda Ann, born July 20, 1849; baptized, Sept. 30, 1849; communicant.
Sarah Jane, born Nov. 9, 1851; baptized, Dec. 1851; communicant.
Martha Joan, born Nov. 25, 1856; baptized, 1857.
James Edward, born June 8, 1859; baptized, 1860; died, Oct. 18, 1927.
Wm. F. Henderson.
His wife, Nancy.
Family:
Dovey, communicant; died, 1867.
Naomi, communicant.
Hugh Brison.

John Thomas, communicant; died, Oct. 13, 1858.
His wife, Anna, received by certificate, Mar. 14, 1839; communicant; died, 1859.
Nancy Gullege, received by certificate, June 14, 1839; communicant; died, 1849.
Margaret Stockard, on certificate, April 13, 1846; communicant; dismissed, 1849.

Elizabeth Thomas, communicant; died, Sept. 7, 1845.
Ann Thomas, communicant.
James Thomas, communicant, Aug. 29, 1852.
Calib Thomas, baptized Aug. 29; communicant, Aug. 29, 1852.*
*The above named person, having some 2 years since expressed to several members of the session that he thought himself deceived in regard to a change of heart, it was thought best, as he continues in the same state of mind, to erase his name from the list of church members, Dec. 20, 1858.

Jonathan Amis, communicant.
His wife, Elizabeth, communicant; died, June 20, 1860.
Family:
Jame C. Amis, communicant.
Nancy Amis, communicant.
Felix Amis.
Darinda Amis.

Jonas E. Thomas.
His wife, Martha.
Family:
Elizabeth, baptized, Aug. 29, 1852; communicant.
Miss Martha Thomas, baptized, Sept. 17, 1858; communicant.

Elisha M. Matthews.
His wife, communicant.

Rev. James Watson, communicant.
His wife, Martha J., communicant.

Solomon P. Maxwell, communicant.
His wife, Elenor, by certificate, Feb. 1, 1847; communicant; died, 1866.

M. B. Henderson, communicant; died,

Bible Records—Tombstone Inscriptions

July 19, 1852.
His wife, Sarah J., received on certificate, 1847; communicant.

John Cheatham.
His wife, Lydia, communicant.

Edward H. Henderson, died, Jan. 16, 1852; dismissed, Oct., 1851.
His wife, Sarah E., by certificate, Aug. 29, 1852.
Family:
Cinthelia Castero, born, Sept. 11, 1840.
Nancy Jame, born Nov. 18, 1843.
Alexander Homes, born June 8, 1848; baptized, Aug. 29, 1852.
Sarah Houston, born May 27, 1852; baptized Aug. 29, 1852.

A. F. Aydlott, received by certificate Nov. 21; communicant; dismissed, Dec. 3, 1865.
Jos. Aydlott, received on examination; baptized, Dec. 19, 1858; communicant.

Wm. W. Ramsey, by certificate May 1, 1859; communicant.
Ezekiel Green Ramsey, by certificate May 1, 1859; communicant.
Ann Ramsey, by examination; communicant.
Wm. W. Ramsey, by examination; communicant.

Mrs. C. Foster Williams, by certificate July 17, 1859; communicant.
Lawrence Smith.

The following is a corrected list of members of Ebenezer Church, made Aug., 1872:

Elders—
Solomon Maxwell; died, 1875.
James T. Thomas; died, May, 1886.
Members:
Miss Ann M. Thomas; died, 1876.
Mrs. Nancy J. Henderson; died, Mar. 16, 1889.
Mrs. Fanny Davis; removal, 1874.
Mrs. Ann Scott.
Miss Sallie J. Henderson.
Mrs. Mollie Henderson; dismissed, Aug. 18, 1873.
Leonidas Henderson; dismissed, Aug. 18, 1873.
Minnie Lee Scott, Oct. 7, 1894.

Lizzie Lenora Scott, Oct. 7, 1894.
Allen H. Smith, Oct. 7, 1894.
Lucy B. Smith, Oct. 7, 1894.
Wm. L. Henderson, by letter, May 23, 1897.
Mrs. Mollie Henderson, by letter, May 23, 1897.
Wm. H. Henderson, by letter, May 23, 1897.
Frank H. Henderson, by letter, May 23, 1897.

Louisa Cummins, Aug., 1896.
Sarah J. Cummins, Aug., 1896.
Mollie Flenning Giddens, Oct. 10, 1897.
Bessie May Giddens, Oct. 10, 1897.
Polly Walker Hanna, Oct. 10, 1897.
J. Ed. Henderson, by letter, Jan. 16, 1898.
Mrs. Sallie Henderson, by letter, Jan. 16, 1898.
Henry Boyd Scott, June 17, 1899; dismissed by letter, 1902.
Frank Henderson Scott, June 17, 1899; dismissed by letter, 1902.
Mrs. Kannon, by examination, Oct. 17, 1902.
Miss Lizzie Hall, by letter, Oct. 17, 1902.
Carrie Brownie Giddings, joined the Church May 23, 1908.
W. L. Henderson, dismissed by letter, Sept. 25, 1904.
Mrs. Mollie Henderson, dismissed by letter, Sept. 25, 1904.
W. Henderson, dismissed by letter, Sept. 25, 1904.
Frank H. Henderson, dismissed by letter, Sept. 25, 1904.
James Woodard, dismissed by letter, Sept. 25, 1904.
Gertrude Henderson, joined the Church May 22, 1904.
Minnie Engram, dismissed by letter, May 10, 1904.
Lizzie Cotham, dismissed by letter, May 10, 1904.
Dismissed by letter by the session of the Ebenezer Church, Nov. 28, 1904:
Florence M. Scott.
Sarah Agnes Scott.
Jessie L. Scott.
Annie L. Scott.
Emma Y. Scott.

S. S. Lusk, Clerk.

Bible Records—Tombstone Inscriptions

Received:
Bruce Kannon, by examination, Sept. 24, 1905.
Horace E. Thomas, M.D., by examination, Feb. 25, 1906.
Mamie Giddens, by examination, April 8, 1906.
Sallie McMillan, by examination, Sept. 23, 1906.
Baptisms:
Mrs. Dora D. Wilkes, Oct. 15, 1871.
Daughters of Mrs. Dora Wilkes:
Katie Irene Wilkes, Oct. 15, 1871.
Mary Emma Wilkes, May 17, 1874.
Mrs. Lizzie Hearn, dismissed, May 17, 1864.
Mrs. Rebecca T. Amis, dismissed by letter, Feb. 26, 1890.
Lawrence Smith, died, Sept., 1880.
Hugh Bryson, died.
James Lusk, dismissed Feb. 19, 1884.
William Ramsey, died.
William W. Ramsey, dismissed, June 6, 1886.
Mrs. Jane Perry, died.
Mrs. Dora D. Wilkes, dismissed.
Mrs. Sarah Henderson, gone.
Mrs. Bettie A. Williams, died.
Mrs. Sallie Spain, died Nov. 23, 1885.
Miss E. B. Birchett, died.
Miss Martha Jo. Henderson, dismissed by letter, Oct. 19, 1890.
J. F. Craig, by letter, May 17, 1874; died, May 10, 1891.
James Edward Henderson, dismissed by letter, Oct. 19, 1890.
Mrs. Tennie Thomas.
Mrs. J. P. Brown, by letter, Sept. 25, 1876.
Mrs. Millie E. Brown, by letter, Sept. 25, 1876; died, Mar. 2, 1885.
Col. William Maxwell, died, April 22, 1877.
Mrs. Allen S. Lusk, by letter, April 27, 1879; dismissed, Feb. 19, 1884.
James F. Henderson, by letter, June 22, 1879.
His wife, by letter, June 22, 1879; died, 1899.
His daughter, Martha Jane, by letter, June 22, 1879.
Miss Belle, by letter, June 22, 1879; dismissed, Nov. 25, 1883.
Miss Samuella Spain, May 23, 1880.
Mrs. Nora Thomas, May 23, 1880.
Mrs. Katy Amis, died, June 11, 1890.
Bruce Amis, Sept. 25, 1880.
Dr. Charles W. Winn, Sept. 17, 1882; dismissed, June, 1885.
Miss Maxey Perry, Sept. 28, 1884; dismissed, Dec., 1899.
Miss Amanda Barnes, by letter, Sept. 28, 1884.
Scott S. Lusk, May 10, 1885.
His wife, Margaret, by letter, June 14, 1885.
Master Thomas E. Lusk, Oct. 11, 1885.
Kirby S. Howlett, Nov. 7, 1886; dismissed, Dec., 1899.
James B. Wagstaff, Nov. 7, 1886.
Miss Annie Green Matthews, Oct. 2, 1887.
Miss Annie Louise Scott, Oct. 2, 1887.
Miss Fanny May Scott, May 6, 1888; dismissed by letter.
Miss Anna Estelle Scott, May 6, 1888; dismissed by letter, 1902.
Miss Louella B. Alexander, Sept. 30, 1888; dismissed, 1899.
Miss Mattie B. Alexander, Sept. 30, 1888.
Mrs. Sarah M. Burchett, Sept. 30, 1888.
Mr. James B. Scott, Sept. 30, 1888; dismissed by letter, 1902.
James Houston Thomas, Sept. 29, 1889.
Miss Alice Gertrude Maxwell, dismissed, Dec., 1899.
James Frank Matthews, baptized, Sept. 21, 1890.
Samuel William Scott, dismissed, 1902.
Emma Young Scott, baptized Sept. 21, 1890; dismissed, 1902.
Ernest Mayberry Lusk, baptized Sept. 21, 1890.
William Lyons Maxwell, Nov. 16, 1890; dismissed, Dec., 1899.
Robert Bruce Atkisson, June 7, 1891; died, June 17, 1891.
Mary E. Henderson, by letter; dismissed by letter Nov. 2, 1903.
Wm. D. Scott, by letter; dismissed by letter, June 18, 1899.
Jessie Scott, by letter.
Florence Scott, by letter.
Agnes Scott, by letter.
Mary Trice, Oct. 7, 1894; dismissed by letter.

Bible Records—Tombstone Inscriptions

St. Johns Church, Ashwood
By Mrs. George McKennon

In the Banner of the Cross, a Philadelphia paper, in 1842 appears the first description of the now famous chapel, St. Johns Church, on the pike leading from Columbia, Tenn., to Mt. Pleasant, with the passing of pikes, now merged into highways, it serves to link its 100 years and more to present route no—Andrew Jackson Highway. I quote:

"It was my privilege in the month of Jan., 1834, to listen to the details of the progress of the church in Tennessee from the lips of Bishop Otey, who had just been consecrated. I did not think then that in God's Providence I should ever witness in person the results of the Bishop's labors in the then far-off country. But yesterday, Sept. 4, 1842, which was a bright beautiful Sabbath, I witnessed a scene gladdening to a churchman's heart. I have thought a sketch of it might be interesting. In this country upon the road leading from Columbia to Mt. Pleasant and about six miles from the former place, in a grove of majestic and towering oaks, may be seen a neat brick church of simple gothic architecture; its interior plain and appropriate, and capable of seating five hundred persons. It has just been completed and is the result of the joint liberality of Bishop Polk and three of his brothers. Without aid from abroad, these gentlemen have erected and paid for this edifice and presented it together with a plot of about six acres of land to the diocese. The lot has been selected from a portion of the Bishop's plantation, within a few hundred yards of whose mansion it stands. It has been erected for the convenience of the few families in the neighborhood who with the large number of Negroes on their plantations will make quite a congregation; for the latter class the Bishop has been in the habit for a long time of holding regular services in his own house."

Thus was the foundation stone of this edifice laid—thus does its history show forth the traditions of the South. It has become a shrine to the annual pilgrimage of the church and the public. Its walls envision the scences of peace and war. The white interior shows forth its high ideals, and amid these peaceful surroundings lie the bodies of those departed who have wrought in their day and with the militant throng gave their life blood for their beloved South and its cause. When Hood's army invaded Tennessee

Bible Records—Tombstone Inscriptions

after the fight around Atlanta, Nov., 1864, the route of the army in its march to Nashville lay on this highway. The army had marched over the hills of Georgia, the barrens of the Highland Rim, when it entered Middle Tennessee in the garden spot of which sat this little church.

General Patrick R. Cleburne, whose great fame as a dashing fighter must have projected his fate, raised his hat to the sacred tranquility of the scene and said: "If I am killed in the coming battle, I would like to be buried yonder." The battle of Franklin followed. Not only Cleburne, but Generals Gist, Strahl, Granbery, and Adams, five of Hood's greatest field officers, were killed. All except General Adams and General Gist were buried in the beautiful cemetery of St. Johns. Years afterwards their bodies were removed to their native hearths. Today a tale in stone shows the name of a boy who fell in battle from home (Texas). These men who gave their lives for the cause, believing as did their sires, they were fighting for self-government, could they awake today would wonder and their sons would not accept the two things these brave lives died for—the institution of slavery and the right of a state to secede.

St. Johns Church, a memorial to the South, St. Johns Churchyard a history in stone, whose grave stones bear unperishable records of more than a century.

St. Johns Episcopal Church

Built by Bishop, afterwards Lieut.-Gen. Leonidas Polk, C. S. A., killed at Pine Mt., Ga., June 14, 1864. In this churchyard is buried Bishop James Hervy Otey and for a number of years before they were removed Generals Cleburne, Gist, Adams, Strahl, and Granbery, Confederate generals killed at the Battle of Franklin, Nov. 30, 1864. Tablet at the entrance. Copied by Mrs. George McKennon, Mrs. Oscar F. Noel, and Mrs. J. H. Acklen.

John William Howard, April 27, 1847-Oct. 14, 1921.
Joseph Branch, Aug. 3, 1817-Nov. 23, 1867; died in Desha County, Ark.
Maria Branch, daughter of A. H. and E. N. Polk, June, 1860-Aug., 1860.
Leonide Polk, daughter of W. E. and L. D. Huger, July 3, 1865-Aug. 11, 1866.
Mary Polk Branch, Nov. 28, 1830-Dec. 2, 1918.
Cleora L. Polk, daughter of Cadwallader and Carrie Polk, July 28, 1866-July 15, 1867; age, 10 months, 18 days.
Maria O., daughter of Wm. J. and M. R. A. Polk, Aug. 17, 1839-April 3, 1840.
Rowan, son of Wm. J. and Mary R. A. Polk, Jan. 10, 1835-April 1, 1844.
Robin Ap. Wm., son of Wm. J. and

Bible Records—Tombstone Inscriptions

Mary R. Polk, April 3, 1842-Nov. 21, 1848.
Mary Polk, daughter of F. B. and M. P. Hemphill, Oct. 10, 1887-Sept. 18, 1889.
Leonidas Polk, son of George W. and Sally L. Polk, born in Maury County, Tenn., Dec. 9, 1856-April 3, 1859.
In memory of the children of Andrew J. and Rebecca Polk.
Kitty Kirkman, Sept. 18, 1852-Feb. 13, 1857; born in Ashwood Hall.
Andrew Jackson, Sept. 26, 1850-April 28, 1852; born in Ashwood Hall.
An infant son, 1846.
George B. M. Polk, son of George W. and Sally L. Polk, born in Maury County, Tenn., Dec. 15, 1848-Mar. 25, 1877.
Rufus K. Polk, son of George W. and Sally L. Polk, Oct. 31, 1843-Aug. 27, 1902; Lieut., 10th Tenn. Inf., C. S. A.
George W. Polk, son of William and Sarah Polk, born in Raleigh, N. C., July 12, 1817-Jan. 8, 1892.
Sally L. Polk, wife of George W. Polk, and daughter of Isaac and Mary M. Hilliard, born in Halifax County, N. C., Nov. 26, 1813-July 2, 1894.
Isaac H., son of Isaac H. and Miriam B. Hilliard, Mar., 1849-June, 1882.
Sally Hawkins, daughter of George W. and Sally L. Polk, June 18, 1845-Nov. 18, 1914.
Mammy Sue, Jan. 24, 1873. Faithful to every trust. The tender loving nurse of the 11 children of George W. and Sally L. Polk.
Annie Pillow, wife of Joseph Branch, and daughter of George W. and Narcissa Martin, Sept. 8, 1829-Sept. 11, 1854; married, Sept. 7, 1848.
Narcissa Pillow, daughter of George W. and Narcissa Martin; died, Dec. 27, 1854; age, 8 years, 3 months, 1 day.
Narcissa Kittrell, wife of T. G. Martin, May 3, 1842-Sept. 5, 1904.
Mary Moore Hilliard, daughted of Col. Hardy Murfee, and wife of Isaac Hilliard, Sen., born in North Carolina, Mar. 9, 1786; died in Mississippi, Mar. 1, 1818.
George W. Hillard, 1822-1864.
William Hardeman, May 8, 1801-Mar. 28, 1863.
Mary M. M. Hardeman, daughter of Isaac and Mary M. Hilliard, Dec. 1, 1805-Sept. 30, 1890.
Edwin S. Hilliard, Oct. 5, 1850-Dec. 12, 1920.
On one monument are these two records:
Isaac H. Hilliard, Sr., Sept. 7, 1811-June 25, 1868.
Mariam Brannin Hilliard, wife of Isaac H. Hilliard, Aug. 5, 1824-Aug. 24, 1853.
Mary Hardeman Hilliard and sister, no dates.
George W. Martin, born in Albermarle County, Va., Feb. 1, 1808-Aug. 19, 1854.
Narcissa Martin, Jan. 17, 1811-April 28, 1883.
Capt. Lucius E. Polk, Co. D, 43rd Reg., U. S. A., Mar. 23, 1870-May 18, 1904.
James Knox Polk, Jan. 14, 1882-Feb. 13, 1812.
Sarah McGavock, daughter of James H. and Eliza D. Otey, June 30, 1830-May 28, 1847. On the same stone is: Frances Jane, daughter of James H. and Eliza D. Otey, Sept. 23, 1838-Feb. 6, 1848.
A very unique and symbolical monument to the memory of Bishop Otey. I. H. S. Harvey Otey, first Bishop of the Holy Catholic Church in Tennessee, Jan. 25, 1800-April 23, 1863.
Harry Yeatman, Jr., Mar. 2, 1866-Dec. 20, 1896.
Russell H. Yeatman, son of Henry C. and Mary B. Yeatman, Aug. 28, 1869-April 16, 1893. Hamilton Place, Maury County.
Mary B. Yeatman, wife of Henry C. Yeatman, born in Maury County, Tenn., Mar. 25, 1835-Mar. 27, 1896; died at Hamilton Place.
Lucia Polk Yeatman, daughter of Mary B. and Henry C. Yeatman, Aug. 7, 1877-May 2, 1908.
Henry C. Yeatman, born in Nashville, 1831; died at Hamilton Place, Aug. 1, 1910.
William J. Polk, born in Mecklenburg, N. C., Mar. 21, 1793; died in Maury County, June 27, 1860.
Mary Rebecca, wife of W. J. Polk, Mar. 10, 1797-Sept. 20, 1885.
Thomas G. Polk, 1825-1877.
Elizabeth J., daughter of Dr. M. R. Douglass, April 8, 1861-June 30, 1857.
In memory of an infant daughter of

Bible Records—Tombstone Inscriptions

David and Mary R. Douglass, born Jan. 28, 1848.
Edward W., son of David and Mary R. Douglass, born Jan. 7, 1848; age, 6 months, 8 days.
Joseph B. Malone, July 14, 1834-Aug. 18, 1849; age, 15 years, 1 month, 4 days.
Mary R. Douglass, wife of David Douglass, Mar. 20, 1820-Oct. 6, 1856.
Joseph Andrew, infant son of James J. and Martha Ann Bryant, Oct. 13, 1849-Oct. 30, 1849.
Joel Tucker Craik entered into rest April 28, 1906.
Gertrude Brashear Craik entered into rest Jan. 31, 1904.
Maude Long, 1860-1908.
Lemuel Long, 1827-1906.
Martha P. Long, 1838-1902.
Mary P. Long, 1871-1879.
Cynthia B. Long, 1868-1869.
Ella Long, wife of M. J. Orr, Mar. 10, 1859-July 7, 1890.
Mary Martin Pillow, wife of Gideon J. Pillow, April 2, 1812-Oct. 4, 1869.
Hattie L. Bethell, Oct. 4, 1866-Oct. 30, 1867.
Synthia Long, Mar. 13, 1868-Sept. 22, 1869.
Mary P. Long, Mar. 29, 1821-April 16, 1829.
George M. Pillow, July 17, 1829-Aug. 30, 1872.
Edward Higgins, July 1, 1819-June 25, 1901.
Anne Brown, daughter of D. F. and Anne P. Wade, born in Maury County, Tenn., Nov. 10, 1880-Nov. 6, 1881.
Frances, infant daughter of W. and F. S. McClinch, born Nov. 14, 1850.
Mary Smith, daughter of James and Mary Dawney, born in Granville, N. C., 1771; married to James W. Smith, Dec. 15, 1791; moved to Tennessee, 1810; died, June 7, 1836, at her daughter's, Mary W. Ridley, in Maury County, Tenn.
Wm., son of Willis and Mary W. Ridley, Aug. 23, 1815-Sept. 30, 1839.
Willis Ridley, Sept. 26, 1786-Nov. 5, 1834.
Mary Webb, wife of Willis Ridley, Sept. 17, 1792-Jan. 28, 1852.
George S. Martin, Jan. 8, 1840-Sept. 28, 1863.
Branch Martin, Dec. 28, 1849-Dec. 21, 1905.

Little Louise, daughter of I. A. and M. A. Johnson, Mar. 6, 1901-June 27, 1902.
Unmarked square box tomb.
Fell asleep in Christ in Memphis, Tenn., June 4, 1861, Eliza Davis, wife of Rt. Rev. James H. Otey, born in Oxford, N. C., Mar. 31, 1800.
Martha Pannhill, died May 18, A. D., 1842; age, 79 years. (Born, 1763.)
Edw. Paine, Jan. 15, A. D., 1836-July 21, 1841.
James Paine, May 1, 1810-July 19, 184—.
Robert Paine, Jan. 2, A. D., 1846-Sept. 2, 1847.
Frank Currey, Sept. 2, 1849-May 8, 1851.
Rev. Richard N. Newell, born in London, Eng., Nov. 30, 1796; died at Hamilton Place, Ashwood, Oct. 9, ——.
George Campbell Brown, Sept. 25, 1871-July 23, 1912.
Lizinka Campbell Brown, only daughter of Campbell and Susan Brown, April 6, 1874-Aug. 28, 1899.
Campbell Brown, Nov. 27, 1840-Aug. 30, 1893.
Susan Brown, July 7, 1847-Feb. 19, 1922.
Eliza Eastman Polk, died in Nashville, July 3, 1897.
Lucius J. Polk, born Mar. 16, 1802, in Raleigh, N. C.; died at Hamilton Place, Tenn., Oct. 3, 1870.
Frances Ann, wife of Lucius J. Polk, born in Bedford County, Tenn., Feb. 23, 1828; died at Hamilton Place, May 28, 1858.
James Plunket Brown, Nov., 1909-Jan., 1913.
Rufus King Polk, born in Raleigh, N. C., May 15, 1814; died in Nashville, Feb. 25, 1843.
Sarah Moore Polk, Sept. 29, 1819-July 19, 1888.
Katie J. Polk, daughter of George W. and Jane Polk, Jan. 13, 1887-Aug. 23, 1888.
Sarah Rachel Polk, wife of Robin A. P. C. Jones, daughter of Lucius J. Polk and Mary Eastman, born in Hamilton Place, Ashwood, Jan. 24, 1833; died at Woodstock, Nashville, June 12, 1905.
Ellen Harrell, daughter of Lucius J.

Bible Records—Tombstone Inscriptions

and Daisy C. Polk, Mar. 15, 1893-May 10, 1895.
Lucius J. Polk, Aug. 14, 1854-Sept. 30, 1923.
Mary Ann, wife of Lucius J. Polk, born in Davidson County, July 25, 1810; died at Hamilton Place, Aug. 1, 1847. Monument by Launitz, N. Y.
Infant twins of L. J. and M. A. Polk, died Mar. 25, 1845.
George W. Polk, 1847-1924.
William Polk, Feb. 1, 1839-April 5, 1906; Major, 48th Tenn. Reg., C. S. A.
Rebecca A., wife of William Polk, died at Columbia, Nov. 30, 1875; age, 26 years.
Infant son of Leonidas and Frances A. Polk, A. D., 1841.
Rosa Jackson Eastman, wife of Hyder Davie Bedon, Mar. 22, 1855-Dec. 11, 1912.
Hyder Davie Bedon, Mar. 5, 1835-Oct. 2, 1897.
"Erected by the Woodmen of the World" (Dum Taget Clamat). William Littlefield, Feb. 1, 1845-Sept. 15, 1899.
George Edward Purvis, Sept. 21, 1836-April 3, 1903.
Susie Eastman Purvis, July 19, 1853-Mar. 24, 1923.
Near this monument rest the mortal remains of Martha Louisa Sheegog, wife of Edward Sheegog, Oct. 15, 1824-Dec. 17, 1847.
Jane Sheegog, infant daughter of Ed. and M. L. Sheegog, Dec. 4, 1847-Dec. 27, 1847.
Edward Sheegog, born in Ireland, May 10, 1810-Nov. 14, 1893.
Lieut. Welborn S. McMurray, born in Columbia, Nov. 24, 1843-Feb. 25, 1864.
Col. —— Young, of Texas, killed at Franklin, Tenn., Nov. 30, 1864.
Lieut. J. H. March, of Hardeman County, Tenn., aid to Gen. Strahl, killed at Franklin, Tenn., Nov. 30, 1864.
Col. Robert F. Beokham, Chief of Artillery, Lieut.-Gen. of Stephen D. Lee's Corps, born in Culpepper County, Va., May 6, 1837; mortally wounded at Columbia, Tenn., Nov. 29, 1864; died, Dec. 5, 1864.
Lieut. John Harper, Co. K, 30th Ala. Regt., wounded in battle at Columbia, Nov. 29, 1864; died at St. John's Church Hospital, Dec. 6, 1864.

J. A. Seymore, Feb. 17, 1837-Nov. 21, 1864; Fayette County, Tenn., Barber's Company, Forrest's old Regt.
Private Joel Dubose, wounded in battle at Columbia, Tenn., Nov. 29, 1864; died, Dec., 1864.
Joseph Granbery, Feb. 14, 1866-July 15, 1903.
Mother—Susan Brown Granbery, Dec. 30, 1841-Aug. 25, 1920.
J. J. Granbery, my beloved husband, died Jan. 2, 1885, in his 44th year.
Robert Lee Granbery, Oct. 3, 1870-Dec. 26, 1922.
James Brown Granbery, Oct. 3, 1861-Jan. 28, 1922.
Kathleen Freret, wife of H. D. Granbery, Nov. 22, 1878-Jan. 15, 1899.
H. D. Granbery died in his 54th year, July 1, 1922.
Margaret Treanor Granberry, ——.
Wm. Langley Granbery, Feb. 11, 1863-Nov. 29, 1927.
Major William Langley Granbery, Jr., July 19, 1889-May 29, 1932.
Robert Meston of the County of Surry, England, died May 17, 1856; age, 45 years. Erected by Andrew J. Polk.
Martha Elizabeth, daughter of Wilson and Susan W. Bland, died April 21, 1853; age, 15 years, 7 months, 7 days.
James Hardin, son of W. and S. W. Bland, died Nov. 5, 1857; age, 16 years, 9 months, 5 days.
Jinny, wife of Manuel Donelson, 1810-April 15, 1864.
Caroline, wife of Henry Anderson, died Oct. 3, 1853, in the 27th year of her age.
Frances Anderson, Aug. 8, 1847-Sept. 17, 1849.
Martha Anderson, daughter of Henry Anderson, Mar. 23, 1853-Aug. 1, 1854.
Eveline, wife of Jefferson Jett, born Oct. 10, 1833, Caswell County, N. C.; died, Oct. 17, 1859.
Dr. Edwin Grant, Feb. 9, 1809-Aug. 22, 1866.
Robert G. Grant, Oct. 3, 1839-Nov. 1, 1868.
Avarilla Thomas, 1828-1917.
James Houston Thomas, born in North Carolina, Sept. 22, 1808; died in Tennessee, Aug. 4, 1876.
Margaret Meeds, wife of James H. Thomas, and daughter of Rev. Daniel

277

Bible Records—Tombstone Inscriptions

Stephens, D.D., Dec. 10, 1810-Aug. 12, 1849.
Kate Paine Roache, daughter of Francis G. and Amanda P. Roche, April 4, 1844-Sept. 29, 1855.
Amanda Paine, wife of Francis G. Roche, born near Roxboro, N. C., July 31, 1813; married Dec. 4, 1854; died in Memphis, Tenn., Oct. 14, 1855; buried here Dec. 4, 1855.
Gen. L. E. Polk, 1833-1892.
Sally Moore Polk, 1844-1925. On the same stone.
Sarah M. Polk, 1864-1865.

GREENWOOD CEMETERY

Record given by Mrs. George McKennon. Compiled by Mrs. McKennon and members of Tenassee Chapter.

Thomas K. Hull, Aug. 6, 1815-Aug. 4, 1856.
Elizabeth Wood, 1781-Feb. 23, 1860.
Nancy Keef, Nov. 24, 1802-Sept. 6, 1871.
Thomas Keef, Sept. 20, 1804-Aug. 24, 1856.
Erastus D. White, Aug. 10, 1832-Dec. 25, 1865; son of J. M. and S. B. White.
James Frierson, born June 18, 1857; lived 8 days; son of Sam D. and Sarah E. White.
Mary J., daughter of Thomas and M. M. O'Neal.
Four unmarked graves.
Broken tomb, "Whom God loveth he calleth unto himself."
Conny, son of Jerry and Mary Shea, born Jan. 25.
Patrick Hand, a native of Ireland, 1806-1853.
J. T., son of E. C. and J. T. Sullivan, 14 months.
Sept. 21, 1859-Mar. 21, 1862; age, 2 years.
James, infant son of H. T. and P. Griffin.
Mary Ann, daughter of Michael and Mary Sherlock.
Henry Wilson, May 15, 1814-Jan., 1852; member of the Methodist Church.
Mary Frances, daughter of John K. and Martha E. McDonald, Oct. 27, 1856-1857.
Daniel, Oct., 1859-1860.
Gideon D. Ham, Mar. 23, 1839-July 8, 1856.
Silas Chappell White, Feb. 1, 1850-Mar., 1851.
James M. White, 1802-1872.
Sarah B. White—James M. White, born 1806, Blountville, East Tennessee; died, 1888.
Mary Elizabeth, daughter of James and

Elizabeth Guest, 1815-1848.
Mary Jane, daughter of Wm. R. and Martha Johnson, 1854-1855.
Charley—Infant—Johnson.
Mrs. Nancy Moore, Andrew Moore, April 16, 1810-Jan. 1852.
My son, Alfred D. Smith, Aug. 3, 1833-Feb. 8, 1852.
Sarah D. Burgess, wife of Thomas Burgess, Dec. 31, 1817-July 8, 1861.
Thomas B., infant son of M. and Mary Straughis, Oct. 22-Nov. 11, 1860.
Jessie Ashton, Aug. 23, 1848-Feb. 2, 1881.
Little Mable, 1880-1885.
Henry C. Chumley, son of John and Virginia Chumley, Dec. 24, 1849-1851.
Edna Scruggs, consort of Thomas, 1790-1876; age, 86 years.
Thomas Scruggs, 1780-1845; age, 65 years.
S. S. Cain, 1803-1877.
Elizabeth Cain, 1807-1898.
Harvey Ketchum, son of Levi and Barsina Ketchum, 1832-1852.
Miss Tempy Ketchum, 1760-1836; age, 76 years.
Nancy Bates, consort of James W. Bates, daughter of Samuel and Elizabeth Paul, 1830-1859.
Charles, son of D. and M. H. Folsome, born 1831; age, 9 years. Charles was a good boy.
Mrs. Rebecca Guffee, 1782-1848; age, 66 years.
Thomas O'Brien, 1855.
Fanny, daughter of W. C. and M. W. Porter, 1855-1857.
John Mckliffe Alderson, Nov. 14, 1830-Mar. 3, 1881.
Nancy White, 1791-1872.
Mrs. Ann Burns, native of North Carolina, April, 1763-April 6, 1854; age, 71 years.

Bible Records—Tombstone Inscriptions

Nancy E. Bates, consort of James W., daughter of Saul and Elizabeth Paul, 1830-1859.
Harvey Ketchum.
Levi Harsena, 1832-1832.
Alice, wife of John Lehman, 1832-1855.
Mary G. Johnson, wife of Gideon Polk, Jan. 22, 1813-April 18, 1893.
Gideon B. Polk, Jan. 30, 1816-Feb. 9, 1890.
Octavine Polk, wife of W. L. Murphy, Nov. 22, 1848-1870.
Hillary Summerfield Young, 17— 1857.
Fanny Forrester Young, Dec., 1848.
James K. P. LeMaster, 1834-1835.
John M. LeMaster, 1832-1833.
James Simpson Walker, 1833; age, 45 years.
Mrs. Maria A. Armstrong, 1802-1855.
David Augustine C. Hays, died Feb., 1824; age, 22 years.
M. LaFayette LeMaster, 1824-1825.
Ophelia Lazinka Walker, daughter of Jane and James Walker, 1857-1859.
Chesley Estes, a native of Ireland, 1762-1857.
Mrs. Patsy Williamson, 1777-1854; age, 77 years.
William Voorhies, born in New Jersey, 1779-1857; age, 78 years.
Miss Nancy Sanderson, Presbyterian, 1/73-1851; age, 78 years.
Jaminia Sanderson, 1750-1849; age, 99 years; Presbyterian.
Thomas Tyerell, born in Eden Derry, King's County, Ireland, 1779-1842.
Ben Henderson, husband of Jenny Herson Henderson, 1858.
Isaac Newban Alderson, born Feb., 1828.
Lucy P. Alderson, 1802-1884.
Taswell S. Alderson, Nov. 2, 1802-1842; born in Virginia.
John Hodge, May, 1783-1825.
Ann C. Hodge, wife of John Hodge, 1797-1848.
R. E. East, son of Thomas, 1844-1847.
Mary Davis, consort of Benj. Davis, 1784-1859; age, 71 years, 24 days.
Benj. Davis, July 28, 1778-1848.
Fanny Graves, 1763-1843.
Andrew C. Hays, died May 15, 1840; age, 12 years.
Lemuel H. Phillips, 1818-1860.
Annie M. Phillips, April 8, 1827-1919.
Elizabeth Green Minter, 1786-1844.
Joseph, son of Wm. and Elizabeth Minter, Jan. 22, 1821-Sept., 1829.
Dr. J. B. Green, 1820-1887; age, 67 years.
Sarah N. Green, 1825-1916; age, 91 years.
Herbert Jones Aydelotte, 1876-1899.
Austin Petway Aydelatte, 1871-1845.
Joseph Burchler, Nov. 14, 1796-1845.
Madison Carruthers, May 28, 1825-1826.
Luciude Caroline, daughter of James W. and Mary J. Moore, 1829.
Nancy Jenkins Moore, daughter of James W. Moore, 1811; age, 22 years.
Infant daughter of Mary and J. W. Moore.
James A. Moore, J. S., S. L. Moore, Mississippi, 1860-1861.
James Wisdom Moore, Past Master in Columbia Lodge No. 31, died 1867.
Dyer Johnson, 1815.
Green W. Maxwell, son of George W. and Maria Maxwell, June, 1845-Oct. 11, 1845.
William H. Williamson, son of Green and P. H. Williamson, April 9, 1797-Oct., 1825.
Maria G. Maxwell, consort of G. W. Maxwell.
Jane Sanderson.
Milla Mitchell, 1827-1849; age, 22 years.
Fanny, servant of W. Voorhies, 1859; age, 45 years.
Terry Hughes, Thomas and Sarah Hodge, 1841-1842.
Thomas George, son of Thomas and Sarah Hodge, 1839-1848.
Sarah, infant daughter of Alfred and Nancy Menfel, 1857-1857.
Andrew Lemuel Cameron, 1856.
James Washington Gamblin, 1842-1844.
Thomas Smith Dale, 1808-1846.
Emily Duncan, wife of Lemuel, 1806-1835.
Charles Dillon, son of C. B. and E. A. Dillon, 1824-1867.
Alexander S. East, son of T. and M. E. East, 1842-1853.
Susan Estes, wife of Bartlett Estes, 1767-1852.
Mary L. Kensey, daughter of W. J. and Elizabeth, 1857-1861.
S. L. and J. T. Pickard, 1858-1861; 1860-1861.
J. W. Satterfield, 1795-1853.
Jane Ferguson, 1821-1842.
Anna Grant, consort of Israel Grant,

Bible Records—Tombstone Inscriptions

mother of Cyrus Webster, 1791-1856.
Peter Holland, 1774-1860.
Ennis Holland, 1779-1859.
W. L. Holland.
Sarah Hodge, 1820-1849.
James Lewis Hodge, 1814-1849.
Julius S. Houston, in Philadelphia, 1733-1853.
Ann Eliza Hayes, daughter of John and Ophelia, 1832-1835.
Adelaide Harris, daughter of Adley D. and Naomi, 1856-1856.
Mittleberry Mangrem, 1783-1837.
Clara Mangrem, wife of Littleberry, 1779-1843.
John W. Nelson, 1797-1859.
John Alexander, Stark County, Ohio, 1825-1851.
Joseph Brantley, 1828-1847.
Lucy Virginia Colquit, daughter of W. L. and Lucy, 1852-1857.
John Wesley Colquit, son of W. L. and Lucy, 1838-1858.
Margaret Collins, wife of L., 1835-1858.
Brantley E. Brantley, 1832-1845.
Joseph Wingfield Byrum, 1839-1861.
Nancy Cameron Brantley, wife of W. D. Brantley, 1813-1845.
Julia A. E. Johnson, 1832-1857.
Sarah Elizabeth Morris, 1832-1862.
William Simpson, son of Thomas and Catherine, 1850-1864.
Lucrecia Long, 1823-1896.
Marie Louisa Titcolm, infant of Samuel and Sara, 1850-1851.
Rev. S. T. Worman, 1799-1839.
Lucy Ann McBrady, daughter of E. W. and Sara, 1831-1832.
Old, babe of C. W. and E. N. Old.
Abraham Looney, 1780-1841.
Elizabeth Looney, wife of Abraham Looney, 1776-1838.
Sarah Hardin McNeill, died Jan. 27, 1794; age, 49 years.
Read Lorenzo Don Overall, son of Nathaniel and Ann Overall, Jan. 8, 1805-Aug. 28, 1854.
Mary O'Rielly, wife of James C. O'Rielly, Sept. 15, 1782-Feb. 6, 1827.
Joseph Alfred Walker, Feb. 8, 1810-Mar. 22, 1882.
Abram Whiteside, Dec. 23, 1778-June 30, 1821.
Jenken Whiteside, Sept., 1822.
Richard C. Whiteside, Aug. 24, 1810-Oct. 5, 1852.
N. Wilson.
Eliza Gill Wilson, Oct. 12, 1796-Sept. 7, 1851.
Major Samuel Polk, Nov. 5, 1771-1827.
Jane Polk, consort of Major Samuel Polk, 1776-1852.
Mary Anna Lanier, 1851-1860.
Mary Osborne, wife of E. R. Osborne, and daughter of Julia Towler, 1816-1831.
Caroline L. B. Reynolds, wife of Samuel Reynolds, Oct. 22, 1817-Sept. 15, 1858.
Margaret L. Duss, died Nov. 17, 1855; age, 3 years.
Joseph Alfred Walker, infant son of Joseph and Adeline, Dec. 11, 1815-Feb. 15, 1817.
Adeline A. E. Walker, wife of Joseph Walker, Jan. 5, 1718-Aug. 17, 1868.
Margaret Brown, native of North Carolina; died, 1844.
Infant daughter of William H. and H. G. Slaughter, 1828; age, 4 hours.
Susan Adaline, Robert C. Mildred, G. Martin, 1842.
David C. Brown, Jan., 1804-1840.
Maria W. Fly, 1817-1873; wife of W. H.
Priscilla Brown, 1838-1853.
Daniel C., William C., James C., Charlotte C., Robert L. C., Mary Thompson; children of Daniel and Susan Brown.
Tusan J. Caperton, 1835-1853.
John T. Moore, Morelumberland County, Pa., 1787-1831.
Phoelie Chaffin, 1760-April 2, 1829; age, 69 years.
Nathan A. Chaffin, April 3, 1819-July 24, 1845.
Joseph Spence, 1788-July, 1829.
Isaac Barr, Sept. 26, 1771-Mar. 21, 1841; erected by his daughter, Eliza.
Ruth M. Chaffin, 1791-May 12, 1847; age, 56 years.
Edward H. Chaffin, 1791-Nov. 6, 1856.
John, son of R. and L. S. White, May 15, 1849.
"Our Little Walter."
Saloma K., daughter of I. S. and S. K. Barr, July 18, 1853-1853.
Name unknown, 1816-1902.
Sarah Boardman, wife of Rev. Wm. Mack, Nov. 24, 1826-1886.
Rev. William Mack, July 29, 1807;

Bible Records—Tombstone Inscriptions

ordained Feb. 5, 1835; died, Jan. 16, 1879.
Elizabeth Scoville, wife of Wm. Mack, Feb. 3, 1813-1815.
Cornelia Mays, Wm. and E. S. Mack, 1848-1887.
Mary Elizabeth Mack, Wm. and E. S. Mack, 1841-1920.
Wm. J. Rankin, born in Lexington, Ky., Jan. 5, 1811; died, 1846.
Mrs. Martha Rankin, consort of Rev. A. Rankin, Lexington, Ky., 1763-1836; age, 73 years.
Tomb broken, unknown.
James Calvin Cohea, son of Perry Cohea, Sept. 5, 1819-1819.
Cohea, 1784-1824.
Martha Cohea, consort of Perry Cohea.
R. E. Tuckness, 1819-1839.
Ann Lewis Dale, consort of E. W. Dale.
Edwin W. Dale, 1825-1825.
E. W. Dale, 1790.
Eliza P. Goff, 1811-1861.
Maria P. McKean, 1870; age, 40 years.
Thomas Goff, Nov. 17, 1802-1830.
James White, 1799-1820; age, 39 years.
William Colthart, native of Scotland, 1787-1822.
Mary Elizabeth McEwen, died, 1820.
Sacred to the memory of Col. John McGumsley, a native of Ireland, who came to America at the age of 16 and was a zealous patriot of the cause of liberty during the Revolution . . . although a youth, unsheated his sword, marched to the . . . and fought and bled for the liberty of his adopted country. He was a Presbyterian for many years, a citizen of respectability of Burke County, N. C. The many virtues were characteristic of indulgent parents, affectionate and devoted Christian. He was born May 22, 1760; died, Sept. 10, 1827, in the 67th year of his age.
Mary Cohea, 1798-1822.
Mrs. Rebecca Guffie, 1848; age, 66 years.
Charles, son of D. and M. H. Folsom, 1831.
Thomas O'Brien, Nov. 7, 1855.
Green Williamson, April 20, 1768-June, 1819.
Anne Dillon (colored), April, 1861-April 28, 1880.
Emeline B. Alderson, Nov. 22, 1811-Oct. 29, 1875.
Elizabeth Johnson, Sept. 27, 1845; age, 57 years. This stone is placed by S. B. White, Polly Polk, and E. Campbell, three daughters.
Sarah, daughter of D. and Elizabeth Campbell, Aug. 29, 1835-1836.
Elisha Sutherlin, died, 1811.
Martha Mangrum, May 15, 1784-Jan. 26, 1852.
Minerva Mangrum, May 5, 1850-May 18, 1850.
Benjamin Mangrum, Oct. 10, 1840-Nov. 5, 1845.
William Mangrum, Mar. 21, 1842-Nov. 5, 1845.
Mary Mangrum, Oct. 8, 1811-Feb. 28, 1883.
Thomas Moore, son of R. B. and Mary Moore, Mar. 11, 1839-June 5, 1840.
James M. McBath, 1827-Aug. 5, 1829.
Col. James McGimsey, May 22, 1760-Sept. 10, 182—.
Elizabeth Nelson, wife of Pleasant Nelson, 1799-Mar. 15, 1870.
Mary Gordon Nicholson, 1837-1841.
Rev. Simeon Norman, July 29, 1799-Mar. 13, 1837.
Pleasant Nelson, June 29, 1792-July 27, 1862.
James C. O'Reilly, Jr., Nov. 18, 1843-July 4, 1866.
Mary O'Reilly, Sept. 3, 1782-Feb. 6, 1827.
Elizabeth N. Pickens, daughter of Joshua and Mary Guest, Dec. 24, 1823-Aug. 23, 1868.
Mary L. Polk, wife of William H. Polk, died April 2, 1851.
William H. Polk, son of Samuel and Jane, May 24, 1815-Dec. 16, 1862.
Andrew J. Plummer, son of J. R. and Eliza, Dec. 15, 1832-Dec. 2, 1852.
Seymour Plummer, son of J. R. and Eliza, Nov. 22, 1850-April 23, 1855.
Samuel Washington Polk, son of Reuren and Laura, 1840-Sept. 9, 1842.
John B. Pursell, son of F. H. and Mary E. July 3, 1860-June 17, 1861.
James Russell, son of Poley Russell, May, 1816-Oct., 1816.
J. B. Russell, 1865-1921.
Poley Russell, step-daughter of L. B. Boyd, Jan. 7, 1789-Mar. 22, 1816.
James Sanderson.
J. T. and C. Smott, 1824.
Thomas Smott, son of John N. and

Bible Records—Tombstone Inscriptions

E. H., 1825-Sept. 1, 1826.
Little son of Eady Sheppard, 1850.
Elizabeth H. Smoot, 1788-April 12, 1827.
Sally Smott.
Edmond D. Steward, Feb. 1-Feb. 12, 1844.
Cony Shea, son of Jerry and Mary, June 25-Mar., 1852.
John Voorhies.
Garrett Voorhies and Jemina Ann Voorhies.
Anthony Pillow White, son of Samuel D. and Sarah C., Jan. 7, 1861-June 12, 1862.
Jane Maria Walker, wife of James Walker, Jan. 14, 1793, ——.
James Walker.
John Chesley Wilson, son of Janius and Maria Jane, Jan. 14, 1846-June 20, 1847.
Eliza Ann Wilson, daughter of Janius and Maria Jane, Dec. 11, 1853-April 1, 1862.
George and Cyrus Webster, sons of Cyrus and Eliza.
Amanda Whaley, 1821-Jan., 1839.
Addison Wilkes, son of Charles and Jane Wilkes, Sept. 26, 1830-Sept. 26, 1871.
Harris Richard, Albert Edmond, and Solomon Philip Webster, sons of Cyrus and Eliza.
Mrs. Clarinda Zellner, wife of Arnold Zellner, 1814-Jan. 18, 1842.
Jeremiah Cherry, April 1, 1766-Jan. 29, 1821.
William Cherry, born Oct. 14, 1824.
Kenneth Cherry, died Dec. 24, 1829; age, 39 years.
Mary Cherry, Jan., 1766-May 15, 1852.
Jane Scott Edmondson, consort of A. J. Edmondson, 1890; age, 18 years.
Sarah E. Guest, Mar. 17, 1828-July 6, 1859.
Joshua Guest, Jan. 12, 1789-Feb. 2, 1831.
Mary Guest, born in North Carolina, July 11, 1814-Feb. 13, 1820.
James L. Gunnels, son of William and Dorothy Gunnels, Nov. 18, 1813-Oct. 17, 1816.
Isaac B. Hardin, died June 24, 1819; age, 34 years.
Isaac B. Hardin, Jr., July 23, 1819; age, 1 year old.
Sarah Hunt, April 11, 1829-Aug. 26, 1845.
G. B. Hunt, consort of F. D. Hunt, Oct. 12, 1824-Nov. 4, 1841.
Nancy Hunt, daughter of F. D. and G. B. Hunt, July 29, 1847-Nov. 11, 1847.
A. E. Hunt, born and died Dec. 1, 1831.
Durinda Jourdan Hunt, wife of F. D. Hunt, Aug. 22, 1820-Dec. 2, 1851.
W. A. Kerr, April 13, 1827-Mar. 22, 1862.
Nancy Hays Kenely, Dec. 25, 1810-Sept. 21, 1855.
James Martin Lewis, born May 7, 1762, in Albermarle County, Va.; died, April 2, 1822.
Sarah Alderson, Dec. 3, 1768-Mar. 15, 1854.
John S. Alderson, native of Virginia, Jan. 16, 1779-May 29, 1852.
Monroe Alford, C. S. A., May 25, 1837-Dec. 14, 1904.
William Henry Ament, Jan. 23, 1850-Jan. 7, 1852.
Mrs. Sarah Alston, wife of Colonel P. D. Franklin, Sept. 4, 1794-April 18, 1862.
Betsy Ann Boyd, Feb. 8, 1814-Sept. 26, 1816.
Land B. Boys, Mar. 10, 1775-Jan. 30, 1843.
Hamilton Brown, son of Dr. Thomas and Eliza, Feb. 14, 1829-April 4, 1838.
Cordelia Brown, daughter of Dr. Thomas and Eliza and wife of Dr. Wm. Watt of Fayette County, Dec. 5, 1825-Sept. 6, 1845.
Dr. Thomas Brown, native of North Carolina, died Aug. 2, 1834.
Eliza Brown, Jan. 17, 1801-Feb. 19, 1841.
Mary E. Bailey, daughter of A. D. and E. N. Bailey, Sept. 18, 1840-Sept. 20, 1841.
Augustus Bailey, Mar. 10, 1815-Feb. 22, 1844.
Lucinda M. Boyd, Dec. 7, 1810-Oct. 22, 1811.
Louisa A. Boyd, May 29, 1809-Sept. 30, 1814.
William D. Bradshaw, son of Americus and Mary, July 24, 1840-Dec. 2, 1851.
William G. Connelly, son of J. M. and M. E. Connelly, Feb. 28, 1876-Sept. 26, 1871.
Mary Collins, July 18, 1841-Feb. 12, 1848.

Bible Records—Tombstone Inscriptions

Demsy Cherry, April 1, 1802-Oct. 24, 1835.
Thomas Colquit, son of William and Lucy E., Sept. 28-Oct. 17, 1842.
Schilde Elizabeth Cherry, 1802-1849.
Samuel Crockett Davis, Dec. 11, 1811-Sept. 6, 1812.
Ellen Duke, Oct. 7, 1874-Nov. 12, 1922.
Nancy Duke, July 6, 1893-May 10, 1931.
Thomas Elmore, Nov. 15, 1817-Feb. 15, 1852.
Augustus Guest, son of J. L. and E. J. Guest, Nov. 10, 1841-Oct. 3, 1866.
Connelly Gillespie, son of G. M. and N. Gillespie, born Mar. 20, 1888.
Eliza Harriet Graham, consort of Charles Graham, daughter of Elizabeth C. McDaniels, 1810-Aug. 5, 1835.
Eliza M. Hitchcock, daughter of L. and J., Dec. 5, 1812-Oct. 27, 1815.
Nancy M. Hitchcock, daughter of L. and J., May 15, 1822-Aug. 9, 1823.
John Elliot Horton, Delaware County, Va., Jan. 1, 1814-Nov. 10, 1836.
Josiah Swanson Harris, Dec. 20, 1818-Mar. 17, 1860.
Winnie M. Hilliard, wife of A. Hilliard, Nov. 13, 1813-Oct. 18, 1815.
Anderson Hilliard, July 12, 1809-April 1, 1831.
Frank Hilliard, June 1, 1841-Feb. 23, 1869.
Lena Hilliard, Aug. 17, 1867-Feb. 21, 1869.
William Warner Harris, son of Adloio and Mary B., Dec. 25, 1838-Mar. 1, 1839.
Samuel Hayes, son of John B. and Ophelia C., Aug. 24, 1812-Oct. 28, 1813.
Joseph Hobson, son of William L. and Lucy E. Colquit, May 12-July 2, 1849.
B. A. and A. H. H., no dates.

Mrs. Ophelia C. Hayes, Sept. 6, 1812-April 18, 1852.
Neoma Leetch Harris, wife of Adlai O., July 2, 1809-Aug. 2, 1836.
Elizabeth Hays, wife of Ausbern, 1822-Feb. 13, 1852.
Alex B. Johnson, Mar. 8, June 12, 1857.
Charlie Johnson, son of H. C. and M. T., July, 1859-July 28, 1860.
Mrs. Martha Jennings, Dec. 6, 1773-May 20, 1844.
Lucy Jordan, wife of John A., Nov. 2, 1812-Mar. 19, 1850.
Julia Johnson, 1820-1848.
Elizabeth Johnson, 1820-1891.
Dyer Johnson, 1815-1871.
Clara King, 1792-1864.
Andrew M. Kerr, Oct. 7, 1820-Dec. 20, 1843.
Ophelia Josephine Kirby, daughter of L. W. and H. A., Aug. 10, Dec. 10, 1813.
Rosanna Knox.
William A. Knox.
Mary E. Knox.
Julia E. Kimbell, Dec., 1822-May 9, 1853.
W. A. Kerr, April 13, 1827-Mar. 22, 1862.
W. O. Kerr, son of W. A. and J. B. Kerr, Aug. 2, 1856-July 31, 1861.
G. W. Langley.
E. J. Langley.
G. S. Langley.
Mrs. Jane Virginia Lee, Sept. 11, 1830-Sept 19, 1857.
Sara Lester, daughter of E. I. and Sara; age, 7 years.
Sallie Betty Looney, daughter of Robert and Louisa Looney, Dec. 25, 1818-Jan. 25, 1850.

Graves on Farm

Graves on the farm of Mrs. T. F. Holden, Eagleville Pike, near Murfreesboro. Copied by Miss Jetton, Mrs. Landis, and Mrs. Elder.

Sally Ransom, June, 1789-June, 1860.
Benjamin C. Ransom, Dec., 1787-1844.
Mrs. Jane P., wife of D. Jarratt, Sept. 18, 1824-April 14, 1869.
John M., son of D. and J. Jarratt, May 26, 1859-April 12, 1867.

Altazeras, wife of James P. Hollowell, Oct. 24, 1844-Feb. 11, 1884.
Daver —ux Jarratt, June 10, 1813-Oct. 25, 1866.
Mrs. Louisa W. Jarratt, Feb. 15, 1816-Jan. 27, 1890.

Bible Records—Tombstone Inscriptions

Thomas J. Jarratt, Sept. 26, 1804-Sept. 27, 1877.
Robert May, Feb. 18, 1781-Nov. 7, 1857.
Susan G. May, Nov. 3, 1794-April 27, 1872.
Robert B. Smotherman, Oct. 17, 1818-May 19, 1869.
Mary N. Manier, Nov. 28, 1824-Dec. 24, 1899.
Lemuel Mame, June 18, 1829-Mar. 20, 1898.
Rev. Jack Holt, Sept. 30, 1854-Nov. 20, 1924.
Wife, Susie Holt, Aug. 25, 1852-Mar. 20, 1924.

FARM OF MRS. C. N. TAYLOR, NEAR EAGLEVILLE

Capt. Robert Wilson, 1760-1819.
Jane Wilson, 1761-1853.
Lucinda W. Calhoon, July 30, 1803-Aug. 20, 1830.
Robert Wilson Hemphill, Dec. 3, 1830-Sept. 11, 1849.
Charles H. Hemphill, Aug. 10, 1826-Aug. 23, 1830.
Thomas Wilson, 1796-1811.
Miss Jetton says that Capt. Robert Wilson was the first man to cross the Cumberland Mountains in a wagon. He was the son of Robert W. and Eleanor Wilson; they had eleven sons; seven sons were in service in the Revolutionary Army. The farm on which these graves are located was given for service. The family came from North Carolina.
Jane Wilson was the daughter of William McDowell and his wife, Ellen.

FARM OF THE REV. MCPHERSON

On the farm of the Rev. McPherson is the grave of William McDowell; born in Scotland; died, Jan. 12, 1864.

FARM OF EARL MCKNIGHT

Near Puckett's Store on Eagleville Pike. Copied by Mrs. Landis and Mrs. Elder.

Mary P. Cole, wife of W. G. Cole, Feb. 5, 1866-Aug. 27, 1913.
J. Edmund Reid, Nov. 22, 1858-May 24, 1913.
Mary Lytle Cooper, Feb. 3, 1901-Oct. 24, 1915.
Jennings Cecil Cooper, Oct. 5, 1897-Oct. 2, 1898.
Susanna L., wife of E. C. Reid, Mar. 15, 1854-Aug. 11, 1878.
Anne E. Hays, July 18, 1865-June 14, 1882.
Minervi Hays, Oct. 11, 1825-Sept. 7, 1888.
J. G. Reid, Sept. 27, 1827-Mar. 18, 1902.
Catharine Reid, wife of J. S. Reid, May 18, 1824-Dec. 3, 1893.
Mary J. Reid, daughter of J. G. and C. Reid, July 27, 1858-July 6, 1884.
Elizabeth L. Reid, daughter of J. G. and C. Reid, Dec. 8, 1855-June 4, 1885.
Cyrene E. Read, June 7, 1854-June 13, 1913.
Tabitha, daughter of H. P. and Rachel Reid, Dec. 25, 1877-Jan. 2, 1881.
Martha G., daughter of C. I. and B. L. Read, April 19, 1862-July 31, 1883.
R. L. Read, Oct. 22, 1824-Dec. 1, 1905.
Infant son of Wm. C. Read, no dates, part gone.
E. C. Reid, April 11, 1884-Sept. 20, 1885.
R. R. Manier, Jan. 16, 1855-Mar. 23, 1916.
J. M. Reid, Mar. 5, 1843-Jan. 10, 1899.
Elvira W., wife of Robert Read, Dec. 4, 1814-Mar. 26, 1891.
Josiah Read, 1768-Mar. 12, 1842.
Mary Read, Oct., 1773-Nov. 11, 1860.
Robert Read, Oct. 28, 1796-Dec. 17, 1883.
Robert F. Read, Sept. 5, 1836; died in the fall of 1843.
Eliza Jane Manire, Oct. 11, 1859-Aug. 27, 1860.

Bible Records—Tombstone Inscriptions

Martha M., wife of D. C. Manire, daughter of Robert Read, Feb. 11, 1800-Aug. 13, 1850.
Robert T. Read, May 4, 1853-July 11, 1883.
Otis O. Read, July 22, 1899-July 27, 1918.
Judith M. Lamb Read, Sept. 8, 1861-May 29, 1923.
James T. Read, Dec. 18, 1857-Feb. 14, 1912.
Richard T., son of C. T. and R. L. Read, Oct. 30, 1855-Sept. 15, 1878.

TAYLOR GRAVEYARD

Off the Eagleville Pike. Copied by Miss Jetton, Mrs. Lloyd Elder, Mrs. W. H. Lambeth, Mrs. Robert Landis.

Mary R. Taylor, wife of Vincent Taylor, Sept. 27, 1802-Sept. 20, 1845.
Tabitha Taylor, wife of Vincent Taylor, Sept. 12, 1800-Oct. 22, 1853.
James R. Taylor, infant son of Charles P. and Elizabeth Taylor, Oct. 13, 1849-July 28, 1850.
John H. Taylor, son of C. P. and E. K. Taylor, June 20, 1851-May 2, 1853.
Isabell T. Taylor, daughter of C. P. and E. K. Taylor, April 3, 1855-April 11, 1859.
Thomas L. Taylor, 1812-1876.
The following two names on the same stone:
F. S. Brown, Aug. 30, 1821-Dec. 19, 1879.
Elizabeth H. Brown, June 3, 1823-Sept. 15, 1876.
W. C. Taylor, husband of Martha J. White, Sept. 6, 1860-Aug. 4, 1907.
Martha Jane, daughter of W. M. and Eliza White, wife of W. C. Taylor, Sept. 16, 1860-Dec. 14, 1896.
John Henry Taylor, son of J. P. T. and M. A. Taylor, July 8, 1858-Aug. 2, 1862.
Infant daughter of J. P. T. and M. A. Taylor, born and died Dec. 12, 1857.
Wm. F. Taylor, son of Wm. C. and Martha J. Taylor, Oct. 26, 1861-Oct. 28, 1862.
Nancy J. Taylor, daughter of N. R. and M. A. Taylor, Nov. 16, 1858-Jan. 24, 1859.
Vincent Taylor, Aug. 1, 1797-Mar. 27, 1861.
Margaret M. Taylor, consort of Vincent Taylor, and daughter of Dr. Wm. and M. Cheatham, Mar. 15, 1816-Dec. 24, 1849.
William V., son of Samuel W. and Amanda B. Brown, Mar. 12, 1852-Oct. 2, 1884.
Vincent Taylor, son of N. R. and M. A. Taylor, June 17, 1857-Sept. 12, 1861.
Infant son of C. P. and E. K. Taylor, Mar. 13, 1866-Mar. 22, 1866.
Nancy Jane Taylor, April 4, 1828-Nov. 1, 1852.
Emeline Taylor, daughter of Vincent and Mary R. Taylor, Nov. 30, 1842-June 16, 1857.

MT. PLEASANT CHURCH CEMETERY

Three miles from Eagleville. Copied by Miss Jetton, Mrs. Lambuth, and Mrs. Landis.

Almary Lamb, July 4, 1833-June 5, 1870; married June 9, 1853.
Jinsey Lamb, wife of David Lamb, no dates.
David Lamb, Feb. 14, 1812-Feb. 12, 1861.
Nancy Morgan, 1812-Mar., 1874.
Martha Jane, wife of David Heath, Dec. 26, 1836-June 18, 1890.
Jane Putman J. Carlton, Jan. 18, 1816-Sept. 21, 1840.
Jebin Putman, 1775-Sept. 26, 1835.
John Crick, June 30, 1799-Sept. 19, 1869.
Nancy Putman, Oct. 31, 1819-Nov. 12, 1824.
Martha Webb, wife of John Webb, 1793-Feb. 11, 1842.

Bible Records—Tombstone Inscriptions

Jennie Lee, daughter of B. H. and M. P. Lamb, Nov. 1, 1898-June 7, 1911.
Bernard, son of N. W: and M. B. Lamb, Mar. 23, 1905-May 20, 1907.
Margaret A., wife of Nathaniel R. Taylor, Jan. 27, 1826-Nov. 21, 1914.
Nathaniel R. Taylor, Sept. 21, 1830-May 11, 1888.
Elizabeth K. Puckett, wife of S. M. Whitehead, 1865-1924.
Roy Orman Whitehead, Feb. 7, 1890-Sept. 10, 1911.
William Spencer Puckett, July 23, 1801-July 20, 1873.
Mrs. Lavenia Bumpas, Mar. 11, 1843-Dec. 20, 1895.
Louisa Rutledge, April 13, 1818-Oct. 11, 1888.
Nancy C. Jackson, Mar. 18, 1820-June 20, 1897.
Eliza B., wife of L. S. Whitehead, May 18, 1831-Dec. 17, 1910.
L. S. Whitehead, Nov. 27, 1830-Nov. 14, 1920.
Infant sons of W. P. and J. P. Ray, 1885-1904.
Katie C., daughter of A. M. and M. A. Vaughn, Mar. 22, 1880-Oct. 8, 1895.
Susie A. Taylor, wife of R. V. Taylor, Oct. 25, 1874-Mar. 11, 1898.
Infant of B. M. and Susie Taylor, no dates.
T. E., wife of R. B. Carlton, Oct. 6, 1869-Jan. 10, 1906.
W. H. Carlton, Nov. 29, 1895-Mar. 14, 1920.
W. C. Puckett, Aug. 11, 1855-May 30, 1923.
S. L. Puckett, June 11, 1859-Oct. 3, 1916.
Sue E. Winn, wife of N. F. Lamb, Oct. 17, 1859-July 14, 1918.
Martha E. Winsett, Aug. 8, 1850-Sept. 8, 1862.
May A. C. Winsett, Sept. 23, 1823-Mar. 23, 1862.
Delpha Ann Winsett, Jan. 21, 1853-Oct. 12, 1854.
Delphe Landrum, died Sept. 10, 1854.
Mary S. Hall, Oct. 11, 1830-June 7, 1848.
John B. Lamb, Aug. 5, 1859-April 1, 1882.
T. A., wife of H. W. Lamb, Oct. 10, 1859-Nov. 21, 1897.
E. E., wife of H. W. Lamb, Sept. 10, 1857-May 2, 1921.
Effie Lamb, Dec. 31, 1891-Nov. 31, 1892.
Mary E. T. Lamb, May 22, 1888-July 22, 1889.
Vidie Lamb, Sept. 23, 1893-Sept. 28, 1894.
Benjamin H. Lamb, Oct. 25, 1895-Aug. 8, 1896.
H. B. Carson, June 6, 1885-July 30, 1885.
Mrs. Mary J. Carson, wife of W. H. Carson, Aug. 21, 1849-June 14, 1885.
The following two names on same stone:
D. L. Manire, June 7, 1859-Dec. 26, 1912.
Mary F. Manire, Oct. 18, 1871; died (to be cut).
W. M. Lamb, Oct. 27, 1827-April 1, 1894.
Tennie, wife of W. M. Lamb, June 30, 1887-April 14, 1892.
S. G., wife of T. H. Carlton, Aug., 1829-July, 1883.
R. M. Taylor, Oct. 14, 1820-June 25, 1897.
Mary, wife of R. M. Taylor, Jan., 1818-Nov. 8, 1889.
James H. Cole, Sept. 11, 1834-Dec. 11, 1896.
Thomas V. Cole, Sept. 16, 1870-May 27, 1890.
Mary F. Cole, Nov. 22, 1888-May 20, 1890.
Peany, wife of Rev. John Landrum, Oct. 26, 1817-Mar. 6, 1883.
Rev. John Landrum, 1800-Sept. 1, 1872; son of Reuben and Mary Landrum.
B. H. Pope, Mar. 26, 1834-Mar. 20, 1884.
Elizabeth Pope, wife of William Jackson, Feb. 4, 1823-Jan. 6, 1903.
Minnie B. Edwards, Oct. 5, 1874-July 27, 1912.
Mollie T., wife of J. T. Daniel, April 23, 1858-Nov. 11, 1898.
John F. K., infant son of J. T. and M. T. Daniel, no dates.
Susie E. Puckett, Oct. 13, 1861-June 23, 1923.
James N. Puckett, Jan. 18, 1845-Mar. 20, 1914.
Mary E., wife of T. J. Puckett, April 17, 1843-Sept. 14, 1896.
Frank C. Puckett, Dec. 25, 1886-Dec. 17, 1892.

Bible Records—Tombstone Inscriptions

James N. Puckett, Jr., Feb. 7, 1874-Dec. 12, 1892.
Thomas Cole, Mar. 25, 1809-Sept. 28, 1817.
John W. Putman, April 30, 1836-Sept. 22, 1837.
Merimon Landrum, July 12, 1784-July 28, 1826.
Mary Ann Manervy Landrum, July 22, 1827-Nov. 26, 1851.
Mary Louisa, infant of W. R. and Delia Taylor, Dec. 10, 1869-Feb. 2, 1870.
T. E. Taylor, son of Mary and P. M. Taylor, June 16, 1851-July 21, 1852.

Cedar Grove Cemetery, Lebanon, Wilson County, Tenn.
Copied by Mrs. W. P. Bouton, Lebanon, Tenn.

Robert L. Caruthers, born in Smith County, Tenn., July 31, 1800; died at Lebanon, Tenn., Oct. 2, 1882.
Sally Sanders Caruthers, wife of Robert L. Caruthers, born Mar. 11, 1807; married, Jan. 16, 1827; died, Oct. 20, 1870.
Mary Jane Caruthers, born May 1, 1828; born again, Oct. 20, 1843; died, Oct. 20, 1845; only child of R. L. and Sally Caruthers.
Judge Abe Caruthers, Jan. 14, 1803-May 5, 1862.
Eliza M., wife of Judge Abe Caruthers, April 9, 1810-Oct. 14, 1859.
Kate Howard, daughter of Judge Abraham and Eliza Caruthers, born Oct. 1, 1851; married L. B. Edwards, May 17, 1875; died at Asheville, N. C., Aug. 27, 1884.
Rev. Robert C. Hatton, born in Charleston, S. C., Dec. 16, 1795-Sept. 1, 1886.
Margaret C. Hatton, wife of Rev. R. C. Hatton, Mar. 6, 1794-Dec. 28, 1868.
Capt. William S. Hatton, May 2, 1820-Oct. 9, 1866.
Maggie H. Riddle, Sept. 18, 1830-Jan. 21, 1881.
Gen. Robert Hatton, born Nov. 2, 1826; fell May 31, 1862, while leading his Tennessee Brigade in the battle of Seven Pines, Va.
Mary E. Hatton, wife of Joseph H. Peyton, 1822-1893.
Mary C. Wharton, wife of J. B. Peyton, Feb. 17, 1848-Jan. 12, 1900.
Margarett J. Crowell, Aug. 5, 1833-June 16, 1896.
Sophie Reily Hatton, May 1, 1827-Mar. 12, 1916.
William Arrington, May 20, 1831-Sept. 23, 1892.
Mrs. Mary Mullins, died Nov. 12, 1899; age, 76 years.
Mary J. Gannaway, consort of E. R. Gannaway, Sept. 29, 1826-Jan. 27, 1848.
George Washington Lewis, Jan. 19, 1819-July 5, 1907.
Sophie Allen Lewis, July 5, 1824-Oct. 6, 1880.
John Lewis, 1816-1895.
Evie Allen Lewis, 1878-1879.
Hannah Lewis Smithwick, 1824-1897.
Ludica Caroline, wife of David Donnell, May 10, 1804-Jan. 31, 1869.
Dr. Thomas Norman, Oct. 15, 1801-Mar. 7, 1873.
Elizabeth Norman, May 5, 1814-May 27, 1857.
D. W. Braden, M.D., 1825-1914.
Caroline M. Braden, 1833-1904.
William B. Tatum, Mar. 2, 1821-Dec. 11, 1903.
John F. Doak, 1833-1909.
A. W. Page, Nov. 5, 1832-Nov. 7, 1908.
Henry A. Trice, Aug. 5, 1827-July 23, 1901.
Cynthia M. Trice, Aug. 12, 1832-Feb. 8, 1921.
Mary A. Franklin, Dec. 17, 1826-Nov. 12, 1904.
Samuel S. Gause, 1839-1901.
Portia D. Gause, 1841-1921.
Martin V. New, Jan. 3, 1839-April 6, 1918.
Elizabeth Young New, Jan. 12, 1839-Jan. 14, 1903.
Dr. Harden Ragland, Nov. 5, 1811-Feb. 6, 1882.
Amelia A., wife of H. Ragland, Dec. 6, 1806-Dec. 13, 1885.
Agnes Ragland, wife of William C. Edwards, Dec. 12, 1839-Dec. 4, 1885.
B. W. G. Winford, Sept. 23, 1814-April 19, 1879.
J. A. Rutherford, 1827-1887.
Sarah Harsh Rutherford, 1829-1912.

Bible Records—Tombstone Inscriptions

Edmund W. Lewis, Dec. 22. 1808-Dec. 15, 1897.
Martha Thompson, wife of E. W. Lewis, Mar. 27, 1830-Oct. 1, 1900.
Thomas Jefferson Thompson, Dec. 24, 1807-Aug. 13, 1873.
Lucy Ann Peace, wife of T. J. Thompson, born June 15, 1814; married, May 20, 1835; died, Sept. 17, 1884.
Mary D. Thompson, died Nov., 1906.
Andrew P. Thompson, died Mar., 1909.
Martha L. Thompson, died Aug., 1910.
Lucy P. Thompson, died Oct., 1927.
Andrew Shorter, July 22, 1884-Jan. 10, 1907.
Col. Robert Allen, born in Pennsylvania, June 19, 1778; died at Greenwood, Tenn., Aug. 19, 1844.
Mrs. Alethia Lapsley, daughter of Archibald and Alethia VanHorn, born in Maryland, Oct. 18, 1804; died at Greenwood, Oct. 31, 1862.
David B. Allen, son of Col. Robert and Alethia, born at Greenwood, Tenn., Jan. 3, 1830; died at Brownsville, Tex., Sept. 5, 1855.
Miss Alethia B. Allen, daughter of Col. Robert and Alethia, June 10, 1835-July 6, 1854; died in Nashville, Tenn.
Sarah Ruston, wife of Jacob Howard, born in Jonesboro, Tenn., May 8, 1800; died in Lebanon, Tenn., Oct. 7, 1863.
John K. Howard, died in Richmond, Va., July 9, 1862.
Mary Ann Burford, wife of John K. Howard, Sept. 26, 1838-Nov. 13, 1916.
Sarah E. Hankins, wife of William Hannah, Feb. 5, 1836-Aug. 20.
Dr. John Owen, born in Granville County, N. C., Aug. 31, 1787; died in Smith County, Tenn., Sept. 5, 1826.
Mary Amis Goodwin, born in Granville County, N. C., Jan. 30, 1787; married Sept. 17, 1812, to Dr. John Owen; died, Jan. 2, 1879.
Dr. John D. Owen, 1825-1889.
His wife, Fannie Jamison, 1835-1886.
J. W. Sory, Feb. 17, 1842-June 2, 1904.
Fannie D. Sory, Aug. 6, 1846-Mar. 8, 1891.
Virginia, wife of Dr. E. Donoho, died April 28, 1867; age, 39 years.
Annie E. Kirkpatrick, wife of D. D. Clayton, May 25, 1831-Mar. 5, 1912.
W. M. Harkreader, 1839-1912.
Ella Coo, wife of W. M. Harkreader, 1859-1901.
William E. Green, died Dec. 19, 1877; age, 52 years.
Amanda E., wife of William E. Green, July 21, 1839-May 17, 1880.
Dr. Miles McCorkle, died April 15, 1869.
Mrs. Kittie Ann McCorkle, died Oct. 26, 1878.
John A. Lester, 1827-1905.
Mattie Lester, wife of John A. Lester, 1833-1904.
William J. Lester, 1825-1901.
Harry A. Dillon, 1813-1897.
Dillon Lester, 1856-1870.
Robert Cantrell, Nov. 9, 1823-Feb. 9, 1903.
Martha Magness, wife of Robert Cantrell, Dec. 15, 1831-Mar. 1, 1897.
Alexander Rush Fonville, Jan. 6, 1828-Dec. 15, 1886.
Elizabeth McClarin Fonville, May 20, 1828-Sept. 15, 1904.
Samantha J. Gribble, June, 1838-Aug. 6, 1892.
Dr. James Barry, brother of Sir Edward Barry of London, born in the North of Ireland, 1779; located in Tennessee in 1805; died, May 12, 1821.
Mary M. Sanders, wife of Dr. James Barry, born in North Carolina, May 18, 1790; died in Tennessee, Oct. 27, 1842.
Martha Wilkinson, a true friend, born in Maryland, 1803; died in Tennessee, A. D., 1865.
Col. M. A. Price, born in Pittsylvania County, Va., Oct. 1, 1800; died in Lebanon, Tenn., Dec. 6, 1878.
Maria J. Barry, wife of Col. M. A. Price, born in Gallatin, Tenn., July 19, 1800; died in Lebanon, Tenn., May 10, 1871.
William Williamson Price, son of M. A. and Maria J. H. Price, born in Lebanon, Feb. 26, 1836-Aug. 12, 1871.
James Barry Price, son of M. A. and Maria J. H. Price, born in Danville, Va., Jan. 19, 1832; died in Denver, Colo., Oct. 10, 1892.
Maru Murphy, wife of James E. Price, born in St. Mary's Parish, La., Feb. 22, 1834; died in Lebanon, Oct. 9, 1870.
Andrew Bennett Martin, 1836-1920; a teacher in Cumberland University Law School, 1878 to 1920.
Alice Ready, wife of Andrew B. Martin, Nov. 9, 1842-Sept. 7, 1890.

Bible Records—Tombstone Inscriptions

Abe Britton, 1827-1901.
Jane Britton, 1820-1915.
Eva Zernes Britton, Oct. 3, 1868-Feb. 12, 1927.
George W. Martin, June 29, 1822-Oct. 10, 1896.
Dr. George Hugh Waters, May 27, 1857-Mar. 3, 1895.
William Gillham, son of Rev. W. T. and L. J. Dale, died at Campblake, Lebanon, Tenn., Jan. 29, 1874.
E. B. Pendleton, July 26, 1833-Sept. 1, 1906.
John P. Grigsby, Jan. 10, 1826-Oct. 12, 1903.
James F. Baird, Feb. 10, 1836-Jan. 2, 1920.
Emeline S. Baird, Oct. 22, 1837-Feb. 23, 1919.
Frank S. Buchanan, 1821-1862.
Anne (Wharton) Buchanan, 1831-1924.
Catharine L. Bailey, June 12, 1836-Aug. 25, 1905.
J. W. Bailey, April 8, 1838-Jan. 4, 1908; Confederate Soldier and belonged to Company C.
R. A. Bailey, Feb. 29, 1840-Jan. 16, 1900; Company G, 4th Tenn. Cavalry, C. S. A., A. McGregor Company.
Eleanor L. Thompson, wife of J. W. Bailey, May 5, 1843-May 15, 1923.
Martha Caroline Bell, wife of Joseph Dozier, June 28, 1827-July 12, 1900.
Eliza Palmer, April 14, 1819-Sept. 17, 1907.
William T. Grissim, Nov. 12, 1843-Sept. 28, 1913.
Conelia Grissim, Sept. 28, 1849-June 20, 1916.
Talitha C. Foster, Sept. 25, 1839-Jan. 11, 1912.
C. D. Barton, wife of Robert A. Barton, May 2, 1837-Sept. 30, 1896.
Wesley Hancock, Oct. 8, 1829-Oct. 25, 1894.
Margaret Hancock, Aug. 3, 1834-Sept. 18, 1915.
J. B. Baird, Aug. 19, 1813-June 11, 1894.
Rebecca Baird, Dec. 23, 1818-Aug. 12, 1896.
Martha B. Blair, Feb. 14, 1839-Sept. 12, 1900.
H. C. Palmer, June 11, 1844-Aug. 14, 1926.
Bettie Blair Palmer, Dec. 11, 1856-Mar. 16, 1899.
Joshua D. Lester, July 27, 1839-April 14, 1893.
Margaret H. Lester, Jan. 4, 1843-Oct. 22, 1903.
J. S. Trice, Dec. 15, 1822-Dec. 3, 1890.
Elizabeth, wife of J. S. Trice, Jan. 11, 1833-July 17, 1890.
Martha McClain Fields, Dec. 25, 1835-Sept. 15, 1918.
James H. McGee, May 18, 1840-Dec. 21, 1904.
Addison Askins, born in Culpepper County, Va., 1803-April 29, 1890.
George M. Carter, 1824-1900.
Emily Carter, 1831- 1903.
John D. Kirkpatrick, July 8, 1832-Aug. 2, 1895. "First Murdock professor of Church History in Cumberland University; soldier, scholar, Christian gentleman, friend, and father to every student."
Mrs. Sue Kirkpatrick, wife of Dr. John D. Kirkpatrick, Mar. 1, 1844-Mar. 24, 1908.
Stanford Guthrie Burney, April 16, 1814-Mar. 1, 1893. "A ripe scholar, a profound philosopher, a forceful writer, an eloquent preacher, an able teacher, a devout Christian, a true friend."
Susan Gray Burney, April 11, 1823-Feb. 28, 1893.
John M. Hamilton, Feb. 20, 1855-Nov. 4, 1889; age, 34 years.
James Madison Goodbar, Aug. 16, 1816-Feb. 2, 1905.
Verlinder Cullom Goodbar, Oct. 11, 1823-Dec. 28, 1893.
Mary Goodbar, Feb. 21, 1848-Nov. 6, 1890.
Lean Goodbar, Dec. 23, 1845-April 15, 1912.
Elizabeth Emma Goodbar Johnston, Dec. 5, 1850-Jan. 31, 1896.
James Horace Goodbar, Aug. 24, 1854-Jan. 29, 1897.
Cassandra Hawks, July 18, 1824-July 24, 1876.
Dan W. Baird, July 29, 1838-Feb. 7, 1913.
Dovie C. Baird, Oct. 2, 1842-Sept. 20, 1890.
W. G. H. Page, Mar. 26, 1830-Jan. 20, 1906.
M. W. Page, April 18, 1832-Nov. 5, 1916.
William J. Cragwall, born in Gooch-

Bible Records—Tombstone Inscriptions

land County, Va., April 21, 1807-June 18, 1888.
Ellen B. Harris, wife of W. J. Cragwall, born in Hanover County, Va., Mar. 2, 1811-July 15, 1861.
Ann Eliza Cragwall, Mar. 29, 1832-Oct. 3, 1893.
W. Temple Cragwall, Aug. 21, 1847-July 22, 1905.
Rufus H. Foster, born in Wilson County, Tenn., Oct. 4, 1814; died, July 3, 1896.
Sarah Spain, wife of R. H. Foster, born in Rutherford County, Tenn., July 1, 1818-Jan. 27, 1876.
Pascal K. Williamson, Dec. 19, 1822-Aug. 23, 1886.
Maria E. Williamson, Nov. 19, 1836-Mar. 20, 1893.
Etheldred Phillips Horn, April 28, 1831-Nov. 4, 1899.
Samuel A. Carter, Feb. 29, 1832-Mar. 27, 1884.
James H. Britton, July 28, 1796-Oct. 5, 1848.
Sallie M. Lauderdale, wife of James H. Britton, May 24, 1786-April 10, 1873.
Clara C., daughter of J. H. and S. M. Britton, Dec. 25, 1829-Jan. 26, 1864.
Sarah A. Slate, mother of W. H. Slate, July 23, 1836-April 3, 1906.
A. W. Clifford, 1830-Aug. 7, 1897.
Jasper R. Ashworth, Dec. 15, 1819-July 26, 1884.
Adelaide Sewell Ashworth, Mar. 21, 1827-April 11, 1902.
N. S. Ashworth, wife of G. H. Smith, June 1, 1845-April 13, 1871.
Jasper R. Ashworth, Mar. 26, 1857-Dec. 12, 1896.
Mason Tiller, April 21, 1800-June 8, 1869.
Jane Weir, 1839-1921.
J. A. Seagraves, 1839-1904.
Nancy Seagraves, 1841-1918.
W. H. Brown, Dec. 18, 1837-Oct. 17, 1907.
Mattie Davis Brown, Sept. 18, 1835-July 4, 1897.
Thomas M. Edwards, June, 1820-Mar. 18, 1902.
Louisa F. Edwards, Jan. 29, 1824-Oct. 2, 1874.
William T. Edwards, Nov. 12, 1842-May 11, 1872.
James R. Edwards, Jan. 27, 1845-April 8, 1869.
Eliza A. Roberts, wife of Thomas J. Shelton, Feb. 29, 1840-Jan. 8, 1881.
Clara Penny; age, 89 years (corner rock, Henry Orr).
John Moxley Goldston, June 14, 1809-July 4, 1892. "A member of the Christian Church for more than 50 years."
Louisa Tatum Stovall, wife of J. M. Goldston, born in Sumner County, Tenn., Mar. 2, 1813; married Dec. 1, 1830; died in Lebanon, Tenn., June 27, 1888. "A member of the Christian Church for 46 years."
William T. Goldston, 1831-1904.
His wife, Martha Ann, eldest daughter of Col. J. H. Allen, 1839-1874; married June 11, 1857.
Richard C. Sanders, born in Sumner County, Tenn., July 23, 1826; died in Orlando, Fla., Feb. 25, 1887.
Rhoda Reeves, wife of Richard C. Sanders, born in Smith County, Tenn., Feb. 17, 1837.
Sarah, wife of Rev. W. W. Suddarth, Feb. 13, 1841-Oct. 8, 1869.
Carrie Young, wife of D. D. Suddarth, Nov. 22, 1867-July 15, 1899.
H. M. Blair, Oct. 20, 1837-April 11, 1907.
Harriet N., wife of H. N. Blair, July 27, 1846-Feb. 26, 1884.
Lucy E. Blair, Feb. 6, 1837-April 19, 1909.
A. F. Blair, Dec. 23, 1805-Jan. 20, 1879.
E. J. Blair, Jan. 23, 1820-Mar. 10, 1905.
John Kanary, died June 16, 1906; age, 66 years (corner post marked Patrick O'Bryan).
William S. Holman, May 26, 1811-April 25, 1864.
Sophia Ann Holman, July 15, 1816-Feb. 5, 1855.
Dr. J. S. Brown, Sept. 10, 1861-Mar. 28, 1896.
Nathan Green, born in Amelia County, Va., 1792; died in Lebanon, Tenn., 1866. "Attorney, legislator, supreme judge, and professor of law; he made a record that will give immortality to his name; he lived and died an exemplary member of the Cumberland Presbyterian Church."
Elizabeth Amelia, wife of Nathan Green, born in Lewisburg, Va., June 11,

Bible Records—Tombstone Inscriptions

1812; died in Henderson, Ky., Mar. 22, 1875.
Mary Field, daughter of N. and E. A. Green, and wife of M. Merritt, Feb. 2, 1852-Jan. 31, 1876.
Ann A. Green, wife of J. C. Bowden, Dec. 22, 1823-Mar. 14, 1911.
Nathan Green, Jr., 1827-1919. "Professor of law in Cumberland University, 1857-1919."
Bettie Green, wife of Nathan Green, Jr., Mar. 30, 1833-July 4, 1893.
Blanch Hunter Green, wife of N. Green, Sept. 14, 1864-Feb. 5, 1910.
Rev. George Donnell, born in Wilson County, Tenn., 1801; died, Mar., 1845. "Entered the ministry of C. P. C., 1822. "Elizabeth Donnell, wife.
Mrs. Rosanna Jones, died May 27, 1856; age, 94 years.
Mrs. Fannie Hager, wife of H. C. Hager, Sept. 28, 1832-Oct. 22, 1902.
I. P. Cox, Aug. 15, 1835-Nov. 16, 1889.
J. T. Cox, July 22, 1836-Dec. 14, 1891.
Mary A. Young, wife of J. T. Cox, Nov. 24, 1855-Sept. 27, 1904.
I. P. Cox, Aug. 15, 1835-Nov. 16, 1889.
R. H. Cartwright, April 15, 1820-Aug. 8, 1891.
N. J. Cartwright, Mar. 12, 1835-Feb. 14, 1922.
Josiah Scott McClain, born in Wilson County, Jan. 1, 1799; died, April 6, 1876. "He was clerk of County Court more than 40 years; a Trustee of Cumberland University, an elder in C. P. Church."
Rufus P. McClain, 1838-1914.
Hettie S. McClain, 1840-1910.
Jennie J. Mackenzie, Sept. 25, 1833-Mar. 21, 1899.
O. G. Finley, May 24, 1787-Mar. 22, 1871.
Sallie J. Finley, consort of O. G. Finley, May 1, 1788-Aug. 22, 1857.
Foster G. Finley, son of O. G. and M. L. Finley, Mar. 22, 1822-July 10, 1906.
Alta Taylor Finley, daughter of Maj. Isaac and Margaret Taylor, Oct. 10, 1826-May 14, 1893.
Charles L. Johns, Sr., April 19, 1818-June 25, 1850.
Elizabeth C. Johns, Jan. 18, 1823-Sept. 20, 1894.
Gov. William Bowen Campbell, Feb. 1, 1807-Aug. 19, 1867.

Fannie Isabella, wife of Gov. William Bowen Campbell, Feb. 5, 1818-Mar. 22, 1864.
William Bowen Campbell, Jr., July 21, 1846-May 29, 1869.
Mary Dicken Morris Smith, wife of Henry Fuller Smith, Nov. 15, 1802-May 29, 1895. "Real daughter of American Revolution."
William R. Allen, Aug. 27, 1837-Aug. 21, 1873.
Theo C. Jarmon, son of Stephen and Eliza Jarmon, born in Hardeman County, Tenn., Oct. 9, 1831; died in Wilson County, June 25, 1854. "Monument erected by students of Cumberland University."
Rev. Richard Beard, Nov. 27, 1799-Dec. 2, 1880. "Professor of Systematic Theology in Cumberland University; ordained in Nashville Presbytery of Cumberland Presbyterian Church, July 29, 1822."
Cynthia E. Castleman, wife of Rev. Richard Beard, Nov. 22, 1804-May 27, 1886.
Edward Ewing Beard, 1850-1924. Professor of Law in Cumberland University.
Sarah Livingston Beard, 1853-1931.
W. B. Cundall, Nov. 17, 1815-Aug. 10, 1889.
Emily C. Cundall, born in Washington County, Va., May 20, 1818; died in Smith County, Tenn., Sept. 8, 1882.
John L. Cundall, Aug. 8, 1843-Jan. 4, 1928.
Bettie, wife of John L. Cundall, born June 23, 1845; married, Nov. 10, 1868; died, Oct. 9, 1899.
Sallie Wiseman, 1799-1877.
Edwin R. Pennybaker, 1833-1875.
Martha L. Pennybaker, 1838-1920.
William M. Cartmell, June 15, 1822-June 19, 1876.
H. H. Cartmell, 1828-1908.
Emma J. Cartmell, his wife, 1831-1909.
W. H. Cartmell, 1846-1923.
Capt. Andrew McGregor, Aug. 13, 1832-Sept. 23, 1910.
Eldora Anderson, wife of Capt. Andrew McGregor, Jan. 8, 1841-Jan. 18, 1908.
Maj. W. W. Carter, July 4, 1798-Dec. 25, 1877.
Isabella N. Carter, born Feb. 15, 1810; married to Maj. W. W. Carter, Nov.

Bible Records—Tombstone Inscriptions

20, 1828; died, April 4, 1883.
Lucy Wynne, wife of S. A. Carter, born April 18, 1847; married, Dec. 18, 1867; died, Nov. 27, 1870.
Angela Carter Solomon, Sept. 14, 1848-Nov. 26, 1874.
Allen Dillard, Aug. 20, 1821-Oct. 30, 1865.
Selety Ann, wife of A. Dillard, Jan. 29, 1827-Jan. 14, 1892.
Mary J. Solomon, Feb. 10, 1827-Jan. 19, 1902.
G. M. Shutt, Mar. 22, 1837-Mar. 24, 1890.
Josephine Shutt Miller, Dec. 29, 1846-April 24, 1927.
Berry Cox, Feb. 3, 1815-Nov. 18, 1889.
Lucy Clifton, wife of Berry Cox, Nov. 5, 1816-April 7, 1891.
R. Alex Graves, Dec. 19, 1835-July 14, 1901.
John Royal Harris, 1869-1926; President of Cumberland University, 1922-1926.
H. A. Chambers, Dec. 23, 1841-Feb. 23, 1896.
Marcia A. Holman Chambers, Aug. 20, 1844-Nov. 3, 1895.
Mary C. Holman, Nov. 19, 1840-Dec. 29, 1902.
Rev. W. W. Suddarth, Jan. 1, 1823-July 1, 1914.
Josie H. Suddarth, Nov. 15, 1848-July 6, 1909.
Rev. John J. Pittman, Feb. 6, 1825-April 6, 1886.
Rev. John T. Pittman, son of Rev. J. J. and L. S. Pittman, Dec. 7, 1850-Aug. 26, 1885.
T. C. Wheeler, M.D., Jan. 15, 1838-Dec. 30, 1909.
S. C. Trigg, Aug. 22, 1837-Oct 22, 1910.
Fanny Trigg, Nov. 19, 1841-Nov. 1, 1918.
J. T. Spears, Jan. 13, 1835-Oct. 29, 1916.
Permelia Ann Ellis, wife of J. T. Spears, 1840-Nov. 9, 1907.
R. B. Nolen, Nov. 2, 1826-May 4, 1911.
Mary C. Nolen, wife of R. B. Nolen, Sept. 30, 1839-Dec. 6, 1920.
William Paisley Bouton, Nov. 26, 1848-Sept. 3, 1917.
H. K. Edgerton, 1865-1914.
S. H. Pate, Feb. 3, 1834-Feb. 2, 1928.
Lucy E. Pate, June 2, 1842-Mar. 29, 1921.
Robert H. Wharton, 1835-1917.
Margaret D. Wharton, 1843-1916.
William A. Skeen, Feb. 20, 1844-Dec. 16, 1926.
Robert W. Skeen, Aug. 11, 1852-Dec. 5, 1918.
William Ewing Graham, Mar. 27, 1830-Mar. 7, 1872.
Annie R. Graham, Dec. 21, 1844-Aug. 25, 1918.
S. T. Green, Oct. 11, 1830-Aug. 25, 1911.
Col. S. G. Shepard, Jan. 28, 1830-June 6, 1917; married, Aug. 3, 1865.
Martha Major Shepard, Nov. 10, 1845-June 20, 1915.
James Houston Hancock, 1832-1915.
D. Turner Hancock, April 3, 1847-Dec. 29, 1921.
Malissa S. Hancock, Oct. 23, 1854-Dec. 24, 1926.
Mary G. Shannon, Jan. 27, 1832-Oct. 22, 1908.
E. K. Shannon, Mar. 22, 1841-Mar. 13, 1921.
M. L. Shannon, Nov. 5, 1847-June 12, 1908.
Emily Holloway, wife of W. W. Grigg, Mar. 31, 1838-July 11, 1912.
Bettie O. Terry, Aug. 6, 1842-Jan. 3, 1916.
Willis J. Settle, Dec. 17, 1847-Mar. 13, 1891.
Jennie S. Rousseau, Mar. 6, 1849-Dec. 7, 1893.
Adjt. R. G. Settle, C. S. A., killed in battle at Dalton, Ga., Aug. 15, 1864; age, about 25 years.
Leroy B. Settle, Jr., April 1, 1841-Aug. 1, 1888; wore the gray during the war.
Mrs. Asenath A. Rutland, wife of James B. Rutland, born in East Windsor, Conn., 1818; married, 1842; died, May 6, 1849; member of the Cumberland Presbyterian Church.
James H. Fisher, Sept. 27, 1808-July 29, 1851.
Ann Catharine, wife of James H. Fisher, Oct. 11, 1824-May 28, 1849.
Edward I. Golladay, Sept. 9, 1830-July 11, 1897.
Lucinda L. Golladay, Feb. 9, 1832-July 9, 1875.
Franceway R. Cossitt, D.D., April 24, 1790-Feb. 3, 1863. First President of

Bible Records—Tombstone Inscriptions

Cumberland College, first President of Cumberland University, a Presbyterian.
George H. Shutt, Feb. 1, 1808-Oct. 9, 1853.
Hannah Hill Shutt, Mar. 13, 1809-Nov. 2, 1873.
Lizzie Shutt, wife of Thomas Miller, Mar. 31, 1833-Feb. 12, 1873.
Virginia Shutt, wife of Rev. C. P. Duvall, born near Lebanon, Tenn., Mar. 31, 1848; died in Fayetteville, Tenn., May 4, 1875.
Henry F. Shutt, Jan. 18, 1843-Sept. 22, 1921.
Almira Bell Shutt, Oct. 17, 1847-Feb. 17, 1928.
Jordan Stokes, born in Chatham County, N. C., Aug. 23, 1817-Nov. 27, 1886.
Martha J. Stokes, born in Wilson County, Tenn., Mar. 9, 1826-June 19, 1883.
Robert Porter Allison, July 24, 1809-Nov. 20, 1896.
Alethia Sanders Allison, April 11, 1820-Nov. 14, 1894.
W. J. Grannis, 1823-1905.
Lucy Grannis, 1828-1895.
Mary P. Williams, June 7, 1818-June 22, 1877.
S. T. Williams, Aug. 13, 1851-Nov. 1, 1888.
Benjamin J. Tarver, 1826-1905.
Sue Shelton White Tarver, 1834-1923.
Haywood Y. Riddle, June 20, 1834-Mar. 28, 1879.
Martha Jefferson Goode Riddle, Mar. 25, 1831-Dec. 19, 1916.
Henry Stevens Lindsley, June 20, 1844-Feb. 19, 1875.
John Irodelle Dillard Hinds, Dec. 13, 1847-Mar. 4, 1921.
Naomi, wife of Isaac Buchanan, April 19, 1805-June 17, 1888.
Andrew Hays Buchanan, June 28, 1828-Aug. 11, 1914.
Malinda A. Buchanan, Sept. 20, 1837-May 29, 1919.
Rena Buchanan, wife of W. D. McLaughlin, Mar. 25, 1849-Mar. 18, 1911.
Jerden Webb, born in Wilson County, Tenn.; died, Feb. 13, 1860; age, 66 years.
W. A. Baird, April 21, 1837-Dec. 26, 1903.
Martin Hancock, Jan. 24, 1827-April 16, 1876.
Martha Hancock, Oct. 21, 1831-May 12, 1910.
Prof. James B. Hancock, July 19, 1847-Oct. 1, 1903.
Julier H. Hancock, 1852-1929.
W. S. Paty, Nov. 14, 1827-Dec. 3, 1886.
E. A. Paty, April 26, 1830-Aug. 10, 1893.
Rev. A. J. Ford, Dec. 13, 1847-Sept. 24, 1882.
Elizabeth Holloway Miller, July 15, 1815-Oct. 12, 1897.
Eldridge Gerry Seawell, Aug. 26, 1822-June 28, 1881.
Sue Miller Seawell, Sept. 2, 1834-Mar. 25, 1916.
Elleonora Price, wife of R. W. Miller, Dec. 29, 1847-April 3, 1923.
Elizabeth Seawell, wife of A. F. Claywell, Jan. 10, 1855-Nov. 14, 1884.
J. L. Castleman, Jan. 15, 1838-Dec. 11, 1915.
S. J. Castleman, Mar. 15, 1837-July 22, 1903.
John G. Powell, April 25, 1816-Feb. 15, 1888.
Sallie M. Powell, April 4, 1833-July 21, 1896.
John M. Fakes, July 21, 1844-Aug. 8, 1921.
Rosa G. Fakes, April 13, 1848-Mar. 26, 1926.
Harriet Henry Winford, Nov. 17, 1820-June 9, 1900.
James W. Hardy, May 27, 1815-Mar. 3, 1883.
John Frank Coles, Sr., 1830-1892.
Susan Hunt Coles, 1833-1894.
Eugenia Barry, 1844-1885.
J. E. Stratton, Feb. 27, 1842-Aug. 17, 1904.
Mary G. Stratton, April 15, 1842-May 28, 1886.
Maj. David L. Wallace, died June 9, 1900; age, 79 years.
Mrs. Caroline O. Wallace, died Sept. 26, 1887; age, 58 years.
Henry Thomas Dawson, July 9, 1822-Jan. 20, 1914.
Martha Rebecca Dawson, Dec. 5, 1826-Dec. 21, 1897.
Alex Shannon, April 16, 1844-June 23, 1920.
Maggie H. Shannon, May 22, 1847-July 15, 1920.
Alice Robertson, wife of Dr. J. W.

Bible Records—Tombstone Inscriptions

Huddleston, born in Nashville, Feb. 3, 1837; died in Lebanon, Feb. 15, 1900.
Joshua Cox, May 24, 1832-July 19, 1887.
William Hays Halbert, 1847-1922.
W. E. Bass, Feb. 4, 1841-June 16, 1905.
R. C. Scobey, May 22, 1827-Feb. 20, 1898.
Annie E. Scobey, wife of R. C. Scobey, Feb. 14, 1833-Oct. 7, 1893.
Green Scobey Hearn, Feb. 1842-Oct. 22, 1899.
Thomas J. Stratton, Aug. 5, 1818-Jan. 18, 1885.
Frances, wife of T. J. Stratton, Jan. 19, 1833-Mar. 23, 1909.
Samuel G. Stratton, Jan. 30, 1844-Aug. 3, 1909.
Alice A. Stratton, Oct. 10, 1844-Oct. 19, 1877.
Mark A. Brinkley, July 4, 1801-July 27, 1849.
Milley Brinkley, Feb. 5, 1800-Sept. 24, 1868.
E. L. Brinkley, June 18, 1822-Aug. 21, 1869.
Sallie, wife of E. L. Brinkley, Mar. 22, 1825-Jan. 8, 1886.
Nathaniel Lawrence Lindsley, Sept. 11, 1816-Oct. 10, 1868.
Julian Stevens, wife of Nathaniel Lawrence Lindsley, July 30, 1828-July 8, 1883.
Zachariah Tolliver, Aug. 24, 1799- Dec. 14, 1875.
Rebecca Tolliver, June 8, 1800-Nov. 6, 1874.
Martha Tolliver, Jan. 5, 1835-Jan. 11, 1851.
Robert Emmet Thompson, Oct. 27, 1822-Nov. 18, 1897.
Mary E. Thompson, Aug. 11, 1827-Dec. 22, 1912.
David Cook, Sr., Sept. 6, 1795-June 17, 1878.
Mary Colbun, wife of David Cook, May 19, 1799-Nov. 27, 1875.
George Warren Cook, July 4, 1826-Jan. 10, 1862; died at New Orleans.
Cora Agness Cook, July 13, 1841-June 5, 1871.
David Cook, Jr., May 18, 1824-Feb. 4, 1872.
Julia A. Cook, wife of A. S. Jones, died Jan. 27, 1897.
Clark Cook, died Dec. 17, 1899.
E. G. Mount, Aug. 6, 1833-Feb., 1903.

Eddie Hankins, June 19, 1849-Oct. 30, 1894.
Arthlean, wife of W. G. Swindell, died Jan. 25, 1878; age, 34 years.
W. H. Bennett, 1844-1903.
Sallie J. Bennett, 1849-1876.
Lizzie W. Bennett, 1856-1928.
Whitson P. Hearn, April 12, 1820-Sept. 14, 1884.
Ann Elizabeth Dickason, wife of Whitson P. Hearn, Aug. 17, 1824-May 30, 1884.
Matilda A. Hearn, wife of J. T. Lane, April 7, 1844-Oct. 14, 1878.
Orin D. Hearn, 1828-1906.
D. L. McClellan, Oct. 24, 1833-May 4, 1881.
Margaret Norman, May 20, 1840-Aug. 24, 1863.
James L. Fite, Jan. 9, 1836-June 18, 1893. Surgeon, 7th Tenn., C. S. A.
Emma Norman, wife of J. L. Fite, April 11, 1845-Sept. 14, 1928.
James Y. Blythe, Oct. 13, 1809-Nov. 6, 1887.
Elizabeth Seawell Blythe, Feb. 11, 1819-Jan. 30, 1883.
Pazzie Cummins, June 3, 1842-July 6, 1929.
William Henry Williamson, Oct. 29, 1828-Mar. 16, 1887.
Martha R. M. Williamson, first the wife of Gen. John H. Morgan, and then the wife of Wm. H. Williamson, died Nov. 16, 1887; age, 47 years.
J. A. Brent, May 16, 1822-Feb. 22, 1896.
Amanda W., wife of Joseph A. Brent, Aug. 11, 1823-Feb. 21, 1891.
Lemuel M. Shaw, April 22, 1827-Aug. 3, 1886.
Levina G., wife of Lemuel M. Shaw, Sept. 7, 1832-Aug. 30, 1901.
A. F. Tatum, Mar. 16, 1849-May 1, 1925.
Elizabeth H. Shaw, wife of A. F. Tatum, Nov. 25, 1850-Feb. 6, 1905.
Mourning S., daughter of Elder William Woods, Oct. 6, 1808-May 13, 1890.
Mary Ann Woods, wife of John M. Miller, Feb. 20, 1819-Feb. 9, 1893.
Polly Woods Miller, wife of J. D. Chambers, Dec. 19, 1849-Aug. 7, 1897.
Capt. A. K. Miller, April 24, 1842-April 17, 1926. Served under Gen.

Bible Records—Tombstone Inscriptions

Robert Hatton, Company D, 7th Tenn. Regiment.
Nannie Solomon, wife of Andrew K. Miller, Nov. 15, 1846-Mar. 15, 1889.
Joe M. Miller, June 5, 1837-July 21, 1919.
Josephine Lash Miller, wife of J. M. Miller, May 8, 1840-Jan. 22, 1888.
Robert Verrell Foster, 1845-1914.
Belle Braden Foster, 1853-1919.
Matthew W. Cowan, Mar. 7, 1828-May 28, 1892.
Adeline L. Cowan, Oct. 12, 1828-Sept. 18, 1908.
S. R. Comer, Aug. 7, 1808-Aug. 27, 1897.
Jane, wife of S. R. Comer, Dec. 16, 1817-Nov. 13, 1900.
Alice Ann Edwards, wife of J. G. Nix, April 5, 1853-Jan. 12, 1908.
N. C. Dunn, Aug. 22, 1837-Sept. 13, 1909.
William H. Smith, 1846-1924.
Sarah J. Smith, 1845-1923.
Nannie Hewgley, Oct. 15, 1815-Mar. 22, 1901.
John W. Hewgley, Feb. 18, 1834-Dec. 24, 1910.
Lucy Jane, wife of J. W. Hewgley, May 12, 1850-Feb. 4, 1919.
Elizabeth Hearn, wife of John A. Shannon, July 18, 1819-Mar. 22, 1899.
W. A. McClain, Dec. 26, 1833-Feb. 25, 1909.
Fannie Vaughan, his wife, Oct. 10, 1837-Sept. 8, 1906.
H. S. Kennedy, Aug. 3, 1839-Dec. 12, 1924.
Mrs. Chloe N. Kennedy, Feb. 17, 1848-Oct. 4, 1901; died at Boulder, Colo.
Aseneth Pickett, wife of Samuel Schockney, Mar. 14, 1840-Nov. 15, 1897.
R. B. Pearce, Nov. 16, 1841-Jan. 14, 1912.
W. J. Gamble, June 9, 1834-Dec. 24, 1914.
J. W. Quaintance, Aug. 20, 1830-Oct. 19, 1908.
M. A. Quaintance, wife of J. W. Quaintance, Feb. 4, 1841-Jan. 19, 1914.
Edmund W. Lewis, Dec. 22, 1808-Dec. 17, 1897.
Martha Thompson, wife of E. W. Lewis, Mar. 27, 1830-Oct. 1, 1900.
Leopold Drifoes, died Oct. 16, 1886; age, 79 years.
Eliza, wife of Leopold Drifoes, died Aug. 23, 1889; age, 69 years.
A. F. Claywell, Jan. 26, 1831-Mar. 18, 1904.
Callie A. Claywell, wife of A. F. Claywell, June 28, 1841-May 13, 1874.
Allen W. Vick, Aug. 21, 1799-Feb. 1, 1876.
Martha A. R. Vick, Mar. 17, 1808-July 4, 1876.
Anna J. Vick, Sept. 30, 1832-Feb. 1, 1885.
Alexander W. Vick, Oct. 26, 1834-Aug. 6, 1901.
Samuel Brown, Feb. 25, 1800-Mar. 17, 1852.
Lucy Chandler Brown, Feb. 1, 1804-Feb. 15, 1872.
Dixon Brown, Sept. 6, 1829-Oct. 10, 1859.
Joseph A. Brown, April 5, 1833-Aug. 15, 1856.
Sophronia A. Brown, Feb. 3, 1835-July 26, 1849.
Robert Andrew Brown, Dec. 20, 1845-Mar. 20, 1865.
Alfred R. Davis, April 16, 1831-Mar. 29, 1889.
Frances Brown Davis, Dec. 3, 1827-Aug. 21, 1849.
T. H. Anderson, 1826-1884.
Mary E. Anderson, 1837-1877.
Thomas J. Smith, May 9, 1816.
Almira Jane, wife of Thomas J. Smith, died Oct. 7, 1873.
Sallie B., wife of Roland T. Foster, died May 6, 1867; age, 22 years.
William Syport, Tennessee Pvt., Harpole's Co., 2nd Tenn. Mtd. Gunman, War of 1812.
William C. Dew, Oct. 27, 1790-Feb. 16, 1868.
Ann Dew, May 10, 1800-Mar. 19, 1871.
James Nesbet Cartwright, Mar. 28, 1818-Oct. 16, 1895.
Nancy Jane Goodner, his wife, April 12, 1827-July 12, 1894.
Matthew Thomas Cartwright, June 13, 1809-Jan. 28, 1848.
Martha Harris Goodner, his wife, May 7, 1818-Nov. 23, 1854.
Ophelia Cartwright, wife of W. P. Turner, Mar. 25, 1837-Oct. 23, 1878.
Robert Donnell Ivy, Feb. 11, 1847-June 3, 1908.
Tennessee Ivy, Aug. 6, 1847-July 5, 1928.
Sarah A. Goldstein, wife of W. B.

Bible Records—Tombstone Inscriptions

Tatum, Sept. 18, 1824-Dec. 14, 1910.
Ellen M. Lash, 1839-1911.
T. C. Anderson, Oct. 21, 1801-Feb. 3, 1881; President of Cumberland University, 1844-1865.
Rachel Asenath, wife of Rev. T. C. Anderson, June 6, 1811-Dec. 5, 1849.
Julian Anderson, July 19, 1813-Oct. 3, 1854.
John Mitchell McMurry, Sept. 30, 1804-April 6, 1875.
Amanda A. Anderson, Nov. 1, 1835-Aug. 2, 1931.
Isaac Golladay, April 10, 1781-Oct. 6, 1848.
Elizabeth Golladay, July 18, 1786-Sept. 8, 1849.
Caroline, wife of Thomas J. Stratton, Mar. 16, 1813-Aug. 15, 1865.
F. W. Golladay, Aug. 22, 1822-May 3, 1900.
Eugenia Stratton, his wife, Mar. 20, 1832-Nov. 16, 1863.
M. Mannie Kelley, born May 23, 1835; married, Jan. 1, 1851; sent as missionary to China, Mar. 19, 1851; died, May 15, 1867.
E. J. Peyton, Dec. 6, 1821-Mar. 28, 1884.
J. M. Peyton, Feb. 27, 1817-Mar. 17, 1857.
Dr. Oliver C. Kidder, Oct. 13, 1831-Dec. 25, 1888.
Sarah Jane, wife of O. C. Kidder, Oct. 5, 1837-Dec. 9, 1892.
Cyrus Kidder, born in Columbia County, Ky., May 15, 1801; died in Wilson County, May 10, 1879.
Margaret Roberts Wilson, April 15, 1832-Sept. 10, 1893.
Thomas Richmond Murphey, 1837-1919.
Alice Gray Wilson Murphey, 1849-1925.
R. P. Baird, Sept. 15, 1821-Mar. 23, 1884.
M. G. Baird, Dec. 29, 1824-Mar. 4, 1885.
Elizabeth C. Davis, Sept. 16, 1799-Feb. 23, 1899.
Mrs. Martha B. McDonnold, Feb. 3, 1807-June 18, 1878.
Rev. B. W. McDonnold, D.D., LL.D., Mar. 24, 1827-Feb. 27, 1889.
Mrs. A. B. McDonnold, June 3, 1833-May 11, 1906.
Z. T. Newbey, Sept. 6, 1820-Dec. 26, 1808.
Mrs. E. E. Newbey, Dec. 28, 1824-April 21, 1890.
A. P. Sherrill, Dec. 26, 1826-Jan. 31, 1891.
M. A. Sherrill, June 20, 1828-Mar. 2, 1905.
Matt. M. Thompson, Sept. 4, 1824-Feb. 12, 1891.
Elizabeth J. Thompson, Dec. 5, 1833-Nov. 25, 1902.
C. N. Cook, Mar. 29, 1826-Jan. 23, 1911.
Cleopatra Cook, Aug. 5, 1834-Oct. 26, 1905.
Newt H. Baird, 1840-1912.
Maggie Bishop Baird, 1851-1929.
Louisa, wife of Henry Mitchell, Aug. 31, 1820-Mar. 8, 1886.
Larkin Robertson, Mar. 5, 1827-Feb. 20, 1876.
Capt. J. H. Martin, 1837-1908, Company D, 7th Tenn.
Mary Jane, wife of John Gavin, July, 1829-Nov. 19, 1883.

NAMES ON CONFEDERATE MONUMENT AND PRIVILEGE

Capt. Brown, Company D, 2nd Ky. Reg.
A. Whitlock, Company A, 2nd Ky. Reg.
P. Whitlock, Company E, 2nd Ky. Reg.
Henry Dorsey, Company A, 2nd Ky. Reg.
"To the memory of Confederate Soldiers who sleep in this cemetery and to their surviving comrades who shall rest here."
Pensioners: Capt. W. M. Harkreader, Capt. A. K. Miller, General Robert Hatton, Colonels J. K. Howard, R. G. Sanders, E. I. Golladay, J. W. Hardy. Majors: W. H. Williamson, S. A. Carter, Dr. J. L. Fite, Dr. O. C. Kidder.
Captains: J. H. Britton, J. R. Lester, J. F. Coe, J. D. Kirkpatrick, J. H. Anderson, Rev. B. W. McDonnold.
Lieutenants: Pat O'Brien, W. H. Barrow, C. T. Burgess, J. T. Lane, W. D. Martin, S. M. Allen, L. A. Trice, A. G. Settle.
Privates: G. M. Shutt, J. D. Lester, G. Stratton, J. Chandler, L. B. Settle, J. T. Hankins, I. P. Cox, E. R. Pennebaker, J. H. Ragland, J. T. Cox, G. R.

Bible Records—Tombstone Inscriptions

Glenn, W. R. Britton, R. A. Davis, D. K. Donnell, Sr., J. A. Rutherford, W. P. Eason, J. M. Martin, O. T. Barbee, G. Donnell, J. L. Hearn, R. Swain, G. R. Allen, D. L. McClellan, B. M. Jackson, W. S. Paty, H. L. Lindsley, J. M. Fowler, C. Scheibe, William J. Lester, R. A. Bailey, J. H. Martin. Majors: A. W. Vick, S. S. Gause. Captains: A. W. Roe, Abe Britton. Lieutenants: T. J. Lea, H. C. Cox, W. H. Bennett, G. A. Carter. Adjt.: A. F. Claywell, R. Alex Graves, J. A. Neal, Howell W. Williams, O. D. Hearn, John Kanary, E. D. Vaughan, H. M. Blair, W. W. Smith, J. A. Sakers, W. P. Skeen, W. A. McClain, Capt. Ellis Harper, J. F. Doak, J. A. Woollard, D. J. Barton, T. C. Wheeler, S. C. Trigg, A. J. Doak, Capt. Andrew McGregor, Capt. W. J. Gamble, Capt. R. P. McClain, Prof. A. H. Buchanan, Prof. R. V. Foster, D. F. Hammon, W. T. Grissim, S. M. Matherly, J. S. Mosley, R. M. Whitescarver, D. C. Donnell, R. Cox, J. T. Spears, J. H. Johnson, Maj. A. W. Page, Joe M. Miller, R. T. Davis, W. H. Halbert, H. H. Harkreader, Benjamin Duggan Rogers, J. M. Fakes, Capt. Brown P. Whitlow, A. Whitlack, H. Dorsey, Andrew B. Martin, P. H. Anderson.

LEEVILLE GRAVEYARD

Eight miles west of Lebanon, on the old Lebanon and Leeville dirt road, Wilson County, Tenn. Sent by Mrs. W. P. Bouton, Lebanon, Tenn.

David Campbell, born Mar. 4, 1781; married Catharine Bowen, April, 1806; died, June 18, 1841. He was not for God took him; trust in God, and inheritance from his parents; he left a legacy to his children.

Catharine, wife of David Campbell, born Mar. 27, 1785; married, April 15, 1806; died, April 15, 1868. Her six children called her blessed.

Dr. John Hamilton Campbell, son of David and Catharine, June 21, 1808-Feb. 16, 1890.

Margaret Hamilton Campbell, daughter of David and Catharine, Aug. 29, 1812-May 9, 1880.

David H. Campbell, June 29, 1826-Sept. 21, 1872.

Lucy G. Campbell, June 14, 1835-Mar. 4, 1921.

Frank G. Campbell, D.D., Mar. 19, 1870-Feb. 9, 1896.

Margaret H. Campbell, June 14, 1866-Sept. 14, 1872.

Lucy G. Campbell, Sept. 29, 1872-Nov. 30, 1888.

Mary E. Campbell, wife of Gen. John Campbell, and daughter of Nathaniel and Sarah Cowan, born in Knoxville, Tenn., Sept. 17, 1798-Oct. 31, 1880.

James Wallace, Oct. 25, 1794-Feb. 5, 1871.

Nancy Wallace, May 11, 1795-Feb. 23, 1879.

Rev. William Barton, Jan. 15, 1814-April 25, 1897.

Margaret Barton, wife of William Barton, April 13, 1815-July 31, 1904.

E. P. Sullivan, Oct. 8, 1812-Oct. 12, 1888.

Martha Mariah Sullivan, Aug. 26, 1810-May 1, 1899.

L. H. Sullivan, April 6, 1832-Jan. 29, 1907.

Mary L. Sullivan, Mar. 9, 1833-Feb. 13, 1894.

Thomas B. Stroud, April 22, 1823-Jan. 10, 1899.

Catharine E., wife of T. B. Stroud, and daughter of Col. J. and Martha Swingley, Oct. 16, 1834-Oct. 14, 1875.

Benjamin D. Pendleton, Sept. 26, 1822-Aug. 13, 1863.

Mrs. Gelie Pendleton, Sept. 5, 1836-June 7, 1917.

Thomas B. Taylor, Mar. 9, 1819-April 13, 1879.

S. A. Sanders, Oct. 5, 1832-Aug. 7, 1899.

To the memory of Col. David Campbell and Jane, his wife. He died Nov. 24, 1832, in the 80th year of his age; she died Sept. 18, 1840, near the age of three score and ten.

Bible Records—Tombstone Inscriptions

John Kelley, Jan. 28, 1801, died May 22, 1864; age, 43 years; an itinerant in the Methodist Church.
Margarett Lavinia Campbell, born Apr. 30, 1805; married John Kelley, Jan. 27, 1833; died, Oct. 29, 1877; perhaps the brightest missionary spirit which has adorned the M. E. Church, South.
Mary Owen Campbell, wife of D. C. Kelley, June 20, 1836-Nov. 11, 1890.
E. T. Grigg, born in Pennsylvania County, Va., Aug. 1, 1827-Oct. 5, 1901.
Martha Thompson, wife of E. T. Grigg, May 12, 1831-April 12, 1885.
John J. Swingley, Sept. 14, 1822-Aug. 20, 1909.
Sarah Swingley, Aug. 31, 1822-July 23, 1868.
William H. Jackson, Sept. 9, 1830-Dec. 28, 1891.
Susan Swingley, wife of W. H. Jackson, Feb. 7, 1836-Nov. 6, 1917.
Edmond Jackson, July 10, 1825-May 2, 1897.
Martha A., wife of Edmond Jackson, April 2, 1828-April 13, 1890.
S. C. Jackson, Nov. 9, 1828-Feb. 4, 1907.
Jane Jackson, wife of S. C. Jackson, Oct. 10, 1835-Nov. 28, 1917.
John J. Jackson, Dec. 6, 1832-June, 1870.
Margaret L. Jackson, Aug. 13, 1833-May 10, 1866.
Sarah H. Baker, Mar. 6, 1809-Feb. 21, 1853.
Elizabeth W., wife of R. A. Rozell, Mar. 6, 1822-April 3, 1880.
Sarah J. Neal, Feb. 8, 1827-July 19, 1857.
Col. Jonas Swingley, Oct. 30, 1800-Sept. 25, 1851.
Martha, wife of Col. Jonas Swingley, Nov. 22, 1805-Nov. 22, 1886.
Archibald Carver, June 3, 1810-Sept. 22, 1865.
Mary A. Watkins, wife of Archibald Carver, Aug. 29, 1823-June 24, 1861.
Jacob S. Horn, Nov. 1, 1814-Feb. 20, 1860.
Margaret J., wife of Jacob S. Horn, Aug. 10, 1827-Oct. 11, 1852.
Mary Purrell McWhirter, consort of Dr. S. C. McWhirter, born in Knoxville, April 30, 1800; born again a child of God, Sept. 16, 1822; she died a Christian, July 31, 1832.
Asa Jackson, Feb. 14, 1792-Aug. 30, 1870.
Nancy Jackson, July 18, 1800-Feb. 28, 1833.
W. B. Guthrie, Nov. 20, 1818-June 25, 1908.
Mary E., wife of W. R. Guthrie, Dec. 18, 1819-May 23, 1881.
J. A. Guthrie, 1844-1929.
W. H. Guthrie, May 13, 1846-July 5, 1909.
S. J. Guthrie, 1855-1923.
J. A. Sullivan, Feb. 6, 1846-July 11, 1924.
Nannie C. Guthrie, wife of J. A. Sullivan, Oct. 3, 1847-July 11, 1921.
Rev. Levi Fisher, Dec. 3, 1803-Sept. 17, 1866.
Susan Guthrie, wife of Rev. Levi Fisher, Oct. 20, 1816-July 31, 1898.
John W. Fisher, Jan. 22, 1845-Sept. 6, 1906.
Louisa C., wife of John W. Fisher, Aug. 11, 1845-June 1, 1911.
John Baker, 1835-July 27, 1886.
Agnes W. Baker, Jan. 22, 1837-June 21, 1873.
A. A. Dillard, Feb. 6, 1827-May 22, 1898.
Sarah J., wife of A. A. Dillard, Dec. 27, 1834-Jan. 31, 1909.
J. W. Clemmons, Oct. 31, 1841-Jan. 24, 1907.
Mary Thompson, wife of J. W. Clemmons, 1840-1901.
Sarah F. Cummings, born May 13, 1846; professed faith in Christ, July 14, 1861; joined the Baptist Church and was baptized Aug. 17, 1862; died, Dec. 22, 1872.
Charity Vincent, wife of Sam C. Stover, June 15, 1814-April 15, 1882.

Bible Records—Tombstone Inscriptions

WILLIAMSON GRAVEYARD

South of Nashville Pike, near Green Hill, on C. R. Williamson estate, Wilson County, Tenn. Sent by Mrs. W. P. Bouton, Lebanon, Tenn.

John Williamson, Green's Company, N. C. Regt., Rev. War.
James Williamson, Jan. 18, 1798-Sept. 3, 1834.
Lucy C., wife of James Williamson, Aug. 1, 1797-Jan. 13, 1864.
Elizabeth B. Williamson, Sept. 17, 1820-July 11, 1823.
William Williamson, Sept. 14, 1806-Aug. 20, 1823.
Nancy Evans Crutchfield, April 4, 1811-Aug. 7, 1853.
George Williamson, Oct. 10, 1793-Dec. 13, 1871.
Thomas E. Williamson, Feb. 15, 1818-June 18, 1870.
Fannie E. Williamson, July 3, 1827-Oct. 17, 1904.
Albert, infant son of Thomas E. and Fannie E. Williamson, Mar. 10, 1861-Jan. 27, 1865.
Maria, daughter of Thomas E. and Fannie E. Williamson, Dec. 15, 1857-Nov. 7, 1864.
Sarah S., wife of Thomas E. Williamson, Aug. 28, 1824-Nov. 7, 1845.
Nancy S. Williamson, May 29, 1837-Feb. 22, 1904.

Pink Maria Williamson, Mar. 10, 1844-Oct. 26, 1900.
George Williamson, Mar. 11, 1859-July 20, 1890.
Maggie, wife of H. L. Robertson, Nov. 3, 1855-May 6, 1888.
Sue Evans Tarbet, Mar. 12, 1857-May 29, 1881.
J. W. Williamson, 1848-1919.
Tabitha Williamson, 1856-1927.
John Kelley Stroud, Mar. 15, 1849-Jan. 4, 1911.
Fannie Stroud Grizzard, May 10, 1880-Nov. 13, 1903.
On one monument:
Nancy Sewell, May 29, 1837-Feb. 22, 1904.
Mary Jane, Mar. 18, 1846-July 2, 1912.
John Vann, July 11, 1830-Mar. 6, 1890.
Maria Mastison, Mar. 10, 1844-Oct. 22, 1900.
Ann Eliza, Mar. 16, 1832-Oct. 6, 1844.
Andrew W. Baird, April 13, 1833-July 6, 1875.
John M. P. Williamson, Aug. (scaled off).
One hundred or more graves, no markers.

MANN GRAVEYARD

North of Lebanon and west of Hunters Point Pike in Wilson County, Tenn. Sent by Mrs. W. P. Bouton, Lebanon, Tenn.

John Coleman Mann, Mar. 26, 1806-June 30, 1887.
A. E. Mann, Oct. 1, 1815-July 11, 1874.
To the memory of Mary W. Allen, June 22, 1813-Oct. 1, 1848.
H. C. Ford, Sept. 11, 1832-Dec. 26, 1916.
Liza Ford, Aug. 9, 1838-Mar. 23, 1907.
Hariett Burke, wife of Logan Burke,

1832-Mar. 5, 1891.
Walter Lee Padgett, April 7, 1877-June, 1903.
H. L. Padgett, April 24, 1881-Feb. 13, 1905.
Fannie J. Hill, Sept. 2, 1859-Feb. 1, 1864.
M. E. Goldston.
W. A. Goldston.

CORUM GRAVEYARD

West of Hunters Point Pike and North of Lebanon, Wilson County, Tenn. Sent by Mrs. W. P. Bouton, Lebanon, Tenn.

Logan Burke, May 3, 1822-April 18, 1877.

Ely Corum, April 11, 1807-Nov. 2, 1881.

Bible Records—Tombstone Inscriptions

Caroline Corum, July 8, 1810-Sept. 2, 1875.
Dollie Lavender, died May 11, 1832.
William Austian Bettis, May 18, 1827-June 15, 1890.
Mary Bettis, Dec. 1, 1830-June 20, 1898.
Sarah Jane Bettis, Oct. 7, 1850-Feb. 1, 1890.
Mary Margaret Bettis, Oct. 2, 1873-June 3, 1879.

HOLMAN GRAVEYARD

North of Lebanon on S. B. Webber Farm, Wilson County, Tenn. Sent by Mrs. W. P. Bouton, Lebanon, Tenn.

Thomas Holman, consort of Anna Holman, Jan., 1817-Jan. 30, 1851.
Thomas Holman, consort of Frances Holman, June 30, 1815-June 17, 1850.
Robert M. Holman, consort of Elizabeth Holman, June 8, 1805-Oct. 3, 1954.
To the memory of Dr. German Y. Holman, consort of Marcia B. Holman, Feb. 20, 1807-Sept. 7, 1871.

WHARTON GRAVEYARD

Three miles east of Lebanon, Wilson County, Tenn., on Peyton Place. Sent by Mrs. W. P. Bouton, Lebanon, Tenn.

Joseph P. Wharton, Oct. 10, 1806-Sept. 26, 1866.
Caroline C. Hewitt, wife of J. P. Wharton, Sept. 8, 1809-Jan. 20, 1881.
Joseph P. Wharton, Jr., Aug. 23, 1837-May 9, 1865, at Rock Island, a Prisoner of War.
Caroline Wharton, infant daughter of J. P. and Caroline Wharton, Jan. 9, 1841-Oct., 1843; age, 2 years, 9 months, 9 days.
Isabella Wharton, Aug. 9, 1845-Mar. 24, 1901.
Robert Hewitt Peyton, Mar. 31, 1882-June 27, 1902.
Emily Hatton Peyton, Sept. 19, 1880-April 13, 1908.
Sallie A. Tutt, died Sept. 20, 1867; age, 32 years.
William Morgan, Sept. 21, 1825-Oct. 31, 1887.

WILLIAM SEAY GRAVEYARD

North of Trousdale Ferry Pike, near Smith County line, Wilson County, Tenn. Sent by Mrs. W. P. Bouton, Lebanon, Tenn.

Maj. W. W. Seay, died Mar. 24, 1874; age, 72 years, 11 months, 21 days.
Ann W., wife of W. W. Seay, died Sept. 21, 1872; age, 67 years, 8 months, 12 days.
Charlie I. Seay, Dec. 18, 1836-July 21, 1890.
Victoria Rives Seay, Mar. 24, 1839-June 2, 1902.
Thomas J. Seay, Jan. 9, 1841-Nov. 30, 1887.
Lelia V. Seay, wife of Thomas J. Seay, Jan. 1, 1845-Oct. 13, 1884; age, 39 years, 9 months, 12 days.
Sidney, son of T. J. and L. V. Seay, died Dec. 11, 1864- age, 8 months.

CLOYD GRAVEYARD

South of Nashville Pike, on Duncan Ligon Place, Wilson County, Tenn. Sent by Mrs. W. P. Bouton, Lebanon, Tenn.

John W. Cloyd, Feb. 7, 1814-Aug. 8, 1880.
Sarah W. Cloyd, wife of J. W. Cloyd, Mar. 26, 1816-Sept. 4, 1887.

Bible Records—Tombstone Inscriptions

Elizabeth, wife of Henry Bullington, Mar. 20, 1807-Feb. 22, 1889.
John W., son of J. W. and S. W. Cloyd, Nov. 28, 1847-July 26, 1854.
Allie W., daughter of J. W. and S. W. Cloyd, Nov. 14, 1854-Nov. 19, 1864.
W. B. Cloyd, Dec. 25, 1854-Oct. 12, 1900.
Dora T. Cloyd, Nov. 6, 1859-April 25, 1916.
Jammie, son of E. B. and I. M. Viverett, Mar. 13, 1869-April 6, 1869.
John W., son of L. I. and E. V. Ligon, May 15, 1879-Mar. 23, 1881.
F. W., son of W. B. and E. V. Ligon, April 30, 1893-July 7, 1894.
Four or five graves, no markers.

Geers Graveyard

South of Nashville Pike, about three miles west of Lebanon, Wilson County, Tenn. Sent by Mrs. W. P. Bouton, Lebanon.

Wm. G. Geers, born in Lunenburgh County, Va., May 23, 1821-Feb. 17, 1895.
Emily Woolard Geers, July 28, 1828-July 12, 1890.
Edward Franklin Geers, Jan. 25, 1851-Sept. 3, 1924.
Narcisus Geers, born in Lunenburgh County, Va., 1819-1903.
Seven names on large monument, no dates.

Carter Graveyard

Near Taylorsville, between Rome and Hartsville Pike, about ten miles from Lebanon, Tenn. Sent by Mrs. W. P. Bouton, Lebanon.

Joseph G. Bell, Dec. 18, 1800-Mar. 23, 1879.
Mary P. Bell, wife of J. G. Bell, Mar. 31, 1804-Mar. 31, 1871.
James Bell, Jan. 26, 1824-Sept. 29, 1841.
Robert D. Bell, Mar. 16, 1826-Aug. 2, 1849.
Martha A. Bell, Dec. 8, 1833-Aug. 23, 1855.
Josephine Bell, July 22, 1848-Sept. 22, 1849.
C. D. Young, May 16, 1861-Feb. 16, 1883.
W. H. Carter, Dec. 4, 1821-Aug. 31, 1902.
Mary W. Dickens, wife of W. H. Carter, Jan. 27, 1843-Oct. 10, 1900.
C. T. Carter, Sept. 11, 1832-Aug. 27, 1902.
Mattie, wife of C. T. Carter, born, 1837.

Bond Graveyard

Ten miles south of Lebanon, Tenn., one mile west of Murfreesboro Pike, on old Bond Place, Wilson County, Tenn. Sent by Mrs. W. P. Bouton, Lebanon, Tenn.

George Washington Cummings Bond, son of John Bond, Nov. 11, 1815-Nov. 8, 1868.
Martha Ann Bond, wife of G. W. C. Bond, Jan. 7, 1823-June 3, 1889.
Mary Cradock, Nov. 27, 1795-Jan. 10, 1869.
William C. Cradock, Nov. 29, 1784-Feb. 16, 1867.
Monroe M. Bond, son of G. W. and Martha Ann Bond, Jan. 31, 1843-Oct. 16, 1883.
Sophronia Jane Bond, daughter of G. W. C. and Martha Ann Bond, April 28, 1844-Dec. 25, 1864.
Nancy Caroline Lannom, Jan. 2, 1834-Mar. 21, 1925.

Bible Records—Tombstone Inscriptions

ROWLAND GRAVEYARD

About seven miles southwest of Lebanon, Tenn. Sent by Mrs. W. P. Bouton, Lebanon, Tenn.

Henry Shannon, Sr., Jan. 10, 1766-Sept. 25, 1844.
Jane Shannon, Mar. 22, 1772-Dec. 10, 1852.
My Ma Sally, consort of Morris Brewer, Feb. 15, 1793-Aug. 8, 1865.
My Pa Morris Brewer, April 7, 1792-Mar. 21, 1866.
Mary Jane Brewer, Mar. 15, 1824-Aug. 26, 1841.
E. J. Shannon, Sept. 29, 1829-July 27, 1894.
F. E. Shannon, Nov. 20, 1814-Mar. 18, 1895.
William B. Shannon, Feb. 9, 1836-July 9, 1862.
R. A. Shannon, Dec. 25, 1826-Aug. 28, 1865.
In memory of James Shannon, Dec. 10, 1795-Aug. 7, 1867.
In memory of Mrs. Mary H. Shannon, wife of James Shannon, Nov. 20, 1794-Aug. 12, 1865.
In memory of Lucinda H., daughter of James and Mary H. Shannon, Aug. 13, 1817-June 25, 1864.
Sacred to the memory of Rachel C. Carraway, consort of James P. Richmond, May 11, 1827-July 12, 1851.
John A. Shannon, Dec. 20, 1804-Dec. 23, 1882.
Jesse L. Moore, Sept. 28, 1805-May 5, 1883.
Caroline M. T., wife of J. L. Moore, June 25, 1820-Aug. 13, 1857.
Sarah Moore, wife of J. L. Moore, Jan. 9, 1807-Jan. 21, 1844.
Cornelia Moore, wife of J. W. Ragsdale, born Jan. 18, 1851; married, Sept. 8, 1870; died, Dec. 11, 1899.
Cyrus J. Moore, April 16, 1847-May 11, 1881.
Barbara Crawford, Feb. 8, 1772-Sept. 15, 1827.
Barbara Crawford, wife of V. G. Haralson, Feb. 10, 1831-July 22, 1896.
In memory of Edmund Crawford, died Sept. 24, 1860, in 75 year of age.
William Haralson, son of Rowland, Dec. 8, 1857-July 25, 1875.
David Rowland, April 12, 1831-Dec. 17, 1888.
Amanda Estell, daughter of M. T. and A. L. Rowland, Nov. 26, 1889-Nov. 18, 1893.
In memory of James H. Osment, June 14, 1821-Nov. 17, 1834.
In memory of Lannora Osment, Feb. 7, 1828-Aug. 31, 1840.
Joseph Swingley, Aug. 14, 1790-June 27, 1820.
Elizabeth Harpole, April 1, 1792-Dec. 28, 1824.
In memory of James Jones, Dec. 22, 1837-Aug. 1, 1852.
In memory of Sarah E. Waters, Dec. 4, 1851-Aug. 1, 1852.
James D. Brown, July 16, 1866-Feb. 24, 1888.
Infant of T. G. and S. C. Cook, died July 15, 1853.
Wilson County, Tenn., between old Franklin Road and Central Pike, on old Wool Factory Road.

EDDINS GRAVEYARD

Seven miles west of Lebanon, Wilson County, Tenn., on Tuckers Gap Road, south of the N. C. R. R. Sent by Mrs. W. P. Bouton.

Rebecca Osment, wife of Richard S. Osment, 1800-Dec., 1845.
Jane Eddins, May 8, 1805-July 29, 1823.
Lucinda Capel, July 2, 1809-July 10, 1835.
B. F. Eddins, July 7, 1829-Oct. 7, 1838.
T. H. Eddins, Sept. 7, 1846-Sept. 3, 1922.
Lila Eddins, born June 26, 1849; living.
Jordan Eddins, Jan. 27, 1857-Oct. 12, 1916.
Nannie Eddins, June 9, 1858-Sept. 15, 1923.
W. M. Eddins, Mar. 19, 1881-Feb. 2, 1918.

Bible Records—Tombstone Inscriptions

Julia G. Eddins, born July 30, 1882; living.
H. P. Eddins, June 29, 1882-Jan. 27, 1912.
Several graves with no markers.

Major Graveyard

Seven miles west of Lebanon, Wilson County, Tenn., on Tuckers Gap Road, north of the N. C. R. R. Sent by Mrs. W. P. Bouton.

James H. Peyton, Oct. 12, 1812-Dec. 7, 1852.
Nancy Maria, wife of James H. Peyton, Nov. 3, 1815-Mar. 9, 1892.
Sarah Jane, wife of Louis Westbrook, Sept. 27, 1838-Nov. 30, 1860.

Perkins Graveyard

Two miles west of Lebanon, Wilson County, Tenn., on Tuckers Gap Road. Sent by Mrs. W. P. Bouton, Lebanon, Tenn.

John Perkins, July 15, 1806-April 11, 1880.
A. M. Perkins, Jan. 27, 1832-Oct. 20, 1898.
Sarah E. Campbell, wife of A. M. Perkins, Aug. 28, 1835-Mar. 6, 1910.
Pheney Ann Cornelia, daughter of A. M. and S. E. Perkins, Aug. 11, 1869-Dec. 4, 1888.
Montgomery Owen, Jan. 23, 1830-Oct. 17, 1898.
Syrena L. Perkins, wife of Montgomery Owen, Oct. 29, 1839-Oct. 16, 1886.
John A. Owen, Jan. 15, 1859-Mar. 4, 1917.
J. D. Bettis, Mar. 15, 1823-July 24, 1889.
Margaret E., wife of J. D. Bettis, Jan. 15, 1830-Sept. 23, 1861.
Mary J. Perkins, wife of J. D. Bettis, June 19, 1836-May 10, 1916.
Winnie L. Bettis, wife of Fil Eatherly, June 8, 1865-Mar. 13, 1897.
Paul W. Eatherly, Nov. 21, 1896-July 16, 1897.
Myra Sanders, July 26, 1870-April 28, 1910.
Allen M. Jones, Oct. 15, 1886-Nov. 15, 1913.
W. N. Morgan, Oct. 6, 1888-Aug. 7, 1913.
Many more graves not marked.

Osment Graveyard

South of Lebanon, Wilson County, Tenn., on Murfreesboro Pike, about three miles from Lebanon. Sent by Mrs. W. P. Bouton.

(On same monument.)
Cam Osment, died Nov. 15, 1890.
Catherine Osment, wife of Cam Osment, died Dec. 13, 1896; age, 77 years.
Luther Osment, died Oct. 10, 1897.
John Osment, died Oct., 1902; age, 48 years.
G. T. Osment, died Nov. 11, 1909; age, 61 years.

———

"Good-by, Aunt Jennie." Jane Drake, 1801-Mar. 25, 1895.
Angie Lain, wife of R. G. Osment, June 17, 1870-Sept. 1, 1894.
Stella Blanch Fields, June 13, 1873-Aug. 31, 1906.
David C. Fields, April 8, 1831-April 26, 1892.
Henry C. Fields, Oct. 9, 1857-Jan. 28, 1890.
John C. Fields, born Oct. 24, 1856; married Mary Skeen, Oct. 5, 1876; died, Mar. 20, 1893.
Gracie Lee Fields, July 17, 1897-June 12, 1898.
Susan M., wife of R. F. Floyd, Mar. 22, 1862-Oct. 18, 1895.

Bible Records—Tombstone Inscriptions

Old box tomb walled up with rock, no inscription, some pioneer.
Mattie Pass, April 29, 1893-May 9, 1893.
Ernest G., son of J. H. and M. J. Pass, Nov. 2, 1884-Dec. 25, 1894.

CASTLEMAN GRAVEYARD

South of Lebanon, Wilson County, Tenn., on Murfreesboro Pike, about four miles from Lebanon. Sent by Mrs. W. P. Bouton.

Aramenta, wife of R. B. Castleman, Mar. 20, 1810-Sept. 2, 1885.
R. B. Castleman, Mar. 12, 1814-April 29, 1896.
Jacob M. Castleman, Sept. 24, 1821-April 17, 1901.
Margaret Ann Castleman, Mar. 29, 1846-Aug. 20, 1908.
Nancy Caroline, wife of William Castleman, Mar. 16, 1848-June 25, 1892.
Claude Liston Clemmons, Sept. 15, 1887-Nov. 21, 1887.

REED GRAVEYARD

South of Lebanon, Tenn., Wilson County, Sent by Mrs. W. P. Bouton, Lebanon, Tenn.

Sallie Reed, May 6, 1808-Sept. 21, 1821.
Eli Reed, Nov. 24, 1813-Dec. 2, 1900.
Sophia Reed,. Mar. 13, 1841-July 2, 1909.
J. S. Reed, Jan. 18, 1848-Aug. 12, 1929.
Mrs. Fannie Graves, died Oct. 19, 1924; age, 86 years. M. F. G.
"Next to this grave is another foot stone with R. M. G. on it."
Kate E. Reed, wife of G. H. Reed, Sept. 24, 1863-July 6, 1901.
Amy L. Shorter, wife of W. B. Shorter, Dec. 22, 1869-June 18, 1907.
Monroe Shorter, Dec. 2, 1892-Dec. 7, 1910.
Two large pine trees in this graveyard.

BAIRD GRAVEYARD

South of Lebanon, Wilson County, Tenn., on road leading east from Murfreesboro Pike. Sent by Mrs. W. P. Bouton.

Dr. Thomas J. Baird, June 6, 1816-Oct. 24, 1841; age, 25 years, 4 months, 18 days.
In memory of Emanuel C. Baird, Feb. 26, 1819-Sept. 2, 1850; age, 30 years, 6 months, 6 days.
Mary G. Baird, wife of W. H. L. Baird, May 15, 1835-Jan. 1, 1854; age, 18 years, 7 months, 16 days.
In memory of Sallie B. Baird, only child of W. H. L. and Mary G. Baird, Oct. 16, 1853-June 8, 1854; age, 7 months, 22 days.
Of sweet memory of Permelia A., wife of W. R. McDaniel, Feb. 13, 1846-Oct. 5, 1874.
Mary C., wife of D. R. Fakes, June 16, 1831-Jan. 31, 1893.
Mary S., wife of F. L. Morton, daughter of C. J. T. and M. Baird, May 11, 1864-Dec. 23, 1888.
In bad condition, stock trampling, stones knocked over and broken in this Baird Graveyard.
Reed being used, some of relations live on place.

BURTON GRAVEYARD

West of Lebanon, Wilson County, Tenn. Sent by Mrs. W. P. Bouton, Lebanon, Tenn.

Dedicated to the memory of James Mingle Burton, who was born in Mecklenburg County, Va., Jan. 23, 1761, and departed this life Feb. 16, 1844; age,

Bible Records—Tombstone Inscriptions

83 years, 23 days. "Rest in Hopes sweet shade till resurrection morn." By his daughter, M. A. B. (Box tomb.)
Mrs. Elizabeth Burton, consort of James Mingle Burton, and daughter of Bondfield Ridle, born 27th day of Aug., A. D., 1771, in Granville County, N. C.; departed this life on the 4th day of Jan., A. D., 1838. (Box tomb.)
Col. Robert Burton, Nov. 20, 1800-Oct. 26, 1843. He entered the bar at Lebanon, a stranger, 1823. By force of his talents he soon won and ever retained distinction. He was a conspicuous member of the Legislature in 1827 and the Convention of 1834. He lived in Lebanon 20 years, a prominent member of the bar and society; died in the Christian faith, a member of the Cumberland Presbyterian Church. (Box tomb.)
Here lies the remains of Robert Burton, son of Ralph and E. C. Martin, June 26, 1846-April 27, 1848; also their infant child, Martha Harris, Feb. 19, 1848-Jan. 14, 1849.

MARTIN

Ralph Martin, 1810-1866.
Elizabeth B. Martin, 1827-1909.
William B. Martin, 1852-1916.
Sallie M. Eastman, 1854-1877.
Eight miles from Lebanon on Nashville Pike. Copied by Mrs. W. P. Bouton, 139 Hatton Avenue, Lebanon, Tenn.

GWYNN FAMILY GRAVEYARD

Eight miles from Lebanon on Nashville Pike. Copied by Mrs. W. P. Bouton, 139 Hatton Avenue, Lebanon, Tenn.

Robert Gwynn, Nov. 18, 1803-May 29, 1888.
Judith P. H., wife of R. Gwynn, Feb. 3, 1813-May 11, 1882.
J. R. Gwynn, Sept. 22, 1848-Jan. 14, 1908.
Rannie, son of J. R. and Alice Gwynn, Nov. 2, 1883-Nov. 27, 1883.
Walter Davis Evertson, April 5, 1819-Mar. 14, 1892.
Ann Mary Fatheree, wife of W. D. Evertson, Aug. 30, 1831-Sept. 1, 1890.
Addie M. Evertson, wife of George C. Oldham, Jan. 13, 1867-Feb. 22, 1892.
(Furnished by Mrs. J. R. Gwynn, whose home is in Wilson County, Tenn.)

CALHOUN GRAVEYARD

On Cedar Creek, Wilson County, Tenn. Sent by Mrs. W. P. Bouton, Lebanon, Tenn.

Sacred to the memory of Hugh Roan and Hannah, his consort. Both professed religion early in life, lived exemplary lives and died in the faith of the gospel.
Hugh Roan was born in the State of Pennsylvania in 1765 and died in May, 1825.
Hannah Roan was born in North Carolina, Aug. 24, 1775-Mar. 18, 1851. (Above is on same monument.)
In memory of James Roane, 1795-Aug. 4, 1859; age, 65 years. (Old box tomb.)
Our father; he was dear to us. Rev. Thomas Calhoun, May 31, 1782-April 13, 1855. (Shaft.)
In memory of Mary R. Calhoun, wife of Rev. Thomas Calhoun, departed this life Mar. 18, 1850; age, 60 years, 7 months. (Shaft broken.)
In memory of Rev. John Provine, Mar. 30, 1784-July 30, 1855. (Box tomb.)
In memory of Jane Provine, consort of John Provine, Jan. 30, 1787-June 11, 1830. (Box tomb.)
In memory of Rebecca Eliza, consort of O. B. Stailey, May 31, 1831-Oct. 29, 1858.
To the memory of Samuel Calhoun, Jr., Mar. 10, 1791- Aug. 2, 1859.
In memory of W. M. Johnston, April 6, 1796-Sept. 2, 1840.
(The above two graves are on Mr. Hamlett Grissim's place in lot in different places, about a mile from Calhoun Graveyard, on Cedar Creek, Wilson County, Tenn.)

Bible Records—Tombstone Inscriptions

CALHOUN OLD GRAVEYARD

On side of hill on Cedar Creek about six miles northeast of Lebanon, Wilson County, Tenn. Sent by Mrs. W. P. Bouton, 139 Hatton Avenue, Lebanon, Tenn.

In bad condition, rocks under sides of box tombs scattered, stock trampling and tombs broken.

WILLIAM PALMER FAMILY GRAVEYARD

Near Linwood, Wilson County, Tenn. Sent by Mrs. W. P. Bouton, Lebanon, Tenn.

Sarah Palmer, died Nov. 4, 1858; age, 78 years.
William Palmer, died Mar. 12, 1857; age, 81 years. (On same.) And his sons:
Francis, died Nov. 30; age, 47 years.
Henry, died Oct. 16.
Henry Palmer, Dec. 24, 1818-1844.
Francis Palmer, April 6, 1815-Nov. 30, 1857.
Robert Palmer, Oct. 27, 1807-July 18, 1855.
Victoria Phelps, Sept. 10, 1807-Nov. 2, 1871.
Emily F. Williams, daughter of Robert and Victoria Phelps, Mar. 2, 1844-May 9, 1872.
Martha J. Williams, daughter of R. and V. Phelps, Jan. 23, 1841-Aug. 17, 1877.
Martha S. Bennett, Dec. 24, 1822-Oct. 28, 1848.
Sarah Phelps, Feb. 11, 1835-Feb. 11, 1868.
Martha J. Bone, July 23, 1855-Oct. 20, 1869.
C. L. Murphy, Nov. 8, 1822-Dec. 17, 1892.
Sarah A. Murphy, Feb. 24, 1825-April 12, 1896.
Infant son of J. W. and S. E. McKee, born Aug. 25, 1888.
Infant son of D. W. and Tabbie Grandstaff, born and died Oct. 26, 1886.
Infant son of J. W. and S. E. McKee, Dec. 6, 1878-Dec. 8, 1878.
(Place now belongs to Mr. Charles Murphy, a descendant.)

JOHN PALMER FAMILY GRAVEYARD

Five miles north of Lebanon, Wilson County, Tenn. Sent by Mrs. W. P. Bouton, 139 Hatton Avenue, Lebanon, Tenn.

John Palmer, April 13, 1804-Feb. 23, 1892.
Margaret Palmer, Jan. 11, 1803-Jan. 5, 1874.
(Both on tall shaft.)
Ellen Palmer, July 30, 1841-Nov. 17, 1895.
Louisa Chambers, Dec. 7, 1833-June, 1900.
(Both of above on same shaft.)
Sarah Chambers, Dec. 31, 1854-Nov. 12, 1882. (Slab.)
(J. L. Chambers owns and lives on plase; is grandson. John Palmer was son of William Palmer.)

RESOLUTIONS OF CONDOLENCE

Sent to Mrs. George Washington Vaughan on the death of her husband by Board of Supervisors of Benton County, Mississippi, 1871. Sent by Mrs. W. P. Bouton, 139 Hatton Avenue, Lebanon.

"At a regular meeting of the Board of Supervisors of Benton County, Miss., held on the 7th day of August, 1871, the following preamble and reso-

Bible Records—Tombstone Inscriptions

lutions were unanimously adopted:
" 'Whereas, it has pleased an allwise and inscrutable Providence, to whose mandate it becomes us all with utmost reverence to bow, to remove from our midst our friend and countryman, Major G. W. Vaughan. Thus in the bloom and vigor of manhood, with a heart filled with desire for the religious and intellectual advancement of society, especially for the permanent establishment and prosperity of his country, he was summoned to meet the stern realities of an unknown future. Had he been spared to enjoy the establishment of the schools and churches in his beloved Ashland, "within sight of his home," an object for the accomplishment of which he labored so indefatigably and spent his means so liberally, it would have been gratifying to those who knew him best; but it was ordained otherwise, and he bowed meekly to the fiat of Him who ruleth all things according to the counsel of His own will; and he is lost to his county, lost to his family, lost to us. Therefore, resolved: That in the death of Major Vaughan this community has lost a generous benefactor, and his family a living and indulgent protector, and his county its warmest and most efficient advocate.
" 'Resolved: That we deeply deplore this dispensation of the divine will, and extend our heart-felt sympathy to the bereaved family and relations of the deceased, with our earnest desire that the great disposer of events who "suffers not a hair of our heads to fall without his notice" will overrule this sad affliction for good, and that it may be the means of leading others to seek that rest that afforded him such sweet composure and joy amidst the throes of dissolving Nature.
" 'Resolved: That the Clerk of this Board be required to furnish the Holly Springs Reporter and Ripley Advertiser with a copy of these resolutions, and request their publication and that he furnish the family of the deceased with a copy also.'
Signed, P. M. Gatlin,
Pres. of Board of Supervisors.
Ashland, Aug. 7, 1871."
State of Mississippi,
Benton County.
By order of the Honorable Board of Supervisors of said county. Passed Aug. 7, 1871.
Ordered that the resolutions relating to the death of Major G. W. Vaughan be received and spread upon the minutes of this Court, and the clerk have same published in Ripley Advertiser and Holly Springs Reporter.
By order of Court.
Signed, John H. Morgan,
Clerk of Board.
(From original sent to my mother which I have.)

Wynne Graveyard

Four miles west of Lebanon, Wilson County, Tenn., one-half mile north of Hickory Ridge Road. Sent by Mrs. W. P. Bouton, 139 Hatton Avenue, Lebanon, Tenn.

Col. John K. Wynne, born Jan. 16, 1765-Jan. 7, 1847. (Box tomb, falling.)
Sacred to the memory of Lucy Wynne, Oct. 13, 1777-June 29, 1853. (Box tomb, falling.)
Sacred to the memory of Dr. John L. Wynne, Aug. 31, 1797-Sept. 24, 1829.
Thomas K. Wynne, Dec. 23, 1807-Aug. 12, 1861.
Wife of Thomas K. Wynne, Jan. 11, 1817-Sept. 23, 1859.
William H. Wynne, born Dec. 23, 1817; married to R. E. Babb, April 1, 1842; died, April 2, 1867.
Sacred to the memory of Matilda A. Bledsoe, wife of O. F. Bledsoe, Jan. 28, A. D., 1835-Feb. 8, A. D., 1837.
"Wynne"—In loving memory of Alanson Gallatin Wynne, July 10, 1850-Aug. 12, 1920.
(Many other graves with only rock markers.)

Bible Records—Tombstone Inscriptions

"ONE GRAVE"

Six miles from Lebanon, west, Wilson County, Tenn., one-half mile north of Hickory Ridge Road. Sent by Mrs. W. P. Bouton.

John Seay, Oct. 9, 1794-Feb. 19, 1885; local minister of the M. E. Church. Grave concreted all over last year.

WHITE GRAVEYARD

North of Bellwood, Wilson County, Tenn. Sent by Mrs. W. P. Bouton, 139 Hatton Avenue, Lebanon, Tenn.

Dr. James Dearing White, 1802-1874; a friend and neighbor.
Mary Eleanor Rogers White, 1816-1865. A good wife and mother.
(Both on same granite monument.)
To the memory of Lucy A. White, Dec. 22, 1810-Nov. 10, 1847; age, 36 years, 10 months, 18 days. (Shaft.)
To the memory of Nathaniel Powell, 1762-1827. A soldier of the American Revolution, 1776-1782.
His wife, Elizabeth Cowper, daughter of Philip Cowper, of the Revolutionary Navy.
(Both on same monument.)
To the memory of Nancy White, Dec. 30, 1838-Dec. 13, 1842; age, 3 years, 11 months, 13 days.
To the memory of James White, Sept. 9, 1833-Dec. 15, 1833.
Mary C., wife of David C. Scales, born April 2, 1844; married May 7, 1873; died, Nov. 21, 1873. "Blessed are the pure in heart, for they shall see God."
(The White Graveyard has a splendid rock wall put up in later years; best condition of any visited.)

TARVER PRIVATE GRAVEYARD

Tuckers Gap, Wilson County, Tenn. Sent by Mrs. W. P. Bouton, 139 Hatton Avenue, Lebanon, Tenn. (Copied by Mrs. H. H. Hagan, nee Nancy Tarver, who is at the home.)

Sacred to the memory of Nancy Harris Tarver, wife of Silas Tarver, Nov. 8, 1799-Feb. 23, 1840.
Silas Tarver, Nov. 10, 1795-June 10, 1862.
Lucinda Burdine, second wife of Silas Tarver, Feb. 20, 1812-May 20, 1868.
Mary Elizabeth, daughter of Silas and Nancy Tarver, May 12, 1829-July 10, 1853.
Lucy Elmira, daughter of Silas and Lucinda Tarver, Feb. 20, 1841-May 10, 1847.
(Above on one large monument.)
Mattie Rowland Tarver, July 2, 1863-Nov. 10, 1887. "Our precious one, asleep in Jesus."
Lucy Hobson, daughter of Lucy and John Tarver, Mar. 5, 1861-Nov. 15, 1873.
Frank Hobson, son of John B. and Lucy Tarver, Mar. 8, 1861-Dec. 29, 1863.
Laurence L. Tarver, Sept. 1, 1869-July 4, 1889.
"Asleep in Jesus precious son,
A sweet unbroken sleep,
Which the hand of death has won,
But there is still a blessed sleep."
"Mother."
J. Eddie Tarver, April 13, 1867-Sept. 2, 1889.
"A precious one from us is gone,
A voice we loved is still,
A place is vacant in our home,
Which never can be filled."
"Mother."
Lucy Hobson, wife of John B. Tarver, born Aug. 9, 1837; married John B. Tarver, Feb. 23, 1856; died, July 26, 1891. "Piously did she live and triumphantly did she die. He last words were: 'Glory, glory.'"
John B. Tarver, June 14, 1835-Aug. 17, 1906.

Bible Records—Tombstone Inscriptions

RUCKS GRAVEYARD

In edge of Smith County, Tenn., west of Rome. Sent by Mrs. Bouton, 139 Hatton Avenue, Lebanon, Tenn.

In memory of Rev. Josiah Rucks, born in Chesterfield County, Va., April 3, 1757; died in Smith County, Tenn., Aug. 5, 1836. He was a soldier of the Revolution; a minister of the gospel in the Baptist Church for sixty years. And, above all, that noblest of the works of God, an honest man. The memory of the just is blest. (Box tomb.)
Mrs. Elizabeth, consort of Josiah Rucks, Jan. 27, 1769-Dec. 6, 1856; age, 86 years. She was a Christian woman. (Box tomb.)
Ben Rucks, Mar. 20, 1805-April 10, 1883.
H. T. Rucks, Nov. 7, 1807-April 3, 1874.
Bertha, wife of H. T. Rucks, Jan. 3, 1813-May 23, 1866.
Lyda, wife of Tarlton, Feb. 15, 1789-Oct. 14, 1878; age, 89 years, 8 months.
W. B. Rucks, Jan. 20, 1847-Mar. 20, 1885.
James T. Rucks, Aug. 6, 1850-Aug. 3, 1919.
H. T. Rucks, 1838-1910.
Sallie Rucks, 1844-1929.
In memory of Mary Toney, wife of Elijah Toney, Feb. 17, 1792-Nov. 23, 1828.
Elizabeth Hubbard, deceased Nov. 21, 1824; age, 25 years, 6 months, 17 days.
S. O. McDonald, Nov. 24, 1830-June 15, 1863.
Sacred to the memory of Rebecah Hibbitt, consort of D. C. Hibbitt, Jan. 16, 1801-July 9, 1842; died the death of the righteous.
(There are five more Hibbitt; rainstorm prevented copying.)

MAJ. ISAAC TAYLOR FAMILY GRAVEYARD

East of Smithville on road to Sparta, Tenn. (This graveyard is on a side road north of highway in White County.) Sent by Mrs. W. P. Bouton.

Maj. Isaac Taylor, Jan. 11, 1781-June 2, 1854.
F. E. J. Taylor, Feb. 7, 1828-May 3, 1876.
John D. Taylor, Feb. 3, 1819-July 9, 1894.
T. E. Taylor, Sept. 22, 1829-June 17, 1909.
F. R. Taylor, May 27, 1863-Dec. 17, 1885.
A. L. Davis, Aug. 17, 1804-Aug. 14, 1871.
C. H. Davis, Sept. 9, 1840-Oct. 6, 1863.
Douglas B. Davis, May 6, 1842-Feb. 13, 1872.
Ammie L. Davis, daughter of I. L. and H. H. Davis, Jan. 29, 1873-Nov. 23, 1888.
Maggie Davis, daughter of I. L. and H. E. Davis, April 28, 1880-July 1, 18—.
(This graveyard is on a side road north of the highway in White County.)

The following two graves are box tombs just over the fence near Centerville on the Beasley Bend Road in Wilson County, Tenn. Sent by Mrs. W. P. Bouton, 139 Hatton Avenue, Lebanon, Tenn.

Sacred to the memory of Samuel Johnson, who was born Jan. 20, 1779, and departed this life June 12, 1857; age, 77 years, 1 month, 17 days.
Sacred to the memory of Rev. Jesse Johnson, June 29, 1777-Oct. 31, 1856.

Bible Records—Tombstone Inscriptions

The following grave is a box tomb and only one at that place about four miles east of Lebanon, Wilson County, Tenn. Sent by Mrs. W. P. Bouton, 139 Hatton Avenue, Lebanon, Tenn.

Sacred to the memory of Maria Edwards who departed this life Oct. 5, 1811; age, 86 years.

BASS

Second District, Wilson County, Tenn., south of Nashville Pike, on Harry Bass farm. Sent by Mrs. W. P. Bouton.

Sion Bass, Aug. 1, 1781-Aug. 20, 1847.
Mary Bass, consort of Sion Bass, July 23, 1789-May 18, 1857.
Cader Bass, Mar., 1790-Oct. 28, 1858.
M. P. Anderson, July 12, 1810-June 24, 1891.
Milberry, wife of M. P. Anderson, Sept. 17, 1823-Jan. 16, 1898.
Sallie Freeman, Jan. 3, 1812-Jan. 5, 1882.
H. T. Bass, Dec. 25, 1809-Oct. 19, 1894.
Nancy W. Bass, April 26, 1817-Oct. 14, 1904.
P. W. Weatherford, April 6, 1826-Nov. 28, 1898.
Louvinia C. Weatherford, Feb. 29, 1830-Dec. 16, 1898.
Elizabeth E. Patton, Sept. 4, 1828-Sept. 2, 1882.
Mary A. M., wife of H. P. Reavis, daughter of Richard and Mary Anderson, Mar. 22, 1827-Sept. 17, 1848.
John E. Graves, Aug. 12, 1823-May 24, 1895.
Ary Ella, wife of J. E. Graves, Sept. 11, 1837-Mar. 29, 1890.
H. L. Bass, July 21, 1834-Oct. 16, 1898.
Almeda V. Bass, 1833-1922.
(A few of the older ones from a large cemetery.)

VIVRETT

Second District, Wilson County, Tenn., south of Nashville Pike, on J. M. Walker place. Sent by Mrs. W. P. Bouton.

Thomas, consort of J. A. Vivrett, Feb. 14, 1826-Oct. 11, 1869.
Jane McWhirter, Sept. 6, 1830-July 3, 1889.
(These are the only old ones that are marked; many other graves not marked.)

SMITH

Second District, Wilson County, on road leading south from Martha to Leeville. Sent by Mrs. W. P. Bouton.

Samuel Smith, Nov. 25, 1800-Feb. 1, 1869.
Dicy B. Smith, April 29, 1808-Nov. 24, 1889.
Nancy A. Smith, Feb. 14, 1845-Aug. 3, 1929.
(These three graves concreted all over; 12 or more graves no markers.)

McFARLAND

Second District, Wilson County, Tenn., on road leading south from Martha to Leeville, on hill southwest of old McFarland home. Sent by Mrs. W. P. Bouton, 139 Hatton Avenue, Lebanon, Tenn.

James McFarland, born in the Fort at Nashville, Jan. 10, 1784-April, 1856.
Dicy Bilbro McFarland, 1784-Feb., 1865.
Dicy Ann Whisitt, Dec., 1818-May, 1872. Her children rise up and call her blessed.
(Several more graves not marked.)

Bible Records—Tombstone Inscriptions

DAVIS

Second District, Wilson County, Tenn., one-half mile north of Beckwith. Sent by Mrs. W. P. Bouton.

Sham F. Davis, June 19, 1800-Jan. 20, 1880.
Sallie Davis, Nov. 10, 1802-Aug. 11, 1887.
Alice Reynolds, wife of R. T. Davis, born July 25, 1844; married, July 14, 1870; died, July 10, 1872.
W. P. Davis, Aug. 19, 1833-Mar. 26, 1902.
Elizabeth Lindsay Davis, Mar. 6, 1834-Jan. 16, 1929.

EATHERLY

Second District, Wilson County, Tenn., on road leading from Beckwith to Nashville Pike, north. Sent by Mrs. W. P. Bouton.

T. E. Eatherly, Dec. 11, 1810-1870.
W. Scott Eatherly, Dec. 15, 1841-Mar. 1, 1889.
Amanda M. Sanders, Sept. 22, 1846-
Oct. 9, 1921.
J. V. Vanhooser, June 2, 1851-May 9, 1919.

EATHERLY

Second District, Laguardo Road, Wilson County, Tenn. Sent by Mrs. W. P. Bouton, 139 Hatton Avenue, Lebanon, Tenn.

J. J. Eatherly, May 20, 1830-April 4, 1912.
Emily E. Eatherly, July 11, 1849-June 1, 1929.
Clarence F. Eatherly, Sept. 23, 1870-April 13, 1892.
Ruby F. Eatherly, Oct. 8, 1887-Mar. 3, 1890.
Eliza S. Enochs, departed this life, Jan. 5, 1834.
Melissa Enochs, departed this life, Feb. 21, 1836.
Price Curd, May 6, 1808-Aug. 19, 1883.
Elizabeth A., wife of Price Curd, July 2, 1818-April 29, 1857.
John T., son of P. and E. Curd, Nov. 27, 1842-Jan. 1, 1863.
(Six graves no markers.)

GRAVES

Third District, Wilson County, Tenn., Laguardo and Gwynne Road. Sent by Mrs. W. P. Bouton, 139 Hatton Avenue, Lebanon.

James M. Graves, April 21, 1817-July 16, 1874.
Elizabeth N. Graves, Aug. 18, 1824-April 28, 1914.
James T. Graves, June 16, 1851-May 4, 1890.
William D. Graves, May 8, 1862-July 18, 1931.
G. W. Graves, Aug. 12, 1845-June 13, 1908.
Mattie, wife of G. W. Graves, Feb. 14, 1847-Feb. 13, 1896.
W. H. Lenning, 1842-1917.
Rebecca M. Lenning, 1835-1888.
Marie Inez G. Wright, Nov. 26, 1895-Sept. 1, 1919.
(Ten or more graves no markers.)

EAGAN

Same field as above

M. R. Eagan, Sept. 5, 1830-Feb. 11, 1912.
M. D. Eagan, July 12, 1844-Feb. 28, 1918.
R. E. Eagan, Aug. 29, 1869-June 18, 1905.

Bible Records—Tombstone Inscriptions

SEWELL

Third District, on road north of pike, known as Horn Springs Road.

Benjamin Sewell, 1742-July 6, 1821; age, 79 years. New marker, Col. Ben J. Sewell, N. C. Mil. Rev. War.
Indiana Sewell Gillespie, June 4, 1805-Feb. 24, 1829. Indiana L. Gillespie was born the 4th of June, 1805, and departed this life in the City of New Orleans, 21st of Feb., 1829.
To the memory of David McMurry and his wife, Ann, who died Aug. 25, 1840; his age, 64 years, 6 months; her age, 62 years, 5 months. They were lovely in their lives and in their deaths they were not divided. (Not inclosed in the Sewell plot.)

COOK

Third District, Wilson County, Tenn., one mile west from Horns Springs. Sent by Mrs. W. P. Bouton.

Dr. L. N. M. Cook, Aug. 15, 1815-Feb., 1896.
Elvira Lasater Cook, Aug. 24, 1824-Feb. 26, 1883.
Eliza J., wife of T. G. Cook, Feb. 26, 1831-Mar. 18, 1854.
Mary A. Cook, 1792-Feb. 26, 1853; age, about 61 years.
Thomas Cook, 1782-June 7, 1851, in the 69th year of his age.
(Six or more graves no inscriptions.)

SMITH

Third District, two miles north of Nashville Pike on Cairo Road, Wilson County, Tenn. Sent by Mrs. W. P. Bouton.

In memory of Sydney J. Smith, born July 16, 1819; married to Mackhenry A. Smith, born April 10, 1822.
Mattie J. Smith, wife of Carrol Cocke, Oct. 19, 1841-April 10, 1903.
Nancy Amanda Hunt, wife of Henry C. Smith, May 19, 1849-Nov. 21, 1897.

WOOD

Fourth District, Wilson County, Tenn., near Wood's Ferry.

Josiah Wood, May 27, 1786-Mar. 28, 1855.
Nancy C. Wood, June 8, 1799-April 16, 1863.
J. J. Wood, Feb. 5, 1828-Dec. 11, 1873.
Archibald B. Wood, Oct. 18, 1821-June 11, 1845.
Elizabeth, wife of G. J. Wood, April 30, 1825-April 21, 1873.
Joseph E. Wood, Dec. 17, 1848-Sept. 1, 1876.
Olivia K. Wood, June 3, 1851-May 22, 1878.
William B., son of G. J. and E. A. Wood, April 16, 1846-Mar. 30, 1868.
India V. Wood, Nov. 15, 1838-June 10, 1911.
Nannie C. Wood, wife of L. R. Kirkpatrick, Aug. 7, 1871-Feb. 7, 1916.
Lottie M. Wood, wife of C. C. Arnold, Jan. 28, 1873-Nov. 27, 1908.
S. V. Motheral, wife of J. B. Arnold, Mar. 15, 1839-Mar. 10, 1913.
Elizabeth Ann Wood, wife of William Motheral, Oct. 16, 1816-July 14, 1891.
Lycurgus Jefferson Motheral, Oct. 14, 1842-June 19, 1890.
George W. Motheral, Aug. 19, 1844-May 4, 1872.
Dora R. Motheral, Nov. 17, 1849-Oct. 10, 1915.
Lycurgus Wood, 1830-1904.
E. A. Williamson, April 6, 1844-Feb. 11, 1881.
Fannie D., wife of T. H. Everett, July 17, 1854-Mar. 21, 1880.

Bible Records—Tombstone Inscriptions

JACKSON
Fourth District, Laguardo Road, Wilson County, Tenn.

Asa Jackson, Oct. 8, 1823-Feb. 14, 1889.
Elizabeth J. Jackson, Sept. 8, 1825-July 8, 1899.
Andrew F. Jackson, Nov. 25, 1847-Oct. 19, 1887.
Nannie J. Jackson, April 16, 1856-Dec. 12, 1892.
James P. Jackson, May 12, 1860-Aug. 11, 1887.
R. L. Jackson, July 16, 1862-Mar. 22, 1922.
Walter E. Jackson, Oct. 1, 1877-Feb. 5, 1896.

DAVIS
Fourth District, Laguardo Road, Wilson County, Tenn.

James Harvey Davis, 1791-1864.
Penelope W. Davis, consort of J. H. Davis, departed this life Aug. 16, 1834; age, 32 years, 7 months, 7 days.
James Harvey Davis, Dec. 25, 1822-Oct. 18, 1899.
Eliza Thomas Davis, 1805-1899.
J. E. Davis, July 18, 1821-Oct. 11, 1896.
J. M. Davis, Jan. 30, 1853-April 12, 1873.
N. G. Davis, July 12, 1855-Mar. 23, 1887.
William Clinton Davis, Dec. 15, 1828-Sept. 26, 1917.
Lamiza Pitts Davis, Jan. 31, 1831-Nov. 17, 1892.
S. Emeline H. Davis, 1839-1917.
Meeky J. Davis, 1847-1882.
Sallie Louisa Harvey, daughter of James and Eliza Davis, Jan. 19, 1837-Sept. 30, 1861.
James Davis, 1866.
J. T. Capers Davis, 1844-1906.
Mary D., wife of John H. Oldham, Jan. 4, 1858-Sept. 21, 1900.
Nellie Graham, daughter of P. W. and Elnora Davis, Feb. 3, 1887-Sept., 1896.
Charles P. Davis, June 24, 1861-Aug. 21, 1890.
Athene Anderson, Feb. 3, 1851-Dec. 5, 1870.
Elizabeth Bridges, departed this life Sept. 13, 1845; age, supposed to be 100 years.

BRADSHAW
Fourth District, Wilson County, Tenn., Laguardo Road. Sent by Mrs. W. P. Bouton, 139 Hatton Avenue, Lebanon, Tenn.

Mary P. Hunt, April 9, 1836-July 26 1913.
Bettie Hunt, Nov. 10, 1861-Sept. 28, 1888.
(Fifty or more graves no markers.)

BLOODWORTH
Fourth District, Wilson County, Tenn., Laguardo Road.

Webb Bloodworth, May 27, 1777-April 16, 1858; married, Dec. 9, 1804.
Mary, wife of Webb Bloodworth, June 5, 1791-Mar. 6, 1863.
Alsa Bloodworth, Sept. 28, 1812-Dec. 24, 1858.
Wilson Bloodworth, Aug. 17, 1813-Nov. 7, 1892.
Harriet E. Bloodworth, Mar. 12, 1838-Aug. 17, 1880.
H. S. Bloodworth, Sept. 1, 1841-Aug. 30, 1872.
William Bloodworth, June 28, 1830, ——.
Lucy F. Bloodworth, May 20, 1840-Jan. 2, 1907.
Mattie Miller Bloodworth, Oct. 10, 1864-June 3, 1889.
Mollie Smith Bloodworth, May 20, 1866-Dec. 10, 1887.
William J. Bloodworth, Aug. 23, 1866-Jan. 11, 1911.

Bible Records—Tombstone Inscriptions

Mary B., wife of J. E. Graves, daughter of Webb and Mary Bloodworth, April 14, 1825-Mar. 15, 1861.
William J. Cocke, Feb. 6, 1806-Mar. 14, 1879.
Minerva Cocke, Aug. 11, 1807-Oct. 7, 1881.
L. S. Cocke, Aug. 28, 1838-Sept. 1, 1883.
M. E. Riggan, wife of S. E. Riggan, Feb. 5, 1867-Mar. 6, 1896.

VAUGHAN

Fourth District, Laguardo Road. Sent by Mrs. W. P. Bouton.

James W. Vaughan, Oct. 15, 1847-July 19, 1903.
Mary P. Vaughan, Jan. 26, 1852-Mar. 2, 1921.
J. Stokes Vaughan, Nov. 18, 1853-Aug. 8, 1886.
Willie Prater Vaughan, Oct. 31, 1885-Jan. 8, 1902.
Eliza G., wife of J. K. Wright, Dec. 28, 1850-April 5, 1888.
Henrietta Gambell, wife of H. C. Cole, June 27, 1850-Jan. 13, 1895.
(Fifty or more graves no markers.)

CHAPMAN

Fifth District, Wilson County, Tenn., west of Hunters Point Pike. Sent by Mrs. W. P. Bouton, Lebanon, Tenn.

James Anderson, June 10, 1778-Nov. 3, 1831.
Elizabeth Chapman, wife of J. Anderson, May 5, 1778-Jan. 11, 1854.
Samuel G. Anderson, Oct. 16, 1802-Mar., 1876.
James Anderson, Feb. 19, 1814-Aug. 12, 1863.
J. N. Chapman, Nov. 24, 1821-Mar. 21, 1906.
John S. Chapman, Sept. 23, 1824-Dec. 15, 1855.
S. J. Chapman, April 22, 1831-June 20, 1915.
Mary F. Chapman, Aug. 14, 1846-May 11, 1928.
(Only a few copied from this large graveyard.)

BUHLER

Fifth District, Wilson County, Tenn., east of Hunters Point Pike. Sent by Mrs. W. P. Bouton, Lebanon, Tenn.

Cordula Buhler, Sept. 29, 1816-Nov. 2, 1892; age, 82 years.
John Buhler, May 1, 1845-June, 20, 1907.
Nannie J., wife of John Buhler, Aug. 29, 1844-Mar. 14, 1905.
Fannie D., daughter of John and Nanny Buhler, Sept. 27, 1874-Feb. 17, 1898.
John M. Rutledge, May 1, 1847-Sept. 4, 1897.
(Twelve or more graves no markers.)

JOLLEY

Fifth District, Wilson County, Tenn., west of Hunters Point Pike. Sent by Mrs. W. P. Bouton, Lebanon, Tenn.

J. T. Jolley, Nov. 18, 1824-Aug. 31, 1915.
S. A. Jolley, Mar. 30, 1828-July 22, 1883.
Emma T. Jolley, June 27, 1853-Jan. 18, 1926.
J. T. Reed, June 15, 1855-Feb. 8, 1917.
Elnora Reed, Dec. 16, 1868-Aug. 12, 1921.

Bible Records—Tombstone Inscriptions

HARRIS
Fifth District, west of Hunters Point Pike, Wilson County, Tenn.

Richard W. Harris, consort of Amelia Harris, Mar. 12, 1801-Dec. 25, 1852.
James B. DeBow, consort of Evaline,
Sept. 30, 1827-Oct. 25, 1855.
(Six or more unmarked graves.)

MABRY
Fifth District, Wilson County, Tenn., Hunters Point Pike.

Vincent Compton, Jan. 28, 1809-Oct. 27, 1889.
Martha Elizabeth A., wife of V. Campton, April 19, 1819-Dec. 10, 1896.
Virginia E. Head, Sept. 5, 1809-July 28, 1886.
John C. Jones, Mar. 22, 1821-Sept. 19, 1881.
Sallie Rutledge, wife of C. H. Mabry, Mar. 8, 1853-Mar. 7, 1902; professed faith in Christ and joined the Baptist Church in 1867.
Mary E. Moser, Oct. 22, 1873-Oct. 22, 1905.
(Twelve or more graves no markers.)

MOSLEY
Fifth District, Wilson County, Tenn.

W. J. Mosley, died Dec. 21, 1924; age, 79 years.
John L. Mosley, 1855-1928.
Mary E. Mosley, 1856-1928.
A. Bettis, Feb. 14, 1828-May 29, 1898.
Jennie L. Bettis, Nov. 9, 1856-Nov. 12, 1896.
Louanna Bettis, June 29, 1889-Dec. 13, 1904.
Mary C. Bettis, died Mar. 7, 1883.
Mary A., wife of R. Cox, June 18, 1834-Feb. 20, 1892.
J. M. Moss, died Aug. 20, 1924; age, 54.
(Twelve or more graves no markers.)

ALLCORN
Tenth District, Wilson County, Tenn., east of Hunters Point Pike, one and one-half mile north of Lebanon, Tenn.

John Allcorn, died Mar. 9, 1829; age, 62 years.
Mrs. Prudence Allcorn, wife of Col. John Allcorn, departed this life Aug. 5, 1854, in the 75th year of her age.
Zuriha Douglass, daughter of John and Prudence Allcorn, Oct. 19, 1800-Feb. 11, 1930; also her infant child who died a few hours after its birth.
James Allcorn, May 3, 1802-Sept. 22, 1831; age, 32 years, 1 month, 30 days.
Mrs. Minerva Wynne, wife of John L. Wynne, and daughter of John and Prudence Allcorn, June 7, 1805-Nov. 2, 1832.
Emily Martin, Sept. 3, 1807-Feb. 14, 1831. Here also lies infant daughter. This is erected to their memory by the husband and father, W. L. Martin.
(Twelve or more graves not marked.)

HARPOLE
Fifth District, east of Hunters Point Pike, Wilson County Tenn., a few hundred yards north of Spring Creek.

Here sleeps the mother and five children, three on the right, and two on the left. Judy Harpole was born Feb. 20, 1814- and departed this life Sept. 3, 1844; age, 30 years, 6 months, 14 days. She was amiable in person.

Bible Records—Tombstone Inscriptions

(Sand stone marker.)
Ann Harpole, Dec. 10, 18— -Aug. 11, 1850; age, 9 years, 7 months, 1 day. (Dim.)
Here rests Martha Harpole, Feb. 20, 1838-Sept. 20, 1841; age, 3 years, 7 months. (Plain rock, hand written.)

The D.—— was born and died, 40 years age, 22 days, and was a member of the Presbyterian Church. (This rock split and part gone.)
Infan boy ——.
(Old brick vault torn down, 75 or 80 graves no markers.)

TURNER

Eleventh District, near Zion Methodist Church.

Frances New, Mar. 5, 1774-Nov. 2, 1857.
Sacred to the memory of Elizabeth Cartwright, Dec. 10, 1786-Oct. 23, 1851.
Thomas Turner, July 15, 1809-Oct. 14, 1871.
Penelope S. (Cartwright), wife of Thomas Turner, Sept. 30, 1813-Aug. 9, 1838.
Mathew James Turner, April 20, 1832-Jan. 29, 1910.
Martha Eliza Turner, Aug. 7, 1838-May 13, 1911.
Amanda J. Turner, Sept. 28, 1836-Aug. 29, 1858.
Edward A. Turner, Aug. 8, 1838-June 21, 1871.
Thomas M. Turner, Jan. 23, 1844-July 3, 1923.
Nancy F. Bryan, wife of Thomas M. Turner, Jan. 4, 1848-July 11, 1875.
Mattie S. F. Fisher, wife of Thomas M. Turner, June 1, 1858-Nov. 27, 1895.
Rufus Wilson Turner, Oct. 5, 1853-June 18, 1877.
Adaline O. Turner, May 25, 1852-July 9, 1852.
Marion H. Turner, Dec. 24, 1847-Dec. 21, 1913.
Sallie F. Turner, May 14, 1875-Dec. 18, 1896.
Francis E. Turner, Feb. 10, 1846- Dec. 1, 1850.
Almira L. Turner, Oct. 12, 1849-Dec. 20, 1850.
Peter C. Turner, April 25, 1856-May 1, 1856.
Laura Bell, infant daughter of E. A. and A. R. Turner, born and died Dec. 7, 1868.
Fannie N., daughter of M. J. and M. E. Turner, Nov. 10, 1872-Aug. 8, 1874.
James Cartwright, June 11, 1848-Oct. 19, 1849.
Annie May, daughter of Thomas W. and Alma M. Turner, 1895-1897.
Beulah L., infant of W. M. and I. N. Turner, 1899-1900.

TRIGG

Seventeenth District, Wilson County, Tenn., three miles south of Norene, and west of Greenvale. Sent by Mrs. W. P. Bouton.

Daniel Trigg, Mar., 1776-April 28, 1830.
Nancy Trigg, Oct. 21, 1785-Sept. 22, 1823.
William Word, Jan. 29, 1786-July 29, 1849.
David B. Word, Jan. 8, 1815-July 3, 1835.
Elizabeth A. Word, Aug. 18, 1833-Sept. 17, 1835.
Sarah A. Word, wife of Thomas C. Word, Aug. 6, 1817-April 12, 1857.
Kittie Word, born Jan. 5, 1811; married to James Dillon, Aug. 2, 1832; died, Nov. 4, 1860.
Samuel T. Williams, Feb. 4, 1814-Oct. 31, 1857.
Miss Sallie Gentry, Aug. 25, 1815-Dec. 11, 1888.
Georgianna Gentry, June 15, 1859-Jan. 5, 1906.
Edward Hansberry, Jan. 19, 1832-Feb. 8, 1887.
Martha J. Hansberry, May 12, 1846-Feb. 20, 1923.
Elmer Hansberry, Mar. 6, 1875-Nov. 11, 1901.
T. J. Adams, died Mar., 1860; age, 38 years.
(Fifty or more graves not marked.)

Bible Records—Tombstone Inscriptions

FOSTER

Doak's Crossroads, Nineteenth District, Wilson County, Tenn., west of Cainsville Road. Sent by Mrs. W. P. Bouton, Lebanon.

J. A. Foster, deceased Oct. 3, 1832, in 84th year of age (1748).
Martha Foster, deceased Mar. 11, 1802, in 58th year of age (1744).
Polly Marrs, Feb. 21, 1833-July 6, 1891.
W. F. McKee, July 22, 1833-June 18, 1834.
(Signs of 2 or 3 graves, no markers. Three cedars in field.)

MARRS

Nineteenth District, Wilson County, Tenn, on Wilson Marrs' place, east of Bairds Mill. Sent by Mrs. W. P. Bouton, Lebanon.

Alexander Marrs, Nov. 29, 1778-Feb. 11, 1850.
Martha, wife of A. Marrs, 1783-June 17, 1868.
Samuel E. Marrs, Nov. 17, 1817-Aug. 9, 1857.
Mary Jane Marrs, Nov. 8, 1828-Dec. 31, 1857.
R. A. Marrs, April 5, 1824-Mar. 24, 1882.
(Twenty graves not marked.)

WILLIAM BAIRD

Twenty-first District, Wilson County, Tenn., east of Bairds Mill.

Ann J. Baird, died July 3, 1859; age, 20 years, 3 days.
Evalina Cason, consort of John M. Cason, daughter of William and Lucinda Baird, May 2, 1836-June 1, 1853.
R. T. Clemmons, Feb. 26, 1833-Mar. 7, 1908.
T. B. Clemmons, Jan. 17, 1839-Feb. 8, 1918.
Bettie Page, daughter of R. T. and T. B. Clemmons, Feb. 14, 1864-Dec. 3, 1888.
(Twelve or more graves not marked.)

MARTIN

Twenty-first District, Wilson County, west of Bairds Mill.

S. W. Martin, Oct. 27, 1822-Jan. 15, 1878.
Mary Martin, July 12, 1832-June 28, 1870.
J. W. Martin, May 23, 1853-Mar. 19, 1891.
Nannie Martin, wife of J. W. Martin, May 31, 1857-Oct. 12, 1907.

SHANNON

Twenty-first District, west of Bairds Mill, north of Central Pike.

Wilson H. Shannon, Sept. 12, 1848-Nov. 21, 1897.
Frances A. Caraway, wife of Wilson Shannon, June 29, 1849-Nov. 25, 1889.
Mary W. Henry, wife of M. A. Thompson, Sept. 28, 1839-May 15, 1895.

BRYAN

Nineteenth District, Wilson County, Tenn., near Shop Springs, on road from Shop Springs to Leeman's Corner.

Nelson J. Bryan, Mar. 15, 1813-Sept. 11, 1897.
Minerva J. Bryan, Dec. 19, 1822-Feb. 19, 1905.
Algernon Bryan, Sept. 20, 1821-Aug. 7, 1884.

Bible Records—Tombstone Inscriptions

Elizabeth Phillips, wife of Algernon Bryan, Jan. 23, 1829-July 18, 1881.
William N. Bryan, April 15, 1853-Sept. 25, 1897.
John Bryan, Jr., July 26, 1852-Jan. 11, 1914.
Laura A. Bryan, Nov. 26, 1863-Jan. 26, 1928.
Eugene Cullen Bryan, June 22, 1859-April 1, 1878.
Walter Bryan, 1865-1930.
Minerva Trammell, Aug. 15, 1816-Feb. 19, 1905.
Sallie Trammell, Aug. 11, 1855-Aug. 4, 1908.
James R. Allen, Feb. 20, 1821-May 12, 1897.
Annie Phillips, wife of James R. Allen, April 1, 1824-Nov. 18, 1897.
John W. Bryan, May 12, 1840-Nov. 28, 1913.
Anna C. Bryan, Jan. 23, 1871-Aug. 15, 1918.
W. T. Bryan, 1849-1918.
Margaret Patton, his wife, 1848, ——.
Minnie M. Simms, 1875-1924.
G. W. Simms, 1870, ——.
M. J. Robman, Dec. 17, 1827-Nov. 25, 1902.
Eva Redman Burns, Nov. 14, 1872-July 11, 1927.
Rev. H. F. Burns, April 25, 1860, ——.
W. A. Rushing, Mar. 18, 1841, ——.
N. T. Rushing, Dec. 29, 1841-Feb. 22, 1910.
Etta T. Rushing, 1862-1923.
W. E. Rushing, 1877-1901.

Thomas H. Stark, 1847-1929.
Nan Berry, his wife, 1844-1915.
Joseph W. Patton, June 2, 1840-Nov. 1, 1925.
Laura B. Patton, Aug. 2, 1852-June 20, 1923.
Millerd F. Donnell, 1851-1921.
Mollie C. Donnell, 1857-1926.
Christine Patton, Jan. 8, 1891-Aug. 20, 1910.
Ermer Simms, Feb. 12, 1886-Dec. 5, 1909.
Millie D. Mitchel, Feb. 17, 1900-Nov. 25, 1916.
Elliott Allen, April 19, 1858-May 7, 1910.
J. T. Young, Nov. 8, 1840-Aug. 12, 1908.
Mallissa Young, Dec. 4, 1845, ——.
Nettie Y. Patton, Aug. 31, 1875-Oct. 10, 1912.
Lena Williams, wife of H. N. Young, Feb. 7, 1887-Oct. 6, 1920.
M. N. Hudson, 1845-1912.
Ann O. Hudson, 1855-1928.
Mary B. Henderson, Feb. 12, 1842-June 5, 1901.
Kate M. Henderson, May 7, 1850-Dec. 15, 1916.
Mattie Ola Sanders, Oct. 2, 1879-May 24, 1916.
Mary A. Leeman, Sept. 20, 1848-June 4, 1911.
Hall Bass, 1878-1920.
Hattie E. Bass, 1879, ——.
Fred B. Bass, 1913-1929.

GREGORY D. JOHNSON

Nineteenth District, Wilson County, Tenn., east of Tater-Peeler Road on Hankins Hill, five and one-half miles from Lebanon.

Rebecca Halbert, May 16, 1773-Sept. 22, 1864.
Richard Cartwright, 1795-Jan. 11, 1842.
Annie Cartwright, April 10, 1793-May 15, 1865; joined the M. E. Church, 1829. (Box tomb down.)
James H. Moxley, April 30, 1812-July 26, 1859.
Nancy L. Moxley, wife of James H. Moxley, Nov. 27, 1817-Mar. 5, 1877.
G. D. Johnson, Jan. 6, 1800-Jan. 23, 1871.
Lucinda M., wife of G. D. Johnson, Nov. 2, 1817-Dec. 27, 1898.

W. A. Johnson, born Nov. 14, 1842; married Dora Johnson, Nov. 19, 1872; joined M. E. Church, 1873; died, May 2, 1893.
T. W. Hankins, Dec. 5, 1842-Sept. 21, 1902; married Mildred H. Johnson, Oct. 4, 1866.
M. H. Hankins, Mar. 10, 1844-Feb. 17, 1920.
G. D. Hankins, Oct. 10, 1875-Nov. 22, 1919.
J. H. Hankins, Sept. 20, 1878-Sept. 5, 1904; married Stella Brown, Oct. 12, 1902.

Bible Records—Tombstone Inscriptions

J. A. Graves, died April 10; born, —— 20, 1883. (Dim sandstone rock; 20 graves not marked.)

DR. WHITE

Twenty-first District, Wilson County, Tenn., west of Tater Peeler Road on P. D. Johnson's place, five miles from Lebanon.

Dr. L. W. White, April 6, 1800-Dec. 1859. (Tall column with Masonic emblem; several children's graves.)

BOSTICK

Twenty-first District, west of Tater Peeler Road, six miles from Lebanon. Sent by Mrs. W. P. Bouton, Lebanon, Tenn.

John S. Bostick, Mar. 12, 1825-Mar. 11, 1898.
Mary Ann Campbell, wife of John Bostick, born Feb. 17, 1832; married, Oct. 5, 1847; died, Feb. 19, 1904.
H. B. Odom, Dec. 11, 1851-Jan. 25, 1890.
(Six graves not marked.)

SKEEN

Nineteenth District, Wilson County, Tenn., east of Tater Peeler Road, three miles from Lebanon, on Bates place.

Martin Skeen, June 5, 1813-June 23, 1880.
Maranda (Hearn) Skeen, Sept. 7, 1813-Oct. 7, 1893.
George H. Campbell, April 1, 1817-Feb. 9, 1910.
Elizabeth (Skeen), wife of G. H. Campbell, Nov. 30, 1817-Jan. 26, 1867.
Hugh L. Campbell, Aug. 8, 1840-Oct. 22, 1876.
America A. Skeen, wife of Henry C. Fields, born near Lebanon, Tenn., May 13, 1852; died at Murfreesboro, Tenn., Mar. 14, 1891.
Walter C. Fields, son of H. C. and America Fields, Mar. 27, 1876-Feb. 25, 1891.
Mary J. Covington, May 19, 1854-Mar. 15, 1900.
(Several graves not marked.)

WILEY RUSSELL

Twenty-first District, west of Tater Peeler Road, Wilson County, Tenn., six miles from Lebanon (Lockey Bostick place).

Wiley Russell, April 18, 1815-Nov. 7, 1882.
Hixey Russell, Dec. 10, 1818-Oct. 21, 1870.
Hugh J. Bostick, Sept. 10, 1849-Dec. 25, 1926.
Dovie Bostick, June 21, 1873-June 3, 1878.
(Six graves not marked.)

HEARN

Nineteenth District, Wilson County, Tenn., Tater Peeler Road, eight miles south of Lebanon. Sent by Mrs. W. P. Bouton.

Stephen H. Hearn, Mar. 2, 1791-Mar. 19, 1863.
Elizabeth M., wife of S. H. Hearn, Mar. 22, 1794-Oct. 21, 1881.
Eveline Hearn, June 3, 1839-May 26, 1907.
Purnell G. Hearn, June 4, 1815-Mar. 11, 1852.
John W. Baird, Mar., 1853-1859.
(15 or 20 graves not marked.)

Bible Records—Tombstone Inscriptions

JONES

Nineteenth District, Wilson County, Tenn., west of Tater Peeler Road, eight miles south of Lebanon. Sent by Mrs. W. P. Bouton.

Richard B. Jones, Aug. 14, 1828-Jan. 27, 1889.
G. G. Jones, Mar. 13, 1839-Oct. 7, 1910.
Rebeccah Ann Williams, wife of G. G. Jones, Dec. 17, 1838-Feb. 28, 1905.
Jincy J. Jones, Richard Jones.
John T. Jones, June 28, 1877-April 9, 1905.
Roe Lea, Oct. 12, 1840-June 6, 1908.
(Thirty-six graves not marked.)

BETHESDA OLD CHURCH GRAVEYARD

Nineteenth District, Wilson County, Tenn. (Being used, only a few copied.) Sent by Mrs. W. P. Bouton, Lebanon, Tenn.

Banister C. Parton, Dec. 23, 1833-Oct. 19, 1907.
Rufina Electa Parton, April 14, 1848-Sept. 2, 1907.
E. C. Marrs, wife of R. A. Marrs, Feb. 8, 1834-July 9, 1918.
M. A. Marrs, April 27, 1863-Sept. 28, 1910.
S. C. Marrs, June 6, 1868-Oct. 13, 1905.
Bobert Bell Donnell, Nov. 20, 1815-Dec. 10, 1884.
Anis Donnell, July 2, 1815-Sept. 24, 1900.
A. J. Climer, Dec. 8, 1822-June, 1887.
Annie C. Climer, Mar. 4, 1862-Nov. 21, 1893.
Aseneth Davis, wife of A. J. Climer, Nov. 7, 1835-July 21, 1905.
Ida F. Jones, wife of John W. Jones, Feb. 15, 1875-Oct. 19, 1894.
(Large graveyard.)

THOMPSON

Nineteenth District, Wilson County, Tenn., Cainsville Road, ten miles south of Lebanon. Sent by Mrs. W. P. Bouton, Lebanon.

G. W. Thompson, Oct. 22, 1822-Feb. 27, 1900.
Martha Baird, wife of G. W. Thompson, July 4, 1825-July 12, 1878.
Charles C., son of G. W. and Martha Thompson, Sept. 20, 1848-July 12, 1890.
Elizabeth Frances, daughter of G. W. and Martha Thompson, wife of William L. Martin, Nov. 20, 1850-June 9, 1889.
Mary F. Thompson, Sept. 12, 1840-Jan. 25, 1932.
G. E. Thompson, May 1, 1863-Dec. 2, 1926.
Nelia P. Thompson, May 19, 1868, —.
J. R. Baird, Dec. 19, 1822-July 24, 1912.
Louisa Baird, Nov. 20, 1831-Oct. 18, 1900.
Edwin Berry, Oct. 8, 1820-June 25, 1897.
M. C. Scott, wife of E. Berry, Jan. 12, 1823-Aug. 4, 1890.
G. D. Berry, July 18, 1846-Oct. 5, 1913.
Nancy Berry, Aug. 31, 1845-Jan. 10, 1931.
Julia A. Martin, 1836-1917.
G. B. Alexander, April 18, 1836-July 18, 1918.
Martha Alexander, April 29, 1835-May 16, 1920.
E. L. Lindsey, April 29, 1833-Oct. 31, 1917.
E. W. Lindsey, Jan. 10, 1871-Oct. 4, 1917.
Agnes W. Lindsey, Mar. 7, 1883-Jan. 10, 1928.
J. P. Paty, Feb. 12, 1837-Mar. 25, 1922.
Minerva Paty, Aug. 9, 1836-April 10, 1912.
Annie Thompson, wife of E. H. Lester, Nov. 14, 1866-June 27, 1902.
W. A. Lester, Jan. 29, 1849-Nov. 17, 1902.
M. L. Lester, wife of W. A. Lester, Feb. 11, 1853-July 7, 1910.
E. R. Warmack, 1857-1914.
Mary L. Warmack, 1858-1922.
Miss E. H. Williams, Oct. 30, 1848-Nov. 30, 1912.

Bible Records—Tombstone Inscriptions

BAIRD

Nineteenth District, Wilson County, Tenn., Cainsville Road, twelve miles south of Lebanon. Sent by Mrs. W. P. Bouton.

Houston Baird, April 16, 1827-Sept. 2, 1896.
Cassandra Baird, Sept. 25, 1831-Oct. 31, 1923.
Christopher Wilburn Baird, Oct. 28, 1829-Aug. 2, 1875.
Martha S. Baird, July 22, 1833-April 26, 1906.
Henrietta Baird Beadle, Aug. 31, 1854-Feb. 2, 1927.
Nim W. Baird, Oct. 29, 1857-Mar. 22, 1929.
M. A. Thompson, April 22, 1829-May 1, 1911.
Martha F., his wife, Nov. 6, 1834-Feb. 27, 1892.
J. H. Thompson, June 23, 1868, ——.
Nancy D. Bass, wife of J. H. Thompson, Sept. 23, 1867-Mar. 7, 1922.
Sarah, wife of G. H. Campbell, Sept. 5, 1836-Nov. 26, 1892.
R. S. Pemberton, Oct. 28, 1837-Jan. 20, 1893.
Margaret F. Pemberton, Mar. 14, 1845-Feb. 26, 1908.
John W. Pemberton, Oct. 1, 1878-Jan. 10, 1900.
B. J. Owen, April 18, 1859-July 10, 1922.
W. F. Cummings, Aug. 29, 1847-June 21, 1878.
M. C. Berry, Oct. 21, 1843, ——.
Attie Berry, June 7, 1877-May 27, 1902.
Robert Berry, April 11, 1866-Oct. 2, 1903.
Ellen Berry, Jan. 3, 1870-Feb. 1, 1929.
Newton Donnell, April 15, 1851-Nov. 3, 1931.

McKEE

Nineteenth District, Wilson County, Tenn., eight miles south of Lebanon. Sent by Mrs. W. P. Bouton, Lebanon, Tenn.

Thomas McKee, June 11, 1812-April 16, 1894.
Margaret McKee, June 15, 1813-Mar. 29, 1892.
(One grave not marked and an infant.)

DONNELL (JOHN ALVA)

Nineteenth District, Wilson County, Tenn., on the road from Shop Springs to Leeman's Corner. Sent by Mrs. W. P. Bouton.

J. A. Donnell, Sept. 2, 1815-Sept. 18, 1898.
Mary Ann, wife of J. A. Donnell, May 1, 1823-Dec. 25, 1888.
Wilson L. Donnell, June 14, 1853-April 17, 1930.
Carrie W. Donnell, Feb. 14, 1867-Feb. 23, 1931.
Etta W. Donnell, Jan. 14, 1866-July 5, 1907.
Eliza Jane Parton, Aug. 9, 1844-Nov. 28, 1893.
Oscar Parton, Aug. 25, 1878-Dec. 11, 1905.
Edgar P. Walker, 1870-1911.

WILLIAMS

Nineteenth District, Wilson County, Tenn., on Sparta Pike at foot of Preuett Hill. Sent by Mrs. W. P. Bouton, Lebanon, Tenn.

A. S. Williams, April 18, 1808-Dec. 7, 1878.
Martha E. Phillips, wife of A. S. Williams, May 30, 1803-Mar. 8, 1895.
Aunt, Martha Williams, April 17, 1825-Dec. 25, 1880.

Bible Records—Tombstone Inscriptions

Mary Phillips, wife of William Vantrease, Mar. 21, 1817-Oct. 28, 1908.
A. P. Williams, Jan. 29, 1845-Oct. 9, 1914.
Shelah D. Williams, 1847-1922.
Emma Tinsley Williams, 1859-1928.
Nannie G. Williams, Sept. 17, 1847-Oct. 17, 1926.
Robert M. Williams, July 27, 1842-June 8, 1924.
Cormelia C. Williams, Nov. 5, 1852-

July 17, 1904.
Charlie A. Williams, May 31, 1871-May 16, 1897.
Pattie L. Williams, 1873-1915.
Mable Williams Reed, wife of Dr. W. A. Reed, Mar. 31, 1890-June 13, 1918.
W. B. Clark, Mar. 10, 1864-Nov. 30, 1922.
L. E. Vanhooser, Nov. 22, 1866-Jan. 8, 1915.

DOAK

Nineteenth District, Wilson County, Tenn., seven miles south of Lebanon, at Doak's Crossroads. Sent by Mrs. W. P. Bouton.

Coley Q. Doak, April 15, 1805-Nov. 8, 1884.
W. H. Doak, July 18, 1828-Sept. 21, 1903.
Mary Doak, Jan. 10, 1841-Jan. 4, 1878.
Sarah A. Doak, Jan. 18, 1843-Oct. 13, 1868.
William P. Doak, Dec. 4, 1873-June 27, 1894.
(Tombstones piled againt the fence, 1933.)

FOSTER

Eighteenth District, Wilson County, Tenn., on S. J. Baskin's place, near Spring Creek Church, Cainsville Road.

Sarah A., wife of R. H. Foster, July 5, 1817-Jan. 27, 1876.
Mary M. Ralston, wife of John S.
Foster, Sept. 8, 1848-Mar. 18, 1884.
Maggie M. Ralston, wife of John S. Foster, Jan. 13, 1856-Dec. 26, 1885.

BARBEE

Nineteenth District, Wilson County, Tenn., between Shop Springs and Leeman's Corner, on Herbert Young's place.

W. H. Barbee, Mar. 7, 1840-June 22, 1900.
James M. Barbee, Jan. 4, 1849-Mar. 30, 1917.
Mary S., wife of J. M. Barbee, July 10, 1864-Oct. 23, 1883.
Mary Smith, wife of John W. Bryan, April 28, 1842-Feb. 12, 1876.
Sarah A. McEachern, wife of John

W. Bryan, Jan. 27, 1842-June 13, 1884.
Emma Allen, wife of M. N. Hudson, Jan. 13, 1847-Sept. 21, 1889.
J. L. Hudson, May 24, 1885-Aug. 28, 1909.
W. W. Lynch, son of G. P. and R. A. Lynch, Nov. 8, 1878-Jan. 29, 1909.
(Two or three graves not marked.)

THOMPSON

Twenty-first District, Wilson County, Tenn., Central Pike.

John D. Martin, Oct. 7, 1818-Oct. 25, 1869.
Mary A. Hunt, wife of John D. Martin, and third wife of W. C. Rutland, April 1, 1822-Oct. 15, 1884.
W. T. Thompson, Aug. 13, 1848-Oct. 4, 1903.
Mary F. Martin, wife of W. T. Thompson, Mar. 19, 1849-Aug. 5, 1876.
Bettie N. Baird, Oct. 18, 1845-Nov. 25, 1871.
Jennie C. Sherrill, wife of W. A. Sherrill, May 5, 1851-Mar. 12, 1875.

Bible Records—Tombstone Inscriptions

REED

Twenty-second District, Wilson County, Tenn., on road leading from Holloway to Central Pike. Sent by Mrs. W. P. Bouton.

Rev. H. W. Reed, Jan. 20, 1827-Feb. 20, 1903.
Rebeccah Moore, wife of H. W. Reed, July 5, 1837-Feb. 10, 1918.
Ollie M. Reed, May 17, 1875-Feb. 12, 1895.

ROGERS

Twenty-second District, Wilson County, Tenn., Wool Factory Road. Sent by Mrs. W. P. Bouton, Lebanon, Tenn.

William James Rogers, April 2, 1819-July 10, 1871.
Elizabeth Rogers, July 22, 1826-July 12, 1907.

GOLDSTON

Twenty-second District, Wilson County, Tenn., Wool Factory Road. Sent by Mrs. W. P. Bouton, Lebanon, Tenn.

William B. Goldston, Oct. 11, 1817-May 30, 1892.
Harriet P., wife of W. B. Goldston, Dec. 11, 1815-May 22, 1892.
(Twelve or more graves no markers.)

BAGWELL

Twenty-second District, Wilson County, Tenn.

(About 40 or 50 graves no inscriptions.)
Daisy M. Hankins, wife of H. C. Hopkins, Aug. 4, 1881-Aug. 11, 1911.
(Only grave marked.)

SULLIVAN

Twenty-second District, Wilson County, Tenn., on north of Steward's Ferry Road, east of Gladeville.

Benjamin T. Sullivan, Sept. 23, 1800-July 19, 1872.
Polly Ann Sullivan, wife of B. T. Sullivan, May 17, 1805-May 8. 1873.
Elizabeth F. Sullivan, consort of H. J. Rogers, Aug. 3, 1830-Jan. 25, 1850.
C. C. Sullivan, May 6, 1826-Sept. 27, 1846.
Mary P., daughter of B. T. and M. A. Sullivan, Sept. 29, 1837-June 10, 1877.
Bat Baird, Aug. 29, 1801-Sept. 12, 1877.
Elizabeth Baird, wife of Bat Baird, Jan. 3, 1804-July 18, 1875.
B. A. Baird, Nov. 30, 1828-Aug. 7, 1898.
Fanny Baird, wife of Rufus Baird, Jan. 16, 1850-April, 1880.
Pinkney C. Baird, Jan. 26, 1826-Dec. 15, 1863.
Josephine Baird, born Mar. 8, 1833; married, May 4, 1854; died, June 23, 1889.
Thomas Gates, Feb. 22, 1821-April 3, 1850.
Amanda, wife of Thomas Gates, Jan. 13, 1825-July 12, 1880.
Martha J. Sullivan, April 2, 1839-Jan. 14, 1884.
Birdie W., wife of T. L. Carpenter, April 26, 1859-Oct. 26, 1895.
(Only a few of the older ones copied, well-kept cemetery.)

Bible Records—Tombstone Inscriptions

CARAWAY

Twenty-third District, Wilson County, Tenn., on road east of Gladeville. Sent by Mrs. W. P. Bouton, Lebanon, Tenn.

Elihu Caraway, Feb. 4, 1813-Nov. 16, 1892.
Polly Caraway, July 20, 1819-June 23, 1894.
Joseph F. Harris, April 20, 1836-Nov. 24, 1920.
Louisa F. Harris, Aug. 7, 1839-Mar. 25, 1928.
(Only a few copied of the older ones; many graves not marked.)

BABB

Fifth District, Wilson County, Tenn., on hill about one mile south of Bethlehem Church and Nashville Pike.

Martha A. C. Winford, Dec. 7, 1744-May 19, 1818.
Mrs. Polly, wife of Bennett Williams, 1784-Jan. 13, 1853.
John Guthrie, 1787-Mar., 1858; age, 71 years, 4 months, 8 days; he died a Christian.
Sterling Brown Peyton, Nov. 22, 1821-Nov. 27, 1866.
Abagail Babb Peyton, Feb. 13, 1828-Sept. 13, 1866.
F. M. Shearon, Mar. 5, 1829-Jan. 21, 1834.
Martha A. Shearon, May 4, 1834-July 8, 1878.
Tennie Shearon, April 5, 1866-July 5, 1881.
H. J. Garland, Oct. 14, 1849-Nov. 15, 1883.
(A number of graves with no inscriptions.)

BURDINE

Twenty-second District, Wilson County, Tenn., on hill south of Tuckers Gap on County Farm. Sent by Mrs. W. P. Bouton.

Martha W. Blacknall, May 6, 1803-April 21, 1847.
Thomas H. Blacknall, Aug. 9, 1823-Aug. 21, 1850.
Floella B. Burdine, July 17, 1829-Feb. 21, 1849.
(This is not the County Farm graveyard, but near it.)

GRAVEYARD ON TUCKER HILL

In front yard of old Tucker home; later the Joe W. Murray place. Sent by Mrs. W. P. Bouton, Lebanon, Tenn.

(Tuckers Gap Railroad Station was named for this Tucker family and located on their land. There are 25 or more graves not marked.)
Mariah Tucker and husband are buried there in unmarked graves.
Elizabeth, daughter of S. J. and E. T. Kidwell, Dec. 22, 1839-Aug. 15, 1859.
Lel F., daughter of E. T. and W. H. Tumblain, Jan. 22, 1856-Sept. 6, 1859.
(Only two markers.)

ROBERT ROSE

Twenty-second District, Wilson County, Tenn., one-half mile west of Barton's Creek Church. Sent by Mrs. W. P. Bouton.

Robert Rose, April 3, 1814-Sept. 13, 1882.
Sabrina Rose, Sept. 25, 1831-Feb. 9, 1912.
M. Johnson, Oct. 6, 1825-July 7, 1905.
Sarah E. Johnson, July 7, 1828-Dec. 4, 1893.
(Eighteen unmarked graves.)

Bible Records—Tombstone Inscriptions

FIELDS

Twenty-second District, one-half mile south of Barton Creek Church. Sent by Mrs. W. P. Bouton, Lebanon, Tenn.

John Fields, July, 1808-Nov. 7, 1895. (Wash Tomlin and wife, Mary Eliza-beth Fields, graves; no inscriptions.)

RUSSELL

Twenty-second District, Wilson County, Tenn., east of road leading from Leeville to Central Pike. Sent by Mrs. W. P. Bouton.

Mrs. Ann Russell departed this life Oct. 3, 1842; age, 27 years. (Twenty-five or thirty graves with no inscriptions.)

ELI SULLIVAN

Twenty-fourth District, Wilson County, Tenn., west of road leading south from Leeville to Gladeville.

Eli Sullivan, born Oct. 14, 1810; married to Lizabeth Spickard, Mar. 10, 1840; died, June 3, 1889.
Elizabeth M. Sullivan, born Feb. 7, 1807; married to Eli Sullivan, Mar. 10, 1840; lived a Christian; died a Christian, Aug. 8, 1875.
Phillip Berry Smart, Sept. 6, 1818-May 27, 1890.
Sallie Smart, about 1814-Mar. 5, 1892.
(This is a large, well-kept graveyard, owned by grandson of Eli Sullivan.)

WRAY

Twenty-second District, Wilson County, Tenn., on Mt. View Hill. Sent by Mrs. W. P. Bouton, Lebanon, Tenn.

Richard E. W. Wray, Oct. 25, 1826-April 11, 1909.
Clementine Wray, June 1, 1838-Oct. 20, 1917.
Elizabeth, daughter of Ben and Sarah Stone, wife of R. E. W. Wray, Feb. 14, 1840-Mar. 31, 1870.
Emma, daughter of R. E. W. and E. Wray, Oct. 31, 1865-April 9, 1889.
Wm. H. Wray, June 12, 1867-Sept. 26, 1895.
(Twelve or more graves not marked.)

CLEMMONS AND GRIGG

Twenty-second District, Wilson County, Tenn., east of Franklin Road. Sent by Mrs. W. P. Bouton, Lebanon, Tenn.

William L. Clemmons, Mar. 10, 1806-July 17, 1874.
Sarah T. Clemmons, Dec. 15, 1807-April 17, 1850.
C. T. Hewgley, Nov. 2, 1835-Feb. 15, 1920.
Cornelia Clemmons, wife of C. T. Hewgley, Mar. 4, 1840-May 28, 1916.
J. B. F. Grigg, Mar. 27, 1832-June 12, 1902.
Ann Dew, wife of J. B. F. Grigg, Dec. 16, 1837-Dec. 6, 1853-July 22, 1887.
Mary Elizabeth Grigg, Sept. 18, 1859-Jan. 3, 1887.
Pattie B. Burke, wife of T. E. Burke, daughter of J. B. F. and A. D. Grigg, Feb. 17, 1868-July 17, 1891.
(Two or three graves not marked.)

Bible Records—Tombstone Inscriptions

GRIGG HOME PLACE

Twenty-second District, Wilson County, Tenn. Sent by Mrs. W. P. Bouton, Lebanon, Tenn.

R. A. Grigg, May 18, 1829-Jan. 3, 1905.
Jane Grigg, July 8, 1835, ——.
Daisy Grigg, wife of S. O. Jennings, May 3, 1883-Nov. 26, 1905.

BAIRD

Twenty-second District, Wilson County, Tenn., one and one-half miles south of Mt. View Hill. Sent by Mrs. W. P. Bouton.

Clinton Baird, April 28, 1800-Dec. 28, 1878.
Martha, wife of Clinton Baird, 1798-Mar. 21, 1861.
Nancy T. Sullivan, born July 7, 1823; married O. Baird, 1862; married J. W. Hewgley, Dec. 1, 1881; died, Feb. 19, 1899.
James W. Hewgley, Oct. 25, 1810-Mar. 27, 1890.
Almeda H. Baird, wife of H. A. Baird, April 22, 1827-Mar. 11, 1899.
(Six or more graves not marked.)

OLD ESKEW

Twenty-second District, Wilson County, Tenn., one mile south of Mt. View Hill, in middle of a plowed field.

Alfred Eskew, Dec. 9, 1806-1869.
Newraney Eskew, June 29, 1809-April 25, 1892.
Thomas Eskew, Nov. 15, 1843-1864.
Tennie Eskew, Jan. 1, 1847-1865.
Eli Goldston, Mar. 19, 1795-Feb. 8, 1875.
Elizabeth Goldston, Feb. 25, 1797-Mar. 4, 1873.
(Twenty-five or more graves not marked.)

CLARK OR GRISSOM

Twenty-second District, Wilson County, Tenn., one-half mile south of Mt. View Hill. Sent by Mrs. W. P. Bouton, Lebanon.

A. H. Grissom, Oct. 21, 1825-July 12, 1902.
Elizabeth S., wife of A. H. Grissom, Nov. 11, 1826-Oct. 30, 1889.
D. E. Clark, July 29, 1839-Oct. 21, 1921.
G. P. Clark, June 4, 1836-Mar. 23, 1922.
Albina E. Chandler, Feb. 20, 1830-June 25, 1896.

HUDSON

Twenty-second District, Wilson County, Tenn., north of Franklin Road. Sent by Mrs. W. P. Bouton, Lebanon, Tenn.

R. W. Hudson, born in Lunenburgh County, Va., Feb. 29, 1824; died in Wilson County, Tenn., Mar. 30, 1894.
Mrs. M. P. Hudson, Jan. 25, 1834-Dec. 30, 1916.
Joshua Hudson, Dec. 22, 1857-Feb., 1923.
Allison May Frizzell, wife of Joshua Hudson, May 1, 1862-Aug. 24, 1901.
James H. Frizzell, Oct. 22, 1833-Dec. 6, 1896.
Sarah J. Frizzell, Feb. 7, 1838-Jan. 7, 1899.
John D. Reed, April 10, 1840-Jan. 12, 1905.
(Twelve graves not marked.)

Bible Records—Tombstone Inscriptions

LIGON

Twenty-second District, Wilson County, Tenn., south side of Franklin Road. Sent by Mrs. W. P. Bouton, Lebanon, Tenn.

Ann P. P. Ligon, daughter of R. L. and Rosaline Ligon, born Mar. 22, 1837; married John R. Gleaves, Jan. 6, 1856; died, Jan. 6, 1857.
(Twelve or more graves no markers.)

CAMPER

Twenty-second District, Wilson County, Tenn., east of Franklin Road. Sent by Mrs. W. P. Bouton, Lebanon, Tenn.

Rev. Joseph Camper, Oct. 31, 1812-Feb. 15, 1894.
Mrs. E. A. Camper, Feb. 15, 1826-May 11, 1901.
Sallie E., daughter of Joseph and Elizabeth A. Camper, born Oct. 4, 1854; married, Sept. 28, 1879; died, Oct. 3, 1889.

SANDY ESKEW

Twenty-second District, Wilson County, Tenn., Franklin Road, on Mt. View Hill. Sent by Mrs. W. P. Bouton, Lebanon, Tenn.

Dr. A. Eskew, Mar. 16, 1811-May 6, 1854.
Matilda Eskew, Aug. 16, 1818-Nov. 27, 1853.
S. J. Eskew, April 28, 1854-Nov. 11, 1922.
Lydia Eskew, July 10, 1871.
Hattie B., wife of J. O. Eskew, Jan. 29, 1875-Oct. 8, 1899.
(Twelve or more graves not marked.)

RICE

Twenty-second District, Wilson County, Tenn., at Gladeville.

Here lies the body of Fletcher Sullivan, who departed this life Nov. 20, 1817. (Sand stone slab.)
Mary Sullivan, July 28, 1750-Aug. 8, 1822. (Sand stone.)
Sacred to the memory of Archibald Sherrill, May 26, 1786-June 27, 1853.
Sallie Sullivan, Jan. 1, 1789-April 15, 1821.
Lucy Sherrill, 1861-Jan. 25, 1880.
Sallie Jackson, 1860-May 19, 1887.
J. H. Rice, Mar. 20, 1839-April 18, 1911.
Virginia H. Rice, June 7, 1858, ——.
(175 or 200 graves no inscriptions.)

CLEMMONS

Twenty-second District, Wilson County, Tenn., east of road leading south from Leeville to Central Pike.

John Clemmons, Nov. 18, 1778-June 26, 1858.
Allen Clemmons, Sept. 18, 1802-Aug. 4, 1840.
Edwin Clemmons, July 21, 1809-Dec. 31, 1857.
S. T. Clemmons, April 14, 1812-Dec. 22, 1842.
Wincey, wife of S. T. Clemmons, Nov. 10, 1813-April 24, 1900.
J. B. Clemmons, Aug. 28, 1818-Mar. 8, 1843.
Nancy G. Clemmons, Dec. 20, 1818-Dec. 23, 1869.

Bible Records—Tombstone Inscriptions

W. Turner Clemmons, Nov. 6, 1837-July 6, 1885.
Emily F. Clemmons, wife of W. T. Clemmons, May 16, 1840-April 30, 1889.
Joe A. Clemmons, July 9, 1853-Nov. 10, 1913.
Nannie E. Clemmons, Mar. 4, 1850-Jan. 16, 1909.
Wincey T. Shannon, wife of J. A. Shannon, Oct. 24, 1813-Oct. 13, 1839.
Louisa E., wife of W. P. Sullivan, Mar. 4, 1836-April 28, 1877.
Alice C. Sullivan, Sept. 15, 1854-Mar. 1, 1927.
George W. Williams, 1844-1920.
Marion Williams, 1881-1920.

CHANDLER

Twenty-second District, Wilson County, Tenn., north of Gladeville. Sent by Mrs. W. P. Bouton, Lebanon, Tenn.

Josiah Chandler, 1805-1880.
Annes Chandler, 1804-1888.
D. W. Chandler, 1836-1890.
A. L. Chandler, 1840-1917.
D. F. Johns, 1850-1919.
S. A. Johns, Aug. 19, 1854-June 21, 1926.

CHANDLER

Twenty-second District, Wilson County, Tenn; present owner, Horace Martin; about two miles south of Leeville, Tenn.

George Avery, 1750-June 10, 1853.
Elizabeth Allen, wife of George Avery, 1750-Nov. 27, 1857.
Josiah Chandler, July 12, 1762-Oct. 16, 1827.
Sallie Eddins, wife of Josiah Chandler, Aug. 24, 1762-July 3, 1848.
Jordan Chandler, Mar. 22, 1797-Oct. 7, 1872.
Elizabeth Avery, wife of Jordan Chandler, Dec. 22, 1797-Aug. 17, 1872.
In memory of John O. Poyner, June 21, 1795-Feb. 22, 1862.
Elizabeth Poyner, Dec. 2, 1795-Nov. 7, 1878.
Mary Hugley, daughter of H. and T. Walker, Mar. 5, 1797-Aug. 21, 1853.
Sacred to the memory of Pollie Haralson, consort of Lea Haralson; age, about 82 years; departed this life, Aug. 17, 1818.
Sacred to the memory of Lea Haralson; age, about 82 years; departed this life, Sept. 5, 1844.
Sacred to the memory of Polly L. Haralson, June 3, 1808-Sept. 15, 1821.
Sallie S. Graves, wife of Henry H. Rogers, Mar. 12, 1793-May 27, 1871.
Asa Graves, son of Henry and Sarah Rogers, Jan. 22, 1818-Dec. 19, 1893.
Pauline Chandler, wife of A. G. Rogers, Oct. 22, 1822-Nov. 27, 1906.
Thomas S., son of A. G. and S. A. P. Rogers, May 16, 1858-Nov. 2, 1876.
Fannie L. Major, wife of E. D. Rogers, Feb. 11, 1842-Feb. 26, 1885.
Jordan M., son of B. D. and F. L. Rogers, Nov. 2, 1875-Sept. 24, 1880.
Thomas M. Major, Jan. 21, 1840-July 9, 1893.
Willie H. Major, Jan. 20, 1875-April 24, 1876.
Daisy; age, 17 years.
Our little Fannie, Dec. 1, 1873-Nov. 15, 1877.

LAND PATENT OR GRANT

From Virginia Patent Office, Richmond, Va. Book 24, page 624.

Jan. 12, 1746, to Edward Colwell, in consideration of the sum of Thirteen Pounds, Fifteen Shillings, good and lawful money, paid to Receiver General of Revenues Colony and Dominion of Virginia, and divers good causes and considerations, grant and confirm tract and parcel land containing 2,740

Bible Records—Tombstone Inscriptions

acres of land in Brunswick County on both sides of Couches Creek. Begin at Hickory on said creek—metes and bounds given—to red oak on Thomas Briggs line—down Branch as meanders to Briggs Corner—thence along his line—to White Oak on Embrys line, thence alone line—along Embrys line north—to Couches Creek, thence down creek to beginning, with all woods, swamps, marshes, lowgrounds, meadows, feedings, and his due share all mines and quarries, rivers and watercourses, hunting, hawking, fishing, farming profits and commodities.

Signed, William Gooch. From copy in possession of Mrs. W. P. Bouton, Lebanon, Tenn. Edward Colwell is maternal great-great-great-great-grandfather of Mrs. W. P. Bouton, nee Mildred T. Vaughan.

FITE

Tenth District, Wilson County, Tenn., three miles south of Lebanon on Cainsville Road (R. D. Bates place).

Peggy, wife of Leonard Fite, April 12, 1761-Nov. 1, 1864. A member of the Methodist Church 55 years; her hundreth birthday was celebrated at her son's, Jacob; her living descendants then numbering 464; her children, 11, all living on that day except one that died in infancy.
Jacob Fite, Nov. 29, 1786-Dec. 5, 1870; a member of the Methodist Church for 49 years.
Matilda M. Baird, wife of Jacob Fite, Nov. 27, 1793-Oct. 18, 1876; married to Jacob Fite, Nov. 26, 1810; a member of the Methodist Church for 56 years.
Dorcas Rowena Scott, born Feb. 16, 1814; married Leander Scott, May 5, 1831; died, Aug. 9, 1893.
George Lee Scott, Feb. 18, 1833-Mar. 24, 1873.
Isabella J. Hearn, daughter of Leander and Dorcas B. Scott, July 2, 1844-Jan. 13, 1866.
Elenora Hearn, April 9, 1846-Jan. 13, 1872.
Rufus K. Scott, died Aug. 29, 1860; age, 20 years.
Sarah A. Melissa Scott, died Jan. 6, 1857; age, 22 years.
Robert K. Scott, died Mar. 5, 1865; age, 15 years.
Amanda S. Burns, died May 31, 1867; age, 25 years, 9 days.

BIRCHETT

Tenth District, Wilson County, Tenn., east of Cainsville Road, four miles from Lebanon. Sent by Mrs. W. P. Bouton, Lebanon.

Mary P. Birchett, May 10, 1827-July 25, 1906.
Isam Birchett, Dec. 25, 1856-Jan. 13, 1874.
Horace R. Birchett, Mar. 10, 1858-Dec. 23, 1926.
Minnie Birchett, June 13, 1862-Nov. 7, 1872.
Minerva M. Waters, Jan. 11, 1835-Feb. 28, 1917.

COMER

Tenth District, Wilson County, Tenn., five miles from Lebanon, Tenn., on J. W. Hawkins' place. (This place is said to have been settled by Mr. Stemridge; he built a log house with rock chimney, which with part of house stills stands; he and wife buried in north-

Bible Records—Tombstone Inscriptions

east corner of front yard, in unmarked graves, but fences have been moved and graves are now orchard or chicken yard, 1933.)

Jesse J. Comer, born Jan. 3, 1845; was killed Sept. 6, 1864 at Battle of Murfreesboro, C. S. A.
Mary E. Comer, Dec. 7, 1842-Feb. 12, 1863.

Jesse M. Donnell, Jan. 6, 1863-May 1, 1889.
Lewis Felure, Mar. 31, 1837-Dec. 11, 1901.
(Two infants, ten graves not marked.)

SIMMS

Nineteenth District, Wilson County Tenn., between Caimsville Road and Sparta Pike. Sent by Mrs. W. P. Bouton, Lebanon, Tenn.

Callie Simms, Nov. 6, 1867-July 30, 1904.

NORMAN WALSH

Nineteenth District, Wilson County, Tenn., Sparta Pike. (Marker, with Walsh, new rock fence, six or eight graves, but no markers, with dates.)

SMITH

Sixteenth District, Wilson County, Tenn., on Pruett Hill, Sparta Pike. Sent by Mrs. W. P. Bouton, Lebanon, Tenn.

John Y. Smith, born Jan. 21, 1793; married, Dec. 10, 1812; died, Mar. 1, 1865.
—— Smith, Dec., 1795-June 9, 1836. (Sandstone dim.)
Mary I. Cable, Feb. 3, 17— -Dec. 17, 1854. (Sandstone dim.)
Sarah L. Smith, Dec. 24, 1833-Nov.

9, 1852.
B. H. Moser, 1843-1927.
His wife, F. L. Moser, 1842-1903
E. M. Moser, June 18, 1868-Jan. 6, 1891.
R. G. Jacobs, April 19, 1850-July 3, 1911.
(25 or more graves not marked.)

COX

Tenth District, Wilson County, Tenn., on road from Sparta Pike to Linwood. Sent by Mrs. W. P. Bouton, Lebanon, Tenn.

John Cox, Oct. 25, 1826-Aug. 18, 1916.
Perlina Cox, wife of John Cox, Jan. 25, 1831-April 29, 1911.
Lauretta Hankins, June 9, 1835-Sept. 24, 1926.

Robert H. Cox, July 6, 1855-Jan. 23, 1879.
J. C. Hankins, 1855-1922.
V. A. Hankins, 1852, ——.
(Several other graves not marked.)

FORBES

Eleventh District, Wilson County, on Linwood Road.

Ben C. Forbes, Nov. 15, 1831-Dec. 1, 1910.
Susan C. Forbes, Aug. 10, 1842-July 15, 1912.
T. A. Johnson, wife of T. G. Johnson,

Sept. 24, 1840-Aug. 19, 1888.
Dr. J. B. Johnson, Nov. 27, 1860-Mar. 14, 1900.
Callie Johnson, Feb. 19, 1863-July 22, 1901.

Bible Records—Tombstone Inscriptions

BEADLE

Eleventh District, Wilson County, Tenn., south side of Commerce Road, near Linwood. Sent by Mrs. W. P. Bouton, Lebanon.

Joseph Beadle, Dec. 3, 1808-June 7, 1895.
Susan A. Beadle, wife of J. Beadle, Jan. 9, 1809-July 20, 1875.
Henry D. Beadle, 1846-1919.
Lelia A., wife of H. D. Beadle, Mar. 22, 1852-Aug. 5, 1896.

CRUTCHFIELD

Eleventh District, Wilson County, on road leading from Linwood to Cherry Valley.

Samuel B. Crutchfield, Nov. 25, 1789-June 26, 1832.
Nancy A., consort of Samuel B. Crutchfield, Mar. 5, 1790-Dec. 12, 1858.
William Crutchfield, Oct. 9, 1815-Aug. 27, 1835.
Thomas C. Grissom, Mar. 23, 1815-Aug. 22, 1845.
Sarah B. Grissom, Sept. 11, 1819-Feb. 9, 1874.
Cynthia Staley, wife of W. G. Staley, Nov. 11, 1841-Feb. 18, 1872.
D. D. Badgett, June 2, 1841-Aug. 10, 1912.
E. J. Badgett, Jan. 27, 1846-Nov. 7, 1913.
Jessie Badgett Maholland, July 14, 1880-Aug. 31, 1910.

HARRIS

Seventh District, Wilson County, Tenn., north of Baptist Church, near Big Springs, on Ben Purnell place.

Levisa Saunders, wife of Maj. Jas. Saunders, 1781-1857; died in peace.
B. W. Harris, April 25, 1814-Jan. 22, 1895.
Tabitha M. Saunders, wife of B. W. Harris, Mar. 11, 1816-Dec. 6, 1844.
Sallie A. Watters, wife of B. W. Harris, Jan. 16, 1828-Feb. 11, 1878.
Mary T. Harris, daughter of B. W. Harris, Nov. 4, 1844-April 19, 1868.
Nellie W. Harris, April 17, 1862-Feb. 15, 1880.
B. F., youngest son of B. W. and S. A. Harris, Oct. 4, 1866-May 2, 1889.

BRADSHAW

Ninth District, Wilson County, Tenn., in front of Dave Terry's.

J. C. Bradshaw, Sept. 15, 1801-May 1, 1888.
Charlotte, wife of J. C. Bradshaw, Dec. 22, 1803, ——.
J. G. Ragland, Feb. 16, 1854-May 25, 1807.
(More than 20 graves no markers.)

MAHOLLAND

Eleventh District, Wilson County, Tenn., on Commerce Road.

William Maholland, July 12, 1791-Jan. 12, 1879.
Sarah G. Maholland, April 27, 1802-April 27, 1840.
Elizabeth E. Maholland, Jan. 29, 1830-July 10, 1884.
W. T. Maholland, Feb. 25, 1836-Nov. 17, 1916.
Patience A., wife of W. T. Maholland, 1842-1915.
Talley Maholland, May 29, 1872-Sept. 22, 1905.

Bible Records—Tombstone Inscriptions

M. H. Andrews, Sept. 3, 1820-Feb. 20, 1894. (Box tomb made of rock, and a box tomb made of cedar slabs, both falling down. Whose graves are they?)

BRYAN

Eleventh District, Wilson County, Tenn., on road between Linwood and Tuckers Crossroads, on R. L. Bryan's farm.

W. M. Bryan, Oct. 7, 1817-Jan. 20, 1902.
Fannie Young, wife of W. M. Bryan, Aug. 10, 1825-Feb. 13, 1901.
James N. Bryan, Aug. 24, 1844-Oct. 9, 1910.
Sallie Bryan, Oct. 5, 1851-April 13, 1875.
William Bryan, Oct. 10, 1853-May 4, 1880.
Julia Hearn, Dec. 25, 1845-Oct. 5, 1872.
(Two or three graves not marked.)

POPLAR HILL

Twelfth District, Wilson County, Tenn., on Commerce Road. (Few copied from large graveyard.) Sent by Mrs. W. P. Bouton.

James Allen, Oct. 27, 1807-Mar. 19, 1876.
Elizabeth Allen, Sept. 21, 1812-Oct. 21, 1886.
Thomas Borum, May 29, 1822-Feb. 10, 1899.
Susan Borum, 1823-Aug. 10, 1895.
William Amzy Wamack, July 5, 1833-June 14, 1896.
J. W. Massey, Sept. 8, 1825-Jan. 27, 1903.
Mary, wife of Samuel McClellan, July 1, 1825-Sept. 30, 1891.
Mary Ann, wife of E. P. Bass, died Dec. 15, 1872; age, 45 years.
M. A., husband of T. B. Wynn, Dec. 28, 1845-Mar. 14, 1878.

REV. WILSON HEARN

Eleventh District, Commerce Road, Wilson County.

Rev. Wilson Hearn, born Aug. 22, 1789, and professed faith in Christ, Sept., 1810; was licensed to preach in the Methodist Episcopal Church in the year 1813; he was married to Lucy Hearn (Cousin), Aug. 22, 1807; he sustained an unblemished Christian and ministerial character up to the day of his death, which took place on the 17th of April, 1855, in the city of Nashville, Tenn.
Asa Andrews, Sept. 22, 1778-Sept. 6, 1862.
Benete R. Andrews, Oct. 22, 1780-Mar. 28, 1857.
S. A. G. Hearn, Sept. 6, 1844-Mar. 22, 1873.
J. W. Hearn, May 14, 1833-Aug. 22, 1879.
John Ewin, son of John and Elizabeth Shannon, Oct. 15, 1855-July 24, 1858.
(Several graves no markers.)

JAMES HEARN

Eleventh District, Commerce Road, Wilson County.

James W. Hearn, Aug. 25, 1787-Nov. 17, 1862.
M. R. Hearn, July 5, 1790-Nov. 20, 1834.
Julia Ann Hearn, Aug. 14, 1816-April 7, 1873.
Purnell Hearn, Mar. 7, 1810-June 23, 1880.
Clarinda E. Hearn, wife of J. P. Hearn, June 10, 1833-July 6, 1861.
Cornelia Ann Hearn, Nov. 13, 1853-Aug. 9, 1876.

Bible Records—Tombstone Inscriptions

Martha R. Hearn, Oct. 17, 1859-June 25, 1875.
H. H. Hearn, Mar. 5, 1850-Dec. 1, 1852.
P. M. Hearn, Jan. 19, 1845-April 5, 1851.
Jesse Hearn, infant son of J. P. and

Martha Hearn, Mar. 11, 1865-Aug., 1865.
T. M. Irby, May 26, 1843-Feb. 19, 1891.
Mankin H. Irby, Feb. 3, 1877-Mar. 27, 1891.
Levander G. Irby, Nov. 24, 1881-Aug. 7, 1882.

OLD HOPE, CUMBERLAND PRESBYTERIAN, BURIAL GROUND

West of Coles Ferry Pike, near Coles Ferry on Dudley Northern's place, Wilson County, Tenn. Sent by Mrs. W. P. Bouton.

Alexander Kirkpatrick departed this life Aug. 14, 1825; age, 84 years (born, 1741).
Ann Kirkpatrick, June 20, 1772-Aug. 6, 1823; age, 51 years.
Col. Joseph Kirkpatrick, June, 1786-Mar. 2, 1852. "A devoted Christian, 55 years a ruling elder, main pillar in the New Hope congregation of the Cumberland Presbyterian Church."
Jane Kirkpatrick, wife of Joseph Kirkpatrick, Aug. 13, 1795-Mar. 16, 1819.
David Kirkpatrick, Feb. 13, 1801-Aug. 17, 1834.
William A. Kirkpatrick, Sept. 17, 1817-Sept. 13, 1848.
Amanda M., wife of J. L. Kirkpatrick, born June 8, 1831; married April 15, 1852; professed in same year; died, May 28, 1853.
Rachel C. L. Kirkpatrick, died Aug. 30, 1837; age, 24 years, 8 months, 2 days.
Sallie Mozella Kirkpatrick, Jan. 8, 1847-July 30, 1864.
James Stewart, 1742-Nov. 7, 1825; age, 83 years.
Mary S. Stewart, Oct. 17, 1797-Oct. 15, 1810.
Jane Stewart, 1799-Aug. 20, 1823; age, 23 years, 11 months.
Elizabeth Stewart, 1801-Oct. 28, 1825; age, 24 years.
Samuel Motherall, Mar. 2, 1757-Feb. 21, 1840.
Sarah Motherall, June 21, 1762-Mar. 23, 1850.
Agnes Motherall, Nov. 2, 1795-Nov. 7, 1833.
Nathan Cartmell, Sept. 22, 1793-Aug. 29, 1866.
Sarah Cartmell, wife of Nathan Cartmell, Oct. 4, 1796-June 18, 1875.
E. S. Cartmell, Nov., 1819-Aug. 14, 1839.
E. J. Cartmell, July 11, 1822-Jan. 20, 1859.
William F. Cartmell, June 12, 1827-May 7, 1854.
S. M. Cartmell, Oct. 28, 1830-Aug. 17, 1859.
Samuel Coles, 1804-Mar. 14, 1867.
John H. B. Coles, Feb. 9, 1807-Dec. 14, 1862.
Phylander Coles, son of Isaac G. and his wife, Mary A. Coles, Mar. 27, 1828-April 10, 1848.
Eliza Coles, daughter of I. G. and Mary A. Coles, July 18, 1830-July 19, 1851.
Eliza Apperson, born June 7, 1809; married George W. Apperson, Mar., 1827; died, April 1, 1827.
James Tipton, Jan. 26, 1788-Mar. 13, 1866.
Mary, wife of James Tipton, Feb. 3, 1794-July 22, 1859.
James A. Campbell, Oct. 15, 1815-July 29, 1849.
George W. Campbell, Sept. 8, 1821-July 13, 1827.
William B. Williams, June 19, 1819-Dec. 6, 1831.

Bible Records—Tombstone Inscriptions

NEW HOPE, CUMBERLAND PRESBYTERIAN CHURCH, BURIAL GROUND

A few hundred yards west of Old Hope Burial Ground, on Dudley Northern's place; no church at either place.

Robert Motherall, May 10, 1793-July 28, 1876.
Jane Motherall, wife of Robert Motherall, July 15, 1795-Mar. 15, 1882.
J. K. Motherall, Mar. 28, 1823-Oct. 17, 1903.
Martha Ann Motherall, Sept. 26, 1837-May 14, 1919.
James K. Motherall, son of J. K. R. and M. A. Motherall, Nov. 17, 1859-April 24, 1909.
Felix H. Taylor, May 3, 1818-Feb. 3, 1870.
Louisa Ann Motherall, born Aug. 6, 1818; married F. H. Taylor, Nov. 14, 1844; died, Nov. 9, 1886.
I. G. Coles, Dec. 28, 1798-Jan. 6, 1879.
Mary A., wife of Isaac G. Coles, Aug. 20, 1805-Oct. 14, 1890.
G. W. Coles, Nov. 29, 1828-June 13, 1876.
Nancy E. Coles, wife of G. W. Coles, Mar. 10, 1838-Mar. 28, 1884.
Anderson Kirkpatrick, Feb. 4, 1808-Jan. 14, 1887.
Emma Eliza Moss, wife of A. Kirkpatrick, Feb. 1, 1812-Aug. 31, 1874.
Mary J. Moss, wife of Joseph C. Johnson, May 21, 1814-July 11, 1878.
Rev. J. B. Jackson, Sept. 8, 1828-Aug. 31, 1894.
Letitia J. Kirkpatrick, wife of Rev. J. B. Jackson, May 24, 1835-May 1, 1892.
Mason Jenkins, Dec. 27, 1817-April 5, 1888.
Sarah Ann Stewart, wife of Mason Jenkins, Jan. 12, 1823-Dec. 26, 1876.
William M. Barrow, died July, 1872; age, 65 years, 9 months, 11 days.
Mary A., wife of W. M. Barrow, Oct. 9, 1817-Nov. 10, 1893.
W. H. Barrow, Oct. 12, 1842-Nov. 2, 1926; C. S. A., 1861-65.
Madora E. Creswell, wife of W. H. Barrow, Jan. 29, 1852-Oct. 28, 1882.
Matilda Jane Corum, wife of W. H. Barrow, Oct. 6, 1852-May 21, 1920; age, 67 years, 5 months, 15 days.
Mary F. Barrow, Dec. 24, 1844-April 25, 1894.
R. D. Cartmell, June 27, 1838-Aug. 1873.
W. B. Lawrence, April 16, 1833-April 20, 1887.
Hannah J., wife of W. B. Lawrence, Sept. 14, 1845-May 31, 1891.
John L. Britton, Oct. 8, 1824-May 1, 1908.
Minerva J. Britton, April 7, 1828-Dec. 16, 1897.
J. T. Dill, Nov. 11, 1846-Jan. 17, 1906.
Roseter Dill, April 5, 1856-Nov. 1, 1930.
Malvina Fitzallen, June 28, 1820-Aug. 22, 1902.
D. D. Clayton, May 28, 1822-Feb. 11, 1888.
Julia Franklin Clayton, 1818-Oct. 3, 1897.
Sarah E. Tatum, died Mar. 9, 1926; age, 98 years.
A. M. F. Tatum, Feb. 20, 1844-Feb. 9, 1909.
Mildred Albina Sullivan, Oct. 29, 1845-June 3, 1880.
L. B. "Tint" Sullivan, May 25, 1848-Oct. 30, 1929.
A. J. Sullivan, Jan. 10, 1851-Dec. 9, 1917.
M. J. Sullivan, born Jan. 24, 1857.
(One hundred or more graves no markers.)

OLD BAPTIST GRAVEYARD

On Rocky River, near the bridge on Spencer Road, ten miles from McMinnville, Tenn. Sent by Mrs. J. M. Elkins, McMinnville.

Mark Mitchell, died April, 1838; a patriot of '76; age, 89 years.
Anna Mitchell, died Oct. 12, 1833; age, 55 years, 10 months, 14 days.
James Wood, died April 25, 1842; age, 52 years, 9 months, 11 days.

IN APPRECIATION OF THE SERVICES OF
COLONEL JOHN DONELSON
BORN IN DELAWARE, 1718.
DIED IN KENTUCKY, 1786.

DISTINGUISHED IN EARLY LIFE IN VIRGINIA AS A CIVIL, INDUSTRIAL AND MILITARY LEADER.

MEMBER OF THE HOUSE OF BURGESSES, IRON MANUFACTURER, LIEUTENANT COLONEL OF PITTSYLVANIA COUNTY, AND DEVOTED VESTRYMAN OF CAMDEN PARISH.

NOTED SURVEYOR OF STATE BOUNDARIES, MAKER OF TREATIES WITH THE INDIANS, AND REVOLUTIONARY PATRIOT. EMIGRATED WEST IN 1779-1780. A LEADER AND "DIARIST" OF THE SETTLERS GOING BY WATER IN:

"THE GOOD BOAT ADVENTURE, FROM FORT PATRICK HENRY TO THE FRENCH SALT SPRING ON CUMBERLAND RIVER."

FOUNDER OF DONELSON'S STATION ON STONE'S RIVER, 1780.

ONE OF THE COMMISSIONERS HOLDING TREATY WITH THE CHICKASAW INDIANS NEAR NASHBOROUGH, 1783.

MEMBER OF "THE TENNESSEE LAND COMPANY" PROJECTING A SETTLEMENT IN THE "GREAT BEND" OF TENNESSEE RIVER, 1785.

LOST HIS LIFE. SUPPOSED TO HAVE BEEN MURDERED BY THE INDIANS - NEAR BIG BARREN RIVER, KENTUCKY, 1786.

"DISTINGUISHED NOT ONLY IN THE ESTIMATION OF HIS FELLOW-CITIZENS, BUT MORE EXCELLENT AT HOME IN THE FAMILY CIRCLE." (PUTNAM)

TABLET IN FORT NASHBOROUGH

Bible Records—Tombstone Inscriptions

F. W. Bright, July 6, 1808-April 1, 1851.
Lucinda Bright, wife of F. W. Bright, died Mar. 5, 1851; age, 67 years.
Rebecca, consort of I. Hillis, died Aug. 30, 1830; age, 17 years.
Wm. W., son of J. and M. Hillis, died Oct. 15, 1848; age, 23 years.
Robert Hillis, died June 1, 1826; age, 71 years, 19 days.
James, son of J. and M. Hillis, died 1840.
Samson Hillis, died Nov. 18, 1851; age, 78 years, 2 months, 20 days.
Ann, daughter of J. and W. Boyd, died April 19, 1832; age, 36 years.
Jane, daughter of W. and I. Boyd, died Aug. 15, 1836; age, 25 years.
William Boyd, died April 4, 1816; age, 58 years, 6 months, 9 days.
James H. Boyd, died April 16, 1858; age, 55 years, 9 days.
Nancy Boyd, consort of H. Boyd, died Aug. 10, 1850; age, 52 years.
Robert Boyd, died Dec. 2, 1857; age, 29 years, 10 months, 19 days.
Sarah Neil, died April 20, 1856; age, 26 years, 11 months, 8 days.
Mary Neil, died Jan. 8, 1825; age, 20 years, 8 months.
Mary, consort of John M. Drake, daughter of J. and M. Hillis, died July 21, 1855; age, 20 years.
(John M. Drake afterwards married Dicy Seitz.)
Wm. W., son of J. and M. Hillis, died Oct. 15, 1848; age, 23 years.
Lavina, consort of J. Dennis, died Aug. 27, 1855; age, 22 years.
Wm. Robison Hillis, Feb. 19, 1837-July 25, 1861.

TOMBSTONE RECORDS

Copied from tombstones at Winchester, Tenn.

Mark Hutchins White, Aug. 26, 1851-Mar. 3, 1933; son of Col. George W. White and Mary Hutchins White.
Whitmel Ransom, Mar. 1, 1824-Nov. 18, 1890.
Martha Jane Ransom, April 20, 1832-Feb. 5, 1912.
Thomas Ransom, Nov. 7, 1849-Jan. 7, 1893.
Nannie Ransom White, April 1, 1852-April 25, 1924.
Mark Hutchins, born in Windsor County, Vermont, Oct. 28, 1793; died at Winchester, Tenn., Jan. 9, 1849.

JACOB BROWN

This grave was located by Judge John H. DeWitt and data given by him. In the valley of the Nolichucky River, about eight miles southeast of Jonesboro, Tenn., is the site of the home of Jacob Brown, the pioneer who came to the Watauga in 1772 from North Carolina and leased from the Cherokees two large tracts of land in what are now Washington and Greene Counties (Ramsey's Annals, pp. 110, 121: Garrett and Goodpasture's History, p. 52). The tombstone over his grave in the graveyard nearby contains the following inscription: "Jacob Brown, born Dec. 11, 1736; died, Dec. 28, 1785. Jacob Brown was a major under Col. John Sevier. He served at King's Mountain (Draper's "King's Mountain and Its Heroes," p. 424) and in expeditions against the Indians.

Bible Records—Tombstone Inscriptions

"Old Gray" Cemetery

Knoxville, Knox County, Tenn. Sent by Louise M. Craig (Mrs. Albert Lyon), 3449 Kingston Pike, Knoxville, Tenn.

John J. Craig, Sept. 20, 1860-Oct. 10, 1904.
Lucy H. Cage, April 18, 1863-June 23, 1927; his wife. "Recompense."
Lucille, daughter of Lucy Cage and John J. Craig, July 18, 1887-Oct. 14, 1903.
John J. Craig, Alabama, Sept. 20, 1820-July 31, 1892, Knoxville, Tenn.
Mary G. Lyon, Oct. 10, 1821-Sept. 9, 1904; his devoted wife. "Blessed are the pure in heart."
Children of John J. Craig and Mary G. Lyon:
Louise, Oct. 10, 1861-May 20, 1862.
Henry, Sept. 17, 1853-Oct. 21, 1853.
Florence, Mar. 1, 1857-Aug. 1, 1860.
Elinor, Sept. 20, 1851-July 10, 1853.
T. C. Lyon, Dec. 10, 1810-Oct. 1, 1864.
W. H. Lyon, Aug. 17, 1808-Feb. 10, 1878.
Charles Lyon, Nov. 23, 1823-Mar. 20, 1828.
William Lyon, Dec. 26, 1819-Sept. 19, 1864.
Robert Lyon, Aug. 25, 1815-Sept. 2, 1830.
Azra Ashley Barnes, Vermont, June 2, 1821-Mar. 18, 1901.
Louisa Lyon Barnes, Tennessee, Aug. 20, 1827-Aug. 4, 1895.
John Russell Ford, Oct. 5, 1860-Feb. 6, 1917.
His wife, Mary Barnes Ford, July 3, 1853-July 24, 1933.
"Thy trials ended, thy rest is won."
Iva McMullen, wife of Hiram C. Wylie, 1878-1931.
Mary Lyon Craig, wife of William Bryson McMullen, April 24, 1847-Aug. 18, 1912; born in Alabama, died in Tennessee.
William Bryson McMullen, Sept. 23, 1848-June 25, 1908; born in Mississippi, died in Tennessee.
William McMullen, son of Thomas O'Conner and Mary Lou House, Mar. 31, 1904-Aug. 2, 1904.
LeRoy S. McMullen, M. D., Oct. 20, 1887-Sept. 3, 1923.
R. M. McPherson, Feb. 8, 1825-May 23, 1868.
R. M. McPherson, Jr., Dec. 25, 1857-Nov. 2, 1881.
Sadie McPherson, July 28, 1863-Oct. 8, 1867; daughter of R. M. and Mary McPherson.
S. A. McCammon, Sr., 1801-1860.
Mrs. E. C. McCammon, 1820-1897.
D. A. McCammon, 1851-1878.
S. McCammon, Jr., 1860-1877.
B. McCammon, 1853-1920.
S. A. McCammon, 1856-1919.
William Heiskell, died Sept. 9, 1871.
In memory of Thomas B. Snow, Mar. 2, 1835-April 4, 1862.
S. B. Cunningham, Sept. 20, 1799-Nov. 11, 1875.
Sarah J. Cunningham, wife of S. B. Cunningham, June 5, 1829-Aug. 20, 1875.
Anna Francillon, wife of Adran Charavannes, 1838-1889. "Fais ce que doil advienneque pours."
Andrew J. Cooley, July 4, 1812-June 7, 1886.
Elizabeth, wife of T. B. Cooley, Feb. 5, 1850-Nov. 25, 1876.
John T. Roberts, Sept. 12, 1836-Mar. 19, 1882.
Daniel Briscoe, 1843-1918.
Catherine C. Earnest, wife of Daniel Briscoe, 1846-1883.
Mattie B. Briscoe, 1865-1884.
John G. Briscoe, 1874-1884.
David Groves, Dec. 26, 1858-Nov. 24, 1885.
Sarah Nichols Groves, Aug. 2, 1823-April 3, 1912.
David Groves, May 12, 1820-Feb. 28, 1894.
Sarah Groves, May 4, 1912-July 2, 1921.
Mary McCutchan Groves, Feb. 18, 1878-July 2, 1921.
Johanna Marie Roehl, born, Copenhagen, Denmark, 1824; died, Knoxville, Tenn., 1885.
Alexander Otto Roehl, Feb. 7, 1856-Oct. 16, 1924.
Ganes M. Harrill, Mar. 14, 1844-Nov. 9, 1921.
Sophie E., wife of G. M. Harrill, and daughter of William D. and L. T. Crawford, July 13, 1849-Mar. 21, 1876.

Bible Records—Tombstone Inscriptions

Rosannah McMullen, wife of Dr. Jas. Rodgers, July 22, 1820-April 2, 1890.
Charles E. Rodgers, Oct. 15, 1853-Feb. 18, 1895.
Dr. James Rodgers, July 2, 1818-Feb. 23, 1898; age, 79 years, 7 months, 21 days.
Dr. Samuel R. Rodgers, Aug. 18, 1851-April 26, 1926.
Hugh M. Rodgers, Jan. 5, 1862-April 21, 1932.
Mary, wife of John Fouche, Nov. 9, 1837-Jan. 9, 1875.
Hugh Craig, son of John and Louisa M. Fouche, Aug. 16, 1847-Mar. 2, 1862.
Louisa Minerva, wife of John Fouche, Dec. 1, 1825-May 7, 1859.
William A. Pitner, April 11, 1854-May 17, 1930.
Elizabeth Haynes, 1823-1919.
Mary A. Thomas, 1859-1878.
Emma McCoy, 1886-1902.
John E. Caldwell, April 15, 1835-Aug. 18, 1888.
Catherine A. Caldwell, Oct. 16, 1840-April 22, 1920.
John S. Caldwell, Sept. 12, 1865-Jan. 28, 1908.
Charles W. Caldwell, April 12, 1871-Oct. 23, 1889.
James P. Caldwell, June 26, 1855-April 19, 1901.

West View Cemetery

Sweetwater, Monroe County, Tenn. Sent by Louise M. Craig (Mrs. Albert Lyon), 3449 Kingston Pike, Knoxville, Tenn.

Mary Ballard Willson, Aug. 24, 1842-April 3, 1886.
J. C. Willson, May 24, 1837-Dec. 29, 1923.
Ida Willson, Mar. 13, 1878-June 9, 1879.
James W. Willson, Jan. 26, 1872-Jan. 28, 1872.
Mary Byrd, 1907-1923.
Mrs. Julia Guthrie, Aug., 1841-1923; age, 83 years.
Jimmie Carter, Nov. 13, 1868.
L. C. Carter, Jan. 20, 1864-May 29, 1930.
Their children: Oscar Cleveland, Ella Franklin, Ethel Jane, Clarie Ann, Pankin Abraham, Elija Crawford, Clara Lee, Erskin Reed.
Charles Allison, son of Ben S. and Bessie M. Farkner, Jan. 12, 1917-April 4, 1917.
Hiram P., husband of Sarah M. Sherlin, Aug. 14, 1840-Aug. 31, 1891.
Sarah Gains Johnston, Mar. 6, 1840-Sept. 15, 1901. "He giveth his beloved sleep."
John Hamilton Johnston, June 28, 1838-Mar. 19, 1901.
J. A. Miller, Sept. 19, 1849-Mar. 14, 1917.
Oscar Cleveland, Feb. 11, 1844-June 15, 1920.
Harriett J. Axley, wife of W. S. Haus, born Aug. 10, 1870.
John Newton Bogart, June 2, 1862-Jan. 22, 1901.
Eliza Payne Miller, May 24, 1854-Feb. 6, 1918.
Anna M. Bogart, Dec. 20, 1864-Feb., 1893.
Frank J. Williams, Aug. 16, 1883-Feb. 14, 1886.
Dr. Franklin King Berry, Dec. 4, 1841-Mar. 20, 1926.
Caroline Cleveland Berry, Feb. 2, 1843-Sept. 16, 1910.
Nina Berry, Oct. 14, 1873-July 29, 1897; "Christ is risen."
Penelope L. Osborne, May 29, 1829-May 18, 1902.
Christin A. Walker, Jan. 9, 1856-Feb. 9, 1898.
Frances Penland, Feb. 13, 1899-Oct. 16, 1900.
G. E. Stooke, June 20, 1845-Mar. 12, 1898.
Annie C., daughter of G. E. and B. K. Stooke, April 24, 1882-June 12, 1902.
James M. Pardue, Jr., Sept. 12, 1900-Mar. 11, 1926.
James M. Pardue, Dec. 30, 1862.
Rebecca Moore Pardue, Dec. 3, 1869-Aug. 15, 1927.
John R. Sherlin, Sept. 22, 1866-May 17, 1910.
Amanda E. Youngblood, Dec. 3, 1841-——— 31, 1903.
Thomas M. Youngblood, July 30, 1840-Aug. 19, 1911.

Bible Records—Tombstone Inscriptions

Coral, daughter of J. M. and M. T. Jones, April 11, 1868-Jan. 30, 1870.
Kate L., daughter of J. M. and M. T. Jones, July 31, 1878-Aug. 3, 1878.
Myrtle, daughter of J. M. and M. T. Jones, Aug. 28, 1886-Oct. 2, 1892.
Martha Tipton Jones, daughter of Albert Jackson Tipton and Catherine Right, Aug. 30, 1864-July 28, 1913.
John Martain Jones, son of Samuel Chandler Jones and Isabella Ann Wilson, Aug. 6, 1835-May 29, 1908.
Mollie T., daughter of J. M. and M. T. Jones, Aug. 13, 1869-Sept. 7, 1870.
Robert C. McKnight, Aug. 19, 1888-May 16, 1924.
Gertrude Patton, wife of John Airheart, Dec. 15, 1875-Sept. 5, 1913.
Levi Thomas, July 29, 1860-Dec. 4, 1921.
Mary C., wife of J. L. Thomas, May 21, 1893; age, 63 years, 11 months, 24 days.
John Lilburn Thomas, Jan. 28, 1826-Jan. 5, 1905.
Eliza Taylor Thomas.
William Thomas, Mar. 22, 1866-Dec. 3, 1915.
Ida Gunter, Nov. 29, 1873-Nov. 19, 1912. "At Rest."
Albert, son of John and Rebecca Edgemon, June 2, 1900-June 22, 1912.
Maggie Edgemon, July 4, 1895-Mar. 21, 1915. "Asleep in Jesus."
Jennie Edgemon, 1890-1925.
Charles Euclid McGuire, Sept 28, 1895-Feb. 1, 1917; son of J. F. and Ethel McGuire.
Halstead McGuire, Oct. 11, 1909-Jan. 16, 1917; son of J. F. and Ethel Berry McGuire.
J. H. Byrd, Jan. 29, 1835-May 10, 1912.
T. J. Byrd, Dec. 19, 1869-Sept. 13, 1887.
C. L. Johnson, Feb. 29, 1859-Nov. 1, 1904.
Mary A. Robinson, Sept. 30, 1880-Dec. 8, 1897.
Emma, daughter of C. L. and Rebecca Johnson, Aug. 16, 1886-Aug. 8, 1904.
Father—Charles Robinson, Oct. 1, 1849 —— 19. "Dying is but going home."
Mother—Nancy M. Robinson, June 1, 1841-Jan. 10, 1913.
Ellen A. Bright, Sept. 24, 1861-June 30, 1918.
Frank Bright, Sept. 27, 1879-Sept. 26, 1903.
George H. Foland, Jan. 9, 1862-April 15, 1909.
Apittae Foland, Feb. 24, 1864-April 7, 1918.
Henry H. Foland, Aug. 29, 1888-Nov., 1913.
William D. Howard, April 10, 1860-April 23, 1907.
Nolie, son of P. E. and L. Bennette, April 3, 1885-Oct. 18, 1892.
"Come, ye blessed." Claude, son of P. and L. Bennette, Dec. 5, 1875-May 26, 1893.
Thomas Bennette, son of J. T. and E. B. Cade, Nov. 9, 1911-July 3, 1912.
Louisa, wife of Perry Bennette, July 4, 1853-Nov. 25, 1909.
Perry Bennette, Feb. 26, 1853-April 8, 1925.
S. J. Presswood, died June 19, 1909; age, 69 years; Company D, R. G. Tenn. Vol., Inf.
Fannie Henderson, May 7, 1898-Nov. 28, 1901.
Father—J. H. Schneider, 1850-1926.
Thomas B. Byrd, Jan. 29, 1835-May 10, 1912.
Elmyra Williams, wife of J. A. Builderback, July 28, 1871-Dec. 13, 1918.
J. L. Kinser, 1852-1905.
M. P. Kinser, 1851-1924.
G. A. Kinser, 1877-1894.
Annie Laura, beloved daughter of J. M. and L. E. Heiskell, April 7, 1889-July 20, 1891. "A treasure in heaven."
Beloved son of J. M. and L. E. Heiskell, June 13, 1883-July 23, 1883.
Mother—Ammanda Meek Martain, April 13, 1835-July 7, 1908.
Father—Robert P. Martain, Aug. 16, 1837-Oct. 20, 1914.
Loua H. Lenoir, Sept. 30, 1851-Feb. 5, 1926.
Mother—Bessie, wife of W. D. Howard, Aug. 12, 1870-Nov. 10, 1908.
Bachman, his wife, Sarah Cunningham, June 14, 1836-July 26, 1864.
Sadie C. Moore, Mar. 15, 1899-Nov. 4, 1899.
G. M. McKnight, Jr., Aug. 21, 1886-Jan. 15, 1915.
G. M. McKnight, June 12, 1844-April 21, 1919.
Sarah L., wife of L. A. Thomas, Sept. 28, 1857-Aug. 18, 1921. "At Rest."

Bible Records—Tombstone Inscriptions

L. A. Thomas, Mar. 1, 1852-May 15, 1932. "At Rest."
C. M. Builderback, May 28, 1867-May 2, 1914.
Josie Builderback, June 2, 1869-Sept. 16, 1912. "At Rest."
Mary J. Roberts, wife of J. E. Builderback, July 11, 1840-Nov. 23, 1916.
J. E. Builderback, June 23, 1837-Mar. 1, 1910.
William H. Smith, Jan. 27, 1860-Jan. 29, 1806.
Amanda W. Smith, Dec. 26, 1842-Aug. 12, 1911.
David Lee Smith, Sept. 20, 1868-Nov. 19, 1911.
Children of Amanda J. Smith and William H. Smith: David Lee, Mary Elizabeth, Margaret Jennie.
James M. Heiskell, Jan. 30, 1845-Mar. 26, 1898. "Blessed are the dead which die in the Lord."
Father—James M. Heiskell, 1845-1898.
Mother—Laura E. Heiskell, 1848-1921.
Charles M. Satterfield, Aug. 15, 1868.
Sarah E. Satterfield, July 4, 1868.
Andrew L. McCampbell, Dec. 19, 1841-Feb. 1, 1928.
Ruthelia Love, wife of Andrew L. McCampbell, Jan. 17, 1842-Oct. 1, 1920.
Vesta J. Satterfield, May 27, 1887-Mar. 6, 1899.
Minnie B. Satterfield, May 27, 1884-July 11, 1910.
Matilda M. Satterfield, Sept. 3, 1849-Mar. 5, 1908.
Levi Satterfield, Sept. 30, 1844-May 23, 1832.
Cynthia J., wife of Olliver McDaniel, May 1, 1879-June 13, 1904.
Ollie McDaniel, Oct. 21, 1874-May 26, 1916.
Ernie Love McCampbell, Dec. 10, 1879-May 22, 1917.
Robert Leon McCampbell, Oct. 7, 1870-Feb. 16, 1901. "We will meet again."
Lizzie Taylor, wife of S. L. Wilson, 1869-1902.
John Lynn Bachman, 1841-1919.
Fannie Rogan Bachman, 1850-1915.
Margaret Ayne, infant daughter of J. I. and Fannie Bachman, Sept. 23, 1882-Oct. 16, 1882. "Of such is the kingdom of heaven."
Rev. Nathan Bachman, Dec. 13, 1832-Dec. 3, 1914.

Rosa Wilcox Brackney, April 12, 1868-July 6, 1897.
Henry Peters, Dec. 1, 1827-Oct. 3, 1899.
Virginia, wife of Henry Peters, Feb. 28, 1840-Mar. 20, 1918.
W. B. Peters, Sept. 5, 1856-July 7, 1915.
Emma H., daughter of W. J. and M. J. Stockston, July 10, 1852-May 20, 1911.
Charles Henry, son of Fannie A. and W. A. Lenoir, Sept. 26, 1793-Nov. 14, 1869.
Della M. Valden, Dec. 3, 1885-June 20, 1907.
Jas. H. Raustin, Company H, 5th Tenn. Inf.
"In loving memory of our dear mother." Mary A. Raustin, Sept. 23, 1888-Dec. 29, 1918.
W. C. Milligan, Mar. 15, 1852-Sept. 3, 1918.
W. M. Jayner, 1864.
His wife, Elizabeth, 1859-1927.
Samuel Munsey, Oct. 10, 1901-Mar. 21, 1902.
John Bryant Pennington, June 7, 1868-June 1, 1822.
Israel Curtis, Nov. 18, 1880-Nov. 28, 1924.
Joseph C. Cobble, Nov. 4, 1865-May 28, 1926.
Goldie Ernestine, daughter of J. C. and Josie Coffer, Feb. 2, 1912-July 30, 1921.
James Franklin Carter, Feb. 10, 1925-Sept. 10, 1927.
Mary Craig Carter, wife of Paul Carter, April 8, 1899-Jan. 1, 1929.
Laura Lane Craig, daughter of William and Seaton Craig, wife of Albert King, mother of Josephine King, Nov. 29, 1830-Oct. 27, 1915.
Frank Alton Carter, Aug. 12, 1829-May 25, 1870.
Robert Carter, Jan. 10, 1860-Sept. 28, 1920.
Mathew Carter, Dec. 15, 1829-April 28, 1885.
Mary Brown Carter, Oct. 17, 1831-May 29, 1906.
Sarah E. Lane, wife of John K. Brown, Jan. 26, 1827-May 3, 1890.
John K. Brown, April 9, 1821-May 3, 1890.
Will A. Brown, Aug. 11, 1845-Feb. 15, 1925.

Bible Records—Tombstone Inscriptions

Mary Neil Brown, wife of W. A. Brown, Aug. 10, 1849-Feb. 9, 1926.
Margaret A. Patton, June 3, 1863-June 28, 1908.
Emma Patton, wife of R. A. Ledford, Oct. 16, 1860-Aug. 8, 1911.
James Harry Patton, Feb. 11, 1886-Aug. 23, 1894.
Albert M. Tredway, Mar. 17, 1855-May 10, 1902.
James W. Clark, Dec. 25, 1825-Oct. 18, 1856.
Mrs. Ida Clark Hutcheson, June 20, 1853-Jan. 28, 1915.
Bland E. Clark, wife of J. W. Clark, Feb. 6, 1834-July 23, 1916.
Steven D. Forkner, Dec. 28, 1858-April 15, 1905.
Mattie A. Forkner, May 26, 1866.
Mary Emma Byrd, wife of David Newton Browder, July 9, 1857-Oct. 1, 1918.
D. M. Browder, July 31, 1853-Feb. 7, 1903.
Amanda McConnell, wife of G. A. McLin, Sept. 3, 1834-Jan. 27, 1914.
George Alexander McLin, May 19, 1819-May 19, 1895.
Josephine King, wife of F. A. Carter, Nov. 19, 1872-May 27, 1903.
Carrol O. Valden, May 25, 1892-Nov. 17, 1911.

Gasta M. Valden, Feb. 4, 1888-April 13, 1906.
Margaret C. McSpadden, wife of James Harvey Patton, Oct. 28, 1836-May 10, 1887.
Infant son, Aug. 6, 1856.
Henrietta Patton, April 5, 1869-Sept. 16, 1870.
J. A. Miller, Sept. 19, 1849-Mar. 14, 1917.
Eliza Payne Miller, May 24, 1854-Feb. 6, 1918.
Elizabeth Ann Presley, wife of J. W. Barnett, born Oct. 28, 1873.
James Wesley Barnett, July 12, 1875-Feb. 18, 1920.
Roscoe K. Plemons, Feb. 1, 1890-Mar. 15, 1920.
G. W. Payne, 1841-1924.
Oren Fain Kyker, Sept. 16, 1908-June 9, 1928.
Carl Cavett, Dec. 3, 1895-Feb. 8, 1925. "Rest, soldier, rest, thy warfare is o'er."
W. A. Harris, Sept. 2, 1844-April 25, 1927.
William J. Richeson, June 18, 1885-April 13, 1930.
J. B. Naylor, Nov. 17, 1879-May 25, 1923.

WOODLAWN CEMETERY

Near Knoxville, Knox County, Tenn. Sent by Louise M. Craig (Mrs. Albert Lyon), 3449 Kingston Pike, Knoxville, Tenn.

John Blair Montgomery, Nov. 27, 1860-Aug. 2, 1918.
Julia Ogle, Nov. 7, 1829-April 10, 1899.
Thomas E. McLean, Mar. 4, 1867-Dec. 19, 1914.
Pearl Boyd, Feb. 8, 1890-Mar. 19, 1900.
Evan A. McLean, Mar. 15, 1893-Jan. 28, 1823 (1923?).
Martha Webber, Aug. 6, 1863-Mar. 5, 1905.
T. L. C. McLean, Sept. 24, 1838-Nov. 15, 1918.
James Calvan Morgan, Nov. 27, 1864-Feb. 2, 1923.
Caroline Carter, wife of T. L. C. McLean, Sept. 17, 1845-April 6, 1907.
Miss Debbie Porter Satterfield, Jan. 22, 1856-June 4, 1909.
James Hampden Moors, 1840-1908.

Ellen C. Toby, wife of J. H. Moors, 1841-1918.
Russell Mays, June 3, 1877-Sept. 17, 1927.
Elizabeth Mays, Aug. 31, 1879-April 22, 1832.
Arthur B., son of A. M. and W. B. Wittenbarger, April 11, 1914-May 7, 1914.
G. S. McGhee, Mar. 14, 1849-May 14, 1904.
Infant son of M. L. and Possela Wolf, Nov. 23, 1903.
Rosella Wolf, Dec. 10, 1866-July 21, 1911.
"My Husband." Jacob T. Forrest, June 22, 1840-Jan. 18, 1906.
"Father and Mother." A. W. Lillard, April 3, 1850-Oct. 20, 1922.

Bible Records—Tombstone Inscriptions

"My Husband." Henry P. Thompson, Mar. 28, 1878-July 20, 1906.
Lou E. Lillard, July 25, 1850-July 11, 1925. "Gone but not forgotten."
"Our Mother." Fannie Irwin, wife of John Irwin, Aug. 29, 1832-Nov. 2, 1912.
"Mother." Mamie A., wife of W. R. Kelly, July 21, 1891-Feb. 2, 1920.
Edward Arning, Nov. 15, 1872-April 15, 1908.
"Mother." Nellie B. Shearl, Aug. 1, 1875-Dec. 18, 1929.
John S. Cross, Jr., Nov. 13, 1925-Mar. 15, 1927.
"Father." Franklin King, Dec. 14, 1861-Aug. 2, 1893.
"Mother." Margaret Rachel Hooper, April 21, 1825-May 24, 1911.
"Mother." E. Elizabeth King, Sept. 21, 1861-Aug. 21, 1910.
Clifford L. McClinton, 1875-1920.
Louis C. Cartwright, April 11, 1858-July 15, 1918.
James M. Hood, Mar. 12, 1848-April 2, 1922.
Mary LeBow, his wife, Jan. 2, 1855-July 11, 1919.
Jacob A. Reep, Dec. 15, 1844-Dec. 2, 1925. Veteran, Company G, 19th Reg. Inf., Ohio Volunteers.
Sarah Craig, wife of Jacob A. Reep, Aug. 29, 1840-July 26, 1923.
Herman Paul Dykes, Sept. 17, 1886-Mar. 10, 1906.
Lilly May Dykes, Oct. 12, 1884-Mar. 21, 1907.
"Mother." Mary A. Henry, died June 14, 1915; age 81 years.
Paulinea Kurth, 1861-1918.
Herman Kurth, Dec. 28, 1820-May 12, 1900.
Johnna Kurth, Dec. 5, 1830-Jan. 27, 1906.
Augusta Kurth, June 11, 1852-April 17, 1900; born in Saxony, Germany.
Pheby Ann Lewis, wife of James A. Davis, born July 20, 1864.
James A. Davis, Oct. 12, 1855-July 16, 1918.
Minnie A. Trotter, wife of J. L. Smoker, Jan. 29, 1875-May 4, 1914.
Dr. R. A. McCallie, April 15, 1859-July 27, 1920.
"Our Darling." Hattie Murtle, daughter of S. A. and R. A. McCallie, June 12, 1889-Oct. 14, 1890.

Dr. T. O. McCallie, Sept. 28, 1868-Dec. 13, 1924.
Thomas McCallie, Nov. 6, 1899-Sept. 24, 1900.
Ruth Elizabeth, daughter of Hugh and Jennie Cox, Dec. 23, 1903-July 17, 1923.
William F. Bean, Dec. 22, 1856-Mar. 25, 1915.
George, husband of Mary E. Glenn, Mar. 9, 1847-Oct. 17, 1903.
In memory of Martha E. Glass Connelly, May 4, 1875-Aug. 28, 1918.
"Mother." Susie Glenn, 1876-1931.
J. W. Burns, Aug. 13, 1848-Jan. 18, 1905; married Sarah J. Blan, Feb. 5, 1871.
Andrew Jackson Lowery, May 15, 1858-Dec. 8, 1928.
Cordellia Lowery, Dec. 8, 1864-Sept. 20, 1928.
"There remaineth a rest for the people of God."
Joseph L. Bonavita, Feb. 4, 1873-April 16, 1915.
Horace Angol, June 28, 1867-Aug. 8, 1925.
Lyda B. Bales, wife of S. A. Miles, Aug. 24, 1814-Oct. 30, 1909.
Mattie P. McTeer, wife of W. J. Cunningham, Nov. 15, 1874-Aug. 28, 1912.
J. A. Umbarger, June 9, 1846-Dec. 14, 1918.
Virginia Katurah, wife of J. A. Umbarger, May 11, 1846-Feb. 28, 1908.
Elizabeth Sterchi, born in Berne, Switzerland, Oct. 14, 1865-Oct. 10, 1931.
Pearl McTeer, wife of John F. Henry, July 1, 1889-Nov. 12, 1910.
H. Stewart, Aug. 28, 1879-May 10, 1908.
Fannie E. Hersey, 1842-1915.
Stella Roberts, wife of William Roberts, 1895-1923.
Sallie LaRue, Dec. 3, 1885-April 9, 1924.
Sarah C. Stiles, Sept. 19, 1857-Feb. 19, 1915.
"Mother." Virginia Stewart, April 5, 1850-Aug. 13, 1918.
Sam Jinks, Mar. 16, 1889-Feb. 21, 1916.
C. M. Davenport, Jan. 12, 1868-Feb. 25, 1925.
Elizabeth Hooper Gossett, Nov. 10, 1855-May 28, 1925.
Calway B. Gossett, Dec. 5, 1844-Jan.

Bible Records—Tombstone Inscriptions

13, 1918. Company A., 6th Tenn. Inf.
Arthur A. Gossett, April 25, 1862-July 30, 1900.
Claude Elmer, son of Mr. and Mrs. C. A. Kelly, Jan. 9, 1905-Jan. 31, 1925.
W. A. Kelly, April 24, 1877-Jan. 31, 1925.
Sidney A. Rose, 1873-1925.
Paul Bently Wittenbarger, Mar. 23, 1905-July 21, 1920.
John T. Farr, son of W. T. Wittenbarger, April 20, 1911-June 26, 1911.
Oscar Cate, Sept. 13, 1877-Mar. 26, 1926.
"Tinsley." May E., born Oct. 1, 1885.
Homer, July 28, 1889-June 24, 1915.
Russel Mays, June 3, 1877-Sept. 17, 1927.
Elizabeth Mays, Aug. 31, 1879-April 22, 1932.
Gertrude Broome, wife of C. A. Moors, 1869-1928.
Luther L. Chesney, Sept. 19, 1882-April 22, 1917.
Robert W. Williams, Nov. 6, 1849-Dec. 19, 1909; born in London, Ont., Canada.
Jessie Williams, Aug. 16, 1867-April 30, 1903; born in Galt, Ont., Canada.
Frances Jannette Gentry, daughter of Mr. and Mrs. H. H. Gentry, Sept. 19, 1912-Jan. 1, 1914.
Horace H. Gentry, April 7, 1884-May 26, 1930.
Annie Louise Cottrell, wife of Charles A. Weaver, Aug. 26, 1880-Sept. 6, 1927.
Samuel H. Cottrell, Aug. 22, 1846-Sept. 9, 1922.
Birtha A. Cottrell, Nov. 26, 1881-Feb. 25, 1903.
Elver H. Cottrell, May 20, 1888-Mar. 3, 1927.
La Venia Halliburton, Mar. 24, 1874-Aug. 4, 1926.
Campbell M. Wolf, Oct. 13, 1845-Feb. 11, 1925.
Rosella Wolf, Dec. 10, 1866-July 21, 1911.
Annie Mae Bean, wife of R. F. Bean, Mar. 28, 1887-Mar. 7, 1825.
Robert S. Bean, Nov. 10, 1857-June 10, 1925.
"His wife;" daughter of Jessie and Lizzie Hall, May 28, 1869.
"Mother." Eliza E. Sexton, July 15, 1851-Feb., 1908.
Alexander R. McBath, Sept., 1832-Aug., 1918.

"Hanna L. Bough," his wife, Oct., 1838-Jan., 1909.
"HORNE"
Martha Miller, July 1, 1810-April 25, 1922.
William Miller, Oct. 14, 1829-Aug. 1, 1903.
Alice Shultz, wife of L. W. Shultz, Dec. 22, 1865-April 5, 1899.
Alice Shultz, July 19, 1890-July 27, 1899.
Edna Shultz, Oct. 4, 1874-Aug. 2, 1909.
"Father." W. D. King, Aug. 18, 1868-Sept. 14, 1926.
"Mother." Rhinam King, Dec. 3, 1873.
"Daughter." Gertrude King Maston, Nov. 6, 1896-June 6, 1922.
Thomas A. Norman, 1849-1896.
Elizabeth Norman Pickens, 1857-1921.
Clarence A. Norman, June 11, 1878-July 30, 1932.
Infant son of Thomas and Elizabeth Norman, June 15, 1877-Jan. 19, 1879.
Mary J. Dawson, Feb. 17, 1844-June 9, 1919.
Elizabeth P. Dawson, Mar. 9, 1840-Mar. 31, 1899.
Alner W. Rose, Feb. 1, 1840-April 19, 1907.
Charles F. Myers, Feb. 22, 1849-May 13, 1909.
Vesta Cryer, Nov. 1, 1878-April 16, 1918.
Mary Cryer, wife of James McGinley, July 11, 1871-Aug. 23, 1917.
Edward Mitchel, May 5, 1874-Dec. 3, 1910.
Susan, wife of W. Coffman, died Sept. 22, 1908. "At Rest."
Walker Mitchel, April 10, 1872-May 12, 1918.
Higgins, son of Walker and Rettie Mitchel, June 30, 1898-Oct. 15, 1918.
Robert Galling, born Aug. 13, 1844, Systen, England, died Dec. 11, 1909; age, 65 years.
John A. Dobson, 1825-1908.
Martha H. Dobson, 1825-1905.
Robert W. Parker, 1848-1929.
A. C. W. Cain, Mar. 10, 1845-Aug. 14, 1908.
Mrs. Louise Sterchi, born in Berne, Switzerland, April 26, 1828-July 17, 1909.
J. J. Province, Mar. 29, 1869-Sept. 3, 1904.

Bible Records—Tombstone Inscriptions

Lucy Ann Rose, Oct. 9, 1844-Nov. 13, 1924.
Mitchel Kaminsta, Dec. 25, 1854-May 19, 1915.
Frank J. Kirby, June 11, 1852-Aug. 18, 1929.
Margaret R. Wilson, wife of Frank J. Kirby, May 10, 1851-May 29, 1920.
Nannie J. Ellis, April 21, 1884-Dec. 29, 1926.
Margaret Ellis, Sept. 12, 1860-Sept. 22, 1922.
Lucille E. Gredig, Nov. 26, 1850-Oct. 8, 1900.
Houston E. Roberts, Nov. 26, 1843-Feb. 3, 1907.
His wife, Elizabeth Atchley Roberts, May 25, 1845-Feb. 6, 1905.
Austin Keith, Feb. 19, 1922-May 28, 1925.
Bobby Dan Keith, April 27, 1924-May 31, 1925.
Martha E. Barry, Mar. 5, 1835-July 3, 1906.
John Mitchel Pickens, 1866-1908.
William Jones, Aug. 22, 1872-Sept. 24, 1904; "killed in New Market wreck."
Samuel C. Russel, May 15, 1846-Feb. 5, 1930.
J. W. Hedgecock, Jan. 14, 1880-May 1, 1933.
Horace L. Jones, Aug. 20, 1874-June 16, 1916.
James Cross, Aug. 17, 1907-Feb. 5, 1910.
James A. Doyle, Jr., April 14, 1882-Oct. 9, 1922.
Lula Umphreys Doyle, Jan. 10, 1891-June 22, 1920.
William C. Doyle, June 22, 1853-Dec. 6, 1917.
Alice Edington Doyle, June 8, 1861-July 16, 1917.
Alvin C. Doyle, June 12, 1874-Dec. 2, 1920.
James A. Doyle, Oct. 10, 1842-Nov. 23, 1921.
Malinda J. Doyle, Jan. 3, 1854-Sept. 19, 1929.
Annie Drake, wife of W. L. Drake, Mar. 16, 1878-Sept. 18, 1916.
George L. Presterfield, died June 3, 1924; age, 52 years.
Sarah J. Kidd, Nov. 30, 1843-Mar. 9, 1932.
Margaret Kidd, Nov. 4, 1837-June 26, 1900.
Robert L. DeArmond, 1869-1920.
Thomas E. Ford, Oct. 30, 1866-Sept. 19, 1931.
Earl C. Ford, M.D., June 26, 1890-April 12, 1932.
William F. Earley, Sept. 15, 1852-June 26, 1905.
Mary Virginia Earley, Aug. 28, 1857-July 19, 1909.
Cora Bundran Jones, 1872-1906.
Adran Davenport, 1839-1904.
William F. Bean, Dec. 22, 1856-Mar. 25, 1915.
"My Husband." Henry P. Thompson, Mar. 28, 1878-July 20, 1906. "Gone but not forgotten."
Charles F. Youngblood, May 2, 1845-June 29, 1899.
E. J. Hill, Sept. 5, 1901-Dec. 1, 1826. "May he rest in peace."
H. M. Bowers, wife of W. F. Bowers, 1877-1917. "Ours, yet remembered."
P. C. Bowers, daughter of W. F. and H. M. Bowers, 1895-1914. "Gone, yet remembered."
W. R. Thompson, Mar. 2, 1851-Feb. 28, 1923.
Taylor Roberts, Nov. 3, 1902-Dec. 20, 1926. "At Rest."
Charles E. Irwin, May 5, 1848-Feb. 2, 1926.
R. B. Bundren, 1842-1909.
William L. Bundren, 1880-1905.
Alcy Johnson Wells, Nov. 25, 1854-Jan. 27, 1921.
Bessie L., wife of C. H. Thomas, 1888-1927.
Naomi Franklin, wife of James Perry Johnson, Sept. 1, 1846-Mar. 5, 1905.
James Perry Johnson, Dec. 22, 1848-Feb. 3, 1929.
James Leroy Boruff, April 2, 1901-April 25, 1931.
James W. Boruff, Jan. 13, 1865-Nov. 16, 1926.
Ruth Boruff, Jan. 19, 1908-April 14, 1925.
Hattie Foster, Aug. 9, 1877-Mar. 20, 1926.
Missouri Gaddis, wife of J. B. Stone, Nov. 1, 1861-Mar. 6, 1910.
Flandia L. Armstrong, Mar. 1, 1889-July 2, 1923.
James Camp Woody, May 22, 1888-May 27, 1927.
Clifford A. Taylor, Aug. 27, 1879-Mar. 27, 1911.

Bible Records—Tombstone Inscriptions

Ida Bell Long, June 29, 1872-Nov. 21, 1926.

J. B. Henly, Mar. 11, 1862-June 28, 1922.

PHILADELPHIA CEMETERY

Philadelphia, Tenn., Monroe County. Sent by Helen Louise McLean Craig (Mrs. Albert Lyon), 3449 Kingston Pike, Knoxville.

Sacred to the memory of James Bacome, who departed from this life this 25th of July, A. D., 1810, in the 60th year of his age, a native of Virginia.
Hiram Glass Bacome, April 18, 1860-Nov. 11, 1874.
Arch Bacome, July 29, 1814-Dec. 7, 1900.
S. C. Johnston, wife of Arch Bacome, Sept. 10, 1836.
Nancy J., wife of Dr. P. Gregory, died May 4, 1865, in the 22nd year of her life.
Mary Martain, April 17, 1819-Feb. 28, 1907.
Hugh Martain, Jan. 19, 1808-Feb. 28, 1857.
William Martain, Aug. 13, 1839-Mar. 3, 1863.
Julia A. E., wife of A. W. Cozart, Sept. 21, 1829-Aug. 16, 1854.
David M., son of E. W. and James E. Cozart, died July 3, 1874; age, 22 years.
Newton Bogart, Oct. 14, 1831-May 26, 1889.
Elizabeth Bogart, Feb. 8, 1838-July 6, 1898.
A. W. Cozart, Feb. 11, 1823-Feb. 20, 1889.
Anna Bogart, wife of Salmon Bogart, Dec. 12, 1801-Nov. 24, 1860.
Salmon Bogart, Jan. 4, 1800-June 9, 1878.
Mary Cornelia Bogart, Sept. 26, 1845-Nov. 21, 1864.
Martha M. Bogart, Jan. 6, 1844-June 30, 1922.
Elizabeth M., wife of E. S. Atkins, Mar. 12, 1841-Nov. 7, 1874.
Lucille Atkins, wife of Henry Atkins, Nov. 6, 1792-Nov. 23, 1869.
Eli S. Adkins, Jan. 6, 1824-Feb. 20, 1887.
M. A. Sparks, Oct. 10, 1830-July 16, 1890.
Thomas J. Moore, Jan. 9, 1824-Mar. 2, 1875.
Mary A., wife of R. A. King, and daughter of J. S. Thomason, Nov. 16, 1854-Nov. 6, 1883.
Martha L., wife of John S. King, Dec. 2, 1813-May 30, 1880.
John Seymour King, May 30, 1811-April 15, 1884.
James Griffen Martain, June 14, 1841-Feb. 21, 1906.
Mary Louise Martain, Oct. 18, 1842-Sept. 10, 1901.
John Lavender, born April 1, 1826; age, 52 years.
Henry C. Call, Company K, S. Mich. Inf.
Emily C. Malleston, Jan. 26, 1860-Oct. 3, 1884; age, 60 years, 8 months.
W. G. Malleston, died Jan. 25, 1872; age, 63 years.
W. A. Allen, Feb. 4, 1859-Mar. 12, 1889.
Zela Cullen, Dec. 5, 1814-April 4, 1839.
Franklin King Berry, Mar. 23, 1809-Oct. 28, 1845.
Charles Owens, Dec. 29, 1793-Sept. 6, 1873.
Louisa Berry, wife of Charles Owens, Mar. 26, 1799-Jan. 18, 1862.
Anna Owens, 1824-July 6, 1839; age, 15 years, 5 months, 26 days.

GLEN ROCK CEMETERY

On Fork Creek, near Sweetwater, Tenn., Monroe County. Sent by Helen Louise McLean Craig (Mrs. Albert Lyon), 3449 Kingston Pike, Knoxville, Tenn.

Martha M. Carter, Dec. 31, 1819-Sept. 28, 1885.
J. F. Montgomery, Feb. 7, 1825-May 26, 1888.
Mary A. F. A. Carter, Aug. 19, 1862-June 20, 1865.

344

Bible Records—Tombstone Inscriptions

George G. Montgomery, Mar. 7, 1866; age, 66 years, 4 days.
Urola Guinn, Mar. 27, 1772-Jan. 18, 1856.
Mrs. Martha Montgomery, May 5, 1833-Feb. 7, 1879.
James Montgomery, Jan. 21, 1791-Feb. 10, 1880.
Jane Carter, wife of Robert Carter, Sept. 5, 1772-Nov. 12, 1880.
Dorcas B. Montgomery, wife of James Montgomery, Feb. 26, 1794-Jan. 20, 1870.
William Carter, Aug. 5, 1882-Mar. 26, 1851.
Sophronia G. Carter, Nov. 16, 1811-Sept. 24, 1827.
James H. Montgomery, Dec. 23, 1851-June 15, 1853.
John Carter, Jan. 12, 1785-Sept. 5, 1827.
Nancy Johnson, daughter of Joe and Polly Walker, and wife of James H. Johnson, Jan. 13, 1809-April 26, 1851.
Opha Jane Montgomery, daughter of J. H. and M. I. Montgomery, Aug. 12, 1859-Oct. 27, 1861.
Ann Johnson, died 18 years of age.
Samuel Johnson, son of Joe Johnson, Aug. 12, 1831- —— 22, 1832.

CLEVELAND FAMILY CEMETERY

Near Philadelphia, Tenn., Monroe County. Sent by Helen Louise McLean Craig (Mrs. Albert Lyon), 3449 Kingston Pike.

Alley Mathis Cleveland, wife of J. D. Jones, May 7, 1813-May 30, 1855.
Elizabeth Pennington, wife of William Pennington, Oct., 1776-Dec., 1844.
Allie Cleveland, Oct. 14, 1816-Nov. 3, 1821.
William Cleveland, Oct. 11, 1820-April 22, 1835.
A. M. Cleveland, Sept. 26, 1833-July 25, 1854.
H. H. Cleveland, Mar. 18, 1830-Sept. 1, 1851.
William Pennington, Dec. 13, 1777-April 22, 1838.
William E. Johnson, April 28, 1823-Sept. 17, 1909.
Louis (or Louise) Johnson (badly worn), Jan. 29, 1799-April 17, 1890.
Nancy Carrie Johnson, April 17, 1876-May 22, 1920.
Louise (or Louis) Johnson (name badly worn), May 29, 1805-Sept. 5, 1865.
Elizabeth Cleveland, wife of David H. Cleveland, Jan. 5, 1827-Dec. 31, 1882.
Catherine Johnson, wife of Louis Johnson, May 29, 1805-Sept. 5, 1865.
William Johnson, May 21, 1766-Dec. 27, 1837.
Elizabeth J. Walker, wife of Joseph Walker, July 25, 1825-Feb. 14, 1846.
Elizabeth Ruth Creed, Sept. 26, 1826-Oct. 30, 1870.
Joseph Walker, July 25, 1825-Feb. 14, 1846.
Alley Mathis, daughter of Joseph Dyche Jones, and Alley Mathis Cleveland, Jan. 8, 1840-Mar. 3, 1857.

WALKER FAMILY CEMETERY

On Fork Creek, near Sweetwater, Tenn. Sent by Helen Louise McLean Craig (Mrs. Albert Lyon), 3449 Kingston Pike.

Annie C. Walker, wife of C. L. Walker, Dec. 25, 1800-June 3, 1830.
Polly Walker, daughter of D. P. and Jane Walker, Feb. 13, 1828-Sept. 26, 1833.
Joseph C. Walker, July 20, 1837-May 24, 1858.
Rebecca Walker, Oct. 4, 1855-Sept. 25, 1856.
Caswell L. Walker, June 18, 1800-April 9, 1886.
Joseph Walker, May 25, 1769-Mar. 22, 1858.
David P. Walker (dates on stone are gone).

Bible Records—Tombstone Inscriptions

COMPLETE RECORD OF THE HEISKELL FAMILY CEMETERY

Near Sweetwater, Tenn., Monroe County, located on the Heiskell farm. Sent by Helen Louise McLean Craig (Mrs. Albert Lyon), 3449 Kingston Pike, Knoxville, Tenn.

"Tommy's Sister." Emily L. Guinn, Feb. 3, 1804-June 30, 1873.
James J. Sheldon, July 1, 1829-Jan. 18, 1868.
Mary, wife of Daniel Heiskell, Jan. 1, 1819-June 4, 1888.
Mrs. Sarah Harris, Oct., 1794-Dec. 11, 1855.

Dorcas Ann, daughter of Daniel and Mary Heiskell, died Jan. 14, 1853; age, 3 years, 9 months.
Daniel Heiskell, Mar. 7, 1799-July 22, 1875.
Elizabeth Heiskell, wife of Daniel Heiskell, died Aug. 1, 1815; age, 37 years.

CUNNINGHAM GRAVEYARD

Two miles south of Viola, Tenn., on Manchester Road. Sent by Mrs. J. M. Cunningham.

In memory of John Cunningham, Revolutionary Soldier, 1748-Dec. 18, 1842; age, 94 years, 10 months, 8 days.
"Hark! hark! What awful tidings soar,
What strains of grief we hear,
The mighty herald is no more,
And Zion drops a tear."

In memory of Kiziah Cunningham, consort of John Cunningham, Mar. 8, 1758-April 22, 1839.
"For why the Lord our God is good
His mercy is forever sure,
His truth at all times firmly stood,
An shall from age to age endure."

OLD CUNNINGHAM GRAVEYARD

At Great Caney Fork Falls, Rock Island, Tenn.

John Cunningham, son of John and Kiziah Cunningham, 1792-1858.
James Cunningham, son of John and Mary Hill Pettepool Cunningham, 1773-1863.

John Cunningham, son of John and Sarah Swingle Cunningham, Jan. 16, 1824-1862.
(Taken from tombstone and Bible records.)

JOHN CUNNINGHAM

Extracts from legal papers in which he or his heirs are referred to.

A
State of Tennessee to John Cunningham, assignee of Daniel Cherry. Grant No. 26115; May 10, 1831. Entry No. 15993; Nov. 10, 1815. Certificate No. 1939; Oct. 27, 1814. Grants 50 acres of land on the Caney Fork River, beginning about one-fourth mile above the mouth of Collins River.

B
State of Tennessee to John Cunningham, assignee of John A. Wilson.

Grant No. 26986; June 18, 1838. Entry No. 19329; Dec. 11, 1817. Certificate No. 2781; Oct. 29, 1817. Surveyed Sept. 20, 1818. Grants 50 acres of land on Caney Fork River adjoining Grant No. 26115.

C
Deed; John Cunningham to Heirs of Thomas Hopkins. Dated Dec. 18, 1838. Reg. Bk. L., p. 262-3-4, Warren County. In compliance with title bond executed to said Hopkins, Dec.

Bible Records—Tombstone Inscriptions

20, 1834, and whereas said Hopkins died intestate about Mar. 20, 1836. Conveys to said heirs, amongst other lands two tracts of 50 acres each. This refers to the above grants.

D

State of Tennessee to Stephen Owens. Grant No. 9565; Aug. 18, 1816. Entry No. 1799; May 21, 1808. Warrant No. 3813; Jan. 11, 1794. Surveyed, Nov. 5, 1814. Grants 180 acres of land in the First District of Warren County. This included all the land between the Collins and Caney Fork Rivers from a point just west of the "Narrow" to the mouth of Collins River.

E

Stephen Owens to Thomas Hopkins. No record.

F

Thomas Hopkins to John Cunningham. Amount, $900.00. Date, Dec. 20, 1834. Reg. Bk. O, p. 382, Warren County. In this deed Cunningham acquired all of the Owens Grant.

G

Thomas Hopkins to John Cunningham. Special Warranty Deed. No consideration. Date, Dec. 20, 1834. Reg. Bk. O, pp. 385-6, Warren County. This deed conveys 96 acres adjoining the first tract purchased from Hopkins and covers the area around and including the "Narrows." Along with the description the deed says, "Corner of the 180-acre tract whereon John Cunningham now lives. . . ."

G

State of Tennessee to John Cunningham. Grant No. 10081; Aug. 25, 1849. Warren County, Entry 3648. Surveyed July 25, 1849. Grants 144 acres of land on the waters of Caney Fork and Collins Rivers.

H

John Cunningham, Sr., John Cunningham, Jr., to John B. Rogers. Date, June 11, 1853. Reg. Bk. R, pp. 546-7. "The full right and privilege in fee simple to erect at the Great Falls of Caney Fork in Warren County, Tenn., on lands of said John Cunningham, any sort of waterworks or machinery with full enjoyment of said privileges, with room for mill yard, out house, etc., for miller, hands, etc., right of way to and from and for a public road not to exceeding 25 feet wide from junction of Caney Fork and Collins River on such grounds as grantor may designate; to erect a bridge across Collins River. Grantor to have use of bridge and grain to be ground free of toll."

I

John Cunningham, Sr., to George Cunningham. Gift. Jan. 10, 1854. Reg. Bk. 2, pp. 131-2, Warren County. Consideration: love and affection. Conveys 90 acres of land on Collins River. This is what was later known as the "Hoover Farm."

J

John Cunningham to John Cunningham. Deed of Gift. Retained life estate to himself and wife. Oct. 22, 1855. Reg. Bk. 1, pp. 346-7, Warren County. This deed conveys a farm of 150 acres and is the old Cunningham place, including the old house, cemetery, spring, etc. It included all not conveyed to George Cunningham.

BANDY GRAVEYARD

One mile west of Laguardo Road. Sent by Mrs. W. P. Bouton.

Epperson Bandy, May 12, 1794-June 6, 1863.
W. P. Bandy, 1823-1891.
Lucinda Bandy, 1830-1857.
Edward Bandy, 1827-1850.
Bennett Bandy, 1851-1853.
Perone Bandy, 1875-1876.
Z. W. Davis, April 7, 1829-Sept. 4, 1910.
H. J. Bandy, wife of Z. W. Davis, Mar. 27, 1836-Dec. 13, 1876.
James, son of Z. W. and H. J. Davis, Aug. 20, 1860-Oct. 5, 1860.
Lizzie W., daughter of Z. W. and H. J. Davis, Sept. 18, 1863-Jan. 8, 1864.
Col. Isaac Green, Mar. 28, 1796-Oct.

Bible Records—Tombstone Inscriptions

9, 1856.
Samuel A. Green, Aug. 19, 1835-July 18, 1868.
N. Green, —— 33 (on sandstone, scaled off).
Thomas Bartholamew; age, about 60 years; died, Nov. 5, 1850.

G. J. Penge, Jan. 6, 1800-Feb. 3, 1852.
P. P. Crutcher, Dec. 3, 1829-April 17, 1887.
Morton Lanius, 1876-1882.
(Three or more graves in rock pen not marked.)

Berry Johnson Graveyard

On road two miles north of Maple Hill, on Robert Shearron place. Sent by Mrs. W. P. Bouton, Lebanon, Tenn.

L. B. Johnson, Jan. 9, 1805-Feb. 27, 1898.
Maranda Johnson, Nov. 10, 1809-Oct. 26, 1884.
Prissila, wife of L. B. Johnson, April 13, 1820-May 9, 1892.
Sarah Malinda, wife of B. L. Johnson, Dec. 8, 1838-May 5, 1868.
W. H. Smith, May 29, 1832-Dec. 26, 1901.

Lucy Jane Johnson, wife of William H. Smith, Mar. 21, 1836-Oct. 10, 1881.
W. H. Johnson, Jan. 6, 1847-Aug. 9, 1905.
Mattie Chamberlain, May 9, 1872-Jan. 22, 1893.
V. Ramsey, Mar. 13, 1840-June 16, 1893.
Synthia E. Ramsey, Dec. 28, 1837-Sept. 8, 1890.

McFarland Graveyard

On Dr. J. J. McFarland's place, on Coles Ferry Pike, Wilson County, Tenn. Sent by Mrs. W. P. Bouton, Lebanon, Tenn.

Dr. James Harvey McFarland, 1816-Aug. 5, 1870; age, 54 years.
Charlotte Walker McFarland, 1812-Oct., 1881; age, 69 years.
Dr. J. W. McFarland, Mar. 22, 1843-Dec. 20, 1917.
James Harvey McFarland, April 18, 1850-Sept. 22, 1901.

Mattie Chambers McFarland, Dec. 17, 1855-July 29, 1911.
Walter James McFarland, Oct. 17, 1877-Aug. 26, 1896.
Sallie McFarland Adams, 1888-1917.
Infant of Dr. J. J. and Kate McFarland, born and died Jan. 9, 1900.

Graves on Hill West of Walter Smith's

On Coles Ferry Pike. Sent by Mrs. W. J. Bouton, Lebanon, Tenn.

Mrs. Elvira Lavender, born in Herice County, Va., April, 1815-Oct. 20, 1880.
Zack Nettles, 1837-1913.
Dr. W. M. Wherry, June 10, 1743-Nov. 3, 1815.
(Several graves in cedar pens not marked.)

McClain Graveyard

On Orville Young's place, between Laguardo Road and Nashville Pike, north of Cooks Church. Sent by Mrs. W. P. Bouton.

John Anderson McClain, Dec. 31, 1806-May 2, 1866.
Manerva Ross, wife of John Anderson McClain, Mar. 22, 1810-Aug. 7, 1867.
J. B. Arnold, Aug. 31, 1845-Mar. 15, 1922.

S. E. Arnold, Mar. 8, 1844-July 3, 1879.
Joe McClain, son of J. B. and S. E. Arnold, Mar. 31, 1877-July 1, 1879.
S. A. Arnold, Sept. 23, 1874-Mar. 28, 1906.

Bible Records—Tombstone Inscriptions

Inscriptions copied at Old City Cemetery at Murfreesboro, Tenn., by Miss Lillian Jetton.

Colonel Robert Jetton served his country faithfully as a soldier and statesman; born 1781; died 1810.

Nancy Jetton, wife of Col. Robert Jetton, born March 13, 178—; died July 22, 1855.

Inscriptions from Vaughan family cemetery, Almaville, in Rutherford County, Tennessee. Sent by Miss Jetton.

Elizabeth Slate, born Sept. 16, 1776; died Aug. 29, 1839.
Richard B. Vaughan, born March 17, 1795; died Dec. 11, 1854.
Ann Vaughan, born Sept. 20, 1788; died Sept. 18, 1845.
John S. Vaughan, son of R. B. and Ann Vaughan, born Feb. 25, 1821; died Sept. 9, 1845.

Martha A. E. (Elliott) Vaughan, born July 27, 1822; died Jan. 27, 1849.
James Vaughan, died Aug. 12, 1889; age 70 years 9 months 29 days.
Mary Lytle Elliott Vaughan, born Jan. 21, 1833; died April 14, 1921.

Sent by Miss Jetton.

Andrew Carnahan, Revolutionary soldier; buried on farm of George Youree, Readyville, Tenn.; location of grave can be seen from the highway; unmarked; only grave there.

Sent by Mrs. Oliver Mann.

Capt. Nat. Allen, killed at Battle of Stones River; carried flag after he was wounded; grave in old Read family burial ground, also called Enon Church Graveyard; unmarked.

Copied from Fosterville Cemetery, by Rebekah Jetton.

Nicholas Woodfin, born Aug. 2, 1759; died Dec. 21, 1832.
Hannah Woodfin, born Aug. 16, 1815; died —— (space left for date which was never cut).
Miss Jane Woodfin, born April 22, 1803; died March 31, 1826.
John Naylor, born Feb. 10, 1855; died in his 68th year.
G. N. Edwards, born Sept. 21, 1828; died Aug. 14, 1851.

OLD CITY CEMETERY AT MURFREESBORO, TENN.
By Miss Rebekah Jetton

The City Cemetery, now called the Old City Cemetery, is on East Vine Street. The plot of three acres was purchased from Mary M. Hilliard, December 28, 1837, by Henderson Yoakum, Mayor, for the City of Murfreesboro. Mary W. Hilliard was represented by her "Attorney in Fact," Moses G. Reeves. Deed was registered by Robert S. Morris, Clerk, December 29, 1837, Deed Book W, Page 494, R. O. R. C., Tenn.

The Presbyterian Church, erected 1819-1820, on the corner lot adjoining the cemetery grounds, was used as a hospital during the Civil War and was demolished by the Federal Army.

Bible Records—Tombstone Inscriptions

A call session of the General Assembly was held in the church, Aug., 1822. The Lower House met on the first floor and the Senate in the gallery. In 1873, the city purchased 20 acres from James Maney for a new cemetery to be called Evergreen Cemetery. Lots were exchanged in the new for those in the old cemetery and many families had their dead removed, but many are still buried in the old cemetery.

The remains of 2,000 Confederate soldiers were moved from the Confederate Cemetery on the Shelbyville Road, to Evergreen Cemetery. The spot is called Confederate Circle. The U. D. C. placed a monument there to the Unknown Dead.

The Lytle family burying ground is at the old home place of Capt. Wm. Lytle, now owned by the Carnation Milk Company. It is about one-fourth of an acre and surrounded by the land of the Carnation Plant. A few of the graves are enclosed by an iron fence. The graves of Capt. Wm. Lytle and his wife, Nancy Taylor Lytle, and others, are not protected. The grave of Tabitha Morton, daughter of James Morton and wife of John Lytle, Revolutionary soldier, is there.

Inscriptions copied from tombstones in the Old City Cemetery in Murfreesboro, Tenn., by Miss Rebekah Jetton Regent.

Mary Williams, born Aug. 9, 1790; died April 15, 1828.

Elisha Williams, Jr., born Oct. 20, 1822; died Oct. 31, 1848.

Sarah J. Ray Childress, born July 31, 1815; died March 14, 1850.

In memory of Joseph John P. Williams, born Dec. 10, 1817; died May 31, 1852.

In memory of Henry J. Williams, youngest son of Elisha and Mary Williams, born June 20, 1825; died April 18, 1855.

Sarah H. Williams, consort of Elisha Williams; born Nov., 1735; departed this life Sept. 1, 1857.

Sacred to the memory of Selina Ann Thomas, born July 16, 1812; died Oct. 25, 1816.

In memory of Mrs. Frances, consort of J. W. Fletcher, born July 19, 1782; died Aug. 21, 1856.

Sacred to the memory of Susan Fuller, born in Culpeper County, Ca., in 1752; died July 22, 1816, being 64 years old. She was a member of the old Baptist Church; lived an exemplary life and died happy in the Lord.

Sacred to the memory of John Fuller, born in Caswell County, N. C., April 28, 1812; died in Rutherford County, Tenn., Dec. 17, 1851, in his 10th year. He professed faith in Christ and died happy.

John M. Watson, M.D., born Nov. 20, 1798; died Sept. 20, 1866.

Lockey S. Watson, wife of Dr. John Watson, and daughter of Col. Bedford and Sally S. Brown of Clark County, Ga.; born Feb. 4, 1814; died July 4, 1850. They were married April 15, 1831.

R. M. Searcy, Lieutenant in 34th Virginia Regiment; born at Tuscaloosa, Ala., March 20, 1844; died at Murfreesboro Jan. 7, 1863.

In memory of Dr. Wm. R. Rucker, born May 20, 1792; died Aug. 8, 1861.

In memory of Delila Petty, wife of John Petty, born April 17, 1790; died Dec. 7, 1855.

John Petty, born in North Carolina in Chatham County, June 22, 1781.

Bible Records—Tombstone Inscriptions

Sacred to the memory of Maj. Samuel H. Hodge, born Jan. 1, 1800; died March 29, 1846.
Sarah Curry Mitchell, born July 3, 1800; died June 25, 1867; married Samuel H. Hodge in 1820.
In memory of John H. Hodge, born July 21, 1829; died April 16, 1851.
Our loved and honored father, Dr. James Maney, born in Hertford County, N. C., Feb. 9, 1790; died at Murfreesboro Nov. 12, 1872; age 82 years 9 months 3 days.
In memory of Sallie H. Maney, consort of Dr. James Maney, born Feb. 12, 1793; died Aug. 12, 1857.
In memory of Thomas H. Maney, Born Jan. 24, 1821; died March 20, 1847; age 26 years 1 month 21 days.
In memory of Fanny Maney, wife of Thomas H. Maney, born Aug. 22, 1820; died Oct. 21, 1847; age 27 years 1 month 29 days.
In memory of Thomas H. Maney, son of Thomas H. Maney and Fanny M. Maney, born Sept. 18, 1844; died Nov. 2, 1845.
In memory of Thomas Henry, son of David and Mary L. Maney, born Dec. 9, 1851; died Jan. 18, 1852; age 3 weeks 6 days.
Lavinia, daughter of L. M. and R. A. Maney, born Oct. 6, 1856; died Nov. 30, 1857.
Here lies the remains of Silas Locks, born Jan. 21, 1791, at Sprinlane, County of Arough ——, Ireland, died at Tyree Springs Aug., 1830.
Sacred to the memory of Harrison Patillo, born in Brunswick County, Va., Jan. 1, 1805; died in Rutherford County, Tenn., —— 11.
Sacred to the memory of S. W. Blankenship, consort of B. Blankenship, died Feb. 4, 1826, in the 42nd year of her age.
Sacred to the memory of Margaret Stewart, born Oct. 15, 1755; died Feb. 12, 1836.
H. Henderson, died Dec. 27, 1824; age 32 years 9 months.
Fanny P. Wallace, born July 7, ——; died Nov. 22, 1833.
Sacred to the memory of Leathy R. Wallace, daughter of John and Mary Wallace, born Dec. 14, 1808; died Feb. 27, 1836.
In memory of John B. Maney, born Sept. 29, 1835; died Jan. 29, 1839.
In memory of William M. Maney, born Feb. 7, 1832; died Nov. 12, 1838.
In memory of Frances E. Maney, born Sept. 16, 1813; died Nov. 12, 1838.
In memory of James H. Maney, born Dec. 2, 1818; died Nov. 13, 1838.
Mrs. Sarah Hooper Cherry, wife of Rev. John M. Cherry and mother of Rev. S. M. and Rev. W. D. Cherry, born Dec. 1, 1796; died June 25, 1870.
In memory of Jeremiah W. Fletcher, born Nov. 11, 1776; died Jan. 13, 1812.
Sacred to the memory of Evander McIver, died Sept., 1828, in the 55th year of his age.
Sacred to the memory of Margaret, consort of John McIver, died Sunday, Nov. 7, 1824.
John McIver, 1770-1830.
To the memory of the lamented Dr. John M. King, died Nov. 23, 1824, in the 30th year of his age.
Marman Spence, a Christian, born May 6, 1798; died Feb. 24, 1847.
Sarah W. Spence, wife of Marman Spence, born in Ireland; died July 12, 1857; age 66 years.
Sacred to the memory of Margaret Wasson, a native of Ireland, died in Murfreesboro, Tenn., Sept. 23, 1834; age 81 years.
Wm. Gilliam, born May 10, 1798; died March 2, 1842.
John L. Jetton, born in Mecklenburg County, N. C., Dec. 11, 1778; died June 25, 1854. (The Masonic emblem appears above the inscription.)
Sacred to the memory of Mrs. Martha M. Moore, consort of James C. Moore, and daughter of Gen. Robt. Purdy, born Oct. 18, 1808; died March 31, 1843.
Sacred to the memory of Margaret W. Johns, daughter of Col. John Thompson and relict of F. E. Johns, born Dec. 31, 1803; died

Bible Records—Tombstone Inscriptions

Oct. 11, 1819. Frederick John. Sacred to the memory of Eliza Leinau, wife of Daniel Leinau; age 52 years; born in the City of Philadelphia, 1803; died Sept. 6, 1855, in Murfreesboro, Tenn.

Sacred to the memory of Lavinia Hilliard, wife of Isaac H. Hilliard Leinau; and only child of Daniel and Eliza Leinau; born in the City of Philadelphia, Pa., Oct. 9, 1817; died at Beersheba Springs, Tenn., Aug. 11, 1837.

Copied from tombstones in the Old City Cemetery, Murfreesboro, Tenn., by Annie E. Campbell.

Ann Eliza Slater, consort of Rev. E. C. Slater and daughter of Thos. W. and Mary Linster, born May 2, 1821; died Jan. 10, 1853.
In memory of Mrs. Mary M. Linster, born Sept. 13, 1802; died May 9, 1859.
Daniel S. Brown, 1845-1931.
Elizabeth Jetton, wife of Wm. Jetton, born Nov. 7, 1824; died Oct. 16, 1850.
Elizabeth Brenard Jetton; born Oct. 13, 1828; died at the age of 42 years 7 months 3 days.
Margaret Jetton, born July 16, 1826; died at the age of 69 years.
Mary E. Jetton, born Feb. 26, 1829; died July 16, 1850.
Rob H. Jetton, born June 2, 1822; died Jan. 5, 1836.
William Jetton, born Jan. 15, 1818; died July 10, 1850.
Margaret C. Kelton, consort of Samuel Kelton, born Feb. 16, 1838; died at the age of 27 years 10 months 10 days.

Hudson Cemetery, near Puckett's Store, Rutherford County, Tenn. Copied by Miss Fanny Berry.

Crockett Hudson, born Jan. 2, 1839; died Oct. 13, 1918.
W. G. Morgan, born 1844; died 1905.

CAPTAIN WILLIAM BATEY, A SOLDIER OF THE AMERICAN REVOLUTION

Captain William Batey is buried on the farm upon which he settled when he came to Tennessee, from Brunswick County, Virginia, in 1807. The stone slab tombs that mark the last resting places of Captain Batey and his wife, Mrs. Anne Bass Batey, are found in the family cemetery, about fifty yards east of the old Batey residence, which stands today their lone sentinel. The inscriptions read:

Capt. Wm. Batey, born May 1, 1760, soldier of the Revolution and for many years a member of the Baptist Church; died Jan. 11, 1836.

Mrs. Ann Batey, relict of Capt. Wm. Batey, born Aug. 23, 1773; died Aug. 3, 1854.

The pioneer home of Capt. Wm. Batey is located seven miles west of Murfreesboro, Tennessee, adjoining the farm of the late Charles Hayes King, and lying one-half mile to the northwest, and one-half mile north of the Franklin Road.

(Signed)   Jeannette Moore King.

Bible Records—Tombstone Inscriptions

Murfreesboro, Tenn., Feb. 5, 1932.
Copied at the Lytle family burial ground by Rebekah Jetton, Capt. Wm. Lytle Chapter, D. A. R., Murfreesboro, Tenn.

Sacred to the memory of Captain William Lytle, an officer of the War of the Revolution. He was born in Pennsylvania Feb. 17, 1755; died on this farm Sept. 9, 1829. Universally beloved for his honesty and firmness in all the relations of life. His youngest son, on whom his name was bestowed, placed this tablet to his memory. Beneath this monumental slab lie entombed the remains of Mrs. Nancy Lytle, wife of Captain William Lytle, Sr., who departed this life Nov. 1, 1825; age 55 years 8 months, 21 days. She lived in the esteem and died with the regard of a large circle of friends and an affectionate family of children and relatives.

Bronze marker:
Nancy Taylor Lytle, daughter and wife of a Revolutionary soldier. erected by Campbell Chapter, D. A. R.
In tender and affectionate recollection of one of the most amiable and kind and virtuous of her sex. Her husband, William F. Lytle, has placed this monument over the remains of Mary Patterson Lytle, his lamented wife. She was born Dec. 2, 1818; died March ——.
In tender loving memory of Richard Ridgely Lytle, born Dec. 29, 1852; died Jan. 31, 1931.
His wife, Ethel Benedict Cox, born Nov. 8, 1887.
Mrs. Tabitha Lytle, born Feb. 17, 1791; died Sept. 22, 1817. Tomb of wife of Wm. F. Lytle. (Notation: Broken, pieces missing, inscription cannot be read.)
Sacred to the memory of Richard W. Caswell, born May 17, 1784, in Lenoir County, N. C.; died May 5, 1810, in Rutherford County, Tenn.; age 25 years 11 months 18 days.
William Lytle Avent, son of B. W. J. and Nancy T. Avent, born April 9, 1812; died Jan. 7, 1815.
James P., infant son of Robt. and Eliza P. Lytle, born Dec. 25, 1858; died July 18, 1859.
Joshuaway Johnson, died April, 1839.
Thomas M. Johnson, died Sept., 1839.

MARRIAGES

Amanda C. C. Wright and Joshua F. Johnson, married March 8, 1846.
Benjamin Johnson and Arrimintia M. L. Wright, married June 28, 1844.
Charles C. Abernathy and Narcissa A. R. Wright, married Jan. 3, 1839.
John H. Hall and Clementine C. Johnson, married Feb. 19, 1840.
J. B. Hall and Narcissa A. R. Abernathy, married March 18, 1849.
W. S. McKnight and Virginia E. Johnson, married —— 15, 1853.

Copied from tombstone in Center Presbyterian Church, Davidson, North Carolina.

Sacred to the memory of Lewis Jetton, died Sept. 21, 1826; age 78 years.
In memory of Priscilla Jetton, died May 13, 1838; age 88 years.

Copied from a tombstone located on the farm of Robert Steelman, on Manson pike, near Murfreesboro, Tenn.

Sacred to the memory of Thomas Blanton, born 1158 (1758; died May 27, 1846; age 88 years. He was a soldier in the Revolution under General Greene and fought in the Battles of Gilford Court House, Camden, Eutau Springs, and several others.

Bible Records—Tombstone Inscriptions

Copied from old Cannon Graveyard, near Smyrna, Tenn., by Miss Mary Robertson, member of Shawnee Chapter.

Major John Sharp, Revolutionary officer, died Nov. 1, 1824; age 72 years.

Other side of tomb: Martha, wife of Major Sharp, died May 8, 1821; age 61 years.

Taken from family graveyard, Franklin Road, near Murfreesboro, Tenn., by Miss Katherine Haley, Capt. Wm. Lytle Chapter, D. A. R.

Sacred to the memory of Nathaniel Puckett, died May 25, 1842; age 78 years.
Sacred to the memory of Thomas S. Berry, died Sept. 10, 1835; age 36 years 6 months.
Mahala P. Batey, born Dec. 30, 1804; died Feb. 14, 1883.
Christopher T. Batey, born Sept. 9, 1792; died April 22, 1849.

In memory of Mrs. Elizabeth Akin Puckett, consort of Charles Puckett, born Oct. 16, 1778; died June 11, 1859; age 80 years 8 months 27 days.
In memory of Charles Puckett, born June 22, 1771; died Jan. 13, 1854; age 82 years 7 months 8 days.

This grave is on the farm of Womack Peebles, Nashville Road, Rutherford County. Sent in by Miss Rebekah Jetton, Murfreesboro, Tennessee.

Sacred to the memory of John Etter, a Revolutionary soldier, born June, 1760; died Feb. 19, 1851.

Tombstone inscriptions sent by Mildred Hord Hicks, Regent, Capt. Wm. Lytle Chapter, D. A. R.

HORD

Col. William Hord, born Aug. 5, 1764; died May 15, 1825.
Nancy Hord, born April 1, 1772; died July 11, 1841.
(Taken from New Providence churchyard, Stoney Point, Tenn., Hawkins County, East Tennessee.)

HOWSE

Ambrose Howse, born in Brunswick County, Va., Feb. 6, 1766; emigrated to Rutherford County in 1815; died June 24, 1855, in full hope of a blissful immortality. He was an exemplary member of the Methodist Episcopal Church for 25 years.
Mrs. Mary Howse, wife of Ambrose Howse, born in Brunswick County, Va., Feb. 9, 1781; died Dec. 3, 1831.
(Howse Family Cemetery.)
George Washington Howse, Sr., born April 22, 1819; died Sept. 4, 1910.
Elizabeth M. Burrus, wife of G. W. Howse, Sr., born Sept. 28, 1823; died July 20, 1892.
(Evergreen Cemetery.)

SIKES

Thomas A. Sikes, born in Virginia, 1760; died in Rutherford County Sept. 5, 1835; served three years as private under the command of Capt. Jno. Winston and Col. Chas. Lewis, in Virginia. He was en-

Bible Records—Tombstone Inscriptions

gaged in the Battle of Paulus Hook.

HORD

Thomas Hord, born Aug. 31, 1802, in Hawkins County; died Sept. 15, 1865.
Mildred Gilmer Hord, born Jan. 28, 1824; died July 16, 1894.
Thomas Hord, married, second, Mildred Gilmer Hord, at the First Presbyterian Church, by Dr. Edgar, Oct. 12, 1859. (Bible record.)
Thomas Hord, son of William and Nancy Hord.
(Evergreen Cemetery, Murfreesboro.)
Mary E. Hord, wife of Thomas Hord and daughter of Benjamin and Sarah McCulloch, died Sept. 16, 1851. (Thomas Hord's first wife.)
Ada B. Hord Ewing, born Oct. 22, 1836; died Aug. 16, 1920.
J. W. Ewing, born Aug. 11, 1836; died Aug. 4, 1890 (tombstone); married Nov. 21, 1855 (Bible record).
Benjamin McCulloch Hord, born March 20, 1842; married Miss Annie Gray Warner, Nov. 15, 1866 (Bible record).

TUCKER

In memory of Elmira Tucker, wife of Silas Tucker, and her two infants.
Elmira, born May 27, 1813; died July 15, 1838.
Her infant, Samuel B., born April 11, 1837; died May 13, 1837.
Her infant, William, was born July 18, 1838; died July 19, 1838.
In memory of Malissa Tucker, born Sept. 15, 1809; died April 22, 1833 (remainder illegible).
(From an old burying ground on the Hord place, Rutherford County.)
Alice Gray Hord, born Feb. 5, 1844; married J. H. Warner of Chattanooga June 20, 1867 (Bible record).
Benjamin McCulloch, died Aug. 10, in the 61st year of his age (Evergreen Cemetery tombstone).
John W. Richardson, born Nov. 23, 1809; died Nov. 19, 1872.
Auousta M. Starnes, wife of John W. Richardson, born Jan. 1, 1814; died July 28, 1900 (tombstone).
James Crichtow, born in North Carolina Sept. 3, 1793; died April 8, 1872; age 78 years 7 months 5 days.
Jane C. Crichtow, born Nov. 29, 1806; died April, 1898.
Col. Richard H. Keeble, killed in the Battle at Petersberg, Va., June 30, 1864; age 33 years.
(Above tombstone records from Evergreen Cemetery.)

The following records were taken from the Old City Cemetery on Vine Street, at Murfreesboro, Tennessee. Copied by Mrs. J. B. Black, Regent, Colonel Hardy Murfree Chapter, D. A. R.

Moses G. Reeves, born in North Carolina, Jan. 5, 1800; died April 22, 1861.
Catherine S., wife of M. G. Reeves, born in Philadelphia, Pa., March 20, 1804; died in Christian triumph Dec. 2, 1894.
Martha Butler, wife of Daniel L. Reeves, born Aug. 25, 1836; died Nov. 12, 1857.
Daniel L. Reeves, born Dec. 24, 1828; died July 7, 1876.
Mary Garner, wife of Daniel Reeves; died Nov. 24, 1872; age 34 years.
Lewis G. Reeves, born Dec. 2, 1862; died Nov. 15, 1865.
Lillian Reeves, born Feb. 15, 1867; died Aug. 20, 1867.
Mary G. Reeves, born Dec. 14, 1859; died Aug. 20, 1876.
Violet L., consort of J. D. Alexander, born Sept. 15, 1807; died April 15, 1853.
Sophia Harrison, born Nov. 24, 1799; died March 3, 1858.
Sacred to the memory of Joshua Harrison, died Dec. 25; age 36

Bible Records—Tombstone Inscriptions

years.
Joshua Harrison; age 5 months.
To the memory of Robert Harrison, died June, 1822.
Sacred to the memory of Samuel Killough, born Sept. 10, 1763, in the State of North Carolina; moved to Tennessee in 1804; died March 20, 1819.
In memory of Sarah Locke, died March 3, 1839; age 81 years.
Sacred to the memory of Mary Kellough, daughter of Samuel Kellough and Mary Kellough, died Feb. 20, 1840; age 27 years 27 days.
Sacred to the memory of Lavena Kellough, daughter of Samuel and Mary Kellough, died Sept. 22, 1840.
In memory of Robert Henderson Kellough, born Jan. 23, 1819; died Jan. 10, 1843.
In memory of Mary Jane Kellough, born Sept. 21, 1827; died Feb. 10, 1844.
In memory of James Pinckney Kellough, son of Matilda, born Jan. 3, 1843; died Jan. 19, 1844.
Susan Kellough, daughter of Samuel and Mary Kellough, died March 3, 1897; age 20 years 2 months 9 days.
Sacred to the memory of Elizabeth W. Huggins, died Aug. 7, 1835; age 53 years.
In memory of Cornelia Anne, consort of E. Warren, born Nov. 13, 1820; died Aug. 25, 1877 (?).
In memory of Mary Elizabeth, consort of Wm. S. Huggins, born Jan. 13, 1831; died March 5, 1832.
Sacred to the memory of Isabella W. Jarman, wife of George W. Jarman, born Jan. 20, 1833; died Nov. 21, 1853.
Nina Lawrence, wife of A. G. Vaughn, born Oct. 11, 1866; died March 24, 1908.
In memory of Louesa B. Finch, consort of J. R. Finch, born Feb. 20, 1833; died Feb. 14, 1855.
Hardy M. Burton, son of F. N. W. Burton and Lavinia Burton, died Dec. 15, 1852, at the Island of St. Thomas; age 34 years 6 months 8 days.

Lavinia B. Murfree Burton, wife of Frank N. W. Burton and daughter of Col. Hardy Murfree; born in North Carolina, April 3, 1795; died in Kentucky, Jan. 24, 1881.
Frank N. W. Burton, born in North Carolina, May 2, 1779; died in Tennessee, June 6, 1813.
Eliza F. Cressthwaite, daughter of F. N. W. and L. Burton, wife of Dr. C. D. Crossthwaite; died Dec. 22, 1860; age 13 years.
This monument was erected to the memory of David Rankin, born June 16, 1768; died Feb. 3, 1830; age 62 years 4 months 13 days.
Anne M. Rankin, born Oct. 22, 1782; died Sept. 9, 1872.
Sacred to the memory of Rev. James Porter, born May 10, 1805; died Sept. 11, 1831; age 26 years 1 month 1 day.
Sacred to the memory of Ermina Rankin, consort of J. P. Rankin, born Jan. 27, 1806; died Nov. 5, 1840; age 34 years 9 months 9 days.
Jane G. Rankin, wife of James Bane, born Sept. 2, 1813; died Jan. 21, 1892.
In memory of Nancy Morgan, wife of Gary Morgan, born Oct. 17, 1794; died May 19, 1860.
Sacred to the memory of Dr. Wm. L. Thompson, died Nov. 10, 1833; age 28 years.
A tribute of respect to the memory of Mrs. Sarah S. Holmes, consort of Dr. Henry Holmes and daughter of Bedford and Sarah Brown; born in Georgia, Nov. 25, 1806; died in this place Aug. 19, 1840.
In memory of Isaac Anderson, born Jan. 13, 1831; died Feb. 19, 1850.
In memory of Sarah B. Anderson, born July 7, 1829; died May 9, 1878 (?).
Lucy Anderson, born Nov. 9, 1823; died April 23, 1874.
Erected by Rutherford Division No. 5, Sons of Temperance, to the memory of Lucas Oslin, born Oct. 25, 1799; died Jan. 18, 1851.
In memory of Loutha W. Haynes, a lovely daughter of I. J. C.

Bible Records—Tombstone Inscriptions

Haynes and E. A. Haynes, born Nov. 3, 1842; died Jan. 25, 1850.
In memory of Ann Trahue, infant daughter of I. J. C. and E. A. Haynes; born July 16, 1857; died July 25, 1857.
Sacred to the memory of Elvira A., consort of I. J. C. Haynes, born May 26, 1820; died Aug. 27, 1858.
Sacred to the memory of Nancy W. Fletcher, born Dec. 1, 1803; died May 24, 1863.
Martha Alice Haynes, 1858-1873.
Julia A. Warren, wife of I. J. C. Haynes.
Martha O. Sutill, wife of I. J. C. Haynes, died 1881.
I. C. J. Haynes, born June 19, 1816; died Nov. 30, 1887.
Sue R. Jetton, wife of P. L. Binford, born Oct. 3, 1853; died Feb. 27, 1881.
Joanna L. Jetton, born Oct. 19, 1822; died Oct. 15, 1853.
In memory of William B., infant son of Robert B. and Joanna Jetton.
In memory of John Blanton, born Jan. 26, 1809; died June 11, 1833.
Sacred to the memory of Elizabeth, consort of Samuel Anderson, born in Amherst, Va., March 5, 1802; died Nov. 17, 1850.
Samuel Anderson, born in Virginia, Jan. 5, 1787; died July 20, 1850.
Sophia B. Ellis, wife of R. G. Ellis, eldest daughter of Samuel Anderson, born Sept. 19, 1821; died April 28, 1851.
In memory of Mrs. Margaret M. Bostick, consort of Dr. Jonathan Bostick, born Aug. 20, 1825; died Nov. 19, 1858.
In memory of Margaret Bostick, born Nov. 10, 1843; died July 28, 1856; daughter of J. and M. M. Bostick.
Marietta Bostick, born June 12, 1852; died July 19, 1852 (daughter of J. and M. M. Bostick).
Algenon Bostick, born Feb. 24, 1855; died July 27, 185—.
Jonathan Bostick, born Oct. 30, 1850; died June 5, 1851.
Mrs. Clemintine Jarrat, born July 18, 1824; died July 3, 1858.
In memory of Mrs. Amanda V. Baird, consort of William Baird and daughter of David M. and Rebecca Jarrat, born Dec. 1, 1833; died Aug. 18, ——.
Sacred to the memory of Thomas Johnson, born Nov. 25, 1796, in Louenberg County, Va.; died April 18, 1837; age 40 years 22 days.
Finie, youngest daughter of F .N. W. Burton and Lavinia B. Burton, born Dec. 15, 1838; died Nov. 18, 1862.
Prisscilla Burton, wife of Joseph E. Carter, 1836-1900.
Robert H. Burton, second son of F. N. W. and Lavinia Burton, born May 2, 1820; died Aug. 31, 1821.
In memory of Mrs. Sally M. Dodson, wife of Prof. P. W. Dodson and daughter of Col. F. N. W. and Lavinia Burton, born Dec. 25, 1833; died Aug. 22, 1858; married July 23, 1858.
Sacred to the memory of Mrs. Mary J. Coldwell, consort of Thos. H. Coldwell, died in Shelbyville, May 2, 1846.
In memory of Hugh Kirk, born in South Carolina in 1785; moved to Tennessee in 1832; died Oct. 22, 1850.
Jane Kirk, consort of Hugh Kirk, died Dec. 25, 1859; age 63 years.
In memory of Jane Oliver, wife of G. W. Oliver, died April 14, 1856; age about 57 years.
James W. Phillips, son of Joseph and Dorothy Phillips, born June 22, 1826; died July 24, 1854.
Megs Sarah Phillips, consort of James W. Phillips and daughter of William B. and Susan Rucker, born Sept. 7, 1828; died June 18, 1853.
Charles Edmund Ready, son of Charles and Martha A. Ready, born Dec. 11, 1830; died Sept. 27, 1856; age 25 years 10 months 18 days.

Bible Records—Tombstone Inscriptions

Inscriptions from cemetery on C. T. Carter's farm, Wilson County, Tenn. Sent by Hazeline Young.

Sallie L. Beasley, born Dec. 7, 1865; died Sept. 18, 1872.
Flora R. Bell, 1847-1917.
James S. Bell, born Jan. 26, 1824; died Sept. 20, 1841.
Josephine Bell, born July 22, 1848; died Sept. 22, 1849.
Josephine G. Bell, born Dec. 18, 1800; died March 23, 1879.
Martha A. Bell, born Dec. 8, 1833; died Aug. 23, 1855.
Mary P. Bell, wife of J. G. Bell, born March 31, 1804; died March 31, 1871.
Robert D. Bell, born March 16, 1826; died Aug. 2, 1849.
William A. Bell, 1839-1917.
Charlie P. Carter, son of C. T. and Mattie Carter, born June 6. 1875; died Sept. 9, 1876.
Charley Hubert Carter, son of W. H. and Mary W. Carter, born July 3, 1874; died March 4, 1884.
C. T. Carter, born Sept. 11, 1832; died Aug. 27, 1902.
Flora Carter, daughter of C. T. and Mattie Carter, born Oct. 30, 1868; died Jan. 9, 1869.
Jessie Lee Carter, son of W. H. and Mary W. Carter, born Sept. 13, 1867; died Jan. 24, 1886.
Juhlice Bell Carter, daughter of C. T. and Mattie Carter, born March 13, 1873; died Sept. 5, 1890.
Laura T. Carter, daughter of C. T. and Mattie Carter, born Feb. 7, 1866; died June 25, 1890.
Mary W. Dickens Carter, wife of W. H. Carter, born Jan. 27, 1843; died Oct. 10, 1900.
W. H. Carter, born Dec. 4, 1821; died Aug. 31, 1902.
Caldona Conatser, born Aug. 17, 1860; died June 27, 1892.
Clementine Conatser, 1840-1917.
Mrs. Fannie Dickens, born Jan. 30, 1827; died age 60.
I. N. Brown Dickens, wife of N. S. Dickens, born Jan. 25, 1843; died March 6, 1889.
James N. Dickens, born Oct. 23, 1869; died Feb. 17, 1882.
Joseph Dickens, born Jan. 3, 1816; died Dec. 9, 1898.
Joseph E. Dickens, born Dec. 15, 1871; died April 15, 1888.
Mrs. Lizzie Dickens, died 1926.
Martha E. Dickens, born June 7, 1868; died Nov. 29, 1890.
Martha S. Melvin Dickens, wife of Joseph Dickens, born Sept. 8, 1841; died Sept. 24, 1916.
Mary Bell Dickens, born Aug. 23, 1844; died May 13, 1891.
N. S. Dickens, died Oct. 28, 1927; age about 75.
Adaline Fuqua, born Oct. 9, 1830; died Aug. 25, 1913.
Infant son of Buford and Pearl Macey, born Jan. 7, 1913; died Jan. 10, 1913.
Mattie B. Fuqua Marshall, wife of W. F. Marshall, born Nov. 6, 1857; died Jan. 15, 1895.
Willie Bell Marshall, son of W. F. and M. E. Marshall, born Jan. 14, 1895; died Oct. 7, 1895.
Archie D. Norris, born Dec. 29, 1838; died Aug. 12, 1911.
Mary E. Norris, born Feb. 5, 1883; died Feb. 7, 1894.
Sarah M. Norris, born March 17, 1843; died Feb. 26, 1920.
Lillie Puryear, wife of Mintlow Puryear, died 1930.
Mintlow Puryear, died 1931.
Lawrence Suite, son of W. E. Suite, born Jan. 16, 1890; died Dec. 10, 1893.
A. J. Tomlinson, born Sept. 16, 1856; died Dec. 2, 1924.
Arizona Tomlinson, born May 3, 1865; died Oct. 13, 1899.
Mrs. Tom Tunstall.
C. D. Young, born May 16, 1861; died Feb. 16, 1883.
Chrysteen B. Young, born June 28, 1905; died June 18, 1906.
Janie Young, born April 8, 1869; died Feb. 3, 1826.
Mary A. Carter Young, wife of Thomas Young, born July 16, 1837; Nora Young, born Oct. 12, 1872; died April 12, 1911.
Thomas Young, born Aug. 22, 1833; died Feb. 9, 1895.
Webb Young, born Feb. 1, 1902; died June 19, 1917.

Bible Records—Tombstone Inscriptions

COPY OF TOMBSTONES
West View Cemetery, Sweetwater, Tenn., Monroe County.
Sent by Mrs. Richard J. Yearwood, Knoxville.

D. B. Yearwood, born March 3, 1862; died Aug. 24, 1928.
F. Carter Yearwood, born Oct. 27, 1864; died Feb. 16, 1832.
Ben Dickerson Jones, born July 9, 1877; died Dec. 9, 1926.
Isabella, daughter of Ben D. and Mary Porter Jones, born March 6, 1915; died Oct. 25, 1918.
Andrew J. Dickey, born Jan. 17, 1846; died April 13, 1923.
Amanda B. Dickey, born April 12, 1849; died Dec. 24, 1929.
Horace Lackey Browder, born May 17, 1868; died March 1, 1918.
Mark H. Pease, born Nov. 1, 1846; died Dec. 13, 1920.
David Carter Young, born Aug. 28, 1866; died July 1, 1917.
Henry Lee Cecil, born March 8, 1865; died April 9, 1917.
Virginia Dickey, daughter of H. L. and L. D. Cecil, born April 30, 1909; died Feb. 28, 1910. "Suffer little children to come unto me."
Laura L. Pardue, wife of U. S. Beard, born March 28, 1874; died Feb. 19, 1928.
Maude Henley, born Nov. 25, 1902; died Sept. 8, 1925.
William Browder, 1870-1919; his wife, Mattie A. Fite, 1869-1928.
William L. Harrison, born Dec. 6, 1863, died Nov. 17, 1928.
Father, W. Y. Wilson, born Jan. 29, 1853; died Feb. 12, 1933.
Mother, Rachel Hudgins, wife of W. Y. Wilson, born April 3, 1855; died June 18, 1925.
Joseph D. Clark, born Dec. 14, 1859; died Nov. 11, 1932; Sarah Jane Edgmon, wife, born Jan. 2, 1864; died April 12, 1919; Iowa Poland Scott, wife, born Oct. 11, 1879.
Joe, son of R. F. and E. H. Scruggs, born July 31, 1874; died Aug. 11, 1875.
Mattie, infant daughter of Dr. R. F. and E. R. Scruggs, died Oct. 20, 1861, age 11 months.
Mary S. Childress, born May 11, 1841; died Dec. 1, 1924.
David E. Childress, born April 14, 1891; died Nov. 9, 1887.
Dr. Richard Francis Scruggs, born Feb. 1, 1834; died Dec. 28, 1904.
Elizabeth Heiskel Scruggs, born Nov. 5, 1839; died Aug. 27, 1920.
Susie N. Scruggs, born Sept. 13, 1871; died Nov. 6, 1890.
Margaret T. Williams, born April 5, 1835; died Jan. 6, 1922.
Col. J. R. Love, born Aug. 19, 1831; died Nov. 10, 1885.
Julia Reagan Love, daughter of Gen. James H. Reagan, wife of Col. James Robert Love, born Sept. 4, 1843; died Jan. 1, 1926.
Maggie Bell, daughter of J. R. and Julia Love, born Aug. 4, 1874; died Jan. 7, 1885.
John M. Reagan, born Feb. 20, 1848; died July 17, 1870.
Mira Ann Reagan, daughter of William Ballard LeNoir and Elizabeth Avery, wife of Gen. James H. Reagan, born April 2, 1810; died March 8, 1879.
Joseph Walker Lowery, Jr., born Aug. 27, 1903; died Sept. 8, 1927.
James N. Heiskell, born July 20, 1856; died June 27, 1930.
Julia Clay Johnson Cosey, born Nov. 1, 1888; died Oct. 3, 1904.
Gideon B. Johnson, born Sept. 15, 1839; died Jan. 18, 1898.
Elizabeth M. Johnson, born March 1, 1854; died Oct. 9, 1902.
Helen Graham Cannon, born ——— 10, 1838; died Dec. 3, 1909.
Chas. Cannon, born March 13, 1827; died June 27, 1889.
Father, W. L. Clark, born Oct. 19, 1829; died April 20, 1909.
Mother, Mary Clark, born Aug. 24, 1834; died April 24, 1934.
Mabel E. Clark, wife of D. W. Dickey, born Jan. 18, 1875; died Aug. 1, 1908.
Frances J. Clark, wife of R. C. Copenhaven, born Oct. 14, 1849; died Nov. 18, 1908.
Father, John Rhea Gaines, born April 22, 1827; died March 7, 1911.

Bible Records—Tombstone Inscriptions

Harriet Craig, wife of John Rhea Gaines, born Jan. 10, 1848; died Feb. 12, 1924.

James V. Walker, born June 17, 1875; died Jan. 9, 1902.

Gus L. Walker, born Dec. 27, 1877; died March 29, 1915.

Father, G. A. Walker, born Aug. 15, 1844; died July 6, 1917.

Alice Browder Hardin, born 1866; died 1919.

Mary Carolyn Walker, wife of James Harrison Lowry, born Jan. 14, 1853; died April 7, 1921.

Wilbur A. Dickey, born July 5, 1855; died Nov. 30, 1910.

Sarah Elizabeth, daughter of Mr. and Mrs. N. A. Dickey, born Aug. 16, 1903; died Sept. 2, 1904.

George W. Lawrence, born March 4, 1830; died Dec. 7, 1917.

Mary A. Lawrence, born March 21, 1824; died Sept. 30, 1898.

Mrs. Allie Newman, born March 21, 1863; died Aug. 28, 1903, age 40 years 5 months 7 days.

Elizie Vaughn, born Sept. 29, 1868; died Jan. 21, 1908.

T. A. Chambers, born April 28, 1821; died July 2, 1903; Eliza McClurg, his wife, born May 4, 1834; died Nov. 23, 1900.

Mrs. W. P. Wilson, died June 14, 1911, age 47 years.

Mina K. Wilson, born April 12, 1894; died April 1, 1928. In God's care.

Sylvester Decker, born Nov. 2, 1845; died —— 28, 1913.

Walter B. Sample, born Nov. 9, 1881; died Dec. 27, 1918; his wife, Stella L. McLendon, born Feb. 15, 1884; died Dec. 31, 1918.

John A. Purdy, born Oct. 17, 1860; died Sept. 8, 1918.

Beulah C. Martin, born March 19, 1902; died Aug. 15, 1910.

Robert Neil Martin, born Jan. 13, 1904; died March 5, 1916.

Alice Trotter, wife of Len. Moore, born Sept. 15, 1888; died Aug. 27, 1910. Come ye blessed.

A. K. Maloy, born March 17, 1867; died July 18, 1911. Grace to you and peace from God our Father and the Lord Jesus Christ, thank my God making mention of the things in my prayers.

Margaret J. Edwards, wife of W. H. Lowry, born Jan. 9, 1842; died Feb. 4, 1892. Her children rise up and call her blessed.

Syntha E. Fite, born Dec. 31, 1845; died May 29, 1909.

J. William Plemons, born Jan. 12, 1884; died Sept. 7, 1908.

Gerene Catherine Pierce Hale, born Dec. 30, 1833; died Sept. 1, 1919.

Thomas C. Seymour, born July 17, 1881; died Feb. 28, 1929.

Elizabeth Mildred, daughter of Thos. and Inez Seymour, born Jan. 4, 1910; died June 17, 1911. Asleep in Jesus.

Charles W. Presley, son of I. P. and Sallie Presley, born Nov. 16, 1885; died June 20, 1905.

I. P. Presley, born May 19, 1865; died Aug. 9, 1930.

Eddie, son of I. P. and Sallie Presley, born Feb. 27, 1891; died May 8, 1909. Though lost to sight to memory dear.

Melvin Scott, born Jan. 7, 1874; died Dec. 14, 1911.

Lucy G. Caldwell, wife of Levi Fox, born Jan. 22, 1855; died May 19, 1899.

Laura A. Sutton, born Dec. 12, 1864; died Sept. 24, 1929.

J. B. Edmonds, born Jan. 16, 1840; died March 28, 1907.

Will J. Honey, born May 3, 1883; died June 14, 1924.

Martha, wife of W. R. Thompson, born Sept. 12, 1861; died Feb. 9, 1920.

James Harrison Lowry, born June 12, 1849; died Sept. 25, 1916.

Joseph Forsyth Swords, born Aug. 8, 1842; died July 9, 1917.

Emma Alice Walker, wife of Joseph Forsyth Swords, died 1918.

Francis Elizabeth, daughter of Chas. N. and Pearl P. Hulvey, born Feb. 6, 1911; died June 27, 1912.

LaFayette Evans, born Aug. 17, 1878; died Oct. 12, 1910.

Jabin Snow Taylor, born in Grainger County, Aug. 10, 1822; died Feb. 22, 1857.

Nancy Fine, consort of Jolin Fine, born Nov. 10, 1782; died Feb. 18,

Bible Records—Tombstone Inscriptions

1859, age 76 years 3 months and 8 days.

Hally Fine, daughter of Jolin and Nancy Fine, born Nov. 30, 1803; died Jan. 29, 1857; age 53 years 2 months 4 days.

Manda Walker, daughter of Jolin and Nancy Fine and consort of N. G. Walker, born Feb. 18, 1817; died Feb. 8, 1859; age 42 years 11 months 18 days.

Abijah F. Boggess, born June 3, 1880; died July 8, 1907.

John T. Boggess, born Jan. 23, 1853; died Feb. 9, 1928.

Nettie Lee, daughter of J. G. and M. A. Holland, died Nov. 24, 1911; age 22 years.

Icem Barnett, born Feb. 2, 1905; died March 12, 1912.

Virgil Barnett, born Dec. 29, 1916; died Aug. 27, 1929.

Jacob Miller, born Aug. 20, 1851; died Dec. 7, 1914.

Margaret A. Hale, beloved wife of J. D. Sanders, born May 5, 1873; died May 2, 1931. Earth has no sorrow that Heaven cannot heal.

Thomas G. Tiller, son of J. F. and A. C. Tiller, born Nov. 28, 1883; died Jan. 1, 1912.

T. W. Mitchell, born Sept. 16, 1846; died March 22, 1900.

Nannie J. Mitchell, born Feb. 21, 1848; died Jan. 28, 1917.

J. E. Mitchell, born Dec. 6, 1879; died June 18, 1902.

Cora Allen, wife of Henry Palmer, born Feb. 20, 1882; died July 2, 1926.

Robert H. Allen, born Feb. 20, 1848; died March 5, 1926.

Louise C. Bowen, wife of Robert H. Allen, born Dec. 19, 1854; died ———.

Della May Allen, born Sept. 28, 1903; died Oct. 26, 1923.

In memory of Addie E. Barden, wife of L. F. Knight, born July 20, 1878; died Oct. 26, 1912. Sleep, dear Mother, peaceful sleep, where no one ever wakes to weep. For blessed is the dead who die in the Lord, Yea sayeth the Spirit, they do rest from their labor and their works do follow them.

Edna Belle Beard, wife of Dr. T. M. Roberts, born March 18, 1875; died Jan. 3, 1910. Blessed rest.

Minnie Lee Young, born Sept. 21, 1882; died May 7, 1906.

H. H. Norris, 1826-1910; his wife, Louisa Owen, 1831-1908.

Harriet Florence Morris, wife of James Forrest Yearwood, 1857-1921.

George W. Hicks, born Sept. 27, 1819; died Nov. 28, 1888.

Martha Whitson Hicks, born July 31, 1827; died March 11, 1900.

Homer E. Thompson, born Sept. 2, 1874; died Feb. 16, 1905.

Mary L. Thompson, born Sept. 5, 1843; died Feb. 26, 1917.

Rufis Gaut, born Jan. 16, 1844; died May 10, 1913.

COPY OF TOMBSTONES

Cemetery, Philadelphia, Tennessee, Loudon County.
Sent by Mrs. Maude Yearwood Fouche, Chicamauga Chapter, D. A. R., Chattanooga, Tennessee.

Minnie B. Bradshaw, born Dec. 14, 1879; died April 6, 1898.

Annie F. Bradshaw, born Nov. 7, 1881; died March 23, 1897.

Pierce Carter, born Aug. 24, 1855; died Oct. 5, 1920.

John Harlin Martin, born Sept. 1, 1846; died Jan. 6, 1912.

Margaret Manda, daughter of J. C. and M. L. Martin, born June 16, 1870; died Dec. 12, 1901.

In memory of Harry Alexander, son of J. W. and Nannie D. Rausin, born Jan. 17, 1884; died Nov. 6, 1901; age 20 years 9 months 19 days. I know that my Redeemer liveth.

Thomas Laughlin, born March 30, 1791; died June 10, 1869.

Nancy P. Maddy, wife of Thomas Laughlin, born Dec. 18, 1800; died Dec. 19, 1876.

Mary E., daughter of Thos. and Jane M. Brown, born Jan. 19

Bible Records—Tombstone Inscriptions

1846; died Aug. 2, 1888.
Jane M., wife of Rev. Thomas Brown, born Nov. 19, 1817; died Jan. 28, 1897.
Thomas Brown, minister of the gospel, born Dec. 27, 1800; died April 21, 1872.
In loving memory of Capitola, wife of Ewd. Marston, passed away Jan. 10, 1894.
John L. Lewis, born June 27, 1832; died March 5, 1894.
William T. McCarroll, born Oct. 24, 1868; died July 19, 1907.
Irby Thompson, born March, 1808; died Aug., 1873.
Frank B. Caldwell, born Aug. 15, 1869; died June 24, 1898.
H. W. Cozart, died Jan. 27, 1917; age 58 years.
J. M. Hodges, born Aug. 27, 1827; died Oct. 18, 1892.
Martha Stuart, wife of Stephen Parshley, born Sept. 21, 1816; died Nov. 19, 1882. We loved her.
Nancy J. Kennedy, born May 12, 1833; died March 17, 1903.
S. J. Sparks, born Oct. 24, 1824; died April 2, 1912.
Mary A. Sparks, born Oct. 28, 1830; died July 16, 1890.
T. J. Sparks, born Jan. 15, 1855; died Jan. 26, 1888.
D. R. Kennedy, born Jan. 1, 1805; died Dec. 21, 1880.
Margery C., wife of D. R. Kennedy, died Nov. 7, 1869; age 66 years 11 months 12 days.
Louisa Cox, wife of R. S. Breeden, born April 6, 1834; died March 7, 1899.
F. J. Hamilton, born Sept. 17, 1836; died Dec. 10, 1880.
Amanda Laughlin, born May 29, 1835; died Oct. 27, 1890.
W. L. Price, born Dec. 1, 1830; died May 25, 1891.
In memory of our sister, Mary J. Robertson, born March 12, 1819; died Sept. 6, 1901; age 82 years.
G. M. Guson, born Oct. 24, 1824; died June 9, 1898.
Sophia Laughlin, wife of G. M. Guson, born Oct. 7, 1831; died April 10, 1906.
Joseph Louis, born Oct. 30, 1824; died Sept. 12, 1896. A friend to his country, and a believer in Christ.
Thomas P. Reynolds, born Feb. 16, 1833; died March 20, 1909.
Elizabeth E., wife of T. P. Reynolds, born Sept. 3, 1833; died Oct. 4, 1894.
Annie Reynolds, born July 1, 1870; died April 29, 1911.
John B. Campbell, 1821-1894.
Mariah E. Campbell, 1837-1894.
William Morris, 1864-1908.
E. Rausin, born June 29, 1837; died Nov. 11, 1889.
P. E. Rausin, born Nov. 7, 1842; died July 12, 1888.
Mary E. Jones, born Jan. 3, 1889; died July 8, 1890.
Francis B. McCauley, born Jan. 7, 1836; died Oct. 14, 1864.
T. McCauley, born May 23, 1810; died Aug. 25, 1864.
Margaret Alexander, died Jan. 20, 1858; age 48 years.
Nancy Alexander, died Nov. 24, 1864; age 42 years.
Sarah Alexander, 1804-1850.
Geo. Alexander, died Nov. 23, 1860; age 77 years.
Nancy Ann, daughter of Gabriel and Miriam Alexander Ragsdale, born Dec. 10, 1850; died July 16, 1912.
Miriam Ragsdale, born July 18, 1815; died Dec. 30, 1852.

EVERGREEN CEMETERY, MURFREESBORO

Capt. Richard Beard, C.S.A., 1842-1931. One of Lee's men of gentle birth and of a goodly presence. A man, noble and true. A soldier, generous and dauntless. A scholar, ripe, exact. Accomplished. A Christian, steadfast, immovable. He filled every position in life with fidelity and honor. Steadfast unto the end. A friend faithful and true. A husband, tender and devoted. A father, indulgent and understanding.
Mrs. Marie L. Beard, wife of Richard Beard, born Nov. 11, 1849; died Dec. 11, 1900. "Blessed are

Bible Records—Tombstone Inscriptions

the pure in heart, for they shall see God."
Dromgoole, R e b e c c a Mildred Blanch, daughter of Col. Ezekiah Alfred Blanch and Mildred Cook Blanch of Brunswick Co., Va., and wife of John Easter Dromgoole.
Richard Beard, Jr., son of Capt. Richard Beard and Marie Louise Dromgoole, born July 12, 1881; died July 27, 1913. To live in hearts we leave behind is not to die.
Richard Beard Faircloth, June 11, 1897; May 4, 1904. Only a mist between silence—and then a song.
Faircloth, Edward Cameron, 1858-1929. Father, friend. In loving memory. His children.
Mary Noailles Murfree, daughter of William Law Murfree and F. Priscilla Murfree, Jan. 24, 1850-July 31, 1922. I know that my Redeemer liveth.
William Law Murfree, born in Murfreesboro, N. C., July 19, 1817; died Aug. 23, 1892. "Blessed are the dead which die in the Lord."
John Williams Burton, born April 18, 1825; died Nov. 16, 1883. The elements so mixed in him that nature might stand up and say to all the world: This was a man. Civilian, statesman, jurist. Having served his generation by the will of God, he fell asleep.
Mary Frierson, wife of John W. Burton, born Dec. 27, 1834; died July 12, 1891. Attractive, graceful, lovely, worthy the respect and affection of friends and the devotion of her family. A sincere, earnest Christian, faithful in Christ and glorifying Him in her body and spirit. She has entered into rest. The heart of her husband did safely trust in her. Her children rise up and call her blessed.
Joseph B. Palmer, born Nov. 1, 1825; died Nov. 4, 1890.
Horace E. Palmer, born Sept. 26, 1855; died June 11, 1912.
Willie Mason Palmer, born May 15, 1855; died Dec. 4, 1916.
Children of H. E. and W. M. Palmer: M. B. Palmer (Margaret), C. M. Palmer (Carrington), W. M. Palmer (William Mason).

Twenty-foot shaft—J. B. Palmer (Gen. Palmer).
Maj. John Woods, born Sept. 11, 1807; died May 23, 1896.
His words were kindness,
His deeds were love,
His spirit humble;
He rests above.
Mrs. Mary Frances Woods, wife of Maj. John Woods and daughter of Thomas and Susanah Jarratt, born in Rutherford County Tenn., Aug: 6, 1815; died Aug. 19, 1884. She was what a woman ought to be.
Mrs. Nanie Woods, wife of Maj. John Woods, daughter of Amon and Nancy Boring, born in Rutherford County, Tenn., April 28, 1828; died May 11, 1890.
Confederate Circle: Our unknown dead, 1861-1865.
(Insignia)
U. S. Military Aviator James Elmo Overall, born Aug. 20, 1888; died Dec. 5, 1918.
Wm. Hatton Baskin, born Jan. 20, 1894; died Oct. 7, 1918. Private of Co. F, 57th Inft. Died en route to France. Buried at Murfreesboro July 31, 1920.
Andrew J. Fletcher, born Feb. 22, 1841; died May 13, 1871. He was one of nature's gentlemen.
James M. Witherspoon, 1832-1900.
Nannie R. Witherspoon, 1846-1931.
Lieut. Edwin E. Witherspoon, 1889-1919. 1 Bat. Co. B 22, Eng.
Geo. G. Hightower, born March 18, 1901; died Sept. 29, 1918. Volunteer M'boro Mch. Co. B., 113 Batallion, 30th Div. Fell on field in Bellcourt, France.
Lieut. Robt. S. Brown, killed in action Oct. 4, 1918, defending Apremont, Argonne Forest, France. Age 21.
Edgar F. Manus, born Jan. 30, 1894; died Sept. 29, 1918. A. R. D. Inft. Died at Dartford Kent, Eng. Buried May 31, 1920.
Private Porter E. Compton, born Dec. 31, 1891; died Feb. 14, 1919. Co. A., 16th Inft., 81st Div.
Charles Ready, born Dec. 22, 1802; died June 4, 1878.
Our father and mother: "I will ransom them from the power of the grave."

Bible Records—Tombstone Inscriptions

Martha Strong, wife of Charles Ready, born March 18, 1807; died Aug. 27, 1877.
Amon Boring, born 1791; died 1839.
Nancy Boring, born 1795; died 1839.
Margaret H. Jordan, daughter of Rev. Ezekiel Blanch, born in Brunswick Co., Va., Sept. 12, 1810; died in Murfreesboro, Tenn., Oct. 20, 1878.
John Jones, born Sept. 3, 1797; died Jan. 24, 1884.
Martha W. Jones, born Sept. 26, 1830; died Sept. 12, 1908.
Betsy M. Jones, born Oct. 30, 1797; died June 3, 1863.

Mary E. Jones, born Dec. 30, 1831; died July 25, 1899.
Col. W. D. Robison, born June 30, 1840; died Sept. 18, 1890.
Chester Fowler Elrod, born Aug. 5, 1899; died Sept. 29, 1918. Corp. of Co. B., 118 Mch. Gun Bat. Killed in action in France.
Samuel F. Coleman, Tenn., Pvt., 328 Inf., 82nd Div. March 25, 1922.
Lewis Crockett, Tenn., Pvt., 105th Trench Mortar Bat., 30th Div. Feb. 3, 1933.
Sam A. Walden, Co. E, 20th Tenn. Inft., C. S. A. Born Jan. 22, 1847; died June 5, 1922.

EVERGREEN CEMETERY, MURFREESBORO
Copied by Rebekah Jetton

James Elliott, born in Orange Co., N. C., Oct. 1, 1795; died in Rutherford Co., Tenn., Oct. 30, 1836.
Adaline Bowman Elliott, born in Roan Co., N. C., June 4, 1803; died March 9, 1886.
William Y. Elliott, born in Murfreesboro, Tenn., July 24, 1871; died Nov. 2, 1899.

William Y. Elliott, born in Rutherford Co., Tenn., Nov. 2, 1827; died in Murfreesboro, Tenn., April 21, 1893.
Thomas A. Elliott, born April 16, 1834; died Sept. 4, 1876.
Margaret G. Elliott, born June 15, 1852; died Sept. 10, 1917.

Copied at Miller Family Cemetery, Shelbyville Road, near Murfreesboro. Copied by Margaret Dann.

Sacred to the memory of Alfred Miller, born at Guilford Courthouse, N. C., Nov. 24, 1796. Removed with his parents to Murfreesboro, Tenn., in the year 1811, near which place he departed this life June 24, 1867, age 70 years and 7 months.
In memory of Narcissa G. Miller, Sr., born Sept. 15, 1821; died April 14, 1875, age 53 years, 6 months, 26 days.
S. H. Miller, born May 1, 1844; died June 26, 1873.
Capt. Richard Ransom, born 1792; died 1827.
Richard Ransom, born March 17, 1802; died March 2, 1835.
Elizabeth Ransom, wife of John Ransom (son of Capt. Richard), born July 1, 1798; died Sept. 3, 1857.

Richard Granville Crockett, son of D. W. Crockett, born Feb. 1, 1855; died 1856.
John Overton Crockett, born December 9, 1842; died Sept. 26, 1857.
Capt. Richard Ransom was born in 1752.

MEMORIAL TABLET

Here lies David Crockett and his wife, grandparents of David Crockett, who were massacred near this spot by Indians, 1777.—Division of the State of Tennessee.
About three miles from New Market are the graves of some of our ancestors on our mother's side, our great-great-grandparents. It was in their home that the "first Sunday school was organized in the State of Tennessee." — Anthony Caldwell.

II

HISTORICAL

PROGRAM OF EXERCISES
ATTENDING THE UNVEILING OF THE STATUE OF
JOHN SEVIER
IN STATUARY HALL, OF THE NATIONAL CAPITAL
WASHINGTON, D. C.

SUNDAY AFTERNOON, APRIL 19, 1931
AT THREE O'CLOCK

MRS. JOSEPH HAYES ACKLEN, *State Regent*, Chairman

Bible Records—Tombstone Inscriptions

JOHN SEVIER
Born September 23, 1745-Died September 24, 1815

MONUMENT AND MEMORIAL COMMISSION

Hon. Henry H. Horton............................Governor of Tennessee
Hon. John F. Nolan.................................Treasurer of the State
Hon. Grafton Green......................Chief Justice of Supreme Court
Hon. E. N. Haston.......................................Secretary of State
Hon. Edgar J. Graham...........................Comptroller of State
Rogers Caldwell
Mrs. George Fort Milton

Bible Records—Tombstone Inscriptions

JOHN SEVIER STATUTE COMMISSION

Mrs. Joseph Acklen..................................State Regent, D. A. R.
Judge John H. DeWitt......President Tennessee Historical Society
Mrs. Eldon Rogers..................................President State Federation
Judge J. P. Young....President West Tennessee Historical Society
Mrs. Flora Myers Gillentine......Historian General, N. S. D. A. R.
Mrs. John Trotwood Moore................State Librarian and Archivist
Mrs. P. M. Hamer......President East Tennessee Historical Society

CONGRESSIONAL DELEGATION FROM TENNESSEE

SENATORS

Hon. Kenneth McKellar   Hon. Cordell Hull

REPRESENTATIVES

Hon. Joseph W. Byrns
Hon. E. E. Eslick
Hon. Sam D. McReynolds
Hon. O. B. Lovette
Hon. J. Ridley Mitchell
Hon. Ewin Davis
Hon. L. Jere Cooper
Hon. J. Will Taylor
Hon. Gordon Browning
Hon. E. H. Crump

CHAIRMEN OF INVITATIONS

Mrs. B. Kirk Rankin   Mrs. Charles Bailey Bryan
Mrs. William Vaught

Bible Records—Tombstone Inscriptions

PROGRAM

NATIONAL STATUARY HALL, SUNDAY, APRIL 19, 1931, P. M.

Music—2:30-3:00   United States Marine Band
                                       Taylor Branson, Leader

Mrs. Joseph Hayes Acklen, State Regent of Tennessee, D. A. R., Presiding

Prayer   Dr. James I. Vance
                        Descendant of Captain Robert Sevier
                        Killed at the Battle of King's Mountain

Introductory Remarks   Presiding Officer

Presentation of Statue   Hon. Henry H. Horton
                                 Governor of Tennessee

Unveling of Statue   Embree Hoss Headman and
                                 Fenton Allen Gentry
                             Descendants of John Sevier

Acceptance Address   Hon. F. Trubee Davison
                                 Assistant Secretary of War

"Star-Spangled Banner"   Marine Band

Greetings   Mrs. Lowell Fletcher Hobart
                    President General N. S. D. A. R.

Selections   Marine Band

Tribute   Mrs. Flora Myers Gillentine
                       Historian General N. S. D. A. R.

"Tennessee"   Marine Band

Presentation of Regents of John Sevier Chapter   Mrs. R. S. Boyd

Bonny Kate Chapter   Mrs. Samuel Arnell

Presentation of Belle Kinney, L. F. Scholtz, Sculptors

Presentation of wreaths

"America"   Marine Band

Benediction   Dr. James I. Vance

Bible Records—Tombstone Inscriptions

INTRODUCTORY REMARKS OF THE CHAIRMAN GENERAL, MRS. ACKLEN

It is a privilege for the Sons and Daughters of Tennessee to come together today to place in the Hall of Fame in their nation's Capitol the statue of Tennessee's first governor, John Sevier, the beau chevalier, the gallant soldier, the hero of King's Mountain.

John Sevier is but one of a galaxy of great men that Tennessee has given to our nation. Here stands our mighty Jackson who forever settled the question of American Independence; James K. Polk, who gave an empire to his country, sleeps in the shadow of our Capitol at Nashville; while our Davy Crockett wrote his name in letters of flame on the walls of the Alamo, and grim Sam Houston became the Governor of two States; while the "gray-eyed man of destiny," William Walker, led his half-clad force to the presidency of a foreign nation.

These tall men gave to our State the name of Volunteer, and we are proud of all that it signifies. Tennessee stretches like a vari-colored ribbon through the center of our Union from where her plains roll down to meet the Father of the Waters through the fertile basin of Middle Tennessee on to the sun-kissed peaks of East Tennessee where John Sevier summoned his mountain men to march to victory and King's Mountain.

His was not only the ability of the warrior, but he was a statesman and possessed rare judgment and knowledge of men. To his comrades he was Nolichucky Jack and when they heard his battle cry, "Here they are! come on, boys," there were no laggards.

Today we are happy to honor his name and to place this son of Tennessee among this distinguished company of men representing the great of our land.

It is my privilege to present to you the President of the Tennessee Historical Society and a man whose word is final in all questions of Tennessee history so great is our trust in Judge John H. DeWitt, who will represent the Governor of Tennessee in presenting this statue to the United States Government.

BIOGRAPHICAL SKETCH

John Sevier, commonwealth builder and Revolutionary hero; born in Rockingham County, Virginia, September 23, 1745.

His father, Valentine Sevier, son of a Huguenot refugee, originally named Xavier, came from London to Baltimore, married Joanna Goode, and settled in Rockingham County. The son John attended schools at Fredericksburg and Staunton. He conducted a store in Dunmore (now Shenandoah) County and traded with

Bible Records—Tombstone Inscriptions

the Indians. In 1761 he was married to Sarah Hawkins, who bore to him ten children. He established a store and there laid out the village of New Market, Virginia. Reports concerning the land to the southwest circulated in the Valley. The Seviers determined to move to that frontier, willing to pay the price in hardship for the benefits from the cheap lands on the Watauga. In 1772 John Sevier was appointed by the colonial governor, Lord Dunmore, as a captain in the Virginia line; but the lure led him to the country where the great drama of his life was to be performed. He made a visit to the Watauga settlements. He was chosen one of the commissioners of government of the Watauga Association; and he was a member of the first court established to maintain order in the settlement. He was afterward the clerk of the court. In 1773, with his father and brothers, he removed permanently to what is now northeastern Tennessee. For three years he lived on the north side of the Holston in the Keywood settlement. In 1776 he moved his family to the Watauga, near the present location of Elizabethton.

Henceforth John Sevier was the unfailing leader and protector of those settlements. For over twenty years they were in peril from murderous Indians. During the Revolution they were menaced by British and Tories. Those settlements were the very cradle of southwestern civilization. For forty years the life of John Sevier was devoted to the service of his people and country. His people gave to him the first place in their hearts and always the primacy in leadership. To him they unfailingly turned in the darkest crises, and they were never unrewarded. Sevier's personal characteristics made him popular with his friends and neighbors, and his success in office was due to his good sense, his affability, and his devotion to the public welfare. The historian Haywood said that he "was endowed by nature with those rare qualities which make the possessor in all places and with all people an object of attention and a depository of their confidence—qualities which cannot be kept from observation." The historian Ramsey said: "He was fluent, colloquial, and gallant—frolicsome, generous, and convivial—well informed rather than well read. Of books he knew little. Men he had studied well and accurately. Oral communications had been the source of his mental culture and his knowledge. He was impulsive, but his impulses were high and honorable. He was without pride—if that feeling is not one of the ingredients that constitute a laudable ambition—for he was ambitious, not of anything low or ignoble; he was ambitious of fame, character, distinction, and achievement."

That year of 1776 became a turning point in the career of John Sevier. He assisted John Carter and James Robertson in managing the defense of Watauga Fort against the elaborate efforts of the Cherokees to destroy this and all the other over-mountain settlements. It was during an attack upon the Watauga Fort that Sevier rescued from the Indians the woman who later became his second wife, Catherine Sherrill.

In that same year Sevier was one of the representatives of the Washington District in the Provincial Congress of North Carolina. He was elected by that body as lieutenant-colonel of the Washington District. He was chosen and served in the convention which framed the first constitution of the State of North Carolina. For some time he lived as a farmer and owner of a water mill five miles from Jonesborough, but finally he removed to a large plantation, "Plum Grove," in the beautiful valley of the Nolichucky River, in Washington County. There he built a comfortable log residence and dispensed a generous hospitality. He became familiarly known as "Nolichucky Jack."

But the terrible Indian warfare continued. All along the frontier from Georgia to Pennsylvania the Cherokees and Chickamaugas committed depredations. Sevier and his frontier soldiers served with Colonel Evan Shelby on a most successful expedition down the Holston and the Tennessee Rivers to the Chickamauga towns near Lookout Mountain. They killed about forty Indians, burned their towns, destroyed their corn and every other article of provision, and drove away their great stocks of cattle. Such methods were necessary for peace and preservation of the white settlements. The Indians were then unable seriously to menace the settlements until they took advantage of the absence of the "over-mountain men" on the King's Mountain expedition in the fall of 1780.

In 1780 Sevier was commissioned by Governor Abner Nash, colonel commandant of Washington County. In that year his wife having died, he was married to Catherine Sherrill, known affectionately as "Bonny Kate" in Tennessee history. Of this union eight children were born.

When the British and Tories, under Major Ferguson, were overruning Western North Carolina and threatening to invade the "over-mountain" country, Sevier joined with Colonels Campbell and Isaac Shelby in assembling the heroic frontiersmen at Sycamore Shoals and planning the expedition to do battle with Ferguson and his men. Sevier commanded a regiment on the long, toilsome march through the mountainous wilderness. In the Battle of King's Mountain, on October 7, 1780, he and his sturdy band were first and foremost in the charge on the left wing of the patriot army. He contributed vitally to that glorious victory which marked the turning of the tide of the American Revolution. But he did not rest on this illustrious record.

Bible Records—Tombstone Inscriptions

On the return march from King's Mountain, Sevier had to deal with a threatened outbreak from the Cherokees in the absence of so many men and guns from the frontier. He had reached home just in time to repel the savage invaders. Without a day's rest he set on foot another expedition.

Placing himself at the head of about one hundred men, he set out in advance of other troops who were assembling. It was according to his method of bold, swift dashes. On the third day they encountered a large force of Indians near Boyd's Creek and by bold charges achieved a decisive victory without one of their number being even wounded. This battle of Boyd's Creek was considered as one of the best fought battles in the border war of Tennessee. The prompt collection of troops and rapid expedition under Sevier saved the frontier from a bloody invasion. Being joined by other forces, Sevier proceeded further into the country of the Cherokees, burned their towns, devastated their fields and effected a treaty of peace with them.

In 1781 Sevier responded to the call of General Nathaniel Greene, led his regiment to South Carolina and served with Marion until the British were driven to the lines of Charleston.

In 1782 the implacable Chickamaugas began again their work of murder and depredation. Sevier led an expedition against them to the Coosa River, destroyed their towns, killed all their warriors they could find, and returned home. He never hesitated to pursue such destructive warfare when the lives of his people and the existence of the settlements were imperiled. Only by such methods could peace be attained. They caused the Indians each time to move to other lands. Sevier, as no other western leaders did, employed the method of using mounted riflemen in small, well-organized bodies, making rapid and telling movements.

In 1784 Sevier was appointed brigadier-general of Washington District by the legislature of North Carolina. When, because of inability of North Carolina to afford governmental protection to the "over-mountain" people, the independent State of Franklin was established, Sevier became its first and only governor, 1785-1788. When that government fell he was arrested for treason, but was never tried, and his disabilities were removed. He was elected to the North Carolina senate. He was elected and he served as a member of the First Congress of the United States—the first congressman west of the Alleghanies. In 1791 he was appointed by President Washington as brigadier-general for the Washington District of the Territory South of the Ohio. He led, in 1793, a punitive expedition as far as Etowah, in Georgia, against the Cherokees and Creeks, with the result that they were never again a menace to the settlements in Tennessee. It is the tradition that he fought in thirty-five battles and skirmishes, and

Bible Records—Tombstone Inscriptions

in all of them was victorious. His battle order was always: *"Here they are! Come on, boys, come on!"*

In 1796 Sevier became the first Governor of Tennessee. He was governor for six terms—1796-1801; 1803-1809. In 1802 he served as a commissioner to run the boundary line between Virginia and Tennessee. In 1809 he served as a state senator from Knox County, Tenn. From 1811 until his death he was a member of the United States Congress. He was a faithful adherent of the Madison administration in all the Second War with Great Britain.

General Sevier died on September 24, 1815, near Fort Decatur, Alabama, where, while a member of Congress, he was serving as a commissioner appointed by President Madison to fix the Creek Indian boundary according to treaty. In 1889 his remains were removed and reinterred in the grounds of the courthouse at Knoxville, and a graceful marble shaft was erected above his grave.

John Sevier was an outstanding pioneer leader who met with perfect courage every duty; who conquered the wilderness, overcame the deadly foes of his people and fashioned the State. He was a hero in an age of heroes. His long and illustrious service was rendered peculiarly to his beloved Tennessee, and it opened the way to the settlement and development of the Southwest.

JOHN H. DEWITT,
President of the Tennessee Historical Society.

ADDRESS OF HONORABLE F. TRUBEE DAVIDSON
Assistant Secretary of War

The War Department is deeply appreciative of the invitation to participate in the unveiling of this memorial to General John Sevier whose illustrious record as a soldier and as a statesman is an inspiration to those familiar with his exceptionally outstanding achievements.

There are some men who through their courage, wisdom, and initiative write chapters in the life of their country which lift the ordinary man out of the rut of the commonplace and spur him on to simulate those who blazed the trail along which this nation has marched to liberty and greatness. Among the men who dedicated their lives to the blazing of that trail the name of John Sevier shines with a brightness that will never fade or be forgotten.

General Sevier lived to the allotted age of seventy and every one of his adult years was devoted to public service and constructive patriotic effort. General Sevier was a soldier; but he was more than that. He was a member of that small but chosen group whose spiritual courage and unselfish zeal made them tireless

KING'S MOUNTAIN MONUMENT
Erected by United States Government at King's Mountain, South Carolina

Bible Records—Tombstone Inscriptions

crusaders in the cause of progress—not for themselves, but for all. He was a statesman, but his statesmanship was not of the kind that found expression in oratory. It was rather that of the pioneer who builds an empire in the wilderness and, once more, not for himself but for posterity.

We cannot but be thrilled by the story of courage and unselfish effort that is the life of John Sevier. I vision those early days on the eastern fringe of the Mississippi Valley which in 1773 was the threshold of the West where, persecuted by the British and harried by Indians, he and his family, friends, and neighbors—hardy and fearless men and women grouped into a frontier community—laid the foundation for what is now the great State of Tennessee.

Almost from the very day he arrived in the Watauga Community on the Holston River, Sevier took an active part in the affairs of the settlement. He was a young man, still under thirty, and yet he was elected one of the five judges who administered the law.

Prior to the time Sevier migrated with his family from Virginia—he married at seventeen—he had had considerable military experience in the French and Indian wars in which he served with rank of Captain and it was through this experience, combined with a natural gift for strategy, that he he won signal military honors.

There were but few occasions, from the early seventies to as late as 1793, when Sevier was not in the field. Between 1777 and 1781, for instance, he participated in thirty-five battles and never lost one. His leadership at King's Mountain was outstanding. Between 1781 and 1784 he waged at least half a dozen brilliant campaigns against the Indians in his effort to push forward and make secure the new empire he helped to erect.

Indeed, John Sevier was a great soldier but a man who took his sword in hand to construct and not to destroy and what the soldier won the statesman improved. It was he who drew the petition asking that the frontier country in which he lived be annexed to North Carolina. This accomplished, he was the first to represent that district in the provincial Congress and one of the framers of the first constitution of North Carolina. Later—from 1796, when Tennessee became a state, until 1801—he was the first Governor of Tennessee and served three terms. He was Major General of the Militia from 1801 to 1803, when he was re-elected Governor—this time to serve until 1810. The following two years he was a member of the State Senate, resigning in 1811 to go to Washington as a member of Congress where he was of singular service as a member of the Military Affairs Committee during the War with England. He was, in fact, offered a general's commission but declined it on account of his advanced age.

In 1815, President Monroe appointed Sevier to head a commission authorized to make a survey in Alabama for the purpose of defining the lines of the Creek Indians. The office was accepted, and he started on his last campaign. He died near Fort Decatur on the Tallapoose River on September 24, 1815, one day after his seventieth birthday.

I have given but a brief outline of a career devoted to exceptional patriotic service and of a life crammed with the romance that most of us succeed in finding only in books. In paying him tribute let me quote what a great American of a later day—President Roosevelt—said of him:

"Sevier was a gentleman by birth and breeding. . . . To the end of his days he was an interested and intelligent observer of men and things both in America and Europe. He corresponded on intimate and equal terms with Madison, Franklin, and other of our most polished statesmen. . . . Sevier was a very handsome man, reputed during his life the very handsomest in Tennessee. He was tall, fair-skinned, blue-eyed, brown-haired, of slender build, with erect, military carriage and commanding bearing. . . . From his French forefathers he had inherited a gay, pleasure-loving temperament that made him the most charming of companions. His manners were polished and easy, and he had great natural dignity."

Such was John Sevier, the man whose memorial we are unveiling today and whose deeds, acts, and thought can best be summarized by saying that he was in truth a gentleman, statesman, a patriot, and a soldier.

The early history of any community is generally the most important, because the initial influences inevitably carry on through the decades that follow and leave an indelible imprint. Sevier's vigorous and effective personality and constructive leadership have unquestionably been dominating factors in the glorious history of the commonwealth of which he was the first Governor. Primarily for that reason, not only the sons and daughters of Tennessee are eternally indebted to him, but likewise the nation as a whole.

REPORT MRS. ALLEN MADE DURING REGENCY OF MRS. ACKLEN

We have celebrated in Tennessee this year three sesqui-centennials which mark notable events in the beginning of the history of our State.

The founding of Jonesboro, the first town in Tennessee, was fittingly celebrated on July 4th, when descendants of the first settlers gathered from all over the United States to do honor to the occasion. The arrangements were in charge of Judge Samuel

Bible Records—Tombstone Inscriptions

C. Williams, our distinguished historian. The Honorable John Q. Tilson and ex-Governor Alf Taylor were speakers, and a program was given in which many descendants of the pioneers of Washington County took part. The hospitable homes of Jonesboro were thrown open to the visitors, and many happy reunions took place among the attendance. It was my pleasure to attend this celebration and join with other Daughters of the American Revolution in honoring Jonesboro.

The one hundred and fiftieth anniversary of the Battle of King's Mountain was observed both in Tennessee and in the Carolinas. On September 25, the day on which the Tennessee pioneers gathered for their march to join the patriots across the mountains, for the attack on Colonel Ferguson's British army, a celebration was held at Sycamore Shoals, the place where this brave and fearless band gathered. Several years ago a monument was erected at this spot by the Sycamore Shoals Chapter, the John Sevier Chapter, and the Bonny Kate Chapter of the Daughters of the American Revolution, because of its significance in Tennessee history. The exercises this year at Sycamore Shoals were planned by the East Tennessee Historical Society as a tribute to the men who set out for that forced march which ended in victory—a victory which is said to have turned the tide of the Revolution.

The celebration at King's Mountain was held on the battlefield on October 7th before a mighty concourse of people that came from all over the nation to celebrate the 150th anniversary of the battle which was described by Thomas Jefferson as the "turning point in the Revolution." President Hoover was the speaker of the day, and his address was worthy of the occasion. Many of you who could not be present heard it over the radio. To us who were privileged to be there it was inspiring and uplifting. In the morning the Daughters of the American Revolution had charge of the program. The Regents of the four states—North and South Carolina, Tennessee, and Georgia—brought greetings; and Virginia was represented by her Vice-Regent. Our own State Regent, Mrs. Joseph H. Acklen, was present and during her address the State flag was held by our former Regent, Mrs. Walter C. Johnson.

We number among our Tennessee Daughters of the American Revolution so many descendants of soldiers who fought at King's Mountain that we feel that we have a particular pride in this celebration.

By appointment of the Governor, Mrs. Acklen and I represented the State of Tennessee.

The third sesqui-centennial which we celebrated this year is the founding of the colony which grew into our State Capital, the colony which Middle Tennessee calls "mother" and which has furnished a long line of distinguished men for Tennessee's up-

Bible Records—Tombstone Inscriptions

building. The exercises incident to this celebration have formed a part of this Conference program.

From 1780, Tennessee has had its part in the building of our nation, and it is our duty and privilege to preserve for all time the memory of those places where the great events in our history have taken place. PENELOPE JOHNSON ALLEN,
National Chairman of Preservation of Historic Spots.
November 17, 1930.

THE 150TH ANNIVERSARY OF THE RENDEZVOUS OF KING'S MOUNTAIN MEN—SYCAMORE SHOALS, ELIZABETHTON
By MRS. WM. VAUGHT

A large crowd was in attendance at the 150th anniversary September 25, 1930, of the rendezvous of the mountain men of this section who led the successful attack on the British forces at King's Mountain held at the monument at Sycamore Shoals, Elizabethton. A fine program had been arranged for the day, the event being sponsored by the East Tennessee Historical Society and the Daughters of the American Revolution. Judge Samuel C. Williams being the presiding chairman of the event, with Mrs. W. M. Vaught of this city serving as local chairman for the East Tennessee Historical Association, also representing the D. A. R. and assisting in every way possible to make it one of the finest celebrations of like nature ever to be held in this entire section.

Music was rendered by the Soldiers' Home Band, playing very softly at the monument at the beginning of the program, "Our Flag," especially composed for the occasion by Iris G. Oster, a D. A. R.

Due to the inclemency of the weather the crowd was directed to the American Bemberg-Glanzstoff Athletic field where the address for the occasion was heard. Invocation rendered by Dr. H. S. Lyle of Washington College. A duet, "The Patriots Hymn," was sung by the Payne Sisters.

Ex-Governor A. A. Taylor gave the welcome address. Governor Taylor always delighted his hearers and on this memorable occasion was better than ever before. He brought to mind instances of the past relating many stories given to him by his father's old slave. The reminiscences of yesterday were so vivid they were pictured almost to realization before the hearers' eyes. Governor Taylor was a resident of the historic Watauga Valley upon whose broad acres his antecedents lived and aided in the historic past.

Governor Taylor said in part: "This meeting today brings afresh to my mind the stirring scenes and tragedy enacted here 150 years ago." With the banding together of men under Colonel Campbell

Bible Records—Tombstone Inscriptions

at Abingdon, John Sevier at his Nolichucky settlement, and Isaac and Evan Shelby from where Bristol now stands 950 men gathered at Sycamore Shoals upon this day, a century and a half ago for the purpose of marching against General Ferguson's army at King's Mountain.

"At this place the first draft in history to keep men at home from battle was issued. It was learned that no one was being left to guard the home, so the officers asked for volunteers; not a single man volunteered to stay at home. The men were then lined up and every eighth man in line was drafted to remain on guard over their fort and pioneer homes." Then 805 men marched across the mountains to meet Ferguson.

The ground on which we stand is holy and sacred to every true American who loves the free institutions of his government, the greatest on earth.

Within a stone's throw of where we are now assembled free government had its birth in the formation of the Watauga Association.

Something had to be done to secure orderly and decent life for civilized people. The pioneers promptly settled the question by forming a free government of their own. This government was the Watauga Association organized in 1772.

At the beginning the Association included only the Watauga and the Carters Valley settlements, but in 1775 it was known that some people of the Nolichucky settlement were "Tories." Men from Wolfs Hill, Carters Valley, and Watauga went down to Brown's Store and made the Nolichucky people, and all other disaffected people, take the "oath of fidelity to the common cause" of American liberty. Nolichucky became part of the Watauga Association, and there was very little more of "Toryism" in Tennessee.

The original paper, called "Articles of Association," that these people all signed and agreed to live by has been lost; but from some other old documents we have learned a good deal about this simple and original form of government.

The germ of Tennessee was the Watauga Association; the first government established on this continent absolutely free of religious tests, class distinctions, kingly dictation, or proprietary interference. It was "a government of the people, by the people, and for the people"; it served its purpose and has passed to its place of honor in the temple of history. Let us honor the memory of the pioneers who had the wisdom to found it and the courage to administer its difficult affairs through six years of toil and hardship on a remote and dangerous frontier.

Our's is indeed a great heritage, "the land of the free and the home of the brave."

Bible Records—Tombstone Inscriptions

The pages of history do not sparkle with greater names than Shelby, Sevier, Robertson, and Carter. They were God-fearing and liberty-loving characters. Their works as well as themselves were immortal.

The governor related the story of the battle which he stated came to him first hand, telling of the defeat of the British and the death of General Ferguson inflicted by a bullet from the rifle of Darling Jones, a resident of this settlement.

Ex-Governor Taylor was born on this historic ground and told interesting incidents of his boyhood days, saying that "Old Solla," an African slave, would say, "As we boys hunted in the fields this is where the men knelt and prayed as they laid their plans for the battle of King's Mountain." Old Solla lived to be 110 years of age.

Governor Taylor, notwithstanding his advanced age, physical infirmities, and the inclement weather, was at his best; and as he stood in a drizzling rain, when he was delivering this hypnotic address, his son, Frank, held an umbrella over him to protect him from the rain. It was one of his last addresses, for he soon passed to the Great Beyond, thus ending a life like his distinguished brother, Robert Love Taylor, rich in achievements and accomplishments for his fellow-men and country.

Alfred A. Taylor was a great American and internationally known as a statesman, orator, philosopher, and above all a profound Christian gentleman. He well proved himself worthy of the men, heroes, and his ancestors that made this historical section of the country famous.

It was suggested from the floor by the Honorable Sherman Grindstaff that the historical societies of Tennessee should get together and see that Governor Taylor's address be printed in the school histories of the State in order that every child may have the privilege of reading and studying same. Mr. Grindstaff stated: "It is the best address I have ever heard the Governor make, and he has made some good ones."

The historical address of Judge Samuel M. Wilson, a famed lawyer and orator of Lexington, Ky., followed Governor Taylor's address. In speaking of the battle of King's Mountain the Judge paid high tribute to General Ferguson, declaring that he was an able, daring, and fearless fighter.

He was a general well worthy of being the foe of our fearless pioneer fathers, and I am glad that this is true. I would rather they had been defeated by a brave man instead of a coward. America has so recognized the bravery of Ferguson that a monument will be unveiled to him at the 150th anniversary of the Battle of King's Mountain on October 7th, 1930.

Bible Records—Tombstone Inscriptions

Judge Wilson declared that the over-mountain men from Sycamore Shoals were entitled to the credit of victory in this memorable battle that turned the tide of the American Revolution. They were victorious because they *knew how to use rifles*, and this more than anything else was responsible for the defeat of Ferguson.

The Judge dwelt at length upon the life of Isaac Shelby, stating that he was a man loved by both Tennessee and Kentucky. He was known there, said the speaker, by the name of "King's Mountain Shelby." He was an Indian fighter and a gentleman. Kentucky and "Tennessee are more like each other than any other states in America" quoted the Judge in paying tribute to Kentucky, his home state, and to Tennessee.

Judge Wilson paid high tribute to this East Tennessee section and spoke of the stalwart men who turned the tide of the Revolution. His discourse was a masterpiece. His audience was spellbound at the wonderful flow of oratory.

Other features of the program was a commemorative poem written and read by Amy May Rogers of Knoxville. A poem written by Adam Mast Dougherty, "Heroes of King's Mountain," was read by the Honorable Sherman Grindstaff.

A FLAG DAY SERVICE

The John Carter Chapter, Elizabethton, held on Flag Day a dedicatory service and members dedicated a tree to an ancestor or a famous person. This is an unsual and interesting list of trees.

No. 1. Abraham Lincoln—D. A. R., by Regent, Mrs. H. L. Frost. This tree came from the farm of Thomas Lincoln, an uncle of Abraham Lincoln. Thomas lived and died on this farm a few miles above Elizabethton, Tennessee.

2. Samuel Tipton—by Mesdames J. R. Boring, W. T. Johnson, George Harden, and L. W. McCowan. Samuel Tipton was born in 1752; died, 1833. Served in Revolution. Was in Battle of King's Mountain. It was in his house, or on his lawn, that the first court south of the Ohio River and east of the Rocky Mountains was held.

No. 3. Col. John Carter—Gen. Landon Carter—by Mrs. J. Frank Seiler. Col. Carter was born in Virginia; died after 1780. This is the man for whom the Chapter is named. He was chairman of the Watauga Association. General Carter, his son, was born in Virginia, 1760. Was the first Secretary of State of the State of Franklin. It is this Landon Carter for whom Carter County is named.

No. 4. Edmond Williams—by Mrs. Dayton Hunter. Edmond Williams was born a native of Wales. Married Lucretia Adams

Bible Records—Tombstone Inscriptions

of Massachusetts about 1775 or 1779. He is buried at Milligan, Tennessee.

No. 5. Andrew Greer—by Mrs. Earle Holly. Andrew Greer was one of the first two white men to come to the Watauga Association. He died about 1806. Fought in the Indian War and the Revolutionary War. He was one of the first magistrates and helped to survey the town of Elizabethton.

No. 6. Alexander Doran—by Mrs. Lon Hendrixon, Mrs. Clarence Miller, and Mrs. Jerry Thomas. Alexander Doran was born, 1760; died, 1814. Served as Ensign at Battle of King's Mountain, and as Major in War of 1812.

No. 7. Michael Hyder—by Mrs. Clint Smith. Michael Hyder died about 1790. He married Elizabeth Wood in 1764. He was one of the signers of Washington Compact in 1762.

No. 8. Jackson Carriger—by Mrs. W. M. Vaught. Jackson Carriger was one of the leading men of the town. Born March 8, 1821; died, 1890.

No. 9. Andrew Taylor—by Mrs. C. P. Toncray. Andrew Taylor was born in Augusta County, Virginia in 1735; died in Washington County, North Carolina, now Carter County, Tennessee, in 1782. Married Ann Wilson.

No. 10. Charles P. Toncray and Margaret Toncray—by grandchildren, Mrs. R. E. Wood. Mr. Toncray was born, 1838; died, 1909. A tree dedicated to this couple was particularly appropiate. Mr. Toncray was a man of sterling worth; a man who was, all during his life time, a promoter and leader in every movement for the upbuilding and betterment of the town of Elizabethton—unselfish and altruistic to the highest degree. Mrs. Toncray was worthy of her husband.

No. 11. W. B. Carter and Samuel P. Carter—by Miss Carrie Carter. W. B. Carter was born, 1820; died, 1902. He was a Presbyterian Minister. Graduate of Princeton. Member of the Constitutional Convention of 1870. His prayer being a part of, and being recorded as part of, the proceedings of February 23, 1780. Samuel P. Carter was the only man in America to attain the rank of General in the Army and Rear Admiral in the Navy. Born in Elizabethton, Tennessee, 1819; died, 1891.

No. 12. Mr. Herbert Hoover—by an Englishman, John N. Shoolbred. Address by J. Frank Seiler. Mr. Hoover (now President Hoover), Southern speech in Elizabethton.

The Chapter has also planted trees to the memory of George Washington and Andrew Johnson. These trees will be dedicated next year.

The John Carter Chapter is sponsoring a monument to be

Bible Records—Tombstone Inscriptions

erected at the grave of Colonel John Tipton, a man who had no small part in the establishment of American Independence.

The stone has been selected, as has the inscription, and arrangements have been completed in every detail; but owing to the temporary closing of the bank, in which the funds were placed, there will be some delay in the unveiling.

This monument is a belated tribute to the loyalty and worth of a Revolutionary Soldier, a pioneer patriot, and a fearless statesman.

The character of no man in the early settlement and organization of Tennessee has been so cunningly and so willfully misrepresented by some of the earlier historians and so atrociously distorted by some of their lesser informed successors as that of Col. John Tipton. Theodore Roosevelt, in his "Winning of the West," thoroughly discredits these historians in this matter; as do the unpublished manuscripts of Lyman Draper, now in the custody of the Historical Society of Wisconsin.

Col. John Tipton was born in Baltimore County, Maryland, in 1730. His father, Edward Tipton, having come to this country on the ship "Friendship" from Tipton, Staffordshire, England, which is centuries old, and whose Parish records date back to 1513.

When in 1772 Dunsmore County, Virginia (the name later being changed to Shenandoah), was cut off from Frederick, John Tipton became prominently identified with political, military, and church history of the new county. From its organization to 1781 he was a justice of her courts. Like his Maryland ancestors, he was a staunch supporter of the church of England, and from the establishment of the parish of Beckford, in Shenandoah, we find him one of the ten vestrymen.

In 1774 Colonel Tipton was elected by the people of Shenandoah County to the House of Burgeeses and was re-elected each succeeding term to this highest position of honor, certainly as late as 1780, and likely until his departure to Tennessee. He was high sheriff of Shenandoah, Lieutenant-Colonel of the militia of the county. He was one of the composers and a signer of the well known spirited and patriotic "Woodstock Resolutions," member of the Committee on Safety and Correspondence, which committee made the Resolution possible. He served as a member of the famous Virginia Convention of 1776.

In 1783 Colonel Tipton came to Washington County, then North Carolina, and the following year we find him elected to the Convention of the Western Counties, a confessed opponent to the separation of this district from the parent State of North Carolina.

Under North Carolina's authority Colonel Tipton was a justice in the courts of Washington County, and in 1786 was the first

Bible Records—Tombstone Inscriptions

Senator from that county to the legislature of that State and continued to be re-elected to that Senate until 1790 when the cession of the Western North Carolina was accepted by the Federal Government and created into "The Territory South of the River Ohio."

He was a member of the Convention which met at Hillsboro, North Carolina, to vote upon the adoption of the Federal Constitution for that State.

In 1776 the Territory was found to have more than the requisite number of inhabitants to authorize the formation of a State Government. As heretofore, Washington County deemed John Tipton one of her ablest men, worthy of trust and honor, and he accordingly was one of the five chosen to represent Washington County to help draft the first Constitution of Tennessee, formed by convention, which Constitution Thomas Jefferson pronounced "The least imperfect and the most republican system of government adopted by any of the American States."

To the first legislature of the State of Tennessee, Col. John Tipton was elected Senator from Washington County. Again to the second Assembly which closed 1779, he was a representative in the Senate.

To Col. John Tipton, Tennessee owes much. The Archives of State and Nation are full of the deeds of valor and heroism of himself and his descendants.

There is a Tipton, Tennessee, also Tiptonville, Tipton Station, and Tipton County in Tennessee. In the United States there are sixteen towns and counties named Tipton.

The name has been preserved in more lasting form than marble. His military record, since his early manhood, has been enviable. He was Lieutenant-Colonel of the Militia in Virginia. He was Colonel of the Militia of Washington County, North Carolina—now Carter County, Tennessee.

The county records of Shenandoah County repeatedly attest his activities in recruiting and maintaining the Continental Army under the authority of both State and United States Government. They tell of his participation in the expedition of 1774, culminating in the Battle of Point Pleasant.

Colonel Tipton, with his seven sons fought all through the Revolutionary War, was in the Battle of King's Mountain.

He served twenty-seven years in the legislatures of Virginia, North Carolina, "Territory South of the River Ohio," and Tennessee. Was repeatedly elected to succeed himself.

What more proof could one desire of Colonel John Tipton's ability, his bravery, his loyalty, his knowledge of government, his very fitness to lead?

Bible Records—Tombstone Inscriptions

He died in his home near Elizabethton, Tennessee, and was buried there, on this spot so rich in history. After his death the farm passed into the hands of the Haynes family, and it was here that Landon C. Haynes, that eloquent Confederate Senator, died.

The house is much as it was then, only the logs are covered with boards, as is the old barn. The occupants of the house will show one the room where Colonel Tipton died, the spot where a famous battle took place; and in walking there voices from the past seem to say, "Cherish your State and Nation, your freedom was bought with a price." Mrs. HORACE L. FROST, *Regent*.

PRIZE ESSAY

Mrs. J. Byron Martin, Chairman, Daughters of American Revolution for Middle Tennessee for the marking of historic spots, has offered a prize of $20.00 to the Daughters of American Revolution Chapter, or any member of a Chapter in Middle Tennessee, writing the best story of an unmarked historic spot, either of battlefields, old forts, sites of early settlements, or treaty grounds and, also, a list of unmarked Revolutionary Soldiers' graves in the community in which the writer lives. This is in accord with the plan of the National Chairman to preserve and record all historic spots and Revolutionary Soldiers' graves. As a result of this announcement many stories were sent in. Mrs. Rhea Garrett of Dixon Springs won Mrs. Martin's prize for two successive years.

THE FORT BLOUNT ROAD TO CUMBERLAND
By Mrs. RHEA GARRETT

This was the first road into the valley of our State, directly from the East; and between the years 1786 and 1796 the only direct road to "the Cumberland Country"; yet a section of it lies today practically unknown; its sacred spots unhonored and unsung.

Rough it was, and narrow, and winding with hills; but it played its vital part in the winning of the West.

The pledge of the Revolutionary heroes was "our lives, our fortunes, and our sacred honor"; their lives and honor saved, but their fortunes somewhat worsted at the ending of the war—what better solution of finances, what happier thought could come than to reprieve on the marvelous Cumberland Bounty Land? The news of its richness was spreading; the Old North State was generous with her grants; the influx of immigration had begun.

Spencer's choice had been made in Sumner; the Bledsoe's had erected their fort near "The Lick"; the Peytons, Colonel Douglass, Maj. Wm. Cage, Captain Blackmore, Robert Desha, Major Hall, and others had come; General Winchester and his brother had

Bible Records—Tombstone Inscriptions

settled Cragfont; and Henderson's vision of Nashboro was now an undoubted achievement.

But the Indians also prized the fertile valleys and richly timbered hills of their hunting ground; and notwithstanding the treaty of Hopewell, they contested the right of the white man to pass without paying toll over the newly opened road through the territory remaining in their possession.

In lieu of other compensation, the Indians exacted human life; and so energetic they became in collecting that in 1787, the year following the opening of the first narrow roadway, the North Carolina legislature deemed it expedient to send for the protection of the Cumberland settlers an armed force known as "Evan's Battalion."

Three of the captains under Major Evans were Joshua Hadley, John Hunter, and Wm. Martin; and one of their duties assigned by the legislature was the leveling and widening of the new Wilderness Road.

No child's play, that of converting an Indian trail into a wagon road, especially through the Red Man's territory and under his unfriendly nose. An arduous and hazardous adventure, and one to try men's mettle; but that courage which threw off the British yoke had faith to "blaze the trail" to Cumberland; and the opening of the finished road September 25, 1788, to a party of sixty immigrant families was the consummation of the first forward step towards good roads in Tennessee.

The Cumberland country was "looking up."

The Indians had as yet never consented to more than one ferry across Clinch River, that at Campbell's Station, Southwest Point, the present Kingston. The Kentucky road used exclusively before this time by Cumberland settlers crossed the Clinch there, and at that point the new road began.

Striking the Cumberland Mountains twelve miles from Clinch, it crossed in turn: Rock Castle, Mammy's Creek, Spencer's Hill, Crab Orchard, Daddy's Creek, Obi River, Drowning Creek, and descended the western side of the mountain. From a point between White Plains, the present Allgood, and the town of Livingston, on the last ledge of the mountain, it was eleven miles to the later location of the house of John Blackburn, who must have been the first settler of the region which lies between Cumberland Mountains and the river.

From Blackburn's down Flinn's Lick Creek the road then ran, missing the present Gainesboro by four miles, and crossed the Cumberland River at the present ferry, where in 1794 Fort Blount

Bible Records—Tombstone Inscriptions

was erected, on the north side of the river,* as a protection against Indians hostile and resentful of travel through their territory.

Williamsburg, the first county seat of Jackson, was in 1805 located at Fort Blount, on the same side of the river, but on the opposite side of the road from the fort and several hundred yards further from the river than the fort. The log jail still stands, its wonderfully preserved old logs marvelously locked together at the corners—only a stone's throw from Sampson Williams' graveyard.

From the fort at the river the road ran westward; crossed Salt Lick Creek a short distance below the old Woodfork place; crossed Defeated Creek (of the noted camp of the Peyton surveying party, where they lost to the Indians their horses and "land stealer") at the site of the Cross Roads Church, at William's Cross Roads; down the Sloan Branch where, in 1799, the "Widow Young" made the Moravian ministers pay dearly for a night's lodging.

Thence across Peyton's Creek below old Herod's Cross Roads, at Pleasant Shade; up the Porter Branch of Peyton's, across Tow Town Branch (named by an early local Presbyterian minister) and to the top of Mace's Hill; down the Mace's Hill Road, leaving the road near the house on the place sold by Sam M. Young about 1920 to Jim Phillips, now owned by Phillips, and passing through his lower field towards the first Baptist Church organized between Station Camp Creek and the settlements in East Tennessee, and across Dixon's Creek about three hundred yards below the church and about one-half mile to the north of the northern boundary of Tilman Dixon's tract; across Lick Creek just south of the old Gillespie house and north of the Othiel Johnson house; across Glasgow Branch where Goodwill Church now stands, winding through the lower side of Greene Wright's farm, by an old log house on his place, and runs south of, and roughly parallel with, the Mongle's Gap road and, with the topography of the land, diagonally down the line of hills to the foot of Stalcup's; by Harts-

---

*This location of the fort on the north side of the river, though in contradiction to some authorities, is corroborated by map of early roads and forts in Tennessee Historical Magazine, in Vol. 7, No. 4, and also by the statements of Mr. E. P. Garrett, Dixon Springs, of Mrs. Jean McClelland, and of Mr. Buddie Smith of Carthage, Tenn., who all remember having seen the logs which were the remains of the fort in close proximity to a spring several hundred yards nearer the river than the Williams Graveyard and on the same side of the road as the graveyard.

Bible Records—Tombstone Inscriptions

ville and Bledsoe's Lick, Station Camp and Mansker's to the river at French Lick.**

This was the route of practically all travel to Cumberland from the year 1786 until the settlement of Col. Wm. Walton at the mouth of the Caney Fork about ten years later, when, by way of Cookeville, Chestnut Mound and Carthage, a new route was opened which diverged from the older Fort Blount route, at the point between Livingston and Allgood, previously mentioned as being eleven miles from the house of John Blackburn. This was known as the Caney Fork Road, and it converged again with the Fort Blount route at the foot of Stalcup's Hill, Trousdale County, three miles east of Hartsville, on the present Tilman Dixon Highway.***

Both routes from that time were in constant use for about five years, and it is only too significant of the condition of each that, regardless of which road a traveler chose first, he usually returned over the other!

In the year 1801 the Caney Fork route from Carthage east was widened and graded and called the Walton Road, and the Fort Blount section of the original road became only a connecting link between the local settlements and landmarks, and some of its stretches now are almost obscured by the intervening century and a half.

But the glories of the old Fort Blount can never fade!

"The Appian Way of the Cumberland Country," it fitly might be called, for along its historic bed are the graves of countless early heroes, whom Rome herself need not have scorned to own— officers and privates of the Colonial wars; members of committees of safety of North Carolina and Virginia; participants in the Battle of Alamance, where Freedom's first blood was shed in 1771; members of Robertson's and Donelson's adventurous parties, and signers of the Cumberland Compact; Watauga settlers, who signed the first independent government west of the Allegheny mountains; signers of the Mecklenburg Declaration; distinguished ministers of the gospel, as McFerrin and the Magees; officers of

---

**The information in regard to the western end of the old 1786 or Ft. Blount Road, from Cumberland River to the foot of Stalcup's Hill, was given me by Mr. Ed P. Garrett, age 75. The route from Glasgow's branch south of (Daniel) Mongle's Gap to foot of Stalcup's Hill has not been traveled for several generations. Its course was impressed on Mr. Garrett when as a young man; he accompanied his father and older men who were surveying in that section, and who pointed out to him the remains of the old roadbed.

***This route by Hartsville (called at first Damascus), by Bledsoe's, Gallatin (?), Shackle Island (?), and Mansker's, to French Lick appears to be generally accepted as the route of the road, but some researchers with whom I have conferred seem somewhat doubtful of it. I hope in the future sometime to verify the old road's course west of Stalcup's Hill as I have done from Southwest Point to Stalcup's Hill.

Bible Records—Tombstone Inscriptions

George Washington's staff, and privates, captains, majors, colonels, generals, in the war for independence—all these were here.

Among them I list the following, whose services for patriotic motive and rich achievement are worthy of a nation's thinks:

Capt. Sampson Williams, the obliging young commander of Fort Blount, who claimed to have preceded Robertson's party to Nashboro and who with Moses Fisk established at Hilham, Overton County, the first female academy in the southwest.

Edmond Jennings, fierce Indian fighter in early settlement of Nashville, who requested that his body be buried at a certain spot near the Fort Blount Road and his grave filled with rocks, "for," he said, "I don't want no d— varmints scratching me out."

Col. Wm. Martin, soldier of the Revolution at fifteen years, and of the Creek War at forty-seven, son of Gen. Joseph Martin, who in Powell's Valley, in March, 1769, made the first, though not permanent, settlement in Tennessee.

Wm. Herod of Stafford County, Va., supposed brother or close relation of James, of Harrodsburg fame; his son Peter, tradition says, was General Washington's godson.

Maj. Wm. Cunningham descended from Abraham Michaux and aide de camp to General Washington during Revolution. His son-in-law.

Col. Wm. Saunders, member of North Carolina Society of Cincinnati, father of the Hon. Romulus Mitchell.

Wm. Cleveland, son of Col. Benjamin of King's Mountain fame, who claimed descent from Oliver Cromwell.

Maj. Tilman Dixon, member of North Carolina Society of Cincinnati, founder of Dixon Springs, first postmaster, first tavern keeper; mentioned by Louis Philippe, Duke of Orleans, and other early travelers. The local tradition, given me by one of his descendants, says that the Duke on being informed that he might share a bed with one of the major's sons said: "But do you realize that I am a prince of the blood?" "Yes," answered the old patriot, "and you'll be sleeping with a prince of the blood when you sleep with one of my boys!"

John Magee, who with his brother William, Rev. McGready, and others, started "the jerks" of the great revival in 1799. First M. E. minister in Smith County.

Andrew Greer, son of Andrew Watauga settler, brother of Alexander who carried the news of King's Mountain to Congress.

John Brevard, Jr., son of John, member of committee of safety and constitutional congress of North Carolina.

Capt. Wm. Alexander, James Hart, and James Lauderdale, and the Bledsoe's.

Bible Records—Tombstone Inscriptions

Halery Malone, who always refused a pension, saying: "I owe that much to my country," and the distinguished Winchesters.

Dr. Wilson Yandell, honored with a degree from Johns Hopkins University for his skill in medicine without ever having attended a lecture. (Died in Rutherford County and buried there.)

James Sanders, member of North Carolina Cincinnati.

Wm. Brandon, the first white child born south of the Yadkin in North Carolina.

Gen. Griffith Rutherford, one of the few Revolutionary generals who came to Middle Tennessee. He was accompanied in 1792 by thirty immigrant wagons, and Dr. Redmond D. Barry who brought the first blue grass to Tennessee.

Col. Wm. Cage and Edward Douglas and the Peyton twins.

Gen. Matthew Locke had four sons in the Revolutionary War at one time. He was, with Herman Husbands, selected by the people to receive the fees of the sheriffs and court officers of the crown. Member of North Carolina Constitutional Congress.

Zaccheus Wilson, Mecklenburg signer.

Gen. Daniel Smith, soldier, scholar, statesman, whose commission as surveyor of the Territory South of the Ohio, is in the Lyman C. Draper collection in Wisconsin.

Yes, the Fort Blount Road has its glories. It served its country well; our oldest homes were built along its course; our finest stories still revolve around it; our bravest pioneers sleep along its way.

May our old traditions keep its memory green!

(Middle Tennessee) Laura Gastin Garrett, Dixon Springs.

FOUNDING OF NASHVILLE
By JUDGE JOHN H. DEWITT

(Read at the dedication of the Fort Nashborough Memorial at the War Memorial Building Thursday afternoon, November 20, 1930, under D. A. R. auspices.)

The history of the founding of Nashville involves the dreams and plans of Richard Henderson and his associates of the Transylvania Company in co-operation with James Robertson, John Donelson, and the adventurous colonists whom they brought to the Cumberland region. The story here briefly given shows a series of causative forces and influences which is our enduring heritage.

On March 17, 1775, at a great council held at the Sycamore Shoals on the Watauga River, a treaty was concluded and signed by Henderson for the Transylvania Company and certain chiefs

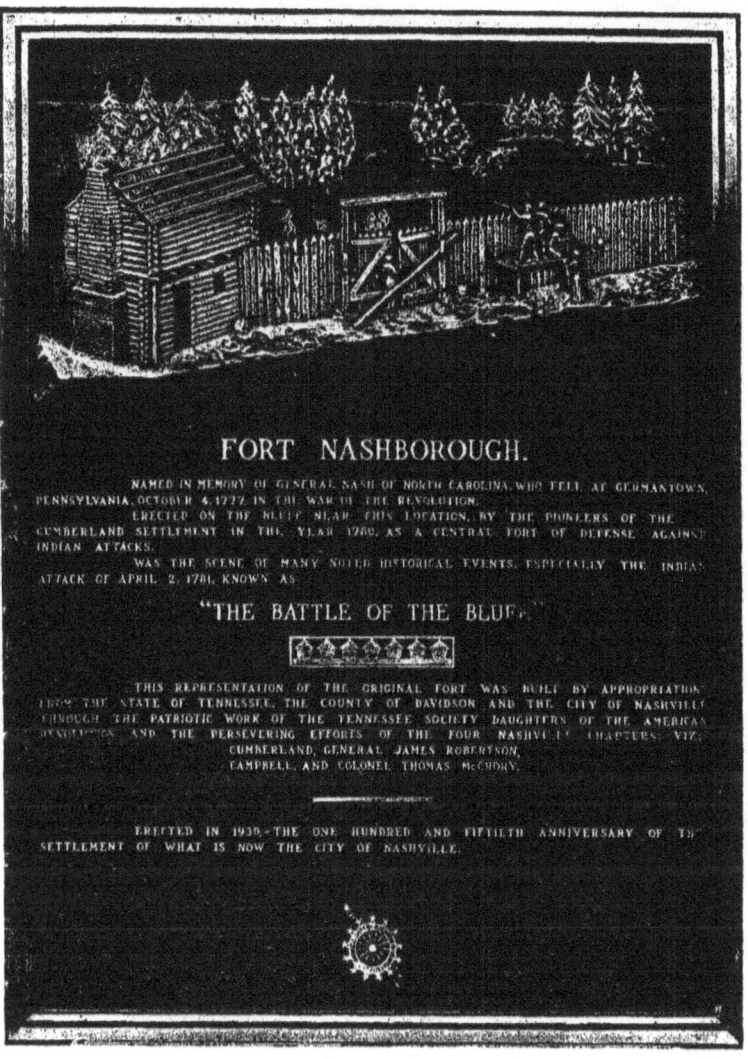

TABLET IN FORT NASHBOROUGH

Bible Records—Tombstone Inscriptions

and warriors in the presence of 1,200 Cherokee Indians. James Robertson, John Sevier, and Isaac Shelby, the three strongest men in the overmountain settlements, were also present. Under this treaty the Cherokees relinquished to the Transylvania Company all their claim of title to two great bodies of land; one, a tract of about twenty million acres comprising the lands lying south of the Ohio and between the Kentucky and Cumberland Rivers—and this deed was construed to include all the lands along the Southern tributaries of the Cumberland; the other tract comprising lands in what is now East Tennessee.

Under this purchase the company caused to be made the first settlements in Kentucky under the leadership of Daniel Boone. But the General Assembly of Virginia (of which Kentucky was then a part) declined to recognize the validity of the Henderson purchase, and the Transylvania Company was foiled in its enterprises in Kentucky, although it was granted a tract of 200,000 acres lying between the Ohio and Green Rivers by way of compensation for services in extinguishment of the Indian title and in helping to settle the country. Another enterprise of colonization was now undertaken by the Transylvania Company with the co-operation of James Robertson and John Donelson.

On July 20, 1777, at the Long Island of the Holston (now Kingsport) commissioners from North Carolina and Virginia, designing to end the bloody warfare of the Cherokees, entered into a treaty of peace with their chiefs. It contained four principal provisions:

1. An enlargement of the boundaries within which white settlers might live without molestation.
2. An enduring peace.
3. Regulations for trade and intercourse.
4. That Col. James Robertson, as Indian agent, should reside in the Indian town of Chota.

Col. Richard Henderson, head of the Transylvania Company, Col. John Donelson, late of Virginia, and Col. James Robertson, a leader in the Watauga Settlement, were present at the making of this treaty of Long Island. It was there that they must have projected the settlement in the distant region of the Cumberland. It was the first time after the Transylvania purchase was made that the dream of its promoters could be projected into a reality, for peace with the Indians was so essential to any colonization. Virginia had repudiated the Transylvania Company's title from the Indians. Colonel Henderson, believing that the Cumberland region was within the boundaries of North Carolina, turned to the plan of establishing settlements in the Cumberland region and selling lands to the settlers. He enlisted the interest and the services of Robertson and Donelson to recruit parties of settlers

Bible Records—Tombstone Inscriptions

and led them to the distant lands. Time must indeed elapse before the wonderful enterprise could be put in motion. Robertson must reside for some time at Chota, to cultivate the friendship of the Cherokees and fulfill the provisions of the treaty. Colonel Henderson must prove that the Cumberland region lay within North Carolina, and to this end he procured the appointment of himeslf as a commissioner to run the boundary line between Virginia and North Carolina.

Stories of the wondrous beauty and fertility of the land had been widely told among the settlements in Virginia and North Carolina as a result of the expeditions of the Long Hunters of the previous decade or more. Eagerly did men and women of courage and boldness yield to the desire to try their fortunes on the lands along the western waters. History is silent as to the very source of supplies for the long and difficult journeys planned; and it is silent as to the exact contractual relations between the Transylvania Company and Robertson and Donelson. But their presence here in the spring of 1789 and their co-operative labors in founding the settlement are matters of history clearly demonstrated.

The plan was to send one party over land and another by water. But, first, bread must be provided for the emigrants upon their arrival. For this presence here in the spring of 1780 James Robertson, with eight white men and one Negro set forth from the Holston settlements to make a preliminary examination and to plant corn. Arriving at French Lick, they erected a few log huts on the high ground near the Lick and planted a crop of corn. A small company of men led by Kasper Mansker arrived, doubtless by pre-arrangement, and all labored together in the field near the sulphur spring. When the crop was laid by three men were left to keep the buffalo out of the corn while the others returned to the settlements for their families.

The overland party of men, goods, horses, and other live stock, after passing through Cumberland Gap coming along Southern Kentucky as far as Red River, came then southward and reached the Cumberland on Christmas Day, 1779. They crossed the river on the ice on the first day of January, 1780. The leader of this part was Col. James Robertson. They were joined by three other parties—one from New River under John Rains, another under Kasper Mansker, and another from South Carolina under John Buchanan.

Some of these settlers unwisely scattered over the country for settlement, but Robertson advised the building of a stockade and fort into which all should come for protection at night. It was agreed that the stockade at the Bluff should be the headquarters for the colony. The erection of this stockade and fort must have

Bible Records—Tombstone Inscriptions

been undertaken and carried on soon after the arrival of these parties. They were composed almost entirely of men.

The other party, led by Col. John Donelson, Robert Cartwright, and Capt. John Blackmore, came in boats down the Tennessee River to the Ohio, and thence up the Cumberland to French Lick. It included the women and children and most of the household goods. The story of this voyage of the adventure and its companion boats, the long contest with the forces of nature, the murderous attacks by Indians, the struggles with hunger and disease, the loss of boats and members of the party, is one of the most heroic and thrilling in all our history. Donelson kept a journal of the voyage and we have it preserved. It shows that Henderson provided for his party a boatload of corn which arrived at the starving time. It also shows that the party arrived at the Bluff on April 24, 1780, where he said they found a few log cabins "which have been built on a cedar bluff above the Lick by Captain Robertson and his company."

How thrilling it is to visualize that joyful meeting and reunion! Long months had passed when the fate of those who were the dearest of earth was not known; and yet they were at last together—husband and wife, father and children, in this place far from all centers of civilized life, the advanced guard of Western civilization. Hither in the boats had come, among others, that noble woman, Charlotte Reeves Robertson, with their children; and here was a girl, Rachel Donelson, destined to become the wife of Andrew Jackson and one of our immortals.

These pioneers then did almost immediately two things most necessary—they completed the stockade and fort, they entered into a compact of government. An eminent historian has given the following very credible account:

"Nashborough, sometimes called the Bluff, or the bluffs, was to be the headquarters. The fort was located in what is now the City of Nashville, at the foot of Church Street, near a bold spring flowing out of the bank of Cumberland River. The main building, which was at first occupied by Robertson and a few companions, was of logs, and two stories high, with portholes around the walls above and below, these being for rifles in case of attack. On top was a lookout station. Other cabins were built near, the whole enclosed by a stockade—cedar pickets sunk firmly into the ground. There was but one entrance to the enclosure, the gate being fastened at night or in times of attack by a heavy log chain. To the west and south beyond Broad Street the scene was much obstructed by a thick growth of cedars. On the uplands around and beyond this was an abundance of forest timber, while the bottom lands along the east and north were covered with cane, ten to twenty feet tall."

Bible Records—Tombstone Inscriptions

The fort was a place of council, of refuge, the seat of government, the center of the life of the people.

Here was drafted and signed the famous Cumberland Compact of Government; Richard Henderson and Nathaniel Hart were present, representing the Transylvania Company. Henderson, lawyer and former judge, drafted in his own handwriting this compact of government. It was signed by 256 persons, nearly all of whom wrote their own names. It is plain from the provisions of the document that the settlers believed that their titles to land must be derived by purchase from the Transylvania Company; but while Henderson and his associates undertook to sell the lands they agreed to take no money for them until the titles should be confirmed by the State of North Carolina. This confirmation was refused in 1783, but inasmuch as by means of the conveyances obtained by Henderson and his associates from the Cherokees, peaceable possession might be obtained from the Indians. Henderson and his associates were granted by North Carolina a tract of 200,000 acres of land in the present counties of Claiborne, Knox, Union, Campbell, and Anderson, in East Tennessee. Henderson and his associates had done a great work in projecting and beginning the colonization of the Cumberland region, but they now faded from the scene. It has been well said that Richard Henderson in all things dealt justly with the pioneers and left among them when he died an honored name. It was left for Robertson to govern and preserve the settlement. He was from the beginning the presiding officer of the body of twelve notables, or general arbitrators, and also the colonel of the militia. Within a few weeks eight forts were built—Fort Nashborough, Freeland's, Asher's, Mansker's, Eaton's, Union, Bledsoe's, and Donelson's. The Cumberland Compact created in this wilderness a small self-governing commonwealth. It established a tribunal of twelve members with certain legislative, judicial, and executive functions. These functions were limited and defined. The tribunal was distributed equitably among the eight settlements in the Cumberland Country. The elective franchise was conferred on all free men over the age of twenty-one years. Careful provisions were made for the entry of lands, for the registration of land titles, and for the descent of lands. The administration of justice, civil and criminal, was provided for and justice was rendered accessible by the institution of inferior courts and courts of appeal, all persons being bound by a solemn agreement to abide by the decision of the Cumberland Courts and to renounce all right of appeal to North Carolina. A commission was provided for to assure the general assembly of North Carolina of the attachment of the Cumberland people to the interests of the country and their obedience to the laws and constitution thereof. And the commission was further instructed

Bible Records—Tombstone Inscriptions

to express the desire of the settlers to meet their ratable share of the expenses of the Revolutionary War as well as the other expenses of the government—to explain that the organization was made to provide for the exigencies of their exposed condition—and to petition North Carolina to establish a county of the settlement and to afford it aid and protection.

Pursuant to the provisions of the Compact the Government was put into operation by the election of military officers and members of the court. The Compact was entered into on May 1, 1780, and was finally ratified on the 13th day of the same month. There are no records of the Court until January 7, 1783, when a meeting was held.

The settlers were soon menaced by Indians. In fact, for fourteen long years the lives of the pioneers were in daily peril. No sooner had the articles of government been adopted than the settlers began in peace to plow their fields and plant their corn, but the Indians deeply resented this sudden advent of so large a number of whites into their hunting grounds.

The British on the north and the Spaniards on the south were busily, but secretly, engaged in urging the savages to open hostilities against the defenseless outposts on the western frontier. In the language of Judge Haywood, it was indeed "a period of danger and hazard; of daring adventure and dangerous exposure." It is a long and tragic story of murderous attacks, of death from ambush, of suffering from hunger and wounds, of distress and discouragement. Only recently have been found the reminiscences of John Cockrill, who married the widowed sister of Robertson, describing the suffering and near starvation of the inhabitants of the Fort and his own successful effort, in the face of dreaded danger from Indians, to bring in bear meat as food.

The list of martyrs is long. The very first year, 1780, was marked by incessant attacks and harrassing warfare by Indians. Two terrible attempts were made to take and destroy the forts—the attack on Freeland's Station, January 15, 1781, and the Battle of the Bluffs, April 2, 1781. These were unsuccessful, but lives were lost and suffering entailed. In their dismay, many settlers returned to their former homes. Finding that they could not take the forts, the Indians resorted to guerilla warfare. It was never abandoned until after the Nicojack expedition conducted by General Robertson in 1794.

Amid all these stressful scenes and circumstances, the noble and courageous spirit of James Robertson prevailed. In 1782, when to many the extinction of settlement and settlers was at hand, a council was held and it was only by the spirit of determination of Robertson that the people decided to stay. It was probably at this council that Robertson said: "The God of crea-

Bible Records—Tombstone Inscriptions

tion and providence never designed these rich and beautiful lands to be given up to wild beasts and savages. They are to be the home of Christianity and civilization."

And Isaac Bledsoe, later a martyr, also said: "If we perish here, others will come to avenge our death and accomplish the work we have begun. They will find our graves, or our scattered bones, and tell to the ages that we deserved a better fate."

How wonderfully prophetic and true were all these heroic words. In this way they met unmoved and extremest perils, and in defiance of starvation, havoc, and death they held this lone and far-flung outpost of civilization.

There were many brave souls, but their great leader, Robertson, shone among them like a beacon light. When in the autumn of 1780 corn was scarce and powder was gone, he made the journey alone through the wilderness to the settlements in Kentucky and brought back a supply of powder. He made journeys to the seat of government in North Carolina and procured military protection for the settlements. He was an able diplomat. He won the enduring friendship of the Chickasaws. He had a taciturn, masterful way of dealing with men and affairs. He had a wonderful combination of cool caution and adventurous daring. Well did Haywood say of him: "He merited all the eulogium, esteem, and affection which the most ardent of his countrymen have ever bestowed on him. He had a sound mind, a healthy constitution, a robust frame, a love of virtue, an intrepid soul, and an emulous desire for honest fame." He lived until the autumn of 1814 and died while still serving his people as commissioner to the Chickasaw Indians.

Amid the sorrows and distresses of the earlier years the institutions of permanent government were created. By act of April 14, 1783, Davidson County was by the legislature of North Carolina established. By Act of 1784, the town of Nashville was established, the original tract of 200 acres being set apart to be laid out into town lots, roads, streets, and public square.

In 1785 Davidson Academy was chartered. A board of trustees was created. A tract of 240 acres of land to the south of the town was granted to the trustees of the Academy. The first school and church were conducted by Rev. Thomas B. Craighead, a graduate of Princeton, who was specially induced by the settlers to come here from North Carolina.

Our beautiful and beloved Nashville is thus a heritage from heroic souls. Today we rear and dedicate this Fort Nashborough on the old bluff as a memorial of our gratitude to them; as a symbol of our belief in the enduring value of the courage, the faith, and the vision which filled the souls of those pioneers; and as an admonition to each on-coming generation that our civilization can only be preserved and can only fulfill its destiny by the exercise

Bible Records—Tombstone Inscriptions

of that faith and rugged virtue which sustained the pioneers in those primitive times one hundred and fifty years ago.

REMINISCENCES RELATIVE TO "UNCLE SOLOMON," AN OLD AFRICAN SLAVE WHO LIVED TO BE 110 YEARS OLD

Sent by Mrs. Wm. Vaught; written at her request by Mr. H. W. Taylor.

During the pioneer days, in what now is Carter County, East Tennessee, there lived a man by the name of Nathaniel Taylor. He was a gentleman of education and refinement, who had migrated from Rockbridge County, Va., in those early days; like many other, daring but cultured, as well as uncultured young men, seeking adventure and new surroundings.

After acquiring a body of land of several thousand acres, located along the Watauga River between Gap Creek and what is now Elizabethton and some other adjacent lands, he had a home built on an eminence not far from the bend of the Watauga River, purchased a number of Negro slaves, and carried on farming operations. But it was not long until he entered a military career and soon became a Lieutenant-General in the army of our *then* young Republic. That was within the period when the early settlers of our country had much trouble with the savage Indians and with the Tories of Great Britain.

General Taylor exercised his military genius and training in several battles with the wild Indians and with the British, and in each battle he was crowned with outstanding success.

When not engaged in a military campaign, the General made a trip to Charleston, S. C., to buy a Negro slave or two, for be it remembered that in that day it was the fashion, especially among owners of plantations, to buy and own many slaves; and General Taylor owned and worked a number of Negro slaves on his Watauga plantation. He was said to have been an exceedingly kind and human master to all his slaves, providing comfortable homes, food, and clothing for them, and allowed no unjust and brutal treatment, or cruelties of *any kind* toward them *by any one*. The writer obtained this information relative to the General's humane treatment from some of the old slaves and ex-slaves of General Taylor when the author of this article was a boy.

On one occasion when General Taylor was at Charleston he purchased a Negro boy who had just arrived on a slave ship from the jungles of the Dark Continent and was being offered for sale by one of the slave dealers. The General brought this boy home with him to work with the other slaves on the big Watauga plantation.

Bible Records—Tombstone Inscriptions

This African boy was found to be so superior by nature and aptitude, so quick of understanding, so shrewd and logical that the General named him Solomon. The boy was then only in his latter teens. He was slender and agile and exceedingly strong *physically* as well as mentally. His fellow workers gave him the nickname of "Bony." Later in life he was sometimes called "Uncle Soller," "Uncle Sol," or "Uncle Solomon."

Such was Solomon's aptitude for learning the English language and was so practical in his ideas and conduct that his master soon made him the plantation *overseer*. From the very outset of his life on the plantation he showed the trait of strictest honesty, truthfulness, and general integrity of character and was never known to do a dishonest act or tell a falsehood.

Moreover, he realy manifested a surprising controlling influence over his subordinates and fellow workers and a remarkable executive ability in planning and getting work done properly and without friction or criticism.

At the death of General Nathaniel Taylor, Solomon with the other slaves of his father, became the property and body-servant of District Attorney-General James P. Taylor, who was one of the heirs to the General's large estate. When the latter died, his *son*, Nathaniel G. Taylor, father of Bob and Alf and the writer and other brothers and sisters, inherited a portion of the Watauga plantation, with several slaves, including Uncle Solomon.

It was customary for slaves to take the surname of their masters, so Solomon was known as Solomon Taylor.

The author of these statements (Hugh L. Taylor) knew *"Uncle Solomon Taylor"* while he (Hugh) was a little boy. Uncle Solomon used to tell of his experiences while hunting lions, tigers, elephants, and boaconstrictors in the jungles of Africa before he was captured in war by another Negro tribe and sold to a white slave dealer. His stories were full of thrilling incidents and hair-breadth escapes, but always bore the rational features of reality and truth. His stories of these adventures among the jungles were as full of thrills as any of those the author heard Henry M. Stanley describe on his search for David Livingston in Africa, and which he so graphically portrays in his wonderful work entitled "Darkest Africa." By close observation and almost daily personal contact with Uncle Solomon, extending through several years of boyhood, while living with parents at the family home on Watauga River, Happy Valley, Tennessee, the writer can testify from personal knowledge that this old, highly respected Negro man, Solomon Taylor, was thoroughly reliable in his statements.

Uncle Solomon used to tell us how that he was present when the soldiers gathered in a field opposite Sycamore Shoals to go to

Bible Records—Tombstone Inscriptions

fight Patrick Ferguson at King's Mountain; that he and others passed buckets of cool spring water to the thirsty soldiers gathered there on their way to King's Mountain; *and how that every eighth man was drafted to stay at home on guard duty and not to march to battle* with the rest of the soldiers; how that he heard the Rev. Samuel Doak speak to all the soldiers there assembled, making them a brilliant, encouraging, and patriotic speech and closed it by saying to them with emphasis, "Take with you the sword of the *Lord and of Gideon!*

It is believed that this was the first time in history that men of any army already organized and on the march to battle were ever drafted to stay at home, even for guard duty.

We think that old Uncle Solomon's statements, coupled with a survey of the military history of the world, will be quite convincing in substantiation of this statement as true and correct.

Uncle Solomon lived on my father's plantation of Watauga River, while a slave and afterwards, and died there in about 1869, at the advanced age of 110 years.

He was my mother's gardener for a little while after slavery was abolished, was paid for his services, was given a good home by my father. Just prior to his death my mother had him brought to a cottage near our home where she furnished him comfortable quarters, a trained nurse and cook and engaged a good doctor for him. But one day, after he had lain ill for some days under the care of the nurse and the doctor, Uncle Solomon sent his nurse to our home and told her to tell "Queen Emmeline," as he always called my mother, and the rest of our family to come and tell him good-by as he was soon going to heaven. My father was not at home at the time, but those of us who were at home, including my mother, sisters, my brother, Alfred A. Taylor, and myself quickly went to the bedside of our beloved, old, faithful, dying servant who had helped to nurse and care for us while we were babies. He seemed so glad to see us and he asked Alfred to read that passage in the Bible, "I have fought a good fight, I have kept the faith," etc., which Alf read aloud to him. The old man listened intently until the closing sentence when he folded his hands across his breast and passed peacefully to the Great Beyond.

Clad in a brand-new, broadcloth suit, and placed in a splendid casket furnished by "Marse Nat" and "Queen Emmeline" and followed by a host of old friends, both white and black, and amid a wilderness of flowers, Uncle Solomon's remains were borne on a funeral hearse to the cemetery and there laid to rest. His skin was black and he was born in the midst of the ignorance and savagery of the jungle; but, nevertheless, his *soul was white* and *pure* by living a pure and blameless life and consecrating his life to God and living a devoted *Christian* life after seeking and find-

Bible Records—Tombstone Inscriptions

ing that change of *heart* and life that comes with forgiveness of sins and receives the indwelling of the Holy Spirit.

HISTORIC HAPPY VALLEY, CARTER COUNTY, TENN.
By HUGH L. TAYLOR
(Written for Mrs. H. L. Frost, Elizabethton)

Facts and fancies that have the lure of novelty, adventure, romance, and heroism always give us pleasure, and often cultural value.

We believe the reader may find some, if not all, of these in the history of Happy Valley, Carter County, Tennessee.

To begin with, the very name is forever associated with the heroic, the romantic, and the beautiful.

The name Happy Valley was given this favored region long before the year 1860 by one who owned, in fee simple, a big slice "of the aforesaid and the same" and whose immediate ancestors were among the first settlers of this valley. His name was Nathaniel G. Taylor, who was the father of Robert Love and Alfred Alexander Taylor (commonly known as Bob and Alf Taylor), the two brothers of opposite politics, who ran against each other for Governor of Tennessee in 1886 in a political contest called "The War of the Roses." Each of these brothers served the State as Governor—Alf, the Republican, was elected thirty-four years after his defeat by his brother Bob.

Nathaniel G. Taylor had four other sons and four daughters, all of whom were natives of Happy Valley, most of whom married, established homes, and added to its population.

Nathaniel Taylor was a man of scholarly attainments, being a graduate of Washington College, Tennessee, and subsequently of Princeton College with honor, and was in public life as Congressman from the first district of Tennessee and subsequently Commissioner of Indian Affairs.

The mother of this Taylor family was a woman of rare culture and refinement and the maker of a happy Christian home and was idolized by her children.

It may not be inappropriate to state that Elizabethton was named for Mrs. Elizabeth Carter, and Carter County, of which Elizabethton is the county seat, was named for Col. Landon Carter, her husband. These were the maternal grandparents of N. G. Taylor.

Landon Carter was one of the heroes of the battle of King's Mountain, and afterwards held positions of honor and trust in which he rendered valuable service to the early settlers of Happy Valley.

Among the direct descendants of Landon and Elizabeth Carter were Samuel P. Carter, Lieutenant-General of the U. S. Army in

Bible Records—Tombstone Inscriptions

the Civil War and afterwards Rear Admiral of the U. S. Navy. He was a scholarly man and an honor graduate of the U. S. Naval Academy and sailed over all the seven seas on his ship of war. Another descendant was the Rev. Wm. B. Carter, Jr., Princeton graduate, preacher, lawyer, congressman, and a man of fine scholarship.

Perhaps the name of Happy Valley was suggested to Nathaniel G. Taylor by the beautiful story of "Rasselas," by Dr. Samuel Johnson of English literary fame, in which he describes the "Happy Valley" of his dreams. It may be that it was suggested by the beauty of the landscapes and of the streams flowing through this Watauga Valley and the happy conditions of its inhabitants through the years following the heroic struggles and perils of its pioneer settlers. But, whatever the origin, the territory bearing the name has a historic background that for beauty, romance, and heroism scarcely has a superior.

Happy Valley extends from the mouth of Stony Creek, east of Elizabethton to the headwaters of the Buffalo, and is not very far from the Great Smoky Mountain National Park now under way of development. From this valley are visible some of the loftiest mountains of the Appalachian System.

It is deemed proper to state that Happy Valley has produced several persons who, in the realm of letters, oratory, poetry, and humor, are justly entitled to distinction, as well as some of whose names will forever illumine the pages of history as military heroes and renowned statesmen.

The life of Nancy Ward, the half-breed Cherokee heroine, would make a volume of thrilling romance, heroic action, and perilous adventure. By her prowess and at the peril to her life, she saved the lives of hundreds of white men, women, and children among the pioneers of Happy Valley by revealing conspiracy of the savage Indians of her tribe. In fact, her life and deeds of valor have inspired one of America's great poets to produce, in Epic form, a poem entitled "The Pocahontas of the West," picturing in graphic style the greatness of her amazing acts of daring and courage in classic verse.

There is a monument erected in Happy Valley by the "Daughters of the American Revolution" not far from Elizabethton and near the famous Sycamore Shoals, which not only commemorates the heroism of Nancy Ward, but also marks the place where stood Fort Watauga and the Parapets, around which cluster so many historic memories of the Tennessee pioneer days.

Happy Valley is bristling with hallowed recollections of great historic interest too numerous to mention in this article.

Allow the writer to quote here a pen picture of Happy Valley, which would best show the genius of one of her native sons for graphic and descriptive style in the statement of facts:

"Happy Valley of the beautiful Watauga and lesser streams—the Doe, the Buffalo, and the Stony—reposing like the Vale of Cashmere in the midst of green hills and towering mountains, half veiled in the purple haze that is born of magnificent distances, is one of those charming spots of earth the like of which it would be difficult to find elsewhere, even within the limits of this vast region of bewitching sceneries.

"When the Divine Architect fashioned it, He embodied His most exquisite ideals of terrestrial beauty and sublimity. Here He wrought also as Sculptor, Painter, Poet, and Musician and harmonized His handiwork with the last touch of Divine perfection. Here we look upon a broad valley, cut like a cameo in low-relief from the rugged upheavels of nature, and flanked on the southeast by a lofty mountain range, notched and fluted and bisected by many a wild gorge and cove, through which rushes many a foaming torrent—a range whose towering crags and peaks lift their sculptured heads into the regions of eternal sunshine. From mighty gorges cut through the mountain-masses emerge two pellucid rivers—the Watauga and the Doe—uniting their waters near the head of the Valley and coursing it westwardly for several miles to the mouth of the Buffalo, a small stream, where the greater river suddenly bends through a gap in the hills and flows through a northwesterly direction to join the Holston.

"Supplementary to these rivers, the Divine Artist has studded the valley with innumerable springs of living crystal and interlaced it with numberless silver streamlets, winding through dell and woodland and meadow, and, thus, subsidiary to the clouds, helping to clothe the land with summer's unfailing garments of leaf and flower and golden harvests and ripening fruits and making it as fair and delightful as the fields and shades of Vallambrosa."

Permit the writer of this article to say further in his own humble style that the Watauga River of legend, song and story, beloved, romantic stream which has loafed through the centuries between its enamored banks of wild bloom, theme of poets, inspiration of orators—has flowed out of its languorous, lazy dream, into the golden channel of industry. Its mobile crystal flood, which erstwhile leisurely serenaded the mountains and idly sang to the stars, has lent the silver of its pure, rare waters to the swift and wholesome current of business, now flowing through wonderful awakened Happy Valley. Here at this moment there are two giant silk mills, manufacturing rayon thread, and these were built and are operated by the American Bemberg and the American Glanzstoff Corporations, employing thousands of workers. These

FANNIE N. F. MURFREE OF MURFREESBORO

mills are the pride of Happy Valley, Tennessee, in a very special sense. Their heart throbs and pulse beats are heard night and day! The whirr of their thousands of mechanical silk worms, the scream of their engines, the rumble and roar of their multiform machinery proclaim the glory of modern industry! This, *this*, is indeed sweet music to the workers and inhabitants of beautiful Happy Valley and her near neighbors!

BACKWARD GLANCES
By FANNY N. F. MURFREE

Dante has declared: *"Nessum magior dolore*
Che recordarsi del tempo felice
Nella miseria."

And many writers have repeated the thought—Chaucer, Marino, Fortiquerra, and others; in our own times Alfred Tennyson also expresses the idea:

" 'Tis a truth the poet sings
That a sorrow's crown of sorrow
Is remembering happier things."

A multiude of wounded hearts has vibrated to the truth of those words. Yet, now and again, like the calm glitter of "heat lightning" across the depths of a mid-summer night sky—lambent, alluring, harmless, a gentle memory gleams along the dusk of a saddened home and brings back a happier time. Such thoughts come to me of our stay in the New England States long ago.

I recall a snowy March morning in 1885 when my sister and I, utterly unprescient of the impending stir to be inaugurated by our action, cheerfully and casually ascended the stairs of a former dwelling in Boston, devoted in later years to the offices of the Atlantic Monthly—the Riverside Press under the same firm control was located in Cambridge, across the river Charles. The story of the ensuing interview has been often "written up" and perhaps nothing additional can be added except the queer ricochet on the consciousness of two of the participants, as they may be termed. They were so much surprised at the surprise and excitement their visit had evoked that they reminded me forcibly of the spectacle of two little boys wildly chasing each other until it occurred to one to conceal himself behind a jutting wall and jump out on his pursuer, the victim being so appalled that the agitation was suddenly mutual, and the dismayed perpetrator was in the grip of his own device.

In the mailing room, once the "double parlors" of the large dwelling, we were received by a blond young man to whom we made known our request.

"We would like to see Mr. Aldrich for a few minutes," said the unknown Charles Egbert Craddock.

"What name?" inquired the young man firmly but very politely.
"I will mention my name to Mr. Aldrich," she replied, also firmly but also very politely.

He turned away and disappeared, evidently with some reluctance, probably thinking that she wished to read a poem to the famous editor and was mentally canvassing methods of sparing his chief. The editor may also have been of this persuasion for he descended from the editorial office to the mailing room, perhaps on the theory that hearing the supposititious poem would be less strenuous in the perlieus of what may be called the marts of trade than in a more rarified literary atmosphere.

When she explained, "I have had some correspondence with you, Mr. Aldrich, and being in Boston I thought I would come and meet you."

His facial expression said (we have no equivalent English phrase), "Plait It?"

"I am Charles Egbert Craddock," she continued, "M. N. Murfree."

Then it was that the simile of the pursuing and pursued little boys on the sidewalk became applicable. She was so surprised by his amazement that she was suddenly almost as much discomposed as he by her own revelation. The limitations of the layman are not easily realized. While she had been for years absorbed by her Craddock works and knew, of course, that they had "arrived" she had not guessed that these were more than episodes; she had not reckoned on the tenseness of the bookish interests.

This was the beginning of a series of delightful events. It has been a cause of wonder why the phrase the "cold New Englander" should have been invented. Surely never was more earnest cordiality, eager hospitality, more warm-hearted friendship extended to strangers within the gates than for weeks and months was lavished on us. And to the hero worshippers that we were the happiness can be appreciated that we experienced, meeting and knowing the writers of books which we loved, and the painters, sculptors, musicians whose dreams had merged into achievements.

I do not recall when I first met Celia Thaxter. I think it was on the occasion of an informal dinner at the house of a friend of hers and of ours. So dominant was her personality, so brilliant her talk, so musical her delightful laughter (that famous laugh of hers I often heard mentioned before I ever saw her) that the thought of her pervades my recollection of much of the time of our stay in Boston, although our actual meetings were few in number and somewhat casual. At the Isle of Shoals, however, where her summer home was situated—on Appledore, the largest of the islands—we were staying at Star Island, we were often with her. Her flower garden at Appledore was much admired, but

Bible Records—Tombstone Inscriptions

I remember more distinctly the "living room" which was indeed a "living room," lined with bookcases and every inch of the walls covered with pictures, most of them executed expressly for her by celebrated artists. Here she received many interesting people. Her poems and her delightful personality commanded more than the usual tribute given to a favorite author. She used to say this room proved that she was a "bower bird"—the wonderful winged creature that bedecks its resort (not its nest but a kind of parlor, a veritable "living room") with many attractive odds and ends. One of her possessions which she greatly valued was a bracelet made of tiny sea shells which she had caused to be mounted on a velvet plaque and placed on one of the walls. This bracelet she had chanced to wear on the evening that she first met Charles Dickens. He noticed it—nothing ever escaped his attention. He asked to examine it and placed it on his own wrist wearing it himself throughout the evening. Thereafter it was sacred and cherished as a precious *objet de vertos*. No one was ever allowed to wear it again.

Mrs. Thaxter and my sister were very congenial and in a short time became devoted friends, notwithstanding the difference in age, environment, and tradition.

She was a fine raconteur, telling a story most vividly. I remember one which had a somewhat eerie quality. At that time New England was a little given to an interest in mystical effects (perhaps it is thus inclined now). We were sitting in "the bower bird's resort"; a number of interesting people were present; among them her uncle who was a famous violinist and his wife. The attention of the party was attracted by the violence of the wind. The sky was black; not a rift, nor a star, and the waves seemed to be tossing mountain high. To land lubbers like my sister and me Appledore was not a pleasant place on that wild night. Here is the story.

On an evening like this Mrs. Thaxter said she was bidding adieu to two young friends who had run over from the hotel near at hand to make inquiry as to the state of her father's health; he was suffering with a severe attack of illness. His room was on the opposite side of the hall. Both doors were closed. Everything was kept extremely quiet. The silence was profound. One of the young visitors said in a whisper, "How the wind blows! I'm afraid to cross the lawn, I might see a ghost!"

Only high histrionic ability could compass such a rendering as Mrs. Thaxter's utterance of these words. The visitors departed with low-voiced adieus and good wishes for the improvement of the invalid. Upstairs she stopped in the room of her young sons—then children—to see that the fire was burning and that they were comfortable. As she stooped to kiss their sleeping little faces one

of them murmured in his sleep: "How the wind blows! She's afraid to cross the lawn. She might see a ghost!"
He could not possibly have heard the words. It was of course evident to the psychical addict that the touch of her lips conveyed to his sleeping mind the thought of her waking mind. What other explanation is possible?

When she told this story with extreme gravity only the quizzical expression of her eyes, which she could not quite suppress, might betray to the very observant the fact that she was surreptitiously laughing at her own story and at the impression she was making on her half credulous audience.

A somewhat similar incident of quasi mysticism occurred one evening at another summer home—at this time at Mount Desert. A full moon, riding high in the deeply blue, cloudless heavens, flooded with white effulgence the scintillating waters of Frenchman's Bay, the far reaches of the distant Atlantic and evoked definite visibility in the bosky recesses of the mountain that rose steeply at the back of the residence. To our inland souls that mountain held a most welcome quality of power and serenity, dominating the ceaseless movement of the infinity of waters about us—wildly turbulent in time of storm, always restless even in calm moments like this. I chanced that the party in the large parlor was engaged in the somewhat absorbing game of Twenty Questions. No one now-a-days could possibly have time for games of that sort, which require much thought and swift mental agility. People seem to care only for bridge, poker, tennis, and golf; the two last mentioned might seem to the uninitiated and quiet of temperament to be aptly described in the dictum of the early historian Adiar in his characterization of the Indian game, chunghe.

"A game? No—no! Running hard labor!"

Twenty Questions requires that one member of the party shall be absent while the crucial proverb, or sometimes only a word, is selected. It chanced that my sister was at one time thus segregated. On her return, summoned from the verandah where she had retired during the deliberations, she chanced to remark, "A Dutch lugger seems to be at anchor in Frenchman's Bay."

A general laugh ensued. A gentleman present, who had been all over the earth many times, "even to Jericho," it was always stipulated, remarked that a Dutch lugger was a very old-fashioned craft and probably one had never before been in these remote waters.

"And how can you—a landsman from the wilds of St. Louis—know a vessel of this kind when you see it?"

She persisted: "It *is* a Dutch lugger."

"But how do you know a Dutch lugger." He was well versed

Bible Records—Tombstone Inscriptions

in nautical affairs—he even said "tops'l" and "mains'l," which seemed to our inland minds very knowing indeed.

He walked out on the verandah to see for himself. But a perverse mist had supervened and interfered; he was obliged to wait until morning. Then he repaired to the fishing village near by for information and came back much puzzled.

"It really is a Dutch lugger. She has discharged her freight and is about to return in ballast. But how did you recognize it as a Dutch lugger?"

She, too, was puzzled. Various interpretations were offered as to the uncanny cognition; the favorite suggestion, in accord with the psychical trend of thought characteristic of the time, was to the effect that some sailor or officer on the craft seeing a lady on the verandah had sent across the quiet moonlit water through that little understood science, telepathy, the information as to the nationality and character of the craft, introducing the stranger, so to speak. My sister did not accept this theory and reflected aimlessly on the problem till suddenly in a flash the solution presented itself.

In an old book of French steel engravings which in her childhood she admired extremely, illustrating the novels of Sir Walter Scott—the literary hero of all the world at that time, there chanced to be a picture of Dirk Hatteraick's lugger, the Youngfrauw Hagenslaapen, pursued by his Majesty's sloop of war, Shark. Through the years this picture remained in her brain. The recognition was complete, and the theory of telepathy was abandoned.

Mysticism, spiritism, hypnotism—any of those obscure, half credited, half understood—in fact, not understood at all, branches of inquiry have a perennial fascination, especially to thinking young people, and there is a certain sense of deprivation in being definitely out of the pale of influence of powers to which one objects and derides. To be assured that you cannot respond because you have no "plane"—or is it "sphere"?—when other people have a "sphere strikes a surprised resentment—though you don't wish to respond and do not want to have a "plane"—or a "sphere."

On a certain evening a notable gentleman well known in the world of letters and science and society tried some simple experiments in the line of psychology, I suppose it might be considered. The time was after a very agreeable dinner party; the place was an ideal library; the company was brilliant and cordial; the fires were blazing cheerfully; the perfume of flowers was on the air of the summer-like apartments. One of the guests was sent into the hall while a small object—a pencil, I think—was hidden in a vase. When he was recalled Mr. J., who was expert with the unseen powers, so to speak, placed two fingers on the shoulders of

Bible Records—Tombstone Inscriptions

the patient—shall he be called?—who walked straight to the table, slipped his hand in the vase and extracted the pencil. Was the expert laughing in his sleeve at the credulity of the spectators or did he unintentionally and unconsciously steer the exponent of the experiment across the room? Perhaps the thought in his mind was conveyed to the mind of the subject through the medium of the man's touch on the shoulder—who can say?

A story is told of Mr. J.—occurring some years after his death— a story which possibly has been sent to the Society for Psychical Research—it should have been sent. A young acquaintance of mine states that one day during his first year at Harvard while alone as he supposed quietly reading, he suddenly became conscious that he was *not* alone. Standing in the doorway was a gentleman he had never before seen—a man of medium height, rather slim, wearing a white beard, looking at the young man with a kindly somewhat quizzical expression, out of bright amiable eyes. He wore a long cloak of a fashion passed away many years before and a broad-brimmed hat. The young student rose hurriedly, but when he glanced up again toward the door the visitor had departed. He mentioned the circumstance and was astounded to hear that he must have been mistaken. Of course he persisted in his account.

"It couldn't have happened and I will prove it was impossible." His interlocutor took him into the hall and pointed to the communicating door through which the visitor seemed to have passed. A heavy bookcase filled with volumes stood against it. There was no gainsaying the question of weight.

However, no one is willing to admit having been the victim of a dream or a delusion or hallucination. Even more positively one repudiates the accusation of manufacturing in detail the appearance of an impossible visitant. The young aspirant for collegiate distinction was reassured some few days later, when on looking at a volume of likenesses of former professors he suddenly proclaimed, "This is the man I saw that afternoon! This is the man!" and pointed to a picture—the bearded face, the long cloak, the wide-brimmed hat, the amiable, yet whimsical face.

"This is the man! And I saw him!"

"That—that is a likeness of Professor W. J.," faltered his friend.

I do not vouch for this story, but *si non è vero è ben trovato*.

One who is unaccustomed to the sea and is in the habit of spending the summer days amid the shadows of Tennessee densely wooded, mountain ranges is apt to find rather glaring the sunshine on the reaches of the Atlantic. But a tree embowered lawn, the overshadowing roof of a wide veranda and the blue expanse of foam-crested waters, judiciously revealed yet screened, especially if very agreeable people are grouped about in cheerful conclave,

Bible Records—Tombstone Inscriptions

combine in an ideal *mise en scène*. On such an occasion the conversation chanced to advert to the production the preceding winter of the play "Ruy Blas." The play "Don Cesar de Bazan" followed on the same evening, which seemed a little strange as the two plots have much in common. This circumstance was commented on and the further remark was made that the opera "Maritana," by Massenet, also is based on much the same story. Oddly enough, Edwin Booth, who was of the party, had never heard this opera, which, although not a great work, is very attractive. One scarcely realizes that a famous actor or singer misses much that infinitely less gifted people are privileged to enjoy. My sister chanced to mention that on the production of that opera about a year previously in St. Louis the tenor scored a brilliant effect in one of the scenes—the moment that the dashing Don Cesar, in his successful personation of the king, is suddenly confronted by the monarch himself. The imposter, from his seat on the improvised throne, surrounded by the humble deluded villagers, calls out imperatively, "Who are you, sir?" The royal catchecumen evidently possessed a definite sense of humor and replied instantly, "I am Don Cesar de Bazan. And who are *you*, Sir?"

The reply also came instantly, "I am the King of Spain." The word Spain, taken on G in alt was accompanied by an imperative wave of the hand toward the new-comer's hat, imperiously commanding its removal. Now this was well done and the applause was very vehement. But the whole episode was so far in advance of anything else in the role, both before and after, that the contrast was inexplicable until the explanation was given by the rendition of the episode in Ruy Blas the preceding March.

The subject seemed to interest Mr. Booth, and he mentioned an incident apropos of that impressive gesture. He said that when he was very young during a rehearsal of Ruy Blas it chanced that Charlotte Cushman who was present objected to this "business." "I will show you, Edwin, how the great Lemaitre played the episode." This she did, but Mr. Booth declared he preferred to use his own interpretation. "When you are older, Edwin," she said, reproachfully, "you will not criticize the methods of the great lights of the profession." But he persisted in his own "reading" with what success the many hundreds who have delighted in the incident.

In these lambent embellishings of the summer "heat lightnings" of the long gone past come now and then memories of boating on the Charles River, and of the many drives through the quiet woods of Mount Desert and Beverly and Manchester by the Sea and Intervale. Of a certain wild rush along the wet sandy beach at Rye when a party unaccustomed to the treachery of the rising of the tide narrowly escaped the culminating disaster that threatened

Bible Records—Tombstone Inscriptions

Sir Arthur Warder and his daughter and Edie Ochletree. Only we had the saving foothold of "Bessie's apron," temporary though it was. The drive had been everything delightful—the air crisp and fresh, the skies blue and cloudless, only a faint flush suggesting sunset, the sand hard and dry beneath the horses' feet—when suddenly—the sand was not hard and dry—it was wet—it was very wet. The water was up to the fetlocks of the horses. With incredible swiftness it reached to their knees. On one side of the way was a steep bluff; on the other side was the illimitable Atlantic, the depths, shoaling with ironic beauty from blue into green, into rose, into vague indiscriminated tints. But for super equine intelligence a party of reckless Western land lubbers would have found watery graves in all that aquatic beauty. For without guidance from rein or voice the intelligent beasts turned sharply and almost overturning the light carriage scrambled up an opening in the high bank and achieved safety.

It is hard to recover from a scare like that. After all, I don't covet the Atlantic. It is big, but it is cruel, and glaring, and cold and very, very restless. With the Great Smokies infinitely solid and calm, and magnetic on the east and the illimitable silent Mississippi on the west and our lovely rolling country between we ought to be satisfied.

MRS. CHARLES BAILEY BRYAN

Mrs. Charles B. Bryan, daughter of the late Admiral Raphael Semmes, of the Confederate's States Navy, has long been a prominent figure in our state activities. Descended from a long line of Colonial and Revolutionary ancestry. She has done much work along historical and patriotic lines. She has always taken great interest in the cause of education in her state.

The outstanding piece of work, when State Regent of the D. A. R. of Tennessee, was the first step taken to preserve the State archives from absolute destruction. She brought the matter to the attention of her organization for sanction and approval, viz: To have presented a bill to our legislature for the appropriation of an adequate sum to remove the records from the basement of the Capitol where they were being destroyed by mold and rats to a suitable place for preservation. She called a meeting of prominent citizens, heads of patriotic societies, educators, churchmen, and high dignitaries to lend their influence to the movement. Our legislature realizing the advisability of such a move, promptly passed the bill. Our valuable State papers were placed in a dry room and properly assorted. That was the nucleus of our splendid Department of Tennessee History today.

MRS. CHARLES BAILEY BRYAN
Past Vice President General, Honorary State Regent

Bible Records—Tombstone Inscriptions

Mrs. Bryan has had many deserved honors conferred upon her in recognition of her valuable services. In 1907 she was appointed by Governor Malcolm Patterson as one of the State Commissioners to the Jamestown Exposition. In 1913 was appointed by Mayor E. H. Crump of Memphis to represent that city at the National Conservation Congress held in Washington. In 1915 was selected by the National President of the D. A. R. to represent that organization at the Centennial Celebration of the Battle of New Orleans. It was a notable occasion, attended by notables from the different States and Canada. Mrs. Bryan worked with zeal and energy to help complete a dormatory at Lincoln Memorial University and was one of the pioneer women workers of her State for the education of our mountain children.

Her work in various lines covered a period of nearly forty years and her influence is still felt by her co-workers in the State, who love and admire her. This little sketch is but a well deserved tribute to our Mrs. Bryan.

TENNESSEE STATE LIBRARY

By MRS. JOHN TROTWOOD MOORE, *Librarian and Archivist*
(Tennessee Libraries, October, 1932)

The Tennessee State Library endeavors to be for the state what the Congressional Library is for the nation. There is no other class of libraries whose field can be so clearly defined, whose character is so unmistakably determined by the needs of the state, and whose service to the state can be so comprehensive and economic.

The library was created by Act of the Tennessee Legislature in 1854 as a law library, especially for the use of the state's official family. It has outgrown this idea of service and now includes an important service to the state and nation.

The real purpose of our State Library is to collect and carefully preserve all material of historic interest, to keep alive and up-to-date its choice law library, the books needed by the highest courts, to provide books needed by members of the General Assembly, different state officials and departments of the state, and to provide a reference library of Tennessee and Southern history, genealogy and literature for readers and researchers for every section of our state, the South, and the United States.

Our collection of Tennesseana is, perhaps, the largest and strongest in existence. It contains many valuable and rare books, pamphlets, maps, prints, broadsides, portraits, scrapbooks, letters and diaries, early newspapers, scattering numbers dating from 1806-70, in constant use as original source material, and manuscript material on every phase of Tennessee history, biography, travel, etc.

The eight leading daily Tennessee newspapers are subscribed

for and bound quarterly, 1,500 volumes, dating from 1870 to date. Subscription is made to the leading law journals, the historical publications of all states, bound annually, important historical information is collected and filed through a clipping bureau service, and the important magazines of genealogical, patriotic, literary, archaeological, and scientific nature.

Our Jacksoniana collection is priceless, as is our collection of early Indian history.

The Southern collection ranks next in importance and is proving a valuable aid to researchers in every subject pertaining to the South. Our collection of southern genealogy is doubtless the strongest in this region, comprising several thousand volumes.

The State Library of Tennessee has recently made a strong effort to complete its already valuable file of state documents, or reports, and leading municipal reports, since the State Library is the logical place where such reports should be filed for present and future use.

This library is a Government Depository and receives such publications as are called for by students. It has also been made a "state centre" for Tennessee state documents.

Here may be found a complete file of the enlistments of Tennessee soldiers in the War of 1812, the Cherokee War, the two Seminole Wars, 75,000 records of Confederate soldiers who enlisted in Tennessee, 3,000 questionnaries returned by living ex-Confederate soldiers, and 3,000 World War Gold Stars from this state.

Our manuscript and typescript collection contains original writings of many of the older and the present-day Tennessee authors and is being added to regularly. Especial effort is being made to collect all original material relating to the Fugitive group.

Much of the material in this library cannot be loaned, but whenever duplicates are available we try to accommodate students and always welcome them as visitors or researchers in the library.

OLD BURIAL GROUNDS OF WARREN COUNTY, TENN.
By Mrs. Blanche Bentley

The movement, inaugurated by the Daughters of the American Revolution, to preserve the names of men and women buried in the early graveyards of the country is a most notable and worthy one, and as the years go by will became increasingly distinguished and historic. Not only will the names so preserved be rescued from forgetfulness, but interesting questions concerning the first settlers of a section will arise and the student of ethnology or genealogy will have only the legends carved on these disintegrating

Bible Records—Tombstone Inscriptions

old stones to tell of the strains of nationality of migrations—perhaps from far countries, of family lineages and kinships.

When settlements were first formed over the country the log church arose almost simultaneously with the log house and around the church was invariably laid off land for a burial ground. This association of the use of the church and the churchyard is an age-old inheritance and brought from countries beyond the seas, the Saxon tongue calling the plot so reserved by a word meaning "God's Acre"; and the church itself, a building now seen by every roadside, river, or mountain top—a simple oblong room with end doors—first came into this country with the Scots from Ulster, and as shown by pictures is an exact replica of the "Meeting House of the Covenanters."

There are many such churches and churchyards in Warren County, some of them much over a century old, and the older the church there is usually found the best care and attention. The neighboring families worshipping in the same church for generations would naturally keep their burial grounds in order.

There are also pathetic cases where old places of interment and worship have been so long abandoned the sites they once occupied are covered with impenetrable thickets of briar and bramble—even the names of families once belonging there forgotten. No one left to remember because all who could do so are dead or gone away.

One of the best known and first organized churches of Warren County was Liberty, a mile or so from McMinnville. As shown by his will, land was given by Thomas Wiltshire (Wilcher), the church house built and the church, Cumberland Presbyterian in doctrine, organized all in 1815. William Cheek Smartt is the reputed founder and he and John Allison, a Revolutionary soldier, were two of its first elders. William C. Smartt, his wives, his venerable mother, and many descendants are buried in this peaceful enclosure which in the springtime, with its level grassy turf, its evergreens, flowers, and waving vines, looks very like a garden of the long ago. William C. Smartt was a commissioned general in the militia, but he won his spurs as a fighting man at Mobile under Jackson where he was promoted to the rank of major. Among the many persons buried at Liberty are John Allison, Revolutionary soldier, the wife, father, and mother of Samuel Hervey Laughlin, and Thomas Hopkins of Virginia, a large land owner of Warren and adjacent counties. So many of his relatives came to Tennessee to settle on land he had given them that numerous families still prominent in Warren and Davidson Counties are included in the number.

Another very early church in Warren County is known as Armstrong Church, the land for the church and churchyard being given by Hugh Armstrong, a Revolutionary soldier from Surry

Bible Records—Tombstone Inscriptions

County, North Carolina. He was closely related to Colonel Martin Armstrong, surveyor general of western lands, and to John Armstrong entry taker at the historic land office, as shown by wills of Surry County, North Carolina. One of the entries of his Bible, placed among the treasured records of births and marriages, was the statement: "I, Hugh Armstrong, was at the surrender of Cornwallis at Yorktown." Old Armstrong stands in one of the beauty spots of the county—fair, sloping land which seems lying asleep in the sunshine, watched by a long line of nearby blue mountains with Towns Creek flowing between the mountains and churchyard. The plantation of Hugh Armstrong stood on Towns Creek and adjoining this land lived Jonathan Tipton from Watauga. Adrian Northcutt, captain of the "Mountain Blues," one of the companies enrolled in Campbell's Regiment in the War with Mexico, is buried at Armstrongs, with his wife, family, and kinspeople. He was later commissioned a general in militia.

Additional land was given to Armstrong by George Etter; and he, with a large connection of his name, and of Woodleys, Moffatts, and related families and many others are buried in this beautiful and well-preserved spot.

In the earliest days of the county there stood on "the Old Kentucky Road" two miles south of Rock Island a log church known as Asbury's Meeting House. The men who built the church were Reuben Roberts, a Revolutionary soldier, his sons and sons-in-law, their neighbors and friends; and if the date is correct of their coming to this section—1796— given in the diary of one of them, they formed one of its oldest settlements. The meeting house, a building of one room, stood in the heart of a great forest and has been described as of most primeval simplicity both as to building and furnishings. The men, however, who built it found it a perfectly satisfactory place in which to worship God. Being devout Methodists and strictly adhering to the forms of worship permitted by that church in early days, but sometimes at meeting house services mingled with the sweet songs of Zion wild scenes of shouting and fierce exhortations would burst upon the forest silence and terrify a little boy present, who seventy-five years afterwards recounted the sights and sounds of Asbury Meeting House revivals.

According to very responsible tradition the pioneers of Asbury Settlement honored and collected the history of Warren County as known to them upon their first arrival. As recounted by Captain John Kelly Roberts, grandson of the patriarch Reuben, he himself remembered three diaries that had been written in the settlement and that as a boy "he was often present when the entire settlement would meet in the evening to hear these diaries read and talked about" and one can imagine how weird and mystical some of these tales must have sounded in the darkening twilight

Bible Records—Tombstone Inscriptions

within sound of the Caney Fork River. One of the diaries was kept by a young Virginian, a school teacher, who came West with Peter Nuckoll, went to New Orleans under Jackson and never returned. All these precious papers have been lost, but from "reading and rereading" much of the history was remembered. As they sat thus together in the quiet evening time, the men and women of the little settlement must have often spoken of a very patriotic service once performed by the older men of the community. Sometime while Jackson and his army were at New Orleans word came to the settlement that the General's powder was running low. Immediately Reuben Roberts, Elijah Drake, Peter Buren, Peter Nuckoll, George Sanders, and others from material gotten from the Big Bone Cave and other places, made a large quantity of powder, packed it in wagons drawn by oxen and cutting a new and direct route as they went, by Short Mountain, Rutherford and Davidson Counties to Nashville, loaded the powder on flat boats and sent it to New Orleans to General Jackson. (Taken from letters of Captain John R. Roberts.) The road so cut and traveled was called the old road to Nashville and is mentioned in Warren County Road Books as late as 1858.

The old meeting house, once so vociferous in its songs and services as remembered by the little boy present, has become very still with the passing years. In fact, the church seems to have disappeared, nor can the graves of those who built it be found. So completely, apparently, have the forest and earth recalled them to themselves.

In the discharge of Reuben Roberts from the Revolutionary Military Service it is said, "He bore himself with honor in seven battles," once serving under Light Horse Harry Lee and once under Campbell at King's Mountain. It is hard to realize that any one once bearing the form of a lusty, daring, young cavalryman charging with Light Horse Harry or a soldier under Campbell, yelling, cheering, and shooting as he forced his way up King's Mountain could be anywhere under that quiet sod.

McMinnville and Its Old Graveyards

That it may be known what manner of men and women are buried in the old cemetery adjoining McMinnville—who they were, from whence they came, what is remembered of their lives in the town, and all the other questions we ask ourselves when wandering through old burial places, a brief sketch of the town will follow. For all that was worthy and honored in citizenship in that early settlement, gracious and lovely in womanhood or kind, gentle and true in friendship and neighborliness were all with few exceptions buried in the old graveyard. So completely is this true that if a

Bible Records—Tombstone Inscriptions

list of all who rest there could be given it would be a census of the residents of the first half century of the town.

McMinnville, founded in 1810, and then one of the frontier towns of Tennessee is situated high up the foothills among the Cumberland Mountains. Soon after its settlement families began to arrive in the town who became permanent residents and in many cases still have descendants there. The men and women who came in this migration were typical of and similar to the early settlers in other sections of Tennessee and adjoining states who came principally from the Scotch Settlements in the Virginia Valley and North Carolina as from the older and longer settled sections of those two states. Also listed among early residents were a few prominent families from New England.

Students of ethics claim that education more than any other factor—honorable character excepted—makes a good citizen and prevents retrogression of families. Cease to educate, we are told, and families and communities lapse.

According to this theory McMinnville started well on its career of citizenship. Of the seven or eight lawyers noted in Tennessee Gazette of 1834, four of those lawyers are shown by family knowledge to have been educated in universities. Princeton, Hampden Sidney, Chapel Hill, and Yale, and two of them during long lives in the town accumulated valuable libraries. Of the two academies listed in same Gazette, one had as principal a graduate of Priceton Theological and the other was taught by a pupil from the Nashville Female Academy. How far-reaching these influences were it is impossible to say. They doubtless gave to McMinnville its antebellum reputation for fine schools and an educated community.

Many of the early homes of the town—after the passing of the first log houses—were of brick, comfortable, commodious, and of dignified aspect, standing along the quiet shady streets, built either against the curb or back in yards filled with locust trees, and very like in appearance other houses of the period which stood—and in many instances still stand—in Virginia, Kentucky, and Tennessee.

No matter what the house was in its fashion or material, the trees shading, beautifying, and guarding it were in nearly all instances locusts. Tree of the pioneer the locust was called, because when tired of the wilderness and its endless succession of forest trees the pioneer when reaching his place of settlement denuded it of growth and planted about his home the tree of his own choosing, the quickly growing, quickly shading, lovely fragrant locust tree.

Many of the men and women of early McMinnville had, in addition to education, advantages of birth and breeding enabling them

Bible Records—Tombstone Inscriptions

to bring to the town the influence of the older civilization from which they came, its customs, speech, dress, manners, and best of all, thoughts, beliefs, and restraints.

In those early homes of the town was exercised a very frequent and very friendly hospitality. Very simple at first was this hospitality, but growing more elaborate with the passing of years and many descriptions come back to us of those "parties." Guests were bidden to them by tiny cards from "Mr. ——— and lady desiring the pleasure of your company at half-past six o'clock" or some other specified hour.

We may be sure at whatever hour bidden that when the guests started to the party the twilight had not yet descended, and as they proceeded along the streets—frequently filled with pools of water—they must have often watched the lovely purple shadows on Ben Lomond turned to crimson and gold by the setting sun.

Conversation was generally the entertainment at such gatherings, only; tradition tells us when the party occurred at the big brick house of John Cain, his wife, Beersheba, varied the entertainment by singing and playing on her "pianoforte from Philadelphia"—the first one in the town; and we know (in letters from his granddaughter) that Doctor William Pitt Lawrence, a genial, social gentleman, often sang "by ear" in melodious voice the songs of Thomas Moore, and we may feel sure these best loved old songs upon occasion were heard floating out of doors and windows when Doctor Lawrence was at the party.*

A host would doubtless hesitate long before resorting to conversation as the sole entertainment of his guests. The host of such social gatherings as those referred to had no misgivings as to the success of his entertainment. He knew the men and women gathered there had interesting things to tell each other, things that would be told in a spirited, forceful, and often charming manner. These people had come to the little mountain town by long and devious ways, often filled by thrilling and dangerous experiences. In that pristine time of the world simply traveling

---

*Surprising tale of the rise of a young Irish emigrant to a position of national influence and importance is found in the history of the family of James Lyon of Lyonville—now Faulkner's—on Charley's Creek in Warren County. James Lyon was son of Colonel Matthew Lyon and his first wife, Mary Horsford.

The career of Colonel Lyon is too well known to give details here: his distinguished Revolutionary service under Colonel Ethan Allen, his ownership and editing of a great newspaper of the country, his imprisonment under the Alien and Sedition Act, and his election to Congress while in prison, and his loyal support of Jefferson during his term of office in Washington. During his life he had founded two manufacturing towns and was believed to be sponsor of a third—an unsuccessful attempt to found the same sort of a town as Lyonville by James Lyon, Pleasant Henderson, and Henry Beidleman.

Bible Records—Tombstone Inscriptions

through the wilderness in a covered wagon was of itself an experience of never-to-be-forgotten sights and sounds.

There were those present who knew fresh details of old historic events learned from immediate forbears who had born a part in those events. Pleasant Henderson, for instance, who, according to Samuel Laughlin, was the "most knowing business man in town," but also of agreeable presence and a fine raconteur could have told of harrowing days during the seige of the old fort at Bonesboro when his father, just lately died in his home a feeble old man, then a stalwart youth distinguished for his tall, upstanding appearance, had shared with Boone and Calloway all the dangers of death and captivity. And the tale, too, he could tell of the spectacular dash of young Samuel to rescue the girl he was to marry, Elizabeth Calloway, from the Indians.

And Margaret Campbell Rogers, who married in the town in 1811, with her husband, James Rogers, could have told them how every memory of her childhood, traveling back to the green valleys and blue mountains of East Tennessee, was haunted by the dark and skulking shadows of Indians always watching and waiting by each tree or roadside or of the part played by her father, Judge David Campbell, in the great turbulent drama of Tennessee, the history of the State of Franklin. Sion of a distinguished family of Scotland and America, Margaret Campbell Rogers long survived her husband before she went to sleep by his side in the old graveyard.

"Matthew Lyon's descendants were distinguished," said Collins in his history of Kentucky. None deserved distinction more than did his granddaughter, Eliza Lyon, who came with her parents, James Lyon and Phila Ann Risley, to Warren County before it was even a county. If a wilderness experience had been desired, she could have told of a long horseback journey she made when a small girl with her father.

They started from Lyonville in Warren County, she on her pony, her carpet bag swinging from the pommel of her saddle, and traveled down a post road that led southeastward, crossed the Cumberland Mountains, forded the lovely Sequatchee River, on over Waldens Ridge into the southern Cherokee country where they often stopped in Indian houses for rest and refreshment. Reaching to the great sweeping Tennessee River, where Chattanooga now stands, but where no Chattanooga stood for many years, this was in the year 1809, they were ferried across by Indians, as Indians were given the right of ferriage along the post roads. Their crossing place was believed to have been the old fording place of the Chickamaugas while they lived in their towns on Chickamauga River. Crossing over, the Lyons passed into the great Federal road which, after traversing Tennessee, penetrated the

Bible Records—Tombstone Inscriptions

State of Georgia. Here Eliza Lyon was placed in a noted southern school for girls.

Phila Risley and Nancy Pomeroy Risley were the wives respectively of James Lyon and William Pitt Lawrence. Soon after his removal to Warren County, Doctor Lawrence enlisted as surgeon under Jackson at New Orleans and during his absence his wife remained at Lyonville. Letters yet exist written by Mrs. Lawrence from Lyonville to her mother, Mrs. Eunice Grant Risley mention the fact that she "is living across the street from Sister Lyon in one of Mr. Lyon's houses." During the absence of Dr. Lawrence, his son, John Marshall Lawrence, was born who became the husband of Rachel Jackson.

Dr. Lawrence later removed into McMinnville and in 1829-30 approximately removed to Nashville. He left one daughter, Mary, in McMinnville. She was the wife of Robert B. Caim; died young and is buried in the old graveyard.

Phila Risley Lyon is said to have been beautiful in her youth and was all her life long the possessor of a magnetic charm that enabled her to enlist the sympathy and help of others in her many fine activities. She and her daughter, Eliza Lyon Mitchell, lived long in the town distinguished as educated, cultured ladies and still remembered and beloved for all their good works.

With her daughter and other members of her family, Phila Risley Lyon sleeps in the old graveyard.

SITUATION OF THE OLD GRAVEYARD AND ITS FIRST USE AS A PLACE OF INTERMENT

In 1812 one hundred and twenty-three years ago, and one year after the first sale of lots in the town, occurred the interment of Samuel Colville in the cemetery adjoining McMinnville and now known for many years as the old graveyard.

Traditionally, Samuel Colville was the first person buried there and as the spot was taken from the land of his father-in-law, Robert Cowan, the tradition is doubtless true.

It was situated about one-quarter of a mile from the main street of the town on the recently opened Winchester road and being almost surrounded by a forest was for that reason regarded as being in the country. Its convenience and perhaps the beauty of its situation being in plain view of the mountains and river influenced others and it soon became what it has remained for about sixty years the one and only burial place of the town.

The original limits remain the same. The western boundary is still a line of picturesque cedar bluffs, rising high above the Barren Fork River flowing at its base; the eastern boundary was and still is the Winchester road, which bounding the entire length of the cemetery descended a hill and crossed the Barren Fork at the ford

Bible Records—Tombstone Inscriptions

of Polly Black, the first woman mentioned in Warren County history.

Traditions from the early days in McMinnville claim that for the first years in its history the dead of the town were not carried to the cemetery in vehicles, but borne on the shoulders of men walking in the streets, the families and friends following in procession behind. Whether there is truth in this old echo from the past is not known or whether if true the custom was local or a hand-down from much older and far-away countries, but one corroboration comes from an eye witness—a very venerable and responsible woman told the writer of this article many years ago that as a very young girl she saw the coffin containing the body of Capt. William White carried on the shoulders of men walking in the street on their way to the old burial ground. Captain William White died in 1816.

A driveway originally intersected the cemetery and on either side and branching off in various directions were lots, some of them enclosed in iron railings or picket fences and one other style, stone pillars standing at intervals about the lot connected by heavy swinging chains. Near the central part of the lot, also the first in use, was a row of square, connected brick enclosure, the walls built several feet above the ground. Evidently burial lots, but whose no one seems to know.

As the years passed on the lots were made the objects of tender care and attention by their owners living in the town. Magnolia trees were planted, rare shrubs and evergreens—a flowering, very fragrant box plant among them—and roses and gradually the spot became beautiful with all the planting and tending, and lovely green things grew everywhere, all bathed in the soft tremulous light of quiet serenity that comes to old loved places tenderly cared for.

This was the appearance of the cemetery remembered by persons now gone, but who in the days preceding the War between the States went there often for the soothing quiet and sweetness of the scene.

We know, too, from those same persons, as well as from early newspaper articles that this beautifications of the graveyard by those old residents of the town was the only permanent work ever done there; that they alone, apparently, felt the urge and desire to make it a fit resting place for an honored and respected people.

And so at last with the passing of time they were all brought to the old graveyard to sleep under the trees they had planted and the sweetness they had created.

During the war, and the years following, perhaps there was so much sorrow in the land only the living were thought of and the cemetery was brought forcibly to mind when some gallant soldier

Bible Records—Tombstone Inscriptions

was brought back from the war. Then came the need for a new cemetery for the town, and after this was established only occasionally interments on family lots were made and none now for many years.

A few old trees still stand guard over forgotten spots and lonely groups of box mark places where some beloved ones are buried. Not so long ago two huge bushes of the very old rose of former times, the Microphylla, still outlined the former driveway.

The list that follows is only a partial one of the persons buried in the old graveyard—perhaps not more than a third, but all that could be gotten from family records, from facts, and the few stones left undisturbed there:

Isham Randolph of Goochland County, Va., married Sally Payne; removed to Warren County, Tenn., in its early organization. Died in Warren County in town of McMinnville. Sally Payne, born in Virginia, descended in two lines from distinguished Payne family, wife of Isham Randolph.

George R. Smartt, born in Tennessee, son of Francis Smartt and wife, Martha Cheek, both of Mecklenburg County, North Carolina, removed early to Warren County, Tenn.; married Athelia Randolph; died at his home, "Woodlawn," in 1855. Athelia, daughter of Isham Randolph and wife, Sally Payne, born in Hawkins County, Tenn., in 1791; married George R. Smartt in McMinnville, Tenn.; died in McMinnville.

One of the last burials in the old graveyard was that of Mrs. Mary V. Hill, daughter of George R. Smartt and wife, Athelia Randolph, and wife of General Benjamin J. Hill. Benjamin J. Hill, born in Warren County, Tenn., son of Benjamin Hill and wife—Pickett; died in McMinnville, Tenn. Brigadier-General in service of C. S. A.

Of the two or three generations of the Payne connection in the old graveyard were two daughters of Rodham Renner and wife, Malinda Payne, of Hawkins County, Tenn., originally from Virginia. Matilda and Elizabeth married respectively to Alexander Shields and George Savage and own cousins of Sally Payne, wife of Isham Randolph. The Savage family was later removed to the new cemetery.

Myra, daughter of Isham Randolph and wife, Sally Payne, married her cousin, Alfred Payne, of a different but connected line, son of Captain William Payne and wife, Orpha. His sister, Paulina Payne, married John Davidson Lusk of Warren County, Tenn., but who died from home and is not buried with the others of Payne connections in old graveyard. One of the last of the family buried there was "Orville Sydenham Payne, infant son of Alfred and Myra Payne," inscribed on a tiny stone, the only clue left of the connection between the Paynes and Sydenham families of Goochland County, Va.

Mary Ann Smith, born near South West Point, Tenn., daughter of Colonel Merriwether Smith, once Commandant of South West Point, was descended through her mother from Payne-Clark families of Virginia, believed to be connected with the family already noted. Colonel Alexander Black died from home.

Stokely Donelson Rowan was born in Overton County, Tenn., son of Major Henry Rowan and wife, Elizabeth Latham; married first to Lucretia Hord of Hawkins County, Tenn., and second to Jane, wife of James (or John) Grundy, son of Felix Grundy; maiden name McCullough and granddaughter of Governor Caswell of North Carolina, a bridesmaid of Mrs. J. K. Polk. Mary Grundy, daughter of James (or John) Grundy and wife, Jane McCullough, married first to Walter

Bible Records—Tombstone Inscriptions

Scott; second, to Colonel Philip Marbury of McMinnville.
Ann Hord was born in Hawkins County, Tenn., in 1821; married Lorenzo Dow Mercer of McMinnville, Tenn., in 1840; died in 1851. Lorenzo Dow Mercer was born in Wayne County, Ky., Nov. 28, 1810, son of Richard and Mary Mercer. Mercer removed to Warren County, Tenn., in 1831; married Ann Hord; died in McMinnville. Lieut. Elza Mercer, son of Richard and Mary Mercer, member of Company of Mountain Blues, Capt. Adrian Northcutt, 1st Tennessee Regiment; died in McMinnville, Tenn. Howard Mercer, wife, Priscilla. Rebecca, daughter of Howard Mercer and wife, Priscilla, first wife of Philip H. Marbury of Warren County, Tenn.
Robert Alexander Campbell was born in Richmond, Va., in 1812, son of James Austin Campbell and wife, Mary Massie Vaughn, of Nelson County, Va., graduate of Yale University; married Sarah Ann Harrison, daughter of Joshua Stone Harrison and wife, Judith Turner Harrison. Lawyer and teacher of McMinnville; died, 1854.
Joshua Stone Harrison, son of Answorth Harrison and wife, Dolly Coleman Stone, of Pittsylvania County, Va., died in McMinnville. Judith Turner Harrison was born in Pittsylvania County, Va.; married Joshua Stone Harrison.
John Cain was born in Kentucky, son of William Cain and wife, Hannah; came to McMinnville about 1815; married Beersheba Porter Sullivan, merchant and land dealer; died in McMinnville about 1837. Beersheba Porter Sullivan, daughter of one of the earliest settlers of Warren County, and wife of John Cain, died at advanced age at home of her daughter, Mrs. Mary Cain Stubblefield. In 1833 discovered the spring on top of Cumberland Mountain named for her.
Hiram B. Stubblefield, son of George Stubblefield and wife, Mary Jeffries, married Mary, daughter of John and Beersheba Cain. This family claimed descent from Colonel George Stubblefield of Spottsylvania County, Va.

John Josiah Morford was born in 1799 in Princeton, N. J., son of Zebulon Morford and wife, Mary Denton; graduate of Princeton University; came to McMinnville about 1820; lawyer and Chancery Court Clerk for many years; married Jane B. Taylor; died in McMinnville in 1869. Jane B. Taylor was born in Warren County, Tenn., daughter of Edmund Taylor and wife, Polly Robards; married John Josiah Morford; died at her home in Warren County, Tenn. Through her father, Jane Taylor Morford was a lineal descendant of the Pendleton family of Virginia, of Charles Lewis of the Byrd and the Howell families of Virginia.
Landon A. Kincannon, grandson of Andrew Kincannon and Catherine McDonald, son of James Kincannon and wife, Elizabeth Armstrong, daughter of Hugh Armstrong and wife, Martha Dismukes. Andrew Kincannon was at King's Mountain. Cyrena Roberson of Rutherford County, Tenn., wife of Landon A. Kincannon and niece of Edward Ward of Davidson County, Tenn.
John Lyle Shaw was born in Augusta County, Va., in 1780, son of Robert Shaw and wife, Esther Blair, both from County Antrim, Ulster Province, Ireland; married Sarah Davidson, daughter of John Davidson, Rockbridge County, Va., and wife, Sarah Roates; came to Tennessee in 1800; was in the War of 1812; died in Warren County, 1852. Sarah Allen Shaw was born in 1810, daughter of John Lyle Shaw and wife, Sarah Davidson, and wife of James Clare Spurlock, son of Drury Spurlock and wife, Olive Clare; died at her home in Warren County, Tenn., in 1844. Drury Clare Spurlock was born in 1833, son of James C. and Sarah A. Spurlock. Captain of Company C. Savage's 16th Tennessee Regiment; killed at battle of Murfreesboro, Tenn. Chamberlayne Spurlock was born on April 7, 1842, son of James C. and Sarah A. Spurlock; died March 10, 1873.

Bible Records—Tombstone Inscriptions

Pleasant Henderson, son of Colonel Samuel Henderson and wife, Elizabeth, came to Warren County about 1807; married Agnes Robards in North Carolina; nephew of Judge Richard Henderson of Transylvania history; died in 1837. Buried in old graveyard by the side of his wife and his father who died in 1810.

Joshua Coffee was born in Smith County, Tenn.; died at his home in Warren County in 1842; age fifty-five years. Wife of Joshua Coffee, Jane Trousdale, daughter or niece of Governor Trousdale. Her burial in old graveyard uncertain.

Rachel Shelley Thompson was born in Davidson County, Tenn., in 1804, daughter of Thomas Edmondson and wife, Martha Buchanan, and wife of James Powell Thompson; died in McMinnville in 1859. John Lucas Thompson, son of James Powell Thompson and wife, Rachel Shelley Thompson, born in McMinnville in 1833; educated in Virginia; lawyer. Captain in Company C, Savage's 16th Tennessee C. S. A., after death of Captain Drury Spurlock in 1862. James Powell Thompson was buried in Riverside Cemetery.

Dr. Thomas Boyd died in McMinnville in 1830; wife, Buchanan.

William Edmondson was born in Washington County, Va., son of John Edmondson and wife, Mary Buchanan; removed to McMinnville in its early settlement; married Myra Coffee, daughter of Ambrose Coffee. William Edmondson and wife, Myra, died of fever in 1832; their deaths occurring close together.

Captain William White, Revolutionary soldier, died in McMinnville in 1816. William White was born in 1800, son of Captain William White and wife, Bathia Lyne; removed to McMinnville about 1810; married Patsy Buchanan; died in McMinnville. Patsy Buchanan was born in Davidson County, Tenn., in 1800, daughter of Thomas Edmondson and wife, Martha Buchanan, wife of William White, Jr.

Sion Spencer Read, son of Captain John Nash Read and wife, Julia Elizabeth Spencer, born in Charlotte County, Va., April 22, 1791; married his cousin, Hardenia Jefferson Spencer, in 1819; died in McMinnville in 1845. Was in the War of 1812 in Gen. John Coffee's Regiment of Cavalry and later in Williamson's Mounted Gunmen of Tennessee. Hardenia Jefferson Spencer was born in Virginia in 1803; married her cousin, Sion Spencer Read, in 1819. Married second to Doctor Melchizadec Hitt in 1849; died Sept. 6, 1889. Sion Spencer Read and his wife, Hardenia, married first, Dillard Thomas Jefferson. Haniel Read, daughter of Sion Spencer Read and wife, Hardenia, married, first, Dillard Stone; second, Samuel Pennybaker. Archibald Stone was born July 12, 1805; died, 1879; wife, Sarah Wood.

Mary French was born in Nelson County, Va., daughter of Colonel John Hopkins and wife, Mary King, wife of Robert French; removed to McMinnville in 1826; died in about 1846.

John S. Young, Secretary of State of Tennessee; married Mrs. Jane Colville Preston in McMinnville; died in 1857; buried in old graveyard. Jane Colville Young was born in McMinnville, daughter of Joseph Colville and second wife, Mrs. Martha Cheek Smartt; married first, James Preston of Washington County, Va.; second, John S. Young.

Thomas North Clark died in 1834, Virginia. Elizabeth Garth Clark died in 1831; buried in old graveyard. Surviving little daughter rode horseback behind the relative who came from Virginia for her. A granddaughter came from Charlottesville, Va., in 1932 searching for graves of her ancestors.

Miss Betsy Langdon died April 7, 1863.

Edward Hoge was born in Virginia; removed early to McMinnville; died in 1844. Said to be descendant of Capt. Peter Hogg of Augusta County, Va. Susan Montgomery Hoge was born in Augusta County, Va.

Bible Records—Tombstone Inscriptions

BITS OF HISTORIC INTEREST IN FRANKLIN COUNTY, TENNESSEE

By ENZENA SMITH WILLIAMS

Ten miles west from Winchester, the county seat of Franklin County, on Memphis Highway Number 15, passing through the section of the country called Belvidere, in a direct line to Old Salem as a road turns south to Maxwell, is a small marker with this inscription:

"Two miles south is buried Polly Finley Crocket. One mile south is the well that David Crocket dug at his old home."

On a small bronze plate attached to the marker is this:

"Erected by the James Lewis Chapter, D. A. R., Franklin County."

Now go about one-fourth mile south to Maxwell, then one and one-half miles east and here is the piece of land on which was located "Old Kentucky," the home of David Crocket, where he lived with his first wife, Polly Finley Crocket. The old well marks the spot near which the house stood. It is now enclosed in a rail pen, and on examination one discovers it to be a well of the long ago. It is not built up at the top as were the latter day wells, but is even with the surface and is not very deep, but the opening is unusually wide; it is walled with large stones and they grow smaller as the well goes deeper. The stones are carpeted with green moss, and they appear like steps leading down, so much so that one feels like stepping down for a drink of its historic water. The well is kept in healthful condition and waters the stock of Boone Templeton, owner of the place, who is a direct descendant of Daniel Boone on his mother's side and a distant kinsman of David Crocket.

Now go on east about three miles and in and out winds Beans Creek among the remnants of woodlands where David Crocket loved to roam. Here the distinguished woodsman—and in my humble opinion the most valiant hero of all time—loved to roam. Here he lived and made merry and gave out vigor of life and strength of character to that great old Beans Creek neighborhood and left in his wake some of the highest type citizens of Tennessee, whom I shall liken to the finest and most splendid stones which when the outer crust is worn away become polished and beautiful as the years go by. I have often heard it said that in this neighborhood have dwelt the "cream of creation." Amid these surroundings on a small rise is a little overgrown cemetery called Brown's cemetery or more commonly called a country graveyard. Here under a pile of huge stones lies the dust of Polly Finley Crocket, a name still held in enhancing memory by the Beans Creek citizens. One would find difficulty in identifying the

Bible Records—Tombstone Inscriptions

grave as it is not marked. Old citizens of the community—some of them, claim they know the exact spot—say it is one of two piles of stone, but since one of these cairns is marked by some other name we are left to choose the unmarked grave as that of Polly Finley Crocket.

When Polly Crocket died David Crocket courted and married a widow Patton who had two sons. Mrs. Katherine Kelly, who was reared in this neighborhood, but now of Memphis, tells this incident as a fact:

"My great grandfather, Richard Callaway, was a magistrate in that community and knew Crocket as a friend, was called to the home of the Widow Patton to perform the wedding ceremony. Mr. Calloway and David Crocket waited in the front room while the bride to be was dressing for the ceremony. A pet pig as was his custom sauntered in and Mr. Crocket, in his native way, with his foot invited him out saying: 'I'm running things here today.' "

This Memphis Highway Number 15, which doubtless should have been named David Crocket Highway, was once the old stage coach road from New Orleans to Philadelphia, but known in the community as "to Huntsville" and later as "Winchester and Huntsville road" or "to Fayetteville."

About twelve miles from Winchester on this road stands an old brick tavern, or a part of it. There are two stories consisting of four rooms. It has been painted gray and the walls are in good state of preservation. Old citizens in the community still visualize the distant notes of the stage coach bugle around the curves or among the hills and hollows as the vibrating, interesting, monstrous conveyance was announced long before its arrival at the inn. And many stories are still extant of the distinguished visitors who were guests there during the stage coach days while Mrs. Cowan and Mrs. Gillispie operated it. About one mile from there at Branchville there were large barns and there was "much water"; and there the horses were taken out, watered and fed; and while the guests were comfortably resting at the tavern a mile away fresh horses were ready and waiting to replace tired ones who had been rushed and even galloped to meet the exigencies of the "rapid transit" of the good old fantastic stage coach days.

ANDREW JACKSON AS I REMEMBER HIM
By MRS. EMILY DONELSON WALTON

I am the only woman and, no doubt, the only living person today who knew Andrew Jackson during his lifetime. Our families have been most intimately associated. His wife, Rachel Donelson, was my father's (Stockly Donelson) aunt and was my great aunt. My home, Cleveland Hall, was possibly a mile from the Hermitage. Of course at that time I was just a little girl, and now in a few days I will be 90 years old, so you see that has been a long time ago.

I first remember General Jackson as he came to our house to visit my grandmother (Mary Pernell Donelson), his sister-in-law, whom he always addressed as "Sister Mary." He was usually received and entertained in my grandmother's room. I can distinctly remember how he looked as he entered my grandmother's room through what was called the back parlor, but what you children of today would call the "living room." He seemed so very tall to me as he came through the doorway. Our families attended the same church, the little Hermitage church that you passed as you came out here today. His pew was just in front of ours, and there I remember seeing him.

I often accompanied my mother on visits to the Hermitage, and I remember seeing the great Jackson, now quite an old man, sitting in his big arm chair covered with brown linen, wearing his flowered dressing gown, the same that is draped on the chair in the same room where I saw him; this must have been a short time before his death. I remember the afternoon he died. I with my sisters were taking a walk through the lane near by our home when we were startled by a "courier" on horseback tearing by, calling out as he went by "General Jackson is dead!" We were terror stricken and hastily returned home. I attended the funeral with my father and mother, which took place here at the Hermitage. The grounds were filled with soldiers and many people from Nashville and all the country around. I remember seeing the metal coffin, which was placed on a pedestal in front of the great doorway. I remember seeing many flags, but do not remember seeing any flowers and that was the last I saw of President Andrew Jackson who did so much for his country. He was a Revolutionary soldier and a great general. He drove the Indians away that were killing the early settlers. He whipped the Spanish in Florida that were helping the Indians. He whipped the British at New Orleans who had never been conquered and ended the Rev-

---

Note.—Mrs. Walton sat on the porch at the Hermitage and talked to the David Crockett Society, C. A. R., and the children were so interested in her story that I asked her to write it for me and she graciously did so. On August 30, 1933, Mrs. Walton will be ninety-six years old. On April 24, 1933, she assisted in unveiling a monument marking the grave of her great-grandmother, Rachel Stockley Donelson, and a memorial to her great-grandfather, Col. John Donelson. This marking was on the anniversary of the landing of Colonel Donelson's boat, "The Good Adventure," at Nashville, or as it was then Fort Nashborough. After the exercises, Mrs. Walton received her large family connection and many friends at a luncheon in her home, Glen Echo, where all were happy to pay tribute to this very remarkable woman who has lived through so much of her country's history and has made such contribution to its progress.   MRS. ACKLEN.

olutionary War. He helped to make America a great nation and next to George Washington he was "our greatest American." As long as you children live I hope you will visit this sacred place where he lived and died and where his body lies buried beside his wife, his beloved Rachel; and always remember what he did for this country, which has become one of the greatest nations on earth. And as children of the American Revolution you must love and serve always and give your loyal support.
Emily Donelson Walton.
Glen Echo, Madison, Tenn., August 9, 1927.

MARKER TO THOMAS SPENCER, PIONEER, UNVEILED AT CASTALIAN SPRINGS

INSCRIPTION ON MARKER

"On this spot stood the hollow sycamore tree in which Thomas Sharpe Spencer spent the winter of 1778-79, deserted by his companions for fear of Indians. Spencer helped build at Bledsoe's Lick, fifty yards south of this spot, the first cabin in Middle Tennessee and planted the first crop of corn. He was killed by Indians April 1, 1794, on the site since known as Spencer's Hill, Van Buren County, Tenn. This marker erected by General James Robertson Chapter, D. A. R., 1927."

This marker was presented to the General James Robertson Chapter during the regency of Mrs. E. B. Stahlman by Mrs. J. Byron Martin.

Judge John H. DeWitt made an address on "The Pioneer" on the unveiling of this marker. The marker stands on the roadside near Castalian Springs in Sumner County.

TRIBUTE TO PIONEERS

"This tablet commemorating the first residence of a white person in Sumner County, Thomas Spencer (who lived here in a hollow tree) expresses our homage to the great and daring pioneers who began civilized life in this beautiful country. The settlements at Bledsoe's Lick (now Castalian Springs) were almost contemporary with the settlements at the French Lick (later Nashville). The settlers were isolated in the heart of the wilderness and their only protection from marauding Indians was their undaunted courage and the stockade enclosures around their cabins. Near this place to the west Col. Isaac Bledsoe built the first block house and stockade. Two and one-half miles northward his brother, Col. Anthony Bledsoe, built a like station. They came from the border of Virginia and what is now Tennessee about the year 1781. On Oct. 8, 1787, there were granted to Anthony Bledsoe the Greenfield tract of 6,280 acres, and to Isaac Bledsoe several adjoining

Bible Records—Tombstone Inscriptions

tracts, including more than 2,000 acres. Col. Anthony Bledsoe was killed by the Indians at Isaac Bledsoe's station on July 20, 1788. Col. Isaac Bledsoe was killed by the Indians near the same place in 1793. Both left large families, and many illustrious people have traced their ancestry to them. Anthony Bledsoe was a colonel in the colonial wars and a major of militia in the Revolution. Col. Isaac Bledsoe was a member of the party of hunters and explorers which penetrated to the Cumberland country in 1771, and on this expedition he discovered the spring to which was given the name Bledsoe's Lick. He it was who in 1781 made a perilous journey with James Robertson to the settlements in Kentucky to secure much-needed ammunition for the Cumberland settlers. The Indians gave to him the name of Tullikoska, the waving corn blade or perpetual motion. Hither came many hearty emigrants from the Watauga, North Carolina, and from Virginia. Many of them were fresh from the battlefields of the Revolution and brought with them the rifles and the muskets with which they had helped to win independence for their country. Most of them were of obscure birth and accustomed to poverty. Both men and women had brave hearts and were determined to withstand all adversities. They were progenitors of as fine a race of people as ever spoke the English language.

"The Cherokees and Creeks waged upon these settlers a long and merciless warfare, which ended only when all danger from Indians was terminated at the Battle of Nickajack Cave in 1794.

"The roll of martyrs to the cause of civilization upon this soil numbers more than seventy-five. These men, women, children, and slaves were murdered by Indians between 1781 and 1794. Some of the outstanding pioneer settlers who had been Revolutionary soldiers were Gen. James Winchester and his two brothers, George and Stephen; Gen. Griffith Rutherford, David Wilson, Anthony and Isaac Bledsoe and William Cage, who had been treasurer of the state of Franklin. In 1840 there were still living in Sumner County at least thirty old Revolutionary soldiers. The martial spirit of the people was strong from the beginning. They and their descendants have fought valiantly in all the wars. Sumner County was established by act of the North Carolina legislature on Nov. 17, 1785, out of Davidson County, as the second county in Middle Tennessee. The first court was held in April, 1787, at the house of John Hamilton, about five miles southwest from where Gallatin now is. The members of that court were Gen. Daniel Smith, Maj. David Wilson, Maj. George Winchester, Isaac Lindsey, William Hall (father of Gov. William Hall), John Hardin, Joseph Kuykendall, Col. Edward Douglas, and Col. Isaac Bledsoe. David Shelby,

Bible Records—Tombstone Inscriptions

son-in-law of Col. Anthony Bledsoe, was appointed clerk and held that position until his death in 1822. They were men of education, sound judgment, good morals, and of good influence in the community. The first town in the county was called Ca Ira, now known as Cairo, on Cumberland River. The original name was taken from a song of the French revolution.

"Gallatin was laid out and finally designated as the county seat under an act passed on November 6, 1801. It was named in honor of Albert Gallatin. It was incorporated on November 7, 1815. From 1787 to 1800 the first court of Sumner County was held at homes of its members. From 1800 to 1802 it was held at Cairo. From October, 1802, to January, 1803, the court was held at the house of James Trousdale in Gallatin. The first court held under the Tennessee state govenment was in July, 1796, at the home of Ezekiel Douglas. It was composed of the following members, commissioned by Gov. John Sevier: William Case, Stephen Cantrell, James Douglas, Edward Douglas, James Gwynn, Wetherel Lattimore, Thomas Masten, Thomas Donald, James Pearce, David Wilson, James Winchester, and Isaac Walton.

"The ground upon which Gallatin was located originally belonged to James Trousdale, father of Gov. William Trousdale. By the year 1830 Sumner County had a population of 20,606.

"The first school in Sumner County was at Bledsoe's Lick, established in 1788. George Hamilton was the schoolmaster. One night the schoolmaster was sitting in Col. Anthony Bledsoe's room at his brother's fort, singing at the top of his voice. Indians were prowling around and one of them found a hole in the back of the chimney, through which he poked his gun and fired, hitting Hamilton in the chin. The teacher recovered, but what became of him afterwards history does not record and tradition is silent."

The speaker quoted from the late Maj. J. G. Cisco in his "Historic Sumner County": "Place one foot of a compass on a line between Gallatin and Bledsoe's Lick, and about six miles east of the first named place, then draw a circle the diameter of which shall be twenty miles, and you will have within that radius a territory in which it would be difficult to find a more beautiful, more fertile, or one richer in historical associations. And, too, it would be hard to find a territory of the same extent in which more men known to fame have had their homes."

"This memorial is dedicated to every exalted sentiment in the hope that the spirit of these devoted people will rest upon us," said Judge DeWitt in conclusion. "About us are the stirring of

Bible Records—Tombstone Inscriptions

unseen wings. May it be a great incentive to noble endeavor and useful achievement."

A sycamore tree has been planted to the rear of the monument. The exactness of the site of the original tree is verified by a tradition in the Wynne family.

QUAINT WYNNE HOME NEAR THE MARKER

A visit to the quaint Wynne homestead was one of the delightful features of the day, and here the guests were welcomed by Mr. and Mrs. George Wynne. The century-old house is of sturdy oak and ash logs, with an L extension, and the typical office nearby, built of cedar logs. The quaint stairway in the enclosed central porch and the woodwork are attractive features, and the furniture includes beautiful old specimens which would delight a collector.

The spacious house was first erected by a stock company as an inn, and a year or so later it became the residence of Col. Alfred R. Wynne, one of the original owners. Colonel Wynne married Almira Winchester, daughter of Gen. James Winchester, Revolutionary soldier and soldier in the War of 1812, close friend of Andrew Jackson, and this pioneer family included fourteen children. The property remains today in the possession of the Wynne family.

In the yard the stately trees include a hickory which was planted by Colonel Wynne on the day of the death of Andrew Jackson to commemorate the great soldier President.

SOUTHWEST POINT, KINGSTON, TENNESSEE
SENT BY MRS. B. C. WATKINS, HARRIMAN

Some historical facts gleaned from the following sources:
1. G. F. Mellen, miscellaneous papers, Vol. 2, page 73.
2. Wells, Roane County.
3. Williams. Early Travels in the Tennessee Country.
4. *The Knoxville Gazette.*

In 1791-1793 *Gen. John Sevier* established a fort on the Clinch River at the present site of Kingston. The main fort was near the famous Clark Springs which now supplies the town with water. General Sevier called the military post *Southwest Point.*

A detachment of United States soldiers, under command of Capt. Abraham McClellan, was stationed there to protect the settlers and travelers from the Indians. Thomas Brown was the first quartermaster; Dr. Daniel Rather was the surgeon.

The troops were stationed there until 1817. It was an important place on the frontier. Those who went from Knoxville and Knox County to the Cumberland settlements were accompanied by a detachment of soldiers from *Southwest Point.* All that country was then a wilderness and was Indian territory.

Bible Records—Tombstone Inscriptions

In 1792 Capt. Samuel Hadley, at the head of his soldiers, went forth from *Southwest Point* and was captured and imprisoned by Indians but later returned.

William Lea was captured but escaped August, 1892. Abraham Byrd was wounded. Samuel Russell, bearing dispatches from the Cumberland settlements to William Blount at Knoxville was wounded by the Indians at *Southwest Point;* the surgeon, Dr. Daniel Rather, dressed his wounds.

In 1794 Thomas Sharp Spencer started from *Southwest Point* to Nashville with money and other valuables and was murdered on the Cumberland road at Spencers Hill.

On March 6, 1796, Andrew Michaux, botanist and agent of Genet, stopped at *Southwest Point* on his way to Knoxville.

In 1797 Capt. John Wade was commandent.

In 1797 Louis Phillippe, Duke of Orleans, afterwards King of France, and his brother, passed through and were entertained at *Southwest Point*. The commandant had bread baked for them.

In 1799 Capt. Thomas Butler was in command at *Southwest Point*.

In 1799 the Tennessee legislature passed an act to establish a town at *Southwest Point* upon the land of Robert King. The town was to be called Kingston. At this time Davis' school for Cherokee Indians was in operation at *Southwest Point*.

In 1800 Bishop Francis Asbury was hospitably entertained at the home of Thomas N. Clark near *Southwest Point*.

In 1801 Roane County was created.

September 21, 1807, the General Assembly of Tennessee met at Kingston. Thus Kingston, formerly *Southwest Point*, was for a time the capital of the state.

John Riley was chief of the Cherokee Indians in this territory; he is buried in an unmarked grave by the side of Highway No. 58. This highway runs through the old Hiawassee Purchase and was Cherokee country.

Kingston was a trading post and was on a beaten trail from New York and Washington to Texas.

HISTORIC SPOTS OF TENNESSEE
COMPILED BY MRS. A. S. BOWEN
State Chairman Historic Spots, Daughters of American Revolution, 1930-1931

JOHNSON COUNTY
Boone Trail.
Home of Andres Taylor (ancestors of Governors Bob and Alf Taylor).
Shoanes Ford.
Lost Lead Mine on Doe Mt.
Boone's Gap, headwaters of Doe River.
Camping Place of Honeycut on Roane Creek
Iron Works of Roane Creek.

CARTER COUNTY
Sycamore Shoals.

Bible Records—Tombstone Inscriptions

Fort Lee.
Where Andrew Johnson died.
The Tipton Home.
Happy Valley Home of Bob Taylor.
The Court Oak Tree.
Watauga Old Fields.

SULLIVAN COUNTY
Long Island.
Fort Patrick Henry.
Kingsport.
Great Indian War Path.
Kings Meadow (Bristol).
Fort Womack (Bluff City).
Weaverville Cemetery.
Rock Holt Campground.
Old Netherland Tavern.
The Doak-Rhea Elm Tree.
Site of Old Silk Mill.
Evan Shelby Fort.
Grave of Gen. George Rutledge.
Cobb House.
Earhart Elm.
Fort Robinson, 1761.
Old Boat Yard.
Buffalo Ridge Baptist Church.
Old Presbyterian Church near Piney Flats.
Choates Ford.
Holston Valley.

WASHINGTON COUNTY
Washington College.
Home of John Sevier.
Jonesboro, oldest town in Tennessee.
Home of William Bean.
William Bean Mill.
Home of Chris Taylor, where Andrew Johnson first lived.
Home of John Sevier (second home).
Site of organization of State of Franklin.
Field where Andrew Jackson fought duel with Colonel Avery.
Tree where Daniel Boone "Killed the Bar."
Grave of Jesse Duncan.
Boone Falls, where Boone hid from Indians.
The Embry House.
Sinking Creek Baptist Church, 1783.
Grave of Samuel Doak.
Site of first Methodist Conference, 1793.
The Brown Settlement.
Duncan's Mill.
Old Jonesboro Cemetery.
Cherokee Baptist Church, 1783.

Buckham Inn.
Old Chester House, 1795.
Gillespie House.
David Dradrick House.

GREENE COUNTY
Home of Andrew Johnson.
Andrew Johnson Tailor Shop.
Site of first capitol of State of Franklin.
Tusculum College.
Birthplace of Davy Crockett.
First log house of Greeneville College, 1794.
Crockett's Landing.
Old Rheatown.
Grave of Hesikaih Blach.
Site of Old Presbyterian Church.

HAWKINS COUNTY
Rogersville, second oldest town.
First newspaper published.
Rogersville Female College, first female college in state.
Indian War Path.
Brown Settlement, second in the state.
Graves of Joseph Crockett and wife, grandparents of Davy Crockett.
Galbreath Springs.
Site of first courthouse, built 1795.
Site of pillary and whipping post.
Old Rogers Tavern.
Home of Gov. Joseph McMinn.
Marble Hall.
Carter's Valley.
Mulberry Grove — Senator Wm. Cocke.
Home of Gov. Joseph McMinn, 1815-21.

UNICIO COUNTY
Greasy Cove Race Track.
Buffalo Spring.
Campground of John Sevier.

HANCOCK COUNTY
Wilderness Road.

HAMBLIN COUNTY
Indian War Path.
Home of Davy Crockett.
Home of Tidence Lane.
"Hayslope."
Home of Gov. DeWitt Center.
Panther Springs.
St. Paul's Presbyterian Church.
Nolichucky Settlement.

Bible Records—Tombstone Inscriptions

Home of David Coffman, 1788.
Mt. Harmony.
Old Brent Creek Baptist Church.

SEVIER COUNTY
Home of Isaac Thomas.
Grave of Spencer Black.
Klingman's Dome.
Indian War Path.
McCroskey Island.
Fort on Dumplin Creek, 1783.
Nancy Academy.

JEFFERSON COUNTY
Indian War Path.
Old Log Meeting House.
Maury Academy, 1806.
Home of Samuel McSpadden.
Dandridge.
Hopewell Presbyterian Church, 1785.

GRAINGER COUNTY
Beans Station.
Tates Springs (Col. James Orr).
Beans Station Gap.
Red House Inn.
Blaines Cross Roads.
Big Springs.
Site of one of first paper mills.
Site of one of first hatters.
Indian Cave.
Massengills Mill.
Cedar tree near Beans Station.

CLAIBORNE COUNTY
Fort Blackmore.
Cumberland Gap.
Log Baptist Church, 1790.
Big Springs on Sycamore Creek.
Bishop Asbury preached at Hunts, 1802.
Clinch River.

UNION COUNTY
Fort Holmack.

CAMPBELL COUNTY
Jacksboro.
Powells Valley.
Early Iron Furnaces.

KNOX COUNTY
Wm. Blount Home.
Lamar House.
John Sevier Home.
W. G. Brawnlaw Home.
Sawyer's Fort.
Farragut's Birthplace.

First Capitol of State.
Grave of John Sevier.
Grave of Bonnie Kate Sevier.
Place where Chief Tullentuski signed treaty.
Campbells Station.
Fort White.
Old Lebanon Church.
Washington Church and graveyard.
Old Washington Pike.
Site of Brakebill Mound.
Chisholm Tavern.
First Presbyterian Church.
Ramsey Home.
Carrick's Ford.
Loew's Ferry.
First block house.
Alexander Rock House.
Fort Adair.
Blount College, University of Tennessee.

BLOUNT COUNTY
Great Indian War Path.
Eusibia.
Graves of Campbell Family.
Tree where first white man camped.
Old Stone House.
Home of Col. David Henley.
Dunkard Church.
Tomotley Ford.
Eusibia Graveyard.
Big Springs Graveyard.
Baker's Creek Graveyard.
Iles Family Graveyard.
Grave of James Henry.
Grave of John Clark.
Birthplace of Ann Elizabeth Thompson, mother of Gen. J. J. Pershing.
Fort McTeer.
Fort Houston.
Fort Magoha.
Fort James Henry.
Fort McCroskey.
Fort Ish.
Fort David Craig.
Fort John Craig.
Fort Thomas.
Fort Hunter.
Fort Samuel Henry.
Fort Tedford.
Fort Kelley.
Fort Gillespie.
Fort Calvin Black.
Fort Martin.
Fort Wells.
Home of Sam Houston.
Sam Houston log schoolhouse.

Bible Records—Tombstone Inscriptions

Home of John Weir.
Montvale Springs.
Niles Ferry.

ROANE COUNTY
Southwest Point Block House.
Kingston (Capital for one day).
Home of Chief Tullentuski.
Home of Tandy Senter.
Post Oak Springs.
Historic Graveyard.
Kendrick Graveyard.
Old Stage Road.
Famous Old Inn.
Rittenhouse Academy, 1806.

LOUDON COUNTY
Old Fort Loudon.
Blairs Ferry.
Grave of Amos Marney.

MONROE COUNTY
Madisonville, site of first printing plant.
Indian War Path.
Chota—Indian town.
Telagua—Indian town.
Madisonville.
Hiawassee College.
Citico and Togua, Indian towns.
Sweetwater College.
Coker Creek Gold Mines.

MEIGS COUNTY
Home of Chief Jolly of the Cherokees.
Jolly's Island at mouth of Hiawcissee.

McMINN COUNTY
Birthplace of U. S. Senator John T. Morgan.
White Cliff Springs.
Graves of Weena and Connestoga.
Grave of Gov. Joseph McMinn.
Grave of Lieut. Isaac Lane.
Site of Home of Return J. Meigs.

POLK COUNTY
Grave of Nancy Ward.
Indian War Path.
Indian towns of old Hiwassee.
Ocowe, Indian town before 1600.
Ocoes Caverns.
Hilderbrands Stand.
Portage House.
McNair's Stand.
Fort Blockhouse, 1814.
Columbus.

Crawford Ford.
Harris Mill.
Old Federal Road.

BRADLEY COUNTY
Indian War Path.
Home of Chief Jack Walker.
Site of Cherokee Agency.
Tucker's Springs.
Indian Campground.

HAMILTON COUNTY
Site of Brainerd Mission.
Joseph Martin's Battle with Indians on Lookout Mountain.
Grave of Robert Patterson.
Citico Mounds.
Grave of Dr. James Cosby.
Ross's Landing.
Home of John Ross at Rossville.
First Cherokee post office.
The Suck of Boiling Pot.
Williams Island, or Tuskegee Island.
Chickamauga Town.
Pow-wow Camping Grounds.
Indian War Path.
First Battle of Chickamauga, 1779. (Col. Evan Shelby).
First three courthouses of Hamilton County: Poe's Tavern, Dallas, and Harrison.
Cross Roads.
Home of Capt. John Brown, Cherokee River pilot.
School at Sale Creek.
Prehistoric Fortification at Mouth of Chickamauga Creek.

RHEA COUNTY
Rhea Springs.
Old town of Washington.
Grave of Judge David Campbell.

CUMBERLAND COUNTY
Old Walton Road.

MORGAN COUNTY
Rugby Colony.

FENTRESS COUNTY
Home of John M. Clemmons, father of Mark Twain.
Home of Alvin York.
Three Forks of Wolf River.
Home of Old Man Stout—a witch.
Obedstown.

OVERTON COUNTY
Site of Fisk Academy, established, 1808.

Bible Records—Tombstone Inscriptions

Site of Alphine Institute, established, 1821.

CLAY COUNTY
The Dale, home of wife of John Sevier.

JACKSON COUNTY
Fort Blount.

PUTNAM COUNTY
Walton Road.
Standing Stone.
Monterey Springs.

WHITE COUNTY
Rock House Tavern.

GRUNDY COUNTY
Beersheba Springs.

BLEDSOE COUNTY
Old Mansion.

MARION COUNTY
Grave of Major Robert Bean.
Nickajack Cave.
Town of Running Water.

FRANKLIN COUNTY
Home of Major Wm. Russell, 1808.
Home of Jesse Bean.

COFFEE COUNTY
Stone Fort.

WARREN COUNTY
Poplar Tavern on Elk River.

DEKALB COUNTY
First mill on Smith's Fork Creek, 1797.

SMITH COUNTY
Walton Road Crossing River.
Home of Col. William Walton.
Dixon Springs.
Home of Peter Turney.

WILSON COUNTY
Red Boiling Springs.
Drake's Lick, 1797.
Spring Creek, 1799.
Home of Neddie Jacobs.
Cumberland University.

RUTHERFORD COUNTY
Home and Grave of Sam Davis.
Old Citizens Cemetery.
Old Indian War Trail.

Camp of Black Fox.
Grave of Gen. Joseph Dickson.
Old Jefferson.
Camp of Uriah Stone.

CANNON COUNTY
Birthplace of Albert B. Fall, former Secretary of Interior.

BEDFORD COUNTY
The "Brick House," built 1796.
Home of Merideth P. Gentry.
Home of J. B. Gowen.
Home of Davy Crockett.
Grave of Wm. Pearson.
Grave of Polly Crockett.
Holly Tree Gap.
Salem Academy, 1820.

MOORE COUNTY
Site of Whipping Post.
Enoch's Campground.

LINCOLN COUNTY
Site where Jackson mobilized troops for Horse Shoe Bend and New Orleans.
Prehistoric Mounds.

GILES COUNTY
Old Indian Reservation Line.
Congressional Reservation Line.
Sam Davis captured.
Half-way House.
Lewis Kirk House.
Home of Aaron V. Brown.
Where Sam Davis was executed.
Latitude Hill.
Pisgah Campground.
Home of Bishop Robert Paine.
Mount Moriah.
Fort Hampton on Elk River.
Ku Klux Klan organized at Pulaski.

MAURY COUNTY
Home of Col. Joseph Brown.
Grave of Col. Joseph Brown.
Home of Abram Maury and Commodore Matthew F. Maury.
Western Boundary Line.
Zion Presbyterian Church.
First home of James K. Polk.
Law offices of James K. Polk.
Burial place of Samuel and Jane Knox Polk.
Home of Senator E. W. Carmack.
Columbia Institute.
Mercer Hall.

Bible Records—Tombstone Inscriptions

Home of A. O. P. Nickalson.
Spring Hill.

WILLIAMSON COUNTY
Grave of Col. Hardy Murfree.
Home of John H. Eaton.
Boyhood home of Thomas H. Benton.
Garrison Fork Creek.
Holly Tree Gap.
Roger's Knob.
Home of Timothy Demonbreun.
Home of Gideon Blackburn, 1811-22.
Harpeth Academy, 1807.

DAVIDSON COUNTY
Fort Nashborough.
Fort Freelands.
Fort Mankcas.
Fort Union.
Fort Eatons.
Clover Bottoms.
The Hermitage.
Grave of Robert Cartwright.
Grave of Capt. John Stark.
Tusculum.
Natchez Trace.
Grave of Col. Berkley Martin.
Site of LaFayette Landing.
Grave of James Robertson.
Hunter's Hill.
Old Stone Tavern at Eaton's Place.
Buchanan Station.
Capt. John Stark's Home.
Old Craighead Place.
Haysboro.

SUMNER COUNTY
Castillian Springs.
The Spencer Tree.
Fort Bledsoe.
Ashers, near Gallatin.
Greenfield.
Manskers Station.
Station Camp Creek, 1787.

CHEATHAM COUNTY
Indian Block House at Half Pone.
Sycamore Mills.

ROBERTSON COUNTY
Kilgore Station.
Kilgore's Cave.
First school at Sulphur Fork, prior to 1805.
Liberty Academy.
Red River Baptist Church, 1791.
Cave Ridge Presbyterian Church, 1793.

Camp Ground at Mt. Zion.
Home of the so-called Bell Witch.

MONTGOMERY COUNTY
Home of John Montgomery.
Home of Martin Armstrong.
Home of Robert Nelson.
Searcy's Ferry.
Moses Renfroe Settlement.
Station of Col. Valentine Sevier.
Battle Creek.
Fort Prince.
Fort Clarksville.
Fort Neville.
Palmeyra, Part of Eutrey.
Tittsworth Massacre, 1794.

DICKSON COUNTY
Cumberland Furnace, first furnaces in the West.
Ruskin Cave.

HICKMAN COUNTY
Edmund Hickman, killed by Indians on Duck River.

LEWIS COUNTY
Natchez Trace.
Grave of Capt. Meriweather Lewis.
Colony of Swiss.

LAWRENCE COUNTY
Big Buffalo River Settlement.
Home of David Crockett.
Mayland Springs.
Monument to Soldiers of Mexican War.

WAYNE COUNTY
Crossing of Natchez Trace.
Fork of Shoal Creek.
Site of first settlement on Pine River.

PERRY COUNTY
First steamboat (General Greene) arrived, 1819).
Town Creek.
Cedar Creek.

HUMPHREYS COUNTY
General Forrest captured Federal gun boats.

BENTON COUNTY
Rustling's Creek.

HOUSTON COUNTY
Stewart Station, 1798.

Bible Records—Tombstone Inscriptions

STEWART COUNTY
First house built in 1795.
Fort Donelson.
"The Drunken Oak."
Indian Mound.
Dover Iron Furnaces, 1820.
Cumberland Rolling Mills, 1828.
Site of a Servile Insurrection.

CARROLL COUNTY
Site where Jackson and Isaac Shelby made treaty with Indians.

HARDIN COUNTY
Home of Col. Joseph Hardin, 1818.
Horse Creek—Savannah.
Old Town.
Battle of Shiloh.

HARDEMAN COUNTY
Home of Col. Ezekiel Polk.
Home of Thomas J. Hardeman.

MADISON COUNTY
Bigelow Female Academy, 1832-37.
Presbyterian Female Academy.
Prehistoric Mounds.

HAYWOOD COUNTY
Nixon Settlement.

GIBSON COUNTY
Gibson's Port.
Andrews College.

WEAKLEY COUNTY
Home of Col. Robert Weakley, 1823.
First cabin built by John Bradshaw.

OBION COUNTY
Last home of David Crockett.
Reel Foot Lake.

LAKE COUNTY
Reel Foot Lake, 1811-1812.

LAUDERDALE COUNTY
Key Corners.

TIPTON COUNTY
Home of Jesse Benton.

SHELBY COUNTY
Chisca Mounds.
DeSota Crossing.
Fort Assumption.
Fort Pickering.
Fort Ferdinando De Barancas.
Fort Adams.
Old Bell Tavern.
Isaac Rawling's Indian Trading Post.
Home of Gen. N. B. Forrest.
One time home of Jefferson Davis.
The Nashoba Venture.

BURIAL PLACES OF FIRST INHABITANTS ON TENNESSEE SOIL

By MRS. A. S. BOWEN

INDIAN MOUNDS

The burial places of the very first inhabitants on what is now Tennessee soil were in large, high heaps known to us as Indian Mounds. In these mounds were placed not only the body of the deceased, but much of his private property such as trinkets, tools, and sacrificial offerings. Many of these mounds remain intact today, although ruthless explorers have unnecessarily demolished many of them at various times. Mounds remain along Little Tennessee River and in the section of the state formerly occupied by towns of the Cherokees. More mounds have been found in Lincoln County than in any other one County. In the western part of the state, especially in Madison County, are many mounds which are said to have existed long before the Chickasaw Indians occupied this section.

Bible Records—Tombstone Inscriptions

The Citico Mound, located in Chattanooga, was originally 110x 145x15 feet in size. In 1914 the greater portion of the mound was leveled in the construction of Riverside Drive, and many interesting relics were unearthed. It is unfortunate that a monument as interesting as the Citico Mound should have been sacrificed to the building of a road *through* it when it was of sufficient historical interest to deserve having a road built *to* and *around* it.

OLD CHURCH GRAVEYARDS

Paperville.—Inscriptions on two of the stones:
Jacob Thomas, born about 1752 (or 56); died May 26, 1824. Jacob Thomas was a private in Capt. Noah Abraham's Company of Militia of Cumberland County, Pa., for the years 1781 and 1782. Reference: Pennsylvania Archives.)
John Thomas, born July 25, 1778; died Aug. 19, 1851.
Pleasant Grove.—Inscriptions:
Adam Thomas, Senior, born April 18, 1794; died, 1865.
Elizabeth McNew Thomas, born April 21, 1797; died June 1, 1855.
Cherokee Baptist Church.—Inscription:
Edward West, born Oct. 29, 1766; died April 8, 1849. (Edward West served in the war against the Cherokees.)
Rutledge Presbyterian.—William Cocke, one of the two first U. S. Senators from Tennessee, was buried here. His grave is unmarked.
Among other unmarked graves in this cemetery is that of Stephen Jones, Revolutionary soldier, who died Jan. 18, 1835. He was one of the first hatters of Tennessee.
Big Springs.—Inscriptions:
"Colonel Hugh Jones, born 1805; died Dec. 19, 1862.
Colonel Daniel Miller, born Dec. 6, 1769; died July 28, 1835.
Sallie Jones, born Jan. 10, 1774; died Oct. 30, 1839.
Shiloh.—The first church was built of logs about 1830 and was still standing in 1875 when the new church was constructed. There are many very old graves in the well-kept cemetery. Among the inscriptions are:
Thomas West, born May 28, 1792; died June 6, 1870.
Rachel Oliphant West, born Sept. 13, 1796; died Jan. 4, 1872.
(Thomas West was in the Battle of Horse Shoe Bend.)

OLD FAMILY GRAVEYARDS

In pioneer days there were no facilities for burying the dead—no roads, no hearse, and there was constant danger of Indians or wild beasts destroying the grave. A family burying lot was arranged near the home for protection and convenience, since the

---

Reference on *Citico Mound*: "History of Hamilton County and Chattanooga," by Zella Armstrong.

IN RECOGNITION OF
COLONEL RICHARD HENDERSON
BORN IN VIRGINIA 1735.
DIED IN NORTH CAROLINA 1785.

FOUNDER AND PROMOTER OF THE NOTED
"TRANSYLVANIA LAND COMPANY"

WHOSE PURCHASE FROM THE CHEROKEE INDIANS COVERED THE TERRITORY FROM THE WATERS OF KENTUCKY RIVER TO THAT OF CUMBERLAND.

  HIS FIRST SETTLEMENT WAS MADE AT BOONESBOROUGH, WHICH FAILED IN LOSS OF TITLE BY ACTION OF VIRGINIA.

  HIS SECOND ATTEMPT AT SETTLEMENT WAS MADE IN 1779-1780, AT THIS PLACE ON CUMBERLAND RIVER,-THEN KNOWN AS "THE FRENCH LICK."

  HE ENLISTED JAMES ROBERTSON OF THE WATAUGA SETTLEMENT TO LEAD THIS PROJECT WHILE HE ACTED AS COMMISSIONER FROM NORTH CAROLINA TO SURVEY THE BOUNDARY LINE BETWEEN THAT STATE AND VIRGINIA IN ORDER TO KNOW IN WHICH STATE THE SETTLEMENT WOULD FALL.

  EARLY IN 1780 COLONEL HENDERSON JOINED THE SETTLEMENT, PROVIDED CORN FOR ITS MAINTENANCE, THE "COMPACT" FOR ITS CIVIL GOVERNMENT AND A LAND-OFFICE FOR THE SALE OF LANDS.

  DISSATISFACTION SOON AROSE AS TO THE VALIDITY OF TITLES, DISCOURAGEMENTS AS TO PROVISIONS, AND DANGER FROM INDIANS. THE LIFE OF THE SETTLEMENT WAS SERIOUSLY THREATENED. COLONEL HENDERSON RETURNED TO NORTH CAROLINA LEAVING JAMES ROBERTSON IN CHARGE, WHO AFTER MANY TRIALS BROUGHT IT TO SUCCESS.

"COLONEL HENDERSON WAS A GENTLEMAN EMINENTLY DISTINGUISHED FOR HIS LEGAL ACQUIREMENTS, BOTH AS AN ADVOCATE AND AS A JUDGE...STILL MORE SO FOR A SOUND JUDGMENT, AS WELL AS MENTAL ENDOWMENTS...WHICH MADE HIM AN OBJECT OF GENERAL ADMIRATION." (HAYWOOD.)

TABLET IN FORT NASHBOROUGH

Bible Records—Tombstone Inscriptions

body must be carried by hand by neighbors or the family to the grave. Very few of these old graveyards have been cared for and preserved, but among those known are the following:

The Bean graveyard is located near Bean Station on the Lee Highway, on land originally granted to Captain William Bean for his services in the Revolutionary War. It is about an eighth of a mile from the old fort established before 1787. No burials have been made there in more than a hundred years. Only one stone bears an inscription and that is made on local field rock, hand carved rudely: "J. Bean, Nov. 24, 1798." . . . It is the grave of Jane Bean who was killed by the Indians while at a spring doing the family washing. Tradition has erroneously been that this might have been for Jesse Bean. There seem to have been only three Jesse Beans; one died on Watauga in 1782, one died in Alabama, and the other in Arkansas. . . . According to family tradition, Capt. William Bean, Revolutionary soldier, was buried at this place in October, 1798. His grave is identified only by a pile of loose stones heaped over it. One Robert Bean, apparently brother of the William Bean of Watauga, was probably buried here in 1806. Court records at Rutledge verify these statements.

The Shields graveyard at Clinchdale is an example of one which has been continually used and well cared for since about 1800. U. S. ex-Senator John K. Shields has recently had the graveyard enclosed by a substantial stone wall and made all provisions possible to preserve it from the ravages of time so that, in the future as in the past, it may be a peaceful resting place for deceased members of the Shields family. (If you wish inscriptions, write to Senator Shields, Bean Station, Tennessee.)

Another well-preserved graveyard is that of the Bowen family. This is in the same community as the Shields graveyard. It is enclosed by a substantial fence and has been in use for a hundred years. The following inscriptions have been copied from monuments there:

Reece Bowen, born Oct. 15, 1801; died Dec. 18, 1881. (He was a great-nephew of the Reece Bowen killed at the battle of King's Mountain.)

Mary Moody Bowen, born Sept. 9, 1805; died June 11, 1865.

Theresa Ann Miller, wife of Hugh Jones, born Oct. 6, 1809; died, 1883.

Hammer's Graveyard, about two miles from Rutledge on the Lee Highway, contains many old, unmarked graves (apparently uncared for). Among these is the grave of John Bowen, born about 1766; died, 1823. He was one of the three John Bowens who served in the battle of King's Mountain.

In an isolated spot in Grainger County, unkept and inaccesible,

Bible Records—Tombstone Inscriptions

is the Collins Graveyard where lies the body of Michael Massengill who served in the Revolutionary War.

Another Bean Cemetery is located in Sweden's Cove, Sequatchee Valley, Tennessee. A picture is enclosed of the mountain stone monument and bronze tablet which contains the following inscription: "Captain Robert Beene, born in Virginia. A captain in Indian wars. A companion of Daniel Boone. A Tennessee Volunteer. A Hero of King's Mountain. An intrepid pioneer patriot. 1750-1824. Erected by his descendants in 1917."

In 1928 an official marker of the National Society of Daughters of American Revolution was placed on this grave by Nancy Ward Chapter, Chattanooga, Tenn.

The Cherokee nation lived in what is now Monroe County. The names of some of their Indian villages were Chota, Tellico, Citico, Toqua, and Echoto. The last the capital and city of Refuge.

Homes

Andres Taylor, a Revolutionary soldier, established his home in Johnson County along with the first settlers. His son, Nathaniel Taylor, was a congressman, and also a well known minister of the gospel. From this same home came the two noted sons of Nathaniel Taylor, Robert and Alfred Taylor, both of whom were governors of the state, members of Congress, and Robert Taylor also a Senator, and a nationally known orator and lecturer.

Oldest Towns in the State

Jonesboro, Blountville, Rogersville, Dandridge, Greeneville, Kingston, and Kingsport.

Old Mills

Massengills, Grainger County, established by Michael Massengill, a Revolutionary soldier, on land granted for military service. This mill was of real service in providing a means for food to the pioneers, as was also the Mossy Creek Mills, located in Jefferson County. Bean's Mill, near Elizabethton, was erected by William Bean, the reputed first white settler, furnished supplies to men under Sevier, who rendevoused six miles away, when starting on the march to King's Mountain. In the will of William Bean this mill is bequeathed to the youngest son of William Bean, Russell Bean, said to be the first white child born in Tennessee.

Trails

The Great War Path, made by the Indians, extending from the northeastern part of the state, southwest, past the Cherokee towns, on into Georgia, and Alabama to Great Creek Crossing.

Cherokee Trail branched off at the Cherokee towns towards the west, on towards the Mississippi districts. These trails were the

Bible Records—Tombstone Inscriptions

foundations of roads maintained from the time of the first coming of pioneers until present, along which traversed the armies of all our wars, the covered wagons and immigrants on their pilgrimages to the west, and all the great and near great travelers through Tennessee.

Boone Trail traversed by Daniel Boone in his journeys to and from Kentucky and North Carolina.

TREES

Boone Tree, known as the tree in which Daniel Boone killed a bear in 1760. Tree was blown down.

Spencer Sycamore, tree in which Spencer lived, 1778-1779, prior to the coming of settlers to the Cumberland District, twelve miles from Nashville.

Large Cedar Tree, still standing near Bean Station. An Indian, who was hidden in this tree, was killed, he being one of the many marauders loitering about this station.

FORTS

Old Fort Loudon, named for Earl of Loudon, Commander-in-chief of British forces in America and Governor of Virginia. This fort was the first structure erected in Tennessee by Anglo-Americans and was established in 1756—surrendered to chief of the Cherokees in 1760, more than three hundred soldiers, women, and children having been promised a safe retreat to another fort—they were overtaken the second day of January and most of the company massacred. The names of only three survivors being known, Captain John Stuart, Jeremiah Jack, and Isaac Thomas.

Fort Patrick Henry, near present Kingsport on Holston River, established about 1774. From this place John Donelson and party launched their boats for the perilous journey to the Cumberland settlements. This fort was a rendezvous for the soldiers accompanying Col. Christian to subdue the Cherokee and Chickamauga Indians in 1776.

Fort Watauga, in which the earliest settlers took refuge before the attack of the Cherokees in July, 1776.

Bean Station was erected in 1776 by William, Robert, George, and Jesse Bean, located in Granger County on what is now the Boone Trail and Lee Highway, formerly called the Baltimore to Nashville Stage Road, crossing the Louisville to Charleston Road at Bean Station. The foundation logs of one corner of the fort remains. The roads crossing at this place were established by the Indians and were branches of the Great War Path.

Sawyer's Fort, established about 1788 by Colonel John Sawyer, located in northern part of Knox County, eighteen miles from Knoxville.

Bible Records—Tombstone Inscriptions

Campbell's Station, erected about 1790 by Colonel Campbell, maintained as a protection from the Indians, the towns of the Cherokees being not more than thirty miles away. Campbell's Station, twenty miles from Knoxville.

MOUNTAINS

Wallen's Ridge, beginning near Chattanooga, running in northeastern direction, was visited by Wallen and a company of Long Hunters before any white settlements in Tennessee.

Missionary Ridge, Chattanooga, named because of the first Mission School for Indians, established on eastern slope in 1819. Missionary Ridge was part of the stragetic ground occupied by armies in Civil War, 1860-1864. Bragg's Tower, an outlook, is still maintained on the crest of the Ridge.

Lookout Mountain, an outlook place used by Chickamauga Indians in watching approach of Donelson party and the boats of pioneers on their way to Cumberland settlements. In the Civil War of 1860 the Battle above the Clouds was fought on Lookout Mountain. Monuments, commemorating the events of the battle, have been erected—the outstanding one being the New York Monument.

Chingman's Mountain, now a part of the new National Park, called the Smoky Mountain Park. In 1776 John Sevier and a few valiant men, with Isaac Thomas as scout, scaled the height of this mountain in order to spy out the lay of the land and towns of Cherokees while on an expedition to repel the Cherokee nations.

THE FIRST PRESBYTERIAN CHURCH, MURFREESBORO, TENN., FROM THE YEAR 1812 TO 1868

COMPILED BY REV. JOHN W. NEEL

(Pastor from 1866 to about 1871)

(Copied from a scrapbook of Joanna L. Rucker, owned by Rebekah Jetton, Murfreesboro. Joanna L. Rucker was born September 19, 1822, and died October 15, 1853. She was the daughter of Susan Childress and Dr. William Reed Rucker, and a niece of Mrs. James K. Polk. She married Robert B. Jetton November 6, 1850.)

The Presbyterian Church of Murfreesboro was organized in April, 1812, by the Rev. Robert Henderson, D.D., under the name of "The Murfree Spring Church," and was the first church organized in the place. It commenced its career with eighteen members, viz: Robert Wasson, Margaret Wasson, John Smith, James C. Smith, Isabella Smith, William D. Baird, Abigail Baird, Joseph Dickson, Margaret Dickson, Mary Dickson, John Henry,

Bible Records—Tombstone Inscriptions

Susanna Henry, Frances Henderson, Mary Stewart, Margaret Jetton, Mrs. Samuel Wilson, Grace Williams, and Elizabeth Kelton. The first ruling elders of the church were Robert Wasson, John Smith, and William D. Baird.

The church was organized in a log schoolhouse, near Murfree Spring, on a site now included in the yard of Mr. James Avent. For some time public services were held in this house. Subsequently services were held in a schoolhouse which stood on the ground now occupied by the residence of Mr. Robert Reed; and still later the courthouse was used for worship. About the time this church was organized the county seat was moved from Old Jefferson to Murfreesboro; the ground was laid off in town lots and offered for sale. Not only was this the first church organized in the place, but it is believed there was no church in striking distance of Murfreesboro for several years afterward. It was, in more senses than one, the mother church.

During the year 1813 Dr. Henderson preached to the church two Sabbaths in the month. He was a man of vigorous intellect and devoted piety. He was earnest in his work and succeeded in impressing himself upon the community as few men do.

In 1814, Dr. Henderson was succeeded in the pastorate of the church by Rev. Thomas I. Hall, who also preached two Sabbaths in the month. During the year 1815 the church received the ministerial services of Rev. James Bowman and Rev. George Newton, each preaching one Sabbath in the month. In 1816 Rev. George Newton and Rev. Jesse Alexander served the church. In 1817 Mr. Newton left, and Mr. Alexander gave the church one-third of his time.

In 1818 Rev. Robert Henderson, D.D., resumed the pastoral charge of the church, and the name was changed to the First Presbyterian Church of Murfreesboro. The church seems now to have entered upon a career of unusual prosperity. A substantial and commodious brick building was erected, the first ever built in the town, and for a number of years the only one.

The records show frequent and powerful outpourings of God's Spirit, which resulted in the awakening of the whole community and the conversion of many souls.

There were giants in the land in those days, and among them stood, PRIMUS INTER PARES, Dr. Gideon Blackburn, who often wrought in the church his labors of love. The high-sounding music of his eloquence has not yet died away in the hearts of God's people, for the eyes of our old women sparkle and the breasts of our old men heave as they tell of the crowds that flocked to hear him through rain and snow and the breathless silence that reigned through his three-hour sermons.

Bible Records—Tombstone Inscriptions

In the hands of such men the word of God was not bound, and the church grew apace. In 1820 Joseph Marlin and Samuel Trott were added to the session. In 1822 the legislature of Tennessee, on account of the destruction of the courthouse by fire, sat in the Presbyterian church. A floor was put in the building on a level with the galleries, thus making two stories. One branch of the legislature sat down stairs and the other above. In 1825 Benjamin McCulloch, James C. Mitchell, and Dr. James Maney were elected and ordained to the office of ruling elder.

On the 3rd of December, 1825, Rev. J. W. Hall commenced his ministerial labors in the church, the membership then being about ninety. On the 7th of April, 1827, thirty-eight persons were received into the church, and among them appear the familiar names of Elder, Killough, Niles, Wilson, Rucker, Wade, Stewart, Black, Tennent, Tandel, Henderson, and Fletcher. The membership had now increased to one hundred and thirty-eight.

In December, 1829, Rev. J. W. Hall resigned the pastoral charge, and in the same month Rev. William Eagleton, D.D., received and accepted a call to the pastoral office. The church now numbered about one hundred and fifty members.

In 1831 a camp meeting was held at Kelton's camp ground. During the ten days it lasted forty-four persons united with the Church. Before the close of the year thirty-six more united with the Church, increasing its membership to two hundred and thirty-eight. The year following, during another meeting at Kelton's, forty-four were again added to the Church.

In October, 1832, Jonathan Curran, James C. Moore, David Mitchell, George Calhoun, James Kelton, and David McGill were elected ruling elders in the Church.

The Church, under the ministry of Dr. Eagleton continued to grow and prosper until it numbered 320 communicants in 1838. The Church was now strong enough to send out her branches, and in 1838 between fifty and sixty members were dismissed to form Mt. Tabor Church at Kelton's.

Up to this time the Church had been under the care of Shiloh Presbytery, in connection with the Synod of West Tennessee, in connection with the General Assembly of the Presbyterian Church of the United States of America. In 1837-8 the Presbyterian Church was divided into New and Old School Presbyterians.

In 1839 the Synod of West Tennessee divided on this issue, and the Church at Murfreesboro went with the New School party, in connection with the New School Assembly, until that assembly divided between North and South on the slavery issue. The southern portion of the New School Church organized and formed the United Synod. When this took place in 1859, the Murfrees-

Bible Records—Tombstone Inscriptions

boro Church returned again to the Old School Assembly. In the year 1840 Samuel Hodge and D. D. Wendel were made ruling elders in the Church.

In November, 1841, the church enjoyed a glorious revival of religion. The pastor was assisted, in a meeting of eighteen days, by Rev. Matt. Marshall and others, when ninety persons were hopefully converted; and as usual, when the spirit of God is poured out upon a church, the difficulties and divisions of the church were all healed. In 1842, the books report 270 members, notwithstanding the large colony which had been sent out to form Mt. Tabor Church.

In 1843 fifty more were added to the church, and for the second time the church numbered over 300 communicants.

In 1844, Samuel Anderson, Wilson L. Watkins, and Gordon W. Shanklin were made Ruling Elders in the church.

The church record contains a brief notice of a camp meeting, held at Sulphur Spring Camp Ground, from the 9th to the 21st of September, 1842, when one hundred and fifty persons made a profession of religion. As is often the case when such large numbers come into the church, many unworthy ones are found among them; but the *grace of discipline* was vigorously applied, and the church kept in a state of comparative purity.

In 1851, the Legislature of Tennessee passed an act of incorporation, by which the pastor and elders of the church, and their successors in office, became a body corporate, by the name and style of the Pastor and Elders of the Presbyterian Church at Murfreesboro, to obtain and hold property of any descriptions, etc.

In 1854, a large colony was sent out to organize the Sulphur Spring Church, the second daughter of the Murfreesboro Church. In the latter part of the same year Mr. J. M. Beard and Wm. P. McFadden were called to the office of Ruling Elder.

For several years now the church diminished in membership. Notwithstanding a goodly number was added every year, the drainage by removals and colonization was so great that the membership in 1857 was only 133.

In 1858, thirty-five were added to the church, and in 1859 forty-two more, bringing up the membership again to over two hundred. During this year the Presbytery of Shiloh, the New School Presbytery to which the church belonged, was dissolved, and the Murfreesboro church united with the Presbytery of Nashville (Old School) with which it has ever since held connection. The losses and gains for the church for the next two years were about equal, so that in the spring of 1861, at the breaking out of the war, the membership of the church was 200. Services in the church were uninterrupted until October, 1862, when the pastor, Dr. Eagleton, on account of ill health, had to leave his home and church.

Bible Records—Tombstone Inscriptions

Among the many deeds of vandalism perpetrated by the Federal army was the pulling down of the Presbyterian Church, a building in which we and our fathers had worshipped for forty-four years. The aged pastor returned in March, 1864, to find his home desolated, his church destroyed and his flock scattered. Many had fled from their homes, never to get back again; many had gone to their final rest, and those that remained were oppressed and discouraged. Dr. Eagleton preached as best he could, from house to house and around in the neighboring country. After the close of the war, in the spring of 1865, the brethren of the Cumberland Presbyterian Church kindly offered Dr. Eagleton the use of their church part of the time, which was the only church, it is believed, at the time, in a condition to be used. He preached there, as occasion offered, until March, 1866, when he fell with his armor on. Thus passed away a man, who, in the providence of God, was permitted to serve one church for thirty-seven years. The memory of this good man is too fresh in the heart of this community to require anything to be said in his favor here. It is not too much to say that Dr. Eagleton, on account of his official position, his guileless life, his noble work and his long ministry, was enabled to accomplish more good than any other man who ever lived in it.

In 1861, the Presbytery of Nashville, to which the Murfreesboro church belongs, in common with all Presbyteries in the Southern States, withdrew from the General Assembly of the Presbyterian Church of the United States, on account of its political differences and in the fall of the same year a Southern General Assembly was formed, called "The General Assembly of the Presbyterian Church in the United States." The name of the Northern Assembly is, "The General Asembly of the Presbyterian Church of the United States of America."

The present pastor of the church commenced his labors in December, 1866. Having no church building, public services were commenced in the upper room of the courthouse, which was fitted up for the purpose. The scattered flock was gathered together again. Mr. A. G. Price, Hon. Charles Ready and Dr. J. E. Wendel were elected Ruling Elders.

Dr. J. B. Murfree, W. D. Killough, Gideon Baskette, Wm. H. McFadden, Dr. A. Hartman and A. C. H. P. Sehorn were elected deacons. A complete system of finance was immediately adopted by the Session, and put into execution by the Board of Deacons. The congregation met on the 16th of May, 1867, and determined to build a house of worship. Hon. E. A. Keeble, D. D. Wendel, E. D. Hancock, Dr. Knight and J. M. Baird were elected a building committee, and invested with plenary powers in the matter of building a church. The services of J. C. Kiddell, of Nashville, were secured as architect, and in August the work was com-

Bible Records—Tombstone Inscriptions

menced. The cornerstone was laid on the 4th of October, 1868; the church was dedicated to the service of God.

The church is now considered to be in a healthy condition and in good working order. During the year ending May 1st, 1869, there were forty-four additions to the church. The Sabbath school is growing rapidly in numbers and organization, and the Sabbath congregations are considered large. The present membership is 208.

It is just now a half century since the first church was built in Murfreesboro (1818). From 1819 to about 1823 there was no other church building in the town. Now (1868) Murfreesboro has nine churches. It is doubtful whether there is another town in this state or any state, of the size of Murfreesboro, that can boast of so many churches, and all of them so well attended. It is pleasant also to add, that nowhere will there be found less of that bigoted and uncharitable spirit which so often characterizes the churches of different denominations.

A tablet is erected in the churchyard where the old church stood.

The Presbyterian Church of Murfreesboro was organized in April, 1812, under the name of the "Murfree Spring Church" with 18 members: Abigail Baird, William D. Baird, Joseph Dickson, Mary Dickson, Margaret Dickson, John Henry, Susanna Henry, Frances Henderson, Margaret Jetton, Elizabeth Kelton, John Smith, James C. Smith, Mary Stewart Isabel, Isabella Smith, Robert Wasson, Margaret Wasson, Grace Williams, Mrs. Samuel Wilson.

In 1818 the name of the Church was changed to the First Presbyterian Church. A brick building was erected; the Legislature sat here in 1822 during the time when Murfreesboro was the Capitol of Tennessee. The Church was demolished by the Federal army in 1864.

This tablet was placed by the Colonel Hardy Murfree Chapter of the Daughters of the American Revolution, July, 1933.

RECORD OF THE STONE'S RIVER CHURCH

The Church of Stone's River was organized April 1, 1816. Members then in communion were: James McKnight, Elenor McKnight, William McKnight, Isabel McKnight, Joseph Knox, Jane Knox, Charles Ready, Polly Ready, Joseph Witherspoon, Jane Witherspoon, Charles Porterfield, Jane Porterfield, Polly Witherspoon, Peggie Andrews, David Andrews, Polly Andrews, John Henderson, Sarah Henderson, John McKnight, Peggie McKnight, Moses McKnight, Rixney McKnight, Peggie McKnight, John M. McKnight, Abigail McKuight, James Bowl, Margret Bowl, Thomas Berry, Sarah Berry, Polly M. Elliot, Margret Ramsy. These

Bible Records—Tombstone Inscriptions

composed the Stone's River Church at its organization, with Charles Ready, David Andrews, James Bowl, John Henderson and John Dickson as elders.

The church received stated supply from Jesse Alexander, licentiate from April, 1816, to April, 1817. During this time there were six more members added to the church. April 7, 1817, Jesse Alexander was ordained pastor of Stone's River Church.

In 1817 the number of members was 72.

S. G. McKNIGHT, *Clerk of Session.*
Readyville, Tenn.

SMYRNA PRESBYTERIAN CHURCH
By ELIZABETH EVERETT LOWRY OF SMYRNA
(Sent by Mary Robertson, member of Capt. Wm. Lytle Chapter, to Rebekah Jetton.)

A note in the minutes of a session meeting of March 2, 1835, states that "former records had been lost, but that the church was organized by Rev. Samuel Hodge about 1820, consisting chiefly of members who formerly composed the church at Jefferson."

The elders were: Theophilus Cannon, William Martin, George Ralston and Samuel Bowman.

Beyond the fact that the first church building, located a mile from where the town of Smyrna now stands, was built of logs, we know little. During the time the congregation worshipped in this church it was customary to have camp meetings in the summer. The members came from miles around, bringing tents, food and Negro slaves, who cooked the meals and camped around the church.

During the war this building was burned by the Federal soldiers and after the war the government paid the church $1,000 (one thousand) for rebuilding. This money was used in building a new brick church which was finished in 1867.

Ministers of the Smyrna Church from 1820 to 1882 were: Samuel Hodge, 1820-1824; Robert Henderson, 1825; Silas Morrison, 1825-1828; Amzi Bradshaw, 1828-1831; Levi Morrison, 1831-1832; Bedford Ryland, 1834-1835; John Allison, 1835-1841; S. H. Henderson, 1842-1843; J. B. Lindsley, 1846-1847; Wm. Bull, 1848-1853; James Hoyte, 1851-1863; J. B. Chapman, 1868-1880; T. D. Latimer, 1881-1882.

PRIMITIVE BAPTIST CHURCH
(Sent by Miss Rebekah Jetton, Murfreesboro)

One of the earliest church organizations in Rutherford County was the Primitive or Regular Baptist Church. Its first members were from North Carolina or Virginia. The first church organ-

Bible Records—Tombstone Inscriptions

ized in the county by the Baptists was McCoy's in the Norman settlement. This was before 1800. Elder William Keel is believed to have been the first minister. In consideration of $1.00, love and affection, Thomas Rucker deeded two acres of land to John Warren and Drury Vaughn, deacons, or their successors in office, of that branch of the Baptist Church who believe in the "final preservation of the Saints in Christ, and Baptism by emersion." This church house was erected near Cumming's mill on the east fork of Stone's River. This was called Providence. Other early members were the Lillards, Claytons, and Clarks, also Dr. Yandell, father of the distinguished Dr. Yandell of Louisville, Ky. Dr. Watson, one of its early ministers, was distinguished as a physician and a minister, and respected as a citizen.

BEASLEY'S CHURCH

Beasley's Church was built four miles west of Murfreesboro about 1820, on the Beasley farm. There is still a house of worship near the same place. Among the early members of this church were Chrishall and wife; Posey, wife and family. Elder Whitesett was one of its first ministers.

ENON CHURCH

"Enon Church was built at a later date. The building is a frame structure and stands about six miles north of Murfreesboro. Early members were the Reads, Barksdales, and Searceys. Peyton Smith was one of its early ministers. He afterwards joined the Methodists and later the Christians." Goodspeed, Vol. II.

There is not a church there now. Enon Church was built on two acres of land given by John Nash Read. Deed recorded in Deed Book, Vol. O, pp. 224-225, R. O. R. C. No. 181. John Nash Read to Daniel Nelson and William A. Sublett, Trustees for the Baptist Church. Deed written "in the presence of Ota Cantrell, John Allen, A. W. Harris, March 1, 1822. Signed John Nash Bond and Blackman Coleman, Clk."

Lett Bond was a later minister of the Church in Murfreesboro. The first church of this denomination was built near the southeast corner of the Public Square, and stood for some years. On the failure of the Bradley Academy early in the decade of 1830, that building was used by these people till the creation of the church which now stands in Murfreesboro.

Prominent among the early families belonging to this church were the Brooks, Powells, Morgans, Lethermans, Ruckers, and Claytons. Capt. Jones conducted the first public prayer meeting at the old Bradley Academy in 1818.

Bible Records—Tombstone Inscriptions

BAPTIST CHURCH

Deed Book K, page 41, State of Tennessee:
This indenture made the 8th day of May in the year of our Lord 1813 between Thomas Rucker of the County of Rutherford and State of Tennessee, of the one part, and John Warren and Drury Vaughan, deacons of the Baptist Church near Cummings mill on the east fork of Stone's River, holding this doctrine of election and final perseverance of the Saints in Christ and Baptism by emersion, of the other part. Witnesseth that for and in consideration of the love and affection which he, the said T. R., has for the Baptist people aforesaid, and believing as aforesaid, and for the further consideration of the sum of $1.00 to him in hand paid, the receipt whereof is hereby acknowledged, he, the said T. R., hath this day given and granted by these presents do give and grant (for a place of worship) unto the said John Warren and Drury Vaughan, deacons in the said Baptist Church and ministers and to their successors in office forever. With this proviso, that no part of said two acres hereby conveyed shall be appropriated as a burying ground, and that whenever it shall be so appropriated it is bargained and understood that the land and premises shall revert to the said T. R., his heirs and assigns.

Signed in the presence of Daniel Elam, John Newman, Joseph B. Johns.
Book No. 1, page 355:

METHODIST EPISCOPAL CHURCH

This indenture made and entered into this 20th day of April in the year of our Lord 1843, between John Etter of the County of Rutherford, State of Tennessee, of the one part, and Cary James, B. W. Goodrich, Samuel M. Copeland, Joseph Watkins, Benjamin Ward, William D. Nelson and William D. Neal, Trustees, for the purpose hereinafter specified of the other part. Witnesseth, that the said John Etter for and in consideration of the sum of $5.00 and in further consideration of an ardent desire of the prosperity of Zion, and having a permanent place of worship in the neighborhood, now give, granted, bargained and sold to the above-named Trustees, a certain piece or parcel of ground on the N. E. corner of the tracts of land I purchased of John Davis, lying on the south side of the turnpike road from Murfreesborough to Nashville, beginning at my N. E. corner, being the corner between me and Jesse Sikes; thence with the line S. between 18 poles to a stake, thence W. 9 pols to a flat rock, thence straight line to turnpike and with the turnpike to the beginning so as to include 1 acre more or less to have and to hold to said Trustees and their successors for the purpose of erecting a house of worship for the use of the Methodist Episcopal Church in the U. S. A., provided they shall permit it to be used

Bible Records—Tombstone Inscriptions

as a house of worship for the ministers and members of said church according to the regulations and discipline that may from time to time be adopted by the General Conference of said Church, and I also grant to them the privilege of water from the Spring nearest the lot; and it is hereby stipulated that if the above described piece of land should (not—was omitted) be occupied for the above purposes it is to revert to me and my heirs. I hereby covenant and agree to warrant and defend the title to the above described acre of land against me and my heirs and all other persons to the said Trustees and their successors that may from time to time be appointed according to discipline of said Church. In testimony whereto I have hereunto set my hand and seal the day and date above written.

Signed, sealed and delivered in the presence of Martin Clark, W. H. Cayse, I. G. Baugh, John (X—His Mark) Etter.

Registered October 17, 1843. Robert S. Morris, Clerk.

CONVEYANCE TO PRESBYTERIAN CHURCH
(Sent by Miss Jetton)

Book M, page 445 of Deed Book in R. O. R. C., Murfreesboro, Tenn. Registered 1st June, 1800, No. 345, William Lytle to Deed of Trust to William D. Baird.

State of Tennessee, Rutherford County Circuit Court, March term, 1815, I, John Coffee, Clk. of the Circuit Court of the County of Rutherford, do certify that the execution of the within deed of conveyance was duly acknowledged in open court at the above term by the within named Robert Weakley, and ordered to be registered. In testimony whereof I have set my hand at office this 2nd day of June, 1820. JOHN COFFEE, *Clerk.*

"Witnesseth that the said William Lytle Senr. to promote the cause of religion and to provide a suitable place for the Society of Christians called Presbyterians on which to erect a Church for the worship of Almighty God," etc.——

Signed and delivered in the presence of Ben McCulloch, W. Douglas. This was "Lot No. 20 as designated in the general plan of the town of Murfreesboro." Mary M. Hilliard, who sold the land to the city for the cemetery, was Mary Moore Hilliard, Dec. 28, 1837. Henderson Yoakum was Mayor of the city.

METHODIST CHURCH HERE WAS ORGANIZED IN 1812
(Sent by Miss Rebekah Jetton, Murfreesboro, Tenn.)

The organization of the Methodist church in Rutherford county dates back to about 1812.

At that time there was held a camp meeting at the Windrow Camp Ground at which time there were many professions of religion. Rev. Robert Paine who became bishop in the Methodist

Episcopal church, was a circuit rider over a district embracing Rutherford county. During the session of the General Assembly, he preached in the courthouse and many members were present and took a part in the exercises, among them Felix Grundy, the distinguished lawyer and statesman.

A class was organized at a house on College street in 1821. The following are charter members: Benjamin Blankenship and wife, Edward Fisher and wife, Thomas Montague and wife, John Lytle and wife, Martin Clark, Willis Reeves, John Jones, William Ledbetter, G. A. Sublett, D. Henry Holmes, Dr. W. R. Rucker, Levi Reeves, J. D. Neugent and David Hannis.

Preaching was furnished by traveling preachers at first, and services were held either in the courthouse or in private dwellings till the year 1823. In 1823 John Lytle deeded a lot, near where Soule College now stands, for the purpose of having a church erected thereon.

The lot was deeded to John R. McLaughlin, Samuel McLaughlin, Simpson Simmons, Benjamin Rucker, S. Ogden, A. Childress and Edmond Jones as trustee.

A brick house, one story high, with gallery for Negroes, and bell, was completed at a cost of about $1,800.

HISTORY OF BETHEL CHURCH

(This paper was given to Miss Rebekah Jetton by J. T. Sanders, Murfreesboro.)

Bethel Church was established by the Rev. Ebenezer McGowan. He was born in London, England, in 1767, and because his father wanted him to become a Catholic priest he ran away from home at the age of 17 years and came to America, settled in Virginia and lived there until 1816, when he moved to Tennessee. He bought a 1,000 acres of ground for the sum of $2,500.00 and gave the lot where the church now stands. The lot was deeded to trustees, John Lane, Joseph Windley, John Jones, Capt. William Smith, and James E. Stockard and their successors in office according to the discipline of the M. E. Church, South. The first church was built in 1817 or 18. It was a cedar log house and is still standing and is being used as a part of the Bethel schoolhouse. The next house was built in 1887, and it is the house we now use.

The first pastor after Rev. Ebenezer McGowan was the Rev. A. Overall. Up to this time there have been 60 different pastors and 22 different presiding elders. Rev. J. W. Cullum, J. C. Keathley, and D. T. Reed stayed four years and J. W. Cullum was back again for three years. Rev. M. J. Mabry stayed three years at one time and two at another. Bethel Church register dated back to 1830. If there was a register previous to that time, it has been lost. Regular services have been held in this church since the

Bible Records—Tombstone Inscriptions

formation, except during the Civil War. Belonging to the church at this time is one grandchild, ten great-grandchildren, and three great-great-grandchildren of the founder, Rev. Ebenezer McGowan and there are a number of great-grandchildren and great-great-grandchildren belonging to Salem Church and also to the church at Murfreesboro. The church now has a membership of 148. Four of the great-grandsons of the Rev. McGowan are members of the official board. Since writing the above the grandchild has died.

THE FIRST CHRISTIAN CHURCH
(Sent by Miss Jetton)

"The first Christian Church was organized in Murfreesboro January 1, 1833, and consisted of twelve members. Steps were immediately taken to build a church. Lot 59 of the original plan of Murfreesboro was purchased of F. E. Bicton (Becton) for $50.00 and deeded to Peyton Smith, George Morris, William Smith, Thomas Rucker, Sr., Joseph Ramsey, Thomas Rucker, Jr., and G. W. Banton." Copied from Goodspeed.

PIONEER MARBLE HALLS
By KATE WHITE

Tennessee is noted in song and story for her log cabins in pioneer romance, but we have many marble halls, intersected in Tennessee that have much to do with the life of our pioneer in his love and death, and tragedy and in romance. Blount County has two of these still standing in all their pristene glory of pioneer days. One is a very large building near Lowe's Ferry on a tract of land that was the original 593 acres. This house is of marble blocks perfectly set, and a large spring house nearby is erected the same way. Above the front door is a large block of marble bearing the inscription, "J. G. and I. G., 1802." It was built by two brothers, James and Isaac Gillespie, ancestors of the Gillespies of Knox and Blount Counties. There were two marble quarries near this place, and no doubt but that is why they built a large marble house instead of logs. Another beautiful marble hall of baronial capacity is the Alexander-Ramsay building on the Asbury Road in Knox County. It, too, was near a marble quarry.

Some three miles above Rogersville on the old stage road is one of the ancient stone houses of East Tennessee, built by Thomas Amis, even before the State of Franklin was organized. Andre Michaux, the eminent French botanist, in his diary of 1793, tells of the beauty of this building, where he stopped on his tour through this country. It was built in 1783. The walls are eighteen inches thick, and the doors are very heavy, of solid oak, the doors being hinged double in the middle, and long hinges above

Bible Records—Tombstone Inscriptions

and below, heavy bolts at the top of the door were made in the blacksmith shop, and were for defense.

Mrs. Jasper C. Barnes, the Historian of Mary Blount Chapter, of Blount County, writes me of another pioneer marble baronial hall of that county, that she is sure it was built while we were still in the State of North Carolina, but as yet, she has not found the name of the man who built it. The construction of the building broke up the man financially who built it, and he lost his farm and house on account of the cost. She does know he sold to David Parkins, but as yet, has not found the title of sale, or the date that Parkins bought the place.

These marble halls of East Tennessee were in most part built near some marble yard. This same Andre Michaux tells of his staying in the magnificent marble baronial hall of Gen. Daniel Smith in Sumner County, Middle Tennessee. This building was commenced in 1784, and finished in 1790. It is a beautiful home today. It was on account of the depredations of the Indians that it took seven years to build. It is constructed of cut stone and has seven large rooms with an ell. I find all these marble houses were built in one style, colonial, like our brick pioneer houses. Another marble home in Middle Tennessee, that David Shelby erected in 1796, was erected on 640 acres one mile south of Gallatin. The place is known as "Spencer's Choice." It is a two full stories of smooth blocks of stone, with a small front porch, still used as a handsome home. Walnut Grove, in Summer County, the home of the pioneer, Charles Elliott, consisted of a square mile of land, devoted to groves and meadows on which stand a beautiful colonial marble castle, built in 1795. It is now called the Boddie Farm. The people who own it have wealth and they keep this beautiful place in perfect order. Mrs. Carrington Mason, of Memphis, now owns it as a summer home, and she is the descendant of Eligh Boddie and Maria Elliott. General James Winchester, who was a member of the Territorial Assembly in Knoxville, 1794, and Speaker of the first State Senate, 1796, married Miss Susan Black, of Sumner County, and his home, "Cragfront," is a large, substantial marble building. He brought stone-masons from the East to do the work. It is still standing and occupied, but like most of these marble halls, has passed away from the possession of the family. These are a few of the marble baronial halls of Tennessee built in her colonial and pioneer days that could give themes to the writers of today in romance and tragedy.

On Fork Creek Road in Monroe County, near the Loudon County line, is an old post office called Eve Mills. There were no mills there, but the name came from an Indian romance. Evaleeka, a daughter of the Indian Cherokee chief, who had his home there, was a beautiful half-breed young girl whom the young Cherokee

Bible Records—Tombstone Inscriptions

warriors wooed. But a white man came along, named Mills, and they loved each other. On the day they were to be married Mills was found dead, murdered by one of the young Cherokee chiefs who loved her. Evaleeka was wild with grief and determined to follow her lover to the "happy hunting ground." She rushed down the banks of the Tulogher, and from a high rock she jumped into the mad current and was borne rapidly to the seething waters of the Tennessee River and was never seen again.

In Monroe County, near the McMinn County line, is still one of the first cabins built by Indians. It was built of logs and covered with bark. It now has a large stone chimney that was added in the early 1800's, and still occupied by people.

An old flint rifle used in the battle of Quebec during the Revolutionary War and in the Civil War is now owned by Mrs. Johnnie E. Troutman, of Corryton, not far from Knoxville. It is four feet nine inches long and six feet with the bayonet attached. The date 1759 is cut into the stock. During the seige of Quebec the rifle was captured from an English soldier, and later came into the possession of P. A. Estes, an officer of the Revolution who used it during that war. He was killed in the battle of King's Mountain and the rifle was picked up by his brother, Joseph Estes, who was beside him. A century later John A. Keener, of Corryton, gained possession of the gun, and when he died it was inherited by his daughter, Mrs. Troutman. Mrs. Troutman also has a cup found on the battlefield of King's Mountain, used by one of Ferguson's soldiers.

The great Indian war path of the Cherokees was the first road in Tennessee. It was about three feet wide and was made by constant travel by the Indians. This trail was used by the Indians from Chickamauga town, now Chattanooga. It came through Ooltewah, leaving Cleveland to the north, crossed the Hiawassee River near its junction with Estanal, crossed the Little Tennessee River near its junction with the Tell, and passed through Maryville, taking what is now known as the Maryville and Sevierville Road on to Sevierville, went along the east prong of the Little Pigeon River, passing by what is known as Harrisburg, Fairgarden, on to Newport, crossed the Big Pigeon River near Stockly Canning factory at War Ford. Then it followed the base of the mountain until it got to Greeneville, crossed the Chucky River near Brown's Settlement, eight miles south of Jonesboro, following what is now called the Cherokee Road, passing Garber's Mill, went on by the south of Johnson City to Sinking Creek to its junction with Watauga River. It was this trail that Chief Abraham took when he made his attack on the settlers in Watauga in 1776. The road from Sapling Grove, now Bristol, to Knoxville was the great highway from Baltimore to the South, and now we know it as the Lee Highway. It is a historical fact that the Knoxville merchants traveled this great road with their six-mule teams, carrying furs, hides, beeswax, ginsing, and all else they could sell in Baltimore and Philadelphia, to bring back to the wilds of Tennessee dry goods and other articles wanted. This traffic of the merchants' wagons, stage coaches, and travelers was a great source of revenue to the farmers along the route, as it enabled them to dispose of their corn, meat, oats and hay to the Inn Keepers.

One of the oldest land marks in Grainger County is the old Joseph Cobbs home, whose wife was a niece of William Bean. It was first built by William Bean; a large full two-story log building, with a chimney on each end. When Joseph Cobb bought it he weather-boarded and put a front porch on it. A large giant cedar tree a little way from this house is where the Indians were hid that William Bean shot out of the tree. The State Historical Society is intending to put a marker at this place. Ocoee Chapter, of Cleveland, is going to mark the grave and the place where the home stood of Chief Jack Walker, where Pryor Lea Farm now is. Chief John Walker was the Lockinvar of the Cherokee Nation. He fell in love and eloped with Emily Meigs, the 13-year-old granddaughter of Return Jonathan Meigs, a Revolutionary soldier, and at this time an Indian agent, located at the historical town of Calhoun. Colonel Meigs and a brother gave chase after the runaways, but "On all the wide border his steed was the best." They made their escape and were married here in Bristol, Va. There was a law against white and red races marrying, the minister would not take them in the house, but married them out on the road in a downpour of rain. Chief Jack Walker was educated at Harvard, and had but three-fourths of an Indian in him. He was said to be very handsome and captivating. His father was Maj. John Walker, who laid out the town of Calhoun, and was part Cherokee. He named the town after the famous South Carolina statesman in 1819.

THE HISTORY OF KNAPP FARM
By JEANNETTE TILLOTSON ACKLEN

Yesterday a pioneer fort; today a demonstration farm. That is the history of the Seamen A. Knapp farm, the demonstration school of Peabody College for Teachers, in Nashville, Tenn.

In 1780, a fort was built on the bluffs of a creek near what was then the town of Nashborough. On the Elm Hill Pike the first water mill in this section was built, and it was this mill that gave Mill Creek its name. Near this mill was erected the old Buchanan Fort to guard the mill while it ground the corn to make bread for those pioneers of civilization.

Bible Records—Tombstone Inscriptions

In the year 1792, the Indians had been gathering for some time, and spies sent out by the settlers said they had formed a plan to attack Buchanan's Fort first and then that of his father-in-law, Ridley Fort, and after taking these two forts to take the other one on the Cumberland and thus rid this section of the white men. Four hundred settlers had gathered at Buchanan's Fort awaiting the Indians, but after waiting some days, most of the men went home because they believed the Indians had given up their intentions. Also they were anxious about their families who were left unprotected.

On Saturday night, only seventeen men, living in the neighborhood, remained in the fort. That night a Frenchman and a half-blood Indian arrived to say that the Indians were on their way and would soon be there. The men did not believe this tale, and the Indian said they might cut off his head if the Indians did not arrive in a few hours. But while he was not believed, however, two men were sent out to reconnoiter. So sure were they that no Indians were about, they fell into an ambush and were both killed and scalped. When these men did not return, the settlers thought they had failed to find any Indians and had gone on further for more information.

The early settlers had little confidence in the half-breeds and the Frenchman who had recently come among them, so the men went to rest, leaving only Mrs. Sally Buchanan to guard. Mrs. Buchanan was sitting in the kitchen listening for any alarming sounds when suddenly she heard a noise in the distance which she thought was a messenger, but when she heard the horses and cows running about in the enclosure, she knew that Indians were in the immediate vicinity, for as Mrs. Ridley, the mother of Mrs. Buchanan, expressed it, "Cows is mortal feared, as well as horses, of them pafect devils, the Indians!" Mrs. Buchanan aroused the men with the cry, "Indians, boys, Indians!"

The men armed themselves instantly and on rushing to the gate found nine hundred warriors of the Cherokees, Choctaws, and Chickasaws attempting to force it. The gate was well secured and the Indians did not try any other point in the stockade, which was fortunate for the frontiersmen, as it would have divided their small force.

Sally Buchanan undertook the task of molding the bullets. One of Mrs. Buchanan's descendants said that her grandmother had molded their pewter plates into bullets and had carried them in her apron to the men. As fast as the bullets were ready and clipped, Sally would run out with them and cry, "Here, boys, here's bullets for you; mind you don't serve them out until you are sure of knocking some of them screaming devils over."

Bible Records—Tombstone Inscriptions

An English traveler, Featherstonehaugh, who visited Nashville in 1835, says that this incident is the equal of anything we read of in history. The men were so much encouraged by the wonderful spirit of Sally Buchanan that they withstood the attack for several hours, after many fruitless attempts on the part of the Indians to force their way in. The reports of the rifles were heard two miles away at the fort where Mrs. Buchanan's mother lived. The Indians drew off before daylight, having lost their chief, Chiachattalla. This defeat doubtless saved the other forts along the Cumberland which were to have been attacked if this one had fallen.

One story told by relatives of Sally Buchanan is quite amusing. During one of the attacks, the men were standing on stools firing through holes in the fort's walls and the women were nearby loading the guns as the men handed them down. One man's gun was not shooting, but he did not know it as the firing was so fast and heavy around him. He handed his gun down several times and it was loaded each time. When it did shoot it had so many loads in it that it knocked him off the stool and the other defenders thought he had been shot by the Indians.

One day Henry Buchanan and his sister left the fort's high walls to go into the woods. Some Indians caught and scalped them. They were left lying unconscious in the woods. Late in the afternoon they were found and carried into the fort. They afterwards recovered, but were compelled to wear wigs to cover their heads.

Today Peabody students get water at the same spring where Sally Buchanan and her brave family went, carrying their handmade cedar buckets. The old fort and blockhouse stood where the present clubhouse of the Knapp Farm now stands and at the foot of the bluff which sloped down to Mill Creek is the same clear cold spring. From under a rock, down a mossy bank, it flows just as it did when redskin and frontiersmen bent over to drink. In the yard of the clubhouse is one of the original log houses. The sides are of yellow poplar and the roof is made of clapboards riveted and split with an axe.

Along the line of the railway are several neglected graves, all that is left of a larger number, for the grave of brave Sally Buchanan has long since been destroyed. One modest headstone marks the resting place of Martha Buchanan who died September 15, 1840, aged twenty-eight years. Three little children of Martha Buchanan lie near their mother, while at a short distance is the grave of T. H. Williams, born August 23, 1826, and died January 7, 1848. The grave myrtle is gently covering these forgotten sleepers, who lived and labored in the early years of struggle and privation in the fertile valley of the Cumberland.

Bible Records—Tombstone Inscriptions

TABLET ON THE PIKE LEADING FROM BRISTOL TO GREENEVILLE

Copied by Mrs. Acklen

Fort Robinson erected near here in 1761. Built by Col. Adam Stephen of Col. William Byrd's Regiment during the campaign against the Cherokees that year.

From this Fort, Henry Timberlake and Thos. Sunter, later General in the Revolutionary War, were sent on a mission to the Cherokee Indian towns.

The Indian Peace treaty of Nov. 19, 1761, was made near this Fort.

DRINKING FOUNTAIN IN JONESBORO

One face of fountain: Washington District, 1776. The first governmental division ever named in honor of George Washington. Washington County, 1777. Jonesborough established by North Carolina Act of 1779, laid out in 1780. Capital of State of Franklin, 1784-1785. Judicial Capital of Washington District Territory south of the River Ohio, 1790-1796.

Opposite face of fountain: A bas relief of Major Jesse Walton. Major Jesse Walton, founder of Jonesborough. An officer throughout the Revolutionary War serving in North Carolina and this region; second in command in Washington District forces under Col. John Sevier; "A man of elemental force and dignity, of essential honor and true worth."

CHESTER INN JONESBOROUGH TABLET

Chester Inn erected, 1798. Andrew Jackson, John Sevier, James K. Polk, Andrew Johnson were guests of this inn. Erected by State of Franklin Chapter, D. A. R.

Inscriptions on Markers at Readyville, Tenn.

(Sent by Miss Jetton)

Charles Ready, Sr., born at Salisbury, Md., April 1, 1770; lived from early childhood in North Carolina and emigrated in 1797 to Tennessee. Settled in what is now Readyville; died Aug. 3, 1859. Mary Ready, consort of Charles Ready, Sr., born in North Carolina, Sept. 4, 1773; died Sept. 3, 1848.

Inscription from grave of John Nash Read, Revolutionary soldier, from the tombstone near Old Jefferson. Sent by Miss Jetton:

Here lie the mortal remains of John Nash Read who was born in Charlotte County, Va., on April 25, 1763; emigrated to Rutherford County, Tenn., in 1806 and departed this life at "Templeton Grove" on Jan. 6, 1826, in the glorious triumph of a living faith; leaving a large and affectionate family to lament their loss.

Bible Records—Tombstone Inscriptions

MONUMENT IN COURTHOUSE YARD, MURFREESBORO

Inscriptions:
In commemoration of the valor of Confederate soldiers who fell in the great battle of Murfreesboro, Dec. 31, 1862, and Jan. 2, 1863, and in minor engagements in this vicinity, this monument is erected.

Lest we forget—1861-1865.
A monument for our soldiers, built of a people's love.
Honor decks the turf that wraps their clay.

WEST ENTRANCE OF COURTHOUSE, MURFREESBORO

This tablet commemorates the fact that Murfreesboro was the capital of the State of Tennessee from Sept. 26, 1819, to Oct. 15, 1825.
(D. A. R. Insignia.)

Erected by the Col. Hardy Murfree Chapter of the Daughters of American Revolution, 1921. "Patriotism is kindled in the hearts of a people by the flaming torch of history."

TABLET AT EAST DOOR OF COURTHOUSE, MURFREESBORO

Erected to the memory of General Nathan Bedford Forrest by the Daughters of the Confederacy for heroic services render the citizens of Murfreesboro on July 13, 1862. July 13, 1912. Placed in memory of the Rutherford County boys who gallantly served in the World War, by the United Daughters of the Confederacy. "The Brave Beget the Brave."

Bronze tablet on boulder at Sam Davis Home (to the left of walkway to house):

Sam Davis, 1842-1863. In the shadow of this great rock Sam Davis hid his horse, fastened to a swinging limb of this old oak on the night of his last visit home just before he was captured, November 19, 1863. Erected by Nashville Chapter No. 1, United Daughters of the Confederacy, 1932.

From marble shaft at grave of Sam Davis, Sam Davis Home, Smyrna, Tenn.:

In memory of Samuel Davis, a member of the First Tennessee Regiment of Volunteers; born Oct. 6, 1842; died Nov. 27, 1863; age, 21 years, 1 month, and 21 days. "He laid down his life for his country. A truer soldier, a purer patriot, a braver man never lived, who suffered death on the gibbet rather than betray his friends and his country."

INSCRIPTION ON BROKEN STONE

John J. Shelby, born Aug. 21, 1—7; died Sept. 11, 1815. (Inscription on broken stone in a field near residence of W. H. King of Smyrna. Given over phone to Rebekah Jetton by Mrs. King.)

Windows (3) in St. Paul's Episcopal Church, Murfreesboro, Tenn. Copied by Rebekah Jetton for Capt. Wm. Lytle Chapter:

To the sacred memory of Mary Noailles Murfree, known in literature as Charles Egbert Craddock, Jan. 24, 1850-July 31, 1922.
In loving memory of our mother, Tempe Swoope Darrow. By Tempe D. S. and Wm. D. Kyser.
In loving memory of my son, Samuel Henry Hodge. By his mother.
In memorium. Rev. Bartow B. Ram-

Bible Records—Tombstone Inscriptions

age, first Rector of this Church; born Aug. 8, 1860; died Sept. 30, 1927. "I believe One Catholic and Apostolic Church."
In memorium. Samuel Henry Hodge; born July 13, 1872; died Nov. 27, 1927; first person confirmed in this church. "Unto the upright there ariseth light."
Inscription on altar: in memorium. Elizabeth T. Swoope; erected Nov. 30, 1893.

Government markers placed by the Capt. Wm. Lytle Chapter in Burlason family burial ground at home place of Mrs. Kate Burlason Talley, Rutherford County:

(Latin Cross.) David Burlason, James Farris Battalion, Col. Wade's Reg., N. C., discharged Oct. 9, 1782; died Aug. 13, 1832.
(Latin Cross.) Isaac Burlason, private in Capt. Thomas Jones' Company, First Regiment of Dyer's Mounted Gunmen, Tennessee Volunteer; died Jan. 24, 1865.

ISAAC LINCOLN FARM BURYING GROUND
(Sent by Mrs. Wm. Vaught)

Sacred to the memory of Isaac Lincoln who departed this life June 10, 1818; age, 64 years.
Sacred to the memory of Mary Lincoln who departed this life Aug. 27, 1831; age, about 76 years.
Daniel Stover, born Aug. 25, 1820; died Nov. 28, 1838.
Note—This farm is now owned by the estate of Dr. J. N. Rasar. (This September 25, 1933.)

THE MICHAEL HYDER, SR., CEMETERY RECORDS
Location: Powder Branch in Carter County, southwest of Elizabethton:

Michael Hyder, Sr., died June 25, 1790; member of the Watauga Association, Watauga Fort, June 21, 1776; took part in all early Indian wars in Tennessee under Shelby, Sevier, and Christian; was in following battles of the Revolution: Thickety Fort, Cedar Springs, Musgroves Mill in South Carolina; was detailed from the King's Mountain expedition to defend the Watauga settlement from Indian evasion.
Martha Hyder, died Aug. 8, 1812; age, 32 years.
Michael Hyder, April 26, 1803-Sept., 1805.
Michael Hyder, died Oct. 6, 1861; age, 94 years.
Sarah H. Hyder died May 6, 1865.
Samuel W. Hyder, Aug. 21, 1870-Sept. 25, 1897.
Lavicia E. Hyder, wife of Samuel W. Hyder, died April 5, 1870; age, 46 years.
Michael E. Hyder, 1796-1864.
Michael E. Hyder, Jr., Oct. 22, 1844-Mar. 19, 1885.
Samuel G. Hyder, Dec. 24, 1863-Sept. 6, 1886.
Joseph Hyder, Jan. 20, 1820-April 14, 1882.

OLD GREEN HILL CEMETERY, ELIZABETHTON, TENN.
Cemetery records:
Sent by Mrs. Wm. Vaught

Mary A., wife of Rev. John Singletary, June 24, 1806-Aug. 21, 1892.
Rev. John Singletary, died Dec. 5, 1851; age, 45 years.

Bible Records—Tombstone Inscriptions

Louisa Isabella, wife of W. G. Hunt, daughter of J. and K. Perry, April 18, 1829-July 30, 1855.
Thomas Springfield Folsom, Dec. 11, 1826-April 16, 1904.
Thomas V. Singletary, Nov. 4, 1832-Aug. 23, 1852.
W. J. Folsom, Feb. 29, 1820-Mar. 5, 1906.
Wife, Eliza F., died May 13, 1891; age, 56 years.
Martha G., wife of Samuel Angel, Dec. 19, 1813-July, 1864.
Ann M., wife of John W. Ellis, Sept. 15, 1838-June 4, 1865.
Mary N. Magee, Dec. 24, 1831-July 30, 1855.
Calloway Roberts, Mar. 20, 1835-Mar. 15, 1915 (Civil War Veteran).
Elizabeth, wife of L. C. Carter, April 5, 1838-May 27, 1876.
M. D. L. Cameron, Feb. 14, 1820-Dec. 23, 1869.
David A. Holly, Aug. 15, 1834-Sept. 9, 1911.
Malcolm Neville Folsom, died Feb. 21, 1878; age, 85 years.
Wife, Nannie Hughes, died April 16, 1877; age, 80 years.
Jane Cameron, April 16, 1801-Nov. 27, 1881.

Jacob Cameron, Feb. 14, 1802-Dec. 29, 1850.
William B. Cameron, Nov. 13, 1828-Dec., 1852.
Sarah Jane Cameron, Mar. 16, 1840-Sept. 19, 1844.
John Tyler Jobe, born Aug. 14, 1841; died in infancy.
Harriett A. Jobe, died June 18, 1842; age 33 years, 10 months, 6 days.
John Jobe, Sept. 29, 1794-June 25, 1857.
Ann P. Tipton, wife of Isaac Tipton, died Sept. 17, 1887; age, 74 years.
Isaac Tipton, May 17, 1809-July 31, 1863.
Col. W. M. Shell, born Jan. 31, 1802; age, 82 years.
Wife, Mary A. Shell, 1825-July 4, 1884.
Joseph Powell, born Nov. 28, 1839; age, ——.
William B. Cameron, Nov. 13, 1828-April 11, 1852.
James I. Tipton, Oct. 14, 1792-Jan. 20, 1861.
Susanna Tipton, consort of Samuel Tipton, died Feb. 10, 1853; age, 85 years, 3 months, 26 days.

HALL CEMETERY RECORDS, HAMPTON, TENN.

Oliver Hall, Company E, 2nd Tennessee Infantry.
A. C. Carden, born April 28, 1843; Company A, 13th Tenn. Cav.
Mary Hester McCloud, wife of Joseph McCloud, July 27, 1860-July 17, 1927.
J. N. Carriger, June 25, 1842-May 29, 1907 (Civil War Veteran).
M. G. Lovelace, Mar. 3, 1870-Nov. 29, 1910.
William T. Casey, Mar. 13, 1845-Oct. 27, 1929.
Louie Casey, wife of William T. Casey, June 25, 1858-Oct. 21, 1929.

Samuel J. Jackson, Oct. 24, 1874-Mar. 23, 1930.
John H. Hardin, Dec. 21, 1844-Jan. 15, 1912.
N. T. Campbell, Company G, 13th Tennessee Cav.
Sarah Campbell, Mar. 9, 1840-Dec. 3, 1893.
Captain David E. Baker, born Mar. 31, 1879.
Andrew J. Shull, Feb. 22, 1827-Feb. 16, 1906; Company K, 14th Regiment, Kentucky Vol.
Elizabeth J. Brown, wife of W. C. Brown, June 11, 1843-Mar. 10, 1901.

MAJOR PHARAOH ARTHUR COBB

Major Pharaoh Arthur Cobb was born November 22, 1827, near Cobb's Ford, now in Hamblen County, Tennessee. His parents were Jesse and Leannah Cobb, whose maiden name was Cox. When eighteen years old he volunteered in the war against Mex-

Bible Records—Tombstone Inscriptions

ico and rode horseback via Memphis, Tenn., and Houston, Texas, to Tampico, in Mexico, where he joined General Scott's army and sailed to Vera Cruz. He was engaged in the battle around Vera Cruz until he was incapacitated by malaria and tropical diseases and compelled to return home. The return trip was by boat to New Orleans and up the Mississippi and Cumberland rivers to Nashville, then by private conveyance to his home.

On September 29th, 1849, he married Catherine Chesnutt, of St. Clair, Tenn., daughter of Samuel Chesnutt, a godly woman and a devoted wife and mother. They made their home at St. Clair, where their seven children were born. Four of these died in one month during the Civil War, two of them being buried in one grave. The three remaining children grew to maturity. The oldest, Mary Leannah, married Dr. N. F. Phillips, a brave young Confederate soldier, who had served in her father's regiment. Dollie married James S. Morrisett and Pharaoh Lee married Miss Cora Nell Crosby of Boston, Mass. Dollie died in 1881. Mary Leannah and Pharaoh Lee are still living.

Major Cobb was among the first volunteers for service in the Confederate army. As a Major in the Second Tennessee Cavalry under Col. Ashby, he fought in the battles of Chickamauga, Missionary Ridge, Shelbyville, Bowling Green, Cumberland Gap, Barboursville, and Fishing Creek. He was known as a good officer and a brave soldier. He was a fine rider and the best pistol shot in the company in which he enlisted. He came of a family of citizen soldiers. His grandfather, for whom he was named, was an officer in the Revolutionary war. The army of King's Mountain was assembled at the home of William Cobb, his great-grandfather, rendezvoused at his grandfather's home at Elizabethton, and marched from there to King's Mountain, where the notable victory was won over the British and Hessian troops. His grandfather enlisted in the War of 1812. It was but natural that Major Cobb should volunteer for the war against Mexico and in the Confederate army and should regret his inability on account of his age to go with Jo Wheeler to help free the Cubans from Spanish rule.

He was an ardent Mason, having been admitted first to Overton Lodge at Rogersville and afterwards becoming one of the charter members of the Kyle Lodge at Whitesburg, Tenn.

Possibly the most far-reaching act of his life was the building, in partnership with Lieut. Jno. A. Walker, of blessed memory, the St. Clair Academy from which have gone out to the ministry, the teaching and medical profession, to agricultural and business life and to the navy, well trained and capable young men who have made their influence felt wherever they have gone.

Bible Records—Tombstone Inscriptions

As a young man he made a profession of religion and joined the Baptist Church; but like so many others he allowed the army life to wean him away. When he was over sixty years of age, having heard Mr. Moody, the great Evangelist, at Knoxville, he was very much impressed and soon after, in a revival at St. Clair, influenced by his son, now Rev. P. L. Cobb, of Chattanooga, he went to the altar and was happily converted, after which he joined the Methodist Episcopal Church, South, to which his wife and children belonged.

After the death of his wife in 1895, he made his home with his daughter, Mrs. Mary L. Phillips. The last year of his life was spent in Whitesburg and Chattanooga. In May of this year, as a result of his blindness, he fell and injured his hip; this was followed by severe chills. He never was able to leave his bed after this and passed peacefully away at 11 o'clock, September 21st, 1915. A strong faith in Jesus Christ enabled him to meet death as a matter of course. He showed no fear, and after arranging his business affairs, calmly awaited the last enemy and conquered him.

"Soldier of Christ well done,
Thy glorious warfare's past;
The race is run, the battle fought,
And thou art crowned at last."

Ancestry of Kate Phillips Cassidy, wife of Rev. E. H. Cassidy. Copied by Mrs. J. M. Ferguson, Registrar Unaka Chapter, D. A. R., Erwin, Tenn.

Tabulation submitted by Mrs. R. E. Garrett, Dixon Springs, 1930. List of historic spots indicated by letters on map:

A—Walton Road, from Cumberland Gap to mouth of Caney Fork at Carthage, which followed from Cookeville, the route of "the Caney Fork Road." It .... extension, to Nashville by Lebanon, has recently been rechristened "The Alvin York Highway." The Walton Road was opened in 1801 by Wm. Walton and was the first wagon road through the wilderness into Middle Tennessee. Approximate route:

B—Battery Hill, Carthage, Federal encampment during War between the States.

C—Old Fort Blount Road from Cookeville to Bledsoe's Lick.

D—Old Fort Blount, built, ..., and commanded by Capt. Sampson Williams, and mentioned in diaries of the Michaux botanist, and other early travelers.

E—Site of Livingstone, in Cage's Bend of north side Cumberland, and selected first and courthouse partly built, for county seat of Smith.

F—Hill with breastworks still to be seen occupied by Federals during and after War between States.

G—Site of Bledsoesborough, selected and town lots sold for county seat of Smith. Vote was taken between Carthage and Bledsoesborough, and the former won—much to the detriment in later development to the county, many think. Near this sit and on this land are buried Col. Wm. Saunders, original member of

Bible Records—Tombstone Inscriptions

the Sons of Cincinnati and, and Major and Lt.-Col. William Cunningham, member of General Washington's staff during the Revolution.

H—House spring and grove of Major Tilghman (or Tilman) Dixon, first settler (1787 or before) in this section, second settler in Smith County, from whom our village gets its name. In his house, still standing, the first court of Smith County was held in 1799. He kept the first tavern and was first postmaster in this section, and contracted to build the first schoolhouse. He was an original member of the Sons of Cincinnati, and in this house entertained Louis Philipe—"two in a bed" and gave him "the luxury of coffee."

I—Site of first Baptist church in county, on Col. Martin's land.

J—Site of first Methodist church in county, on John Magee's land, near Capt. Grant Allen house.

K—Hartsville, where Morgan's Cavalry, in an hour's fierce fighting, with the thermometer below zero, took 1,500 Federal prisoners.

L—Hilham, site of first female academy in Tennessee, and perhaps in entire Southwest, established by Sampson Williams and Moses Fisk.

M—Bledsoe's Lick, site of Bledsoe's Fort, Bledsoe Monument, and where Thomas Sharpe Spencer spent the winter in a Sycamore tree, and first corn was raised by white man in Middle Tennessee, and site of Thomas Sharpe Spencer Monument erected by Mrs. Martin.

N—Approximate vicinity of hill where Thomas Sharpe Spencer was killed by Indians.

O—Tomb of Robert Wright, Revolutionary soldier, near Lafayette.

Locations of Revolutionary graves, submitted by Mrs. R. E. Garrett, Dixon Springs, 1930. Key to numbers on map:

* following name is to indicate that it is on a list of fifty Revolutionary soldiers living in Smith County, Tenn., in year 1812.

** following name indicates soldier to have had Colonial as well as Revolutionary service.

*** following name indicates general opinion that he had Revolutionary service, but I have not the proof at hand.

1—Capt. Wm. Alexander,*** born Dec. 25, 1748, Cecil County, Md.; died Aug. 4, 1930. Buried on original grant one-half mile southeast of Hartsville, Trousdale (formerly Sumner) County, known as the Gleaves place. Graves marked with upright slabs now falling, though moderately well preserved. Wall which surrounded graves is scattered and removed.

2—Capt. Grant Allen,* born in North Carolina; died in Smith County; married Tabitha. Buried on original grant near four-story brick house built by him. In this house was held the first Baptist religious meeting in Smith County; the members organized as an arm of the Station Camp Church. On this land the "Smith County Revolutionary Volunteers" mustered to be reviewed by General Winchester to whom they had tendered their services as a home guard for the War of 1812.

3—Richard Banks,* "of Wake County, N. C." Died before Sept., 1814. Supposed to be buried on his original tract, below the mouth of Dixon's Creek, on south side of Cumberland River.

4—John Barkley,*** b——; died, 1831. March 7th. Married Margaret. Buried most probably on graveyard near "Barkley's Bar," now owned by Mrs. Dillon. Came from Virginia.

5—Jacob Benton.*

6—Anthony Bledsoe,** born about 1735; died April, 1793. Buried near

Bible Records—Tombstone Inscriptions

site of old fort at Bledsoe's Lick, Sumner County, on hill near old Academy, northeast of new public school.

7—Isaac Bledsoe,** born, 1700, in Virginia; died July 20, 1788. Buried by his brother.

8—Capt. James Bradley,* born in North Carolina; died, ——. Buried on original grant on hill a few hundred yards northwest of old brick house built by him. Tombstones not inscribed, but surrounded by heavy rock wall on corner stone of which is cut: "James Bradley Family Graves."

9—Wm. Brandon, born, 1748; died in Smith County, 1836.

10—John Brevard,*** born ——; died before 1828. Buried on original grant on Goose Creek, now Macon County. Stone wall surrounding graves, but all markers missing except one handsome tomb marked, "Oolythenia Brevard." Land owned for years by Daniel Goad, bought from Johnson, now owned by Goad's son-in-law.

11—Jacob Burrus,* born in Virginia; died, 1832. Buried in Col. Martin graveyard on Dixon's Creek.

12—Daniel Campbell.*

13—Caleb Carmen,* born ——; died, 1831-2. Probably buried in Harris graveyard in Shady Grove neighborhood, Trousdale County, on land now owned by Leland and Lillard Carmen.

14—Walter Caroth.*

15—Wm. Carter, 1760-1847. Buried on old Prior Carter place on Carter Branch, west side of Goose Creek. Land now owned by Jarrel Burrow, Confederate soldier.

16—David Cockran.*

17—Wm. Collee.* Most probably buried on old Collee place on Tow Town Branch of Peyton's Creek, near Edward Settle's old home.

18—Major Wm. Cunningham,** 1741-1806. Married Elizabeth Watkins. Buried in Wm. Saunders graveyard, on Rome Road from Dixon's Spring. His and wife's tombstones have been removed as well as rock wall surrounding graveyard by vandals. Land now owned by Millard Lynch and sisters. Stones were removed when owned by H. B. Wright.

19—Philip Day.* Possibly buried on Lick Creek, Trousdale County, on old Day place, formerly owned by Tom Reece Merryman. Stones gone.

20—Major Tilghman Dixon,* 1750-1816. Buried on original grant, short distance northeast of house built by him, still standing, continuously occupied since its erection, not later than 1787.

21—Charles Donaho,* I understand, buried in graveyard on Donaho place on Goose Creek, still owned by the family.

22—John Fergueson,* possibly one-fourth miles northeast of village of Riddleton, Smith County.

23—John Gammons,* probably on Dry Branch of Goose.

24—Wm Goodall,* born ——; died, 1813. I am told buried in cemetery at Hartsville. I do not know.

25—Andrew Greer,* born ——; died, 1817. Lived on Goose Creek.

26—Harris Grisham, born ——; died about 1830. Buried, I feel sure, on old Tom Walker place, south side of Cumberland, opposite Col. Wm. Saunders' original grant, as he lived near there and his wife had previously been buried there.

27—Daniel Hammock,* 1762-1829. Buried in Col. Wm. Martin graveyard.

28—John Hargis.* Family have always lived "on the Ridge," Macon County.

29. John Harris,*** buried in Harris graveyard in Shady Grove, now owned by Leland and Lillard Carmen.

30—James Hart, buried in Hartsville cemetery.

Bible Records—Tombstone Inscriptions

31—Wm. Haynie,* born ——; died, 1849. Died on Jack Hackett place on Peyton's Creek which he settled in 1799 and lived on for half a century.

32—Wm. Herod, 1748-1836. Buried on part of his tract which was owned by his son, William, now owned by Ellis Porter, Peyton's Creek.

33—James Hibbetts,*** 1760-1821. Buried on Carter Branch of Goose Creek near house he built, now owned by Lon Burrow.

34—Andrew Hoover.*

35—Parish Lankford,* settled on Brush Creek, or in Goose Creek neighborhood near Mongle's Gap, where several old Lankford graves are.

36—Wm. Ligon,* most probably in graveyard on place originally settled by him on Dixon's Creek. Born in Virginia; died, 1828-9.

37—John Lovelady,* settled on Peyton's Creek near head of Dixon. His wife also served as bullet molder during Revolutionary War.

38—Charles McMurry,* born ——; died, 1820. Buried in graveyard now owned by Gilbert Porter, Trousdale County, near Monglis Gap.

39—Champ Madden.* Probably buried in graveyard on Madden place on Goose, joining Donaho place.

40—Rev. John Magee, 1761-1836. Buried near house built by Ellis Beasley and occupied for last fifty years by W. Y. Jenkins, Trousdale County.

41—James Martin,*** born ——; died, 1853. Buried on place he lived on in Cage's Bend, Smith County, on which land town of Livingston was planned.

42—Col. Wm. Martin, 1765-1846. Buried on original settlement on Dixon's Creek, now owned by Robert Cormwell.

43—Daniel Mongle,*** born ——; died before 1809. Long Hunter, signer of Cumberland Compact, settled early on Glasgow Branch of Goose and built house, still standing, now owned by Greene Wright. Buried on place near McMurry graveyard where some of the Pipers are also buried.

44—Francis Moore.*

45—Col. Wm. Moore, *** born ——; died, 1828. Died at Carthage, probably buried in oldest of the three Carthage cemeteries.

46. John Oakley.

47—Joseph Paine. Will recorded in Smith County in 1828. Was living on original settlement in Payne's Bend on south side of Cumberland at time of death. Probably buried in graveyard there, enclosed by rock wall, the stones of which, I understand, were sold some years ago to be used as foundation for a house. A protest was made, however, by some descendants, and wall was left intact.

48—Wm. Roper,* in graveyard on old Roper place on Goose Creek, on Roper Road out from Hartsville, now owned by Robert Cornwell.

49—Johann Roseby.*

50—Obediah Sanders,' was living in Smith County in 1806.

51—Col. Wm. Saunders, born, 1759, in North Carolina; died, 1803, in Smith County, Tenn. Buried in graveyard on original grant one-eighth mile due south of present residence of Charlie Alexander, which is original site of old Bledsoesborough. Land where graveyard now owned by Millard Lynch and sisters.

52—Capt. Edward Settle, born ——; died, 1839. Buried on land he settled on Tow Town Branch of Peyton's Creek, on or very near old Fort Blount Road, near Mace's Hill.

53—Hugh Shaw,* near Chestnut Mound.

54—John Shelton,* built rock house before year 1796, on Highway 25, half way between Hartsville and Dixon Springs. His grand-nephew, by marriage, Wm. Neeley, says Shelton moved to Cornersville in Maury or Giles County in the fifties.

Bible Records—Tombstone Inscriptions

55—Nicholus Shrum,* possibly buried on Dry Fork of Goose.

56—Shelton Smith.*

57—Wm. Stalcup,*** buried on place he originally settled on Stalcup's Hill between Hartsville and Dixon Springs, on Highway 25, where Negro graveyard now is.

58—Francis Surles,* inventory of his estate recorded in Smith County in 1835.

59—Thomas Talbot.*

60—Wm. Thompson.*

61—Frederick Turner.*

62—Peter Turney,** born ———; died, 1804-5. Buried on original settlement on old Fort Blount Road near Mace's Hill now owned by O. H. Garrett. Sam M. Young born and reared on place was always told that mulberry tree in graveyard stands at head of Peter Turney's grave, otherwise unmarked.

63—Freak Whiles (Frank Uhles?)

64—Warren Walker.* One Warren Walker was living in Smith County in 1848.

65—Col. Wm. Walton,* born, 1760, in North Carolina; died, Mar. 6, 1816. Buried on original settlement on Cumberland River, north side, at mouth of Caney Fork. Rock wall surrounds graves.

66—Philip Watson* died in Smith County before May, 1816.

67—Sampson Williams, born ———; died about 1840. Buried on land he lived and died on, near old Fort Blount, in the garden.

68—James Wilson.* His grandson, Jarrel Burrow, Confederate soldier, says he thinks he is buried on Wilson place on Dry Fork of Goose.

69—Robert Wright, born in Virginia, 1759; died in Smith County, 1831. Buried on road leading from Brattentown, Macon County, Tenn., to Thompkinsville, Ky., about one-quarter mile from Brattentown, 100 yards from road on left side.

70—Wm. Young, probably buried on land now owned by Wm. A. Allen, a few hundred yards due north of present residence. He is said to have died here en route from Nashville or New Orleans to his home on Peyton's Creek, and was buried on Tilman Dixon's land. Grave not marked, and rocks of surrounding wall being gradually removed few at a time. Some of the Yaters also buried there.

71—Wm. Cage, 1745-1811. "A major in the Revolutionary War." Buried on original settlement in Cage's Bend, Sumner County.

72—Edward Douglas, born Oct. 3, 1713; died Feb. 2, 1795; married Sarah, daughter; buried in Wm. Cage graveyard, who was his son-in-law. Land now owned by ——— Moss.

73—Gen. Griffith Rutherford is buried somewhere in Sumner County, perhaps at Shiloh Church, near Bledsoe's Lick.

74—Gen. James Winchester, buried on the Grag Font estate on Bledsoe's Creek, also most probably his brother George.

Graves of Revolutionary soldiers, located in 1931:

1—Andrew Alexander, buried in orchard of Dan Carr's place on Middle Fork of Goose Creek, Trousdale County.

2—Isham (Isom) Beasley, buried on place now owned by John Jellicorse, in Sullivan's Bend, Smith Sounty.

3—Richard (or Samuel?) Bradley, buried on land now owned by Richard Payne, near Templow.

4—Jeremiah Brown, buried between Hilham, Overton County, and Gainesboro.

5—Francis Corley, buried in Corley graveyard on old Corley place, between John Shelton's Rock House and Grant Allen place, Trousdale County.

6— .... Dale, father of Adam Dale, came to Liberty, DeKalb County, in

Bible Records—Tombstone Inscriptions

1791; buried on old Givens place, near Liberty.

7—Jeremiah Dixon lived and probably buried at foot of ridge, at the head of Middle Fork of Goose.

8—Jonathan Fares, buried at Brush Creek Church, Smith County.

9—Jacob Fite, buried in Alexandria, DeKalb County, cemetery.

10—Bryan Gregory, settled and died on Tow Town Branch of Peyton's Creek.

11—Berry (Bray) Gregory, buried on Piper place on Nickajack Branch, Smith County.

12—Thomas Gregory, father of Berry and William, buried somewhere in the Peyton's Creek neighborhood.

13—William Gregory, on Wm. Nixon place on Peyton's Creek.

14—Arthur Hesson, on Tow Town Branch, of Peyton's.

15—John Hill, in Willow Grove Cemetery.

16—Joseph Jared, on ridge in Putnam County at "The Low Gap."

17—Wm. Jared, on place owned by John B. Denny, near Cookeville, on Indian Creek.

18—Jonathan Key, on Robert K. Nesbitt, near Monoville, Smith County.

19—James Lauderdale, in Lauderdale graveyard, near Templow, Trousdale County.

20—Green B. Low, in graveyard on original Low settlement, south side of Cumberland at Harts Ferry.

21—Hallery Malone, Lauderdale graveyard, near Templow.

22—Capt. Job Morgan, on his settlement on Spring Creek, now Putnam County.

23—Josiah Paine, supposed buried beside his brother Joseph, in Payne's Bend, south side of Cumberland, Smith County.

24— .... Porter, at Brush Creek Baptist Church.

25—Marcus Rickman, Willow Grove Cemetery, Templow.

26—Maj. Wm. Quarles, on Mrs. C. M. Huddleston's place, near White Plains.

27—Bartholomew Stovall, at Templow, Trousdale County, on hill opposite site of his residence.

28—Wm. Thompson, lived on Goose Creek near Thomas Donaho and John Brevard.

29—Henry Wakefield, in year 1809 owned land on ridge between Cumberland and Barren Rivers.

30—James or Daniel Witcher, on Salt Lick, Jackson County, in Witcher graveyard.

31—Henry McAden, buried on Little Goose Creek, in old McAden graveyard, about one-half mile west of Lytle Dalton's residence, on land owned several years ago by a Negro by the name of Dalton. Grave enclosed by rock wall. Information given me by Mr. Jim Freedle of Hartsville, Confederate soldier, who is his grandson.

Graves of Revolutionary soldiers unlocated on list sent in by me last year, 1930, which I have since located, or verified, or learned something more of:

Richard Banks, buried in Banks or Turner graveyard, south side of Cumberland below mouth of Dixon's Creek, near Cedar Bluff. Very bad condition.

Christopher Boston; one Christopher Boston buried in graveyard opposite old Boston house site; unable to learn whether he was the Revolutionary soldier or the son or grandson of the soldier. Though I still think he was the soldier.

David Cockran, back of house built "in North Carolina," one-half mile

Bible Records—Tombstone Inscriptions

east of Dixon Springs, on Tilman Dixon Highway, formerly and for many years owned by G. F. Bransford.

Wm. Denny, on old Wm. Denny place, south side of Cumberland above the mouth of Dixon's Creek.

Maj. Thomas Draper and wife, Sarah Lyle, in the old graveyard, back of and to the left of old house built by him. The two graves enclosed by rock wall. Place now owned by Millard Holland.

Harris Grisham, not buried by his wife on south side of Cumberland, but in graveyard in Anderson Beasley's place, right on river, on right side of road leading from Dixon Springs to Rome.

John Hargis, I was told by Mrs. Mary E. Rowark, age 91 years, at the time, recently deceased, that there are old soldiers buried in graveyard on old Hargis place, one-half mile from LaFayette on the Brattontown Road, and that John Hargis possibly was buried there.

John Shelton, I am told by Wm. Neely, Confederate soldier, descended from John Shelton's sister-in-law, that he did not die here but moved to Maury or Giles County, Tenn., and died there.

Nicholas Shrum, from Smith County Deed Books, I find that he lived near the head of Dixon's Creek. Most probably buried on Dry Fork of Goose, where Shrums have lived for generations.

William Stalcup is not buried in Negro graveyard on Stalcup's Hill, but on the Mongle's Gap Road, on land originally owned by Stalcup, now owned by Jim Tom Cunningham, opposite side of the road from Cunningham's entrance. Enclosed by rock wall, almost entirely down; no inscriptions.

Berryman Turner, in Turner-Banks graveyard below mouth of Dixon's Creek, south side of Cumberland, near Cedar Bluff.

Graves of Revolutionary soldiers buried in Sumner County which have come within my knowledge in my inquiries for old graves. Thinking it probable that these same graves will appear on lists sent in from D. A. R.'s living in Sumner County, I am listing them separately:

Dr. Redmond D. Barry, cousin of Barry O'Meara, Napoleon's Physician at St. Helena; graduate of Dublin University; resigned a commission in the British Navy to come to America and fight on our side; skilled surgeon; lawyer; and brought the first bluegrass and thoroughbreds to Tennessee. Buried under handsome elms on west side of East Station Camp Creek, a few hundred yards northwest of Miller Harris' residence, on Andrew Jackson Highway.

James Bryson, 1745-1833. Buried in Bethpage Cemetery on Andrew Jackson Highway.

James Hanna, 1765-1833, also wife, in Bethpage Cemetery.

Maj. George D. Blackmore, in old Presbyterian graveyard, about four miles east of Gallatin on Tilman Dixon Highway. on hill above and behind the Branham place. Gen.

Griffith Rutherford also supposed to be buried there, though no sign of his tombstone, though I am told that there are probably stones there not visible because covered with layers of soil washed on them or accumulated.

Nathaniel Parker, on Dr. Johnson place near Greenfield, north of Bledsoe.

Frank Weathered, Willow Grove Cemetery.

Zaccheus Wilson, Mecklenburger signer, near Gallatin on site of old cotton factory, or near, south of Gallatin.

Bill Edwards, buried on Green place, on Salem Road, which connects the Red River and the Douglass Pikes, north of Gallatin. Edwards, I am told, had a lawsuit with Andrew Jackson which was tried three times, Edwards winning all three suits.

Bible Records—Tombstone Inscriptions

THE SESQUI-CENTENNIAL OF DAVIDSON COUNTY.

DR. W. A. PROVINE,

Curator of the Tennessee Historical Society.

The year 1783 contained many events bearing on the general history of the United States and her Western borders. The one of most importance in the annals of nations was the final Treaty with England that forever defined and recognized the freedom of the American Colonies and the firm establishment of the United States among the world's governments.

We can picture no more interesting scene than that presented by the General Assembly of North Carolina at its sessions in Hillsboro, April, 1783, when on Friday the 19th a message was received from Governor Alexander Martin, by both Houses as follows:

"To the Honourable General Assembly;

Gentlemen:

A number of great events of the most interesting nature to the United States having intervened since the last meeting of the Legislature, I feel myself too much impressed with the General Joy that must be occasioned to confine to the dull formality of a message.

I therefore propose to wait upon the Honourable the General Assembly and communicate the same in person, and those matters and things I have to lay before them, and for this purpose request the attendance of both Houses in the Conference Chamber tomorrow, or such a time as shall be most acceptable to them."

Whereupon the Commons sent to the Senate the following message:

"Mr. Speaker and Gentlemen this accompanying message desiring the attendance of both Houses of the General Assembly in Conference, in order that he may in person communicate such matters, and things as he may have to inform them of.

In consequence thereof, this House agrees to receive his Excellency, the Governor, at the Church at 4 o'clock this evening, and desire your concurrence. . . .

The Senate and Commons in Conference, appointed each member of their body to wait upon His Excellency the Governor and request his attendance in the Conference Room. . . . Whereupon His Excellency, attended by the said gentlemen, waited upon the General Assembly in Conference and addressed them as follows:

"Gentlemen of the General Assembly:

Since the last meeting of the Legislature a Train of great and interesting events have intervened in our political system which, added to those of the preceding year, have, under Almighty God, led at length the power of the United States to the summit of her wishes.

With highest pleasure I present you with those communications I have been honoured with for your information, announcing this importance occurence. [1st, the withdrawing of the enemy from Charleston and Savannah, 2nd, the Treaty concluded by the United States with the New Netherlands.]

Bible Records—Tombstone Inscriptions

With impatience I hasten to communicate the most important intelligence that has yet arrived in the American Continent.

His British Majesty having acknowledged the United States of America Free, Sovereign and Independent, and for Himself, his Heirs and Successors relinquished all Claims to the Government, proprietary and territorial rights of the same at Paris, the thirtieth of November last, by His Commissioners appointed to treat of Peace with the Commissioners of the United States, though not to be concluded until terms of peace should be agreed upon between Great Britain and France, which peace between Great Britain and France was signed the twentieth day of January last, (1783) that renders the former conclusive, as certified by papers now before you transmitted to me from the Minister of Foreign Affairs and our Delegates in Congress.

For this most happy and auspicious event, which involves in it a most precious inheritance for ages and all the blessings that can flow from Independent Empire, with the most lively, fervent and heartfelt joy.

I congratulate you, and thro' you, all my fellow-citizens of the State of North Carolina."[1]

THE REVIVING OF THE CUMBERLAND RIVER DISTRICT GOVERNMENT.

Just about the time the above heartening news was spread abroad in the Colonies, the far-away struggling settlement of North Carolina on Cumberland River at the "French Lick" began to re-assert itself and come out of the shadows of its early three uncertain years of life. L

"The three years following the first settlement in Cumberland, were years of great privation, losses and gloom, —insomuch that the Stations were abandoned, and the people were assembled at Nashborough and Eaton's, a few at Freeland's.

They had no corn or wheat, and were compelled to live on fresh and dried meat. Some would leave the Country and risk a journey to the Stations in Kentucky, others were ready and preferred to undertake the perils and hardships of a voyage to the settlements in Illinois, —then a County of Virginia.

Col. Robertson and others earnestly remonstrated against such desertions,—but in vain. By these removals and the massacre of the Indians,— the number of settlers was reduced more than half."[2]

From the time of the organization of the Compact Government, May, 1780, down to January, 1783, there remains in existence no record whatever with reference to the functioning of any government or attempt at same in the Cumberland River District— not even a fugitive scrap or sheet to reveal the progress of the settlement in law and order. It has been said that the people were so greatly exposed and kept in such constant alarm, some leaving, and many others agitating the propriety or possibility of remaining—all admitting that their perils were eminent and were likely so to continue for an indefinite period—that we may presume there were no regular meetings of the Judges, and no

---
[1](N. C. State Records. XIX. p. 239-244.)
[2]Putnam.

Bible Records—Tombstone Inscriptions

official Minutes made, and in all probability there were no consultations, decisions or acts requiring a record.

However, at the beginning of 1783 the sun seemed to have somewhat shined out with a more promising day. About this period accessions came to the withered colony and a new life and spirit sprang up, of which we do have an official record, viz:

North Carolina, Cumberland River, Jan'y 7th, 1783.[1]

The Manifold Sufferings & Destresses That The Settlers here have From Time To Time / Undergone, Even Almost From our First Settling; With the Desertion of the Greater / Number of the First Adventures, Being So Discouraging To the Remaining / Few; That All Administration of Justice Seemed to Cease Amongst us; Which / however Weak, in Constitution, Administration, Or Execution; Yet has been / Construed in our Favour; Against Those Whose Malice, or Interest, Would Insinuate / Us a People Fled To a Hiding Place from Justice; And the Revival of them / Again Earnestly Recommended;

And now having a little Respite granted; / And Numbers Returning To is; It appears highly Necessary That for the / Common Weal of the Whole; The Securing of the Peace; The Performance / of Contract Between Man & Men; Together with the Suppression of Vice, /—Again To Revive our former Manner of Proceedings Pursuant To the Plan / Agreed Upon at our first Settling here; And To Proceed Accordingly, Until / Such Times as it Shall Please the Legislature To grant us the Salutary / Benefit of The law Duly Administered Amongst (us) by Their Authority.

To this End, Previous Notice having been given To the Several Stations / To Erect Twelve Men of Their Several Stations Whom They Thought Most Proper / For the Business And being Elected To Meet At Nashborough the &th. day / of Jan'y 1783, Accordingly There met at The Time And Place Affore'sd /

    COL. JAS. ROBERTSON
    CAPT. GEO. FREELAND
    THOS. MOLLOY
    ISAAC LINSEY
    DAVID ROUNSEVALL
    HEYDON WELLS
    JAS. MAULDING
    EBENEZER TITUS
    SAM'L BARTON
    ANDREW ERWIN

Constituting Themselves into a Committee For The Purpose Affor'sd / By Voluntarily Taking The Following Oath, Viz; /

I, A. B. Do Solemnly Swear That as a Member of Committee, / I will do Equal Rights & Justice To The best of My Skill and / Judgement on the Decision of All causes that shall be laid before Me / Without Fear, Favour, or Partiality,———So help me God———

The Committee So Constituted, Proceeded To Elect Andrew Erwin / To be Their Clerk. John Montgomery To be Sheriff of the District, / And Col. James Robertson to be Their Chair-Man."

[1] Original Revue in Tenn. Hist. Society.

Bible Records—Tombstone Inscriptions

ARRIVAL OF THE COMMISSIONERS AND GUARD.

Just about this time there arrived in the settlement the Commissioners appointed by North Carolina to lay off the reservation in lands for the soldiers of the Continental Line of that State. This was a great company and indeed was the event of the early days of 1783. A "Call Meeting" of the Committee was held on January 18th to present to these Commissioners a petition in behalf of certain of the early settlers whose situation was not provided for in the above Act for the reserving of lands. The petition was sympathetically heard, but it was necessary that same be referred to the Legislature of North Carolina for approval.

PETITION FOR LOCAL GOVERNMENT.

The next important action of the Committee was on March 15th, 1783, the record of which is as follows:[4]

"On Motion made, the Committee agree that an address be sent to the Assembly, acknowledging our grateful sense of their late favour in granting us lands: praying them to grant us the salutary benefit of government in all its various branches; and that a land-office may be opened on such a plan as may encourage the settling of the country; that the protection of it may be less burdensome;

And that Col. James Robertson present the same, being elected thereto by the people."

The North Carolina Assembly as has been noted, convened at Hillsboro, April the 18th, 1783. There is no record concerning the personal appearance of Col. James Robertson at Hillsboro during this sitting of the Assembly, and such was the uncertain situation in the little colony on Cumberland it is quite reasonable to suppose that it was not expedient for him personally to take a long journey to the east just then, and this item is rather confirmed by the local records of the Committee showing his presence at each meeting during this period, thus he was hardly giving time for so long and tedious a journey as that required in an attendant on the assembly.

A FRIEND OF THE WESTERN DISTRICT.

The Western District, however, had present in that Assembly one whose life-record was that of favor and personal interest in the farther settlements. This was the Hon. Waighstill Avery, a representative in the Commons from Burke—one of the western frontier counties of the State. While a New-Englander by birth and rearing, yet Mr. Avery had chosen to settle in the South, and from the first was notably a champion of the people in democracy, education and all humanitarian efforts.

---

[4]Original Record,—Tenn. Hist. Society.

Bible Records—Tombstone Inscriptions

TWIN COUNTIES.

The Counties of Greene and Davidson are twin counties so far as having their birth through the action of the same session of the Assembly of North Carolina, and Mr. Avery stood sponsor in the case of each of them.

The North Carolina State Records give the Journals of both the Senate and House of Commons for this April Sessions of the Assembly, and the introduction and progress of the creating bills for both counties progress together, save the action with reference to Greene runs a little ahead of that of Davidson.

"1783. April 21. Monday. Mr. Avery presented a Petition from a number of inhabitants of Washington County, praying a division thereof. Mr. Avery presented a Bill agreeable to the prayer of said Petition, which was read the first time, passed and sent to the Senate."[5]

The final action on this Bill was taken in the Senate on April 26, when the same was passed on third reading and ordered engrossed.

The Act as published is as follows:

LAWS OF NORTH CAROLINA[6]
Chapter LI.

AN ACT FOR DIVIDING WASHINGTON COUNTY INTO TWO DISTINCT COUNTIES, AND ERECTING A COUNTY BY THE NAME OF GREEN.

I. WHEREAS the large extent of the County of Washington, renders the attendance of the inhabitants on the extreme parts of the said county to do public duties, extremely difficult and expensive;

II. Be it therefore Enacted by the General Assembly of the State of North Carolina, and it is hereby Enacted by the authority of the same, that from and after the passing of this Act the county of Washington shall be divided into two distinct counties, by a direct line beginning at William Williams' in the Fork of Horse Creek, at the foot of the Iron Mountain, thence a direct course to George Gallaspie's house, at or near the mouth of Big Limestone, thence a north course to the line which divides the counties of Washington and Sullivan, thence from the said line, to the Chimney-Top Mountain, thence a direct course to the mouth of Cloud's Creek in Holstein River; and all that part of Washington county westward of the said line, from and after the passing of this Act, shall be and is hereby declared to be a distinct county by the name of Greene.

(The remainder unnecessary to be inserted).

Mention has been made of the improbability of Col. James Robertson having attended in person on the sessions of this Assembly. If he did not, it is supposedly true that he had prepared the regular type of Petition usual in such cases and had same forwarded by trustworthy messengers to the Assembly. Anyhow, the Records show that the Petition safely arrived and was duly introduced into the Assembly, etc.:
1783. April /30.

[5] N. C. State Records—XIX. p. 288.
[6] N. C. State Records. Vol. XXIV. p. 539.

Bible Records—Tombstone Inscriptions

"Mr. Avery presented a Petition from a number of inhabitants on Cumberland River, praying to have Courts of Justice established,—&c. which being read, Mr. Avery moved for leave to prepare and bring in a Bill agreeable to the prayer of said Petition. Ordered that he have leave accordingly."[7]

Tuesday, May 5th. "Mr. Avery according to order, presented a Bill to erect a County adjoining the Line of Virginia, including a part of Cumberland River, which was read the first time, passed and sent to the Senate."

Wednesday, May 6th. Senate passed the Bill on first reading.

Thursday, May 15th. Commons passed Bill on second reading.

Thursday, May 15th. Senate passed Bill on second reading.

Friday, May 17. (last day of the Sessions.) Commons passed Bill on third and final reading, & sent to the Senate.

Friday, May 17. (Senate.) "Received from the Commons a Bill to erect a County adjoining the Line of Virginia, including a part of Cumberland River. . . Ordered that the Bill be read, The same being read was amended by consent of the Commons, passed the third time, and ordered engrossed."

On this same day of the Sessions of the Assembly the following last action is recorded:

(Senate.)[8]

"Ordered that writs of Election issue to the Counties of Greene and Davidson, that the election for the first mentioned County be held on the first Monday and Tuesday in August, and for the latter, on the second Monday and Tuesday of the same month."

(Commons.)[9]

"Resolved, that a writ of election issue to the County of Davidson, to elect two members of this House; that the said Election be held on the second Monday and Tuesday in August / next."

LAWS OF NORTH CAROLINA. 1788.
Chapter LII.[10]

AN ACT TO ERECT A COUNTY ADJOINING THE LINE OF VIRGINIA, INCLUDING A PART OF CUMBERLAND RIVER.

I. WHEREAS a considerable number of inhabitants have settled on the lands on Cumberland River in this State, at a very great distance from any place where county courts are held, and it is represented that erecting a county to include the said inhabitants, and appointing courts to be held among them, would be very beneficial and advantageous: THEREFORE for the general good of the said inhabitants,

II. BE IT ENACTED by the General Assembly of the State of North Carolina, and it is hereby enacted by the authority of the same, that all that part of this State lying west of the Cumberland mountain and south of the Virginia line, beginning on the top of Cumberland mountain where the Virginia line crosses, extending westward along the said line to the Tennessee River, thence up said river to the mouth of Duck River, then up Duck River to where the line of marked trees run by the Commissioners for laying off land granted the Continental line of this State intersects said river (which said line is supposed to be in thirty-five degrees fifty minutes north latitude) thence east along said line to the top of Cumberland mountain, thence northwardly along said mountain to the beginning, shall after

---
[7] Ibid. pgs.—224, 288, 308, 314, 356, 360.
[8] Ibid. 231.
[9] Ibid. 368.
[10] N. C. State Records. Vol. XXIV. p. 540.

Bible Records—Tombstone Inscriptions

the passing of this Act be, and is hereby declared to be a distinct county by the name of Davidson.

III. (Unnecessary to be inserted.)[11]

IV. And be it further enacted by the authority aforesaid, that the County Court of Davidson shall appoint an entry-taker for the purpose of receiving entries of lands for those who are allowed pre-emptions by the law for laying off lands granted to the Continental line of this State; And as it has been suggested that the inhabitants of the said county have no specie certificates they shall be at liberty to pay at the rate of ten pounds specie or specie certificates per hundred acres, for the aforesaid pre-emptions, and shall be allowed the term of eighteen months to pay the same, and that the heirs of all such persons who have died, having rights of pre-emptions as aforesaid, shall be allowed the term of one year after coming of lawful age, to secure their pre-emptions.

Provided, that no grants shall be made for said lands until the purchase money shall be paid into the proper office.

NORTH CAROLINA SETTLES WITH RICHARD HENDERSON & CO.

Just here it may be mentioned as an integral factor in the further stabilizing of land tenures and clearing of titles in the Cumberland River District, was the action of the North Carolina Assembly at this same session of forever outlawing the claims of Richard Henderson and Company of their interest in this section, following the course of Virginia of some years ago, by vesting a large grant of land in them to cover their expenses, etc.; the action was as follows:

"(Senate.) May 7th, 1783;[12]

Gen'l. Rutherford from the Committee to whom was referred the Memorial in behalf of Richard Henderson & Company, reported as follows:

'That the Memorialists ought to have a compensation for Their Expenses, Troubles and Risque in settling the lands in the said Memorial mentioned, 400,000. Acres, to be laid off in Powell's Valley, Beginning on the dividing line between North Carolina and Virginia where the same is nearest to the Old Indian Town, extending down Powell's River on both sides and four miles wide to the mouth of said River, then down Clinch River on both sides thereof twelve miles wide so far as to compleat the complement of 400,000. Acres.'

"The House taking this report into consideration, resolved that they do concur therewith, and ordered that the same be sent to the Commons."

By later action this land grant was reduced, first from 400,000 to 200,000 and still later, finally to 100,000 acres.

OPENING OF THE LAND OFFICE.

A further and a far-reaching action of this Assembly was the prōvision made for the opening of a Land-Office where the thous-

---

[11]Research by the Sec. of State of N. C. fails to throw any light on the omitted section.
[12]Ibid. 354.

Bible Records—Tombstone Inscriptions

ands of acres already located west of Cumberland Mountain could be duly entered as the basis of future grants.

No record is preserved as to the carrying out of the order issued for "writs of election" to be held on the second Monday and Tuesday in August, 1883. It is supposed that the election was duly held. Provision for the due organization of the County Court was made and the date of October 6th, 1783, set for its first meeting.

While these first recorded meetings have at times been put in print, yet in preparation for the contemplated Sesqui-Centennial it will be interesting to read them again:

(FIRST RECORDS OF DAVIDSON COUNTY.)[13]

State of No. Carolina.
Oct. 6th. 1783.

Davidson County,

Whereas an Act Was Made at Hillsbourough, the Ap'l Session past For laying off of a Distinct County Westward of Cumberland Mountain, to be known by the name of Davidson County and to include the Settlement on Cumberland River, &c; and for Establishing and Inferior Court of Pleas and Quarter Sessions therein, to be held on the first Monday of Janr'y, Apr'l, July and Oct. Appointing and Commisoning The Following Gentlemen, Viz:

Anthony Bledsoe, Daniel Smith, James Robertson, Isaac Bledsoe, Samuel Barton, Thomas Molloy, Francis Prince, And Isaac Linsey, Esq's. Members of said Court . . .

Be it Therefore Remembered that Pursuant to the Afforesaid Act of Assembly; Isaac Bledsoe, Samuel Barton, Francis Prince and Isaac Linsey, Esq'rs Named in the Commission Afforesaid Meet, this 6th. Day of Oct. In the Seventh Year of the American Independence, and in the Year of Our Lord, One Thousand Seven Hundred and Eighty Three; Quallifying themselves for the Purpose Afforsaid by taking the Oath by Law Prescribed for the Qualifying of Public Officers, And Likewise the Oath of Office; In the Following manner, Viz; the next Jun'r Member to the Sen'r Present Mentioned in the Commission, Administered the Afforsaid Oath to the Sen'r Member Present, and then he to the Other Members Present, Which Proceedings was Immediately Signed by Isaac Bledsoe.

The Court then Proceeded to Elect a Clerk Agreeable to the Act of the General Assembly, And made choice of Mathew Talbot, Esq. Which was Likewise Signed by Isaac Bledsoe . . .

The Court then Proceeded to Elect a Sheriff for the Court of Davidson, Agreeable to Act of Assembly, and made Choice of Daniel Williams, Esq. Who give Bond of Five Thousand Pounds, With James Mulherin, Isaac Linsey and William Overall, Securities for the Faithfull Discharge of his Office, And took the Oath by law Prescribed for the Qualifycation of Officers, And Likewise the Oath of Office.

[13]Original Records in Tenn. Hist. Society.

Bible Records—Tombstone Inscriptions

(page 2.)

Court then Adjourned untill Tomorrow Morning at 8 O'clock.
Tuesday Morning, 7th. of Oct. 1783.
The Court Meet According to Adjournment.

Mathew Talbot, Jun'r. Esq, Who was Yesterday Elected Clerk of the Court, And having been Indulged by the Court untill this Morning to find Sufficient Securities for his Faithful Performance of office. And failing therein; he Relinquished his Claim to the Place, on which the Court declared the Place of the Clerk Vacant, and Proceed to Elect Andrew Ewin there Clerk, Who gave Bond of Two Thousand Pounds, With William Overall, James Shaw, Julius Sanders and Jonathan Drake Securities for his Faithfull Performance of Office; And took the Oath Prescribed by Law for Public Officers, and Likewise the Oath of Office.

The Court then Proceeded to Elect by ballot and Entry Taker for the County of Davidson; The Candidates for the Place were Major Samuel Barton and Major John Reed, When the Vote of the Court were Unanimous for Major Barton. Who Entered into Bond of Fifty Thousand Pounds, With John Buchanan, Jun'r, Robert Espey, James Mulherin and Andrew Lucas Securities for the Faithfull return of the Money by him Received to the Treasurer.

And Likewise into Bond of Ten Thousand Pounds, with Robert Espey, Daniel Williams And John Buchanan, Jun'r. Surities for the Faithfull Discharge of his Office; And Likewise took the Oath of Office, Having Immediately before, as a Justice of the Peace, taken the Oath by Law Prescribed to be taken by Public Officers.

The Court Proceeded to Elect by Ballot a Surveyor for the County of Davidson. The Candidates for the Place were: Col. Anthony Bledsoe and James Mulherin, when the Votes being Two for Each of the Candidates, the Court Agreed to Pospone the Determination to the Ensuing Court.

(page 3.)

The Court then Proceeded to Elect by Ballot a Register for the County of Davidson; The Candidates for the Place were Capt. Francis Prince and Andrew Erwin; When the Votes were for Erwin, one, & for Capt. Francis Prince, two, Who Entered into Bond of One Thousand Pounds, With Isaac Linsey and Daniel Williams, Securities for his Faithful Performance of his Office; And Likewise took the Oath of Office, having before as a Justice of the Peace take the Oath by Law Prescribed for the Qualifycation of Public Officers.

The Court then Nominated and Appointed Constables in the several Stations, Samuel Mason at Maulding's, James McCain at Mansco's, Stephen Ray at Heatonsburg, John McAdams at Nashborough, and Edward Swanson At Freeland's Station.

The Court then Proceeded to fix on a Place for Building of a Court-house & Prison, And Agree that in the Present Situation of the Settlement, they be builded at Nashborough At the Expence of the Public; And that the size of the Court-house be Eighteen feet Square in the Body, with a Lentoe Space On One Side of Twelve feet in Breadth, And in Length Equal to the house. And that the said house be Furnished with the Necessary Benches, Bar, Table &c.

Bible Records—Tombstone Inscriptions

Also a Prison of Fourteen feet Square of Hewed Logs of A Foot Square And that both Walls, Loft and Floor be Done with the Same Materials, Unless Builded on the Surface of A Rock, and that the Doing of Both be let by way of Public Vandue on the Fourteenth of this Inst. to the Lowest Bidder; And if not then Lett, that Major Barton Lett the Same on the Lowest Terms he can, to any Who will Undertake the Doing of them. To be Compleated by the first Monday of Jan'y Ensuing.

On motion made by Heydon Wells, Ordered that he have Leave to build a Water Grist Mill on Thomas's Creek, up Said Creek from the Mouth, About a Quarter of a Mile.

(page 4.)

Ordered that the Road from Nashbourough to Mansco's Station as Marked off heretofore by an Order of our Late Committee be Cleared out, And that James Freeland be Overseer from Nashbourough as far as opposite to Mr. Buchanan's Spring, And that James Shaw Oversee from Mansco's this Way to the Afforsaid Spring. And that they Call Together as many of the Inhabitants of there Respective Stations as shall be Necessary for Perfiteing of the Same.

The Court then Nominated for Grand Jury at the Ensuing Court, James Shaw, Ebenezer Titus, James Mulherin, Isaac Johnson, Daniel Williams, Sen'r, Robert Espey, John Buchanan, Sen'r, William Gowen, James Freeland, Capt. George Freeland, Francis Hodge, John Thomas, Heydon Wells, David Rounsevall, James Hollis, Sen'r, John Hamilton, Capt. Gasper Mansco, Benj'n Kuykendall, Elmore Douglass, James Maulding, Capt. McFadden, Capt. Solomon White, Charles Tomson, and Benj'm Drake, Sen'r.

The Court then Adjourned untill Court in Course, and the Proceeding was Signed by Isaac Bledsoe, Samuel Barton, Capt. Francis (Prince) and Isaac Linsey. Test. Andrew Erwin. C. D. C.

As to what will be done toward a proper observation of the Sesqui-Centennial of Davidson County during the coming months, remains with the future action of the County Court. The attention of the Honorable County Judge, Litton Hickman, has been called to this important and immediate matter by a representative of the Tennessee Historical Society, and Judge Hickman at once invited the representative to appear before the October meeting of the Court and present the same for their consideration.

It is to be noted that already, some weeks ago, the County of Greene celebrated in a most worthy way its Sesqui-Centennial and it can but be hoped that Davidson County will follow sooth.

Memorial Building, Nashville, Tenn.   Sept. 26, 1933.

Bible Records—Tombstone Inscriptions

THE DREAM

On May 16, 1897 the *Nashville American* announced the solution of a prize contest entitled The Dream.

Having spent an afternoon in wandering about the Centennial grounds, I had devoted the evening to Haywood, Ramsey, and other chroniclers of early Tennessee history. These two circumstances combined were doubtless the cause of a singular dream which I had that night. I thought that I stood in the Auditorium and saw congregated within its walls many of the famous men and women of the past whose names are closely interwoven with the history of our state. They seemed to constitute a convention of some kind; and, although the assemblage had not yet been called to order, the chair had already been taken, very appropriately, by the illustrious patriot whom Andrew Jackson styled "the Father of Tennessee" (1), while the publisher of the first newspaper issued in the state (2) acted as secretary, assisted by the first native historian of Tennessee (3), the founder of the first "campaign paper" established west of the Alleghanies (4), and the editor of the first Abolition paper issued in the South (5).

Seated upon the platform were several persons who seemed to have been designated as vice presidents of the meeting. There were the statesman who defeated another eminent Tennessean for Speaker of the National House of Representatives, and was in turn defeated by him (6); the only two United States Senators from Tennessee who were ever expelled (7, 8); the only Confederate States Senators from Tennessee (9, 10); the man of whom an ex-President of the United States said that he was "the greatest natural orator in Congress" (11); the United States Senator who published the first map of Tennessee (12); "Old Bullion" (13); and the patriot who, on resigning his seat in the Senate because he could not conscientiously obey the instructions of the Legislature, said: "For myself, I am proud that my state can, in my person, yet produce one man willing to be made a sacrifice rather than sacrifice his principles," (14).

An interesting quartet, near the stage, consisted of the member of the first Constitutional Convention who proposed the name "Tennessee" for the infant Commonwealth (15); the eminent statesman who said of the first Constitution of Tennessee that it was "the least imperfect and most republican" of any which had been adopted up to that time (16); and the Presidents respectfully of the second and third Constitutional Conventions (17, 18).

Seated together, a little farther back, were the two men who signed the act ceding "the territory south of the Ohio" to the United States (19, 20); the Virginia statesman in whose honor, at the suggestion of Andrew Jackson, a county was named, in

Bible Records—Tombstone Inscriptions

recognition of his earnest advocacy of the admission of Tennessee to the Union (21); the man who gave in the Senate the casting vote which secured that admission (22); and the commissioner who was sent by the Confederate Government to effect the withdrawal of Tennessee from the Union (23).

Chatting pleasantly together, in one corner of the hall, was a notable group of women, comprising the wife of whom her husband left the record that she was "a being so gentle and yet so virtuous, slander might wound, but could not dishonor" (24); the only female for whom a Tennessee county has ever been named (25); the pioneer maiden who, in endeavoring to escape from Indians, fell into the arms of the soldier who afterwards became her husband (26); and the beautiful Irish girl who was the cause of the disruption of a President's Cabinet (27); while near them "the Pocahontas of the West" (28) stood silently listening.

A remarkable group was composed of the famous general whose name was bestowed on the largest area ever embraced within the limits of a single county (29); a nobleman whose ancestral name, in abbreviated form, is borne by a Tennessee County (30); the explorer who named the Cumberland Mountains and river (31); the Governor by whose misspelled name a large part of Tennessee was known for many years (32); the Revolutionary soldier in whose honor the first settlement on the Cumberland was called (33); and the famous explorer whose mysterious death, within the limits of the county which now bears his name, has never been satisfactorily explained (34).

A picturesque trio consisted of the leader of the first body of white men who ever set foot on the soil of Tennessee (35); the first white man who erected an edifice within its limits (36); and the nobleman whose titular name was given to the first structure built therein by English-speaking people (37).

Grouped modestly in the rear of the hall were several men whose dress and accoutrements proclaimed them pioneers. There were the famous "big-foot hunter" who lived in a hollow tree (38); the man whom the Indians called "the fool warrior" on account of his reckless bravery (39); the commander of a marvelous expedition by water of which it has been said that "it has no parallel in modern history" (40); the man for whom the oldest town in the state was named (41); the first white child born in Tennessee (42); the first white child born in Nashville (43); and the bridegroom of the first marriage ceremony performed west of the Cumberland Mountains (44).

Just beyond these, leaning on their Deckhard rifles, stood three men who would have attracted attention anywhere—the celebrated backwoodsman who left an engraved record to designate the spot where he had "cilled a bar" (45); another, equally fa-

Bible Records—Tombstone Inscriptions

mous, who relates in his autobiography that he killed one hundred and five bears in less than a year (46); and still another who shot thirty-two of these "varmints" during one winter within seven miles of Nashville (47).

I was much interested in the appearance of a number of intellectual-looking men who sat together, engaged in earnest conversation. There were the men who founded the first educational institution in the Mississippi valley (48); the first minister who preached regularly to a Tennessee congregation (49); the bishop whose journal forms a valuable contribution to the history of early times in this State (50); the president of the first nonsectarian college chartered in the United States (51); the classmate of Daniel Webster who founded the first academy for females in Tennessee (52); and the eminent educator who declined successively the presidency of seven universities and colleges in other states in order that he might continue his chosen work in this (53).

Immediately in rear of these were the illustrious savant who first mapped the Gulf Stream and demonstrated the feasibility of a submarine cable (54); the first State Geologist of Tennessee (55); a distinguished surgeon who served professionally in the armies of three countries (56); and the young physician who, while perishing in a snow-storm on Mont Blanc, kept a record of his sensations for the benefit of science (57).

Just across the aisle sat the first Chief Justice of Tennessee (58); the judge who, after having been Chief Justice of Kentucky, removed to this state and became the greatest criminal advocate in the history of its bar (59); the first judge who was ever impeached in Tennessee (60); the eminent jurist who wrote President Jackson's farewell address (61); and the judge whose singular death from the attack of an infuriated turkey-gobbler was regarded by the early settlers as retributive justice for official oppression (62).

A literary group was composed of "the father of Tennessee history" (63); the famous printer whose name a short-lived commonwealth once bore (64); the English author who founded a colony in this state which was named for the scene of his best-known book (65); a Tennessee editor who was afterward elected to a seat in the British Parliament (66); the author of "Hymns to the Gods" (67); and "Sut Lovengood" (68).

In a prominent position in the center of the hall was a man who was Governor of two states of the Union (69); a Governor of Tennessee who was buried in two states (70); the first man who became Governor by virtue of his position as Speaker of the Senate (71); one who was elected Governor, but never inaugurated (72); a Governor who was presented by a grand jury as a public nuisance (73); one to whom a celebrated author referred as having given his official station "the ill-savor of a corner grocery" (74); the only person present at the death of Henry Clay except the members of his immediate household (75); the editor famous as "the fighting parson" (76); and the man who, by casting the entire vote of the state at a national convention, although he was merely a chance bystander, gave a new word to Tennessee politics (77).

A distinguished looking body was composed of the revolutionary general to whom 25,000 acres of land in Tennessee were granted by legislative enactment (78); a famous fighter under Jackson who was said to have been "a great general without knowing it" (79); a naval officer who was master of a vessel at twelve years of age, and whom one of the best-known of American poets has styled

"The sea-king of the sovereign west
Who made his mast a throne" (80);

the Tennessee postmaster to whom Andrew Jackson bequeathed a sword (81); the Colonel of the famous "Bloody First" (82); and the "grey-eyed man of destiny" (83).

Elsewhere were to be seen the man who supplied the funds which equipped John Sevier for King's Mountain (84); the man who furnished Jackson all the cannon-balls used by him at New Orleans (85); the first man who coined silver money in Tennessee (86); the owner of the first steamboat that ever landed at Nashville (87); the man who inaugurated the movement for building the first railroad in Tennessee, and was long known as "Old Chattanooga" in consequence (88); the man who exchanged a cow and calf for the hill on which the State Capitol was afterwards built (89); the man who bought the ground on which a large part of one of the most important cities in the state now stands for a rifle, a mare, and a pair of leather breeches (90); the discoverer of the Yosemite valley (91); the famous philanthropist who was chiefly instrumental in the founding of a state asylum for the insane (92); the author of the first bill for the establishment of a normal school in Tennessee (93); and the patriotic citizen who erected, at his own expense, the first monument to the memory of John Sevier (94).

A striking pair was composed of the man in whose veins circulated the blood of four races, and who simultaneously held commissions in the armies of three countries and was loyal to none (95); and the Choctaw chief who was graduated at the University of Nashville, and of whom Charles Dickens has said that he was "as stately and complete a gentleman, of nature's making," as he had ever met (96). Another pair, quite as striking, consisted of the first permanent settler at French Lick (97), convers-

Bible Records—Tombstone Inscriptions

ing volubly in his own tongue with a royal personage who visited Nashville in his youth, and afterwards became a king (98).

Just then the presiding officer arose and gave a premonitory rap with his gavel. As he did so I saw slipping furtively out of a rear door "the great western land pirate" (99); closely followed by the man who was instrumental in bringing him to justice (100).

THE INTERPRETATION

1. James Robertson.
2. George Roulstone.
3. James Gattys McGregor Ramsey.
4. Allen Anderson Hall.
5. Elihu Embree.
6. John Bell.
7. William Blount.
8. Alfred Osborn Pope Nicholson.
9. Landon Carter Haynes.
10. Gustavus Adolphus Henry.
11. Meredith Poindexter Gentry.
12. Daniel Smith.
13. Thomas Hart Benton.
14. Hugh Lawson White.
15. Andrew Jackson.
16. Thomas Jefferson.
17. William Blount Carter.
18. John Calvin Brown.
19. Charles Johnson.
20. Stephen Cabarrus.
21. William Branch Giles.
22. Samuel Livermore.
23. Henry Washington Hillard.
24. Rachel Jackson.
25. Mary Grainger.
26. Catharine (or Katherine) Sherrill.
27. Margaret O'Neill (or O'Neal).
28. Nancy Ward.
29. George Washington.
30. Marie Jean Paul Roche Yves Gilbert Motier de Lafayette.
31. Thomas Walker.
32. Estevan Miro.
33. Francis Nash.
34. Meriwether Lewis.
35. Fernando (or Ferdinand or Hernando) De Soto.
36. Robert Cavelier De La Salle.
37. John Campbell, Earl of Loudoun.
38. Thomas Sharpe (or Sharp) Spencer.
39. Abraham Castleman.
40. John Donelson.
41. Willie Jones.
42. Russell Bean.
43. Felix Robertson.
44. James Leiper (or Leeper).
45. Daniel Boone (or Boon).
46. David Crockett.
47. John Rains.
48. Samuel Doak.
49. Tidence Lane.
50. Francis Asbury.
51. Samuel Carrick.
52. Moses Fisk (or Fiske).
53. Philip Lindsley.
54. Matthew Fontaine Maury.
55. Gerard Troost.
56. Paul Fitzsimmons Eve.
57. James Baxter Bean.
58. John Catron.
59. Felix Grundy.
60. David Campbell.
61. Roger Brooke Taney.
62. Samuel Spencer.
63. John Haywood.
64. Benjamin Franklin.
65. Thomas Hughes.
66. John Mitchell.
67. Albert Pike.
68. George Washington Harris.
69. Hamuel Houston.
70. John Sevier.
71. William Hall.
72. Robert Looney Caruthers.
73. James Knox Polk.
74. Andrew Johnson.
75. James Chamberlain Jones.
76. William Gannaway Brownlow.
77. Edmund Rucker.
78. Nathanael (or Nathaniel) Greene.
79. John Coffee.
80. David Glasgow (or Glascoe) Farragut.
81. Robert Armstrong.
82. William Bowen Campbell.
83. William Walker.
84. John Adair.
85. Montgomery Bell.
86. Charles Roberson.
87. William Carroll.
88. James Overton.
89. George Washington Campbell.

Bible Records—Tombstone Inscriptions

90. David Shelby.
91. Joseph Reddeford Walker.
92. Dorothea Lynde Dix.
93. Robert Hatton.
94. Albigence Waldo Putnam.
95. Alexander McGillivray (or McGilvery).
96. Peter P. Pitchlynn.
97. Timote (or Timothy) Demonbreun.
98. Louis Phillipe.
99. John Arnold Murrell.
100. Virgil Adam Stewart.

A WORD FROM THE AUTHOR

To The American:

Some years ago certain circumstances caused me to form the opinion that the amount of time and attention given by our schools to the teaching of the history of our State was lamentably insufficient. This idea lay dormant for a time, until the Centennial enthusiasm which began to take hold upon all of us quickened it into activity; and the "Centennial Dream" was the result. My intention, at first, was merely to endeavor to have the questions which it embraces submitted, as a kind of competitive examination, to the pupils of that one of our city public schools in which I was personally interested as a patron, but your suggestion of giving it larger publicity through the medium of your columns, and your liberality in offering generous prizes as an additional incentive to contestants, broadened the scope of the undertaking, and so made it a state instead of a local competition.

It is proper here to say that, in preparing the "Dream," my intention was not so much to present those prominent and important events in Tennessee annals which are familiar to all well-informed persons as it was to collate such curious and comparatively little known facts as would, from their very obscurity, attract attention and incite study of the history of our State, knowing as I did that its investigation, once begun, would inevitably lead the student on and on until the charm of a history which is surpassed in brilliant and romantic features by that of none of the American commonwealths would compel him to master all its details. The result has amply justified your and my expectations. It is not too much to say that no similar undertaking has ever excited such general and widespread interest, and it is certainly true that more people of all classes have given diligent and painstaking care to the investigation of Tennessee history than ever before. Letters from many eminent men and women in all parts of the state, the printing of which your space would not permit, afford gratifying evidence of the general favor with which the "Dream" has been regarded as an educational aid of permanent value.

Notes on some of the questions are here added, both for the better elucidation of certain obscure matters and for the behoof of those critical contestants who, apprehensive that certain of

Bible Records—Tombstone Inscriptions

their answers might prove to be wrong, have taken pains in advance to present epistolary argumentation to demonstate that they are right.

By way of preface, I desire to say that, when the manuscript of the "Dream" was given to "The American," the "interpretation" which appears above was placed in an envelope, which was sealed and deposited in the safe of the business office, where it remained until the close of the contest, and that the names given above are printed precisely as they appear on that paper. In this way the decision of the contest was intentionally made altogether a matter of clerical comparison, with no opportunity for the exercise of critical judgment or discretion—if the name submitted by a contestant was identical with that appended to the corresponding number on the list referred to above, it was counted as correct; otherwise it was rejected. This was evidently the only method absolutely fair to all concerned.

In the matter of orthography, latitude was allowed wherever it was proper to do so. For example, the famous "backwoodsman of Kentucky" was in the habit of signing his name "Boon" or "Boone," as the fancy struck him; Capt. Leiper was known as "Leiper" or "Leeper" indifferently, the latter having been the signature to the Cumberland Compact; the surname of "Bonnie Kate" is always printed as "Sherrill" by historians (the "Sherril" of Putnam being manifestly a typographical error), although her father wrote his name "Sherrell"; that romantic scoundrel, Alexander McGillivray, was almost as versatile in the matter of autographic variants of his family name as was Shakespeare—Capt. Allison, in his "Dropped Stitches in Tennessee History," speaks of having examined two autograph letters, one of which is signed "McGillivray" and the other "McGilvery"; the middle name of the "big-foot hunter" is "Sharpe" or "Sharp," as may be; the Moses Fisk of history appears in the catalog of Dartmouth College as "Fiske," and while the actual name of the "pretty Peggy" of Jackson's time seems unquestionably to have been Margaret O'Neill, Patton invariably prints it "O'Neal." Any one of the foregoing variations was counted as correct. On the other hand, there were several cases in which contestants might easily have decided for themselves the absolutely accurate orthography, and in which consequently no variation was allowed. Instances are the Christian name of Meriwether Lewis, a fac-simile of whose autograph may be found in Appleton's Cyclopedia of American Biography, and who invariably signed his name as it is here given, although the Tennessee Legislature, with that faculty for blundering which seems an inevitable characteristic of Tennessee Legislatures at all periods, inscribed his tombstone "Merriwether"; the Earl of Loudoun, for any other spelling of whose name there is no shadow of authority; John Mitchel, the Irish

Bible Records—Tombstone Inscriptions

patriot; Willie (pronounced "Wylie") Jones, whose Christian name many contestants seem to have regarded as a diminutive of William (even Phelan makes this error); Demonbreun, which is the form the name of the pioneer of French Lick assumed when its bearer, who was "De Mont Breun" in France, came to America—the various curious shapes in which the name is given by Haywood and Ramsey being merely vagaries of the fancy of these worthies, who had an ingenuous habit where proper names were concerned of "spelling by ear" and notably the "misspelled names" referred to in 32—in this case most of the contestants, warned by the form in which the question was presented, usually succeeded in getting the surname correctly as "Miro," but many of them blundered as to the Christian name, misled by Haywood, Ramsey, and Putnam, although they might have found it rightly given in Martin's History of Louisiana—unquestionable authority in all matters relating to that period—and, to "make assurance double sure," could have seen a photographic reproduction of his autograph signature in a recent issue of that valuable publication. Prof. Garrett's Magazine of American History, a periodical which is worth many times its price to all historical students. One name which no single competitor gave correctly was that of Charles Roberson, although the spelling "Robertson" was not counted as incorrect, for the reason that the name is invariably so printed. Capt. John Allison informs me, however, that the old court records at Jonesboro show that he invariably signed his name as I have given it above. It may be well here to state that the general belief that Charles Roberson was a relative of Gen. James Robertson is incorrect.

Many competitors would have made better scores if they had examined their lists with care before submitting them. There were numerous cases in which the errors apparent had doubtless been made by the typewriter, but here no discretion could be allowed—if a contestant wrote "Danuel" when he meant "Daniel," the former was regarded as the orthography which he preferred.

The identity of the editor referred to in 4 seems to have puzzled a large majority of contestants. This doubtless originated from two causes—first, the erroneous idea that "campaign paper" and "political paper" are synonymous terms, in consequence of which the names of George Wilson, Thomas Phœbus, and other old-time political editors were presented by a number of competitors; and, second, a remarkable blunder in Crew's History of Nashville, where the positive assertion is made that Jeremiah George Harris, in 1840, "issued the first campaign paper ever issued west of the Alleghanies, named 'Advance Guard of the Democracy,' and this occasioned the issue from the office of the Banner of 'The Spirit of '76,' a Whig campaign paper." This statement is the exact reverse of the fact, the first issue of "The Spirit of '76" (Allen A.

Bible Records—Tombstone Inscriptions

Hall's paper) having made its appearance March 14, 1840, while Harris's paper did not see the light until the 23rd of the following April, it having evidently been suggested by instead of suggesting, the rival campaign paper. This blunder is the more singular from the fact that bound volumes of both papers were easily accessible to the writer in the library of the Tennessee Historical Society—and he does not even give the name of Harris's paper correctly!

No. 5 seems also to have occasioned some confusion, although a majority of investigators eventually succeeded in discovering—thanks, probably, to Dr. Hoss's interesting article in the April American Magazine of American History—that Elihu Embree was really the first Abolition editor. To settle definitely a matter which all of the histories and biographical dictionaries (so far as I have examined, without exception) misstate—they invariably call Benjamin Lundy the pioneer in anti-slavery journalism—I quote here a passage from an extremely rare book—Lundy's Autobiography. After narrating his experiences in St. Louis, in 1819, which caused his determination to return to his home in Ohio, Lundy says: "Before I left St. Louis I heard that Elihu Embree had commenced the publication of an anti-slavery paper called 'The Emancipator' at Jonesborough, in Tennessee; but on my way home I was informed of the death of Embree, and I determined immediately to establish a periodical of my own. I therefore removed to Mount Pleasant (Ohio) and commenced the publication of 'The Genius of Universal Emancipation,' in January, 1821. * * * When the friends of the deceased Embree heard of my paper they urged me to remove to Tennessee and use the press on which his had been printed. I assented, and after having issued eight monthly numbers of the 'Genius' I started for Tennessee. On my arrival I rented the printing office and immediately went to work with the paper."

Want of care in differentiating the meaning of words has led many contestants into error as to 19 and 20. A majority of them identified the "two men" therein referred to as Samuel Johnston and Benjamin Hawkins. This would have been correct if the question had been as to the men who signed the deed ceding to the United States the territory south of the Ohio; but the phrase used was "the two men who signed the act," meaning, of course, the act of the Legislature of North Carolina by which that state ceded the territory in question to the general government—that is to say, Charles Johnson and Stephen Cabarrus, Speakers, respectively, of the two houses. The technical differences between a "deed" and an "act" is very marked.

Careless reading of Ramsey led astray a large number of contestants with regard to the minister referred to in 49. Speaking

Bible Records—Tombstone Inscriptions

of the expedition of Col. Christian for the relief of the Watauga settlers in 1772, Ramsey says: "The Rev. Charles Cummings accompanied the expedition as chaplain, and was thus the first Christian minister that ever preached in Tennessee." Granted—but while this is doubtless true, the question is not who "first preached in Tennessee," but who first preached regularly to a Tennessee congregation," and that this was Tidence Lane, in 1779, is clearly demonstrated elsewhere by Ramsey. Goodspeed, indeed, using Ramsey's fact, but changing his language, asserts in terms that Cummings had charge of a congregation "within the limits of the state," but Goodspeed is in error in this, as he is in very many other statements. In Park's "historical discourse," a work which is the result of the most careful and painstaking original research, the statement is explicitly made that the congregation to which Goodspeed refers as having enjoyed the ministrations of Cummings "in the Holston valley as early as 1772," was really not located in Tennessee at all. It was "in Virginia, near the site of the present town of Abingdon." Dr. Park, himself a Presbyterian, would not be likely to fail to claim for a minister of his own denomination any credit justly due him.

In order to be absolutely frank, I desire to correct an error—the only one, I believe, in the "Dream," and one fortunately of little moment. The man who "founded the first academy for females in Tennessee" (52) was not a classmate of Daniel Webster, as stated; but as nearly all the contestants succeeded in discovering the identity of Moses Fisk, no harm was done by this misstatement, which was made on what I considered good authority.

In conclusion, I desire to tender my congratulations to the prize winners in this friendly contest, while to those who were not so fortunate I proffer the consolation which may be found in the reflection that, although they may have gained no pecuniary reward, the zealous and persistent investigation of Tennessee history which they necessarily undertook will inevitably prove of large and lasting benefit. The knowledge that I have in some sort been able to rouse hundreds of my fellow-Tennesseans to a study of the annals of our splendid commonwealth amply rewards me for my "labor of love." R. L. C. WHITE.

Bible Records—Tombstone Inscriptions

INDEX

A

Abball, 228.
Abbey, 93.
Abbott, 64, 222.
Abernathy, 13, 83, 194, 268, 353.
Abston, 13.
Acklen, 165, 224.
Achor, 13.
Acres, 188.
Adair, 225, 495.
Adam, 157.
Adama, 93.
Adams, 13, 50, 51, 53, 54, 91, 93, 102, 128, 131, 157, 194, 195, 274, 316, 348, 381.
Adcock, 13, 81.
Adkins, 344.
Aecorn, 151.
Agnew, 175, 224, 234.
Ahearn, 72.
Aiken, 136.
Ainsworth, 117.
Akeman, 155, 156.
Akin, 13, 264.
Akers, 222.
Akroyd, 93.
Albertson, 13.
Albritton, 143.
Alderman, 10.
Alderson, 278, 279, 281, 282.
Aldrich, 403, 404.
Alexander, 13, 54, 77, 81, 84, 87, 93, 100, 133, 135, 138, 148, 173, 174, 175, 182, 183, 201, 203, 222, 223, 234, 259, 267, 268, 269, 272, 280, 320, 355, 362, 389, 443, 448, 465, 468.
Alford, 93, 282.
Alison, 133.
Allcorn, 315.
Allen, 13, 49, 51, 56, 58, 63, 67, 74, 76, 80, 93, 105, 113, 174, 180, 181, 215, 219, 264, 288, 290, 291, 296, 297, 318, 322, 328, 332, 344, 349, 361, 449, 465.
Alley, 13, 52, 78, 85, 203.

Allison, 8, 11, 13, 14, 83, 93, 172, 173, 293, 413, 448.
Alloway, 14.
Alston, 282.
Altmeyer, 14.
Ambrister, 228, 231.
Ambrose, 93.
Ambush, 73.
Ambuster, 236.
Ament, 14, 93, 282.
Ames, 267.
Amis, 250, 260, 262, 270, 272, 453.
Amos, 188.
Anderson, 14, 51, 82, 85, 88, 93, 101, 122, 140, 151, 166, 175, 188, 192, 198, 199, 201, 219, 222, 225, 229, 233, 234, 264, 277, 291, 295, 296, 297, 310, 313, 314, 348, 356, 357, 445.
Andes, 196.
Andrews, 14, 57, 58, 81, 93, 184, 215, 219, 332, 447, 448.
Angel, 462.
Anglea, 121.
Angol, 341.
Ankenbaner, 63, 64, 66, 71, 72, 73.
Annan, 160.
Anthony, 93, 121, 166, 224.
Apperson, 333.
Aprangler, 233.
Arbeely, 201.
Arbuthnot, 76.
Archibald, 56.
Argo, 14, 47, 49, 54, 144, 147.
Armstead, 208.
Armstrong, 8, 11, 12, 14, 50, 93, 95, 110, 145, 146, 149, 221, 227, 235, 243, 244, 246, 247, 248, 249, 250, 251, 255, 256, 279, 343, 413, 414, 422, 436, 495.
Arnell, 243, 245.
Arning, 341.
Arnold, 60, 135, 312, 348.
Arrington, 287.
Arthur, 49, 82, 166.

Arthurs, 82.
Asberry, 152.
Asbury, 431, 495.
Asher, 137.
Ashley, 14.
Ashton, 278.
Ashworth, 290.
Askew, 256.
Askins, 289.
Asite, 72.
Aslin, 203.
Atkins, 86, 203, 344.
Atkinson, 78, 208, 209, 219.
Atkisson, 272.
Atlee, 175.
Atnip, 145.
Attry, 203.
Aultmeyer, 90.
Austin, 14, 93, 193.
Avent, 353, 443.
Avery, 328, 359, 474, 475.
Avrill, 84.
Axley, 130, 337.
Aydelotte, 279.
Aydlott, 271.
Aykloyd, 14.

B

Babb, 307.
Bachman, 339.
Bacome, 344.
Bacon, 129.
Badgett, 231, 235, 331.
Badger, 150, 215.
Badgers, 140.
Baggarly, 121.
Bagiotte, 225.
Bagwell, 117.
Bailey, 14, 48, 73, 93, 120, 206, 215, 282.
Baily, 289, 297.
Bain, 105, 146, 215.
Baine, 59.
Baines, 67.
Bains, 61, 64.
Baird, 14, 113, 160, 161, 222, 223, 289, 293, 296, 299, 304, 317, 319, 320, 321, 322, 323, 326, 329, 357, 442, 443, 446, 447, 451.
Bakean, 67.

Bible Records—Tombstone Inscriptions

Baker, 14, 20, 78, 85, 90, 113, 134, 175, 180, 205, 222, 224, 237, 298, 462.
Balch, 132, 135, 432.
Baldridge, 258, 265, 270.
Baldwin, 229.
Bales, 136, 341.
Balfour, 178.
Ball, 14, 175.
Ballard, 128, 231.
Baltishweiler, 215.
Bandy, 14, 347.
Banke, 93.
Banks, 175, 181, 465, 469.
Banner, 205, 206.
Banton, 453.
Barbee, 161, 297, 322.
Barbour, 14, 47.
Barden, 361.
Barem, 226.
Bargozie, 14.
Barham, 215.
Barker, 14, 51, 116, 203.
Barkley, 465.
Barksdale, 449.
Barner, 14.
Barnes, 153, 155, 172, 248, 254, 272, 336, 454.
Barnett, 86, 258, 340, 361.
Barnhill, 169.
Barr, 14, 101, 280.
Barrell, 14.
Barrett, 14, 58, 60, 63, 203.
Barrow, 14, 263, 296, 334.
Barry, 14, 128, 138, 183, 288, 293, 343, 390, 470.
Bartee, 92.
Barthell, 88.
Bartholamew, 348.
Bartlett, 86.
Barton, 289, 297, 473, 477, 479, 480.
Baskette, 446.
Baskin, 363.
Bass, 14, 15, 53, 55, 82, 90, 93, 95, 106, 151, 219, 294, 310, 318, 321, 332.
Basson, 15.
Bassow, 54.
Bateman, 15, 53, 169.
Bates, 15, 47, 48, 278, 279.
Batey, 168, 352, 354, 364.
Batson, 85.
Batter, 61.
Batts, 159, 160.
Bauer, 15.
Baugh, 173, 451.
Bauman, 15, 59, 61, 221.

Baxendale, 87.
Baxter, 2, 7, 12, 15, 92.
Bayers, 85.
Bayless, 137, 234.
Beach, 15.
Beadford, 150.
Beadle, 107, 321, 331.
Bealer, 62.
Beals, 230.
Bean, 47, 188, 225, 341, 342, 343, 432, 435, 439, 441, 456, 495.
Bear, 15.
Beard, 84, 87, 180, 219, 291, 359, 361, 362, 445.
Bearden, 166, 221, 224, 233.
Beardsley, 130.
Beasley, 15, 54, 184, 358, 468.
Beaton, 170.
Beauregard, 260.
Beck, 15.
Becker, 15.
Becton, 453.
Beckwith, 15.
Bedford, 15.
Bedon, 277.
Beech, 215.
Beecher, 250.
Beeham, 73.
Beene, 440.
Beguin, 15.
Beidleman, 417.
Belcher, 15.
Belfield, 15.
Bell, 15, 48, 75, 76, 84, 93, 116, 147, 149, 158, 160, 220, 289, 301, 316, 358, 495.
Bellsnyder, 2, 12, 15.
Bender, 15, 104.
Benderman, 258, 267.
Bengiff, 15.
Benner, 58.
Bennett, 15, 51, 203, 294, 297, 306.
Bennette, 338.
Benoit, 15.
Benson, 15.
Bentley, 15, 68, 69, 149.
Benton, 15, 77, 436, 437, 465, 495.
Beokham, 277.
Bender, 15.
Berger, 81.
Bergin, 55, 56.
Bergman, 87.

Berry, 59, 87, 98, 128, 142, 158, 165, 189, 318, 320, 337, 344, 354, 447.
Berryhill, 15.
Berson, 215.
Bertheal, 58, 66.
Bertrand, 15.
Beth, 15.
Bethell, 276.
Betts, 259.
Bettis, 300, 303, 315.
Bevington, 64.
Bezier, 17.
Bienter, 223.
Biggs, 15, 86.
Bigley, 15, 51.
Biglow, 15.
Bilderlock, 232.
Billings, 79.
Bills, 259.
Binford, 215, 230, 357.
Bingham, 257.
Binkley, 86, 106, 107.
Bipe, 15.
Birchett, 15, 47, 272, 329.
Birchfield, 205, 206.
Birmingham, 203.
Bishop, 92.
Bitts, 119.
Black, 15, 144, 146, 147, 175, 206, 207, 215, 227, 420, 421, 433, 444, 454.
Blackburn, 199, 215, 386, 388, 436, 443.
Blackman, 116, 168.
Blackmore, 15, 100, 114, 203, 385, 393, 470.
Blacknall, 324.
Blackwell, 52, 138, 175.
Blair, 117, 136, 137, 188, 229, 230, 289, 290, 297, 422.
Blake, 255.
Blakely, 250, 252, 265.
Blakemore, 88, 203.
Blan, 341.
Blanch, 363, 364.
Blanchi, 52.
Bland, 15, 49, 84, 208, 277.
Blanghard, 175.
Blankenship, 167, 192, 351, 452.
Blanton, 353, 357.
Bledsoe, 15, 16, 76, 115, 254, 255, 307, 385, 388, 389, 396, 427, 428, 429, 465, 466, 478, 479, 480.
Blizard, 175.

492

Bible Records—Tombstone Inscriptions

Bloodworth, 16, 76, 77, 313, 314.
Blount, 52, 165, 166, 224, 431, 433, 495.
Blunt, 95.
Blythe, 294.
Boardman, 16, 280.
Bobbett, 16.
Bobbitt, 75.
Bochms, 207, 209.
Boddie, 263, 454.
Bodily, 121.
Bochms, 209.
Boehms, 216.
Bogart, 337, 344.
Boggess, 361.
Bogle, 150, 235.
Boham, 231.
Bohan, 66, 71.
Bohme, 93.
Bohney, 16.
Bolton, 16.
Bomar, 121.
Bon, 16.
Bonavita, 341.
Bond, 123, 153, 301, 449.
Bonds, 243.
Bondurant, 79.
Bone, 306.
Bonfuerlo, 71.
Bonner, 140, 141, 148, 149.
Booher, 225, 226.
Boon, 216.
Boone, 55, 86, 391, 424, 440, 441, 495, 497.
Booth, 86, 137, 216, 407, 409, 418.
Borcroft, 136.
Boren, 157.
Boring, 363, 364.
Borsch, 203.
Borthick, 161.
Boruff, 343.
Borum, 332.
Boseley, 53.
Bosher, 16.
Bosley, 16.
Bost, 153.
Bostick, 16, 51, 264, 319, 357.
Boston, 469.
Bosworth, 16.
Bottom, 157.
Bough, 342.
Boughton, 247.
Bounds, 151, 233.
Bouton, 292.
Bowdis, 16.

Bowen, 5, 11, 16, 118, 119, 125, 126, 127, 188, 297, 361, 439.
Bowerman, 231.
Bowers, 77, 81, 82, 84, 196, 343.
Bowie, 145.
Bowl, 447, 448.
Bowling, 16, 160.
Bowman, 78, 80, 108, 111, 112, 206, 266, 443, 448.
Boyd, 16, 53, 69, 78, 81, 145, 166, 175, 178, 180, 216, 221, 222, 224, 229, 236, 237, 264, 266, 268, 282, 335, 340, 423.
Boyle, 69, 75.
Boys, 282.
Boyton, 222.
Brace, 78.
Brackley, 58.
Brackney, 339.
Brackwell, 236.
Bradbury, 234.
Braden, 287.
Bradford, 7, 11, 16, 52, 84, 89, 106, 150, 157, 171, 175.
Bradfute, 16.
Bradley, 47, 68, 69, 70, 116, 215, 466, 468.
Bradshaw, 16, 54, 175, 282, 331, 361, 448.
Bradsute, 33
Brady, 16, 56, 57, 58, 59, 67, 68, 73, 91.
Bragg, 150.
Brakbill, 236.
Brallom, 244.
Branan, 176.
Branch, 215, 216, 274.
Brandon, 16, 17, 138, 390, 466.
Bransford, 17.
Brantley, 2, 280.
Bratton, 254.
Breathitt, 17.
Brawley, 157.
Brawnlaw, 433.
Brazier, 17.
Brazzelton, 175, 177.
Brazzleton, 89, 176.
Breck, 135.
Breeden, 362.
Breen, 55, 57, 58, 61, 69, 70.
Brennan, 66.

Brent, 76, 294.
Brett, 58, 62, 104, 203.
Brevard, 186, 269, 389, 466.
Brew, 58, 61, 63.
Brewer, 80, 146, 150, 195, 228, 302.
Briant, 175.
Brice, 59.
Brickley, 228.
Bridges, 17, 74, 79, 123, 175, 176, 180, 313.
Briggs, 86.
Bright, 138, 139, 230, 335, 338.
Brinkley, 294.
Brionatk, 69.
Brisbo, 60, 61.
Brisboe, 68.
Briscoe, 336.
Brison, 270.
Britt, 17, 54, 58, 81, 206.
Brittain, 146.
Britten, 181.
Britton, 135, 289, 290, 296, 297, 334.
Brixley, 140.
Broadway, 167, 192.
Broady, 229.
Brock, 236, 237.
Brockley, 71.
Brockman, 64.
Broderick, 62, 69, 71, 72.
Brook, 265.
Brooke, 162.
Brooks, 15, 16, 86, 87, 89, 125, 148, 187, 250, 449.
Broome, 342.
Browder, 129, 130, 340, 359.
Brown, 12, 16, 17, 52, 55, 57, 60, 64, 65, 74, 76, 80, 82, 85, 93, 113, 125, 133, 136, 140, 142, 145, 146, 147, 148, 150, 152, 160, 166, 172, 175, 190, 203, 205, 216, 224, 233, 243, 245, 253, 255, 257, 272, 276, 280, 282, 285, 290, 295, 296, 302, 318, 335, 339, 340, 350, 352, 356, 361, 362, 363, 430, 433, 435, 462, 468, 495.
Browne, 16, 60, 67, 139.
Brownlow, 222, 495.
Broyles, 136, 237.
Bruce, 16, 93, 123.
Bruhold, 16.

493

Bible Records—Tombstone Inscriptions

Bryan, 16, 92, 100, 139, 316, 317, 318, 322, 332, 410.
Bryant, 16, 52, 80, 143, 151, 276.
Bryson, 114, 115, 272, 470.
Buchanan, 74, 80, 82, 88, 114, 125, 126, 127, 137, 144, 146, 289, 293, 297, 392, 423, 457, 458, 479, 480.
Buchi, 85.
Buck, 16, 55, 203.
Buckingham, 84.
Buckle, 54.
Buckley, 56, 59, 68.
Buckner, 16.
Buddeke, 16, 89.
Buehan, 62.
Buford, 210.
Bugg, 82, 99.
Buhler, 60, 314.
Builderback, 339.
Buist, 16.
Bull, 448.
Bullard, 101.
Bullen, 155.
Bullington, 301.
Bullock, 264.
Bumpass, 193, 286.
Bunch, 252, 253.
Bundren, 343.
Burchett, 272.
Burchfield, 188.
Burchler, 279.
Burdine, 308, 324.
Burem, 231, 236.
Buren, 415.
Burford, 181, 182, 185, 288.
Burger, 175, 180.
Burgess, 16, 278, 296.
Burgie, 174.
Burke, 17, 56, 58, 59, 61, 62, 68, 69, 70, 71, 72, 81, 219, 299, 325.
Burks, 79, 80.
Burkhalter, 85.
Burkhard, 62.
Burkinbine, 78.
Burlason, 461.
Burlington, 16.
Burlison, 156.
Burnell, 211.
Burnet, 193.
Burnett, 16, 17, 47, 128, 172, 232.
Burney, 260, 289.

Burns, 17, 55, 56, 57, 58, 59, 63, 67, 69, 130, 159, 175, 228, 247, 278, 318, 329, 341.
Burr, 99, 100.
Burrall, 65.
Burrow, 466.
Burrows, 73.
Burrough, 184.
Burroughs, 17, 147.
Burrus, 187, 354, 466.
Burton, 17, 47, 62, 63, 98, 225, 244, 304, 305, 356, 363.
Burwell, 211.
Bushing, 130.
Bust, 17.
Bustard, 59.
Butcher, 88.
Butler, 17, 70, 127, 189, 190, 355, 431.
Buttersworth, 83.
Butney, 289.
Byars, 87, 138, 139, 143, 151.
Byers, 136.
Byram, 17.
Byrum, 280.
Byrd, 17, 337, 338, 340, 422, 431, 459.
Byrne, 58, 61.

C

Cabarrus, 495.
Cable, 330.
Cabler, 17, 90.
Cady, 60.
Caffery, 63.
Caffey, 61.
Cage, 93, 98, 137, 138, 336, 385, 390, 428, 468.
Cagle, 152.
Cahal, 10, 12, 17.
Caim, 419.
Cain, 17, 47, 63, 73, 74, 79, 93, 144, 145, 153, 278, 342, 417, 422.
Cairns, 66, 68, 73.
Calcote, 17.
Caldwell, 93, 176, 191, 203, 216, 337, 360, 362.
Calhoun, 30, 176, 284, 305, 444.
Call, 344.
Callaghan, 49, 52, 59.
Callahan, 56, 57, 60, 61, 62, 65, 71.
Callaway, 425.

Callender, 17, 97.
Calloway, 131, 144, 418.
Calvin, 58.
Cameron, 18, 216, 279, 462.
Camp, 146.
Campbell, 5, 8, 9, 12, 13, 17, 18, 50, 51, 52, 54, 80, 85, 87, 92, 93, 146, 166, 193, 216, 224, 225, 281, 291, 297, 298, 303, 319, 321, 333, 362, 378, 415, 418, 422, 433, 442, 462, 466, 495.
Campen, 239.
Camper, 122, 327.
Cannody, 69.
Cannon, 18, 93, 100, 201, 211, 219, 359, 448.
Canon, 62.
Cantrall, 116.
Cantrel, 18.
Cantrell, 75, 76, 138, 148, 150, 187, 288, 429, 449.
Canzaty, 132.
Capel, 302.
Caperton, 280.
Capington, 18.
Capps, 18, 58.
Caral, 12.
Card, 18.
Carden, 462.
Cardin, 176.
Cardwell, 120, 157.
Carland, 61.
Carley, 195.
Carlile, 82.
Carlisle, 18, 74, 75.
Carlin, 71, 73.
Carlton, 285, 286.
Carmack, 107, 176, 435.
Carmen, 466.
Carmichael, 136.
Carnahan, 349.
Carne, 203.
Carney, 57, 61, 63, 69.
Carns, 18.
Caroth, 466.
Carpenter, 18, 48, 172, 323.
Carper, 50.
Carr, 65, 67, 116, 176, 224.
Carrack, 239.
Carraway, 302, 317, 324.
Carroway, 18.
Carrell, 87.
Carroll, 3, 7, 9, 12, 18, 47, 52, 90, 91, 102, 232, 495.

494

Bible Records—Tombstone Inscriptions

Carrick, 134, 199, 223, 224, 239, 495.
Carriger, 382, 462.
Carruthers, 279.
Caruthers, 81, 287, 495.
Carson, 18, 120, 137, 286.
Carter, 18, 53, 87, 93, 98, 154, 165, 184, 185, 203, 216, 232, 289, 290, 291, 292, 296, 297, 298, 301, 337, 339, 340, 344, 345, 357, 358, 361, 380, 381, 382, 400, 401, 462, 466, 495.
Carthel, 203.
Carthell, 253.
Carthy, 66.
Cartmell, 18, 291, 333, 334.
Cartwright, 50, 78, 108, 111, 114, 152, 155, 172, 193, 291, 295, 316, 318, 341, 393, 436.
Carver, 122, 123, 298.
Carvin, 63.
Case, 77, 429.
Caseday, 18.
Casey, 58, 67, 462.
Cason, 317.
Casper, 18.
Cass, 237.
Cassidy, 85, 464.
Caster, 18.
Castleman, 8, 11, 18, 172, 173, 291, 293, 304, 495.
Caswell, 110, 353.
Cate, 342.
Cates, 246, 253.
Catlett, 196.
Cato, 77.
Catron, 18, 495.
Caulfield, 59.
Cauvin, 18.
Cavett, 340.
Cavender, 18.
Cayce, 251, 255.
Cayse, 451.
Cecil, 244, 246, 359.
Center, 432.
Chadwell, 77.
Chadwick, 147.
Chaemar, 18.
Chaffin, 280.
Chairs, 201.
Chamberlain, 348.
Chambers, 169, 292, 306, 360.
Champion, 47.

Chandler, 121, 196, 231, 296, 326, 328.
Channaberry, 227.
Chapel, 216.
Chapman, 7, 11, 18, 57, 63, 113, 140, 314, 448.
Charavannes, 336.
Chavannes, 221.
Cheatham, 53, 93, 113, 271, 285.
Cheek, 18, 55, 207, 421.
Chemault, 18.
Chenault, 138, 197.
Cherry, 282, 283, 346, 351.
Chesney, 342.
Chesnutt, 463.
Chester, 136, 203.
Chestnut, 87.
Childress, 18, 83, 116, 159, 350, 359, 442, 452.
Chiles, 211, 213.
Chilton, 47, 49.
Choate, 203.
Chrishall, 449.
Christian, 18, 138, 157, 461.
Chumley, 278.
Church, 176.
Churchill, 18.
Churchwell, 221.
Cisco, 429.
Clack, 196, 197.
Claiborne, 18, 19, 53, 54.
Clapp, 225.
Clare, 149.
Clark, 7, 19, 50, 59, 69, 71, 82, 84, 93, 107, 144, 145, 146, 198, 213, 222, 228, 229, 238, 322, 326, 340, 359, 421, 423, 431, 433, 449, 451, 452.
Clarke, 263.
Claus, 75.
Clay, 19, 182, 246.
Clayton, 19, 293, 334, 449.
Claywell, 293, 295, 297.
Cleage, 176, 180.
Clees, 60.
Cleanevsil, 66.
Cleburne, 274.
Clements, 19, 47, 66, 195.
Clemmons, 298, 304, 317, 325, 327, 328, 434.
Clendenen, 152, 156.
Clendenning, 146.
Cleveland, 81, 86, 131, 164, 165, 176, 187, 334, 345, 389.

Click, 19.
Clifford, 290.
Clife, 148.
Clift, 148.
Clifton, 81.
Climer, 320.
Clinard, 19, 191.
Clinton, 19, 81.
Clonan, 57.
Clooar, 93.
Cloud, 19.
Clour, 120.
Clower, 84.
Clowson, 134.
Cloyd, 236, 300, 301.
Clunan, 59.
Coatney, 86.
Cobb, 19, 456, 462, 463, 464.
Cobble, 339.
Cobleigh, 176.
Cochran, 59, 137, 187, 466, 469.
Cochrane, 211.
Cocke, 188, 221, 314, 432, 438.
Cockerill, 19.
Cockrell, 11, 12.
Cockrill, 19, 53, 85, 90, 395.
Cockrane, 19, 211.
Cockson, 19.
Cody, 72, 216.
Coe, 296.
Coen, 50, 64.
Coer, 73.
Coffee, 112, 145, 146, 423, 451, 466, 495.
Coffer, 339.
Coffey, 257.
Coffin, 132, 135.
Coffing, 65.
Coffman, 19, 342, 433.
Coggin, 83.
Cogswell, 19.
Cohea, 281.
Colborn, 50.
Colbun, 294.
Coldwell, 357.
Cole, 9, 19, 86, 90, 158, 190, 225, 226, 284, 286, 287, 314.
Coles, 88, 293, 333, 334.
Coleburn, 260, 264.
Coleman, 8, 11, 19, 49, 57, 253, 364, 449.
Coley, 203.
Colladay, 19.

495

Bible Records—Tombstone Inscriptions

Collier, 19.
Collinge, 19.
Collins, 19, 56, 222, 225, 264, 280, 282.
Collon, 262.
Colquitt, 280, 283.
Coltart, 9, 11, 19, 52.
Colthart, 281.
Colvert, 19.
Colville, 143, 144, 147, 148, 153, 419, 423.
Colwell, 19, 328, 329.
Combs, 47, 84.
Comer, 140, 295, 330.
Commander, 53.
Compton, 315, 363.
Conatser, 358.
Condon, 19, 78.
Condra, 75.
Conely, 63.
Conkey, 268, 269.
Conlon, 72.
Conn, 20.
Connally, 95.
Connell, 148.
Connelley, 19.
Connelly, 60, 69, 282, 341.
Conner, 166, 203.
Connor, 19, 47, 58, 61, 62, 63, 64, 67, 264.
Connors, 57, 72.
Connolly, 60, 223.
Consadine, 72.
Constable, 205.
Conway, 54.
Cook, 70, 91, 105, 122, 123, 157, 159, 176, 187, 219, 294, 296, 302, 312.
Cooke, 19, 176.
Cooley, 7, 336.
Coon, 163.
Cooney, 20, 174.
Cooper, 20, 47, 50, 53, 54, 126, 243, 244, 247, 257, 265, 284.
Cope, 138, 141, 151, 237.
Corley, 468.
Copeland, 20, 119, 450.
Coppinger, 152, 153.
Corbitt, 20, 55, 113.
Corcoran, 58, 66, 67, 68, 71.
Corley, 185, 230.
Correy, 20.
Corsaw, 52.
Corum, 299, 300, 334.
Cosby, 187, 434.
Cosey, 359.

Cosgrove, 69.
Cossitt, 292.
Costella, 63.
Costello, 58, 60.
Cotham, 271.
Cotton, 18, 20, 49, 55, 145, 192, 193, 194.
Cottrell, 342.
Couch, 20, 174.
Couchm, 49.
Coughlin, 59, 63, 64.
Courfman, 58.
Courtney, 216, 259.
Coussens, 20.
Covington, 319.
Cowan, 20, 166, 167, 192, 203, 223, 224, 228, 295, 297, 419, 425.
Cowley, 78.
Cowper, 308.
Cox, 55, 56, 57, 58, 60, 61, 67, 71, 84, 176, 193, 231, 291, 292, 294, 296, 297, 315, 330, 341, 353, 362, 462.
Cozart, 344, 362.
Crabb, 20.
Crabtree, 124.
Craddock, 20, 118, 403, 404, 460.
Cradock, 301.
Craft, 20, 48.
Cragwall, 289, 290.
Craig, 77, 201, 216, 259, 262, 272, 336, 337, 339, 341, 360.
Craighead, 20, 73, 74, 78, 79, 223, 396.
Craik, 276.
Crain, 139.
Crandall, 20.
Cranor, 158.
Cravendel, 208, 209.
Crawford, 20, 93, 128, 152, 175, 176, 203, 225, 226, 268, 302, 336.
Credon, 60.
Creed, 345.
Cregger, 135.
Crehan, 59.
Creighan, 58.
Crenshaw, 20.
Cress, 128.
Cressen, 57.
Cressthwaite, 356.
Creswell, 236, 334.
Crick, 285.
Crichtow, 355.

Cridden, 57.
Criddle, 216.
Crier, 105.
Crimmons, 62.
Crisp, 144, 203.
Crittenden, 97.
Crocket, 424, 425.
Crockett, 13, 20, 160, 161, 191, 193, 216, 219, 220, 364, 370, 432, 435, 437, 495.
Crocking, 71.
Crommins, 69.
Crommons, 64.
Cronin, 56, 58.
Cronswell, 389.
Cronk, 20.
Crosby, 463.
Cross, 2, 20, 47, 49, 70, 81, 85, 341, 343.
Crossthwaite, 356.
Crosswait, 47, 49.
Crosswhite, 127, 128, 206.
Crosthwait, 20.
Crouch, 176, 216.
Crow, 20, 176.
Crowder, 81.
Crowell, 287.
Crozier, 135, 166, 222, 224.
Crush, 165, 166, 224.
Crutcher, 2, 8, 11, 20, 216, 219, 348.
Cruthcer, 216.
Crutchfield, 299, 331.
Cryer, 121, 342.
Cuffman, 119.
Cullen, 58, 62, 68, 344.
Cullum, 452.
Culton, 229.
Cummings, 298, 321.
Cummins, 67, 107, 271, 294.
Cundall, 291.
Cunning, 234.
Cunnining, 236.
Cunningham, 47, 59, 76, 83, 88, 93, 124, 134, 142, 143, 149, 166, 167, 183, 193, 216, 233, 234, 239, 336, 341, 346, 347, 389, 465, 466.
Curd, 311.
Curlin, 62.
Curran, 7, 10, 11, 59, 444.
Curren, 59.
Currin, 49, 66.
Currey, 20, 35, 91, 276.

Bible Records—Tombstone Inscriptions

Curry, 8, 11, 12, 117, 203, 268.
Curtis, 155, 339.
Cushman, 407.
Cutchin, 194.
Cutrell, 83.
Cuvney, 20.
Cuzzort, 87.

D

Dale, 58, 279, 281, 289, 468.
Dallas, 54.
Dallinger, 68.
Dally, 48.
Dalton, 20, 56, 57, 64, 116, 209, 211, 213.
Dameron, 226.
Dance, 20, 50.
Dancy, 164.
Danger, 68.
Daniel, 20, 286.
Daniels, 21.
Dannaher, 61, 70.
Darcy, 64.
Darden, 43, 159, 191.
Darlington, 106.
Darnaby, 198.
Darnell, 141.
Darrow, 460.
Dashazer, 21.
Dashiel, 21.
Daughal, 93.
Daughney, 69.
Daughtery, 60, 84.
Daughtry, 102.
Dautel, 78.
Davenport, 341, 343.
Daveon, 64.
Davey, 73, 148.
David, 93.
Davidson, 21, 142, 145, 195, 257, 268, 422.
Davies, 92.
Davis, 21, 47, 55, 56, 62, 66, 69, 70, 75, 76, 87, 89, 92, 93, 139, 142, 147, 149, 151, 158, 160, 166, 167, 176, 180, 203, 205, 216, 232, 236, 237, 239, 258, 259, 260, 261, 262, 271, 276, 279, 283, 295, 296, 297, 309, 311, 313, 320, 341, 347, 435, 437, 450, 460.
Davy, 58, 71.
Dawney, 276.

Dawson, 60, 263, 265, 293, 342.
Day, 466.
Deadrick, 21, 50, 222.
Dearmond, 228.
DeArmond, 343.
Deartin, 88.
Deason, 203.
Deaver, 80.
DeBard, 146, 147.
Deberry, 21.
De Bow, 76, 315.
Decker, 360.
Degraffenreidt, 255, 256.
DeGrove, 21.
DeKalb, 86.
DeLozier, 235.
Delworth, 21.
Dement, 107, 123.
DeMonbreum, 114, 436, 496, 498.
DeMoville, 21, 91, 92.
Dempsey, 138, 216.
Dennis, 47.
Denny, 470.
Denton, 51, 139, 194, 422.
Deprew, 209.
Derr, 59.
Derrick, 21.
Desha, 385.
Deshazer, 54.
DeSoto, 495.
Deubler, 69.
Devany, 60.
Deveny, 64, 66, 71, 73.
Devine, 60, 66, 68.
Devinney, 21.
Dew, 203, 295, 325.
DeWitt, 85, 427.
Diamond, 73.
Dibrell, 238.
Dickason, 294.
Dickens, 47, 301, 358, 405.
Dickerson, 85.
Dickey, 196, 248, 251, 256, 257, 359, 360.
Dickinson, 21, 54.
Dickrey, 228.
Dicks, 234.
Dickson, 21, 51, 119, 133, 244, 263, 435, 442, 447, 448.
Diffee, 21.
Diggins, 8, 21.
Diggons, 8, 13, 21, 175.
Dill, 334.
Dilla, 246.
Dillahunty, 169, 170.

Dillard, 85, 86, 292, 298.
Dillen, 49.
Dillon, 21, 57, 70, 279, 288, 316, 465.
Dillworth, 136.
Dismukes, 79, 80, 422.
Dittmer, 21.
Dix, 21, 496.
Dixon, 80, 93, 176, 180, 246, 254, 387, 389, 466, 469.
Doak, 137, 199, 268, 287, 297, 322, 399, 432, 495.
Dobbin, 255.
Dobbins, 244, 248, 249, 250, 251, 255, 263, 264.
Dobie, 86.
Dobson, 21, 135, 342.
Dodd, 58.
Dodson, 47, 155, 176, 357.
Doherty, 57.
Dohoney, 67, 68, 73.
Doke, 21.
Domido, 52.
Donagan, 226.
Donald, 429.
Donaldson, 212, 232, 236.
Donavan, 58.
Donelson, 188, 277, 390, 391, 392, 393, 425, 426, 441, 495.
Donelly, 56.
Donahue, 71.
Donnard, 63.
Donnell, 287, 291, 297, 318, 320, 321, 330.
Donnelly, 56, 61, 127, 128, 189, 190, 191.
Donoho, 288, 466.
Donovan, 64, 67.
Dooley, 72.
Doran, 382.
Dorgan, 57, 60.
Dorris, 21.
Dorsey, 60, 67, 296, 297.
Doubleday, 75.
Dougal, 21.
Dougherty, 68, 72, 132, 206.
Doughty, 21.
Douglas, 21, 98, 104, 105, 108, 137, 182, 187, 211, 428, 429, 451, 468.
Douglass, 21, 22, 247, 249, 275, 276, 315, 385, 390.
Dougle, 21, 175.
Dowell, 201.
Dowd, 22, 62, 70, 72.

Bible Records—Tombstone Inscriptions

Dowling, 72.
Downs, 113.
Dowyers, 22.
Doyle, 57, 59, 150, 203, 216, 233, 343.
Dozier, 289.
Drain, 22.
Drake, 48, 92, 93, 108, 112, 139, 156, 187, 216, 303, 335, 343, 415, 479, 480.
Draper, 76, 124, 185, 470.
Drew, 127.
Drifoes, 295.
Driscoll, 56, 59.
Driver, 9, 12, 22, 52, 89.
Dromgoole, 363.
Dryden, 134.
Dubose, 277.
Duckworth, 22.
Dudley, 208, 209, 216, 219.
Duff, 22, 47.
Duffy, 70, 73, 75, 189.
Dugan, 59, 153.
Duglas, 256.
Duke, 257, 283.
Duling, 93.
Dumont, 89.
Dunagon, 226.
Duncan, 22, 52, 82, 97, 137, 201, 226, 279, 432.
Dunlap, 151, 227, 239.
Dunn, 62, 63, 73, 165, 194, 195, 229, 234, 295.
Dunton, 22.
Dutton, 86.
Duss, 280.
Duval, 22.
Duvall, 293.
Dwyer, 55, 58, 60, 63, 67, 170, 216.
Dyas, 22.
Dye, 85.
Dyer, 22.
Dykes, 152, 153, 341.

E

Eady, 156.
Eakin, 22, 136.
Eagan, 64, 311.
Eagleton, 201, 228, 444, 445, 446.
Earborhart, 22.
Earl, 102.
Earley, 343.
Earnest, 336.
Eason, 297.
East, 22, 98, 127, 279.
Eastham, 22, 51.
Eastman, 276, 277, 305.
Eastin, 91.
Eatherly, 303, 311.
Eaton, 208, 436.
Echols, 219.
Ecklecamp, 65.
Eclbeck, 216.
Eddins, 302, 303, 328.
Edens, 86, 188.
Edgar, 58, 61, 64.
Edgerton, 292.
Edgemon, 338.
Edgmon, 359.
Edley, 59.
Edmiston, 246.
Edmonds, 360.
Edmondson, 22, 47, 144, 146, 226, 282, 423.
Edmundson, 22, 48, 149.
Edwards, 84, 93, 105, 120, 129, 140, 147, 205, 286, 287, 290, 295, 310, 349, 360, 470.
Eelbeck, 216.
Egan, 22, 58, 62, 64, 66, 70.
Eggansperger, 64.
Eggleston, 22.
Eglone, 67.
Egly, 59.
Eisenborg, 64.
Ekhart, 74.
Elam, 81, 87, 89, 450.
Elder, 203, 444.
Eldredge, 129.
Eldridge, 129.
Elliot, 22, 58.
Elliott, 9, 11, 12, 22, 47, 49, 52, 116, 127, 201, 219, 234, 364, 447, 454.
Ellis, 22, 123, 226, 292, 343, 357, 462.
Ellison, 22, 47.
Elliston, 51, 92, 93.
Elmore, 22, 283.
Elrod, 364.
Elsworth, 22.
Embree, 48, 136, 495.
Embric, 22.
Embry, 244, 251.
Embush, 67.
Emerson, 136.
Emmerson, 22.
Emmie, 22.
Emmitt, 127.
Empson, 159.
England, 223, 342.
Engledow, 176.
English, 216.
Engram, 271.
Engrim, 208, 209.
Enoch, 44, 47.
Enochs, 311.
Ensley, 22.
Eperson, 156.
Epps, 194.
Erb, 68, 71.
Erhard, 93.
Erskin, 10.
Erskine, 5, 12, 22.
Erwin, 93, 128, 216, 236, 237, 473, 479, 480.
Eskew, 326, 327.
Espey, 479, 480.
Estell, 22, 50, 302.
Ester, 176.
Esters, 22.
Estes, 84, 105, 216, 279, 455.
Etheridge, 83, 89.
Etter, 154, 155, 354, 414, 450, 451.
Eubanks, 47.
Eugenie, 59.
Evans, 22, 47, 60, 86, 87, 92, 138, 145, 176, 219, 239, 360, 386.
Eve, 495.
Everett, 22, 47, 114, 312.
Evers, 54, 58.
Evertson, 305.
Eves, 22.
Evins, 22.
Ewell, 8, 12, 22, 52.
Ewin, 23, 52, 210, 332, 479.
Ewing, 2, 4, 10, 11, 12, 13, 22, 23, 48, 108, 112, 168, 169, 216, 234, 355.

F

Fachtzehner, 23.
Fagalay, 50.
Fahey, 60, 61, 65, 69, 70, 73.
Fahy, 61, 71.
Fain, 251, 252.
Fairbanks, 155.
Faircloth, 363.
Fakes, 293, 297, 304.
Fall, 23, 435.
Fallon, 65.
Falpz, 23.
Fancher, 236, 237.
Fanning, 168.

Bible Records—Tombstone Inscriptions

Fant, 61, 62, 71.
Fares, 469.
Farkner, 337.
Farley, 193.
Farmer, 113, 160, 161.
Farner, 159.
Farquharson, 23.
Farr, 342.
Farragut, 433, 495.
Farrar, 23.
Farrell, 23, 56, 57, 58, 59, 60, 61, 62, 69, 71, 86.
Farrington, 216.
Farris, 93.
Farriss, 23.
Fatheree, 305.
Faulkner, 141, 146, 147, 148.
Faw, 189.
Fawcett, 47.
Fay, 57.
Feathers, 205.
Fell, 50.
Felts, 23, 47.
Felure, 330.
Fennell, 70.
Fergeson, 219.
Ferguson, 23, 76, 94, 216, 248, 279, 364, 372, 380, 399.
Fergueson, 466.
Feris, 247.
Ferns, 50.
Ferrell, 101.
Ferrick, 61.
Ferring, 63.
Ferriss, 94.
Fetter, 137.
Fetz, 90, 94.
Field, 291.
Fields, 23, 135, 289, 303, 319, 325.
Figuers, 216.
Finch, 356.
Fine, 360, 361.
Finger, 140, 230.
Finley, 291.
Finnegan, 57.
Finney, 59.
Fisher, 23, 51, 151, 176, 179, 216, 292, 298, 316, 452.
Fisk, 238, 389, 465, 495.
Fite, 23, 91, 146, 294, 296, 329, 359, 360, 469.
Fitzallin, 334.
Fitzgerald, 53, 56, 57, 61, 63, 65, 67, 68, 70.

Fitzgibbon, 56, 62.
Fitzgibbons, 63, 65, 70, 72.
Fitzpatrick, 60.
Fitzsimmons, 69.
Fitzwilliam, 61.
Fitzwilliams, 61.
Flack, 87.
Flanders, 151.
Flanagan, 56, 60, 73.
Flannagan, 56.
Flanigan, 57, 61, 68.
Fleming, 23, 125, 126, 243, 245, 246, 247, 250, 251, 252, 253, 257.
Flenz, 23.
Flenniken, 166.
Fletcher, 23, 142, 157, 350, 351, 357, 363, 444.
Floersh, 60.
Floeck, 49.
Flournow, 146.
Floyd, 303.
Fluker, 23.
Fly, 23, 52, 113, 114, 280.
Flyn, 57.
Flynn, 60, 71.
Fogarty, 60, 62.
Fogg, 9, 11, 12, 23, 91.
Foland, 338.
Foley, 56, 59, 66, 68, 71.
Folsom, 278, 281, 462.
Folsome, 278.
Foltz, 48.
Fontine, 73.
Fonville, 288.
Foot, 63.
Foote, 162.
Forbes, 23, 330.
Ford, 23, 54, 60, 67, 69, 71, 72, 83, 84, 155, 201, 233, 293, 299, 336, 343.
Fore, 176.
Forgey, 226, 267.
Forkner, 340.
Forest, 23, 156.
Forrest, 11, 340, 437, 460.
Formalt, 166.
Formwalt, 224.
Forster, 100.
Fort, 164.
Fortner, 232.
Foster, 8, 10, 12, 23, 53, 75, 176, 216, 217, 224, 257, 269, 289, 290, 295, 297, 317, 322, 343.
Foresyth, 8.
Forsyth, 11, 23, 50.
Fouche, 221, 337.

Foust, 226.
Foutch, 122.
Fowler, 87, 92, 94, 133, 297.
Fowlkes, 118.
Fox, 65, 176.
Foy, 11, 23.
Fraley, 23.
Francis, 264.
Francisco, 135.
Frank, 69, 131.
Franklin, 23, 54, 64, 75, 101, 107, 282, 495.
Frasch, 24.
Frazer, 24.
Frazier, 82, 87, 125, 130.
Fredale, 89.
Freeland, 473, 480.
Freeman, 24, 310.
Freese, 82.
French, 57, 145, 223, 423.
Frensley, 24, 55.
Frick, 24.
Frickster, 67.
Friel, 72.
Frierson, 85, 240, 241, 243, 244, 246, 248, 249, 250, 251, 252, 253, 254, 255, 256, 257, 263, 264, 278, 363.
Frindsley, 24.
Fritts, 128.
Frizzell, 87, 326.
Frost, 119, 192.
Frow, 229.
Fry, 24, 217.
Fugaggi, 61.
Fulcher, 92, 94.
Fuller, 24, 54, 128, 350.
Fulton, 226, 245, 247, 248, 251, 255.
Funk, 47.
Fuqua, 81, 358.
Furguson, 24.
Furman, 145.
Furtwangle, 24.
Furtwangler, 52.
Fuston, 138.
Fyffe, 190.

G

Gabler, 55.
Gaddis, 343.
Gadsey, 217.
Gaffney, 60.
Galbraith, 132.
Galbreth, 269.
Gaines, 24, 47, 359, 360.

499

Bible Records—Tombstone Inscriptions

Gaither, 24.
Gale, 24.
Gallaghan, 24.
Gallagher, 24, 60, 67, 94.
Gallaher, 24.
Galling, 342.
Galloway, 259, 261.
Gally, 24.
Galt, 342.
Galvin, 58, 61.
Gamble, 179, 234, 235, 295, 297.
Gambell, 116, 314.
Gambert, 72.
Gamblin, 279.
Gammill, 167, 192.
Gammons, 466.
Gannaway, 24, 150, 287.
Gannon, 84.
Garber, 136.
Gardiner, 177.
Gardner, 85, 94, 142, 194.
Garen, 130.
Garland, 103, 324.
Garner, 92, 169, 355.
Garolin, 58.
Garrett, 24, 54, 148, 149, 219, 387, 388.
Garriston, 157.
Garretson, 157.
Garritson, 142.
Gary, 58.
Gash, 24.
Gaskin, 58.
Gass, 176.
Gasser, 86.
Gaston, 176, 177.
Gates, 323.
Gatlen, 171.
Gatlin, 171, 307.
Gault, 217.
Gause, 287, 297.
Gaut, 361.
Gavin, 296.
Gay, 194, 195.
Geary, 56, 67.
Gee, 77, 81, 86, 253.
Geenan, 65.
Geers, 301.
Gegan, 56.
Geiger, 24.
Gennett, 24, 92.
Genette, 105.
Gent, 162.
Gentry, 219, 316, 342, 435, 495.
George, 24, 181, 228, 231.
Gerraty, 65.

Gerstle, 81, 87.
Gettys, 175, 176.
Gibb, 120.
Gibbs, 83, 201.
Gibson, 24, 50, 76, 136, 176, 188.
Giddens, 271, 272.
Giddings, 271.
Gierr, 94.
Giffin, 233.
Gifford, 186.
Gigily, 91.
Gilbert, 24, 51, 176, 177, 206, 233.
Gilchrist, 24, 53.
Gilea, 68.
Giles, 495.
Gilkie, 2.
Gill, 24.
Gillen, 61.
Gillespie, 56, 57, 64, 115, 147, 176, 228, 229, 230, 283, 312, 425, 453.
Gilliam, 10, 13, 24, 76, 217, 351.
Gilliland, 82.
Gillman, 24.
Gilliner, 54.
Gilmore, 58, 64, 121.
Gilride, 56.
Gilvain, 58.
Gingrich, 149.
Gist, 143, 274.
Glasgow, 78, 86.
Glass, 217.
Glasser, 69.
Glasscock, 50.
Glaze, 130, 131.
Gleaves, 108, 114, 327.
Glenn, 24, 56, 71, 83, 139, 151, 174, 236, 297, 341.
Glennon, 58, 66.
Gloster, 58, 59.
Glouster, 60.
Glover, 24, 100, 191.
Glutingers, 87.
Glymp, 83, 87.
Goad, 24, 260, 466.
Goarley, 117.
Godard, 236.
Goddard, 129, 130, 131.
Godfrey, 201.
Godshall, 24.
Goff, 219, 281.
Gohlson, 217.
Golden, 68, 138.
Goldstein, 295.

Goldston, 290, 299, 323, 326.
Golladay, 52, 292, 296.
Gooch, 24.
Good, 82.
Goodall, 466.
Goodbar, 148, 289.
Goodlet, 125.
Goodloe, 24, 262, 263.
Goodner, 295.
Goodrich, 59, 81, 450.
Goodson, 86, 150.
Goodwin, 24, 25, 47, 49, 53, 113, 236, 237, 288.
Gooley, 119.
Gordon, 25, 94, 217.
Gore, 25.
Gorman, 57, 61, 63, 69.
Gory, 77.
Goss, 25.
Gossett, 341, 342.
Gough, 56.
Gould, 11, 12, 25, 98.
Gowan, 86, 435, 480.
Gowans, 85.
Gowen, 140.
Gowdey, 25.
Gowdy, 25, 94.
Gower, 25, 171.
Grady, 58, 61, 64, 66, 70, 71, 72.
Graft, 83.
Graham, 25, 90, 283, 292, 313.
Grainger, 495.
Granbery, 274, 277.
Grandstaff, 306.
Granger, 25, 29.
Grannis, 293.
Grant, 25, 145, 176, 190, 277, 279.
Grassham, 128.
Graves, 47, 75, 81, 83, 87, 124, 186, 279, 292, 297, 304, 310, 311, 314, 319, 328.
Gray, 10, 25, 49, 68, 84, 88, 167, 192, 217, 262, 296.
Gredig, 343.
Greig, 94.
Green, 25, 47, 54, 55, 84, 94, 130, 138, 143, 147, 148, 151, 157, 265, 279, 288, 290, 291, 292, 347, 348, 373.
Greene, 25, 241, 495.
Greenfield, 25, 65.

Bible Records—Tombstone Inscriptions

Greenhalgh, 25.
Greenwood, 25, 180.
Greer, 25, 141, 173, 174, 187, 201, 382, 389, 466.
Greers, 25.
Greeway, 137, 201.
Gregory, 182, 207, 344, 469.
Gregsby, 75.
Gresham, 176.
Gresiac, 60.
Gribble, 151, 288.
Griffice, 25, 83.
Griffin, 25, 59, 63, 66, 84, 177, 278.
Griffith, 230, 232.
Griffis, 25, 47.
Grigg, 80, 298, 325, 326.
Griggs, 194.
Grigsby, 167, 192, 289.
Grimm, 103.
Grimmer, 219.
Grindstaff, 206.
Grisham, 181, 201, 466, 470.
Grissim, 289, 297, 305.
Grissom, 150, 326, 331.
Griswold, 147, 157.
Grizzard, 25, 76, 87, 88, 299.
Grizzell, 151.
Croome, 86.
Groomes, 25.
Gross, 148, 153.
Grosse, 25.
Groves, 336.
Growdis, 55.
Grubb, 176, 180.
Grubbs, 25.
Grundy, 144, 421, 452, 495.
Guest, 278, 281, 282, 283.
Guffee, 278.
Guffie, 281.
Guinn, 345, 346.
Gunn, 51, 113, 160, 164, 256.
Gunnels, 282.
Gunter, 217, 338.
Guntrie, 150.
Guthrie, 88, 219, 298, 324, 337.
Gussman, 25.
Guson, 362.
Gwyn, 142.
Gwynn, 305.

H

Habert, 51, 297.
Hackett, 153.
Hacky, 230.
Hackl, 204.
Hadley, 25, 76, 386, 431.
Hadly, 76.
Hagar, 123, 291.
Hagen, 94.
Hager, 25.
Hagerty, 56, 58, 72.
Haggard, 147.
Haggart, 25.
Hagon, 117.
Hail, 263.
Haile, 25.
Hailey, 25, 47, 85.
Hainbly, 64.
Haines, 201.
Halberd, 294, 318.
Hale, 26, 47, 81, 222, 234, 360, 361.
Haley, 68, 150, 177.
Halfer, 26.
Halfly, 236.
Hall, 25, 26, 48, 50, 78, 138, 217, 226, 269, 271, 342, 353, 385, 428, 443, 444, 462, 495.
Haller, 53.
Halley, 25.
Halliburton, 342.
Halliday, 52.
Halloran, 56, 57, 58, 59, 60, 63, 65, 73.
Halloway, 264.
Hallum, 26, 121.
Ham, 113, 278.
Hamblen, 83, 117, 118, 122, 124.
Hamill, 83.
Hamilton, 26, 47, 60, 91, 183, 210, 362, 428, 480.
Hamington, 66.
Hammack, 187.
Hammer, 145, 147.
Hammers, 83.
Hammock, 466.
Hammon, 297.
Hammontree, 228.
Hampton, 144.
Hancock, 289, 292, 293, 446.
Hand, 278.
Hanifin, 63.
Hankal, 135.
Hankins, 140, 288, 294, 296, 318, 323, 330.
Hank, 51.
Hanks, 26.
Hanley, 62.
Hanlon, 217.
Hanly, 65.
Hanna, 78, 80, 258, 259, 261, 271, 288, 470.
Hannah, 203.
Hannapen, 61.
Hanner, 217.
Hannis, 452.
Hannon, 65.
Hansard, 130.
Hansberry, 316.
Hansbrough, 217.
Hanson, 57, 58, 73.
Happel, 204.
Harahan, 60, 69.
Haralson, 302, 328.
Harbert, 80, 203.
Harbin, 72.
Harbison, 177.
Hard, 26, 52.
Hardeman, 54, 56, 62, 217, 275, 437.
Harden, 151, 265.
Hardenband, 155.
Hardin, 167, 188, 260, 282, 360, 428, 437, 462.
Harding, 66, 79, 85, 93, 171.
Hardy, 263, 264, 293, 296.
Hare, 26, 82, 85.
Hargis, 466, 470.
Harkreader, 288, 296, 297.
Harlam, 264.
Harlan, 203, 253, 254, 264.
Harlen, 207.
Harley, 49.
Harlow, 26, 259.
Harman, 26, 47.
Harmey, 26.
Harmon, 49, 76, 86, 134.
Harper, 51, 97, 161, 204, 207, 256, 267, 268, 277, 397.
Harpole, 302, 315, 316.
Harrahan, 69.
Harrell, 276.
Harrill, 326.
Harry, 207.
Harrington, 64, 82.

Bible Records—Tombstone Inscriptions

Harris, 11, 12, 26, 47, 49, 54, 67, 68, 75, 78, 84, 88, 92, 116, 125, 136, 166, 177, 178, 188, 205, 206, 224, 225, 226, 229, 231, 248, 263, 280, 283, 290, 292, 315, 324, 331, 340, 346, 449, 466, 470, 495.
Harrison, 26, 65, 83, 85, 131, 146, 156, 172, 204, 210, 355, 356, 359, 422.
Harsena, 279.
Harsh, 10, 26, 138.
Hart, 108, 112, 113, 138, 160, 161, 201, 254, 260, 389, 394, 466.
Hartley, 219.
Hartman, 446.
Hartnett, 62.
Hartsell, 229.
Hartshorn, 26.
Harvey, 95, 224, 313.
Harwell, 88, 148.
Harwood, 113, 204.
Hash, 152, 239.
Haskins, 256.
Haslam, 26, 50.
Hatchett, 116.
Hatham, 26.
Hatton, 116, 287, 295, 296, 496.
Haun, 201.
Haury, 90, 94.
Hauser, 52.
Hawes, 246.
Hawkins, 26, 51, 275, 371.
Hawks, 47, 289.
Hay, 2, 26, 51.
Hayes, 26, 56, 62, 64, 82, 90, 94, 155, 172, 280, 283.
Hays, 51, 90, 94, 123, 169, 203, 279, 283, 284.
Haynes, 217, 337, 356, 357, 382, 495.
Haynie, 26, 467.
Haywood, 245, 495.
Head, 92, 120, 315.
Hearn, 85, 272, 294, 295, 297, 319, 329, 332, 333.
Heartsell, 229.
Heath, 85, 285.
Hedgecock, 343.
Hefferman, 26, 57, 62.
Hefy, 60
Hegherty, 64.
Heheir, 56, 60, 73.

Heiskell, 133, 166, 224, 336, 338, 339, 346, 359.
Heiss, 26.
Helfer, 53.
Helm, 177.
Helphenstine, 206.
Hembree, 84.
Hemphill, 275, 284.
Henderson, 26, 144, 177, 180, 196, 209, 210, 211, 212, 213, 219, 230, 235, 260, 265, 266, 268, 270, 271, 272, 279, 318, 338, 351, 385, 390, 391, 392, 393, 394, 417, 418, 423, 442, 443, 444, 447, 448, 477.
Hendrick, 245, 246, 251, 257.
Hendrix, 85.
Henegar, 140.
Henley, 58, 137, 359, 433.
Henly, 344.
Henness, 26.
Hennessee, 236, 237.
Henniger, 177.
Henning, 26, 27, 75, 94.
Hennot, 56.
Henry, 67, 116, 117, 162, 163, 188, 229, 341, 433, 442, 443, 447, 495.
Hensley, 26, 70, 71, 206, 265.
Herdel, 61.
Hergel, 27.
Herndon, 27, 144.
Herriges, 27.
Herod, 389, 467.
Herron, 84, 203, 204.
Hersey, 341.
Hess, 59, 204.
Hession, 58.
Hesson, 469.
Heston, 67, 68, 93.
Heverin, 57.
Hewgley, 295, 325, 326.
Hewitt, 300.
Hewlett, 27.
Hibbitt, 309.
Hibbitts, 467.
Hickey, 56.
Hickox, 177.
Hicks, 27, 52, 92, 177, 203, 217, 236, 361.
Higginbotham, 27.
Higgins, 27, 276.
Hightower, 217, 363.
Hildebrand, 27.

Hildreth, 217.
Hill, 27, 53, 75, 76, 99, 140, 144, 145, 156, 170, 194, 195, 203, 204, 217, 219, 244, 245, 250, 299, 343, 421, 469.
Hiller, 256.
Hilliard, 108, 275, 283, 349, 352, 451, 495.
Hillis, 335.
Hillman, 27.
Hillsman, 204.
Hiltson, 149.
Hinds, 293.
Hines, 27, 57, 67, 129.
Hipkins, 91.
Hitch, 85, 228.
Hitchcock, 283.
Hite, 81, 113, 125.
Hitt, 77.
Hixey, 138.
Hobbs, 27, 153, 217.
Hobson, 283, 308.
Hodge, 27, 49, 54, 100, 114, 205, 279, 280, 351, 445, 448, 460, 461, 480.
Hodges, 166, 224, 362.
Hoffmeister, 234.
Hogan, 27, 61, 62, 68, 72, 174, 208, 209.
Hoge, 177, 252, 264, 423.
Hogg, 10, 12, 27, 423.
Hoggatt, 98.
Hogue, 252, 253.
Holderfield, 86.
Holland, 61, 66, 106, 280, 361.
Holley, 27.
Holliday, 27, 229.
Hollingsworth, 27, 207.
Hollins, 94, 217.
Hollis, 140, 158, 480.
Holloway, 292.
Hollowell, 49, 283.
Holly, 462.
Holman, 51, 85, 162, 290, 292, 300.
Holmes, 27, 204, 356, 452.
Holony, 58.
Holston, 131.
Holt, 51, 130, 284.
Holzappel, 76.
Homes, 27.
Honey, 360.
Hood, 27, 47, 53, 71, 140, 201, 221, 341.
Hoodenpyl, 145, 146, 148.
Hook, 130.

Bible Records—Tombstone Inscriptions

Hooke, 201.
Hooper, 27, 108, 109, 110, 341.
Hoover, 157, 158, 231, 382, 467.
Hope, 80, 232.
Hopert, 60.
Hopkins, 27, 119, 128, 145, 153, 323, 346, 347, 413, 423.
Hopman, 256.
Horan, 58, 64, 67.
Hord, 144, 354, 355, 422.
Horn, 27, 76, 80, 82, 83, 102, 290, 298.
Hornsby, 177.
Horsford, 417.
Horton, 27, 177, 194, 210, 213, 283.
Hosale, 87.
Hoskins, 364.
Hoss, 137.
Hossbein, 27.
Hotchkiss, 167.
Hotten, 27.
Houchens, 27.
Hough, 27.
Hougins, 54.
Houser, 27, 233, 256, 257.
Houstan, 235.
Houston, 105, 201, 202, 235, 266, 267, 280, 433, 495.
Howard, 10, 11, 27, 128, 135, 147, 176, 177, 264, 265, 274, 288, 296, 338.
Howe, 54.
Howell, 11, 27, 51, 127, 145, 422.
Howington, 86.
Howlett, 272.
Hows, 88.
Howse, 168, 354.
Hoyt, 201.
Hoyte, 448.
Hubbard, 9, 27, 309.
Hubble, 149.
Huckman, 89.
Huddleston, 93, 120, 294, 364.
Hudgens, 237, 238.
Hudgins, 28, 359.
Hudson, 71, 78, 80, 85, 100, 237, 267, 318, 322, 326, 352.
Huff, 28, 47.
Huger, 274.
Huggins, 356.

Hughes, 28, 56, 58, 59, 65, 66, 82, 84, 86, 148, 150, 154, 173, 206, 209, 210, 211, 213, 252, 279, 462, 495.
Hugley, 328.
Hull, 28, 278.
Hulme, 209, 219.
Hulvey, 360.
Humble, 154.
Hume, 4, 7, 11, 12, 13, 28, 47, 52, 221.
Humes, 166, 221, 222, 224.
Hummer, 28.
Humphrey, 228.
Humphreys, 82, 177, 180.
Humphries, 232.
Hundley, 28.
Huneycutt, 73.
Hunt, 28, 51, 75, 160, 177, 204, 231, 282, 312, 313, 322, 364, 462.
Hunter, 28, 82, 244, 245, 253, 386.
Huppert, 71.
Hurley, 91.
Hurly, 80.
Hurry, 28.
Hurst, 28, 60.
Hurston, 58.
Hurt, 28, 126.
Hurton, 90.
Husbands, 390.
Huse, 28.
Huskins, 206.
Husle, 10, 12.
Hussey, 57, 70, 71.
Hutcheson, 340.
Hutchison, 28.
Hutchings, 108, 112.
Hutchinson, 77.
Hutson, 237.
Hutton, 217, 219.
Hyde, 57, 65, 94, 108, 110, 111.
Hyden, 177.
Hyder, 188, 382, 461.
Hyler, 188.
Hynes, 10, 11, 28, 58, 59, 60, 61, 63, 65, 72.
Hyronemous, 61.

I

Ignatz, 28.
Ingram, 263, 264.
Irby, 333.
Irvin, 177.

Irwin, 28, 50, 52, 201, 264, 265, 341, 343.
Isabel, 447.
Isman, 59.
Isom, 245.
Ivey, 106, 195.
Ivy, 295.
Ivins, 177.

J

Jack, 441.
Jackson, 28, 52, 76, 85, 87, 89, 91, 94, 101, 102, 121, 127, 161, 177, 194, 195, 251, 275, 286, 297, 298, 313, 327, 334, 364, 393, 425, 426, 459, 462, 470.
Jacobs, 56, 64, 330.
Jacobson, 47.
James, 28, 83, 450.
Jamison, 288.
Janeway, 130.
Jared, 469.
Jarman, 356.
Jarmon, 291.
Jarnagin, 225.
Jarrell, 86, 195, 204.
Jarrat, 357.
Jarratt, 283, 284, 363.
Jarrett, 195.
Jarvis, 237.
Jayner, 339.
Jean, 167.
Jeck, 94.
Jefferson, 13, 28, 54, 495.
Jefferies, 235, 236.
Jeffreys, 84.
Jeffries, 231, 422.
Jenkins, 28, 105, 124, 127, 128, 131, 182, 190, 217, 334.
Jennings, 8, 13, 28, 54, 56, 62, 66, 71, 92, 93, 156, 265, 283, 326, 389.
Jett, 166, 277.
Jetton, 204, 349, 351, 352, 353, 357, 442, 443, 447.
Jettun, 81.
Jewell, 167.
Jewett, 28.
Jinkins, 183.
Jinks, 341.
Jobe, 28, 462.
Johns, 94, 181, 291, 328, 351, 352, 450.

Bible Records—Tombstone Inscriptions

Johnson, 7, 9, 12, 28, 29, 47, 49, 54, 59, 64, 75, 78, 80, 81, 86, 87, 94, 101, 128, 132, 134, 155, 161, 162, 165, 171, 177, 193, 204, 205, 206, 217, 226, 227, 231, 233, 234, 235, 246, 257, 264, 276, 278, 279, 280, 281, 283, 289, 297, 305, 309, 318, 324, 330, 334, 338, 343, 345, 348, 353, 357, 359, 382, 387, 432, 459, 466, 470, 480, 495.
Johnston, 54, 83, 134, 193, 204, 337, 344.
Joice, 60, 61.
Joins, 177.
Jolley, 195, 314.
Jones, 29, 49, 53, 58, 60, 63, 68, 76, 81, 82, 84, 87, 88, 94, 116, 121, 127, 135, 136, 145, 146, 147, 148, 152, 156, 162, 163, 165, 167, 172, 177, 183, 195, 204, 205, 234, 236, 237, 238, 239, 244, 246, 247, 252, 253, 254, 255, 263, 264, 276, 278, 279, 280, 281, 291, 302, 303, 315, 320, 338, 343, 345, 353, 359, 362, 364, 438, 449, 452, 495, 498.
Jonnard, 69.
Jonte, 7, 49, 90.
Jonti, 29.
Jordan, 117, 137, 264, 283, 364.
Joseph, 88.
Joslin, 174.
Jourdan, 282.
Joyce, 57, 58, 60, 64.
Judkins, 57.
Julee, 71.
Julius, 29.

K

Kaiser, 29.
Kaminsta, 343.
Kanary, 290, 297.
Kannon, 271, 272.
Kane, 10, 12, 29, 59, 63.
Karl, 75.
Karsh, 89.
Keanan, 61.
Keanon, 58.
Kearns, 59, 60, 71.
Keathley, 452.
Kedy, 66.
Keeble, 355, 446.
Keef, 276.
Keefen, 69.
Keegan, 58, 61, 72.
Keel, 449.
Keeling, 108, 109, 110.
Keenan, 65, 69, 204.
Keener, 455.
Keesee, 54
Keezer, 47.
Keith, 343.
Kell, 140.
Kelley, 29, 56, 59, 60, 61, 67, 177, 296, 298.
Kelly, 29, 58, 66, 70, 71, 72, 73, 238, 341, 342, 425.
Kellough, 356.
Kellum, 87.
Kelton, 352, 443, 444, 447.
Kemes, 64, 65.
Kemmess, 61.
Kemper, 77, 79.
Kemphan, 94.
Kempkau, 90.
Kendrick, 29.
Kendrickan, 58.
Kendrickson, 58.
Kenely, 282.
Kenelly, 57.
Kennelly, 64.
Kennedy, 55, 167, 192, 219, 221, 222, 245, 247, 260, 295, 362.
Kenny, 57, 61, 62.
Kenning, 76.
Kensey, 279.
Kenson, 232.
Kerbey, 94.
Keogh, 73.
Keon, 71.
Kerby, 94.
Kercheval, 167, 192.
Kernel, 87.
Kernell, 86.
Kerney, 64.
Kerr, 184, 259, 282, 283.
Kerrigan, 56, 57, 62, 63.
Kesey, 155.
Kessling, 29.
Ketchum, 278, 279.
Ketrine, 96.
Key, 469.
Keyes, 177.
Keys, 177, 189.
Kezer, 9, 11, 12.
Kidd, 231, 235, 343.
Kiddell, 446.
Kidder, 296.
Kidwell, 150, 324.
Kierman, 47.
Kiger, 81, 83.
Kiggins, 65.
Kilcoin, 70.
Kilgore, 158, 163, 164.
Killea, 60.
Killian, 153.
Killough, 356, 444, 446.
Kilzoe, 177.
Kimbell, 283.
Kimberly, 187.
Kimbro, 87, 171.
Kincannon, 145, 422.
Kindel, 264.
Kinefie, 67.
Kinder, 180.
King, 29, 47, 50, 84, 86, 94, 115, 117, 150, 175, 177, 190, 221, 233, 253, 283, 339, 340, 341, 342, 344, 351, 352, 460.
Kingsley, 12, 29, 58.
Kingsly, 9.
Kinnard, 143.
Kinney, 56, 65, 72, 94.
Kinsey, 177, 338.
Kirban, 63.
Kirby, 29, 117, 283, 343, 364.
Kirk, 9, 11, 13, 29, 357.
Kirkman, 29, 91, 275.
Kirkpatrick, 29, 94, 96, 236, 248, 288, 289, 296, 312, 333, 334.
Kirkwood, 88.
Kiser, 128, 228.
Kissing, 53.
Kittrell, 263, 264, 265, 275.
Klein, 70.
Kleiser, 29.
Klooz, 29.
Klugman, 86.
Knapp, 49, 456.
Knight, 29, 64, 90, 361, 446.
Knootz, 235, 236.
Knop, 69.
Knott, 157.
Knowles, 10, 11, 29, 30, 104.
Knox, 30, 85, 283, 447.
Kobbs, 69.
Kohee, 63.
Kohlie, 69.
Kohlis, 69.

Bible Records—Tombstone Inscriptions

Kountz, 235.
Kruder, 76.
Kughn, 94.
Kuhn, 30, 60, 62.
Kuigley, 59.
Kurth, 341.
Kusle, 159.
Kuykendall, 480.
Kyker, 177, 340.
Kyle, 30, 204.
Kyser, 460.

L

Lackey, 130.
Lafayette, 495.
Lafferty, 178.
Laffey, 57, 70.
Laffy, 58.
Lain, 303.
Laird, 30.
Lallemand, 84.
Lally, 56, 57.
Lamb, 285, 286.
Lancaster, 86, 87.
Landers, 60, 62, 70.
Landis, 204.
Landrum, 286, 287.
Lane, 134, 135, 153, 177, 187, 194, 195, 196, 294, 296, 339, 452, 490, 495.
Langan, 60, 61, 62.
Langdon, 145.
Langford, 30.
Langham, 76.
Langley, 30, 283.
Lanier, 30, 88, 89, 92, 99, 170, 280.
Lanius, 348.
Lankford, 467.
Lanning, 196.
Lanny, 217.
Lanon, 65.
Lannom, 301.
Lansden, 236.
Lanston, 131.
Laporing, 61.
Lapsley, 30, 288.
Larkin, 61, 85.
LaRue, 341.
Larvis, 57.
Lasater, 178.
Lash, 296.
Lasky, 59.
Lassiter, 30, 47, 204.
Latelle, 57.
Latham, 116, 154, 421.
Latsch, 87.
Latta, 78.

Latimer, 448.
Lattimore, 429.
Lattiner, 30.
Lauderdale, 116, 167, 290, 389, 469.
Lauflin, 153.
Laughlin, 361, 362, 413, 418.
Laughters, 135.
Laurence, 150, 239.
Laurent, 30.
Lavender, 300, 344, 348.
Lavelle, 68.
Law, 30, 469.
Lawrence, 17, 30, 47, 53, 55, 75, 102, 144, 150, 228, 239, 262, 263, 334, 356, 360, 417, 419.
Lawson, 177.
Laycock, 130.
Layne, 142.
Lea, 226, 297, 320, 431.
Leach, 87, 259.
Leagania, 157.
Leahy, 67.
Leaird, 157.
Leake, 30.
Leath, 113.
LeBow, 30, 34.
Leche, 68.
Lechliton, 62.
Leck, 57.
Leckey, 67.
Lecky, 59, 63.
Ledbetter, 452.
Ledford, 340.
Leddy, 117.
Lee, 30, 49, 57, 61, 63, 71, 78, 89, 125, 130, 162, 164, 204, 283, 463.
Leeahy, 72.
Leehe, 65.
Leeman, 318.
Leffering, 61.
Lefler, 128, 190.
Leftwich, 146, 238.
Lehart, 62.
Lehman, 279.
Lehmann, 30.
Leichleiter, 60.
Leinau, 352.
Leiper, 231, 495, 497.
LeMaster, 279.
Lemmons, 228.
Lemons, 117.
Lenden, 75.
Lenning, 311.
Lenoir, 165, 338, 339, 359.

Leonard, 62, 64, 77, 78.
Leslie, 219.
Lester, 30, 85, 177, 217, 283, 288, 289, 296, 297, 320.
Lesueur, 30.
Letherman, 449.
Levene, 94.
Levi, 54.
Levin, 30, 175.
Levy, 204.
Lewis, 12, 30, 84, 91, 96, 107, 128, 139, 146, 217, 282, 287, 288, 295, 341, 354, 362, 422, 424, 495, 497.
Lide, 178.
Lienert, 92.
Lightfoot, 219.
Ligon, 264, 301, 327, 467.
Lillard, 340, 341, 449.
Linert, 30.
Lincoln, 30, 133, 188, 238, 381, 461.
Lindsay, 97.
Lindsey, 320, 428.
Lindsley, 30, 53, 119, 219, 293, 294, 297, 448, 495.
Lingrow, 81.
Linker, 83.
Linn, 243, 247, 257.
Linsey, 473, 478, 479, 480.
Linster, 352.
Linton, 173, 174.
Lipscomb, 178, 244, 252, 254.
Lipton, 187.
Lischey, 78, 83, 88.
Lisk, 237.
Lister, 148.
Little, 204.
Littlefield, 30, 34, 257, 277.
Litton, 30, 31, 51.
Lively, 145.
Livermore, 495.
Livingston, 31.
Lloyd, 105.
Lockalier, 31.
Lockart, 78.
Locke, 154, 356, 390.
Locks, 351.
Locken, 94.
Locket, 31.
Lockett, 31.
Lockhart, 31, 153.
Lockridge, 219.
Loftin, 89.
Logan, 94, 141, 229.

505

Bible Records—Tombstone Inscriptions

Loger, 67.
Loman, 51.
Lomas, 31.
Lomasney, 58, 60, 63, 64, 69.
Lonas, 235.
Lone, 145.
Long, 31, 94, 159, 162, 178, 195, 217, 222, 257, 262, 263, 276, 280, 344.
Longenotti, 10, 12.
Longinotti, 31.
Loomis, 31.
Looney, 234, 235, 280, 283.
Loser, 76.
Lotspeich, 129.
Loubheimes, 72.
Louis, 362.
Louis Philippe, 389, 431.
Love, 77, 78, 80, 82, 88, 205, 206, 226, 233, 359.
Lovelace, 462.
Lovelady, 467.
Lovelard, 152.
Lovell, 31, 47, 75.
Loving, 31.
Lovisson, 31.
Lowe, 55, 56, 88, 130, 131, 182.
Lowery, 138, 139, 167, 341, 359.
Lowrey, 31, 237, 238.
Lowry, 167, 168, 360.
Lucas, 479.
Lumsden, 94.
Lurner, 76.
Lusk, 139, 144, 146, 157, 158, 271, 272, 421.
Luster, 31, 78.
Luton, 75.
Lybarger, 130, 131.
Lyda, 237.
Lyle, 470.
Lynam, 65.
Lyne, 144.
Lynn, 147.
Lynch, 31, 59, 61, 64, 67, 73, 80, 184, 322, 466.
Lyon, 31, 94, 137, 145, 223, 336, 417, 418, 419.
Lyston, 62.
Lytle, 59, 92, 209, 350, 353, 451, 452.
Lytton, 94.

M

Mabry, 142, 143, 145, 315, 452.
Mabury, 85.
MacCarrell, 129.
Mace, 31.
Macey, 358.
MacGuire, 131.
Mack, 57, 260, 280, 281.
Mackenzie, 51, 291.
MacNabb, 128.
Macon, 150, 243, 257.
Madden, 57, 59, 94, 95, 185, 467.
Maddin, 58.
Maddis, 12.
Maddox, 82.
Maddux, 31.
Maddy, 361.
Madewell, 152.
Maeher, 57.
Magar, 31.
Magee, 388, 389, 462, 465, 467.
Magill, 178, 234.
Magness, 147, 149, 288.
Magown, 269.
Maguire, 146.
Mahan, 31, 62.
Maher, 57.
Maholland, 331.
Mahoney, 61, 62, 67, 70, 73.
Major, 328.
Maleaby, 73.
Malfour, 175.
Malay, 360.
Mallory, 47, 93, 219.
Malloy, 58, 59.
Malleston, 344.
Malone, 31, 66, 276, 390, 469.
Maloney, 57, 59, 66.
Mame, 284.
Mandley, 31.
Maney, 94, 108, 220, 350, 351, 444.
Mangrem, 280.
Mangrum, 281.
Manhard, 62.
Manier, 94, 284, 285.
Manere, 284, 285, 286.
Mann, 76, 299.
Manning, 31, 55, 58, 59, 63, 217.
Mannion, 68.
Mansco, 480.

Mansker, 392.
Manus, 363.
Marable, 87.
Marah, 61.
Marbury, 422.
March, 50, 277.
Marchbanks, 146, 149.
Mardith, 178.
Marfield, 82.
Markham, 107.
Marks, 183.
Marlin, 7, 8, 12, 31, 55, 444.
Marling, 9, 12, 31.
Marlow, 32, 53, 85.
Marney, 129, 434.
Marquet, 70.
Marr, 217.
Marrs, 317, 320.
Marsh, 32, 50, 136.
Marshall, 31, 32, 86, 116, 135, 198, 204, 217, 219, 246, 358, 445.
Marston, 178, 362.
Martain, 338, 344.
Martin, 31, 50, 51, 57, 58, 59, 60, 61, 63, 66, 69, 74, 79, 87, 91, 94, 97, 114, 116, 130, 134, 148, 154, 155, 158, 159, 181, 186, 187, 194, 209, 210, 211, 212, 213, 217, 219, 232, 235, 237, 238, 244, 245, 246, 249, 253, 262, 263, 275, 276, 288, 289, 296, 297, 305, 315, 317, 320, 322, 360, 361, 386, 389, 436, 448, 465, 467, 471.
Marton, 58.
Mary, 235.
Masey, 154, 155.
Mason, 64, 134, 152, 454, 479.
Massengill, 32, 439, 440.
Massey, 332.
Masterson, 32.
Masten, 429.
Mastison, 299.
Maston, 342.
Matherly, 297.
Mathes, 134.
Mathis, 193.
Matlock, 128, 129, 230.
Mathews, 180.
Matthews, 32, 57, 76, 178, 230, 233, 243, 248, 258, 259, 260, 261, 270, 272.
Mattimore, 65, 72.

Bible Records—Tombstone Inscriptions

Maulding, 473, 480.
Maurey, 82.
Maury, 435, 495.
Maxey, 8, 11, 32, 51.
Maxwell, 32, 270, 271, 272, 279.
May, 55, 69, 136, 178, 223, 284.
Mayberry, 74, 80, 173.
Mayer, 32.
Mayes, 69, 174, 243, 244, 246, 249, 251, 257, 281.
Mays, 174, 217, 340, 342.
Maynard, 87.
Maynor, 32, 89.
Mayo, 32, 131, 178, 188.
Mayson, 32.
McAbee, 195, 226, 469.
McAdams, 136, 479.
McAfee, 141, 148.
McAffrey, 178.
McAlister, 32, 51, 87, 217.
McAllister, 32, 57.
McAmis, 135, 188.
McAnderson, 71.
McAndrews, 72.
McBath, 281, 342.
McBrady, 280.
McBride, 32.
McCabe, 61, 63.
McCain, 479.
McCall, 94, 149.
McCallie, 235, 341.
McCallum, 152.
McCamey, 232.
McCammon, 233, 336.
McCampbell, 32, 225, 226, 234, 235, 339.
McCance, 78.
McCarmock, 59.
McCarroll, 362.
McCarthy, 59, 63, 64, 65, 66, 67.
McCarty, 267.
McCaslin, 47, 233.
McCauley, 62, 247, 362.
McClain, 291, 295, 297, 348.
McClannahan, 165, 166, 224.
McClarty, 147.
McClaskey, 178.
McClellan, 32, 135, 217, 294, 297, 332, 430.
McClelland, 134, 387.
McCelen, 224.
McCleod, 198.
McCluggager, 32.

McClinch, 276.
McClinton, 341.
McCloud, 462.
McClung, 32, 166, 221, 222, 223, 224, 228.
McClure, 89.
McClurg, 360.
McColloch, 157, 158.
McComb, 32, 246.
McConnell, 32, 229, 237, 340.
McConnico, 76, 217.
McCook, 71.
McCool, 85.
McCorkle, 132, 133, 288.
McCormack, 57, 65, 71.
McCowan, 196, 208.
McCown, 209, 217.
McCoy, 76, 135, 260, 337.
McCrory, 2, 32, 55, 193.
McCroy, 32, 194.
McCroskey, 235, 236.
McCroskley, 228.
McCue, 67, 70.
McCulloch, 35, 202, 204, 228, 229, 355, 444, 451.
McCullough, 229, 236, 421.
McCullen, 234.
McCulley, 178.
McCurdy, 32.
McCutcheon, 83, 219.
McDade, 128.
McDaniel, 32, 155, 184, 217, 283, 304, 339.
McDannel, 134.
McDearmon, 204.
McDonald, 64, 66, 71, 278, 309.
McDonate, 68.
McDonnold, 296.
McDonnell, 60.
McDougall, 87.
McDowell, 178, 284.
McDoyle, 64.
McDuffee, 269.
McEachern, 322.
McElwain, 263.
McElwee, 178.
McEwen, 32, 53, 74, 94, 178, 281.
McFadden, 32, 60, 170, 247, 445, 446, 480.
McFall, 244, 246, 248, 254.
McFarland, 32, 310, 348.
McFerin, 188.
McFerrin, 90, 126, 388.
McFillen, 32.
McGann, 217.

McGar, 32.
McGarry, 70.
McGath, 57.
McGaughey, 178.
McGavock, 32, 53, 89, 90, 94, 209, 210, 264, 265.
McGaw, 254, 255, 256.
McGee, 107, 156, 181, 182, 204, 289.
McGhee, 142, 201, 222, 340.
McGill, 168, 444.
McGilvery, 496, 497.
McGimsey, 281.
McGinley, 201, 202, 342.
McGinnis, 70, 89.
McGonage, 64.
McGonegal, 62.
McGonnegle, 66.
McGonigoe, 64.
McGonnigoe, 65.
McGovern, 57, 61, 63, 64, 69, 70, 73.
McGowan, 16, 452, 453.
McGowias, 32.
McGrath, 60, 62.
McGready, 389.
McGregor, 49, 81, 92, 155, 291, 297.
McGuire, 32, 57, 63, 81, 338.
McGumsley, 281.
McHenry, 76.
McHugh, 65, 66.
McIlhaney, 127.
McIndoe, 32.
McIndole, 52.
McIntire, 32, 52.
McIntosch, 33.
McIntosh, 33, 36, 49, 166, 224, 226.
McInturff, 81, 205, 206.
McIver, 48, 170, 351.
McKamey, 178.
McKay, 33, 187.
McKean, 281.
McKee, 59, 60, 70, 133, 265, 306, 317, 321.
McKeehan, 229.
McKendree, 103.
McKenzie, 9, 13, 33, 68, 92, 201.
McKeon, 33, 62, 65, 67, 71.
McKeldin, 178.
McKierman, 47.
McKinley, 65, 67, 68.
McKinly, 63.

507

Bible Records—Tombstone Inscriptions

McKinney, 132, 167, 178.
McKinnie, 88.
McKnight, 47, 257, 338, 353, 447, 448.
McKnitt, 135.
McLane, 168.
McLaughlin, 33, 66, 68, 69, 293, 452.
McLoughlin, 63.
McLean, 33, 94, 153, 340.
McLemore, 33, 50, 154.
McLendon, 360.
McLin, 221, 233, 340.
McMahan, 196.
McMahon, 72, 197, 219.
McManus, 68.
McMenaway, 121.
McMillan, 68, 73, 253, 272.
McMillian, 224.
McMillin, 244.
McMinn, 33, 432, 434.
McMullen, 58, 248, 336, 337.
McMullin, 64.
McMurray, 126, 178, 277, 296.
McMurry, 105, 312, 467.
McMurtrye, 96.
McNabb, 51, 228, 229.
McNairy, 7, 12, 94.
McNamara, 60, 94.
McNeal, 33.
McNeill, 172, 280.
McNish, 76.
McNulty, 57, 58, 63.
McNutt, 221, 223, 229.
McO'Nawry, 167, 190.
McPhail, 209, 217.
McPherson, 33, 84, 174, 336.
McQuade, 33.
McQuown, 128.
McRamsey, 153.
McRee, 204.
McRoberts, 178.
McSpadden, 231, 340, 433.
McTague, 61.
McTigue, 59, 69.
McTeer, 200, 221, 224, 225, 235, 236, 341.
McTyeire, 102.
McVeigh, 159.
McWharter, 195.
McWhirter, 94, 298, 310.
McWhorter, 195.
McWilliams, 78.

McWright, 33.
Mead, 33.
Meadows, 33, 132, 147.
Meaghen, 68.
Meagher, 71.
Meeds, 277.
Meek, 178, 226, 227.
Mehne, 69.
Meigs, 187, 456.
Meier, 69.
Meir, 57.
Melody, 67.
Menees, 117.
Menfel, 279.
Mercer, 145, 422.
Merri, 72.
Merrick, 131.
Merriman, 33.
Merry, 33.
Merryman, 466.
Merritt, 33, 94, 291.
Meston, 277.
Metz, 62.
Meyer, 33, 68, 69, 70.
Meyers, 155.
Michaux, 389, 431.
Mickels, 233.
Middleton, 9.
Milan, 101.
Miles, 33, 341.
Mille, 164.
Miller, 33, 47, 48, 54, 73, 79, 82, 146, 178, 217, 223, 236, 292, 293, 294, 295, 296, 297, 337, 340, 342, 361, 438, 439.
Milligan, 133, 339.
Million, 137.
Millitt, 62, 72.
Mills, 33, 455.
Mims, 194.
Milner, 246, 247.
Minnick, 33.
Minor, 33, 94.
Minter, 279.
Minton, 85.
Miro, 495.
Mitchel, 342, 497.
Mitchell, 33, 61, 63, 67, 68, 73, 77, 133, 141, 145, 149, 150, 154, 221, 229, 279, 296, 318, 334, 351, 361, 389, 444, 495.
Mitchner, 120, 121, 253.
Mizell, 110.
Mocker, 59, 60.
Moffat, 33.
Moffatt, 414.

Moffett, 133.
Moffitt, 153, 154, 155, 156.
Mogan, 59, 71.
Moggiana, 58, 61.
Molloy, 57, 65, 66, 473, 478.
Moncrief, 52.
Monday, 33.
Mone, 140.
Mongle, 467.
Monnahan, 33.
Monohan, 65.
Monroe, 76.
Montague, 452.
Montgomery, 90, 115, 196, 197, 201, 229, 230, 234, 340, 344, 345, 436.
Moody, 204.
Mooney, 63, 68.
Moonyham, 239.
Moore, 33, 34, 59, 75, 76, 85, 86, 94, 110, 127, 150, 152, 154, 161, 164 174, 175, 183, 193, 204, 231, 268, 276, 278, 280, 281, 302, 323, 338, 344, 351, 360, 444, 467.
Moors, 340, 342.
Mooreland, 47.
Mooring, 86.
Moran, 55, 60, 64, 65, 68, 70.
Morefield, 34.
Moreland, 124.
Morey, 135.
Morford, 144, 146, 422.
Morgan, 9, 12, 34, 60, 61, 71, 77, 87, 94, 103, 138, 166, 204, 224, 261, 285, 294, 300, 303, 307, 340, 352, 356, 434, 449, 469.
Moriarity, 58.
Morissey, 59.
Morrissey, 56, 63, 69, 72.
Morrell, 137.
Morris, 34, 92, 135, 280, 349, 361, 362, 453.
Morrisett, 463.
Morrison, 34, 62, 65, 68, 448.
Morristown, 68.
Morrow, 88, 107, 147, 207, 221.
Mory, 67.
Morse, 63.
Mortimore, 34.
Morton, 34, 83, 153, 194, 201, 210, 304, 350.

Bible Records—Tombstone Inscriptions

Mosby, 34.
Moseley, 34, 239.
Mosher, 34.
Mosley, 34, 193, 194, 297, 315.
Moser, 34, 222, 315, 330.
Moss, 34, 84, 107, 122, 125, 173, 178, 179, 180, 315, 334.
Motheral, 100, 312.
Motherall, 333, 334.
Motherwell, 114.
Motlow, 167.
Moulton, 49, 52.
Mount, 86, 294.
Moxley, 318.
Mulhall, 34.
Mulherin, 478, 479, 480.
Mulherrin, 251.
Mullican, 151.
Mullen, 83, 194, 235.
Mullin, 62.
Mullins, 144, 287.
Mullendores, 196.
Muller, 70, 94.
Mulligan, 72.
Mulloy, 59, 60, 62, 65, 66, 67.
Mulray, 58, 66.
Mulvihill, 63, 65.
Mumford, 113, 147, 160.
Mundy, 66.
Munroe, 34.
Munsey, 339.
Murfee, 275.
Murfree, 108, 109, 219, 220, 356, 363, 403, 436, 446, 460.
Murphey, 77, 127, 296, 306.
Murphy, 34, 56, 57, 58, 59, 61, 62, 65, 66, 67, 69, 70, 72, 279, 288, 306.
Murphree, 141.
Murray, 34, 54, 57, 60, 61, 66, 69, 70, 71, 73, 99, 148, 149, 239.
Murry, 71.
Murrell, 34, 91, 178, 496.
Myers, 34, 47, 48, 63, 68, 69, 71, 87, 94, 155, 236, 342.

N

Naff, 135.
Nailling, 219.
Naive, 85.

Napier, 7, 12, 34, 49, 51, 94.
Napper, 84.
Nash, 372, 495.
Naughton, 58.
Naulty, 135.
Nave, 61.
Naylor, 84, 340, 349.
Neal, 34, 55, 58, 174, 297, 298, 450.
Neely, 34, 78, 88, 217, 219, 470.
Neil, 178, 234, 335.
Neill, 61.
Neilson, 204.
Nell, 34.
Nellums, 84.
Nelson, 81, 95, 136, 205, 208, 224, 261, 280, 281, 449, 450.
Neman, 60.
Nenon, 65, 72.
Nestor, 68.
Nettles, 348.
Neugent, 452.
Nevins, 47.
New, 34, 81, 287, 316.
Newbern, 34.
Newbey, 296.
Newburn, 48.
Newell, 34, 48, 50, 276.
Newherne, 55.
Newman, 34, 51, 360, 450.
Newsom, 172, 173, 257.
Newton, 146, 187, 443.
Neylan, 60, 70, 72.
Nice, 178.
Nichol, 34, 35, 50, 90, 92, 94, 196, 217.
Nicholls, 245.
Nichols, 196, 197, 209, 217.
Nicholson, 60, 61, 65, 281, 495.
Nickalson, 436.
Night, 119.
Niles, 444.
Nimmo, 204.
Nimon, 232.
Nix, 295.
Nogan, 60.
Nogianna, 56.
Nokes, 35, 87.
Nolan, 58, 63, 66, 68, 70, 71.
Nolen, 86, 87, 292.
Noles, 35.
Noonan, 73.
Norfleet, 92.

Norman, 55, 81, 281, 287, 294, 342.
Norment, 77.
Norris, 127, 358, 361.
Northcut, 148, 154, 155, 156.
Northcutt, 414, 422.
Norvell, 7, 11, 13, 35, 90.
Notgrass, 81.
Nuckoll, 415.
Nuckolls, 162.
Nuebert, 227.
Nunelly, 153.
Nunn, 202.
Nutt, 94.

O

Oakley, 467.
Oaks, 227.
Oatman, 250, 256.
O'Brien, 57, 63, 70, 222, 278, 281, 296.
O'Brine, 61.
O'Bryan, 35, 57, 217, 290.
Ochrle, 35.
O'Callahan, 57.
O'Connell, 56, 67, 68.
O'Connor, 57, 58, 63, 66, 72.
O'Donahue, 72.
O'Donnell, 56, 59, 63, 64, 65, 68, 71.
Odom, 319.
Odum, 150.
Ogden, 73, 108, 111, 112, 452.
Ogle, 340.
O'Hagerty, 57.
O'Harris, 35.
O'Keefe, 62, 64.
Old, 280.
Oldham, 86, 197, 207, 313.
O'Leary, 57, 63.
Oliphant, 83, 84, 129, 188.
Oliver, 35, 357.
Olwill, 56, 67.
O'Maley, 73.
O'Meara, 470.
Omohundro, 35.
O'Neal, 195, 278, 495, 497.
O'Neill, 60, 495, 497.
Oney, 35.
O'Reilly, 251, 280, 281.
O'Rilley, 35.
O'Rourke, 69.
Orr, 130, 232, 263, 276, 433.
Orvyl, 80.

Bible Records—Tombstone Inscriptions

Osborn, 82, 193, 219.
Osborne, 280, 337.
Oscar, 35.
O'Shaughnessy, 59, 62, 72.
O'Shea, 67, 68.
Oslin, 356.
Osment, 113, 302, 303.
Osmon, 265.
Otey, 217, 273, 274, 275, 276.
Otis, 48.
Ottenville, 59, 64.
Otto, 35.
Overall, 280, 363, 452, 478, 479.
Overby, 86.
Overton, 94, 186, 223, 495.
Owen, 35, 141, 146, 217, 288, 303, 321, 361.
Owens, 35, 344, 347.
Owsley, 82.

P

Padgett, 74, 299.
Page, 35, 52, 76, 79, 82, 209, 212, 287, 289, 297.
Paine, 144, 276, 467, 469.
Palmer, 149, 289, 306, 361, 363.
Pankey, 218.
Pannell, 213.
Pannhill, 276.
Paradise, 84.
Paragan, 48.
Pardue, 337, 359.
Parish, 35, 54, 100, 114.
Park, 35, 148, 218, 223.
Parker, 35, 55, 58, 128, 140, 193, 222, 229, 263, 342, 470.
Parkes, 48, 218.
Parks, 83, 157, 164, 228.
Parkerville, 189.
Parkins, 454.
Parkison, 178.
Parmantick, 50.
Parmer, 35, 147.
Parminter, 35.
Parnell, 103.
Parriah, 48.
Parrish, 35, 48, 51, 105, 193, 218.
Parry, 127.
Parshley, 362.
Parsons, 178.
Partee, 204.
Parton, 320, 321.
Paschall, 82.

Pass, 304.
Pate, 87, 124, 292.
Patillo, 252, 351.
Patrick, 36, 82, 153, 222.
Patteon, 138.
Patterson, 56, 92, 139, 148, 160, 187, 258.
Patton, 35, 36, 80, 83, 85, 94, 138, 202, 204, 310, 318, 338, 340, 425.
Paty, 140, 293, 297, 320.
Paul, 10, 11, 36, 278, 279.
Pavatt, 119.
Paxendale, 36.
Payne, 36, 88, 120, 134, 144, 146, 149, 164, 340, 421.
Peabody, 54.
Peace, 288.
Peach, 36, 172.
Peacock, 36, 49, 83.
Pearce, 295.
Pearl, 36, 94.
Pearre, 219.
Pearsoll, 86.
Pearson, 36.
Pease, 359.
Peay, 36, 140.
Peck, 178, 187.
Peebles, 85, 218, 261, 262.
Peek, 123, 229.
Peeler, 257.
Peeples, 204.
Pemberton, 321.
Pendergast, 63.
Pendleton, 289, 297.
Penge, 348.
Penland, 337.
Pennebaker, 141, 145.
Pennington, 165, 339, 345.
Penny, 290.
Pennybaker, 291, 296.
Pentecost, 36, 54.
Pepper, 160.
Perkins, 36, 184, 209, 210, 211, 218, 219, 303.
Perry, 36, 88, 104, 114, 116, 152, 192, 257, 258, 272, 462.
Person, 36, 53, 55.
Petit, 36.
Pettibone, 221.
Petty, 36, 350.
Peters, 339.
Petre, 36.
Pew, 36.
Peyton, 101, 223, 287, 296, 300, 303, 324, 385, 390.

Pfeiffer, 36.
Phelps, 36, 55, 94, 306.
Philbin, 72.
Philips, 142, 150, 170, 171.
Phillips, 36, 67, 69, 155, 219, 279, 290, 318, 321, 322, 357, 387, 463, 464.
Phillipe, 496.
Phipps, 87.
Pickard, 279.
Pickett, 36, 49, 295, 421.
Pickel, 129.
Pickens, 281, 342, 343.
Pickering, 135.
Pickford, 194.
Pierce, 191.
Piete, 94.
Pike, 36, 495.
Pilcher, 36.
Pillow, 36, 276.
Pinchum, 36.
Pinegar, 151.
Pippin, 206.
Pirtle, 78, 80.
Pitcairn, 36, 53.
Pitchlynn, 496.
Pitner, 235, 236, 337.
Pitt, 86, 120.
Pitts, 88.
Pittard, 85.
Pittman, 36, 292.
Plemons, 340, 360.
Pless, 128.
Plum, 60.
Plummer, 36, 48, 52, 56, 61, 66, 72, 73, 281.
Plunkett, 218.
Poindexter, 198.
Pointer, 218.
Polk, 10, 36, 53, 97, 273, 274, 275, 276, 277, 278, 279, 280, 281, 370, 421, 422, 459, 495.
Pollak, 72.
Pollard, 36.
Pomphrett, 252.
Pomroy, 144.
Poole, 48.
P'Pool, 37.
Pope, 202, 286.
Porch, 135.
Porter, 8, 12, 36, 37, 79, 80, 91, 128, 157, 171, 196, 218, 229, 231, 246, 278, 356, 469.
Porterfield, 6, 37, 48, 91, 244, 253, 447.
Posey, 449.

510

Bible Records—Tombstone Inscriptions

Post, 37.
Poteet, 36, 53.
Potter, 138, 148, 151.
Potts, 172, 218, 219.
Powell, 37, 134, 145, 149, 155, 160, 222, 234, 293, 308, 449, 462.
Power, 66.
Powers, 37, 57, 59, 62, 70, 239.
Poyner, 328.
Prater, 149, 230.
Presley, 340, 360.
Presswood, 338.
Presterfield, 343.
Preston, 80.
Preuett, 121.
Price, 37, 48, 49, 51, 83, 86, 148, 161, 288, 293, 362, 446.
Pride, 202.
Prichett, 173.
Prichitt, 195.
Priest, 86, 219.
Prige, 37.
Prince, 86, 478, 479, 480.
Pritchet, 37.
Probart, 37, 90.
Province, 305, 342.
Pruner, 202.
Prunty, 66.
Pryor, 89, 116, 166, 224.
Puckett, 219, 286, 287, 354, 364.
Puccetti, 62.
Pugsley, 37, 94.
Purdy, 129, 351, 360.
Pursell, 281.
Purvis, 144, 277.
Puryear, 358.
Putnam, 13, 37, 92, 285, 287, 496.
Pyle, 37.

Q

Quaintance, 295.
Quarles, 86, 469.
Queener, 230.
Quick, 156.
Quimby, 119.
Quin, 56.
Quinn, 37, 56, 57, 59, 60, 65, 66, 68, 72, 73.
Quisenberry, 197.

R

Rabe, 133.
Rader, 195.
Radford, 37.
Rafferty, 59.
Ragan, 174, 195.
Ragland, 287, 296, 331.
Ragon, 165.
Ragsdale, 78, 80, 218, 219, 302, 362.
Rahm, 37.
Railly, 71.
Raines, 239.
Rains, 10, 13, 37, 114, 119, 392, 495.
Rainey, 81, 83.
Ralphfile, 116.
Ralston, 322, 448.
Ramage, 37, 460.
Rambo, 128, 129.
Rambos, 196.
Ramsay, 205, 221, 224.
Ramsey, 8, 12, 37, 50, 134, 135, 141, 147, 149, 150, 166, 205, 260, 265, 266, 268, 269, 271, 272, 283, 348, 433, 447, 453, 495.
Randall, 143.
Randolph, 144, 146, 149, 421.
Rankin, 178, 281, 356.
Ransom, 37, 283, 335.
Raser, 461.
Rather, 431.
Rausin, 361, 362.
Raustin, 339.
Rawley, 37.
Rawlings, 37.
Rawls, 89.
Rawson, 37.
Ray, 37, 127, 172, 286, 479.
Rayburn, 50.
Rayl, 222.
Read, 37, 38, 97, 145, 284, 285, 449.
Ready, 146, 149, 288, 357, 363, 364, 446, 447, 448, 459.
Reagan, 129, 130, 131, 359.
Reams, 252.
Reany, 268.
Reavis, 310.
Record, 178.
Reddy, 38.
Reddick, 38.
Redford, 219.
Redmond, 84, 195.
Reece, 9, 12, 128, 189, 265.
Reed, 38, 76, 84, 179, 221, 222, 304, 314, 322, 323, 326, 443, 452, 479.
Reeder, 138, 150, 179, 232.
Reep, 341.
Reese, 38, 48, 127, 204, 221, 268.
Reeves, 38, 290, 349, 355, 452.
Regan, 56, 59, 60.
Regenold, 264.
Reid, 38, 60, 179, 284.
Reilly, 60, 61.
Reinberger, 38.
Renfro, 167.
Renick, 253.
Renner, 421.
Reyburn, 38.
Reynolds, 38, 57, 68, 71, 73, 84, 93, 148, 151, 280, 311, 362.
Rhea, 158, 190, 222.
Rhodes, 117, 226.
Rice, 83, 104, 137, 160, 179, 218, 327.
Richards, 38, 78, 94.
Richardson, 38, 53, 84, 93, 124, 125, 138, 218, 355.
Richeson, 131, 340.
Richie, 38.
Richmond, 87, 302.
Rickman, 108, 114, 469.
Riddle, 38, 178, 287, 293.
Rider, 178, 180.
Ridge, 81, 88.
Ridle, 305.
Ridley, 94, 113, 114, 125, 276, 457.
Rieff, 38.
Rieves, 194, 195.
Riggan, 314.
Riggs, 38.
Right, 338.
Riley, 56, 64, 431.
Rimberger, 54.
Ring, 87.
Ripley, 218.
Rippy, 265.
Risely, 38.
Risley, 418, 419.
Rissel, 84, 85.
Ritchey, 147.
Ritchie, 130.
Riva, 38.
Rives, 38, 193, 198.
Rivin, 61.
Rix, 49.
Rizzetto, 72.

511

Bible Records—Tombstone Inscriptions

Roach, 84, 278.
Roan, 305.
Roane, 38.
Roates, 422.
Robards, 144, 422.
Robb, 38, 100, 114.
Robbins, 236.
Roberts, 38, 78, 84, 86, 166, 205, 222, 223, 224, 225, 227, 290, 336, 339, 341, 343, 361, 414, 415, 462.
Robertson, 3, 4, 7, 8, 11, 12, 13, 38, 49, 52, 53, 112, 113, 117, 120, 160, 171, 188, 212, 244, 293, 296, 299, 362, 370, 380, 389, 390, 391, 392, 393, 395, 396, 428, 473, 474, 475, 478, 495.
Roberson, 422, 495, 498.
Robeson, 38, 179.
Robinson, 38, 76, 121, 129, 131, 135, 154, 202, 218, 247, 254, 258, 338.
Robison, 364.
Robman, 318.
Robterb, 71.
Roche, 278.
Rockwood, 38.
Rodes, 58, 70.
Rodger, 61.
Rodgers, 140, 146, 154, 218, 231, 337.
Roe, 297.
Roehl, 336.
Rogan, 189, 222.
Roger, 39, 84.
Rogers, 38, 71, 79, 140, 143, 155, 179, 191, 196, 198, 221, 231, 234, 297, 323, 328, 347, 418.
Roland, 39, 139, 163.
Roler, 39, 87.
Romans, 138.
Rooney, 67.
Rooney, 58, 61.
Roper, 467.
Rosacher, 66.
Roseby, 467.
Rose, 48, 52, 66, 128, 129, 179, 180, 324, 342, 343.
Roser, 39.
Ross, 93, 126, 147, 154, 180, 188, 230, 348, 434.
Rothenberg, 69.
Rothrock, 218.
Rotterman, 72.

Roulstone, 495.
Rousseau, 292.
Rowan, 39, 144, 421.
Rowark, 470.
Rowe, 39, 206.
Rowland, 239, 302.
Rowley, 58.
Roy, 193, 198.
Royle, 39.
Royster, 39, 50.
Rozell, 191, 298.
Rounsevall, 480.
Rucker, 350, 357, 442, 444, 449, 450, 452, 453, 495.
Ruckle, 39.
Rucks, 309.
Rue, 64.
Ruff, 87.
Ruhm, 39, 263.
Rule, 222.
Rumbough, 135.
Rumple, 179.
Rusber, 147.
Rush, 194.
Rushing, 318.
Russel, 204.
Russell, 64, 77, 83, 85, 94, 134, 179, 230, 231, 281, 319, 325, 343, 431, 435.
Russey, 61.
Ruster, 147.
Ruston, 288.
Ruten, 256.
Ruth, 39.
Rutherford, 39, 83, 85, 287, 297, 390, 428, 468, 470.
Rutland, 50, 104, 292, 322.
Rutledge, 9, 39, 141, 150, 187, 286, 314, 315, 432.
Ryan, 55, 56, 57, 58, 60, 61, 64, 66, 67, 68, 70, 72, 94.
Ryland, 448.
Ryman, 39, 63, 64, 72.
Rymer, 39.
Ryckman, 212.

S

Sacott, 224.
Sadler, 39.
Saffell, 230.
Saffrans, 39.
Safley, 138, 155.
Sagalay, 39.
Sain, 140, 149, 157.
Sakers, 297.
Sample, 179, 218, 360.

Sanders, 39, 55, 65, 69, 70, 80, 83, 94, 98, 99, 113, 138, 139, 192, 288, 290, 296, 297, 303, 311, 318, 361, 390, 415, 467, 479.
Sanderson, 39, 86, 228, 279, 281.
Sandhouse, 39.
Sanford, 221.
Sansom, 247.
Sargent, 155.
Satterfield, 279, 339, 340.
Saunders, 51, 84, 97, 116, 125, 182, 183, 331, 389, 464, 466, 467.
Sautel, 179.
Savage, 48, 49, 145, 146, 149, 154, 156, 421, 422.
Sawyer, 39.
Sawyers, 222, 225, 226, 227, 441.
Sayers, 39, 62.
Sayres, 39.
Sayrs, 39.
Scales, 308.
Scally, 67.
Scalon, 63.
Scanlan, 61.
Scanlon, 64.
Scharenberger, 39.
Scheibe, 297.
Schields, 57.
Schendier, 221.
Scheuerman, 53.
Schnell, 39, 117.
Schio, 62.
Schloss, 39.
Schneider, 57, 65, 76, 131, 338.
Schnelder, 83.
Schockney, 295.
Schorr, 53.
Schreider, 57.
Schumann, 180.
Schund, 56.
Schwartz, 90.
Scobey, 294.
Scott, 39, 75, 84, 94, 128, 152, 166, 179, 202, 218, 219, 222, 223, 224, 230, 238, 258, 259, 260, 261, 271, 272, 320, 329, 359, 360, 422.
Scoville, 281.
Scroggs, 230.
Scruggs, 39, 165, 218, 231, 278, 359.

Bible Records—Tombstone Inscriptions

Scruthin, 202.
Seabury, 39.
Seagraves, 290.
Searcy, 350.
Searcey, 449.
Searight, 218.
Seawell, 170, 293.
Seat, 204.
Seay, 39, 81, 300, 308.
Secrest, 219.
Seek, 39.
Seever, 179.
Sehorn, 175, 179, 446.
Seibert, 39, 53.
Seifried, 59, 67, 89.
Seitz, 149.
Selleck, 39.
Sellers, 244, 249, 254, 256, 259.
Semmes, 410.
Sennett, 57.
Senter, 204, 434.
Sesler, 88.
Sessions, 218.
Sesson, 152.
Settle, 144, 292, 296, 467.
Sevell, 244.
Sevier, 10, 12, 13, 48, 95, 132, 136, 222, 234, 335, 367, 370, 371, 372, 373, 374, 375, 376, 377, 379, 380, 391, 428, 430, 432, 433, 442, 459, 461, 495.
Sewanski, 39.
Sewell, 99, 299, 312.
Sexton, 342.
Seymore, 277.
Seymour, 360.
Shackelford, 204.
Shaeffer, 48.
Shaffer, 39.
Shan, 84.
Shanklin, 445.
Shannon, 39, 84, 86, 120, 127, 140, 292, 293, 295, 302, 317, 328, 332.
Shapard, 11, 12, 40, 91.
Sharenberger, 59.
Sharp, 169, 208, 209, 219, 229, 234, 354.
Sharpe, 40, 70, 495, 497.
Shaw, 40, 145, 149, 294, 442, 467, 479, 480.
Shea, 56, 58, 278, 282.
Shearl, 341.
Shearon, 40, 48, 324.
Sheddan, 235.
Sheegog, 277.

Sheehan, 70.
Sheets, 125.
Sheetz, 71.
Shehan, 218.
Sheffield, 40.
Sheilds, 57.
Shelby, 10, 12, 40, 372, 379, 380, 381, 391, 496, 428, 434, 454, 460, 461.
Sheldon, 346.
Shell, 157, 462.
Shelton, 40, 48, 109, 290, 346, 467, 470.
Shepard, 9, 11, 92, 222, 292.
Shephard, 40.
Shepherd, 86.
Sheppard, 40, 142, 219, 282.
Sherell, 152.
Sherfly, 60.
Sherlin, 179, 337.
Sherlock, 278.
Shermin, 58.
Sherrell, 152.
Sherrill, 121, 122, 296, 322, 327, 372, 495, 497.
Sherritz, 227.
Sherwood, 40.
Shey, 62.
Shields, 40, 235, 421.
Shipe, 227.
Shirley, 8, 12, 40.
Shivers, 40.
Shockney, 81.
Shoemaker, 179.
Shorferk, 63.
Short, 218.
Shorter, 288, 304.
Shouman, 40.
Shoun, 190.
Show, 128.
Shrum, 468, 470.
Shryer, 77, 88.
Shugart, 179.
Shull, 190, 462.
Shultz, 342.
Shute, 89, 106.
Shutt, 292, 293, 296.
Sigler, 40.
Sikes, 239, 240, 354, 450.
Simmons, 94, 129, 139, 157, 218, 452.
Simms, 40, 318, 330.
Sims, 149, 154, 179, 237, 238.
Simpkins, 84.

Simpson, 40, 166, 195, 222, 233, 234, 238, 280.
Sinclair, 48, 55, 218.
Singletary, 461, 462.
Singleton, 70, 231.
Sinnot, 57, 58.
Sinnott, 57.
Sinsebaugh, 164.
Sippy, 40.
Sitten, 181.
Skeen, 292, 297, 303, 319.
Skeggs, 40, 48.
Skelly, 65.
Skiles, 204.
Slack, 49.
Slade, 40.
Slaman, 58.
Slate, 290, 349.
Slater, 84, 352.
Slatton, 151, 236.
Slaughter, 218, 280.
Sleage, 40.
Sledge, 219.
Slimp, 127.
Slinkard, 92.
Sloan, 40.
Slocum, 40.
Slonaker, 137.
Slonecker, 84.
Sluder, 169.
Slover, 179.
Smallman, 147.
Smart, 66, 123, 325.
Smartt, 144, 148, 150, 153, 154, 413, 421.
Smiley, 40, 90.
Smelling, 159.
Smiley, 40, 90.
Smith, 8, 10, 12, 40, 41, 48, 49, 50, 51, 52, 60, 68, 71, 72, 75, 85, 87, 92, 94, 98, 99, 138, 139, 144, 146, 148, 150, 153, 156, 157, 169, 174, 179, 192, 204, 205, 213, 218, 219, 221, 223, 227, 236, 237, 248, 252, 263, 271, 272, 275, 276, 278, 290, 291, 295, 297, 310, 312, 322, 330, 339, 348, 387, 390, 421, 428, 442, 443, 447, 449, 452, 453, 454, 468, 495.
Smithson, 210.
Smithwick, 287.
Smoker, 341.
Smoot, 141, 282.
Smotherman, 284.

Bible Records—Tombstone Inscriptions

Smott, 281, 282.
Smythe, 128, 189, 282.
Snead, 41.
Snedekum, 41.
Sneed, 12, 41, 52, 84.
Snell, 41.
Snider, 41.
Snyder, 83.
Snipes, 140, 256.
Snoddy, 236.
Snodgrass, 238.
Snow, 41, 336.
Sobrina, 75.
Solan, 72.
Solen, 68.
Soloman, 155, 292, 295.
Somerville, 12.
Soper, 116.
Sory, 288.
Soule, 103.
Sowell, 246.
Spain, 41, 258, 272, 290.
Spann, 84, 87, 218.
Sparkman, 151.
Sparks, 344, 362.
Spear, 61.
Spears, 172, 292, 297.
Speece, 41.
Spence, 50, 94, 280, 351.
Spencer, 145, 202, 385, 427, 431, 441, 465, 495.
Spenge, 41.
Spiegelhalter, 41.
Spivey, 218.
Spong, 155.
Spottswood, 41.
Springfield, 41.
Springs, 140.
Sprowell, 225.
Spurlock, 145, 146, 149, 422.
Squier, 218.
Squires, 219.
Stacey, 87.
Stack, 58.
Stagg, 41.
Stailey, 305.
Stainback, 41.
Stair, 227.
Stairs, 227.
Stalcup, 41, 468, 470.
Staley, 331.
Stall, 41.
Stamger, 234.
Stanfield, 82.
Stanfill, 246.
Stanley, 41, 70.
Stanton, 235.

Stargel, 77.
Stark, 108, 109, 120, 159, 161, 318, 436.
Starnes, 82, 355.
Staton, 41.
Staub, 41.
Steane, 41.
Stearns, 41.
Steed, 122.
Steel, 48
Steele, 107, 122, 126, 127, 224.
Stegall, 269.
Steger, 95.
Steillinger (Stamger), 234.
Stelle, 166.
Stemridge, 329.
Stephen, 459.
Stephens, 41, 234, 278.
Stephenson, 88, 90, 222, 241, 242, 243, 244, 245, 250, 251, 252, 258.
Stepp, 152.
Sterchi, 341, 342.
Sterling, 230.
Stevens, 11, 41, 42, 49, 93, 150, 179, 294.
Stevenson, 42, 90, 104.
Steward, 282.
Stewart, 5, 42, 48, 49, 75, 100, 174, 236, 333, 334, 341, 351, 443, 444, 496.
Stiles, 131, 341.
Stine, 91.
Stites, 82.
St. John, 141, 150.
Stockard, 263, 266, 270, 452.
Stockell, 94.
Stockston, 339.
Stoddard, 27.
Stodder, 42.
Stoddert, 51, 52.
Stodhard, 42.
Stokes, 91, 293.
Stall, 53.
Stone, 42, 82, 93, 128, 144, 145, 146, 325, 343, 422, 435.
Stones, 53.
Stooke, 337.
Stothard, 42.
Stotts, 157.
Stout, 42, 52, 53, 59, 86, 205.
Stovall, 218, 290, 469.
Stover, 298, 461.

Strahl, 264, 277.
Strange, 82.
Stratton, 80, 102, 293, 294, 296.
Straughis, 278.
Strayhorn, 256.
Stretch, 42.
Strickland, 12, 103.
Strobel, 57.
Strong, 118, 204, 364.
Strother, 158, 164.
Stroud, 141, 148, 297, 298, 299.
Stuart, 218, 222, 362, 441.
Stubblefield, 140, 141, 145, 149, 156, 422.
Studley, 42.
Stull, 92.
Sublett, 449, 452.
Suddarth, 290, 292.
Sugart, 179.
Suit, 82.
Suite, 358.
Suiter, 63.
Sullivan, 42, 57, 58, 60, 64, 66, 69, 70, 72, 73, 145, 150, 278, 297, 298, 323, 325, 326, 327, 328, 334, 422.
Summers, 103.
Summerville, 42.
Sumner, 42, 82, 89, 171.
Sunter, 459.
Surles, 468.
Sutfin, 49.
Sutherland, 56, 66, 128, 189.
Sutherlin, 281.
Sutill, 357.
Sutton, 360.
Swadler, 84.
Swah, 239.
Swain, 119, 297.
Swan, 148, 222, 223, 224.
Swann, 81, 140.
Swanson, 219.
Sweeney, 42, 85, 122.
Sweezy, 124.
Swenson, 247.
Swiney, 51, 174.
Swindell, 294.
Swingley, 297, 298, 302.
Swoope, 461.
Swords, 59, 360.
Sydenham, 421.
Syers, 72.
Synoh, 184.
Syport, 295.

Bible Records—Tombstone Inscriptions

T

Taggart, 193.
Tait, 42, 53.
Talbot, 468, 478, 479.
Taliaferro, 128, 129.
Talleferro, 230.
Talley, 75, 84.
Tandel, 444.
Taney, 495.
Tanksley, 94, 113, 193.
Tannehill, 8, 11, 12, 42.
Tansey, 72.
Tarbet, 299.
Tarbett, 230.
Tardiff, 42.
Tarver, 42, 50, 293, 308.
Tassi, 63, 71.
Tate, 42, 153, 154.
Tatum, 287, 294, 296, 334.
Taylor, 42, 56, 65, 76, 80, 81, 85, 94, 144, 146, 149, 179, 180, 188, 204, 205, 218, 222, 231, 285, 286, 287, 291, 297, 309, 334, 339, 343, 360, 377, 378, 382, 397, 398, 399, 400, 401, 431, 432, 440, 442.
Teal, 42.
Tebow, 42.
Tedford, 202, 229.
Teele, 124, 125.
Telton, 42.
Temple, 42, 221, 263.
Templeton, 237, 424.
Tennent, 444.
Tennison, 116.
Terrass, 42, 54.
Terry, 42, 75, 83, 292.
Tessier, 43.
Thaxter, 404, 405.
Thaxton, 149, 157.
Therrhis, 269.
Thomas, 43, 55, 94, 103, 128, 130, 154, 183, 196, 244, 254, 258, 265, 270, 271, 272, 277, 282, 337, 338, 339, 343, 350, 356, 433, 438, 441, 442, 480.
Thomason, 344.
Thomison, 167, 191, 192.
Thomm, 54.
Thomson, 197.
Thompkins, 185.
Thompson, 43, 48, 50, 52, 84, 85, 87, 88, 94, 123, 140, 146, 149, 156, 194, 195, 202, 204, 219, 227, 228, 229, 239, 244, 245, 250, 252, 264, 270, 288, 289, 294, 295, 296, 298, 317, 320, 321, 322, 341, 343, 351, 356, 360, 361, 362, 433, 468, 469.
Thornburg, 43, 48.
Thurman, 147, 148, 194.
Thurston, 197.
Tilford, 43, 141.
Tiller, 290, 361.
Tillett, 218.
Tilman, 465.
Tilson, 377.
Timberlake, 459.
Timon, 59, 62, 69, 71.
Tindall, 43, 254.
Tiner, 204.
Tipton, 8, 12, 13, 43, 188, 205, 333, 338, 381, 382, 414, 462.
Titcolm, 280.
Tittsworth, 151.
Titus, 43, 145, 473, 480.
Toby, 340.
Todd, 43.
Tolburt, 234.
Toller, 161.
Tolliver, 294.
Tomlin, 325.
Tomlinson, 358.
Tomson, 480.
Toombs, 43.
Tompkins, 139.
Tooms, 43.
Toncray, 382.
Tongray, 177, 180.
Toney, 43, 49, 309.
Tools, 202.
Toon, 218.
Topp, 114.
Torhit, 254.
Torrence, 205.
Towler, 280.
Towles, 143.
Townsend, 43, 87, 102.
Trabue, 8, 11, 43, 94.
Tracey, 59.
Tracy, 64.
Trail, 195.
Trammel, 318.
Traughber, 88.
Treacy, 58.
Tredway, 340.
Treber, 60.
Trent, 222.
Trice, 272, 287, 289, 296.
Trigg, 224, 292, 297, 316.
Trihy, 61.
Trimble, 43.
Troost, 10, 11, 43, 495.
Trott, 444.
Trotter, 341, 360.
Trousdale, 94, 145, 429.
Trout, 227.
Troutman, 455.
Trull, 79.
Tubb, 138.
Tuck, 95, 147.
Tucker, 172, 179, 202, 228, 324, 355.
Tuckness, 281.
Tuell, 179.
Tulbert, 128.
Tulley, 80, 88.
Tullifield, 243.
Tulloch, 187.
Tully, 43, 53.
Tumblain, 324.
Tunstall, 358.
Tuberville, 113.
Turbeville, 43.
Turnbow, 258.
Turner, 43, 48, 60, 78, 82, 85, 87, 97, 117, 148, 150, 159, 179, 191, 204, 219, 295, 316, 468, 470.
Turney, 435, 468.
Turpin, 43, 253.
Turvines, 269, 270.
Tutt, 300.
Twain, 434.
Tyerell, 279.
Tyler, 84.
Tyne, 60.
Tyrell, 62.

U

Uhleo(?), 468.
Ullian, 43.
Umbarger, 157, 341.
Uncell, 208.
Utley, 75.

V

Vaden, 205.
Valden, 339, 340.
Valentine, 43, 60.
Valentino, 61.
Vance, 43, 101, 228.
Vandervart, 85.
Van Dyke, 179.

Bible Records—Tombstone Inscriptions

Van Hooser, 151, 311, 322.
Van Horn, 288.
Van Lear, 91.
Vanleer, 50, 54.
Van Leer, 91.
Vann, 299.
Vanney, 55.
Vanpelt, 218.
Vantrease, 322.
Varley, 62.
Vasser, 16.
Vaughn, 43, 48, 56, 58, 62, 82, 83, 85, 146, 174, 178, 286, 295, 297, 307, 314, 329, 349, 356, 360, 422, 449, 450.
Vaulx, 9, 12, 43, 169.
Vaupelt, 218.
Veader, 43.
Venable, 173.
Vernon, 207, 219.
Vick, 84, 113, 120, 194, 205, 295, 297.
Villines, 158.
Vines, 43.
Vitetoe, 87.
Vivrett, 301, 310.
Vogel, 44.
Vollinco, 71.
Voorhies, 279, 282.

W

Wade, 44, 65, 192, 205, 276, 431, 444.
Waggoner, 44, 76, 87, 156.
Wagner, 127, 155, 189, 190.
Wagstaff, 272.
Waid, 269.
Waits, 79.
Wakefield, 469.
Walden, 364.
Waldron, 44, 48.
Walford, 62.
Walker, 10, 30, 44, 49, 78, 80, 87, 88, 95, 97, 98, 135, 153, 163, 164, 180, 202, 205, 207, 233, 234, 244, 250, 251, 254, 259, 260, 261, 265, 279, 280, 282, 321, 328, 337, 345, 360, 361, 370, 456, 463, 466, 468, 495, 496.
Walkup, 195.
Wall, 82.
Wallace, 44, 53, 146, 175, 202, 230, 293, 297, 351.
Waller, 44, 83, 193.

Walling, 44, 143, 146, 147.
Wallis, 130.
Walsh, 56, 58, 59, 60, 61, 62, 70, 72, 73, 330.
Walston, 243, 258.
Walter, 136, 207.
Walters, 78.
Walton, 44, 48, 95, 120, 121, 161, 162, 163, 388, 429, 435, 459, 468.
Wamack, 332.
Wand, 44.
Wanna, 270.
Wanamaker, 152.
Ward, 44, 55, 56, 61, 264, 401, 422, 450, 495.
Warden, 192.
Warder, 44, 48.
Ware, 155.
Warfield, 44.
Warmack, 85, 320.
Warnack, 83.
Warner, 90, 355.
Warren, 44, 84, 161, 210, 230, 356, 357, 449, 450.
Washington, 44, 46, 382, 459, 495.
Wasson, 178, 351, 442, 443, 447.
Waterhouse, 154.
Waters, 44, 51, 92, 145, 232, 289, 302, 329.
Watkins, 44, 48, 49, 81, 87, 90, 95, 125, 205, 218, 244, 245, 246, 252, 263, 298, 445, 450, 466.
Watson, 44, 62, 81, 116, 270, 350, 449, 468.
Watters, 331.
Wattles, 179.
Watt, 282.
Wayman, 231.
Weakley, 92, 437, 451.
Wear, 202, 229, 232.
Weathered, 470.
Weatherford, 95, 310.
Weatherly, 364.
Weaver, 44, 55, 83, 265, 342.
Webb, 44, 50, 139, 150, 151, 221, 224, 252, 276, 285, 293.
Webber, 44, 174, 175, 340.
Webster, 280, 282.
Ween, 44.
Wehrley, 45.
Weir, 61, 180, 290, 434.

Weiss, 84.
Welborn, 44, 205.
Welcher, 44.
Welcker, 130.
Weller, 44, 54.
Wells, 45, 85, 162, 218, 343, 473, 480.
Wendel, 445, 446.
Wernet, 67.
Wersner, 45.
Wessel, 65.
Wessells, 48.
West, 8, 12, 45, 137, 150, 151, 159, 218, 438.
Westbrook, 303.
Wester, 180.
Western, 174.
Weston, 45, 174.
Wetterou, 45.
Wetzel, 45, 90.
Whaley, 55, 282.
Wharton, 45, 145, 287, 289, 292, 300.
Wheat, 45.
Wheeler, 49, 74, 86, 140, 194, 195, 196, 292, 297, 463.
Wheeless, 45.
Whelan, 56, 65, 71.
Wherry, 99, 348.
Whiles(?), 468.
White, 45, 54, 84, 88, 92, 95, 96, 101, 104, 108, 111, 112, 117, 144, 162, 165, 166, 188, 197, 205, 218, 219, 223, 224, 227, 237, 238, 244, 278, 280, 281, 282, 285, 308, 319, 335, 420, 480, 495.
Whitehead, 286.
Whiteley, 85.
Whitley, 195.
Whiteman, 10, 45, 48, 49.
Whitescarver, 297.
Whitesett, 449.
Whiteside, 280.
Whitesides, 134.
Whitlack, 297.
Whitley, 237.
Whitlock, 296.
Whitlow, 297.
Whitsitt, 310.
Whitson, 146.
Whittle, 79.
Whitworth, 120, 125, 255.
Whyte, 10, 12, 45.
Wiatt, 95.
Wilds, 180.

516

Bible Records—Tombstone Inscriptions

Wiles, 45.
Wiley, 71.
Wilkerson, 11, 45, 95.
Wilkes, 113, 258, 272, 282.
Wilkins, 97.
Wilkinson, 9, 45, 48, 288.
Willard, 194, 195.
Williams, 45, 48, 51, 54, 55, 63, 82, 84, 87, 88, 89, 90, 133, 135, 143, 153, 156, 170, 171, 179, 188, 212, 213, 218, 221, 222, 223, 224, 230, 231, 232, 235, 243, 244, 246, 252, 253, 258, 263, 271, 272, 293, 297, 306, 316, 320, 321, 322, 324, 328, 333, 337, 338, 342, 350, 359, 378, 381, 387, 389, 443, 447, 464, 465, 468, 478, 479, 480.
Williamson, 279, 281, 290, 294, 296, 299, 312.
Willis, 45, 92, 106, 205, 246.
Willock, 205.
Willoughby, 233.
Wills, 48, 75, 127, 189, 190.
Willson, 337.
Willy, 49, 69.
Wilson, 9, 11, 12, 45, 48, 51, 53, 84, 88, 95, 116, 129, 134, 148, 160, 161, 175, 179, 202, 218, 219, 228, 233, 234, 244, 245, 248, 250, 252, 262, 263, 278, 280, 282, 284, 296, 338, 339, 343, 346, 359, 360, 382, 390, 428, 429, 443, 444, 447, 468, 470, 498.
Wiltshire (Wilcher), 413.
Wimberly, 153.
Winbourn, 12, 13, 45, 46.
Winbourne, 11, 46, 80, 88.
Winchester, 385, 390, 428, 429, 454, 465, 468.
Winder, 46.
Windley, 452.
Winfield, 158.
Winford, 287, 293, 294, 324.
Winfred, 36.
Wing, 46.
Wingfield, 46, 249.

Winham, 90.
Winn, 102, 272, 286.
Winnie, 65.
Winningham, 67.
Winsett, 286.
Winstead, 46, 210.
Winston, 2, 11, 46, 81, 354.
Winter, 61.
Winters, 66.
Wintermutt, 221.
Winton, 150, 157, 158.
Wise, 46.
Wiseman, 291.
Wiser, 227.
Witcher, 180, 469.
Witherspoon, 150, 244, 249, 250, 363, 447.
Witt, 188.
Witten, 148.
Wittenbarger, 340, 342.
Witty, 46.
Wofford, 205.
Woehrle, 53.
Woldridge, 218.
Wolf, 46, 340, 342.
Womack, 147, 148.
Wood, 46, 84, 85, 87, 134, 137, 149, 205, 278, 312, 334, 382.
Woodall, 195.
Woodard, 87, 121, 160, 271.
Woodfin, 46, 174, 349.
Woodfolk, 46.
Woodford, 92.
Woodhead, 46.
Woodlee, 154, 156.
Woodley, 414.
Woods, 12, 18, 46, 48, 50, 62, 95, 130, 228, 294, 363.
Woodward, 46, 121.
Woody, 343.
Woollard, 297.
Wooten, 142, 150.
Word, 316.
Work, 25, 46.
Worley, 94.
Worman, 280.
Wortham, 89.
Wray, 46, 117, 118, 171, 325.
Wren, 218.
Wrenn, 218.
Wrigglesworth, 46.

Wright, 46, 56, 58, 59, 81, 89, 101, 122, 159, 179, 182, 184, 202, 205, 218, 234, 264, 311, 314, 353, 364, 387, 465, 466, 468.
Wrinkle, 233.
Writesman, 62.
Wyatt, 46, 48.
Wyche, 92.
Wylie, 130, 336.
Wymer, 56, 65.
Wynne, 46.
Wynn, 332.
Wynns, 196.
Wynne, 46, 292, 307, 315, 430.

Y

Yandell, 390, 449.
Yarbrough, 46, 127, 143, 205.
Yarlin, 46.
Yates, 161, 163, 164.
Yeargan, 364.
Yeargin, 50, 74, 80, 83.
Yearout, 95.
Yearwood, 165, 180, 359, 361.
Yeatman, 46, 47, 48, 50, 95, 275.
Yetts, 196.
Yoakman, 234.
Yoakum, 349, 451.
York, 83, 364.
Yost, 135.
Young, 47, 48, 84, 86, 110, 116, 117, 144, 147, 166, 172, 181, 232, 238, 258, 277, 279, 287, 290, 291, 301, 318, 332, 358, 359, 361, 387.
Youngblood, 337, 343, 468.
Youree, 244, 253, 349.

Z

Zachary, 47.
Zachery, 95.
Zarecor, 117.
Zeck, 158.
Zellner, 282.
Ziegler, 180.
Zollicoffer, 9, 12, 47.
Zula, 86.
Zwingle, 141.

www.ingramcontent.com/pod-product-compliance
Lightning Source LLC
Chambersburg PA
CBHW031539300426
44111CB00006BA/113